EQUITY AND THE LAW OF TRUSTS IN IRELAND

AUSTRALIA
Law Book Co.
Sydney

CANADA and USA
Carswell
Toronto

HONG KONG
Sweet & Maxwell Asia

NEW ZEALAND
Brookers
Wellington

SINGAPORE and MALAYSIA
Sweet & Maxwell Asia
Singapore and Kuala Lumpur

Equity and the Law of Trusts in Ireland

3rd edition

Hilary Delany

B.A. (Mod.), M.Litt., Ph.D, Barrister-at-Law
Fellow of Trinity College, Dublin
Senior Lecturer in Law, Trinity College, Dublin

THOMSON ™
ROUND HALL

Published in 2003 by
Round Hall Ltd
43 Fitzwilliam Place
Dublin 2
Ireland

Typeset by
Gough Typesetting Services
Dublin

Printed by
MPG Books, Cornwall

ISBN 1-85800-345-8 pbk
ISBN 1-85800-346-6 hbk

A catalogue record for this book
is available from the British Library

To my Mother,
and in memory of Douglas

Preface to the First Edition

The aim of this book is to provide a comprehensive modern text dealing with Equity and the Law of Trusts in Ireland. Although it is designed primarily to fulfil the needs of students in this area of the law, it is hoped that it will also prove to be of value to practitioners and others who for one reason or another need to acquaint themselves with the principles of equity.

While I have sought to set out and analyse the law as it presently exists in Ireland, this analysis extends to consideration of case law in other jurisdictions, particularly England, in areas where this is necessary to supplement our own developing jurisprudence. Indeed some aspects of equitable jurisdiction have yet to be considered adequately or at all here and in such instances I have endeavoured to provide an insight into approaches adopted elsewhere in the common law world. While a number of excellent English texts cover this area, particularly Hanbury and Martin's *Modern Equity*, since the book written by Mr Justice Ronan Keane on the subject, *Equity and the Law of Trusts in the Republic of Ireland* went out of print, there has been no text available dealing specifically with equity and the law of trusts in this jurisdiction. Although developments here have tended to a great extent to mirror those in England, this trend is far from universal and equitable principles as they exist in Ireland today differ in some important respects from those applied in other common law jurisdictions, e.g. in relation to secret trusts and trusts of family property.

A number of significant decisions have been handed down in areas covered by the text over the past year or so. In particular, the judgment of Keane J in *Re Worth Library* [1994] 1 ILRM 161 has provided a detailed and most useful overview of the general principles relating to charitable trusts and the exercise of cy-près jurisdiction. The scope of a trustee's powers of investment (*Stacey v. Branch* [1995] 2 ILRM 136) and the jurisdiction of our courts to grant Mareva injunctions, both on a domestic and extra-territorial basis (*Deutsche Bank Atkiengesellschaft v. Murtagh* [1995] 1 ILRM 381 and *Countyglen plc v. Carway* [1995] 1 ILRM 481), have also been addressed by the High Court in decisions delivered over the past year.

I have made every effort to include developments in this area up to 20 October 1995 although in some cases (e.g. the decision of Kinlen J in *Premier Dairies Ltd v. Doyle* (High Court 1995 No. 7008P, 29 September 1995) it was only possible to include a brief reference to this new material in a footnote. In addition, it should be noted that at the time of writing, judgment has been reserved by the Supreme Court in two important cases, *Lynch v. Burke* and

Bank of Ireland v. Smyth.

I would like to record my thanks to a number of individuals who have greatly assisted me at various stages in the preparation of this book. First, I would like to thank Michael Adams of Four Courts Press and Terri McDonnell and Eilis Maguire of Round Hall Sweet & Maxwell for their guidance and practical advice and expertise. I am also most grateful to Gilbert Gough for his trojan work in typesetting the book so quickly and efficiently and to Julitta Clancy for preparing the tables and index in such a professional and user friendly manner. In addition, I would like to thank my colleagues in the Law School, Trinity College, Dublin for their advice and support and the staff of the Berkeley Library at Trinity College for their assistance while I was researching the book.

I wish particularly to thank my colleague and friend Paul Coughlan who read a draft of the text and made many useful suggestions and Ruth Heard, who also read the manuscript and greatly assisted me in the unenviable and rather laborious task of proofreading. I am greatly indebted to them both and to my friends, particularly Niall, for their support and encouragement in what proved to be a rather more time-consuming project than I had perhaps envisaged!

Hilary Delany
20 October 1995

Preface to the Third Edition

While equity may be regarded by some people as an area of the law in which principles laid down long ago continue to apply, in reality it is an increasingly dynamic subject which has adapted to meet the changing needs of litigants. In the four years since the publication of the second edition of this book, there have been a number of significant decisions, particularly in England, which now justify a further edition.

While the number of decisions of real significance handed down in this jurisdiction during this time is relatively small, some merit mention. The decision of Barr J in *Kelly v. Cahill* [2001] 1 IR 56 illustrates that the 'new model constructive trust', now discarded in some other common law jurisdictions, continues to play a role here and the consideration given to the Rule in *Clayton's Case* which applies to tracing into a bank account by Laffoy J in *Re Money Markets International Stockbrokers Ltd* [1999] 4 IR 267 illustrates the willingness of our judiciary to reappraise traditional principles in this area. A number of significant judgments have also been delivered relating to the circumstances in which an interlocutory injunction may be granted particularly in an employment context (e.g *Moore v. Xnet Information Systems Ltd* [2002] 2 ILRM 278) and the circumstances in which an Anton Piller order and Bayer injunction will be granted were discussed in *Microsoft Corporation v. Brightpoint Ireland Ltd* [2001] 1 ILRM 540 and *O'Neill v. O'Keeffe* [2002] 2 IR 1 respectively. In addition, some useful *dicta* in relation to the circumstances in which specific performance may be granted of a contract for the sale of land are contained in the judgments of the Supreme Court in *Jodifern Ltd v. Fitzgerald* [2000] 3 IR 321 and *Supermacs Ireland Ltd v. Katesan (Naas) Ltd* [2000] 4 IR 273.

It is fair to say that there have been a considerable number of judgments delivered by the courts in England over the past few years which are of significance and it is useful to highlight some of them. The decisions of the House of Lords in *Foskett v. McKeown* [2001] 1 AC 102 and in *Royal Bank of Scotland v. Etridge (No. 2)* [2002] 2 AC 773 are of real importance in the context of tracing and undue influence respectively, as is the decision in *Twinsectra Ltd v. Yardley* [2002] 2 AC 164 which develops the principles relating to the imposition of a constructive trust on a stranger who has assisted in the misappropriation of trust property. A number of decisions of the Court of Appeal are also noteworthy; *Pennington v. Waine* [2002] 1 WLR 2075 (constitution of trusts); *Bank of Credit and Commerce International (Overseas) Ltd v. Akindele* [2001] Ch 437 (knowing receipt of trust property) *Yaxley v. Gotts* (constructive trusts/proprietary estoppel) and *Gillett v. Holt* [2001] Ch 211 and *Jennings v. Rice* [2002] EWCA Civ 159 (proprietary estoppel). The controversial decision of the Court of Appeal in *Great Peace Shipping Ltd v. Tsavliris Salvage (International) Ltd* [2002] 3 WLR 1617 is also examined, and if not reversed in the future by the House of Lords, it may have implications for equitable jurisdiction generally and not just in relation to rescission of a contract on grounds of mistake.

I would like to thank a number of people who have helped me in various ways in the preparation of this new edition. First, I would like to thank the staff at Round Hall Sweet and Maxwell and in particular Terri McDonnell and Catherine Dolan. I would also like to express my appreciation to Gilbert Gough who as ever did a superb job of typesetting and to Nessa Cahill who read the text in proof form. Finally, I would particularly like to thank Patricia Brazil who compiled the tables and index in addition to proofreading the text; I am greatly indebted to her.

I have endeavoured to state the law as of 1 May 2003.

Hilary Delany
1 May 2003

Contents

Table of Contents

CHAPTER 3 TRUSTS — AN INTRODUCTION

CHAPTER 4 TRUSTS — FORMALITIES AND ESSENTIAL ELEMENTS

CHAPTER 5 SECRET TRUSTS

CHAPTER 6 CONSTITUTION OF TRUSTS

CHAPTER 7 RESULTING TRUSTS

CHAPTER 8 CONSTRUCTIVE TRUSTS

CHAPTER 9 PURPOSE TRUSTS

CHAPTER 10 CHARITABLE TRUSTS

CHAPTER 11 VOID AND VOIDABLE TRUSTS

CHAPTER 12 THE ADMINISTRATION OF TRUSTS

CHAPTER 13 INJUNCTIONS

CHAPTER 14 SPECIFIC PERFORMANCE

CHAPTER 15 RECTIFICATION

CHAPTER 16 RESCISSION

CHAPTER 17 EQUITABLE ESTOPPEL

CHAPTER 18 TRACING

CHAPTER 19 EQUITABLE DOCTRINES

Table of Cases

Other Tables

Constitutution

Table of Statutes

Table of Statutory Instruments

Table of European Legislation

Table of European Conventions

CHAPTER 1

Introduction

GENERAL PRINCIPLES

Equity can be described as the branch of the law administered by the Court of Chancery prior to the enactment of the Judicature (Ireland) Act 1877 and is the body of principles which evolved with the aim of mitigating the severity of the rules of the common law. The original objective of the Court of Chancery which operated as a 'court of conscience' was to achieve a fair and equitable result in all cases which came before it and the principles which it developed became known as 'equity'. The court sought to avoid the injustice which might result from a strict application of the common law[1] and to provide a remedy where an existing one might be inappropriate or even lacking altogether.[2]

While equitable jurisdiction developed as a means of mitigating the harshness of the common law, it is important to stress that it is still dependent on the existence of the framework which the common law provides. Equity is essentially a supplementary and fragmentary jurisdiction and as Maitland[3] has suggested it should be regarded as a gloss added to the common law and statute law, rather than as an independent system.[4] More recently Kenny J spoke in similar terms in the course of his judgment in *Hynes Ltd v. Independent Newspapers*[5] and referred to equity as being 'a gloss on or an improvement and reform of the common law'. For this reason it is difficult to define its scope and a more useful exercise is to point out the main areas in which equity operates today. However, it should be stressed that equity plays a role

---

1. As Lord Denning MR commented in *Crabb v. Arun District Council* [1976] Ch 179, 187: 'Equity comes in true to form, to mitigate the rigours of strict law.'
2. As Sir Anthony Mason, the former Chief Justice of Australia has commented, writing extra-judicially, 'equitable principles were shaped with a view to inhibiting unconscientious conduct and providing for relief against it.' (1997-98) 8 KCLJ 1.
3. *Lectures on Equity* Lecture II. See also the comment of Lord Evershed MR to the effect that 'equity never denied the existence of the legal right. It said that the legal position was not the whole position, and added something to it.' (1954) 70 LQR 326, 329.
4. As Kiely states in *Principles of Equity as Applied in Ireland* (1936) p.7 'If a conglomeration of miscellaneous rules can be called a system then it is such'.
5. [1980] IR 204, 218.

in a wide range of different situations and it would not be possible to delimit these in a fully comprehensive manner. Lord Upjohn's statement in the course of his speech in *Boardman v. Phipps*[6] should also be borne in mind, namely that: 'Rules of equity have to be applied to such a great diversity of circumstances that they can be stated only in the most general terms.'

One of the most enduring and still one of its most important creations is the trust, which is the relationship which arises whenever a person, called a trustee, is compelled in equity to hold property for the benefit of some person or persons, termed beneficiaries, or for some object permitted by law, in such a way that the real benefit accrues, not to the trustee, but to the beneficiaries or other objects of the trust.[7] This device is still of enormous practical significance today, particularly in view of the wide-ranging nature of taxation statutes and the desire to avoid or postpone their application whenever this is legally possible. The other area in which the influence of equity can be seen most clearly is in relation to the grant of equitable remedies such as injunctions and specific performance. Such remedies which are discretionary in nature continue to play an important role in increasingly diverse areas of the law.

One of the hallmarks of equitable jurisdiction is that it is discretionary in nature, as Black LJ made clear in *Conlon v. Murray*[8] in relation to the remedy of specific performance, although his comments could be interpreted as being of more general application: 'This discretion is not, of course, the arbitrary discretion of the individual judge but is a discretion to be exercised on the principles which have been worked out in a multitude of decided cases'. Similar sentiments were expressed by Greene MR in *Re Diplock*[9] where he said that 'if [a] claim in equity exists, it must be shown to have an ancestry, founded in history and in the practice and precedents of courts administering equity jurisdiction.' To ensure that equitable jurisdiction is not exercised in an arbitrary and unfair manner the courts must strive to reconcile the conflicting aims of achieving justice in an individual case and ensuring an element of consistency in decision making. It could be argued that the very nature of equitable jurisdiction lends credence to the belief that there is some concept of fairness in equity which renders precedent superfluous. The temptation to seek to do justice in an individual case may be great, but as Lord Evershed has pointed out, 'there is, I venture to think, great danger in practice in what is, in truth, palm tree justice'.[10] He is correct to the extent that the principles of certainty and consistency form an integral part of the fair administration of

---

6. [1967] 2 AC 46, 123.
7. See Keeton and Sheridan, *The Law of Trusts* (12th ed., 1993) p. 3 and *infra*, Chapter 3.
8. [1958] NI 17, 25. See also the *dicta* of O'Higgins CJ in *Smelter Corporation v. O'Driscoll* [1977] IR 305, 310–311.
9. [1948] Ch 465, 481–482.
10. (1954) 70 LQR 326, 329. See Halliwell (1994) 14 LS 15, 17.

justice and the sacrificing of settled principles and precedents in specific cases to meet the demands of justice in the name of equity would result ultimately in the development of an arbitrary and therefore unfair legal system.

Another important aspect of the overall development of equity, although it may have been lacking at certain stages of its development, is that equitable principles have been 'altered, improved, and refined from time to time'.[11] Certain areas, such as constructive trusts and the equitable remedy of tracing, have developed considerably in significance over recent decades and are both now of primary importance as devices to combat increasingly sophisticated transnational fraud. The extent to which equity itself is still developing is a less straightforward question to answer. Although there have been signs of judicial willingness to extend the reach of existing doctrines in some areas,[12] in others there has been a marked reluctance to do so.[13]

Article 73 of the Irish Free State Constitution and Article 50 of the Constitution of Ireland 1937 made provision for the carrying forward of existing laws to the extent to which they were not inconsistent with these Constitutions and the practice has been to treat the established principles of equity as being applicable in our courts. It is fair to say that since the foundation of the State the attitude of the judiciary in this jurisdiction has generally been to follow the approach adopted by their counterparts in England — although there have been notable exceptions to this principle[14] — and equity as it exists in Ireland today plays an ever-increasing role across a broad range of activities, including commercial ones.

As Sir Peter Millett[15] has commented in an important recent article on the way forward for equity in England: 'It can no longer be doubted that equity has moved out of the family home[16] and the settled estate and into the marketplace' and in his view 'the intervention of equity in commercial transactions, long resisted by common lawyers, can no longer be withstood'. However, it is also fair to say that while the circumstances in which equity intervenes are changing and developing, the underlying rationale for its intervention remains essentially the same. Millett usefully summarizes the basis for equity's role as follows:

---

11. *Re Hallett's Estate* (1880) 13 Ch D 696, 710 *per* Jessel MR.
12. *H.K.N. Invest Oy v. Incotrade Pvt Ltd* [1993] 3 IR 152.
13. See e.g. the attitude of the Supreme Court in *L. v. L.* [1992] 2 IR 77 in relation to extending the reach of the purchase money resulting trust.
14. E.g. in relation to half secret trusts (Chapter 5) and the division of family property (Chapter 7).
15. At the time a Lord Justice of Appeal in England, writing extra-judicially. See (1995) 9 Trust Law Int 35.
16. However, it should be noted that equity still plays an important role in resolving property disputes between co-habitees, between spouses and third parties e.g. financial institutions and between spouses outside the context of separation and divorce proceedings. See further Chapter 7.

The traditional objects of equity have not changed: to relieve against mistake, fraud, accident and surprise; to protect the weak from exploitation and trust and confidence from betrayal; to prevent the unconscionable assertion of legal rights; and to give relief against every kind of unconscionable conduct. It demands not merely honesty and a willingness to meet one's commitments, but integrity, good conscience and fidelity.[17]

HISTORICAL BACKGROUND

The 13th century saw considerable progress being made in the development of the common law in England. However, by the end of that century it had grown into a rigid set of principles which were slow to adapt to meet the needs of a developing system of justice and hardship frequently arose as a result. A number of major defects had become apparent, principally that under the common law, many wrongs could not be remedied. An injured party could only bring an action at common law if his claim came within a recognised form of writ. To compound this difficulty, the *in consimili causa* clause in the Statute of Westminster II 1285 was interpreted very restrictively and was confined to varying the form of existing writs.

In addition, even where a remedy was available, it was frequently inappropriate or inadequate. The only remedy available at common law was damages and orders which are of such importance in our modern system of justice, such as specific performance and injunctions, were unknown. A defendant might also suffer because a plaintiff might be entitled to a judgment at common law regardless of mitigating factors which would be relevant to the exercise of equitable jurisdiction as we know it today. A further shortcoming of the common law system as it existed at the end of the thirteenth century was its numerous procedural defects and inadequacies. Often a defendant might not be allowed to give evidence or a jury might be subject to outside influences.

As a result of these defects in the system a practice developed of petitioning the king in situations where a litigant complained that he could not obtain an adequate remedy within the framework of the common law. The Lord Chancellor was the officer responsible for overseeing such matters and as the number of petitions increased, the king delegated his functions to the chancellor with the direction that a petitioner should be given a legal remedy if a litigant was entitled to one and where none existed, to give such a remedy as would be just. As the number of petitions increased, the chancellor and his office took on the role of a court which became known as the Court of Chancery.

---

17. (1995) 9 Trust Law Int 35, 36–37.

The office of Lord Chancellor of Ireland was created in the early thirteenth century,[18] although it should be pointed out that until the seventeenth century Brehon law tended to prevail outside the settled areas in the country. The early chancellors in both jurisdictions were predominantly ecclesiastics and many of the principles which date from this time have their origins in canon law or, to a lesser extent, in Roman law. During the Middle Ages, the Irish parliament seems to have played a significant role in exercising equity jurisdiction and it was not until the sixteenth century that the Lord Chancellor of Ireland started to play a meaningful role in dispensing justice on the basis of equitable principles.

The Court of Chancery never sought to deny a litigant's legal rights but rather aimed to ensure that such rights were not exercised in a manner which would cause undue prejudice to the other party or bring about an unjust or inequitable result to a dispute. The court began to issue injunctions to restrain a party from exercising his legal rights, a practice which effectively curtailed the authority of the common law courts. This caused increasing ill-feeling and matters came to a head during the reign of James I in the *Earl of Oxford's Case*[19] when a bitter dispute about the validity of these 'common injunctions' between the Chief Justice of England, Edward Coke and the Lord Chancellor, Lord Ellesmere, was resolved in favour of the Court of Chancery.

While in theory the early chancellors acted on a number of settled principles in granting or refusing relief, there was little uniformity in the judgments handed down and the types of remedies varied from one chancellor to the next. By the beginning of the 17th century the chancellors were generally common lawyers, rather than ecclesiastics and while the court of chancery remained a 'court of conscience', a system of precedent did begin to develop. Much of this systemisation took place from the time of the chancellorship of Lord Nottingham (1673–1682), sometimes referred to as the 'Father of Equity',[20] until the time of Lord Eldon (1801–1806 and 1807–1827). However, the price of systemisation was that by the beginning of the nineteenth century, the principles of equity were nearly as rigid as the common law rules. As Lord Eldon commented in *Gee v. Pritchard:*[21] 'Nothing would inflict on me greater pain, in quitting this place [the office of chancellor] than the recollection that I had done any thing to justify the reproach that the equity of this Court

---

18. There is some dispute about the identity and the date of appointment of the first Lord Chancellor. Kiely suggests in *Principles of Equity as Applied In Ireland* (1936) p. 6 that it was John de Worchley appointed in 1219, but other commentators suggest that it was Ralph Neville, appointed in 1232. See Hand (1970) Ir Jur (ns) 291; Ball, *The Judges in Ireland* (1926) pp. 6-7; Wylie, *Irish Land Law* (3rd ed., 1997) p. 84 and Keane, *Equity and the Law of Trusts in the Republic of Ireland* (1988) p.13.
19. (1615) 1 Rep Ch 1. See Baker (1969) 4 Ir Jur (ns) 368.
20. *Kemp v. Kemp* (1801) 5 Ves 849, 858 *per* Arden MR.
21. (1818) 2 Swans 402, 414.

varies like the Chancellor's foot.'[22] A further difficulty which had come to the fore by this time was the inconvenience of the fact that two distinct court systems had developed, each applying its own often inconsistent principles. Reforms aimed at tackling this problem were begun in the mid-nineteenth century. In 1856 the Common Law Procedure Amendment Act, Ireland,[23] was passed which gave the common law courts power to grant equitable remedies in limited situations. Subsequently the Chancery Amendment Act 1858 (Lord Cairns' Act) gave the Court of Chancery power to award the common law remedy of damages either in substitution for or in addition to an injunction or a decree for specific performance.

A major reform of the system of the administration of justice was effected in England by the Supreme Court of Judicature Acts 1873 and 1875 (followed in Ireland by the Supreme Court of Judicature (Ireland) Act 1877) which established one Supreme Court of Judicature and replaced the system of separate courts exercising common law and equitable jurisdiction.[24] This court had two divisions, the High Court of Justice, which possessed both original and appellate jurisdiction and the Court of Appeal which exercised a purely appellate function. The High Court itself was initially divided into five divisions — Chancery, Queen's Bench, Common Pleas, Exchequer and Probate and Matrimonial. In 1887 the Common Pleas Division was merged with the Queen's Bench and in 1897 so were the Exchequer and Probate and Matrimonial Divisions so that by the end of the century, only the Chancery and Queen's Bench Divisions remained.

Palles CB summarised the effect of the Judicature Act as follows in *Barber v. Houston*,[25] a decision of the Exchequer Division:

> The same system of Jurisprudence now prevails in all Divisions of the High Court; and if, upon the facts pleaded, the Plaintiff could, before the Judicature Act, have had in Equity the relief which he seeks in this action, he is now entitled to it in this Court. That Act changed forms of procedure, but did not alter rights or remedies.

The fusion of the administration of legal and equitable jurisdiction was continued with the enactment of the Courts of Justice Act 1924 which established a High Court and Supreme Court to take the place of the Supreme

---

22. Note that in *Taylor v. Dickens* [1998] 1 FLR 806, 820 Judge Weeks in rejecting the suggestion that the court might intervene merely because the assertion of strict legal rights was unconscionable, commented that if it were to do so, 'the days of justice varying with the size of the Lord Chancellor's foot would have returned.'
23. The equivalent legislation in England was the Common Law Procedure Act 1854.
24. See the comments of Palles CB in *Antrim County Land, Building and Investment Co. Ltd v. Stewart* [1904] 2 IR 357, 364.
25. (1884) 14 LR Ir 273, 276.

Court of Judicature and this structure was continued by the Courts (Establishment and Constitution) Act 1961. However, as Kiely[26] has stated: 'The intrinsic difference between legal and equitable rights and remedies remains unaffected'.

One issue which was bound to lead to difficulties in practice was how this new court system was to deal with any potential conflict between legal and equitable principles. Section 28(11) of the Supreme Court of Judicature (Ireland) Act 1877 addressed this problem by providing that where any conflict arose between the rules of equity and common law that the equitable rule was to prevail. An illustration of how this provision operated in practice is provided by the decision of the English Court of Appeal in *Walsh v. Lonsdale*.[27] The defendant landlord agreed in writing to grant the plaintiff a lease of a mill for seven years although no deed was executed as required by law. The agreement provided that the rent would be paid quarterly in arrears but that a year's rent would be payable in advance if demanded. The plaintiff tenant fell into arrears; the defendant demanded a year's rent in advance and when the plaintiff refused to pay, purported to exercise a right of distress. The plaintiff claimed an injunction and damages for illegal distress but the action failed. At law, the distress would have been illegal, as there was no deed in relation to the seven year lease[28] and the yearly legal tenancy which had arisen because of the entering into possession and the payment of rent by the plaintiff would not have permitted the landlord to demand the payment of a year's rent in advance. However, in equity the agreement for the lease was treated as being as good as a lease and the Court of Appeal, in reliance on section 28(11), which required that in the event of conflict, the equitable rule must prevail, held that the distress was lawful. As Jessel MR stated: 'There are not two estates as there were formerly, one estate at common law by reason of the payment of rent from year to year and an estate in equity under the agreement. There is only one court and equity rules prevail in it.'[29]

FUSION OF LAW AND EQUITY — A PROCEDURAL FUSION ONLY?

The generally accepted opinion at the time of the enactment of the Judicature Acts was that the result of the legislation was to effect a fusion of administration

---

26. *Principles of Equity as Applied in Ireland* (1936) p.9.
27. (1882) 21 Ch D 9. In this case the equivalent provision, s.25(11) of the Supreme Court of Judicature Act 1873, was at issue. See Sparkes (1988) 8 OJLS 350.
28. S. 1 of the Statute of Frauds 1677 as amended by s. 3 of the Real Property Act 1845 provided that a lease for a period of time greater than three years would be void unless it was executed by deed.
29. (1882) 21 Ch D 9, 14.

rather than a fusion of the principles of the common law and equity. Jessel MR remarked in *Salt v. Cooper*[30] in relation to this issue: 'but it was not any fusion, or anything of the kind, it was the vesting in one tribunal the administration of law and equity in every cause, action or dispute which should come before that tribunal.' Similarly, Ashburner[31] has commented: '[t]he two streams of jurisdiction, though they run in the same channel, run side by side and do not mingle their waters.' This view is also well summarised by Delany[32] in the following terms:

> The Judicature Acts fused the courts of law and equity; they created a substantially uniform system of procedure and pleading; and they provided that in case of 'conflict or variance' the rules of equity should prevail. But there was nothing more than a fusion of jurisdiction, procedure and pleading; the substantive rules themselves remained.

While the development of common law rules since the enactment of the Judicature Acts have in some instances been influenced by equitable principles, there is no doubt that the distinctions between legal and equitable rights and remedies remain today. For example, to obtain an equitable remedy a litigant must rely on the court's discretion whereas if he seeks a common law remedy, once he has established that a right existing at common law has been breached, a remedy will be granted. In recent decades there has undoubtedly been greater interaction in this area and it has been accepted that a legal remedy may be given for breach of an equitable right, as in *Seager v. Copydex Ltd*[33] in which damages were assessed in respect of a breach of confidence, which is a right protected by equity. However, as a general rule the courts in England have been reluctant to apply this principle, as in *Metall und Rohstoff AG v. Donaldson Lufkin & Jenrette Inc*[34] in which the Court of Appeal held that damages could not be awarded for a breach of trust. This reluctance has not been evident in some other common law jurisdictions, particularly New Zealand, where damages have been awarded in respect of breach of confidence[35] and breach of fiduciary duty.[36] This more radical view is well

---

30. (1880) 16 Ch D 544, 549. See also *Joseph v. Lyons* (1884) 15 QBD 280.
31. *Principles of Equity* (2nd ed., 1933) p.18.
32. (1961) 24 MLR 116, 117. Delany referred to Maitland's point that equity is not a self sufficient system in itself and presupposes the existence of the common law. He stressed that the so called 'fusion' effected by the Judicature Acts has not reduced the dependence of equity on the common law. See also the comments of Baker in (1977) 93 LQR 529, 531 that 'we may . . . conclude that it was the intention of the Judicature Acts to preserve the distinction between the rules of law and equity'.
33. [1967] 1 WLR 923.
34. [1990] 1 QB 391, 473.
35. *Attorney General for the United Kingdom v. Wellington Newspapers Ltd* [1988] 1 NZLR 129; *Aquaculture Corporation v. New Zealand Green Mussel Co. Ltd* [1990] 3

summarised by the comments of Cooke P in *Attorney General for the United Kingdom v. Wellington Newspapers Ltd*:[37]

> As law and equity are now mingled … it does not seem to me to matter whether the duty be classified as equitable or not. The full range of remedies deriving historically from either common law or equity should be available.

Such an expansive approach would tend to suggest that the fusion effected by the Judicature Acts was more than merely procedural in nature and that the systems of law and equity themselves have merged as a result. This view was put forward by the House of Lords, and particularly forcefully by Lord Diplock, in *United Scientific Holdings Ltd v. Burnley Borough Council*[38] in which the essential issue was whether a landlord who had failed to adhere strictly to the time requirements laid down by a rent review clause should be deprived of the right to increase the rent. The Supreme Court of Judicature Act provided that stipulations in contracts which would have been deemed to be of the essence in a court of equity prior to the enactment of the legislation should henceforth receive that construction in all courts. The lessee argued that as this question had not arisen prior to this, the relevant section[39] could not apply and that time was of the essence. The House of Lords held that the position prior to the enactment of the legislation was not of relevance and that since then a fusion of the rules of law and equity had occurred. It therefore held that the council was entitled to invoke the rent review provisions notwithstanding the fact that the time limits prescribed had expired as time was not normally of the essence under the rules of equity.

In reaching this conclusion Lord Diplock stated that Ashburner's metaphor has become 'both mischievous and deceptive' and if that 'fluvial metaphor is to be retained at all, the waters of the confluent streams of law and equity have surely mingled now'.[40] In his view as a result of the Judicature Acts 'the two systems of substantive and adjectival law formerly administered by courts of law and courts of chancery … were fused.'[41]

NZLR 299. See also the Canadian decision of *Lac Minerals Ltd v. International Corona Resources Ltd* (1989) 61 DLR (4th) 14.

36. *Day v. Mead* [1987] 2 NZLR 443; *Mouat v. Clarke Boyce* [1992] 2 NZLR 559.
37. [1988] 1 NZLR 129, 172. See also his comments in *Day v. Mead* [1987] 2 NZLR 443, 451.
38. [1978] AC 904.
39. S.25(7) of the Supreme Court of Judicature Act 1873. The equivalent provision under the Supreme Court of Judicature (Ireland) Act 1877 was s. 28(7).
40. [1978] AC 904, 925. See also the comments of Lord Denning MR in *Federal Commerce & Navigation Co Ltd v. Molena Alpha Inc* [1978] QB 927, 974.
41. *Ibid*. See also the speeches of Lord Simon at 944–945 and of Lord Fraser at 957–958.

The finding in this case appears to have been applied by a number of the members of the Supreme Court in *Hynes Ltd v. Independent Newspapers Ltd.*[42] The question at issue was a similar one, namely whether time was of the essence with regard to a rent review provision in a contract. The Supreme Court held that if the time stipulation would not have been deemed to be of the essence of the contract in a court of equity prior to the enactment of the Judicature Act then it would still receive the same construction. As there were no grounds for implying a term that time was of the essence, the plaintiff tenant's appeal against the validity of the late service of a rent review notice was disallowed. O'Higgins CJ stated that in Ireland 'the fusion of common law and equitable rules ... initiated by the Supreme Court of Judicature Act (Ireland) 1877 . . . was completed by the Courts of Justice Act 1924 and the Courts (Establishment and Constitution) Act 1961.'[43] Kenny J also spoke in terms of the decision of the House of Lords in *United Scientific* as being the 'restoration of a fundamental equitable principle which, unfortunately, has tended to be ignored in many recent decisions.'[44]

However, it would be a mistake to read too much into these comments. Coughlan[45] points out that the statement of O'Higgins CJ quoted above, in which he refers to the legal basis for the existing court structure, may suggest that he was referring instead 'to the uncontroversial principle of procedural fusion'. Keane comments that the opinions expressed by the Law Lords in *United Scientific* must be regarded as *obiter*[46] and argues that it would be unwise to assume that *Hynes* indicates that these views have necessarily been accepted in this jurisdiction.

The better view would certainly seem to be that the substantive distinctions between the two systems of law and equity are still valid and there have been signs of this approach being reasserted recently in England.[47] So, in *Downsview Nominees Ltd v. First City Corporation Ltd*[48] the Privy Council refused to replace or supplement the equitable duties of a mortgagee and a receiver

---

42. [1980] IR 204.
43. *Ibid.* at 216.
44. *Ibid.* at 221.
45. *Property Law* (2nd ed., 1998) p. 49.
46. *Equity and the Law of Trusts in the Republic of Ireland* (1988) p.25. Keane suggests that until the question is unequivocally resolved, the views expressed 'are most safely regarded as in the nature of premature funeral orations'.
47. *Bank of Boston Connecticut v. European Grain and Shipping Ltd* [1989] 1 All ER 545, 557 *per* Lord Brandon. Although it has been argued by Duggan that 'contrary to the new equity rhetoric' there is no sharp difference in values between equity and the common law, see (1997) 113 LQR 601, 603.
48. [1993] AC 295. See also the *dicta* of Lord Browne-Wilkinson in *Target Holdings Ltd v. Redferns* [1996] AC 421, 434 who, in considering the principles relating to equitable compensation for breach of a traditional trust, stated that the common law rules of remoteness of damage and causation do not apply in this context, although he did not concede that 'the principles underlying both systems are the same' (at 432).

appointed by him by liability in negligence, holding that such a result would lead to 'confusion and injustice'.[49] Similar reluctance to apply the principle of substantive fusion can be discerned from the approach of the House of Lords in *Lord Napier and Ettrick v. Hunter*,[50] in which Lord Goff stated that he could see no 'justification for sweeping the line of equity cases under the carpet as though it did not exist'.[51] In addition, in *Tinsley v. Milligan*,[52] Lord Browne-Wilkinson although he spoke of the fusion of law and equity[53] seemed to rely on common law and equitable principles which had developed side by side. This approach is also borne out by the *dicta* of Rimer J in *Clarion Ltd v. National Provident Institution*,[54] who, in commenting on the type of mistake which will entitle a party to a contract to avoid it described this as 'an area of law in which even by the end of the twentieth century there has been little merging of the streams of common law and equity'.

Millett[55] has quite rightly suggested that the opinion that the Judicature Acts had the effect of fusing law and equity to the extent that they have become a single body of law rather than two separate systems of law administered together has been widely discredited, both in England and Australia.[56] In

---

49. *Ibid.* at 316. However, it should be noted that in *Medforth v. Blake* [2000] Ch 86 Scott VC held that a receiver managing mortgaged property not only owed a duty to the mortgagor to exercise his powers in good faith and for proper purposes but also owed a duty to manage the mortgaged property with due diligence, which he characterized as an equitable duty of care. This approach avoided the objections to imposing liability in negligence based on the fusion fallacy argument, but the view has also been put forward that 'a self standing equitable duty of care remediable in damages is a novelty – surely tort masquerading under a false label', see Sealy [2000] CLJ 31, 33. See also Frisby (2000) 63 MLR 413.
50. [1993] AC 713.
51. *Ibid.* at 59. Although the language employed by Lord Browne-Wilkinson who spoke in terms of 'the fusion of law and equity' (at 65, 66) might have suggested support for the alternative approach, the conclusion which he reached did not.
52. [1994] 1 AC 340.
53. *Ibid.* at 147, 151. Although note that this first reference appears in the All England Reports as 'the fusion of the administration of law and equity', see [1993] 3 All ER 65, 86.
54. [2000] 1 WLR 1888, 1898.
55. (1995) 9 Trust Law Int 35, 37.
56. See Mason (1994) 110 LQR 238. Mason also warns that over-concentration on the effect of the Judicature Acts is likely to result in undue emphasis being placed on the state of equitable doctrine as it existed at the time of their enactment. Similarly Millett asserts that not only did the Judicature Acts not fuse law and equity, 'they did not freeze them in their then state of development either'. See (1995) 9 Trust Law Int 35, 37. Note that while the 'mingled' doctrine has been favoured by some judges in New Zealand (see the *dicta* of Thomas J in *Powell v. Thompson* [1991] 1 NZLR 597, 615 where he spoke of the 'happy mingling of law and equity') this approach has been far from universal in that jurisdiction, see the *dicta* of Wylie J in *Equiticorp Industries Group Ltd v. Hawkins* [1991] 3 NZLR 700, 727. A more balanced view is that following put forward by Somers J in *Elders Pastoral Ltd v. Bank of New Zealand* [1989] 2

reviewing the recent English decisions, Martin[57] argues that the view that flexibility and capacity for development is best achieved by disregarding the legal or equitable origins of causes of action, remedies or defences is misconceived. She asserts that it does not seem that the fusion fallacy evidenced in cases such as *United Scientific* has become established in England; on the contrary she claims that there has been a return to orthodoxy. In her view, this is apparent from recent decisions of the House of Lords in *Napier* and *Tinsley* which, she says, contain 'meticulous analyses of the separate common law and equitable origins and principles' in the areas concerned. Hanbury and Martin's[58] concluding comments on this subject probably come closest to summing up the existing position:

> What can be said is that a century of fused jurisdiction has seen the two systems working more closely together; each changing and developing and improving from contact with the other; and each willing to accept new ideas and developments, regardless of their origin. They are coming closer together. <u>But they are not yet fused.</u>

NZLR 180, 193: 'Neither law nor equity is now stifled by its origin and the fact that both are administered by one court has inevitably meant that each has borrowed from the other in furthering the harmonious development of the law as a whole'.
57. [1994] Conv 13.
58. *Modern Equity* (16th ed., 2001) p. 26.

CHAPTER 2

Maxims of Equity

INTRODUCTION

The maxims of equity constitute the general principles developed by the Court of Chancery over the years; as Mason CJ stated in *Corin v. Patton*[1] an equitable maxim is 'a summary statement of a broad theme which underlies equitable concepts and principles'. While they are not to be interpreted as positive rules of law which should always be applied in their literal sense, they do reflect general trends which can be discerned from the manner in which the equitable jurisdiction of the courts has been exercised. It is important to realize that some of these maxims overlap or may even appear to contradict one another and they should be treated with a certain degree of caution. Nevertheless a brief examination of the maxims and what they mean in practice provides a useful introduction to the manner in which equity operates.

EQUITY WILL NOT SUFFER A WRONG TO BE WITHOUT A REMEDY

The principle which lies behind this maxim is that equity will intervene to protect a recognised right which for some reason is not enforceable at common law and it reflects the basis for the origins of the equitable jurisdiction of the chancellor. However, as equitable jurisdiction became more established, it also grew increasingly formalised and based on precedent. As Greene MR commented in *Re Diplock*:[2] 'if a claim in equity exists it must be shown to have an ancestry founded in history and in the practice and precedents of the courts administering equity jurisdiction'.

Textbook writers have pointed out that this maxim should be treated with considerable caution today; Wylie[3] has commented that 'it is a grossly inaccurate statement of equity's approach in modern times' and Meagher, Gummow and Lehane[4] stress that it is misleading unless one realises that the

---

1. (1990) 169 CLR 540, 557.
2. [1948] Ch 465, 481–482.
3. *Irish Land Law* (3rd ed., 1997) p. 121.
4. *Equity Doctrines and Remedies* (3rd ed., 1992) p. 71.

maxim is now of 'purely historical importance'. It should also be made clear
at the outset that in this context the word 'wrong' refers to conduct contrary
to the law rather than simply immoral.

Despite its potentially misleading nature, there are nevertheless some
important practical illustrations of the operation of the maxim which can still
be seen today. Perhaps the most far-reaching of these is the recognition given
by equity to the concept of the trust by virtue of which a beneficiary can
enforce equitable rights which the common law would not recognise, as it
simply regarded the trustee as the legal owner. Other notable illustrations of
the maxim can be found in relation to the grant of equitable remedies. The
injunction developed as a means of achieving justice where the common law
remedy of damages could not provide an adequate remedy and will now issue
e.g. to restrain an ongoing nuisance[5] or in *quia timet* form to prevent a
threatened wrong from occurring.[6] Similarly, where specific performance of
a contract for the sale of land is sought, it can be granted despite non-
compliance with the necessary statutory formalities provided sufficient acts
of part performance can be established.[7] Another illustration is the appointment
of a receiver by way of equitable execution which can operate where a creditor
is unable to levy execution at law owing to the equitable nature of the property
concerned.

Despite the frequency with which the above illustrations of the maxim
occur in practice, it would be fair to say that more recent attempts to develop
the principle that equity will not suffer a wrong to be without a remedy have
proved less successful. As Lindley LJ commented in *Holmes v. Millage*:[8] 'It
is an old mistake to suppose that, because there is no effectual remedy at law,
there must be one in equity'. A classic example of how an attempt to develop
a new form of equitable relief has met with mixed fortunes is provided by the
new model constructive trust,[9] a creature first devised by Lord Denning to be
imposed 'whenever justice and good conscience require it'.[10] Maudsley[11]
criticised this development saying that it was possible to read into the decisions
the principle that 'in cases in which the plaintiff ought to win, but has no legal
doctrine or authority to support him, a constructive trust in his favour will do
the trick.' More recent judgments in England show a considerable retrenchment
from the position laid down in the early decisions[12] and it has been rejected

---

5. *Patterson v. Murphy* [1978] ILRM 85; *Kennaway v. Thompson* [1981] QB 88.
6. *Whelan v. Madigan* [1978] ILRM 136.
7. *Lowry v. Reid* [1927] NI 142.
8. [1893] 1 QB 551, 555.
9. See *infra* Chapter 8.
10. *Hussey v. Palmer* [1972] 1 WLR 1286, 1290. See also *N.A.D. v. T.D.* [1985] ILRM
    153, 160.
11. (1977) 28 NILQ 123. See also Oakley (1973) 26 CLP 17, 39.
12. E.g. *Ashburn Anstalt v. Arnold* [1988] 2 WLR 706.

outright in some common law jurisdictions.[13] While there is still evidence of its existence in this jurisdiction,[14] there is certainly no sign of any wholesale adoption of Lord Denning's constructive trust of a 'new model'.

There is also evidence of a reluctance to further extend existing equitable devices for achieving justice between parties which is well illustrated by examining the concept of the purchase money resulting trust and the manner in which it has been used to confer interests in the family home. This type of trust has traditionally been employed to give relief to a party who has no legal interest in the property but has nevertheless contributed financially either directly or indirectly to its purchase. When the Supreme Court was faced with the argument in *L. v. L.*[15] that contributions of a non-financial kind, such as work in the home, should also give rise to a resulting trust, it declined to accept this proposition on the basis that such a step would involve the creation of an entirely new right and instead decided that the issue was one for the legislature.

EQUITY FOLLOWS THE LAW

This maxim might be more accurately stated as: 'Equity follows the law, but not slavishly nor always'[16] and it would be inaccurate to interpret it too strictly. It would be fair to say that although equity does not seek to question the existence of legal rights it will attempt to mitigate the often harsh results caused by their strict enforcement. Equity restricted or modified the application of common law principles where it was in the interests of fairness to do so. A classic illustration of this modification is the principle that equity will not allow a statute to be used as an instrument of fraud.[17] So, for example, equity would not permit a beneficiary to be deprived of an interest in land under the terms of a trust where this would amount to fraud even if there was insufficient compliance with the requisite statutory formalities,[18] provided that there was some other evidence to establish the nature of his interest.[19] Equally, equity would recognise the existence of secret or half secret trusts[20] by waiving the

---

13. E.g. in Australia, *Muschinski v. Dodds* (1985) 160 CLR 583, 615.
14. *H.K.N. Invest Oy v. Incotrade Pvt Ltd* [1993] 3 IR 152; *Kelly v. Cahill* [2000] 1 IR 56.
15. [1992] 2 IR 77.
16. *Graf v. Hope Building Corporation* (1930) 254 NY 1, 9 *per* Cardozo CJ.
17. *McCormick v. Grogan* (1869) LR 4 HL 82, 97 *per* Lord Westbury. See further Chapter 4.
18. S.4 of the Statute of Frauds (Ireland) 1695 requires that express trusts of land be evidenced in writing and signed by a person able to declare the trust, or by his will.
19. *Rochefoucauld v. Boustead* [1897] 1 Ch 196; *McGillycuddy v. Joy* [1959] IR 189; *Gilmurray v. Corr* [1978] NI 99.
20. See *infra* Chapter 5.

requirement of strict compliance with the necessary testamentary formalities in the interests of preventing fraud.[21]

Having referred briefly to some of the equitable modifications to common law principles, it should be pointed out that in numerous situations, equity does indeed follow the law and as a general principle, equitable interests in land correspond with legal estates and interests.[22] This point is well illustrated by the manner in which equity tends to follow the law in relation to executed as opposed to executory trusts. These expressions refer to the creation of a trust and not to its performance. A trust is said to be executed where the settlor has specified precisely the limits under which the trust property is to be held and where no further instrument is required as the trust has been finally declared in the first instance. A trust is said to be executory where, although a valid trust is created, the settlor has only indicated his general intentions as to how the trust property is to be disposed of and the execution of a further instrument is required to define the beneficial interests with precision.[23]

In the case of executed trusts, equity follows the law and generally requires the same precise words of limitation in relation to an equitable interest as would be required for a legal estate. This proposition can be seen from the decision of the English Court of Appeal in *Re Bostock's Settlement*[24] in which it was held that where an executed trust is created, the requisite legal words of limitation must be used and a general intent to confer an interest in fee simple will not suffice. A similar finding was made by the Supreme Court in *Jameson v. McGovern*[25] where Murnaghan J cited with approval the following *dicta* of Lord Eldon in *Jervoise v. Duke of Northumberland*[26] in relation to executed trusts: 'These are cases where the testator has clearly decided what the trust is to be; and as equity follows the law, where the testator has left nothing to be done, but has himself expressed it, there the effect must be the same, whether the estate is legal or equitable.' In *Jameson* by virtue of a marriage settlement freehold premises had been conveyed to a husband for life, to his wife for life, then to any children, or if there were none, to those appointed by the husband and in default of appointment, for the survivor of the husband and wife absolutely. The parties had no children and no appointment was made by the husband. After his death, the question of the extent of the wife's interest under the settlement arose. The Supreme Court held, following *Re Bostock's Settlement*, that the wife only derived a life interest from it, although the court

---

21. E.g. *Riordan v. Banon* (1876) IR 10 Eq 469.
22. There are exceptions to this general principle, see Megarry and Wade, *The Law of Real Property* (5th ed., 1984) p.120. This list is omitted from the 6th ed., 2000.
23. See *Davis v. Richards and Wallington Ltd* [1990] 1 WLR 1511, 1537–1538.
24. [1921] 2 Ch 469.
25. [1934] IR 758.
26. (1821) 1 Jac & W 559.

went on to hold that she had an equity independent of the settlement sufficient to give her an equitable fee simple in the property. A similar approach of requiring the necessary words of limitation was followed by Costello J in *Savage v. Nolan*,[27] although as in *Jameson* the court was able to find that the parties in question, in this instance children under a marriage settlement, were entitled to an absolute interest independent of the settlement. As Keane[28] points out it would be interesting to see whether the courts in this jurisdiction would adopt such a strict approach if a case arose in which there was no such 'escape route'.

HE WHO SEEKS EQUITY MUST DO EQUITY

Equity will only grant relief on terms which ensure that a defendant is treated fairly and to obtain equitable relief, a plaintiff must be prepared to act in an honourable manner. This maxim has many different applications and reflects the fact that equitable remedies are discretionary in nature. It is one of the few maxims that can be interpreted fairly literally; as Meagher, Gummow and Lehane[29] point out 'there are many illustrations of, and almost no exceptions to, the maxim'. It in a sense complements the maxim that 'he who comes to equity must come with clean hands' and while the latter principle focuses on the past conduct of the party seeking the intervention of the court, the maxim that 'he who seeks equity must do equity' is concerned with his likely future conduct.

The effect of the maxim is noticeable in the approach of equity towards the granting of remedies and is a feature of equitable jurisdiction which distinguishes it from the common law. An illustration of this is the manner in which equity approaches a claim for rescission of a contract. Rescission will be granted to a plaintiff on such terms which the court considers just[30] and relief of an unconditional nature may not achieve this aim. So, in *Cheese v. Thomas*[31] an elderly plaintiff who had given the defendant, his great-nephew, approximately half of the purchase price of a house on the understanding that he could live there until he died, sought to have the transaction set aside on grounds of undue influence. Nicholls VC ordered that the property should be sold and that both parties should bear the loss on the sale in the same proportions as they had contributed to the purchase price. He pointed out that the court was concerned to achieve practical justice for both parties and not

---

27. High Court 1976 No. 2395 P (Costello J) 20 July 1978.
28. *Equity and the Law of Trusts in the Republic of Ireland* (1988) p. 29.
29. *Equity Doctrines and Remedies* (3rd ed., 1992) p. 77.
30. *Cooper v. Phibbs* (1867) LR 2 HL 149; *Solle v. Butcher* [1950] 1 KB 671.
31. [1994] 1 WLR 129.

for the plaintiff alone and stated that 'the plaintiff is seeking the assistance of a court of equity and he who seeks equity must do equity'.[32]

Another example of the application of the maxim is that an interlocutory injunction will not be granted unless a plaintiff is prepared to give an undertaking as to damages in order to ensure that a defendant may be compensated in the event of the former being successful at the interlocutory stage but ultimately failing at the trial of the action. In addition, in specific cases a court may choose to withhold interlocutory relief where a claimant is unwilling to carry out his side of a contract or arrangement which may exist between the parties. So, in *Chappell v. Times Newspapers Ltd,*[33] the plaintiffs sought an interim injunction to restrain their employers from terminating their contracts of employment, although they refused to give the undertakings sought by the employers not to engage in disruptive behaviour. Although the plaintiffs themselves had not previously been directly involved in these activities, the Court of Appeal refused to grant the relief sought on the grounds that the plaintiffs had failed to establish that they intended to act equitably by abiding by the terms of their contracts of employment. As Lord Denning MR said: 'if one party seeks relief, he must be ready and willing to do his part in it.'[34]

Equally, a claimant will not be granted specific performance of a contract unless he can establish to the satisfaction of the court that he is willing and able to carry out his own contractual obligations. Specific performance may also be refused on the grounds of a lack of mutuality between the parties, a principle set out as follows by O'Connor LJ in *O'Regan v. White*:[35] 'Generally speaking, at any rate, it would not be even-handed justice to compel specific performance against the one party, where the same remedy would not be available against the other party in respect of matters to be by him performed under the contract.'

In deciding whether to grant or withhold equitable relief, a court will have regard to the conduct of both parties if it 'is truly to act as a court of conscience'.[36] This principle can be seen in the context of claims which may be defeated by a plea of estoppel and, where it would be unconscionable for a plaintiff to renege on an assumption which he has permitted a defendant to make, he will be estopped from asserting his claim.[37]

The operation of this maxim can also be seen in relation to the mortgagor's equity of redemption. If the mortgagor wishes to use the extension of time permitted by equity to exercise the right of redemption, it can only be exercised

---

32. *Ibid.* at 136.
33. [1975] 1 WLR 482.
34. *Ibid.* at 502.
35. [1919] 2 IR 339, 393.
36. *McMahon v. Kerry County Council* [1981] ILRM 419, 421.
37. E.g. *Lim Teng Huan v. Ang Swee Chuan* [1992] 1 WLR 113; *Gillett v. Holt* [2001] Ch 210. See further Chapter 17.

on equitable terms; he must be willing to pay all arrears of interest due to the mortgagee and to give him reasonable notice of his intention to redeem.

Finally, the maxim is the basis for the doctrine of election, i.e. that a person cannot take a benefit and reject an associated burden, which will be considered in detail in a later chapter.[38]

HE WHO COMES TO EQUITY MUST COME WITH CLEAN HANDS

This maxim also reflects the discretionary nature of equity and requires that a person seeking equitable relief must refrain from fraud, misrepresentation or any other form of dishonest or disreputable conduct if he wishes to be granted a remedy.[39] However unlike the maxim just considered, it refers principally to the past conduct of the plaintiff. The general principle which the maxim lays down was stated by Eyre LCB in *Dering v. Earl of Winchelsea*[40] as follows:

> A man must come into a court of equity with clean hands; but when this is said, it does not mean a general depravity; it must have an immediate and necessary relation to the equity sued for; it must be a depravity in a legal as well as in the moral sense.

One classic illustration of the maxim in operation is the decision of Wigram VC in *Overton v. Banister*.[41] An infant beneficiary fraudulently misrepresented herself as being of age, although she was only 19, and thereby induced the trustees to give her possession of assets to which she should only have been entitled when she reached the age of 21. When she reached this age, she instituted a suit against the trustees to compel them to reimburse to the trust fund the assets which they had improperly paid to her. Although at common law, her deceit was ineffectual to discharge the trustees of their duty, her claim was disallowed in equity because she had misrepresented her age. It is clear that where a beneficiary has instigated, participated in or even consented to a

---

38. See *infra* Chapter 19.
39. See generally, Chafee (1949) 47 Mich L Rev 1065 and Pettit [1990] Conv 416. Pettit suggests (at 424) that unclean hands seems to be a 'last resort defence' to be invoked where none of the so called nominate defences are applicable but where it would be unconscionable for the plaintiff to be granted relief by the court. For a recent restatement of the fact that this maxim applies to a plaintiff seeking equitable relief, see the judgment of Keane J in *National Irish Bank Ltd v. RTE* [1998] 2 IR 465, 481–482.
40. (1787) 1 Cox 318, 319-320. Cited with approval by Issacs J in *Meyers v. Casey* (1913) 17 CLR 90, 123. See also *Tinker v. Tinker* [1970] P 136, 143 *per* Salmon LJ and *NZ Netherlands Society 'Oranje' Inc v. Kuys* [1973] 2 All ER 1222, 1227 *per* Lord Wilberforce.
41. (1844) 3 Hare 503. See also *Cory v. Gertcken* (1816) 2 Madd 49.

breach of trust, as the decision in *Overton* shows, the beneficiary will not succeed in any action brought against a trustee in respect of this breach.[42] Even where a beneficiary is not involved prior to the breach being committed, he may still be unable to bring a successful action against the trustees if he subsequently acquiesces in the breach,[43] provided that he does so with full knowledge of the surrounding facts and circumstances.

It is well established that a plaintiff will be refused a decree of specific performance if his conduct towards the defendant has been less than honest. This point was made in a general way by Black LJ in *Conlon v. Murray*[44] where he stressed that the remedy may be withheld in a situation where the conduct of the parties and the circumstances of the case demand it. It was also stressed by the Supreme Court in *Smelter Corporation v. O'Driscoll*[45] in which the plaintiff claimed an order of specific performance of a contract to sell lands. The plaintiff's agent had told the defendant that if she did not sell the land in question, the property would be compulsorily acquired, although, unknown to the agent, this was not in fact the case. The Supreme Court refused a decree of specific performance. O'Higgins CJ stressed that the remedy was a discretionary one and concluded that by reason of the plaintiff's misrepresentation, the defendant was under a fundamental misapprehension as to the true facts and that it would be unjust to grant specific performance in the circumstances. While the type of conduct which will disentitle a plaintiff to equitable relief will usually amount to impropriety of a fairly serious nature, because of the discretionary nature of the court's jurisdiction, a claimant would be well advised to follow the advice given by Barr J in the course of his judgment in *O'Connor v. Harrington Ltd*[46] where he concluded that the 'clean hands' principle applies with equal force to applications for injunctions made under section 27 of the Local Government (Planning and Development) Act 1976. Barr J stated that '[i]n seeking such relief an applicant should put before the court fairly and with candour all facts known to him which are relevant to the exercise of the court's discretion and he should satisfy it about his *bona fides* and the true purpose of his application.'[47]

It has been established that equitable relief may be refused to a plaintiff where his conduct in relation to the transaction at issue has been less than honest even where this conduct has not directly prejudiced the defendant. This proposition is well illustrated by the decision of Costello J in <u>*Parkes v. Parkes.*</u>[48] A husband bought land and the conveyance was taken in his wife's

---

42. *French v. Graham* (1860) 10 Ir Ch R 522; *Re Pauling's Settlement Trusts* [1964] Ch 303, 335 *per* Wilmer LJ.
43. *Walker v. Symonds* (1818) 3 Swans 1, 64 *per* Lord Eldon.
44. [1958] NI 17, 25.
45. [1977] IR 305.
46. High Court 1984 No. 69 MCA (Barr J) 28 May 1987.
47. *Ibid.* at 14.
48. [1980] ILRM 137.

name to obviate the need for Land Commission consent.[49] After the parties divorced, the husband registered an inhibition on the land and the wife instituted proceedings claiming that it had been wrongly registered. The husband counter-claimed that he was entitled to the beneficial ownership in the property. It was claimed on behalf of the wife that the husband should not be able to obtain relief in equity 'by setting up his own illegality or fraud'. Costello J referred to other cases where a husband had bought a house and put it in his wife's name to protect it from creditors[50] and where a father had deposited money in his son's name to avoid death duties,[51] and concluded as follows:

> Just as the courts will not grant relief to a person who has allowed property to be placed in a wife's or son's name for the fraudulent purpose of defeating creditors ... or for the illegal purpose of evading liability to tax ... so it seems to me that the court should not grant relief to a purchaser who has placed property in his wife's name dishonestly and by means of an illegal act performed for the purpose of evading the law relating to the transfer of land.[52]

Therefore, although the husband's dishonest conduct had in no way prejudiced the wife in this instance, it sufficed to disentitle him to the equitable relief which he sought.

One important aspect of the application of this maxim which must be stressed is that a court will decline to intervene on the basis of the 'unclean hands' principle unless there is a sufficient connection between the inequitable conduct and the subject-matter of the dispute. This point was made by Eyre LCB in *Dering v. Earl of Winchelsea*[53] and re-iterated in the following terms by Scrutton LJ in *Moody v. Cox*:[54] 'Equity will not apply the principle about clean hands unless the depravity, the dirt in question on the hand has an "immediate and necessary relation" to the equity sued for.' Or, as Hollinrake JA stated in the recent decision of the British Columbia Court of Appeal in *Rowland v. Vancouver College Ltd*[55] 'the "clean hands" doctrine relates only

---

49. Under s.45 of the Land Act 1965 this consent would have been required had the conveyance been taken in the husband's name, but as the wife was an Irish citizen, it was not necessary.
50. *Gascoigne v. Gascoigne* [1918] 1 KB 223.
51. *McEvoy v. Belfast Banking Co.* [1934] NI 67.
52. [1980] ILRM 137, 144.
53. (1787) 1 Cox 318, 319-320.
54. [1917] 2 Ch 71, 87-88. The plaintiff's claim for rescission of a contract succeeded despite the fact that he had given a bribe to the vendor's solicitor, although admittedly in an unconnected matter.
55. (2001) 205 DLR 193, 213. See also *Polai v. Toronto (City)* (1970) 8 DLR (3d) 689 *per* Schroeder JA.

to situations in which the alleged act of impropriety being raised against the plaintiff is linked to the very subject matter of the dispute.' The effect of this proposition is well illustrated by the decision of Ungoed-Thomas J in *Argyll v. Argyll*[56] where he held that the alleged immorality of the plaintiff's conduct which had led to divorce did not deprive her of her entitlement to an injunction to restrain a breach of confidence by her husband. Ungoed-Thomas J stated that 'the plaintiff's adultery, repugnant though it be, should not in my view license the husband to broadcast unchecked the most intimate confidences of earlier and happier days' and he continued 'a person coming to equity must come with clean hands but the cleanliness required is to be judged in relation to the relief that is sought.'

The so-called 'clean hands' principle has been applied in a wide variety of situations where equitable remedies have been sought e.g. where the plaintiff has acted unfairly and unreasonably,[57] or where he has attempted to mislead the court.[58] It is clear from the decision of Lavan J in *Fanning v. University College Cork*[59] that the manner in which a plaintiff puts forward his case to the court may suffice to disentitle him to relief on the grounds that he has failed to come to equity with clean hands. The plaintiff sought to restrain the defendant from taking any steps to discipline, suspend or dismiss him from his post as a professor in the university arising out of an alleged incident which had taken place between the plaintiff and another member of staff. At the outset of his judgment, Lavan J said that the plaintiff's evidence was totally lacking in candour and clarity and that it was delivered in a defensive and limited fashion. He stated that it is an essential rule of law that he who seeks equity must come with clean hands and that with great regret he had to conclude that the plaintiff had signally failed to do this. Lavan J said that for the purpose of completeness he would set out the various submissions made on behalf of the plaintiff and rejected by the defendant, although he added that these seemed to be moot having regard to the findings he had made in relation to the plaintiff and the evidence which he had given. He concluded that the plaintiff had not come to equity with clean hands and that in the circumstances he had disentitled himself to the equitable relief sought. However, the Supreme Court allowed the plaintiff's appeal, quashing the judgment and order of Lavan J and remitting the matter to the High Court to be heard by another judge.[60] Keane CJ concluded that the judgment was entirely unsatisfactory as a judgment of a

---

56. [1967] Ch 302. However, note that in *O'Doherty v. West Limerick Resources Ltd* Supreme Court, 14 May 1999 the connection between the appellant's previous convictions for fraud and the relief which he sought was not clearcut.
57. *Shell U.K. Ltd v. Lostock Garages Ltd* [1976] 1 WLR 1187, 1199 *per* Lord Denning MR.
58. *Armstrong v. Shepherd & Short Ltd* [1959] 2 QB 384, 397.
59. High Court 2001 No. 15653P (Lavan J), 25 July 2002.
60. Supreme Court 2002 No. 284, 30 January 2003.

trial judge disposing of issues between the parties; in his view it was clear that no case had been made that the plaintiff had not come to court with clean hands and this was not the basis on which the case was defended in the High Court.

The Supreme Court gave some consideration to the type of conduct which is necessary to bring the 'clean hands' maxim into operation in *Curust Financial Services Ltd v. Loewe-Lack-Werk Otto Loewe GmbH & Co. KG.*[61] There, it had to decide whether the alleged breach by the plaintiff of an exclusive licensing agreement, consisting of its sub-contracting the manufacture of a product without the prior written consent of the first named defendant, should disentitle the plaintiff to relief. As a general principle, Finlay CJ accepted that the court has a discretion, where it is satisfied that a person has come to court otherwise than with 'clean hands,' to refuse equitable relief in the form of an injunction on that ground alone. However, he stated: 'It seems to me that this phrase must of necessity involve an element of turpitude and cannot necessarily be equated with a mere breach of contract.'[62] Finlay CJ made reference to the fact that what might be established as a breach by the plaintiff of the agreement not to sub-contract, namely the entering into an arrangement with a third party for this purpose, might also be established as having been provoked by a wrongful repudiation on the part of the first named defendant of its own contractual obligations under the licensing agreement. He therefore concluded that it would be unreasonable that such conduct should disentitle the plaintiff to an injunction to which it would otherwise be entitled and he held that this should not constitute a ground for rejecting the claim for relief.

This more flexible approach to the application of the maxim has also been adopted by the majority of the Court of Appeal and the House of Lords in *Tinsley v. Milligan.*[63] This case concerned a dispute in relation to the beneficial ownership of property registered in the sole name of the plaintiff but bought by the parties as part of a business venture on the tacit understanding that both should be joint beneficial owners of the house. The purpose of this arrangement was to assist in the perpetration of fraud on the Department of Social Security, although the defendant subsequently decided to disclose these irregularities to the department. The plaintiff sought possession of the property and the defendant counter-claimed seeking a declaration that the house was held by the plaintiff on trust for both parties in equal shares. The majority of

---

61. [1994] 1 IR 450.
62. *Ibid.* at 467. Quoted with approval by Roderick Murphy J in *Kavanagh v. Caulfield* High Court 1999 No. 9769P, 19 June 2002 at 9.
63. [1992] Ch 310 (CA); [1994] 1 AC 340 (HL). See further, Lunney (1992) 6 Trust Law Int 110; Martin [1992] Conv 153, 161-166; Halliwell [1994] Conv 62; Buckley (1994) 110 LQR 3. For further analysis of the decision in *Tinsley*, see Thornton [1993] CLJ 394; Stowe (1994) 57 MLR 441; Enonchong (1995) 111 LQR 135; Rose (1996) 112 LQR 386.

the Court of Appeal held that since both the plaintiff and the defendant had been party to the fraud and since the illegality was not of a continuing nature, it would not be an affront to the public conscience to grant the relief sought by the defendant and that her counterclaim did not arise *ex turpi causa* so as to deny her relief.[64] Lloyd LJ in considering the possible relevance of the maxim 'he who comes to equity must come with clean hands' seemed to countenance a flexible application of the principle and said that he saw no reason why the court should not in the exercise of its equitable jurisdiction, follow and adopt the more adaptable attitude shown by the common law in cases where issues of public policy have arisen. He continued:

> If the common law can discriminate, so can equity. So far as the joint fraud on the D.S.S. is concerned, the parties were admittedly *in pari delicto*. But when one looks at the overall equities, the balance comes down strongly in favour of the defendant. I do not think that the clean hands maxim should prevent us from giving effect to that balance. We are not obliged to draw up our skirts and refuse all relief.[65]

The majority of the House of Lords agreed with this more flexible approach to the issues of 'clean hands'[66] and illegality.[67] In the opinion of Lord Browne-Wilkinson, illegality may render a proprietary interest unenforceable in certain circumstances but only where the claimant had to rely on the illegality to prove the equitable right and this was not the case in this instance. Lord Goff in his dissenting judgment took a stricter approach towards the equitable maxim and said that '[i]t is founded on the principle that he who has committed iniquity shall not have equity'. In his view, it was not desirable to distinguish between varying degrees of iniquity and he felt that to adopt a more flexible approach would 'open the door to far more unmeritorious cases'.[68]

---

64. Lunney comments in (1992) 6 Trust Law Int 110 that the basis of both the maxims *ex turpi causa* and 'he who comes to equity must come with clean hands' is public policy and that it is desirable that public policy achieves the same result whether the interest sought to be protected is legal or equitable.
65. [1992] Ch 310, 341.
66. Council suggests that the decision of the House of Lords in *Tinsley* leads one to ask whether the maxim 'He who comes to equity must come with clean hands' has now been modified to read 'He who comes to equity should keep unclean hands in his pockets', see (1993) 143 NLJ 1577.
67. Some commentators have sought to distinguish the 'clean hands' principle from the notion of illegality on the basis that the former merely operates to deprive the plaintiff of his entitlement to equitable relief whereas the latter may destroy all his rights, whether legal or equitable. See Meagher, Gummow and Lehane *Equity Doctrines and Remedies* (3rd ed., 1992) p.82 footnote 15.
68. [1994] 1 AC 340, 362. Buckley (1994) 110 LQR 3, 5-6 has asserted that many of the cases relied on by Lord Goff in support of the view that the 'clean hands' principle applied in this case were distinguishable as they involved unsuccessful attempts by

While Roderick Murphy J has recently referred to the speech of Lord Goff in *Tinsley* in *Kavanagh v. Caulfield*,[69] the tenor of his judgment does not suggest an unduly strict approach to the concept of illegality. Roderick Murphy J stated that the underlying principle is the so called public conscience test and that the court must weigh up or balance the adverse consequences of granting relief against those which will ensue if relief is refused. In his view the ultimate decision requires the making of a value judgment.[70] On the facts, Roderick Murphy J concluded that there had been no illegality such as to render the contract in relation to which specific performance was sought unenforceable and held that he could find no evidence of turpitude on the part of the plaintiff.

In conclusion it is fair to say that while the earlier authorities suggested a rather rigid approach to the application of the 'clean hands' principle, there is now increasing evidence both in England, in this jurisdiction and elsewhere in the common law world[71] of a more flexible attitude being adopted.[72] However, one point which should be made about *Curust* and *Tinsley* is that both parties in these cases had been involved in some form of impropriety. It would be interesting to consider whether if one party alone had been guilty of this impropriety, the court would have taken such a benevolent attitude towards the wrongdoing.

DELAY DEFEATS EQUITY

This maxim is enshrined in the phrase *vigilantibus, non dormientibus jura subveniunt*; the law assists the vigilant not those who sleep, so delay is well established as a discretionary factor which may influence a court's decision to grant or withhold equitable relief.[73] A well known summary of its effect is provided by Lord Camden LC in *Smith v. Clay*[74] where he stated: 'A court of equity ... has always refused its aid to stale demands, where a party has slept

---

participants in unlawful schemes to refer to these schemes so as to rebut the presumption of advancement to which their contribution has given rise.

69. High Court 1999 No. 9769P (Roderick Murphy J) 19 June 2002.
70. *Per* Nicholas LJ in the decision of the Court of Appeal in *Tinsley v. Milligan* [1992] Ch 310, 319.
71. See *Equiticorp Industries Group v. The Crown* [1998] 2 NZLR 480, 527–529; *Unilever plc v. Cussons* [1997] 1 NZLR 433, 442.
72. However, Halliwell suggests [1994] Conv 62, 67 that neither the dissenting speech of Lord Goff, nor the majority satisfactorily determined the scope of the underlying principle of unclean hands. She asserts that 'justice…was achieved in the case but the achievement was purely pragmatic and not purposeful'.
73. See e.g. *Lennon v. Ganly* [1981] ILRM 84; *Howard v. Commissioners of Public Works in Ireland* High Court 1992 No. 331JR (O'Hanlon J) 3 December 1992.
74. (1767) 3 Bro CC 639, 640n. See also the *dicta* of Lord Blackburn in *Erlanger v. New Sombrero Phosphate Co.* (1878) 3 App Cas 1218, 1279.

upon his right and acquiesced for a great length of time. Nothing can call forth this court into activity but conscience, good faith and reasonable diligence.'

Two concepts are of relevance in examining the application of this maxim in practice, namely, laches and acquiescence. The effect of the doctrine of laches is that where there has been unreasonable delay in the bringing of proceedings which would render it unjust to grant relief, a plaintiff may find his claim barred in equity. Acquiescence on the other hand means that where one party infringes another's rights and that other party does nothing, equity infers that the latter has acquiesced in the former's actions and he may not be permitted to pursue his claim. However, before examining these doctrines in more detail, it is first necessary to explain the effect of statutory limitation periods.

As a general principle equitable doctrines will have no application to cases to which the Statute of Limitations 1957 applies,[75] although as is pointed out below, the constitutional right to fair procedures may lead to a claim being dismissed even where it is brought within the requisite period of limitation.[76] In addition, it should be noted that the statute lays down express limitation periods in relation to a number of equitable rights. A six year limitation period is laid down with respect to actions by beneficiaries to recover trust property or in respect of any breach of trust or to recover the estates of deceased persons.[77] A 12 year limitation period is laid down for actions for the recovery of land[78] and actions by a mortgagor to redeem a mortgage.[79] It was held by the Supreme Court in *Gleeson v. Feehan*[80] that a limitation period of 12 years as provided for under section 13 of the statute applies to an action by a personal representative of a deceased owner of land seeking recovery of such land in succession to the owner, rather than a period of six years as laid down by section 45 as amended, which would apply to an action against a personal representative by a person claiming to be entitled to a share in a deceased's estate. As McMahon J had pointed out in *Drohan v. Drohan*,[81] section 45 applied to claims against, and not claims by, personal representatives and it had no application to a claim by a personal representative to recover a deceased's assets against a person holding adversely to the estate.

---

75. S. 5 of the statute provides that 'Nothing in this Act shall afford any equitable jurisdiction to refuse relief on the ground of acquiescence or otherwise' and it would seem in England that where a limitation period is prescribed by statute and a claim is brought within this period a person cannot rely on the doctrine of laches to defeat the claim, see *Re Pauling's Settlement Trusts* [1964] Ch 303.
76. E.g. *O Domhnaill v. Merrick* [1984] IR 151.
77. Ss. 43 and 45 of the Statute of Limitations 1957. Note that a new s. 45 was inserted by s. 126 of the Succession Act 1965.
78. S. 13 of the Statute of Limitations 1957.
79. S. 34 of the Statute of Limitations 1957.
80. [1993] 2 IR 113.
81. [1981] ILRM 473.

Section 43 provides that subject to section 44, an action in respect of a breach of trust, not being an action in respect of which a period of limitation is fixed by any other provision of the legislation, shall not be brought against a trustee[82] after the expiration of six years from the date on which the right of action accrued. However, section 44 excludes from the application of limitation periods a claim founded on any fraud or fraudulent breach of trust to which the trustee was party or where the claim is to recover trust property or the proceeds of trust property retained by the trustee or received by him and converted to his own use.[83]

The only exception to the principle that non-statutory considerations will have no application to cases to which the Statute of Limitations 1957 applies, is the reasoning employed by Henchy J in *O Domhnaill v. Merrick*[84] based on the constitutional right to fair procedures to the effect that in certain circumstances 'inordinate and inexcusable delay' will bar a claim brought within the relevant limitation period where this will place an unfair burden on the person sued. The principle in *O Domhnaill* was applied by the Supreme Court in *Toal v. Duignan (No.2)*[85] where Finlay CJ said that the courts have an inherent jurisdiction to dismiss a claim in the interests of justice where the length of time which has elapsed between the events out of which it arises and the time when it comes for hearing is in all the circumstances so great that it would be unjust to call upon a particular defendant to defend himself.[86] However, as Keane[87] has pointed out, these principles are likely to apply only in a small number of cases, namely those relating to personal injuries claims by minors, in which the limitation period may be particularly long, and the recollection of witnesses of considerable importance.

While some of the most common situations to which express statutory limitation periods apply have been considered, it is important to stress that the principles of laches and acquiescence may also not operate in cases in

---

82. See s.2(2) of the Statute of Limitations 1957.
83. It was suggested by Chatterton VC in *Collings v. Wade* [1896] 1 IR 340, 343-344 in considering the earlier provision contained in s. 8 of the Trustee Act 1888 that the scope of the exception 'must be restricted to breaches of trust induced by some corrupt motive of personal gain or advantage to the trustee,' or as Fitzgibbon LJ commented (at 349) 'fraud...must amount to dishonesty.' See also *Murphy v. Allied Irish Banks Ltd* [1994] 2 ILRM 220, 228 and *Jobling-Purser v. Jackson* High Court (Kinlen J) 27 November 2002 at 39.
84. [1984] IR 151.
85. [1991] ILRM 140.
86. Finlay CJ stated that while the existence of culpable negligence on the part of a plaintiff whose claim has been delayed is of considerable relevance, it is not an essential ingredient for the exercise of the court's inherent jurisdiction to dismiss a claim (at 143). McCarthy J dissented in part by saying that without culpable delay on the part of a plaintiff, the court's inherent jurisdiction to dismiss a claim may not be exercised. (at 159).
87. *Equity and the Law of Trusts in the Republic of Ireland* (1988) at pp. 35–36.

which limitation periods are applied by analogy.[88] While section 9(a) of the
Statute of Limitations 1957 provides that the limitation periods laid down in
section 11 for claims in contract and tort shall not apply to any claims for
equitable relief, section 9(b) goes on to provide that the provision shall not be
construed as preventing a court 'from applying by analogy' any provision of
the section. One question which remains to be satisfactorily resolved is what
the position will be where the cause of action in contract or tort is not statute
barred. In *Cahill v. Irish Motor Traders Association*[89] Budd J stated: 'Mere
delay will not of itself disentitle a plaintiff to an injunction in aid of his legal
rights unless the claim to enforce the right is barred by a statute of limitations.'
The effect of this approach would seem to be that where a cause of action is
not statute barred and equitable relief is sought in relation to a common law
right, the doctrine of laches cannot be applied. This approach seems to have
been also followed in Australia and in *Orr v. Ford*[90] Deane J said that 'laches
. . . is not available in answer to a legal claim'. However, in England it was
held by the Court of Appeal in *Habib Bank Ltd v. Habib Bank AG Zurich*[91]
that laches is always relevant where equitable relief is sought and that no
distinction should be made between cases where such relief is sought to give
effect to legal as opposed to equitable rights. This is borne out by the approach
taken by Nourse LJ in *Gafford v. Graham*[92] where he stated that he doubted
whether a distinction ought to be made between a legal and an equitable right
when considering a defence of acquiescence.

Laches and Acquiescence

The doctrine of laches which may operate to bar a claim in equity where no
statutory period of limitation applies, either expressly or by analogy, was
described as follows by Lord Selborne LC in *Lindsay Petroleum v. Hurd*:[93]

> [T]he doctrine of laches in Courts of Equity is not an arbitrary or a
> technical doctrine. Where it would be practically unjust to give a remedy,
> either because the party has, by his conduct, done that which might
> fairly be regarded as equivalent to a waiver of it, or where by his conduct
> or neglect he has, though perhaps not waiving that remedy, yet put the
> other party in a situation in which it would not be reasonable to place
> him if the remedy were afterwards to be asserted, in either of these
> cases, lapse of time and delay are most material.

---

88. This question was left open by the court in *Hampton v. Minns* [2002] 1 WLR 1, 33.
89. [1966] IR 430, 449.
90. (1989) 167 CLR 316, 340.
91. [1981] 1 WLR 1265.
92. (1998) 77 P & CR 73, 80.
93. (1874) LR 5 PC 221, 239–240.

In deciding whether the defence of laches has been established, a court must consider first, whether the plaintiff has delayed unreasonably in bringing his claim and secondly, assess whether prejudice or detriment has been suffered by the defendant as a result. Delay of itself is insufficient and clearly, the period of time necessary to invalidate a claim will vary according to the circumstances of each case. Often delay may be interpreted as evidence of an agreement by the plaintiff not to pursue his claim and where a plaintiff had acted in a manner which has induced the defendant to alter his position, it would be inequitable to allow the claim to proceed. A good example of how the doctrine of laches operates in practice is provided by the decision of Keane J in *J.H. v. W.J.H.*[94] The plaintiff signed a document in which she agreed to compromise her rights to her late husband's farm under the Succession Act 1965 in favour of her son. While Keane J accepted that the transaction was an improvident one which the courts would in the normal course of events have set aside, he refused to grant her relief in the circumstances. Keane J referred to the delay by the plaintiff for a period of four years in seeking to assert her claim and the time and money invested in the running of the farm by the defendant on the basis that she had abandoned her rights, and concluded that the lapse of time coupled with circumstances which made it inequitable to enforce the claim was sufficient to bar the plaintiff's action. Another illustration of the doctrine of laches is provided by the decision of the English Court of Appeal in *Allcard v. Skinner*.[95] The plaintiff, who joined a sisterhood of nuns, made her will in favour of the superior of the order and also transferred large amounts of money and stock to her. When she left the order, she revoked her will but made no attempt to reclaim her property until five or six years later when she instituted proceedings claiming that it had been transferred as a result of undue influence. The majority of the Court of Appeal held that the claim was barred by laches and acquiescence. As Lindley LJ stated it was a case which by no means rested on mere lapse of time and the plaintiff's conduct amounted in effect to confirmation of the gift.

Acquiescence arises where a plaintiff either expressly or impliedly represents that he does not intend to enforce a claim and as a result of this representation, it becomes unjust in all the circumstances to grant the relief which he subsequently seeks. The principle was summarised as follows by Lord Wensleydale in *Archbold v. Scully*:[96]

> If a party, who could object, lies by and knowingly permits another to incur an expense in doing an act under the belief that it would not be objected to, and so a kind of permission may be said to be given to another to alter his condition, he may be said to acquiesce.

---

94. High Court 1977 No. 5831P (Keane J) 20 December 1979.
95. (1887) 36 Ch D 145.
96. (1861) 9 HLC 360, 383.

It is well established that acquiescence may bar a claim for equitable relief[97] and it usually arises in circumstances where a party fails to seek a remedy when a violation of his rights is brought to his attention.[98]

Consideration was given by Laddie J in his judgment in *Nelson v. Rye*[99] to the circumstances in which the equitable defences of laches and acquiescence operate, although he stressed that it can be misleading to approach them as if they consisted of 'a series of precisely defined hurdles over each of which a litigant must struggle before the defence is made out'. The plaintiff musician sought an account of the moneys received by the defendant, his manager, during the ten year period from 1980–1990 in which the latter had managed his business affairs. Laddie J accepted that the plaintiff's delay in instituting proceedings was such that it would be unreasonable and unjust to allow the plaintiff to assert his right to an account against the defendant for the period prior to December 1985 and that the defences of laches and acquiescence were made out in relation to that part of the claim. Laddie J made the following comment about the circumstances in which the defences will operate:

> [T]hese defences are not technical or arbitrary. The courts have indicated over the years some of the factors which must be taken into consideration in deciding whether the defence runs. Those factors include the period of the delay, the extent to which the defendant's position has been prejudiced by the delay, and the extent to which that prejudice was caused by the actions of the plaintiff. I accept that mere delay alone will almost never suffice, but the court has to look at all the circumstances, including in particular those factors set out above, and then decide whether the balance of justice or injustice is in favour of granting the remedy or withholding it.[100]

This tendency to treat laches and acquiescence as a single defence has been continued in the decision of the Court of Appeal in *Gafford v. Graham*[101] and Milne has recently commented that there is 'no reason for continuing to treat laches and acquiescence as two separate equitable defences'.[102] In *Gafford*, Nourse LJ said that the question which the court must ask is whether in all the circumstances, it would be unconscionable for the plaintiff to continue to seek to enforce the rights which he undoubtedly had. Similar language was

---

97. See e.g. *Irwin v. O'Connell* [1936] IR 44; *Sayers v. Collyer* (1884) 28 Ch D 103; *Shaw v. Applegate* [1977] 1 WLR 970.
98. *McCausland v. Young* [1949] NI 49, 88-89 *per* Andrews LCJ.
99. [1996] 1 WLR 1378.
100. *Ibid*. at 1392.
101. (1998) 77 P & CR 73.
102. (1998) 114 LQR 555, 557.

used by Aldous LJ in *Frawley v. Neill*[103] where he commented that a modern approach to laches and acquiescence should not require an exhaustive inquiry into whether the circumstances fit within the principles established in previous cases but should instead involve asking whether it would be unconscionable for the party concerned to be permitted to assert his beneficial rights.[104]

EQUALITY IS EQUITY

In circumstances where more than one person is entitled to property, equity favours a principle of equal division. The most common illustration of the maxim in practice is the attitude adopted by equity towards the joint tenancy as a method of holding property. In this case the right of survivorship operates and on the death of a joint tenant, the estate belongs to the surviving joint tenant(s) to the exclusion of the deceased's successors. This can be distinguished from the position in relation to a tenancy in common where the interest of each party devolves upon his personal representatives on his death. Equity tends to lean in favour of a tenancy in common and in certain circumstances, even where persons are joint tenants at law, they may be regarded by equity as tenants in common of the beneficial interest. In such cases while the survivor(s) may be entitled to the entire estate, he will hold part of it as trustee for the deceased's personal representatives.

This presumption of a tenancy in common in equity arises in three recognised situations. First, where the purchase money for property is provided in unequal shares, equity presumes a tenancy in common proportionate to the contributions made. On the other hand, where the purchase money is advanced equally, the survivor becomes entitled to the entire estate in equity as well as in law. Secondly, where parties lend money on a mortgage, whether equally or unequally, the mortgagees are presumed to be entitled as tenants in common and the survivor is regarded as a trustee for the representatives of the deceased mortgagee to the extent of the amount of the loan advanced by the deceased.[105] Thirdly, where partners acquire property, they are presumed by equity to hold it as tenants in common on the basis that the principle of survivorship is inconsistent with the nature of the partnership relationship.[106] However, these three situations are not the only ones in which equity will presume a tenancy in common, a point made by the Privy Council in *Malayan Credit Ltd v. Jack*

---

103. Court of Appeal, 1 March 1999.
104. See also *Schulman v. Hewson* [2002] EWHC 855 (Ch) 3 May 2002 and *Experience Hendrix LLC v. PPX Enterprises Inc* [2002] EWHC 1353 (QB) 5 July 2002.
105. *Morley v. Bird* (1798) 3 Ves 628, 631.
106. *Lake v. Craddock* (1732) 3 P Wms 158. Although see *Barton v. Morris* [1985] 1 WLR 1257.

Chia-MPH Ltd[107] where it was held that this result will follow where grantees hold premises for several individual business purposes.

Even where an equitable interest in property is held jointly, for example where the purchase money is advanced equally, equity leans in favour of severance and an act of alienation by one tenant or even an agreement to alienate will be sufficient to sever the joint tenancy and create a tenancy in common.[108]

The maxim that equality is equity can also be seen in operation in a number of other circumstances. It has generally been applied where surplus funds remain on the dissolution of an unincorporated association as in *Re Bucks. Constabulary Widows' and Orphans' Fund Friendly Society (No.2)*,[109] where Walton J held that the surplus funds remaining should be distributed equally amongst the members of the association alive at the date of dissolution. There is still a lack of consensus in this jurisdiction on the issue of whether the distribution of surplus funds should be carried out on the basis of equal division or in accordance with the proportion of contributions made and in *Tierney v. Tough*[110] O'Connor MR favoured the latter approach. However, subsequently in *Feeney v. MacManus*,[111] Johnston J supported the principle of distribution on an equal basis and this is the approach which is more likely to be followed.

In addition, there was for some time a tendency in England to apply the maxim in relation to the division of matrimonial property in the absence of any other clear basis for carrying out this exercise. However, this approach never found favour with the judiciary in this jurisdiction and instead division is carried out on the basis of the respective contributions of the spouses or partners, and the non-owning partner has been held to be entitled to a beneficial interest to the extent of his or her contributions.[112] While the principle of equal division is still applied in England where there is evidence that it was the common intention of the parties that this should be the case,[113] Waite LJ has recently stressed in *Hammond v. Mitchell*[114] that 'this is not an area where the maxim that equality is equity falls to be applied unthinkingly'.

More recently Waite LJ delivering his judgment in the Court of Appeal in *Midland Bank plc v. Cooke*[115] stated that when the court is determining what proportions the parties must be assumed to have intended for their beneficial ownership, the duty of the judge is to undertake a survey of the whole course

---

107. [1986] AC 549.
108. *Burgess v. Rawnsley* [1975] Ch 429.
109. [1979] 1 WLR 936. See also *Re GKN Bolts & Nuts Ltd (Automotive Division) Birmingham Works, Sports and Social Club* [1982] 1 WLR 774.
110. [1914] 1 IR 142.
111. [1937] IR 23.
112. *C. v. C.* [1976] IR 254; *W. v. W.* [1981] ILRM 202; *McC. v. McC.* [1986] ILRM 1.
113. *Grant v. Edwards* [1986] Ch 638.
114. [1991] 1 WLR 1127, 1137.
115. [1995] 4 All ER 562.

of dealing between the parties relevant to their ownership and occupation of the property. Waite LJ said that the court will take into account all conduct which throws light on the question of what shares were intended and that it is 'only if that search proves inconclusive does the court fall back on the maxim that "equality is equity"'.[116] It should be noted that an attempt to pass legislation providing for automatic joint ownership of the matrimonial home in this jurisdiction proved unsuccessful,[117] and it is fair to say that the maxim no longer plays a role in this area and has been superseded by more precise methods of distribution in both jurisdictions.

The Supreme Court has recently commented in *E.B. v. S.S.*[118] that the maxim that 'equality is equity' should not necessarily apply where an application is brought under section 117 of the Succession Act 1965 by a child claiming that a parent has failed in his moral duty to make proper provision for the child in accordance with his means. Although the plaintiff's application was dismissed in this case, Keane J stated that it was not necessarily an answer to an application under section 117 that the testator had simply treated all his or her children equally. As he stated 'the maxim "equality is equity" can have no application where the testator has, by dividing his estate in that manner, disregarded the special needs . . . of one of the children to such an extent that he could be said to have failed in his moral duty to that child.'[119] However, Keane J acknowledged that the understandable desire of parents to avoid any friction amongst their children by effecting, so far as possible, an equal distribution of their property must also be recognised. In the circumstances the Supreme Court held that the defendant, who had divided her property equally between all her children, had not failed in her moral duty towards the plaintiff.

One other area in which the principle that equality is equity may be of relevance is where a 'trust power' is implied in default of any appointment being made by the donee of a power of appointment. So where a general intention in favour of a class of persons is expressed and no selection is made, a trust in favour of the members of the class in equal shares may be implied.[120]

---

116. *Ibid.* at 574.
117. *Re Article 26 of the Constitution and the Matrimonial Home Bill 1993* [1994] 1 IR 305.
118. [1998] 2 ILRM 141.
119. *Ibid.* at 150.
120. See e.g. *Re Kieran* [1916] 1 IR 289. Although note the comments of Lord Wilberforce in *McPhail v. Doulton* [1971] AC 424, 452 to the effect that 'a discretionary trust can, in a suitable case be executed according to its merits and otherwise than by equal division'.

EQUITY LOOKS TO THE INTENT RATHER THAN THE FORM

While this maxim does not mean that legal formalities will not be required by equity, it looks to the substance rather than the form of a transaction and does not require 'unnecessary formalities'[121] to be observed. Lord Romilly MR laid down this principle in *Parkin v. Thorold*[122] in the following terms:

> Courts of Equity make a distinction in all cases between that which is matter of substance and that which is matter of form; and if it find that by insisting on the form, the substance will be defeated, it holds it to be inequitable to allow a person to insist on such form, and thereby defeat the substance.

This maxim was applied in a number of situations. First, where land was used as security for a loan, equity regarded the transaction as a mortgage even though it might not be described as such.[123] In addition, equity provided relief against the payment of penalties on this basis. Where the parties to a contract agreed that in the event of its breach, a named sum of money would be paid by the defaulting party, equity would ask whether it was a genuine estimate of the damage which would result from the breach or whether it was a penalty to be held over the head of the other party. In deciding this, equity would look at the parties' intention rather than the form of the instrument. Another example of the operation of this maxim is where there has been a failure to complete a contract for the sale of land within the time stipulated. While at law the party who failed to complete was in breach of contract, in equity he would be permitted to complete the contract within a reasonable time thereafter, provided time was not expressed to be of the essence in relation to completion of the contract.[124]

Another illustration of this maxim is the fact that a valid trust may be created without actually using the word 'trust'.[125] In limited circumstances a trust may be created by the use of 'precatory words' where a gift is made and the donee expresses the wish or hope that the property be dealt with in a particular manner. However, the use of such words will only be held to be sufficient to create a trust if this intention is clear from the language used in the instrument as a whole,[126] and they are more usually interpreted as being insufficient to achieve this result.[127]

---

121. *Sprange v. Lee* [1908] 1 Ch 424, 430 *per* Neville J.
122. (1852) 16 Beav 59, 66–67.
123. *Grangeside Properties Ltd v. Collingswood Securities Ltd* [1964] 1 WLR 140.
124. *Tilley v. Thomas* (1867) 3 Ch App 61, 67.
125. *Page v. Cox* (1852) 10 Hare 163, 169 *per* Turner VC.
126. *Comiskey v. Bowring-Hanbury* [1905] AC 84.
127. *Re Humphrey's Estate* [1916] 1 IR 21; *Re Sweeney* [1976–77] ILRM 88.

This maxim is also the basis for the equitable remedy of rectification which allows an instrument to be rectified or corrected where it fails to record the actual intention of the parties to a contract.[128] Equity looks at the substance of the transaction and allows rectification in circumstances where it would be inequitable to allow a party to retain a benefit obtained e.g. as a result of mistake.[129]

EQUITY LOOKS ON THAT AS DONE WHICH OUGHT TO HAVE BEEN DONE

Where a specifically enforceable obligation exists, equity regards the parties as being in the position in which they would have been had the obligation been performed, and their legal rights and duties are assessed by reference to this position. So, in equity, a specifically enforceable contract for a lease is treated as being equivalent to a lease and the rights and duties of the parties are regarded as being the same as if the lease had actually been executed.[130] Similarly, a specifically enforceable contract for the sale of land transfers the equitable interest to the purchaser to the extent to which the purchase price is paid, and the vendor holds the legal title on a constructive trust until completion.[131]

It has traditionally been assumed that the maxim cannot be relied on in this context by a volunteer and equity will regard the obligation as carried out only in favour of persons who are entitled to specifically enforce the contract. Lindley LJ made this point as follows in *Re Anstis*:[132]

> Equity no doubt, looks on that as done which ought to be done; but this rule, although usually expressed in general terms, is by no means universally true. Where the obligation to do what ought to be done is not an absolute duty, but only an obligation arising from contract, that which ought to be done is only treated as done in favour of some person entitled to enforce the contract as against the person liable to perform it.

A similar approach seems to have been adopted by Scott J in *Davis v. Richards and Wallington Ltd*[133] in which he applied the maxim that 'equity looks on that as done which ought to be done' in considering the validity of a definitive trust deed establishing a pension scheme. Scott J said that the effect of the

---

128. See *infra* Chapter 15.
129. *Irish Life Assurance Co. Ltd v. Dublin Land Securities Ltd* [1989] IR 253.
130. *Walsh v. Lonsdale* (1882) 21 Ch D 9.
131. *Tempany v. Hynes* [1976] IR 101, 114 *per* Kenny J, O'Higgins CJ concurring.
132. (1886) 31 Ch D 596, 605.
133. [1990] 1 WLR 1511.

maxim was explained in the following terms in *Snell's Equity*,[134] namely: 'Equity treats a contract to do a thing as if the thing were already done, though only in favour of persons entitled to enforce the contract specifically and not in favour of volunteers.'

However, this requirement does not appear to have been enforced by Carroll J in *Shanahan v. Redmond*.[135] The deceased named his cousin as sole beneficiary of a trust, the assets of which comprised a life insurance policy. The parties fell out and the deceased attempted unsuccessfully to exercise a power of appointment over the trust funds in his own favour. Subsequently he instructed the insurance company to cancel the policy and to replace it with a similar one under which he would be the sole beneficiary. Although this direction had not been carried out when the testator died, Carroll J applied the maxim that equity looks on that as done which ought to be done and held that the existing policy should be treated as if it were a substitute policy in which the deceased was named as sole beneficiary.

Another controversial application of the maxim is contained in the decision of the Privy Council in *Attorney General for Hong Kong v. Reid*[136] where it held that when a fiduciary receives a bribe he holds it under a constructive trust for his principal. Lord Templeman explained this conclusion on the basis of the fiduciary's obligation to account to his principal for the bribe. As he stated: 'Equity considers as done that which ought to have been done. As soon as the bribe was received, whether in cash or in kind, the false fiduciary held the bribe on a constructive trust for the person injured.'[137]

The maxim that equity looks on that as done which ought to be done also underlies the doctrine of conversion which operates by regarding one form of property as being another where there is an obligation to convert it.[138] The effect of the doctrine is that in certain circumstances the nature of property is notionally changed so that realty may be treated as personalty with the legal incidents of personalty and *vice versa*. The reasoning behind this is that where a person is under a duty to convert one form of property into another, it will not be regarded as still being in its original form because the person concerned has failed to perform his obligations.

---

134. (28th ed., 1982) p. 41. Now see McGhee (30th ed., 2000) p.40.
135. High Court 1994 No. 129 Sp (Carroll J) 21 June 1994.
136. [1994] 1 AC 324.
137. *Ibid.* at 331. This reasoning has been criticised by a number of commentators. Gardner [1995] CLJ 60, 61 has suggested that 'the maxim's cryptic form has apparently led it to be applied in a fashion which cannot be squared with a proper articulation of the law in question.' See also Oakley [1994] CLJ 31 and Watts (1994) 110 LQR 178.
138. See further Chapter 19.

EQUITY IMPUTES AN INTENTION TO FULFIL AN OBLIGATION

Where a person is under an obligation to perform an act and does some other act which could be regarded as fulfilment of that original obligation, it will be regarded as such. This maxim forms the basis for the equitable doctrines of satisfaction and performance.[139] The effect of the first doctrine is that if a person is under an obligation to another person and subsequently gives that person a benefit, it is presumed that the benefit is intended to satisfy the obligation or debt. Similarly, where a party is under an obligation to carry out a particular act and subsequently does an act which can be considered as performance of his obligation, equity will presume that this subsequent act was carried out in order to fulfil the earlier obligation.

EQUITY ACTS IN PERSONAM

This maxim has been described by Meagher, Gummow and Lehane[140] as 'historically of the greatest importance, theoretically the most elusive and practically of the most dubious significance'. While it has been acknowledged that the 'rights and interests evolved in equity were originally conceived as purely personal'[141] it has also been recognised that the view that equitable interests convey no right *in rem* cannot be reconciled with the right of a beneficiary to follow trust property.[142] While it is still fair to say that equitable relief tends to be of a personal rather than a proprietary nature, this maxim must increasingly be read with some degree of caution.

It was originally one of the most fundamental principles of equity that equitable jurisdiction was exercised against the person of the defendant rather than against his property. This is illustrated by the fact that failure to comply with an order granting equitable relief constitutes contempt of court. Where such a remedy was insufficient, the Court of Chancery had recourse to the writ of sequestration and since the enactment of the Judicature Act, orders can be enforced by any of the legal writs of execution e.g. *fieri facias*.

As Lord Selborne LC stated in *Ewing v. Orr Ewing (No.1)*:[143] 'The Courts of Equity in England are, and always have been, courts of conscience, operating *in personam* and not *in rem*; and in the exercise of this personal jurisdiction they have always been accustomed to compel the performance of contracts

---

139. See *infra* Chapter 19.
140. *Equity Doctrines and Remedies* (3rd ed., 1992) p.96.
141. *Re Cuff Knox* [1963] IR 263, 289 *per* Kingsmill Moore J.
142. *Ibid.*
143. (1883) 9 App Cas 34, 40.

and trusts as to subjects which were not either locally or *ratione domicilli* within their jurisdiction.'

The maxim also had relevance to disputes relating to property outside the jurisdiction and it was immaterial that the property in question was not within a court's jurisdiction provided that the defendant himself was within its jurisdiction or could be served outside the jurisdiction. So, in *Penn v. Lord Baltimore*[144] an English court ordered specific performance of an agreement relating to land boundaries of property in the US although the defendant was in England. When the defendant objected to the jurisdiction of the court, Lord Hardwicke replied that the conscience of the defendant was bound by the agreement and that the dispute was a matter within the jurisdiction of the court which acted *in personam*.

A similar point was made by the Irish Court of Appeal in *Lett v. Lett*[145] in which an injunction was granted to restrain proceedings taken in an Argentine court which amounted to a repudiation of a settlement of divorce proceedings by virtue of which a wife had undertaken not to pursue any further claim against her husband. As Sir Samuel Walker stated: 'The jurisdiction asserted is not against the foreign tribunal, but against the person within the jurisdiction, who has made a contract not to resort to proceedings; and whether such proceedings are in a foreign court or not, is immaterial for the purpose of the equity on which the jurisdiction rests — an equity *in personam*.'[146]

An issue which has provoked considerable controversy in recent years is whether an interest in land arising under a trust is to be characterized as a right of an *in rem* or *in personam* nature. The practical significance of this classification becomes apparent in the context of the provisions of Article 16 of the Convention on Jurisdiction and the Enforcement of Judgments in Civil and Commercial Matters 1968[147] which provides, *inter alia,* that in proceedings which have as their object rights *in rem* in immovable property, the courts of the state in which the property is situated shall have exclusive jurisdiction. The failure to clarify the nature of such rights has led to inconsistencies in the application of the Convention, as an examination of the decisions of the European Court of Justice in *Webb v. Webb*[148] and of Rattee J in *Re Hayward*[149] reveals. In *Webb* the claim of a beneficiary under a trust was classifed as a right *in personam* rather than *in rem*. A father had bought a flat in France in his son's name and subsequently sought a declaration that the son held the property as a trustee for him. In accordance with the provisions of Article 16 of the Convention if the action had been designated as involving rights *in*

---

144. (1750) 1 Ves Sen 444.
145. [1906] 1 IR 618.
146. *Ibid*. at 635.
147. Now see Article 22 of Council Regulation EC No. 44/2001.
148. [1994] QB 696.
149. [1997] Ch 45.

rem, the French courts would have had exclusive jurisdiction in the matter. However, the European Court of Justice concluded that an action for a declaration that a person holds immovable property as a trustee did not constitute an action *in rem* within the meaning of Article 16 of the Convention which meant that the father was entitled to sue in the English courts.[150]

However, this decision is difficult to reconcile with that of Rattee J in *Re Hayward*[151] in which he characterized the claim of a trustee in bankruptcy of a deceased co-owner to a half share of a villa in Spain as of *in rem* nature. As it was a right *in rem* in immovable property within the meaning of Article 16 of the Convention, it was held that the Spanish courts had exclusive jurisdiction in the matter. Rattee J distinguished the decision in *Webb*, asserting that the trustee was in effect claiming the right to legal ownership of half of the villa and said that it was 'difficult to contemplate any right more clearly a right *in rem*'. Stevens[152] has asserted that while the result in *Hayward* was consistent with the policy of the Convention, namely that matters relating to the ownership of land should be determined by the court of the country in which that land is situated, the inconsistency with the decision in *Webb* is open to criticism. In his view, it was by no means clear that the claim of the father in *Webb* was any different in substance to that of the trustee in bankruptcy in *Hayward* and the suggestion of Rattee J that the latter was seeking an essentially different right was 'entirely artificial'. However, Stevens concludes that it is only when it is acknowledged that beneficial interests 'are true proprietary rights *in rem*, albeit of less durability that their legal equivalent'[153] that it will be possible to adopt a consistent approach to issues of jurisdiction. It is difficult to fault the reasoning adopted by Stevens and it will clearly be necessary for the courts to clarify the position of equitable proprietary rights for the purposes of private international law. Despite the traditional classification of such rights as being of an *in personam* nature, this will need to be reassessed in order to achieve a consistency of approach towards issues of jurisdiction where ownership of land is at stake.

---

150. The decision in *Webb* was criticised by Briggs (1994) 110 LQR 526. However, MacMillan [1996] Conv 125, 129 is more supportive of the conclusion reached, asking 'is it not preferable that the determination of a trust created in England be made by an English court'.
151. [1997] Ch 45.
152. [1998] Conv 144.
153. *Ibid.* at 152.

WHERE THE EQUITIES ARE EQUAL, THE FIRST IN TIME
PREVAILS

WHERE THE EQUITIES ARE EQUAL, THE LAW PREVAILS

These two related maxims are relevant to the question of priorities as between competing interests in land. However, they cannot be looked at in isolation; it is necessary to examine the distinction between equitable interests as opposed to mere equities and the effect of the doctrine of notice on the operation of the maxims. Finally, it is also necessary to consider the impact which registration has had on the question of priorities between competing interests in land.

Equitable Interests and Mere Equities

It is difficult to define the concept of a 'mere equity' with any degree of clarity or to explain the characteristics which distinguish mere equities from equitable interests properly so called. Equitable interests can be categorised as actual rights in property and include interests arising under a trust, equitable mortgages, equities of redemption, restrictive covenants and contracts to convey or create a legal estate in land. On the other hand, mere equities are better described as rights of a procedural nature which are ancillary to a property right and include e.g. the right to have a transaction set aside for fraud or undue influence or a right to have a document rectified for mistake.[154] Delany[155] has suggested that the term extends 'to all personal claims which *may* be converted into equitable estates and interests' and Everton has said that a mere equity might be defined as 'a right of an exclusively personal nature to pursue an equitable remedy'.[156] She suggests that many of the difficulties which have been encountered in endeavouring to distinguish between equities and equitable interests could be overcome if it were accepted that equitable interests can be variable in character and of different quality. Not all mere equities can bind third parties and a category sometimes referred to as a 'naked equity' was identified by the House of Lords in *National Provincial Bank Ltd v. Ainsworth*.[157] In the Court of Appeal, Lord Denning MR had held that a deserted wife had a 'licence coupled with an equity' entitling her to remain in possession of the family home and that this took precedence over the rights of the plaintiff bank which had taken a mortgage

---

154. See Everton (1976) 40 Conv 209, 210.
155. (1957) 21 Conv 195, 201.
156. *Ibid.* at 220. Wade [1955] CLJ 158, 160 has suggested that another distinction between equitable interests and mere equities lies in the fact that mere equities are discretionary in character but he concedes that a purchaser's right under a contract for the sale of land which must surely amount to more than a mere equity depends on the willingness of a court to award specific performance (at 161).
157. [1965] AC 1175.

on the house. However, the House of Lords reversed this decision; as Lord Upjohn stated, the wife was seeking to assert rights over the land of another in relation to which she had no beneficial ownership. He said that he could not see how it was possible for a mere equity to bind a purchaser unless it was ancillary to or dependent on an equitable estate or interest in land. In the case before him the right of the wife was not ancillary to or dependent on an equitable interest and could not bind purchasers; it was a right of a purely personal nature.[158]

The most practical significance of the distinction between mere equities and equitable estates can be seen where a question of priorities arises. As the maxim makes clear, where the equities are equal, the first in time prevails, but where one equity is superior to another, the time of their creation cannot govern priority. It would appear that the maxim should only be applied where the equities are in all respects equal. On this point Kindersley VC stated as follows in *Rice v. Rice*:[159]

> [I]n a contest between persons having only equitable interests, priority of time is the ground of preference last resorted to; i.e. . . . . a Court of Equity will not prefer the one to the other, on the mere ground of priority of time, until it finds upon an examination of the relative merits that there is no other sufficient ground of preference between them, or in other words that their equities are in all other respects equal; and that, if the one has on other grounds a better equity than the other, priority of time is immaterial.

While a *bona fide* purchaser of a legal estate for value and without notice of an earlier equitable interest may take the property free of that interest, a *bona fide* purchaser of an equitable interest without notice of an earlier equitable interest will take subject to it on the basis of the maxim that where the equities are equal the first in time prevails. However, while such a purchaser does not take free of prior equitable interests, he will take free of any prior mere equities on the basis that the 'equities' are not equal. An example of how this distinction may be of practical importance is provided by the decision of Lord Sugden LC in *Bowen v. Evans*.[160] There a dispute arose between the plaintiff, who sought to have a deed set aside for fraud and one of the defendants, who claimed under a settlement for value of the lands which constituted an equitable

---

158. As Keane points out in *Equity and the Law of Trusts in the Republic of Ireland* (1988) p. 44 the point decided in *Ainsworth* is now academic in this jurisdiction as a result of the enactment of the Family Home Protection Act 1976, s. 3 of which renders invalid any disposition of the family home by one spouse without the written consent of the other.
159. (1853) 2 Drew 73, 77. Quoted with approval by Porter MR in *Bank of Ireland v. Cogry Flax Spinning Co* [1900] 1 IR 219, 230.
160. (1844) 6 Ir Eq R 569.

interest. Sugden LC held that this defendant could raise a plea of purchaser for value against the plaintiff on the basis that the plaintiff's right to have the transaction impeached for fraud was a mere equity and so could not take priority over the defendant's equitable estate acquired for value and without notice of the plaintiff's claim.

This decision is difficult to reconcile with his subsequent judgment as Lord St Leonards in *Stump v. Gaby*[161] in which he found that where a person makes a conveyance in circumstances where it may be set aside for fraud, his equitable right to rescind amounts to a beneficial interest in the land conveyed that is capable of being devised by will. The better view would seem to be that expressed subsequently by Lord Westbury in *Phillips v. Phillips*[162] where he confirmed that the right to set aside a deed for fraud or correct it for mistake was a mere equity as distinct from an equitable interest. A similar conclusion was reached more recently in this jurisdiction by Kenny J in *Allied Irish Banks v. Glynn*.[163] The first named defendant conveyed land to his son, the second named defendant, subject to the former's right to remain in residence in a house on the lands. The son deposited the land certificate with the plaintiff bank as security for monies advanced to him by the bank. As a result of proceedings brought by the father, the conveyance was set aside on the grounds of undue influence. The plaintiff bank which was not aware of these proceedings, then brought a claim to enforce the equitable mortgage. Kenny J held, in giving priority to the bank, that the equitable mortgage took precedence over the prior right of the father to have the deed set aside, a right which was described as a chose in action rather than an equitable interest.

Similarly, there has been some dispute about the status of a beneficiary's equitable right to trace trust property into the hands of third parties and specifically about whether it should be categorised as an equitable interest or as a mere equity. The position in England would appear to be that it is recognised as an equitable interest. In *Cave v. Cave*[164] trustees improperly invested trust moneys in the purchase of land, the legal estate in which was conveyed to another party who created both legal and equitable mortgages. Fry J held that the mortgagees took without notice and that as between the beneficiaries and the equitable mortgagee, the beneficiaries took priority because they had a prior equitable estate as opposed to a mere equity. Therefore, although the equitable mortgagee was acting in good faith and took without notice of the beneficiaries' interest, he could not take priority over the prior equitable interest of the beneficiaries. The result in this case is a good illustration of the maxim that where the equities are equal, the first in time

---

161. (1852) 2 De GM & G 623.
162. (1862) 4 De G F & J 208.
163. [1973] IR 188. See also *Latec Investments Ltd v. Hotel Terrigal Pty Ltd* (1965) 113 CLR 265 *per* Kitto and Menzies JJ.
164. (1880) 15 Ch D 639.

prevails, although as the decision of the Irish Court of Appeal in *Re Ffrench's Estate*[165] shows, the result will be different where the equities are not considered to be equal. That decision also concerned a contest as between the right of beneficiaries to trace and that of an equitable mortgagee, although Porter MR reached the opposite conclusion on this issue to that arrived at by Fry J in *Cave v. Cave*. Trust funds were mixed by an equitable tenant for life with his own funds and used to buy property. A question of priorities arose between the right of the beneficiaries to trace the trust funds and a bank in whose favour an equitable mortgage had been created, which had no knowledge of the fact that the trust funds had been converted. It was held that the rights of the equitable mortgagee must prevail over the rights of the beneficiaries who possessed a mere equity only i.e. the right of tracing. Porter MR said that the equity of the mortgagees was a 'superior equity' to that of the beneficiaries. In his view, the primary right of a beneficiary was against his own trustees and the right to trace the trust fund into its improper investment was ancillary to this. He concluded that such an ancillary right should not prevail against innocent purchasers and said that in this instance he was unable to regard the equities as equal. Porter MR regarded the beneficiaries' right as 'rather in the nature of a chose in action than an estate — an equity as distinguished from an equitable interest and inferior to the equitable interest of the mortgagees.' While Porter MR was the only member of the court who decided the case on the basis that a right to trace was a mere equity, this view has been applied in several decisions in this jurisdiction.[166] In *Scott v. Scott*,[167] the administratrix of an estate and her son had invested certain assets of the estate in a house and deposited the title deeds with a bank by way of mortgage. When a dispute over priorities arose between the next of kin and the bank, it was held that the former's right was a mere equity which could not prevail over an equitable estate such as was possessed by the bank which amounted to an equitable mortgage on specific items of property.

While this approach to the status of a beneficiary's right to trace appears to be established in Ireland, Wylie[168] has questioned its soundness on the basis that it seems to involve an 'unjustifiable limitation' of the beneficiaries' interests.

---

165. (1887) 21 LR Ir 283.
166. See *Re Sloane's Estate* [1895] 1 IR 146 in which Monroe J confirmed (at 165) that the right to trace was a 'lower one' than the right created by an equitable mortgage by deposit. See also *Bourke v. Lee* [1904] 1 IR 280 and *Re Bobbett's Estate* [1904] 1 IR 461.
167. [1924] 1 IR 141.
168. See Wylie, *Irish Land Law* (3rd ed., 1997) pp. 129–130.

Priorities and the Doctrine of Notice[169]

The basic rule at law as in equity is that estates and interests rank in priority according to the order of their creation where they are otherwise equal and so it is important to distinguish legal estates, equitable estates and mere equities for this purpose. The other important factor which affects the question of priorities is the doctrine of notice. This in turn has been affected and to some extent displaced by the modern systems of registration. As regards notice, the rule developed by equity was that a *bona fide* purchaser for value without notice of a legal estate or interest in land would take free of an equitable interest of which he had no notice. Similarly, a *bona fide* purchaser for value of an equitable interest without notice will take free of a mere equity. As Keane[170] points out, there are two exceptions to this principle, first that a naked equity, such as the right of a spouse to possession considered in *National Provincial Bank v. Ainsworth*,[171] will not be binding on a subsequent purchaser irrespective of the question of notice as the right is purely personal in nature and cannot be binding on third parties. In addition, a purchaser for value of registered land will not be affected by an unregistered equitable claim even if he has notice of it.

For the doctrine of the *bona fide* purchaser without notice to come into effect, the purchaser must be *bona fide* i.e. there must have been no fraud on his part in relation to the purchase. Secondly, he must have been a purchaser for value although there is authority for the proposition that it need not be shown that the consideration given was adequate. Finally, the purchaser must establish that he took the estate without notice of any prior interest.

It is generally accepted that there are three forms of notice — actual, constructive and imputed — and these can be identified in section 3(1) of the Conveyancing Act 1882 which provides as follows:

A purchaser shall not be prejudicially affected by notice of any instrument, fact or thing unless:

(i) It is within his own knowledge, or would have come to his knowledge if such inquiries and inspections had been made as ought reasonably to have been made by him; or

(ii) In the same transaction with respect to which a question of notice to the purchaser arises, it has come to the knowledge of his counsel, as such, or of his solicitor, or other agent, as such, or would have come to the knowledge of his solicitor, or other agent as such, if such inquiries and inspections had been made as ought reasonably to have been made by the solicitor or other agent.

---

169. Sheridan (1950) 9 NILQ 33.
170. *Equity and the Law of Trusts in the Republic of Ireland* (1988) p. 55.
171. [1965] AC 1175.

Actual Notice

A person will be considered to have actual notice where he discovers information himself, so a subjective standard is imposed. The wording of section 3(1)(i) shows that unlike in the case of imputed knowledge referred to in paragraph (ii), it is not necessary that the actual knowledge was obtained in the course of the transaction in question. However, it is clear that merely hearing a rumour will not amount to actual notice.[172]

The question of actual notice was considered by the Supreme Court in *Bank of Ireland Finance Ltd v. Rockfield*[173] although in a different context. The question at issue was whether the plaintiff bank had notice of the fact that monies advanced to a company had been used to purchase its own shares in breach of section 60 of the Companies Act 1963, subsection 14 of which provides that any transaction in breach of section 60 is voidable at the instance of the company against any person who had notice of the facts that constituted the breach of the statute. The Supreme Court held that the company could not invoke section 60(14) as they had failed to establish that the plaintiff had actual notice of the facts alleged to constitute a breach of the section prior to the transaction in question. Kenny J stated that the notice referred to in the subsection was actual notice and not constructive notice and said that there was strong authority to support the view that the doctrine of constructive notice should not be extended to commercial transactions. He said that he was using the term 'actual notice' 'as meaning in this case that the plaintiff bank, or any of its officials, had been informed, either verbally or in writing, that part of the advance was to be applied in the purchase of shares in the defendant company, or that they knew facts from which they *must* have inferred that part of the advance was to be applied for this purpose.'[174]

Constructive Notice

A person will be deemed to have constructive notice where he fails to make the inquiries and inspections which he ought reasonably to have made, judged by reference to standard conveyancing procedures. It is stated in *Snell's Equity*[175] that a purchaser will be treated as having constructive notice 'of all that a reasonably prudent purchaser, acting on skilled advice, would have discovered'. The question of constructive notice was considered by Henchy J in the Supreme Court in the context of the application of the Family Home Protection Act 1976 in *Somers v. W.*[176]

---

172. *O'Connor v. McCarthy* [1982] IR 161, 174. See also *Lloyd v. Banks* (1868) 3 Ch App 488, 491 *per* Lord Cairns.
173. [1979] IR 21.
174. *Ibid.* at 37.
175. McGhee (30th ed., 2000) pp. 53–54.
176. [1979] IR 94.

The plaintiff had purchased a house from the defendant's husband without the defendant's consent and sought to sell it to a purchaser who insisted on obtaining her written consent. The plaintiff then sought an order dispensing with the defendant's consent under section 4 of the Family Home Protection Act 1976. In finding for the defendant, the Supreme Court held that at the date of the purported assignment, the plaintiff was affected by constructive notice of the defendant's statutory rights as these would have come to the knowledge of the plaintiff's solicitor if such inquiries had been made as ought reasonably to have been made. The Supreme Court therefore concluded that the purported assignment by the defendant's husband to the plaintiff was void. Henchy J stated as follows:

> In earlier times the tendency was to judge a purchaser solely by the facts that actually came to his knowledge. In the course of time it came to be held in the Court of Chancery that it would be unconscionable for the purchaser to take his stand on the facts that had come to his notice to the exclusion of those which ordinary prudence or circumspection or skill should have called to his attention. When the facts at his command beckoned him to look and inquire further, and he refrained from doing so, equity fixed him with constructive notice of what he would have ascertained if he had pursued the further investigation which a person with reasonable care and skill would have felt proper to make in the circumstances.[177]

Further consideration was given to the question of what will constitute making reasonable inquiries by the Supreme Court in *Northern Bank Ltd v. Henry*.[178] The second named defendant purchased the leasehold interest in a house with money which belonged to the first named defendant, his wife, but the assignment of the interest was made to him alone. The wife sought a declaration that she was entitled in equity to the leasehold interest. On the same day the husband mortgaged the house to the plaintiff bank which apart from making a search in the Registry of Deeds, made no investigation of the husband's title. The wife succeeded in obtaining a declaration that her husband held the leasehold interest in trust for her and claimed that her interest prevailed over that of the plaintiff bank because, she contended, it had constructive notice of her interest. Henchy J emphasized that section 3(1) of the Conveyancing Act 1882 gave statutory force to the 'existing judicial insistence that constructive notice could be found only when lack of knowledge was due to such careless inactivity as would not be expected in the circumstances from a reasonable man'. He stated:

---

177. *Ibid.* at 108.
178. [1981] IR 1.

In my judgment, the test of what inquiries and inspections ought reasonably to have been made by the plaintiffs is an objective test which depends not on what the particular purchaser thought proper to do in the particular circumstances but on what a purchaser of the particular property ought reasonably to have done to acquire title to it.... . [Section 3(1)] because it is laying down the circumstances in which a purchaser is not to be prejudicially affected by notice of any instrument, fact or thing, is setting as a standard of conduct that which is expected from a reasonable purchaser. Reasonableness in this context must be judged by reference to what should be done to acquire the estate or interest being purchased, rather than by the motive for or the purpose of the particular purchase.[179]

Imputed Notice

This type of notice is referred to in section 3(1)(ii) of the Act of 1882. The effect of the subsection is that all knowledge, of which an agent of a purchaser is actually aware or of which he would have been aware if he had made the inquiries and inspections which he ought reasonably to have made, will be attributed to the purchaser. However, the subsection also stipulates that this notice must have been acquired 'in the same transaction' if it is to bind the purchaser and so any knowledge which an agent may have obtained from previous dealings will not be relevant in this context.

Onus of Proof

Finally, it should be noted that the onus of proving that a person had no notice of a prior interest lies on the party claiming that he took without notice. This was confirmed by O'Byrne J in *Heneghan v. Davitt*.[180] The plaintiff entered into an agreement for the purchase of lands and while the agreement was awaiting completion the vendors entered into a further agreement for sale with another person which was carried into effect by a conveyance. The plaintiff brought a claim for specific performance. In the Circuit Court, the third party's plea of purchaser for value without notice was upheld but in the High Court it was held that it had been incorrect to impose the onus of proving that the other person had not been a *bona fide* purchaser without notice on the plaintiff. The onus rested instead on the defendant to prove that he was a purchaser for value without notice and since he had not discharged this onus, the plaintiff was granted specific performance of the agreement. O'Byrne J stated as follows:

---

179. *Ibid.* at 9.
180. [1933] IR 375.

In order to defeat a plea of purchaser for value without notice, it is not, in my opinion, necessary that the purchaser should have actual notice. If he has sufficient notice or knowledge to put him upon enquiry, and if he deliberately refrains from making such enquiry, he is thereupon deemed to have constructive notice of such facts as would have come to his knowledge if he had made proper enquiry; and such constructive notice is, in my opinion, sufficient to defeat the plea.[181]

Registration of Deeds, Priorities and Notice

There are two main systems of registration affecting land in Ireland; the registration of deeds system introduced by the Registration of Deeds Act (Ireland) 1707 which provided for the registration of memorials of deeds and conveyances affecting lands, tenements and hereditaments, and the registration of title system which provides for the registration of ownership of land.

The registration of deeds system did not have any kind of comprehensive application; it was not compulsory and where there was no memorial or written document in existence relating to a disposition, there was nothing to register. However two provisions of the Act of 1707 are still of considerable importance to the question of priorities where a deed has been registered and must be examined. Section 4 provides that registered dispositions rank in priority according to their date of registration not according to their date of execution, so the maxim that where the equities are equal the first in time prevails has no application in this instance. Section 5 provides that a deed or conveyance of which a memorial is not registered will be deemed 'fraudulent and void' against a deed or conveyance, a memorial of which has been registered and effectively provides that a registered disposition will take priority over a registrable but unregistered disposition.

However, the Act did not govern priorities where an unregistrable disposition was involved e.g. the deposit of the title deeds of land to create an equitable mortgage. In this case such a disposition will take priority over a subsequent equitable interest even though the latter is registered. So in *Re Burke's Estate*[182] it was held that the holder of an equitable mortgage by deposit of title deeds, unaccompanied by any memorandum in writing, took priority over a purchaser for value claiming under a subsequent registered deed, without knowledge of the mortgage.

Where two registered dispositions are involved in a conflict as to priorities, the provisions of section 4 of the 1707 Act will apply and they will rank according to the date of registration of the memorials of the transactions. The question of notice will not be relevant and a purchaser for value without notice

---

181. *Ibid.* at 379.
182. (1882) 9 LR Ir 24.

cannot claim priority over a prior registered deed irrespective of whether the estates or interests created are legal or equitable.[183] However, where there is a conflict between a prior unregistered deed and a subsequent registered deed, the issue of notice does become relevant. It was held in *Forbes v. Deniston*[184] that the 1707 Act which was intended to prevent fraud should not be used to provide a means of achieving fraud. So, where a purchaser who registers a deed has notice of a prior unregistered deed he will not be permitted to obtain priority. In *Forbes* a subsequent lessee, whose lease was registered and who knew of a prior unregistered lease, was not permitted by the House of Lords to take priority over the holder of the earlier lease.

It has been established that for this qualification to the statutory scheme to operate, the purchaser/lessee must have actual notice of the existence of the prior unregistered deed at the time of the subsequent deed's execution or at least at the time of its registration or else have notice imputed to him by reason of the actual notice of his agent. Therefore, in this context constructive notice will be insufficient, a point re-affirmed by Costello J in *O'Connor v. McCarthy*.[185] A company contracted in writing to sell premises to a purchaser although the memorial of the contract was not registered in accordance with the provisions of the Registration of Deeds Act 1707. It subsequently contracted in writing to sell the premises to a second purchaser and this contract was registered in the Registry of Deeds. The second purchaser's solicitor had no knowledge of the existence of the first contract when he registered the second. However, the second purchaser had heard rumours of a previous contract, but being satisfied that he had in fact bought the premises, did not inform his solicitor of this. Costello J held that the registration of the memorial of the second contract in accordance with the provisions of the 1707 Act conferred priority on it subject to the equitable doctrine of notice. He held that neither the second purchaser nor his solicitor had actual notice of the existence or nature of the first contract and that therefore the second contract must be given its statutory priority. Costello J effectively held that constructive notice was insufficient to defeat the statutory scheme. However, he proceeded to refer to the *dicta* of Lord Cairns in *Agra Bank Ltd v. Barry*[186] and suggested that where a purchaser has not acted in good faith e.g. where he has deliberately refrained from making inquiries, the court might not give effect to the statutory priority even though the purchaser only has constructive notice. In this instance, Costello J was satisfied that neither the second purchaser nor his solicitor had acted in any way *mala fide* and there was no reason to consider whether constructive notice might have sufficed to displace the statutory priority accorded to the second contract.

---

183. *Eyre v. Dolphin* (1813) 2 Ba & B 290.
184. (1722) 4 Bro PC 189.
185. [1982] IR 161.
186. (1874) LR 7 HL 135, 149.

Registration of Title and Priorities[187]

Under the registration of title system, title to any land may be registered. In general the system operates on a voluntary basis although registration of title of certain types of land and of land situated in specified counties is compulsory,[188] and once land is registered, all dealings relating to it must be effected through the Land Registry. Where title has been registered, the register will to a large extent govern the question of priorities as between competing interests in land. However, certain types of rights and burdens listed in section 72 of the Registration of Title Act 1964 can affect registered land without being registered. In addition, other unregistered rights apart from those referred to in section 72 may be created in or over registered land, although these will not affect the registered owner of a charge created on land for valuable consideration and will only be effective where the transferee is a volunteer.[189] So, where an equitable mortgage is created by the deposit of the land certificate, this equitable charge is subject to any prior equitable interests in accordance with the maxim that where the equities are equal the first in time prevails. In *Tench v. Molyneux*[190] the equitable interest of a purchaser of registered land who had failed to take the necessary steps to effect his registration as owner was held to take priority over a party with whom the vendor had subsequently deposited the land certificate to secure a loan. As the equities were equal in this case, the interest of the purchaser being prior in time prevailed.

---

187. For more detailed consideration of the registration of title system, see Wylie, *Irish Land Law* (3rd ed., 1997) Chapter 21 and Coughlan, *Property Law* (2nd ed., 1998) Chapter 7.
188. Counties Carlow, Laois and Meath.
189. *Devoy v. Hanlon* [1929] IR 246.
190. (1914) 48 ILTR 48.

CHAPTER 3

Trusts — An Introduction

GENERAL PRINCIPLES

The Origins of the Trust Concept

The modern trust developed out of the medieval concept of the use whereby
the owner of land would give it to another to hold on his behalf.[1] Initially
where the owner of property put his land in the possession of another person
a mere moral obligation was imposed and the original owner had no remedy
if his wishes were not carried out. However, the Court of Chancery intervened
to provide for the enforcement of the use of land on the grounds that it would
be unconscionable not to recognise the device.

The system of the use was adopted for a number of reasons. Perhaps the
most significant of these, and the one which ultimately led to legislative
intervention to curb its predominance, was that it facilitated the avoidance of
certain feudal dues and incidents e.g. payments to a lord where an heir
succeeded to land or the right of escheat where there was no heir. In addition,
until the enactment of the Mortmain Act 1391, the concept also enabled
property to be effectively transferred to bodies corporate, usually religious
institutions, a practice which the earlier mortmain legislation had been designed
to prevent. A further advantage was that despite the fact that it was not possible
to make a devise of land in Ireland until after the passing of the Statute of
Wills (Ireland) Act 1634, a landowner could effectively achieve this result by
employing the device of the use. Another often fraudulent practice which
grew up was to grant lands to the use of another to defeat the claims of a
creditor or to delay actions for the recovery of land.

While the intervention of the Court of Chancery to give effect to the use
proved a most useful and beneficial practice from the point of view of tenants
of land, it grew increasingly unpopular with feudal lords and especially with
the ultimate overlord, the King of England. As a result the Statute of Uses
was passed in England in 1535 and the equivalent legislation, the Statute of

---

1. It became the practice to convey land 'to A to the use of B'. While B had no legal
    estate in the lands which remained at common law the property of A, the Court of
    Chancery would recognise B's beneficial or 'equitable' ownership of the land.

Uses (Ireland) 1634, was passed by the Irish parliament.[2] The statute provided that where any person or persons were seised of any lands or other hereditaments to the use, confidence or trust of any person(s) or of any corporation, the person or corporation having such use, confidence or trust in fee simple, fee tail, for term of life or for years, or otherwise, should be deemed in lawful seisin and possession of the lands or hereditaments for the same estate as he or they had in the use, confidence or trust.

Prior to the enactment of the statute, it was usual to grant land 'unto A and his heirs to the use of B and his heirs'. Its effect was to provide that the use should be immediately executed with the result that B would become the legal owner and A would have no further interest. As the Statute of Uses (Ireland) 1634 was not passed until nearly a century after the equivalent legislation had taken effect in England, it was recognised by the time of its enactment here that the legislation was far from comprehensive in nature. First, it applied only where a person was seised of land to the use of another, which effectively confined its application to freehold land. Secondly, it did not apply where the person to whom the freehold was conveyed had an active duty to perform e.g. to collect rent and pay it over.[3] Thirdly, the statute had no application where a body corporate, rather than a person or persons, was seised of lands to the 'use, trust or confidence' of any other person or corporation. However, the most important exclusion, and the one which ultimately led to the creation of the modern concept of the trust as we know it, was that a use upon a use did not come within the ambit of the statute. At common law there could not be a second use in a conveyance of freehold land so if the land was conveyed 'unto A and his heirs to the use of B and his heirs to the use of C and his heirs', the common law would not give effect to the use to C. This was established in *Tyrrel's* case[4] where it was held that where there was a use upon a use, the second use would not be executed by the statute.

However, the Court of Chancery in England gradually came around to the idea of enforcing this second use in a manner similar to that in which the first

---

2. 10 Chas. I, sess. 2, c.1. It should be noted that this statute has never been repealed. Pearce suggested in an article written in 1990 (see (1990) 41 NILQ 43) that the Statute of Uses could still have effect and that interests in freehold land arising from a contribution to its purchase price should in many cases be treated as executed by the statute. However, in a reply to this article published in 1996 (see (1996) 47 NILQ 367) Mee argued convincingly against such a proposition and submitted (at 376) 'that there is no possibility of the courts in Ireland deciding that the Statute of Uses should execute modern resulting or constructive trusts'.

3. If the statute executed the use in such a case, this person would be left with no interest in the property and would therefore be unable to carry out the duties imposed on him. However, the statute did apply if the use or trust was purely passive e.g. where land was conveyed to A on trust to permit B to receive the rents, A took no estate since there was no active duty to perform.

4. (1557) 2 Dy 1555a.

use had been enforced prior to the enactment of the Statute of Uses. While some controversy remains about when this practice became established,[5] in time the second use became known as a trust and it became common to simply convey property 'unto and to the use of B (the trustee) in trust for C' (the beneficiary).

Definition of a Trust

Since the concept of a trust came to be recognised, numerous attempts have been made both by members of the judiciary and various academic commentators to define in precise terms the nature of the rights and obligations which it gives rise to, often with only a limited degree of success.[6] Underhill and Hayton[7] provides the following definition:

> [A]n equitable obligation, binding a person (who is called a trustee) to deal with the property over which he has control (which is called the trust property) for the benefit of persons (who are called the beneficiaries or *cestuis que trust*) of whom he may himself be one, and any one of whom may enforce the obligation.[8]

This definition is insufficient to cover trusts for various purposes other than for the benefit of persons, so Pettit[9] makes the following addition 'or for a charitable purpose, which may be enforced at the instance of the Attorney General, or for some other purpose permitted by law though unenforceable'.

Perhaps the most comprehensive definition and one approved of in *Snell's Equity*[10] is that suggested by Keeton and Sheridan:

> A trust is the relationship which arises wherever a person (called the trustee) is compelled in equity to hold property, whether real or personal, and whether by legal or equitable title, for the benefit of some persons (of whom he may be one and who are termed beneficiaries) or for some

---

5. One view is that the courts had adopted this approach by the time of the enactment of the Statute of Uses (Ireland) 1634, (see Wylie, *Irish Land Law* (3rd ed., 1997) p. 171 and Baker (1977) 93 LQR 33, who relies on the authority of *Sambach v. Dalston* (1634) Toth 188), while another view is that the position was not clarified until later that century (see Strathdene (1958) 74 LQR 550 and Yale (1957) 15 CLJ 72).
6. See Hart (1899) 15 LQR 294 where a number of attempts at definitions dating back to 1734 are set out and analysed.
7. *Law Relating to Trusts and Trustees* (16th ed., 2003) p. 3.
8. This was quoted with approval by Cohen J in *Re Marshall's Will Trusts* [1945] 1 Ch 217, 219 and by Romer LJ in *Green v. Russell* [1959] 2 QB 226, 241.
9. *Equity and the Law of Trusts* (9th ed., 2001) p.25.
10. (30th ed., 2000, McGhee), p.110.

object permitted by law, in such a way that the real benefit accrues, not to the trustee, but to the beneficiaries or other objects of the trust.[11]

It is not always correct to refer to the trustee as the legal owner and the beneficiary as the equitable owner as the trustee's interest may be equitable only as where for instance a beneficiary under a settlement makes a settlement of his interest where the legal interest remains in the trustees of the original settlement. So it is more correct to refer to the trustee as the nominal owner of the property and the beneficiary as the beneficial owner.

TRUSTS DISTINGUISHED FROM OTHER FORMS OF LEGAL INSTITUTION

Before examining the trust concept in any detail it is useful to distinguish it from other legal institutions. Some of these may in certain circumstances resemble a trust and the duties and obligations which it gives rise to, although none of them contain all the essential elements necessary to constitute a trust and it is therefore important to be able to distinguish them. It is proposed to examine these in turn.

1. Trusts and Bailment

Pettit[12] suggests the following definition of bailment:

> delivery of personal chattels upon a condition, express or implied, that they shall be redelivered to the bailor, or according to his directions, when the purpose of the bailment has been carried out.

There are certain similarities between the position of a trustee and bailee in that both are subject to fiduciary obligations, albeit of varying degrees, in relation to the property which is within their control.[13] However, there are a number of basic distinctions between the concepts of a trust and a bailment. The first is that bailment is a creature of common law while trusts are equitable in nature and their enforcement is based on equitable rather than common law principles. Secondly, bailment applies only to personal property whereas a trust can apply to any type of property. Thirdly, while a bailor can enforce or vary the bailment, a settlor cannot carry out the same function in relation to a

---

11. *The Law of Trusts* (12th ed., 1993) p. 3.
12. *Equity and the Law of Trusts* (9th ed., 2001) p. 27.
13. See the judgment of Mason J in *Hospital Products Ltd v. United States Surgical Corporation* (1984) 156 CLR 41 for a discussion of the nature of the fiduciary obligation owed by a bailee to a bailor.

trust unless he has specifically reserved such a power to himself when setting it up. However, the most important practical significance of the distinction between the concepts of trust and bailment is where the person to whom possession of the property is given disposes of it to a third party. A bailee merely has special property in the goods which constitute the subject-matter of the bailment and cannot generally pass good title to the property which will be valid against the bailor.[14] On the other hand, a trustee can give good title in these circumstances to a person who acquires the legal ownership *bona fide* for value without notice of the trust.

2. Trusts and Agency

There are some similarities between the relationship of principal and agent and that of trustee and beneficiary to the extent that both the agent and the trustee have fiduciary obligations and must act in the interests of their principal or beneficiaries and not for their own benefit. While the agency relationship is governed mainly by common law principles, equity will intervene in certain circumstances. First, it will impose fiduciary obligations on an agent to make him liable to account where he has made a personal profit out of his position without the consent of his principal. In addition, he will be regarded as a constructive trustee where property has been entrusted to him by his principal for investment or safekeeping.

However, there are also a number of significant ways in which the relationships can be distinguished. First, the agency relationship is personal in nature, whereas the trust is proprietary. Secondly, there must be some form of agreement between an agent and his principal which forms the basis of their relationship, whereas this will hardly ever be either necessary or desirable between a trustee and the beneficiaries of a trust. Thirdly, the agency arrangement is normally terminated by the death of either the principal or the agent; this is not the case in relation to a trust where either a trustee or beneficiary dies. Fourthly, a trustee cannot commit the beneficiaries of a trust to liabilities towards third parties whereas an agent can commit his principal to such liabilities. Fifthly, an agent is bound to carry out his principal's instructions yet a trustee is not subject to such control either by the settlor or the beneficiaries and is simply bound to carry out the terms of the trust and discharge his functions as trustee according to law. A final essential element present in a trust relationship which is lacking in an agency agreement is that while an agent may have his principal's property in his possession, he will not usually have title to it.[15]

---

14. There are exceptions to this general principle, e.g. sale in market overt.
15. *Cave v. Mackenzie* (1877) 46 LJ Ch 564, 567 *per* Jessel MR.

3. Trusts and Contract

From one perspective, contracts and trusts would appear to be completely distinct concepts with few characteristics in common; the former is a creation of the common law, an arrangement which requires valuable consideration for its validity and one which only the parties to it can enforce. A trust, on the other hand, is a species of equitable obligation which can be perfectly valid without the element of consideration being present,[16] and which can be enforced by a beneficiary who is not party to the original arrangement between the testator/settlor and the trustees.

However, in practice it is often difficult to draw a distinction between these concepts and the same transaction may even give rise to both a contract and a trust. Yet important practical consequences may flow from characterizing a relationship between parties as either a contract or a trust. For example, where property is vested in A, who then becomes insolvent, the likelihood of B recovering whatever is owed to him is substantially higher if A held the property in trust for him than if he is A's debtor and can only claim in A's bankruptcy. The most far-reaching consequence of the distinction is that beneficiaries can enforce a trust even though not party to its creation whereas only the actual parties to a contract can enforce it.[17] Although the wisdom of not recognising the right of a third party to a contract to enforce it has often been questioned,[18] it has been reasserted on a number of occasions by the House of Lords[19] and there has been no sign of any move away from that position in this jurisdiction. Instead there have been sporadic instances of the courts employing the concept of a constructive trust to provide a third party with a remedy by finding that one of the parties to a contract entered into it as a trustee with the intention of benefiting the third party. In *Drimmie v. Davies*[20] by virtue of a deed a dentist and his son agreed to become partners for five years; in the event of a dissolution the son was to have the right to purchase

---

16. E.g. where a testator creates a trust in his will or a settlor declares himself trustee of named trusts for the benefit of a volunteer.
17. This latter principle has long been an accepted feature of the law in this jurisdiction and in England, see e.g. *Tweddle v. Atkinson* (1861) 1 B & S 393; *Dunlop Pneumatic Tyre Co. Ltd v. Selridge & Co. Ltd* [1915] AC 847 and has been the subject-matter of much academic debate. See Dowrick (1956) 19 MLR 374; Wylie (1966) 17 NILQ 351; Yates (1977) 41 Conv 49; Andrews (1988) LS 14.
18. See Corbin (1930) 46 LQR 12 and the recommendations of the Law Revision Committee in 1937 Cmd 5449, section D paragraph 48. In addition, Lord Denning has often advocated a more liberal view, see *Smith & Snipes Hall Farm Ltd v. River Douglas Catchment Board* [1949] 2 KB 500; *Drive Yourself Hire Co. (London) Ltd v. Strutt* [1954] 1 QB 250; *Adler v. Dickson* [1955] 1 QB 158; Denning (1960) 3 Syd Law Rev 209, 214.
19. *Scruttons Ltd v. Midland Silicones Ltd* [1962] AC 446; *Beswick v. Beswick* [1968] AC 58.
20. [1899] 1 IR 176.

the property and, in the event of his father's death, was to pay certain annuities to his brothers and sisters. The father died and his executors and the brothers and sisters succeeded in an action to enforce payment of the annuities on the grounds that the son was bound by the obligation to his father which was now being enforced by his executors. It is clear from the judgment of Chatterton VC, which was upheld by the Irish Court of Appeal, that he felt it was not necessary to decide whether a fiduciary relationship existed between the executors and the beneficiaries for the purpose of maintaining the action. However, Chatterton VC referred to the *dicta* of Cotton LJ in *Gandy v. Gandy*[21] to the effect that the rule that a contract cannot be enforced except by a party to it is subject to an exception:

> [I]f the contract, although in form it is with A, is intended to secure a benefit to B, so that B is entitled to say that he has a beneficial right as *cestui que trust* under that contract; then B would, in a Court of Equity, be allowed to insist upon and enforce the contract.[22]

This statement was also quoted with approval in *Kelly v. Larkin*[23] by Andrews J who stated that, while he did not seek to question the common law doctrine that a contract cannot be enforced except by a party to it, he considered that the facts of the case before him came within the 'equitable exception' to this doctrine expounded in *Gandy*.

It can be argued that such an approach may often be called for to ensure that justice is achieved yet the courts both in this jurisdiction and elsewhere have shown a marked reluctance to infer the existence of a trust in these circumstances, unless it is clear both from the language used in creating the arrangement and from the surrounding circumstances that this was the clear intention of the parties.[24] In *Cadbury Ireland Ltd v. Kerry Co-operative Creamery Ltd*[25] the plaintiffs claimed an entitlement to a quantity of milk at a price to be determined in accordance with a clause in a contract which had been concluded between the defendants because, it claimed, the second named defendants were trustees of the benefit of the clause in question on behalf of the plaintiffs. The defendants pleaded that the plaintiffs were not party to the

---

21. (1885) 30 Ch D 57.
22. *Ibid.* at 67. Also approved by Walker LJ in *Kenney v. Employers' Liability Assurance Corporation* [1901] 1 IR 301.
23. [1910] 2 IR 550, 557. Andrews J held that a person who is not named as a party to a covenant was nevertheless entitled to maintain an action upon it on the basis that he was in a position akin to that of a beneficiary under the covenant.
24. See *Re Webb* [1941] 1 Ch 225, 234 *per* Farwell J; *Re Schebsman* [1944] 1 Ch 83, 104 *per* du Parcq LJ and *Green v. Russell* [1959] 2 QB 226, 231 *per* Romer LJ: 'an intention to provide benefits for someone else and to pay for them does not in itself give rise to a trusteeship.'
25. [1982] ILRM 77. See also *Bula Ltd v. Tara Mines Ltd (No. 2)* [1987] IR 95, 101.

agreement and denied that they had any rights thereunder. Barrington J held that while the principle that parties to a contract can create a trust of contractual rights for the benefit of a third party which can be enforced by that third party is well established, in the circumstances, the plaintiffs had failed to establish that the second named defendants were trustees of any contractual rights on their behalf. A similarly unsuccessful attempt to rely on this principle was made by the plaintiffs in *Inspector of Taxes Association v. Minister for the Public Service.*[26] Murphy J referred to the judgment of Barrington J in the *Cadbury* case and to the 'well established proposition that parties to a contract can create a trust of contractual rights for the benefit of a third party'.[27] However, he said that he would find it very difficult to infer that the various staff associations, which were parties to the original conciliation and arbitration agreement on which the plaintiffs sought to rely, had purported to contract by implication as trustees for the plaintiff association which had been formed subsequently.

Finally, it is worth noting that in some jurisdictions, third parties are given statutory rights against the promisor in a contract, which as Jacobs[28] has noted, may even put them in a more favourable position than if they had been recognised as beneficiaries under a trust implied by the courts. Section 1 of the Contracts (Rights of Third Parties) Act 1999 in England now provides that a third party may enforce a term of a contract in his own right if the contract provides that he may or if the term purports to confer a benefit on him, unless on a proper construction of the contract it appears that the parties did not intend such term to be enforceable by a third party.

4. Trusts and Powers

There is a fundamental distinction between trusts and powers; while trusts are of an imperative nature, powers are discretionary. A trustee must carry out his functions according to the terms of a trust whereas the donee of a power has considerable discretion as to the manner in which he exercises the power, if indeed he exercises it at all. The beneficiaries under a trust are the owners in equity of the trust property while the objects of a power have only the expectation that the power may be exercised in their favour. The most usual type of power and the one which is relevant in this context is a power of appointment, which authorizes the creation or grant of beneficial interests in property and which gives authority to the donee to nominate objects of the

---

26. High Court 1981 No. 2846P (Murphy J) 24 March 1983.
27. *Ibid.* at 35.
28. *Jacobs' Law of Trusts in Australia* (6th ed., 1997, Meagher and Gummow) p. 27. See e.g. the position in Western Australia and Queensland. In Ireland, ss. 7 and 8 of the Married Women's Status Act 1957 confer rights on spouses and children to enforce certain types of contracts entered into for their benefit.

power who will generally be chosen from a defined class. It is also relevant at this juncture to draw a distinction between general and special powers of appointment. A power will be characterized as general if the donee may designate any person even himself as the object(s) of the power, otherwise it will be termed a special power of appointment.

While these basic distinctions seem clear in theory, they are confused by the fact that a trust may confer a measure of discretion on a trustee e.g. he may be given a discretion to select beneficiaries from a specified class or to decide the proportions in accordance with which the trust property is to be divided, and this is known as a discretionary trust. While the beneficiaries under a discretionary trust cannot demand that trustees exercise their discretion in their favour, they can seek to ensure that the trustees make a selection as to who will benefit under the terms of the trust. This compares with the situation in relation to a power of appointment where the donee of the power cannot be compelled to make a selection.

To confuse matters further, there is also a concept known as a power in the nature of a trust or a 'trust power'[29]. This essentially denotes the situation which arises where a court infers the existence of a trust in default of any appointment being made by the donee of a power.[30] A gift over in default of appointment negatives the existence of a trust of this nature for the objects of a power.[31] Where there is no gift over in the event of non-exercise of a power, it may be construed as a trust for all the members of the specified class equally.[32] However, the absence of a gift over is not conclusive[33] and there must be a clear indication that the testator or settlor intended the power to be in the nature of a trust. Where the court is not satisfied that such a trust power exists and the person to whom the power is given has died without exercising it, there will be a resulting trust in favour of the testator's estate.[34]

---

29. For a detailed consideration of these various distinctions, see Unwin (1962) 26 Conv 92; Hopkins [1971] CLJ 68; Cullity (1976) 54 Can Bar Rev 229 and Bartlett & Stebbings [1984] Conv 227.
30. Explained in the following terms by Lord Eldon in *Brown v. Higgs* (1803) 8 Ves 561, 570: 'there are [sic] not only a mere trust and a mere power, but there is also known to this court a power, which the party, to whom it is given, is entrusted and required to execute; and with regard to that species of power the court consider it as partaking so much of the nature and qualities of a trust, that if the person, who has that duty imposed upon him, does not discharge it, the Court will, to a certain extent, discharge the duty in his room and place.' Quoted with approval by Budd J in *Re Parker's Will* [1966] IR 309, 319.
31. *Re Mills* [1930] 1 Ch 654. Note that an ordinary residuary gift is not considered to be a gift over for this purpose, see *Re Hall* [1899] 1 IR 308, 320.
32. See *Re Llewellyn's Settlement* [1921] 2 Ch 281; *Re Arnold's Trusts* [1947] Ch 131.
33. *Re Weekes' Settlement* [1897] 1 Ch 289 applied in *Re Combe* [1925] Ch 210 and *Re Perowne* [1951] Ch 785.
34. See e.g. *Bank of Ireland v. O'Toole*, High Court 1979 No. 671Sp (Barrington J) 26 June 1980; *Tuite v. Tuite* [1978] ILRM 197.

The manner in which a court should determine whether a mere power or a trust power exists in circumstances where there has been a failure to exercise a power of appointment is in the words of Evershed MR a question of deducing the 'intention or presumed intention to be derived from the language of the instrument'.[35] Perhaps the most frequently cited example of such an intention being found by the courts is *Burrough v. Philcox*[36] where Lord Cottenham laid down the following principle:

> When there appears a general intention in favour of a class, and a particular intention in favour of individuals of a class to be selected by another person, and the particular intention fails, from that selection not being made, the court will carry into effect the general intention in favour of the class.[37]

A testator gave life estates in certain stock and property to his two children with remainder to their issue and provided that if they should both die without leaving lawful issue, the survivor of the children should have power to dispose by will of the estate amongst his nephews and nieces, or their children, either all to one of them or to as many of them as his surviving child should think proper. There was no gift over in default and it was held by Lord Cottenham that a trust was thereby created in favour of the testator's nephews and nieces and their children, subject to a power of selection and distribution in the surviving child.

A similar result was achieved in *Re Kieran*,[38] where a testator devised and bequeathed his farm and the rest of his property to his brother on trust for the latter's eldest son and, if this son should die before attaining the age of 21, to such of his other sons as his brother should appoint. The testator's brother's eldest son died before he reached the age of 21 and his brother died without making any appointment amongst his three surviving sons. Pim J held that in the circumstances these three surviving sons were entitled to the farm in equal shares as tenants in common. He commented that 'it is the recognized duty of every court to carry out a trust if it is possible to do so, and if it is possible, a court will avoid a construction which must result in an intestacy and in the carrying of the property, possibly wholly, probably largely, to persons whom the testator never meant to get it.'[39]

---

35. *Re Scarisbrick* [1951] Ch 622, 635. See also the *dicta* of Buckley J in *Re Leek* [1967] Ch 1061, 1073.
36. (1840) 5 My & Cr 72.
37. *Ibid.* at 92. Note also the *dicta* of Lord Eldon in *Brown v. Higgs* (1803) 8 Ves 561, 574.
38. [1916] 1 IR 289. This was also the approach adopted by Budd J in *Re Parker* [1966] IR 309.
39. [1916] 1 IR 289, 297. See also *Rorke v. Abraham* [1895] 1 IR 334.

The intention of the testator appears to have emerged as the paramount consideration which will influence a court in deciding whether a gift should arise by implication in the absence of any appointment being made in these cases. In *Robinson v. Moore*[40] Dixon J was satisfied that the testator intended to deal exhaustively and completely with the property which formed the subject-matter of the power and did not intend that it should devolve as on intestacy or lapse into residue. In these circumstances, he was satisfied that there was an implied gift to the objects of the power in default of appointment.

The rationale behind this approach is that the failure on the part of the donee to exercise the apparent power should not prejudice the donor's intended objects. Instead, the court will substitute its own discretion for that of the donee and in doing so seek to give effect as far as possible to the donor's original intentions.[41] Where the donor of the power has subsequently died, arguably this approach will come much closer to carrying his wishes into effect than if the property were to become the subject-matter of a resulting trust. Despite the existence of the fundamental principle that the courts will seek as far as possible to ascertain and give effect to a testator's intentions, the courts have on a number of occasions decided in such circumstances that no 'trust power' arises and that a resulting trust in favour of a testator's estate should take effect.

In *Healy v. Donnery*[42] a testator devised freehold property to his daughter for life and gave her power to dispose of it amongst her children in such shares as she might consider proper. Pennefather B rejected the argument that the power to appoint amongst the children was tantamount to creating a trust in their favour and stated that the power was not coupled with a trust. This approach was confirmed by the English decision of *Re Weekes' Settlement*[43] in which the following statement of principle was made by Romer J:

> The authorities do not shew . . . that there is a hard and fast rule that a gift to A for life, with a power to A to appoint among a class and nothing more, must, if there is no gift over in the will, be held a gift by implication to the class in default of the power being exercised. In my opinion, the cases shew ... that you must find in the will an indication that the testatrix did intend the class or some of the class to take — intended in fact that this power should be regarded in the nature of a trust — only a power of selection being given, as, for example, a gift to A for life, with a gift over to such a class as A shall appoint.[44]

---

40. [1962-3] Ir Jur Rep 29.
41. Where the court intervenes the objects of the power will take in equal shares as tenants in common whereas the actual donee might well have exercised his discretion to divide the property in unequal shares.
42. (1853) 3 ICLR 213. See also *Re Hall* [1899] 1 IR 308.
43. [1897] 1 Ch 289.
44. *Ibid.* at 292.

Here a testatrix bequeathed property to her husband for life and granted him a power of appointment over this property to be exercised in favour of their children. The husband died intestate without having exercised the power and Romer J found that there was no implied gift to the children in default of appointment. A similar result was arrived at in *Clibborn v. Horan*,[45] where O'Connor MR stated that 'there must be something in the instrument creating the power from which the intention that the objects shall take in default of appointment can be gathered'.[46] He concluded that no intention that there should be a trust in favour of the objects of the power was expressed or could be gleaned from the will and in the circumstances there could be no gift by implication to these objects. This principle of giving effect as far as possible to the testator's intentions where these can be extracted from the will resulted in a similar conclusion being reached by McWilliam J in *Tuite v. Tuite*.[47] In this instance the testator's intention appeared to the court to be to seek to benefit those persons to whom he had bequeathed his residuary estate and McWilliam J concluded that the proceeds of the property in question should pass under the residuary clause in the will.

A further example of a situation in which a court was satisfied that a testator did not intend a power to operate by implication as a gift to all the potential objects equally in default of appointment is *Bank of Ireland v. O'Toole*.[48] A testator had conferred a power of appointment over his property on his widow intending her to exercise it in favour of one of his sons subject to the payment of a number of legacies to the other children. His widow died without exercising the power and Barrington J rejected the argument that it should be construed as a power in the nature of a trust and that the property, which was principally comprised of a farm, should go to the sons equally. He reiterated that the fundamental duty of the court was to attempt to ascertain and give effect to the testator's intentions and that it was clear that the testator intended that the farm should pass to one of his sons alone; it was quite inconsistent with any intention which could be gathered from the will that the sons should take equally.

Despite the conflicting results arrived at by the courts in this jurisdiction even in comparatively recent cases it is possible to deduce some general principles from these decisions. First, it seems clear that the court will seek to give effect as far as possible to the testator's intentions, which will usually[49] be achieved by construing a power as being in the nature of a trust in default

---

45. [1921] 1 IR 93.
46. *Ibid.* at 97. This statement was quoted with approval by Dixon J in *Robinson v. Moore* [1962-3] Ir Jur Rep 29, 38 a case in which the opposite conclusion was reached.
47. [1978] ILRM 197.
48. High Court 1979 No. 671Sp (Barrington J) 26 June 1980.
49. As in decisions such as *Re Kieran* [1916] 1 IR 289 although, as shown above, not in *Tuite v. Tuite* [1978] ILRM 197.

of appointment. However, there must be some intention either expressed or implied in the will that the objects of the power should take a gift by implication in these circumstances. The question which is difficult to answer with certainty is what will constitute sufficient evidence of such intention and this problem of interpretation is to an extent responsible for the divergence in recent authorities in this area.

A final matter of considerable practical significance is that whether one is dealing with powers or trusts it is necessary for the objects or beneficiaries to be defined with a sufficient degree of certainty to enable the donees or trustees to carry out their functions in relation to distribution. The position in both England and in this jurisdiction in relation to the test of certainty used to differ as between mere powers, on the one hand and trusts, whether fixed, discretionary or trust powers on the other hand. In the former case the test was whether it could be said with certainty that any given individual was or was not a member of the class.[50] In the latter case the trust was void for uncertainty unless a comprehensive list of the beneficiaries could be drawn up.[51] However, the majority of the House of Lords decided in *McPhail v. Doulton*[52] that the test to be applied in ascertaining the validity of a discretionary trust should be the same as that outlined above in relation to mere powers. Clearly the assimilation of the test of certainty in relation to discretionary trusts and powers has from a practical perspective removed to a great extent the need to distinguish between them. It had been presumed in some quarters[53] that the approach of the House of Lords in *McPhail* would be followed in this jurisdiction but it now appears that this will not necessarily be the case. In *O'Byrne v. Davoren*[54] Murphy J stated, albeit *obiter*, that a trust for the division of income between members of a class to be selected by trustees will be invalid unless the entire class of potential beneficiaries is ascertainable. This issue will be considered in more detail below in the context of the requirement of certainty of objects in relation to express trusts, but for present purposes it suffices to make the point that in this jurisdiction at any rate the distinction between mere powers and discretionary trusts or trust powers may yet be of considerable significance in determining the validity of the trust or power in question.

---

50. *Re Gestetner Settlement* [1953] Ch 672; *Re Gulbenkian's Settlement* [1970] AC 508.
51. *IRC v. Broadway Cottages' Trust* [1955] Ch 20, 35-36. Approved by Budd J in *Re Parker* [1966] IR 309.
52. [1971] AC 424. It is interesting to note that a differently constituted House of Lords has confirmed the earlier approach only three years earlier in *Re Gulbenkian's Settlement* [1970] AC 508.
53. See Keane, *Equity and the Law of Trusts in the Republic of Ireland* (1988) at p.81.
54. [1994] 3 IR 373.

5. Trusts and the Administration of a Deceased's Estate

While the roles of a personal representative and trustee are often confused in practice, their origins are quite distinct; the position of the former was regulated by the Ecclesiastical Courts whereas the latter as we have seen was a product of the developments brought about by the Court of Chancery. While the task of the personal representative could be said to be the limited one of realizing and distributing assets whereas the trustee's function is ordinarily of considerably more lasting duration in terms of administering the trust on an ongoing basis, there are nevertheless considerable similarities between the offices.[55]

Both trustees and personal representatives are subject to fiduciary obligations in the performance of their functions and often the same individuals will fulfil both roles at different stages. In the first instance, an individual may act as an executor and once the deceased's estate is administered may take over the role of trustee of the trusts established under the testator's will. It is often difficult to determine precisely when one role ceases and the other commences but having said this, the individual concerned will rarely act in both capacities at the same time. Legislative provisions may cause confusion as for example section 10(3) of the Succession Act 1965 which provides that a personal representative holds a deceased's estate as a 'trustee' for those entitled to it. Despite the use of such terminology, until the estate is fully administered, the residuary legatee or next of kin will not be regarded as the beneficial owner of the testator's assets and a personal representative does not become a trustee in the strict sense of the word.[56] So when acting as a personal representative, he must be regarded as such for the purposes of deciding on the application of relevant limitation periods to any actions which these parties may take or which may be taken against them.[57]

A distinction between the offices which may have considerable practical significance is that while trustees only have joint authority to deal with or dispose of personal property, personal representatives have joint and several authority to do so and the lawful actions of one will be binding on all.[58] This is illustrated by *Attenborough & Son v. Solomon*,[59] where an executor, over thirteen years after the testator's death but before the distribution of the

---

55. *Re Speight* (1883) 22 Ch D 727, 742 *per* Jessel MR.
56. See the *dicta* of Sargant J in *Re Ponder* [1921] 2 Ch 59, 61: 'when the estate has been wound up and the residue ascertained, the executor has ceased to be an executor and has become a trustee for the persons entitled to the residue.' See also *Eaton v. Daines* [1894] WN 32 and Ker (1955) 19 Conv 199.
57. See e.g. *Vaughan v. Cottingham* [1961] IR 184.
58. *Jacomb v. Harwood* (1751) 2 Ves Sen 265, 267. Although note that where one administrator purports to sign a contract on behalf of himself and his co-administrator and warrants that he has the authority to do so when this is in fact lacking, no specifically enforceable contract will exist, see *Fountain Forestry Ltd v. Edwards* [1975] Ch 1.
59. [1913] AC 76. See also *Astbury v. Astbury* [1898] 2 Ch 111.

residuary estate had been completed, pledged property which formed part of this residuary estate to a pawnbroker without the knowledge of his co-executor/co-trustee. The pledgor died and when the transaction was discovered an action was brought to recover the property. The result of the case turned on whether the pledgor had been acting as an executor or trustee; if he was adjudged to have been still acting as executor, the pawnbrokers would have obtained good title. However, the House of Lords held that at the relevant date the executors had assented to the trust dispositions under the testator's will taking effect and that the property was held by the pledgor as a trustee. Accordingly he had no authority to act without the assent of his co-trustee and the property could be recovered.

A further distinction which can be made is that a personal representative holds his office for life except where the grant of probate or letters of administration is for a limited period or the court releases him from such duties.[60] However, by virtue of section 11 of the Trustee Act 1893, provided that there will be at least two trustees remaining to administer the trust, a trustee may by deed declare that he wishes to retire and if the consent of his co-trustees is forthcoming, he will be permitted to do so.

CLASSIFICATION OF TRUSTS

Trusts can be classified in a number of different ways; e.g. according to the manner of their creation, by virtue of the objects which they seek to benefit or from the perspective of the nature of the duties which they impose on the trustee. It is proposed at this point to set out briefly the main classifications which are recognised but it is important to note that these categories are not always mutually exclusive.

Public and Private Trusts

This classification is based on the reason for the creation of a trust. Private trusts are created for the benefit of an individual or a class of individuals irrespective of the benefit which they may confer on the public at large. Public trusts, otherwise known as charitable trusts, are set up for purposes beneficial to the community in general although in most cases they will incidentally confer a benefit on a specific person or class of persons. In the case of the former type of trust the so-called 'beneficiary principle' applies i.e. there 'must be somebody in whose favour the court can decree specific performance'.[61] However, there is no such requirement in the case of public trusts which may be enforced by the Attorney General.

---

60. *Re Timmis* [1902] 1 Ch 176, 183 *per* Kekewich J.
61. *Morice v. Bishop of Durham* (1804) 9 Ves 399, 405 *per* Grant MR. Note that there is

Express, Resulting and Constructive Trusts

Express Trusts

An express trust is one created by express declaration of the settlor or testator either by instrument *inter vivos* or by will. Certain formalities must be observed in the creation of *inter vivos* trusts of land and all trusts which are set up by means of a will. In addition, all express trusts must contain a number of essential elements known as 'the three certainties', and these issues will be considered in detail in the following chapter. Further subdivisions in the classification of express trusts can be made; first, according to the form in which the declaration of trust is effected, which can give rise to either executed or executory trusts. A trust is said to be executed where the settlor or testator has delimited precisely the circumstances under which the trust property is to be held and no further instrument is required to effect this. However, in the case of an executory trust, although a valid trust has been created the settlor or testator has only indicated his general intentions as to how the trust property is to be disposed of and a further instrument is required to define the beneficial interests with precision.[62]

Secondly, a subdivision can be made between completely and incompletely constituted trusts. A trust is said to be completely constituted when the trust property has actually been vested in the trustees for the benefit of the beneficiaries; until this has been done the trust remains incompletely constituted. The distinction between these categories and their practical implications will be considered in more detail below in Chapter 6.

Resulting Trusts

A resulting trust[63] is one which arises from the unexpressed but presumed intention of the settlor or testator. They are known as resulting trusts because the beneficial interest in the property reverts or 'results' to the settlor (or if he is dead, to his estate) who transferred the property to the trustee in the first instance. Resulting trusts are often divided into two categories:[64] automatically resulting trusts which arise where a trust has been declared but the beneficial interest fails for some reason or is not disposed of in its entirety and presumed resulting trusts which occur as a result of the inference drawn by the law with

---

also an anomalous category of 'purpose trusts' which have been upheld as valid despite their failure to adhere to the beneficiary principle. See further, Chapter 9.

62. *Egerton v. Earl Brownlow* (1853) HLC 1, 210 and see further *supra* Chapter 2.
63. The term 'implied trust' is sometimes used interchangeably with the term 'resulting trust'; alternatively resulting trusts may be considered to be merely examples of a wider category of implied trusts, see Wylie, *Irish Land Law* (3rd ed., 1997) p. 543.
64. *Re Vandervell's Trusts (No. 2)* [1974] Ch 269, 294 *per* Megarry J. See further Chapter 7.

regard to the donor's intentions. Due to the informal manner in which they come into being, resulting trusts are exempt from the formalities required in relation to the creation of express trusts.

Constructive Trusts

A constructive trust is a form of trust which arises by operation of law and which comes into being irrespective of the intentions of the parties concerned. The main distinction between resulting and constructive trusts is that in the case of the former, the courts assume that the creation of the trust was intended by the parties whereas in the latter instance a trust is imposed to satisfy the demands of justice and good conscience and may often be imposed in a manner contrary to the intentions of the individuals concerned. To the extent that there is no requirement to observe the formalities necessary in relation to express trusts in either case, there is often little practical significance in drawing a distinction between the two categories. Constructive trusts are generally regarded as constituting a residual category of trust but as we shall see they are adaptable and often dynamic in nature.

Simple and Special Trusts

This classification distinguishes between different types of trust according to the nature of the duties which are imposed on the trustees in each case. A simple trust[65] is one in which property is vested in a trustee but the trustee is given no active duties[66] to perform and merely holds the legal title to the trust property. A special trust is one in which a trustee is required to carry out duties imposed on him by the settlor or testator which necessitates him taking an active as opposed to a passive role in administering the affairs of the trust.

Fixed and Discretionary Trusts

In a fixed trust each beneficiary has a fixed current entitlement to a specific share or interest in the trust property. However, in the case of a discretionary trust, a beneficiary has no actual entitlement to any part of the trust property; instead the trustees are given the discretion to apply the property for the benefit of specified persons or classes of persons. Therefore in the latter case a potential beneficiary cannot compel a trustee to exercise his discretion in his favour.[67]

---

65. Also known as a bare trust, see *Tomlinson v. Glyn's Executor & Trustee Co.* [1970] Ch 112, 125-126.
66. This has been construed as meaning that a simple or bare trustee is given no specific duties by the settlor and must merely carry out whatever duties are imposed on him by law. See McGhee, *Snell's Equity* (30th ed., 2000) p. 124.
67. Although such a trustee can be compelled to at least make a selection amongst the beneficiaries.

Within this category a distinction is sometimes drawn between 'exhaustive discretionary trusts' which impose an obligation on the trustees to dispose of the entire trust income and 'non-exhaustive discretionary trusts' which leave the issue of the extent of any distribution to the trustee.

Protective Trusts

A further category of trust which should be mentioned at this juncture is a protective trust.[68] The essence of such a trust is that the interest of a beneficiary is made determinable on the happening of certain events, usually bankruptcy or an attempt to alienate the trust property. This determinable interest is then followed by the establishment of a discretionary trust, usually in favour of the beneficiary and members of his family or some other class of persons.

While a settlor cannot set up a protective trust to guard against his own bankruptcy,[69] he may do so to protect himself against alienation which will usually be of an involuntary nature. However, the most common type of protective trust will be one in which the interest of a beneficiary, other than the settlor, becomes determinable.[70] It is important to distinguish between such a determinable interest and an interest subject to a condition subsequent. A condition subsequent designed to terminate an interest in the event of bankruptcy or alienation will be void whereas an interest determinable in such cases will be valid.

Although there has been no legislative intervention in this area in Ireland, in a number of other jurisdictions legislation now provides a means whereby a settlor may direct that property be held on protective trusts without the necessity of setting out in detail the circumstances in which the interest will become determinable and the manner in which the discretionary trusts should operate.[71]

---

68. Sheridan (1957) 21 Conv 110.
69. *Re Burroughs-Fowler* [1916] 2 Ch 251.
70. *Billson v. Crofts* (1873) LR 15 Eq 314 and *Re Ashby* [1892] 1 QB 872.
71. E.g. s. 33 of the Trustee Act 1925 in England; s. 42 of the Trustee Act 1956 in New Zealand and s. 45 of the Trustee Act 1925 in New South Wales.

CHAPTER 4

Trusts — Formalities and Essential Elements

FORMALITIES

Creation of Trusts Inter Vivos

Primarily with a view to preventing fraud, legislation has intervened to provide that in specific cases certain formalities must be observed in the creation of express trusts. However, no formalities are required for the creation of an *inter vivos* express trust of personalty and provided that the settlor manifests the intention of creating such a trust[1] it may be established orally.[2] In relation to the creation of express trusts of land, whether freehold or leasehold,[3] section 4 of the Statute of Frauds (Ireland) 1695 requires that the trust be evidenced in writing and signed by a person able to declare the trust, or by his will.[4] It is important to note that the declaration of trust itself does not need to be in writing but written evidence must exist to prove the declaration and its essential terms.[5] This written evidence need not be in any precise form,[6] and can even be extracted from two or more separate documents.[7] It has also been established that this written evidence need not come into existence at the time the trust is

---

1. *Paul v. Constance* [1977] 1 WLR 521, 531 *per* Scarman LJ.
2. While the courts have accepted that such a trust may be validly created in this manner (*M'Fadden v. Jenkins* (1842) 1 Ph 153; *Re Kayford* [1975] 1 WLR 279, 281-282; *Paul v. Constance* [1977] 1 WLR 521) in most cases fairly strong evidence will be required to establish this, see *Paterson v. Murphy* (1853) 11 Hare 88, 91-2; *Maguire v. Dodd* (1859) 9 Ir Ch R 452, 458.
3. *Forster v. Hale* (1798) 3 Ves 696; *Donohue v. Conrahy* (1845) 8 Ir Eq R 679.
4. See Bridge (1986) 64 Can Bar Rev 58 for a comprehensive review of the authorities relevant to the similar evidential requirements imposed by the Statute of Frauds in relation to contracts for the sale of land.
5. *Morton v. Tewart* (1842) 2 Y & C Cas Ch 67, 80; *Smith v. Matthews* (1861) 3 De G F & J 139, 151.
6. E.g. it can be contained in correspondence *Forster v. Hale* (1798) 3 Ves 696; *Childers v. Childers* (1857) 1 De G & J 482 or in a telegram *McBlain v. Cross* (1871) 25 LT 804.
7. *Forster v. Hale* (1798) 3 Ves 696. See also *Timmins v. Moreland Street Property Co.* [1958] Ch 110 (Fridman (1958) 22 Conv 275) and *Elias v. George Sahely & Co. (Barbados) Ltd* [1983] 1 AC 646 which relate to the requirements imposed by s. 40 of the Law of Property Act 1925 in England in relation to contracts for the sale of land.

declared provided that it exists before the commencement of any action in which the validity of the trust is questioned.[8]

The generally accepted view is that section 4 of the Statute of Frauds (Ireland) 1695, or its equivalent,[9] only provides an evidential requirement which will affect the enforceability and not the validity of trusts, so in the absence of any written evidence to prove its existence, such a trust will be valid although unenforceable.[10]

In addition, it should be noted that section 2 of the Statute of Frauds (Ireland) 1695 requires that contracts to create a trust in consideration of marriage must also be evidenced in writing.

Statute Not to be Used as an Instrument of Fraud

Notwithstanding these statutory requirements, the courts will not always insist on strict compliance with the provisions of the Statute of Frauds.[11] Possibly for the reason that these formality provisions which can be considered as merely a means towards an end should be used purposively,[12] the principle has been established that equity will not permit the statute to be used as an instrument of fraud. As Lord Westbury stated in *McCormick v. Grogan*:[13]

> The Court of Equity has, from a very early period, decided that even an Act of Parliament shall not be used as an instrument of fraud; and if in the machinery of perpetrating a fraud an Act of Parliament intervenes, the Court of Equity, it is true, does not set aside the Act of Parliament, but it fastens on the individual who gets a title under that Act, and imposes upon him a personal obligation, because he applies the Act as an instrument for accomplishing a fraud.

So, the court will not permit a beneficiary to be deprived of an interest in land under a trust in the absence of written evidence of the trust if such a result would amount to a fraud providing that there is some other evidence to establish the existence and nature of the trust. Where there has been a failure to comply with the statutory requirements the court must weigh up the desirability of ensuring adherence to these requirements against the likelihood of injustice being caused by insisting on their observance. This balancing exercise is

---

8. *Rochefoucauld v. Boustead* [1897] 1 Ch 196, 206; *Re Holland* [1902] 2 Ch 360, 382.
9. S. 7 of the Statute of Frauds 1677, replaced by s. 53(1)(b) of the Law of Property Act 1925.
10. See Youdan (1984) 43 CLJ 306, 320-1.
11. See generally, Thompson (1985) 36 NILQ 358.
12. Langbein (1975) 88 Harv L Rev 489, 491-498 and Youdan (1984) 43 CLJ 306, 315.
13. (1869) LR 4 HL 82, 97.

illustrated by the decision in *Re Duke of Marlborough*.[14] The Duchess of Marlborough assigned a leasehold interest in property to the duke and after his death asserted that the transfer was made solely to enable her husband to raise money by mortgaging the lease and that they had agreed that the property would ultimately be re-assigned to her. It was held that the provisions of the Statute of Frauds could not be successfully pleaded in opposition to the duchess's claim to the interest on the basis that the duke's estate would benefit unjustly had the obligation to re-assign the lease not been enforced owing to non-compliance with the statute. Stirling J stated that 'the general principle that the statute is not to be used as a protection to fraud has long been recognised by the courts of equity'[15] but commented that this principle has not always been applied in a uniform manner.

Perhaps the most frequently cited example of the operation of this doctrine is the decision of the English Court of Appeal in *Rochefoucauld v. Boustead*.[16] The plaintiff was the owner of mortgaged property which was sold by the mortgagee to the defendant. The defendant had orally agreed to hold the property on trust for the plaintiff subject to repayment to the defendant of the purchase price and other expenses incurred in the transaction. The defendant subsequently sold the land and the plaintiff, who claimed that the land had been conveyed to the defendant as trustee for her, was held to be entitled to obtain an order for an account. Lindley LJ stated:

> [I]t is a fraud on the part of a person to whom land is conveyed as a trustee, and who knows it was so conveyed, to deny the trust and claim the land himself. Consequently, notwithstanding the statute, it is competent for a person claiming land conveyed to another to prove by parol evidence that it was so conveyed upon trust for the claimant, and that the grantee, knowing the facts, is denying the trust and relying upon the form of conveyance and the statute, in order to keep the land himself.[17]

This principle was applied in Ireland in *McGillycuddy v. Joy*.[18] The plaintiff and the defendants agreed to purchase a farm jointly and the contract was signed by one of the defendants. The plaintiff paid one-third of the purchase price and the defendants then reneged on the agreement. The plaintiff sought a declaration that the defendant, who had signed the agreement, held the benefit of the contract in trust for him. Budd J held that the principle in *Rochefoucauld* applied even though here there was only a contract of sale, as opposed to a

---

14. [1894] 2 Ch 133.
15. *Ibid.* at 141.
16. [1897] 1 Ch 196.
17. *Ibid.* at 206.
18. [1959] IR 189.

conveyance. He concluded that the defendant had purchased that part of the lands previously agreed between them in trust for the plaintiff and that the former's repudiation of that trust constituted a fraud.

Similarly, in *Gilmurray v. Corr*,[19] the plaintiff had a leasehold interest in lands part of which were used as a golf driving range. After an unsuccessful attempt to buy the freehold, he came to an oral agreement with the defendant whereby the latter would purchase the lands with the plaintiff providing part of the purchase money, on the understanding that the defendant would then transfer the driving range to the plaintiff. The defendant subsequently told the plaintiff that he wished to incorporate in the transfer of the driving range a restrictive covenant that would prevent the use of the site for a licensed restaurant which might compete with the defendant's own premises. The plaintiff would not agree to this and the defendant proceeded with the purchase of the lands and refused to transfer the driving range to the plaintiff. Lowry LCJ held that when the defendant offered to purchase the lands he was acting as a trustee for himself and the plaintiff and that the plaintiff was entitled to prove by parol evidence that the land was conveyed to the defendant as a trustee. Lowry LCJ referred to *Rochefoucauld* and said that the decision had established that it is a fraud in equity for a person to whom land is conveyed as a trustee and who knows that it was so conveyed to deny the trust and claim the land as his own. This principle clearly applied to the facts of the case before him and the defendant could not rely on non-compliance with the statutory requirements to defeat the plaintiff's claim.

A question which has provoked considerable debate in recent years is whether a third party beneficiary can rely on the principle enunciated in *Rochefoucauld* to enforce such an informal trust. Feltham[20] has argued that there is a strong line of authority against allowing a third party to rely on the doctrine and has stated that 'neither precedent nor policy' support the extension of the principle in this way. However, Youdan[21] has asserted that the relevant authorities[22] favour the view that such trusts can be enforced at the instance of a third party beneficiary and on balance this would seem to be the fairer approach.

Dispositions of Equitable Interests Held Under a Trust

Section 6 of the Statute of Frauds (Ireland) 1695 provides that all subsequent dispositions of the beneficial interests held under a trust must be in writing and signed by the person making the disposition, or be included in a will.

---

19. [1978] NI 99.
20. [1987] Conv 246.
21. (1984) 43 CLJ 306; [1988] Conv 267.
22. *Neale v. Willis* [1968] 19 P & CR 839; *Binions v. Evans* [1972] Ch 359; *Lyus v. Prowsa Developments Ltd* [1982] 1 WLR 1044.

Two important points should be noted in relation to this requirement. First, it must be remembered that the requirement relating to the creation of trusts of land laid down in section 4 of the statute is that they must be evidenced in writing whereas this provision, which relates to the subsequent disposition of such interests, requires that the disposition actually be in writing. Secondly, section 6 applies to both personal and real property held under a trust and so while a trust of pure personalty can be created orally and subsequently be enforced, any disposition of this interest must be in writing.

Considerable uncertainty has surrounded the ambit of section 53(1)(c)of the English Law of Property Act 1925[23] and the circumstances in which a 'disposition'[24] takes place within the meaning of the subsection are far from clear.[25] It has been accepted that where a trustee is directed by a beneficiary to hold his interest on other trusts that this is sufficient to constitute a disposition of the beneficiary's interest.[26] However, the statutory requirement will not apply where the trustee conveys the legal interest to a third party on the instructions of or with the consent of the beneficiary.[27]

Creation of Trusts by Will

Where a trust is created by will, the testator must comply with the statutory requirements laid down by section 78 of the Succession Act 1965 in relation to the making of statutory dispositions i.e. that the will be in writing, signed at the foot thereof by the testator or by some other person in his presence and at his direction and the testator's signature must be made or acknowledged in the presence of two or more witnesses present at the same time, each of whom must attest that signature by his own signature.

However, as with trusts created *inter vivos*, equity will not always strictly enforce the statutory formalities required where the statute is being used as an instrument of fraud and it was in obedience to this principle that so called 'secret trusts', which will be considered in Chapter 5, came to be recognised.

ESSENTIAL ELEMENTS

Essential Elements of a Trust

Apart from ensuring compliance with the formalities outlined above, no

---

23. This replaced the original equivalent to s. 6 of the 1695 statute, s. 9 of the Statute of Frauds 1677.
24. This phrase replaced the formula used in s. 6 of 'grants and assignments of any trust or confidence'.
25. See e.g. *Oughtred v. IRC* [1960] AC 206.
26. *Grey v. IRC* [1960] AC 1; Green (1984) 47 MLR 385.
27. *Vandervell v. IRC* [1967] 2 AC 291.

technical or precise language is necessary to create a valid express trust. However, certain essential elements which have come to be known as 'the three certainties' must be present if such a trust is to be created. These three conditions of substance are as follows: certainty of intention or words, certainty of subject-matter and certainty of objects. These requirements were laid down by O'Byrne J in the decision of *Chambers v. Fahy*:[28]

> [I]t has been established that, in order that a trust may be created, the subject matter must be certain, the objects of the trust must be certain and the words relied on as creating the trust must have been used in an imperative sense so as to show that the testator intends to create an obligation.

Certainty of Intention or Words

The requirement that the words used to create a trust be imperative does not mean that any precise form of wording must be used,[29] so a trust may be validly created without actually using the word 'trust' and conversely the use of that word does not conclusively indicate the existence of a trust.[30] In determining whether this requirement of certainty has been met, the court will examine the substance and effect of the words used and a finding that a trust has been created will not be made unless it is satisfied that this was the settlor or testator's actual intention. So even where there is certainty of subject-matter and of objects, no trust can be created unless there is also certainty of intention.[31]

The words used must be examined with a view to ascertaining whether the intention was to make an absolute gift to the donee which he might, in the exercise of his discretion, dispose of in accordance with the settlor or testator's wishes, or whether the latter intended the donee to hold the property on trust.

This question of construction arises most frequently in relation to wills and historically the courts readily inferred the existence of a trust where the words used were hardly of an imperative nature,[32] as for example, where a

---

28. [1931] IR 17, 21. This essentially reiterated the statement of Lord Langdale MR in *Knight v. Knight* (1840) 3 Beav 148, 173.
29. *La Have Equipment Ltd v. Nova Scotia* (1994) 121 DLR (4th) 67, 77 *per* Chipman JA.
30. *Hunter v. Public Trustee* [1924] NZLR 882. See also the *dicta* of Salmon J in *Thexton v. Thexton* [2001] 1 NZLR 237, 247: 'A declaration of trust does not require a technical form of expression, it is a question of construction whether the words used, taking into account the surrounding circumstances, amount to a clear declaration of trust.'
31. *Crownx Inc v. Edwards* (1994) 120 DLR (4th) 270, 280.
32. The reason for this approach, as suggested in Hanbury & Martin, *Modern Equity* (16th ed., 2001) p. 95 is that prior to the enactment of the Executors Act 1830 in England, the undisposed of residue which remained after an estate was administered

gift was made by a testator who expressed the hope, wish, expectation or desire that the donee would deal with the property in a particular manner.[33] However, more recently these so called 'precatory words'[34] have usually been interpreted as being insufficient to create a trust. Before examining some of the authorities in this area in more detail, it is important to bear in mind that the type of language used is of itself not conclusive and the question of certainty of intention must be resolved by construing the whole of the instrument in question and thereby endeavouring to ascertain the intention of the settlor or testator.[35]

An examination of the decisions of the courts in this jurisdiction since the last quarter of the nineteenth century shows that the majority favour the conclusion that precatory words will not suffice to create an express trust.[36] Instead they may often be interpreted as merely expressing the motive for the gift[37] or as imposing some form of moral obligation on the donee to carry out the testator's wishes. Certainly there have been numerous statements to the effect that the 'tide has turned'[38] and which support the view that the trend is now against permitting the creation of a trust by the use of precatory words.[39] The position now appears to be that such words will not *prima facie* create a trust,[40] so any intention to the contrary must be clearly and unequivocally expressed by the testator. The statement of Monroe J in *Re Byrne's Estate*[41] provides a useful summary of the position:

---

might be retained by an executor. Thereafter, the residue was held on trust for the next of kin.

33. *Palmer v. Simmonds* (1854) 2 Drew 221; *Moriarty v. Martin* (1852) 3 Ir Ch R 26; *Gray v. Gray* (1860) 11 Ir Ch R 218.
34. Trusts created by the use of precatory words have sometimes been referred to as 'precatory trusts', although they are in fact ordinary express trusts and the use of this terminology has been criticised as 'misleading' by Rigby LJ in *Re Williams* [1897] 2 Ch 12, 27.
35. *Re Adams and the Kensington Vestry* (1884) 27 Ch D 394, 410 *per* Cotton LJ; *Re Hamilton* [1895] 2 Ch 370, 373 *per* Lindley LJ; *Re Williams* [1897] 2 Ch 12, 14 *per* Romer J.
36. *McAlinden v. McAlinden* (1877) IR 11 Eq 219; *Morrin v. Morrin* (1886) 19 LR Ir 37; *Murtagh v. Murtagh* (1902) 36 ILTR 129; *Berryman v. Berryman* [1913] 1 IR 390; *Re Humphrey's Estate* [1916] 1 IR 21; *Re Walker and Elgie's Contract* (1919) 53 ILTR 22; *Re McIntosh* [1933] IR 69; *Re Coulson* (1953) 87 ILTR 93; *Re Fitzgibbon* (1959) 93 ILTR 56; *Re Sweeney* [1976-77] ILRM 88. However, the opposite conclusion was reached in *Re Finnerty* [1970] IR 221.
37. *Re Fitzgibbon* (1959) 93 ILTR 56, 59 *per* Budd J.
38. *Re Humphrey's Estate* [1916] 1 IR 21, 24 *per* Ross J.
39. *Re Hamilton* [1895] 2 Ch 370, 374 *per* Lopes LJ; *Mussoorie Bank Ltd v. Raynor* (1882) 7 App Cas 321, 330 *per* Sir Arthur Hobhouse; *Murtagh v. Murtagh* (1902) 36 ILTR 129, 130 *per* Porter MR; *Re Coulson* (1953) 87 ILTR 93, 94 *per* Dixon J.
40. *Re Walker & Elgee's Contract* (1919) 53 ILTR 22, 23.
41. (1892) 29 LR Ir 250. Note also the *dicta* of Chatterton VC in *Morrin v. Morrin* (1886) 19 LR Ir 37 where he stated that where these 'superadded words' do not cut down the interest given, it will not be held without more evidence that a trust has been created.

[I]t is impossible to lay down any general rule by which all the cases on this subject can be reconciled; but I think it will be found that, in the great majority of cases where the Court of Chancery has refused to establish a precatory trust, there is, in the first place, an absolute gift to a particular individual, the terms of which are sought to be qualified by subsequent words in a subsequent clause. No trust will be established unless the words of qualification are clear and definite, and so expressed as to be regarded as imperative.

In *Re Humphrey's Estate*[42] a testator devised and bequeathed all his property, real and personal, to his wife and added that he wished that she should leave by will or transfer during her life a house and demesne to his son and that the remainder of his property should be left or transferred to his daughters. Ross J held that in the circumstances, the wife took an absolute interest. Similarly, in *Re Coulson*,[43] a testatrix left a farm and the furnishings of the farmhouse to her cousin in her will and went on to state that it was her wish that it should not be sold or divided but should be retained by the cousin for whichever of her children she thought fit. In these circumstances, Dixon J said that while the words used in the will were capable of being imperative they were not necessarily so and that the determining factor was 'what could be gathered from the will as a whole'. He was satisfied that the wording used amounted to no more than an expression of the hope that the cousin would act in the manner intended by the testatrix and held that in the circumstances, she took an absolute interest in the farm and furnishings.

The most recent case to be decided in this area would appear to confirm the approach established in decisions such as *Re Humphrey's Estate* and *Re Coulson*. In *Re Sweeney*[44] the testator devised and bequeathed all his assets to his wife for her own absolute use and benefit 'subject to the express wish' that she make provision for the payment of certain legacies after her death. The question arose whether the words of the gift to the wife of all the testator's assets could be cut down by these subsequent words. Hamilton J commented that while they were capable of being imperative, if he were to so hold, he would be cutting down considerably the clear words of the gift and quoted with approval the statement of Ross J in *Re Humphrey's Estate*[45] to the effect that 'after a devise and bequest in clear and express terms, if a trust is intended to be created one would expect that this would be done in terms equally clear and explicit'. He concluded that it was the testator's intention that his wife should enjoy the assets for her own absolute use and benefit and that the

---

42. [1916] 1 IR 21.
43. (1953) 87 ILTR 93.
44. [1976-77] ILRM 88.
45. [1916] 1 IR 21, 24.

words were not intended to create any trust in favour of the other defendants but were merely the expression of his wish for the guidance of his wife as to the manner in which she should dispose of her assets after her death.

Despite the general trend illustrated by these decisions, precatory words may be sufficient to create a trust if it is clear from the language used in the will as a whole that this was the testator's intention.[46] In *Comiskey v. Bowring-Hanbury*[47] a testator devised and bequeathed all his real and personal property to his wife absolutely 'in full confidence' that she would make such use of it as he would have made himself and that at her death she would devise it to one or more of the testator's nieces as she might think fit. The majority of the House of Lords held that on the true construction of the will there was an absolute gift of the testator's real and personal estate subject to an executory gift of the same at her death to such of his nieces as survived her, either in accordance with the shares provided for in the wife's will or otherwise equally.

So, it would be incorrect to assume that the use of any particular form of words may or may not be sufficient to create a trust[48] and in any event the courts may find expressions used in other parts of the will which may be employed as a guide in construing the precatory words.[49] Romer J summarized the position aptly in *Re Williams*:[50]

> [T]he rule you have to observe is simply this: 'In considering whether a precatory trust is attached to any legacy, the Court will be guided by the intention of the testator apparent in the will, and not by any particular words in which the wishes of the testator are expressed.'

The only situation where the use of identical language to that employed in a previous case may be decisive is where a testator can be shown to have used this particular language as a precedent with the intention of creating a trust. Where this is shown to be the case, it has been held that a trust may be created even though the words themselves, given a modern interpretation, might not otherwise have been held to be sufficient to create a trust.[51]

---

46. *Comiskey v. Bowring-Hanbury* [1905] AC 84, 89 *per* Lord Davey.
47. [1905] AC 84. See also *Re Burley* [1910] 1 Ch 215.
48. *Re Hamilton* [1895] 2 Ch 370, 373 *per* Lindley LJ and *Re McIntosh* [1933] IR 69, 71 *per* Kennedy CJ. Contrast the decisions of *Re Williams* [1897] 2 Ch 12 where the words 'in the fullest trust and confidence' were insufficient to create a trust in this case, and *Comiskey v. Bowring-Hanbury* [1905] AC 84 where the opposite conclusion was reached where the words 'in full confidence' were employed.
49. *Re Blackwood* [1953] NI 32, 46 *per* Black LJ.
50. [1897] 2 Ch 12, 14.
51. *Re Steele's Will Trusts* [1948] Ch 603. This decision should not be interpreted as authority for the proposition that if a particular form of wording has been held to create a trust, the use of this wording will necessarily without further evidence also create a trust. See the statement in *Snell's Equity* McGhee (30th ed. 2000) pp.138-139 and (1968) 32 Conv 361.

Where the test of certainty of intention is not complied with, as where precatory words are interpreted as being insufficient to create a trust, the donee will take an absolute gift of the property.[52] This should be contrasted with the situation which arises where the test relating to certainty of objects is not met, in which case a resulting trust arises in favour of the settlor or testator's estate.

Finally it should be noted that even where a settlor executes a declaration of trust, the courts may look behind such a declaration at the settlor's intention to ensure that he genuinely meant to create a trust. In *Midland Bank plc v. Wyatt*[53] the defendant and his wife purchased a property in their joint names and the defendant subsequently executed a trust deed giving the equity in the house to his wife and daughters. After the defendant's business ran into difficulties he sought to resist the making absolute of a charging order on the property obtained by the bank relying on the declaration of trust. However, the court held that the declaration upon which the plaintiff sought to rely was void and unenforceable on the basis that it was a sham and that the deed had been executed by the plaintiff 'not to be acted upon but to be put in the safe for a rainy day'.[54] The court was satisfied that the plaintiff had never intended to give his children any interest in the property but had merely sought to protect his family from commercial risk. If this approach is followed in this jurisdiction, it opens up the possibility of the courts looking behind a whole range of trust declarations with a view to examining the settlor's motives in such cases. It should be noted that in *Wyatt* it was stated that even if the deed was executed without any dishonest or fraudulent motive but was merely entered into on the basis of mistaken advice, it would still be an unenforceable transaction if it was entered into for some ulterior motive.

Certainty of Subject-Matter

To ensure the creation of a valid express trust, the subject-matter of the trust must be defined with sufficient certainty. This principle applies not just in a general way to the property which should form the subject-matter of the trust, but also requires that the beneficial interests to be taken by the beneficiaries are defined with sufficient clarity except in a situation where the trustees are given a discretion to decide what the extent of these beneficial interests should be.

While a testator may leave his residuary estate on trust, where a phrase such as 'the bulk of my … residuary estate' is used no trust will be created.[55] One of the most common examples of a trust failing due to lack of certainty

---

52. *Lassence v. Tierney* (1849) 1 Mac & G 551.
53. [1995] 1 FLR 696.
54. *Ibid.* at 707.
55. *Palmer v. Simmonds* (1854) 2 Drew 221.

of subject-matter is where a testator gives property to an individual and directs that whatever is not required during that individual's lifetime and remains at the time of his death should go to another person or persons.[56] So, where phrases such as 'the remaining part of what is left'[57] or 'such parts of my ... estate as she shall not have sold or disposed of'[58] are employed, these gifts will usually fail to take effect.

However, it would be incorrect to assume that gifts described in this way will invariably be considered too uncertain. As Karminski J commented in *Re Last's Estate*:[59]

> In a matter of construction of this kind, it is clearly essential to pay particular attention to the terms of the instrument which is being construed and to avoid too close comparisons with words used in wills in other cases.

There a testatrix left all her property to her brother and directed that 'anything that is left' should go to her late husband's grandchildren. Karminski J quoted with approval the statement of Joyce J in *Re Sanford*[60] to the effect that 'it is better to effectuate than to frustrate the testator's intentions' and held that when the testatrix's brother died intestate, her husband's grandchildren were entitled to the estate in equal shares.

It must be possible to determine with certainty what will constitute the trust property, so vague expressions such as 'the bulk of my ... residuary estate'[61] and 'remembering always ... the Church of God and the poor'[62] will be insufficient. The most usual result where a purported trust attached to an absolute gift fails due to the uncertainty of its subject-matter is that the donee takes beneficially,[63] but if it is clear that a trust was intended and the only uncertainty relates to the precise shares which the beneficiaries are to take, the trustees will hold the property on a resulting trust. In *Boyce v. Boyce*,[64] a testator devised all his houses in a particular location in trust to his wife for life and after her death in trust to convey whichever of these houses was chosen by her to one of his daughters, the other houses to go to another daughter. The daughter who was to have made the selection predeceased the

---

56. *Mussoorie Bank Ltd v. Raynor* (1882) 7 App Cas 321.
57. *Sprange v. Barnard* (1789) 2 Bro CC 585.
58. *Re Jones* [1898] 1 Ch 438.
59. [1958] P 137.
60. [1901] 1 Ch 939, 944.
61. *Palmer v. Simmonds* (1854) 2 Drew 221.
62. *Curtis v. Rippon* (1820) 5 Madd 434.
63. E.g. *Re Jones* [1898] 1 Ch 438; *Mussoorie Bank Ltd v. Raynor* (1882) 7 App Cas 321; *Curtis v. Rippon* (1820) 5 Madd 434.
64. (1849) 16 Sim 476.

testator and it was held that the trust failed for uncertainty. Had the trustees been given the authority to make the selection this problem could have been averted but in the circumstances the court felt that it had no choice but to find that all the properties should be held on a resulting trust for the testator's estate.

Where an objective criterion which can be applied by the court is provided by a settlor or testator, a failure to quantify precisely the extent of the subject-matter of a trust will not prove fatal to its validity. In *Re Golay's Will Trusts*[65] Ungoed-Thomas J upheld the validity of a gift directing the testator's executors to allow a beneficiary to use a flat during her lifetime and to receive 'a reasonable income' from his other properties. The question which the court had to consider in such a case was 'whether the testator by the words "reasonable income" has given a sufficient indication of his intention to provide an effective determinant of what he intends so that the court in applying that determinant can give effect to the testator's intention.' Ungoed-Thomas J concluded that the yardstick indicated by the testator is what has been objectively identified as a 'reasonable income' and as the court was constantly involved in making such objective assessments, the direction in the will, in his view, could not be defeated on the grounds of uncertainty.

Difficulties have always arisen where a settlor seeks to create a trust of a definite but yet unidentified portion of an asset or assets. It was held by Oliver J in *Re London Wine Co. Ltd*[66] that where wine beneficially owned by certain purchasers and stored in a warehouse had not been segregated no trust could arise over it and the purchasers could therefore not assert proprietary rights over the stock against the holders of a floating charge. The view that where the purported subject-matter of a trust is comprised of goods or chattels these must be properly segregated before there can be a valid trust is borne out by the decision of the Privy Council in *Re Goldcorp Exchange Ltd.*[67] In this case the purchasers of bullion which had not been specifically allocated to them failed to establish proprietary rights over it after the company which had possession of it was put into receivership on the basis that there was no ascertained property to which a trust could attach. As Lord Mustill commented: 'It makes no difference what the parties intended, if what they intend is impossible: as is the case with an immediate transfer of title to goods whose identity is not yet known'.[68]

However, where the asset in question is of an intangible nature, the courts in England have accepted that a trust may arise in these circumstances. In *Hunter v. Moss*[69] it was confirmed that the requirement of certainty of subject-

---

65. [1965] 1 WLR 969.
66. [1986] PCC 121.
67. [1995] 1 AC 74.
68. *Ibid.* at 90.
69. [1993] 1 WLR 934 (DC); [1994] 1 WLR 452 (CA).

matter in relation to a trust of intangible assets is not based on any immutable principle which demands segregation or appropriation of the specific property which is to form this subject-matter. The trust in that case was comprised of a number of shares in a company which were of their nature indistinguishable from other shares in the same company. They were all equally capable of satisfying the trust and it was unnecessary to identify any particular shares before determining that the subject-matter requirement was satisfied. In these circumstances, Colin Rimmer QC, giving the judgment of the Divisional Court in *Hunter*, was of the view that 'any suggested uncertainty as to subject matter appears to me to be theoretical and conceptual rather than real and practical'[70] and his finding that the trust was not void on the grounds of uncertainty of subject-matter was upheld by the Court of Appeal.[71] However, Dillon LJ made no reference to the distinction drawn between tangible and intangible assets at first instance and simply reasoned that 'just as a person can give by will a specified number of his shares in a certain company, so equally, in my judgment, he can declare himself a trustee of 50 of his ordinary shares'.[72]

The decision in *Hunter* was applied by Neuberger J in *Holland v. Newbury*[73] in which he held that it was possible to create a trust of a specified number of shares which constituted a part of unidentified shares of a particular class in a company. While Neuberger J pointed out that the decision in *Hunter* was binding on him unless he was satisfied that it was *per incuriam*, he seemed to accept that a distinction might be drawn between tangible and intangible assets for this purpose.[74] In his view the description of the client's wine in *Re London Wine Co. Ltd*[75] and the customer's bullion in *Re Goldcorp*[76] as 'an unascertained part of a mass of goods' was quite apt whereas it would not be an accurate description of the 50 shares in *Hunter* or those in the case before him.

Prior to the decision in *Hunter* it had been assumed in England that trusts of intangible property would only be valid if the settlor declared a trust of his entire interest in the *chose in action* or of a fixed proportion thereof. The

---

70. [1993] 1 WLR 934, 946.
71. [1994] 1 WLR 452. It would appear that the decision of the Court of Appeal was made after argument had been concluded but before the decision had been given in *Re Goldcorp* [1995] 1 AC 74, see the decision of Neuberger J in *Holland v. Newbury* [1997] 2 BCLC 369, 380.
72. *Ibid.* at 459.
73. [1997] 2 BCLC 369.
74. Although Villiers suggests that he was 'lukewarm' in his support for such a distinction, see (1998-99) 9 KCLJ 112, 113.
75. [1986] PCC 121.
76. [1995] 1 AC 74. It could be argued that the bars of gold bullion in *Goldcorp* were indistinguishable from each other. Villiers has suggested that it might be preferable to reconcile *Hunter* with *Goldcorp* on the basis that the latter concerned generic rather than bulk goods, see (1998-99) 9 KCLJ 112, 114.

decision has provoked controversy; Hayton is particularly critical of the reasoning employed by Dillon LJ and suggests that the latter's judgment 'should not be regarded as the last word on the subject'.[77] He suggests that *Hunter* should not be followed and that there is no sound reason for distinguishing trusts of goods from trusts of intangibles.[78]

Martin[79] states that critics of the *Hunter* decision do not claim that there is any difference between one ordinary share in a company and another but difficulties could arise in relation to subsequent dealings with the shareholding of which an unsegregated part is subject to a trust. However, she submits that the solution achieved in *Hunter* is 'fair, sensible and workable'[80] and welcomes the decision as an example of the court's policy of preventing a clearly intended trust from failing for uncertainty. However, as Oakley[81] rightly suggests *Hunter v. Moss* has left the law in a somewhat uncertain state in England and it is quite possible that the courts in this jurisdiction will not follow it.

A final point which should be made about this certainty requirement is that it should not be regarded as existing in isolation and is often closely connected with the requirement of certainty of words. Sir Arthur Hobhouse made this point in *Mussoorie Bank Ltd v. Raynor*[82] in the following terms:

> [T]he uncertainty of the subject of the gift has a reflex action upon the previous words, and throws doubt upon the intention of the testator, and seems to shew that he could not possibly have intended his words of confidence, hope, or whatever they may be ... to be imperative.

Certainty of Objects

The general principle that 'in order to be valid, a trust must be one which the court can control and execute'[83] has led to the development of a considerable body of case law and academic criticism[84] in relation to the objects of a trust. The fundamental rule which must be observed in this context is that the objects or beneficiaries of a trust must be defined with a sufficient degree of certainty to enable the trustees, or if necessary the court, to administer the trust according to the settlor or testator's intentions. The reason that this area of the law remains clouded by such a degree of uncertainty is that the requirements which must

---

77. (1994) 110 LQR 335, 340. Although as he points out, the House of Lords refused leave to appeal in *Hunter*, see [1994] 1 WLR 614.
78. See *The Law Relating to Trusts and Trustees* (16th ed., 2003) p. 79.
79. [1996] Conv 223.
80. *Ibid.* at 227. See also Hanbury and Martin, *Modern Equity* (16th ed., 2001) p. 101.
81. Parker and Mellows, *The Modern Law of Trusts* (7th ed., 1998) pp. 89-90.
82. (1882) 7 App Cas 321, 330.
83. *IRC v. Broadway Cottages Trust* [1955] Ch 20, 30.
84. See in particular, Hopkins (1971) 29 CLJ 68; Emery (1982) 98 LQR 551. See also Harris (1971) 87 LQR 31; Grbich (1974) 37 MLR 643.

be satisfied will depend on whether the instrument being construed is characterised as a trust or a power and in addition may vary according to the nature of the trust involved.

Test for Fixed Trusts

Under the terms of a fixed trust, the interest which each beneficiary is to take is specified in the trust instrument and the trustees have no discretion to determine either who will benefit or the extent of that individual's share. The requirement in this case is that the persons who are to benefit under a trust must be clearly identified or identifiable by the time it comes into operation; 'the trust must have ascertained or ascertainable beneficiaries'.[85] Clearly where property is to be held on trust to be divided amongst the members of a class either in equal or other specified shares, this task cannot be carried out unless it is possible to draw up a complete list of the members of that class.[86] In addition, the class must be defined with sufficient conceptual certainty to enable the trustees or if they fail to act, the court, to be able to decide in principle whether or not a given individual is or is not a member of the class.[87] Where this requirement is met it will not be fatal to the validity of a fixed trust that the whereabouts and even the continued existence of a beneficiary cannot be ascertained; provided that their identity as a member of the class is established, their share can be paid into court.[88]

Test for Mere Powers

The donee of a power of appointment is under no duty to exercise it in a particular manner, if indeed he exercises it at all and to this extent his position differs from that of a trustee.[89] Such a donee can only make a distribution

---

85. *Re Endacott* [1960] Ch 232, 246 *per* Evershed MR.
86. *IRC v. Broadway Cottages Trust* [1955] Ch 20, 29 *per* Jenkins LJ. While Matthews argued in [1984] Conv 22 that there should be no requirement that all the objects be known in the case of a fixed trust and that the proper test should instead be that the description of the beneficiaries be conceptually certain, there is no sign of any judicial or even academic acceptance of this idea. Hayton argues ([1984] Conv 307) that this suggestion is based on a misunderstanding of Lord Upjohn's judgment in *Re Gulbenkian's Settlements* [1970] AC 508 and Martin ([1984] Conv 304) also disputes Matthews' suggestion and instead insists that the test for the validity of a fixed trust should continue to be that it should be possible to draw up a list of potential beneficiaries which is on the balance of probabilities complete.
87. See *infra* pp. 88-89.
88. *Re Gulbenkian's Settlements* [1970] AC 508, 524 *per* Lord Upjohn.
89. Although note the *dicta* of Lord Reid in *Re Gulbenkian's Settlements* [1970] AC 508, 518 in relation to the situation which arises where a power is given to trustees as such and where a settlor or testator must be taken to be relying on them in their fiduciary capacity, sometimes referred to as a 'power fiduciary'. See Emery (1982) 98 LQR 551, 580.

amongst the classes of individuals specified by the settlor and the validity of special powers of appointment depends upon the objects of the power being defined with sufficient certainty. While Harman J sought to lay down a test of certainty in *Re Gestetner Settlement*,[90] it gave rise to some confusion as to the precise meaning intended and in subsequent cases the requirement was variously stated as being that a power would be valid if it could be said with certainty whether any given individual fell within the class of objects,[91] or that it was sufficient that any person should be found who clearly came within the class.[92] Much needed clarification of the position came in the form of Lord Upjohn's judgment in the House of Lords in *Re Gulbenkian's Settlements*[93] where his lordship formulated the test as follows:

> A mere or bare power of appointment among a class is valid if you can with certainty say whether any given individual is or is not a member of the class; you do not have to be able to ascertain every member of the class.

In *Gulbenkian* a settlement contained a power of appointment in favour of an individual 'any wife and his children or remoter issue ... and any person or persons in whose house or apartments or in whose company or under whose care and control or by or with whom [he] may from time to time be employed or residing.' The validity of this power was unanimously upheld by the House of Lords, although four of the law lords[94] rejected the broader view which had been put forward by Lord Denning MR and Winn LJ in the Court of Appeal to the effect that a power is valid if any one individual clearly falls within its scope. As Lord Upjohn stated: 'the trustees or the court must be able to say with certainty who is within and who is without the power'.[95]

A similar viewpoint was put forward by Murnaghan J in the Supreme Court in *Re Bayley*,[96] where a power of appointment amongst such of the testator's 'Irish relatives' as his sister should appoint was upheld as valid. Murnaghan J stated:

> It is not, I think, necessary for the valid exercise of a power of

---

90. [1953] Ch 672, 688.
91. *Re Gresham's Settlement* [1956] 1 WLR 573.
92. *Re Gibbard's Settlement Trusts* [1967] 1 WLR 42 and see the judgments of Lord Denning MR and Winn LJ in *Re Gulbenkian's Settlements* [1968] Ch 126, where the former stated at p. 134: 'if the trustees can say of any particular person that he is clearly within the category the gift is good.'
93. [1970] AC 508, 521.
94. Lord Donovan reserved his opinion on the issue although he stated that he was inclined to share this view. (at 526)
95. [1970] AC 508, 525.
96. [1945] IR 224.

appointment that the donee should be able to range in his mind every person capable of taking under the power. It is sufficient if the person chosen as an object comes properly within the description of the class amongst which an appointment may be made.[97]

While the Supreme Court did not go as far as following the broader approach adopted by the members of the Court of Appeal and rejected by the House of Lords in *Re Gulbenkian's Settlements*, Murnaghan J did show his willingness to adopt a flexible attitude by stating that the words of Lord Brougham in *Winter v. Perratt*[98] laid down in that case with reference to a devise, were equally applicable to the construction of a power; namely: 'we ought not, without absolute necessity, to let ourselves embrace the alternative of holding a devise void for uncertainty. Where it is possible to give a meaning, we should give it, that the will of the testator may be operative.'[99]

Test for Discretionary Trusts

In the case of a discretionary trust, trustees are under an obligation to distribute the trust property to the beneficiaries, although they have a discretion to select which members of the class should benefit and to what extent. Trusts in this category are usually created by a settlor with a view to deriving the tax advantages which result from divesting himself absolutely of the property and often confer a discretion on trustees to benefit a wide class of potential beneficiaries. Another similar concept, although much less common today, is that of a trust power,[100] which involves the court implying the existence of a trust in default of any appointment being made by a donee of a power.

Considerable doubt still surrounds the question of the correct test of certainty in relation to objects to apply to such discretionary trusts in this jurisdiction. Should the test laid down in *Re Gulbenkian's Settlements* in relation to mere powers apply or must the entire class of potential beneficiaries be ascertained or ascertainable in order for the trust to be valid? The test originally applied in England was as formulated by Jenkins LJ in *IRC v. Broadway Cottages Trust*,[101] namely that 'a trust for such members of a given class of objects as the trustees shall select is void for uncertainty unless the whole range of objects eligible for selection is ascertained or capable of ascertainment.' Where this test is applied the validity of a disposition may therefore depend on whether it is classified as a trust or a power.[102] The

---

97. *Ibid*. at 229. See also the *dicta* of Budd J in *Re Parker* [1966] IR 308, 318.
98. (1843) 9 Cl & F 606, 687.
99. *Ibid*. at 230.
100. Considered *supra* pp. 58–63.
101. [1955] Ch 20, 35–36.
102. Criticised by Harman LJ in *Re Baden's Deed Trusts* [1969] 2 Ch 388, 397 as 'an absurd and embarrassing result'.

rationale behind such an approach was twofold: first, that a trustee's duty to distribute could only properly be carried out if he had before him a comprehensive list of the potential beneficiaries,[103] and secondly, that if the court was required to make a distribution where the trustees failed to act, it could only do so on the basis of equal division and this would not be possible without a complete list of the potential beneficiaries.[104]

Although the traditional *Broadway Cottages Trust* test for discretionary trusts was approved *obiter* by the majority of the House of Lords in *Re Gulbenkian's Settlements*,[105] a differently constituted House took the opportunity to reformulate the test of certainty the following year in *McPhail v. Doulton*.[106] A deed executed by the settlor provided that a fund was to be held on certain trusts for the benefit of the staff of a company and their 'relatives and dependants'. The House of Lords held that the deed created a trust rather than a power and Lord Wilberforce concluded that the test for discretionary trusts 'ought to be similar to that accepted by this House in *Re Gulbenkian's Settlements* for powers, namely, that the trust is valid if it can be said with certainty that any given individual is or is not a member of the class.'[107] When the matter was remitted to the Court of Appeal,[108] the court concluded that the test of certainty had been satisfied in the circumstances of the case and the trust was valid.

Despite these far-reaching developments in England, there is good reason for supposing that in this jurisdiction, certainly in relation to specific types of discretionary trusts, the law remains as formulated in *IRC v. Broadway Cottages Trust*. In *Re Parker*[109] the testator's will provided that certain income from a trust was to be divided amongst his 'necessitous nieces and nephews' and their children in such manner as his executors might think fit. Budd J, in holding that the trust was not void for uncertainty, stated that where trustees

---

103. This rationale was rejected by Stamp LJ in *Re Baden's Deed Trusts (No. 2)* [1973] Ch 9, 27. Although he accepted as Lord Wilberforce had indicated in *McPhail v. Doulton* that a 'wider and more comprehensive range of inquiry' was necessary in the case of a discretionary trust than in the case of a mere power, he said that provided an appropriate survey was made it did not matter that it was not absolutely complete.

104. This reasoning was adverted to by Lord Hodson in *McPhail v. Doulton* [1971] AC 424, 442, although as he pointed out, such a basis for division may lead to absurdity, particularly in the context of a typical modern discretionary trust. Note also the comments of Lord Wilberforce in *McPhail* at p. 451 where his lordship pointed out that in the case before him equal division was 'surely the last thing the settlor ever intended.'

105. [1970] AC 508, although not by Lord Reid.

106. [1971] AC 424. Lord Wilberforce, Lord Reid and Viscount Dilhorne formed the majority. Lord Guest and Lord Hodson, who had supported the view of the House in *Re Gulbenkian's Settlements*, dissented.

107. *Ibid.* at 456.

108. *Re Baden's Deed Trusts (No. 2)* [1973] Ch 9.

109. [1966] IR 308.

have a duty to distribute income under a trust it is essential that they know before performing this duty who the beneficiaries are. He formulated the test as follows:

> [A]n imperative trust for the division of income between such members of the class as the trustees may select is invalid unless the whole class of potential beneficiaries can be ascertained.[110]

This view has recently been approved, albeit in an *obiter* context, by Murphy J in *O'Byrne v. Davoren*.[111] The testatrix's will provided that the residue of her estate should be held on trust for the post-primary education of such members of a class consisting of the children, grandchildren and direct descendants of named persons whom the trustees in their discretion should decide would be most likely to benefit therefrom. Murphy J was satisfied that the gift was sufficiently certain but held that it was void because it infringed the rule against perpetuities and the rule against perpetual trusts. Nevertheless, it is interesting to compare the view which he expressed on the question of certainty with those put forward by the House of Lords in *McPhail v. Doulton*. Murphy J commented that not only was the judgment of Budd J a precedent of greater authority than that of the House of Lords but he also preferred the reasoning in the former case, namely that an imperative trust for the division of income between such members of a class as the trustees may select is invalid unless the whole class of potential beneficiaries can be ascertained. Murphy J also said that he approved Budd J's view to the effect that difficulties in interpretation should not be sufficient to render a gift void for uncertainty; as Budd J had said 'to be void for this reason it must be utterly impossible to put a meaning on it'.[112] So Murphy J concluded that the court should endeavour to resolve ambiguities and uncertainties where this was compatible with the expressed or implied wishes of the testator and concluded that this view would have been of decisive importance in upholding the validity of the residuary bequest if the class of relatives had been confined to those living at the date of the testatrix's death.

It can be argued that from a global perspective the *McPhail* approach is much more likely to lead to at least partial fulfilment of a testator's intentions in these circumstances, for the alternative is that the trust will fail for uncertainty. As against this it can also be said that the approach adopted in this jurisdiction, provided an effort is made to give effect to a testator's intentions in as liberal a manner as possible, is more likely to lead to a division of the trust property or income in equal shares amongst *all* potential

---

110. *Ibid.* at 318.
111. [1994] 3 IR 373.
112. [1966] IR 308, 320.

beneficiaries. However, it is submitted that for a court in this jurisdiction to consider itself faced with a stark choice between the *McPhail* and *Parker* approaches, irrespective of the nature of the discretionary trust involved, is unduly simplistic. As noted above, the rationale of the need for equal division which seems to lie behind *Parker* is far from suitable in the case of many modern discretionary trusts and is based rather on the type of 'trust powers' so common in the last century.[113] Perhaps before deciding which test is to be preferred in a given case, the question of how the court would exercise its discretion where the trustees fail to do so should be addressed.[114] Where the testator's intentions are likely to be fulfilled by equal division amongst all the potential beneficiaries, clearly the certainty requirement laid down in *Parker* is to be preferred. However, as the judgment of Lord Wilberforce in *McPhail* made clear, this is no longer the case in relation to many modern discretionary trusts which are designed to benefit a much wider class of beneficiary and it is difficult to fault the conclusion reached in the latter case on the basis of the nature of the trust involved.

Clearly such a flexible approach will itself lead to uncertainty and may be as undesirable as a rigid application of principle which fails to take into account the nature and circumstances of a discretionary trust. While it would be impossible to predict how the courts in this jurisdiction will resolve the dilemma, it is to be hoped that they will at least have regard to some of the pragmatic arguments advanced above.

Conceptual and Evidential Certainty

Irrespective of the nature of the trust or power involved,[115] the description used to define the class of potential beneficiaries must be conceptually certain. In some instances, the concepts employed to describe this class may be so precise that it is most unlikely that any uncertainty could arise, e.g. 'son' or 'daughter'. On the other hand there will be many cases where the terminology used is far from being free from some element of uncertainty e.g.'relative' or 'friend'. So, as a general rule, whether one is dealing with a fixed or discretionary trust, the class must be defined with sufficient conceptual certainty to enable the trustees, or if necessary the court, to determine theoretically whether any given individual is or is not a member of that class. Where the words used are sufficiently precise to satisfy this test of conceptual certainty in principle, the question of who falls within this description is a matter of fact. As Sachs LJ commented in *Re Baden's Deed Trusts (No.2)*,[116] 'it is essential to bear in mind the differences between conceptual uncertainty

---

113. E.g. *Burrough v. Philcox* (1840) 5 My & Cr 72.
114. See Emery (1982) 98 LQR 551, 569.
115. *Re Sayer* [1957] Ch 423, 432 *per* Upjohn J.
116. [1973] Ch 9, 19.

and evidential difficulties'. This latter concept of evidential certainty relates to the practical question of whether it is possible to establish as a matter of fact that a given individual does or does not fall within the defined class; in the words of Sachs LJ: 'once the class of persons to be benefited is conceptually certain it then becomes a question of fact to be determined on the evidence whether any postulant has on inquiry been proved to be within it; if he is not so proved then he is not in it.'[117]

The point has been made by Martin[118] that 'to insist on complete certainty would be to defeat most gifts' and the courts have displayed a relatively flexible attitude towards this issue, as for instance in *Re Baden's Deed Trusts (No.2)*,[119] where the Court of Appeal accepted that there was no conceptual uncertainty in the words 'relatives' and 'dependants'. Similarly, in *Gold v. Hill*[120] Carnwath J rejected the submission that a trust for a named woman with whom the deceased had lived and 'the kids' was insufficiently precise. While he acknowledged that there was potential ambiguity in the words used as the deceased had a number of children from different relationships, in his view the general intention was clear, namely to provide for his partner and her children.

It would appear that the conceptual certainty required in the case of trusts for members of a class subject to the fulfilment of a condition precedent is not as strict, although arguably this is difficult to justify. In *Re Barlow's Will Trusts*[121] a testatrix directed her executors 'to allow any members of my family and any friends of mine who may wish to do so' to purchase any of her paintings at a reduced price. Browne-Wilkinson J upheld the validity of the gift as it was 'possible to say of one or more persons that he or they undoubtedly qualify even though it may be difficult to say of others whether or not they qualify.'[122]

Administrative Unworkability and Capriciousness

Even where a class is defined with sufficient conceptual certainty a trust may still fail for uncertainty 'where the definition of the beneficiaries is so hopelessly wide as not to form "anything like a class" so that the trust is administratively unworkable.'[123] This ground of uncertainty was put forward by Lord Wilberforce in *McPhail v. Doulton*,[124] where he suggested that perhaps

---

117. *Re Baden's Deed Trusts (No. 2)* [1973] Ch 9, 20.
118. Hanbury and Martin, *Modern Equity* (16th ed., 2001) p. 107.
119. [1973] Ch 9.
120. [1999] 1 FLR 54.
121. [1979] 1 WLR 278.
122. *Ibid.* at 281.
123. *McPhail v. Doulton* [1971] AC 424, 457 *per* Lord Wilberforce.
124. [1971] AC 424. See also the *dicta* of Lord Eldon in *Morice v. Bishop of Durham* (1805) 10 Ves 522, 527.

a discretionary trust for 'all the residents of Greater London' might prove invalid for this reason. While there is no conceptual uncertainty in such a description and it would be theoretically possible to make a complete list of such persons, it would arguably not be possible for trustees to exercise their discretion in such a manner so as to give effect to a settlor's intentions when dealing with such a huge number of potential beneficiaries. A discretionary trust in favour of 'any or all or some of the inhabitants of the County of West Yorkshire' was found to be invalid for this reason in *R. v. District Auditor, ex p. West Yorkshire Metropolitan County Council*,[125] on the grounds that the definition of the beneficiaries was, in the phraseology used by Lord Wilberforce, so hopelessly wide as to be incapable of forming anything like a class.

It should be noted that while administrative unworkability can invalidate a discretionary trust, the weight of authority[126] supports the view that it will not affect the validity of a mere power. The statement of Templeman J in *Re Manisty's Settlement Trusts*[127] that 'a power cannot be uncertain merely because it is wide in ambit' found favour with Megarry VC in *Re Hay's Settlement Trusts*,[128] where the latter concluded that he did not see how mere numbers could inhibit the donees of a power from considering whether or not to exercise it.

While it has been argued that this notion of basing a finding of uncertainty on the concept of administrative unworkability is 'incapable of solid justification on the basis of either administrative feasibility or judicial execution',[129] the better view would seem to be that it is a logical and necessary extension of the requirement of evidential certainty. Hardcastle has put forward the suggestion that while the court will not normally permit difficulties in ascertainment to defeat execution of a trust, a point may be reached where its performance 'becomes an exercise in futility … when a potentially innumerable class of beneficiaries is coupled with a total lack of provable definitional criteria'.[130]

Another related concept which may form the basis for a finding of uncertainty is that of capriciousness. While the same set of circumstances, such as Lord Wilberforce's example of all the residents of Greater London may at the same time give rise to a finding of administrative unworkability and capriciousness, the latter concept has no necessary connection with width of numbers which is an essential characteristic of the former. A further

---

125. (1986) 26 RVR 24.
126. Although note the contrary view expressed by Buckley LJ in *Blausten v. IRC* [1972] Ch 256.
127. [1974] Ch 17.
128. [1982] 1 WLR 202.
129. See McKay (1974) 38 Conv 269, 284.
130. [1990] Conv 24, 33.

important distinction which should be drawn is that the notion of capriciousness has been held to apply to mere powers. In *Re Manisty's Settlement Trusts*[131] Templeman J commented that 'a capricious power negatives a sensible consideration by the trustees of the exercise of the power' and contrasted this with a 'wide power' which 'does not negative or prohibit a sensible approach by the trustees to the consideration and exercise of their powers.' So where a settlor seeks to benefit 'an accidental conglomeration of persons'[132] who have no discernible link with him, it may be unrealistic to seek to give effect to his intentions and the instrument, whether construed as a trust or a power, may be found to be invalid on the grounds of capriciousness.

---

131. [1974] Ch 17, 27.
132. *Re Manisty's Settlement Trusts* [1974] Ch 24, 27 *per* Templeman J.

CHAPTER 5

Secret Trusts

INTRODUCTION

As we have already seen in relation to trusts created *inter vivos*, equity will not always insist on strict compliance with the statutory formalities required when this would result in a statute being used as an instrument of fraud.[1] Similarly, the statutory formalities which must normally be complied with to create a valid trust which is to take effect after a testator's death may in some circumstances be waived to give effect to what has become known as a 'secret trust'. A fully secret trust usually arises where a testator makes a gift of property to a named person in his will without expressly stating that the latter is to hold it on trust. If either before or after making his will, but during his lifetime, he informs the legatee that he wishes him to hold the property on trust for a third party or for a particular purpose and the legatee either expressly or by his silence impliedly agrees to do so, he will be bound by the trust.[2] A half secret trust on the other hand is said to exist where it is clear from the will that the legatee is to hold the property on trust but neither the terms of the trust nor the identity of the beneficiaries are disclosed in the will.

Historically, the reason for the creation of such trusts was to allow a testator to make provision for a mistress or an illegitimate child or another person whom he wished to benefit for some reason without his family or the world at large being aware of the gift. While this is rarely necessary today, a testator may still employ this device, often to prevent having to specify with precision at the time of making a will how he intends his property to be distributed. The practice of giving effect to secret trusts created for such a purpose has been criticised[3] as it effectively allows a testator to bypass the statutory requirements laid down in relation to the execution of wills where the need for secrecy is not present. However, certainly in the case of a fully secret trust, fraud may

---

1. See *supra Rochefoucauld v. Boustead* [1897] 1 Ch 196; *McGillycuddy v. Joy* [1959] IR 189; *Gilmurray v. Corr* [1978] NI 99.
2. Such a trust can also arise where an individual refrains from making a will on the basis of a promise made by his intestate successor that he will carry out the former's wishes, see *Sellack v. Harris* (1708) 5 Vin Abr 521 and note the comments of Lord Westbury in *McCormick v. Grogan* (1869) LR 4 HL 82, 97.
3. Watkin [1981] Conv 335, 338.

still result if effect is not given to these trusts and the principles governing their enforcement are likely to be considered as being too firmly established now to be disregarded for policy reasons.

FULLY SECRET TRUSTS

Historically, the dilemma faced by the courts in deciding whether to enforce a fully secret trust was this; should it be permissible for a testator to disregard or bypass the statutory formalities laid down in relation to testamentary dispositions or should a legatee be permitted to take a gift beneficially when it was clearly intended by a testator to be held on trust? The conclusion reached was that equity should intervene to prevent the perpetration of a fraud[4] and the practice of giving effect to secret trusts developed. The next question was, should the legatee merely hold the property on a resulting trust for the testator's estate, which would be sufficient to prevent fraud, or should the courts go a step further and actually enforce the trust in favour of the beneficiary? It was decided to adopt the latter course and while the avoidance of fraud probably formed the basis for such a development, it is now often justified on the grounds that the testator had declared a valid trust *inter vivos* which merely became constituted on his death by virtue of the testamentary gift to the legatee.[5]

From a practical perspective, it may be of relevance to note that where a testator leaves property to A in his will on the understanding that he will hold it for the benefit of B on a secret trust, B's interest is not considered to have arisen by virtue of the will. This is illustrated in *Cullen v. Attorney General for Ireland*,[6] where a residuary legacy was left to an individual to hold it on a secret trust for the benefit of a charity. Although a testamentary gift in favour of a charity would have qualified for an exemption from certain taxes, the House of Lords held that this tax was payable because the testamentary gift was construed as having been made to the individual; 'the charity has no place, and is not to be found either in anything that is expressed in the will, or in anything that is so referred to in the will.'[7] The most important practical result of this principle that such a trust is not regarded as being a testamentary disposition is that a beneficiary will not forfeit his interest merely because he

---

4. See *McCormick v. Grogan* (1869) LR 4 HL 82, 97; *French v. French* [1902] 1 IR 172, 230.
5. However, as Kincaid points out [2000] Conv 420, 442 a secret trust relies on the death of the settlor to constitute the trust and the terms of the will or the rules of intestate succession to vest the property in the hands of the secret trustee or legatee.
6. (1866) LR 1 HL 190. See also *Revenue Commissioners v. Stapleton* [1937] IR 225.
7. *Ibid.* at 199 *per* Lord Westbury. However, see Critchley's criticism of this decision (1999) 115 LQR 631, 641.

has witnessed the testator's will.[8] Therefore in *O'Brien v. Condon*[9] it was held that a witness to a will was not precluded from benefiting from a secret trust on the grounds that 'what she takes under the trust is something not under the will, but solely by virtue of the secret trust, not disclosed on the will.'[10]

Despite this theoretical independence from the will, the beneficiaries' interests are still dependent on the validity of the initial testamentary disposition.[11] If a testator makes a gift to a legatee in his will intending him to hold it on trust for another and the legatee predeceases the testator, the legacy and therefore the secret trust will fail.[12] However, there is some authority to support the proposition that even if the beneficiary predeceases the testator, his heirs will take the interest created by the secret trust on the testator's death provided that he was alive at the time when the undertaking to enforce the trust was given by the legatee.[13]

To create a valid fully secret trust, the testator must intend to create a trust and its terms must be communicated to the legatee and accepted by him during the testator's lifetime.[14] Brightman J expressed these requirements in the following terms in *Ottaway v. Norman*:[15]

> The essential elements which must be proved to exist are: (i) the intention of the testator to subject the primary donee to an obligation in favour of the secondary donee; (ii) communication of that intention to the primary donee; and (iii) the acceptance of that obligation by the primary donee either expressly or by acquiescence.

As Hammond J commented in the recent New Zealand decision of *Brown v.*

---

8. S. 82 of the Succession Act 1965 provides that a witness to a will may not take a benefit under it.
9. [1905] 1 IR 51. See also *Re Young* [1951] Ch 344, 350 *per* Danckwerts J: 'the whole theory of the formation of a secret trust is that the Wills Act 1837 has nothing to do with the matter.'
10. *Ibid.* at 58 *per* Porter MR.
11. As Viscount Sumner commented in *Blackwell v. Blackwell* [1929] AC 318, 334: 'the doctrine must in principle rest on the assumption that the will has first operated according to its terms.'
12. *Re Maddock* [1902] 2 Ch 220, 231 *per* Cozens-Hardy LJ. See further Kincaid [2000] Conv 420, 439-440.
13. *Re Gardner* [1923] 2 Ch 230. As Wylie has pointed out (see *Irish Land Law* (3rd ed., 1997) p. 532) the reasoning in *Gardner* seems to ignore the fact that the trust is unlikely to be completely constituted at this point and some doubt must be cast on the validity of such a proposition for this reason. See also Kincaid [2000] Conv 420, 431-439.
14. In the words of Viscount Sumner in *Blackwell v. Blackwell* [1929] AC 318, 334 there must be 'intention, communication and acquiescence'.
15. [1972] Ch 698, 711. See also *Kasperbauer v. Griffith* Court of Appeal, 21 November 1997; *Margulies v. Margulies* Court of Appeal, 16 March 2000.

Pourau,[16] communication of the deceased's intention to create a secret trust is an essential factor because otherwise the devisee can quite reasonably argue that he took the will to mean precisely what it said on its face. Hammond J was of the view that once communication was established, acceptance, though also crucial, could in an appropriate case be inferred from the silence of the devisee. This principle had been laid down in the following terms by Lord Davey in *French v. French*,[17] from whose judgment Hammond J quoted with approval:

> It is now well established, and has been settled since the time of Lord Hardwicke, that if a testator communicates in his lifetime to a proposed devisee or legatee that he has left him his property, and expresses a wish that the property should be disposed of in a particular manner, and the legatee or devisee by acquiescence, or even by silence accepts that communication, and the testator dies without any repudiation, a trust is fastened upon his conscience.

Any attempt to communicate the testator's intention after his death, for example by written instructions, will be ineffective as the legatee's conscience will not be affected by the trust at the time the will becomes effective. As Fleming[18] has stated: 'it is not the unilaterally expressed intention of the testator, but the conduct of the legatee in inducing the former, on the faith of his promise, to make or revoke his will, which calls the equitable doctrine into operation.' However, where a testator gives the legatee a sealed envelope during his lifetime containing precise instructions about the terms of the trust and it is not opened until after the testator's death, this will be sufficient to give rise to a trust provided the legatee agrees in principle to carry out its terms during the testator's lifetime.[19] On the other hand, where a testator merely informs the legatee that he intends him to hold the property on trust but does not disclose its terms prior to his death, no secret trust will be created. This will also be the case where it is established that the testator intended to create a trust and the trustee accepted the obligation but the trust fails for some other reason, e.g. because the beneficiaries are unascertainable.[20] Similarly where a legatee agrees to comply with a testator's directions with regard to a trust during the latter's lifetime, but these instructions only come to light following the testator's death.[21] In these situations where the evidence establishes that

---

16. [1995] 1 NZLR 352. See further Rickett [1996] Conv 302.
17. [1902] 1 IR 172, 230.
18. (1947) 12 Conv 28, 29.
19. *Re Boyes* (1884) 26 Ch D 531, 536 and *Re Keen* [1937] Ch 236, 242. See also where the legatee had signed the document containing the testator's instructions although she had not seen its contents; *Morrison v. McFerran* [1901] 1 IR 360.
20. See *Brown v. Pourau* [1995] 1 NZLR 352.
21. *Re Boyes* (1884) 26 Ch D 531.

the testator intended a trust and that the legatee undertook to give effect to it, the legatee will hold the gift on a resulting trust for the testator's estate.[22] However, where the testator never communicated any intention to the legatee during his lifetime that the latter was to hold the legacy on trust, the legatee will take beneficially.[23]

The onus lies on the person seeking to show the existence of a secret trust[24] to establish this on the balance of probabilities. While earlier authorities suggested that a higher standard of proof would be required,[25] it was established in *Re Snowden*[26] that the ordinary civil standard of proof applies. In that case Megarry VC suggested *obiter* that this standard might be higher if any question of fraud arose,[27] although as Keane[28] points out the Supreme Court has rejected the suggestion that any higher burden of proof should be placed on a plaintiff where an allegation of fraud is made in a civil case.[29]

Secret Trusts Involving Joint Tenants and Tenants in Common

A question which must also be addressed is whether a secret trust will arise and who will be bound by it where a testamentary gift is made to more than one person but the testator's intentions with regard to the creation of a trust are not communicated to all of these persons during his lifetime. The traditional approach as set out by Farwell J in *Re Stead*[30] involves drawing a distinction between the position of legatees who hold as joint tenants and as tenants in common.

> If A. induces B. either to make, or to leave unrevoked, a will leaving property to A. and C. as tenants in common, by expressly promising or tacitly consenting, that he and C. will carry out the testator's wishes, and C. knows nothing of the matter until after B.'s death, A. is bound,

---

22. For the residuary devisees or legatees or if there is no residuary gift, assuming that the residue is the subject-matter of a secret trust, for those entitled on an intestacy.
23. *Wallgrave v. Tebbs* (1855) 2 K & J 313.
24. *Jones v. Badley* (1868) 3 Ch App 362.
25. *McCormick v. Grogan* (1869) LR 4 HL 82, 97 *per* Lord Westbury.
26. [1979] Ch 528. This standard seems to have been accepted elsewhere in the common law world, e.g. see *Quinn v. Dean* High Court, Wellington, A 123/84 30 July 1986. The formula adopted by Dixon CJ in his dissenting judgment in *Voges v. Monaghan* (1954) 94 CLR 231, 233 was of establishing the elements of the trust 'to the reasonable satisfaction of the court'. Both these formulae were recently considered by Hammond J in the New Zealand High Court decision of *Brown v. Pourau* [1995] 1 NZLR 352.
27. For a criticism of this suggestion, see Rickett [1979] CLJ 260. See also Rickett [1996] Conv 302, 307.
28. *Equity and the Law of Trusts in the Republic of Ireland* (1988) p. 92.
29. *Banco Ambrosiano SPA v. Ansbacher & Co.Ltd* [1987] ILRM 669.
30. [1900] 1 Ch 237, 241. See also the *dicta* of Monroe J in *Re King's Estate* (1888) 21 LR Ir 273, 278.

but C. is not bound. ... If however the gift were to A. and C. as joint
tenants, the authorities have established a distinction between those cases
in which the will is made on the faith of an antecedent promise by A.
and those in which the will is left unrevoked on the faith of a subsequent
promise. In the former case the trust binds both A. and C., ... the reason
stated being that no person can claim an interest under a fraud committed
by another; in the latter case, A. and not C. is bound, ... the reason
stated being that the gift is not tainted with any fraud in procuring the
execution of the will.

On the basis of this statement it seemed that in the case of tenants in common,
only those to whom the testator's intentions were communicated during his
lifetime were bound and that any other person took free of the trust and was
entitled to his share beneficially. However, in the case of joint tenants, a
distinction was drawn between a situation where one or more of these joint
tenants had accepted the trust prior to the execution of the will and where the
acceptance did not take place until after this. In the former case, all the joint
tenants were bound and in the latter case only those who had accepted the
secret trust were affected by it. Farwell J himself appeared unconvinced by
the drawing of such a seemingly arbitrary distinction and admitted that he
was unable to see the difference between 'a gift left unrevoked on the faith of
antecedent promise and a gift left unrevoked on the faith of a subsequent
promise'.[31]

Similar sentiments were expressed by Walker LJ in the Irish Court of
Appeal in *Geddis v. Semple*,[32] although as the case before him concerned
tenants in common, it was not necessary for him to reach any conclusion on
the issue. At the time the testator in *Geddis* executed his will, the effect of
section 16 of the Charitable Donations and Bequests (Ireland) Act 1844 was
to render void gifts of land for charitable purposes unless the testator's will
had been executed at least three months prior to his death.[33] With the intention
of avoiding this statutory restriction, the testator devised certain houses and a
pecuniary legacy charged on land to three individuals as tenants in common,
although at the time the will was executed only one of these individuals was
aware of the testator's intention to create a secret trust for a charitable purpose.
The Irish Court of Appeal held that while the gift to the individual who knew
of the testator's wishes must fail, the other tenants in common, who knew
nothing of the intended trust until after the testator's death, became beneficially
entitled to their shares. However, there is a suggestion in the judgment of
Walker LJ that an 'innocent' tenant in common might be bound in such

31. *Ibid.* at 241.
32. [1903] 1 IR 73.
33. This provision was repealed by s. 4 of the Charities Act 1961.

circumstances if it could be established that the testator was induced to make the gift by the promise of a co-tenant on the basis of the principle laid down in *Huguenin v. Baseley*[34] that 'no man may profit by the fraud of another'.

This inducement theory was developed by Perrins[35] who has suggested that Farwell J in *Re Stead* misinterpreted the authorities relied on to support the general principles set out above. In Perrins' view, the only question to which the court must address itself in such circumstances is whether the gift to the legatee who was unaware of the testator's intention to create a secret trust was induced by the promise of the legatee who knew of his intentions in this regard to carry out his wishes. If this approach is accepted, issues such as whether the legatees take as joint tenants or tenants in common and whether the promise was made prior to or after the execution of the will are merely matters of evidence which may be of assistance to the court in deciding on the question of inducement but will not of themselves determine the issue.[36]

There is certainly considerable merit in Perrins' views,[37] and on the basis of the comments of Walker LJ in *Geddis v. Semple* they will probably be followed in relation to a situation of tenants in common. Although there is no authority to support this approach in the case of joint tenants, Wylie[38] puts forward the suggestion that a court might regard the creation of a secret trust as severing a joint tenancy, thus allowing the principle of inducement to operate in any event. Until this question is resolved by the courts the result must remain a matter of speculation, but it is submitted that the most equitable result would certainly be to follow the approach laid down by Perrins.

HALF SECRET TRUSTS

A half secret trust arises where a testator leaves property to an individual in a will and expressly directs that this individual is to hold the property on trust without specifying the terms of the trust. The principal advantage to be gained from employing this form of secret trust is that the possibility of the legatee taking the property beneficially and successfully perpetrating a fraud is avoided as it is clear from the face of the will that a trust was intended. However,

---

34. (1807) 14 Ves 273.
35. (1972) 82 LQR 225.
36. As Perrins points out, as a matter of evidence it may be easier to show inducement in the case of a gift to joint tenants and clearly where a secret trust is not communicated to any of the co-tenants until after the testator's death it will be difficult, if not impossible, to show that the gift to the other was induced by any promise made.
37. This is the approach taken in both McGhee, *Snell's Equity* (30th ed., 2000) p. 134 and Underhill and Hayton, *The Law Relating to Trusts and Trustees* (16th ed., 2003) p. 263 although the view is expressed in Hanbury & Martin, *Modern Equity* (16th ed., 2001) p. 158 that while the argument is persuasive the case law suggests otherwise.
38. *Irish Land Law* (3rd ed., 1997) p. 529.

where a testator manifests his intention to create a trust in this way, the historical justification for non-compliance with the statutory formalities required in the case of secret trusts, namely the prevention of fraud, does not apply as it is clear from the face of the will that a trust is intended. Perhaps for this reason, the courts have adopted a more stringent attitude towards the enforcement of half secret trusts and an examination of the case law in this area in the last century, particularly in England, shows a marked reluctance on the part of the judiciary to overlook non-compliance with the provisions of the Wills Act in the absence of any likelihood of fraud.

This trend was reversed in Ireland by the decision of *Riordan v. Banon*[39] and although Chatterton VC acknowledged that 'the same kind of fraud cannot operate'[40] in the case of trusts which appear on the face of the will, he was prepared to extend this principle to half secret trusts as the result of a refusal to enforce such trusts would be to defeat the expressed intention of the testator. In *Riordan*, the testator's will directed that a legacy be disposed by the legatee 'in a manner of which he alone shall be cognizant, and as contained in a memorandum which I shall leave with him'. Prior to executing his will the testator had verbally informed the legatee that he intended to leave the legacy for a named person whom he did not wish to identify in his will and it was accepted that the legatee had agreed to carry out this obligation.[41] Chatterton VC held that a valid secret trust had been created.[42] He stated:

> The result of the cases appears to me to be that a testator cannot by his will reserve to himself the right of disposing subsequently of property by an instrument not executed as required by the statute, or by parol; but that when, at the time of making his will, he has formed the intention that a legacy thereby given shall be disposed of by the legatee in a particular manner, not thereby disclosed, but communicated to the legatee and assented to by him, at or before the making of the will, or probably, according to *Moss v. Cooper*, subsequently to the making of it, the Court will allow such trust to be proved by admission of the legatee, or other parol evidence and will, if it be legal, give effect to it.[43]

---

39. (1876) IR 10 Eq 469.
40. *Ibid.* at 473. Although Chatterton VC also commented (at 478) that the principle which led the courts to hold that the Statute of Frauds and the Wills Act were not to be used as instruments of fraud appeared to apply to cases such as that before him where the will showed that some form of trust was intended.
41. One difficulty with this interpretation to which Chatterton VC did not refer was the possibility of inconsistency between the terms of the statement in the will which pointed to some form of subsequent communication and what the court accepted had actually transpired i.e. communication and acceptance prior to the execution of the will. This ground of inconsistency is considered in more detail *infra*.
42. See also *Re Ellis* (1919) 53 ILTR 6.
43. *Ibid.* at 477–478.

To be valid a half secret trust, like a fully secret trust, must be communicated to and accepted by the legatee prior to the testator's death.[44] This requirement has been strictly enforced as in *Re Watters' Will Trusts*,[45] where a testator directed that his property should be applied for 'charitable purposes and objects known to my executors'. After executing his will but during his lifetime, the testator had a number of general conversations with one of his executors about the manner in which he wished his assets to be applied but failed to specify precisely the particular purposes or objects which he intended to benefit. A memorandum found after his death which contained such specific directions was held not to be admissible as there had not been sufficient communication and acceptance of the trust prior to the testator's death.[46]

One question which has led to considerable controversy and to an apparent divergence in the law as it applies in England and Ireland is whether there can be effective communication and acceptance of a half secret trust after the execution of the testator's will. As can be observed from the portion of Chatterton VC's judgment in *Riordan* set out above, he commented in that decision that such subsequent communication was 'probably' acceptable and this principle was reiterated by Monroe J in the course of his judgment in *Re King's Estate*.[47] While on the facts of that case no secret trust of any nature arose, Monroe J laid down a number of propositions, drawn from the relevant authorities,[48] which it is useful to set out in full:

1. A testator cannot reserve to himself the right of declaring trusts by an instrument informally executed subsequent to the execution of his will. This would be to repeal the statute of wills.
2. If a testator at or before the execution of his will communicate to a person to whom he proposes to give a legacy that the legacy is given upon trust to be applied in a particular way, and if the legatee expressly or tacitly consents to take the legacy on these terms, the Court of Chancery will not permit him to be guilty of a fraud, but will compel the execution of the trust so communicated.
3. This rule applies whether the existence of the trust be indicated on the face of the will, or the legacy by the terms of the instrument be given absolutely.

---

44. *Scott v. Brownrigg* (1881) 9 LR Ir 246.
45. (1928) 62 ILTR 61.There was no evidence to suggest that the trust failed on the grounds of inconsistency. See further *infra* pp. 104–105.
46. Although in the circumstances as a general charitable intention had been manifested by the verbal communication an order was made that a scheme for the application of the assets should be directed by the court.
47. (1888) 21 LR Ir 273.
48. *Riordan v. Banon* (1867) IR 10 Eq 469; *Re Fleetwood* (1880) 15 Ch D 594; *Scott v. Brownrigg* (1881) 9 LR Ir 246; *Re Boyes* (1884) 26 Ch D 531.

4. The rule applies when the communication is made subsequently to the execution of the will: *Moss v. Taylor.*[49]
5. It is essential to the creation of a valid trust that the communication should be made to the legatee in the testator's lifetime, and that the legatee should not object to execute the trust.
6. If the bequest be to two or more legatees, a valid trust is created if the communication be made to any one of them, before or at the time of the execution of the will. If the communication be made after the execution of the will, it must be made to all the legatees on whom the trust is sought to be imposed.
7. The terms in which the trust is expressed must not be vague or uncertain.[50]

Further confirmation that communication and acceptance of a half secret trust may validly occur after execution of a testator's will provided this is done during his lifetime can be found in the judgment of Overend J in *Re Browne.*[51] Although Overend J found that the reference in the will before the court to the testator's wishes was too ambiguous to disclose a trust on the face of the will and instead decided to enforce a fully secret trust on the basis of the latter's wishes expressed to the legatee during his lifetime, he suggested *obiter* that that even if he had found the existence of a half secret trust, it would have been immaterial that the trusts in question were communicated to the legatee after the execution of the will so long as they were communicated to him and accepted by him during the testator's lifetime.

The courts in England have not accepted the principle of subsequent communication and indeed it was not until the decision of the House of Lords in *Blackwell v. Blackwell*[52] that the validity of half secret trusts was finally recognised in that jurisdiction. A testator gave a sum of money on trust to legatees to apply the income thereof 'for the purposes indicated by me to them' in a codicil to his will. Detailed instructions were given to one of the trustees and the others accepted these terms in outline before execution of the codicil. Viscount Sumner recognised that a half secret trust existed which arose independently of the will: 'it is communication of the purpose to the legatee, coupled with acquiescence or promise on his part, that removes the matter from the provision of the Wills Act and brings it within the law of trusts'.[53] In the course of his speech Viscount Sumner also laid down the

---

49. More commonly known as *Moss v. Cooper* (1861) 1 J & H 367.
50. (1888) 21 LR Ir 273, 277-278. Quoted with approval by Barron J in *Prendiville v. Prendiville* [1995] 2 ILRM 578, 583.
51. [1944] IR 90. Although note the conclusion reached in *Balfe v. Halpenny* [1904] 1 IR 486.
52. [1929] AC 318.
53. *Ibid.* at 339. Quoted with approval by Barron J in *Prendiville v. Prendiville* [1995] 2 ILRM 578, 583.

following fundamental principle:

> A testator cannot reserve to himself a power of making future unwitnessed dispositions by merely naming a trustee and leaving the purposes of the trust to be supplied afterwards, nor can a legatee give testamentary validity to an unexecuted codicil by accepting an indefinite trust, never communicated to him in the testator's lifetime. ... To hold otherwise would indeed enable the testator to 'give the go-by' to the requirements of the Wills Act, because he did not choose to comply with them.[54]

This statement although it is in some respects in line with a number of the propositions set out by Monroe J in *Re King's Estate*, has been subsequently interpreted in England as authority for the proposition that the communication and acceptance of a half secret trust cannot be effective if made after the execution of a will. In *Re Keen*[55] a testator gave a legacy to trustees 'to be held upon trust and disposed of among such person, persons or charities as may be notified by me to them or either of them during my lifetime'. Before executing this will the testator had given a sealed envelope to one of the trustees containing the name of the intended beneficiary which the court accepted as 'notification'. The provision in the will was interpreted as the reservation of a power by the testator to make future testamentary dispositions in a manner which would be contrary to section 9 of the Wills Act 1837. However, in the view of Lord Wright MR, even if such subsequent communication had been permitted the trust would have failed independently on the grounds of inconsistency. On the facts of the case, communication and acceptance of the trust had taken place prior to the execution of the will, when the sealed envelope was handed over, and this was plainly inconsistent with its terms which provided for a future definition of the terms of the trust. While there has been a certain amount of confusion and academic debate about the true *ratio* of *Re Keen*,[56] it was re-affirmed in England in *Re Bateman's Will Trusts*[57] that communication and acceptance of a half secret trust must take place prior to the execution of the will.[58]

---

54. *Ibid.* at 339. See also the *dicta* of Parker VC in *Johnson v. Ball* (1851) 5 De G & Sm 85, 91.
55. [1937] Ch 236.
56. See the judgment of Barron J in *Prendiville v. Prendiville* [1995] 2 ILRM 578; Coughlan (1991) 5 Trust Law Int 69; Mee [1992] Conv 202. Huband JA suggests in the course of his dissenting judgment in *Jankowski v. Pelek Estate* (1995) 131 DLR (4th) 717 that *Re Keen* is authority for the proposition that the nature of trust instructions must be consistent with the wording of the will.
57. [1970] 1 WLR 1463. However, it should be noted that in *Gold v. Hill* [1999] 1 FLR 54, which concerned the analogous situation of a nomination under a life insurance policy, Carnwath J was prepared to treat communication effected after the execution

It is interesting to note that a refusal to accept the principle of subsequent communication in the context of a half secret trust has recently manifested itself elsewhere in the common law world. In *Jankowski v. Pelek Estate*[59] the majority of the Manitoba Court of Appeal found that the evidence disclosed the existence of a fully secret trust which in their view was valid as communication and acceptance of it had taken place during the testator's lifetime. However, Huband JA was satisfied that any trust intended was a half secret one as there was no possibility that the intended legatee might fraudulently retain the legacy as his own and in his view the rules relating to the enforcement of such trusts are 'much more stringent'. He continued as follows:

> Specifically there must be communication of the terms of the trust to the proposed trustee before or contemporaneously with the making of the will. The word 'contemporaneously' in this context means 'at the same time'. It cannot include 'shortly after'. To have it otherwise would allow the testator to add to the terms of the will after its execution, in a form which does not comply with statutory requirements.[60]

He concluded that in the case before him the fact that the instructions regarding the trust were given after the will was executed was fatal to its enforcement and said that this could not be redeemed by the fact that these instructions were communicated only minutes after the execution of the will. In his view 'the effect is the same whether the time differential is a few minutes, a few hours, a few weeks or a few years'. This seemed a particularly harsh conclusion to reach and resulted, as Huband JA himself acknowledged, in the intentions of the testatrix being frustrated by purely technical reasons.

The opportunity to resolve the question of whether communication and acceptance of a half secret trust must take place before the execution of the will in order for it to be valid in this jurisdiction was presented to the High Court in the case of *Prendiville v. Prendiville*.[61] There, the testator left his

---

of the will as valid. He stated that: '[s]uch doubts as there may be, in the case of testamentary dispositions, as to the effectiveness of an intention communicated *after* the execution of the will, appear to be derived from the particular rules applying to wills.'

58. This has been justified by Perrins [1985] Conv 248 on the basis that extrinsic evidence of prior communication is admissible as it does not contradict the terms of the will whereas to allow evidence of subsequent communication would be 'to give the go-by' to the Wills Act even where there is no danger of fraud. The suggestion has even been made that this stricter requirement should also apply to fully secret trusts, see Watkin [1981] Conv 335, 340. See also Wilde [1995] Conv 366.

59. (1995) 131 DLR (4th) 717.

60. *Ibid.* at 730.

61. [1995] 2 ILRM 578.

estate to his wife for life 'to be used by her according to my wishes — as she has been advised'. Before he died the testator had told one of his sons that he had written out his wishes as to the passing of his estate after his wife's death and had shown him a document containing these instructions which included the provision that a named residence and lands were to be offered for sale to another son at a reasonable valuation. Following the testator's death, his wife made a statutory declaration acknowledging that her husband's instructions had been communicated to and accepted by her. After her death a dispute arose between the next of kin of the testator and the son in whose favour the option to purchase had been made as to whether an enforceable secret or half secret trust existed. Barron J said that *Re Keen* had been relied on as an authority for the proposition that a half secret trust could not be established unless its terms were communicated and accepted prior to the execution of the will. He felt that this proposition could not be taken from that case, which, in his opinion, turned on the construction of the particular clause in the will and the issue of inconsistency. Barron J concluded that the principles of law to be applied to secret and half secret trusts are the same and were those as set out by Monroe J in *Re King's Estate*.[62] He held that in the case before him, a trust existed on the face of the will and found there was sufficient evidence that the terms of the trust in relation to the option to purchase the house had been communicated by the testator to his wife and accepted by her during his lifetime.

Although this judgment would appear to confirm the correctness of the *obiter* views on the timing of communication and acceptance of a half secret trust referred to above, *Prendiville* is not an entirely satisfactory authority for a number of reasons. Barron J failed to identify precisely the time at which communication and acceptance of the trust occurred although he did find that this had taken place at some stage during the testator's lifetime. The use of the words 'as she has been advised' would suggest that such communication was intended to take place either before or at the time of execution of the will and yet one must ask why Barron J took the trouble to refute the suggestion that *Re Keen* was authority for the proposition that communication must occur prior to the will, unless on the facts of the case before him, communication did not take place until after its execution. Because of his failure to be more specific about the timing of these events, it is therefore still not clear whether Barron J's rejection of the need for prior communication forms part of the *ratio* of the case. A further possible flaw in his judgment is the failure to address the potential problem of inconsistency. As Andrews[63] has pointed out, the most important requirement with regard to half secret trusts is the

---

62. (1881) 21 LR Ir 273. Note that Wilde has asserted in [1995] Conv 366 that there is a justification for the distinctions drawn by the courts between secret and half secret trusts.

63. (1963) 27 Conv 92, 99.

need for careful construction and communication in some other form or at a time other than that contemplated in the will cannot be permissible as it will lead to an attempt to contradict its express terms. Barron J appeared to endorse this ground of inconsistency as being the basis for the decision in *Re Keen* and yet, if as his rejection of the wider ground for that decision suggests, communication in the case before him took place after the execution of the will, this would itself lead to inconsistency with the terms of the instrument.[64] While it is unfortunate that the Supreme Court was not given the opportunity of further clarifying these issues, the High Court decision in *Prendiville* does appear to confirm that in Ireland it is permissible for communication and acceptance of a half secret trust to take place after the execution of a will but during a testator's lifetime provided it does not contradict the terms of the will. Certainly, the view of Barron J that the principles to be applied to fully and half secret trusts should be the same has much to commend it and is based on sound practical arguments.[65] The passing of the beneficial interest in respect of either type of trust is not a testamentary disposition and so it should not be relevant whether communication and acceptance of the trust occurs prior to the execution of the will.[66] This argument is reinforced if one accepts the modern justification for the enforcement of secret trusts and on this basis the approach of the Irish courts cannot be faulted either on policy grounds.[67]

---

64. See Coughlan (1991) 5 Trust Law Int 69, 73; Mee [1992] Conv 202, 205. It would appear that the possibility of inconsistency was also effectively ignored by Chatterton VC in *Riordan v. Banon* (1876) IR 10 Eq 469 and by Meredith J in *Re Watters' Will Trusts* (1928) 62 ILTR 61. However, it appeared to be accepted by Huband JA in his dissenting judgment in *Jankowski v. Pelek Estate* (1995) 131 DLR (4th) 717 that inconsistency between the instructions given and the scheme of the will would be fatal.There is probably merit in Mee's argument that inconsistency should be overlooked where it is merely inadvertent (see *infra* n. 66).

65. It would seem arbitrary to draw a distinction when the overriding reason for enforcing such half secret trusts is to give effect as far as possible to the testator's intention to create a trust. For a view of the academic arguments favouring such an approach, see Holdsworth (1937) 53 LQR 501 and Sheridan (1951) 67 LQR 413.

66. Mee [1992] Conv 202, 206 suggests that where inconsistency occurs as a result of mere inadvertence it would be 'unnecessary and unjust' to base a finding of invalidity on this ground.

67 It is interesting to note that Young J in a decision of the Supreme Court of New South Wales in *Ledgerwood v. Perpetual Trustee Co. Ltd* (1997) 41 NSWLR 532 followed *Re Prendiville* rather than *Re Keen*. Having considered the relevant authorities and academic commentary in some detail, he concluded that 'I cannot get away from the view that the Irish position is the one which carries out the policy of this part of the law, that is, that it is against the conscience of the donee that the donee should be permitted to have undertaken to the testatrix to carry out her wishes and then not to have done so.'

THE JURIDICIAL NATURE OF SECRET TRUSTS

As we have already seen,[68] a secret trust is not considered to have arisen by virtue of a testator's will. While to an extent its existence is dependent on the validity of this instrument and in particular on the disposition which is to form the subject-matter of the trust, it is considered to arise 'dehors' the will.[69] A related question which has provoked considerable debate, and which can have practical significance is whether secret trusts are express or constructive in nature. Clearly, if they are characterised as express, where land forms the subject-matter of the trust there must be compliance with the statutory formalities.[70] Fully secret trusts have been variously characterised as implied[71] or sometimes express[72] in nature but the most acceptable view would seem to be that they are constructive and are imposed on a legatee to prevent him from abusing the fiduciary obligations which he assumed on giving an undertaking to the testator that he would enforce the trust.[73] This conclusion would appear to be supported by the decision in *Ottaway v. Norman,*[74] where a fully secret trust of land was upheld as valid on the basis of oral evidence. However, it would be incorrect to place too much emphasis on this decision as the issue of the nature of the trust and the need for compliance with the statutory formalities was not discussed.

Half secret trusts on the other hand are usually accepted as being a species of express trust. Support for this proposition is derived from *Re Baillie*[75] where a half secret trust was held not to be enforceable in the absence of adequate written evidence. Burgess[76] has argued that this decision actually turned on the lack of evidence to establish the terms of the trust and that the very essence of a secret trust is that it operates in spite of the requirements as to form. While there is some merit in the arguments put forward by Burgess, the most widely held view is that half secret trusts are express in nature.

The issue of the classification of secret trusts as express or constructive was raised again recently in the New Zealand decision of *Brown v. Pourau*[77] in which Hammond J had to consider whether an oral secret trust of land

---

68. See *supra* p. 93.
69. However, note that Critchley (1999) 115 LQR 631, 641 has suggested that the 'dehors' theory seems to be fatally flawed and that the mistake is to confuse 'outside the will' with 'outside the Wills Act'.
70. See *supra* Chapter 4.
71. Burgess (1972) 23 NILQ 263, 268-273.
72. Perrins [1985] Conv 248, 254. See also Wilde [1995] Conv 366, 371 and Rickett [1996] Conv 302, 305 and 308.
73. Andrews (1963) 27 Conv 92, 98. See also Sheridan (1951) 67 LQR 314, 327.
74. [1972] Ch 698.
75. (1886) 2 TLR 660.
76. (1972) 23 NILQ 263.
77. [1995] 1 NZLR 352.

could be valid. He stated that whatever the correct theoretical explanation, the reported English decisions appeared to recognise that a fully secret trust of land could be valid independent of any requirement of written evidence. In his view contemporary New Zealand jurisprudence required the court to inquire into the obligation which it was being asked to uphold and then make an evaluation of the remedy which would best support or advance that obligation. Applying this reasoning he concluded that the court should support the intended trust by using a constructive trust as a remedy. While Hammond J's judgment therefore fails to resolve the express/constructive issue in the context in which it has arisen in England and in this jurisdiction, it confirms the practical point that for the purposes of compliance with the Statute of Frauds, fully secret trusts can be treated as constructive in nature.[78]

So although this issue of the juridicial basis of secret trusts remains to an extent uncertain, it should be remembered that even if a secret trust is characterised as express, compliance with the formality requirements will not be enforced where this would lead to the perpetration of a fraud.

---

78. It should be noted that Rickett [1996] Conv 302 is critical of Hammond J's reasoning and asserts that a secret trust is express in nature and therefore where necessary must satisfy the formal requirements in relation to trusts of land. She points out quite correctly (at 306) that if judges persist – as Hammond J did in *Brown v. Pourau* – in applying the test of certainty laid down for express private trusts, it is a strong argument in favour of using the express rather than the constructive trust label.

CHAPTER 6

Constitution of Trusts

INTRODUCTION

A trust is said to be completely constituted when the trust property has been vested in the trustees for the benefit of the beneficiaries; a trust remains incompletely constituted until this is done. The practical importance of identifying when a trust has been completely constituted lies in the fact that equity will not enforce or perfect an incompletely constituted trust in favour of a volunteer.[1] However a completely constituted trust will be enforceable at the suit of the beneficiaries irrespective of whether or not they are mere volunteers. This different attitude adopted by equity towards the enforcement of completely and incompletely constituted trusts was summed up by Lord Eldon in *Ellison v. Ellison*[2] as follows:

> I take the distinction to be, that if you want the assistance of the Court to constitute you *cestui que trust*, and the instrument is voluntary, you shall not have that assistance for the purpose of constituting you *cestui que trust*; as upon a covenant to transfer stock etc., if it rests in covenant, and is purely voluntary, this Court will not execute that voluntary covenant; but if the party has completely transferred stock etc., although it is voluntary, yet the legal conveyance being effectually made, the equitable interest will be enforced by this Court.

To fully understand the practical implications of this distinction a number of issues must be examined. First, the circumstances in which a trust may be regarded as completely constituted must be clarified and secondly, the question of who will be regarded as a volunteer has to be addressed. Finally, it is necessary to examine the alternative remedies open to beneficiaries of an incompletely constituted trust who are regarded as mere volunteers.

---

1. *McArdle v. O'Donohoe* High Court 1997 No. 13426P (O'Donovan J) 8 June 1999 at 17. See also *Re Wilson* [1933] IR 729, 739.
2. (1802) 6 Ves 656, 662.

COMPLETE CONSTITUTION OF A TRUST

An express trust may be completely constituted either by a transfer of property to trustees to be held on certain trusts, by will or *inter vivos*, or by a settlor declaring himself to be trustee of his own property for the benefit of specified beneficiaries. Since it is necessary to recognise whether a voluntary trust has been completely constituted if it is to be enforced, it is necessary to set out in some detail the manner in which this may be achieved. These principles were summarized by Turner LJ in the decision of *Milroy v. Lord*[3] as follows:

> I take the law of this Court to be well settled, that, in order to render a voluntary settlement valid and effectual, the settlor must have done everything which, according to the nature of the property comprised in the settlement, was necessary to be done in order to transfer the property and render the settlement binding upon him. He may of course, do this by actually transferring the property to the persons for whom he intends to provide, and the provision will then be effectual, and it will be equally effectual if he transfers the property to a trustee for the purposes of the settlement, or declares that he himself holds it in trust for those purposes; and if the property be personal, the trust may, as I apprehend, be declared either in writing or by parol, but in order to render the settlement binding, one or other of these modes must, as I understand the law of this Court, be resorted to, for there is no equity in this Court to perfect an imperfect gift.

Transfer of Trust Property

In order to completely constitute a trust by this method, there must be an effective transfer of the property to be included in the trust and an intention on the settlor's part to bring about such a transfer will not suffice. This is illustrated by the decision of O'Donovan J in *McArdle v. O'Donohoe*,[4] in which the settlor purported to execute a deed of settlement to make provision for his adopted daughter and her children. O'Donovan J stated that he was satisfied that at the time the deed was executed, it was the settlor's intention that £200,000 invested in a bond would form part of the trust fund. The issue which O'Donovan J had to decide was whether this sum invested in the bond constituted part of the trust fund as defined in the deed of settlement or whether it remained the personal property of the defendant settlor. He concluded that the settlor had never effectively transferred any monies or property which might be included in the 'trust fund' as defined in the deed of settlement and

---

3. (1862) 4 De GF & J 264, 274.
4. High Court 1997 No. 13426P (O'Donovan J) 8 June 1999.

that the trust created by the deed of settlement was not completely constituted. O'Donovan J quoted with approval the following *dicta* of Johnston J in *Re Wilson:*[5]

> A gift is a gift, and, of course if a donor, while expressing an intention to give something and taking certain steps in the direction of giving it, has not gone the whole way, the expectant donee has no equity to compel the completion of the gift. It is good sense and good law.

O'Donovan J held that as the trust was not completely constituted,[6] equity would not compel the completion of an incompletely constituted trust in the absence of valuable consideration. He therefore concluded that the sum of £200,000 invested by the settlor in the bond did not constitute part of the trust fund as defined by the deed of settlement but remained his personal property.

If a trust is to be validly constituted by transfer, it is necessary to comply with whatever formalities apply to the method employed to effect this. A trust created by will can only be regarded as completely constituted provided that the relevant statutory formalities have been complied with. Similarly, where the transfer is effected *inter vivos*, the formalities applicable to the type of interest being transferred must be observed. So where for example the subject-matter of the trust is a legal estate in unregistered land the transfer must be effective to vest this interest in the trustee and will therefore usually require the execution of a deed. Where the trust property comprises an equitable interest, it will be completely constituted provided that a valid assignment of that interest to the trustees takes place.[7]

In *Milroy v. Lord*[8] a settlor executed a voluntary deed purporting to transfer shares in a bank to be held on trust for the plaintiff. Such a transfer could only be properly effected by registration of the name of the transferee in the bank's records. While the trustee held a power of attorney to act on the settlor's behalf, he failed to register the transfer. The Court of Appeal held that no enforceable trust in favour of the plaintiffs had been created.

It should be noted that the statement of Turner LJ in *Milroy* set out above to the effect, *inter alia*, that in order to ensure that a trust is completely constituted, the settlor must have done everything which it is necessary to do to effect the transfer,[9] is subject to some qualification in the following

---

5. [1933] IR 729, 739.
6. O'Donovan J also held that the settlor had never expressed an intention to constitute himself a trustee. See further *infra*, p. 113 *et seq.*
7. *Kekewich v. Manning* (1851) 1 De GM & G 176; *Re McArdle* [1951] Ch 669.
8. (1862) 4 De GF & J 264.
9. It was suggested by Griffiths CJ in *Anning v. Anning* (1907) 4 CLR 1049, 1057 that the words 'necessary to be done' as used by Turner LJ in *Milroy v. Lord* mean necessary to be done by the donor.

circumstances. Where the settlor has done everything in his power to transfer the title to the property but cannot ensure compliance with some formality which is outside his control, the trust will nevertheless be regarded as completely constituted. In *Re Rose*,[10] a settlor executed a voluntary deed which purported to transfer shares in a private company to trustees but died before the transfer was registered by the company's directors. The question arose whether the settlor was still the owner of the shares at the time of his death for the purpose of determining whether estate duty was payable. The Court of Appeal held that as the settlor had done all in his power to divest himself of the shares, although he remained in law the owner until the transfer was registered, in equity the transfer was regarded as being effective from the date of the deed. The reasoning in *Re Rose* has been criticised[11] and it has been argued that it is difficult to distinguish the circumstances of the case from those in *Re Fry*,[12] in which a donor was not regarded as having done everything in his power to effect a transfer of shares as it could not be registered without treasury consent. Nevertheless, the principle laid down in *Re Rose* has been applied subsequently in England in *Mascall v. Mascall*[13] in the context of a transfer of registered land and more recently in *Brown & Root Technology Ltd v. Sun Alliance and London Assurance Co. Ltd*[14] which concerned the assignment of a leasehold interest which had not yet been registered. In *Mascall* the plaintiff had executed a transfer of a property with registered title to his son but before the necessary documents had been sent to the Land Registry for registration, the plaintiff changed his mind about the transfer. The Court of Appeal held that there had been an effective gift to the son; as Lawton LJ commented 'the plaintiff had done everything in his power to transfer the house to the defendant'.[15] In *Brown & Root* the first named plaintiff, the original lessee, served a notice purporting to terminate the lease after an assignment to the second named plaintiff, its parent company, had taken place but before it had been registered at the Land Registry. The court refused the first named plaintiff a declaration that the notice served was valid to terminate the lease on the basis that the date on which the assignment took place was the date upon which it was completed and so the lease could not have been determined by a notice served by this plaintiff. Judge Paul Barker QC reiterated that the leading case in this area is *Milroy v. Lord* but pointed out that there are exceptions to the rule that 'an attempted but ineffectual or uncompleted conveyance or transfer of property to trustees to hold on certain

---

10. [1952] Ch 499.
11. Sheridan (1955) 33 Can Bar Rev 284 and McKay (1976) 40 Conv 139. See also Lowrie and Todd [1998] CLJ 46.
12. [1946] Ch 312. See also *Pehrsson v. Von Greyerz* Privy Council, 16 June 1999.
13. (1984) 50 P & CR 119.
14. [1996] Ch 51.
15. (1984) 50 P & CR 119, 125.

trusts would not be enforced at the suit of a volunteer'. He accepted the
defendant's submission that if it was necessary to fix a date on which the
assignment took place, this was the date upon which it was completed. As he
pointed out 'the tenant/assignor gives up the property on that date; he has no
control over the stamping of the transfer, or its submission to the Land
Registry'.

Recently in *Pennington v. Waine*[16] the Court of Appeal has taken the
opportunity to consider the exception to the principle in *Milroy v. Lord* set out
in cases such as *Re Rose*[17] in some detail. The donor wanted to transfer shares
in a company to her nephew, the second named defendant and to make him a
director of it. The articles of association of this company required that in
order for an individual to become a director he must hold at least one share in
it. The company's auditors informed the second named defendant of the share
transfer and he signed a form of consent to act as a director which was
countersigned by the donor. The donor signed a share transfer form but it was
retained by the company's auditors and was not sent to the second named
defendant. Following the donor's death in an action brought by her executors,
the residuary beneficiaries under her will sought a determination of whether
there had been a valid equitable transfer of the shares. Howarth J held that the
gift had become effective once the share transfer form was signed and that it
was not necessary for the form to have been delivered either to the second
named defendant or the company for the gift to be complete. The Court of
Appeal agreed that delivery of the share transfer certificate to the donee or
the company was not required for there to have been a valid equitable
assignment of the shares to the second named defendant. Arden LJ stated that
there was a clear finding that the donor intended to make an immediate gift
and that a stage had been reached when it would have been unconscionable
for her to recall it. In his view delivery of the share transfer before the donor's
death was unnecessary so far as the perfection of the gift was concerned.
Clarke LJ agreed and said that he did not think that this conclusion was
inconsistent with any of the decided cases like *Milroy v. Lord* as in those
cases there were no completed documents evidencing a present transfer of
the donor's beneficial interest. He referred to the decision of the Privy Council
in *T. Choithram International SA v. Pagarini*[18] in which Lord Browne-
Wilkinson had highlighted the contrast between the maxims that equity will
not aid a volunteer and that it will not strive officiously to defeat a gift. In his
view, if equity refused to help the second named defendant in the case before
the court, it would be preferring the former maxim to the latter in a situation
where all the circumstances of the case led to the conclusion that it should
give effect to the gift which the donor intended. Clearly both judges were in

---

16. [2002] 1 WLR 2075.
17. [1952] Ch 499.
18. [2001] 1 WLR 1.

favour of a flexible interpretation being given to the exception to the proposition set out in *Milroy v. Lord* and as Arden LJ noted 'the principle against imperfectly constituted gifts [has] led to harsh and seemingly paradoxical results'.[19]

The approach taken in these English decisions appears to confirm the *obiter* view expressed in this jurisdiction in *Devoy v. Hanlon*.[20] There the owner of registered land executed a voluntary deed transferring land to his son, but the transfer was not registered and was therefore ineffective. He subsequently devised the land to his daughter in his will and she was then registered as the owner. The son's claim to the land failed but only because he could not prove that the deed of transfer was ever delivered. The implication was that the court would have been willing to hold that the son, who was a volunteer and to whom the legal interest had not been transferred, would have been entitled to the land if he could have proved that the deed had been delivered. Once registered, the gift would have been completely constituted and could have been enforced even by a volunteer.

It follows from the proposition that a completely constituted trust is enforceable by a volunteer that such a trust is binding on a settlor and his personal representatives and will be irrevocable unless an express power of revocation is reserved at the time of its constitution. In *Re Bowden*,[21] a settlor by means of a voluntary settlement agreed to convey to trustees all the property to which she might become entitled under her father's will. She knowingly allowed this transfer to take place and it was held by Bennett J that she could not subsequently reclaim the property held on trust. As the trust was completely constituted, the fact that the settlement was voluntary did not affect its validity or enforceability. It should also be noted that in England there appears to be authority to support the proposition that a trust may be considered as completely constituted when property is vested in trustees although it did not come into their possession in their capacity as trustees of that particular trust.[22]

Declaration of Trust by Settlor

The alternative method of completely constituting a trust is for a settlor to declare himself a trustee of property for the benefit of third parties. Neville J summarised the requirements which must be satisfied to achieve this in *Re Cozens*[23] as follows: 'where a declaration of trust is relied on the Court must be satisfied that a present irrevocable declaration of trust has been made.'

---

19. [2002] 1 WLR 2075, 2087.
20. [1929] IR 246.
21. [1936] Ch 71. See also *Paul v. Paul* (1882) 20 Ch D 742.
22. *Re Ralli's Will Trusts* [1964] Ch 288. However, note the conclusion reached by Farwell J in *Re Brooks' Settlement Trusts* [1939] Ch 993 which was not referred to in *Ralli*.
23. [1913] 2 Ch 478, 486.

There must therefore be a clear manifestation of the intention to create a trust in this way and where it appears that a settlor's intention was to bring a trust into operation by transfer in the manner outlined above but he fails to achieve this objective, this ineffective attempt to transfer the property will not be construed as a declaration of trust. The general principle was set out by Turner LJ in *Milroy v. Lord* as follows:

> [I]f the settlement is intended to be effectuated by one of the modes to which I have referred,[24] the Court will not give effect to it by applying another of those modes. If it is intended to take effect by transfer, the Court will not hold the intended transfer to operate as a declaration of trust, for then every imperfect instrument would be made effectual by being converted into a perfect trust.[25]

This was also made clear by O'Donovan J in his judgment in *McArdle v. O'Donohoe*,[26] where he stated that in the absence of a stated intention on the part of the settlor to constitute himself a trustee of trust property, and where there has been no effective transfer of the property to trustees, equity will not construe the ineffective transfer as a declaration of trust by the settlor.

Similar sentiments were expressed by Fitzgibbon LJ in the Irish Court of Appeal in *O'Flaherty v. Browne*:[27]

> A voluntary trust may be created by a declaration of trust, or by a complete assignment of the legal ownership to a trustee; but it is impossible to turn an incomplete, conditional, or postponed gift into a trust, where there is no intention to create the relationship of trustee and *cestui que trust*.

This proposition is aptly illustrated by the decision of *Richards v. Delbridge*,[28] in which the deceased who was the owner of leasehold premises endorsed and signed on the lease a memorandum in the following terms: 'this deed and all thereto belonging I give to Edwards Benetto Richards from this time forth, with all the stock-in-trade'. He delivered this document to the mother of the intended transferee and after his death the question arose whether the purported transfer was effective. The Court of Appeal concluded that there had been no

---

24. See *supra* n. 3.
25. (1862) 4 De GF & J 264, 274-275. Quoted with approval by Lawson J in *Hayes v. Alliance British & Foreign Life & Fire Assurance Co.* (1881) 8 LR Ir 149, 153. See also *T. Choithram International SA v. Pagarani* [2001] 1 WLR 1, 11.
26. High Court 1997 No. 13426P (O'Donovan J) 8 June 1999 at 19.
27. [1907] 2 IR 416, 434.
28. (1874) LR 18 Eq 11.

proper assignment of the lease and in addition, that this ineffective attempt to transfer the interest could not be interpreted as a declaration of trust.[29]

It should be noted that the decision of the Privy Council in *T. Choithram International SA v. Pagarani*[30] makes it clear that where the settlor is one of a number of co-trustees the trust may be completely constituted by a declaration of trust made by him even though the property has still to be vested in the co-trustees. The donor executed a trust deed establishing a philanthropic foundation appointing himself one of the trustees and stated orally that he was giving all his wealth to the foundation. This property was expressed to include his deposit balances and shares in the first to fourth named defendants and the donor told the accountant to those companies that he was to transfer the deposit balances and shares to the foundation although in some instances his shares in the companies had not been transferred before he died. Some of the other trustees signed the trust deed the day the declaration of trust was made and the others subsequently did so. The Court of Appeal of the British Virgin Islands held that the plaintiffs, who claimed to be entitled to the donor's estate on his intestacy, had succeeded in establishing that the donor had not made a valid gift of the deposit balances and shares to the foundation. However, the defendants' appeal to the Privy Council was allowed. Lord Browne-Wilkinson conceded that while it was understandable that the courts below should have reached the conclusion which they had since the case did not fall squarely within either of the methods normally stated as being the only possible ways of making a gift, he did not agree with this conclusion. In his view, while the words 'I give to the foundation' appeared to be words of outright gift, they were essentially words of gift on trust. He held that there could be no difference in principle between a case where a donor declares himself to be sole trustee and where he declares himself to be one of a number of trustees; in both cases his conscience is affected and it would be unconscionable to allow the donor to resile from the gift. Lord Browne-Wilkinson concluded that in the absence of special factors, where one out of a larger body of trustees has trust property vested in him he is bound by the trust and must give effect to it by transferring the trust property into the name of all the trustees. Therefore, in the view of the Privy Council, the assets included in the gift to the foundation had been properly vested in the trustees.

There has been some criticism of this decision on the grounds, *inter alia*, that it may breach the principle laid down in *Milroy v. Lord*[31] to the effect that a failed transfer will not be interpreted as a successful declaration of the settlor

---

29. Jessel MR stated at 15: 'The true distinction appears to me to be plain, and beyond dispute: for a man to make himself a trustee there must be an expression of intention to become a trustee, whereas words of present gift shew an intention to give over property to another, and not retain it in the donor's own hands for any purpose, fiduciary or otherwise.'

30. [2001] 1 WLR 1.

31. (1862) 4 De GF & J 264. See *supra* n. 25.

as trustee.[32] However, it has also been welcomed as showing a willingness to depart from strict legal formalities[33] and it is difficult to argue with the conclusion reached by Lord Browne-Wilkinson that it would be unconscionable to allow a donor to resile from his intention to make a gift in such circumstances.[34]

Where the trust property is comprised of realty, the declaration of trust must be evidenced in writing and while strictly speaking this is not necessary in relation to personalty,[35] it is clearly desirable from an evidential point of view. While the settlor 'need not use the words "I declare myself a trustee"',[36] he must unequivocally convey that this was his intention. As Lord O'Hagan LC commented in *Miller v. Harrison*[37] the effect of the declaration of trust must be to leave no reasonable doubt about the reason for its execution. In this case a dispute arose about the distribution on intestacy of the property of an individual who had died in America a naturalized US citizen. One of the next of kin executed a deed in which he agreed to share the property equally with the other next of kin and in reliance on this deed, these other individuals allowed a decree in the former's favour to be given by an American court in proceedings to determine ownership of the property. The Court of Appeal held that a subsequent attempt by this person to revoke the deed was invalid as its execution in the first instance had constituted a declaration of trust. As Lord O'Hagan LC stated:

> No future act is contemplated; no promise remains to be fulfilled; there is a gift, and not an engagement to give. The words of the donor denude him equitably of the shares which he bestows, save as a trustee for those so obtaining the beneficial interest, while the legal interest remains in himself ... and therefore it binds him, though it states no consideration, and uses no language expressly creating trusts.[38]

In some cases the courts have adopted a fairly rigorous interpretation of this requirement that the intention to declare a trust must be clearly shown. In *Jones v. Lock*[39] a father who had been reproved by his family for failing to bring home a present for his baby son on his return from a trip, placed a cheque in the child's hand having expressed the intention that the latter should

---

32. Rickett [2001] Conv 515, 519.
33. Hopkins [2001] CLJ 483, 485.
34. A possible alternative approach would have been to find that the donor held the property on a constructive trust in which case the requirements in relation to the constitution of an express trust need not have been complied with.
35. See e.g. *Rowe v. Prance* [1999] 2 FLR 787.
36. *Richards v. Delbridge* (1874) LR 18 Eq 11, 14 *per* Jessel MR.
37. (1871) IR 5 Eq 324.
38. *Ibid.* at 344.
39. (1865) 1 Ch App 25.

have the money. The cheque was placed in a safe and six days later the father died. Lord Cranworth LC found that no valid transfer had been effected and stated that there was no evidence of an intention on the father's part to declare himself trustee on his child's behalf.

However, there has been some evidence of a relaxation of this rather restrictive attitude and a more liberal view of the evidence necessary to establish a declaration of trust has been taken in more recent decisions.[40] In *Paul v. Constance*,[41] Scarman LJ acknowledged that on the facts it might be thought to be a 'borderline case' as it was not easy to identify a specific moment when the trust was declared. However, the court concluded that the repetition of the words 'the money is as much yours as mine' in relation to funds in a bank account was sufficient to constitute the deceased as trustee of these monies for the plaintiff. Similarly in *Rowe v. Prance*[42] Nicholas Warren QC held that the regular use of the word 'our' in relation to a boat owned by the defendant and the latter's statement that the plaintiff's security was her interest in it was sufficient to establish that he had effectively constituted himself as an express trustee of the boat for himself and the plaintiff equally.

EXCEPTIONS TO THE PRINCIPLE THAT EQUITY WILL NOT PERFECT AN INCOMPLETELY CONSTITUTED TRUST IN FAVOUR OF A VOLUNTEER

1. The Rule in Strong v. Bird

The effect of the rule in *Strong v. Bird*[43] is that where an incomplete gift is made during a donor's lifetime and the legal title to this property subsequently becomes vested in the donee, the donor's prior intention to make the gift is regarded as having been perfected provided that the intention has continued until the date of the donor's death. The result of the decision in *Strong* itself was that an executor did not have to account for a debt where a testator had manifested an intention to forgive the debt during her lifetime and this intention had continued until her death. This was extended to a positive application of the principle in *Re Stewart*[44] by a finding that an imperfect gift made by a testator *inter vivos* to his wife was subsequently perfected by her appointment as one of his executors. Neville J stated:

---

40. As Lord Browne-Wilkinson stated in *T. Choithram International SA v. Pagarani* [2001] 1 WLR 1, 11: 'Although equity will not aid a volunteer, it will not strive officiously to defeat a gift.'
41. [1977] 1 WLR 527.
42. [1999] 2 FLR 787.
43. (1874) LR 18 Eq 315.
44. [1908] 2 Ch 251.

[W]here a testator has expressed the intention of making a gift of personal estate belonging to him to one who upon his death becomes his executor, the intention continuing unchanged, the executor is entitled to hold the property for his own benefit. The reasoning by which the conclusion is reached is of a double character – first, that the vesting of the property in the executor at the testator's death completes the imperfect gift made in the lifetime and secondly, that the intention of the testator to give the beneficial interest to the executor is sufficient to counterveil the equity of beneficiaries under the will, the testator having vested the legal estate in the executor. The whole of the property in the eye of the law vesting in each executor, it seems to me immaterial whether the donee is the only executor or one of several; nor do I think the rule is confined to cases of the release of a debt owing by the donee.[45]

A number of aspects of the principle must be considered in more detail. The legal vesting of the property in the donee commonly occurs when this individual is appointed a personal representative of the donor. So the rule applies where a donee acquires legal title to the property by becoming an executor[46] of the deceased's estate and has been also held to extend to a situation where the donee is appointed administrator. While the latter principle was laid down in *Re James*[47] and now seems to be accepted, it has been criticised[48] on the basis that the identity of an administrator is often a matter of chance and it would seem unfair that such a person should obtain an advantage over the other beneficiaries by reason of this position.

An intention to make a gift in the future[49] or to make a future testamentary gift[50] will not come within the rule in *Strong v. Bird*. The distinction between a present intention to make an immediate gift of property and the intention to make a testamentary gift is well illustrated by the decision in *Re Wilson*.[51] The testator had manifested an intention to make an immediate gift of certain securities to his son, who was the executor of his will, although he did not complete or perfect this gift during his lifetime. Johnston J was satisfied that this intention had been proved and that the principle in *Strong v. Bird* applied to perfect the gift. However, the rule did not apply to other properties which the testator had promised to transfer to his son during his lifetime or by his

---

45. *Ibid.* at 254.
46. It suffices if a donee is appointed as one of a number of executors. See *supra Re Stewart* [1908] 2 Ch 251, 254.
47. [1935] Ch 449.
48. See the judgment of Walton J in *Re Gonin* [1979] Ch 16, although he did apply the principle as both counsel had accepted it.
49. *Re Freeland* [1952] Ch 110.
50. *Re Innes* [1910] 1 Ch 188.
51. [1933] IR 729.

will. In relation to the intended testamentary disposition, Johnston J quoted with approval[52] the words of Neville J in *Re Stewart*[53] as follows:

> [T]he intention to give, however, must not be an intention of testamentary benefaction, although the intended donee is the executor, for, in that case the rule cannot apply, the prescribed formalities for testamentary disposition not having been observed.

It is also important that the intention relates to specific property[54] and the gift must be perfected in all respects save for the formalities necessary to effect the proper transfer of the property. In addition, for the rule to apply the intention to make the gift must have continued until the time of the donor's death,[55] and it cannot have any application in cases such as *Re Wale*,[56] where the evidence showed that the settlor appeared to have forgotten the very existence of the settlement and had continued to treat the property as if it were her own.

The practical significance of the rule in *Strong v. Bird* is that the claim of beneficiaries under a will will be displaced by the donee's prior equity, although it is not clear in this jurisdiction or in England whether this priority will be effective as against creditors.

2. Donatio Mortis Causa

A *donatio mortis causa* is the delivery of property to a donee in contemplation of the donor's death which is conditional on this event occurring and the gift is not regarded as complete until the donor dies. It should be regarded as a conditional present gift and must be distinguished from a straightforward gift *inter vivos* which is an absolute present gift, and from a testamentary gift which is a future gift. Buckley J described a *donatio mortis causa* in the following terms in *Re Beaumont*:[57]

> It is an act *inter vivos* by which the donee is to have absolute title to the subject of the gift not at once but if the donor dies. If the donor dies the title becomes absolute not under but as against his executor. In order to make the gift valid it must be made so as to take complete effect on the donor's death.

The general principle that equity will not perfect an imperfect or incomplete

---

52. *Ibid.* at 748.
53. [1908] 2 Ch 251, 255.
54. *Re Innes* [1910] 1 Ch 188, 193 *per* Parker J.
55. See *Re Gonin* [1979] Ch 16 where the lack of a continuing intention to make the gift resulted in the court's refusal to apply the rule in *Strong v. Bird*.
56. [1956] 1 WLR 1346.
57. [1902] 1 Ch 889, 892.

gift in favour of a volunteer does not apply to a *donatio mortis causa*, although in practice the assistance of equity will only be required in limited circumstances. Where the subject-matter of the *donatio mortis causa* is a chattel which has been delivered to the donee, title to this object is regarded as being complete on the donor's death. However, where the subject-matter is a chose in action or land, the legal title to this property will vest in the donor's personal representatives on his death. It is in these circumstances that the exception to the general principle becomes important as equity will compel the donee's personal representatives to take whatever steps are necessary to complete the donor's title.

The essential elements of a *donatio mortis causa* have been laid down in a number of decisions and are now clearly established.[58] There must have been a gift made in contemplation of the donor's death, the subject-matter of the gift must have been delivered to the donee and the gift must have been made on the basis that it becomes absolute only on the donor's death and therefore remains revocable during his lifetime. It is also necessary to consider whether the property is capable of forming the subject matter of a *donatio mortis causa*.

The attitude of the court in relation to these requirements has tended to be quite strict and they must all be satisfied to establish a valid *donatio mortis causa*. As Gallen J has recently commented in the New Zealand High Court decision of *Wilson v. Paniani*:[59]

> It is important . . . that there ought to be stringent requirements in respect of such claims since they are frequently made without any independent evidence to support them and in circumstances where they would be difficult to refute. Accordingly the law ensures that for such a claim to succeed the strict requirements of the law must be adhered to and satisfied.

Another reason why a strict approach has been taken in such cases is that the upholding of a *donatio mortis causa* may mean that the court is giving effect to a distribution of the deceased's property in a manner which may differ considerably from that set out by the deceased in his will. This point is well illustrated by the judgment of Barr J in *Bentham v. Potterton*,[60] the most recent decision in this jurisdiction on *donatio mortis causa*. The deceased in

---

58. See *Cain v. Moon* [1896] 2 QB 283, 286 *per* Russell LJ quoted with approval by Molony CJ in *Re Mulroy* [1924] 1 IR 98, 103; *Re Craven's Estate (No. 1)* [1937] Ch 423, 426 *per* Farwell J.
59. [1996] 3 NZLR 378, 384. The court held that on the facts the conditions necessary to establish the existence of a *donatio mortis causa* had not been made out by the plaintiff despite the fact that Gallen J was satisfied that the deceased had wished to benefit her.
60. High Court (Barr J) 28 May 1998.

her will bequeathed cash legacies varying in amount from £1,000 to £3,000 to nine beneficiaries, including the first and second named plaintiffs, her grandnieces, and a residuary clause provided for the division of the remainder of the estate equally between all but one of the named beneficiaries. The deceased was hospitalised two months before her death and it was discovered that she was suffering from inoperable cancer. The trial judge was satisfied that there was no evidence that she had ever been told that her condition was terminal and it was not until a week before she died that she told her niece that she knew she was in fact dying. Three and a half weeks before her death the deceased asked the first named plaintiff to retrieve bank books from her home and put them in a safe in the latter's house, which she did. The following day, the first named plaintiff informed her great-aunt that she had carried out her wishes and the former deposed that the deceased had then told her that if anything was to happen to her, she was 'to keep the contents of the books and give [her sister] a few bob out of it'. After the deceased's death, an issue arose about whether this transaction amounted to a valid *donatio mortis causa* made in favour of the plaintiffs. Barr J stressed that the onus lay on the party claiming the gift to prove to the court that the requirements for *donatio mortis causa* had been satisfied. In the first instance, he said that the facts fell short of establishing on the balance of probabilities that the gift had been made by the donor in contemplation of her death. He suggested that if it had been the deceased's intention to make a gift of the funds on deposit to the plaintiffs it seemed probable that she would either have made this clear on the first occasion on which she had referred to the deposit books or alternatively would have made a new will or codicil to give effect to her revised intentions. Barr J concluded that he was not satisfied that the deceased 'positively intended to make a radical change in the disposition of her property in contemplation of her death'. Although this might have been her intention, he said that the surrounding facts raised considerable doubt in this regard and in the circumstances he held that the plaintiffs had not established the validity of the alleged gift on the balance of probabilities.

(i) *In Contemplation of Death*

The gift must have been made in contemplation, although not necessarily in the expectation of death, but not simply in circumstances where the donor is acknowledging the general inevitability of death. So it is usually made where 'death for some reason [is] believed to be impending'[61] as a result of some form of serious illness or because the donor intends to embark on a particularly hazardous journey.[62] However, it is essential that the court is satisfied that the

---

61. *Re Craven's Estate (No. 1)* [1937] Ch 423, 426 *per* Farwell J.
62. The ordinary risks of travel by air will not suffice, see *Thompson v. Mechan* [1958] 13 DLR (2d) 103.

donor knew that he was dying at the time the transaction took place and this point is illustrated by the High Court decision in *Bentham v. Potterton*,[63] the facts of which are set out above. Barr J said that he had substantial doubts about whether the donor appreciated the gravity of her medical condition when the transaction in question took place. Although she was elderly and had been gravely ill two years previously, he adverted to the fact that there was no evidence that the deceased had been told that her condition was terminal and pointed out that it was only some two and a half weeks after the transaction had taken place that she had admitted to her niece that she thought she was dying. In these circumstances he said that the facts fell short of establishing on the balance of probabilities that the gift had been made by the donor in contemplation of her death.

Provided that death actually occurs it appears to be immaterial that it does so as a result of a cause different to that contemplated at the time of the gift. This is illustrated by *Wilkes v. Allington*,[64] in which a donor made a gift knowing that he was suffering from an incurable disease and then died two months later from pneumonia. It was held that the gift remained valid in such circumstances. A similar result ensued in *Mills v. Shields (No. 1)*,[65] where a donor made a gift while suffering from an oppressive form of neurosis and subsequently took his own life while travelling to obtain treatment for this condition. Gavan Duffy P stressed that a *donatio mortis causa* is not defeated by the fact that the donor did not die in the manner he had feared and held that the case was not one of 'intended suicide' within the meaning of that phrase as set out in *Agnew v. Belfast Banking Co.*[66] It is therefore important to distinguish *Mills* from the decision in *Agnew* in which it was held that a gift actually made in contemplation of suicide could not form the subject-matter of a valid *donatio mortis causa*. Porter MR commented that as suicide was recognised as a crime, it was 'fundamentally opposed to the first principles of our law ... that legal rights should be created by the intention to commit suicide followed by the actual commission of it'.[67] Fitzgibbon LJ agreed that it would be contrary to public policy to uphold a gift which was intended to take effect as a result of suicide and the policy arguments which lay behind the *Agnew* decision may still be recognised as valid.

(ii) *Delivery of the Subject-Matter of the Gift*

There must be delivery of the subject-matter of the *donatio mortis causa* made

---

63. High Court (Barr J) 28 May 1998.
64. [1931] 2 Ch 104.
65. [1948] IR 367.
66. [1896] 2 IR 204.
67. *Ibid.* at 216. Note that suicide is no longer regarded as a crime; see s. 2 of the Criminal Law (Suicide) Act 1993.

by the donor with the intention of parting with dominion over the property[68] and not just mere physical possession.[69] It is insufficient if the property is simply handed over for safe keeping and the result of such delivery must be that the donor can no longer exercise any control over the subject-matter of the gift.[70] As Evershed MR commented in *Birch v. Treasury Solicitor*[71] delivery must be made 'of the essential indicia or evidence of title, possession or production of which entitles the possessor to the money or property, purported to be given'.

Delivery may be made before[72] or after[73] the appropriate words of gift[74] are used and provided that it is achieved in an effective manner there is no requirement of any written evidence to substantiate it. It was held in *Mills v. Shields (No.1)*[75] that where delivery is made to an agent of the donor as trustee for the donee this will suffice. However this can be contrasted with the finding made in the earlier case of *Re Thompson's Estate*[76] that where the deceased simply handed her servant the property to keep for the donee this was not sufficient delivery. Meredith J quoted with approval the *dicta* of Knight Bruce VC in *Farquharson v. Cave*[77] to the effect that 'a mere delivery to an agent, in the character of agent for the giver, would amount to nothing' and concluded that in the circumstances where insufficient instructions had been given to the agent, no delivery, either actual or constructive, had taken place.

Where the subject-matter of the *donatio mortis causa* is a chattel, there must be either delivery of the chattel itself or of something which will enable the donee to obtain effective control over it. So the handing over of a key to a locked container or safe deposit box will constitute delivery,[78] although the reverse is not the case and delivery of a locked box without the key does not meet the requirements of a valid *donatio mortis causa*.[79] A good example of a case where no delivery was found to have taken place was *Re Mulroy*.[80]

---

68. There must be 'a complete parting with the dominion over the subject matter by the donor' *per* Molony CJ in *Re Mulroy* [1924] 1 IR 98, 100. See also *Hawkins v. Blewitt* (1798) 2 Esp 663.
69. *Birch v. Treasury Solicitor* [1951] 1 Ch 298.
70. *Re Craven's Estate (No. 1)* [1937] Ch 423, 427.
71. [1951] Ch 298, 311.
72. *Cain v. Moon* [1896] 2 QB 283.
73. *Re Weston* [1902] 1 Ch 680.
74. Note that words of gift are clearly not in themselves sufficient without actual delivery taking place, see *Re Mulroy* [1924] 1 IR 98, 104 *per* Molony CJ.
75. [1948] IR 367.
76. [1928] IR 606.
77. (1846) 2 Coll 356, 367.
78. *Re Wasserberg* [1915] 1 Ch 195; *Re Lillingston* [1952] 2 All ER 184. Although if the donor retains another key, it will probably not suffice, see *Re Craven's Estate (No. 1)* [1937] Ch 423, 428 *per* Farwell J.
79. *Re Johnson* (1905) 92 LT 357.
80. [1924] 1 IR 98.

Shortly before his death, the deceased opened a cash box in the presence of the defendant and took out a deposit receipt and two 'stale' cheques and said to him: 'Here is all belonging to me; I am sorry I have no more to give you. You were very good to me.' He then replaced the documents and locked the box, putting the key in his pocket. The deceased subsequently died intestate and the Irish Court of Appeal held that there was no valid *donatio mortis causa* on the grounds that the deceased, by replacing the documents, had led the court to believe that he had never intended to part with them in such a manner as to lose dominion over them during his lifetime.

(iii) *The Gift Must be Conditional upon Death and Revocable*

The gift must have been made on the basis that although it is in form a present gift it is nevertheless conditional on the donor's death and it will remain revocable during his lifetime. As Lord Porter MR stated in *Agnew v. Belfast Banking Co.*:[81] 'A *donatio mortis causa* is incomplete till death, and depends upon it. If the sick man recovers it is of no avail. No property passes until death.' Such revocation may occur automatically where for example the donor recovers from the illness which led him to make the gift.[82] Equally, the donor may expressly inform the donee that the gift is being revoked, or may recover dominion over it, although recovery of possession for the purposes of safe keeping will not amount to revocation.[83] Clearly a purported revocation by will cannot be achieved as the instrument will not come into effect until the donor's death at which stage the donee's gift will be regarded as complete.

(iv) *The Property Must be Capable of Forming the Subject-Matter of a Donatio Mortis Causa*

Clearly, any property transferable by mere delivery can form the subject matter of a valid gift by way of *donatio mortis causa* and delivery of the documentation appropriate to effect a transfer of property will also suffice.[84] Until recently it had been thought that realty could not form the subject matter of a valid *donatio mortis causa*[85] but the Court of Appeal in *Sen v. Headley*[86] made it clear that a gift of land by the delivery of deeds should not be excluded. The deceased and the plaintiff lived together for ten years and remained on

---

81. [1896] 2 IR 204, 216.
82. *Keys v. Hore* (1879) 13 ILTR 58.
83. *Re Hawkins* [1924] 2 Ch 47.
84. *Birch v. Treasury Solicitor* [1951] Ch 298, 311.
85. See the *dicta* of Lord Eldon in *Duffield v. Elwes* (1827) 1 Bli 497 and the Australian decisions of *Watts v. Public Trustee* (1949) 50 SR 130 and *Bayliss v. Public Trustee* (1988) 12 NSWLR 540.
86. [1991] Ch 425. See Halliwell [1991] Conv 307; Thornley [1991] CLJ 404; Baker (1993) 109 LQR 19.

close terms thereafter. When the deceased was very ill he told the plaintiff that his house was hers and that the deeds to it were in a steel box to which she had the keys. He died intestate and the plaintiff claimed that he had made a valid gift to her in contemplation of death. The defendant, who was the deceased's nephew and the administrator of his estate, counterclaimed for the return of the deeds to the house. The Court of Appeal upheld the plaintiff's claim.

There is some authority to the effect that stocks and shares cannot form the subject matter of a *donatio mortis causa*[87] on the basis that a share certificate although it will constitute *prima facie* evidence of good title, is not the vital document which forms 'the fundamental contract between a company and its members'.[88] Similar uncertainty surrounds the position of a savings bank book. In *M'Gonnell v. Murray*[89] Walsh MR rejected the argument that it could validly form the subject-matter of a *donatio mortis causa* on the grounds that the book did not embody the terms of the contract between the depositer and the bank. However, in the more recent Circuit Court decision of *Hearty v. Coleman*,[90] it was held by Judge Sheehy that the handing of a post office savings bank book by the testator to the defendant constituted a valid *donatio mortis causa* of the money standing to her credit in the account and other authorities seem to support this conclusion.[91] It would seem that neither an IOU[92] nor a donor's own cheque or promissory note can come within the ambit of the doctrine on the basis that these are respectively merely a revocable instrument and a gratuitous promise.[93]

In the last analysis perhaps the most useful test is that proposed by Evershed MR in *Birch v. Treasury Solicitor*,[94] which was set out above; namely whether delivery of the documents concerned amounts to a transfer 'of the essential indicia or evidence of title, possession or production of which entitles the possessor to the money or property, purported to be given'.

---

87. *Moore v. Moore* (1874) LR 18 Eq 474; *Re Weston* [1902] 1 Ch 680, although note *Staniland v. Willot* (1852) 3 Mac & G 664.
88. *Mills v. Shields (No. 2)* [1950] IR 21, 31 *per* Gavan Duffy J.
89. (1869) IR 3 Eq 460.
90. [1953-54] Ir Jur Rep 73.
91. *Re Weston* [1902] 1 Ch 680; *Birch v. Treasury Solicitor* [1951] Ch 298. In addition, in *Re Thompson's Estate* [1928] IR 606 Meredith J while he held on the facts that there was no valid *donatio mortis causa* on the grounds that there had been no delivery, did not raise any issue as to whether a Post Office savings bank book could have formed the subject-matter of such a gift.
92. *Duckworth v. Lee* [1899] 1 IR 405.
93. *Re Beaumont* [1902] 1 Ch 889; *Re Leaper* [1916] 1 Ch 579. However there might be a valid gift if the cheque was paid during the donor's lifetime or even after his death if the bank was not aware of the fact that he had died.
94. [1951] Ch 298, 311.

3. Proprietary Estoppel

Where an imperfect gift has been made and the donor knowingly allows the donee to improve the property or act to his detriment in some manner, equity may compel the donor to perfect the gift even where the donee is a volunteer. This will be considered *infra*.[95]

THE POSITION OF A VOLUNTEER

As we have seen, once a trust is completely constituted it can be enforced by any beneficiary, even if he is a mere volunteer. However, where a trust is still incompletely constituted, it may be of crucial importance to determine whether the beneficiaries are volunteers or have given consideration; in these circumstances 'equity will not assist a volunteer' although it will enforce such an incompletely constituted trust if valuable consideration has been given by the beneficiaries.

A beneficiary will be regarded as a volunteer unless he had provided valuable consideration in the sense recognised at common law or he comes within the scope of marriage consideration. It is important to note that what is referred to as 'good consideration' comprised of natural love and affection is not considered to be valuable consideration and will not suffice to make an incompletely constituted trust enforceable in equity. A settlement made before and in consideration of marriage is regarded as being one for valuable consideration. However, a settlement made after marriage will only suffice provided it is made in fulfilment of a pre-nuptial agreement.[96] In any other circumstances a settlement made in consideration of a past marriage will not be regarded as one for valuable consideration. This is illustrated by the decision of *Re Greer*,[97] in which a settlement executed for the benefit of children of a former marriage on the occasion of a second marriage was not found to be a settlement for valuable consideration. The spouses[98] and issue[99] of the marriage are regarded as coming within the marriage consideration. The latter phrase has been variously interpreted as being confined to children[100] and as extending to grandchildren[101] but the better view would seem to be that it is usually confined to the children of the marriage.[102]

---

95. See Chapter 17.
96. *Re Holland* [1902] 2 Ch 360.
97. (1877) IR 11 Eq 502.
98. *Dennehy v. Delany* (1876) IR 10 Eq 377.
99. *Greenwood v. Lutman* [1915] 1 IR 266.
100. *Re Dixon's Trusts* (1869) IR 4 Eq 1.
101. *McDonald v. Scott* [1893] AC 642.
102. *Re Bromhead's Trusts* [1922] 1 IR 75. While some early authorities suggested a wider definition of those falling within the marriage consideration, these decisions are now explained on the basis that in the special circumstances of these cases the

It has been clearly established that persons coming within the marriage consideration can enforce the settlement even though they might otherwise be regarded as volunteers. In *Pullan v. Koe*[103] as part of a marriage settlement in which property was settled on a husband and wife and their prospective children, the wife covenanted to settle after acquired property to the value of £100 or upwards. She subsequently received a gift of £285 which was ultimately used to buy bonds which remained in her husband's name until his death. The question arose whether these bonds could be recovered from his estate and held on the trusts of the settlement. It was held by Swinfen Eady J that the trustees, acting on behalf of the wife and children, could succeed in reclaiming the bonds on the grounds that the money had been subject to a trust in favour of those coming within the marriage consideration. Swinfen Eady J distinguished the circumstances of the case before him from those where it had been held that a court would not intervene to assist a volunteer who did not come within the marriage consideration. In *Re Plumptre's Marriage Settlement*[104] a settlement in consideration of marriage contained a covenant providing for the settlement of property subsequently acquired by the wife on trust for herself and her husband for life, their issue and in default, for their next of kin. The husband gave some stock to his wife and it was held that after her death the covenant could not be enforced by their next of kin against her personal representative, her husband, on the grounds that the next of kin were volunteers and did not come within the marriage consideration.[105]

POSSIBLE ALTERNATIVE REMEDIES FOR A BENEFICIARY WHERE A TRUST IS INCOMPLETELY CONSTITUTED

Where a beneficiary is a volunteer and does not come within any of the exceptions outlined above, it is necessary to examine whether there are any other means of enforcing an incompletely constituted trust in his favour. A settlor may commonly enter into a covenant to create a trust by transferring existing or so called after acquired property to trustees. This is particularly common in the case of a marriage settlement where the parties may covenant to settle any property which they may subsequently acquire on the trusts of

---

interests of these parties, often illegitimate children or children of a former marriage, were so closely interwoven with the interests of the children of the marriage that they could not be separated.

103. [1913] 1 Ch 9.
104. [1910] 1 Ch 609. See also *Re D'Angibau* (1880) 15 Ch D 228.
105. It should be noted that a volunteer beneficiary who is party to a covenant may bring an action on the covenant at common law for damages, see *Cannon v. Hartley* [1949] Ch 213.

the settlement.[106] Where such a covenant is entered into other than for valuable consideration, there are two main alternatives relating to its possible enforcement which must be examined. First, it may be possible to establish that there is a completely constituted trust of the benefit of the covenant in their favour and secondly indirect enforcement by means of an action by the trustees on the covenant at common law against the settlor may be explored.

The principal difficulty with the first option is in determining the circumstances when such a trust will arise and in particular in assessing whether sufficient intention to create a trust has been established. In the early decision of *Fletcher v. Fletcher*[107] a settlor entered into a voluntary covenant with trustees to the effect that if either or both of his natural sons should survive him, his executors should, within twelve months of his death pay a sum of £60,000 to the trustees to hold on trust for both or such one of them as might attain the age of 21. One of these sons survived the settlor and reached the age of 21 when he sought to enforce the covenant against the executors who had refused to take any action. The effect of the decision of Wright VC was that there was a completely constituted trust of the benefit of the covenant which could be enforced by the son. On the facts the court in *Fletcher* was satisfied that the testator had manifested a sufficient intention to create a trust, although it has been argued that these same facts would hardly satisfy a more modern approach to the question of certainty of intention.[108] A further difficulty is that *Fletcher* has been distinguished in the case of after acquired property and it has been held in a number of decisions that there can be no enforceable trust of the benefit of the covenant in such cases.[109] In *Re Cook's Settlement Trusts*,[110] by virtue of an agreement and subsequent settlement entered into by Sir Herbert Cook and his son, certain pictures became the absolute property of the son, who covenanted that if any of these pictures were to be sold during his lifetime the proceeds of sale should be held on the trusts of the settlement. The son gave one of the pictures to his wife who wished to sell it and the question arose whether the trustees were obliged to take any steps to ensure performance of the covenant. Buckley J distinguished *Fletcher v. Fletcher* as follows:

> The covenant with which I am concerned did not, in my opinion, create a debt enforceable at law, that is to say a property right, which, although

---

106. See *supra Re Plumptre's Marriage Settlement* [1910] 1 Ch 609; *Pullan v. Koe* [1913] 1 Ch 9.
107. (1844) 4 Hare 67.
108. See *supra* Chapter 4. While at the time *Fletcher* was decided the use of precatory words was considered to be sufficient to show intention to create a trust, a more stringent approach is now applied.
109. *Re Pryce* [1917] 1 Ch 234; *Re Kay's Settlement* [1939] Ch 329; *Re Cook's Settlement Trusts* [1965] Ch 902.
110. [1965] Ch 902.

to bear fruit only in the future and upon a contingency, was capable of being made the subject of an immediate trust, as was held to be the case in *Fletcher v. Fletcher*. ... In contrast ... this covenant on its true construction is, in my opinion, an executory contract to settle a particular fund or particular funds of money which at the date of the covenant did not exist and which might never come into existence. It is analogous to a covenant to settle an expectation or to settle after-acquired property. The case in my judgment, involves the law of contract, not the law of trusts.[111]

It has been argued that there is no good reason for drawing such a distinction[112] and perhaps the decision in *Cook* is better explained on the grounds that there was clearly no intention to create a trust of the benefit of the covenant in that case.

So, in theory a completely constituted trust of the benefit of a covenant to settle either existing or after acquired property may be found provided the settlor has manifested the appropriate intention and it is likely that in the absence of such a clearly expressed intention no trust will exist. This would allow voluntary covenants to settle property to be enforced where there is sufficient evidence of the settlor's intention to create a trust of the benefit of the covenant; any more radical approach would seem inconsistent with a considerable number of authorities.

A second option, which derives little or no support from the relevant case law, is that where a beneficiary is unable to enforce a covenant to settle in the manner outlined above it might be possible to secure enforcement of the covenant by means of an action on it at common law by the trustees against the settlor. However, the authorities in this area have clearly established that there is no obligation on the trustees to take action in such circumstances; *a fortiori* it has been suggested that they should be restrained from taking any such proceedings.[113] In *Re Kay's Settlement*[114] a spinster executed a voluntary settlement in favour of herself for life and after her death for her issue which contained a covenant to settle after acquired property. She subsequently married, had children and acquired further property and then refused to comply with the trustees' request to bring this additional property into the settlement. The trustees sought the direction of the court on the issue of whether they should take proceedings against the settlor to compel performance of the covenant or to recover damages for her failure to implement it. Simonds J

---

111. *Ibid.* at 913-914.
112. Barton (1975) 91 LQR 236; Meagher & Lehane (1976) 92 LQR 427; Goddard [1988] Conv 19.
113. *Re Pryce* [1917] 1 Ch 234.
114. [1939] Ch 329.

followed the decision of Eve J in *Re Pryce*[115] and directed the trustees not to take any steps either to compel performance of the covenant or to seek damages in respect of the settlor's failure to implement its terms.

However, even if the courts were to re-appraise their approach, there would be difficulties from the point of view of the beneficiaries in having recourse to this option. First, the extent of the damages to which the trustees would be entitled in these circumstances is far from clear and in any event, any damages which might be recovered would in all likelihood be held by the trustees on a resulting trust for the settlor rather than for the beneficiaries. Therefore, unless a beneficiary is recognised as being an actual party to the covenant, in which case he can maintain an action at common law for its breach,[116] he will not be able to secure a remedy at law for failure to give effect to the terms of the covenant.

---

115. [1917] 1 Ch 234. Criticised in *Jacobs' Law of Trusts in Australia* (6th ed., 1997, Meagher and Gummow) pp. 101-102.
116. *Cannon v. Hartley* [1949] Ch 213.

CHAPTER 7

Resulting Trusts

INTRODUCTION

Resulting trusts can be said to arise by implication and are founded on the unexpressed but presumed intention of the settlor.[1] This label is used to describe such trusts because the beneficial interest in the property in question comes back or results to the settlor, or, if he is dead, to those entitled to his estate, where the law presumes that this was the settlor's intention. They are also sometimes referred to as implied trusts because they are presumed to arise as a result of the settlor's implied intention. Due to the informal manner in which they come into being, such trusts are exempt from the formalities required in relation to the creation of express trusts.

While there are a number of possible bases for the rationale behind resulting trusts, in practice they tend to arise in two distinct factual situations; first, where there has been an apparent gift of property and secondly, where an express trust has failed to dispose of the trust property. Traditionally, a distinction has been made between categories of resulting trusts as suggested by Megarry J in *Re Vandervell's Trusts (No. 2)*[2] in the following terms:

   (a) The first class of case is where the transfer to B is not made on any trust. If, of course, it appears from the transfer that B is intended to hold on certain trusts, that will be decisive, and the case is not within this category; and similarly if it appears that B is intended to take beneficially. But in other cases there is a rebuttable presumption that B holds on a resulting trust for A. . . . The presumption thus establishes both that B is to take on trust and also what that trust is. Such resulting trusts may be called 'presumed resulting trusts'.

   (b) The second class of case is where the transfer to B is made on trusts which leave some or all of the beneficial interest undisposed of. Here B automatically holds on a resulting trust for A to the extent that the beneficial interest has not been carried to him or others. The resulting trust here does not depend on any intentions or

---

1.   See generally Chambers, *Resulting Trusts* (1997).
2.   [1974] Ch 269, 294. See Clarke (1974) 38 Conv 405; Harris (1975) 38 MLR 557.

presumptions, but is the automatic consequence of A's failure to dispose of what is vested in him. . . . Such resulting trusts may be called 'automatic resulting trusts'.

The extent to which the trusts which may arise by implication in either of these two categories will actually reflect the settlor's real intentions in a given case is open to question and particularly in the context of automatically resulting trusts, the result, which the law presumes, is often quite contrary to that which a settlor could be said to have intended.[3]

More recently a number of potentially unifying theories have been put forward to challenge the orthodoxy of Megarry J's distinction between presumed and automatic resulting trusts. In his speech in *Westdeutsche Landesbank Girozentrale v. Islington Borough Council*[4] Lord Browne-Wilkinson suggested that Megarry J was incorrect in his assumption that trusts in category (b) set out above do not depend on intention but operate automatically; in his view all resulting trusts give effect to the presumed intention of the transferor.[5] A further alternative analysis which has been developed in recent years is that resulting trusts arise by virtue of the absence of any intention on the part of the transferor to benefit the transferee. While suggested in the first instance by Birks,[6] this theory has been developed by Chambers,[7] who has stated as follows:

[A]ll resulting trusts operate on precisely the same principles regardless of the situations in which they arise. They do not depend on an implied intention to create a trust, but neither do they arise completely independently of intention. All resulting trusts come into being because the provider of property did not intend to benefit the recipient.

Similar views were expressed by Lord Millett in *Air Jamaica Ltd v. Charlton*[8] in the following terms:

3. *Vandervell v. IRC* [1967] 2 AC 291. See *infra* pp. 134–135.
4. [1996] AC 669.
5. As Rickett and Grantham comment (2000) 116 LQR 15, 'While....describing two sets of circumstances, his Lordship was not convinced that there were two types of resulting trust'.
6. 'Restitution and Resulting Trusts' in *Equity: Contemporary Legal Developments* (ed., Goldstein, 1992) p. 335 *et seq*.
7. *Resulting Trusts* (1997) at p. 2. As Lord Millett commented in *Twinsectra Ltd v. Yardley* [2002] 2 AC 164, 190: 'The central thesis of Dr Chambers' book is that a resulting trust arises whenever there is a transfer of property in circumstances in which the transferor (or more accurately the person at whose expense the property was provided) did not intend to benefit the recipient. It responds to the absence of an intention on the part of the transferor to pass the entire beneficial interest, not to a positive intention to retain it.'
8. [1999] 1 WLR 1399, 1412. See also the *dicta* of Potter LJ in *Twinsectra Ltd v. Yardley* [1999] Lloyd's Rep Bank 438, 457.

Like a constructive trust, a resulting trust arises by operation of law, though unlike a constructive trust it gives effect to intention. But it arises whether or not the transferor intended to retain a beneficial interest – he almost always does not – since it responds to the absence of any intention on his part to pass a beneficial interest to the recipient.

Once this view of a resulting trust is accepted, the link with a restitutionary response is easy to make[9] and this in itself has led to controversy. Birks has suggested that if and so far as personal restitutionary claims are backed by equitable proprietary claims, we should learn to attribute those proprietary rights to the resulting trust.[10] Similarly, Chambers[11] has put forward the view that the existing resulting trust is capable of a far greater role in proprietary restitution. However, Lord Browne-Wilkinson in *Westdeutsche Landesbank Girozentrale v. Islington Borough Council*[12] characterized the resulting trust as an unsuitable basis for developing proprietary restitutionary remedies, and Swadling[13] has rejected such an approach concluding that 'the resulting trust has little or no part to play in the law of restitution'. While Rickett and Grantham are also sceptical of a restitutionary based approach,[14] they put forward an alternative explanation for the role of resulting trusts and suggest that such trusts and the presumptions associated with them operate as part of the law of property, simply as a series of default rules which identify the beneficial interest where the transfer is either ambiguous as to the location of that interest or ineffective to dispose of it.[15]

While there has been little discussion of these competing theories outside academic circles, the views put forward by Birks and Chambers, if adopted, could have far-reaching practical implications and the academic community undoubtedly awaits with interest discussion of these views by the judiciary.

---

9. See Simpson 'On the Nature of Resulting Trusts' in *Restitution and Equity Volume One: Resulting Trusts and Equitable Compensation* (eds. Birks and Rose, 2000) p. 19. He states that 'In such circumstances, where the evidence (or the reinterpreted presumption) shows that a transfer was made without any intention to benefit the recipient, then the retention of the corresponding enrichment by the recipient will be unjust, in just the same way as in all cases where restitution is the legal response to circumstances of non-voluntary transfer.'

10. 'Restitution and Resulting Trusts' in *Equity: Contemporary Legal Developments* (ed., Goldstein, 1992) pp. 368-369.

11. *Resulting Trusts* (1997) at p. 7.

12. [1996] AC 669, 716.

13. (1996) 16 LS 110, 111.

14. 'Resulting Trusts – A Rather Limited Doctrine' in *Restitution and Equity Volume One: Resulting Trusts and Equitable Compensation* (eds. Birks and Rose, 2000) p. 57-59.

15. *Ibid.* at p. 48.

AUTOMATICALLY RESULTING TRUSTS

Failure of the Trust

Where an express trust fails completely for any reason, a resulting trust of the trust property will arise in favour of the settlor or his estate. This may occur for a variety of reasons; there may have been a total failure of the beneficiaries, the settlement deed defining the scope of the trust may have been lost,[16] the trust may be void for uncertainty,[17] or may fail to qualify for charitable status in circumstances where it cannot operate as a valid purpose trust.[18] In *Re Ames' Settlement*[19] property was settled on the trusts of a marriage settlement by the husband's father. The marriage was subsequently declared void and it was held that this property should be held on a resulting trust for the settlor's estate after the husband's death, rather than passing to those entitled under the settlement in default of issue.

Another situation in which a resulting trust will arise is where property is given to trustees and yet no trusts are defined. This can arise in the context of a half secret trust,[20] where a testator makes it clear on the face of a will that property is to be held on trust without specifying the nature and extent of the trust and the identity of the beneficiaries. In those circumstances where such a trust fails because there has been no adequate communication and acceptance of the terms of the trust during the testator's lifetime,[21] or if it were to fail on the grounds of inconsistency between the terms of the will and the events which transpired,[22] a resulting trust in favour of the testator's estate would arise. A similar result will ensue where a testator makes an unsuccessful attempt to create a fully secret trust and the intended trustee admits that it was not the testator's intention that he should take as a beneficiary.[23]

One of the most important cases in this area is that of *Vandervell v. IRC*,[24] in which the appellant transferred shares in a private company to a college which he wished to endow with the intention of declaring dividends on the shares. The effect of the arrangement was that the college would grant an

---

16. *Cummins v. Hall* [1933] IR 419.
17. *Re Pugh's Will Trusts* [1967] 1 WLR 1262; *Re Atkinson's Will Trusts* [1978] 1 WLR 586.
18. *Re Diplock* [1948] Ch 465.
19. [1946] Ch 217.
20. See *supra* Chapter 5.
21. See *Scott v. Brownrigg* (1881) 9 LR Ir 246; *Re Watters' Will Trusts* (1928) 62 ILTR 61. This seems to be now accepted as being the requirement in Ireland rather than communication and acceptance prior to the testator's will which still appears to be the position in England, see *supra* Chapter 5.
22. *Re Keen* [1937] Ch 236.
23. *Re Boyes* (1884) 26 Ch D 531.
24. [1967] 2 AC 291.

option to a company which acted as trustee for various family trusts enabling the shares to be acquired by the company, although it was not stated on what trusts these shares were to be held. The House of Lords held that the option was held on a resulting trust for the appellant with the result that not having divested himself completely of his interest in the shares, he was liable for surtax on the dividends paid to the college. As Lord Wilberforce stated: 'the conclusion on the facts found, is simply that the option was vested in the trustee company as a trustee on trusts, not defined at the time, possibly to be defined later. But the equitable, or beneficial interest, cannot remain in the air: the consequence in law must be that it remains in the settlor'.[25]

Failure to Exhaust the Beneficial Interest

In practice a trust does not often fail completely but a situation may quite frequently arise where there has been an incomplete disposal of the beneficial interest under a trust. Even though it may appear at the time a trust instrument or will is executed that this interest has been fully disposed of, subsequent events may occur, or fail to occur, which may change this position. In *Re Lane's Trusts*[26] by virtue of a marriage settlement a husband and wife each contributed the sum of £1,000 to a fund to be held on certain trusts with the intention that it would ultimately benefit their children. No issue of the marriage survived the husband and he died before his wife. On her death, it was held that a resulting trust in favour of the husband's administrator and the wife's executor arose. The resulting trust which will arise in such circumstances has been described as 'the last resort to which the law has recourse when the draftsman has made a blunder or failed to dispose of that which he has set out to dispose of'.[27] In *Re Cochrane*[28] a marriage settlement provided that assets were to be held on trust for the wife for life 'so long as she shall reside with [her husband]' and after her death for her husband and then for their issue as they should jointly appoint or in default of appointment at the age of 21, or in the case of daughters, on their marriage. The wife ceased to reside with her husband and her interest under the trust terminated. The income was thereafter paid to the husband until his death and the question then arose whether their children should become entitled to the income during the wife's lifetime. Harman J found that an omission had clearly been made by the draftsman of the settlement as there had been no provision to cover the events which had transpired. In the circumstances he held that a resulting trust should arise for the wife's lifetime.

---

25. *Ibid.* at 329.
26. (1863) 14 Ir Ch R 523.
27. *Re Cochrane* [1955] Ch 309, 316.
28. [1955] Ch 309.

It may often be difficult to distinguish a gift to a trustee on trust solely to carry out a specified purpose, the implication being that any remaining surplus will be held on a resulting trust, from a situation where a gift is made to a donee subject to the carrying out of some obligation in which case he will be permitted to keep whatever remains after this obligation has been fulfilled. Kekewich J commented in *Re West*[29] that '[i]t is impossible to say that because property is given to persons as trustees they therefore take no beneficial interest … [n]evertheless, there is a presumption that a gift in trust is not a beneficial gift.' This question must be resolved by seeking to ascertain the true intentions of the donor but where the non-beneficial character of the gift is clear from the face of the trust instrument or will, it will be difficult to rebut the presumption of a trust.[30] A good example of a case falling into the latter category outlined above is *Re Foord*,[31] in which a testator left his estate to his sister absolutely on trust to pay his widow an annuity. Sargant J held that the sister was beneficially entitled to the balance when the income of the estate exceeded the amount of the annuity and that no resulting trust arose.

A number of cases have dealt with the circumstances where property is given on trust for the maintenance or education of specified persons and the difficulties which arise when these purposes are fulfilled. Should the intended beneficiaries be permitted to keep the remaining trust property or should a resulting trust in favour of the donor arise once the stated objective has been achieved? Where the specified purposes can be regarded as merely constituting the testator's motive for making the gift, the donee will be permitted to retain the property, but this may be difficult to establish particularly where it is the donee's estate, rather than the donee personally, who stands to benefit. In *Re Trusts of the Abbott Fund*[32] contributions were made to a fund to be used for the maintenance of two distressed ladies. No provision had been made in relation to the disposal of the fund on the death of the survivor and Stirling J held that on her death the balance of the fund should be held on a resulting trust for the subscribers. This can be contrasted with *Re Andrew's Trust*,[33] where a fund was subscribed to by the friends of a deceased clergyman for the education of his children. Kekewich J held that when their formal education was complete, no resulting trust of the remaining balance should arise and that it should instead be divided equally amongst the children. He quoted with approval the following passage from the judgment of Wood VC in *Re Sanderson's Trusts*:[34]

---

29. [1900] 1 Ch 84, 87.
30. *Re Rees' Will Trusts* [1950] Ch 204.
31. [1922] 2 Ch 519.
32. [1900]-2 Ch 326.
33. [1905] 2 Ch 48.
34. (1857) 3 K & J 497, 503.

If a gross sum be given, or if the whole income of the property be given, and a special purpose be assigned for that gift, this Court always regards the gift as absolute, and the purpose merely as the motive of the gift, and therefore holds that the gift must take effect as to the whole sum or the whole income, as the case may be.

Kekewich J felt that he was entitled to construe 'education' in the broadest possible manner and even if a narrow interpretation were to be placed on the meaning of that word, it could be interpreted as being merely the 'motive of the gift' in the sense outlined in the passage above. This approach of treating the trust as being for the benefit of the beneficiaries generally with special reference to a particular purpose was followed in *Re Osoba*,[35] where a testator left property to his widow on trust to be used for her maintenance and 'for the training of my daughter up to university grade and for the maintenance of my aged mother'. The testator's mother predeceased him and his widow died some years later. When the daughter completed her university education the issue of whether the testator's children from a previous marriage could claim the residue on intestacy arose. Megarry VC set out the a number of general principles as follows:

I think that you have to look at the persons intended to benefit, and be ready, if they can still benefit, to treat the stated method of benefit as merely indicating purpose, and no doubt, as indicating the means of benefit which are to be in the forefront. In short, if a trust is constituted for the assistance of certain persons by certain stated means there is a sharp distinction between cases where the beneficiaries have died and cases where they are still living. If they are dead, the court is ready to hold that there is a resulting trust for the donors; for the major purpose of the trust, that of providing help and benefit for the beneficiaries comes to an end when the beneficiaries are all dead and are beyond earthly help, whether by the stated means or otherwise. But if the beneficiaries are still living, the major purpose of providing help and benefit for the beneficiaries can still be carried out even after the stated means have all been accomplished, and so the court will be ready to treat the stated means as being merely indicative and not restrictive.[36]

The Court of Appeal agreed that the testator's overriding intention was to provide for his wife and daughter and that the specified purposes should be merely regarded as an expression of his motives. In these circumstances no resulting trust arose and it was held by the Court of Appeal, varying the order

---

35. [1978] 1 WLR 791 (ChD); [1979] 1 WLR 247 (CA).
36. [1978] 1 WLR 791, 795-796.

of Megarry VC, that the beneficiaries took as joint tenants with the result that on her mother's death, the daughter became entitled to the whole of the residue.[37]

It has been argued that there has been a certain lack of consistency in the case law in this area, although some distinguishing features can be identified. While in *Abbott* it was no longer possible to use the funds for the benefit of the beneficiaries, this was clearly not the case in *Andrews* and *Osoba*, where the beneficiaries were still alive. So while it would be difficult to distinguish between the motives of the subscribers in *Abbott* and *Andrews*, the results in these cases do seem to be justified by the surrounding circumstances.

A further difficulty may arise where a fund is comprised mainly of anonymous contributions. In *Re Gillingham Bus Disaster Fund*[38] donations were made to a fund set up to benefit those injured in an accident and to provide a memorial for those who had been killed. Some of this fund was derived from contributions made by known individuals but it was comprised mainly of donations of an anonymous nature raised by street collections and other means. Harman J concluded that a resulting trust arose despite the obvious practical difficulties involved in drawing such a conclusion and that the Crown's claim to *bona vacantia* could not succeed merely because there were a number of donors whose identity could not be ascertained. He stated:

> The general principle must be that where money is held on trusts and the trusts declared do not exhaust the fund it will revert to the donor or settlor under what is called a resulting trust. The reasoning behind this is that the settlor or donor did not part with his money absolutely out and out but only *sub modo* to the intent that his wishes as declared by the declaration of trust should be carried into effect.[39]

This result was not followed in the later decision of *Re West Sussex Constabulary's Widows, Children & Benevolent (1930) Fund Trusts*,[40] in which Goff J had to determine the manner of distribution of a fund made up partly from the proceeds of entertainments and raffles, from collecting boxes, and from donations and legacies. While Goff J concluded that the gifts in the latter category were to be held on a resulting trust for the donors or their estates, he held that gifts in the first two categories went as *bona vacantia* on the basis that they were absolute out and out gifts. While the logic of the approach in *Gillingham* cannot really be faulted the practical result of such a

---

37. Megarry VC had held that the daughter and the mother's personal representatives were beneficially entitled to the residue in equal shares.
38. [1958] Ch 300. See Atiyah (1958) 74 LQR 190.
39. *Ibid.* at 310.
40. [1971] Ch 1.

finding is often wholly unsatisfactory and to this extent the conclusion reached by Goff J may therefore be preferable.[41]

The Distribution of Surplus Funds on the Dissolution of Unincorporated Associations[42]

Where surplus funds remain on the dissolution of an unincorporated association, some method of distributing these funds must be determined. In *Re Printers and Transferrers Amalgamated Trades Protection Society*[43] on the dissolution of a society formed to provide support for its members and their families, surplus funds were distributed amongst the surviving members in proportion to their contributions by way of a resulting trust. This decision has been criticised on the basis that a proper application of resulting trust principles would have ensured that such distribution would not have been confined to the surviving members on the grounds that 'death does not deprive a man of his beneficial interest'.[44] A less convenient although more principled solution was accepted by Cohen J in *Re Trusts of Hobourn Aero Components Ltd's Air Raid Distress Fund*,[45] in which he held that on the dissolution of the association the assets should be distributed amongst all the members, past and present, in shares proportionate to their contributions.

More recent case law in England has tended to lay considerably more emphasis on the manner in which an association's assets are held prior to its dissolution. Where the funds are considered as being held on trust for the association's purposes, particularly where persons other than members have also contributed, this will usually give rise to a resulting trust in the event of dissolution,[46] or where the donor effectively disclaims it, the assets will go to the Crown as *bona vacantia*.[47] Where on the other hand the donor has parted with his money on an absolute basis pursuant to a form of contract, the manner in which any surplus funds will be disposed of in the event of a dissolution will be governed by contract. This may either take the form of an express

---

41. Although to the extent that it involved the distribution of funds on the dissolution of a club or association, it is not in line with more recent authorities e.g. *Re Bucks. Constabulary Widows' and Orphans' Fund Friendly Society (No. 2)* [1979] 1 WLR 936, see *infra*.
42. For a recent article which addresses some of the issues raised in this area, see Matthews [1995] Conv 302.
43. [1899] 2 Ch 184.
44. *Re Sick and Funeral Society of St John's Sunday School, Golcar* [1973] Ch 51, 59 *per* Megarry J.
45. [1946] Ch 86.
46. E.g. the category of donations and legacies in *West Sussex Constabulary's Widows Childrens & Benevolent (1930) Fund Trusts* [1971] Ch 1.
47. E.g. the category of the proceeds of collection boxes in *West Sussex Constabulary's Widows, Childrens & Benevolent (1930) Fund Trusts* [1971] Ch 1.

provision contained in the association's rules or in the absence of such a provision, in accordance with an implied term, usually to the effect that the surplus is to be divided equally amongst those individuals who are members of the association at the time of the dissolution. In circumstances where an association may have been dissolved due to lack of members this will be impractical and the remaining assets will pass as *bona vacantia*.

The most important case in this area which seems to confirm that the modern trend is to favour a contractual approach is *Re Bucks. Constabulary Widows' and Orphans' Fund Friendly Society (No. 2)*,[48] which concerned the distribution of a fund established to provide benefits to the widows and orphans of deceased police officers and for the relief of members of the force during sickness or ill-health. When the Bucks. constabulary was amalgamated with others the issue of the proper distribution of the association's assets arose. Walton J held that the surplus funds should be distributed equally amongst the members of the association alive at the date of dissolution.[49] He also expressed the view that it is only where a club or association has become moribund that its assets should go as *bona vacantia*. This approach was followed in *Re GKN Bolts & Nuts Ltd (Automotive Division) Birmingham Works, Sports and Social Club*[50] and now seems to be generally recognised as the most practical way of resolving this question. However, it has not met with universal approval and in *Davis v. Richards & Wallington Industries Ltd*,[51] Scott J departed from the more recognised approach of analysing the manner in which the funds are held prior to dissolution and concluded that a resulting trust might still provide the correct solution in certain circumstances.[52]

The approach favoured in this jurisdiction seems to involve the rejection of the concept of a resulting trust in favour of a contractually based solution. However, there is still a lack of consensus on the issue of whether the distribution of surplus funds should be carried out on the basis of equal division or in accordance with the proportion of contributions made. In *Tierney v. Tough*[53] the manner of distribution of a fund established to provide benefits for the employees of the Grand Canal Company and their families had to be considered. O'Connor MR rejected the suitability of the resulting trust approach to the facts of the case before him in the following terms:

---

48. [1979] 1 WLR 936.
49. Contrast this with the approach taken in *Cunnack v. Edwards* [1896] 2 Ch 679 where it was held that the personal representatives of the members of an association were not entitled to a share in the society's funds when it was dissolved after the death of the widow of the last surviving member on the basis that its members had received all that for which they had contracted. See also *West Sussex Constabulary's Widows, Childrens and Benevolent (1930) Fund Trusts* [1971] Ch 1.
50. [1982] 1 WLR 774.
51. [1990] 1 WLR 1511.
52. See Gardner [1992] Conv 41 for an analysis of this decision. See also the comments of Lord Millett in *Air Jamaica Ltd v. Charlton* [1999] 1 WLR 1399, 1412.
53. [1914] 1 IR 142.

As I understand that doctrine, it applies only to a case where the trusts or purposes to which a fund or property is dedicated do not exhaust the whole interest, whereupon such part of the fund or property as is not required for carrying out the trusts or the purposes of the settlor results, or, in other words, goes back to the settlor. Now, this principle would give back to the existing members only so much of the funds as represented their own contributions to it. . . . A resulting trust would have given the fund, so far as subscribed by deceased members, to their personal representatives, and not to other parties.[54]

He concluded instead that the assets were the property of the society which was composed of individual members and that the funds should be distributed amongst the existing members in proportion to the contributions which they had made. In these circumstances he found that the fund could not be regarded as *bona vacantia* and that the Attorney General had no claim to the society's assets. While the basis for O'Connor MR's decision has been upheld as 'wholly convincing' by Walton J in *Re Bucks. Constabulary Widows' and Orphans' Fund Friendly Society (No. 2)*,[55] the manner which he prescribed for distribution of the funds has not met with similar approval.[56] Another relevant authority is the decision of Johnston J in *Feeney v. MacManus*,[57] which concerned the dissolution of the General Post Office (Dublin) Dining Club which had a membership comprised of certain classes of post office officials. The club, which provided subsidized refreshments, ceased to function following the destruction of the GPO in 1916 and when the building was re-opened in 1929, a new club was formed with similar objectives and membership. The plaintiffs, who were the secretary and treasurer of the original club, sought directions from the court in relation to the distribution of its remaining property. It was held by Johnston J that the entire fund must be distributed in equal shares amongst the individuals who were members of the club at the time of its dissolution and the personal representatives of those who had died since that date. He concluded that it would be impossible to ascertain the proportions in which each of the members had subscribed to the club's funds and assets and that accordingly, distribution had to be on an equal basis.

---

54. *Ibid.* at 155.
55. [1979] 1 WLR 936, 947. Although it could be argued that he decided simply that the inevitable consequence of following resulting trust principles would not yield the result desired, and that an approach which would allow him to distribute proportionately amongst existing members must therefore be arrived at.
56. Rickett [1980] CLJ 88, 116 suggests that it is 'an attempted half-way house which has no basis' and argues that once the manner in which the property was to be held was determined, division on the dissolution of the society ought to have been in accordance with that finding.
57. [1937] IR 23.

This principle of equal distribution would appear to be firmly entrenched in England. In *Re Sick and Funeral Society of St John's Sunday School, Golcar*[58] Megarry J agreed that membership of a club or association is primarily a question of contract and that the sums paid by members cease to be their individual property and capable of forming the subject-matter of a resulting trust. He concluded that on dissolution the only interested persons should be the existing members of the club and 'reject[ed] the basis of proportionate division in favour of equality, or division per capita.' Similarly in *Re Bucks. Constabulary Widows' and Orphans' Fund Friendly Society (No. 2)*[59] Walton J accepted that, provided that there is no other method of distribution prescribed by the terms of the contract, it should be on the basis of equality amongst the existing members. Certainly this manner of distribution seems to be more in line with the principle of a contractual relationship which governs members' entitlements and it is likely that the basis of division adopted by the High Court in *Feeney v. MacManus* will be applied in Ireland in the absence of any express provision requiring an alternative approach.

Quistclose Trusts

Considerable debate has surrounded the manner in which the so called 'Quistclose'[60] trust should be classified. While it may be considered to be a form of express trust, the secondary trust which will arise in some circumstances can be classified as an automatically resulting trust and for this reason it is convenient to deal with them at this point. Although there has been little consideration given to the type of trust recognised in the *Quistclose* case in this jurisdiction,[61] trusts of this nature are likely to assume increasing significance in the future and it is proposed to outline the basic principles which relate to them.

While it is possible to identify significant differences between the concepts of a debt and a trust, they are not always mutually exclusive. As Bingham J pointed out in *Neste Oy v. Lloyds Bank plc*[62] the existence of a contractual obligation to pay a debt is not necessarily inconsistent with the parallel existence of a trust in favour of the creditor. If a lender loans money to a borrower subject to the conditions that it is to be kept in a separate bank account and employed for a specified purpose, such an agreement may give

---

58. [1973] Ch 51.
59. [1979] 1 WLR 936.
60. Named after *Barclays Bank Ltd v. Quistclose Investments Ltd* [1970] AC 567.
61. Although an argument based on the principles set out in *Barclay's Bank Ltd v. Quistclose Investments Ltd* was put forward and rejected in *Re Money Markets International Stockbrokers Ltd* [2001] 2 IR 17.
62. [1983] 2 Lloyd's Rep 658, 663.

rise to a trust.[63] A further question arises when, for whatever reason, the money cannot be used for the purpose laid down. It would appear that in these circumstances, a primary purpose trust coupled with a secondary resulting trust for the benefit of the lender will arise.[64] This reasoning follows from the decision of the House of Lords in *Barclays Bank Ltd v. Quistclose Investments Ltd*.[65] A company, R. Ltd, which was in serious financial difficulties, borrowed a sum of money from Quistclose for the purpose of paying a dividend to shareholders under an arrangement which spelt out that the money was only to be used for this purpose and which involved this money being paid into a separate bank account in Barclays Bank, to whom R. Ltd was indebted. Before the dividend was paid, R. Ltd went into liquidation and the money in the account was claimed by both Quistclose and Barclays. The House of Lords held that the money had been paid into the account on trust for the purpose of paying the dividend and that since this purpose could not now be carried out, it was held on a resulting trust for Quistclose. As Lord Wilberforce said, the loan for the express purpose of ensuring the payment of the dividend gave rise 'to a relationship of a fiduciary character or trust, in favour, as a primary trust, of the creditors, and secondarily, if the primary trust fail[ed], of the third person',[66] namely the institution which had made the loan.

A useful summary of the circumstances giving rise to a Quistclose trust was provided by Lord Millett in *Twinsectra Ltd v. Yardley*:[67]

> [I]t is well established that a loan to a borrower for a specific purpose where the borrower is not free to apply the money for any other purpose gives rise to fiduciary obligations on the part of the borrower which a court of equity will enforce. In earlier cases the purpose was to enable the borrower to pay his creditors or some of them, but the principle is not limited to such cases.

> Such arrangements are commonly described as creating 'a Quistclose trust'. ... When the money is advanced, the lender acquires a right, enforceable in equity, to see that it is applied for the stated purpose, or more accurately to prevent its application for any other purpose. This

---

63. Where the money is used for the authorised purpose, the trust will determine and only the relationship of debtor/creditor, which involves personal liability, will remain. However, where the borrower uses the money for an unauthorised purpose, the lender will be able to employ a proprietary tracing remedy.
64. See Rickett (1991) 107 LQR 608, 617.
65. [1970] AC 567.
66. *Ibid.* at 580. This approach has been applied in other jurisdictions, e.g. in Australia (*Re Groom* (1977) 16 ALR 278) and New Zealand (by the New Zealand Court of Appeal in *General Communications Ltd v. DFC New Zealand Ltd* [1990] 3 NZLR 406).
67. [2002] 2 AC 164, 184. See further Richardson (2002) 16 Trust Law Int 165; Glister (2002) 16 Trust Law Int 223; Yeo and Tijo (2003) 119 LQR 8.

prevents the borrower from obtaining any beneficial interest in the money, at least while the designated purpose is still capable of being carried out.

In *Twinsectra*, the plaintiff lent money for the purchase of property after a solicitor gave a personal undertaking that it would be retained by his firm until applied in the acquisition of the property and would not be used for any other purpose. The solicitor who had given the undertaking went bankrupt and the lender commenced proceedings against a number of defendants, including another solicitor, on the grounds that he had dishonestly assisted in a breach of trust. The majority of the House of Lords held that a trust arose because the money had been paid into a solicitor's client account although it did not impose accessory liability. However, Lord Millett concluded that the money was held on a Quistclose trust and went on to hold the solicitor liable for assisting in a breach of trust.

In such cases, it is not necessary that the term 'trust' is used provided the conditions outlined above, namely in relation to segregation of the funds and specifying the purpose for their use, have been complied with. This point was made clear by Lord MacDermott in the Northern Ireland decision of *Re McKeown*.[68] Here the applicant loaned a sum of money to McKeown, in whose favour an arbitration award had been made, so that the latter might pay the necessary fees and costs to enable him to recover the award. The loan was made on the condition that it would only be used for the purpose of paying these fees and costs and that the applicant would be paid out of the award. McKeown was adjudicated bankrupt before he received payment of the award and the applicant sought a declaration that the official assignee held the sum of the loan on trust for him. Lord MacDermott upheld the applicant's claim and did not appear to be deterred by the lack of the type of language usually associated with the creation of trusts. However, the words used must be sufficiently certain in nature and must show a sufficient intention to create a trust.[69]

The principle laid down in *Quistclose* was applied by the English Court of Appeal in *Re EVTR*[70] in a situation where the loan was made in order that a company might purchase new equipment rather than to ensure payment of a debt. Dillon LJ concluded that: 'On *Quistclose* principles, a resulting trust in favour of the provider of the money arises when money is provided for a particular purpose only, and that purpose fails.'

It is important to point out that in the *Quistclose* case itself, the primary purpose of the trust was no longer capable of being carried out and the question of what the outcome will be where this obligation can still be fulfilled must

68. [1974] NI 226.
69. *Re Multi Guarantee Co. Ltd* [1987] BCLC 257.
70. [1987] BCLC 646.

be considered. Where a trust of this nature is created, a right to compel performance may also be vested in the 'beneficiaries' i.e. those contemplated as the ultimate recipients of the fund. This was the situation which arose in *Re Northern Development Holdings Ltd*[71] where funds were paid into a segregated account for the specific purpose of providing money for the unsecured creditors of a company which was in financial difficulties so that it might continue trading. When the company went into receivership, the question arose of who was entitled to the balance remaining in the account, the banks who had provided the funds, or the company's unsecured creditors. While as Millett[72] points out, Megarry VC might have distinguished the *Quistclose* decision on a number of grounds,[73] he held that the arrangement gave rise to a trust in that mould which might be enforced both by the banks and by the company and its unsecured creditors. This approach was followed by Peter Gibson J in *Carreras Rothmans Ltd v. Freeman Matthews Treasure Ltd*,[74] so considerable importance may attach to the question of whether the ultimate beneficiaries are in a position to enforce the obligation involved in the arrangement.

The true nature of a Quistclose trust has given rise to considerable judicial and academic debate and it is possible to identify a number of alternative theories concerning the location of the beneficial interest pending the application of the money for the stated purpose or the failure of that purpose. In *Twinsectra Ltd v. Yardley*[75] Lord Millett examined a number of possibilities although he clearly favoured the position that the beneficial interest remained in the lender throughout. An alternative view put forward by Chambers[76] is that the borrower receives the entire beneficial ownership of the money subject to a contractual right in the lender to prevent its misapplication and if the purpose for which it was lent fails a resulting trust in the latter's favour will come into being. A further alternative adopted by Peter Gibson J in *Carreras Rothmans Ltd v. Freeman Matthews Treasure Ltd*[77] is that the beneficial

---

71. Chancery Division, 6 October 1978.
72. (1985) 101 LQR 269.
73. *Ibid.* at 278. He suggested that the distinctions were that the fund in *Northern Developments* was established to enable the company to continue trading which would necessarily involve it in incurring further liabilities and because the creditors were told of the existence, size and purpose of the fund, unlike in *Quistclose* where the contemplated recipients did not even know of its existence.
74. [1984] 3 WLR 1016.
75. [2002] 2 AC 164.
76. *Resulting Trusts* (1997) Chapter 3. See Millett [1998] RLR 283. Lord Millett comments (at p. 828) that he does not believe that Chambers' analysis can survive the criticism levelled against it by Ho and Smart (2001) 21 OJLS 267.
77. [1985] Ch 207, 223. See also the *dicta* of Potter LJ in the Court of Appeal in *Twinsectra* [1999] 1 Lloyd's Rep Bank 438, 456, although he went on to consider what is effectively Chambers' analysis of the position (see *supra*), namely that the beneficial interest was in the borrower. See Tettenborn [2000] LMCLQ 459.

interest remains in suspense until the stated purpose is carried out or fails. However, Lord Millett concludes as follows:

> I would reject all the alternative analyses…and hold the Quistclose trust to be an entirely orthodox example of the kind of default trust known as a resulting trust. The lender pays the money to the borrower by way of loan, but he does not part with the entire beneficial interest in the money, and in so far as he does not it is held on a resulting trust for the lender from the outset.[78]

PRESUMED RESULTING TRUSTS

As a general principle, where the ownership of property is transferred to a grantee who gives no consideration, an inference arises that the grantee holds the property by way of a resulting trust for the grantor. However, it must be stressed that is only a presumption which can be rebutted by evidence that a contrary result was intended[79] or by the presumption of advancement,[80] which involves the inference being drawn that a gift of property was intended rather than that it should be held on a resulting trust because of the relationship between the parties.[81]

Voluntary Conveyance or Transfer

Where the owner of property makes a voluntary transfer of it to another person, a presumption of a resulting trust arises unless there is sufficient evidence of a contrary intention to rebut the presumption[82] or the presumption of advancement dictates otherwise. The presumption of a resulting trust in these circumstances applies both to voluntary conveyances and transfers of personal property. The law relating to the transfer of freehold land is now affected by statute in England, so it is advisable to examine it separately.

---

78. [2002] 2 AC 164, 192-193. However, this view has not won universal acceptance. See Payne 'Quistclose and Resulting Trusts' in *Restitution and Equity Volume One: Resulting Trusts and Equitable Compensation* (eds. Birks and Rose, 2000) pp. 88-89.
79. *McEneaney v. Shevlin* [1912] 1 IR 32; [1912] 1 IR 278. This is the essence of the distinction between automatically and presumed resulting trusts. As Swadling points out (see (1996) 16 LS 110, 113) 'an automatic resulting trust cannot be rebutted by evidence of an intention to give'.
80. *Hepworth v. Hepworth* (1870) LR 11 Eq 10.
81. Considered *infra* pp. 161-169.
82. Swadling suggests (see (1996) 16 LS 110, 111) that an examination of the historical origins of the resulting trust reveals that '*any* evidence which is inconsistent with the presumption that the transferee is to be a trustee will suffice'.

Conveyance of Land

A voluntary conveyance of freehold land 'unto the grantee and his heirs' raised a resulting use to the grantor which was executed by the Statute of Uses, with the result that the legal estate reverted to the grantor. As Wylie states: 'Since the 1634 Statute a voluntary conveyance of land in Ireland without any uses expressed is ineffective and leaves the legal estate in the land in the grantor.'[83] If the gift of land was 'unto and to the use of the grantee and his heirs' this prevented a resulting use arising and the legal estate became effectively vested in the grantee. While there is no unanimity on this question, it is likely that the express reference to the use for the grantee rebuts the presumption that he holds it for the benefit of the grantor.

In England, the Law of Property Act 1925 repealed the Statute of Uses and section 60(3) provides that 'in a voluntary conveyance a resulting trust for the grantor shall not be implied merely by reason that the property is not expressed to be conveyed for the use or benefit of the grantee.' The effect of this subsection would appear to be that a voluntary conveyance of land takes effect as expressed unless there is evidence of a contrary intention, although in view of the fact that this question has not been finally determined by the courts[84] it may still be advisable to make it clear that a gift was intended. Russell LJ remarked in *Hodgson v. Marks*[85] that it is now a 'debatable question whether on a voluntary transfer of land by A to stranger B there is a presumption of a resulting trust'. Subsequently in *Lohia v. Lohia*,[86] Nicholas Strauss QC, sitting as a Deputy High Court judge, stated that on a plain reading of section 60, the presumption of a resulting trust has been abolished in relation to voluntary conveyances of land. In his view section 60(3) provides in effect that a voluntary conveyance means what it says and that it is not necessary to use additional words to make it effective.[87] On appeal, the Court of Appeal[88] held that the trial judge's findings that a transfer of the appellant's beneficial interest to his father was intended as part of a family arrangement would rebut any presumption of a resulting trust in any event.[89] For this reason, Mummery LJ and Sir Christopher Slade stated that they would prefer to express no views on the difficult question of whether the presumption of a resulting

---

83. *Irish Land Law* (3rd ed., 1997) p. 545.
84. See the judgments of the Court of Appeal in *Lohia v. Lohia* [2001] EWCA Civ 1691, 25 October 2001.
85. [1971] Ch 892, 933. See Sweeney (1979) 14 Ir Jur (ns) 282.
86. [2001] WTLR 101.
87. See Chambers (2001) 15 Trust Law Int 26. As he points out: (at 32) '[T]he conclusion that the presumption of a resulting trust does not apply to a gratuitous transfer of land means only that the donor of land bears the onus of disproving her or his intention to give.'
88. [2001] EWCA Civ 1691, Court of Appeal, 25 October 2001.
89. Hanbury and Martin, *Modern Equity* (16th ed., 2001) p. 254.

trust on the voluntary conveyance of land survived the enactment of the section 60(3).

Transfer of Personalty

Where there is a voluntary transfer of personalty, the transferee is presumed to hold this property on a resulting trust for the transferor. This presumption will arise most often where there is a voluntary transfer into the joint names of the transferor and transferee but it may also be raised where a transfer is made solely to the transferee.[90] In *Re Vinogradoff*[91] a testatrix had transferred an £800 war loan into the joint names of herself and her four year old granddaughter but continued to receive the dividends until her death. Farwell J held that after her death, the granddaughter held the loan on a resulting trust for the testatrix's estate. This decision illustrates well that presumed resulting trusts can often arise in circumstances where it is highly questionable whether this result would actually reflect the settlor's real intentions, if he had been given an opportunity to decide on the ultimate destination of the property concerned. The importance of the principle that this presumption is rebuttable, and to this extent only operates where no evidence to the contrary has been adduced, was adverted to by Lord Upjohn in *Vandervell v. IRC*[92] in the following terms:

> Where A transfers, or directs a trustee for him, to transfer the legal estate in property to B otherwise than for valuable consideration it is a question of the intention of A in making the transfer whether B was to take beneficially or on trust, and if the latter, on what trusts. If, as a matter of construction of the document transferring the legal estate, it is possible to discern A's intentions, that is an end of the matter and no extraneous evidence is admissible to correct and qualify his intentions so ascertained.
>
> But if, as in this case (a common form share transfer) the document is silent, then there is said to arise a resulting trust in favour of A. But this is only a presumption and is easily rebutted.

This point is well illustrated in *Standing v. Bowring*,[93] where the plaintiff widow transferred stock into the joint names of herself and her godson, the defendant, having been warned that if she made the transfer she could not revoke it. It was held that the plaintiff could not claim a re-transfer on equitable grounds because she had not intended to make the defendant a mere trustee

---

90. *Re Howes* (1905) 21 TLR 501; *Re Muller* [1953] NZLR 879.
91. [1935] WN 68.
92. [1967] 2 AC 291, 312.
93. (1885) 31 Ch D 282.

except in relation to the dividends payable on the stock. On the contrary, there was ample evidence to suggest that at the time of the transfer she intended to benefit the defendant and the presumption of a resulting trust was therefore rebutted. Cotton LJ stated:

> [T]he rule is well settled that where there is a transfer by a person into his own name jointly with that of a person who is not his child, or his adopted child, then there is *prima facie* a resulting trust for the transferor. But that is a presumption capable of being rebutted by shewing that at the time the transferor intended a benefit to the transferee.[94]

Joint Deposit Accounts[95]

One of the most common situations in which a transfer of property takes place into the joint names of the transferor and transferee is where a joint deposit account is opened. This is usually done in a manner which allows the transferor or depositor alone to retain dominion over the money in the account during his lifetime but which displays the intention that the balance should go to the other party should he survive him. Where such an arrangement is put in place the question arises whether the money which remains in the account on the depositor's death should be subject to a resulting trust in favour of his estate or whether it can be paid over to the other party. The approach traditionally followed was set out by Gordon J in *Doyle v. Byrne*[96] as follows:

> Where there is a transfer by a person into his own name jointly with that of a person who is not his child or adopted child, of money on deposit receipt there is, *prima facie*, a resulting trust to the transferor.

If this presumption is to be rebutted, the onus lies on the transferee to show that the transferor intended that the beneficial interest should pass to him.[97] The main policy argument against allowing the survivor or transferee to take a beneficial interest in circumstances where he has made no contribution to the monies in the account is that such an interest arguably passes as a form of testamentary disposition which has not complied with the formalities required by the Succession Act 1965. As we have seen above in relation to secret trusts, the courts in this jurisdiction have not always taken such a strict approach

---

94. *Ibid.* at 287.
95. See generally Sheridan (1950-52) 9 NILQ 101; Montrose (1950-52) 9 NILQ 148; Delany (1957) 23 Ir Jur 31; Brady (1990) 12 DULJ (ns) 155; Miller (1992) 6 Trust Law Int 57.
96. (1922) 56 ILTR 125, 126-127.
97. *McEneaney v. Shevlin* [1912] 1 IR 32, 36 *per* Ross J; *Owens v. Greene* [1932] IR 225, 237 *per* Kennedy CJ.

to this issue. It is ironic then that in the area of presumed resulting trusts, which are in theory supposed to give effect to a settlor or testator's intentions, the judiciary had, until the recent Supreme Court decision in *Lynch v. Burke*,[98] adopted a more restrictive approach to this policy question and often succeeded in arriving at a result which might be quite contrary to the transferor's actual intentions.

Although it was held in *Diver v. McCrea*[99] that no resulting trust arose even in circumstances where the depositer had kept control and dominion over the monies in a joint account during his lifetime, the Supreme Court in *Owens v. Greene*[100] declined to follow this approach. In that case, the deceased kept sums of money on deposit in the joint names of himself and a nephew, and of himself and a distant relative. He retained control over these funds during his lifetime but made it clear that he wished the money to go to his co-depositors in the event of his death. The Supreme Court held that these persons, who were volunteers, had failed to rebut the presumption of a resulting trust in favour of the deceased's personal representatives. Kennedy CJ stated the while it was open to the plaintiffs to seek to rebut the presumption of a resulting trust which arose in the circumstances this could only be done by establishing that it was the deceased's intention when putting the money in the accounts to give to the plaintiffs 'then and there and by that act, a right, that is to say an immediate present right to take the monies with which he associated their respective names by survivorship'.[101] It would not suffice to show a testamentary intention on the part of the deceased as a disposition of a testamentary nature could, in the opinion of the Chief Justice, only be made by will. Fitzgibbon J came to the same conclusion on the facts:

> In my opinion the plaintiffs have failed to establish any present intention on the part of [the deceased] to part with his property in, and absolute dominion over, the deposited money during his lifetime, and a disposition, to take effect only upon his death, if he should not have previously disposed of the money, cannot be effected except by a declaration of trust, which is admitted not to have been made by him.[102]

The reasoning in *Owens* was applied by Judge Sheridan in the Circuit Court decision of *Daniels v. Dunne*.[103] The deceased opened a joint account in the names of himself and the defendant. Although the words 'payable to either or survivor' appeared in the deposit account book, the customer history card

---

98.   [1995] 2 IR 159.
99.   (1908) 42 ILTR 249.
100. [1932] IR 225.
101. *Ibid.* at 237-238.
102. *Ibid.* at 251-252.
103. (1990) 8 ILT 35 (Circuit Court, 2 February 1989).

stated that withdrawals were to be signed by the deceased only or his survivor. Judge Sheridan found that the deceased had retained in law total dominion over the money in the account until the time of his death and that *prima facie* the defendant held the monies in the account on a resulting trust in favour of the deceased's estate.

The most interesting recent case in this area is that of *Lynch v. Burke*[104] and both the High Court judgment of O'Hanlon J and that of O'Flaherty J in the Supreme Court include a useful analysis of the law in certain other common law jurisdictions in relation to the ownership of monies remaining in a joint deposit account on the death of the depositer. The Supreme Court decision is particularly noteworthy as it reversed the position taken by the courts in this jurisdiction for over six decades. Before examining the reasoning of the Supreme Court in more detail it is useful to explain how pressure to take such a step built up over the preceding years. In *Lynch* the deceased opened a joint account in the names of herself and the first named defendant, her niece. The latter had travelled from Scotland at her aunt's request and both signed the necessary documentation for opening the account. All lodgments were made by the deceased and the account deposit book was endorsed payable to the deceased only or survivor. The deceased bequeathed all her property to the plaintiff and O'Hanlon J held that a resulting trust arose and that therefore the plaintiff was entitled to the money remaining in the joint account. However, it is necessary to examine in more detail precisely how O'Hanlon J arrived at this conclusion. He stated that as a general principle where money is deposited in a joint account by a person who subsequently dies, there is an equitable presumption of a resulting trust against the survivor in favour of the estate of the deceased in respect of the beneficial interest in the monies remaining on deposit at the time of death. On the facts, O'Hanlon J held that the deceased had intended that the first named defendant would be entitled by right of survivorship to the beneficial interest in this money and the equitable presumption in favour of the deceased's estate was therefore rebutted. However, he felt obliged on the authority of the *Owens* decision to hold that the transaction was an invalid gift and an unsuccessful attempt to make a testamentary disposition otherwise than by will. Despite this conclusion there are definite signs in O'Hanlon J's judgment that he was unhappy with the reasoning in the earlier Supreme Court decision. As he stated:

> I consider that in the present case I am bound to follow and apply [*Owens v. Greene*] but having regard to the fact that it is a decision which appears to conflict with the interpretation of this branch of the law in so many other common law jurisdictions it might well be a case where the

---

104. [1990] 1 IR 1 (HC); [1995] 2 IR 159 (SC).

Supreme Court would be disposed to review again the correctness of that decision, if a suitable opportunity arose for so doing.[105]

This statement was quoted with approval by Morris J in *AIB Finance Ltd v. Sligo County Council*,[106] although once again the result in that case was similar to that reached in *Owens v. Greene*. The deceased, a priest who wished to benefit his home town in Co. Sligo, had lodged a sum of money in a bank account in the joint names of himself and Sligo County Council with the intention that the money should be used to carry out a specific project under an urban renewal scheme. The priest died and the question arose whether his executor or the county council was entitled to the monies in the account. Although the mandate executed in favour of the bank contained a provision that these monies should be paid to the county council as survivor on the priest's death, there was evidence that the deceased had intended to and had in fact retained control over these funds during his lifetime. Morris J concluded that there was at most an incomplete gift and that the relationship of trustee and beneficiary had not existed as between the deceased and the county council. Therefore he found that a resulting trust in favour of the deceased's executor arose.

In the circumstances it was not necessary for Morris J to decide whether the reasoning in *Owens* was correct as there was insufficient evidence to rebut the presumption of a resulting trust in favour of the deceased's estate. Nevertheless it is interesting that he saw fit to expressly approve of O'Hanlon J's *dicta* in *Lynch* set out above[107] and this could be construed as evidence of the fact that the courts were increasingly dissatisfied with the *Owens* approach which was certainly out of line with the view taken in relation to this question in most other common law jurisdictions.

While some earlier Canadian cases had been decided on the basis of the approach laid down in *Owens*,[108] different reasoning was employed by the Supreme Court of Ontario in *Re Reid*[109] and by the High Court of Australia in *Russell v. Scott*.[110] In the latter case an elderly lady transferred money into an account in the joint names of herself and her nephew. Although Dixon and Evatt JJ found that she did not intend her nephew to benefit during her lifetime, they concluded that 'by placing the money in the joint names, the deceased did then and there and by that act give a present right of survivorship'. The court therefore interpreted her actions as giving the nephew an immediate

105. [1990] 1 IR 1, 13.
106. [1995] 1 ILRM 81.
107. See *supra* n. 105.
108. *Hill v. Hill* (1904) 8 OLR 710; *Shortill v. Grannan* (1920) 55 DLR 416; *Larondeau v. Laurendeau* [1954] 4 DLR 293.
109. (1921) 50 OLR 595. See also *Re Aylward* [1955] 5 DLR 753.
110. (1936) 55 CLR 440.

beneficial interest which, however, did not fall into possession until her death and which might be revoked up until that time. This approach, which involved regarding both parties upon the opening of the account as being jointly entitled at common law to a chose in action consisting of their contractual right against the bank which would accrue to the survivor, was a plausible alternative to the reasoning employed in *Owens* and avoided the difficulties inherent in regarding the transaction as a testamentary disposition, namely the need for compliance with the requisite statutory formalities.

O'Hanlon J in *Lynch* certainly seemed to favour this reasoning and Miller[111] suggested that the Supreme Court in *Owens* might not have ruled out reliance on such an approach by speaking in terms of rebutting the presumption of a resulting trust if the plaintiffs had been given 'then and there, a right, that is to say an immediate present right, to take the moneys.'

The position in England would appear to be as set out in Halsbury as follows:

> [T]he fact that the transferor retains control during his lifetime over the property transferred into the joint names does not prevent the gift, even where it appears to be of a testamentary nature and not in conformity with the Wills Act 1837, from being an effective and complete gift *inter vivos* from the time of making, so as to vest the legal title to the property in the donee by survivorship on the death of the transferor.[112]

In *Young v. Sealey*,[113] Romer J, although he confessed that the reasoning in *Owens* appealed to him, concluded that the survivor should take free of a resulting trust in these circumstances, an approach which was followed in *Re Figgis*.[114]

So, by the time the Supreme Court was called upon to make a decision in *Lynch*, it was faced with persuasive arguments requiring it to re-examine the judgment of the former Supreme Court in *Owens*. While it could have been argued that the approach favoured in England and Australia and more latterly in Canada seemed to allow the making of so-called 'nuncupative wills' where there was no real justification for such a course of action, such as avoiding fraud, any policy argument against a more flexible approach was not easily reconcilable with the rationale of a resulting trust which might be said to

---

111. (1992) 6 Trust Law Int 57, 59.
112. *Laws of England*, 4th edition, Volume 20 paragraph 40. As quoted by O'Hanlon J in *Lynch v. Burke* [1990] 1 IR 1, 13.
113. [1949] Ch 278.
114. [1969] 1 Ch 123. See also *Aroso v. Coutts & Co.* [2002] 1 All ER (Comm) 241 where Collins J held that sufficient evidence had been adduced to displace the presumption of a resulting trust and to prove that the deceased intended to give his co-depositor a beneficial interest in the assets in the bank account. See further Walford (2001) 31 Tr & Est LJ 9.

depend on the implied intention of the donor.[115] It was certainly arguable that insistence on strict compliance with statutory provisions designed to prevent fraud was not necessary or even desirable where no danger of fraud would arise in bypassing their requirements, and where such an approach gave effect to a donor's real intentions about the disposition of his property on his death.

Delivering the judgment of the Supreme Court,[116] O'Flaherty J considered the legal effect of opening a deposit account in joint names. He said that by her presence and signature, it was manifest that the first named defendant was a party to the contract from the outset and she must be entitled to claim as a party to the contract under its terms. He quoted with approval from the judgment of Dixon and Evatt JJ in *Russell v. Scott* and stated that since historically, the concept of a resulting trust was an invention of equity to defeat the misappropriation of property as a consequence of potentially fraudulent or improvident transactions, it would be paradoxical if the doctrine was allowed to defeat the clear intention of the donor as found by the trial judge. O'Flaherty J pointed out that in *Owens v. Greene,* the Supreme Court had been concerned to emphasize the importance of testamentary dispositions being required to comply with statutory requirements. He commented that if the arrangement in the case before him was not testamentary, which in his view it was not, these statutory requirements had no application. O'Flaherty J also stated that *Owens* had given cause for unease on a number of grounds and concluded that it was wrongly decided and should be overruled. He said that at law the defendant had a legal interest in the monies on deposit either by reason of the contractual relationship of the parties or in the alternative as a gift, which admittedly was not a completed gift in the conventional sense but was one which should be upheld as being a gift subject to a contingency, namely, the donor's death.

One cannot but agree with O'Flaherty J's conclusion that the result arrived at by the Supreme Court will introduce a measure of consistency into this area of the law, and as he stated 'restore.. equity to the high ground which it should properly occupy to ameliorate the harshness of common law rules on occasion rather than itself be an instrument of injustice'.[117] However, as Capper points out, there are conceptual difficulties with both the 'gift theory' and the 'contract theory' and as he comments, 'the underlying doctrinal principles remain very unclear'.[118] Capper is probably correct in suggesting that the 'contract theory' is preferable, and on this basis, provided that the survivor has signed the necessary contractual documents and there is sufficient evidence of the donor's intention to rebut the presumption of a resulting trust, the

---

115. See Brady (1990) 12 DULJ (ns) 155, 164-165.
116. [1995] 2 IR 159. See further Capper (1996) 47 NILQ 281; Breslin [1996] Comm LP 12; O'Doherty (1996) 14 ILT 167; Mee (1996) 90 GILSI 70.
117. *Ibid.* at 168.
118. (1996) 47 NILQ 281, 293.

outcome in similar cases in the future should be the same as in *Lynch*. So, while in some respects the manner in which this result was achieved was somewhat convoluted, it can be said with some degree of certainty that the Supreme Court judgment should have laid to rest the rather paradoxical decision of *Owens v. Greene* once and for all.

Joint Bank Accounts of Husband and Wife

In the light of the Supreme Court's decision in *Lynch v. Burke*[119] it should be possible for either spouse to rebut the presumption of a resulting trust where an account has been opened in their joint names and the contributing spouse subsequently dies. Where the sole contributing spouse is a husband, this issue may in any event be resolved by the application of the presumption of advancement, which will be considered in more detail below.[120] So the fact that this presumption might be applied in cases where the sole contributing spouse was a husband led to different principles being applied by the courts even prior to the decision of the Supreme Court in *Lynch* which are worth noting. Dixon and Evatt JJ summarized the position as follows in *Russell v. Scott*:[121]

> [T]here is much authority to the effect that where a joint bank account is opened by husband and wife with the intention that the survivor shall take beneficially the balance at credit on the death of one of them that intention prevails, and, on the death of the husband, the wife takes the balance beneficially, although the deceased husband supplied all the money paid in and during his life the property was used exclusively for his own purposes.

So, where money is deposited by a husband in an account in their joint names the presumption of a resulting trust in these circumstances may be rebutted by the presumption of advancement and *prima facie* the relationship between the parties will usually result in the wife taking the balance remaining in the account beneficially.[122] So, in *Talbot v. Cody*,[123] where a man lodged sums of money in a number of accounts in the joint names of himself and his wife, it was held that his wife, who survived him, was beneficially entitled to these funds. Similarly, in *Colohan v. Condrin*,[124] it was held by O'Connor MR that the presumption that a wife should be beneficially entitled to monies in an

---

119. [1995] 2 IR 159.
120. See *infra* pp. 161-169.
121. (1936) 55 CLR 440, 451.
122. *Re Young* (1885) 28 Ch D 705.
123. (1874) IR 10 Eq 138. See also *Re Hood* [1923] 1 IR 109.
124. [1914] 1 IR 89.

account in these circumstances was not affected by the fact that the name of her husband's brother was also included on the deposit receipt. As he stated: 'It is well settled that if a deposit is made with a bank by a husband of his own money in the names of himself and his wife, there is a presumption that it is intended as an advancement in the event of her surviving her husband.'[125]

However, such a result should not always be assumed and one question which must be addressed is whether the account was opened merely for the parties' mutual convenience or whether it was intended as a means of making provision for the other spouse.[126] In certain circumstances the presumption that the surviving spouse was to benefit may be rebutted by showing that this was not the intention of the spouse who deposited the money, so in *Marshal v. Crutwell*[127] it was held that a wife was not beneficially entitled to monies remaining in a joint account arranged by her husband solely as a matter of convenience to enable her to sign cheques because of his failing health. Alternatively the depositing spouse may subsequently take some action which will effectively prevent the other from taking a beneficial interest, as in *M'Dowell v. McNeilly*,[128] where a husband endorsed a deposit receipt in favour of a third party who subsequently cashed it.

One related matter which will more usually be of importance where spouses separate is that where a husband and wife open a joint bank account with the intention of pooling their resources, the monies in this account will not be divided in accordance with their respective contributions but rather on an equal basis.[129] However, either spouse can acquire sole beneficial ownership of assets purchased with monies from such a joint account.[130]

Purchase in the Name of Another

A variation of the principle considered above in relation to voluntary conveyances or transfers of property applies where property is purchased in the name of another. So, where a person provides the purchase money for property, whether real or personal, which is conveyed or transferred to another person or to himself and the other person jointly, it is presumed that the latter holds the property on a resulting trust for the person who provided the purchase money.[131] This principle was set out by Eyre CB in *Dyer v. Dyer*[132] as follows:

---

125. *Ibid.* at 94-95.
126. *Re Figgis* [1969] 1 Ch 123.
127. (1875) LR 20 Eq 328.
128. [1917] 1 IR 117.
129. *Jones v. Maynard* [1951] Ch 572.
130. *Re Bishop* [1965] Ch 450, 456.
131. It was suggested by Pearce (see (1990) 41 NILQ 43) that the Statute of Uses might still have a role to play in this area and that the Act might execute the trust under which a person with no documentary title to property is held to have a beneficial interest by reason of a contribution to its acquisition. However, Mee argues

The clear result of all the cases, without a single exception, is, that the trust of a legal estate ... whether taken in the names of the purchasers and others jointly, or in the names of others without that of the purchaser; whether in one name or several, whether jointly or *successive*, results to the man who advances the purchase money.

The operation of this principle is well illustrated by the decision of Pim J in *Re Slattery*.[133] A policy of insurance was taken out by Lawrence Slattery in the name of and on the life of his brother. He paid the premiums on the policy and retained it in his possession and at no time did his brother have any interest in the policy or make any claim to it. When his brother died it was held that Lawrence Slattery was entitled to the monies payable on the policy; there was no evidence of any intention to make a gift of the interest under the policy to his brother and a resulting trust therefore arose.

The presumption of a resulting trust applies equally where two or more persons advance purchase money jointly but the property is conveyed or transferred to only one of them, in which case there will be a resulting trust in favour of the other party or parties proportionate to the extent of the contributions made.[134] This principle has proved to be extremely important in resolving disputes relating to the beneficial ownership of family property, which will be considered in detail below.[135]

However, it must be stressed that the presumption which arises in any of the above circumstances is liable to be rebutted, either by evidence that the purchaser intended to benefit the other party or because 'the purchaser is under a species of natural obligation to provide for the nominee',[136] known as the presumption of advancement.[137] These two factors, which may lead to the rebuttal of the presumption of a resulting trust in the case of a voluntary

---

convincingly against such a proposition (see (1996) 47 NILQ 367) pointing out that the doctrine of the purchase money resulting trust was developed by the courts after the enactment of the Statute of Uses and after the statute had been made a dead letter through the creation of trusts by means of a 'use upon a use'.

132. (1788) 2 Cox Eq Cas 92, 93.
133. [1917] 2 IR 278. See also *Re Scottish Equitable Life Assurance Society* [1902] 1 Ch 282 which concerned a similar factual situation and in which the *dicta* of Eyre CB in *Dyer* was cited with approval by Joyce J.
134. E.g. *McGillycuddy v. Joy* [1959] IR 189.
135. See *infra* pp. 177-194.
136. *Murless v. Franklin* (1818) 1 Swans 13, 17.
137. It should be pointed out that there is in any event increasing unease about the manner in which these presumptions, particularly the presumption of advancement, operate. Chambers has recently suggested (2001) 15 Trust Law Int 26, 32 that the courts should rely on a presumption only when it is otherwise impossible to ascertain the intention of the donor and that if all the circumstances of a case indicate the probable intention of the apparent donor, a presumption is unnecessary.

conveyance or transfer or where property is purchased in the name of another, will now be considered.

Rebutting the Presumption of a Resulting Trust

Evidence of an Intention to Benefit

Where evidence establishes that the transferor or purchaser intended to benefit the donee, no resulting trust will arise. This is well illustrated by *Standing v. Bowring*,[138] where evidence showed that the plaintiff transferor had intended to benefit her godson when she transferred stock into his name. The judgment of the Court of Appeal also makes it clear that the relevant time for establishing evidence of intention to make a gift is the time of the transfer and once this is shown, a donor cannot subsequently change his mind and withdraw this intention. A good illustration of this principle is provided by the recent decision of the British Columbia Court of Appeal in *Romaine Estate v. Romaine*[139] in which an uncle transferred property to his nephew before his death in order to save taxes and subsequently regretted his decision. Levine JA confirmed that 'all of the evidence of the donor's intention, written or oral, at the time a transfer that is claimed to be a gift was made, is admissible to determine whether the transfer was a gift.'[140] However, the Court of Appeal ruled that the trial judge had erred in admitting statements made after the parties fell out to support the presumption of a resulting trust. All the evidence of the uncle's intentions up to that time suggested that he intended to transfer the property to his nephew and it was held that when all the admissible evidence was considered it rebutted the presumption of a resulting trust.

Another decision which casts light on how the presumption of a resulting trust may be rebutted is *Fowkes v. Pascoe*,[141] where a Mrs Baker made various purchases of stock in the joint names of herself and the son of her daughter-in-law. After her death, the Court of Appeal upheld this individual's claim to be entitled to the stock on the basis that the purchase had been intended as a gift and the presumption of a resulting trust had therefore been rebutted. The general principle was well set out by Mellish LJ:

> [A] man may make an investment of stock in the name of himself and some other person, although not a child or wife, yet in such a position to him as to make it extremely probable that the investment was intended

---

138. (1885) 31 Ch D 282 considered above in the context of voluntary transfers. See also *Dewar v. Dewar* [1975] 1 WLR 1532 where the presumption was likewise rebutted by evidence of an intention to make a gift.
139. (2001) 205 DLR (4th) 320.
140. *Ibid.* at 335.
141. (1875) 10 Ch App 343.

as a gift. In such a case, although the rule of law, if there was evidence at all, would compel the Court to say that the presumption of trust must prevail, even if the Court might not believe that the fact was in accordance with the presumption, yet, if there is evidence to rebut the presumption, then, in my opinion, the Court must go into the actual facts.[142]

Where Fraud or Illegality Exists

Where a trust is intentionally created for an illegal purpose, a resulting trust in favour of the settlor or testator will not arise unless there is a failure to carry out this illegal purpose.[143] In *Ayerst v. Jenkins*,[144] a settlor's personal representatives claimed that a resulting trust arose in circumstances where a settlement had been founded on an illegal consideration, namely the settlor's marriage to his deceased wife's sister, which both parties knew to be illegal at that time. Lord Selborne refused the claim on the basis that a settlor was not entitled to relief in this form on the grounds of illegality of his own intention or purpose unless the direct result of refusing such relief would be 'to effectuate an unlawful object or to defeat a legal prohibition or to protect a fraud.'[145]

It should be noted that where a transferor does not carry out the illegal purpose which was intended at the time of making the transfer, he may adduce evidence of his repudiated intention so as to recover the property.[146] This principle was confirmed by the decision of Hoffman J in *Sekhon v. Alissa*,[147] where a property was conveyed into the sole name of her daughter by a mother with the intention of avoiding liability to capital gains tax when the property was ultimately sold. Hoffman J held that as this unlawful purpose had not yet been carried out, the mother could rely on evidence of this purpose and found that the presumption of a resulting trust in the mother's favour had not been rebutted.[148]

It would appear that even where a transfer of property occurs for an illegal purpose, this will not prevent a resulting trust arising in favour of the transferee where the claim can be made without reliance on this unlawful purpose, sometimes referred to as the 'reliance principle'. This point is illustrated by the important decision of the House of Lords in *Tinsley v. Milligan*.[149] Two

---

142. *Ibid.* at 352–353.
143. *Symes v. Hughes* (1870) LR 9 Eq 475.
144. (1873) LR 16 Eq 275.
145. *Ibid.* at 283.
146. Although not where his illegal purpose has merely been frustrated by circumstances beyond his control; *Bigos v. Boustead* [1951] 1 All ER 92.
147. [1989] 2 FLR 94. See Kodilinye [1990] Conv 213.
148. A similar principle now operates in relation to rebutting the presumption of advancement. See *Tribe v. Tribe* [1996] Ch 107.
149. [1994] 1 AC 340.

women purchased a house in the plaintiff's sole name but on the understanding that they should be joint beneficial owners of the property in order to assist in the perpetration of a fraud on the Department of Social Security. When the parties quarrelled, the defendant disclosed the fraud to the department and the plaintiff moved out and brought proceedings against the defendant claiming possession and sole ownership of the property. The defendant counter-claimed and sought a declaration that the property was held on trust for the parties in equal shares. The majority of the House of Lords held that a party to an illegality can recover by virtue of a legal or equitable interest in property provided that he can establish his title without relying on his own illegality. In the circumstances it was held that the defendant had established a presumption of a resulting trust by showing that she had contributed to the purchase price of the house and that there was a common understanding between the parties that they owned it jointly. There was no need for her to establish the reason why the house had been conveyed solely into the plaintiff's name and it was held that there was no evidence to rebut the presumption of a resulting trust.[150]

The principles established by the House of Lords in *Tinsley*, although regarded as controversial, have been applied by the Court of Appeal on a number of occasions. In *Silverwood v. Silverwood*,[151] an elderly lady transferred monies into bank accounts in the names of two of her grandchildren and then applied for and received income support from the DSS without disclosing the fact she had made the transfer. After her death her executor claimed that the grandchildren held the monies on a resulting trust for her estate. The Court of Appeal upheld the claim as the executor had not been forced to rely on any illegality in order to establish a resulting trust in favour of the estate.[152] A similar result ensued in *Lowson v. Coombes*[153] in which the plaintiff and defendant both contributed to the purchase price of a house but it was conveyed into the defendant's sole name in order to avoid the plaintiff's wife having any claim on it. The Court of Appeal found that although the house had been conveyed into the defendant's sole name with the illegal purpose of frustrating any potential claim by the plaintiff's wife pursuant to section 37(2)(b) of the

---

150. However, as we will see *infra* (see p. 175), the position is different where the relationship between the parties gives rise to the presumption of advancement. As Lord Browne-Wilkinson made clear (at 372) in such cases in order to establish any claim, the plaintiff will have to adduce evidence sufficient to rebut the presumption of a gift and in so doing will normally have to plead, and give evidence of, the underlying illegal purpose.
151. (1997) 74 P & CR 453.
152. However, it should be noted that Peter Gibson LJ accepted (at 457) that 'it would be absurd as well as unjust if a claimant, claiming a resulting trust, could not lead evidence of fraud in order to disprove a spurious defence.'
153. [1999] Ch 373.

Matrimonial Causes Act 1973, the plaintiff was entitled to a declaration that the defendant held half the beneficial interest on a resulting trust for him. In the view of Nourse LJ the case before the court was 'in all material respects ... on all fours with [*Tinsley v. Milligan*]' and the plaintiff was entitled to relief as he had not been forced to rely on the illegality in order to establish a resulting trust in his favour.

The Presumption of Advancement

The presumption of advancement arises where because of the relationship which exists between the parties, the donor or purchaser is under an obligation recognised in equity to provide for the person to whom the property is given.[154] Just as the presumption of a resulting trust can be rebutted by evidence showing that a gift was intended, so the presumption of advancement can be rebutted by evidence which establishes that the donor did not intend to benefit or make provision for the donee.[155] The manner in which these presumptions operate was summarised by Viscount Simonds in *Shephard v. Cartwright*:[156]

> The law is clear that on the one hand where a man purchases shares and they are registered in the name of a stranger there is a resulting trust in favour of the purchaser; on the other hand, if they are registered in the name of a child or one to whom the purchaser then stood *in loco parentis*, there is no such resulting trust, but a presumption of advancement. Equally it is clear that the presumption [of advancement] may be rebutted but should not . . . give way to slight circumstances.

It should be noted that the presumption of advancement has been regarded in various quarters in more recent times as being an outdated concept which can operate in an anomalous and arbitrary manner and which may be constitutionally suspect. As a result it is fair to say that in circumstances where it has traditionally been held to exist, it has become easier to rebut and where a relationship exists which does not give rise to the presumption on the basis of established principles, evidence which shows that a gift was intended will be readily accepted by a court. However, despite this erosion of traditional principles, it has recently been confirmed by the courts in this jurisdiction that the presumption has the status of an equitable doctrine rather than a mere rule of evidence[157] and must be recognised as such. Traditionally the

---

154. *Bennet v. Bennet* (1879) 10 Ch D 474, 476 *per* Jessel MR.
155. *Anson v. Anson* [1953] 1 QB 636; *Re Gooch* (1890) 62 LT 384. See *infra* pp.169-176.
156. [1955] AC 431, 445.
157. *Per* Henchy J in *R.F. v. M.F.* [1995] 2 ILRM 572 and *per* O'Sullivan J in *Malone v. McQuaid* High Court 1996 No. 392 Sp, 28 May 1998.

presumption of advancement has operated in three types of relationship which will be examined in turn before consideration is given to the question of whether its ambit might be extended further.

Husband and Wife

The presumption of advancement arises where a husband transfers property to his wife or purchases it in her name.[158] However, traditionally where a wife bought property and put it in her husband's name, this did not give rise to the presumption of advancement and instead a resulting trust was presumed.[159] The general principle was set out by Malins VC in *Re Eykyn's Trusts*:[160] 'The law of this Court is perfectly settled that when a husband transfers money or other property into the name of his wife only, then the presumption is, that it is intended as a gift or advancement to the wife absolutely at once. ...' As we have seen above in the context of joint bank accounts, this principle traditionally operated where a husband placed money in a bank account in the joint names of himself and his wife.[161] It appears to apply even if the marriage is subsequently dissolved or declared voidable,[162] but not where the marriage is later declared void *ab initio*.[163] The presumption will apply as between engaged couples who subsequently marry,[164] but not between co-habitees.[165]

Lord Diplock in *Pettitt v. Pettitt*[166] expressed his view that the presumption was an anachronistic concept in the following terms:

> It would, in my view, be an abuse of the legal technique for ascertaining or imputing intention to apply to transactions between the post war generation of married couples 'presumptions' which are based upon inferences of fact which an earlier generation of judges drew as the most likely intentions of earlier generations of spouses belonging to the propertied classes of a different social era.

Certainly, in this jurisdiction, in view of the constitutional guarantee of equality, it would seem difficult to justify the continued existence of a principle which undoubtedly seems to benefit a wife and not a husband. However, in *W. v.*

---

158. See e.g. *Irwin v. O'Connell* [1936] IR 44.
159. *Mercier v. Mercier* [1903] 2 Ch 98.
160. (1877) 6 Ch D 115, 118.
161. *Talbot v. Cody* (1874) IR 10 Eq 138; *Colohan v. Condrin* [1914] 1 IR 89, 94.
162. *Dunbar v. Dunbar* [1909] 2 Ch 639.
163. See *Re D'Altroy's Will Trusts* [1968] 1 WLR 120 which establishes this point in another context.
164. *Moate v. Moate* [1948] 2 All ER 486; *Ulrich v. Ulrich* [1968] 1 WLR 180.
165. *Calverley v. Green* (1984) 56 ALR 483; *Lowson v. Coombes* [1999] Ch 373.
166. [1970] AC 777, 824.

W.,[167] although it was not strictly necessary for his decision, Finlay P took the opportunity to reiterate that where a husband makes a contribution to the purchase of property in his wife's sole name, he will be presumed to have intended to advance his wife unless that presumption is rebutted.

In *J.C. v. J.H.C.*[168] Keane J held that a husband and wife should share the beneficial interest in property, which although conveyed to them both as joint tenants was purchased entirely out of monies provided by the husband. Keane J stated as follows:

> Where property is taken in the joint names of two or more persons, but the purchase money is advanced by one of them alone, the law presumes a resulting trust in favour of the person who advanced the purchase money. This presumption may however be rebutted; and in particular the circumstance of the person into whose name the property is conveyed being the wife of the person advancing the money may be sufficient to rebut the presumption under the doctrine of advancement.[169]

However, Keane J went on to refer to the remarks of Lord Diplock in *Pettitt v. Pettitt*,[170] which cast doubt on the relevance of the presumption, and he appeared to base his decision on the fact that the evidence 'overwhelmingly' reinforced the presumption of advancement, which he said would arise had there been no other evidence as to the parties' intentions. Therefore, one could argue that Keane J appeared to regard the presumption of advancement as being relevant only where evidence to establish the parties' true intentions was lacking.

One of the most important authorities in the area is the Supreme Court decision of *R.F. v M.F.*,[171] which also concerned a dispute about ownership of property purchased by a husband in the parties' joint names. Henchy J appeared to accept the relevance of the presumption of advancement but went on to hold that it had been clearly rebutted in the circumstances of the case. The evidence established that the wife had refused to live in the house unless it was in their joint names and despite her promise to live there, which Henchy J considered to be an integral part of the arrangement, she had never done so.

The most recent decision dealing with the application of the presumption of advancement in this context is that of O'Sullivan J in *Malone v. McQuaid*.[172] The defendant was the liquidator of a company in which the first and second named plaintiffs, a wife and husband respectively, were one-third shareholders.

---

167. [1981] ILRM 202, 204.
168. High Court 1982 No. 4931P (Keane J) 4 August 1982.
169. *Ibid*. at 3.
170. [1970] AC 777, 824.
171. [1995] 2 ILRM 572.
172. High Court 1996 No. 392 Sp, 28 May 1998.

The defendant obtained a judgment against the husband and registered that judgment as a mortgage against the latter's alleged equitable interest in a property, which was not the family home. This house was registered in his wife's name and she was at the time negotiating a sale to a purchaser which subsequently fell through. In considering the plaintiffs' claim for damages against the defendant in relation to the loss of the sale, it became necessary for the court to establish whether the husband had an equitable interest in the house. O'Sullivan J accepted that assuming that the husband had provided some or all of the monies for the purchase of the house, 'whatever about the [husband's] obligation to provide [the house] for the benefit of his wife, he was clearly under an obligation to provide for his children'.[173] Accordingly he considered that he should apply the presumption of advancement unless it had been rebutted on the facts. O'Sullivan J pointed to the fact that there was some evidence that the husband had not intended to confer a beneficial interest on his wife and he had allegedly told a third party that he wanted to put the property in her name so that the tenants would not know that he owned the building. However, O'Sullivan J stated that the evidence which tended to rebut the presumption of advancement was of an indirect nature and he concluded that on the overall balance of the evidence it had not been rebutted and applied to the case before him. He therefore held that the entire beneficial interest in the property was vested in the wife, although he found that the registration of the judgment had not caused the abandonment of the sale and accordingly he refused to award damages against the defendant.

An examination of these decisions would suggest that the courts still tend to proceed on the basis that the presumption of advancement will *prima facie* apply where a husband transfers property to his wife or purchases it in her name. However, as the decision in *R.F. v. M.F.* makes clear, the presumption can readily be rebutted by evidence establishing a contrary intention and in practice, it is only likely to directly influence the outcome of a case where there is little or no evidence to show what the parties' intentions in relation to ownership of the property actually were.

One further issue which can no longer be ignored is the lack of equality inherent in the principle that the presumption of advancement does not extend to circumstances where a wife purchases property in her husband's name. The point has recently been made by Hogan and Whyte[174] that 'the courts have ... identified a principle of equality of spouses within marriage implicit in Articles 41 and 42 which has sounded the death-knell for a number of common law rules reflecting a dominant role for the husband.' It is submitted that the presumption of advancement, albeit a creature of equity, cannot itself remain immune from constitutional developments over the last decade in this

---

173. *Ibid.* at 18.
174. Kelly, *The Irish Constitution* (3rd ed., 1994) p. 713.

area of equality of spouses within marriage and the traditional principles referred to above must be regarded with a degree of caution.

Father and Child

Where a father purchases property in the name of his child or transfers it into the child's name, the presumption of advancement will apply. This is illustrated by the decision in *Hepworth v. Hepworth*,[175] in which it was held that the voluntary transfer of stock into his son's name by a father operated as an absolute gift to the son. As Malins VC commented: 'The law is not doubtful that if this had been a transfer to a stranger it would have operated as a trust, but if a gift is made in favour of a child the presumption of law is that it is intended as an advancement or provision for the child'.[176] An important authority in this area is the judgment of Sullivan MR in *O'Brien v. Sheil*.[177] There a father lodged securities in a bank in the joint names of himself and his daughter which was held after his death to be an advancement in the daughter's favour, despite evidence which suggested that the father had subsequently intended the securities to be applied to different purposes. Sullivan MR stated that it was 'now settled law that a lodgment by a father in the joint names of himself and his child is as powerful and strong an indication of advancement as a lodgment in the name of the child alone'[178] and stressed that declarations made by the father which were subsequent to the advancement could not constitute evidence to rebut the presumption.[179]

There have been conflicting views expressed on the question of the strength of the presumption of advancement in the case of a father/child relationship. It was suggested by Viscount Simonds in *Shephard v. Cartwright*[180] that it should not 'give way to slight circumstances' and recently by O'Sullivan J in *Malone v. McQuaid*[181] that the presumption in such relationships is stronger than in the case of a husband and wife. However, the views of the Law Lords expressed in *Pettitt v. Pettitt*[182] would suggest that the presumption of advancement is no longer as strong as it was in any context and it has been acknowledged recently by the Court of Appeal in *McGrath v. Wallis*[183] that in the context of a father/son relationship the presumption may be rebutted by 'comparatively slight evidence'.

---

175. (1870) LR 11 Eq 10. See also *Crabb v. Crabb* (1834) 1 My & K 511; *Re Roberts* [1946] Ch 1; *B. v. B* (1976) 65 DLR (3d) 460.
176. *Ibid.* at 12.
177. (1873) IR 7 Eq 255.
178. *Ibid.* at 259.
179. See further *infra* pp. 169-176.
180. [1955] AC 431, 445.
181. High Court 1996 No. 392 Sp, 28 May 1998.
182. [1970] AC 777, 815.
183. [1995] 2 FLR 114.

Persons in Loco Parentis to a Child

The presumption also applies where the donor or purchaser of property stands *in loco parentis* to the person in whose name this property is held or bought.[184] This principle was explained by Jessel MR in *Bennet v. Bennet*[185] in the following terms: 'nothing is better established than this, that as regards a child, a person not the father of the child may put himself in the position of one *in loco parentis*[186] to the child and so incur the obligation to make a provision for the child.' Jessel MR stressed that while the presumption of advancement applies to a father because he is under an obligation to provide for his child by virtue of the relationship between the parties, in the case of someone who stands *in loco parentis*, 'you must prove that he took upon himself the obligation.' This principle has been held to apply, *inter alia*, to the relationship between a father and an illegitimate child,[187] or his stepson[188] but not to that between an uncle and his nephew where there was no evidence of the former being *in loco parentis*.[189] It has been suggested by Martin[190] that the principle that the presumption of advancement did not extend to illegitimate children 'seems unaffected' by the provisions of the English Family Law Reform Act 1987 which to a large extent removed the disadvantages in terms of succession rights which affected the children of unmarried parents. If this is the case, it must be assumed that the provisions of the Status of Children Act 1987 which effected similar reforms in this jurisdiction have not altered the position in relation to the operation of the presumption. In fact, this should have no practical effect, as such individuals would in all likelihood be deemed to come within the category of persons acting *in loco parentis* and would therefore in any event be affected by the presumption.

Does the Presumption Apply in other Circumstances?

The position in relation to gifts made by a mother to her child is still far from settled. The leading English authority of *Bennet v. Bennet*[191] is based on the reasoning that there is 'no moral legal obligation . . . no obligation according to the rules of equity . . . on a mother to provide for her child'.[192] More recent

---

184. *Shephard v. Cartwright* [1955] AC 431, 445.
185. (1879) 10 Ch D 474, 477.
186. Defined by Jessel MR as 'a person taking upon himself the duty of a father of a child to make provision for that child' (at 477).
187. *Soar v. Foster* (1858) 4 K & J 152.
188. *Re Paradise Motor Co.* [1968] 1 WLR 1125.
189. *Romaine Estate v. Romaine* (2001) 205 DLR (4th) 320, 334.
190. Hanbury and Martin, *Modern Equity* (16th ed., 2001) p. 258, n.10.
191. [1879] 10 Ch D 474. See also *Re De Visme* (1863) 2 De GJ & S 17. However, note that the contrary conclusion was reached in *Sayre v. Hughes* (1868) LR 5 Eq 376.
192. *Ibid.* at 478 *per* Jessel MR.

decisions there have tended to follow this approach[193] although there is also growing academic criticism of what is perceived to be an outdated view on this question.[194]

An analysis of decisions elsewhere in the common law world would suggest that the general trend is towards recognising that the relationship of mother and child does give rise to the presumption of advancement. While the authorities in Canada conflict on this point,[195] the courts in New Zealand[196] and Australia[197] seem to have come down in favour of the proposition that the presumption should apply to such relationships.

The position in this jurisdiction is somewhat unsatisfactory as there have been no recent decisions in this area which might take account of changing perceptions of the parent/child relationship. In *Re Grimes*[198] Johnston J found that the presumption of advancement applied to a gift by a widowed mother to her son, and described the reasoning in *Bennet* as 'singularly unconvincing'. He went on to hold that even if the presumption did not apply, the former's intention to benefit the son in the circumstances of the case was sufficiently strong to rebut any presumption of a resulting trust. However a different conclusion was reached on this question by the Supreme Court in *McCabe v. Ulster Bank Ltd.*[199] The evidence surrounding the circumstances of the gift, which consisted of the lodgment by a widowed mother of sums in a bank account in the names of herself and her three daughters was in the words of Murnaghan J 'very meagre'. After an extensive review of the relevant authorities in the area both in this jurisdiction and in England, Murnaghan J concluded that the application of the presumption of advancement to the

---

193. See *Sekhon v. Alissa* [1989] 2 FLR 94. However, note that in *Gross v. French* (1976) 238 EG 39, while the Court of Appeal failed to resolve the issue as a result of the finding by the court that even if the presumption of advancement did exist between a mother and daughter, it was rebutted on the facts of the case, the *dicta* of Scarman LJ suggested that the presumption should operate in such cases.

194. See Dowling [1996] Conv 274. Dowling suggests (at 283) that the presumption should be 'updated to reflect the realities of life towards the beginning of the twenty-first century rather than left as a reminder of attitudes prevailing in the eighteenth'. Enonchong [1993] RLR 78, 84 points out that today's society has embraced the concept of equality of the sexes – he cites the decision of the House of Lords in *Barclays Bank plc v. O'Brien* [1994] 1 AC 180, 188 in support of this proposition - and says that it would be odd for the law to maintain a distinction which rests on a discredited concept.

195. *Re Dagle* (1990) 70 DLR (4th) 201 supports the position that the presumption applies, while *Mehta v. Canada Trust* (1993) 104 DLR (4th) 24 is evidence of the contrary view.

196. See *Re Brownlee* [1990] 3 NZLR 243.

197. *Dullow v. Dullow* (1985) 3 NSWLR 531; *Brown v. Brown* (1993) 31 NSWLR 582; *Nelson v. Nelson* (1995) 132 ALR 133.

198. [1937] IR 470.

199. [1939] IR 1.

relationship between a mother and her child could not be based on any sound principle. He continued:

> I have come to the conclusion that the presumption must be based upon the obligation to make provision which a Court of Equity recognises in the case of a father, or of one who has assumed his obligation in this respect.
>
> In many cases of widowed mothers very slight circumstances may be sufficient to place the widow *in loco parentis*, i.e., of having assumed the father's obligation to provide. In such cases there will be a basis for the presumption, but in a case such as the present, where there are no circumstances to go upon save the mere relationship of mother and child, there is, in my opinion, no ground for an equitable presumption which will rebut a resulting trust.[200]

On the basis of the facts before the court, the Supreme Court concluded that there was insufficient evidence of the mother's intention to confer a benefit on her daughters to rebut the presumption of a resulting trust. On the one hand it is difficult to fault the reasoning of Murnaghan J having regard to the historical origins of the doctrine of advancement and if one were to follow his approach it is certainly true that in the majority of cases 'very slight circumstances' would suffice to establish that a widowed mother had assumed the father's traditional obligation to provide for the child. However, it could also be said that the rationale which originally justified the imposition of the presumption as between father and child, namely that the former was under a moral obligation[201] to provide for the latter, is arguably today just as relevant to the position of a mother as to that of a father and it is difficult to justify a principle which continues to result in the drawing of such anomalous and arbitrary distinctions. Equally, if the courts in this jurisdiction were to apply the reasoning employed by the Supreme Court of South Australia in *Callaghan v. Callaghan*,[202] namely that the presumption of advancement is based on the relationship between the parties rather than on any obligation on the part of the transferor, it should make no difference whether the parent is a father or a mother.[203]

Keane[204] is correct in suggesting that it is also difficult to reconcile a

---

200. *Ibid.* at 15.
201. See *Bennet v. Bennet* (1879) 10 Ch D 474.
202. 5 May 1995.
203. Although the language employed by O'Sullivan J in *Malone v. McQuaid* High Court 1996 No. 392 Sp, 28 May 1998 at 18 would suggest that the rationale of obligation still subsists.
204. *Equity and the Law of Trusts in the Republic of Ireland* (1988) p. 158. See further Kelly, *The Irish Constitution* (3rd ed., 1994, eds. Hogan and Whyte) p. 713.

reluctance to extend the presumption of advancement to mother/child relationships in the light of the position adopted by the Supreme Court in decisions such as *Re Tilson*[205] which stress the concept of joint parental responsibility towards children. Finally, it can be said with a fair degree of certainty that even if the courts in this jurisdiction were to continue to draw such a theoretical distinction between the position of a mother and father in applying the presumption of advancement, it is likely that the evidence available to them in any particular case would suffice to ensure that any unjustified presumptions would be rebutted.

As pointed out above, there has been no evidence of a willingness on the part of the judiciary to extend the presumption of advancement to co-habitees, whether of different sexes,[206] or of the same sex.[207]

Finally, it should be noted that in the recent decision of *Fitzpatrick v. Criminal Assets Bureau*,[208] which concerned a dispute about whether a car seized by the first named defendant was in fact the property of an individual or of a company, the High Court refused to contemplate the extension of the presumption of advancement to a relationship of a commercial nature. As Shanley J stated:

> I know of no decided case, and none was opened to me, which suggests that the relationships to which the presumption of advancement extend include those of a shareholder and the company in which he owns shares or the relationship between an individual and the company which he manages, controls or operates.[209]

Rebutting the Presumption of Advancement

As noted above, there has been some erosion of judicial confidence in the concept of the presumption of advancement due in part to the rather anomalous results which it may produce and to significant constitutional developments in the area of equality. In circumstances where the presumption has traditionally been held to exist, it has generally become easier to rebut[210] and where a relationship exists which does not give rise to the presumption on the basis of

---

205. [1951] IR 1.
206. *Calverley v. Green* (1984) 155 CLR 242. See also *Lowson v. Coombes* [1999] Ch 373.
207. *Tinsley v. Milligan* [1994] 1 AC 340. See also Thornton [1993] CLJ 394, 395.
208. High Court 1997 No. 426 Sp (Shanley J) 27 February 1998.
209. *Ibid.* at 28.
210. *Pettitt v. Pettitt* [1970] AC 777, 824 *per* Lord Diplock (quoted with approval by Keane J in *J.C. v. J.H.C.*, High Court, 1982 No.4931P, 4 August 1982). See also *McGrath v. Wallis* [1995] 2 FLR 114. However, there have also been examples of cases where the presumption has not been held to have been rebutted, see *Malone v. McQuaid* High Court 1996 No. 392 Sp (O'Sullivan J) 28 May 1998.

established principles, evidence which shows that a gift was intended will now be more readily accepted by a court. However, in addition to this general development, it is still important to note the circumstances in which the presumption has traditionally been rebutted.

Evidence that no Gift Intended

The presumption of advancement will be rebutted if evidence is adduced to show that no gift was intended by the donor or transferor.[211] As Henchy J stated in *R.F. v. M.F.*:[212]

> If the relevant circumstances show that the paper result achieved by the conveyance conceals the real intention of the husband in entering into the transaction, so that the benefit contended for by the wife was not intended, the court will hold that the presumption of advancement has been rebutted.

In *Anson v. Anson*[213] a husband guaranteed his wife's bank account and was obliged to pay a sum of money to the bank on foot of this guarantee. It was held that the husband could recover this amount from the wife and that there was no presumption of advancement in a transaction of this nature. Pearson J stated that the husband had made it clear to his wife that his intention was not to relieve her of the debt, but to solve the immediate problem in which she found herself. Therefore it would appear that a transaction of this nature cannot be presumed to be an advancement unless the donor makes it clear to the donee at the time of making the guarantee that he does not expect to be reimbursed.

Where the relationship at issue is that of father and child it may be more difficult to identify with any degree of certainty the types of circumstances in which the presumption may be rebutted, particularly where the child is a minor as the father may be more likely to retain some element of control over the property.[214] However, it was held in *Re Gooch*[215] that, where a father bought shares in a company purely to enable the son to become a director, with the

---

211. The contesting party must prove on the balance of probabilities that the person who is presumed to have intended a gift actually intended not to make it, see *Pasko v. Pasko* British Columbia Supreme Court, 12 April 2002 paragraph 50.
212. [1995] 2 ILRM 572, 577.
213. [1953] 1 QB 636. See also *Re Salisbury-Jones* [1938] 3 All ER 459.
214. See e.g. *Grey v. Grey* (1677) 2 Swans 594 where it was held that the fact that a son continued to allow his father receive the rents on a property was insufficient to rebut the presumption of advancement as it was 'an act of reverence and good manners' (at 600).
215. (1890) 62 LT 384.

latter handing over the dividends received on these shares, and subsequently the share certificates, the presumption of advancement had been rebutted. Similarly in *Warren v. Guerney*,[216] where a father arranged for a house to be conveyed into his daughter's name, it was held by the Court of Appeal that the presumption of advancement was rebutted by the fact that the father had retained the title deeds to the property,[217] and by the contemporaneous declarations made by him that it was not his intention that his daughter should be the sole beneficial owner of the house.

Nature of Evidence Admissible to Rebut Presumption

A further important question which must be considered is the type of evidence which will suffice to rebut the presumption of advancement. As Sullivan MR stated in *O'Brien v. Sheil*:[218] 'declarations of the [transferor], subsequent to the advancement, if they are not so connected with it as to be reasonably regarded as contemporaneous, cannot be evidence to rebut the presumption of advancement.' In that case, a memorandum found among a father's papers after his death was not admissible in evidence to rebut the presumption of advancement in favour of his daughter in relation to a transfer of securities into their joint names during the father's lifetime.

The most important authority in this area is the decision of the House of Lords in *Shephard v. Cartwright*.[219] A father arranged for shares in certain private companies to be allotted to his children. He subsequently dealt with the shares, at one point crediting the profits of these dealings to a bank account in the children's names, but later appropriating these funds to his own purposes. After his death, the children succeeded in establishing that the shares registered in their names must be regarded as an advancement which had not been rebutted by their father's conduct. The House of Lords held that the father's conduct after allotting the shares could not go to prove that he had not intended to make an advancement to his children and laid down a number of important general principles in this regard. Viscount Simonds quoted with approval the following passage from *Snell's Equity*:[220]

> The acts and declarations of the parties before or at the time of the purchase, or so immediately after it as to constitute a part of the trans-action, are admissible in evidence either for or against the party who did

---

216. [1944] 2 All ER 472.
217. It would appear that retention of title deeds alone might be insufficient to rebut the presumption.
218. (1873) IR 7 Eq 255. See also the decisions of *Fox v. Fox* (1863) 15 Ir Ch R 89 and *Sidmouth v. Sidmouth* (1840) 2 Beav 447 to which Sullivan MR referred.
219. [1955] AC 431.
220. 24th ed., p. 153. Now see McGhee (30th ed., 2000) p. 180.

the act or made the declaration. . . . But subsequent declarations are admissible as evidence only against the party who made them, and not in his favour.

These principles would seem to mean that an act or declaration by a donor or transferor at the time of or prior to the transaction may be used by him to rebut the presumption while subsequent acts or declarations cannot be admitted to support his claim but may be used against him by the donee in order to support the application of the presumption. In addition, as pointed out by Oakley,[221] evidence of subsequent acts and declarations by the transferee can be admitted against him in order to enable the transferor to rebut the presumption of advancement. These principles were recently confirmed by the Supreme Court in *R.F. v. M. F.*,[222] where Henchy J stated as follows:

> The presumption of advancement . . . is, of course, rebuttable. For a rebuttal to be made out, it is for the husband to show, by reference to acts or statements before or around the transaction, that a beneficial interest was not intended to be conveyed in the circumstances relied on. As to subsequent acts or statements, the authorities show that they are admissible in evidence against the party making them, but not in his or her favour. Thus, subsequent acts or statements on the part of the wife are admissible in evidence to rebut the presumption of advancement.

Unlawful or Fraudulent Conduct

It would appear that the presumption of advancement cannot be rebutted by evidence that the transfer was made for a fraudulent or illegal purpose where this purpose has been wholly or partly carried out.[223] So, where for example, a father transfers land into his son's name with a view to achieving an unlawful purpose or where a husband puts property into his wife's name in order to evade the payment of taxes,[224] the transferor cannot adduce evidence of the improper purpose to rebut the presumption of advancement. In *Chettiar v. Chettiar*[225] a father transferred land into his son's name for an illegal purpose,

---

221. Parker and Mellows, *The Modern Law of Trusts* (7th ed., 1998) p. 248.
222. [1995] 2 ILRM 572, 576-577.
223. The decision of the English Court of Appeal in *Tribe v. Tribe* [1996] Ch 107 is to the effect that evidence of an illegal purpose can be relied upon where it has not been either wholly or partly carried into effect. This decision is considered in more detail *infra*. See also the *dicta* of Lord Denning MR in *Chettiar v. Chettiar* [1962] AC 294, 302. It should be noted at this point that the High Court of Australia has recently rejected this principle in *Nelson v. Nelson* (1995) 132 ALR 133 also considered below.
224. *Re Emery's Investment Trusts* [1959] Ch 410.
225. [1962] AC 294.

namely to avoid certain regulations applying to the holding. The Privy Council concluded that the illegal purpose had been carried into effect and held that the father could not rely on evidence of this illegality to rebut the presumption of advancement in order to recover the land. It is not necessary to prove that the transferee was entirely unaware of the illegality in order to prevent the transferor relying on such rebuttal evidence. In *Gascoigne v. Gascoigne*[226] a man conveyed property into his wife's name to protect it from his creditors. It was held that he could not rely on this fact to rebut the presumption of advancement and that the wife could retain the property for her own benefit, notwithstanding the fact that she had been aware of the fraudulent purpose behind the transaction.

This principle has also been applied in Ireland. In *Parkes v. Parkes*[227] the defendant husband wanted to buy land and arranged for it to be conveyed into his wife's name to obviate the need for Land Commission consent, which would have been necessary had he purchased the property in his own name as he was not an Irish citizen.[228] After the parties divorced, the husband registered an inhibition on the land and the wife instituted proceedings claiming that it had been wrongly registered. The husband counterclaimed that he was entitled to the beneficial ownership in the land and the wife put forward the argument that he should not be able to obtain relief in equity by setting up his own illegality or fraud. Costello J referred to *Gascoigne v. Gascoigne* and to *McEvoy v. Belfast Banking Co.*,[229] where a father had deposited money in his son's name to avoid death duties, and stated:

> Just as the courts will not grant relief to a person who has allowed property to be placed in a wife's or son's name for the fraudulent purpose of defeating creditors ... or for the illegal purpose of evading liability to tax so it seems to me that the court should not grant relief to a purchaser who has placed property in his wife's name dishonestly and by means of an illegal act performed for the purpose of evading the law relating to the transfer of land.[230]

Therefore, the husband was not allowed to adduce evidence of his motives for conveying the land into his wife's name and could not rebut the presumption of advancement which operated in her favour.

---

226. [1918] 1 KB 223. Equally, it is not necessary to establish that the transferor acted fraudulently, and his honest motives may even help to strengthen the presumption against him, see *Tinker v. Tinker* [1970] P 136.
227. [1980] ILRM 137.
228. S.45 of the Land Act 1965 required that the consent of the Land Commission be obtained for the purchase of land to which the section applied by anyone other than a qualified person which means, *inter alia*, an Irish citizen.
229. [1934] NI 67.
230. [1980] ILRM 137, 144.

However, it would appear that different considerations apply where the illegal purpose has not been carried out.[231] As Millett LJ stated in *Tribe v. Tribe*:[232]

> [A] person who has transferred property for an illegal purpose can nevertheless recover his property provided that he withdraws from the transaction before the illegal purpose has been wholly or partly performed. This is the doctrine of the *locus poenitentiae* and it applies in equity as well as at law.

In *Tribe* this principle was applied specifically to a situation where the presumption of advancement arose.[233] The plaintiff had transferred shares in a family company to his son with a view to defrauding his creditors. The difficulties which might have led to claims being made against him were resolved and when the plaintiff sought to recover the shares from the defendant, the latter resisted his claim. The Court of Appeal held that the plaintiff transferor was entitled to adduce evidence of his intention in order to rebut the presumption of advancement in favour of his son, which he successfully did. Effectively this decision means that a plaintiff who has made a transfer of property to a person in whose favour the presumption of advancement arises, can withdraw from the transaction before the illegal purpose has been wholly or partly carried out[234] and then recover the property by adducing evidence of his illegal purpose in order to rebut the presumption. However, as Millett LJ stressed, the transferor 'must have withdrawn from the transaction while his dishonesty still lay in intention only. The law draws the line once the intention has been wholly or partly carried into effect.'[235] Millett LJ was of the view that while the withdrawal from the transaction must have been voluntary, genuine repentance in relation to the illegal purpose was unnecessary; as

---

231. Note the comments of Denning MR in *Chettiar v. Chettiar* [1962] AC 294, 302 to the effect that 'if the fraudulent purpose had not been carried out there might well have been room for repentance and the father might have been allowed to have the land retransferred to him'.
232. [1996] Ch 107, 124. This is one of the exceptions to the general rule against relying on one's own illegality and is known as the doctrine of *locus poenitentiae*.
233. See further Enonchong [1996] RLR 78; Pettitt (1996) 10 Trust Law Int 51; Virgo [1996] CLJ 23; Rose (1996) 112 LQR 386.
234. Virgo argues in [1996] CLJ 23, 25 that in *Tribe* although nobody was actually deceived, the father had done all that he could to carry his illegal purpose into effect and that therefore the court should have concluded that his purpose had been partly carried out.
235. [1996] Ch 107, 133. So, in *Collier v. Collier* [2002] EWCA Civ 1095, Court of Appeal, 17 May 2002 a father could not rely on the principle accepted by the Court of Appeal in *Tribe* in relation to a transfer to his daughter because he had given effect to his dishonest intention and the doctrine of the *locus poenitentiae* described by Millett LJ could not assist him.

Nourse LJ stated, all that mattered was that no deception should have been practised on the plaintiff's creditors.

While it is likely that the courts in this jurisdiction will follow *Tribe,* it is less likely given the approach adopted by Costello J in *Parkes* that they would find that a transferor should be able to rely on an illegal purpose which has been carried into effect to rebut the presumption of advancement. However, it must be pointed out that the High Court of Australia has recently reached this conclusion in its decision in *Nelson v. Nelson*[236] which for the sake of completeness we should briefly consider. Mrs Nelson transferred a house into the names of her son and daughter so that she could obtain a subsidy for the purchase of a subsequent house. After the sale of the original house her daughter claimed a half-share in it and argued that Mrs Nelson could not adduce evidence of her illegal purpose in order to rebut the presumption of advancement.[237] However, the High Court of Australia accepted evidence to rebut the presumption of advancement even though it was tainted with illegality and despite the fact that the illegal purpose had been carried into effect.[238] In reaching this conclusion the court effectively rejected the distinction drawn by the House of Lords in *Tinsley v. Milligan*[239] between cases where the presumption of advancement did or did not apply. As Lord Browne-Wilkinson had stated 'in cases where the presumption of advancement does not apply, a plaintiff can establish his equitable interest in the property without relying in any way on the underlying illegal transaction'.[240] However, in cases where the presumption of advancement applies, in Lord Browne-Wilkinson's view 'in order to establish any claim, the plaintiff has himself to lead evidence sufficient to rebut the presumption of gift and in so doing will normally have to plead, and give evidence of, the underlying illegal purpose.'[241] This so called *Tinsley* distinction has been criticised by academics[242] and while the Court of Appeal in *Tribe* clearly felt bound to follow this reasoning,

---

236. (1995) 132 ALR 133.
237. The court in Australia had already accepted that the presumption of advancement applies between a mother and her child. See *Dullow v. Dullow* (1985) 3 NSWLR 531; *Brown v. Brown* (1993) 31 NSWLR 582.
238. Rose has suggested (1996) 112 LQR 386, 388 that the rules which deny relief to a plaintiff who has been involved in illegality 'are crude and capricious, generally fail to discriminate between the relative demerits of the parties and may penalise a plaintiff disproportionately to the relevant wrongdoing'. It should be pointed out that Mance LJ has recently commented in *Collier v. Collier* [2002] EWCA 1095, Court of Appeal, 17 May 2002, paragraph 106 that while he had been tempted to take the same approach as Dawson J in *Nelson*, he decided that this was not a course open to him. He concluded that: 'If English law in this area is to be further refashioned judicially after *Tinsley v. Milligan*, it seems to me that it should be at the highest level.'
239. [1994] 1 AC 340.
240. *Ibid.* at 371-372.
241. *Ibid.* at 372. See also *Tribe v. Tribe* [1996] Ch 107, 117-118 *per* Nourse LJ.
242. See e.g. Enonchong (1995) 111 LQR 133; [1996] RLR 78.

dissatisfaction at what is a rather arbitrary distinction is evident particularly in the judgment of Nourse LJ.[243] In the view of Dawson J in *Nelson*, the distinction had no basis in principle and was unjustifiable on policy grounds.[244] As he pointed out the distinction could not logically be based on the policy of discouraging the transfer of property for an illegal purpose 'because a knowledgeable transferor would choose a transferee other than one who could take advantage of the presumption of advancement'.[245]

As we have seen above, the principles laid down in *Tinsley v. Milligan* have been applied in *Silverwood v. Silverwood*[246] and *Lowson v. Coombes*,[247] although as Thompson[248] has commented in relation to the latter decision, it was central to the result in that case that the relationship between the parties did not give rise to the presumption of advancement. Had it done so, the plaintiff could not have relied on his real motive for putting the house into the defendant's name in order to rebut the presumption and the latter would have retained full beneficial ownership of the property. As Nourse LJ commented in *Tribe v. Tribe*[249] there seems to be some perversity in the elevation of the presumption of advancement to a decisive status in the context of illegality, or as Mance LJ put it in *Collier v. Collier*:[250] 'Why should the presumption of advancement, which depends upon the precise family relationship ... play so potentially important a role in determining the enforceability of a transaction between two parties implicated in illegal purpose.' In addition, as Virgo and O'Sullivan[251] point out, the elevation of the presumption of advancement to such a conclusive status is problematic because there is no consensus as to which relationships attract it and because it is questionable whether a presumption based on such outdated assumptions should play any role in determining property rights.

The arbitrariness of the distinction between cases where the presumption of advancement does and does not apply has also been criticized by the Law Commission in England, which has provisionally recommended that the reliance principle should be abandoned.[252] Instead the Commission recommends that there should be a statutory discretion to declare an illegal trust to be invalid taking into account such factors as the seriousness of the illegality, the knowledge and intention of the beneficiary, principles relating

---

243. [1996] Ch 107, 118.
244. (1995) 132 CLR 133, 166.
245. *Ibid.* at 164.
246. (1997) 74 P & CR 453.
247. [1999] Ch 373.
248. [1999] Conv 242, 246. See also Cotteril [1999] LMCLQ 465.
249. [1996] Ch 107, 118.
250. [2002] EWCA 1095, Court of Appeal, 17 May 2002, paragraph 97.
251. 'Resulting Trusts and Illegality' in *Restitution and Equity Volume One: Resulting Trusts and Equitable Compensation* (eds. Birks and Rose, 2000) pp. 103-104.
252. Law Com CP No. 154 (1999) *Illegal Transactions: The Effect of Illegality on Contracts and Trusts*, paragraph 8.12.

to deterrence and policy and whether the invalidity would be a proportionate response to the illegality.[253]

Trusts of Family Property

Introduction

The circumstances which give rise to a resulting trust when property is voluntarily conveyed into the name of another or where it is purchased in another party's name have in general terms been outlined above. By far the most common application of these principles today occurs in relation to the question of ownership of the family home when cohabitees,[254] or in certain limited circumstances spouses, separate and it is therefore useful to examine the case law in this area in some detail.

In the context of property disputes between spouses, section 12 of the Married Women's Status Act 1957 provided a statutory framework for the resolution of such issues, although it made no specific provision in relation to the principles to be applied in carrying out this function. Therefore until the enactment of the Judicial Separation and Family Law Reform Act 1989, equitable principles still governed the manner in which property disputes between spouses who separated were resolved. The 1989 Act provided a scheme for making property adjustment orders in the context of separation proceedings[255] and section 20(2) laid down specific factors which the court should have regard to in resolving these disputes.[256] This legislation was largely re-enacted in the Family Law Act 1995 and the provisions of section 16(2) of the latter Act replace those in section 20(2) of the earlier legislation. In addition, the Family Law (Divorce) Act 1996 has introduced a similar scheme for the making of property adjustment orders in the context of divorce proceedings.[257] Where this legislation applies, equitable principles need no longer be relied upon, but there are still a number of situations involving spouses where it may be necessary to determine ownership of matrimonial property to which the legislative provisions referred to above will not be relevant. In the first instance, where spouses decide to separate without obtaining a divorce or judicial separation or where they obtain a civil annulment, equitable principles will still govern any property dispute which may arise. Similarly, where one

---

253. *Ibid.* at paragraphs 8.49 and 8.63.
254. See Mee (2001) 6 CPLJ 43.
255. S. 15.
256. Note that the constitutionality of other provisions of this legislation was challenged unsuccessfully in *F. v. F.* [1994] 2 ILRM 401(HC); *F. v. Ireland* [1995] 2 ILRM 321(SC).
257. S.14 of the Act of 1996 provides that a court may make a property adjustment order on granting a decree of divorce or at any time thereafter and s.20 sets out the factors which the court should have regard to.

spouse dies,[258] or is adjudicated bankrupt,[259] or where a judgment mortgage is registered against the interest of one spouse in a property,[260] it may be necessary to rely on equitable principles to determine the respective beneficial shares of the spouses. So, bearing in mind the limited circumstances in which equity still plays a role in resolving disputes concerning matrimonial property, it is useful to reiterate the following general principles.

Where a husband buys property in his wife's name or transfers it into her name, by virtue of the presumption of advancement, she will be regarded as the sole beneficial owner of the property provided that the presumption is not rebutted.[261] Where it is purchased solely by the husband but conveyed or transferred into their joint names, the same presumption of advancement will usually ensure that the parties are beneficially entitled as joint tenants.[262] However, where it is the wife who purchases the property and it is conveyed either solely into the husband's name or into their joint names, in the absence of rebutting evidence, the husband will hold any interest on a resulting trust for his wife. It should be noted that different considerations apply where the parties are not married as the presumption of advancement does not come into play.[263] In such cases the presumption of a resulting trust will operate and unless it is rebutted, a partner who contributes to the purchase price will acquire a beneficial interest where the property is in the other party's name.

Situations in which property is purchased outright are relatively unusual in practice; more commonly it will be purchased by way of a mortgage and both parties will effectively contribute to the instalments payable. In the context of co-habitees, it is important to bear in mind that even where the property is in their joint names, this will not necessarily lead to joint beneficial ownership. If one partner works and pays the mortgage instalments this will lead to him or her acquiring an increased beneficial interest. Such an arrangement will give rise to a resulting trust in favour of the contributing partner, which if not rebutted, will lead to the conferral of a beneficial interest proportionate to the contribution. It is also quite common for a house to be conveyed solely into one partner's name in these circumstances and a question which may arise in practice is whether the other partner should have any beneficial interest in the property arising from his or her contributions.

There are fundamental difficulties in employing the traditional concept of the purchase money resulting trust in these circumstances. In theory the beneficial interests of the parties should be assessed at the time the purchase occurs but such an assessment could not accommodate the practical reality of

---

258. *E.N. v. R.N.* [1992] 2 IR 116.
259. *Wall v. Wall* High Court 1983 No. 402 Sp (Hamilton P)10 September 1986.
260. See e.g *Malone v. McQuaid* High Court 1996 No. 392 Sp, 28 May 1998.
261. *Re Eykyn's Trusts* (1877) 6 Ch D 115, 118.
262. *J.C. v. J.H.C.*, High Court 1982 No. 4931P (Keane J) 4 August 1982.
263. *Calverley v. Green* (1984) 56 ALR 483; *Lowson v. Coombes* [1999] Ch 373.

the situation which may involve the repayment of a mortgage loan over a period of years subsequent to the actual purchase. The Irish courts have tended to deal with this difficulty by treating mortgage repayments as the practical equivalent to paying the initial purchase price and as capable of giving rise to a proportionate beneficial interest under a resulting trust. An alternative approach suggested by Finlay P in *W. v. W.*[264] is to treat the repayment of the mortgage as the buying back of the equity of redemption from the mortgagee. As he stated:

> [T]he fundamental principle underlying this rule of law is that the redemption of any form of charge or mortgage on property in truth consists of the acquisition by the owner or mortgagor of an estate in the property with which he parted at the time of the creating of the mortgage or charge and ... there can be no distinction in principle between a contribution made to the acquisition of that interest and a contribution made to the acquisition of an interest in property by an original purchase.[265]

As a result it would appear that contributions towards the redemption of any mortgage over property, even if the money was not borrowed to purchase the property, can give rise to a resulting trust.[266] This latter approach in particular could give rise to serious anomalies[267] and the more straightforward former theory, although also technically flawed, is less likely to lead to difficulties in its application.

While most of the case law in this jurisdiction in relation to the purchase money resulting trust deals with property disputes between spouses, the rationale behind such a trust as interpreted by the courts is that it should apply because of the circumstances in which the contributions are made, rather than because of the nature of the relationship between the parties. There was no suggestion made in either of the cases decided in this jurisdiction which related

---

264. [1981] ILRM 202.
265. *Ibid.* at 204-205. Quoted with approval by Finlay CJ in *E.N. v. R.N* [1992] 2 IR 116, 123.
266. As Mee points out in [1993] Conv 359, 363 this reasoning leads to the result that where a person contributes to the repayment of a loan he gains a share, not in what was purchased with the help of the loan, but in the security for the loan.
267. See further Mee [1993] Conv 359, 363. He points to the anomaly that a share will be gained by a woman who pays off a mortgage raised to finance improvements to a man's property, whereas a woman who pays for the same improvements in cash will not gain anything. In addition, Mee highlights the difficulty which would arise if someone repaid an unsecured loan which represents a portion of the purchase price of property. He argues that in such cases no trust could arise as there could be no question of buying back an estate transferred to the lender in the absence of any security for the loan.

to cohabitees[268] that different principles should apply to property disputes between co-habiting partners as opposed to spouses. However, it should be borne in mind that unmarried cohabitees may not necessarily have the same intentions about sharing beneficial ownership in property as married couples and for this reason the presumption of a resulting trust will probably be more readily rebutted in such cases.

Subject to this caveat, it would appear that the principles established in case law are relevant today in the limited circumstances set out above where matrimonial property issues between spouses are not governed by legislation, and also to property disputes between cohabitees and between spouses or cohabitees and third parties. The difficulties which have arisen in relation to deciding in what circumstances a beneficial interest may arise have largely centred on assessing the worth or suitability of the various types of contributions which can be made and it is proposed to examine these in turn.

Direct Contributions

It has been clearly established that where property is purchased in one spouse or partner's name but the other party has made direct contributions to the purchase price or the payment of instalments on the mortgage, the property will be held on a resulting trust to the extent of these contributions. The first signs that the concept of a trust would be employed by the courts to resolve disputes about the ownership of matrimonial property emerged from the decision of Kenny J in *Heavey v. Heavey*,[269] and subsequently in *C. v. C.*,[270] in which he applied this reasoning to the issue of direct contributions. The spouses purchased a family home in the husband's sole name although the wife made a direct contribution to the purchase price by paying the deposit and some of the mortgage repayments. When the parties' marriage broke down, the wife made an application pursuant to section 12 of the Married Women's Status Act 1957 claiming that she was entitled to half the beneficial interest in the house. Kenny J said that the correct approach was to apply the concept of a trust to the legal relationship which arises when a wife makes payments towards the purchase of a house or the repayment of mortgage instalments when the house is in the sole name of the husband. He continued by saying that when this is done, the husband then becomes a trustee for her of a share in the house proportionate to the size of her contributions. In view of the size of her contributions, Kenny J therefore granted a declaration that the wife was in the circumstances entitled to one-half of the beneficial interest in the family home.

The principle enunciated in *C. v. C.* was re-iterated in *W. v. W.*[271] by Finlay

---

268. *Power v. Conroy* [1980] ILRM 31; *McGill v. S.* [1979] IR 238.
269. (1974) 111 ILTR 1.
270. [1976] IR 254.
271. [1981] ILRM 202, 204.

P in a comprehensive judgment in which he laid down a number of general principles. These included the following:

> Where a wife contributes by money to the purchase of property by her husband in his sole name in the absence of evidence of some inconsistent agreement or arrangement the court will decide that the wife is entitled to an equitable interest in that property approximately proportionate to the extent of her contribution as against the total value of the property at the time the contribution was made.

The position was confirmed by Henchy J in the Supreme Court in *McC. v. McC.* [272] and it now seems indisputable in this jurisdiction that contributions of a direct nature towards the acquisition of the family home will give rise to an equitable interest in the absence of evidence of an agreement to the contrary.

The principle of proportionate interest which derives from the rationale behind the resulting trust has continued to be applied in this jurisdiction, and has ensured a degree of consistency in decision-making although perhaps at the expense of an element of flexibility which might be preferable in certain circumstances. In England, where there has been uncertainty about whether contributions of a direct nature will give rise to a resulting or a constructive trust based on the parties' common intentions,[273] a claimant's share may be measured by reference to such intentions and may in some circumstances give rise to a share in excess of the actual financial contributions made.[274] Recently in *Midland Bank plc v. Cooke*[275] the Court of Appeal accepted that once a common intention has been established on the basis of direct financial contributions to the purchase price of property, the court should 'undertake a survey of the whole course of dealing between the parties relevant to their ownership and occupation of the property' and 'the scrutiny will not confine itself to the limited range of acts of direct contribution of the sort that are needed to found a beneficial interest in the first place'.[276] So, in this case,

---

272. [1986] ILRM 1, 2 *per* Henchy J.
273. In *Lloyds Bank plc v. Rosset* [1991] 1 AC 107, 133. Lord Bridge stated that 'direct contributions to the purchase price by the partner who is not the legal owner ... will readily justify the inference necessary to the creation of a constructive trust.' However, contributions of a direct nature should under traditional principles give rise to a resulting trust. See further O'Hagan (1991) 42 NILQ 238, 244.
274. *Grant v. Edwards* [1986] Ch 638.
275. [1995] 4 All ER 562. See O'Hagan (1997) 60 MLR 420; Gardner (1996) 112 LQR 378; Oldham [1996] CLJ 194; Dixon [1997] Conv 66; Wragg [1996] Fam Law 298; Pawlowski [1996] Fam Law 484.
276. *Ibid.* at 574. See also *Drake v. Whipp* [1996] 1 FLR 826 where the Court of Appeal found that the female partner's contribution to the actual expenditure on the property amounted to 19.4% of its value, but held on the basis of other contributions which she had made, that she was entitled to a one-third interest in it. See Dunn [1997] Conv 467.

although the wife's initial direct contribution had been only 6.4% of the value of the property,[277] the Court of Appeal took into account 'the whole course of dealing between the parties' and held that she should be entitled to a one-half share in the house. As O'Hagan has commented: 'If a spouse or cohabitee contributes a proportionately trifling sum directly to the purchase of property, the initial direct contribution opens the door for the scrutiny of the relationship'.[278]

However, this difference in the approach adopted in England can in part be explained by the fact that the courts in that jurisdiction have recently taken a much more restrictive view of the circumstances in which contributions, if they are only of an indirect nature, can give rise to a trust.[279] To this extent, by allowing contributions of a direct nature to trigger interests proportionately greater than those which might arise in this jurisdiction, the courts could be said to be merely seeking to avoid the hardship which might otherwise be caused by the application of such a stringent approach.

Indirect Contributions

The issue of whether contributions of a indirect nature, either to the purchase price of property or to mortgage repayments, can give rise to a beneficial interest is one which was the subject-matter of considerable uncertainty for a time but now appears to be fairly settled in this jurisdiction. A substantial number of cases relating to this issue also came before the High Court in this jurisdiction in the late 1970s and early 1980s. Two distinct approaches can be identified, the first of which is well illustrated by the decision of Keane J in *M.G. v. R.D.*[280] The family home had been purchased in the sole name of the husband and all mortgage repayments and other expenses directly referable to the house were paid by him. The wife used her salary to purchase items for the house and a car which was used by both parties but Keane J could find no evidence of an agreement of any kind that these outgoings should give her an interest in the property. He concluded that there must be evidence of a common intention that indirect contributions will give the contributor a share in the beneficial interest in property before the court would make such an order and in the circumstances of the case he dismissed the wife's claim. The alternative approach, and the one which has now found favour with the Supreme Court,

---

277. A wedding gift of £1,100 was made jointly to Mrs Cooke and her husband by his parents and the court accepted that she had made a direct contribution to the purchase price of the house in the form of her half of the gift. This conclusion was based on the reasoning of the Court of Appeal in *McHardy v. Warren* [1994] 2 FLR 338.
278. (1997) 60 MLR 420, 427.
279. See *infra Lloyds Bank plc v. Rosset* [1991] 1 AC 107.
280. High Court 1980 No. 423 Sp (Keane J) 28 April 1981. See also *McGill v. S.* [1979] IR 283; *S.D. v. B.D.* High Court 1981 No. 194 Sp (Murphy J) 19 March 1982; *B. v. B.* High Court (MacKenzie J) 22 April 1986.

can be found in the judgment of Finlay P in *W. v. W.* [281] referred to above. The wife claimed a beneficial interest in the family farm on the basis of the fact that mortgages to which the property was subject had been paid off partly as a result of her contributions and she had also contributed to the carrying out of improvements to the property. Finlay P directed an issue to be tried as to the extent to which the wife had contributed to the repayment of the mortgages but rejected a claim to an equitable interest relating to improvements to which she had contributed after the property had been acquired. In relation to the issue of indirect contributions, he stated as follows:

> Where a wife contributes ... to a general family fund thus releasing her husband from an obligation which he otherwise would have permitting him to discharge liabilities out of that fund and permitting him to repay mortgage instalments, she will in the absence of proof of an inconsistent agreement or arrangement be entitled to an equitable share in the property which had been mortgaged and in respect of which the mortgage was redeemed approximately proportionate to her contribution to the mortgage repayments, to the value of the mortgage thus redeemed and to the total value of the property at the relevant time. [282]

This approach of assuming that the wife should be entitled to a beneficial interest proportionate to the extent of her indirect contributions 'in the absence of proof of an inconsistent agreement or arrangement' also found favour with the Supreme Court in *McC. v. McC.* [283] The wife had contributed to the cost of a previous family home and when it was sold this amount was put towards the cost of furniture in the new house, the purchase of which was financed by her husband's employers and secured by a mortgage. It was held by the Supreme Court that this original contribution was not applied to the purchase of the second house either directly or indirectly and had not been part of a general family fund. The court upheld the finding of Costello J that the wife was only entitled to a one-third share in the furniture and fittings. However, Henchy J made the following statement about the general effect of indirect contributions:

> When the wife's contribution has been indirect (such as contributing, by means of her earnings, to a general family fund) the court will in the absence of any express or implied agreement to the contrary, infer a trust in favour of the wife, on the grounds that she has to that extent

---

281. [1981] ILRM 202. See also *R. v. R.*, High Court 1978 No.574 Sp (McMahon J) 12 January 1979; *M.B. v. E.B.*, High Court 1979 No. 556 Sp (Barrington J) 19 February 1980; *C.R. v. D.R.* High Court 1983 No. 228 Sp (Lynch J) 5 April 1984, although on the facts the wife's claim did not succeed in this case.
282. *Ibid.* at 204.
233. [1986] ILRM 1.

relieved the husband of the financial burden he incurred in purchasing the house.[284]

Therefore, it would seem that where one partner makes an indirect contribution of a financial nature to the purchase of the property in a manner which can be identified as relieving the other party of a burden which he would otherwise bear in relation to these outgoings and thereby allows him to pay the mortgage instalments, this contribution will be recognised in the form of a proportionate beneficial interest. This is a sensible and pragmatic approach which recognises the reality that few spouses or partners will think of making any specific agreement about the effect which any contributions which they might make should have.[285] It is interesting to note that the Supreme Court's approach in *McC.* is diametrically opposed to the requirement laid down by Lord McDermott LCJ in the decision of the Northern Ireland Court of Appeal in *McFarlane v. McFarlane*,[286] in which the Lord Chief Justice said that if an indirect contribution is to result in a wife acquiring a beneficial interest, it must be the subject of a proper arrangement between the spouses.

The law in England relating to the status of indirect contributions is at present considerably more restrictive than in this jurisdiction and while there are no signs of any move by the judiciary here towards such an approach it is nevertheless interesting to note these developments. A number of decisions of the English Court of Appeal in the late 1960s had established the so-called doctrine of 'family assets' described by Lord Denning MR in the Court of Appeal decision in *Gissing v. Gissing*[287] as follows:

> Where a couple, by their joint efforts, get a house and furniture, intending it to be a continuing provision for them for their joint lives, it is the *prima facie* inference from their conduct that the house and furniture is a 'family asset' in which each is entitled to an equal share. It matters not in whose name it stands: or who pays for what: or who goes out to work and who stays at home. If they both contribute to it by their joint efforts, the *prima facie* inference is that it belongs to them both equally: at any rate when each makes a financial contribution which is substantial.

---

284. *Ibid.* at 2. This principle was accepted by Finlay CJ in *L. v. L.* [1992] 2 IR 77, 107-108 and by McGuinness J in *C.D. v. W.D.* High Court 1995 No. 587 Sp, 5 February 1997.

285. As was pointed out above, the same principles should in theory apply to contributions made by either spouses or cohabitees. Some consideration should perhaps be given to the fact that there is a greater likelihood in the case of unmarried couples that the legal owner did not intend his or her partner to derive an equitable interest in the property by making contributions to joint expenses. However, the present position would seem to be that unless there is evidence of an express or implied agreement to this effect, such contributions will be taken into account.

286. [1972] NI 59.

287. [1969] 2 Ch 85, 93.

However, the validity of the doctrine of family assets was questioned by the House of Lords in *Pettitt v. Pettitt*[288] where it was held that section 17 of the Married Women's Property Act 1882 on which Lord Denning had relied, was purely procedural in nature and that the courts did not derive authority from it to transfer property rights from one spouse to another. So, by the time the *Gissing* case reached the House of Lords, the doctrine of family assets had been effectively discredited. While Lord Reid considered that there was no real reason to distinguish between direct and indirect contributions, a distinction which he felt in many cases would be 'unworkable', it was Lord Diplock's more restrictive attitude based on common intention which found favour with the English Court of Appeal during the 1980s.[289] A more flexible approach was adopted in the decision of *Grant v. Edwards*,[290] in which a woman was held to be entitled to half the beneficial interest in a house in circumstances where she had made substantial contributions to the household expenses in excess of what would be expected as normal and without which, it was accepted, the defendant would not have been able to pay the mortgage instalments. The Court of Appeal held that in such circumstances, equity would infer a trust where although a house was purchased in the name of one party, there was a common intention that both parties should have a beneficial interest and the non-proprietary owner had acted to his detriment[291] on the basis of that intention. However, the more recent decision of the House of Lords in *Lloyds Bank plc v. Rosset*,[292] although founded on the same principles of common intention and detriment, was considerably more restrictive and seems to have set a fairly uncompromising precedent in this area. Lord Bridge stated that the fundamental question was whether, independently of any inference which might be drawn from the parties' conduct, there had been at any time prior to the acquisition of the house, or exceptionally at a later date, any agreement, arrangement or understanding reached between them that the property was to be shared beneficially. Such a finding of agreement could only be based on evidence of express discussions between the partners and once this was established it would be necessary for the partner asserting the claim to the beneficial interest to show that he or she had acted to his or her

---

288. [1970] AC 777. See further Brady (1984) 6 DULJ 1, 7-9.
289. See e.g. *Burns v. Burns* [1984] Ch 317 where it was held by the Court of Appeal that since the plaintiff had not made any substantial financial contribution to the acquisition of the house (although she had used her earnings to pay rates, telephone bills etc) the court could not impute a common intention that she should acquire a beneficial interest.
290. [1986] Ch 638.
291. The importance of this element of detriment was stressed by the Court of Appeal in *Midland Bank Ltd v. Dobson* [1986] 1 FLR 171.
292. [1991] 1 AC 107.

detriment or significantly altered his or her position in reliance on the agreement in such a manner as to give rise to a constructive trust.[293]

While such an approach could in limited circumstances result in a more extensive interest being granted to the contributing partner than the application of the straightforward Irish purchase money resulting trust, in the majority of cases it will lead to a more restrictive result and it can be criticised on a number of grounds. It is unclear why Lord Bridge saw fit to depart from the resulting trust approach even in the case of a direct contribution. In doing so, Lord Bridge has seemingly introduced the idea that any common intention must be founded on *express* agreement or representation, requirements which have traditionally not been associated with resulting trusts which are founded rather on the *presumed* intention of the parties. While the elements of common intention and detriment were well-established requirements in the case of indirect contributions, certainly in *Grant v. Edwards*, the requisite intention was implied rather than being founded on express agreement. As O'Hagan[294] has commented, Lord Bridge's requirement of express agreement or representation appears to flow from a confusion as to the nature of resulting and constructive trusts.

As the consideration of the recent decision of the Court of Appeal in *Midland Bank plc v. Cooke*[295] above shows, some of the rather harsh consequences of the decision of the House of Lords in *Lloyds Bank plc v. Rosset* have been mitigated by a willingness to take into account contributions of an indirect nature even in the absence of evidence of express agreement to do so, provided that an initial direct contribution has been made. As we have seen such a payment may trigger an analysis of 'the whole course of dealing between the parties' and allow a broad range of other forms of contribution to be taken into account. However, as O'Hagan has pointed out, where the contribution has only been indirect, no interest will arise under the *Lloyds Bank* principle in the absence of express discussions,[296] and this will be particularly unfair to claimants who have made very large indirect contributions towards the purchase of a property. For this reason, the approach adopted by the courts in this jurisdiction towards contributions of an indirect nature would seem to be fairer and more consistent.

---

293. This approach has been applied in *Hammond v. Mitchell* [1991] 1 WLR 1127 (see Lawson [1992] Conv 218). See also *Chan v. Leung* [2002] EWCA Civ 1075 Court of Appeal, 29 July 2002 where Jonathan Parker LJ reiterated that it was necessary for a claimant to establish that he had acted to his detriment or significantly altered his position in reliance on an alleged promise or agreement in order to establish a constructive trust in such circumstances.
294. (1991) 42 NILQ 238, 244. See further Wong (1998) 18 LS 369, 372.
295. [1995] 4 All ER 562. See *supra* 'Direct Contributions'.
296. (1997) 60 MLR 420, 427.

Improvements to Property

In *W. v. W.*[297] Finlay P stated that where a wife expends monies or carries out work in the improvement of a property, the legal ownership of which is vested solely in the husband, she will not be entitled to an equitable share in this property by reason of such contributions unless she can establish that it was specifically agreed or that she was led to believe by virtue of the surrounding circumstances, that she would be recompensed for it. In addition, he stressed that any claim which she might have was limited to a right to monetary compensation and could not give rise to any beneficial interest. This *dictum* was applied by Barron J in *N.A.D. v. T.D.*,[298] a case which shows the limitations of the device of the resulting trust in circumstances where a house is built on land which is solely the property of one partner. As Barron J commented:

> The circumstances in which a wife may contribute to the improvement of the property of her husband may obviously vary considerably between minor decorative improvements at the one end of the scale and payment for the erection of an entire dwelling-house at the other end. In each case, since the legal and beneficial ownership of the property was already vested in her husband he is entitled at law in the absence of a contrary agreement to take the entire benefit of the improvement.[299]

So, despite the fact that the plaintiff wife had contributed over one-third of the building costs of the family home, it was held that she was not entitled to any beneficial interest in the property. Barron J also considered the possible application of a constructive trust, which he said was a concept 'imposed by operation of law independent of intention in order to satisfy the demands of justice and good conscience'. However, he was satisfied that there was no evidence of any conduct on the husband's part which would make it inequitable for him to deny his wife's claim and he rejected the argument that she should have any share in the beneficial ownership of the family home.

A slightly less restrictive attitude was adopted by Finlay CJ in his judgment in *N. v. N.*,[300] in which the plaintiff widow claimed a beneficial interest in the family home on a number of different grounds. She had for a time applied her earnings from part time work towards family purposes and had managed bedsitter flats into which part of the house had been converted, the rental income from which was applied either directly or indirectly towards the mortgage repayments. In addition, she claimed that her work in the home as a wife and mother should give her a beneficial interest, an argument which will

---

297. [1981] ILRM 202.
298. [1985] ILRM 153.
299. *Ibid.* at 162.
300. [1992] 2 IR 116.

be considered in more detail below. On the issue of improvements, Finlay CJ rejected the claim that the wife should have any additional percentage increase by virtue of her indirect contributions to a mortgage which was taken out to finance an extension to the property. He stated as follows:

> I do not consider as I indicated in my decision in *W.v.W.*, that a direct contribution, even in money's worth, to an improvement made on a family home by a wife, where the husband is the sole owner of it, can, in the absence of express or readily implied agreement, constitute a claim for a beneficial interest in it.[301]

So, while Finlay CJ's statement shows that some form of agreement is necessary if any claim in relation to improvements is to succeed, he at least seems to accept that provided evidence of such an agreement can be established, contributions can give rise to a beneficial interest rather than just an entitlement to monetary recompense. However, it must be pointed out that in the majority of cases it is unlikely that the partner claiming a share as a result of his or her contribution to improvements to the property will be able to provide evidence of the necessary agreement.

There is one situation according to Mee[302] in which a beneficial share may be obtained by a claimant because of contributions to improvements in the absence of an agreement to this effect. Mee suggests that on the basis of the reasoning of Finlay P in *W. v. W.*[303] and *E.N. v. R.N.*,[304] a partner who pays off a mortgage raised to finance improvements will gain a share but is of the view that an individual who pays for the same improvements in cash will be awarded nothing. This result is indeed anomalous and highlights the fact that consideration should be given to addressing the whole question of how to compensate partners who may contribute, often in a significant way, to improving property in which they have no legal ownership.

One possible solution is to allow claimants to rely on estoppel principles or alternatively to follow the 'common intention' analysis developed by the English courts. As we have seen this approach has led to a degree of inconsistency when applied to direct and indirect contributions but it does open up some possibilities in relation to contributions towards improvements, as the recent decision of the Court of Appeal in *Midland Bank plc v. Cooke*[305]

---

301. *Ibid.* at 122. Contrast the position in England, where s. 37 of the Matrimonial Proceedings and Property Act 1970 provides that a substantial contribution in money or money's worth to an improvement to property will give rise to a beneficial interest in the absence of evidence of any agreement to the contrary.
302. [1993] Conv 359.
303. [1981] ILRM 202.
304. [1992] 2 IR 116.
305. [1995] 4 All ER 562. Dixon points out ([1997] Conv 66, 72) that Mrs Cooke had made substantial improvements to the property and suggested that the case was a

shows. Provided that there is evidence of some initial direct contribution to the purchase price, the whole course of dealing between the parties will be scrutinised and the court will take into account 'all conduct which throws light on the question of what shares were intended'.[306]

Other Forms of Contribution

Traditionally the courts in this jurisdiction refused to accept that a partner's contribution by working in the home, whether in performing housework or looking after children, may give rise to a beneficial interest.[307] As Brady[308] has commented, while the attitude of the Supreme Court in *McC. v. McC.*[309] in relation to the issue of indirect contributions was evidence of a shift towards pragmatism, relief for a wife remained dependent on the fact that she has made a financial contribution to the acquisition of the property and no cognisance was taken of her work in the home. While this rather arbitrary approach was called into question by the High Court, the Supreme Court has to date declined to change its view on this issue.

In *B.L. v. M.L.*[310] the plaintiff wife had made no direct contributions to the purchase of the family home and her only indirect contribution was to its refurbishment and redecoration. However she spent most of her time running the household and looking after the children of the marriage. Barr J said that it was well settled that a wife's work in the home and in the care of her children did not amount to an indirect contribution entitling her to a beneficial interest in the family home, nor did work done by her in the maintenance or enhancement of the property. However, Barr J held that having regard to Article 41.2 of the Constitution, a woman who elected to adopt the full time role of wife and mother and was thus precluded from contributing directly or indirectly in money or money's worth from independent employment towards the acquisition by the husband of the family home and contents, should have her work in the home taken into account. In these circumstances Barr J held that the wife was entitled to a 50% beneficial interest in the family home and its

---

suitable one for an application under s. 37 of the Matrimonial Proceedings and Property Act 1970 which allows a court to award a beneficial interest consequent upon spousal improvements to property which he says 'could have been used to generate a sizeable interest for Mrs Cooke without any violence to the principles of resulting or constructive trusts'. However, the operation of this section is subject to the existence of an 'express or implied agreement' between the parties and so is as limited in its application in the same manner as the principle laid down by Finlay CJ in *E.N. v. R.N.* [1992] 2 IR 116.

306. *Ibid.* at 574.
307. *R.K. v. M.K.* High Court 1978 No. 330 Sp (Finlay P) 24 October 1978.
308. (1991) 42 NILQ 1, 9.
309. [1986] ILRM 1.
310. [1992] 2 IR 77.

contents.[311] However, in *E.N. v. R.N.*[312] Barron J said that while he could see the equity in recognising the contribution made by the plaintiff towards the welfare of the family, he did not see Article 41.2.2° as supporting her claim to a share in the family home and said that insofar as that provision might be construed as a guarantee of financial reward to mothers working in the home, it seemed to him that it must be construed as 'a guarantee of reward from outside the family rather than a re-distribution within the family'. Clearly in view of the differing opinions expressed by High Court judges on the issue, clarification was necessary and this came in the Supreme Court's decision in *L. v. L.*,[313] in which the appeal of the appellant husband from the decision of Barr J was allowed. Finlay CJ concluded that to allow the courts to extend the circumstances in which a wife may claim a beneficial interest in the family home to a situation where she has made no direct or indirect financial contribution to the acquisition of the property or to a family fund but has performed the constitutionally preferred role of wife and mother in the home would not be to develop any principle known to the common law but rather would involve the creation of an entirely new right. As he said, unless this result was 'clearly and unambiguously warranted by the Constitution or made necessary for the protection of a specified or unspecified right under it, it must constitute legislation and be a usurpation by the courts of the function of the legislature.'[314]

This reasoning was applied by the Supreme Court in the judgment which it delivered on the same day in *E.N. v. R.N.*[315] One further anomaly to emerge from this decision was that the court recognised that the wife's activities in managing the bedsitter flats were 'different from and not to be identified with the activities of a wife and mother in the home' and that the income earned from this enterprise which went directly or indirectly towards paying off the various mortgages taken out on the property should be recognised as a contribution which would give her a beneficial interest. Taking all the wife's contributions into account, the Supreme Court held that she was entitled to a half-share in the beneficial interest in the house. As Mee[316] has commented, it is difficult to justify an approach which differentiates between unpaid work in the home which will not give rise to an interest and unpaid work in the legal owner's business which may be recognised.

Although the provisions of the Judicial Separation and Family Law Reform Act 1989 came into effect too late to assist the plaintiff in *L.*, that Act, the provisions of which were substantially re-enacted in the Family Law Act 1995,

---

311. This reasoning was approved *obiter* by Barrington J in *A.H. v. P.H.* High Court, 20 June 1989.
312. [1990] 1 IR 383. See also *J.F. v. B.F.* High Court (Lardner J) 21 December 1988.
313. [1992] 2 IR 77. See Jackson (1992) 14 DULJ (ns) 153.
314. *Ibid.* at 107.
315. [1992] 2 IR 116.
316. [1993] Conv 359, 366.

became relevant where the courts were called upon to make a property adjustment order, on the granting of a decree of judicial separation. Section 16(1) of the Family Law Act 1995 now sets out the matters which the court is required to take into consideration in making certain orders including a property adjustment order and these include, by virtue of section 16(2)(f), 'contributions by looking after the home and caring for the family'. Section 20 of the Family Law (Divorce) Act 1996 sets out the same list of factors which the court is required to take into account in making, *inter alia*, property adjustment orders on the granting of a decree of divorce.

While the legislature has therefore now intervened to provide wider recognition of the contribution made by spouses who remain at home, the position of cohabitees in these circumstances remains far from satisfactory. One further point which is interesting to note about *L. v. L.*, is that McCarthy J referred to Article 41.2 and said that while the issue did not arise in the case before him, he wished to make it clear that he was not to be taken as holding that the guarantees provided for in that article were restricted to mothers of families based on the institution of marriage. However, having regard to the point made by Finlay CJ in *L.* that to follow the approach suggested by Barr J would be to develop existing law beyond the permissible limits of judicial interpretation, it is unlikely that McCarthy J's comment will hold out any hope for a cohabitee seeking to rely on any constitutional guarantee, which in any event would only extend to mothers.

As is the case in relation to contributions towards improvements, the English 'common intention' approach would, if applied in this jurisdiction, afford some protection to claimants and in *Grant v. Edwards*[317] Browne-Wilkinson VC accepted that 'labour or other unquantifiable actions' might be taken into account. However, as we have seen above, it would be necessary that the individual concerned had made some initial direct contribution to trigger the court's analysis of the 'whole course of dealing between the parties' or alternatively that there was evidence of some 'agreement, arrangement or understanding' that the contribution should be recognised, as required by the House of Lords in *Lloyds Bank plc v. Rosset*.[318]

Possible Future Developments

As can be seen from the above summary of the manner in which recognition is or is not given to different forms of contribution to the purchase price of family property, the principles applied by both the English and Irish courts each have their respective advantages and disadvantages. The English principles have the advantage of flexibility; there is certainly merit in the 'broad brush' approach adopted by Waite LJ in *Midland Bank plc v.*

---

317. [1986] Ch 638, 658.
318. [1991] 1 AC 107.

Cooke[319] which allows consideration of 'all conduct which throws light on the question of what shares are intended'. In addition, it allows for quantification based on common intention rather than on the amount of the actual contributions made. However, the English approach also lacks consistency and can lead to arbitrary and unfair results e.g. where no direct contribution has been made and no evidence of express agreement can be found, indirect contributions even on a large scale will be insufficient to establish a beneficial interest. It is difficult to justify the imposition of this stringent initial hurdle of direct contributions or express agreement on which evidence of common intention may be based and it is also fair to say that common intention is 'in most cases no more than a fiction'.[320] In addition, the detrimental reliance requirement set out by the House of Lords in *Lloyds Bank plc v. Rosset*[321] has been labelled problematic and inappropriate in the context of disputes between cohabitees,[322] and confusion about the nature of the trust concept being employed in such cases is not a sound basis for reasoned development of the law in this area in England.

The Irish approach on the other hand has the merit of consistency and comparative simplicity but is also based on reasoning which is theoretically flawed to varying degrees and the limited nature of the contributions which are recognised as giving rise to a beneficial interest is a serious shortcoming. In particular the lack of recognition given to claimants in relation to contributions to improvements to property in the absence of an express or readily implied agreement that this should be the case and the unequivocal rejection of the principle that work in the home can give rise to a beneficial interest need to be addressed. As further judicial development of the resulting trust concept appears to have been ruled out by the Supreme Court's decision in *L. v. L.*, it would seem that if the rights of cohabitees in this area are to be extended by virtue of equitable principles then the possibility of other approaches must be explored.

The potential of using the constructive trust as a device which will provide a remedy where 'justice and good conscience' demand was explored by Barron J in *Murray v. Murray*.[323] The defendant was the legal owner of premises in respect of which he had paid the initial deposit; the remainder, approximately three-quarters of the price, was paid by way of a mortgage. The plaintiff, his nephew, had lived in the premises with his aunt, the defendant's sister, for many years and it was accepted by Barron J that the defendant had intended

319. [1995] 4 All ER 562, 574.
320. Riniker [1998] Conv 202, 207. See also the comment of Wong (1998) 18 LS 369, 388 that it has led some to argue that the process of awarding a proprietary remedy depends on the willingness of the courts to manipulate the facts in order to find the relevant intent. See further Glover and Todd (1996) 16 LS 325.
321. [1991] 1 AC 107.
322. Lawson (1996) 16 LS 218.
323. [1996] 3 IR 251.

to transfer the house to his sister. While she was alive she paid the mortgage instalments and most of the outgoings on the property, although there was evidence that she had at one point refused to accept a transfer of the property. After her death the plaintiff claimed a declaration that the entire beneficial ownership in the house was vested in his aunt at the date of her death and the defendant claimed the legal and beneficial ownership himself. The plaintiff claimed that the circumstances were such that it would be unconscionable for the defendant to rely on his legal title and he relied on the decision of *Hussey v. Palmer*[324] to support this claim. Barron J stated: 'It is I think quite clear that the law will impose a constructive trust in all circumstances where it would be unjust and unconscionable not to do so.' In his view *Hussey* was authority for the proposition that in certain circumstances where equity so required, 'a debt may be secured by the device of a constructive trust on the property created by the money involved'. He said that in the case before him the equity to create a constructive trust arose from the payment of monies which had resulted in the property being freed from the mortgage and the owner being relieved of other outgoings. Barron J concluded that the aunt was at the date of her death entitled to three-quarters of the beneficial interest in the property so the plaintiff, being her next of kin, was a tenant in common of the premises with the defendant.

It is interesting that the High Court decided not to seek to apply conventional purchase money resulting trust principles to this case. It is probably due to the uncertainty surrounding the issue of whether the plaintiff's aunt made her contributions intending that she would thereby acquire a beneficial interest in the property. Barron J pointed out that there was evidence of the fact that she had not wanted to take a transfer of the legal ownership of the property during her lifetime and so arguably the presumption of a resulting trust might have been rebutted in the circumstances if the court had sought to apply such reasoning. The question remains whether the constructive trust principles employed by the High Court could usefully be employed in other situations involving family property disputes where a claimant will not gain a beneficial share on the basis of traditional purchase money resulting trust principles. Mee suggests not and argues that a 'simple appeal to abstract notions of equity and fairness will not suffice'.[325] Given the almost universally unfavourable reaction to Lord Denning's new model constructive trust, to which Barron J's trust in *Murray* is undoubtedly related, this is probably an accurate prediction and it is likely that our courts will have to look elsewhere for more acceptable solutions.

It is interesting at this point to briefly consider the means employed elsewhere in the common law world to resolve family property disputes.[326]

---

324. [1972] 1 WLR 1286.
325. (1996) 1 CPLJ 9, 13.
326. See Gardner (1993) 109 LQR 263 for an excellent summary of these approaches. See also Wong (1998) 18 LS 369, 380-388.

The Canadian Supreme Court relies on the concept of 'unjust enrichment' and will intervene where there is 'an enrichment, a corresponding deprivation and the absence of any juristic reason for the enrichment'.[327] The Australian approach is founded on the concept of unconscionability and is based on the principles which might apply where a commercial joint venture is terminated.[328] In New Zealand the reasonable expectation principle is applied and where a claimant has contributed to the acquisition of the legal owner's property a constructive trust will be imposed on the basis that this must have been what the parties intended.[329] However, as Gardner points out, in all these jurisdictions there has tended to be 'a gap between the articulated doctrines and the manner in which cases are actually decided'.[330] He quite correctly asserts that all the doctrines make reference to the parties' own ideas but there is often little such thought on their part and in most jurisdictions 'the circle is squared by fabricating the necessary facts'.

Mee suggests that all these Commonwealth doctrines look to the parties' respective contributions to the wealth generated by the relationship rather than merely focussing on the financial contributions to the purchase of property which is the limitation inherent in the traditional purchase money resulting trust.[331] While none of these doctrines are ideal in themselves, Mee feels that it might be possible to develop a hybrid version which would share their broad scope but which would be founded on a principle consistent with the result which it generates. To achieve this, he suggests resorting to the concept of pooling, which already plays a significant role in the method employed in this jurisdiction, but instead to treat the relationship as an economic partnership and allow the courts to take into account 'all forms of contributions and all forms of wealth accumulation'.[332] However, Mee also identifies difficulties with such an 'ideal' doctrine and on balance would prefer a solution based on legislation. Indeed, given the Supreme Court's attitude in *L. v. L.* further judicial initiatives in this area are unlikely and it remains to be seen whether the legislature will be prepared to intervene further in what is undoubtedly a particularly problematic area.[333]

---

327. *Pettkus v. Becker* (1980) 117 DLR (3d) 257, 269 *per* Dickson J. See also *Sorochan v. Sorochan* (1986) 29 DLR (4th) 1; *Wilcox v. Wilcox* (2000) 190 DLR (4th) 324.
328. See *Muschinski v. Dodds* (1985) 160 CLR 583; *Baumgartner v. Baumgartner* (1987) 164 CLR 137.
329. *Lankow v. Rose* [1995] 1 NZLR 277. See also *Gillies v. Keogh* [1989] 2 NZLR 327.
330. (1993) 109 LQR 263, 279.
331. *The Property Rights of Cohabitees* (1999).
332. *Ibid.* p. 309.
333. It should be noted that an attempt to pass legislation providing for automatic joint ownership of the matrimonial home proved unsuccessful. The Bill was declared unconstitutional by the Supreme Court in a reference under Article 26 of the Constitution in *Re Article 26 of the Constitution and the Matrimonial Home Bill 1993* [1994] 1 IR 350.

CHAPTER 8

Constructive Trusts

INTRODUCTION

A constructive trust is one which arises by operation of law and which comes into being as a result of conduct and irrespective of the intention of the parties. In general terms it can be described as a trust which is imposed by equity in order to satisfy the demands of 'justice and good conscience'[1] and to prevent a person deriving profit from fraudulent conduct or taking unfair advantage of a fiduciary position. As Deane J stated in the Australian decision of *Muschinski v. Dodds*:[2]

> Viewed in its modern context, the constructive trust can properly be described as a remedial institution which equity imposes regardless of actual or presumed agreement or intention (and subsequently protects) to preclude the retention or assertion of beneficial ownership of property to the extent that such retention or assertion would be contrary to equitable principle.

There can be some degree of overlap between the circumstances in which resulting and constructive trusts can arise[3] and from a practical perspective it makes little difference whether a trust is described as resulting or constructive as there is no requirement that the formalities which apply to express trusts be complied with in either case. In addition, it should be noted that the obligations and liabilities imposed on a constructive trustee will not necessarily be as extensive as those demanded of the trustee of an express trust and may tend to vary according to the nature of the circumstances giving rise to the imposition of the trust. It would appear that a constructive trust will take effect from the moment the conduct giving rise to the need for its imposition occurs,[4] which

---

1. *Hussey v. Palmer* [1972] 1 WLR 1286, 1290 *per* Denning MR. See also *Kelly v. Cahill* [2000] 1 IR 56, 61.
2. (1985) 160 CLR 583, 614.
3. This can be seen primarily in relation to determining the beneficial interest in family property. See *infra* pp. 177-194.
4. *Re Sharpe (a Bankrupt)* [1980] 1 WLR 219, 225 *per* Browne-Wilkinson J.

may be of crucial importance when the trustee is liable to account for profits derived from the activities which led the court to impose the trust.

It is also important not to consider the imposition of a constructive trust in isolation; it must often be considered in conjunction with the proprietary remedy of tracing trust property or the personal remedy against a trustee for breach of trust. While these remedies may sometimes prove to be equally effective, where the constructive trustee is insolvent, it will be important to pursue a proprietary rather than a personal remedy which will ensure that the beneficiary ranks ahead of the trustee's general creditors.

The constructive trust is often regarded as a residual category which arises where fairness demands it,[5] although it has also been said that equity's intervention in imposing such trusts 'must be based on principle; there must be some relationship between the relief granted and the circumstances which give rise to it.'[6] While it is possible to delimit several categories in which constructive trusts will arise, it would never be possible, nor indeed desirable, to define exhaustively the circumstances which might give rise to the imposition of such a trust. It is therefore proposed to examine the traditionally recognised categories in turn and then to consider where future developments in this area may lead.

ADVANTAGES GAINED BY PERSONS IN FIDUCIARY POSITIONS

General Principles

It is a fundamental principle that a trustee or other party in a fiduciary position will not be permitted to take advantage of his position to make a personal profit and any profit which he makes in this manner will be held by him as a constructive trustee for the benefit of the persons equitably entitled to the property. This principle was laid down as follows by Chatterton VC in *Gabbett v. Lawder*:[7]

> The fundamental position upon which the doctrine of constructive trusts proceeds is, that no person in a fiduciary capacity shall be allowed to retain any advantage gained by him in his character as trustee. His *cestuis*

---

5.   Recent examples of the imposition of a constructive trust include *Ord v. Upton* [2000] Ch 352 and *Banner Homes Group plc v. Luff Developments Ltd* [2000] Ch 372.

6.   *Lonrho plc v. Fayed (No. 2)* [1992] 1 WLR 1, 9.

7.   (1883) 11 LR Ir 295, 299. See also the *dicta* of Chatterton VC in *Kelly v. Kelly* (1874) 8 IR Eq 403, 406: 'It is the great principle that no person in a fiduciary position accepting any benefit attributable in any degree to that fiduciary position can be allowed to enjoy such benefit for himself.' See also *M'Cracken v. M'Clelland* (1877) IR 11 Eq 172, 176 and *Armstrong v. Armstrong* (1880) 7 LR Ir 207, 218 *per* Lord O'Hagan LC.

> *que trusts* are entitled to the benefit of any advantage so gained by him,
> to any addition or accretion to the trust estate which he may have
> acquired, and to all profit which he may have made by any dealing with
> it.

While it is not possible to provide an exhaustive definition of the categories
of persons who occupy fiduciary positions, generally speaking such individuals
can be distinguished from those who are merely bound by contractual
obligations by the fact that those in the former category are obliged to act in a
completely selfless manner. The most commonly encountered examples of
fiduciary relationships are those existing between trustee and beneficiary, agent
and principal, director and company and between partners, and although these
categories are not closed, some limitations have been imposed on the extension
of these obligations.[8] There has been a considerable divergence between the
views expressed in England and in other common law jurisdictions on the
question of the extent to which fiduciary obligations should be extended to
commercial transactions. Certainly in England there are increasing signs of a
reluctance on the part of the judiciary to impose the higher standards of conduct
demanded by equity on transactions where the parties are dealing with each
other at arm's length and on a relatively equal footing.[9] This attitude is
exemplified by the following statement of Lord Mustill in the decision of the
Privy Council in *Re Goldcorp Exchange*:[10]

> No doubt the fact that one person is placed in a particular position *vis-
> à-vis* another through the medium of a contract does not necessarily
> mean that he does not also owe fiduciary duties to that other by virtue of
> being in that position. But the essence of a fiduciary relationship is that
> it creates obligations of a different character from those deriving from
> the contract itself. Their Lordships have not heard in argument any
> submission which went beyond suggesting that by virtue of being a
> fiduciary the company was obliged honestly and conscientiously to do
> what it had by contract promised to do. Many commercial relationships
> involve just such a reliance by one party on the other, and to introduce
> the whole new dimension into such relationships which would flow from
> giving them a fiduciary character would (as it seems to their Lordships)
> have adverse consequences far exceeding those foreseen by Atkin LJ in
> *Re Wait* [1927] 1 Ch 606.

While the vast majority of cases decided in this jurisdiction where a

---

8. See e.g. *Tito v. Wadell (No. 2)* [1977] Ch 106; *Swain v. The Law Society* [1982] 3
   WLR 261.
9. See the comments of Mason (1994) 110 LQR 238, 245.
10. [1995] 1 AC 74, 98.

constructive trust has been held to arise due to a breach of fiduciary obligations have related to non-commercial transactions, this policy question is bound to have increased significance before our courts in the not too distant future, and it will be interesting to see whether the sentiments expressed by Lord Mustill will find favour here.

The Fiduciary Position of Trustees

The 'fundamental position' referred to above by Chatterton VC in *Gabbett v. Lawder*[11] applies strictly to trustees and personal representatives. These principles also apply to a varying degree to other categories of persons who act in a fiduciary capacity. It is not possible to state with certainty the extent to which these principles will apply to or be treated as irrebuttable presumptions of law in relation to such other categories and it is proposed to examine a number of situations which are relevant primarily, although not exclusively, to persons acting as trustees and personal representatives, and then to consider some of the circumstances in which liability will be imposed in the context of other types of fiduciaries.

Renewal of a Lease

A common situation which will give rise to the creation of a constructive trust is where a trustee of leasehold property obtains a renewal of the lease in his own name. It was circumstances such as these which led to the formulation of the so called rule in *Keech v. Sandford*,[12] which has formed the basis for the rather wider principle enunciated by Chatterton VC in *Gabbett v. Lawder* above. In *Keech*, a trustee held a lease of the profits of Romford Market on trust for an infant. Before the expiration of the lease he applied for a renewal for the infant's benefit but the lessor refused to renew on the grounds that the infant could not enter into the usual covenants. The lessor indicated that he would be willing to give the trustee the lease instead and the latter accepted the renewal in his own name. It was held that despite the trustee's attempt to obtain a renewal for the infant's benefit, he must be regarded as holding the lease for the latter's benefit and was obliged to pay over to the infant the profits which he received. King LC stated: 'This may seem hard, that the trustee is the only person of all mankind who might not have the lease; but it is very proper that the rule should be strictly pursued'.[13]

   This precise principle was outlined as follows by Chatterton VC in *Gabbett v. Lawder*,[14] albeit in an *obiter* capacity:

---

11. (1883) 11 LR Ir 295.
12. (1726) Sel Cas T King 61.
13. *Ibid.* at 62.
14. (1883) 11 LR Ir 295, 299.

> It has long been settled by a current of authorities that a trustee of a leasehold interest who obtains a renewal of the lease, whether by covenant or custom, or by the voluntary act of the reversioner, comes within this principle, and that he cannot hold the interest he so acquired for his own benefit, but as a constructive trustee of it for his *cestuis que trusts.*

In this context any advantage or profit derived by a trustee is deemed by equity to be engrafted onto the property held on trust, a process known in this jurisdiction as the doctrine of graft. The effect and ambit of this doctrine was discussed by Fitzgibbon LJ in *Dempsey v. Ward*[15] and it is clear that it extends beyond trustees to other classes of individuals, with executors and administrators being specifically mentioned by Fitzgibbon LJ. Under the rule in *Keech v. Sandford*, where a trustee or person in a fiduciary position surrenders an old lease with a view to obtaining a new one, he will be held to be a constructive trustee, and this principle was illustrated in the context of an executor by the decision of *M'Cracken v. M'Clelland.*[16] There, an executor surrendered a holding which was subject to the Ulster Custom while the old tenancy was still in existence and, in compliance with the custom, was given a new tenancy on his own behalf. Chatterton VC commented that he was at a loss to understand how the defendant, by virtue of the position which he occupied as executor of the testator's estate, could contend that he was entitled to retain the benefit of the new tenancy for himself and concluded that it was held on a constructive trust for the persons entitled under the will.

The doctrine of graft was also applied in the context of an administrator of an estate in *Kelly v. Kelly*,[17] where a widow and administratrix of her husband's estate continued in possession of land held on a tenancy from year to year. The landlord determined the tenancy by serving a notice to quit and the administratrix did not oppose this and was left in occupation at the same rent. It was held that while her conduct did not amount to fraud, the new tenancy was a graft on the old one and she was regarded as being in occupation of the premises as constructive trustee for the next of kin who would have been entitled to the original tenancy on her husband's death. Similarly, the doctrine of graft has been held to apply to the guardian of an infant,[18] and to a person managing the property of a lunatic.[19] A further category of persons to whom the doctrine applies is that of a limited owner, which is illustrated by the decision of the Irish Court of Appeal in *Re Brady's Estate.*[20] A testator

---

15. [1899] 1 IR 463, 474-475.
16. (1877) IR 11 Eq 172. See also *Re Egan* [1906] 1 IR 320.
17. (1874) IR 8 Eq 403.
18. *Quinton v. Frith* (1868) IR 2 Eq 396, 494.
19. *Smyth v. Byrne* [1914] 1 IR 53.
20. [1920] 1 IR 170.

bequeathed leasehold premises on trust to permit his wife to use and enjoy these for the remainder of the term so long as she should live and continue to be his widow. The widow, who did not remarry, remained on in beneficial possession of the lands for a period of three years after the expiry of the lease and then obtained a new lease of the premises in her own name. The Court of Appeal held that the widow was necessarily in the position of a limited owner only, in addition to being the executor and trustee under the will, and that the renewal of the lease which she obtained in her own name must be deemed to be a graft on the former one.

However, the doctrine of graft is not unlimited in its ambit;[21] although it was applied in *Hunter v. Allen*[22] to a case of tenants in common, Barton J commented that *Dempsey v. Ward*[23] was a useful decision in that 'it served to remind us that the frontiers of the doctrine of graft have in this country been reached; and that the doctrine should be cautiously applied.' In *Dempsey* it was held that there was no graft when the widow of a previous tenant of an expired lease obtained a new tenancy on her own behalf on the basis that there was nothing to connect these tenancies. Fitzgibbon LJ commented that 'to have a graft at all, there must still be life in the old stock'[24] and said that he entertained grave doubts about the extent to which the doctrine had been developed in this jurisdiction.

The crucial question which must be addressed in determining whether the new interest will be engrafted onto the old is whether the person obtaining the renewal occupies a fiduciary position. In the case of a trustee, there appears to be an almost irrebuttable presumption of a constructive trust arising.[25] This has been confirmed by the following *dicta* of Chatterton VC in *Gabbett v. Lawder*:[26]

> Where a trustee obtains a renewal of a lease this Court will not allow the trustee to say that he did not obtain the additional interest as trustee, or that he procured it from personal favour to himself, or from the refusal of the landlord to deal with the *cestuis que trusts*, or for any similar reason. If his position could have caused or even contributed to his obtaining the advantage, it is in my opinion enough; and the Court will not undertake the difficult and often impossible task of investigating the motives of the parties to the transaction. If it results in either gain to the trustee or loss to the *cestuis que trusts*, the trustee is liable to hand over to them the one or make good the other.

---

21. *Robinson v. Crosse & Blackwell Ltd* [1940] IR 56.
22. [1907] 1 IR 212.
23. [1899] 1 IR 463.
24. *Ibid.* at 474.
25. *Re Biss* [1903] 2 Ch 40, 56 *per* Collins MR.
26. (1883) 11 LR Ir 295, 299-300.

However, as Romer LJ stated in *Re Biss*,[27] 'where the person renewing the lease does not clearly occupy a fiduciary position [he] is only held to be a constructive trustee of the renewed lease if, in respect of the old lease, he occupied some special position and owed, by virtue of that position, a duty towards the other persons interested,' and so the presumption of a constructive trust will ordinarily be rebuttable.[28] Where the person taking the renewal owes neither a fiduciary obligation nor a special duty, clearly no constructive trust will arise.[29]

Cretney[30] has commented that the distinction between persons who act in a fiduciary capacity and those who do not is a difficult one to draw and while he accepts that it may be justifiable to impose a special onus on trustees, asks 'why should it be contrary to public policy to allow a trustee to rebut a presumption of misbehaviour?' He argues that while it is quite acceptable that there should be a high onus on a trustee who has obtained a renewal of a lease which may only be discharged in rare cases, this does not justify the principle that the rule in *Keech v. Sandford* should be an absolute one. However as Oakley[31] has commented, although such a 'stringent penal rule' is difficult to justify in a modern context so far removed from the conditions which gave rise to it, there is no evidence of any retrenchment from this position by the judiciary either in England or in this jurisdiction.

Purchase of the Reversion in a Lease

The question of whether a trustee or other person in a fiduciary position may purchase the reversion of a lease held in trust or for his principal for his own benefit has been the subject of some controversy. Traditionally, the rule in *Keech v. Sandford* was applied in a limited way to such a purchase and a constructive trust would arise if the lease was renewable by contract or custom or where the trustee obtained the reversion by virtue of his position as lessee.[32] This principle was applied by Chatterton VC in *Gabbett v. Lawder*,[33] where the administrator of the estate of an intestate held lands under a lease as trustee. The fee simple reversion of these lands became vested in the Church

---

27. [1903] 2 Ch 40, 61.
28. *Chan v. Zacharia* (1984) 154 CLR 178, 201-202 *per* Deane J.
29. *Robinson v. Crosse & Blackwell Ltd* [1940] IR 56, where Johnston J found that the defendants occupied neither a fiduciary nor 'quasi fiduciary' relationship. See also *Savage v. Dunningham* [1974] Ch 181.
30. (1969) 33 Conv 161.
31. Parker and Mellows, *The Modern Law of Trusts* (7th ed., 1998) p. 308.
32. See Cretney (1969) 33 Conv 161, 162. See also Jackson (1968) 31 MLR 707, 709. This seems to have been the position originally accepted in England, see *Randall v. Russell* (1817) 3 Mer 190; *Longton v. Wilsby* (1897) 76 LT 770 and see the *dicta* of Wilberforce J in *Phipps v. Boardman* [1964] 2 All ER 187, 201-202.
33. (1883) 11 LR Ir 295.

Temporalities Commissioners who were authorized to sell it but before doing so they were bound to offer it to the lessee at a price to be named by them. The reversion was offered to the lessee who declined to buy it on the ground that the price was too high but he then bought it for himself at a public auction for a lower sum. It was held by Chatterton VC that in the circumstances the administrator became a constructive trustee of the reversion for the persons beneficially entitled to the personal estate of the deceased although he was entitled to the costs incurred by him in purchasing the reversion.

The authorities in England now appear to support the imposition of an absolute prohibition against the purchase of the reversion by a fiduciary irrespective of the circumstances in which this occurs and even where the fiduciary is not a trustee or personal representative. In *Protheroe v. Protheroe*[34] a husband held the leasehold interest in the family home, which it was agreed he held on trust for himself and his wife in equal shares. After the parties had separated, the husband bought the freehold reversion and it was held by the Court of Appeal that the wife was entitled equally with the husband to the proceeds of sale of the freehold. While it has been argued[35] that this conclusion was reached more as a result of a desire on the part of the court to do justice between the spouses rather than by way of application of strict principles which should apply as between trustee and beneficiary, Lord Denning MR made the following general statement: 'There is a long established rule of equity from *Keech v. Sandford* downwards that if a trustee, who owns the leasehold, gets in the freehold, that freehold belongs to the trust and he cannot take the property for himself.'[36] This principle was followed without reference to the earlier authorities in this area in *Thompson's Trustee v. Heaton*,[37] where Pennycuick VC described Lord Denning's *dicta* as 'an application of the broad principle that a trustee must not make a profit out of the trust estate'.[38]

It is unlikely that the courts in this jurisdiction will take quite such a restrictive view of this position where a fiduciary purchases the reversion on a lease and it is probable that a trust will only arise in the circumstances outlined by Chatterton VC in *Gabbett v. Lawder* or where the fiduciary has clearly taken advantage of his position as lessee to obtain this benefit. However, having regard to the tenor of the authorities in the area, the onus will

---

34. [1968] 1 All ER 1111.
35. Underhill & Hayton, *The Law Relating to Trusts and Trustees* (16th ed., 2003) p.384.
36. *Ibid.* at 1112.
37. [1974] 1 WLR 605.
38. *Ibid.* at 612. Jackson has criticised this decision on the grounds that in view of the categorisation laid down by Collins MR in *Re Biss* [1903] 2 Ch 40 of the types of relationships which will give rise to an irrebuttable presumption of a constructive trust arising, there should be at most a rebuttable presumption of a trust where a partner as opposed to a trustee obtains the reversion on a partnership lease. See (1975) 38 MLR 226.

undoubtedly lie on the fiduciary to establish that he has not acted improperly, particularly where he occupies the position of trustee.

Competition with Trust Business

As we have seen above, a fundamental principle exists which prevents a trustee or other party in a fiduciary position from taking advantage of his position to make a personal profit and he will be required to hold any profit which he makes in this manner as a constructive trustee for the benefit of the persons equitably entitled to the property. In addition, a trustee must not place himself in a situation where his duty to the trust and his own personal interest may conflict,[39] in circumstances where he is likely to derive a profit by virtue of his fiduciary position. One situation which will obviously give rise to concern is where a trustee derives profits from a business which can be said to be in competition with any business carried on by the trust and this question was considered in detail by Chatterton VC in *Moore v. McGlynn.*[40] The testator who was a shopkeeper and postmaster bequeathed all his property to his brother and son to be held on trust and managed by them for the benefit of his wife and children, and he directed that his brother should be entitled to a salary for managing the business. The brother was appointed postmaster and carried on this role in the same premises for a number of years. Subsequently, he set up his own business in the same town and opened the post office there. The question which had to be determined by the court was whether a trust could be imposed for the benefit of the testator's estate in relation to the new premises and business carried on by the testator's brother. Chatterton VC rejected this argument in the following terms: 'I am not prepared to hold that a trustee is guilty of a breach of trust in setting up for himself in a similar line of business in the neighbourhood, provided that he does not resort to deception, or solicitation of custom from persons dealing at the old shop'. However, he continued by saying:

> It is plain that the setting up a shop in a small town to a certain extent in rivalry with another must tend more or less to injure the business of any similar shop in the locality, and I think there would be an inconsistency between the duties of the defendant ... as trustee and manager of the testator's business, and the necessary personal interest which he must take in his own. ... I am of opinion that his new position disqualifies him from remaining any longer a trustee, and it would have been better for him to have procured his removal from the trusteeship before setting up for himself. He should not be continued in a position where his duties and his self interest may conflict.[41]

---

39. *Re Jarvis* [1958] 1 WLR 815, 819 *per* Upjohn J.
40. [1894] 1 IR 74.
41. *Ibid.* at 89-90.

This rather lenient approach has met with some criticism and can be contrasted with the stricter view taken by Clauson J in *Re Thomson*,[42] where an injunction was granted restraining a trustee from carrying on a yacht brokerage business in the same town as that in which a similar business had been managed by him and his co-trustees on behalf of the trust. Clauson J said that having regard to the special nature of the business which he was pursuing, the defendant trustee would have been entering into engagements which would or might conflict with the interests of the beneficiaries as he would be obtaining commission for himself which might otherwise have been obtained on the beneficiaries' behalf. It can be argued that the decision in *Thomson* was influenced by the extremely specialized nature of the business in question, and Goff and Jones have commented that it is doubtful whether there is an absolute rule against a trustee or executor carrying on a business in competition with his beneficiary.[43] Certainly it would seem unduly restrictive to impose a constructive trust where a trustee continues to carry on an existing business in competition with one to which he is subsequently appointed trustee. However, it is also doubtful whether it should be necessary to establish a motive of 'deception, or solicitation of custom' in order for a constructive trust to arise and it is arguable that the approach of Chatterton VC in *Moore* was unduly lenient and might not be followed.

Other Types of Fiduciary Relationships

Introduction

As Lord Herschell stated in *Bray v. Ford*:[44] 'It is an inflexible rule of a Court of Equity that a person in a fiduciary position … is not, unless otherwise expressly provided, entitled to make a profit; he is not allowed to put himself in a position where his interest and duty conflict.'[45] The rationale behind the imposition of a constructive trust in such circumstances was well summarised by McLachlin J delivering the judgment of the majority of the Supreme Court of Canada in *Soulos v. Korkontzilas*[46] in the following terms:

> The constructive trust imposed for breach of fiduciary relationship thus

---

42. [1930] 1 Ch 203.
43. *The Law of Restitution* (6th ed., 2002) p. 722.
44. [1896] AC 44, 51. Quoted with approval by Lindsay J in *Re Drexel Burnham Lambert UK Pension Plan* [1995] 1 WLR 32, 37. See also *Swain v. The Law Society* [1982] 1 WLR 17, 37 *per* Oliver J.
45. A recent definition of a fiduciary is provided by Millett LJ in *Bristol and West Building Society v. Mothew* [1998] Ch 1, 18 in the following terms: 'A fiduciary is someone who has undertaken to act for or on behalf of another in a particular matter in circumstances which give rise to a relationship of trust and confidence'.
46. (1997) 147 DLR (4th) 214, 227.

serves not only to do the justice between the parties that good conscience requires, but to hold fiduciaries and people in positions of trust to the high standards of trust and probity that commercial and other social institutions require if they are to function effectively.

Clearly where a fiduciary has been unjustly enriched at his principal's expense, the imposition of liability is fully justified. However, where the fiduciary has acted in an honest manner and the principal has not suffered any loss as a result of the former's conduct, the question of whether the fiduciary should be liable to account for any profit made is, in principle, less straightforward. The authorities would suggest that unjust enrichment is not a prerequisite for the imposition of liability and that a fiduciary will be liable unless he acts with the knowledge and consent of his principal.[47] The extent of the rather restrictive approach taken by the courts in this area is well summarised by Jones:[48]

> Once a fiduciary is shown to be in breach of his duty of loyalty he must disgorge any benefit gained even though he acted honestly and in his principal's best interests, even though his principal could not otherwise have obtained the benefit, and even though the benefit was obtained through the use of the fiduciary's own assets and in consequence of his personal skill and judgment.

A number of academic commentators have questioned the fairness of such a rigid application of the principle in *Keech v. Sandford*, which Finn[49] has stated is applied 'in an arbitrary and technical fashion irrespective of any actual conflict of duty and interest, or of any actual misuse of a position of trust.' Similarly, Lowry[50] has questioned the correctness of applying a 'uniform set of inflexible rules to govern all fiduciaries irrespective of the particular circumstances in which they are operating', but the fact remains that the courts seem intent on continuing to apply the established principles in what may appear a rather arbitrary manner.[51]

---

47. This view is supported by the conclusion reached by the majority of the Supreme Court of Canada in *Soulos v. Korkontzilas* (1997) 147 DLR (4th) 214.
48. (1968) 84 LQR 472, 474.
49. *Fiduciary Obligations* (1977) p. 261.
50. (1994) 45 NILQ 1, 2. Note also the comments of the English Law Commission in Consultation Paper No. 124 (1992) paragraph 2.4.2.
51. Although note the slightly more flexible approach adopted by Lindsay J in *Re Drexel Burnham Lambert UK Pension Plan* [1995] 1 WLR 32 where he held that the court had jurisdiction to give directions in relation to the winding up of a pension proposed by trustees who were themselves beneficiaries, notwithstanding this conflict between duty and interest.

Another question which must also be addressed is whether the opportunity for profit actually derived from the fiduciary relationship. In order to found liability it will be necessary to establish a connection between the fiduciary position and the profit made. Another important issue is the nature of the liability which should be imposed; the proprietary remedy of a constructive trust may have far-reaching consequences for third parties particularly where the fiduciary has insufficient funds to meet his creditors' demands and while there is no sign of an acceptance of such an approach by the judiciary in this area, it is possible that personal liability to account for any profits made might be a preferable form of remedy where a fiduciary has acted honestly and has not been unjustly enriched at his principal's expense. Finally it should be borne in mind that 'there is more than one category of fiduciary relationship and the different categories possess different characteristics and attract different kinds of fiduciary obligation'.[52] Subject to this caveat, it is now proposed to examine some of the general principles which may apply in more detail, both in relation to the circumstances in which liability may be imposed and with reference to some specific types of fiduciary relationships.

The Liability of a Fiduciary to Account for Secret Commissions and Bribes

As a general principle, a fiduciary may not accept secret commissions or bribes arising out of a transaction in which he is acting on behalf of a principal without the knowledge and consent of his principal. An examination of the authorities in this area shows that the boundaries of the types of relationships which can be categorised as fiduciary are not clear and that such a classification may to an extent depend on the remedy which a court feels is justified in the circumstances of a case. For the purposes of imposing liability to account for any secret profits or commissions received, the interpretation placed on the term 'fiduciary' has always been a fairly liberal one. This is illustrated by the decision in *Reading v. Attorney-General*,[53] in which a British Army sergeant was held to be liable to account to the Crown in relation to monies which he received for assisting in the smuggling of goods on the grounds that he had used his uniform and the privileges which attached to it to carry out these activities.

Traditionally, where a fiduciary received a secret commission as a result of his position, he was liable as a constructive trustee of these monies. In *Williams v. Barton*[54] a trustee was employed by a stockbroking firm on terms

---

52. *Per* Woolf MR in *Attorney General v. Blake* [1998] 1 All ER 833, 842. As Lord Browne-Wilkinson commented in *Henderson v. Merrett Syndicates Ltd* [1995] 2 AC 145, 206: 'the phrase "fiduciary duties" is a dangerous one, giving rise to a mistaken assumption that all fiduciaries owe the same duties in all circumstances'.
53. [1951] AC 507. See also *Attorney-General v. Goddard* (1929) 98 LJ KB 743.
54. [1927] 2 Ch 9.

which entitled him to half the commission earned by the firm on business introduced by him. His recommendation that the firm be used to value trust securities was followed and he was held liable to account to the trust as a constructive trustee in respect of the commission which he earned from this business. However, it was generally accepted on the authority of the decision of *Lister & Co. v. Stubbs*[55] that where a fiduciary received a bribe from a third party, although he was liable to account, he was not regarded as a constructive trustee of this sum.[56] Attempts were made to justify this position on the grounds that the use of the fiduciary position to exact a bribe in these circumstances did not deprive the beneficiary or principal of property which belonged or ought to have belonged to him.[57] The imposition of a personal as opposed to a proprietary remedy has important practical consequences; namely that the funds cannot be traced into property into which they might be converted and the beneficiary or principal cannot recover any profit made through the use of the money or acquire any preferential rights should the fiduciary become bankrupt. The rather anomalous result that a person who obtained a bribe might be merely obliged to account for its value, whereas a fiduciary who had earned a commission in good faith might be held to be a constructive trustee of this sum, was frequently criticised and it has been suggested that the cases of *Williams* and *Lister* should have been decided in the same way.[58] One view was that the imposition of a proprietary remedy should be confined to situations where a beneficiary has been deprived of property which he would otherwise have obtained. However, the alternative argument is that a constructive trust should have been imposed in both sets of circumstances on the grounds that a fiduciary should not be allowed to derive *any* advantage from acting in a manner contrary to his fiduciary obligations or from placing himself in a situation where his duties and personal interests might conflict.

While the questions have yet to be addressed by the courts in this jurisdiction, the decision of the Privy Council in *Attorney-General for Hong Kong v. Reid*[59] has gone some way towards resolving many of the anomalies which have developed in this area. While employed by the legal service of the government of Hong Kong in various capacities, ultimately as acting Director of Public Prosecutions, the first named respondent accepted bribes

---

55. (1890) 45 Ch D 1. Although note that there has been a certain amount of confusion about the precise *ratio* of the case, see *Jacobs' Law of Trusts in Australia* (6th ed., 1997, Meagher and Gummow) pp. 321-323 and Cope, *Constructive Trusts* (1992) pp. 263-264.
56. See also *Metropolitan Bank v. Heiron* (1880) 5 Ex D 319.
57. Note that Millett has commented that the decision in *Lister* could not be supported 'as matter of policy, principle or authority' [1993] RLR 7, 29.
58. See Parker & Mellows, *The Modern Law of Trusts* (7th ed., 1998, Oakley) p. 294; Millett [1993] RLR 7; Oakley [1994] CLJ 31.
59. [1994] 1 AC 324. See also Oakley [1995] CLJ 377.

in breach of his fiduciary duty. He pleaded guilty to a number of bribery offences and was sentenced to eight years' imprisonment and ordered to pay a sum equivalent to the value of his assets which could only have been derived from bribes. These sums were not paid over and the Attorney-General for Hong Kong lodged caveats in New Zealand against the titles to properties in that jurisdiction which it was alleged had been purchased with monies received as bribes. The application of the Attorney-General for Hong Kong to renew the caveats was refused by the Court of Appeal of New Zealand but was allowed on appeal by the Privy Council. It was held that when a bribe is accepted by a fiduciary in breach of his duty, he holds it on a constructive trust for the person to whom that duty is owed and to the extent to which they represented bribes received by the first named respondent, the New Zealand properties were held in trust for the Crown. As Lord Templeman stated:

> The rule must be that property which a trustee obtains by use of knowledge acquired as trustee becomes trust property. The rule must, *a fortiori*, apply to a bribe accepted by a trustee for a guilty criminal purpose which injures the *cestui que trust*. The trustee is only one example of a fiduciary and the same rule applies to all other fiduciaries who accept bribes.[60]

Lord Templeman added that if the property representing the bribe decreases in value the fiduciary must pay the difference between that value and the initial amount of the bribe. If the property increases in value, the fiduciary is not entitled to any surplus in excess of the initial value of the bribe because he is not allowed by any means to make a profit out of a breach of duty. The decision of *Lister & Co. v. Stubbs* was rejected as being inconsistent with the principle that a fiduciary should not benefit from his own breach of duty and that he should account for the bribe as soon as he receives it.[61] Lord Templeman therefore concluded that: 'From these principles it would appear to follow that the bribe and the property from time to time representing the bribe are held on a constructive trust for the person injured.'[62]

This decision has been welcomed as it resolves the rather arbitrary inconsistency between the remedies imposed in circumstances where a fiduciary received a bribe and earned a commission.[63] However, while it may

---

60. *Ibid.* at 332.
61. In *Attorney General v. Blake* [1997] Ch 84, 96 Sir Richard Scott VC suggested that he would still be bound to follow *Lister & Co. v. Stubbs* but said that he was persuaded by the reasoning of Lord Templeman in *Reid* that *Lister* ought no longer to be regarded as good law. No reference to this point was made by the Court of Appeal [1998] Ch 439 or by the House of Lords [2000] 1 AC 268.
62. *Ibid.* at 336.
63. Oakley [1994] CLJ 31.

be reasonable that a fiduciary should not profit from a breach of duty even if this means that the principal receives a windfall, it has been argued by Jones[64] that it is not so obvious that a windfall is justified where the contest is between creditors who have given value and a principal who has not. There is certainly merit in the argument that in circumstances where a recipient of a bribe is insolvent the imposition of a more limited form of remedy, such as a claim merely to secure the sum which represents the value of the bribe might be more equitable, given the enormous significance of proprietary remedies and their potential impact on creditors and third parties.

The Position of Agents

Where an agent puts himself in a position where his duty to his principal and his own interests may conflict and makes a profit out of his fiduciary position, he will be liable to account for this. Moore LJ summarised the nature of the fiduciary duty owed by an agent to his principal in *Sherrard v. Barron*[65] as follows:

> There is no dispute about the law, which is that an agent cannot without the knowledge of his principal make any profit for himself out of services rendered to his principal. Should he do so, he must account. It is equally settled law that it is the duty of the agent to make the fullest disclosure to his principal of all transactions in which the agent is making, directly or indirectly, a profit out of his principal. If this is done and the principal, expressly or by course of conduct, impliedly assents, the agent can retain his profit.

The requirement of disclosure and consent is strictly applied as can be seen from *Patten v. Hamilton*,[66] where an agent purchased a charge on his principal's estate at an undervalue and continued to collect the interest on the face value of the charge. It was held by the Irish Court of Appeal that in the absence of evidence that the principal had consented to the agent retaining the full benefit of the transaction, the agent should be treated as a trustee for the principal and the extra interest should be applied towards extinguishing the charge.

As Andrews LJ made it clear in *Sherrard v. Barron*, it is of paramount importance in all transactions between agent and principal and between other

---

64. [1994] Conv 156.
65. [1923] 1 IR 21, 24. Note also the *dicta* of James LJ in *Parker v. McKenna* (1874) 10 Ch App 96, 124 to the effect that 'no agent in the course of his agency, in the matter of his agency, can be allowed to make any profit without the knowledge and consent of his principal.' See also *Re Canadian Oil Works Corporation* (1875) 10 Ch App 593, 601 *per* Mellish LJ.
66. [1911] 1 IR 46. See the general principle set out by Cherry LJ at 60.

parties who stand in a fiduciary relationship to one another that 'there should be nothing in the nature of underhand dealing.'[67] However, liability does not depend on any finding of fraud and applies equally even where it has not been shown that any advantage has been taken. It has also been established that it is irrelevant that the principal does not suffer any loss as a result of the agent's actions and in fact may have benefited, although in such circumstances, the agent may be entitled to remuneration for his endeavours. The best illustration of the rigour with which these principles have been applied is the decision of the House of Lords in *Boardman v. Phipps*.[68] Assets were held on trust for the benefit of a testator's children, the trustees being his widow, who was senile, his daughter and an accountant. The trust had a sizable minority shareholding in a textile company and with the consent of the two active trustees, Boardman, the trustees' solicitor, and one of the beneficiaries, set about acquiring a majority shareholding in the company in order to make it more profitable. By purporting to act on behalf of the trust they obtained detailed information about the company and succeeded in gaining control of it, making a considerable profit as a result. The House of Lords held that Boardman and the beneficiary were liable to account to the trust for the profits which they had made, although it was held that they were entitled to payment for the work which they had carried out.

The majority view was that the defendants had placed themselves in a position in which their duty and self-interest might conflict and had abused their fiduciary position by utilizing information acquired in a fiduciary capacity. Lord Hodson and Lord Guest agreed that information could be characterized as trust property and found that since the defendants had made a profit out of using this information, they were liable to account for it. Lord Cohen felt that information was not property in the strict sense, and said that the mere use of knowledge which comes to an agent in the course of his agency does not necessarily make him liable,[69] but he will be required to account where, as in the case before him, he purported to act on behalf of the trust. Viscount Dilhorne and Lord Upjohn dissented, holding that the information obtained by the defendants when purporting to act as agents of the trust was not trust property and they found that in the circumstances there was no conflict between their private interests and their fiduciary duty to the trust.

The distinction between the views expressed by the majority and minority members of the House of Lords is well summarized by Underhill and Hayton[70] as follows:

> The essential difference between the majority and the minority was that

---

67. [1923] 1 IR 21, 26.
68. [1967] 2 AC 46.
69. *Ibid.* at 102-103.
70. *Law Relating to Trusts and Trustees* (16th ed., 2003) p. 396.

the majority favoured the traditional strict deterrent approach, so that (*non de minimis*) possibility of a conflict between private interest and fiduciary duty arising out of use of information received in a fiduciary capacity should give rise to constructive trusteeship of the shares purchased as a result of such information, whilst the minority favoured a liberal reasonable approach that only a real sensible possibility of a conflict should give rise to a constructive trusteeship of the shares and there was not such a real sensible possibility.

It should be stated that the existence of the conflict of interest identified by the majority has been doubted by some commentators.[71] However, it has been argued that the majority view is preferable as it is more likely to protect the position of a principal or beneficiary who may be unaware of the agent's activities and in any event the agent can avoid liability if he obtains consent for the course of action which he intends to pursue before embarking upon it.

Finally, it is interesting to note that the majority of the Canadian Supreme Court has recently held in *Soulos v. Korkontzilas*[72] that an agent who acquires property from a third party in breach of his fiduciary obligations to his principal holds this property on a constructive trust despite the fact that the agent had not thereby realized any financial gain.[73] As McLachlin J stated: '[A] constructive trust is required in cases such as this to ensure that agents and others in positions of trust remain faithful to their duty of loyalty'.[74] In her view if the courts did not intervene by imposing a constructive trust in such circumstances the message which that would send out would be that agents might breach their fiduciary duties and the courts would do nothing unless the agent had made a profit. In the opinion of McLachlin J 'this will not do'; as she stated 'courts of equity have always been concerned to keep the person who acts on behalf of others to his ethical mark'.[75]

If the views of the majority of the House of Lords in *Boardman* and of the Supreme Court of Canada in *Soulos* are followed in this jurisdiction, it will lead to particularly strict standards being applied to the conduct of agents and a constructive trust will be imposed even where the principal has not sustained any loss as a result of the agent's actions or where the agent himself has not profited financially from any transaction entered into. It would seem likely that the view of the majority in *Boardman*, which is so firmly entrenched in

---

71. Jones (1968) 84 LQR 472.
72. (1997) 146 DLR (4th) 214. See further Smith (1997) Can Bar Rev 539; (1998) 114 LQR 14.
73. The view of the minority was that to impose a constructive trust where there had been no unjust enrichment would depart from settled principles, see the judgment of Sopinka J at 236.
74. *Ibid.* at 231.
75. *Ibid.* at 232.

England, will be followed here. Perhaps more uncertain is whether the slightly controversial principle of imposing a constructive trust in the absence of unjust enrichment will find favour with the courts in this jurisdiction.

The Position of Company Directors[76]

Company directors are treated as being fiduciaries insofar as they owe a duty to their company and they will not be permitted to place themselves in a position where their duty to the company and their personal interests will conflict or to derive a profit from their fiduciary relationship. As Swinfen Eady J stated in *Transvaal Lands Co. v. New Belgium (Transvaal) Land & Development Co.*,[77] referring to the judgment of Lord Cranworth in *Aberdeen Railway Co. v. Blaikie*:[78]

> It was there decided that directors of a company have duties to discharge of a fiduciary nature towards their principal, and that it is a rule of universal application, that no one, having such duties to discharge, shall be allowed to enter into engagements in which he has, or can have, a personal interest conflicting, or which possibly may conflict, with the interests of those he is bound to protect.

This view has been echoed recently by Lightman J in *Neptune (Vehicle Washing Equipment) Ltd v. Fitzgerald*[79] where he stated that 'a director of a company owes a fiduciary duty to the company to act *bona fide* in the best interests of the company and to prefer its interests to his own where they conflict'.

While it has been argued that the rule in *Keech v. Sandford* should only apply to trustees in the strict sense, as Lowry[80] has noted, 'it has been taken to be of equal applicability to all types of fiduciaries including company directors, irrespective of the equity of a particular case.' There is no question that liability will be imposed where a director abuses his fiduciary position by diverting to himself a contract which could have been taken up on the company's behalf. So in *Cook v. Deeks*,[81] the Privy Council held that directors who had engaged in such conduct held the benefit of those contracts on a constructive trust for the benefit of the company. This principle was succinctly set out by Laskin J in *Canadian Aero Service Ltd v. O'Malley*:[82]

> A director or a senior officer ... is precluded from obtaining for himself,

---

76. See generally Sealy [1967] CLJ 83; Lowry (1994) 45 NILQ 1.
77. [1914] 2 Ch 488, 502.
78. (1854) 1 Macq 461.
79. [1996] Ch 274, 279.
80. (1994) 45 NILQ 1, 2.
81. [1916] 1 AC 554.
82. (1974) 40 DLR (3d) 371, 382.

either secretly or without the approval of the company (which would have to be properly manifested upon full disclosure of the facts), any property or business advantage either belonging to the company or for which it has been negotiating; and especially is this so where the director or officer is a participant in the negotiations on behalf of the company.

Liability will also be imposed where the company itself was not in a position to take on a contract secured by a director where he takes advantage of his fiduciary position to achieve this. So in *Industrial Development Consultants v. Cooley*,[83] the defendant managing director of a company which provided construction consultancy services learnt in the course of negotiations with a gas board on its behalf that the board would not enter into an agreement with the company but that it would consider awarding the contract to him in a personal capacity. He secured a release from his employment by falsely claiming ill health and then entered into a contract with the board on his own behalf. Roskill J held that the defendant was a constructive trustee of the benefit of the contract and liable to account for the profits derived from it. As he stated: 'if the defendant is not required to account he will have made a large profit, as a result of having deliberately put himself into a position in which his duty to the plaintiffs who were employing him and his personal interests conflicted.'[84]

In some cases this general principle that a director must not profit from his fiduciary relationship with the company has been inflexibly applied and if a director takes advantage of his position and makes a profit, the court will not look behind his motives for so doing.[85] So even where a director has acted in an honest and *bona fide* manner in what he believes are the best interests of the company, he will nevertheless be liable to account for any personal profit made as a result of his fiduciary relationship with the company. The harshness of this rule is well illustrated by the decision of the House of Lords in *Regal (Hastings) Ltd v. Gulliver.*[86] A company which owned a cinema formed a subsidiary to take up the lease of two additional cinemas so that they might be all sold as a going concern. The landlord insisted on the subsidiary company having a paid up share capital of 5,000 ordinary £1 shares and as the parent company had insufficient resources to subscribe for more than 2,000, the directors of the company agreed to take up the remainder. When the business

---

83. [1972] 1 WLR 443.
84. *Ibid.* at 453. However compare this finding with the decision of the Canadian Supreme Court in *Peso Silver Mines Ltd (NPL) v. Cropper* (1966) 58 DLR (2d) 1 in which the court appeared to lay down the principle that it should not penalise a director in circumstances where he had acted in a *bona fide* manner and had taken up an opportunity which his company had been unable or unwilling to accept.
85. *Furs Ltd v. Tomkies* (1936) 54 CLR 583, 592 *per* Rich, Dixon and Evatt JJ.
86. [1967] 2 AC 134. (Initially reported at [1942] 1 All ER 378).

was transferred to new controllers the directors made a personal profit on the transaction. The purchaser successfully brought an action in the company's name to account for this profit on the grounds that the directors had derived such profit by virtue of their office. Lord Russell stated:

> The rule of equity which insists on those, who by use of a fiduciary position make a profit, being liable to account for that profit, in no way depends on fraud, or absence of *bona fides*; or upon such questions or considerations as whether the profit would or should otherwise have gone to the plaintiff, or whether the profiteer was under a duty to obtain the source of the profit for the plaintiff, or whether he took a risk or acted as he did for the benefit of the plaintiff, or whether the plaintiff has in fact been damaged or benefited by his action. The liability arises from the mere fact of a profit having, in the stated circumstances, been made. The profiteer, however honest and well intentioned, cannot escape the risk of being called upon to account.[87]

This decision seems unduly harsh in that the directors had acted honestly and in the best interests of the company, particularly as the company itself could not have obtained the benefit of the transactions which ultimately took place without the financial input of the directors. As Jones[88] has commented, while the policy issues in *Regal Hastings* were finely balanced the unquestioning adherence to the inexorable rule of equity by the House of Lords meant that these factors were never properly weighed against each other.

The fact that a director's liability to account for any profit made as a result of his fiduciary relationship with the company does not depend on *mala fides* but 'on the mere fact of a profit having been made' was restated by the House of Lords in *Guinness plc v. Saunders*,[89] in which the court had to consider the question of whether a director might be entitled to remuneration in circumstances where he had made a profit for the company. A committee of the board of directors of the plaintiff company had paid the second named defendant £5.2 million for his services in connection with a takeover bid being made by the plaintiff. Recovery of the money was claimed on the grounds that the second named defendant had received it in breach of his fiduciary duty as director in that he had not disclosed his interest in the agreement to the plaintiff company. The House of Lords agreed that he had failed to disclose his interest and ordered him to repay the money to the plaintiff. In relation to the second named defendant's claim for remuneration, it was argued that *Boardman v. Phipps* was authority for the proposition that in exceptional circumstances a court of equity might award remuneration to a trustee and

---

87. *Ibid.* at 144.
88. (1968) 84 LQR 472, 497.
89. [1990] 2 AC 663. See Goulding [1990] Conv 296.

that therefore it might make such payments to a director. However, Lord Goff concluded that the present case was 'very different' to *Boardman* and continued: 'Whether any such an allowance might ever be granted by a court of equity in the case of a director of a company, as opposed to a trustee, is a point which has yet to be decided. ... In any event I cannot see any possibility of such jurisdiction being exercised in the present case.'[90]

A more flexible approach was adopted by Hutchison J in *Island Export Finance Ltd v. Umunna*[91] in which he held that a former director of a company might secure a contract to supply materials, supplied by the company on a previous occasion, in circumstances where the company was not actively seeking the new contract and where there was no connection between his resignation and the securing of this contract. Hutchison J stated that it would be surprising to find that directors were restrained from exploiting any opportunity of which they had acquired knowledge as directors after they ceased to be such. In his view 'directors, no less than employees, acquire a general fund of knowledge and expertise in the course of their work, and it is plainly in the public interest that they should be free to exploit it in a new position.'[92] Subsequently in *CMS Dolphin Ltd v. Simonet*,[93] while Lawrence Collins J acknowledged that a director is not precluded following his resignation from a company from using his general fund of skill and knowledge or his personal connections, he also made it clear that where he exploits a maturing business opportunity liability will be imposed. The first named defendant who was the director of an advertising agency resigned and set up a new business, recruiting all the agency's staff which resulted in its principal clients also switching their business to his new venture. In imposing liability to account Lawrence Collins J stated as follows:

> In my judgment the underlying basis of the liability of a director who exploits after his resignation a maturing business opportunity of the company is that the opportunity is to be treated as if it were property of the company in relation to which the director had fiduciary duties. By seeking to exploit the opportunity after resignation he is appropriating for himself that property. He is just as accountable as a trustee who retires without properly accounting for trust property. In the case of a director he becomes a constructive trustee of the fruits of his abuse of the company's property, which he has acquired in the circumstances where he knowingly has a conflict of interest, and exploited it by resigning from the company.[94]

---

90. *Ibid.* at 701.
91. [1986] BCLC 460.
92. *Ibid.* at 482.
93. [2001] 2 BCLC 704.
94. *Ibid.* at 733.

It is clear from the recent decision of the Court of Appeal in *In Plus Group Ltd v. Pyke*[95] that 'there is no completely rigid rule that a director may not be involved in the business of a company which is in competition with another company of which he was a director'. In this case the court was satisfied that the defendant had been effectively excluded from the claimant companies of which he was a director some months before he entered into business with one of their customers and that in so doing he was not making use of confidential information which had come to him in his role as director of these companies. In these circumstances the Court of Appeal concluded that the defendant had committed no breach of fiduciary duty in trading with the companies' former customer.

Finally it should be noted that in *Neptune (Vehicle Washing Equipment) Ltd v. Fitzgerald*,[96] while Lightman J reiterated that where a director enters into an arrangement or transaction with himself or with a company in which he is interested, that arrangement may be set aside irrespective of whether the company has suffered as a result, he stated that it is a defence to such a claim that the company's shareholders have consented to the transaction or the articles of association allow it.

Therefore it is fair to say that the general tenor of more recent decisions in England would seem to be more flexible and in many cases directors have escaped liability. The result in *CMS Dolphin Ltd* seemed almost inevitable given the conduct of the defendant and even in this decision the attitude of Lawrence Collins J towards the difficulties faced by ex-directors was a realistic one. So, the courts now appear to be taking a more pragmatic approach and recognising the practical reality that a director will inevitably acquire a general fund of knowledge in the course of carrying out his duties and that he cannot be expected to desist from all activities of a commercial nature on leaving his position or even to refrain from going into competition with the former company.

While it can be argued that it is necessary to apply the relevant principles in this area in a rigid manner to deter those in positions of trust who might otherwise seek to take advantage of their positions, it is equally clear that an arbitrary application of the rule in *Keech v. Sandford* is not the answer and for this reason a more flexible approach in this area is to be welcomed.

---

95. [2002] 2 BCLC 201, 220.
96. [1996] Ch 274.

THE LIABILITY OF STRANGERS AS CONSTRUCTIVE TRUSTEES

Introduction

Persons who are not appointed as trustees may nevertheless be liable to account to beneficiaries and be found to hold trust property as constructive trustees in certain circumstances, where they are found to possess the requisite degree of knowledge about the nature and consequences of their activities. So, where a stranger to the trust takes it upon himself to act as a trustee and subsequently commits a breach of trust, he will be liable for such a breach. In addition, a third party may incur liability where he receives or deals with trust property or where he dishonestly assists in a breach of trust in circumstances where the law is satisfied that he possesses a degree of knowledge[97] sufficient to justify the imposition of liability.

Before considering these principles in more detail, it is important to bear in mind that the imposition of constructive trusteeship on a stranger to a trust is not the only possible cause of action which may be pursued by a beneficiary where trust property is misappropriated. The alternatives are either a proprietary remedy at law or in equity to trace the trust property,[98] or a personal claim against the party responsible for effecting the breach of trust, either at law in the form of an action for money had and received, or in equity.[99] However, often the imposition of constructive trusteeship on a stranger may be the most useful form of remedy. In circumstances where a third party, increasingly a financial institution or professional, has assisted in a breach of trust, experience has shown that such defendants are far more likely to be in a position to meet any claim than the individual who was initially responsible for committing the breach.[100] In addition, where the wrongdoing involves receipt or dealing with trust property, the imposition of constructive trusteeship may in many circumstances be a much more satisfactory remedy than pursuing a tracing claim. Obviously in some situations it will no longer be possible to trace the trust property and the imposition of a constructive trust may also allow for a more extensive form of recovery where there has been a reduction in the value of the trust property or an incidental profit made.

It is important to stress at this point that constructive trusteeship can only

---

97. The question of the degree of knowledge required to impose liability in either of these circumstances is a very uncertain and complex one, which will be considered in detail below.

98. Considered *infra* Chapter 18.

99. As La Forest J pointed out in the Canadian Supreme Court decision of *Citadel General Assurance Co. v. Lloyds Bank Canada* (1997) 152 DLR (4th) 411, 438 'where more than one remedy is available on the facts, the plaintiff should be able to choose the one that is most advantageous'.

100. See Parker and Mellows, *The Modern Law of Trusts* (7th ed., 1998, Oakley) p. 321.

be imposed where the recipient or assister displays the degree of knowledge or dishonesty necessary to justify the imposition of liability. It should therefore be borne in mind that while a beneficiary may be able to trace trust property into the hands of an innocent volunteer, the latter's liability will be confined to the return of the property or its proceeds while still in his possession, and a constructive trust with its additional proprietary consequences cannot be imposed in these circumstances.

There has been an ongoing debate about the circumstances in which liability in the form of constructive trusteeship should be imposed for assisting in a breach of trust or where trust property is received with some degree of knowledge.[101] These issues will be examined in detail below under separate headings but for the present it should be noted that it has been suggested that 'a person who has intermeddled by assisting in [a] breach [of trust] should be less exposed to liability than one who, with knowledge of the breach, has actually received the trust property to his or her benefit'.[102] It has been argued that while 'recipient liability is restitution-based, accessory liability is not'[103] and that, given the fundamental distinction between the nature of liability in assistance and receipt cases, it makes sense to impose a different threshold of liability in each category.[104] Specifically it has been suggested that in cases of assistance in the misappropriation of trust property, which are concerned with the furtherance of fraud, there should be a higher threshold of liability required of the stranger to the trust.[105] However, in knowing receipt cases, which are concerned with the receipt of trust property for the benefit of the recipient, it has been argued that there should be a lower threshold required to found liability.

Before examining these heads of liability in more detail, reference should be made to a suggestion, made largely by Lord Millett, about whether the labels 'constructive trust' and 'constructive trustee' are appropriate in this context. In the course of his judgment as a member of the Court of Appeal in *Paragon Finance plc v. D.B. Thakerar & Co.*,[106] Millett LJ said that these

---

101. It has been suggested that the label 'trustee' is inappropriate in this context and that such persons are 'in reality neither trustees nor fiduciaries, but merely wrongdoers', see *Paragon Finance plc v. D.B. Thakerar & Co.* [1999] 1 All ER 400, 412 *per* Millett LJ.
102. *Per* Smellie J in *Equiticorp Industries Group Ltd v. The Crown* [1998] 2 NZLR 480, 640.
103. *Royal Brunei Airlines Sdn Bhd v. Tan Kok Ming* [1995] 2 AC 378, 386 *per* Lord Nicholls. See also the *dicta* of Lord Millett in *Twinsectra Ltd v. Yardley* [2002] 2 AC 164, 194.
104. *Citadel General Assurance Co v. Lloyds Bank Canada* (1997) 152 DLR (4th) 411, 433 *per* La Forest J and *Gold v. Rosenberg* (1997) 152 DLR (4th) 385, 399 *per* Iacobucci J. See also *Agip Africa Ltd v. Jackson* [1990] Ch 265, 292 per Millett J.
105. (1997) 152 DLR (4th) 411, 434.
106. [1999] 1 All ER 400, 408-409. See also *Coulthard v. Disco Mix Club Ltd* [2000] 1 WLR 707, 731.

phrases have been used by equity lawyers to describe two entirely different situations. The first covers cases where the defendant, although not expressly appointed as a trustee, has assumed the duties of a trustee by a lawful transaction which was independent of and preceded the breach of trust and is not impeached by the plaintiff. In such situations the constructive trustee really is a trustee; he does not receive the trust property in his own right but by a transaction by which both parties intend to create a trust from the outset. The second type of case is where the trust obligation arises as a direct consequence of the unlawful transaction which is impeached by the plaintiff. These cases arise when the defendant is implicated in a fraud and in such a case the defendant is traditionally, although in the view of Millett LJ, unfortunately, described as a 'constructive trustee'. However, in his opinion, 'such a person is not in fact a trustee at all, even though he may be liable to account as if he were. He never assumes the position of trustee, and if he received the trust property at all it is adversely to the plaintiff by an unlawful transaction which is impugned by the plaintiff.'[107]

Rickett[108] supports this view and has said that in cases of dishonest assistance and knowing receipt, constructive trusteeship has no place at all in defining the liability of the defendant and that the equitable liability of third parties who become involved in a breach of trust or fiduciary duty has nothing to do with 'constructive trusts'. In his view 'it is time to come clean on this and avoid the gobbledegook of that terminology.'[109] Lord Millett returned to this theme in the course of his speech in *Dubai Aluminium Co. Ltd v. Salaam*[110] in which he repeated much of what he had said earlier in *Paragon* in relation to the second class of case which he had described in that judgment. In his opinion in this class of case the expressions 'constructive trust' and 'constructive trusteeship' create a trap and are 'nothing more than a formula for equitable relief'.[111] Lord Millett concluded that he thought the courts should now discard the words 'accountable as a constructive trustee' in this context and substitute the words 'accountable in equity'.[112] It remains to be seen whether the views of Lord Millett will win wider support but there is a certain logic in his argument and as the decision of the House of Lords illustrates,[113] failure to distinguish between the two classes of cases described by him may lead to difficulties.

While there has been little case law in relation to the liability of strangers to a trust in Ireland, a wealth of authorities has emerged over recent years in

---

107. *Ibid.* at 409. See also *Fyffes Group Ltd v. Templeman* [2000] 2 Lloyd's Rep 643, 671
108. (1999) 18 NZULR 305.
109. *Ibid.* at 324.
110. [2002] 3 WLR 1913.
111. *Per* Ungoed-Thomas J in *Selangor United Rubber Estates Ltd v. Craddock (No. 3)* [1968] 1 WLR 1555, 1582.
112. [2002] 3 WLR 1913, 1947.
113. See further *infra* pp. 244-245.

other jurisdictions, particularly in England, Canada and New Zealand. This has been attributed in part to a growth in corporate fraud and to a greater willingness on the part of the judiciary to utilize equitable concepts in a commercial context. However, it has also been argued that advances in the law of restitution must necessarily lead to a fundamental reappraisal of the circumstances in which a stranger can be made liable for receiving trust property transferred in breach of trust.[114] To date, while some tentative steps towards such a 'fundamental reappraisal' have been taken in England,[115] there is still no sign of any wholesale departure on the part of the judiciary there from the equitable principles relating to the imposition of constructive trusts, although these principles themselves have undergone considerable change in recent years. While it remains to be seen whether the judiciary in Ireland will seek to take any radical steps in this area, it is probable that in the short term at least, they are more likely to follow the principles developed in England and for this reason it is proposed to examine this case law in some detail before considering briefly some of the alternative options which may be pursued in the future.

Intermeddling in a Trust — the Trustee de son Tort

Where a person intermeddles in the affairs of a trust or performs acts characteristic of a trustee he will become a trustee de son tort i.e. because of his wrong.This principle was set out by Smith LJ in *Mara v. Browne*[116] as follows:

> [I]f one, not being a trustee and not having authority from a trustee, takes upon himself to intermeddle with trust matters or to do acts characteristic of the office of trustee he may thereby make himself what is called in law a trustee of his own wrong — i.e., a trustee de son tort, or as it is also termed, a constructive trustee.

In essence liability under this heading depends on the voluntary assumption of the obligations of trusteeship followed by actions which amount to a breach of trust. A stranger who purports to act as a trustee will be subject to all the liabilities usually imposed on an expressly appointed trustee and to the fiduciary obligations which preclude him from profiting from his position or from placing himself in a situation where his duty and interests may conflict.

In *Selangor United Rubber Estates Ltd v. Craddock (No. 3)*[117] Ungoed-Thomas J identified the following distinguishing features of a trustee de son

---

114. Harpum in *Frontiers of Liability* (ed. Birks, 1993) Volume 1, p. 9.
115. See e.g. *Lipkin Gorman v. Karpanale Ltd* [1991] 2 AC 548.
116. [1896] 1 Ch 199, 209.
117. [1968] 1 WLR 1555, 1579.

tort: such persons do not claim to act in their own right but rather for the beneficiaries; their assumption to act is not of itself a ground of liability, except in the sense of liability to account for any failure in the duty so assumed, and their status as trustees precedes the occurrence which may be the subject of a claim against them. This can be contrasted with the situations which will be considered below where no trusteeship arises before, but only by reason of the action complained of, and where the trustees claim to act in their own right and not for the beneficiaries.

Assisting in the Misappropriation of Trust Property

Dishonesty of the Person Assisting in the Breach of Trust

It was accepted by Lord Selborne in *Barnes v. Addy*[118] that strangers will be made liable as constructive trustees where 'they assist with knowledge in a dishonest and fraudulent design on the part of trustees'.[119] A more recent formulation of the circumstances in which liability may be imposed under this heading is set out by Lord Nicholls delivering the judgment of the Privy Council in *Royal Brunei Airlines Sdn Bhd v. Tan Kok Ming*[120] as follows: 'A liability in equity to make good resulting loss attaches to a person who dishonestly procures or assists in a breach of trust or fiduciary obligation'. This latter formulation focuses on the dishonesty of the person assisting in the breach of trust rather than requiring dishonesty on the part of the trustees as Lord Selborne's principle had done.[121] As Lord Nicholls stated: 'In this

---

118. (1874) LR 9 Ch App 244, 252.
119. The requirement of the existence of a fraudulent or dishonest design, which was set out by Lord Selborne in *Barnes v. Addy* (1874) LR 9 Ch App 244, 252 meant that the conduct necessary to constitute a person as a constructive trustee under this heading had to be tainted with some kind of fraud or dishonesty. While Ungoed-Thomas J expressed the view in *Selangor United Rubber Estates Ltd v. Craddock (No. 3)* [1968] 1 WLR 1555, 1591 that conduct which is morally reprehensible would suffice, this more flexible approach was rejected by the Court of Appeal in *Belmont Finance Corporation v. Williams Furniture Ltd* [1979] Ch 250 where the claim in relation to knowing assistance failed on the grounds, *inter alia*, that no sufficiently clear allegations of fraud or dishonesty had been established. This view was echoed by Peter Gibson J in *Baden v. Societe Generale pour Favoriser le Developpement du Commerce et de l'Industrie en France SA* [1993] 1 WLR 509, 574 where he stated that 'the relevant design ... must be dishonest and fraudulent'.
120. [1995] 2 AC 378, 392.
121. However, when the Supreme Court of Canada considered this issue in *Air Canada v. M. & L. Travel Ltd* (1993) 108 DLR (4th) 592, 617 Iacobucci J made it clear that 'generally there are good reasons for requiring participation in a fraudulent and dishonest breach of trust before imposing liability on agents of the trustees' and the focus seemed to be on whether the breach of trust was itself fraudulent and dishonest rather than the accessory's actions.

regard dishonesty on the part of the third party would seem to be a sufficient basis for his liability, irrespective of the state of mind of the trustee who was in breach of trust.'[122] In his opinion it was difficult to see why, if a third party dishonestly assisted in a breach of trust, there should be a further prerequisite to his liability, namely that the trustee must also be shown to have been acting dishonestly.

The academic reaction to the approach adopted by the Privy Council in *Royal Brunei Airlines* has been overwhelmingly favourable,[123] and it has been welcomed as clarifying a number of uncertainties in this area in a purposeful manner. While these issues have not been directly addressed by the courts in this jurisdiction, it seems likely that they would follow the principles laid down by Lord Nicholls and apply the requirement that dishonesty on the part of the accessory must be shown in order to impose liability.

The Requirement of Knowledge/Dishonesty

The decision of the Privy Council in *Royal Brunei Airlines Sdn Bhd v. Tan Kok Ming*[124] is also significant in that it marks a shift away from the concept of 'knowledge' being the primary focus of the court's inquiry in weighing up whether liability under this heading may be imposed. Prior to this a consideration of the degree of knowledge possessed by the assister was crucial to the imposition of liability although the courts in England were far from consistent in their attitude towards this issue over the last few decades.

In his judgment in *Baden v. Societe Generale pour Favoriser le Developpement du Commerce et de l'Industrie en France SA*[125] Peter Gibson J set out five categories of knowledge, which have been referred to in numerous decisions in this area over the last decade or so. While considerable reservations have been expressed in relation to this categorisation,[126] and the Privy Council suggested in *Royal Brunei Airlines* that 'the *Baden* scale of knowledge is best forgotten',[127] it would be difficult to examine the relevant authorities without setting out these five categories of knowledge.

---

122. *Ibid.* at 385. See also *Powell v. Thompson* [1991] 1 NZLR 597, 613.
123. See Nolan [1995] CLJ 505; Harpum (1995) 111 LQR 545; Halliwell [1995] Conv 339; McCormack (1995) 9 Trust Law Int 102; Podzebenko (1996) 18 Syd Law Rev 234. However, Berg's reaction is less favourable, see (1996) 59 MLR 443.
124. [1995] 2 AC 378.
125. [1993] 1 WLR 509, 575-576.
126. See the comments of Millett J in *Agip (Africa) Ltd v. Jackson* [1990] Ch 265, 293 and of Knox J in *Cowan de Groot Properties v. Eagle Trust plc* [1992] 4 All ER 700, 761; and it has been described in *Nimmo v. Westpac Banking Ltd* [1993] 3 NZLR 218, 228 by Blanchard J as 'unhelpful and ... unrememberable'.
127. [1995] 2 AC 378, 392. Although it was suggested by the Court of Appeal in *Heinl v. Jyske Bank (Gibraltar) Ltd* [1999] Lloyd's Rep Bank 511, 523 that the classification laid down in *Baden* might well remain a useful guide in identifying different states of knowledge which might or might not result in a finding of dishonesty.

(i)   actual knowledge;

(ii) wilfully shutting one's eyes to the obvious;

(iii) wilfully and recklessly failing to make such inquiries as an honest and reasonable man would make;

(iv) knowledge of circumstances which would indicate the facts to an honest and reasonable man;

(v)   knowledge of circumstances which would put an honest and reasonable man on inquiry.

While many of the early authorities[128] restricted liability to a stranger who possessed knowledge in one of the first three categories outlined above, a number of first instance decisions in England in the 1960s and 1970s did not follow this approach. So, in *Selangor United Rubber Estates Ltd v. Craddock (No. 3)*[129] Ungoed–Thomas J described the type of knowledge which was required to found liability in the following terms: 'knowledge of circumstances which would indicate to an honest reasonable man that such a design was being committed or would put him on inquiry, which the stranger failed to make, whether it was being committed.' However, doubts were expressed about the unfair burden which such a requirement could place on innocent defendants and an alternative view was put forward by the Court of Appeal in *Carl Zeiss Stiftung v. Herbert Smith & Co. (No. 2)*,[130] where it was stressed that want of probity should be required to establish liability and the suggestion was made that constructive notice of the impropriety was insufficient.

One of the most important judgments in this area is that of Millett J in *Agip (Africa) Ltd v. Jackson.*[131] Although he confirmed that knowledge within the first three categories laid down in the *Baden* case is required, he also suggested that an important distinction must be made between honesty and dishonesty. A senior officer in the plaintiff company fraudulently altered a payment order for £500,000 to a creditor by substituting the name of a company managed by the defendants which had been set up in order to launder the money. The money was credited to the company's bank account and following a series of transactions in which the money was transferred to various recipients, the company was wound up. The plaintiffs brought an action against the defendants to recover the money claiming, *inter alia*, that the defendants

---

128. E.g. *Barnes v. Addy* (1874) LR 9 Ch App 244; *Williams-Ashman v. Price* [1942] 1 Ch 219.

129. [1968] 1 WLR 1555, 1590. See also *Karak Rubber Co. Ltd v. Burden (No. 2)* [1972] 1 WLR 602.

130. [1969] 2 Ch 276.

131. [1990] Ch 265. See Birks (1989) 105 LQR 528; Harpum [1990] CLJ 217; Millett (1991) 107 LQR 71.

were constructive trustees of the funds on the basis of knowing receipt and knowing assistance. Millett J held that none of the defendants could be held liable on the basis of knowingly receiving trust funds for their own benefit but that the defendants were liable under the heading of knowing assistance as 'they were at best indifferent to the possibility of fraud'. On the question of knowledge, Millett J said that constructive notice of the fraud is not sufficient to make a defendant liable and that 'the true distinction is between honesty and dishonesty'. Millett J continued:

> If a man does not draw the obvious inferences or make the obvious inquiries, the question is: why not? If it is because, however foolishly, he did not suspect wrongdoing or, having suspected it, had his suspicions allayed, however unreasonably, that is one thing. But if he did suspect wrongdoing yet failed to make inquiries because 'he did not want to know' (category (ii)) or because he regarded it as none of his business (category (iii)), that is quite another. Such conduct is dishonest, and those who are guilty of it cannot complain if, for the purpose of civil liability, they are treated as if they had actual knowledge.[132]

The judgment of Fox LJ in the Court of Appeal in *Agip* temporarily confused the issue somewhat and he appeared to accept that all five categories of knowledge as set out in the *Baden* case were relevant.[133] However subsequently in *Eagle Trust plc v. SBC Securities Ltd,*[134] Vinelott J commented that it is implicit in Fox LJ's judgment in *Agip* that he accepted Millett J's conclusion that to establish liability for knowing assistance something amounting to dishonesty and want of probity must be shown.[135] In the view of Vinelott J: 'Constructive notice is not enough, though ... knowledge may be inferred in the absence of evidence by the defendant if such knowledge would have been imputed to an honest and reasonable man.'[136]

---

132. *Ibid.* at 293. This approach was also advocated by May LJ in *Lipkin Gorman v. Karpanale Ltd* [1989] 1 WLR 1340, 1355 in the following terms: 'there is at least strong persuasive authority for the proposition that nothing less than knowledge, as defined in one of the first three categories stated by Peter Gibson J in the *Baden* case, of an underlying dishonest design is sufficient to make a stranger a constructive trustee of the consequences of that design.'
133. The reasoning of the Court of Appeal has been criticised, see Harpum [1991] CLJ 409, 411.
134. [1993] 1 WLR 484.
135. *Ibid.* at 495.
136. *Ibid.* at 496. The position as set out by Vinelott J has recently been confirmed by Scott LJ in the English Court of Appeal in *Polly Peck International plc v. Nadir (No. 2)* [1992] 4 All ER 769, which concerned a claim that the plaintiff company's funds had been misappropriated by the defendant, its former chief executive. The court dismissed the plaintiff's claim for a Mareva injunction against the bank into which these funds had been transferred and Scott LJ approved the statement of

Similar views have also been adopted in a number of other common law jurisdictions. In *Air Canada v. M. & L. Travel Ltd*,[137] a decision of the Canadian Supreme Court, Iacobucci J stated: 'The knowledge requirement for this type of liability is actual knowledge; recklessness or wilful blindness will also suffice'. This approach was approved, albeit in an *obiter* context, by La Forest J in the more recent Supreme Court decision of *Citadel General Assurance Co. v. Lloyds Bank Canada*[138] where it was stated that in this context 'constructive knowledge will not suffice'.

Recent decisions in New Zealand show that there has been an increasing movement towards a test of want of probity[139] or dishonesty.[140] While it has been acknowledged that the decision of the Privy Council in *Royal Brunei* strongly discouraged further reference to the *Baden* scale of knowledge,[141] it has tended to be accepted that nothing less than knowledge in categories (i), (ii) or (iii) will suffice in order to establish liability.[142]

The decision of the Privy Council in *Royal Brunei Airlines Sdn Bhd v. Tan Kok Ming*[143] is undoubtedly the most important recent authority on this issue and requires to be examined in some detail. Lord Nicholls stated that '"knowingly" is better avoided as a defining ingredient of the principle' and that it is 'inapt as a criterion when applied to the gradually darkening spectrum where the differences are of degree and not kind.'[144] Berg has questioned why the Privy Council saw fit to require dishonesty and reject the concept of 'knowingly' as a test of liability[145] and he points out that Lord Nicholls

---

Vinelott J that 'a stranger cannot be made liable for knowing assistance in a fraudulent breach of trust unless knowledge of the fraudulent design can be imputed to him'.

137. (1993) 108 DLR (4th) 592, 608.
138. (1997) 152 DLR (4th) 411, 421. See also *Gold v. Rosenberg* (1997) 152 DLR (4th) 365, 394 *per* Iacobucci J.
139. *Equiticorp Industries Group Ltd v. Hawkins* [1991] 3 NZLR 700, 728.
140. *Marshall Futures Ltd v. Marshall* [1992] 1 NZLR 316, 326; *Nimmo v. Westpac Banking Corporation* [1993] 3 NZLR 218, 228; *Cigna Life Insurance New Zealand Ltd v. Westpac Securities Ltd* [1996] 1 NZLR 80, 87; *Equiticorp Industries Group Ltd v. The Crown* [1998] 2 NZLR 481, 640.
141. *Equiticorp Industries Group Ltd v. The Crown* [1998] 2 NZLR 481, 640. See also *Nimmo v. Westpac Banking Corporation* [1993] 3 NZLR 218, 228,
142. Although the statements made by Cooke P in *Gathergood v. Blundell & Brown Ltd* [1992] 3 NZLR 643 could be said to be open to a broader interpretation than this.
143. [1995] 2 AC 378. See Halliwell [1995] Conv 339. See also Ashe and Reid (1997) 4 Comm LP 188.
144. *Ibid.* at 391. In the view of Lord Nicholls the *Baden* scale of knowledge should be forgotten and as Halliwell has suggested this might be a particularly welcome development in the context of the proper role of equity in commercial transactions, see [1995] Conv 339, 343.
145. (1996) 59 MLR 443, 451. He argues that it appears that an accessory's liability for assisting in a breach of trust is now based on the same principles as the liability of a third party who induces a breach of contract and that liability for inducing a breach of contract depends not on dishonesty but on knowledge of the existence of the plaintiff's contract and an intention to interfere with its performance.

acknowledged that honesty has to be assessed in the light of what a person actually knew at the time.[146] In delivering his speech in the recent decision of the House of Lords in *Twinsectra Ltd v. Yardley*,[147] Lord Hutton acknowledged that it was open to their lordships to depart from the principles laid down by Lord Nicholls and to hold that knowledge was a sufficient ingredient of accessory liability. However, he accepted that the latter's statements have been 'widely regarded as clarifying this area of the law'[148] and stated that the principles laid down in *Royal Brunei* should continue to be applied.[149] As we will see below, this issue is far from settled and the use of knowledge as a touchstone of liability may not have been relegated to the extent to which Lord Nicholls clearly intended.

One aspect of the principles set out by Lord Nicholls in *Royal Brunei* which has proved controversial and may continue to be problematic is whether he intended the concept of 'dishonesty' to be interpreted in a purely objective manner or whether it must be established that a defendant was aware that his conduct was dishonest. He stated as follows:

> [I]n the context of the accessory liability principle acting dishonestly, or with a lack of probity, which is synonymous, means simply not acting as an honest person would in the circumstances. This is an objective standard. At first sight this may seem surprising. Honesty has a connotation of subjectivity, as distinct from the objectivity of negligence. Honesty, indeed, does have a strong subjective element in that it is a description of a type of conduct assessed in the light of what a person actually knew at the time, as distinct from what a reasonable person would have known or appreciated. Further, honesty and its counterpart dishonesty are mostly concerned with advertent conduct, not inadvertent conduct. Carelessness is not dishonesty. Thus for the most part dishonesty is to be equated with conscious impropriety.
>
> However, these subjective characteristics of honesty do not mean that individuals are free to set their own standards of honesty in particular circumstances. The standard of what constitutes honest conduct is not

---

146. As Gardner points out (1996) 112 LQR 56, 67: 'It is doubtful then, that the new law of direct reference to a concept of dishonesty obviates any need for an exegesis upon cognisance'. Berg quite rightly asserts (1996) 59 MLR 443 that the conclusion reached in the subsequent first instance decision of Rimer J in *Brinks Ltd v. Abu-Saleh (No.3)* [1996] CLC 133 (see Stevens [1996] Conv 447) shows that not only must it be established that the accessory was dishonest, but also that he knew or had reason to suspect that he was assisting a trustee in a manner contrary to the terms of the trust.

147. [2002] 2 AC 164.

148. *Ibid.* at 174. Although this statement must be questioned in the light of the different interpretations placed on Lord Nicholls' *dicta* by the majority and minority in *Twinsectra Ltd v. Yardley.*

149. See e.g. *Satnam Investments Ltd v. Dunlop Heywood Ltd* [1999] 3 All ER 652, 671.

subjective. Honesty is not an optional scale, with higher or lower values according to the moral standards of each individual. If a person knowingly appropriates another's property, he will not escape a finding of dishonesty simply because he sees nothing wrong in such behaviour.[150]

Lord Nicholls went on to say that when a court is called upon to decide whether a person is acting honestly, it will look at all the circumstances known to the third party at the time and to personal attributes such as his experience and intelligence. He added that if the concept of honesty is to be judged by objective standards, an accessory will not be able to escape liability by claiming that he did not 'know' that his actions were wrong.

However, when the House of Lords was called upon to apply this reasoning in *Twinsectra Ltd v. Yardley*[151] serious differences of opinion arose in relation to whether Lord Nicholls had intended to lay down a purely objective test in relation to dishonesty.[152] In *Twinsectra* a solicitor who was acting for a client in connection with the purchase of land had been unwilling to secure a loan for the client by giving a personal undertaking. A second solicitor was prepared to do so and received the money after the firm gave an undertaking that it would be used solely for the acquisition of property on behalf of the client. The money was released to the first solicitor who paid it out on the client's instructions although he took no steps to ensure that it was only applied in the acquisition of property and a substantial part of it was used for other purposes. The loan was not repaid and the lender sought to impose liability on the first solicitor alleging that he had dishonestly assisted in the breach of trust of the second solicitor, who had gone bankrupt. Carnwath J found that the first solicitor had not been dishonest although he accepted that he had deliberately shut his eyes to the implications of the undertaking. The Court of Appeal reversed this finding, giving judgment against the first solicitor for the proportion of the loan which had not been applied in the acquisition of property, but an appeal against this decision was allowed by the majority of the House of Lords.[153] Lord Hutton stated that there were three possible standards which could be applied to determine whether a person had acted dishonestly, namely a purely subjective standard, a purely objective standard and a combined test

---

150. [1995] 2 AC 378, 389.
151. [2002] 2 AC 164. It should be noted that in *Niru Battery Manufacturing Co. v. Milestone Trading Ltd* [2002] 2 All ER (Comm) 705, 739 Moore-Bick J stated that the *dicta* of Lord Nicholls in *Royal Brunei* might have been taken to suggest that in this context dishonesty is to be judged in objective terms but that the majority of the House of Lords in *Twinsectra* held that that was not what Lord Nicholls intended.
152. As Garton stated (2001) 15 Trust Law Int 93, 98 – before the decision of the House of Lords was delivered – even if the courts prefer the test of dishonesty, if they are not careful it can involve a similar degree of linguistic confusion as the *Baden* test.
153. Lords Slynn, Steyn, Hoffmann and Hutton.

which requires that before there can be a finding of dishonesty, it must be established that the defendant's conduct was dishonest by the ordinary standards of reasonable and honest people, and that he himself realised that by those standards his conduct was dishonest. In favouring the third option, the combined objective and subjective test, Lord Hutton said that it would be less than just for the law to permit a finding that a defendant had been dishonest in assisting in a breach of trust where he had not been aware that what he was doing would be regarded by honest men as being dishonest. In his view:

> [D]ishonesty requires knowledge by the defendant that what he was doing would be regarded as dishonest by honest people, although he should not escape a finding of dishonesty because he sets his own standards of honesty and does not regard as dishonest what he knows would offend the normally accepted standards of honest conduct.[154]

However, Lord Millett dissented and said that in his opinion Lord Nicholls had adopted an objective standard in *Royal Brunei* according to which the defendant was expected to attain the standard which would be observed by an honest person placed in similar circumstances.[155] While account must be taken of subjective considerations such as the defendant's experience and intelligence and his actual state of knowledge at the relevant time, it was not necessary that he should actually have appreciated that he was acting dishonestly; it was sufficient that he was. So, in the view of Lord Millett, it was unnecessary to consider whether the solicitor realised that honest people would regard his conduct as dishonest and his knowledge that he was assisting the other solicitor to default in his undertaking to the plaintiff was sufficient.

It remains to be seen which approach will be favoured in the future, although it must be said that academic comment has come down on the side of the approach of Lord Millett.[156] Yeo and Tijo comment that if the concerns of equity can be adequately addressed by a careful application of the

---

154. [2002] 2 AC 164, 174. Yeo and Tijo suggest (2002) 118 LQR 502, 507 that the application of a purely objective assessment in this first limb of the combined test can be counter-intuitive and it may be difficult to determine whether a defendant's conduct has breached the objective standard of dishonesty without regard being had to his knowledge and personal attributes.

155. It should be noted that in his judgment in *Bank of Credit and Commerce International (Overseas) Ltd v. Akindele* [2001] Ch 437, 447, Nourse LJ spoke about the trial judge in the case before him determining whether the defendant was 'dishonest by the objective standard explained by the Privy Council in *Royal Brunei Airlines Sdn Bhd v. Tan*'.

156. See Yeo and Tijo (2002) 118 LQR 502; Richardson (2002) 16 Trust Law Int 174, 181. Baughen [2000] Conv 351, 356 expressed the view that 'dishonesty' as defined by Lord Nicholls is 'an objective test tailored to the circumstances of the particular defendant'.

requirements of knowledge in individual circumstances, there should not be cause for regret in a transition from 'dishonesty' to 'knowledge'.[157] The courts in this jurisdiction have yet to properly address this question[158] and it remains to be seen whether the approach adopted by Lord Hutton or Lord Millett in *Twinsectra* would be favoured. Lord Millett's reasoning is in many respects more convincing and the conclusion which he reached arguably preferable but it is difficult to predict which point of view is more likely to win favour with the judiciary in this jurisdiction.

Knowing Receipt of and Inconsistent Dealing with Trust Property

General Principles

A recipient of property which has been misappropriated in breach of trust may be liable as a constructive trustee of this property provided that he possesses the necessary degree of knowledge of the breach of trust. Similarly, where a recipient of trust property deals with it in a manner which he knows to be inconsistent with the terms of the trust, he will be regarded as a constructive trustee of the property. This second category of liability covers situations in which the recipient might not be liable for 'receipt' as such, because he does not possess the requisite degree of knowledge, but subsequently deals with the property in a manner inconsistent with the trust after acquiring such knowledge. Millett J described these categories in his judgment in *Agip (Africa) Ltd v. Jackson*[159] as follows:

> [I]t is necessary to distinguish between two main classes of case under this heading.

---

157. Yeo and Tijo (2002) 118 LQR 502, 508. Certainly the decisions of the Court of Appeal in *Heinl v. Jyske Bank (Gibralter) Ltd* [1999] Lloyd's Rep Bank 511 and *Grupo Torras SA v. Al-Sabah* [2001] Lloyd's Rep Bank 36 show that knowledge still has a useful role to play.

158. O'Dell has suggested in *Annual Review of Irish Law 1997* p. 632 that the decision of McCracken J in *Taxback Ltd v. Revenue Commissioners* High Court 1996 No. 325 JR, 21 January 1997 'might well constitute the Irish adoption of the principle in *Tan*'. Although *Royal Brunei Airlines Sdn Bhd v.Tan Kok Ming* is referred to in the course of the judgment, it is submitted that there are no real grounds for O'Dell's assertion. The case concerned a dispute between the parties about the withholding by the Revenue Commissioners of refunds payable to the applicant VAT refunding agency. The Revenue contended on the authority of *Royal Brunei Airlines* that if they made payments to the applicant they might be assisting in the applicant's dishonesty and incur liability themselves. However, McCracken J rejected this argument and stated that unless they had statutory authority to withhold monies during an investigation of this type they must discharge their statutory obligations in relation to payment.

159. [1990] Ch 265, 291.

The first is concerned with the person who receives for his own benefit trust property transferred to him in breach of trust. He is liable as a constructive trustee if he received it with notice, actual or constructive, that it was trust property and that the transfer to him was a breach of trust; or if he received it without such notice but subsequently discovered the facts.

The second and in my judgment distinct class of case is that of the person, usually an agent of the trustees, who receives the trust property lawfully and not for his own benefit but who then either misappropriates it or otherwise deals with it in a manner which is inconsistent with the trust. He is liable to account as a constructive trustee if he received the property knowing it to be such, though he will not necessarily be required in all circumstances to have known the exact terms of the trust.

As Millett J pointed out, in either class of case outlined it is immaterial whether the breach of trust was fraudulent or not and the most controversial question associated with these categories of liability is the degree of knowledge required.

Before examining this question in more detail, it should be pointed out that the principles which apply in this area are still far from certain, and given their increasing use in a commercial context, this has become a cause for considerable concern. Furthermore there have recently been signs of a move away from equitable principles as a means of resolving questions of this nature.[160] The irony of such a development was not lost on Lord Nicholls as a recent comment shows:

Whatever may ultimately emerge either from the courts or from the legislature, one point is clear. Traditionally equity has supplemented the common law, giving a remedy where the common law was rigid and harsh. With its emphasis on conscience and flexibility, equity went to the heart of the matter affording new rights, new remedies, new procedures. Now, ironically, part of the heartland of equity is itself under siege from the encroaching influence of the common law in the guise of restitution. A vigorous new force is at large.[161]

The Degree of Knowledge Required

There is a fundamental difference between the nature of liability in cases of assistance in the misappropriation of trust property and knowing receipt[162]

---

160. E.g. see the decision of the House of Lords in *Lipkin Gorman v. Karpanale Ltd* [1991] 2 AC 548.
161. Lord Nicholls 'Knowing Receipt: the Need for a New Landmark' in *Restitution: Past, Present and Future* ed. Cornish (1998) p. 243.
162. As Iacobucci J stated in the Canadian Supreme Court decision of *Gold v. Rosenberg*

and it has been argued that given this distinction, it makes sense to impose liability on a different basis in each category.[163] Traditionally, it has been accepted that in cases of knowing receipt, which are concerned with the receipt of trust property for the benefit of the recipient, there should be a lower threshold of knowledge required than in cases of assistance in the misappropriation of trust property in order to found liability.[164] However, the principles in this area are far from settled and it is proposed to trace developments in a number of jurisdictions with a view to suggesting the attitude which the courts are likely to take in the future.

It was held by Buckley LJ in *Belmont Finance Corporation v. Williams Furniture Ltd (No. 2)*,[165] that where a stranger to a trust receives trust property with either actual or constructive knowledge of the breach of trust, he will be regarded as a constructive trustee of this property. Liability was imposed in that case on the basis of a receipt of trust monies by a company, the directors of which knew or ought to have known belonged to the trust.[166]

However, subsequently in *Re Montagu's Settlement Trusts*,[167] Megarry VC favoured the imposition of liability only in circumstances where the recipient possessed actual knowledge of the breach of trust. The trustees in that case had transferred certain chattels to a beneficiary (the tenth Duke of Manchester) in breach of trust and he had disposed of a number of these during his lifetime although his solicitor had been aware of the terms of the settlement. After his death, the eleventh duke claimed that the tenth duke was a constructive trustee of the chattels. Megarry VC held that while the estate of the tenth duke was liable to return any remaining chattels or their traceable proceeds, the duke himself was not liable as constructive trustee as he had no actual knowledge that the chattels were trust property transferred in breach of trust.

Megarry VC was of the view that the imposition of a constructive trust should depend primarily on the actual knowledge of the recipient and not on whether he is deemed to have constructive notice of the trust. He stated:

> I do not see why one of the touchstones for determining the burdens on property should be the same as that for deciding whether to impose a

---

(1997) 152 DLR (4th) 385, 396: 'participation in a fraud underlies liability in cases of knowing assistance; unjust enrichment is the essence of a claim in knowing receipt'.

163. *Citadel General Assurance Co v. Lloyds Bank Canada* (1997) 152 DLR (4th) 411, 433 *per* La Forest J and *Gold v. Rosenberg* (1997) 152 DLR (4th) 385, 396 *per* Iacobucci J. See also *Agip Africa Ltd v. Jackson* [1990] Ch 265, 292 *per* Millett J.

164. See the *dicta* of La Forest J in *Citadel General Assurance Co v. Lloyds Bank Canada* (1997) 152 DLR (4th) 411, 434 to the effect that 'more is expected of the recipient, who unlike the accessory, is necessarily enriched at the plaintiff's expense'.

165. [1980] 1 All ER 393.

166. See also *Karak Rubber Co. Ltd v. Burden (No. 2)* [1972] 1 WLR 602.

167. [1987] Ch 264. See Hayton [1987] CLJ 395; Harpum (1987) 50 MLR 217.

personal obligation on a man. The cold calculus of constructive and imputed notice does not seem to me to be an appropriate instrument for deciding whether a man's conscience is sufficiently affected for it to be right to bind him by the obligations of a constructive trustee.[168]

Megarry VC held that in considering whether a constructive trust has arisen in the context of the knowing receipt of trust property, the basic question is whether the conscience of the recipient is sufficiently affected to justify the imposition of such a trust.[169] He stated that for this purpose, knowledge extends to the first three categories outlined in *Baden* for in such cases there is a want of probity which justifies the imposition of a constructive trust.

A similar view was taken by Alliot J at first instance in *Lipkin Gorman v. Karpanale Ltd*,[170] in which liability for both knowing assistance and knowing receipt was at issue. A partner in the plaintiff firm of solicitors had withdrawn money mostly from the clients' account and lost it gambling at a club. The plaintiff firm brought an action against the club on the basis of knowing receipt and against their bank on the grounds of knowing assistance. The plaintiff failed to establish liability on the part of the club on this basis and the finding of liability against the bank was reversed on appeal to the Court of Appeal. The solicitors' appeal from the dismissal of their claim against the club was ultimately allowed by the House of Lords[171] but on a different basis. It was held that the innocent recipient of stolen money was obliged to pay an equivalent sum to the true owner where full consideration for it had not been given and where this party had been unjustly enriched at the expense of the true owner. Although the solicitors had no proprietary rights in the money in their bank account, at common law they were owners of a chose in action constituted by the indebtedness of the bank to them and could trace their property into its direct product, namely, the money drawn from the bank account by the gambler, and follow it into the hands of the club.

In *Agip (Africa) Ltd v. Jackson*[172] Millett J stated at one point in his judgment that a person who receives for his own benefit trust property transferred to him in breach of trust is liable as a constructive trustee if he received it 'with notice, actual or constructive' that it was trust property transferred in breach of trust. Later in his judgment he refers to the doubts expressed by Megarry VC in *Montagu* about whether constructive notice is sufficient in relation to knowing receipt and appears to reserve the question

---

168. *Ibid*. at 273.
169. This approach has recently been approved by Knox J in *Hillsdown Holdings plc v. Pensions Ombudsman* [1997] 1 All ER 862, 902-903.
170. [1987] 1 WLR 987.
171. [1991] 2 AC 548. See Birks [1991] LMCLQ 473; McKendrick (1992) 55 MLR 377.
172. [1990] Ch 265, 293.

of whether these doubts were well-founded. However, Gardner's suggestion that 'taken with Millett J's other remarks, this passage seems a reflection rather of courtesy towards a brother judge than of uncertainty on Millett J's part over his own view'[173] is probably accurate.

Subsequent decisions in England have failed to satisfactorily resolve this question. In *Polly Peck International plc v. Nadir (No. 2)*[174] Scott LJ suggested that the real question was whether the circumstances in which the transfers of trust monies were made should have made the recipient suspicious as to the propriety of what was being done. While he accepted that a defendant would be liable if he was shown to have wilfully and recklessly failed to make such inquiries as an honest and reasonable man would have made, Scott LJ expressed doubts about whether it would suffice if a defendant could be shown to have had knowledge of facts which would have put an honest and reasonable man on inquiry.

It has been argued that the principle of constructive notice imposes too high a burden in a commercial context and in *Eagle Trust plc v. SBC Securities Ltd*[175] Vinelott J distinguished between the type of knowledge which would be required to found liability in commercial and non-commercial[176] types of transactions. In relation to the former category he stated that in order to make a defendant liable as a constructive trustee, it must be shown that he knew in one of the senses set out in the first three categories identified in *Baden* that the property was misapplied trust property, or the circumstances must be such that, in the absence of any evidence or explanation by the defendant, that knowledge can be inferred.[177] In the view of Vinelott J this inference may be drawn 'if the circumstances are such that an honest and reasonable man would have inferred that the moneys were probably trust moneys and were being misapplied, and would either not have accepted them or would have kept them separate until he had satisfied himself that the payer was entitled to use them in discharge of the liability'.[178] However, it has been argued by Millett J that judges who have warned against extending constructive notice to commercial dealings 'were obviously referring to the doctrine in its strict

---

173. (1996) 112 LQR 64, 69-70.
174. [1992] 4 All ER 769.
175. [1993] 1 WLR 484.
176. Oakley suggests that for non-commercial transactions, Vinelott J appeared to favour the broader based view of liability for knowing receipt rather than that favoured by Megarry VC in *Re Montagu's Settlement Trusts*, see Parker and Mellows, *The Modern Law of Trusts* (7th ed., 1998, Oakley) p. 345.
177. Vinelott J was of the opinion that a difference remains between inferred knowledge and notice and stated (at 494) that 'the term "notice" is often used in a sense or in contexts where the facts do not support the inference of knowledge'.
178. [1993] 1 WLR 484, 506. See also the judgment of Knox J in *Cowan de Groot Properties Ltd v. Eagle Trust plc* [1992] 4 All ER 700, 759 although in the circumstances of the case, no liability arose.

conveyancing sense'.[179] Fox has suggested that this longstanding policy against extending constructive notice to commercial transactions[180] can be circumvented and that the same objections would not necessarily apply to an 'appropriately adjusted commercial standard of notice'.[181] In his view 'there are no compelling economic reasons why constructive notice, set at the proper commercial standard, should not become a basis of liability for knowing receipt arising out of a commercial transaction'. Certainly there have been decisions in other jurisdictions which have not displayed the same unwillingness to confine the basis of liability for knowing receipt in commercial cases to knowledge in the sense of the first three categories set out in *Baden*. In *Citadel General Assurance Co v. Lloyds Bank Canada*[182] the Canadian Supreme Court was willing to impose liability on a banker in respect of knowing receipt where he only possessed constructive knowledge of the breach of trust.

Indeed in one of the few authorities on the issue of knowing receipt in this jurisdiction, the Supreme Court appeared to be prepared to accept that constructive notice would suffice to ground liability even in a commercial context. In *Re Frederick Inns Ltd*,[183] payments were made by a group of associated companies to the Revenue Commissioners in the six months immediately preceding the commencement of the winding up of four of these companies out of the proceeds of sale of various licensed premises which had belonged to these four companies. This sum was appropriated by the commissioners in reduction of the tax liabilities of not only the four companies involved in the proceedings but also those of six other companies in the group. The liquidator challenged these payments as being *ultra vires* insofar as they had effected an alienation of the companies' assets when they were insolvent. Lardner J held that the payments made by the companies which exceeded their liabilities and were intended to reduce the liabilities of the other companies in the same group were *ultra vires* on the grounds that each company was a separate entity. The commissioners' appeal was dismissed by the Supreme Court which held that no clause in the memoranda of association of any of the companies, properly construed, gave them power to pay the debts of an associated company and that the payments were therefore *ultra vires*. Blayney J held that the *ultra vires* payments constituted a misapplication by the directors of company funds in breach of their fiduciary duties. These monies had been received by the Revenue Commissioners with constructive knowledge of this breach as the memoranda of association of the four companies, which were documents of public record, revealed the absence of capacity. So, apart from

---

179. *MacMillan Inc v. Bishopsgate Investment Trust plc (No. 3)* [1995] 1 WLR 978, 1000.
180. See *Manchester Trust v. Furness* [1895] 2 QB 539.
181. [1998] CLJ 391, 396.
182. (1997) 152 DLR (4th) 411.
183. [1994] 1 ILRM 387.

the monies which the Revenue Commissioners had originally appropriated towards the discharge of the respective tax liabilities of the four companies involved in the proceedings, the payments made were held by them on a constructive trust and had to be repaid to the official liquidator. The Supreme Court therefore ordered that the sums involved should be repaid by the Revenue Commissioners.

One disappointing aspect of the judgment from an academic perspective is the lack of consideration given to the question of the degree of knowledge required in a case of knowing receipt.[184] O'Dell has correctly asserted that the application of principle by Blayney J in *Re Frederick Inns Ltd* seemed to go even further than the fifth point on the *Baden* scale and he has commented that 'even if the *Baden* scale does not reach notice properly so-called, *Frederick Inns* certainly seems to'.[185]

The question of the degree of knowledge required to establish liability for knowing receipt has also been considered recently by the High Court in *Ulster Factors Ltd v. Entoglen Ltd.*[186] The first named defendant entered into a factoring agreement with the plaintiff whereby the first named defendant agreed to assign all its debts to the plaintiff by way of sale or assignment and the plaintiff agreed to make payment to or to the order of the first named defendant of a sum not exceeding the 'availability balance' as defined in the agreement. After the first named defendant went into liquidation, the plaintiff instituted proceedings against the company and its liquidator, the second named defendant, claiming the balance which it alleged was due to it. What remained at issue at the hearing of action was one payment made to a third party by the plaintiff which the liquidator claimed had not been properly paid. The defendants submitted that this payment was *ultra vires* the company and that it had been made without the company's authority. Laffoy J did not accept that the payment by the plaintiff was *ultra vires* the company. However, she went on to say that even if the liquidator had established that the payment was *ultra vires*, he had not made out any basis on which the plaintiff should be required in effect to make restitution of this payment. Laffoy J quoted with approval from the judgment of Blayney J in *Re Frederick Inns Ltd* in which he had applied the principle set out in *Belmont Finance Corporation Ltd v. Williams Furniture Ltd (No.2)*[187] and stated that 'what renders the recipient of or the dealer with funds which are being misapplied in breach of the fiduciary duties of the directors of a company liable as a constructive trustee is knowledge, actual or constructive, of the breach of trust'.[188] She found that

---

184. O'Dell has commented that 'the requirement of knowledge as an ingredient was so easily satisfied that it was all but abandoned.' (See [1994] RLR 161).
185. *Annual Review of Irish Law 1997* p. 644.
186. High Court 1992 No. 1060P (Laffoy J) 21 February 1997.
187. [1980] 1 All ER 393.
188. High Court 1992 No. 1060P (Laffoy J) 21 February 1997 at 8.

the plaintiff did not have actual knowledge of any breach of duty and concluded that 'there was no obligation on the plaintiff to enquire as to the purpose for which any payment which the company requested the plaintiff to make to a third party was being made or to satisfy itself that the payment was *intra vires* the company and, even if the payment was *ultra vires*, constructive knowledge of a breach of trust cannot be imputed to the plaintiff for failure to make such inquiries'. Laffoy J also rejected the liquidator's contention that the payment was made without the company's authority and she held that the plaintiff was entitled to judgment in the amount claimed.

There seems little doubt that the judgment of the Supreme Court in *Re Frederick Inns* and the *dicta* of Laffoy J in *Ulster Factors* purport at the least to follow the principle laid down in *Belmont* that either actual or constructive knowledge suffices to establish liability for knowing receipt. Whether the approach adopted by the Supreme Court, which was effectively to accept that constructive notice suffices even in a commercial context, will be followed remains to be seen. Arguably it imposes an unnecessarily high onus on persons or bodies dealing with a company and it is interesting to note that the Supreme Court made no attempt to distinguish the standard required in relation to commercial and non-commercial transactions. While the argument put forward by Fox that there is no reason 'why constructive notice, set at the proper commercial standard, should not become a basis of liability for knowing receipt arising out of a commercial transaction' is a sound one, in the absence of a more detailed consideration of the knowledge/notice requirement in this jurisdiction, some doubt must still surround this question.[189]

It is interesting that there has also been a marked lack of consistency in other common law jurisdictions in relation to the circumstances in which liability will be imposed in cases of knowing receipt. In the New Zealand decision of *Marshall Futures Ltd v. Marshall*[190] Tipping J stated that in cases of knowing receipt 'where the person alleged to be a constructive trustee will usually have benefited personally from the breach of trust there are good

---

189. It is interesting to note the divergence of opinion on the meaning of the term 'notice' between Vinelott J in *Eagle Trust plc v. SBC Securities Ltd* [1993] 1 WLR 484 and Millett J in *El Ajou v. Dollar Holdings plc* [1993] 3 All ER 717. While the approach of Vinelott J appears to assume that a reasonable person 'must always behave as rigourously as he does in the land transfer context', Millett J accepts the idea that 'the reasonable person behaves differently in different contexts' (see Gardner (1996) 112 LQR 56, 62). Gardner believes that Millett J's approach is probably the better founded (at p. 63) and suggests that it is the formula to the effect that 'notice is a function of how the reasonable person would have behaved in the relevant circumstances . . . rather than the standards set in the land transfer cases, that truly defines notice'. It would certainly be useful if the courts in this jurisdiction were to consider this question and clarify what their understanding of 'notice' is, particularly in a commercial context.
190. [1992] 1 NZLR 316, 326.

policy reasons for allowing constructive knowledge in the form of categories (iv) and (v) to be sufficient to make him responsible'.[191] In the subsequent decision of *Equiticorp Industries Group v. The Crown*[192] Smellie J found that the defendant had either wilfully shut its eyes to the obvious or if not, had wilfully and recklessly failed to make the inquiries which a reasonable and honest commercial party would have made and therefore the need to make a decision about the knowledge of types (iv) and (v) on the *Baden* scale did not arise.

The issue has also been considered in detail in two recent decisions of the Canadian Supreme Court. In *Citadel General Assurance Co v. Lloyds Bank Canada*[193] La Forest J expressed the view that in cases of knowing receipt there should be a lower threshold of knowledge required of the stranger to the trust than in cases of knowing assistance. As he stated: 'More is expected of the recipient, who unlike the accessory, is necessarily enriched at the plaintiff's expense. Because the recipient is held to this higher standard, constructive knowledge (that is, knowledge of facts sufficient to put a reasonable person on notice or inquiry) will suffice as the basis for restitutionary liability.'[194] Similarly in *Gold v. Rosenberg*[195] Iacobucci J, albeit in a dissenting judgment,[196] stated that in cases of knowing receipt, a person need not have actual knowledge and that notice would suffice.

The recent decision of the Court of Appeal in *Bank of Credit and Commerce International (Overseas) Ltd v. Akindele*[197] has sought to clarify and simplify the law in this area and in general it has received a cautious welcome.[198] The claimants, who were the liquidators of two banking companies, contended that the defendant was liable to account to them for a sum of money as a constructive trustee on the basis that he had knowingly assisted in a breach of trust or had received trust monies with knowledge of the breaches. Carnwath J dismissed the claim on the basis that dishonesty by the defendant, which in

---

191. A similar view was expressed by Wylie J in *Equiticorp Industries Group v. Hawkins* [1991] 3 NZLR 700, 728.
192. [1998] 2 NZLR 480.
193. (1997) 152 DLR (4th) 411. See Smith (1998) 114 LQR 394.
194. *Ibid.* at 434. See also *Carl B. Potter Ltd v. Mercantile Bank of Canada* (1980) 112 DLR (3d) 88; *Arthur Andersen Inc v. Toronto-Dominion Bank* (1994) 17 OR (3d) 363; *Glenko Enterprises Ltd v. Ernie Keller Contractors Ltd* (1996) 134 DLR (4th) 161; *Real Estate and Business Brokers (Director) v. NRS Mississauga Inc* (2000) 194 DLR (4th) 526.
195. (1997) 152 DLR (4th) 385.
196. The view of the majority was that the bank had not actually received the trust property. However, the minority found that there had been receipt and went on to consider whether the requisite degree of knowledge existed.
197. [2001] Ch 437.
198. Nolan [2000] CLJ 447, Jaffey (2001) 15 Trust Law Int 151; Barkehall Thomas (2001) 21 OJLS 239. However, other commentators e.g. Penner (2000) 14 Trust Law Int 229, are more critical of this new approach.

his view was the essential foundation of the claimants' case, whether under the head of knowing assistance or knowing receipt, had not been established. The claimants' appeal to the Court of Appeal was dismissed, although Nourse LJ clarified the basis for establishing liability on the grounds of knowing receipt and held that Carnwath J had erred in insisting on dishonesty in this context.[199]

Nourse LJ agreed that as the defendant had not acted dishonestly, the claim of knowing assistance was bound to fail. However, he stated that dishonesty was not a prerequisite to liability under the head of knowing receipt and that the trial judge had been incorrect to proceed on this assumption. He referred to *Belmont Finance Corporation Ltd v. Williams Furniture (No.2)*[200] which he said was clear authority for the proposition that dishonesty is not a necessary ingredient of liability for knowing receipt. Nourse LJ stated that while the categorization of knowledge laid down in the *Baden* case has been influential in many decisions relating to knowing receipt, it was not formulated with that head of liability in mind. While he acknowledged that it might often be helpful in identifying different states of knowledge which may or may not lead to a finding of dishonesty for the purpose of establishing liability for knowing assistance, he stated that he had 'grave doubts' about its utility in cases of knowing receipt. Nourse LJ then posed the question of what purpose could be served by a categorization of knowledge in the context of knowing receipt. In his view it could only be to enable the court to determine, in the words of Megarry VC in *Re Montagu's Settlement Trusts*,[201] whether the claimant's conscience was sufficiently affected for it to be right to bind him with the obligations of a constructive trustee. So, if this were the purpose, there was no need for categorization and all that was necessary was that 'the recipient's state of knowledge should be such as to make it unconscionable for him to retain the benefit of the receipt.'[202] In his view such a test although it could not any more than any other avoid difficulties of application, ought to deal with the problems of definition and allocation which previous categorizations had given rise to. Nourse LJ concluded that Carnwath J's findings of fact supported the conclusion that the defendant's knowledge was

---

199. Confusion appears to have arisen in relation to whether dishonesty was a prerequisite to establishing liability for knowing receipt as a result of a number of recent decisions. (see *Twinsectra Ltd v. Yardley* [1999] Lloyd's Rep Bank 438, 466-467 *per* Potter LJ; *Bank of America v. Arnell* [1999] Lloyd's Rep Bank 399, 406-407 *per* Aikens J; *Dubai Aluminium Co. Ltd v. Salaam* [1999] 1 Lloyd's Rep 415, 453 *per* Rix J). However, in *Houghton v. Fayers* [2000] 1 BCLC 511 Nourse LJ reaffirmed that knowledge was the determining factor.
200. [1980] 1 All ER 393. This proposition was supported by other more recent *dicta* e.g. *per* Millett J in *Agip (Africa) Ltd v. Jackson* [1990] Ch 265, 292; Vinelott J in *Eagle Trust plc v. SBC Securities Ltd* [1993] 1 WLR 484, 497.
201. [1987] Ch 264, 273.
202. [2001] Ch 437, 455.

not such as to make it unconscionable for him to retain the benefit of the receipt and dismissed the appeal.

Possible Future Developments

It has been argued that neither the restricted view of fault set out in *Re Montagu's Settlement Trusts*[203] nor the broader view of liability encompassing constructive knowledge provides 'a wholly satisfactory answer and that 'each will produce an unattractive result in some situations'.[204] In addition, it has been suggested that in the light of the approach taken by the House of Lords in *Lipkin Gorman v. Karpanale Ltd*,[205] liability in this area might in future be decided in terms of common law principles in an action for money had and received, based on the concept of strict liability but subject to the defence of change of position. As Oakley[206] points out, such a remedy possesses the distinct advantage that its imposition does not depend on the state of mind or degree of knowledge of the recipient.

An interesting alternative theory has also recently been put forward by Lord Nicholls writing extra-judicially, who suggested that personal liability should be based on a combination of two separate principles.[207] First, recipient liability should cover all third party recipients. This would be a principle of strict liability in that it would apply to every recipient with an impeachable title irrespective of fault, but it would be restitutionary in nature. It would be confined to restoring an unjust gain. Change of position would accordingly be available as a defence. Secondly, dishonest recipients should be personally liable to make good losses as well as accounting for benefits. Harpum has welcomed this model for future development of the law as seeking to reconcile the views of those who consider that receipt-based liability should be founded on restitutionary principles and those who consider that it should be based upon equitable wrongdoing.[208] As he points out, it would involve a move away from fault-based liability, which would be a welcome step in view of the present uncertainties in the area, but this would be balanced by the availability of the defences of change of position and *bona fide* purchase.

However, both judicial and academic opinion is divided about the wisdom of a movement away from a fault-based approach in this area. It was suggested

---

203. [1987] Ch 264.
204. *Per* Lord Nicholls 'Knowing Receipt: the Need for a New Landmark' in *Restitution: Past, Present and Future* ed. Cornish (1998) p. 241.
205. [1991] 2 AC 548.
206. Parker and Mellows, *The Modern Law of Trusts* (7th ed., 1998) p. 348.
207. 'Knowing Receipt: the Need for a New Landmark' in *Restitution: Past, Present and Future* ed. Cornish (1998) p. 244.
208. *Ibid.* at 248.

by Thomas J in the New Zealand decision of *Powell v. Thompson*[209] that liability in the knowing receipt category is based on the concept of unjust enrichment, which is receipt-based and not fault-based.[210] If one accepts this approach, it should therefore follow that the degree of knowledge possessed by the recipient should not be the decisive factor.[211] Similar views have been expressed recently by Lord Millett in the course of his speech in *Twinsectra Ltd v. Yardley*[212] in which he stressed that liability for knowing receipt is receipt-based and does not depend on fault. He added that there is powerful academic support for the proposition that the liability of the recipient is the same as in other cases of restitution, that is to say strict but subject to a defence of change of position. In *Bank of Credit and Commerce International (Overseas) Ltd v. Akindele*[213] Nourse LJ admitted that no argument had been made before the court based on the views put forward by Lord Nicholls[214] and acknowledged that at Court of Appeal level this would have been a fruitless exercise. However, he stated that he doubted whether strict liability coupled with a change of position defence would be preferable to fault-based liability in many commercial transactions. In his view the courts must continue to do their best with the accepted formulation of liability for knowing receipt, simplifying and improving it where possible. Recent academic opinion has tended to support the views put forward by Nourse LJ and Jaffey[215] has commented that it is fortunate that the Court of Appeal in *Akindele* resisted the temptation to effect a radical reform of the law on the basis of a restitutionary analysis of knowing receipt. In addition, Smith[216] has concluded that fault-based liability in equity is the appropriate vehicle for the courts to apply in this context; in his opinion 'knowing receipt counts as equitable wrongdoing and cannot be made to fit into the mould of unjust enrichment'.[217]

It should be stressed that this debate is far from over and it is entirely possible that given the opportunity, the House of Lords might decide to favour a restitutionary model in this area. However, for the present, equitable principles are still relevant and as recent judgments such as that of Nourse LJ in *Akindele* show, still developing. It should also be borne in mind that as the

---

209. [1991] 1 NZLR 597, 607.
210. See also *Royal Brunei Airlines Sdn Bhd v. Tan* [1995] 2 AC 378, 386; *Dublin Corporation v. Ancient Guild of Incorporated Brick and Stone Layers and Allied Trades Union* High Court 1991 No. 1556P (Budd J) 6 March 1996 at 51.
211. McGrath suggests [1999] LMCLQ 343, 351 that 'the flood waters are clearly amassing behind the fault-based barrier for knowing receipt claims'.
212. [2002] 2 AC 164, 194.
213. [2001] Ch 437.
214. See *supra*, 'Knowing Receipt; The Need for a New Landmark' in *Restitution: Past, Present and Future* ed. Cornish (1998).
215. (2001) 15 Trust Law In 151, 152.
216. (2000) 116 LQR 412. See also Barkehall Thomas (2001) 21 OJLS 239, 250.
217. *Ibid.* at 430.

law stands at present in this jurisdiction, knowledge, or if the approach in *Re Frederick Inns* is followed, at least some form of notice, is still required before liability under the heading of knowing receipt can be imposed.[218]

Liability of Agents of Trustees

An agent of a trustee will not be liable as a constructive trustee provided that in receiving trust property or in dealing with it, he has acted honestly and within the scope of his usual authority as an agent. So where he is acting in the capacity of agent, he will not be accountable to the beneficiaries, but only to his principal, provided that he does not act outside the scope of his authority. This general rule was laid down by Lord Selborne in *Barnes v. Addy*[219] as follows:

> [S]trangers are not to be made constructive trustees merely because they act as the agents of trustees in transactions within their legal powers, transactions, perhaps of which a Court of Equity may disapprove, unless those agents receive and become chargeable with some part of the trust property, or unless they assist with knowledge in a dishonest and fraudulent design on the part of the trustees.

In that case solicitors advised against the appointment of a sole trustee although they prepared the documentation necessary for his appointment. When the trustee in question sold the trust property and misapplied the proceeds it was held that the solicitors could not be treated as constructive trustees as they had acted honestly in the course of their agency and had merely carried out the instructions of the trustees.

One of the most important recent authorities in this area is the decision of the Court of Appeal in *Carl Zeiss Stiftung v. Herbert Smith & Co. (No. 2)*,[220] in which a solicitor who was given money by a client which the plaintiff claimed was held by the client on trust for the plaintiff, was found not to be accountable for this money since there had been no want of probity on the

---

218. O'Dell has correctly suggested in *Annual Review of Irish Law 1997* p. 644 that the approach adopted by the Supreme Court in *Re Frederick Inns* makes the traditional knowledge requirement very easy to satisfy. He continues: '[I]t is tantamount to emptying it of all content, and comes close to the imposition of strict liability. On this view, the express adoption of a restitutionary analysis would not work a large change in the law'. Indeed, while there is logic in such an argument, it is still unclear how favourably the courts in this jurisdiction would look upon it. O'Dell himself acknowledges that in this area 'academic discourse has raced well ahead of the caselaw, and might well be exploring routes which as the law develops may not even open up'. *Ibid.* p. 645.
219. (1874) 9 Ch App 244, 251-252.
220. [1969] 2 Ch 276.

solicitor's part. Edmund Davies LJ summarized his view of an agent's position as follows:

> A solicitor or other agent who receives money from his principal which belongs at law or in equity to a third party is not accountable as a constructive trustee to that third party unless he has been guilty of some wrongful act in relation to that money. ... To act 'wrongfully' he must be guilty of (i) knowingly participating in a breach of trust by his principal; or (ii) intermeddling with the trust property otherwise than merely as an agent and thereby becomes a trustee *de son tort*; or (iii) receiving or dealing with the money knowing that his principal has no right to pay it over or to instruct him to deal with it in the manner indicated; or (iv) some dishonest act relating to the money.[221]

It would appear that agents of trustees who are in receipt of trust property or who deal inconsistently with it, are to an extent regarded more favourably than a beneficial recipient of trust property and an agent's duty to inquire is less strictly interpreted.[222] This point is well illustrated by the decision of Kay J in *Williams v. Williams*,[223] in which a solicitor disposed of lands which were subject to a settlement on the settlor's behalf in accordance with the latter's instructions. It was held that the solicitor was not liable to account since he neither knew of the settlement nor had wilfully shut his eyes to its existence although the facts disclosed that he should have been put on inquiry as to its existence. So where an agent acts honestly in following his principal's instructions, he will not be liable. This was confirmed by the judgment of Bennett J in *Williams-Ashman v. Price*,[224] in which solicitors who had followed the instructions of a trustee in making an unauthorized loan and other investments were found not to be liable as constructive trustees as they had acted honestly on the trustee's instructions and had not intermeddled in the affairs of the trust.

However, where an agent receives trust property and, knowing that he is acting in breach of trust, deals with it in a manner inconsistent with its terms, he may be personally liable as a constructive trustee. This is evident from the decision of *Lee v. Sankey*,[225] in which Bacon VC made it clear that where an agent receives trust monies and deals with them in a manner inconsistent with the trust of which he is aware, he is personally liable for the consequences. Solicitors who were employed by trustees to receive the proceeds of the sale of a testator's property and improperly paid over the money to only one of the

---

221. *Ibid.* at 303-304.
222. *Carl Zeiss Stiftung v. Herbert Smith & Co. (No. 2)* [1969] 2 Ch 276, 297.
223. (1881) 17 Ch D 437.
224. [1942] Ch 219.
225. (1873) LR 15 Eq 204. See also *Soar v. Ashwell* [1893] 2 QB 390.

two trustees, who dissipated the fund and subsequently died insolvent, were held liable to account to the beneficiaries in respect of the loss which had occurred.

Liability of Partners

The recent decision of the House of Lords in *Dubai Aluminium Co. Ltd v. Salaam*[226] has clarified a number of issues which had led to difficulties in this area and it is clear that earlier authorities on this issue must now be treated with caution.

In *Mara v. Browne*[227] it was suggested *obiter* by Lord Herschell that it was not within the scope of the implied authority of a solicitor who is a partner in a firm to act so as to make himself a constructive trustee and thereby subject his partner to the same liability. This *dicta* was applied by Vinelott J in *Re Bell's Indenture*[228] in which it was sought to impose liability on a partner in a firm of solicitors whose co-partner had knowingly assisted in a breach of trust. Although in this case the monies had actually passed through the firm's client account, it was held that the innocent partner was not liable as a constructive trustee and it was further held that no liability could arise under the Partnership Act 1890.[229] Subsequently, it was held by Millett J and the Court of Appeal in *Agip (Africa) Ltd v. Jackson*,[230] that where the court found that an accountant had dishonestly assisted in a breach of trust, that liability could also be imposed on his partner, although there was no discussion of the basis for such a finding.

The terms of section 10 of the Partnership Act 1890 which provide as follows should be noted:

> Where, by any wrongful act or omission of any partner acting in the ordinary course of business of the firm, or with the authority of his co-partners, loss or injury is caused to any person not being a partner in the firm, or any penalty is incurred, the firm is liable therefor to the same extent as the partner so acting or omitting to act.

---

226. [2002] 3 WLR 1913.
227. [1896] 1 Ch 199.
228. [1980] 1 WLR 1217.
229. Vinelott J distinguished the earlier decision in *Blythe v. Fladgate* [1891] Ch 337 on the basis that in that case there had been no trustees at the time the breach of trust had been committed and the partners in the firm of solicitors could not claim that they had received the moneys as agents of the trustees. Luxton [1981] Conv 310 is critical of *Re Bell's Indenture* and suggests that as a result of that decision, the liability of the partners of a solicitor who is liable as a constructive trustee, depends on whether there were validly appointed trustees at the time, a distinction which he argues should not be relevant to the co-partner's liability.
230. [1990] Ch 265, 296; [1991] Ch 547.

It was held by the majority of the Court of Appeal and by Lord Millett in *Dubai Aluminium Co. Ltd v. Salaam*[231] that the words 'any wrongful act or omission' in section 10 of the Act of 1890 are not limited to tortious acts or wrongs actionable at common law but are wide enough to encompass all wrongful acts or omissions. In the view of Aldous LJ the conclusion reached in *Agip Africa* could only have been arrived at on the basis that section 10 applied to the facts of that case. In *Dubai* the Court of Appeal concluded that the partner's acts could not have been carried out 'in the ordinary course of business' within the meaning of the section and that vicarious liability could not be imposed on other partners in the circumstances of the case. This approach was followed by the Court of Appeal in *Walker v. Stones*,[232] in which Sir Christopher Slade further accepted that breaches of trust committed by a trustee-partner would fall outside the ordinary business of any partnership and would be incapable of giving rise to vicarious liability under section 10.

However, it is clear in the light of the conclusions reached by the House of Lords in *Dubai*, which overturned the findings of the Court of Appeal[233] and upheld the decision of the trial judge,[234] that the *dicta* of Lord Herschell which has been relied upon on so many occasions must be reassessed. Lord Nicholls stated that the acts done by the partner were so closely connected with the acts he was authorized to do that they might properly and fairly be regarded as having been done by him while he was acting in the ordinary course of the firm's business. He made it clear that the liability of a firm of solicitors in respect of acts of a partner which render him liable depends on an application of the ordinary principles relating to vicarious liability and that there is no special rule of law applicable to this head of equitable liability. He stated that he did not think that Lord Herschell or the other members of the Court of Appeal in *Mara* could be taken to have suggested otherwise,[235] and in so far as Vinelott J did so in *Re Bell's Indenture*, that he must have fallen into error. Lord Millett expressed the view that deliberate and dishonest conduct committed by a partner for his sole benefit is legally capable of being in the ordinary course of the business of his firm and that the conclusion that the solicitor was acting in the ordinary course of the firm's business would have been open to the trial judge. In his opinion, Lord Herschell had used the expression 'constructive trustee' to mean 'trustee de son tort'. However, unlike the solicitor in *Mara*, the partner allegedly guilty of wrongdoing in this case had not assumed the position of trustee on behalf of others. Lord Millett continued as follows:

---

231. [2001] QB 113 (CA); [2002] 3 WLR 1913 (HL).
232. [2001] 2 WLR 623.
233. See Mitchell (2001) 15 Trust Law Int 164.
234. [1999] Lloyd's Rep Bank 415. See McGrath [1999] LMCLQ 343.
235. In the view of Lord Nicholls the statements in *Mara* were directed at a different question, namely whether acting as a trustee, although not having been so appointed, can be regarded as conduct within the scope of the business of a solicitor.

The distinction between the two kinds of constructive trustee is of crucial importance in the present context. If, as I think, it is still not within the ordinary scope of a solicitor's practice to act as a trustee of an express trust, it is obviously not within the scope of such a practice voluntarily to assume the obligations of a trustee and so incur liability as a *de facto* trustee or a constructive trustee of the first kind. But given that a solicitor may be guilty of deliberate and dishonest conduct while acting within the ordinary scope of his practice, there is no conceivable reason why his firm should not thereby incur vicarious liability for loss caused by the conduct which constituted him a constructive trustee of the second kind.[236]

Lord Millett agreed that *Re Bell's Indenture* had been wrongly decided and concluded that the order of the Court of Appeal should be set aside and the decision of the trial judge upheld.

THE VENDOR AS CONSTRUCTIVE TRUSTEE

Traditionally it has been accepted that where a vendor enters into a specifically enforceable contract for sale, equity regards him as a constructive trustee of the property which forms the subject-matter of the contract until completion.[237] This is an example of the equitable doctrine of conversion and the purchaser is regarded as the owner of the property while the vendor is looked upon as the owner of the purchase monies. Contracts which are capable of being specifically enforced are predominantly contracts for the sale of land, as specific performance will only be granted where a breach of contract cannot be adequately compensated by an award of damages.[238]

The position in England was set out by Jessel MR in *Lysaght v. Edwards*[239] in the following terms: 'The moment you have a valid contract for sale the vendor becomes in equity a trustee for the purchaser of the estate sold, and the beneficial ownership passes to the purchaser.' This was also the position accepted by Henchy J in a minority judgment delivered in *Tempany v. Hynes.*[240]

---

236. [2002] 3 WLR 1913, 1947.
237. Although note how this point has been modified by the view taken by the majority of the Supreme Court in *Tempany v. Hynes* [1976] IR 101 considered *infra*, to the effect that the vendor only becomes a trustee of the beneficial interest to the extent to which the purchase price is paid.
238. See further *infra* Chapter 14.
239. (1876) 2 Ch D 499, 506.
240. [1976] IR 101, 109. Henchy J stated: 'When a binding contract for the sale of land has been made, the law treats the beneficial ownership as having passed to the purchaser from the time the contract was made ... from then until the time of completion, regardless of whether the purchase money has been paid or not, the

However the view of the majority[241] of the Supreme Court as set out by Kenny J was as follows:

> [A] vendor who signs a contract with a purchaser for the sale of land becomes a trustee in the sense that he is bound to take reasonable care of the property until the sale is completed, but he becomes a trustee of the beneficial interest to the extent only to which the purchase price is paid. He is not a trustee of the beneficial interest merely because he signs a contract.[242]

The Law Reform Commission considered the issue of the interests of vendors and purchasers of land during the period between contract and completion in a report published in 1995[243] and concluded that the approach adopted by Henchy J in his minority judgment in *Tempany* was the 'only means by which the purchaser's interests prior to completion may be adequately protected'. The Commission therefore recommended the enactment of a statutory provision providing that when a binding contract for the sale of land has been entered into, the law should treat the beneficial ownership as having passed to the purchaser from the time the contract was made, subject to the condition that the sale be completed.

Once the beneficial interest passes, whether it is on contract as the Commission has recommended, or on payment of the purchase money, as the majority of the Supreme Court held in *Tempany*, the vendor is recognised as being a trustee of the property in the sense that he must take reasonable care of it. A vendor must maintain the property in a reasonable state of repair,[244] and will undoubtedly incur liability if he wilfully damages the property.[245] The obligation has been described by Lord Coleridge in *Clarke v. Ramuz*[246] as being 'to use reasonable care to preserve the property in a reasonable state of preservation and so far as may be, as it was when the contract was made.' In that case while the vendor remained in possession of property, a trespasser removed all the surface soil. It was held that the purchaser could maintain an action against the vendor for breach of trust by reason of the fact that he had taken no care to prevent the removal of the soil. However, it is only where the vendor acts in breach of his trust obligations or fails to

---

vendor, in whom the legal estate is still vested, is treated for certain purposes as a trustee for the purchaser.' This also seems to be the view accepted in Australia, see *Legione v. Hateley* (1983) 57 ALJ 292 and *KLDE Pty Ltd v. Commissioner of Stamp Duties* (1984) 58 ALJR 545.

241. See the judgment of Kenny J, with whom O'Higgins CJ concurred.
242. *Ibid.* at 114.
243. LRC 49 -1995.
244. *Royal Bristol Permanent Building Society v. Bomash* (1887) 35 Ch D 390.
245. *Lysaght v. Edwards* (1876) 2 Ch D 499, 507.
246. [1891] 2 QB 456, 459-460.

take reasonable care that he can be made liable and any damage to the property which occurs without any fault on the part of the vendor is the responsibility of the purchaser. So when a purchaser enters into a specifically enforceable contract for sale, the risk of accidental damage to the property passes to him and he should insure against such risk.[247] As Jessel MR stated in *Lysaght v. Edwards*:[248]

> [If] anything happens to the estate between the time of the sale and the time of completion of the purchase it is at the risk of the purchaser. If it is a house that is sold, and the house is burnt down the purchaser loses the house. He must insure it himself if he wants to provide against such an accident.

This principle is well illustrated by the decision in *Rayner v. Preston*,[249] in which a vendor contracted with a purchaser for the sale of a house which had been insured by the vendor against fire. After the date of the contract but before completion, the property was damaged by fire and the vendor received insurance money in respect of it. It was held that the purchaser was not entitled as against the vendor to the benefit of the insurance money; the risk had passed to the purchaser and it was therefore his responsibility to ensure that the premises were insured.[250] This decision also illustrates the qualified nature of the constructive trusteeship which arises in such cases; while the vendor is a constructive trustee of the land, he is not trustee of anything substituted for the land such as insurance money paid to him under his own insurance policy in relation to damage to the land caused by fire. This point was made by

---

247. This position was regarded as being unfair to purchasers and the Law Reform Commission pointed out in a report published in 1991 (LRC 39-1991) that it was unsatisfactory that the law as to the passing of risk did not accord with the reasonable expectations of the ordinary person. It recommended (p. 19) that the risk should instead pass to the purchaser 'in all situations where the purchaser goes into possession of the premises, or on completion of the purchase, whichever is the earlier'. Note the provisions of clause 43 of the Incorporated Law Society Standard Conditions of Sale (2001 Edition) the effect of which is to provide that the risk remains with the vendor until completion.

248. (1876) 2 Ch D 499, 507. Although, see Thompson [1984] Conv 43. Note also that the Law Commission in England recommended that the risk should only pass on completion (See Law Commission Report No. 191 Paragraph 2.25 (1990)) and such a provision has also been incorporated in the Standard Conditions of Sale in that jurisdiction.

249. (1881) 18 Ch D 1. See also *Re Hamilton-Snowball's Conveyance* [1958] 2 WLR 951.

250. Although note that the law on this point has been changed in England by the provisions of s. 47 of the Law of Property Act 1925 which provides that a purchaser may, on completion of the contract, recover from the vendor any insurance money paid in respect of any damage or destruction of the property. See Wellings (1959) 23 Conv 173, 174.

Cotton LJ in *Rayner*, where he said that a vendor was a trustee 'in a qualified sense only'.[251] This fact was also noted by Lord Cairns in *Shaw v. Foster*[252] in the following terms:

> [T]he vendor, whom I have called the trustee, was not a mere dormant trustee, he was a trustee having a personal and substantial interest in the property, a right to protect that interest and an active right to assert that interest if anything should be done in derogation of it. The relation therefore, of trustee and *cestui que trust* subsisted, but subsisted subject to the paramount right of the vendor and trustee to protect his own interest as vendor of the property.

The qualified nature of the trust relationship existing between a vendor and purchaser in these circumstances is further illustrated by the fact that the vendor is entitled to keep the rents and profits of the land until completion and is under a duty to discharge all outgoings such as rates and taxes which may be payable in respect of the property until this date.[253] In addition, the vendor may retain possession of the land until the purchase price is paid and if the land is conveyed before this, he will have a lien on the land for the balance of the unpaid purchase money.[254]

The relationship which arises in these circumstances has been described as 'a highly self-interested modified form of trusteeship'[255] and some commentators have questioned whether the terms trustee and beneficiary should be used at all to describe the relationship between the vendor and the purchaser in such situations.[256] However it is also recognised that it is arguably

---

251. (1881) 18 Ch D 1, 6.
252. (1872) LR 5 HL 321, 338. As Oakley comments 'the inevitable self interest of the vendor in the successful conclusion of the transaction does not sit very easily with his classification as a trustee.' (See Parker and Mellows, *The Modern Law of Trusts* (7th ed., 1998) p. 376).
253. *Re Highett and Bird's Contract* [1902] 2 Ch 214. However, it would appear that the purchaser is entitled to take the benefit and burden of any gains or losses of a capital nature accruing to the property.
254. *Mackreth v. Symmons* (1808) 15 Ves 329. This vendor's lien can be registered as a burden under s. 69(1) of the Registration of Title Act 1964. Similarly the purchaser will have a lien on the land in respect of any purchase money paid prior to completion *Re Strong* [1940] IR 382.
255. Underhill and Hayton, *Law Relating to Trusts and Trustees* (16th ed., 2003) p. 438.
256. See Waters, *The Constructive Trust* (1964) where the opinion is expressed that until the purchase price is paid in full, the operation of a relationship of trustee and beneficiary is excluded by the fact that each party continues to guard their own position in a manner quite inconsistent with a trust relationship. Cope has commented in *Constructive Trusts* (1992) p. 970 that the use of the term 'constructive trust' in the context of vendor and purchaser is an 'anomalous and inappropriate analogy'.

too late to recast the nature of this relationship,[257] and the best approach is to regard the use of such terminology with a certain degree of caution.

THE MORTGAGEE AS CONSTRUCTIVE TRUSTEE

To a limited extent the liability of a mortgagee to a mortgagor has been described in terms of a trust relationship, although for a number of reasons the drawing of comparisons between the position of a mortgagee and that of a trustee has been described as inappropriate. The strength of the trust analogy was never as strong in relation to mortgagees as it was in respect of vendors of property, particularly in view of the fact that a mortgagee did not usually enter into possession of the mortgaged property, while the vendor tended to remain in possession until completion. In addition, the mortgagee's natural desire to protect his own interests in the mortgage transaction and the trustee's obligation to act in the best interests of the beneficiaries were generally regarded as being incompatible.

However, traditionally where a mortgagee retained a surplus after exercising a power of sale over the mortgaged property, he held this on a constructive trust for whoever was entitled to the equity of redemption. This constructive trust was given statutory force and effectively superseded by section 21(3) of the Conveyancing Act 1881 which gave effect to previous practice.[258] Cope[259] suggests that one further aspect of the mortgagees's exercise of his power of sale may still give rise to a liability in equity to account as a constructive trustee, namely where a mortgagee purports to exercise this power in favour of himself without the fully informed consent of the mortgagor.

MUTUAL WILLS

Prerequisites for the Imposition of a Constructive Trust

Where two people, usually although not necessarily husband and wife, make an arrangement concerning the disposal of their property and execute mutual wills which are intended to be irrevocable and the survivor subsequently alters his will, his estate will be held by his personal representatives on a constructive

---

257. Hanbury and Martin, *Modern Equity* (16th ed., 2001) p. 328 and Cope, *Constructive Trusts* (1992) p. 970.
258. In England, this subsection has been replaced by s. 105 of the Law of Property Act 1925.
259. *Constructive Trusts* (1992) p. 976.

trust to give effect to the arrangement provided for in the mutual wills.[260] However, before such a trust will arise, there must be evidence of an agreement to make mutual wills in substantially similar form and not to revoke them. As McPherson J stated in *Bigg v. Queensland Trustees Ltd*:[261] 'What matters is proof that the parties made an agreement to execute their wills in that form and that, expressly or by implication, they contracted not to revoke them.'[262]

In determining whether the necessary agreement exists, the court will have regard to the terms of the wills but may also infer evidence of an agreement from the conduct of the parties and the surrounding circumstances. The mere fact that the wills were made simultaneously and in substantially similar terms is not of itself sufficient proof that the parties have entered into a legally binding agreement not to revoke them. This is illustrated by the decision of Astbury J in *Re Oldham*,[263] in which a husband and wife executed mutual wills with similar provisions although there was no evidence of any agreement that they should be irrevocable. After the husband's death the wife remarried and made a new will. Astbury J upheld the second will and stated that the fact that the two wills were made in identical terms did not necessarily mean any agreement that they should be irrevocable by the survivor.[264]

While the fact that the wills are made simultaneously and in the same form is not *per se* proof of an agreement sufficient to justify the imposition of a constructive trust, it is a relevant factor to be taken into account in determining whether such an agreement exists. In *Re Cleaver*,[265] where a husband and wife made similar wills at the same time and subsequently altered them in the same manner, it was held that the trusts set out in these wills would be enforced rather than those set out by the survivor, the wife, in a will made subsequent to her husband's death. In the circumstances, Nourse J was satisfied that there was sufficient evidence of an agreement shown by the similarity of the provisions and the fact that the changes were made simultaneously.

However, in *Re Goodchild*,[266] a more recent decision on this question, *Re Cleaver* was distinguished and the importance of having specific evidence as to the testator's mutual intentions at the time of the execution of the wills was stressed.[267] In this case the testator and his wife both simultaneously executed

---

260. This principle can be traced to the decision of Lord Camden in *Dufour v. Pereira* (1769) 1 Dick 419. See generally Harper [1997] Conv 182, 188-193.
261. [1990] 2 Qd R 11, 13. See Rickett (1991) 54 MLR 581.
262. See also *Re Newey (deceased)* [1994] 2 NZLR 590, 593 *per* Hammond J.
263. [1925] Ch 75.
264. *Ibid.* at 88. See also *Birmingham v. Renfrew* (1937) 57 CLR 666, 675 *per* Latham CJ.
265. [1981] 1 WLR 939.
266. [1996] 1 WLR 694 (ChD); [1997] 1 WLR 1216 (CA). See Grattan [1997] Conv 153; Richardson (1996) 10 Trust Law Int 88.
267. See also *Fisher v. Mansfield* [1997] 2 NZLR 230 where Heron J found that there was evidence of a mutual agreement between the parties at the time of the execution of the wills.

wills in identical terms leaving their estates to each other and after their deaths to the first named plaintiff, their only son. After his wife's death, the testator married the defendant and six weeks after making a new will in which he left his entire estate to her, he died. The plaintiff brought an action seeking, *inter alia*, a declaration that after the death of his first wife, the testator held her estate on trust for the plaintiff, and that after the testator's death, the defendant held his estate similarly on trust. Carnwath J accepted that where there is a clear agreement or other evidence that wills are intended to be mutually binding, the law will give effect to that intention by way of a 'floating trust' which becomes irrevocable after the death of the first testator and crystallises on the death of the second. However, he held that in the circumstances, the evidence fell short of establishing such an agreement between the testator and his first wife and the wills were not mutually binding. Carnwath J stressed that the onus of proof lay on the plaintiff and said that there must be evidence of 'a specific agreement outside the wills not just some loose understanding or sense of moral obligation'.[268] He characterised *Re Cleaver* as an extreme example of the circumstances in which an agreement may be found on the basis of oral evidence but stated that in his view it did not provide any precedent for the case before him.[269]

The Court of Appeal upheld the conclusion that the wills were not mutually binding and affirmed the decision made by Carnwath J. Legatt LJ also distinguished *Re Cleaver* in which he said there had been specific evidence as to the testator's mutual intentions at the time the wills were made, whereas in the case before him, he was satisfied that there was not. He was of the opinion that 'for the doctrine to apply there must be a contract'[270] and stated that a key feature of the concept of mutual wills was the 'irrevocability of the mutual intentions'.[271] In his view what was missing in the case before him was evidence of a mutual intention that both wills should remain unaltered and that the survivor should be bound to leave the combined estates to his son. The decision of the Court of Appeal would seem to mark a return to the stricter approach of Astbury J in *Re Oldham* and shows that the evidential

---

268. [1996] 1 WLR 694, 706.
269. However, Carnwath J went on to hold that the testator's wife's mistaken belief that the terms of the will were mutually binding imposed a moral obligation on him which justified the plaintiff's claim under the Inheritance (Provision for Family and Dependents) Act 1975 and that part of the estate which constituted her share should be available to meet the plaintiff's claim under the Act.
270. Although it should be noted that in the recent decision of the New Zealand Court of Appeal in *Lewis v. Cotton* [2001] 2 NZLR 21, 32 Blanchard J stated that a formal legal contract is not needed and that 'a contract made without formality is enough'. However, on the facts he concluded that there was insufficient evidence to sustain the mutual wills claim. See further Richardson (2001) 15 Trust Law Int 100.
271. [1997] 1 WLR 1216, 1225.

difficulties facing a litigant who seeks to establish that the doctrine of mutual wills applies are not inconsiderable.[272]

The importance of establishing evidence of an agreement that the parties should not revoke their will without the knowledge of the other was stressed again by Rimer J in *Curtis v. Birch*[273] in rejecting a claim based on the doctrine of mutual wills. In this case the wills in question had been made less than three months before the death of the wife at a time when both parties knew that she was terminally ill and did not have long to live. However, Rimer J was quite satisfied that this fact in itself did not justify a finding that both testators must be taken to have agreed that the husband's will was to be irrevocable after his wife's impending death. In his view it was essential that there was evidence of an agreement not to revoke their respective wills save with the agreement of the other and this could not be implied by the mere fact that the spouses had agreed to make wills in particular terms.

An interesting point was raised in the recent judgment of David Donaldson QC sitting as a Deputy High Court judge in *Healey v. Brown*[274] where the surviving spouse, instead of revoking his will, transferred property into the joint names of himself and the first named defendant which led to the property passing to this defendant by right of survivorship on his death. The wills of the spouses had been made in identical form leaving a named property to the survivor and then to the claimant, who was the wife's niece, with the remainder of the estate going to the first named defendant, the husband's son by an earlier marriage. While it was accepted by the first named defendant that there was sufficient evidence of an agreement that the survivor should not revoke his or her will after the other's death, it was necessary for the court to decide what if any obligations and restrictions in relation to the property were imposed on a surviving testator who has executed a mutual will and undertaken not to revoke it. Although this point had not been developed in earlier cases, David Donaldson QC was satisfied that where a fiduciary duty is breached by a voluntary disposition *inter vivos* of the property in question, the crystallization of the fiduciary obligation occurs at the moment of that disposition. In his view gifts or settlements *inter vivos*, if calculated to defeat the intention of the agreement would be in breach of it and he held that, subject to the provisions of section 2 of the Law of Property (Miscellaneous Provisions) Act 1989,[275]

---

272. Grattan has pointed out [1997] Conv 153, 159 that it has frequently been advocated that those seeking to execute mutual wills 'would be well advised to ensure that the agreement is recited in the body of the instruments'.
273. (2002) 29 EG 139.
274. [2002] 2 WTLR 849.
275. David Donaldson QC held that the claimant was prevented by the provisions of s. 2 of the Act of 1989 from establishing the contract which *Re Goodchild* [1997] 1 WLR 1216 makes clear is necessary for the mutual wills doctrine to apply. However, he concluded that the husband had accepted a trust in favour of the claimant to pass

the doctrine of mutual wills would apply so as to impose a constructive trust attaching to the property in the claimant's favour.

The Time at which the Trust Arises

While some commentators have argued that the trust may arise either at the date of the agreement or at the time when the survivor dies, the correct view would seem to be that it arises on the death of the first party to die. This means that the interest of a beneficiary will not lapse if he predeceases the survivor. In *Re Hagger*[276] a husband and wife made joint wills leaving a life interest in their property to the survivor and after that party's death on trust for sale for nine beneficiaries. One of these beneficiaries survived the wife, but predeceased the husband who left the property on different trusts. Clauson J held that the will operated as a trust from the date of the wife's death and that all the beneficiaries, including the one who had predeceased the husband, could claim their interests under the will.

Until recently it was unclear whether the trust only arose when the survivor received a benefit under the will of the first party to die.[277] As O'Hagan has pointed out, academic opinion favoured the requirement of benefit 'because to benefit under an agreement and afterwards renege on that same agreement is manifestly fraudulent'.[278] However, the decision of Morritt J in *Re Dale*[279] resolved this question by making it clear that a constructive trust can arise even where the survivor does not take any benefit from the will of the first testator. A husband and wife executed identical wills which both contained a bequest of their property in favour of their daughter and son in equal shares or to the survivor of them. Two months later the husband died and subsequently the wife made a new will in which she revoked all previous wills and bequeathed to the daughter the sum of £300, leaving the son the remainder of her property. The daughter claimed that the mutual wills had been made pursuant to a binding and irrevocable agreement and that the son held the estate of the mother as trustee for both of them in equal shares. The court had to consider as a preliminary issue the question of whether, for the doctrine of mutual wills to apply, it was necessary for the second testator to die to have obtained a personal financial benefit under the will of the first testator to die. In answering this question in the negative, Morritt J held that since the aim of the principle underlying the doctrine of mutual wills was to prevent fraud on the first testator to die, it was not confined to cases in which the surviving

---

his wife's half share in the property under his will and that the first named defendant held it for himself and the claimant in equal shares.
276. [1930] 2 Ch 190.
277. See Graham (1951) 15 Conv 28, 35-36.
278. (1994) 144 NLJ 1272.
279. [1994] Ch 31. See O'Hagan (1994) 144 NLJ 1272.

testator had benefited under the will of the first testator but extended to cases
where the two testators had left their property to beneficiaries other than
themselves.[280]

This approach has recently been confirmed by the decision of the Court of
Appeal of British Columbia in *University of Manitoba v. Sanderson Estate*[281]
in which it was held that the doctrine of mutual wills applied whether or not
the survivor received a benefit under the will of the first to die.

Conclusions

Judicial and academic opinion has varied on the issue of the usefulness or
otherwise of the doctrine of mutual wills. Morritt LJ recently described the
doctrine as 'anomalous' in the course of his judgment in *Re Goodchild*[282]
while Martin[283] has commented that 'the imposition by law of a trust in cases
of mutual wills is a clumsy and inadequate way of dealing with a complicated
problem' and can be regarded as being 'a kind of salvage operation'. In
addition, Friel has suggested that there is an emerging judicial reluctance to
use the device of the constructive trust to resolve 'what are inherently problems
within the law of contract'.[284] However, O'Hagan[285] has stated that 'it is in
this sphere that the constructive trust is seen in one of its most flexible forms'
and the doctrine of mutual wills remains for the present a useful example of
how a constructive trust will be imposed by equity to prevent unconscionable
or fraudulent conduct.

FUTURE DEVELOPMENT OF THE CONSTRUCTIVE TRUST

Introduction – The Remedial Constructive Trust

Traditionally the courts in England and in this jurisdiction have labelled the
constructive trust as a substantive institution although there have been some
signs recently of a willingness to regard it more as a remedial concept. The
institutional approach involves treating the constructive trust as a device which

280. Note that Friel has commented (1996) 1 CPLJ 2, 4 that where a survivor takes no
     benefit under a mutual will, the use of a constructive trust on property is 'inappropriate
     and cannot be justified by legal theory'. Instead he suggests that a trust should be
     imposed not on the property but on the implementation of the contract between the
     parties.
281. (1998) 155 DLR (4th) 40.
282. [1997] 1 WLR 1216, 1230.
283. Hanbury and Martin, *Modern Equity* (16th ed., 2001), p. 325.
284. (1996) 1 CPLJ 2, 4.
285. (1994) 144 NLJ 1272.

arises in certain defined situations e.g. where there has been a breach of fiduciary duty or the wrongful assumption of trust duties by a stranger to the trust.[286] The following explanation of a remedial constructive trust has been provided by Paciocco:[287]

> A plaintiff who requests a 'remedial constructive trust' seeks a declaration that he has a beneficial interest in specific property owned, or in the possession of, a defendant who has been unjustly enriched by that ownership or possession. If successful, the relief that the plaintiff obtains is proprietary in the sense that it gives the successful plaintiff rights in the specific property which are good, not only against the defendant, but also against most others, including and most especially, the general creditors of the defendant.

The distinctions between the institutional and remedial constructive trust have been explored by Tipping J in the decision of the New Zealand Court of Appeal in *Fortex Group Ltd v. MacIntosh*.[288] He stated that an institutional constructive trust is one which arises by operation of the principles of equity and whose existence the court simply recognises in a declaratory way, whereas a remedial constructive trust is one which is imposed by the court in circumstances where before the order of the court, no trust of any kind existed. The difference between the two types of trust in his view is that the former arises upon the happening of the events which bring it into being and its existence is not dependent on any order of the court whereas the latter depends for its very existence on such an order.[289]

While Deane J in *Muschinski v. Dodds*[290] has commented that 'for the student of equity there can be no true dichotomy between the two notions' of 'institution' and 'remedy,' the question of whether there should be lines of demarcation between them has provoked considerable academic comment.[291]

---

286. According to Lord Browne-Wilkinson in *Westdeutsche Landesbank Girozentrale v. Islington Borough Council* [1996] AC 669, 714: 'Under an institutional constructive trust the trust arises by operation of law as from the date of the circumstances which give rise to it; the function of the court is merely to declare that such trust has arisen in the past. The consequences that flow from such trust having arisen ... are also determined by rules of law, not under a discretion.'
287. (1989) 68 Can Bar Rev 315.
288. [1998] 3 NZLR 171, 172.
289. See also the comments of Glazebrook J in *Commonwealth Reserves I v. Chodar* [2001] 2 NZLR 374, 383-384 that generally the institutional constructive trust is a mandatory consequence of certain events while the remedial constructive trust is a discretionary remedy. In addition, while the former exists from the time the events giving rise to it occur, the latter becomes effective at the time of the court order.
290. (1985) 160 CLR 583, 614.
291. See e.g. Gardner in *Frontiers of Liability* (ed., Birks, 1993) Volume 2 pp. 186-192; Cope, *Constructive Trusts* (1992) pp. 868-870. Lord Millett has recently commented,

It is certainly fair to say that a difference exists between the traditional institutional trust which is so well-established in England and the newer breed of remedial constructive trust which has developed elsewhere in the common law world, particularly in Canada, as the following passage from the judgment of McLachlin J in the Canadian Supreme Court decision of *Soulos v. Korkontzilas*[292] illustrates:

> The situations which the judge may consider in deciding whether good conscience requires imposition of a constructive trust may be seen as falling into two general categories. The first category concerns property obtained by a wrongful act of the defendant, notably breach of fiduciary obligation or breach of duty of loyalty. The traditional English institutional trusts largely fall under but may not exhaust (at least in Canada) this category. The second category concerns situation where the defendant has not acted wrongfully in obtaining the property, but where he would be unjustly enriched to the plaintiff's detriment by being permitted to keep the property for himself.

The reluctance to embrace the concept of the remedial constructive trust stems from two main sources. First as Millett J, as he then was, made clear in *Lonrho plc v. Fayed (No. 2)*,[293] while equity must be flexible, its intervention must be based on principle and fears have been expressed that the development of this doctrine might lead to a form of 'palm tree justice'.[294] This argument was addressed by Deane J in *Muschinski v. Dodds*[295] in the following manner:

> The fact that the constructive trust remains predominantly remedial does not, however, mean that it represents a medium for the indulgence of idiosyncratic notions of fairness and justice. As an equitable remedy, it is available only when warranted by established equitable principles or by the legitimate processes of legal reasoning, by analogy, induction and deduction, from the starting point of a proper understanding of the conceptual foundation of such principles.

The other main concern about the imposition of a remedial constructive trust relates to the fundamental distinction between the effect of personal and

---

writing extra-judicially, that 'while we still insist on the institutional character of the constructive trust, however, we undoubtedly use it as a remedial instrument' (1998) 114 LQR 399.
292. (1997) 146 DLR (4th) 214, 227.
293. [1992] 1 WLR 1, 9.
294. See the dissenting judgments in the Canadian Supreme Court decision of *Pettkus v. Becker* (1980) 117 DLR (3d) 254.
295. (1985) 160 CLR 583, 615.

proprietary rights in the context of insolvency.[296] As Lord Millett has commented, speaking extra-judicially: 'The potential effect of a proprietary claim on creditors makes it unacceptable that rights of property should depend on vague and ill-defined notions of fairness'.[297]

As we shall see the judiciary in this jurisdiction have failed consistently to address directly the issue of whether imposing a remedial constructive trust would be a welcome development here although it would appear to have been applied in a number of cases.[298] Before examining these decisions in more detail it is proposed to trace how an earlier form of what is now recognised as the remedial constructive trust has fared and then to return to consider how it may develop in the future.

New Model Constructive Trusts

While it has generally been acknowledged throughout the common law world that the concept of 'justice' is too uncertain a basis on which to found a constructive trust which will create proprietary rights which may operate in a wider context than anticipated or required, Lord Denning pioneered just such a development in the English Court of Appeal in the late 1960s and early 1970s. In *Hussey v. Palmer*[299] Denning MR stated that a constructive trust would be imposed 'whenever justice and good conscience require it' and he subsequently described this extension of the existing law in *Eves v. Eves*[300] as 'a constructive trust of a new model'. These 'new model constructive trusts' were applied in a number of areas, particularly in relation to contractual licences and to family property but almost from the outset they met with academic criticism. Oakley[301] commented that: 'It is unsatisfactory for a constructive trust to be imposed whenever the courts feel, on their own individual ideas of justice, that such a remedy will bring about the "right" result' and Maudsley[302] said that it was possible to read into the decisions the principle that 'in cases in which the plaintiff ought to win, but has no legal doctrine or authority to support him, a constructive trust in his favour will do the trick.' Nevertheless it is interesting to note how this device was utilised in a manner which usually succeeded not only in providing a plaintiff with a remedy but also in creating proprietary rights which had a consequential effect on third parties.

For a number of years the new model constructive trust played an important

---

296. See further *infra* p. 270.
297. (1998) 114 LQR 399.
298. *Re Irish Shipping Ltd* [1986] ILRM 518; *H.K.N. Invest Oy v. Incotrade Pvt Ltd* [1993] 3 IR 152; *Kelly v. Cahill* [2001] 1 IR 57.
299. [1972] 1 WLR 1286, 1290.
300. [1975] 1 WLR 1338, 1341.
301. (1973) CLP 17, 39.
302. (1977) 28 NILQ 123.

role in determining the rights of contractual licensees in a series of cases which attracted considerable criticism. In *Binions v. Evans*[303] an employer consented to allowing the defendant, the widow of a former employee, to live rent-free in a cottage for the remainder of her life. The property was sold to the plaintiffs expressly subject to her interest at a lower price than would otherwise have been payable. The plaintiffs then purported to determine the tenancy and the Court of Appeal held that they could not do so. While Megaw and Stephenson LJJ found that the defendant was entitled to a tenancy for life, Lord Denning MR regarded her interest as a licence which was binding on the purchaser under a constructive trust. This approach was endorsed by the Court of Appeal in *DHN Food Distributors Ltd v. Tower Hamlets LBC*,[304] where a constructive trust was imposed by the court so as to enable it to make a finding that a contractual licensee had a sufficient interest to qualify for compensation in respect of land which had been compulsorily purchased.

However, the use of the constructive trust as a form of equitable remedy to do justice *inter partes* in order to protect the licensee's possession or occupation of the premises as against third parties was difficult to justify as they 'let in by the back door contractual licences as full equitable proprietary interests.'[305] As a result of the decision of the Court of Appeal in *Ashburn Anstalt v. Arnold*,[306] the ambit of the earlier judgments has been considerably restricted and Fox LJ made it clear that the court would not impose a constructive trust unless it was satisfied that the conscience of the owner of the land had been affected so that it would be inequitable to allow him to deny the claimant an interest. Therefore it was only in circumstances where a third party sought to renege on the undertaking to honour the licence that he would be liable as a constructive trustee and there was in the circumstances insufficient evidence to infer the existence of a constructive trust. It has been argued that the influence of the new model constructive trust in this area has now 'been almost wholly negated'[307] and in view of the rather arbitrary effect which its application has on property rights, it is unlikely to be rekindled in that jurisdiction.

The Attitude of the Irish Courts to the New Model Constructive Trust

Lord Denning's creation has met with some degree of limited approval in this jurisdiction, although recent authority suggests that a more precisely defined

---

303. [1972] Ch 359. See Martin (1972) 36 Conv 266; Hayton (1972) 36 Conv 277.
304. [1976] 1 WLR 852.
305. See Underhill & Hayton, *Law Relating to Trusts and Trustees* (14th ed., 1987) p. 328. Note that the passage was omitted from the 15th and 16th editions.
306. [1988] 2 WLR 706.
307. Parker & Mellows, *The Modern Law of Trusts* (7th ed., 1998, Oakley) p. 360.

doctrine would be preferable.[308] In *N.A.D. v. T.D.*[309] Barron J appeared to speak in similar terms to Lord Denning when he made the following statement:

> The constructive trust is imposed by operation of law independently of intention in order to satisfy the demands of justice and good conscience. Its imposition is dependent upon the conduct of the person upon whom the trust is imposed and prevents him from acting in breach of good faith. There is no fixed set of circumstances in which such a trust is imposed.

The case before Barron J concerned a claim relating to contributions allegedly made by the plaintiff towards the building of a house on a site bought in her husband's name. Barron J said that the essential prerequisite for the imposition of a constructive trust of the type under consideration was that there must be an element in the conduct of the person upon whom it is imposed which would make it inequitable for him to assert his legal rights. He concluded that there was no evidence of conduct on the part of the husband which would make it inequitable to deny the wife's claim and her claim to a share in the house therefore failed. So while Barron J spoke in general terms in language not dissimilar to that employed by Lord Denning, there was no real sign in his judgment of the flexibility which was the hallmark of this type of trust in England.

More recently in *H.K.N. Invest Oy v. Incotrade Pvt Ltd*[310] Costello J stated that a constructive trust will arise when the circumstances of the case are such as to render it inequitable for the legal owner of property to deny another's title to it and agreed that 'where a person . . . holds property in circumstances which in equity and good conscience should be held or enjoyed by another he will be compelled to hold the property in trust for another'.[311] The case concerned a claim by the plaintiffs who had obtained judgment against the defendants, namely a company and the individuals responsible for conducting its affairs, and who sought to be allowed to complete execution of this judgment. In relation to monies received by way of commission on pre-incorporation contracts, Costello J held that although the individual defendants concerned might not have been fiduciaries at the time they received this commission, these funds were held on trust for the company and could not be the subject of a garnishee order. Costello J held that the monies received after incorporation were held by the individual defendants as fiduciaries on a constructive trust for the company and he made an order declaring that the

---

308. See *Dublin Corporation v. Ancient Guild of Incorporated Brick and Stone Layers and Allied Trade Union* High Court 1991 No. 1556P (Budd J) 6 March 1996.
309. [1985] ILRM 153, 160.
310. [1993] 3 IR 152.
311. *Ibid.* at 162.

liquidator was beneficially entitled to the proceeds of both sets of contracts as the assets of the company.

While arguably the result arrived at by Costello J was a just one in the circumstances of the case and ironically had the effect of strengthening the position of the general body of creditors, a class who often fare rather worse where a constructive trust is imposed,[312] it must be said that the reasoning is in some respects open to criticism. Principally, it is difficult to accept the fact that the individual defendants could be constructive trustees of funds which in theory belonged to a company which had not at the time come into existence. In addition, while the ready acceptance of the 'good conscience' approach by Costello J, reminiscent of Lord Denning's 'new model', as already stated, achieved what would be considered by most to be a just result, it is not a development which will ease the task of those who seek to establish consistent principles in this area of the law.

There have been a number of further recent examples of constructive trusts being imposed because 'justice and good conscience' demand it. In *Murray v. Murray*,[313] considered above in the context of resulting trusts and family property,[314] the plaintiff, the defendant's nephew, had lived in a property belonging to the defendant — who had paid the initial deposit on it — for many years with his aunt, the defendant's sister, who during her lifetime had paid the mortgage instalments and most of the outgoings on the property. After her death the plaintiff, who was her next of kin, claimed that he was entitled to the beneficial interest in the property and argued that in the circumstances it would be unconscionable for the defendant to rely on his legal title. Barron J stated: 'It is I think quite clear that the law will impose a constructive trust in all circumstances where it would be unjust and unconscionable not to do so.' In his view *Hussey* was authority for the proposition that in certain circumstances where equity so required, 'a debt may be secured by the device of a constructive trust on the property created by the money involved'. He concluded that in the circumstances the plaintiff was entitled to three-quarters of the beneficial interest in the property and that he was a tenant in common of the premises with the defendant.

As noted earlier,[315] the lack of any evidence of the fact that the aunt intended to earn a beneficial interest for herself as a result of the contributions she had made seemed to preclude Barron J from finding that these contributions gave rise to a resulting trust and instead he turned to the more flexible constructive trust to provide a remedy. Mee is critical of this approach, stating

---

312. See e.g. *Attorney-General for Hong Kong v. Reid* [1994] 1 AC 324; Jones [1994] Conv 156.
313. [1996] 3 IR 251.
314. See Chapter 7, pp. 177-194.
315. See Chapter 7, pp. 192-193.

that *Murray* shows the new model constructive trust in its worst light;[316] in his view the absence of intention should probably have precluded even a constructive trust arising, but its 'inherent vagueness' made it more plausible for Barron J to provide the plaintiff with a remedy.

Further detailed attention was given to the concept of the new model constructive trust in *Dublin Corporation v. Ancient Guild of Incorporated Brick and Stone Layers and Allied Trades Union*[317] although it should be noted that when the case came before the Supreme Court, the decision was reversed and the court did not find it necessary to explore the constructive trust issue.[318] The plaintiff corporation issued a compulsory purchase order which affected a hall owned by the defendants. An arbitrator made an award on the basis of the cost of reinstatement of the building and the defendants then substantially demolished the premises making reinstatement impractical. The plaintiff sought a declaration that the union held the sum awarded in trust for the reconstruction of the building and a mandatory injunction requiring the money to be applied for this purpose, or in the alternative, repayment of a sum which represented the difference between the figure awarded and that which would have represented the market value of the premises if reinstatement had not been envisaged. Budd J proceeded to examine the plaintiff's claim for restitution of part of the award on the basis of unjust enrichment. He also considered whether the sum awarded by the arbitrator was impressed with a trust for the plaintiff's benefit. Budd J rejected the contention that a resulting trust arose as he was satisfied that it was the intention of the corporation that the defendants should take the sum awarded beneficially.

In relation to the possibility of a constructive trust arising, the defendants sought to argue that a trust could not be inferred as monies which were not held on a constructive trust at the outset could not subsequently become impressed with such a trust at the behest of the donor on account of some event which occurred after the giving of the money. However, Budd J pointed to Denning MR's statement in *Hussey v. Palmer* to the effect that the trust may arise 'later on, as the circumstances require'. Budd J identified two types of constructive trust, one which arises where there is a fiduciary relationship and the other which arises because of the particular circumstances in which a person holds property. While this latter form of constructive trust has been described as arising 'whenever justice and good conscience require it', Budd J commented that the Irish courts have been cautious about adopting such a nebulous touchstone as 'justice and good conscience'. He stated that traditional doctrines of equity permit the imposition of a constructive trust to prevent a person from asserting or exercising a legal right in circumstances where this

---

316. (1996) 1 CPLJ 9, 13.
317. High Court 1991 No. 1556P (Budd J) 6 March 1996.
318. *Sub nom Dublin Corporation v. Building and Allied Trade Union* [1996] 1 IR 468. See further O'Dell (1997) 113 LQR 245.

would amount to unconscionable conduct. In the view of Budd J 'a system of rules has been evolved which, on the whole, is both practical and just but which cannot claim scientific precision as a whole.' Accordingly he held that the extra money was paid to the defendant under a mistaken assumption and said that while the case was on the outer margins of the circumstances in which the law will imply a constructive trust, it seemed to him that there was strong justification for holding that a constructive trust had arisen.

On appeal to the Supreme Court, the defendants argued that by virtue of the doctrine of *res judicata*, the finality of the arbitration award could not be attacked and submitted that they had not at any stage represented that the hall would be reinstated. The Supreme Court allowed the defendants' appeal and held that the award was final and binding on both parties. Keane J accepted that in certain circumstances a person can be obliged to effect restitution where it would be unjust to retain the property but held that the doctrine of *res judicata* could not be significantly abridged by the invocation of the concept of unjust enrichment.

While Budd J accepted that a constructive trust should 'be imposed by operation of law and independent of the intention of the parties to satisfy the demands of justice and good conscience',[319] he also stressed that the courts in this jurisdiction have been cautious about 'the nebulous touchstone' of justice and good conscience and that the imposition of a constructive trust 'does not leave it open to the court to indulge random notions of what is fair and just as a matter of abstract morality'.[320] Budd J also made it clear that he was conscious of the far-reaching effect which the imposition of a constructive trust might have on third parties. For these reasons, it is fair to say that while Budd J undoubtedly favoured the use of the constructive trust as a remedy for unjust enrichment, it would appear that he was not endorsing the type of 'palm tree justice' with which Lord Denning's new model has often been associated.

The most recent decision in this area, *Kelly v. Cahill*,[321] which although it was nominally based on the *dicta* laid down in decisions such as *H.K.N. Invest Oy v. Incotrade Pvt Ltd*, seemed to involve an even further expansion of existing principles in order to achieve a 'just' result. The deceased informed his solicitor that he wanted to alter his will since he no longer wished to benefit his nephew, the second named defendant, but intended to leave all his property to his wife, the first named defendant. His solicitor advised him to execute a deed transferring his property into the joint names of himself and his wife to avoid a charge to probate tax subsequently arising and the parties believed that the deed executed included all of the lands owned by the deceased. However, through the inadvertence of the solicitor, some of the lands had not

---

319. *Ibid.* at 119.
320. *Ibid.* at 116.
321. [2001] 1 IR 56. See O'Dell (2001) 23 DULJ 71 and Hourican (2001) 6 CPLJ 49.

been transferred and would pass on the deceased's death to the first named defendant for life with remainder to the second named defendant, subject to her legal right to half of the lands concerned. Barr J stated that the net issue in the case before him was whether a constructive trust arose in relation to the lands which were not transferred into joint ownership as intended by the testator. This raised the question of whether a 'new model' constructive trust had been established, and if so whether such a trust had a place in Irish law.

Barr J said that the kernel of the question was whether the evidence established a clear, positive intention on the part of the testator that his wife should inherit all his property, that he took appropriate steps to bring this about and that he could not reasonably have known that through his solicitor's error, the deed of transfer which had been duly executed did not include all his lands. Barr J concluded that it had been established that the deceased had expressed the necessary intention to his solicitor and that he had good reason for believing that the deed of transfer had achieved this intention; in his view it was irrelevant that the second named defendant was neither aware of or had any responsibility for the error which had been made. Barr J expressed the view that 'a "new model" constructive trust...the purpose of which is to prevent unjust enrichment is an equitable concept which deserves recognition in Irish law.'[322] In these circumstances 'justice and good conscience' required that the second named defendant should not be allowed to inherit the property and the interest in remainder under the will should be deemed to be subject to a constructive trust in favour of the first named defendant.

O'Dell[323] is particularly critical of Barr J's judgment and describes the statement referred to above as 'yet another example of the unfortunate conflation of unjust enrichment and the remedial constructive trust', which has the effect of collapsing the distinction between personal and proprietary claims. In his view the remedial constructive trust upon which the decision was based, although clearly established in Irish law, is still 'too unfocussed and insensitive to issues of policy, priority and timing'[324] and should be deployed with more caution.

Developments Elsewhere in the Common Law World

In Canada new model constructive trusts met with some degree of approval although in a 'much modified and more acceptable form'.[325] In *Rathwell v. Rathwell*[326] Dickson J approved of the *dicta* of Lord Denning in *Hussey v. Palmer*, but the formulation of the circumstances in which a constructive trust

---

322. *Ibid.* at 62.
323. (2001) 23 DULJ 71, 83.
324. *Ibid.* at 95.
325. Hodkinson [1983] Conv 420, 429.
326. [1978] 2 SCR 436.

should be imposed depended on the concept of unjust enrichment. As he stated 'for the principle to succeed, the facts must display an enrichment, a corresponding deprivation, and the absence of any juristic reason . . . for the enrichment'.[327] This reasoning was further developed by Dickson J in *Pettkus v. Becker*[328] in which he stated that 'the principle of unjust enrichment lies at the heart of the constructive trust'. However, as the views of the majority in the decision of the Supreme Court of Canada in *Soulos v. Korkont-zilas*[329] illustrate, the fact that a remedial constructive trust lies to prevent unjust enrichment does not prevent such trusts being imposed in other circumstances. McLachlin J made it clear that she subscribed to the view that while the constructive trust may appropriately apply to prevent unjust enrichment, it is not confined to that role and may be employed even in the absence of an established loss to condemn a wrongful act and maintain the integrity of relationships of trust. She concluded that 'in Canada, under the broad umbrella of good conscience, constructive trusts are recognized both for wrongful acts like fraud and breach of duty of loyalty, as well as to remedy unjust enrichment and corresponding deprivation.'[330]

However, the Canadian courts have also recognised the reality that 'the constructive trust does not lie at the heart of restitution'.[331] So, in *Sorochan v. Sorochan*[332] Dickson CJ stated that in determining whether unjust enrichment requires the imposition of the proprietary remedy of a constructive trust, the court must address itself to the specific question of 'whether the claimant reasonably expected to receive an actual interest in property and whether the respondent was or reasonably ought to have been cognizant of that expectation.' Whatever approach is adopted it is important to bear in mind that 'there will be many cases where a plaintiff establishes a cause of action based upon the formula of unjust enrichment but where it will be unjust to remedy a breach of his rights with a remedial constructive trust order.'[333]

The new model constructive trust also met with limited success in Australia. In *Allen v. Snyder*[334] a majority of the Court of Appeal of New South Wales rejected it, commenting that 'the legitimacy of the new model is at least suspect: at best it is a mutant from which further breeding should be discouraged'. In

---

327. *Ibid.* at 455.
328. (1980) 117 DLR (3d) 254, 273. See also the *dicta* of Lambert JA in the decision of the British Columbia Court of Appeal in *Ellingsen (Trustee of) v. Hallmark Ford Sales Ltd* (2000) 190 DLR (4th) 47, 70.
329. (1997) 146 DLR 214. See Smith (1997) 76 Can Bar Rev 539.
330. *Ibid.* at 229.
331. *Per* La Forest J in *Lac Minerals Ltd v. International Corona Resources Ltd* (1989) 61 DLR (4th) 14, 48.
332. (1986) 29 DLR (4th) 1, 12.
333. Paciocco (1989) 68 Can Bar Rev 315, 350.
334. [1977] 2 NSWLR 685, 701.

Muschinski v. Dodds[335] Deane J commented that 'there is no place in the law of this country for the notion of a "constructive trust of a new model"' and while the Australian Chief Justice, Mason CJ, has conceded extra-judicially[336] that Lord Denning's creation may have been a 'shorthand version' of the type of remedial constructive trust now recognised in that jurisdiction, it is arguable that the latter owes little to earlier principles. It is therefore likely that henceforth the new model constructive trust, the underlying objective of which was to prevent a result which was 'inequitable' or contrary to the demands of good conscience, will no longer be applied in this rather flexible form.[337] In *Muschinski*, while Deane J rejected the argument that a constructive trust should be imposed based on broad notions of fairness or unjust enrichment, he found a more specific basis for the imposition of a trust, namely that equity would not permit a person to retain the benefit of property to the extent to which it would be unconscionable for him to do so. This approach was followed in *Baumgartner v. Baumgartner*[338] and the notion of unconscionability is now firmly established as the basis for the imposition of what might be termed a 'remedial constructive trust' in Australia.[339]

In New Zealand, Lord Denning's version of the constructive trust met with a rather hostile reaction almost immediately. In *Carly v. Farrell*[340] Mahon J commented as follows:

> I am being asked to apply a supposed rule of equity which is not only vague in its outline but which must disqualify itself from acceptance as a valid principle of jurisprudence by its total uncertainty of application and result. It cannot be sufficient to say that wide and varying notions of fairness and conscience shall be the legal determinant. No stable system of jurisprudence could permit a litigant's claim to justice to be consigned to the formless void of individual moral opinion. . .

Similarly in *Avondale Printers and Stationers Ltd v. Haggie*[341] Mahon J

---

335. (1985) 160 CLR 583, 615. See also the comment of Glass JA in the New South Wales Court of Appeal in *Allen v. Snyder* [1977] 2 NSWLR 685, 694 that the new model constructive trust was 'without authoritative backing and contrary to principle and authority'.
336. (1994) 110 LQR 238, 250.
337. See Evans [1989] Conv 418.
338. (1987) 164 CLR 137.
339. See further Mason (1997-98) 8 KCLJ 1, 18. Although note that Lord Millett has recently suggested that such trusts are unlikely to take root in Australia, see (1998) 114 LQR 399. The better view is probably that put forward by O'Dell (2001) 23 DULJ 71, 76 that the form of constructive trust which has developed in that jurisdiction, while distinct from Lord Denning's model 'plainly has affinities with it'.
340. [1975] 1 NZLR 356.
341. [1979] 2 NZLR 124.

doubted the correctness of *Hussey v. Palmer* and said that the reasoning which Lord Denning had developed was 'vindicated neither by principle nor authority'. However, more recently in *Lankow v. Rose*[342] Gault J stated that criticisms of Lord Denning's approach have been 'overstated' and in that decision the court confirmed that a constructive trust may be imposed based on the reasonable expectations of the parties.[343]

The recent decision of the New Zealand Court of Appeal in *Fortex Group Ltd v. MacIntosh*[344] contains some useful discussion of the concept of the remedial constructive trust, although the court held that there were no grounds for its imposition on the facts of the case before it. Tipping J stated that in order to defeat the rights of secured creditors by the imposition of a remedial constructive trust, the plaintiffs must be able to point to something which could be said to make it unconscionable for the secured creditors to rely on their rights in law. He concluded that whether the power to impose a remedial constructive trust exists in New Zealand and if so, on what basis and in what circumstances, must await consideration in another case. The issue was considered again in the decision of Glazebrook J in *Commonwealth Reserves I v. Chodar*[345] in which he commented that as the Court of Appeal in *Fortex* had left open the question of whether a remedial constructive trust should be confirmed in New Zealand law, this suggested to him that 'the doctrine has at least a foot in the door'.[346] He stated that a remedial constructive trust is potentially available as a remedy in cases of unconscionability and unjust enrichment although he stressed that the court must carefully examine whether proprietary relief can be justified in a given case. Glazebrook J was satisfied that there had been unjust enrichment and that retention of the assets in question would be unconscionable and he concluded that it was a suitable case for the imposition of a remedial constructive trust.

The remedial constructive trust has not fared so well in England, although there is some *dicta* which would appear to suggest that it might be imposed in a suitable case. Slade LJ accepted in the decision of the Court of Appeal *Metall und Rohstoff AG v. Donaldson Lufkin & Jenrette*[347] that there is a 'good arguable case' for the existence of the remedial constructive trust in that jurisdiction and Lord Browne-Wilkinson has commented in *Westdeutsche Landesbank Girozentrale v. Islington LBC*[348] that 'the remedial constructive trust, if introduced into English law [might] provide a more satisfactory road

---

342. [1995] 1 NZLR 277, 288.
343. See also *Gillies v. Keogh* [1989] 2 NZLR 327. Note also the *dicta* of Thomas J in *Powell v. Thompson* [1991] 1 NZLR 597 that 'the constructive trust has become a broad equitable remedy for reversing that which is inequitable or unconscionable'.
344. [1998] 3 NZLR 171. See Rickett and Grantham [1999] LMCLQ 111.
345. [2001] 2 NZLR 374.
346. *Ibid.* at 383.
347. [1989] 3 WLR 563, 621.
348. [1996] AC 669, 715.

forward'. However, Waters has expressed the view that in England 'the constructive trust continues to be seen as an institutional obligation attaching to property in certain specified circumstances'[349] and Lord Millett has recently commented extra-judicially that the remedial constructive trust is unlikely to take root in England.[350] This view is supported by the *dicta* of Mummery and Nourse LJJ in the decision of the Court of Appeal in *Re Polly Peck International plc (No. 2)*.[351] Mummery LJ referred to the decisions in *Metall und Rohstoff AG* and *Westdeutsche* but said that later cases did not take the matter of remedial constructive trusts any further. He concluded that the claim of the applicants that the court should retrospectively confer a proprietary interest on them in the form of a remedial constructive trust in respect of the assets of an insolvent firm was 'not seriously arguable in English law'.[352]

Commenting on the decisions in *Re Polly Peck International plc (No. 2)* and *Fortex Group Ltd v. MacIntosh*, Birks[353] has stated that they stop short of saying that the remedial constructive trust has no future at all, although he is clearly skeptical about the chance of the concept being developed. Wright[354] in turn is highly critical of Birks' views and suggests that these decisions do not indicate the demise of the remedial constructive trust. He argues that Birks places undue emphasis on aspects of the judgments which further his demise thesis and points out that Mummery LJ in *Polly Peck* explicitly confined his comments to an insolvency context.[355] It is difficult to disagree that in such a context the remedial constructive trust would appear to have little future in that jurisdiction, but as developments elsewhere show, it has significant potential if employed in a cautious manner and with due regard to the rights of third parties.

---

349. In Goldstein ed., *Equity and Contemporary Legal Developments* (1992) p. 463.
350. (1998) 114 LQR 399. See also 'Restitution and Constructive Trusts' in *Restitution, Past Present and Future* (1998) p. 199. See further *Satnam Ltd v. Dunlop Heywood Ltd* [1999] 3 All ER 652, 670.
351. [1998] 3 All ER 812.
352. *Ibid.* at 823. As he stated: 'The insolvency road is blocked off to remedial constructive trusts, at least when judge driven in a vehicle of discretion'. (at 827).
353. (1998) 12 Trust Law Int 202. Although he has also stated ((1999) 28 UWALR 13, 57) that these decisions can be interpreted 'not merely as throwing cold water on remedial proprietary interests, but as killing them stone dead'. These comments were made prior to the decision in *Commonwealth Reserves I v. Chodar* [2001] 2 NZLR 374.
354. [1999] RLR 128. See also (1999-99) 9 KCLJ 140.
355. Rickett and Grantham suggest [1999] LMCLQ 111, 117 that the particularity of the facts in *Polly Peck* coupled with the nature of the judgments mean the case 'cannot be taken to have excluded altogether the remedial constructive trust from the judicial remedial armoury in England.'

Possible Future Developments Relating to the Constructive Trust

In addition to the traditionally recognised circumstances which may give rise to a constructive trust, it now seems clear from developments in various parts of the common law world that unjust enrichment and unconscionable conduct can also lead to the imposition of such a trust.[356] Unjust enrichment, which is a firmly established basis of liability in Canada,[357] presupposes '(1) receipt by the defendant of a benefit, (2) at the plaintiff's expense, (3) in such circumstances that it would be unjust to allow the defendant to retain the benefit'.[358] Although Lord Diplock in his judgment in *Orakpo v. Manson Investments Ltd*[359] denied that the principle was recognised in English law, it has clearly been recognized in that jurisdiction as a basis for actions at common law for money had and received.[360]

In this jurisdiction, while the judgment of Finlay P in *Hickey & Co. v. Roches Stores (No. 1)*[361] did little to clarify whether the principle should be recognised as part of our jurisprudence, it seems to have been accepted by Henchy J in the Supreme Court decisions of *East Cork Foods Ltd v. O'Dwyer Steel Co. Ltd*[362] and *Murphy v. Attorney General*,[363] albeit in another context. While no express reference was made to the concept of unjust enrichment it seems to underlie the decision of Carroll J in *Re Irish Shipping Ltd*,[364] which concerned the imposition of a constructive trust. The former bankers of the company, Citibank, claimed a right of set off in respect of monies paid into the company's account in error by another bank, the Korean Exchange Bank. Carroll J held that Citibank was not entitled to claim such a right and that the money paid in error was subject to a constructive trust and could therefore be

---

356. As Glazebrook J stated in the New Zealand decision of *Commonwealth Reserves I v. Chodar* [2001] 2 NZLR 374, 383: 'There appear to be two potential triggers for the exercise of the court's discretion to grant a remedial constructive trust. One is unjust enrichment. The other is unconscionability.'

357. *Pettkus v. Becker* (1980) 117 DLR (3d) 257; *Sorochan v. Sorochan* (1986) 29 DLR (4th) 1; *Soulos v. Korkontzilas* (1997) 146 DLR (4th) 214.

358. *B.P. Exploration Co. (Libya) Ltd v. Hunt (No. 2)* [1979] 1 WLR 783, 839. See also the formulation put forward by McLachlin J in *Soulos v. Korkontzilas* (1997) 146 DLR (4th) 214, 222 '(1) the enrichment of the defendant; (2) the corresponding deprivation of the plaintiff; and (3) the absence of a juristic reason for the enrichment'.

359. [1978] AC 95, 104. Quoted by Murphy J in *Highland Finance Ireland Ltd v. Sacred Heart College of Agriculture Ltd* [1992] 1 IR 472, 477. See also the comments of Mahon J in the New Zealand decision of *Avondale Printers and Stationers Ltd v. Haggie* [1979] 2 NZLR 124, 148-155.

360. *Lipkin Gorman v. Karpanale Ltd* [1991] 2 AC 548; *Woolwich Equitable Building Society v. Inland Revenue Commissioners* [1992] 3 WLR 366 and *Re PMPA Garages Ltd (No. 2)* [1992] 1 IR 332.

361. High Court 1975 No. 1007P (Finlay P) 14 July 1976.

362. [1978] IR 103.

363. [1982] IR 241. See O'Dell (1993) 15 DULJ 27, 29-30.

364. [1986] ILRM 518.

traced by the Korean bank. Carroll J quoted with approval the *dicta* of Vinson CJ in the American Supreme Court decision of *Healy v. Commissioner of Internal Revenue*[365] to the effect that a 'constructive trust is a fiction imposed as an equitable device for achieving justice'; therefore in the words of Carroll J 'it should not work an injustice'.[366] In addition, the judgment of Budd J in *Dublin Corporation v. Ancient Guild of Incorporated Brick and Stone Layers and Allied Trades Union*[367] clearly shows that he favoured the use of a constructive trust as a remedy for unjust enrichment.[368]

As noted above, O'Dell[369] has been particularly critical of what he terms 'the erroneous equation' of the concepts of unjust enrichment and the remedial constructive trust on the basis that liability in respect of the former in his view should be strict and personal whereas the latter is a form of equitable proprietary remedy. He expresses the view that unjust enrichment is no basis for a constructive trust although it may be that a further element in conjunction with that concept will be sufficient to generate a proprietary remedy of this nature.[370]

As the Australian decisions considered above illustrate, it is clear that the need to remedy unconscionable conduct may also justify the imposition of a remedial constructive trust.[371] In *Reidy v. McGreevy*[372] Barron J appeared to accept that unconscionable behaviour could give rise to a constructive trust, although the matter before him merely concerned the preliminary issue of whether the plaintiff's claim was statute barred and his brief judgment contains no reasoning on this point.

It should be noted that the Chief Justice of Australia, Mason CJ, commenting extra-judicially, has identified one significant difference between the notions of unconscionable conduct and unjust enrichment. In his view:

---

365. (1953) 345 US 278. Also approved by Goulding J in the English case of *Chase Manhattan Bank NA v. Israel British Bank (London) Ltd* [1981] Ch 105.
366. [1986] ILRM 518, 522.
367. High Court 1991 No. 1556P (Budd J) 6 March 1996.
368. However, as O'Dell has pointed out (see (1993) 15 DULJ (ns) 27, 45) 'even if an action for restitution in equity is apt, the constructive trust is not the only remedy'.
369. (2001) 23 DULJ 71. In his view (at 79) 'much of the misplaced criticism of the principle against unjust enrichment is crossfire from similar but much less misguided critique of the open-textured nature of the remedial constructive trust.'
370. This view is not wholly in line with the authorities in Canada in particular. See the *dicta* of McLachlin J in *Soulos v. Korkontzilas* (1997) 146 DLR 214, 229-230. See also the *dicta* of Henry J in *Fortex Group Ltd v. MacIntosh* [1998] 3 NZLR 171, 180.
371. *Muschinski v. Dodds* (1985) 160 CLR 583; *Baumgartner v. Baumgartner* (1987) 164 CLR 137.
372. High Court 1990 No. 11804P (Barron J) 19 March 1993. Note that O'Dell has commented (1993) 15 DULJ 27, 50 that 'equity can impose a remedial constructive trust in circumstances other than where the defendant has been unjustly enriched, if the defendant's conduct has nevertheless been unconscionable'.

The former looks to the conduct of the person who takes unconscientious advantage of the person in the position of disadvantage and requires an assessment of that conduct whereas the latter looks to the expectations of the parties and inquires whether there was an enrichment, and corresponding deprivation, and the absence of any juristic reason for the enrichment.[373]

Whichever formula is employed as the basis on which liability should be imposed, clearly this post-Denning version of the remedial constructive trust is recognised as being a powerful form of remedy which should be applied only where the circumstances clearly warrant such a course of action,[374] and specifically only where the plaintiff has a higher claim in equity to the property in question than the general creditors of the proposed constructive trustee.[375] Any analysis of the circumstances justifying the imposition of a remedial constructive trust must include a consideration of the position of third parties, particularly unsecured creditors, who may be affected by this form of remedy.[376] As Glazebrook J commented in the recent decision of the New Zealand High Court in *Commonwealth Reserves I v. Chodar*[377] 'reliability and certainty are primary considerations of any system of property rights, and the unprovoked alteration of those rights is to be avoided where possible. ... The court must carefully examine the reasons why other forms of relief are inadequate, the interests of any third parties and the other circumstances of the case, and consider whether proprietary relief can be justified.' So, as he made clear in his judgment in *Chodar* a remedial constructive trust should only be imposed where other available remedies are inadequate and the courts will not impose such a remedy if there is an appropriate equitable remedy which falls short of the imposition of a trust.[378]

However, in the last analysis the overriding preoccupation of judges and academic commentators alike is the perennial dilemma of choosing between 'predictability in the law and justice in the individual case' and the importance of steering a middle course 'between the extremes of inflexible rules and case-by-case "palm tree" justice'.[379]

The difficulties facing the courts in utilising the concept of the remedial

---

373. (1994) 110 LQR 238, 251.
374. Rickett [1991] Conv 125 and see also Fridman (1992) 11 LS 304, 310.
375. Note the criticisms made by Jones [1994] Conv 156 of the decision of the Privy Council in *Attorney-General for Hong Kong v. Reid* [1994] 1 AC 324 in relation to the consequences of the imposition of a constructive trust on a fiduciary.
376. See e.g. Goode 'Proprietary Restitutionary Claims' in *Restitution: Past, Present and Future* eds. Cornish et al. (1998) p. 63.
377. [2001] 2 NZLR 374, 384.
378. *Giumelli v. Giumelli* (1999) 161 ALR 473, 476.
379. *Peel v. Canada* (1992) 98 DLR (4th) 140, 164 *per* McLachlin J.

constructive trust in a manner which will achieve this objective cannot be under estimated. However, it is submitted that the following statement of Deane J in *Muschinski v. Dodds*[380] comes close to summarising present attitudes towards the imposition of such trusts:

> The mere fact that it would be unjust or unfair in a situation of discord for the owner of a legal estate to assert his ownership against another provides, of itself, no mandate for a judicial declaration that the ownership in whole or in part lies, in equity, in that other: cf. *Hepworth v. Hepworth* (1963) 110 CLR 309, at pp. 317–318. Such equitable relief by way of constructive trust will only properly be available if applicable principles of the law of equity require that the person in whom the ownership of property is vested should hold it to the use or for the benefit of another. That is not to say that general notions of fairness and justice have become irrelevant to the content and application of equity. They remain relevant to the traditional equitable notion of unconscionable conduct which persists as an operative component of some fundamental rules or principles of modern equity.

---

380. (1985) 160 CLR 385, 616.

CHAPTER 9

Purpose Trusts

INTRODUCTION

As we have seen a private trust may be established in favour of specified or ascertainable individuals. In addition, a trust for purposes which are treated in law as charitable will be recognised as valid. The distinctive feature of such trusts is that they are regarded as being for the public benefit and are enforceable by the Attorney General. However, trusts for non-charitable purposes will not generally be regarded as valid as they are considered to lack the human beneficiaries necessary to secure their enforcement, to be too uncertain in nature, and will often offend the rules against perpetuities and inalienability. These potential difficulties do not prevent attempts being made to establish so called 'purpose trusts'; as Sheridan[1] has commented: 'distributors of largesse … generally give because they want to, and not because giving can be accomplished with legal ease.' In certain limited circumstances purpose trusts have been recognised as valid, although these cases have tended to be regarded as 'concessions to human weakness or sentiment'[2] which 'ought not to be increased in number, nor indeed followed, except where the one is exactly like another'.[3] Therefore it is necessary first to consider the objections raised in relation to the enforcement of non-charitable purpose trusts and then to consider the limited exceptions to the general rule that they will not be enforced.

RATIONALE FOR POLICY OF NON-ENFORCEMENT OF PURPOSE TRUSTS

Enforceability — The Beneficiary Principle[4]

As stated above the Attorney General is charged with the responsibility of enforcing charitable trusts, and private trusts in favour of individuals can be

---

1. (1953) 17 Conv 46.
2. *Re Astor's Settlement Trusts* [1952] Ch 534, 547 *per* Roxburgh J.
3. *Re Endacott* [1960] Ch 232, 251 *per* Harman LJ.
4. See generally McKay (1973) 37 Conv 420.

enforced by the beneficiaries themselves. One of the principal objections to non-charitable purpose trusts is that there is no one who can ensure that the court will secure performance of the trust if this should become necessary. As Grant MR stated in *Morice v. Bishop of Durham*:[5] 'there must be somebody in whose favour the court can decree performance'. This principle was explained by Roxburgh J in *Re Astor's Settlement Trusts*[6] in the following terms: that a trustee would not be expected to be subject to an equitable obligation unless there was somebody who could enforce a correlative equitable right.

There seems little doubt about the relevance of the beneficiary principle in this jurisdiction, although some anomalous exceptions to the requirement that there should be human beneficiaries capable of enforcing the trust remain. These are largely confined to the categories of gifts for tombs and monuments and for specific animals which will be considered below, although occasionally decisions have been made which are difficult to justify and for this reason are unlikely to be followed. In *Re Gibbons*,[7] a testator directed that the residue of his estate should be disposed of by his executors, who were fellow priests 'to my best spiritual advantage, as conscience and sense of duty may direct'. While Barton J held that the bequest was not charitable in nature he found that it could be upheld as a valid private trust and rejected arguments that it was too indefinite and lacked the beneficiaries necessary for it to be so regarded. The rationale employed by Barton J in reaching this decision is far from clear and the decision could be said to fall within the category of 'troublesome, anomalous and aberrant cases' which Harman LJ suggested in *Re Endacott*[8] should not be added to.

It is important to note that the objection raised in this regard is not that the trust is for a purpose or object *per se* but rather that there is a lack of beneficiaries in whose favour the court can enforce the trust obligations.[9] Often it may be a matter of construction to determine whether a given trust is for the benefit of persons or purposes and what might appear at first glance as a purpose trust may be upheld as a discretionary trust for the benefit of

---

5. (1804) 9 Ves 399. This principle was reiterated by Lord Parker in *Bowman v. Secular Society Ltd* [1917] AC 406, 441 where he said that with the exception of charitable trusts 'a trust to be valid must be for the benefit of individuals'. See also *Re Wood* [1949] Ch 498, 501 *per* Harman J; *Re Endacott* [1960] Ch 232, 246 and *Re Recher's Will Trusts* [1972] Ch 526, 538.
6. [1952] Ch 534, 541. See also *Armitage v. Nurse* [1998] Ch 241, 253.
7. [1917] 1 IR 448.
8. [1960] Ch 232, 251.
9. *Re Denley's Trust Deed* [1969] 1 Ch 373, 383. Although note the comments of Barton J in *Re Gibbons* [1917] 1 IR 448, 453 in reply to such an argument that: 'The Court is not asked to compel enforcement of this trust. The executors are willing to carry it out; and I see no sufficient ground for refusing to allow them to effectuate, as they propose to do, the expressed intentions of the testator.'

individuals. So for example, a trust for the education of certain children might be construed as a trust of which these children are the beneficiaries, with the purpose of providing for their education being interpreted merely as an expression of motive for the gift.[10] This reasoning was developed by Goff J in *Re Denley's Trust Deed*[11] in a manner which resulted in the following principle being laid down:

> Where, then, the trust, though expressed as a purpose, is directly or indirectly for the benefit of an individual or individuals, it seems to me that it is in general outside the mischief of the beneficiary principle.

However, such a construction will not always be possible and Goff J stressed that there were limitations to the application of such a principle:

> I think that there may be a purpose or object trust, the carrying out of which would benefit an individual or individuals, where that benefit is so indirect or intangible or which is otherwise so framed as not to give those persons any *locus standi* to apply to the court to enforce the trust, in which case the beneficiary principle would, as it seems to me, apply to invalidate the trust, quite apart from any question of uncertainty or perpetuity.[12]

Therefore it would seem that a trust even if it is expressed in terms of a purpose may be valid and enforceable provided that it can be construed as directly or indirectly confering a benefit on an ascertained or ascertainable individual or individuals and provided that it does not fall foul of the other objections to the enforcement of such trusts which will now be considered.

Enforceability — Clarity and Certainty

If non-charitable purpose trusts are to be recognised as valid they must be expressed in terms which are sufficiently clear and certain to enable a court to oversee their performance. So, for example in *Morice v. Bishop of Durham*,[13] a gift for 'such objects of benevolence and liberality as the Bishop of Durham in his own discretion shall most approve of' was considered to be too uncertain. As Grant MR stated: 'there can be no trust over the exercise of which this

---

10. This type of approach can be found in *Re Andrew's Trust* [1905] 2 Ch 48; *Re Osoba* [1979] 1 WLR 247.
11. [1969] 1 Ch 373, 383-384.
12. *Ibid.* at 382-383.
13. (1804) 9 Ves 399.

Court will not assume a control; for an uncontrollable power of disposition would be ownership, and not trust'.[14]

This principle is well illustrated by the decision in *Re Astor's Settlement Trusts*,[15] where an *inter vivos* settlement, expressly limited to the perpetuity period, provided that shares were to be held on trust for specified non-charitable objects including 'the establishment, maintenance and improvement of good understanding, sympathy and co-operation between nations' and 'the preservation of the independence and integrity of newspapers'. Roxburgh J held that the trusts fell foul of the beneficiary principle but he also made it clear that they would have failed as being too uncertain in nature. He stated:

> If (contrary to my view) an enumeration of purposes outside the realm of charities can take the place of an enumeration of beneficiaries, the purposes must, in my judgment, be stated in phrases which embody definite concepts and the means by which the trustees are to try to attain them must also be prescribed with a sufficient degree of certainty.[16]

The question of what will constitute a sufficient degree of certainty is itself not a issue altogether free from doubt. In *Re Gibbons*[17] Barton J described the direction that a gift should be applied to the best spiritual advantage of the testator, 'as conscience and sense of duty may direct' as 'wide' but 'not indefinite'. While Barton J may have been influenced by the willingness of the executors to carry out the testator's wishes in a manner which they were satisfied would comply with his intentions, a decision of this nature does little to clarify the approach which should be followed in this area.

It might be argued on the basis of *Re Thompson*[18] that there is authority to support the proposition that where the purposes or object of a trust are defined with sufficient clarity and certainty, a lack of human beneficiaries will not be fatal. There the testator gave a legacy of £1,000 to a friend to be applied towards the promotion and furtherance of fox hunting. Clauson J said that 'the object of the gift has been defined with sufficient clearness and is of a nature to which effect can be given'[19] and upheld its validity. However such a view appears to be directly in conflict with the principles laid down by

---

14. *Ibid.* at 404-405. On appeal Lord Eldon stated as follows (1805) 10 Ves 522, 539: 'As it is a maxim, that the execution of a trust shall be under the control of the Court, it must be of such a nature, that it can be under that control; so that the administration of it can be reviewed by the Court.' See also *Chichester Diocesan Fund and Board of Finance v. Simpson* [1944] AC 341.
15. [1952] Ch 534. See Marshall (1953) 6 CLP 151.
16. *Ibid.* at 547.
17. [1917] 1 IR 448.
18. [1934] Ch 342.
19. *Ibid.* at 344. See also *Re Douglas* (1887) 35 Ch D 472, 486 *per* Cotton LJ.

Roxburgh J in *Re Astor's Settlement Trusts*,[20] and the better view would seem to be that unless the beneficiary principle can be overcome in the manner suggested by Goff J in *Re Denley's Trust Deed*,[21] the certainty of any purposes expressed will not cure the difficulty caused by the lack of beneficiaries. For this reason *Re Thompson* is perhaps best considered as a rather anomalous decision which is unlikely to be followed.

The Need for Compliance with the Rules against Perpetuities and Inalienability

While the first two objections to the enforcement of purpose trusts arise out of the principle that a trust for non-charitable purposes should fail if it cannot be properly controlled and if necessary administered by the court, this objection is based on considerations of public policy, which dictate that property should not be tied up for excessive periods of time. Essentially before a purpose trust will be enforced the court must be satisfied that its terms will not offend the rule against perpetuities and that the property included in the trust will not be rendered inalienable.[22] So even where a purpose trust might be interpreted as complying with the requirements of the beneficiary principle and as being sufficiently certain, it must be limited to the period of perpetuity[23] if it is to be valid.

It should be noted at this point that the terminology employed by judges in this area can be confusing. In this context what is at issue is essentially an application of the rule against inalienability or the rule against perpetual trusts rather than the rule against perpetuities, although an examination of the authorities shows that judges tend to employ these phrases interchangeably.[24] The effect of the rule against inalienability is to render void a trust which comprises property which might remain inalienable beyond the perpetuity period and it is concerned with the duration of an interest which is already vested rather than with the time at which vesting occurs.[25]

Clearly one of the most important factors in determining whether a gift is

---

20. [1952] Ch 534.
21. [1969] 1 Ch 373.
22. It was for this reason that numerous bequests for the saying of masses (now recognised as a valid charitable purpose, see *O'Hanlon v. Logue* [1906] 1 IR 247 and s. 45(2) of the Charities Act 1961) were held to be void in the last century. See *Dillon v. Reilly* (1875) IR 10 Eq 152; *Beresford v. Jarvis* (1877) 11 ILTR 128; *M'Court v. Burnett* (1877) 11 ILTR 130; *Morrow v. M'Conville* (1883) 11 LR Ir 236 and *Small v. Torley* (1890) 25 LR Ir 388. Although note that the contrary conclusion was reached in *Phelan v. Slattery* (1887) 19 LR Ir 177 and *Reichenbach v. Quinn* (1888) 21 LR Ir 138.
23. The period of a life or lives in being plus 21 years or, if there is no life in being, a period of 21 years only.
24. E.g. *O'Byrne v. Davoren* [1994] 3 IR 373.
25. See Coughlan, *Property Law in Ireland* (2nd ed., 1998) p. 178.

void on these grounds will be whether the obligation involves merely the application of the income from the gift to the stated purpose. However, even where the application of the gift is not limited to income only and there is no direction that the capital be maintained indefinitely, it may still offend the rule against inalienability. This is illustrated by the decision of the Supreme Court in *Re Fossitt's Estate*,[26] in which a bequest to the 'Orange Institution of Ireland' for the upkeep of a hall was held to be void for perpetuity, despite the fact that there was no evidence that the income alone was to be employed for this purpose. Fitzgibbon J stated:

> In my opinion it was the intention of the testator that the capital might be applied from time to time, if occasion should arise and the income of the fund was insufficient, towards the upkeep of the Hall, but I am satisfied that the testator contemplated the continued existence of the fund, in whole or in part, for an absolutely indefinite period, which might far exceed that fixed by law of a life or lives in being and twenty-one years after.[27]

Where a phrase such as 'so long as the law allows' or 'such period as the law permits' has been employed, a gift will be regarded as being valid for a period of 21 years. However, where no such qualification is included, a gift will be void unless it comes to a determination before the end of the perpetuity period. On the other hand, in some respects a fairly flexible attitude has been taken towards the need for compliance with the rule against inalienability and the courts have assumed that the requirements of the rule will be met where it appears that this is a reasonable interpretation of a gift. So, in *Mussett v. Bingle*[28] where a testator gave a legacy of £300 to be applied in the erection of a monument to his wife's first husband and a further sum of £200, the interest on which was to be used for its maintenance, Hall VC upheld the validity of the former gift presumably on the assumption that the monument would be erected within the perpetuity period. The latter gift was clearly of a perpetual nature and therefore void.

Finally, it should be noted that the Law Reform Commission in its Report on *The Rule Against Perpetuities and Cognate Rules*[29] considered the effect of the rule against trusts of undue duration but did not recommend its abolition. The Commission noted that the rule is just one of the devices employed to

---

26. [1934] IR 504. This can be compared to the decision of Haugh J in *Re Conner* [1960] IR 67, in which a gift to a cemetery company for the upkeep of a family vault was upheld in circumstances where there was nothing to prevent the company 'resorting to the capital if and when, they think proper in their discretion to do so'.
27. *Ibid.* at 513.
28. [1876] WN 170. See also *Re Filshie* [1939] NZLR 91.
29. LRC 62-2000 paragraphs 5.08-5.13.

regulate non-charitable purpose trusts and concluded that it would be preferable to postpone any detailed consideration of the rule until it could be examined in the context of a review of the entire area of unincorporated associations.[30]

EXCEPTIONAL CASES IN WHICH PURPOSE TRUSTS HAVE BEEN ENFORCED

Tombs and Monuments

At common law a trust for the erection of a tomb, gravestone or monument was not regarded as being charitable in nature. In this jurisdiction legislation has intervened in a limited way and section 50 of the Charities Act 1961 now provides that gifts for the maintenance or improvement of a tomb, vault, grave, tombstone or any other memorial to a deceased person are deemed to be charitable gifts insofar as they do not exceed £60 a year in the case of income and £1,000 in any other case. However, these monetary limits have not been increased in the years since the enactment of the legislation and in many cases gifts for such purposes will exceed these limits.[31] In these circumstances a bequest for such a purpose will have to come within the rather anomalous exception which has developed at common law, the effect of which is that gifts for the erection of a tomb or monument or for its maintenance will be upheld as valid purpose trusts provided that they do not offend the rule against inalienability.

As illustrated by the decision of Hall VC in *Mussett v. Bingle*,[32] the courts appear to assume that directions of this nature will be carried out within the perpetuity period. However to come within this limited exception the trust must also be expressed with sufficient certainty to be carried out. In *Re Endacott*[33] a testator bequeathed his residuary estate valued at £20,000 to a specified parish council 'for the purpose of providing some useful memorial

---

30. This echoes the view put forward by the Law Commission of England and Wales in its Report on the *Rules Against Perpetuities and Excessive Accumulations* (1998 Law Com No. 251) at paragraph 1.14 to the effect that the rule against inalienability is in reality just one of the devices that is employed to keep the development of non-charitable purpose trusts in check. In the view of the Commission, any consideration of the rule belongs more properly to a review of the law governing such trusts and unincorporated associations.

31. The Law Reform Commission has recommended (*The Rule Against Perpetuities and Cognate Rules* LRC 62-2000 paragraph 5.15) that these sums be increased to a limit of £1,000 (€1,270) per year in the case of income and to a limit of £16,000 (€20, 316) on the capital sum (as of the year 2000).

32. [1876] WN 170. See also *Trimmer v. Danby* (1856) LJ Ch 424 where a bequest of £1,000 to erect a monument to the testator in St Paul's Cathedral was upheld.

33. [1960] Ch 232.

to myself'. The gift was held void by the Court of Appeal; Harman LJ stating 'I cannot think a case of this kind, the case of providing outside a church an unspecified and unidentified memorial, is the kind of instance which should be allowed to add to those troublesome, anomalous and aberrant cases'.[34]

In circumstances where the statutory limits specified above have been exceeded, the issue of compliance with the rule against inalienability becomes of crucial importance in relation to gifts for the maintenance of graves and monuments, and if trusts of this nature are to be regarded as valid at common law they must be confined to the perpetuity period. *Mussett v. Bingle* illustrates that a gift for the maintenance of a monument without any words of qualification will be void and in *Toole v. Hamilton*[35] it was held by Porter MR that a bequest which was to be invested and the income thereof applied in maintaining an enclosure around a grave was also void. However, in *Pirbright v. Salwey*[36] a gift for the upkeep of a grave for so long as the law for the time being permitted was upheld as valid for a period of 21 years. Similarly, in *Re Hooper*[37] a testator bequeathed a sum of money to trustees to apply the income to the maintenance of family graves and monuments 'as far as they can legally do so'. Maugham J held that this trust was valid for a period of 21 years from the testator's death.

A number of devices can be employed to avoid the difficulty of complying with the rule against inalienability. Where a gift is given for the maintenance of an entire churchyard, this will be upheld as a valid charitable gift and so not subject to the rule,[38] and at common law this will provide an effective means of indirectly securing the maintenance of a particular grave or monument.[39] A further method appears to be to make a gift to a cemetery company, where one exists, to be applied for the maintenance of a grave or tomb.[40] In *Re Conner*[41] a bequest of £1,000 was made 'to the General Cemetery Company of Dublin to be applied for the maintenance and care of the family vault at Mount Jerome'. Haugh J said that the testatrix clearly bequeathed the money to the company with the sole limitation that it should be spent in the maintenance of the family vault and concluded that there was nothing to

---

34. *Ibid.* at 251.
35. [1901] 1 IR 383. See also *Beresford v. Jarvis* (1877) 11 ILTR 128.
36. [1896] WN 86.
37. [1932] 1 Ch 38.
38. *Re Vaughan* (1886) 33 Ch D 187.
39. *Re Eighmie* [1935] Ch 524.
40. Such an approach seems to have been justified in England in *Re Chardon* [1928] 1 Ch 464 on the basis that a determinable interest was not subject to the rule against perpetuities although by virtue of s. 12 of the Perpetuities and Accumulations Act 1964 this is no longer the case. Note that s. 1 of the Parish Councils and Burial Authorities (Miscellaneous Provisions) Act 1970 now authorises local and burial authorities to conclude agreements for the maintenance of graves for a period of up to 99 years.
41. [1960] IR 67.

prevent the company from resorting to the capital if and when it was found necessary to do so for the purposes outlined in the will. In the circumstances, he was satisfied that the gift was a valid non-charitable one which did not offend the rule against inalienability and which should therefore be enforced.

Animals

A gift to provide for the welfare of animals generally or for the care and maintenance of a class of animals is regarded as being charitable in law.[42] Gifts to provide for the care of specified animals while they are admittedly not of a charitable nature and would *prima facie* seem to fall foul of the beneficiary principle have been upheld as coming within the limited class of exceptions to the principle that non-charitable purpose trusts will not be enforced. In *Pettingall v. Pettingall*[43] a gift of £50 a year for the maintenance of the testator's favourite black mare was upheld as valid. In *Re Dean*[44] North J upheld a gift of £750 per annum for a period of 50 years for the care and maintenance of the testator's horses and hounds. He rejected the view that the court would not recognise the validity of a trust unless it is capable of being enforced by someone. In what has been recognised as a rather unsatisfactory judgment, North J then proceeded to virtually ignore the potential problem of violating the rule against inalienability and remarked that he would uphold a gift of this nature 'provided that it is not to last for too long a period'.[45] Such an approach to the perpetuity question is unlikely to be followed in England and has been rejected in this jurisdiction. In *Re Kelly*[46] a testator bequeathed a sum of money to be applied in the care and maintenance of his dogs with a gift over should any surplus remain on the death of the last dog. Meredith J upheld the gift as being valid for a period of 21 years following the testator's death, although it would have been technically void thereafter and the gift over was found to be void for remoteness. A number of points in his judgment are worth noting. It clearly emerges that only a human life can be used as a measuring life for the purpose of applying the rule against perpetuities. Meredith J expressed this point unequivocally in colourful language:

> If the lives of the dogs or other animals could be taken into account in reckoning the maximum period of lives in being and twenty-one years afterwards any contingent or executory interest might be properly limited, so as only to vest within the lives of specified carp, or tortoises, or other

---

42. *Re Douglas* (1887) 35 Ch D 472; *Swifte v. Attorney General* [1912] 1 IR 133; *Armstrong v. Reeves* (1890) 25 LR Ir 325. See further *infra* Chapter 10.
43. (1842) 11 LJ Ch 176.
44. (1889) 41 Ch D 552.
45. *Ibid.* at 557.
46. [1932] IR 255.

animals that might live for over a hundred years, and for twenty-one years afterwards, which of course is absurd. 'Lives' means human lives. It was suggested that the last of the dogs could in fact not outlive the testator by more than twenty-one years. I know nothing of that. The Court does not enter into the question of a dog's expectation of life. In point of fact neighbour's dogs and cats are unpleasantly long-lived; but I have no knowledge of their precise expectation of life ... there can be no doubt that 'lives' means lives of human beings, not of animals or trees in California.[47]

On the basis of this statement it would also appear that the court will not take judicial notice of the fact that certain animals will not live for a period of more than 21 years although authority in England suggests the contrary.[48] Meredith J rejected the suggestion that he should read into the will an implied limitation to a period of 21 years or 'so long as the law permits'. However he stressed that this did not prevent him from analysing a provision which was 'manifestly not good in its entirety' for the purpose of determining whether it included a severable part which did not offend the rule against perpetuities, which in the case before him, amounted to expenditure for a period of 21 years. Therefore, in the light of *Re Kelly* it can be said with a fair degree of certainty that in this jurisdiction purpose trusts for the care and maintenance of specified animals will be upheld for a period of 21 years provided that they are expressed with sufficient clarity. In the interests of certainty it is probably preferable that such trusts are clearly limited to a period of 21 years or 'so long as the law allows,' although if one accepts the approach of Meredith J such an omission will not be fatal.

Gifts to Unincorporated Associations[49]

An unincorporated association has been defined by Lawton LJ in *Conservative and Unionist Central Office v. Burrell*[50] as follows:

[T]wo or more persons bound together for one or more common purposes, not being business purposes, by mutual undertakings, each having mutual duties and obligations, in an organisation which has rules which identify in whom control of it and its funds rests and on what terms and which can be joined or left at will.

While a gift to a body corporate even for non-charitable purposes will be

---

47. *Ibid.* at 260-261.
48. *Re Haines, The Times*, 7 November 1952. See Sheridan (1953) 17 Conv 46, 60.
49. See generally Rickett [1980] CLJ 88, 90-111.
50. [1982] 1 WLR 522, 525.

valid because such a body has a separate legal personality and therefore can enforce it, difficulties arise where it is sought to confer a gift of a non-charitable nature on an unincorporated association. An unincorporated association has no separate personality in law and is regarded as a collection of individuals and the potential difficulties which must be considered are that gifts of this nature may fall foul of the beneficiary principle or may contravene the rule against inalienability.

A number of different methods of conferring a benefit on unincorporated associations have been devised, the latter two of which have been recognised as essentially overcoming the potential problems referred to above.

A Gift by Way of Endowment for the Benefit of the Association

Where a gift is construed as an endowment for the benefit of the association, it will almost inevitably be found to be void as infringing the rule against inalienability. This point emerged from the decisions of the House of Lords in *Re Macaulay*[51] and of the Privy Council in *Leahy v. Attorney-General for New South Wales*.[52] However, if the wording of the gift is such that it satisfies the requirement of the rule against inalienability, the decision of Goff J in *Re Denley's Trust Deed*[53] would seem to confirm that the difficulties posed by the beneficiary principle can be overcome.

A Gift to the Members of the Association for the Time Being

A gift to an unincorporated association may be enforced if it is recognised as a gift to the members of the association alive at the time of the disposition, or in the case of a will, at the date of the testator's death. The beneficiary principle is satisfied as it is possible to ascertain who these members are and the rule against inalienability will not be infringed provided that the members are free to dispose of the property, both income and capital, at any time. This principle is explained as follows by Lovell:[54]

> In the context of trusts for unincorporated associations, it is submitted that the fact that the association can last forever is of no significance. ... Once there has been an effectual dedication to the purpose or enterprise, and provided that there is no restriction on the use of the capital, then there is no reason to argue that any principle of perpetuity is offended. Quite clearly the association may last for a period of time longer than

---

51. [1943] Ch 435n.
52. [1959] AC 457. Although note that on the facts of the case the gift was saved by the provisions of a New South Wales statute.
53. [1969] 1 Ch 373.
54. (1970) 34 Conv 77, 96.

the perpetuity period, but the property together with all other association assets is vested according to the trusts of the association and the latter can dissolve at any time if the members so wish it.

However it must be possible to construe the gift as being for the individual members of the association for the time being and as some of the authorities have shown such an interpretation is not always possible. So, in *Hogan v. Byrne*,[55] Christian J held that to put such a construction on the testator's bequest to 'monks named Christian Brothers' would be to defeat his real intention. He stated: 'If you do that you disappoint the testator's intentions. He intended that the land should be held by one body, and not that it should be divided into an indefinite number of parts each to belong to a different person.' As Christian LJ subsequently stated in *Stewart v. Green*,[56] sitting as Lord Justice of Appeal, two distinct interpretations of gifts of this nature are possible:

> First a trust for the [individuals] who happened to compose the community at the moment of the testator's death in their natural capacities. Second, a trust for the community in its communal character, of whomsoever it should from time to time and for ever consist. The first would, of course, be good and effectual in law; and ... practically his purpose would be achieved. ... The other intent — that of giving to the community in a communal or quasi corporate character — would mean the *form* undoubtedly most accordant with the testator's ideas; but would labour under the disadvantage of being utterly incapable of legal realization; for as the community, as such, has no legal personality, it is incapable of taking in that character.

In the case before the court, counsel arguing in favour of the validity of the gift repudiated the first possible construction, relying instead on an argument based on its charitable nature which was not made out, and as a result the bequest was declared void.[57] Similarly in *Morris v. M'Conville*,[58] Chatterton VC stressed that 'the court must act upon the intention of the testator as expressed in the words he has used'.[59] The Vice-Chancellor said that he found the terms of the testator's will impossible to reconcile with the theory of the gift in the case before him being to the individual members of a convent, and found that it was instead intended as a 'permanent contribution *de anno in*

55. (1863) 13 ICLR 166.
56. (1871) IR 5 Eq 470, 481.
57. As Porter MR commented in *Bradshaw v. Jackman* (1887) 21 LR Ir 12, 22 the decision in *Stewart v. Green* might well have been different if counsel had insisted upon rather than repudiated the first of the two possible constructions of the will.
58. (1883) 11 LR Ir 236.
59. *Ibid.* at 247.

annum to the funds of the convent in its aggregate and quasi corporate capacity'[60] which he held to be void.

Despite such setbacks this approach of construing a gift to an association as being for the benefit of the members for the time being was successfully employed on a number of occasions towards the end of the nineteenth century particularly in the context of gifts to associations of a religious nature which were not considered at the time to be charitable in law. It was of particular importance in relation to gifts to contemplative religious orders, which were considered not to possess the necessary element of public benefit to qualify for charitable status. The decision of Gavan Duffy J in *Maguire v. Attorney General*[61] marked a change in judicial attitudes to the question of the public benefit inherent in gifts of this nature, and the provisions of section 45 of the Charities Act 1961 would now seem to confirm that gifts to contemplative religious orders are valid charitable gifts.[62] However, the principles developed in these decisions are important and can be considered as being of general application.

In *Cocks v. Manners*[63] a gift to a contemplative order of nuns was treated as a gift to the superior of the community for the time being and in this manner was upheld on the basis that it did not infringe the rule against inalienability. This principle was applied in Ireland in *Re Delany's Estate*,[64] where a gift to a convent was upheld as being for the benefit of the nuns who comprised the community at the time of the testator's death. A useful summary of this reasoning was set out in *Morrow v. M'Conville*,[65] although as noted above, it was not accepted as applying in the case before the court:

> [A] gift, not charitable, to a religious community, including not only the existing members, but also all persons who should be, or become thereafter members of it, during a period capable of extending beyond the legal limits prescribed by the rule against perpetuities is void; but ... if such gift, according to its true construction, is one to the individuals composing the community at the death of the testator, or some other time, within legal limits, appointed for ascertaining the class of such individuals, the gift is valid.[66]

---

60. *Ibid.* at 250.
61. [1943] IR 238. Although note the decision of Overend J in *Re Keogh's Estate* [1945] IR 13.
62. S. 45(1) provides: 'In determining whether or not a gift for the purpose of the advancement of religion is a valid charitable gift it shall be conclusively presumed that the purpose includes and will occasion public benefit.'
63. (1871) LR 12 Eq 574.
64. (1882) 9 LR Ir 226. See also *Re Wilkinson's Trusts* (1887) 19 LR Ir 531 and *Bradshaw v. Jackman* (1887) 21 LR Ir 12.
65. (1883) 11 LR Ir 236.
66. *Ibid.* at 246-247.

The main consideration which must be taken into account by a court in applying this approach is that there must be nothing to indicate that any form of 'perpetual endowment' was contemplated and this was one of the major difficulties faced by Chatterton VC in *Morrow*, where the trust was clearly treated as being 'a continuing one'. This point was stressed by Overend J in his decision in *Re Keogh's Estate*,[67] where a testator made a bequest to the superioress for the time being of a convent and left the residue of his estate to the prior of an order, neither of which qualified as charitable gifts. Overend J was satisfied that there was nothing in the testator's will which suggested that he had contemplated that the money would be applied for a perpetual endowment and he upheld the gifts to the superioress and the prior to be used for the purposes of their orders.

This principle was applied in a different context in *Re Clarke*,[68] where a bequest was made to the Committee of the Corps of Comissionaires in London to aid in the purchase of a barracks or in any other way beneficial to the corps. Byrne J upheld the bequest as a valid gift to the members of the corps for the time being as they could at any time dispose of it. He stated:

> The test, or one test, appears to be, will the legacy when paid be subject to any trust which will prevent the existing members of the association from spending it as they please? If not, the gift is good. So also if the gift is to be construed as a gift to or for the benefit of the individual members of the association. On the other hand, if it appears that the legacy is one which by the terms of the gift, or which by reason of the constitution of the association in whose favour it is made, tends to a perpetuity, the gift is bad.[69]

The Supreme Court considered this issue in *Re Byrne*,[70] in which a testator left his residuary estate for the use and benefit of the Jesuit Order in Ireland. The majority of the Supreme Court[71] held that the work of the order, while largely charitable in nature, was not exclusively so and that it did not qualify as a charitable gift. As Murnaghan J stated, if the testator meant his gift to enure for the benefit of 'a continuing body whose existence has not received legal recognition', it would fail. If on the other hand, his intention was to divide the money amongst individuals forming a class, there would be no legal objection to its validity. Murnaghan J reiterated the point that 'the language of the testator must in each case be the guide' and upheld the bequest

---

67. [1945] IR 13.
68. [1901] 2 Ch 110. See *Re Smith* [1914] 1 Ch 937.
69. *Ibid.* at 114.
70. [1935] IR 782.
71. Murnaghan and Fitzgibbon JJ. Kennedy CJ dissented and held that the gift was charitable in nature.

as a valid gift of a non-charitable nature for the benefit of an ascertainable class of persons.

The only real theoretical difficulty with such an approach is that any member who leaves the association can take his share with him unless he assigns it to the other members and a new member will have no share in the property. More recently in England an alternative theory has been developed which has found favour with the courts in that jurisdiction and which may well also prove to be the most suitable approach for the courts here to employ.

Property Held on Trust to be Applied in Accordance with the Contract Between the Members

This manner of construing a gift was summarised by Cross J as follows in *Neville Estates Ltd v. Madden*:[72]

> [I]t may be a gift to the existing members not as joint tenants, but subject to their respective contractual rights and liabilities towards one another as members of the association. In such a case a member cannot sever his share. It will accrue to the other members on his death or resignation, even though such members include persons who became members after the gift took effect. If this is the effect of the gift it will not be open to objection on the score of perpetuity or uncertainty unless there is something in its terms or circumstances or in the rules of the association which precludes the members at any given time from dividing the subject of the gift between them on the footing that they are solely entitled to it in equity.

This 'contract-holding theory' was applied by Brightman J in *Re Recher's Will Trusts*,[73] which concerned the validity of a gift to the 'London and Provincial Anti-Vivisection Society'. Brightman J concluded that it was not a gift to the members of the society at the date of the testator's death, nor an attempted gift to present and future members beneficially, nor a gift in trust for the purposes of the society. Instead he held that the legacy ought to be construed as a gift to the members beneficially as an accretion to their funds subject to the contract which they made between themselves. As he stated: 'In the absence of words which purport to impose a trust, the legacy is a gift to the members beneficially, not as joint tenants or as tenants in common so as to entitle each member to an immediate distributive share, but as an accretion to the funds which are the subject matter of the contract which the members have made *inter se*.'[74] A similar approach was applied by Oliver J in *Re*

---

72. [1962] Ch 832, 849. See Warburton [1985] Conv 318, 322-325.
73. [1972] Ch 526.
74. *Ibid.* at 539.

Lipinski's Will Trusts,[75] where a testator bequeathed half of his residuary estate to trustees to the 'Hull Judaeans (Maccabi) Association' in memory of his late wife, to be used in the work of constructing new buildings for the association and/or improving them. Oliver J held the gift valid as an absolute gift to the members of the association beneficially as an accretion to its funds subject to the rules of the association. It was not open to objection on the grounds of perpetuity as Oliver J was satisfied that there was nothing in the will which suggested any intention to create a permanent endowment and he pointed out that the members could if they wished divide the gift between themselves. In this regard he distinguished the decision of the House of Lords in *Re Macaulay*,[76] where a gift was made for the 'maintenance and improvement' of a building on the grounds that in the case before him it was in his view quite evident that the association was free to spend the capital of the legacy if it chose to do so.

Essentially this contract-holding theory involves the idea of property being held on trust to be applied in accordance with the contract existing between the members contained in the rules of the association and it will satisfy the requirements of the rule against inalienability provided that the members are entitled to wind up the association and divide its property between them at any time. One clear advantage of this approach is that compliance with the beneficiary principle is not an issue as the property is held subject to the terms of a contract rather than on trust. In addition, a member who leaves the association or dies will lose his share in the property and any new member will automatically acquire one without the need for any formalities. However, it is important to emphasise that the rules of the association must provide the necessary contractual element in the relationship between the members[77] and it is also necessary that the members have the requisite authority to divide the assets between themselves.[78]

Conclusion

While the categories of trusts for the erection and maintenance of tombs and monuments and for the care of specified animals seem to be accepted as enforceable provided that they do not offend the rule against inalienability, doubt remains about the validity of other forms of non-charitable purpose trusts. Provided that the certainty requirement is met it would appear that trusts for unincorporated associations can be enforced if one of the constructions outlined above is applied, and the reasoning of Goff J in *Re*

---

75. [1976] Ch 235. See Widdows (1977) 41 Conv 179 and Gravells (1977) 40 MLR 231.
76. [1943] Ch 435n.
77. *Conservative and Unionist Central Office v. Burrell* [1982] 1 WLR 522, 525.
78. *Re Grant's Will Trusts* [1980] 1 WLR 360.

Denley's Trust Deed[79] should ensure that difficulties raised by the need for compliance with the beneficiary principle and the rule against inalienability will effectively be overcome. As the cases make clear, if a construction is to be applied which will result in the gift being legally enforceable, it is important that such a construction can be ascertained from the words used by a donor or testator.[80] While recent decisions show a greater willingness to place a favourable construction on gifts of this nature, the warning given by the Court of Appeal in *Re Endacott*[81] that the categories of these 'anomalous' cases should not be extended should also be heeded.

In a general context the suggestion has been made that what might appear as an invalid purpose trust could be saved if it were construed as a power rather than a trust on the basis that there is no requirement that the beneficiary principle be satisfied in relation to powers. While this option has been explored,[82] it has been rejected on the basis that a valid power cannot 'be spelt out of an invalid trust'.[83]

Apart from in the exceptional cases of tombs and monuments and specified animals, the lack of beneficiaries has proved to be a major stumbling block to the enforcement of non-charitable purpose trusts. As Lord Evershed MR commented in *Re Endacott*:[84] 'No principle, perhaps, has greater sanction or authority behind it than the general proposition that a trust by English law, not being a charitable trust, in order to be effective must have ascertained or ascertainable beneficiaries.' However, Hayton[85] has put forward the suggestion that an 'enforcer' might be appointed under the terms of a trust in order to oversee its enforcement and he suggests that there is no reason why equity should not permit a settlor to confer additional enforcement rights on other persons, including himself. If such an approach were approved, non-charitable purpose trusts would not be automatically void and would be valid if the settlor had appointed an enforcer as long as they were administratively workable and restricted to a valid perpetuity period. Hayton's suggestion is an interesting one and may be developed, particularly given that the courts cannot legitimately refuse to give effect to a foreign non-charitable purpose trust which is valid in another jurisdiction where trust instruments may expressly provide for the appointment of an enforcer.[86]

From a practical perspective, where advance planning is feasible, the

---

79. [1969] 1 Ch 373.
80. E.g. *Morrow v. M'Conville* (1883) 11 LR Ir 236, 247; *Re Byrne* [1935] IR 782, 818.
81. [1960] Ch 232.
82. By Harman J in *Re Shaw* [1957] 1 WLR 729, 746.
83. *IRC v. Broadway Cottages Trust* [1955] Ch 20, 36 *per* Jenkins LJ; *Re Shaw* [1957] 1 WLR 729, 746; *Re Endacott* [1960] Ch 232, 246.
84. [1960] Ch 232, 246.
85. (2001) 117 LQR 96.
86. See further *ibid.* at 100.

incorporation of an association which a donor or testator wishes to benefit will undoubtedly provide a method of ensuring that the gift will be carried into effect. However, in the majority of cases, this will not be achieved and the courts will still be faced with the difficult policy question of whether to continue to extend the principle which allows for the enforcement of non-charitable purpose trusts in limited circumstances. While it could be argued that a refusal to enforce non-charitable purpose trusts should in theory at any rate lead to a greater preponderance of gifts of a charitable nature more likely to provide real benefit to the community, as Martin[87] comments 'capricious trusts are the rare ones'. She continues: 'The fact that they do exist is no reason for failing to establish a rational method of validating the useful ones.' Certainly the present approach is in many respects far from rational and lacks any real consistency.[88] In the final analysis, in the absence of any legislative intervention in this area, we must continue to rely on the rather haphazard principles and devices developed at common law when it is sought to establish the validity of a non-charitable purpose trust.

---

87. Hanbury and Martin, *Modern Equity* (16th ed., 2001) p. 388.
88. See the views expressed by Baxendale-Walker in *Purpose Trusts* (1999). He criticises the present legal position as 'uncertain and unsatisfactory' (at p. 284) and contends that the rule against purpose trusts was unknown in earlier centuries and that the authorities which support such a view have largely been ignored in more recent decisions.

CHAPTER 10

Charitable Trusts

INTRODUCTION

Advantages of Charitable Status

While as a general rule, subject to the exceptions examined above,[1] trusts for purposes rather than for the benefit of persons are invalid, charitable trusts which are considered to be for the public benefit are an exception to this principle. Charitable trusts are considered to be for the benefit of the public generally or at least for an appreciable section of it and for this reason have traditionally enjoyed a number of advantages over other types of trust.[2] Before examining in more detail the types of trusts which will qualify for such favourable treatment it is useful to set out briefly the advantages to be gained from establishing charitable status.

Charitable trusts do not depend on the existence of beneficiaries to enforce them; they are considered to be of a public nature and as such are enforceable by the Attorney General.[3] The corollary of this proposition is that those individuals who might benefit from a trust considered to be legally charitable will not be recognised as having the right to enforce such trusts.[4]

A further advantage is that charitable trusts are not subject to the same requirements relating to certainty of objects which must be complied with if a private trust is to be considered valid.[5] Originally, provided that a trust could be identified as being exclusively[6] charitable in nature, such a trust would be

---

1. *Supra* Chapter 9.
2. As Mummery LJ has recently commented in the Court of Appeal decision in *Gaudiya Mission v. Brahmachary* [1997] 4 All ER 957, 963 'Under English law charity has always received special treatment. . . . It is, therefore, subject to special rules governing registration, administration, taxation and duration'. See also Warburton [1999] Conv 20, who states (at 29) that 'charitable trusts operate in a different legal, fiscal and social environment from family and commercial trusts'.
3. While the decision in *Re Denley's Trust Deed* [1969] 1 Ch 373 has made it possible for the beneficiary principle to be effectively by-passed in certain circumstances, a considerable number of purpose trusts will still fall foul of this principle.
4. *Re Belling* [1967] Ch 425.
5. See the *dicta* of Porter MR in *Re Brown* [1898] 1 IR 423, 427.
6. Note that s. 49(1) of the Charities Act 1961 now provides as follows: 'Where any of

enforced even if the nature of these charitable objects was not expressly delimited.[7] In such circumstances a cy-près scheme[8] could be framed to ensure that the charitable intention of the donor or testator was given effect to. From a general perspective, charitable status is also desirable as it will facilitate the operation of cy-près jurisdiction should this become necessary. If a trust fails to qualify as charitable, this jurisdiction cannot be exercised and a bequest may fail, allowing a resulting trust to operate in favour of the donor or his estate. While resulting trusts are intended in theory to give effect to the unexpressed but presumed intention of the donor, this may not always be the case,[9] and it is certainly preferable to find a means of perpetuating the donor's charitable intention in as close a form as possible to that originally expressed by him.

Another crucial distinction is that charitable trusts may be perpetual in nature in so far as the rule against inalienability which has proved such a major stumbling block in any attempts to enforce non-charitable purpose trusts, does not apply to them. However, although charitable trusts may be of perpetual duration, they are subject to the rule against perpetuities to the extent that the initial vesting must be bound to take place within the relevant perpetuity period. This principle is subject to the limited exception that a gift over from one charity to another is not subject to the rule.[10]

It should be noted that charitable trusts also enjoy a number of significant fiscal immunities in terms of exemptions from liability to various forms of taxation. Section 207(1) and (2) and section 208 of the Taxes Consolidation Act 1997 grant certain exemptions from income tax under Schedules C, D and F in respect of income accruing to charitable bodies or trusts established for charitable purposes to the extent that such income is applied for charitable purposes.[11] Section 76(6) of the Taxes Consolidation Act 1997 provides for

---

the purposes of a gift include, or could be deemed to include, both charitable and non-charitable objects, its terms shall be so construed and given effect to as to exclude the non-charitable objects and the purpose shall, accordingly, be treated as charitable.'

7. *Re Koepplar's Will Trusts* [1986] Ch 423.
8. Where a gift is made to charity, it may be impossible to give effect to the intentions of the donor in the precise terms that he intended or it may be impractical or inconvenient to do so. The cy-près doctrine, where it applies, allows for the making of a scheme for the application of such property for other charitable purposes as near as possible to those intended by the donor. This is considered in detail below.
9. E.g. *Re Vinogradoff* [1935] WN 68. See also the approach taken by the former Supreme Court in *Owens v. Greene* [1932] IR 225 in relation to the question of the beneficial ownership of money held in joint deposit accounts which persisted until it was reversed in the recent Supreme Court decision in *Lynch v. Burke* [1995] 2 IR 159.
10. *Christ's Hospital v. Grainger* (1849) 1 Mac & G 460; *Re Tyler* [1891] 3 Ch 252. Although clearly a gift over to a charity after a gift to an individual will be subject to the rule against perpetuities.
11. See further Judge, *Irish Income Tax* (2001, Ward) pp. 2083–2099 and Corrigan, *Revenue Law* (2000) pp. 757–770.

the carrying over of any exemptions which would apply under income tax provisions to corporation tax. Exemptions also apply in respect of capital taxes, and a capital gain which accrues to a charity is not chargeable to capital gains tax provided that it is applied for charitable purposes.[12] In addition, section 76(2) of the Capital Acquisitions Consolidation Tax Act 2003 provides that a gift or inheritance taken for public or charitable purposes will be exempt from capital acquisitions tax provided that the Revenue Commissioners are satisfied that it has been or will be applied to such purposes. Finally, it should be noted that by virtue of section 848A of the Taxes Consolidation Act 1997, inserted by section 45 of the Finance Act 2001, charities or the individuals making donations can now reclaim the tax paid on such donations.

The scope of the exemption from income tax provided by sections 333 and 334 of the Income Tax Act 1967, which have been replaced by sections 207 and 208 of the Taxes Consolidation Act 1997 was considered by the High Court in *Revenue Commissioners v. Sisters of Charity of the Incarnate Word*.[13] The appellants contended that sections 333 and 334 applied to bodies or persons established for charitable purposes but only if they were established within the State and they claimed that the respondents in this case were not established within the State. The respondents claimed that there was no justification for giving the exemption provisions the restricted interpretation contended for by the appellants and argued that even if the appellants' interpretation was correct, the charity was in fact established within the State through one of its branches. Geoghegan J accepted the conclusions reached by the Court of Appeal and the House of Lords in *Camille and Henry Dreyfus Foundation v. IRC*[14] in relation to the equivalent English provisions to the effect that a limited geographical meaning should be given to the expression 'established'. Geoghegan J then went on to consider whether the charity was in fact established in the State. He stated that 'a foreign charity with no activities base (for want of a better expression) in Ireland is not entitled to an exemption but a foreign charity which does have such a base is entitled to it in respect of funds applied towards Irish charitable activities'. Geoghegan J concluded that having regard to the fact that the respondents owned and managed a nursing home in the State there was sufficient 'establishment' in Ireland to give rise to the exemption and he upheld the decision of the Circuit Court that the respondents were entitled to the benefit of the provisions of sections 333 and 334 of the Income Tax Act 1967 as amended.

In view of the extensive advantages enjoyed by charitable trusts, it has been argued that some limitation must be placed on their proliferation. While certain judicial statements show a tendency to adopt a benign attitude to this

12. S. 609(1) of the Taxes Consolidation Act 1997.
13. [1998] 2 IR 553.
14. [1956] AC 39.

question,[15] the perceived benefit of undeserved fiscal immunity has proved a rather thorny issue over the years. An examination of the case law in England would suggest that this motive has led to a restrictive attitude being adopted to the wider question of whether certain trusts should qualify as being legally charitable.[16] For the present at least the concepts of fiscal immunity and charitable status continue to 'march hand in hand'[17] although, as Lord Cross has commented in *Dingle v. Turner*,[18] such a state of affairs is 'unfortunate' given that the question of whether a trust was so unlikely to benefit the public that it ought to be declared invalid and the question of whether it was likely to confer such substantial benefits to the community that it ought to enjoy fiscal immunity are, in his view, two distinct questions.[19] A better approach might be to do as the Radcliffe Commission[20] suggested and sever the connection, which would allow a more liberal approach to develop towards the question of the type of trusts which should qualify as being legally charitable unhindered by the baggage of perceived undeserved fiscal immunity.

The recommendations of the Scottish Charity Law Review Commission,[21] if implemented, would lead to the issues of charitable status and eligibility for tax exemption being determined by separate bodies, although it was stressed in the report that the proposed regulatory body would work closely with the Inland Revenue to ensure the adoption of a consistent approach.[22] The Law Reform Committee of the Law Society of Ireland in its recent report *Charity Law: The Case for Reform*[23] recommended that tax relief should continue to be an automatic consequence of obtaining charitable status, subject to the Revenue Commissioners' right of appeal to the High Court. However, it was also suggested that the option of tiered tax relief[24] depending on the type of charitable purpose being undertaken should be given further consideration. Arguably it is wrong that considerations of undeserved fiscal immunity should

---

15. *Weir v. Crum-Brown* [1908] AC 162, 167 *per* Lord Loreburn; *IRC v. McMullen* [1981] AC 1, 14 *per* Lord Hailsham.
16. See the comment of Lord Cross in *Dingle v. Turner* [1972] AC 601, 624 to the effect that such considerations 'pretty obviously influenced' the decisions of the courts in *Re Compton* [1945] Ch 123 and *Oppenheim v. Tobacco Securities Trust Co. Ltd* [1951] AC 297.
17. *Dingle v. Turner* [1972] AC 601, 624 *per* Lord Cross.
18. [1972] AC 601.
19. Note also the comments of Lord MacDermott in *Dingle v. Turner* [1972] AC 601, 614 in which he doubted whether consequential fiscal privileges had much relevance to the substantive question of whether a trust should be considered charitable in law. (A view shared by Viscount Dilhorne and Lord Hodson.)
20. Cmd. 9474. See Chapter 9, paragraphs 170 and 173. These recommendations were not implemented.
21. May 2001 (The McFadden Report).
22. *Ibid.* at 3.15-3.16.
23. July 2002, p. 94.
24. See also Chesterman (1999) 62 MLR 333, 340.

influence judicial decisions about charitable status to too great an extent, but such policy questions must be borne in mind when embarking on an examination of the legal definition of charitable status.

Administration of Charities

While the Attorney General has the function of overseeing the enforcement of charities in Ireland and will be joined in any court proceedings brought in relation to such matters to ensure that the interests of charities are safeguarded, a statutory body ensures the proper administration of trusts on a day-to-day basis. This body, known as the Commissioners of Charitable Donations and Bequests, was initially established in Ireland in 1844. Its role is now governed by the provisions of Part II of the Charities Act 1961 and its jurisdiction and powers are set out in Chapter II of Part II of the Act of 1961 as amended by the Charities Act 1973. The commissioners, who shall be not more than eleven in number, are appointed by the government and hold office for life unless they retire or are removed from office.[25] They have power to advise charity trustees in relation to the administration of trusts[26] and can authorize the compromise of any proceedings brought by or against such trustees.[27] The commissioners may, with the consent of the Attorney General, sue for the recovery of any charitable gift which has been improperly withheld, concealed or misapplied,[28] and they have a general power to authorise or direct the institution of legal proceedings in relation to any charitable matter.[29] In addition, the commissioners have powers in relation to the investment of funds held on charitable trusts,[30] and as outlined below,[31] have powers to frame a scheme applying property cy-près.[32] A further power, the exercise of which has recently been considered by the High Court, is that contained in section 43 of the Charities Act 1961 as substituted by section 14 of the Charities Act 1973, by virtue of which the Commissioners may appoint new trustees to a charity. In *Eastern Health Board v. Commissioners for Charitable Donations and Bequests*[33] an order was made by the Commissioners pursuant to section 43 of the Charities Act 1961 as amended appointing new trustees of trusts established in respect of the Worth Library which had been housed in Dr Steeven's Hospital under the terms of a will which directed that the books

---

25. Ss. 7 and 8 of the Charities Act 1961.
26. S. 21 of the Charities Act 1961.
27. S. 22 of the Charities Act 1961.
28. S. 23 of the Charities Act 1961.
29. S. 25 of the Charities Act 1961.
30. S. 32 of the Charities Act 1961 as substituted by s. 9 of the Charities Act 1973.
31. See *infra* p. 368.
32. S. 29 of the Charities Act 1961 as amended by s. 8 of the Act of 1973.
33. High Court 1991 No. 207 Sp (Denham J) 17 December 1991.

concerned should not be removed from the room in the hospital in which they were kept. The hospital was closed in 1988 and while the Commissioners prepared a cy-près scheme, the books were temporarily housed in Trinity College Dublin. The plaintiff subsequently purchased the hospital and sought an order annulling the order of the Commissioners appointing Trinity College and the director of the National Library to be trustees in place of the existing trustees. Denham J held that the appointment of the new trustees was not premature and had not prejudiced the plaintiff's position and stated that she was satisfied that it was the correct decision to move the books to Trinity College for safekeeping at the time when the hospital was being sold. She also rejected the claim that the Commissioners had not complied with the procedures laid down by section 43 and held that the notice of the intention to appoint new trustees had been adequate.

Definition of Charity

Gavan Duffy J remarked in *Re Howley's Estate*[34] that '"charity" is in law an artificial conception, which during some 300 years, under the guidance of pedantic technicians, seems to have strayed rather far from the intelligent realm of plain common sense'. Whether such a colourful comment can be justified is open to debate but it is certainly arguable that the meaning of the term 'charity' in law bears no necessary relationship to a lay person's conception of the word.[35]

The first point to note is that no attempt has ever been made by the legislature, either here or in England, to actually define what is legally charitable. A list of charitable purposes was contained in legislation passed in both jurisdictions in the seventeenth century, although these statutes were never intended to define charitable objects in a legal sense but rather to enumerate a variety of purposes recognised as being legally charitable.[36] In addition, this list was never intended to be exhaustive and as Keane J has recently reiterated in *Re Worth Library*,[37] a trust might be considered charitable

---

34. [1940] IR 109, 114.
35. See also the comments of Lord Sterndale MR in *Re Tetley* [1923] 1 Ch 258, 266.
36. As Lord Sugden LC commented in *Incorporated Society v. Richards* (1841) 4 Ir Eq R 177, 202: 'I consider that the object of the statute of Elizabeth was to remedy the abuses that then existed in the management of charitable property ...' and he accepted that the legislation in both jurisdictions was of similar effect. The comment has also been made by Lord Morton in *Royal College of Surgeons of England v. National Provincial Bank Ltd* [1952] AC 631, 650-651 that this was directed towards reforming abuses in the application of property devoted to charitable uses, rather than to defining the concept of a charity.
37. [1995] 2 IR 301, 333. See generally Delany (1994) 45 NILQ 364; Brady (1994) 16 DULJ (ns) 153.

if it fell within the 'spirit or intendment'[38] of the statute. While the Irish Statute of Charitable Uses 1634[39] was repealed by the Statute Law Revision Act (Ireland) 1878, it is nevertheless useful to set out the terms of the Preamble as the decisions given regarding its scope provide a useful insight into the question of what is legally charitable.[40]

> [T]he erection, maintenance, or support of any college, schoole, lecture in divinity or in any of the liberall arts or sciences; or for the reliefe of any manner of poore, succourlesse, distressed, or impotent persons; or for the building, re-edifying, or maintaining in repaire any church, college, schoole or hospitall; or for the maintenance of any minister and preacher of the Holy Word of God; or for the erection, building, maintenance, or repair of any bridges, causeyes, cashes, paces and highways within this realme; or for any other like lawfull and charitable use and uses, warranted by the laws of this realme now established and in force....

Although these words have provided a useful guide over the years, as Bright[41] has commented: its wording 'is clearly not tailored to current social problems.' Thomas J has recently stated in the decision of the New Zealand Court of Appeal in *Commissioner of Inland Revenue v. Medical Council of New Zealand*[42] that in applying the 'spirit and intendment' of the Preamble, it is important to be guided by principle rather than by a detailed analysis of decisions in particular cases, and it should be pointed out that judicial perceptions of what is charitable in law may have altered over the years.[43]

---

38. See *Morice v. Bishop of Durham* (1804) 9 Ves 399, 405. This phrase has also been interpreted on occasion in a negative way to mean that a purpose might only be considered charitable if it fell within the 'spirit or intendment of the legislation'. See *Williams' Trustees v. IRC* [1947] AC 447, 455.

39. 10 Char 1, Sess. 3, c. 1. The English version, the Statute of Charitable Uses 1601, 43 Eliz. 1, c.4., preserved in subsequent legislation, was also finally repealed by the Charities Act 1961.

40. In the context of the English statute, see the comments of Lord Wilberforce in *Scottish Burial Reform and Cremation Society v. Glasgow City Corporation* [1968] AC 138, 154.

41. [1989] Conv 28, 31.

42. [1997] 2 NZLR 297, 314. See also the *dicta* of Sachs LJ in *Incorporated Council of Law Reporting for England and Wales v. Attorney General* [1972] Ch 73, 95.

43. Contrast for example *Re Hummeltenberg* [1923] 1 Ch 237 and *Funnell v. Stewart* [1996] 1 WLR 288. The former case, according to Fletcher (1996) 112 LQR 557 'tended to indicate that "faith healing" was not a charitable purpose'. By the time that the latter case was decided in 1996 it was accepted by the court that faith healing 'had become a recognised activity of public benefit' (at 297) although as Hazel Williamson QC acknowledged 'this would not necessarily have been the case when *Re Hummeltenberg* was decided'. She held in the alternative that the purpose in any event qualified as charitable on the basis of the religious nature of the faith healing movement.

Now a claim to charitable status is generally determined by considering whether a particular purpose comes within one of the four broad categories identified by Lord Macnaghten in *Commissioners for Special Purposes of Income Tax v. Pemsel*,[44] which are as follows:

1. Trusts for the relief of poverty

2. Trusts for the advancement of education

3. Trusts for the advancement of religion

4. Trusts for other purposes beneficial to the community.

It is now generally accepted that trusts which are considered to be charitable in law fall into these four separate, although not necessarily mutually exclusive, categories. While it has been recognised that this classification is one of convenience only and that there may be purposes which do not fit neatly into one or other of these categories,[45] or which fit into one or more categories at the same time,[46] over the last century it has nevertheless provided the basis on which the courts both in this jurisdiction and in England have approached the question of whether a trust should be accorded charitable status. Some consideration has been given in recent years in England to the question of providing further statutory guidance in this area.[47] Legislation enacted in England in 1993 provided that "'charity'[48] means any institution, corporate or not, which is established for charitable purposes and is subject to the control of the High Court'[49] and 'charitable purposes' was defined to mean 'purposes which are exclusively charitable according to the law of England and Wales'.[50] However, no attempt has been made in that jurisdiction to set out in legislation what is charitable in law or to define what constitutes 'charitable purposes'.

---

44. [1891] AC 531, 583. These categories were approved by Keane J in *Re Worth Library* [1995] 2 IR 301, 334. See also *In re Article 26 of the Constitution and the Employment Equality Bill 1996* [1997] 2 IR 321, 355.
45. *Scottish Burial Reform and Cremation Society Ltd v. Glasgow Corporation* [1968] AC 138, 154 *per* Lord Wilberforce.
46. See e.g. *Incorporated Council of Law Reporting for England and Wales v. Attorney General* [1972] Ch 73.
47. See the Report of the Committee on the Law and Practice Relating to Charities 1952 Cmd. 8710 (The Nathan Report) at paragraph 697. Note that the Committee on Charity Law and Voluntary Organizations 1976 (The Goodman Committee) suggested 'guidelines' which might be followed.
48. It was held by the English Court of Appeal in *Gaudiya Mission v. Brahmachary* [1997] 4 All ER 957 that the term 'charity' as contained in s. 33 of the 1993 Act which deals with the taking of charity proceedings, did not include an institution established under the laws of another legal system.
49. S. 96(1) of the Charities Act 1993.
50. S. 97 of the Charities Act 1993.

In 'Charities: A Framework for the Future'[51] the view was expressed that 'the government considers that any attempt to define charity by any of [the suggested means] would be fraught with difficulty and might put at risk the flexibility of the present law which is both its greatest strength and its most valuable feature.'[52] It should be noted that in Australia the Report of the *Inquiry into the Definition of Charities and Related Organisations*[53] recommended the introduction of a statutory definition of charity comprising seven distinct headings including that of 'other purposes beneficial to the community'. However, there are no signs of a movement towards the introduction of a statutory definition of charitable purposes in this jurisdiction at present and there may be merit in Delany's comment that 'there is little to be gained by definitions, legislative or otherwise in charity matters. The social conscience of the judiciary working in the light of contemporary conditions will do more for the fair administration of charities than any definition.'[54] The Law Reform Committee of the Law Society of Ireland in its recent report *Charity Law: The Case for Reform*[55] stopped short of recommending a statutory definition although it did favour the introduction of guidelines in statutory form in order to facilitate decision making in this area whether by the courts or bodies such as the Revenue Commissioners.

The Macnaghten Classification and the Public Benefit Requirement

What this classification fails to make clear explicitly is that for a trust to be regarded as legally charitable, it must be of a public character and must contain some element of benefit to the public generally.[56] An examination of the various judicial interpretations of the types of trust which are legally charitable show that there are in effect two hurdles to be overcome, first, an element of benefit, e.g. the relief of poverty and secondly, an element of *public* benefit.[57] Viscount

---

51. 1989 Cmd. 694. See particularly paragraphs 2.07- 2.17.
52. *Ibid.* at paragraph 2.11. Note that the report of the UK Council of Voluntary Organisations in 2001 *For the Public Benefit?: A Consultation Document on Charity Law Reform* also stressed the importance of flexibility, although it favoured a public benefit test of uniform application.
53. June 2001.
54. *The Law Relating to Charities in Ireland* (1957) p. 20. See also the comments of Sachs LJ in *Incorporated Council of Law Reporting for England and Wales v. Attorney General* [1972] Ch 73, 94.
55. July 2002 at p. 85.
56. See O'Halloran (2001) 23 DULJ 97 where the differences in approach towards the public benefit test as between this jurisdiction and Northern Ireland are analysed.
57. In *Tudor on Charities*, Warburton (8th ed., 1995) at p. 5 it is pointed out that this requirement may involve the consideration of two related questions viz. whether the purposes of the trust confer a benefit on the public or a section of the public and whether the class of persons eligible to benefit constitutes the public or a section of it.

Simonds commented in *IRC v. Baddeley*[58] that it is necessary to distinguish 'between a form of relief extended to the whole community, yet by its very nature advantageous only to a few and a form of relief accorded to a selected few out of a larger number equally willing and able to take advantage of it.' However, as Plowright[59] has pointed out, this type of formula has limitations if it is to be used as a practical criterion of assessment and is moreover not entirely accurate in defining the boundaries between private and charitable trusts.

This concept of public benefit varies considerably as between the different categories of charitable trusts;[60] in the case of trusts for the relief of poverty it has been greatly modified as a result of judicial intervention,[61] and in the Republic of Ireland in the case of trusts for the advancement of religion, section 45(1) of the Charities Act 1961 now provides that it shall be conclusively presumed that such a trust will occasion public benefit.[62] In addition, the requirement may differ as between different types of trusts in the fourth category and the point has even been made that it may seem anomalous to speak in terms of a public benefit requirement in this category as it is defined in terms of trusts for the benefit of the community.[63] It may appear therefore to be in some respects surprising that it is to this residual category that the most rigourous interpretation of the public benefit test has been applied.[64]

Perhaps due to the apparent latitude which this category allows for, the courts have traditionally taken a relatively strict view in interpreting what constitutes a trust for 'other purposes beneficial to the community'.[65] Greater

---

58. [1955] AC 572, 592.
59. (1975) 39 Conv 183, 184.
60. See the statements of Lord Simonds in *Gilmour v. Coats* [1949] AC 426, 437, Lord Somervell in *IRC v. Baddeley* [1955] AC 572, 615 (see further Atiyah (1958) 21 MLR 138, 139) and Carswell J in *Re Dunlop* [1984] NI 408, 425-426.
61. The so-called 'poor relations' trusts were recognised in a number of decisions handed down in the eighteenth century, see e.g. *Issac v. Defriez* (1754) Amb 595, and the modification of the public benefit requirement in this category is well recognised today, see *Gibson v. South American Stores (Gath & Chaves) Ltd* [1950] Ch 177; *Re Scarisbrick* [1951] Ch 622; *Dingle v. Turner* [1972] AC 601; *Re Cohen* [1973] 1 WLR 415 and *Re Segelman deceased* [1996] Ch 171.
62. See the recent *dicta* of Keane J in *Campaign to Separate Church and State Ltd v. Minister for Education* [1998] 2 ILRM 81, 83.
63. Hanbury & Martin, *Modern Equity* (16th ed., 2001) pp. 427-428.
64. See the comments of Babington LJ in *Trustees of the Londonderry Presbyterian Church House v. Commissioners of Inland Revenue* [1946] NI 178, 196, of Viscount Simonds in *IRC v. Baddeley* [1955] AC 572, 592 and of Lord Somervell in *Baddeley* (at 615), although note the different conclusion reached by Lord Reid in *Baddeley* at 612-613.
65. As Viscount Cave pointed out in *Attorney General v. National Provincial and Union Bank of England Ltd* [1924] AC 262, 265: 'Lord Macnaghten did not mean that all trusts beneficial to the community are charitable, but there are certain charitable trusts which fall within that category, and accordingly to argue that because a trust is for a purpose beneficial to the community it is therefore a charitable trust is to turn round

flexibility towards this question can be seen in more recent decisions[66] but evidence of the more demanding approach can still be identified in terms of the application of the public benefit requirement to this category. On the other hand the courts have increasingly inferred that trusts falling within the other three categories will be 'assumed to be for the benefit of the community and therefore, charitable unless the contrary is shown'.[67] While this comment certainly reflects the position in relation to trusts falling within the first and third categories, trusts for the advancement of education have quite often not qualified for charitable status because of failure to satisfy the public benefit requirement. In England, the factors which will prevent the public benefit test being satisfied in the context of trusts for the advancement of education have extended beyond blood ties or a personal nexus to a 'nexus of contract',[68] and trusts for the education of persons, or relatives of persons, in common employment have been found not to be charitable in nature.[69]

THE MACNAGHTEN CLASSIFICATION

1. Trusts for the Relief of Poverty

The point has been made in *Tudor on Charities* that '"poor" is a relative term'[70] and the authorities have shown that it is not necessary for a class of persons to be destitute in order for a trust for their relief to qualify as charitable in nature. This point was made by Evershed MR in *Re Coulthurst*[71] as follows:

---

his sentence and give it a different meaning. . . . It is not enough to say that a trust is for public purposes beneficial to the community or for the public welfare, you must also show it to be a charitable trust.' See also the comments of Lindley LJ (at 466-467) and Rigby LJ (at 476) in *Re Macduff* [1896] 2 Ch 451 and Andrews LJ in *Trustees of the Londonderry Presbyterian Church House v. Commissioners of Inland Revenue* [1946] NI 178, 187.

66. See e.g. the *dicta* of Lord Russell in *Incorporated Council for Law Reporting for England and Wales v. Attorney General* [1972] Ch 73, 88 where he suggested that if a purpose is beneficial to the community it is *prima facie* charitable in law.

67. *Per* Lord Simonds in *National Anti-Vivisection Society v. IRC* [1948] AC 31, 65. Quoted with approval by Keane J in *Re Worth Library* [1995] 2 IR 301, 335.

68. Plowright (1975) 39 Conv 183, 185.

69. *Oppenheim v. Tobacco Securities Trust Co. Ltd* [1951] AC 297. See also *George Drexler Ofrex Foundation Trustees v. IRC* [1966] Ch 673 and *IRC v. Educational Grants Association Ltd* [1967] Ch 993. This approach was in line with the recommendations of the Goodman Committee Report on Charity Law and Voluntary Organisations (1976) paragraphs 38 and 50(b).

70. Warburton (8th ed., 1995) p. 29.

71. [1951] Ch 661, 665-6. See also *Re De Carteret* [1933] Ch 103, 108; *Re Bethal* (1971) 17 DLR (3d) 652, 666 and *DV Bryant Trust Board v. Hamilton City Council* [1997] 3 NZLR 342, 349.

It is quite clearly established that poverty does not mean destitution; it is a word of wide and somewhat indefinite import; it may not unfairly be paraphrased for present purposes as meaning persons who have to 'go short' in the ordinary acceptation of that term, due regard being had to their status in life and so forth.

There the Court of Appeal held that a trust for the benefit of the widows and children of deceased officers of a bank, who by reason of their financial circumstances were the most deserving, was a valid charitable trust. As Viscount Simonds commented in *IRC v. Baddeley*[72] 'there may be a good charity for the relief of persons who are not in grinding need or utter destitution' and a trust to provide for persons of limited or reduced means may come within the ambit of this category. So in *Re Gardom*,[73] a gift for the provision of a temporary residence for 'ladies of limited means' was held to be charitable. As Eve J commented, although such persons were not destitute, 'there are degrees of poverty less acute than abject poverty or destitution.'[74] However, there is often a fine line to be drawn between cases which will satisfy the requirement as being for the relief of poverty and those which will not. In *Re Sanders' Will Trusts*[75] Harman J held that a bequest to provide housing for the 'working classes' and their families resident in a certain district did not qualify, while in *Re Niyazi's Will Trusts*,[76] Megarry VC upheld as a valid charitable trust a gift 'for the construction of or as a contribution towards the cost of a working men's hostel' in the town of Famagusta in Cyprus. The most recent pronouncement on this issue would suggest that a more flexible attitude is now being taken towards the degree of poverty which must be established. In *Re Segelman deceased*[77] Chadwick J accepted that a gift to poor and needy members of a class of the testator's relatives was a valid charitable gift for the relief of poverty. He stated that the evidence suggested that 'most members of the class are comfortably off, in the sense that they are able to meet their day-to day expenses out of income, but not affluent' and that 'like many others in similar circumstances, they need a helping hand from time to time in order to overcome an unforeseen crisis'. Histed has commented that 'the court has come perilously close to implying that an occasional problem of expenditure exceeding income is sufficient to qualify a class member as "poor"'.[78] She states that even though this was presumably not the implication intended, she goes on to comment that 'the tone of the

---

72. [1955] AC 572, 585.
73. [1914] 1 Ch 662.
74. *Ibid.* at 668.
75. [1954] Ch 265. The case was settled on appeal (see *The Times*, 22 July 1954).
76. [1978] 1 WLR 910.
77. [1996] Ch 171.
78. [1996] Conv 379, 386.

judgment does suggest a more flexible approach to the poverty requirement than has obtained in earlier cases'.[79]

A further limitation which should be noted is that the need which is to be relieved by the charitable gift must be attributable to the condition of the person to be benefited. This point was made by Peter Gibson J in *Joseph Rowntree Memorial Trust Housing Association Ltd v. Attorney General*[80] in the context of schemes to provide accommodation for disabled and elderly people, but it would have equal application to trusts for the poor and would seem to rule out any gift which does not go towards alleviating their condition of poverty. An earlier illustration of this principle was provided by Harman J in *Baddeley v. IRC*,[81] where he commented that a gift to amuse the poor would not relieve them and therefore would not be considered charitable. A further consideration is the fact that potential beneficiaries are young and therefore may not themselves have a means of support does not necessarily fulfil the poverty requirement. In *Browne v. King*[82] a gift to be applied for the benefit of the children of the tenantry of an estate under the age of twelve years did not qualify as charitable. As Porter MR stated: 'There is nothing to guide me in deciding that the gift is for children of poor persons, or persons in great need. The law imposes on parents the duty of supporting their children and there is nothing to satisfy me that the tenantry ... are not able to fulfil that obligation.'[83]

A gift of this kind may be expressed in either general or particular terms. So a gift to the poor in a general way will be upheld,[84] or a gift to the poor of a particular area,[85] or a particular religious denomination.[86] It has been established[87] that the fact that the recipients of the testator or donor's bounty are to be chosen by his executors or trustees does not present any difficulties. Similarly, in *Brett v. Attorney General*[88] it was held by the Supreme Court that a trust for 'such poor persons in the County of M. as the executor shall select and consider worthy of assistance' was charitable and that the power of

---

79. This approach can also be discerned in other jurisdictions, e.g. in New Zealand, where in *Re Centrepoint Community Growth Trust* [2000] 2 NZLR 325, Cartwright J stated that 'in contemporary New Zealand poverty can quite readily be equated with lack of affordable accommodation.'

80. [1983] Ch 159, 171 See also *Re Dunlop* [1984] NI 408, 414-416.

81. [1953] 1 WLR 84, 88. As he stated: 'Relief seems to connote need of some sort ... and not merely an amusement however healthy it is.'

82. (1885) 17 LR Ir 448.

83. *Ibid.* at 456.

84. *Attorney General v. Matthews* (1677) 2 Lev 167.

85. *Attorney General v. Exeter Corporation* (1826) 2 Russ 45.

86. *Attorney General v. Wansay* (1808) 15 Ves 231; *Dawson v. Small* (1874) LR 18 Eq 114; *Re Wall* (1889) 42 Ch D 510.

87. *Re Scarisbrick* [1951] Ch 622 and *Re Cohen* [1973] 1 WLR 415 where a trust 'for the maintenance and benefit of any relative of mine whom my trustees shall consider to be in special need' was upheld as charitable.

88. [1945] IR 526.

selection conferred on the executor could not alter the essentially charitable nature of the gift.

It is important to distinguish a gift to specified poor individuals from a gift to a class of the poor. Trusts in the former category are not charitable in nature, while those in the latter are, even where this class is of limited scope.[89] At this point it becomes necessary to consider the public benefit requirement in trusts for the relief of poverty in more detail and it is fair to say that the comment made by Martin[90] that the requirement in this category has been 'reduced ... almost to vanishing point' is an accurate one. This position has come about largely as a result of the development of the category of so called 'poor relations' trusts, whereby a donor or testator may create a valid charitable trust to benefit those of his relatives who are in straightened financial circumstances.[91] These cases are recognised as forming an exception to the general principle laid down by Lord Greene MR in *Re Compton*[92] that 'a gift under which the beneficiaries are defined by reference to a purely personal relationship to a named *propositus*, cannot on principle be a valid charitable gift.'

A justification for these types of trust has been suggested by Evershed MR in *Re Scarisbrick*[93] in the following terms:

> The 'poor relations' cases may be justified on the basis that the relief of poverty is of so altruistic a character that the public element may necessarily be inferred thereby; or they may be accepted as a hallowed, if illogical, exception.

An examination of the authorities suggests that the second rationale is the more likely and these types of trusts have come to be regarded as anomalous exceptions to the public benefit requirement which attaches to charitable trusts generally.[94] A good illustration of such a trust is provided in the *Scarisbrick* case itself, where a trust to benefit such relations of the testatrix's son and daughters who in the opinion of the survivor of her children 'shall be in needy circumstances' was upheld as a valid charitable trust. Jenkins LJ, having set out the general requirement of public benefit in charitable trusts, continued as follows:

---

89. Although as Dunn has commented (2000) 20 LS 222, 233 with reference to the decision in *Re Segelman deceased* [1996] Ch 171 'it takes little to turn a private gift for the poor into a charitable trust.'
90. Hanbury and Martin, *Modern Equity* (16th ed., 2001) p. 428.
91. See *Mahon v. Savage* (1803) 1 Sch & Lef 111.
92. [1945] Ch 123, 131.
93. [1951] Ch 622, 639 and *Gibson v. South American Stores (Gath & Chaves) Ltd* [1950] Ch 177, 197 *per* Evershed MR.
94. See *Re Compton* [1945] Ch 123, 139 *per* Lord Greene MR.

There is, however, an exception to the general rule, in that trusts or gifts for the relief of poverty have been held to be charitable even though they are limited in their application to some aggregate of individuals ascertained as above, and are, therefore, not trusts or gifts for the benefit of the public or a section thereof. The exception operates whether the personal tie is one of blood (as in the numerous so called 'poor relations' cases) or of contract, e.g., the relief of poverty amongst the members of a particular society ... or amongst employees of a particular company or their dependants.[95]

A further point which was made by the Court of Appeal in *Scarisbrick* is that no distinction should be drawn between trusts for the poor which are to have perpetual continuance and those which provide for immediate distribution amongst the recipients.[96] As Jenkins LJ stated: 'I see no sufficient ground in the authorities for holding that a gift for the benefit of poor relations qualifies as charitable only if it is perpetual in character.'[97]

Another recent example of a trust for poor relations being upheld is *Re Segelman deceased*[98] in which Chadwick J accepted that a gift to poor and needy members of a class of the testator's relatives, which was not to close until 21 years after his death, was a valid charitable gift for the relief of poverty and that it was not disqualified from being such by the restricted nature of the class. At the time of the hearing, there were 26 members of the class and Chadwick J stated that it was reasonable to assume that at the end of the period of 21 years from the testator's death, the class would be substantially larger. Chadwick J stated that *prima facie* a gift for the benefit of poor and needy persons is a gift for the relief of poverty and that such a gift is no less charitable because those whose poverty is to be relieved are confined to a particular class limited by ties of blood or employment. He quoted a statement from the judgment of Jenkins LJ in *Scarisbrick,* which had been approved by the House of Lords in *Dingle v. Turner,*[99] to the effect that the true question must be whether the gift was really for the relief of poverty amongst a class of persons or merely a gift to individuals, albeit with the relief of poverty amongst those individuals as the motive for the gift. Chadwick J continued by saying that the basis for disqualification as a charitable gift must be that the restricted

---

95. [1951] Ch 622, 649.
96. In so doing the Court of Appeal reversed the finding of Roxburgh J at first instance in which he had held that the bequest was not charitable on the basis that a gift for immediate distribution lacked the necessary public character to render it charitable. (This finding was in the opinion of the Court of Appeal based on a mistaken interpretation of the decision of Grant MR in *Attorney General v. Price* (1810) 17 Ves 371).
97. *Ibid.* at 655.
98. [1996] Ch 171.
99. [1972] AC 601.

nature of the class leads to the conclusion that the gift is really one to the individual members of a class. In his view the gift which he was required to consider was not of that character and had, in common with the gift in *Scarisbrick,* the feature that the class of those eligible to benefit was not closed on the testator's death but remained open for a further period of 21 years. Chadwick J stated that during that period issue of the named individuals born after the testator's death would become members of the class. In his opinion it was impossible to attribute to the testator an intention to make a gift to those after-born issue as such and his intention must therefore be taken to have been the relief of poverty amongst the class of which they would become members.

While Chadwick J did not address this point directly, the implication might be taken from his judgment that if the class of persons to benefit was confined to those of the testator's relatives living at the date of his death, the gift might have been construed as one to individual members of the class which would not qualify as being for the relief of poverty. Histed has commented that Chadwick J's opinion seemed to be that 'the more restricted the class, the more probable that the gift was one to individuals' and in her view the gift was saved by the inclusion of potential after-born issue.[100] She also expressed the view that the basis for the selection of the class appeared to depend not so much on the degree of relationship to the testator but on the possibility of future need and suggested that this factor also influenced the court's decision that the gift was a charitable one.

The relaxation of the public benefit requirement has been extended to other categories or classes of persons and so trusts for 'poor employees'[101] and 'poor members'[102] have also been recognised despite the existence of some personal nexus between the donor or testator and those whom he seeks to benefit. However the existence of the quality of poverty amongst those whom it is sought to benefit must be clear and trusts for employees have failed to qualify as charitable where this has not been evident.[103] So in *Re Cullimore's Trusts,*[104] a trust for the benefit and maintenance of the families of employees of a firm was found not to be charitable. As Porter MR stated:

Mere kindness, generosity, or benevolence on the testator's part is not

---

100. [1996] Conv 379, 385.
101. The validity of such trusts was recognised in England in *Re Gosling* (1900) 48 WR 300. See also *Gibson v. South American Stores (Gath & Chaves) Ltd* [1950] Ch 177.
102. *Spiller v. Maude* (1881) 32 Ch D 158n (members of mutual benefit society); *Re Young* [1955] 1 WLR 1269 (members of a social club).
103. See *Re Drummond* [1914] 2 Ch 90 where a trust to provide for the holiday expenses of employees in a department in a certain company was found not to be charitable. See also *Re Hobourn Aero Components Ltd's Air Raid Distress Fund* [1946] Ch 194.
104. (1891) 27 LR Ir 18.

enough to constitute a charitable purpose; there must also be an element of poverty or need on the part of the object, or else the gift must be dedicated to some purpose, such as education, religion or the like which the law regards as charitable. There is nothing here to show that the persons whom the testator meant to benefit were to be poor persons.[105]

However, the decision of the House of Lords in *Dingle v. Turner*[106] has clearly confirmed that trusts for the benefit of 'poor employees' will be recognised as valid charitable trusts. The testator directed trustees to apply the income of a fund for the purpose of paying pensions to poor employees of a firm who were at least 60 years of age, or who were at least 45 years of age and incapacitated from earning a living and the House of Lords upheld the gift as being a charitable trust. Lord Cross rejected the argument that the trust in the case before him should not be recognised as charitable despite the fact that the company was in some respects relatively small, employing around 600 people at the date of the testator's death. He stated:

> [T]he 'poor members' and 'poor employees' decisions were a natural development of the 'poor relations' decisions and to draw a distinction between different sorts of 'poverty' trusts would be quite illogical and could certainly not be said to be introducing 'greater harmony' into the law of charity. Moreover, though not as old as the 'poor relations' trusts, 'poor employees' trusts have been recognised as charities for many years; there are now a large number of such trusts in existence; and assuming, as one must, that they are properly administered in the sense that the benefits under them are only given to people who can fairly be said to be according to current standards, 'poor persons', to treat such trusts as charitable is not open to any practical objection.[107]

The principle laid down by Lord Cross is now well established and has been extended to include poor members of a profession. In *Re Denison*[108] the High Court of Ontario found that a bequest for the relief of 'impoverished or indigent members of the Law Society [of Upper Canada] and of their wives and widows and children' was charitable. While the extension of the exception to the public benefit requirement in cases of this nature has been criticised,[109] it is

---

105. *Ibid.* at 24.
106. [1972] AC 601. The point is made by Warburton in *Tudor on Charities* (8th ed., 1995) p.35 that the decision not only removed any 'lingering doubts' about the validity of poor relations trusts but also confirmed the charitable nature of trusts for the relief of poverty amongst other classes of persons having a personal nexus in the form of a common employer.
107. *Ibid.* at 623.
108. (1974) 42 DLR (3d) 652.
109. E.g. by the Report of the Goodman Committee on Charity Law and Voluntary Organisations, Chapter II, paragraph 37.

submitted that it is too firmly entrenched to be overturned at this stage, certainly in England, and it is most unlikely that the courts in this jurisdiction would see fit to depart from this position.

It should be noted that the preamble to the English Statute of Charitable Uses referred to 'the relief of aged, impotent and poor people'.[110] While it has been recognised that these purposes are to be construed in a disjunctive manner,[111] some academics[112] and judges[113] have tended to consider them as being grouped under one heading. In the UK, trusts for the aged and the sick may still be characterised as falling into the first rather than the fourth category in Lord Macnaghten's classification and some residual doubt remained until recently about whether the exception to the public benefit requirement could be extended to such trusts. This question seems to have been settled by Carswell J in *Re Dunlop*,[114] where he stated that the House of Lords in *Dingle v. Turner* intended to circumscribe the scope of the exception and 'to confine it to cases concerning the relief of actual poverty.'[115]

It can be argued that it is unrealistic to enforce the requirement that there should be no personal tie or nexus between a donor or testator and the class of individuals which he seeks to benefit, in that a charitable gift will usually be motivated by such factors, and to strictly enforce it would not be practicable. This issue will be considered in more detail below, but for present purposes, it suffices to say that the requirement of public benefit has all but disappeared in the context of trusts for the relief of poverty.[116]

2. Trusts for the Advancement of Education

While trusts for the advancement of education in the formal sense have long

---

110. The version contained in the Statute of Charitable Uses (Ireland) 1634 referred to 'the relief ... of poor, succourless, distressed or impotent persons'.
111. *Joseph Rowntree Memorial Trust Housing Association Ltd v. Attorney General* [1983] Ch 159 and *DV Bryant Trust Board v. Hamilton City Council* [1997] 3 NZLR 342, 349.
112. Warburton, *Tudor on Charities* (8th ed., 1995) pp. 20-39.
113. Lord Simonds in *Oppenheim v. Tobacco Securities Trust Co. Ltd* [1955] AC 297, 308.
114. [1984] NI 408. Considered in more detail *infra* pp. 332-333.
115. *Ibid.* at 424. The judgment of Carswell J, considered in more detail below, would suggest that while potential beneficiaries of trusts for the aged and the sick must constitute 'a particular section of the community at large', a less strict public benefit test is applied to such categories than that which he suggested should apply to the fourth category.
116. Although as Plowright comments (1975) 39 Conv 183, 187 'there are limits to the acceptable width of class even within this exception beyond which the court will not allow that the trust can properly be regarded as a charitable trust, but will conclude that it is nothing more than a private trust. It is this ... qualification that makes it unwise to assert that trusts for the relief of poverty form a complete exception to the requirement of public benefit.'

been recognised as charitable in nature,[117] the concept of what is 'educational' in the sense of what will be recognised as legally charitable has been widened considerably over the last fifty years by a process of judicial interpretation. A gift for the advancement of education in a general manner will be recognised as charitable; so a bequest for 'educational ... purposes',[118] or a gift 'for the benefit, and advancement, and propagation of education and learning in every part of the world'[119] will be upheld. Similarly, a gift to schools,[120] or to colleges, either generally or to found a scholarship,[121] will be recognised as charitable under this heading. In addition, more recent authorities have established that the ambit of trusts recognised as being for the advancement of education is not confined to those which are educational in the formal sense of the word.

In England it is possible to discern two distinct approaches to the question of what constitutes 'education'. A rather narrow view was taken by Harman J in *Re Shaw*,[122] which concerned a direction under the will of George Bernard Shaw that his trustees should use his residuary estate to provide for research, *inter alia*, into the advantages of reform of the alphabet. Harman J stated that 'if the object be merely the increase of knowledge that is not in itself a charitable object unless it be combined with teaching or education'.[123] He found that these latter elements were lacking in the case before him and also concluded that the objects were not beneficial to the community in a way regarded as charitable in law.

A more expansive interpretation of what should qualify as 'education' was put forward by Wilberforce J in *Re Hopkins' Will Trusts*,[124] where a gift to a society to be applied to the task of finding the Bacon-Shakespeare manuscripts was held to be a valid charitable trust. Wilberforce J stated:

> I think, therefore, that the word 'education' as used by Harman J in *Re Shaw* must be used in a wide sense, certainly extending beyond teaching, and that the requirement is that, in order to be charitable, research must either be of educational value to the researcher or must be directed as to lead to something which will pass into the store of educational material, or so as to improve the sum of communicable knowledge in an area

---

117. The Preamble to the Statute of Charitable Uses (Ireland) 1634 made reference to 'the erection, maintenance or support of any college, school, lecture in divinity, or on any of the liberal arts or sciences, the building, re-edifying, or maintaining in repair any college [or] school'.
118. *Re Ward* [1941] Ch 308.
119. *Whicker v. Hume* (1858) 7 HLC 124.
120. *Incorporated Society v. Richards* (1841) 4 Ir Eq R 177.
121. *R. v. Newman* (1684) 1 Lev 284.
122. [1957] 1 WLR 729.
123. *Ibid.* at 737. See also *Re Macduff* [1896] 2 Ch 451, 472-3 *per* Rigby LJ.
124. [1965] Ch 669.

which education may cover — education in this last context extending to the formation of literary taste and appreciation.[125]

Wilberforce J said that he would be unwilling to treat Harman J's words as meaning that the promotion of academic research is not a charitable purpose unless the researcher were engaged in teaching or education in the conventional sense. While he accepted that research of a purely private nature would not normally be educational, research of the character proposed in the case before him did not fall into this category as it was 'inherently inevitable and manifestly intended' that the results of such research should fall into the public domain. This point that education requires more than just the accumulation of knowledge and must involve some element of sharing or publication was reiterated by Buckley LJ in *Incorporated Council for Law Reporting for England and Wales v. Attorney General*.[126] The majority of the Court of Appeal found that the activities of the council fell within the second head of Lord Macnaghten's classification[127] and Buckley LJ commented in the course of his judgment that the concept of the advancement of education must extend 'to the improvement of a useful branch of human knowledge and its public dissemination'.[128]

In considering these divergent approaches in *Re Shaw* and *Re Hopkins* in *Re Worth Library*[129] Keane J commented that the views of Harman J in *Re Shaw* might not command universal acceptance today and that it was possible that they would exclude from the legal definition of charity certain trusts for the encouragement of academic research which might reasonably be regarded as being for the public benefit. Keane J concluded by saying that if this was the likely interpretation of the views of Harman J, he would prefer those of Wilberforce J.

A closer examination of the judgment of Keane J in *Worth* confirms that he favours an interpretation at the liberal end of the spectrum. In this important decision, the High Court was called upon to decide whether to approve a cyprès scheme proposed by the trustees of the 'Worth Library' which consisted of a bequest of a large and valuable collection of books originally made in the eighteenth century to Dr Steevens' Hospital in Dublin. When the hospital was closed in 1988, the trustees of the library decided to transfer it temporarily to Trinity College, Dublin for safekeeping and appointed the college as trustees in their place.[130] The Eastern Health Board which had purchased the hospital

---

125. *Ibid.* at 680.
126. [1972] 1 Ch 73.
127. Sachs and Buckley LJJ. Russell LJ found that the purposes were charitable under the fourth heading alone.
128. [1972] 1 Ch 73, 102.
129. [1995] 2 IR 301, 337.
130. The Attorney General took the view that an appropriately qualified independent

premises that year took the view that the library should be returned to its original location and when the Attorney General gave his consent to the trustees' application to the High Court for an order framing a cy-près scheme,[131] the board was joined as a defendant to the proceedings. At the outset of legal arguments in the case, Keane J indicated to counsel for the various parties the fundamental issues which he felt required resolution, namely the question of whether the initial bequest of the Worth Library was in law a charitable trust, and if so, the type of charitable bequest which it represented. If this first question was answered in the affirmative, the court would then proceed to consider whether the conditions necessary for the exercise of its cy-près jurisdiction had been satisfied and decide what form of scheme should be approved. In considering the first submission of counsel on behalf of the plaintiff, that the initial bequest should qualify as being for the advancement of education, Keane J made the following general statement:

> [G]ifts for the advancement of education ... would embrace, not merely gifts to schools and universities and the endowment of university chairs and scholarships: 'education' has been given a broad meaning so as to encompass gifts for the establishment of theatres, art galleries and museums and the promotion of literature and music. In every case, however, the element of public benefit must be present and, if the benefit extends to a section of the community only, that section must not be numerically negligible.[132]

Keane J rejected the argument that the trust might qualify as being one for the advancement of education on the basis of the lack of an element of public benefit but it is interesting to note that he stated that in any event a finding that the library was for educational purposes would involve 'some straining of the concept of "education" even beyond the liberal limits of the modern decisions,' given the insignificant portion of the library devoted to topics of medical interest.

A number of decisions have illustrated that the ambit of education for this purpose is not limited to education of the mind and extends to the physical education of those attending a school or college. So, in *IRC v. McMullen*[133] the House of Lords upheld as charitable under this heading a trust 'to organise or provide or assist in the organisation or provision of facilities which will enable and encourage pupils at schools and universities in any part of the United Kingdom to play association football and other games or sports and

---

person should also be appointed as a trustee and the Director of the National Library
agreed to act in that capacity.
131. As he was required to do by s. 51(1) of the Irish Charities Act 1961.
132. [1995] 2 IR 301, 336.
133. [1981] AC 1. See also *Re Mariette* [1915] 2 Ch 284.

thereby to assist in ensuring that due attention is given to the physical education and development of their minds'.

Similarly, the concept of education has been found to extend to aesthetic education and to such purposes as the support of museums[134] and the promotion of an appreciation of art[135] and music.[136] In *Re Shaw's Will Trusts*[137] Vaisey J upheld the validity of a gift for 'bringing the masterpieces of fine art within the reach of the people of Ireland of all classes in their own country,' and stated that he thought that 'education' included 'not only teaching, but the promotion and encouragement of those arts and graces of life which are after all, perhaps the finest and best part of the human character.'[138] In *Royal Choral Society v. IRC*[139] the English Court of Appeal upheld a trust to promote the performance of choral works. Lord Greene MR said that he disagreed with the narrow conception of education as meaning a teacher instructing a class and concluded that in his opinion 'a body of persons established for the purpose of raising the artistic state of the country … is established for educational purposes.'[140]

A broad approach towards the meaning of 'educational' in this context was also adopted by Lavan J in *Magee v. Attorney General*[141] which concerned a cy-près application. Having referred to the *dicta* of Keane J in *Re Worth Library*[142] to the effect that the word 'education' has been given a broad meaning and to the words of Vaisey J in *Re Shaw's Will Trusts*[143] set out above, Lavan J stated that 'these…sentiments tend to confer a stamp of approval on attempts to contribute to the betterment of a class of persons or a community, even if not in a classroom setting.'[144] He concluded that the activities carried on in the local community hall which largely consisted of the running of a number of self-help groups must be deemed to be 'educational' in nature.

Gifts to professional bodies can qualify as being for the advancement of education provided that their objects are truly educational in nature rather than being the promotion of the status of the profession or the safeguarding of the welfare of its members. However, in practice such bodies and associations will frequently have ancillary objects which fall into the latter

---

134. *British Museum v. White* (1826) 2 Sim & St 594.
135. *Re Shaw's Will Trusts* [1952] Ch 163.
136. *Re Delius* [1957] Ch 299.
137. [1952] Ch 163.
138. *Ibid.* at 172.
139. [1943] 2 All ER 101.
140. *Ibid.* at 105.
141. High Court 2000 No. 377Sp (Lavan J) 25 July 2002.
142. [1995] 2 IR 301, 337.
143. [1952] Ch 163, 172.
144. High Court 2000 No. 377Sp (Lavan J) 25 July 2002 at 24.

category. In *Miley v. Attorney General for Ireland*[145] the Irish Court of Appeal was required to determine whether a legacy to the Royal College of Surgeons in Ireland was one for 'charitable uses' within the meaning of section 16 of the Charitable Donations and Bequests Act 1844.[146] The court found that there were two main objects contemplated by the charter of the college, one being the promotion of the science of surgery, and the other being the regulation of the profession and the promotion of the interests of those practising it. The court concluded that the latter object was not a charitable one and that as the testatrix had not impressed her gift with a charitable purpose, the bequest should not be considered to be one for 'charitable uses' within the meaning of section 16 of the Act of 1844.

However, the courts in England have tended to take a more pragmatic approach to this issue by adopting reasoning well summarised by Greer LJ in *Geologists Association v. IRC*:[147]

> If you come to the conclusion, as you may in many cases, that one of the ways in which the public objects of an association can be served is by giving special advantages to the members of the association, then the association does not cease to be an association with a charitable object because incidentally and in order to carry out the charitable object it is both necessary and desirable to confer special benefits upon the members.

A similar principle was applied by the House of Lords in *Royal College of Surgeons of England v. National Provincial Bank Ltd.*[148] It was held that the main object of the college was the promotion and encouragement of the study and practice of surgery and that the professional protection of its members was ancillary to this overall objective and did not alter the charitable status of the college.

It can be said with a fair degree of certainty that the decision of the Irish Court of Appeal in *Miley* is now unlikely to be followed for a number of reasons. First, the surrounding circumstances of the case and the consequences of a finding of charitable status to the outcome must be borne in mind. Secondly, the court laid considerable emphasis on the earlier English decision

---

145. [1918] 1 IR 455.
146. S. 16 (now repealed by the Charities Act 1961) rendered void gifts of land for charitable uses unless the instrument conferring the gift was executed at least three months prior to the death of the donor. The testatrix had died four days after the execution of her will and therefore the validity of her bequest, which would have been payable partly out of realty, would have been affected by the provisions of s.16 if it had been found to be charitable in nature.
147. (1928) 14 TC 271, 283. See also *Royal College of Nursing v. St Marylebone Borough Council* [1959] 1 WLR 1077, 1085.
148. [1952] AC 631.

in *Re Royal College of Surgeons of England*,[149] which was subsequently distinguished by the House of Lords in *Royal College of Surgeons of England v. National Provincial Bank Ltd*. In any event, legislation would seem to have resolved the question in a manner which should ensure that the decision in *Miley* would not now be followed. Section 49(1) of Charities Act 1961 provides that where the purposes of a gift include charitable and non-charitable objects, its terms will be construed so as to exclude the non-charitable objects. On this basis gifts such as that considered in *Miley* would probably be interpreted in such a way that they would be applied solely in furtherance of the charitable purposes of such a professional body.

The Element of Public Benefit

It is important to stress that a gift for the advancement of education will only qualify as charitable provided that it is for the benefit of the public generally or of an 'appreciably important class'[150] of the public. This principle was stressed in *Re Compton*,[151] in which the Court of Appeal held that a trust for the education of the descendants of three named individuals was not a valid charitable trust. As Lord Greene MR stated 'a gift under which the beneficiaries are defined by reference to a purely personal relationship to a named *propositus* cannot on principle be a valid charitable gift.'[152]

One of the most important English authorities in this area is the decision of the House of Lords in *Oppenheim v. Tobacco Securities Trust Co. Ltd*,[153] which concerned the validity of a trust set up to provide for the education of the children of employees or former employees of a tobacco company and its subsidiaries. Despite the fact that the number of such employees exceeded 110,000 at the date of the settlement, it was held that the trust must fail as the distinguishing quality of the class of beneficiaries was a relationship with a named *propositus* and for this reason they could not constitute a section of the public. Lord Simonds stated as follows:

> These words 'section of the community' have no special sanctity, but they conveniently indicate first, that the possible (I emphasise the word 'possible') beneficiaries must not be numerically negligible, and secondly, that the quality which distinguishes them from other members of the community, so that they form by themselves a section of it, must

---

149. [1899] 1 QB 871.
150. *Verge v. Sommerville* [1924] AC 496, 499 *per* Lord Westbury.
151. [1945] Ch 123. See also *Re Hobourn Aero Components Ltd's Air Raid Distress Fund* [1946] Ch 86.
152. *Ibid.* at 131.
153. [1951] AC 297.

be a quality which does not depend on their relationship to a particular individual.[154]

Lord MacDermott in his dissenting judgment considered that the '*Compton* test',[155] while it might often prove of value might equally, if a personal or impersonal relationship remained the criterion, prove to be 'a very arbitrary and artificial rule'. The reasoning of the majority in *Oppenheim* has not met with universal approval[156] and the decision of Lord Cross in *Dingle v. Turner*[157] shows an element of empathy with the views expressed by Lord MacDermott. In the view of Lord Cross the question of whether the beneficiaries under a trust constitute a section of the community is essentially one of degree and cannot of itself prove decisive in determining whether the trust is charitable in nature.[158] A further important reason for questioning the validity of the majority view in *Oppenheim* put forward by Lord Cross in *Dingle v. Turner* was his view that the decisions in both *Compton* and *Oppenheim* appeared to him to have been 'pretty obviously influenced by considerations of a perceived undeserved fiscal immunity which would be the result of a finding of charitable status.' Such concerns can also be seen to lie behind the comments made by Harman LJ in the course of his judgment in *IRC v. Educational Grants Association*[159] that 'it is an admirable thing that the children of employees should have a higher education, but I do not see why it should be at the expense of the taxpayer.' While this issue will be considered in more detail below, for the present it suffices to say that the decision in *Oppenheim* should not be accepted unquestioningly as the basis for the decision may itself be reassessed in the future.

Despite these doubts, there is no evidence in any decisions made by the courts in this jurisdiction of a more relaxed attitude being applied towards this question of public benefit in the context of trusts for the advancement of education, although it should be pointed out that the authorities here have involved a considerably smaller number of potential beneficiaries than those considered in *Oppenheim*. In *Re McEnery*,[160] Gavan Duffy J concluded that a bequest to enable the nephews and nieces of the testator and their male

---

154. *Ibid.* at 306.
155. See *supra* n. 152.
156. See e.g. the comments of Blanchard J in the decision of the New Zealand Court of Appeal in *Latimer v. Commissioner of Inland Revenue* [2002] 3 NZLR 195.
157. [1972] AC 601.
158. It is interesting to note that Lord Simonds in *Oppenheim* criticised the dissenting judgment of Lord MacDermott for the very reason that it made the question one of degree; an objection which Geoffrey Cross QC (later Lord Cross) writing in (1956) 72 LQR 189-190 said was not an objection which he believed to be very cogent.
159. [1967] Ch 993, 1013.
160. [1941] IR 323.

descendants to obtain professions was too narrow in scope to be charitable and that the intention of the testator was to benefit specific individuals. As he stated: 'Courts of Equity generally have been consistently insistent on the public character of legal charity, importing a benefit to the community, or a section of the community. ...'[161]

When the question came before Keane J in *Re Worth Library*, he had no hesitation in finding that the trust could not qualify as being for the advancement of education as the library was clearly expressed to be for the use and benefit of three named office holders in the hospital alone. It is to an extent unfortunate that the question of whether a gift framed in slightly wider terms might have satisfied this requirement did not arise for consideration. Keane J nevertheless expressed some views on the issue which are of relevance, although he failed to clarify the position in any meaningful way. On the one hand, Keane J quoted with approval the statement of Lord Simonds in *National Anti-Vivisection Society v. I.R.C.*[162] to the effect that 'if the purpose is within one of the heads of charity forming the first three classes in [Lord Macnaghten's] ... classification ... the court will easily conclude that it is a charitable purpose' and stated that it has been accepted in England that gifts in the first three 'Pemsel' categories are presumed to be for the public benefit.[163] However, he went on to comment that in the context of trusts for the advancement of education 'in every case ... the element of public benefit must be present and, if the benefit extends to a section of the community only, that section must not be numerically negligible.'[164]

Therefore it is fair to say that the question of the extent of the public benefit requirement is no closer to being resolved in this jurisdiction than it is in England, and while some support for a more lenient approach can be discerned from a portion of the judgment of Keane J in *Re Worth Library*, the overall effect of his decision is probably to maintain the *status quo* as it exists post-*Oppenheim*.

The effect of such an inflexible approach has been mitigated in both jurisdictions to a limited degree, by what are sometimes referred to as the 'founder's kin' decisions. So while a trust simply to educate a donor's relatives will not qualify as being charitable in nature,[165] a gift to an educational institution which contains a direction that preference be given to the 'founder's kin' may constitute a charitable trust. The effect of this principle was summarised in a general context as follows by Atiyah:[166]

---

161. *Ibid.* at 326.
162. [1948] AC 31, 65.
163. [1995] 2 IR 301, 334. A statement which is difficult to justify in the light of the decision of the House of Lords in *Oppenheim*.
164. [1995] 2 IR 301, 336.
165. E.g. *Re McEnery* [1941] IR 323.
166. (1958) 21 MLR 138, 148.

> Where there is a charitable trust for the benefit of a section of the community the trust is not invalidated because the trustees are directed to give preference to certain beneficiaries who would not by themselves have constituted a section of the community.

This principle would seem to be supported by two English decisions, *Spencer v. All Soul's College*[167] and *Attorney General v. Sidney Sussex College*.[168] One example of a particularly liberal construction of this principle is the decision of O'Connor MR in *Re Lavelle*,[169] in which he upheld a bequest to a college which contained a direction that the income should be used to educate the testator's relatives there. While the facts of this case arguably fit within the 'founder's kin' exception established in the cases referred to above, the language employed by O'Connor MR should be treated with a degree of caution. In the course of his judgment he stated that 'gifts for the advancement of education are undoubtedly charitable and it has been decided that bequests for the education of the donor's descendants and kinsman are also charitable,' referring to the English authorities. This is misleading and as Lord Greene MR made clear in *Re Compton*,[170] for a gift to come within this limited exception, the primary object of the donor must be to endow a college for educational purposes and the preference afforded to his own family must be 'merely a method of giving effect to this intention'. This interpretation is supported by the *dicta* of Barton J in *Laverty v. Laverty*,[171] to the extent that he stated that in his opinion 'a valid charitable trust might be created for the advancement of education, with a preference for persons of a particular surname, either by the endowment of, or gift to, a school or college'.[172] He continued by saying *obiter* that such a trust might also be created by means of a gift to trustees, provided that it was sufficiently definite in nature. However, on the facts of the case before him, Barton J held that, having regard to the discretion vested in the trustees, a gift for the support and education in Ireland of Roman Catholic boys and men with specified surnames was not charitable in nature as it 'might have been intended to work, as a mere matter of private bounty'. On the basis that the comments of O'Connor MR in *Lavelle* do not seem to be supported by the authorities on which he placed reliance, and having regard to the fact that Barton J provided no justification for his *obiter* suggestion, there is a distinct possibility that the 'founder's kin' exception may still only be valid in this jurisdiction provided that the gift is expressed in the terms suggested by Lord Greene in *Re Compton*.

---

167. (1762) Wilm 163.
168. (1869) LR 4 Ch App 722.
169. [1914] 1 IR 194.
170. [1945] Ch 123, 132.
171. [1907] 1 IR 9.
172. *Ibid.* at 13.

The principle to which Atiyah referred was given recognition by Upjohn J in *Re Koettgen's Will Trusts*,[173] where a trust established to further the commercial education of British born persons which included a direction that preference be given to employees of a particular firm, was upheld as charitable. However, subsequently in *Caffoor v. Commissioner of Income Tax, Columbo*,[174] the Privy Council showed a reluctance to adopt such an approach and found that the trust before them conferred such a priority on the donor's own relatives and descendants that 'the only fair way to describe [it was] as a family trust'.[175] Lord Radcliffe commented that *Koettegen* 'edges very near to being inconsistent with *Oppenheim*'[176] and Atiyah similarly comments that the decision of Upjohn J 'opens the way to serious evasion of the *Oppenheim* ruling'.[177] Often the result of such cases will turn on a matter of construction and the approach in *Koettgen* might well be embraced by the courts in this jurisdiction as a means of mitigating the severity of *Oppenheim* without giving consideration to the thorny question of the separation of the issues of fiscal immunity and charitable status which a full scale review of that decision might require.

3. Trusts for the Advancement of Religion

Introduction

Trusts purporting to fall into this category have always been numerous in this jurisdiction and the historical aspect of these trusts in particular has been well charted elsewhere.[178] More recently legislative intervention has helped to clarify what had been a most complex and uncertain area of the law which until comparatively recently was notable for the significant divergences which existed between the attitudes adopted in England and in this jurisdiction in relation to certain types of trusts which fall into this category.

The advancement of religion has been described by Lord Hanworth MR in *Keren Kayemeth Le Jisroel Ltd v. IRC*[179] as 'the promotion of spiritual teaching in a wide sense, and the maintenance of the doctrines on which it rests and the observances that serve to promote and manifest it. ...'

---

173. [1954] Ch 252.
174. [1961] AC 584.
175. *Ibid.* at 603.
176. *Ibid.* at 604. See also *IRC v. Educational Grants Association Ltd* [1967] Ch 993, 1010 *per* Denning MR.
177. (1958) 21 MLR 138, 148.
178. Delany, *The Law Relating to Charities in Ireland* (1957) and Brady, *Religion and the Law of Charities in Ireland* (1976).
179. [1931] 2 KB 465, 477. See also the *dicta* of Donovan J in *United Grand Lodge of Ancient Free and Accepted Masons of England v. Holborn Borough Council* [1957] 1 WLR 1080, 1090.

Certainly in England the judiciary has not tended to prefer one religion to another in determining the question of whether a trust falls into this category,[180] and as Cross J has commented: 'As between different religions, the law stands neutral, but it assumes that any religion is at least better than none'.[181] An examination of recent authorities would suggest that judicial attitudes are becoming increasingly flexible and that, provided the religion in question is considered to be *bona fide*, the limited nature of its support or following will not preclude it from qualifying for charitable status.[182] The predominant view in other common law jurisdictions is that it is not necessary that a religion be monotheistic,[183] and it remains to be seen whether the courts in this jurisdiction would take a similarly progressive approach. Certainly, Walsh J made it clear in *Quinn's Supermarket v. Attorney General*[184] that, despite the references to the Christian nature of the State in Article 44 of the Constitution, religion is not confined to the Christian faith. However, it would be unwise to speculate unduly on the question of whether the courts in this jurisdiction would be prepared to stretch the meaning of 'religion' to the extent to which their counterparts elsewhere in the common law world have done.

Gifts in General Terms

A gift for 'religious purposes' has been held to be charitable on the basis that this will *prima facie* mean charitable purposes unless the context suggests otherwise. As O'Connor MR stated in *Arnott v. Arnott (No. 2)*,[185] it has been held that 'a gift for religious purposes and not more will be construed by the court as confined to such religious purposes as are in their nature charitable.' On the basis of this reasoning, it had been argued that a gift for 'charitable or religious purposes' should fail on the grounds that the use of the word 'charitable' shows that the word 'religious' means something distinct from charitable.[186] However, such an interpretation has been rejected in this jurisdiction and it was held by Barton J in *Re Salter*[187] that a gift framed in

---

180. See *Gilmour v. Coats* [1949] AC 426, 458-459 *per* Lord Reid.
181. *Neville Estates Ltd v. Madden* [1962] Ch 832, 853.
182. *Re Watson* [1973] 1 WLR 1472; *Centrepoint Community Growth Trust v. Commissioner of Inland Revenue* [1985] 1 NZLR 673.
183. Despite the views expressed by Lord Parker in *Bowman v. Secular Society* [1917] AC 406, 449. See further Edge and Loughrey (2001) 21 LS 36, 38-40.
184. [1972] IR 1, 23.
185. [1906] 1 IR 127, 134. See also the *dicta* of Ross J in *Rickerby v. Nicholson* [1912] 1 IR 343, 347 that 'according to our law a bequest for a religious purpose is *prima facie* charitable'.
186. See *Rickerby v. Nicholson* [1912] 1 IR 343, 348. See also *Grimond v. Grimond* [1905] AC 124 which relates to an interpretation of Scots law.
187. [1911] 1 IR 289. See also *Rickerby v. Nicholson* [1912] 1 IR 343; *Re Lloyd* (1893) 10 TLR 66.

these terms will be charitable in nature. This can be distinguished from the wording employed in *Re Davidson*,[188] where a gift for 'charitable, religious or other societies, institutions, persons or objects' was found not to be charitable on the grounds that the words 'or other societies' would have enabled the trustees to apply the gift to societies or institutions which were neither charitable nor religious in character. A gift confined to a specified religion may also be charitable, so in *Copinger v. Crehane*,[189] a gift for 'the advancement and benefit of the Roman Catholic religion' was upheld as a valid charitable bequest on the grounds that its terms limited it strictly and exclusively to charitable purposes. The test in determining the validity of such bequests would appear to be that laid down by Grant MR in *Morice v. Bishop of Durham*,[190] which was summarised as follows by Chatterton VC in *Copinger*:[191] '[W]here the trustee is bound to apply the bequest to charitable purposes, the bequest shall not fail on account of the uncertainty of the object, but ... where there is a discretion to apply it to charitable purposes or to other purposes not charitable, and the trust is indefinite, the gift fails.'

The latter interpretation was placed on a bequest for 'such Roman Catholic purposes in the parish of Coleraine and elsewhere' as the trustees might deem proper by the Irish Court of Appeal in *MacLaughlin v. Campbell*,[192] and the gift was held to be void on the basis that it might be applied for a purpose other than a charitable one. The distinction is a fine one as the *dicta* of Fitzgibbon LJ makes clear:

> If the gift were made to 'the Church' e.g. the 'Church of Rome' or the 'Church of Ireland', I should think that it would import — at least *prima facie* — the operative institution which ministered religion and gave spiritual edification to its members; a gift in such terms would exclude objects which would be included in a gift for the 'purposes' of the individual members of a religious body.[193]

A bequest to 'the Christian Brethren' has been upheld as charitable,[194] as has a gift to 'foreign missions',[195] and 'to Presbyterian missions and orphans'.[196] However a gift for 'missionary purposes' was held by Sullivan MR in *Scott v. Brownrigg*[197] to be too vague and wide to be upheld, although it would appear

---

188. [1909] 1 Ch 567.
189. (1877) LR 11 Eq 429.
190. (1804) 9 Ves 399.
191. (1877) LR 11 Eq 429, 431.
192. [1906] 1 IR 588.
193. *Ibid.* at 597.
194. *Re Brown* [1898] 1 IR 423.
195. *Dunne v. Duignan* [1908] 1 IR 228.
196. *Jackson v. Attorney General* [1917] 1 IR 332.
197. (1881) 9 LR Ir 246.

that where there is sufficient evidence to connect the words 'purposes' or 'objects' with the preaching of religion, such a gift may be charitable.[198]

Gifts to Ecclesiastical Office Holders

It would appear that a gift for the benefit of the incumbent of an ecclesiastical office for the time being is charitable, whereas a gift for the particular individual who happens to hold that office at the time of the gift will not be. So, in *Gibson v. Representative Church Body*,[199] a bequest to the chaplain of the Rotunda chapel at the time of the testatrix's death and his successors was upheld as charitable. This can be contrasted with a separate gift in a codicil to the testatrix's will to the chaplain for his own personal use and with the decision in *Donnellan v. O'Neill*,[200] in which a bequest to a cardinal absolutely for his own use and benefit was held to be a gift to the latter in his private capacity and not to be charitable in nature. The test was described by Kindersley VC in *Thornber v. Wilson*[201] as being 'whether the testator designates the individual as such, or as being the person who happens to fill the office'.

So, a gift to a minister for the time being or to a minister for the time being and his successors without more will be considered charitable in nature on the basis that the character of the office holder is such that it is inevitable that he will apply the gift for strictly charitable purposes. As Cozens-Hardy MR stated in *Re Davidson*,[202] while a court does not hold a trust charitable merely because the trustee has a religious office, 'if you find in a will words indicating that a distribution is to be made by persons in succession as holders of a particular religious or charitable office, that goes far to establish — and, it may be, goes sufficiently far to establish — the fact that the whole gift is charitable.' So, in *Reddy v. Fitzmaurice*[203] a residuary gift to a bishop for the time being and his successors without any further words of qualification was interpreted as being of a charitable nature. However, where additional words were attached to the gift which indicated the trusts on which the donee was to hold the property, the gift would fail at common law if the purposes could be construed as not being exclusively charitable ones.

A gift to an ecclesiastical office holder followed by words which did no more than confer a complete discretion on him or impose a specific limitation

---

198. *Re Kenny* (1907) 97 LT 130; *Re Rees* [1920] 2 Ch 59. See also *Jackson v. Attorney General* [1917] 1 IR 332, 335.
199. (1881) 9 LR Ir 1. See also *Robb v. Dorrian* (1877) IR 11 CL 292; *Re Corcoran* [1913] 1 IR 1.
200. (1870) IR 5 Eq 523.
201. (1858) 4 Dr 350, 351. Quoted with approval by Barton J in *Re Corcoran* [1913] 1 IR 1, 6.
202. [1909] 1 Ch 567, 569. Quoted by Gavan Duffy J in *Re Howley* [1940] IR 109. See also the *dicta* of Black J in *Halpin v. Hannon* (1947) 82 ILTR 74, 77.
203. (1952) 86 ILTR 127.

which fell within the scope of the charitable nature of his office would be charitable. This is illustrated by the decision of Joyce J in *Re Garrard*,[204] where a gift to the vicar and churchwardens for the time being of a certain parish 'to be applied by them in such manner as they shall in their sole discretion think fit' was upheld as a valid charitable gift. Similarly, in *Halpin v. Hannon*[205] a bequest to a named priest or his successor 'for such purposes in the diocese as he wishes' was found to be charitable. In the course of his judgment, after a consideration of some of the English authorities, Maguire CJ is reported as saying:

> From these decisions it was clear that it was necessary to distinguish the case where a gift to the holder of a religious office was followed by words which made it clear that the gift might be applied to non-charitable purposes and that such was the testator's intention, and cases where later words do not clearly indicate an intention to widen a field of selection so as to include non-charitable objects. . . .[206]

However, where the words of qualification are wide enough to include purposes which might not be charitable in law, the position at common law was that the gift must fail, notwithstanding the charitable nature of the office generally. This proposition was established in a number of cases including *Dunne v. Byrne*,[207] where a residuary bequest to an archbishop and his successors to be applied wholly or in part as the archbishop might judge 'most conducive to the good of religion' in the diocese was held by the Privy Council to be void. Similarly, in *Farley v. Westminster Bank*,[208] the House of Lords held that a gift to the vicar and churchwardens of a parish for 'parish work' was too wide to be valid.

Therefore unless the gift was given in unqualified terms or on trusts which were unequivocally charitable in nature, the gift might fail. It is likely that the provisions of section 49(1) of the Charities Act 1961 which provides that 'where any of the purposes of a gift include, or could be deemed to include, both charitable and non-charitable objects, its terms shall be so construed and given effect to as to exclude the non-charitable objects and the purpose shall, accordingly be treated as charitable' may now have resolved this problem of construction.

---

204. [1907] 1 Ch 382. See also *Re Flinn* [1948] Ch 241; *Re Rumball* [1956] Ch 105.
205. (1947) 82 ILTR 74.
206. *Ibid.* at 75.
207. [1912] AC 407. See also *Re Davidson* [1909] 1 Ch 567.
208. [1939] AC 430. However note that this decision was distinguished by Romer J in *Re Simson* [1946] Ch 299.

Gifts for the Celebration of Masses

As Delany[209] has commented: 'So much property is devoted to this type of gift in Ireland that it has become by far the most common object of benevolence.' Whether this statement is as accurate today is open to question, but gifts of this nature have led to an extensive amount of litigation over the last century. The charitable nature of such gifts was confirmed by section 45(2) of the Charities Act 1961, but it is an area which for a long time provoked considerable uncertainty and controversy.

Historically the legal principles applicable differed considerably between England and Ireland. The legality of such gifts was doubtful in England as a result of the interpretation placed on the Statute of Chantries 1547 but a majority of the House of Lords held in *Bourne v. Keane*[210] that gifts for the saying of masses were not illegal without holding that they were charitable bequests. Subsequently, in *Re Caus*,[211] Luxmoore J held that such gifts were charitable, although the findings of the House of Lords in *Gilmour v. Coats*[212] led to doubts being expressed about the validity of this decision. However, more recently in *Re Hetherington*,[213] Browne-Wilkinson VC confirmed that a gift for the saying of masses is *prima facie* charitable since it is for a religious purpose and contained the necessary element of public benefit because in practice the masses would be celebrated in public. While he stressed that the celebration of a religious rite in private would not contain this essential public element, the Vice Chancellor made it clear that where either construction was possible, the gift was to be construed as one to be carried out only by charitable means, viz., celebrated in public.

In Ireland the Statute of Chantries never applied and the validity of a gift for the saying of masses was recognised by Lord Manners LC in *Commissioners of Charitable Donations and Bequests v. Walsh*,[214] a finding confirmed by the judgment of Blackburne MR in *Read v. Hodgins*.[215] However, the charitable nature of such gifts was examined in detail by the Court of Exchequer in *Attorney General v. Delaney*,[216] in which it was held that a bequest for masses to be said for the repose of the soul of the testatrix and her brother was not charitable on the basis that there was no stipulation that the masses be said in public. Palles CB commented that if the will had prescribed that the masses should be celebrated in public, he would have accepted them as being charitable. This reasoning suggested that the charitable nature of

---

209. *The Law Relating to Charities in Ireland* (1957) p. 53.
210. [1919] AC 815.
211. [1934] Ch 162.
212. [1949] AC 426.
213. [1990] Ch 1. See Hopkins [1989] CLJ 373; Parry [1989] Conv 453.
214. (1828) 7 Ir Eq R 34n.
215. (1844) 7 Ir Eq R 17.
216. (1875) IR 10 CL 104.

such gifts depended on whether a stipulation was made that they be said in public, although in a number of subsequent cases, gifts of this nature failed even where the inference was that they should be celebrated in public.[217] This misinterpretation of the judgment of Palles CB was particularly evident in the decision of *Kehoe v. Wilson*,[218] where a bequest for masses 'to be celebrated in Ireland in a church open for public worship at the time of such celebration' was held not to be charitable. The view that where a gift contained a direction that the masses be celebrated in public such gifts should be regarded as charitable was however re-affirmed by the decision of the Irish Court of Appeal in *Attorney General v. Hall*.[219]

The question of the charitable nature of gifts for the saying of masses, whether in private or in public was finally resolved by the Irish Court of Appeal in *O'Hanlon v. Logue*.[220] A testatrix devised and bequeathed her property on certain trusts and then on trust to sell it and invest the proceeds and pay the income thereof from time to time to the Roman Catholic Primate of all Ireland for the time being for the celebration of masses for the repose of the souls of her late husband, her children and herself, the will containing no direction that these masses be said in public. The Court of Appeal upheld the charitable nature of the gift and made it clear that a bequest for the saying of masses, whether in public or not, constituted a valid charitable gift. In what was described by Brady[221] as 'a remarkable *volte face*' since his judgment in *Delaney*, Palles CB concluded that the view which he had expressed in the earlier case, that the only element of public benefit in the celebration of the mass is the edification of the congregation, was too narrow and failed to appreciate it 'as a gift from God'. This decision has been followed on a number of occasions,[222] and the issue was put beyond doubt by the enactment of section 45(2) of the Charities Act 1961, which reads as follows:

> For the avoidance of the difficulties which arise in giving effect to the intentions of donors of certain gifts for the purpose of the advancement of religion and in order not to frustrate those intentions and notwith-

---

217. *Beresford v. Jarvis* (1877) 11 ILTR 128; *M'Court v. Burnett* (1877) 11 ILTR 130.
218. (1880) 7 LR Ir 10. This decision was followed, albeit unwillingly, by Porter MR in *Perry v. Twomey* (1888) 21 LR Ir 480 although Chatterton VC subsequently pointed out in *Healy v. Attorney General* [1902] 1 IR 342, that it was never his intention to depart from the view expressed by Palles CB in *Delaney's* case in relation to the validity of masses celebrated in public.
219. [1897] 2 IR 426.
220. [1906] 1 IR 247.
221. *Religion and the Law of Charities in Ireland* (1976) p. 81.
222. *Re Gibbons* [1917] 1 IR 448 and *Re Howley* [1940] IR 109, although in *Re Howley* Gavan Duffy J made some rather confusing remarks (at 116) to the effect that a gift for masses, though charitable, might nonetheless fail if too remote. This suggestion would seem to be at odds with the charitable nature of the gift.

standing that certain gifts for the purpose aforesaid, including gifts for the celebration of Masses, whether in public or private, are valid charitable gifts, it is hereby enacted that a valid charitable gift for the purpose of the advancement of religion shall have effect and as respects it having effect, shall be construed in accordance with the laws, canons, ordinances and tenets of the religion concerned.

Gifts to Religious Orders

Historically there were a number of differences between gifts in favour of male religious orders and female ones. The effect of section 28 of the Roman Catholic Relief Act 1829 was that certain male religious orders such as the Jesuits were regarded as illegal, with the consequence that any gift to these orders was also tainted with illegality and void at law. These disabilities were not removed until the enactment of section 5 of the Government of Ireland Act 1920, which impliedly repealed them. The question of whether gifts to such orders could be considered charitable in nature arose in the case of *Re Byrne*,[223] where a testator directed that his residuary estate be given 'for the absolute use and benefit of the Jesuit Order in Ireland.' It was held by Johnston J that the bequest was not illegal but that it was not a charitable bequest and was void for uncertainty. On appeal, the majority of the Supreme Court held that the gift to the order was not a charitable legacy on the basis that the work of the order while largely charitable, was not exclusively so, although the gift was upheld as a valid gift of a non-charitable nature for the benefit of an ascertainable class of persons.[224] Kennedy CJ dissented, stating that bequests to religious institutions for religious purposes were *prima facie* charitable and concluded that the activities carried out by the Jesuits were clearly charitable in a legal sense.

While the disabilities imposed by the Roman Catholic Relief Act 1829 did not apply to religious orders of women,[225] gifts to such orders of a continuing nature might still fail at common law if the purposes of the order were not exclusively charitable. This problem was particularly evident in relation to contemplative orders on the grounds that they did not fulfil the necessary public benefit requirement. In these circumstances, the only possible solution was to uphold the gift on the basis that it was a valid gift for the benefit of those members of the community alive at the time of the testator's death. This point is well illustrated by the decision of Wickens VC in the English case of *Cocks v. Manners*,[226] which also proved to be of considerable

---

223. [1935] IR 782. See also *Re Keogh's Estate* [1945] IR 13.
224. See further *supra* Chapter 9. This result would now probably be avoided as a result of the operation of s. 49(1) of the Charities Act 1961.
225. See s. 37 of the Act of 1829.
226. (1871) LR 12 Eq 574.

importance in this jurisdiction. A testatrix directed that her property should be sold and after the payment of certain legacies that the proceeds should be distributed among certain specified religious institutions. Wickens VC held that a gift to the Sisters of Charity at a specified place payable to the superior for the time being was a good charitable gift. He considered that it was a 'voluntary association for the purpose of teaching the ignorant and nursing the sick' and said that it could not be distinguished in this respect from other types of voluntary associations performing charitable functions. However, the other bequest to a Dominican convent payable to the superior for the time being was not held to be charitable on the basis that the community had 'none of the requisites of a charitable institution' whether the word was used in its popular or legal sense. As Wickens VC commented: 'It is said ... that religious purposes are charitable, but that can only be true as to religious services tending directly or indirectly towards the instruction or the edification of the public'.[227] However, he held that this gift was valid as a good non-charitable gift, payable to the superior for the time being for the benefit of the existing members of the order, on the grounds that there was nothing to prevent them spending it as they pleased.

This finding that contemplative religious orders were not charitable in nature was applied in Ireland. As O'Connor MR stated in *Commissioners of Charitable Donations and Bequests v. McCartan*:[228]

> Monasteries of men and women are often, if not mostly, institutions, the members of which devote their lives exclusively to acts of piety such as pious meditation, prayer and self denial. Such institutions, however praiseworthy, are not charitable in the sense recognised by this Court.

In view of this approach the only way of establishing the validity of gifts to contemplative orders at that time was to apply the reasoning of Wickens VC in *Cocks v. Manners* and to interpret them as being to the community as it existed at the time of the testator's death, i.e. as a gift to the individual nuns of whom the community happened to consist at that time. This approach can be seen in *Re Wilkinson's Trusts*,[229] where the Irish Court of Appeal upheld a bequest to a superioress of a convent solely for the purposes of the convent on this basis. However, as has been seen, it was not always possible to place such a construction on a gift and where it is interpreted as being a gift to those

---

227. *Ibid.* at 585. See also the *dicta* of Fitzgibbon LJ in *Re Wilkinson's Trusts* (1857)19 LR Ir 531, 539.
228. [1917] 1 IR 388, 396.
229. (1887) 19 LR Ir 531. See also *Re Delany's Estate* (1882) 9 LR Ir 226; *Bradshaw v. Jackman* (1887) 21 LR Ir 12.

individuals who may successively become members of the community it will be void on the grounds of perpetuity.[230]

However, the view that contemplative religious orders did not provide some benefit to the community was questioned by Black J in *Munster and Leinster Bank Ltd v. Attorney General*,[231] and the issue arose directly before the High Court in the case of *Maguire v. Attorney General*.[232] The testatrix directed in her will that a sum of money be spent founding a convent 'of perpetual adoration' in a specified place or elsewhere as the trustees might determine. In the course of a detailed examination of the issues involved, Gavan Duffy J stated that it was a 'grave discredit to the law that there should, in this Catholic country, be any doubt about the validity of [such a bequest].'[233] He said that it had been assumed that the decision in *Cocks v. Manners* had decided as a matter of law that a testamentary gift to a contemplative order of nuns could not be charitable on the grounds that the public was not edified by the gift. However, Gavan Duffy J regarded it as a decision on a question of fact; that while at that time the public would not have been edified by private prayer unaccompanied by external works of charity, there was no reason for attributing the same outlook to public opinion in Ireland at the time when he was considering the case. As he stated: 'The finding, or assumption, in *Cocks v. Manners* that the convent of a contemplative community tended neither directly nor indirectly towards public edification has no scintilla of authority as a determinant of the actual position among us.'[234] Gavan Duffy J therefore upheld the gift as charitable by employing the reasoning of Palles CB in *O'Hanlon v. Logue*, without directly overruling *Cocks v. Manners*.[235]

Doubts were raised about the validity of the decision of Gavan Duffy J when the House of Lords held in *Gilmour v. Coats*[236] that a gift to a Carmelite priory which consisted of a community of cloistered nuns was not charitable as it lacked the necessary element of public benefit.[237] In addition, in *Re*

---

230. *Stewart v. Green* (1871) IR 5 Eq 470. See also *Morrow v. M'Conville* (1883) 11 LR Ir 236. See further *supra* Chapter 9.
231. [1940] IR 19, 30.
232. [1943] IR 238.
233. *Ibid.* at 244.
234. *Ibid.* at 248-249.
235. It is interesting to note that Brady, while acknowledging the provisions of Article 44.1.2 of the Constitution as it then existed, has commented that 'It is difficult to avoid the inference that while all recognised religions might now be equal before the law, the Roman Catholic religion, in Gavan Duffy J's view, was more equal than all the others.' *Religion and the Law of Charities in Ireland* (1976) p. 92.
236. [1949] AC 426.
237. This approach was applied by Lord MacDermott LCJ in *Trustees of the Congregation of Poor Clares v. Commissioner of Valuation* [1971] NI 174, 176. See also the *dicta* of Lowry J in *Commissioner of Valuation v. Trustees of the Redemptorist Order* [1971] NI 114, 169 that '[i]t is....clear that an order which has no other purpose than to achieve its own sanctification by private prayer and contemplation is not an

Keogh's Estate,[238] in considering the validity of gifts to the superioress of a Carmelite convent and to the prior of an order of Carmelite fathers, Overend J said that whether or not these gifts could be supported as charitable gifts, they could be upheld as valid gifts to the individuals comprising the communities in the manner laid down in *Re Wilkinson's Trusts*.[239] As a result of this uncertainty, legislation drafted in 1954 included a provision to confirm the charitable status of contemplative religious orders, although as Brady[240] points out, the legislation never progressed beyond its formal introduction in the Dáil.

The subsequent decision of Dixon J in *Bank of Ireland Trustee Co. Ltd v. Attorney General*[241] allayed these fears to an extent when he declined to follow the decision in *Gilmour* and held that a gift to be applied to the repair and/or improvement of a convent of a contemplative order of nuns was charitable. However, it was still felt that the matter should be put beyond doubt by legislation and section 45(1) of the Charities Act 1961 now provides as follows:

> In determining whether or not a gift for the purpose of the advancement of religion is a valid charitable gift it shall be conclusively presumed that the purpose includes and will occasion public benefit.

Gifts for Churches and Other Miscellaneous Purposes

Gifts for the erection or maintenance of the fabric of a church building or its fixtures and fittings will be upheld as charitable. So a gift to a named church,[242] or to build a parsonage in connection with a church,[243] or for such purposes as the erection of a new altar and altar rails,[244] or the provision and maintenance of seating in a church will be regarded as valid.[245] It was held by O'Connor MR in *Re Greene*[246] that a gift 'for the decoration or improvement of the Roman Catholic Church of the Carmelite Fathers at Clarendon Street, in the

---

association with charitable objects'. However, it should be noted that the majority of the Court of Appeal (Lord MacDermott LCJ and Lowry J; Curran LJ dissented) held that the apostolic functions carried out by the orders in question possessed the necessary public quality.

238. [1945] IR 13.
239. (1887) 19 LR Ir 531.
240. *Religion and The Law of Charities in Ireland* (1976) p. 92. See 184 *Dáil Debates* cols 555-557.
241. [1957] IR 257.
242. *Re Gare* [1952] Ch 80.
243. *Cresswell v. Cresswell* (1868) LR 6 Eq 69.
244. *Re Hawe* (1955) 93 ILTR 175. Although on the facts, the gift failed for remoteness it was contemplated as taking effect on the occurrence of events which might not necessarily occur within the perpetuity period.
245. *Re Raine* [1956] Ch 417.
246. [1914] 1 IR 305.

City of Dublin' was charitable, although difficulties still existed at that time about gifts to benefit such purposes,[247] and in a number of earlier cases gifts for the repair and maintenance of churches belonging to monastic orders had been declared void.[248] O'Connor MR reasoned that the gift in the case before him was not a gift to a monastic community for its own purposes but rather was 'given for the decoration or improvement of a church whose purpose is public worship.'[249] Certainly today there would be no doubts about the legality or charitable nature of such gifts and they would undoubtedly be recognised as valid.

Similarly, gifts for the upkeep of a churchyard or cemetery will be regarded as charitable in nature,[250] whether it is open to persons of all denominations,[251] or possibly, as has been held in England, confined to those of a specific religion.[252] In *Re Quinn*[253] Budd J stated that he could see no real distinction between a gift for the repair and improvement of a church and for a churchyard and concluded that a gift given for the upkeep of a cemetery, open to persons of all denominations, was a gift for the advancement of religion. Even if this were not the case, Budd J was satisfied that the bequest would fall into the fourth category of Lord Macnaghten's classification, as being a gift for other purposes beneficial to the community.

Often this device of making a bequest for the upkeep of an entire churchyard is used as an indirect means of achieving an object of a more specific nature which might otherwise fail.[254] The general view is that gifts for the maintenance or repair of specific vaults or tombs if these are not part of the fabric of a church will not be regarded as charitable at common law. As we have seen above,[255] these may be upheld as valid purpose trusts provided they do not infringe the rule against inalienability or if they are of limited nature and fall within the statutory limits they will be regarded as charitable by virtue of section 50 of the Charities Act 1961.[256]

---

247. See *supra* on gifts to male religious orders at p. 324.
248. *Kehoe v. Wilson* (1880) 7 LR Ir 10; *Liston v. Keegan* (1881) 9 LR Ir 539.
249. [1914] 1 IR 305, 319.
250. *Re Vaughan* (1886) 33 Ch D 187; *Re Pardoe* [1906] 2 Ch 184.
251. *Re Quinn* (1953) 88 ILTR 161.
252. *Re Manser* [1905] 1 Ch 68.
253. (1953) 88 ILTR 161.
254. E.g. *Re Eighmie* [1935] Ch 524. Although often where a gift is given for such a general purpose there will be no means of enforcing any specific direction regarding the upkeep of family graves or tombs. See the *dicta* of Budd J in *Re Quinn* (1953) 88 ILTR 161, 166 and *Re Manser* [1905] 1 Ch 68.
255. Chapter 9.
256. These limits are £60 per year in the case of income, or in any other case, £1,000. The Law Reform Commission has recommended (*The Rule Against Perpetuities and Cognate Rules* LRC 62-2000 paragraph 5.15) that these sums be increased to a limit of £1,000 (€1,270) per year in the case of income and to a limit of £16,000 (€20, 316) on the capital sum (as of the year 2000).

The question of whether residences for priests, clergy and other persons connected with the church qualify as charitable is a difficult one to answer with accuracy, primarily because many of the cases in this area have arisen in the context of whether these premises should be exempt from rates. As Wylie[257] has commented, 'the tests for exemption from rates on the ground of charity are much narrower than those for determining whether or not an object is otherwise charitable.' There is limited authority to support the proposition that gifts for the repair or upkeep of a residence of this nature may be charitable,[258] but the decisions made in a rating context would suggest otherwise. So in *Commissioner of Valuation v. O'Connell*,[259] Palles CB held that a house built by parishioners and used as a residence by a Roman Catholic priest was not exclusively used for charitable purposes so as to be exempt from rates. A similar finding was made in respect of a convent[260] and a basement portion of a church, used as a residence for a sexton on the grounds that it was a separate unit and not indispensably part of the fabric of the church.[261] It should be noted that the changes made by the Valuation Act 2001 to the rating exemptions enjoyed by charities should ensure that a more flexible attitude will be adopted in such cases in the future. 'Charitable organisation' as defined in section 3 of the Act extends to bodies the main objects of which are charitable provided any secondary objects are the attainment of the main objects and an extensive list of property which is not rateable is set out in the Fourth Schedule to the legislation.

4. Trusts for Other Purposes Beneficial to the Community

Introduction

This category can be described as the most difficult of Lord Macnaghten's classes of charitable trust to define and delimit, and embraces purposes which do not fall within any of the three categories already considered but which are nevertheless beneficial to the community in a way recognised by the law as charitable. The view was expressed by Lindley LJ in *Re MacDuff*[262] that Lord Macnaghten did not intend to lay down in *Pemsel's* case that every object of 'public general utility' must necessarily be charitable and this point was developed by Viscount Cave in *Attorney General v. National Provincial and Union Bank of England Ltd*[263] in the following terms:

---

257. *Irish Land Law* (3rd ed., 1997) p. 576. See also Brady (1968) 3 Ir Jur (ns) 215.
258. *Attorney General v. Bishop of Chester* (1785) 1 Bro CC 444.
259. [1906] 2 IR 479.
260. *Good Shepherd Nuns v. Commissioner of Valuation* [1930] IR 646.
261. *Mulholland v. Commissioner of Valuation* (1936) 70 ILTR 253.
262. [1896] 2 Ch 451, 466.
263. [1924] AC 262, 265. See also *Williams v. IRC* [1947] AC 447, 455 *per* Lord Simonds.

Lord Macnaghten did not mean that all trusts beneficial to the community are charitable, but that there were certain charitable trusts which fell within that category; and accordingly to argue that because a trust is for a purpose beneficial to the community it is therefore a charitable trust is to turn round his sentence and to give it a different meaning. So here it is not enough to say that the trust in question is for public purposes beneficial to the community or is for the public welfare; you must also show it to be a charitable trust.

A more flexible interpretation was placed on the *dicta* of Lord Macnaghten more recently by Russell LJ in *Incorporated Council for Law Reporting for England and Wales v. A.G.*,[264] where he suggested that in substance the position is that if a purpose is shown to be of sufficient benefit or utility to the community, it is *prima facie* charitable in law.[265] Here the Court of Appeal held unanimously that the purpose of providing law reports was charitable under the fourth head of Lord Macnaghten's classification; as Russell LJ commented such an object 'cannot be thought otherwise than beneficial to the community and of general public utility'.

However, the view expressed by Russell LJ has not met with universal approval and Dillon J subsequently commented in *Re South Place Ethical Society*[266] that it was not in line with earlier judicial statements[267] and that the approach to be adopted in considering whether something is within the fourth category 'is the approach of analogy from what is already stated in the preamble to the Statute of Elizabeth or from what has already been held to be charitable within the fourth category.'

Public Benefit

One of the primary difficulties in laying down guidelines as to the type of trust which may qualify under this heading is the perennial question of the necessary element of public benefit. A trust may appear to be one of general public utility but difficulties may arise when its application is confined to a limited group of persons. Hart J drew attention to this difficulty when he commented in *Bath & North Eastern Somerset Council v. Attorney General*[268] that in order to satisfy the public benefit test in this fourth category '[f]irst,

---

264. [1972] Ch 73.
265. As Gault J recently commented in *Commissioner of Inland Revenue v. Medical Council of New Zealand* [1997] 2 NZLR 297, 302 few institutions having objects of general public utility have been held not to be within the 'spirit and intendment' of the Preamble of the Statute of Charitable Uses Act 1601.
266. [1980] 1 WLR 1565, 1574.
267. Dillon J referred to the *dicta* of Lord Simonds in *Williams v. IRC* [1947] AC 447, 455.
268. [2002] EWCA 1623 (Ch), 31 July 2002.

the purpose itself must be beneficial as one of public utililty; and secondly, the benefit of the purpose must be available to a sufficient section of the community.' As we have seen above the test laid down by Viscount Simonds in *Oppenheim v. Tobacco Securities Trust Co. Ltd*[269] required that for a group of persons to constitute a 'section of the community', it must not be numerically negligible, and the quality which distinguishes these persons from other members of the community must be one which does not depend on their relationship to a particular individual.[270]

One view is that the application of the public benefit requirement to trusts falling within this fourth category should be more strictly enforced than in the other categories. This view is illustrated by a statement made by Babington LJ in *Trustees of the Londonderry Presbyterian Church House v. Commissioners of Inland Revenue* [271] to the effect that in this category 'there can be no charity until it is shown that the gift is to or for the benefit of the public or a section of the public'. Similar sentiments were expressed by Lord Somervell and Viscount Simonds in *IRC v. Baddeley*,[272] in which the majority of the House of Lords held that a trust to provide, *inter alia*, for recreational facilities for Methodists resident in a particular area of London did not fulfil the public benefit requirement and so was not a valid trust. Lord Somervell stated as follows:

> I cannot accept the principle submitted by the respondents that a section of the public sufficient to support a valid trust in one category must as a matter of law be sufficient to support a trust in any other category. I think that difficulties are apt to arise if one seeks to consider the class apart from the particular nature of the charitable purpose. They are, in my opinion, interdependent. There might well be a valid trust for the promotion of religion benefiting a very small class. It would not follow that a recreation ground for the exclusive use of the same class would be a valid charity. ...[273]

An alternative view was favoured by Lord Reid in his dissenting speech which

---

269. [1951] AC 297, 306. See also the *dicta* of Lord Greene MR in *Re Compton* [1945] Ch 123, 131.

270. It should be noted that in the decision of the New Zealand Court of Appeal in *Latimer v. Commissioner of Inland Revenue* [2002] 3 NZLR 195 Blanchard J stated that the common descent of the Maoris was 'a relationship poles away from the kind of connection which the House of Lords must have been thinking of in the *Oppenheim* case'. In his view there was no indication that the House of Lords had tribal or clan groups in contemplation when laying down this test and the Court of Appeal was satisfied that the Maori beneficiaries constituted a section of the community.

271. [1946] NI 178, 196-197.

272. [1955] AC 572.

273. *Ibid.* at 615. See also the *dicta* of Viscount Simonds at 592.

is founded on the premise that the definition of the class of persons necessary to constitute a sufficient section of the community to satisfy the public benefit requirement should not vary from one category to the other.[274] Lord Reid rejected the suggestion that, for example, the members of one particular religion might constitute a 'section of the community' for one charitable purpose and yet be regarded merely as 'a fluctuating body of private individuals' for another charitable purpose.

An attempt to rationalize this whole question was made by Lord Cross in *Dingle v. Turner*,[275] where he stated as follows:

> In truth, the question of whether or not the potential beneficiaries of a trust can fairly be said to constitute a section of the public is a question of degree and cannot be, by itself, decisive of the question whether the trust is a charity. Much must depend on the purpose of the trust. It may well be that, on the one hand, a trust to promote some purpose, *prima facie* charitable, will constitute a charity even though the class of potential beneficiaries might fairly be called a private class, and that on the other hand, a trust to promote another purpose, also *prima facie* charitable, will not constitute a charity even though the class of potential beneficiaries might seem to some people fairly describable as a section of the public.[276]

This approach has met with both academic[277] and judicial approval and as Carswell J stated in *Re Dunlop*,[278] if it is recognised that the manner in which the essential benefit to the public is effected varies as between the different categories of charity, it becomes easier to determine the existence of this element when examining a trust. Carswell J continued:

> The essence of the charitable nature [of trusts within Lord Macnaghten's fourth category] is that the beneficiaries should not be a private class, nor should any limitations be placed upon the gift which would prevent the public as a whole from enjoying the advantage which the donor intends to provide for the benefit of all of the public. It would be quite consonant with this concept that it should be more difficult for a trust under the fourth head to satisfy the requirements of public benefit, and

---

274. See also the judgment of Andrews LCJ in *Trustees of the Londonderry Presbyterian Church House v. Commissioners of Inland Revenue* [1946] NI 178, 190.
275. [1972] AC 601. See also the dissenting judgment of Lord MacDermott in *Oppenheim v. Tobacco Securities Trust Co. Ltd* [1955] AC 297.
276. *Ibid.* at 624. Quoted with approval by Gibson LJ in *Springhill Housing Action Committee v. Commissioner of Valuation* [1983] NI 184, 191.
277. See Jones [1974] CLJ 63, 65.
278. [1984] NI 408. See Dawson [1987] Conv 114.

that a bridge to be used only by Methodists should fail to qualify where a gift for the education of the children of members of that church might be a valid charity.[279]

In *Dunlop* Carswell J was required to consider the validity of a trust to found or assist in the founding of a home for 'Old Presbyterian Persons'. He held that the object was, subject to the satisfaction of the requirement of public benefit, a valid charitable gift for the relief of the aged as it relieved a need attributable to the condition of the persons to be benefited. Carswell J concluded that the public benefit requirement had been satisfied and that the gift could not be regarded as a private benefaction. The fact that the people who would derive benefit from the trust were to be Presbyterians rather than any other denomination did not, in his view, negative the paramountcy of the public purpose of assistance for the aged.[280] In the opinion of Carswell J, the members of the Presbyterian Church were 'sufficiently defined and identifiable by a common quality of a public nature' and accordingly constituted a section of the public at large 'certainly for the purposes of a gift under Lord Macnaghten's first head'. It should be pointed out that in England the words aged, impotent and poor in the Preamble to the Statute of Charitable Uses have been read disjunctively and Carswell J had earlier expressed the view that the almost non-existent public benefit test in relation to trusts for poor relations and poor employees should not extend 'to the whole of Lord Macnaghten's first head' viz., trusts for the aged and impotent as well. However, the manner in which he stated his conclusion would suggest that the gift in the case before him probably qualified as a charitable trust under this first heading, to which a less strict public benefit test applied than that which he had suggested should be employed in relation to trusts falling into Lord Macnaghten's fourth category.

The extent of the public benefit requirement in this fourth category of charitable trusts has been considered in this jurisdiction in *Re Worth Library*,[281] in which Keane J examined two alternative submissions advanced by counsel for the plaintiff as to why the original gift should qualify as being within the fourth category of Lord Macnaghten's classification. While Keane J accepted that a gift for a library might be charitable in nature as being for the public benefit, he was satisfied that the relevant authorities had made it clear that such a gift was not charitable *per se*.[282] The bequest therefore failed to satisfy

---

279. *Ibid.* at 426.
280. It should be noted that by the time of the testator's death it was no longer practicable to use the properties envisaged by him for the purpose suggested and the court directed the preparation of a cy-près scheme.
281. [1995] 2 IR 301.
282. In this context, he referred to *Carne v. Long* (1860) 2 De GF & J 75 and *Re Prevost* [1930] 2 Ch 383.

the public benefit requirement as it was to provide a library for the physician, surgeon and chaplain of the hospital 'who alone would have access to the room in which the library was housed'.[283] Keane J then proceeded to consider whether a gift of a library such as the one at issue which was expressed to be for the benefit of named office holders in the hospital only, could be regarded as being for the benefit of the hospital generally and hence charitable.[284] Keane J rejected counsel's suggestion that the directions contained in the will regarding access to the books being restricted to named office holders was a precatory condition only, and concluded that these were directions 'which the testator wished to be complied with to the letter'.

Given the tenor of his approach to the whole question of public benefit, Keane J then reached a somewhat surprising conclusion. While the library itself would not have been of significant practical benefit to the office holders given the nature of the topics to which these books related, Keane J was of the view that the library itself 'in its beautiful setting would have provided a haven of quiet intellectual relaxation for the beneficiaries.'[285] He therefore concluded that the bequest of the library played a role in the advancement of the charity represented by the hospital and as such constituted a valid charitable bequest for the benefit of that institution within the fourth category of Lord Macnaghten's classification.

It is fair to say that this conclusion is certainly not in keeping with the general principles laid down by Carswell J in *Re Dunlop*, and that the result in that decision, as in *Worth*, was not altogether in line with the strictness of the public benefit requirement which it is theoretically necessary to overcome. One must question the reason why Keane J saw fit effectively to modify this stringent public benefit requirement in relation to trusts 'for other purposes beneficial to the community' in finding that the bequest in *Re Worth Library* was a valid charitable bequest for the benefit of the hospital. At this point the question of the rationale behind applying such a stringent public benefit requirement might also be raised. The answer probably lies in the statement made by Lord Cross in the course of his judgment in *Dingle v. Turner*,[286] that 'in answering the question whether any given trust is a charitable trust, the courts ... cannot avoid having regard to the fiscal privileges accorded to charities'. As we have seen above, Lord Cross commented that the issues of

---

283. Keane J concluded that the wording used by Dr Worth in directing that catalogues of the books contained in the library be compiled suggested that his primary concern was to ensure the security of the books rather than to facilitate scholars who might wish to peruse them.

284. It has been accepted that a gift for the benefit of a hospital is charitable in nature. See *Barrington's Hospital v. Commissioner of Valuation* [1957] IR 299; *Re McCarthy* [1958] IR 311; *Gleeson v. Attorney General* High Court 1972 No. 2664 Sp (Kenny J) 6 April 1973.

285. *Ibid.* at 340.

286. [1972] AC 601, 624.

validity and fiscal immunity were closely connected and he seemed to accept that the decisions in cases such as *Re Compton*[287] and *Oppenheim v. Tobacco Securities Trust Co. Ltd*[288] were influenced by the fact that if the trusts at issue had been declared valid charitable trusts, they would have enjoyed a perceived 'undeserved fiscal immunity'.

Certainly it would appear that the overriding consideration in the mind of Keane J when deciding the question of the charitable status of the bequest in *Worth* seemed to be the desirability of finding it to be a charitable trust so that the court could apply the property cy-près rather than the issue of the fiscal privileges which would accompany such status. In view of the rather artificial straining of the traditional understanding of what is legally charitable which was necessary to reach such a result, a better approach might be the adoption of the solution proposed by the Radcliffe Commission,[289] namely to provide that only certain charities, which were clearly of obvious benefit to the public at large, should enjoy the fiscal privileges associated with charitable status.[290] On balance the suggestion of the Radcliffe Commission, if it were to avoid the distortion of the concept of public benefit in cases such as *Worth*, might lead to a more consistent application of principle. Even if one were to accept that the public benefit test in relation to trusts in the fourth *Pemsel* category is no more stringent than in the others, it is difficult to justify the finding that a bequest for the benefit of three named office holders in a hospital could be of real benefit to the community generally. The 'charitable' nature of the bequest in a popular as opposed to a legal sense and the desirability of framing a cy-près scheme in the *Worth* case was never called into question and yet the fact that Keane J found it necessary to go through the motions of applying and ultimately satisfying the public benefit requirement illustrate the anomalies which the current legal position may create.

---

287. [1945] Ch 123.
288. [1951] AC 297.
289. Cmnd 9474, Chapter 7. The Commission stated: 'In our view what is amiss in the present system is not the idea of giving income tax relief in respect of charity but the undue width of the range of what ranks as a charity for this purpose.' (Paragraph 170). 'We conclude ... that there would be no insuperable difficulty in producing a statutory definition of charity for tax purposes that would at any rate correspond more closely than the present with the accepted idea of what charity is.' (Paragraph 173)
290. Bright in [1989] Conv 28, 41 argued that 'the way ahead is to separate entitlement to fiscal privilege from entitlement to essential validity and charitable status'. It is also interesting to note that Brady, writing over 20 years ago, remarked that the effect of the comments of the Law Lords in *Dingle v. Turner* might prompt legislation separating the fiscal and non-fiscal privileges consequent upon charitable status, but this has not occurred. See Brady (1976) 27 NILQ 198, 214. The alternative argument, expressed by the Newark Committee (Cmnd 396, paragraph 18) that such a separation would be 'manifestly inconvenient' must also be considered.

*'For Other Purposes Beneficial to the Community' — an Objective or
Subjective Test?*

There has traditionally been a divergence in the position adopted by the
judiciary in Ireland and England in relation to the test which should be applied
by the courts in determining whether a purpose satisfies the requirement of
being 'beneficial to the community' to the extent that it may be regarded as
being charitable in law. The Irish authorities suggest that a subjective test
should be applied and that due weight should be given to the donor's view of
the charitable nature of his bequest provided that this purpose is not obviously
illegal or immoral. However, the accepted approach now in England and
Northern Ireland is to adopt an objective test and allow the court to form an
opinion on the issue based upon the evidence before it. Keane J remarked in
Re Worth Library that as the objects under consideration in the case before
him were such that an appreciable number of reasonable people would consider
them to be charitable, it was not necessary for him to express any firm view
on the divergence of opinion referred to above. However, it is interesting to
note that the comments which he made would support the view that the court
should give due weight to a donor's intentions in these circumstances.

The most important authority in the area in an Irish context is the decision
of *Re Cranston*,[291] in which the Irish Court of Appeal was required to decide
whether gifts for certain vegetarian societies were charitable in nature. The
majority of the court upheld the conclusion reached by Porter MR that the
objects of the societies could be said to be charitable within the legal sense of
the term. Fitzgibbon LJ clearly believed that the view of the donor should be
decisive in determining whether a gift fell within the category of 'other
purposes beneficial to the community', provided that this purpose is not
immoral nor illegal. He stated:

> What is the tribunal which is to decide whether the object is a beneficent
> one? It cannot be the individual mind of a judge, for he may disagree,
> *toto caelo*, from the testator as to what is or is not beneficial. On the
> other hand, it cannot be the *vox populi*, for charities have been upheld
> for the benefit of insignificant sects, and of peculiar people. It occurs to
> me that the answer must be — that the benefit must be one which *the
> founder* believes to be of public advantage, and his belief must be at
> least rational, and not contrary either to the general law of the land, or to
> the principles of morality. A gift of such a character, dictated by
> benevolence, believed to be beneficent, devoted to an appreciably
> important object, and neither *contra bonos mores* nor *contra legem*,
> will in my opinion, be charitable in the eye of the law, as settled by

---

291. [1898] 1 IR 431.

decisions which bind us. It is not for us to say that these have gone too far.[292]

A similar view was taken by Barton J in *Shillington v. Portadown UDC*,[293] in which he concluded that benefits which the testator wished to confer on residents of his native town and its locality were 'such as he believed to be of public advantage'. As, in his view, this belief was rational and not illegal nor immoral, Barton J accepted that the bequest constituted a valid charitable gift.

While this subjective approach was at one time favoured in England,[294] it would now appear in that jurisdiction at any rate that the donor's intentions and beliefs as to the charitable nature of the bequest which he is making are not factors which a court may take into consideration. This view is well illustrated by the statements made by Russell J in *Re Hummeltenberg*.[295] He referred to the views of the majority judges in the Irish Court of Appeal in *Re Cranston*, and stated that although he agreed with them in so far as they declared that the personal or private opinion of the judge was immaterial, he disagreed with them to the extent that they suggested that it was for the creator of the trust to determine whether the purpose is beneficial to the public. In the view of Russell J 'the question whether a gift is or may be operative for the public benefit is a question to be answered by the court by forming an opinion upon the evidence before it.'[296] This approach was endorsed by Lord Hanworth MR in *Re Grove-Grady*,[297] where he said that the court must decide whether benefit to the community had been established and the courts in Northern Ireland have also adopted this objective approach.[298]

Although the views expressed by Keane J in *Re Worth Library* on this question were merely *obiter* and the objects put forward to the court, of the advancement of learning and of hospitals, would probably have been seen as

---

292. *Ibid.* at 446-447. Walker LJ also placed emphasis on the fact that the motive of the donor in making the bequest was to benefit mankind generally. He did comment that there may be cases in which the court might allow its own views to override those of a donor, even where the gift was not illegal, immoral or contrary to public policy, but he was satisfied that this was not such a case (at 450).
293. [1911] 1 IR 247. See also *Attorney General v. Becher* [1910] 2 IR 251; *Re Ni Brudair* High Court 1976 No. 93 Sp (Gannon J) 5 February 1979.
294. *Re Foveaux* [1895] 2 Ch 501, 507.
295. [1923] 1 Ch 237.
296. *Ibid.* at 242. Cited with approval by Megaw J in *Re Lester* [1940] NI 92,103. See also the *dicta* of Lord Simonds in *National Anti-Vivisection Society v. IRC* [1948] AC 31, 65-66.
297. [1929] 1 Ch 557, 572. In this regard he cited with approval the statement made by Holmes LJ in his dissenting judgment in *Re Cranston* that the issue 'does not depend on the view entertained by any individual — either by the judge who is to decide the question, or by the person who makes the gift'.
298. *Re Lester* [1940] NI 92, 101-105.

being of benefit to the community irrespective of whether a subjective or objective approach had been applied, it is nevertheless of interest to note his views because the same result will not always be arrived at by applying these divergent tests. Keane J stated:

> In every case, the intention of the testator is of paramount importance. If he intended to advance a charitable object recognised as such by the law, his gift will be a charitable gift. In the case of gifts which do not come within the first three categories, the fact that the testator's view as to the public utility of his favoured object — e.g. vegetarianism — is not shared by many people will not of itself prevent it from being, in the eyes of the law, a valid charitable object within the fourth category, provided it is not illegal, irrational or *contra bonos mores*.That, as I understand is the effect of the majority decision of the Irish Court of Appeal in *In re Cranston*.[299]

It is not difficult to envisage circumstances in which a donor's intentions and motives cannot be easily reconciled with those of the court, and public policy and an appreciation of what may be immoral are concepts which may undergo significant change over a period of time. This is aptly illustrated by changing judicial attitudes towards trusts created for the purpose of seeking to bring about the abolition of vivisection.[300]

While the courts in this jurisdiction are unlikely to take a liberal attitude towards the question of what types of trusts might be of an illegal or immoral nature, it would appear that they will continue to apply the *dicta* of Fitzgibbon LJ in *Re Cranston* and give due weight to a donor's intention in deciding the question of whether a trust is likely to benefit the community. This may yet prove to be of crucial importance if they are called upon to make a pronouncement on the charitable nature of bequests to organisations which an appreciable number of so called 'objective' members of society would not consider charitable. Clearly in such circumstances, the divergence of view which Keane J rightly characterised as 'not material' in *Worth* might become highly relevant.

Specific Types of Trusts which may Qualify as being 'For Other Purposes Beneficial to the Community'

The range of trusts which may qualify under this heading is enormous and while it is not possible to classify them strictly under different headings, or to rule out the emergence of previously unrecognised heads of charity, by and

---

299. [1995] 2 IR 301, 335.
300. Considered in detail below, see *Armstrong v. Reeves* (1890) 25 LR Ir 325; *National Anti-Vivisection Society v. IRC* [1948] AC 31.

large the types of trusts which will be enforced fall into one of a number of categories which will be considered below. One general point which was clarified by Lord Macnaghten in *Pemsel's*[301] case in a manner which seems to have met with subsequent judicial approval is that 'trusts [in this fourth category] are not the less charitable in the eye of the law, because incidentally they benefit the rich as well as the poor. ...' This approach was confirmed in this jurisdiction by the Irish Court of Appeal in *Re Cranston*.[302] So while it would appear that a trust which will benefit a category of persons under the fourth heading does not need to benefit the poor to the exclusion of the rich,[303] and the fact that rich and poor alike may benefit does not generally appear to be an issue,[304] a trust of this nature which will exclusively benefit the rich will not be charitable.[305]

Gifts for the Aged, the Disabled and the Sick

While the preamble to the English Statute of Charitable Uses refers to 'the relief of aged, impotent and poor people' the Irish statute specifically mentions 'the relief or maintenance of any manner of poor, succourless, distressed or impotent persons.' In the context of the English statute, it has been held that these words should be read disjunctively[306] and this approach now appears to be well established. In *Re Robinson*[307] Vaisey J upheld the validity of a bequest to 'old people over 65 years' in a certain district on the basis that 'old people over 65 years in a particular parish are a class of persons just as much objects of charity as the poor of the parish or the sick of the parish.'[308] Similarly, in *Re Glyn's Will Trusts*,[309] Danckwerts J confirmed that elderly people need not necessarily be poor to benefit from a charitable trust.

This issue does not arise in relation to the interpretation of the Irish statute

---

301. [1891] AC 531, 583.
302. [1898] 1 IR 431. See also *Barrington's Hospital v. Commissioner of Valuation* [1957] IR 299.
303. See *Keren Kayemeth le Jisroel Ltd v IRC* [1931] 2 KB 465, 492. Provided that the poor are not excluded from the ambit of the trust, *Re MacDuff* [1896] 2 Ch 451, 464 *per* Lindley LJ.
304. Although note the findings of Palles CB in *Clancy v. Commissioner of Valuation* [1911] 2 IR 173.
305. *Re MacDuff* [1896] 2 Ch 451, 471 *per* Rigby LJ.
306. *Joseph Rowntree Memorial Trust Hospital Association Ltd v. Attorney General* [1983] Ch 159, 171. As Peter Gibson J commented: 'It would be as absurd to require that the aged must be impotent or poor as it would be to require the impotent to be aged or poor, or the poor to be aged or impotent.' See also *Re Dunlop* [1984] NI 408, 414.
307. [1951] Ch 198.
308. *Ibid.* at 201.
309. [1950] 2 All ER 1150n; [1950] 2 TLR 510.

as the words themselves are framed disjunctively.[310] Although some decisions appear to support the view that it is a sufficient charitable purpose simply to benefit the aged or the sick without more,[311] it is generally accepted that the trust must be for the relief of a need attributable to the condition of the persons to be benefited,[312] a point emphasized by Peter Gibson J in *Joseph Rowntree Memorial Trust Hospital Association Ltd v. Attorney General*,[313] in which a scheme to build self-contained dwellings for the elderly was found to be charitable in nature. Carswell J laid similar stress on the concept of 'relief' in *Re Dunlop*[314] in considering the charitable nature of a trust to the Presbyterian Residential Trust to found or help to found a home for 'Old Presbyterian persons'. Carswell J emphasized that the concept of relief and its connotation of meeting a need was in his view 'preferable to one which would admit as beneficiaries any aged persons, whatever may be the amount of their resources and irrespective of their needs arising from their condition of advancing years'.[315] He concluded that the gift was designed to serve the purpose of benefiting the public by providing accommodation for the relief of a class of persons who require it by reason of their age and it was therefore charitable in nature.

Similarly it has been held that gifts for the relief of the disabled or the sick will qualify under this fourth head of Lord Macnaghten's classification. In *Re Lewis*[316] a bequest to 10 blind girls and 10 blind boys resident in a certain area was upheld by Roxburgh J who stressed that poverty was not an essential ingredient in order for the bequest to qualify as charitable in nature. A gift to the 'sick and wounded' has been found to be charitable[317] and in *Re Chaplin*[318] a gift 'to provide a home of rest that shall afford the means of physical and/or mental recuperation to persons in need of rest by reason of the stress and strain caused or partly caused by the conditions in which they ordinarily live and/or work' was accepted as being charitable as was a gift to a hospital to be applied for the purposes of providing a 'home of rest' for the nurses who worked there.[319]

In *Funnell v. Stewart*[320] the testatrix left her residuary estate to the first

---

310. *Barrington's Hospital v. Commissioner of Valuation* [1957] IR 299, 320 *per* Kingsmill Moore J. See also *Gleeson v. Attorney General* High Court 1972 No.2664 Sp (Kenny J) 6 April 1973 at 11; *Re Worth Library* [1995] 2 IR 301, 339.
311. E.g. *Re Robinson* [1951] Ch 198.
312. E.g. *Re Neal* (1966) 110 SJ 549; *Re Resch's Will Trusts* [1969] 1 AC 514.
313. [1983] Ch 159. See also *DV Bryant Trust Board v. Hamilton City Council* [1997] 3 NZLR 342.
314. [1984] NI 408.
315. *Ibid.* at 414.
316. [1955] Ch 104. See also *Re Elliott* (1910) 102 LT 528.
317. *Re Hillier* [1944] 1 All ER 480.
318. [1933] Ch 115.
319. *Re White's Will Trusts* [1951] 1 All ER 528.
320. [1996] 1 WLR 288.

and second named defendants to further the spiritual work of a faith healing group. Her executors sought to determine whether the disposition created a valid charitable trust. Hazel Williamson QC was satisfied that the substance of the group's work was faith healing. She accepted that it was charitable, either on the basis that faith healing has become a recognised activity of public benefit (although she acknowledged that this might not necessarily have been the case when *Re Hummeltenberg* was decided), or on the basis that the religious nature of the faith healing movement renders its purposes charitable and a sufficient element of public benefit is assumed so as to enable the charity to be recognised by law. On the issue of religion and public/private services she stated that the inclusion of the possibility of private services, 'which could clearly not themselves be charitable' did not prevent the gift from being charitable.

A number of cases in this jurisdiction have established that gifts for the sick or to hospitals are charitable in nature. In *Re McCarthy's Will Trusts*[321] Budd J upheld as valid charitable gifts under this heading a bequest to a society which had as its principal object the care of the sick making pilgrimages to Lourdes and a bequest to a hospital at Lourdes which he described as being for the benefit of the sick and therefore 'clearly charitable'. The most important authority in this area is that of *Barrington's Hospital v. Commissioner of Valuation*,[322] in which the plaintiff hospital sought to challenge the changing of its exemption from rating valuation on the basis that its purposes were exclusively charitable in nature within the meaning of section 63 of the Poor Relief (Ireland) Act 1838. While Kingsmill Moore J accepted that 'charitable purposes' within the meaning of the section has a less extensive meaning than that given to those words in *Pemsel's* case,[323] his judgment nevertheless contains some important statements of general principle. He found that the term 'impotent' includes sick and injured persons and that 'a trust for the care of the sick or the maintenance of a hospital is a charity in the legal meaning of that term.'[324] The real issue which had to be resolved by the Supreme Court was whether the fact that the hospital admitted a number of fee-paying patients could alter this position. The court found that the presence in the hospital of a limited number of patients falling into this category did not detract from the charitable purpose of the institution and concluded that it was used exclusively for charitable purposes within the meaning of the section.[325] However, it is interesting to note that in the course of his judgment Kingsmill Moore J

---

321. [1958] IR 311.
322. [1957] IR 299.
323. *Ibid.* at 333.
324. *Ibid.* at 321.
325. See also *Re Worth Library* [1995] 2 IR 301, 339-340. Although note the findings made by Palles CB in *Clancy v. Commissioner of Valuation* [1911] 2 IR 137 in relation to the charitable status of a hall where a majority of the persons using it paid for the use of the facilities.

commented that 'if a hospital is being conducted exclusively for the well-to-do it ceases to be charitable'[326] and later in his judgment he modified this statement to read 'exclusively or predominantly'.[327]

In practice, the more important issue is probably the destination of any profits which may be derived from the hospital's activities and O'Daly J laid emphasis in *Barrington's* case on the fact that no private profit was derived from the premises by its occupiers. The non-profit making nature of a private hospital also proved to be of relevance in *Re Resch's Will Trusts*,[328] where a gift of the testator's residuary estate to a private non-profit making hospital was upheld as charitable despite the objection that it only provided for 'persons of means'. Lord Wilberforce confirmed that a hospital does not lose its charitable status 'because charges are made to the recipients of benefits' but stressed that a certain type of hospital might not qualify as charitable in nature, either because it 'is carried on commercially, i.e. with a view to making profits for private individuals, or that the benefits it provides are not for the public, or a sufficiently large section of the public to satisfy the necessary tests of public character.'[329] The destination of the profits derived from a private hospital also appeared to be of relevance in *Gleeson v. Attorney General*,[330] which concerned the charitable status of St Vincent's Private Hospital in Dublin which operated in conjunction with a public hospital. Kenny J stated that 'there is ... much to be said for the view that a private nursing home which charges fees and which is run in conjunction with a hospital and whose profits are applied for the purposes of the hospital is a legal charity'.[331] He reiterated that an institution does not cease to be charitable in nature because its activities benefit 'the rich as well as the poor' and concluded that the private hospital was a legally charitable institution.

Finally, it should be noted that Keane J placed a fairly flexible interpretation on the concept of a gift for the benefit of a hospital in *Re Worth Library*.[332] As noted above, Keane J concluded that the bequest of the library played a role in the advancement of the charity represented by the hospital by providing 'a haven of quiet intellectual relaxation' for the named office holders and as such constituted a valid charitable bequest for the benefit of that institution within the fourth category of Lord Macnaghten's classification. While Keane J commented that he did not feel that there was any ground for scepticism as to the capacity of Dr Worth's bequest to play a part in the advancement of the charity represented by the hospital, his conclusion is difficult to reconcile

---

326. [1957] IR 299, 322.
327. *Ibid.* at 334. Relying on *Governors of Royal Victoria Hospital v. Commissioner of Valuation* (1939) 73 ILTR 236.
328. [1969] 1 AC 514.
329. *Ibid.* at 540-541.
330. High Court 1972 No. 2664Sp (Kenny J) 6 April 1973.
331. *Ibid.* at 11.
332. [1995] 2 IR 301.

with his earlier attitude towards the public benefit question and undoubtedly extends present understanding of what might constitute a gift for the benefit of a hospital.

Gifts for Sporting and Recreational Purposes and for the Benefit of a Locality

In this context it may be necessary to draw a distinction between trusts to promote and encourage a particular sport or sports, which have traditionally not been regarded as charitable, and trusts to provide facilities for recreational purposes, which will almost invariably be upheld. So in *Re Nottage*,[333] where a testator had sought to establish a trust to provide a prize for the most successful yacht of the season in order to encourage the sport of yacht racing, the Court of Appeal emphasised that a gift to encourage sport for its own sake was not in itself a charitable one. However a gift of this nature may be upheld where it is part of a more general charitable purpose such as improving the effectiveness of the armed forces. In *Re Gray*[334] a gift to a regimental fund for the promotion of sport[335] was upheld on the basis that it would improve the efficiency of the army. As Romer J commented 'it is to be observed that the particular sports specified were all healthy outdoor sports, indulgence in which might reasonably be supposed to encourage physical efficiency.'[336] Similarly gifts to provide for the promotion of sport in a school,[337] or in educational institutions generally,[338] as we have seen will be regarded as being for the advancement of education.[339] The Goodman Committee[340] in England recommended that the encouragement of sport and recreation should in itself be recognised as a charitable object, provided that the requirement of benefit to the community is satisfied and in Canada it was held in *Re Laidlaw Foundation*[341] that the promotion of amateur athletic sports was charitable as it tended to both promote good health and advance education. It would appear that despite the earlier English authorities, trusts of this nature are likely to be upheld in this jurisdiction, particularly if they can be linked with the provision of recreational facilities.

---

333. [1895] 2 Ch 649. See also *Re Patten* [1929] 2 Ch 276 (a gift to encourage the playing of cricket) and *Laing v. Commissioner of Stamp Duties* [1948] NZLR 154 (rowing, swimming and athletics).
334. [1925] Ch 362.
335. Limited to shooting, fishing, cricket, football and polo.
336. [1925] Ch 362, 365.
337. *Re Mariette* [1915] 2 Ch 284.
338. *IRC v. McMullen* [1981] AC 1.
339. See *supra* pp. 310-311.
340. The Goodman Committee Report on Charity Law and Voluntary Organisations (1976).
341. (1984) 13 DLR (4th) 491. See further Breen (2001) 6 CPLJ 76.

The provision of recreational or leisure facilities such as parks[342] or playing fields[343] have been recognised as charitable objectives and in *Re Morgan*[344] a gift for 'a public recreation ground for amateur activities' for the benefit of a particular parish was upheld. The suggestion was made by Lord MacDermott LCJ in *Commissioner of Valuation v. Lurgan Borough Council*[345] that a distinction must be drawn between the provision of indoor and outdoor facilities and he commented that 'the law does not regard the mere provision of recreational facilities charitable unless they are provided in the open air on land dedicated to the use and enjoyment of the public.' However, this distinction is not supported by authority in this jurisdiction as an examination of the decision of a Divisional Court in *Clancy v. Commissioner of Valuation*[346] shows. The point at issue was whether a hall built with the object of 'promoting temperance among the poor and labouring classes of the town of Sligo and neighbouring districts' and used for such diverse activities as playing billiards and cards and taking baths, was used for exclusively charitable purposes. Persons using the hall were expected to pay an entrance fee; thereafter they were 'put on their honour' to make small contributions if they could afford to do so and the evidence established that more than half of the patrons made such contributions. Palles CB expressed the view that while the user of the hall might have been regarded as being exclusively charitable, the fact that its facilities were open to all, rich and poor alike posed a difficulty, and he concluded that its use by persons not falling within the ambit of the charitable purpose was not 'insignificant or insubstantial'. Gibson J found that the primary object of the institution was charitable as being 'for the moral and educational improvement of its visitors' but he agreed with the finding of Palles CB that its user was not exclusively charitable in nature. While the question was not expressly considered, it would appear that the court implicitly recognised that the provision of recreational facilities for the benefit of the public, whether outdoor or indoor, would be regarded as charitable.

A number of points should be noted about *Clancy's* case which would suggest its general value as a precedent is now limited. First, it was made in the context of a decision on rating, which as has been acknowledged,[347] often involves a more restrictive view of the concept of charitable status than might be employed in relation to a trust or gift. In addition, the fact that certain patrons of the hall paid for the use of the facilities should no longer appear to cause the same difficulty if one accepts by analogy the reasoning employed

---

342. *Brisbane City Council v. Attorney-General for Queensland* [1979] AC 411.
343. *Re Hadden* [1932] 1 Ch 133. The gift was for 'playing fields, parks, gymnasiums or other plans which will give recreation to an many people as possible'.
344. [1955] 1 WLR 738.
345. [1968] NI 104, 125.
346. [1911] 2 IR 173.
347. *Barrington's Hospital v. Commissioner of Valuation* [1957] IR 299, 333.

by the Supreme Court in the context of a hospital which took in fee-paying patients in *Barrington's Hospital v. Commissioner of Valuation*,[348] although it must be acknowledged that these individuals constituted a smaller percentage of the whole than the paying patrons in *Clancy*. A further consideration which would now be of relevance is the potential application to such cases of section 49(1) of the Charities Act 1961 which provides that where the purposes of a gift include charitable and non-charitable objects, its terms shall be construed so as to exclude the non-charitable objects.

It should also be noted that legislation has been introduced in England to regulate the status of trusts for recreational purposes, partly to restore the perceived *status quo* which was threatened by a number of restrictive decisions such as those of the House of Lords in *IRC v. Baddeley*[349] and by the Court of Appeal in Northern Ireland in *Trustees of the Londonderry Presbyterian Church House v. IRC*.[350] Section 1(1) of the Recreational Charities Act 1958 provides that subject to the provisions of the Act, 'it shall be and be deemed always to have been charitable to provide, or assist in the provision of facilities for recreation or other leisure time occupation if the facilities are provided in the interests of social welfare'. The latter requirement will be met if the facilities are provided 'with the object of improving the conditions of life' of those whom they are primarily intended[351] for and 'either (i) those persons have need of such facilities by reason of their youth, age, infirmity or disablement, poverty or social and economic circumstances or (ii) the facilities are to be available to the members or female members of the public at large.'[352] The meaning of these provisions was considered by the House of Lords in *Guild v. IRC*,[353] in which a testator left the residue of his estate to a town council for use in connection with the town's sport centre or for some similar purpose in connection with sport. The House of Lords held that on the true construction of section 1(2)(a) of the Recreational Charities Act 1958, facilities for recreation or other leisure time activities could be provided with the object of improving people's conditions of life notwithstanding that such people were not in a position of relative social disadvantage or suffering from some degree of deprivation. They concluded that the testator's bequest would come within the ambit of section 1(2) of the Act of 1958 and was therefore charitable in nature on the basis that people from all walks of life may have their condition of life improved by the provision of suitable recreational facilities. Similar legislation was introduced in Northern Ireland and was applied in *Springhill Housing Action Committee v. Commissioner of Valuation*,[354] in which a

---

348. [1957] IR 299.
349. [1955] AC 572.
350. [1946] NI 178.
351. S.1(2)(a).
352. S.1(2)(b).
353. [1992] 2 WLR 397.
354. [1983] NI 184.

community centre in the Springhill estate in Belfast was found to be used wholly or mainly for charitable purposes. Gibson LJ stated that he was satisfied that the centre was occupied for a purpose which is normally charitable and the class of persons for whose benefit it was occupied, being the residents of a sizeable estate, was not so insignificant in number as to deprive it of its *prima facie* public character.

Trusts which make provision for the carrying out of public works or the provision of public facilities such as a village club and reading room in a specified area,[355] are recognised as charitable. In addition gifts to a particular locality have traditionally been upheld provided they are of a general character or, where purposes are specified, where these are exclusively charitable in nature. A gift to a church council,[356] or to a town[357] will be upheld where the purposes are confined to general or public purposes beneficial to the community, although a gift to a parish to be applied to 'such public, benevolent or charitable purposes' as the trustees might think proper was construed disjunctively and was not regarded as charitable in nature.[358]

It has recently been suggested by Lord Browne-Wilkinson delivering the judgment of the Privy Council in *Attorney-General of the Cayman Islands v. Wahr-Hansen*[359] that gifts for the benefit of a named locality or its inhabitants have been 'benevolently construed'. The Privy Council rejected the submission that a gift for 'organisations or institutions operating for the public good' not limited to a particular locality should attract such a benevolent construction. In the view of Lord Browne-Wilkinson to apply the principles developed in relation to gifts to a locality to all cases where there are general statements of benevolent or philanthropic objectives so as to restrict the meaning of the words to such objects as are in law charitable would not be permissible.

A decision in this jurisdiction which shows a more flexible approach is *Shillington v. Portadown UDC*,[360] where a gift to an urban council for the purpose of encouraging and providing 'means of healthy recreation' for the residents of an area was found to be charitable, aided by the application of a subjective test to the question of whether the trust was one beneficial to the community. As Barton J stated:

> The testator's purpose was a charitable or public purpose. He wished to benefit the residents of his native town and of its immediate neighbourhood. The benefits which he intended to confer on them were such as

355. *Re Scowcroft* [1898] 2 Ch 638.
356. *Re Norton's Will Trusts* [1948] 2 All ER 842.
357. *Re Allen* [1905] 2 Ch 400.
358. *Houston v. Burns* [1918] AC 337.
359. [2001] 1 AC 75.
360. [1911] 1 IR 247.

he believed to be of public advantage. That belief was rational and not contrary to the laws of the land or the principles of morality.[361]

This broader approach is to be welcomed and an application of the provisions of section 49(1) of the Charities Act 1961 would appear to ensure that trusts of this nature will be upheld in this jurisdiction.

Gifts for the Benefit of Animals

Gifts for the benefit of particular animals are not considered charitable, although as we have seen above,[362] they may be upheld if limited to the perpetuity period as an anomalous exception to the principle that purpose trusts will not be enforced. However, gifts for the welfare of animals generally or for a particular type of animal are recognised as charitable in law.

The rationale behind this finding has varied. In England, the motive of public utility appeared to underlie some of the early decisions in this area,[363] but more recently the idea that kindness towards animals tends to promote the morality of human beings seems to be fundamental to the reasoning employed. In *Re Wedgewood*[364] Swinfen Eady LJ stated as follows:

> A gift for the benefit and protection of animals tends to promote and encourage kindness towards them, to discourage cruelty, and to ameliorate the condition of the brute creation, and thus to stimulate humane and generous sentiments in man towards the lower animals, and by these means promote feelings of humanity and morality generally, repress brutality and thus elevate the human race.

In an Irish context, there is evidence in the judgment of Chatterton VC in *Armstrong v. Reeves*[365] that the motive of safeguarding the welfare of the animals themselves might be sufficient to bring such trusts within the fourth heading of Lord Macnaghten's classification, although the approach in *Wedgewood* appears to have been taken by members of the Irish Court of Appeal in *Re Cranston*,[366] in which Holmes LJ commented: 'If it is beneficial to the community to promote virtue and to discourage vice, it must be beneficial to teach the duty of justice and fair treatment to the brute creation, and to

---

361. [1911] 1 IR 247, 256-257.
362. See *supra* Chapter 9.
363. *London University v. Yarrow* (1857) 1 De G & J 72.
364. [1915] 1 Ch 113, 122. See also the comments of Cozens-Hardy MR to the effect that a trust of this nature tends to 'promote public morality by checking the innate tendency to cruelty.' (at 117)
365. (1890) 25 LR Ir 325.
366. [1898] 1 IR 431.

repress one of the most revolting kinds of cruelty.'[367] Certainly in England the establishment of some benefit to human beings is of paramount importance as was stressed by Russell LJ in *Re Grove-Grady*,[368] where he said that the validity of gifts in favour of animals depends on the question of whether they produce a benefit to mankind.

Whatever the rationale for enforcing trusts of this nature, a variety of different types of gifts have been upheld. These include trusts for the care of specific categories of domestic animals, for example, gifts to a 'Home for Lost Dogs',[369] to 'the Dublin Home for Starving and Forsaken Cats',[370] and 'for the welfare of cats and kittens needing care and attention'[371] have been upheld as charitable. Similarly gifts of a general nature for the protection and benefit of animals,[372] or to a society which possesses such aims,[373] will be upheld, irrespective of whether its activities are confined to the protection of domestic animals or of animals useful to man.[374] In addition, a gift to institutions such as a sanctuary which provides refuge for sick and unwanted animals[375] will be regarded as charitable in nature. However, it is important that such institutions are not intended to be profit-making if they are to qualify for charitable status. As Russell LJ stated in *Re Satterthwaite's Will Trusts*:[376] '*prima facie*, an animal hospital is a charity, as being calculated to promote public morality by encouraging kindness, discouraging cruelty and stimulating humane sentiments to the benefit of mankind; but it lacks the quality of legal charity if it be carried on for private profit as a profession or occupation or trade.'

The object of promoting vegetarianism has been recognised as charitable and in *Re Cranston*[377] the Irish Court of Appeal upheld a gift to named vegetarian societies on the basis of a subjective test as to the element of public benefit which these involved.[378] Clearly the members of the Court of Appeal were not fully convinced of the benefit of such organisations but were satisfied

---

367. *Ibid*. at 457.
368. [1929] 1 Ch 557, 582. See also *National Anti-Vivisection Society v. IRC* [1948] AC 31, 45.
369. *Re Douglas* (1887) 35 Ch D 472.
370. *Swifte v. Attorney General* [1912] 1 IR 133.
371. *Re Moss* [1949] 1 All ER 495.
372. *Re Wedgewood* [1915] 1 Ch 113. See also *Re Green's Will Trusts* [1985] 3 All ER 455.
373. *Armstrong v. Reeves* (1890) 25 LR Ir 325.
374. *Ibid*. at 341 *per* Chatterton VC.
375. *Re Murawski's Will Trusts* [1971] 1 WLR 707.
376. [1966] 1 WLR 277, 284.
377. [1898] 1 IR 431.
378. This finding that vegetarianism was a charitable object was applied in England by Joyce J in *Re Slatter* (1905) 21 TLR 295, without any reference to the different nature of the test employed in this jurisdiction.

that the testator appreciated the benefit to be derived from their activities. As Fitzgibbon LJ commented:

> It is hard to see why the promotion of total abstinence from flesh should not be a 'charitable' object in the legal sense, if we are at liberty to recognise the promotion of total abstinence from intoxicants as charitable; moderation and temperance may be carried to excess, and though the benefits and drawbacks may differ in degree, they seem to be the same in kind. The motives of the promoters of teetotalism and of vegetarianism are equally unselfish, and equally benevolent, and the efforts of vegetarians, so far as I can form a judgment, seem less likely to do mischief than those of anti-vivisectionists, or even than those of the promulgators of the works of Joanna Southcote.[379]

In certain cases trusts which might appear to benefit animals have not been found to be charitable in nature. In *Re Grove-Grady*[380] a testatrix left her residuary estate on trust to found an animal benevolent society the objects of which included the provision of a refuge for the preservation of 'all animals, birds and other creatures not human'. The majority of the Court of Appeal held that the trust was not charitable as it lacked the necessary element of benefit to the community, Russell LJ stating that 'it is merely a trust to secure that all animals within the area shall be free from molestation or destruction by man. It is not a trust directed to ensure absence or diminution of pain or cruelty in the destruction of animal life.'[381] It is possible that such a decision would not be followed in this jurisdiction, particularly in view of the increased importance attached to preserving different species of wildlife,[382] or that alternatively such a trust might be upheld on the basis of its educational value.

Another category of trust which might be said to be of direct benefit to animals and which has met with differing judicial reaction over the last century is that of trusts which aim to abolish vivisection. In *Armstrong v. Reeves*[383] a legacy to the Society for the Abolition of Vivisection was held to be charitable on the grounds that the society was for the public benefit as it tended to correct and prevent cruelty to animals. Chatterton VC rejected the argument that there was something illegal in the nature of the society as one of its aims was to secure the suppression of vivisection by changing the law. In his view it was instead 'a society for the purpose of inducing the legislature by legitimate means, by bringing public opinion to bear, to make certain alterations in the

---

379. *Ibid.* at 447.
380. [1929] 1 Ch 557.
381. *Ibid.* at 585.
382. Note the more recent decision of Holland J in *Attorney General of New South Wales v. Satwell* [1978] 2 NSWLR 200.
383. (1890) 25 LR Ir 325.

law. ...'[384] A similar view was taken by Chitty J in *Re Foveaux*,[385] although more recently in England the House of Lords held in *National Anti-Vivisection Society v. IRC*[386] that the society was not entitled to income tax relief on the grounds that its object was not a charitable one. Faced with a finding of fact made in the lower court that the benefit to humanity in allowing vivisection outweighed the incidental suffering to animals, the House of Lords concluded that a trust which had been found to be detrimental to society could not be charitable merely because of the testator's opinion. The reasoning behind such a conclusion would seem to be that while the protection of animals from cruelty is a charitable purpose, vivisection is a necessary element in medical research and its suppression could not therefore be considered to be beneficial to the community. This point is evident in the judgment of Buckley J in *Re Jenkins's Will Trusts*,[387] where he stated as follows:

> [T]he prohibiting of any forms of cruelty inherent in vivisection, however admirable that may be from an ethical point of view, is not a charitable activity in the contemplation of the law because the court cannot weigh the benefits to the community which result from using animals for vivisection and research against the benefits which would result to the community from preventing such practices.

Gifts for Political Purposes

It is well-established that trusts for the advancement of political purposes are not charitable and as a result gifts for the benefit of specific political parties will clearly not qualify for charitable status.[388] It is often not easy to distinguish trusts which will be accepted as being *bona fide* for the advancement of education from those which are merely disguised as being for such a purpose and are in fact designed to promote political purposes. In *Re Trusts of the Arthur McDougall Fund*[389] a trust for the teaching of political theory was accepted as being educational in nature and in *Re Koeppler's Will Trusts*[390] a bequest to fund the holding of conferences with political themes was also

---

384. *Ibid.* at 339.
385. [1895] 2 Ch 501.
386. [1948] AC 31.
387. [1966] Ch 249, 255.
388. In relation to trusts to support a political party Hammond J has recently commented in the New Zealand decision of *Re Collier* [1998] 1 NZLR 81, 90 that the conclusion that trusts for their benefit are not charitable 'appears to be the agreed position throughout the common law world' and he has stated that he is not aware of any suggestion that any change to this position should be effected.
389. [1957] 1 WLR 81.
390. [1986] Ch 423.

upheld. However, a more borderline case is *Re Scowcroft*[391] in which a gift for the maintenance of a village club and reading room 'for the furtherance of Conservative principles and religious and mental improvement' was found to be charitable, the reasoning employed by Stirling J suggesting that he felt able to make this finding because the purposes of the trust were not predominantly political. A different conclusion was reached in *Re Hopkinson*,[392] where a trust for the advancement of adult education with particular reference to education in the Labour Party's doctrines was found not to be charitable. As Vaisey J commented: 'Political propaganda masquerading — I do not use that word in any sinister sense — as education is not education within the statute of Elizabeth. ... In other words it is not charitable.'[393] This reasoning was applied by Goulding J in *Re Bushnell*,[394] in which a bequest for 'the advancement and propagation of the teaching of socialised medicine' was found to have predominantly political rather than educational objectives and was therefore not charitable in nature. Provided that the predominant motive for a trust is not political, it may often be upheld and as Goulding J commented: 'The existence of some political motive is not necessarily fatal to a good charitable trust'.[395] An excellent summary of what appear to be the applicable principles is provided in *Tudor on Charities*[396] as follows:

> If ... a trust is predominantly political or propagandist, as where the furtherance of the principles of one particular party is, on the true construction of the trust instrument, the main object of the trust, then though it is worded in the terms of an educational trust, and there is provision for lectures and/or discussion classes which are in themselves of an educational character, but subsidiary to the main object, the trust will fail to qualify as a charitable trust for the advancement of education.

The principle that a trust which essentially has political objectives will not be regarded as charitable was confirmed in this jurisdiction in *Re Ní Brudair*,[397] where a gift for the benefit of republicans according to the objects of that movement as they were in the years 1919–1921 was found to be too vague and uncertain to constitute a valid charitable gift. Gannon J concluded that

---

391. [1898] 2 Ch 638.
392. [1949] 1 All ER 346. See also *Bonar Law Memorial Trust v. IRC* (1933) 49 TLR 220.
393. *Ibid.* at 350.
394. [1975] 1 WLR 1596.
395. *Ibid.* at 1603. Approved by Slade J in *McGovern v. Attorney General* [1982] Ch 321, 343. See also *Re Scowcroft* [1898] 2 Ch 638.
396. (8th ed., 1995, Warburton) p. 51.
397. High Court 1976 No. 93 Sp (Gannon J) 5 February 1979. See also *Ganly v. Goff* [1983] ILRM 425.

taking an overall view of the express directions of the testatrix and the 'latitude of apparent duty imposed on her trustees' he was satisfied that there was no charitable intention nor charitable gift in the legal sense in her will. He also commented that even if the testatrix had presented her trustees with the democratic programme of the Dáil of January 1919 by way of directions as to how the money was to be spent this was essentially a statement of broad political objectives and would not constitute a valid charitable trust.

Often trusts for the advancement of political purposes will involve advocating a change in the law and this latter objective provides one of the primary reasons why trusts of this nature will not be regarded as charitable.[398] Lord Parker laid down the reasons for this general principle in *Bowman v. Secular Society Ltd*[399] as follows:

> [A] trust for the attainment of political objects has always been held invalid, not because it is illegal, for everyone is at liberty to advocate or promote by any lawful means a change in the law, but because the court has no means of judging whether a proposed change in the law will or will not be for the public benefit, and therefore cannot say that a gift to secure the change is a charitable gift.

This principle was approved by Lord Simonds in *National Anti-Vivisection Society v. IRC*,[400] where it was held by the House of Lords that the main object of the society was political, namely the abolition of vivisection by means of an alteration in the law, and that for this reason it could not be considered as a body established for charitable purposes only. Similarly, in *R. v. Radio Authority, ex p. Bull*[401] it was held by the Court of Appeal that the promotion the observance of fundamental human rights by campaigning to change the law or government policy was a political object within the meaning of section 92(2)(a)(i) of the Broadcasting Act 1990.[402]

The *dicta* of Lord Parker in *Bowman v. Secular Society Ltd* was analysed further by Slade J in *McGovern v. Attorney General*,[403] which concerned the question of whether a trust created by Amnesty International to achieve certain stated purposes could be registered as a charity. These purposes included the relief of needy persons who were or had been prisoners of conscience and

---

398. As Hammond J recently stated in the New Zealand decision of *Re Collier* [1998] 1 NZLR 81, 89 'the conventional view in the British Commonwealth is that charitable trusts to change the law itself are invalid'.
399. [1917] AC 406, 442.
400. [1948] AC 31.
401. [1998] QB 294.
402. S. 92(2)(a)(i) of the Act of 1990 provided that a licensed independent radio service could not include advertisements inserted by or on behalf of a body whose objects were wholly or mainly of a political character.
403. [1982] Ch 321. See Watkin [1982] Conv 387; Nobles (1982) 45 MLR 704.

their families, attempting to secure the release of such prisoners, procuring the abolition of torture or inhuman or degrading treatment or punishment, the promotion of research into the maintenance and observance of human rights and the dissemination of the results of such research. Slade J concluded that a trust the main objective of which was to secure a change in the laws of a foreign country could not be regarded as charitable because the court would have no means of knowing whether such a change would be for the public benefit and because of public policy considerations based on the risk of prejudicing relations between the countries concerned. Slade J laid down the following general principles:

(1) Even if it otherwise appears to fall within the spirit and intendment of the preamble to the Statute of Elizabeth, a trust for political purposes falling within the spirit of Lord Parker's pronouncement in *Bowman's* case, can never be regarded as being for the public benefit in the manner which the law regards as charitable.

(2) Trusts for political purposes falling within the spirit of this pronouncement include, *inter alia*, trusts of which a direct and principal purpose is either (i) to further the interests of a particular political party; or (ii) to procure changes in the laws of this country; or (iii) to procure changes in the law of a foreign country; or (iv) to procure a reversal of government policy or of particular decisions of governmental authorities in this country; or (v) to procure a reversal of government policy or of particular decisions of governmental authorities in a foreign country.[404]

One further point of importance to be derived from the judgment of Slade J is his comment that if all the main objects of a trust are exclusively charitable, the fact that the trustees may have incidental powers to employ political means to further these objects will not deprive the trust of its charitable status. This approach might allow for some qualification of Lord Parker's *dicta* in *Bowman*, although it should be pointed out that its continued acceptance in England is bound to limit the possibilities of new types of trusts qualifying for charitable status.

A number of recent decisions would suggest that the purpose of aiming to secure peace by a particular means will not be considered charitable as it is political in nature. In the New Zealand decision of *Re Collier*[405] a bequest for the promotion of world peace failed as being overtly political, Hammond J adding that to the extent that soldiers were being encouraged to 'down arms' it also pursued an unlawful aim. In *Southwood v. Attorney General*[406] the

---

404. *Ibid.* at 340.
405. [1998] 1 NZLR 81.
406. Court of Appeal, 28 June 2000. See Garton (2000) 14 Trust Law Int 233.

Court of Appeal held that 'the advancement of education of the public in the subject of militarism and disarmament' was not a charitable purpose. Referring to the *dicta* of Slade J in *McGovern v. Attorney General*, Chadwick LJ stated that cases in which the court will regard the element of public benefit as incapable of proof one way or the other include gifts for 'political objects'. He said that while he would have no difficulty in accepting the proposition that it promotes public benefit for the public to be educated in the differing means of securing peace and avoiding war, there are divergent views on how best to achieve this aim. Chadwick LJ stated as follows:

> The court is in no position to determine that promotion of one view rather than the other is for the public benefit. Not only does the court have no material on which to make that choice; to attempt to do so would be to usurp the role of government. So the court cannot recognize a charitable trust to educate the public to an acceptance that peace is best secured by demilitarization...Nor conversely could the court recognize a charitable trust to educate the public to an acceptance that war is best avoided by collective security through the membership of a military alliance...[407]

Santow's[408] comment that the line between educational and political has become blurred in this context is a fair one. In addition as Martin points out 'it is difficult to answer the criticism that organisations campaigning for improvements in the law cannot be registered as charities, while existing charities can and do campaign for and against change.'[409] This point has been echoed by Hammond J in *Re Collier*[410] where he stated 'why is it that the law allows existing charities to make "political" statements; yet it impugns *ab initio* those which are proposed to be set up to campaign for reform'. Clearly the notion that a 'coherent system of law can scarcely admit that objects which are inconsistent with its own provisions are for the public welfare'[411] is being increasingly called into question and as Hammond J pointed out in *Re Collier* judges themselves often make suggestions for changes in the law. It has been suggested that provided a purpose does not seek to secure a reversal of government policy but rather aims to achieve incremental change in the law in a manner consistent with the direction in which it is going, it may not be treated as political.[412] The Law Reform Committee of the Law Society has

---

407. Paragraph 29.
408. (1999) 52 CLP 255, 276.
409. Hanbury and Martin, *Modern Equity* (16th ed., 2001) p. 424.
410. [1998] 1 NZLR 81, 90.
411. *Per* Dixon J in *Royal North Shore Hospital of Sydney v. Attorney General for New South Wales* (1938) 60 CLR 396, 426.
412. Santow (1999) 52 CLP 255, 282.

also recently recommended that the current absolute prohibition on political advocacy should be reviewed.[413] It is recommended that 'a charity should be able to advocate a change in the law or public policy which can reasonably be expected to help it to achieve its charitable purposes and be allowed to oppose a change in the law or public policy which can reasonably be expected to hinder its ability to do so.'[414] There is clearly increasing dissatisfaction with the scope of Slade J's description of political purposes laid down in *McGovern v. Attorney General* and for this reason groups and organisations which advocate reform of the law should not rule out the possibility that they may qualify for charitable status in the future if these suggestions for reform take root.

CY-PRÈS JURISDICTION

Introduction

Where a gift is made to charity, it may be impossible or impracticable to give effect to the intentions of the donor in the precise terms which he intended. The cy-près doctrine, where it applies, allows for the making of a scheme for the application of such property for other charitable purposes as near as possible to those intended by the donor. As Budd J stated in *Re Royal Kilmainham Hospital*:[415] 'The principle is applied where the method indicated by the donor of carrying out his charitable intentions becomes impracticable, or his intentions cannot be executed literally, most frequently owing to altered circumstances.' The rationale behind the operation of this doctrine is that provided a clear charitable intention is expressed, a gift should not be allowed to fail because the mode of effecting this intention, if specified, cannot be carried out, or no longer provides the most useful and effective manner of applying the bequest. From a practical perspective it will not be possible for a donor to forecast how circumstances affecting his gift will change over a period of time and this difficulty can be also said to underlie the cy-près doctrine. As Meredith J stated in *Governors of Erasmus Smith's Schools v. Attorney General*:[416]

---

413. July 2002 at p. 85.
414. *Ibid.* at p. 86.
415. [1966] IR 451, 469.
416. (1931) 66 ILTR 57, 61. See also the *dicta* of Lord Eldon in *Moggridge v. Thackwell* (1803) 7 Ves 36, 69 as follows: 'If the testator has manifested a general intention to give to charity, the failure of the particular mode in which the charity is to be effectuated shall not destroy the charity; but if the substantial/general intention is charity, the law will substitute another mode of devoting the property to charitable purposes, though the formal intention as to the mode cannot be accomplished.'

To apply without modification a charitable intention that is only expressed in relation to assumed facts and under different conditions is obviously not to carry out the real intention at all. It is on this principle that Courts of Law adapt the statement of a charitable intention to suit altered circumstances and conditions with a view to giving effect to the real intention. Donors cannot be expected to provide expressly for more than the world and the times with which they are familiar.

Therefore for a trust to attain charitable status is a most desirable aim, not only because of the advantages already considered, but also because it will facilitate the operation of cy-près jurisdiction should this become necessary. If a trust does not qualify as charitable, this jurisdiction cannot be exercised and a bequest may fail as contravening the rule against perpetuities, allowing a resulting trust to operate in favour of the donor or his representatives. Such resulting trusts will often not reflect the donor's wishes, and it is certainly preferable to find a means of perpetuating the donor's charitable intention in as close a form as possible to that originally expressed by him. An examination of the judgment of Keane J in *Re Worth Library*[417] would seem to confirm that, as a prerequisite to the exercise of cy-près jurisdiction, a court must satisfy itself that the purpose for which the bequest was originally made was charitable. Despite the fact that counsel were in agreement that the bequest in question was a charitable one, Keane J expressed the view that, as the court was being invited to exercise its jurisdiction to approve a cy-près scheme, a jurisdiction which could only operate in relation to charitable bequests, he felt it necessary to investigate the issue of the charitable status of the original bequest fully. However, it is interesting to note that in another recent case of a similar nature, *Representative Church Body v. Attorney General*,[418] in which O'Hanlon J was called upon to approve a cy-près application in relation to a collection of books in the Old Library of St. Canice's Cathedral, Kilkenny, he proceeded to grant the order sought without raising the question of the charitable nature of the bequest.

In practice, an important distinction must be drawn between circumstances where the gift fails *ab initio*, in which case the property can only be applied cy-près where the donor has manifested a general charitable intention, and cases of subsequent failure where it is not necessary to show such an intention provided that the donor has made an absolute and perpetual gift to a particular charity. This distinction has been well summarised by Murray J in *Re Dunwoodie*[419] in the following terms:

---

417. [1995] 2 IR 301.
418. [1988] IR 19. See further Osborough (1989) 24 Ir Jur (ns) 50.
419. [1977] NI 141, 145. This principle was expressed in a different manner by Budd J in *Re Royal Kilmainham Hospital* [1966] IR 451, 469 although the effect is the same. 'The cy-près principle is confined ... to cases where property is given with a general

There is an important distinction between a charitable trust which is initially impossible or impracticable, i.e. impossible or impracticable as at the death of the testator, and a charitable trust which becomes impossible or impracticable after his death. As regards the former type, the property involved will not be applied cy-près unless the court finds that the testator had a general charitable intention, but as regards the latter type — usually referred to as a case of supervening impossibility — the court will direct a cy-près application whether or not a general charitable intention on the part of the testator can be found in the relevant will.

Initial Failure of Charitable Purposes

In cases where the charitable purposes of a gift fail for one of the reasons which will be examined below, the doctrine of cy-près can be applied 'where, in form, the gift is given for a particular charitable purpose, but it is possible, taking the will as a whole, to say that, notwithstanding the form of the gift, the paramount intention, according to the true construction of the will, is to give the property in the first instance for a general charitable purpose rather than a particular charitable purpose. . . .'[420] Numerous attempts have been made by the judiciary to describe the meaning of the phrase 'general charitable intention'. In *Re Templemoyle Agricultural School*[421] Chatterton VC commented as follows:

It does not mean merely an intention to give charity [sic] generally, without reference to any specified object, but it means an intention the substance of which is charitable, whether generally and without any specified object, in which case the Crown will prescribe the mode of effectuating it, or for an object more or less accurately specified, but with a mode of benefiting that object superadded, which cannot be lawfully or at all carried into execution, in which case the Court will carry out the substantial intention.

An alternative formulation was put forward by Kay J in *Re Taylor*:[422] 'if upon

---

intention to charity with this exception, that where property is given absolutely and perpetually to charity for a particular purpose and has vested in the charity the fund can be applied cy-près irrespective of the donor's particular intention.' Quoted with approval by Keane J in *Re Worth Library* [1995] 2 IR 301, 341.

420. *Re Wilson* [1913] 1 Ch 314, 320-321 *per* Parker J. Quoted with approval by Budd J in *Munster and Leinster Bank Ltd v. Attorney General* (1954) 91 ILTR 34, 39.

421. (1869) IR 4 Eq 295, 301. It should be noted that this decision concerned a case of supervening failure, where arguably it was not necessary to establish a general charitable intent. See *infra* pp. 361-362.

422. (1888) 58 LT 538, 543. See *Re Royal Kilmainham Hospital* [1966] IR 451, 469.

the whole scope and intent of the will you discern the paramount object of the testator was to benefit not a particular institution, but to effect a particular form of charity, independently of any special institution or mode, then, although he may have indicated the mode in which he desires that to be carried out, you are to regard the primary paramount intention chiefly. . . .' A useful distinction was made by Dixon and Evatt JJ in *Attorney General for New South Wales v. Perpetual Trustee Co. Ltd*[423] between cases in which every element in the description of the trust is indispensable to its validity and operation and cases 'where a further and more general purpose is disclosed as the true and substantial object of the trust'. A good example of a case falling into the former category is the decision of the New Zealand Court of Appeal in *Alacoque v. Roche*[424] in which the court concluded that the benefit to the convent named by the testatrix, which had closed some months before her death, was 'the sole and indispensable purpose of the gift' and that no general charitable intention could be found.

While the view has been expressed that in seeking to ascertain whether a general charitable intention can be found in a will, the court should look only at the particular gift,[425] the position would seem to be that such an intention may be discerned from other gifts contained in the will.[426] This was made clear in *Re McGwire*[427] by Black J who stressed that 'a general charitable intention may be collected from the will as a whole'. It has also been suggested recently that because of a reluctance to establish a construction which will lead to intestacy, the courts may lean in favour of finding a general charitable intention.[428]

Whether a donor has displayed sufficient charitable intention is inevitably a question of construction of the relevant document;[429] clearly the more detailed the donor's directions, the less likely it will be that a general charitable intention can be discerned from the terms of the instrument. However, the English decision of *Re Lysaght*[430] would appear to have widened considerably the scope of the concept of general charitable intention. A testatrix made provision in her will for funds to be applied for medical studentships within the gift of the Royal College of Surgeons of England. One of the clauses provided that qualifying students must be male, British-born subjects, the sons of British-

---

423. (1940) 63 CLR 209, 225. Quoted with approval by Murray J in *Re Stewart's Will Trusts* [1983] NI 283, 297.
424. [1998] 2 NZLR 250.
425. *Mayor of Lyons v. Advocate-General of Bengal* (1876) 1 App Cas 91, 114.
426. *Re Satterthwaite's Will Trusts* [1966] 1 WLR 277, 286 *per* Russell LJ.
427. [1941] IR 33, 38.
428. *Per* Hammond J in *Re Collier* [1998] 1 NZLR 81, 95.
429. Dixon and Evatt JJ suggested in *Attorney General for New South Wales v. Perpetual Trustee Co. Ltd* (1940) 63 CLR 209, 226 that this question must be approached on the basis of the circumstances of the failure of the initial trust.
430. [1966] 1 Ch 191.

born doctors registered in the UK 'and not of the Jewish or Roman Catholic faith'. The college declined to accept the bequest in the terms set out in the will but expressed its willingness to do so provided the offending clause was deleted. It was held by Buckley J that to insist on enforcing the discriminatory provision would defeat the paramount intention of the testatrix, and a scheme was ordered which would enable implementation of the trust omitting the words 'and not of the Jewish or Roman Catholic faith'.[431] As Buckley J commented: 'A general charitable intention, then, may be said to be a paramount intention on the part of a donor to effect some charitable purpose which the court can find a method of putting into operation, notwithstanding that it is impracticable to give effect to some direction by the donor which is not an essential part of his true intention — not that is to say, part of his paramount intention.'[432] As Warburton[433] has commented, this reasoning involves asking whether the impugned direction is essential to the donor's purpose and 'allows a far narrower and more detailed intention to amount to a "general" intention'. Although this more liberal approach will be beneficial in circumstances where a good charitable gift might otherwise fail, it is not so justifiable where it appears to defeat the real intention of a donor.

The former consideration applied in *Re Stewart's Will Trusts*,[434] in which a liberal approach to the concept of general charitable intention can also be discerned. The testator left the residue of his estate to a fund established by the Non-Subscribing Presbyterian Church of Ireland for the purpose of supplementing the income of ministers of that church and directed that the income from the residue of his estate should be used for the support of ministers whose congregations complied with certain conditions, one of which, relating to the use of unaltered and unabridged hymn books, was impossible to fulfil. Murray J ordered a cy-près scheme to remove this condition from the trust, holding that the paramount intention of the testator was to increase the salary of ministers of a Christian church. He stated that he could not see how it would be right to regard such an 'ill-considered' provision as an essential part of the charitable scheme particularly when the result of so doing would be to make the trust completely unworkable and frustrate the testator's paramount intention.

This can be contrasted with a decision of the High Court in this jurisdiction which suggests that a more restrictive approach may be applied, although there was no discernible attempt to lay down any such general principle. In

---

431. A similar approach was taken by Vinelott J in *Re Woodhams* [1981] 1 WLR 493 where a scheme to found music scholarships confined to orphans from named homes was altered to omit the latter restriction.
432. [1966] 1 Ch 191, 202. Quoted with approval by Carswell J in *Re Currie* [1985] NI 299, 306.
433. [1981] Conv 231, 232.
434. [1983] NI 283.

Re Prescott[435] a testatrix bequeathed her house to a Dublin parish of the 'Russian Orthodox Church abroad' and directed that if there were no parishioners or members of that church living in Ireland that it should be sold and the proceeds applied for the general purposes of the said church in England. At the time of the testatrix's death, the parish had ceased to exist and the executor applied to the court for directions as to the manner in which the proceeds of the sale of the house were to be distributed. MacKenzie J held that the gift of the house had lapsed as it was to a body which did not exist either at the time of making the will or at the death of the testatrix and the gift over, being dependent on the validity of this gift, also lapsed. While MacKenzie J accepted that there may be cases where a court can find a general charitable intention even in a case of a single gift,[436] he concluded that there was no indication that the testatrix had any intention other than to benefit the named institution in the case before him and he held that the doctrine of cy-près could not be applied. This appears to be a rather restrictive decision given the terms of the gift over in the testatrix's will and it would certainly appear to be out of line with other authorities in this area. On the whole it would be fair to say that the Irish courts have generally leaned in favour of a fairly flexible attitude to this issue.[437]

Initial impossibility in relation to a charitable trust may arise in any one of a number of circumstances. The gift may have been made to a non-existent institution and as Buckley J commented in *Re Davis*:[438] 'where you find a gift to a charitable institution which never existed, the Court, which always leans in favour of charity, is more ready to infer a general charitable intention than to infer the contrary.' While such an intention will not always be found in cases of non-existent institutions,[439] it would appear to be more difficult to establish in circumstances where the object once existed but ceased to do so before the gift took effect.[440] This point was made by Megarry VC in *Re Spence*,[441] where he commented that 'the court is far less ready to find [a general charitable] intention where the gift is to a body which existed at the

---

435. [1990] 2 IR 342.
436. See e.g. *Biscoe v Jackson* (1887) 35 Ch D 460; *Re Currie* [1985] NI 299.
437. A general charitable intention was found in the following cases: *Daly v. Attorney General* (1860) 11 ICR 41; *Munster and Leinster Bank Ltd v. Attorney General* (1954) 91 ILTR 34; *Re Templemoyle Agricultural School* (1869) IR 4 Eq 295; *Re McGwire* [1941] IR 33; *Re Quinn* (1953) 88 ILTR 161; *Re Fitzgerald's Estate* (1957) 92 ILTR 192; *Re Currie* [1985] NI 299. Cases where no such intention was found include *Re Ffrench* [1941] IR 49n; *Attorney General for Northern Ireland v. Forde* [1932] NI 1; *McCormick v. Queen's University of Belfast* [1958] NI 1.
438. [1902] 1 Ch 876, 881. See e.g. *Daly v. Attorney General* (1860) 11 I C R 41.
439. *Re Goldschmidt* [1957] 1 WLR 524.
440. *Re Harwood* [1936] Ch 285, 287 *per* Farwell J. See also *Makeown v. Ardagh* (1876) IR 10 Eq 445, 452; *Re Prescott* [1990] 2 IR 342.
441. [1979] 1 Ch 483, 495.

date of the will but ceased to exist before the testator died, or as I have already held, where the gift is for a purpose which, though possible and practicable at the date of the will, has ceased to be so before the testator's death.' Another reason for initial failure of a gift is that the body or institution which the testator intended to benefit may have been amalgamated with or absorbed into another institution by the time the gift is to take effect. Such a gift may lapse if the court considers that on its true construction it is intended to have been for the originally specified purpose or institution alone.[442] However, it has been established that where a named parish ceases to exist as a separate entity and amalgamates with another, a gift to such a parish may be applied for the purposes of the new unit.[443] Another common difficulty which arises is that the institution may be misdescribed. As Chatterton VC commented in *Re Geary's Trusts*:[444] 'The Court, however, will not allow a charitable legacy to fail because of misdescription, but will endeavour to carry out the testator's intention as nearly as possible.'

Finally, the possibility that the consent of the intended recipient to an acceptance of the trust in its original terms may not be forthcoming must be considered. In *Re Dunwoodie*[445] the testatrix bequeathed the residue of her estate on trust for a particular Presbyterian Church with a direction that the bequest should be used for the installation of bells at that church. The committee of the church decided not to install the bells and the question arose whether the residuary bequest should devolve as on an intestacy or be applied cy-près. Murray J held that the trust for the installation of the bells must be treated as initially impossible to fulfil because the consent of the relevant church authority which was essential to the fulfilment of the trust had never been given. However, he was satisfied that the testatrix had shown a general intention to further the general purposes of the particular church and that the initial failure of the trust in no way invalidated the general trust for the church which remained perfectly good. In the circumstances, he ordered that the property should be applied cy-près.

Subsequent Failure of Charitable Purposes

A gift may be capable of being carried out in the precise terms laid down by the donor or testator at the time it takes effect but may subsequently fail or become impossible or impracticable to enforce. In such circumstances, it is

---

442. *Re Rymer* [1895] 1 Ch 19.
443. *Corbally v. Representative Church Body* [1938] IR 35. See also *Re Bloomfield's Bequest* (1920) 54 ILTR 213 where a clergyman was found to be entitled to an endowment originally intended for the incumbent of a parish which had merged with his.
444. (1890) 25 LR Ir 171.
445. [1977] NI 141.

not necessary to establish a general charitable intention provided that the gift is given 'absolutely and perpetually to charity'. The material date for deciding whether a general charitable intention is necessary is therefore the date on which the trust comes into effect, which in the case of a will, is the date of the testator's death.[446] The effect of the distinction between initial and supervening impossibility was set out by Evershed MR in *Re Tacon*[447] as follows:

> It is well established that in the case of a gift to charity ... where no general charitable intention is present, then (1) if the charity has ceased to exist before the will comes into operation the gift lapses, but (2) if the charity is still in existence at the date mentioned, it is effective as a gift to the extent that the interests of the next-of-kin (or of whoever else take in default of the charitable interest taking effect) are for ever excluded, notwithstanding the later dissolution or disappearance of the charity.

One of the most important decisions establishing this principle in this jurisdiction is that of Budd J in *Re Royal Kilmainham Hospital*.[448] A hospital founded by Charles II in 1684 for the support and maintenance of old soldiers of his army and those of his successors gradually ceased to function after the setting up of the Irish Free State and the Irish government took over control of the lands and buildings. In 1961, the Royal Kilmainham Hospital Act was passed which provided, *inter alia*, for the settling of a scheme for some specified charitable purposes or purpose for the benefit of some classes of members of the defence forces. It was held by Budd J that since it was no longer possible to carry out the founder's intentions the available funds should be applied cy-près and he directed that they should be used to benefit organizations of former members of the defence forces and the British Army. Budd J stated as follows:

> There was no controversy as to the general principles applicable when charitable gifts, which have taken effect, subsequently fail for want of objects. If there is an absolute perpetual gift to a charity, even though the trusts declared are only for the accomplishment of a particular charitable purpose, the subject-matter is applicable cy-près upon failure of the trusts.[449]

---

446. *Re Wright* [1954] Ch 347.
447. [1958] Ch 447, 453.
448. [1966] IR 451.
449. *Ibid.* at 472.

Similarly, in *Re Worth Library*[450] Keane J found that the original bequest of the library in the will of Dr Worth was 'undoubtedly an absolute and perpetual gift' and for this reason could be applied cy-près when the hospital ceased to exist, notwithstanding his finding that no general charitable intention could be inferred on the facts before him.

In certain circumstances surplus funds may remain where a charitable purpose has been completed or where full provision has been made for its requirements and provided that it is an absolute and perpetual gift to charity, these funds may be applied cy-près. In *Trusts of the Rectory of St John*[451] a surplus remained after providing for the maintenance of the choir and choral service at a cathedral church in Cork City as required by the terms of a trust. Chatterton VC held that as part of these monies was not required for the literal fulfilment of the donor's intentions, some of the fund might be applied cy-près in the purchase of an organ for the church, a purpose which was essential for carrying that intention into effect.

Finally, it should be pointed out that there have been sporadic examples throughout the common law world of courts determining whether general charitable intent exists in cases of supervening failure,[452] although Picarda[453] has characterised such judgments as examples of the courts searching unnecessarily for such an intent and finding it. In the recent decision of the Newfoundland Court of Appeal in *Boy Scouts of Canada v. Doyle*,[454] which was a case of supervening failure, Marshall JA still went on to consider whether the requirement of general charitable intent was satisfied. However, he also considered the arguments in favour of dispensing with this latter requirement and concluded that whichever approach was followed, the conditions for cy-près were satisfied in the case before him. His judgment certainly cannot be taken as authority for the proposition that he was insisting on a requirement of general charitable intent even in cases of supervening impossibility or failure and the overwhelming weight of opinion is against such a proposition.[455]

---

450. [1995] 2 IR 301, 342.
451. (1869) IR 3 Eq 335.
452. E.g. *Re Templemoyle Agricultural School* (1869) IR 4 Eq 295 (Ireland); *Re North Devon and West Somerset Relief Fund Trusts* [1953] 1 WLR 1260 (England); *Parker v. Moseley* [1965] VR 580 (Australia); *Hay v. Murdoch* [1952] WN 145 where the House of Lords suggested that in Scotland a general charitable intent was required in all cases.
453. *The Law and Practice Relating to Charities* (3rd ed., 1999) p. 315.
454. (1997) 149 DLR (4th) 22.
455. See e.g. the statement in *Tudor on Charities* by Warburton (8th ed., 1995) p. 409 to the effect that 'the requirement of a general or paramount charitable intention is irrelevant in the case of a subsequent failure of a gift for charitable purposes'.

Legislative Reform of the Cy-près Doctrine

At common law this jurisdiction could only be exercised where it was impossible or impracticable to give effect to the wishes of a donor in the precise terms which he intended. However, the doctrine as it developed at common law was criticised as being too restrictive in nature and section 47 of the Irish Charities Act 1961 laid down much broader parameters for the exercise of this jurisdiction,[456] allowing a cy-près order to be made in circumstances where there were difficulties in implementing the original terms or where more effective use might be made of the trust property by framing an alternative scheme. It is helpful to set out in full the terms of section 47(1) which enumerates the circumstances in which a cy-près order may now be made.

(1) Subject to subsection (2), the circumstances in which the original purposes of a charitable gift may be altered to allow the property given or part of it to be applied cy-près shall be as follows:—
   (a) where the original purposes, in whole or in part—
      (i) have been as far as may be fulfilled; or
      (ii) cannot be carried out, or cannot be carried out according to the directions given and to the spirit of the gift; or
   (b) where the original purposes provide a use for part only of the property available by virtue of the gift; or
   (c) where the property available by virtue of the gift and other property applicable for similar purposes can be more effectively used in conjunction, and to that end can suitably, regard being had to the spirit of the gift, be made applicable for common purposes; or
   (d) where the original purposes were laid down by reference to an area which then was but has since ceased to be a unit for some other purpose, or by reference to a class of persons or to an area which has for any reason since ceased, either to be suitable, regard being had to the spirit of the gift, or to be practical in administering the gift; or
   (e) where the original purposes, in whole or in part, have since they were laid down—
      (i) been adequately provided for by other means; or
      (ii) ceased as being useless or harmful to the community or for other reasons, to be in law charitable; or
      (iii) ceased in any other way to provide a suitable and effective method of using the property available by virtue of the gift, regard being had to the spirit of the gift.

---

456. See also s. 13 of the Charities Act 1960 in England and s. 22 of the Charities Act (Northern Ireland) 1964 which introduced similar reforms.

Lavan J noted in his judgment in *Magee v. Attorney General*[457] that although section 47 of the Charities Act 1961 has caused substantial inroads to be made into the restrictive common law approach to the cy-près doctrine, it was still desirable and necessary to have due regard to the wishes of the donor 'so as to avoid the threat of making the practice of donating to charity a veritable shot in the dark'.[458] He stated that the primary rule to be observed in the application of the cy-près doctrine is that the intention of the donor must be served as far as possible and regard must be had to the spirit of the gift. Thus, he added, if the donor names a particular object which is capable of taking effect any application cy-près which becomes necessary must be restricted to the limits of that object and the mode of application must as far as possible coincide with the donor's wishes.

The provisions of section 47(1) have been applied in a number of cases. In *Re Royal Kilmainham Hospital* Budd J found that the original purposes of the gift could no longer be carried out according to the directions given and the spirit of the gift and that these original purposes had at least in part ceased to provide a suitable and effective method of using the property available. Subsection (1)(e)(iii) was again considered by O'Hanlon J in *Representative Church Body v. Attorney General*[459] in which the plaintiff sought a cy-près order under section 47 in relation to a collection of books kept in the Old Library attached to St Canice's Cathedral, Kilkenny. The plaintiff claimed ownership of the books and wished to sell them and apply the proceeds to the maintenance and repair of the cathedral. It was argued that the books were no longer used in the manner envisaged in the original bequests but the application was opposed by the Attorney General on the grounds that the collection was an important cultural asset for Kilkenny and that if it were sold there was no effective legal restriction on its exportation. O'Hanlon J held that the original purposes of the charitable gifts had ceased to provide a suitable or effective method of using the property available, regard being had to the spirit of the gift. He held further that it was permissible to alter the original purposes of the bequests and to allow the property to be applied cy-près and he made an order authorizing the sale of the collection by the plaintiff so that the proceeds might be applied to the repair and maintenance of the cathedral.

This decision provides a good illustration of how the original common law requirements in relation to the exercise of cy-près jurisdiction have now been relaxed. While it could be argued that section 47 was applied in an unduly lenient manner in this case, the requirement that the property be applied

457. High Court 2000 No. 377 Sp (Lavan J) 25 July 2002.
458. *Ibid.* at 3.
459. [1988] IR 19. See further Osborough (1989) 24 Ir Jur (ns) 50. The equivalent provision in s.22 of the Charities Act (Northern Ireland) 1964 was applied in *Re Steele* [1976] NI 66.

in conformity with the 'spirit of the gift' should ensure that due regard should be given to the wishes of a donor.

However, where the original purposes, or those substituted by a subsequent cy-près scheme, have not been fulfilled and have not ceased to provide a suitable and effective method of using the property available, section 47 will not permit the further application of the property cy-près. This is made clear by the decision of Lavan J in *Magee v. Attorney General*[460] in which the plaintiff trustees brought an application seeking to have the proceeds of sale of trust property, originally given to provide primary Catholic education for male Catholics in an area, applied cy-près. The plaintiffs contended that the original purposes of the charitable trust had been fulfilled as there was adequate schooling for Catholics in the area and sought to have the proceeds of sale of a monastery, the remainder of the trust property, applied cy-près in order to discharge part of the parish debt. The Attorney General contended that the scheme proposed by the plaintiffs was not as close as possible to the original objects of the donor as it had failed to have sufficient regard to the educational nature of those objects and it was further submitted that the proposed scheme had been framed without sufficient consideration being given to the educational needs of the locality. In 1997 the trustees had reluctantly agreed with the Commissioners of Charitable Donations and Bequests to the framing of a cy-près scheme concerning the sale of a school, which together with the monastery, made up the trust property. This provided that the trustees should retain the money received from the sale strictly for educational use for all children attending primary or secondary schools in the parish. In the light of this, the question which the court had to decide was whether the proceeds of sale, the subject-matter of the application before it, could now be used for the purposes advanced by the plaintiffs. In the view of Lavan J it was therefore necessary to answer the question of whether the advancement of educational facilities in all the schools of the parish was closer to the spirit of the gift than the discharge of a parish debt incurred in the pursuit of enhancing the community. He accepted that the activities carried on in the local community hall, the refurbishment of which had contributed so significantly to the incurring of the parish debt, must be deemed to be 'educational' in nature. However, he added that this view of the activities and functions did not solve the very complicated issues raised by the application. Lavan J stated that there was no evidence before him that the cy-près scheme of 1997 was sufficient to meet the needs of all the schools in the parish and added that he considered that there were various types of educational aids which these schools might need. However, he noted that given his acceptance that the activities carried on in the community centre were educational in nature, the court might otherwise have been sympathetic to the plaintiffs' case. Lavan J was satisfied that the

---

460. High Court 2000 No. 377 Sp (Lavan J) 25 July 2002.

trust established in 1892 had been superseded by the cy-près scheme of 1997 and that the application to apply the proceeds of the sale of the monastery could not be severed from the latter scheme. In these circumstances, Lavan J concluded that he was unable to grant the plaintiffs the relief which they sought.

The equivalent English provision, section 13(1)(e)(iii) of the Charities Act 1993 has recently been considered by the Court of Appeal in *Varsani v. Jesani*.[461] A charitable trust had been established with the purpose of promoting the faith of a particular Hindu sect and the charity's assets included a temple in London. Subsequently the members of the sect split into two groups and this produced a situation in which neither group would worship in the same temple as the other. Carnwath J held that the court had jurisdiction under section 13 of the Charities Act 1993 to make a regulatory scheme and ordered that the sect's assets be held on separate trusts for the furtherance of the faith as practised by each group.

The minority group's appeal was dismissed by the Court of Appeal. Morritt LJ concluded that if the original purposes of the charity had led to the impasse which in his view could not be resolved as a matter of faith, then it was self-evident that the original purposes had ceased to be a suitable and effective method of using the available property. He concluded that the spirit of the gift supported the submission that the court should exercise the jurisdiction conferred on it by section 13(1)(e)(iii) of the 1993 Act by directing a scheme for the division of the property of the charity as between the majority and minority groups. Chadwick LJ agreed that the appeal should be dismissed for the reasons set out by Morritt LJ. In relation to the manner in which the spirit of the gift could be identified, he stated as follows:

> The need to have regard to the spirit of the gift requires the court to look beyond the original purposes as defined by the objects specified in the declaration of trust and to seek to identify the spirit in which the donors gave property upon trust for those purposes. That can be done, as it seems to me, with the assistance of the document as a whole and any relevant evidence as to the circumstances in which the gift was made.[462]

Section 47(2) of the 1961 Act provides that its provisions are not 'to affect the conditions which must be satisfied in order that property given for charitable purposes may be applied cy-près except insofar as these conditions require a failure of the original purposes'. Therefore the importance of the distinction between initial and subsequent failure remains, to the extent that a general charitable intention must be established in the former category, and the

---

461. [1999] Ch 219.
462. *Ibid.* at 238.

legislation has merely extended the circumstances in which a cy-près application may successfully be brought.

Finally, it should be noted that the Commissioners of Charitable Donations and Bequests now have jurisdiction to frame a cy-près scheme without being subject to any financial limits in this regard.[463]

The Manner in Which Cy-près Jurisdiction Should be Exercised

As the word 'cy-près' suggests, in determining new purposes for which property should be applied, the court should seek to ensure that these purposes are as near as possible to those originally set out in the gift. In addition, as Keane J stated in *Re Worth Library*[464] it is also 'desirable that the original intentions of the testator should be adhered to so far as is possible', although as Keane J himself acknowledged, the difficulties in both ascertaining and giving effect to such intentions will be obvious where there has been a considerable lapse of time since the making of the initial gift. In the context of the facts in the case before him, he therefore stated that it would be futile to transport the donor in some form of time machine from the early eighteenth century to the present day and all that the court could do was 'to apply the gift as it might be applied by a late twentieth century equivalent of [the donor]'. In the circumstances, Keane J concluded that any cy-près scheme framed by the court must provide for the retention of the books and portraits which formed the subject-matter of the gift in their original setting, which after it ceased to be a hospital, became a health board headquarters.

Another recent example illustrating the importance of adhering to the original purposes as closely as possible is provided by the decision of Carroll J in *Doyle v. Attorney General*.[465] A fund was set up to benefit a child who suffered from a rare genetic skin disease and some of the money raised was used for her benefit. Following her death, the plaintiffs proposed the division of the funds between seven named charities which were institutions, all but one of which were located in the area in which the funds were raised, which treated the sick, the elderly and the handicapped. The scheme was opposed by the Attorney General on the grounds that many of the proposed beneficiaries were not as near as possible to the original purposes of the fund. Carroll J stated that the care of the elderly, the handicapped and the sick was not sufficiently close to the original purpose of the fund and said that she agreed

---

463. S.16 and Schedule, Part 2 of the Social Welfare (Miscellaneous Provisions) Act 2002. S. 29 of the Charities Act 1961 originally limited the jurisdiction of the Commissioners to circumstances where the value of the charitable gift did not exceed £5,000, a figure extended by s. 8 of the Charities Act 1973 to £25,000, and by s. 52(a) of the Court and Court Officers Act 1995 to £250,000.
464. [1995] 2 IR 301, 343.
465. High Court 1993 No. 612 Sp (Carroll J) 22 February 1995.

with the submission that there should be some connection with the disease from which the original beneficiary had suffered, 'either by way of research, or treatment, or palliative care'. In her opinion, the requirement that regard should be had to the wishes of the trustees or other persons in charge of the property did not override the requirement that the property should be applied cy-près. Carroll J concluded that a proportion of the fund should be spent on a specialist clinic set up to treat sufferers of the disease and that a lesser proportion should be given to research into the disease, which was being carried out in a specified location, on condition that the court could be provided with information as to what would constitute a meaningful contribution to research. Carroll J suggested that the plaintiffs might give their opinion as to the division of the fund as between these two purposes but added that if it was not possible to provide a meaningful sum for research, then the entire fund should go the specialist clinic.

Further light was thrown on the process of deciding how to apply property cy-près by the judgment of Marshall JA in the decision of the Newfoundland Court of Appeal in *Boy Scouts of Canada v. Doyle*.[466] The court had to determine how trust property should be applied cy-près when a particular boy scout troop in whose favour it had been established ceased to exist.[467] Marshall JA stated that the first step in the process required 'an examination of the trust settlement's general intent as a prelude to defining the mode which in substance will as nearly as possible execute the general charitable intent'.[468] He concluded that as the particular troop no longer existed, the trust should be applied for the benefit of the local scouting movement which was represented by the provincial council. In his view by making it possible for all scouting to benefit in place of one particular troop, the court could ensure that 'the general object will not be defeated but will continue to be executed in substance through the offices of the scouting movement'.[469]

Sign Manual Procedure

Where money or property is given to charity generally without provision being made for the appointment of trustees the government is considered to be the trustee and is required to ensure the administration of the gift under the 'sign manual procedure'. In *Felan v. Russell*[470] property was bequeathed for 'pious purposes' and although it was accepted as being for charitable purposes, the

---

466. (1997) 149 DLR (4th) 22.
467. The court accepted that there was no difficulty in holding that a trust for the benefit of a scouting troop fell within the parameters of the advancement of education and referred to the decision of Vaisey J in *Re Webber* [1954] 1 WLR 1500 on this point.
468. *Ibid.* at 79.
469. *Ibid.* at 81.
470. (1842) 4 Ir Eq R 701. See also *Kane v. Cosgrave* (1873) IR 10 Eq 211.

trustee died before a scheme to apply the gift was settled. It was held that the gift vested in the Crown and that it should be disposed of under the sign manual procedure. Similarly, in *Merrins v. Attorney General*[471] Black J held that a gift in remainder to charity generally in relation to which no trustee had been appointed, should be applied at the 'will and pleasure' of the government.

---

471. (1945) 79 ILTR 121.

CHAPTER 11

Void and Voidable Trusts

A private trust may fail in circumstances where although it appears to be otherwise valid, it is in fact illegal or contrary to public policy. In such cases, where the trust is void, it is regarded as being invalid *ab initio* and never comes into effect. Alternatively, a trust may be voidable in certain circumstances; these trusts are not void *ab initio* and will remain in operation unless or until their validity is successfully challenged.

VOID TRUSTS

A trust may be void because it offends statutory provisions or the common law or because it may be contrary to public policy. Where a trust is declared void, the property which it was intended to include in it will be held on a resulting trust for the settlor or where such a trust arises under a will, it will lapse into the testator's residuary estate.

Where a trust involves the creation of a future interest it is subject to the rules against perpetuities and inalienability. So, a trust will be void *ab initio* where it might vest outside the perpetuity period i.e. that of a life or lives in being plus a further period of 21 years allowing additionally for periods of gestation or where the property is tied to a specific purpose for a period of time in excess of the perpetuity period. These issues are considered in detail elsewhere and it is not proposed to consider them in this context.[1]

Conditions Precedent and Subsequent

Often the question of whether a trust is void relates to the issue of the validity of any condition to which the trust may be made subject and illegality often arises as a result of a condition imposed on what might otherwise be a valid gift. Such conditions fall into two categories; conditions precedent, which effectively preclude the trust from coming into effect unless and until the

---

1. Wylie, *Irish Land Law* (3rd ed., 1997) Chapter 5; Coughlan, *Property Law* (2nd ed., 1998) Chapter 10. On the rule against inalienability, see *infra* Chapter 9 in relation to purpose trusts.

condition is fulfilled and conditions subsequent which do not prevent the gift vesting but render it liable to be divested if and when the condition is satisfied. Gifts which incorporate a void condition subsequent can still be enforced without the application of this condition,[2] whereas traditionally certain distinctions have to be made in the case of conditions precedent. Generally where a gift of realty is made dependent on a condition precedent which is found to be void, the gift will fail in its entirety.[3] In England a distinction was drawn in the case of gifts of personalty between situations where the condition was *malum in se* (intrinsically wrong in itself) as opposed to *malum prohibitum* (wrong in the eyes of the law).[4] In the former case, the gift would fail but in the latter case, the gift would be considered good and would pass unfettered by the terms of the invalid condition. This distinction was applied in that jurisdiction in cases such as *Re Piper,*[5] where a condition that children should not reside with their father was categorised as *malum prohibitum* with the result that the gift took effect free of the illegal condition.

However, this principle was described as 'archaic' by Dixon J in *Re Blake*[6] who commented as follows: 'this is a curious and somewhat pedantic distinction to introduce in ascertaining the wishes of testators who, in the vast majority of cases, would be quite unaware of the existence of the distinction, and, even if they were aware of it, might be unable to obtain from lawyers any very precise idea of the nature and limits of the distinction.'[7] In the circumstances of the case, Dixon J found that the condition precedent which he was required to consider fell into neither category and concluded that the gift failed in its entirety. However, some doubt still surrounds the effect of an invalid condition precedent attached to a gift in this jurisdiction, particularly as Kenny J appears to have held subsequently in *Re Doyle*[8] that 'when a condition precedent attached to a gift is in violation of the donees's constitutional rights ... the donee takes the benefit of the gift without complying with the condition'.

Trusts Contrary to Public Policy

Trusts which have as their object an illegal or immoral aim will be regarded as void on this ground. So trusts for such diverse objects as to provide for the

---

2. *Duddy v. Gresham* (1878) 2 LR Ir 442.
3. *Re Turton* [1926] Ch 96.
4. See Delany (1955) 19 Conv 176.
5. [1946] 2 All ER 503.
6. [1955] IR 89.
7. *Ibid.* at 100. See the comments of Delany in (1955) 19 Conv 176, 177 that 'the distinction ... is both obsolete and inherently unsound' and 'can no longer be said to be based on any rational foundation — if indeed, it ever possessed one.'
8. High Court, 1972 (Kenny J). See Wylie, *Irish Land Law* (3rd ed., 1997) p. 555.

payment of fines of convicted poachers[9] have been held to be void. Trusts in favour of future illegitimate children were considered to be void at common law as tending to promote immoral conduct[10] and were regarded as being contrary to public policy. However, this is no longer the case as a result of the intervention of statute and section 27(5) of the Status of Children Act 1987 repealed the common law rule which rendered trusts in favour of future illegitimate children void in relation to wills or settlements made after the commencement of the Act.

In addition, many trusts will be of doubtful validity because they contain conditions which may be vulnerable on public policy grounds and it is now proposed to examine some of these categories in greater detail.

Trusts in Restraint of Marriage

A condition in a trust which amounts to a general restraint on marriage is *prima facie* void.[11] However, it was made clear by Mellish LJ in *Allen v. Jackson*[12] that this principle does not apply to conditions which come into effect only upon a second marriage. It would also appear that in England at any rate, conditions which operate as a partial restraint on marriage, for example prohibiting marriage with certain classes of persons,[13] may be valid. Traditionally, a distinction has been drawn in that jurisdiction between a partial restraint imposed in relation to realty on the one hand and to personalty on the other hand. In the case of realty a partial restraint never appears to be regarded as invalid, whereas in respect of personalty, the condition is considered to be *in terrorem* only and invalid if there is no gift over on the happening of the marriage.[14]

In view of the fact that the right to marry has been recognised as an unspecified personal right which derives from Article 40.3 of the Constitution,[15] it is likely that even partial restraints on marriage would now be considered void in this jurisdiction and on the basis of the *dicta* of Kenny J in *Re Doyle* referred to above, it would appear that a donee would take the gift free from any such condition.

A corollary of this principle is that trusts made in contemplation of or

---

9. *Thrupp v. Collett* (1858) 26 Beav 125.
10. *Thompson v. Thomas* (1891) 27 LR Ir 457. As Keane comments in *Equity and the Law of Trusts in the Republic of Ireland* (1988) at p. 192 it was doubtful whether this common law rule survived the enactment of the Constitution.
11. *Lloyd v. Lloyd* (1852) 2 Sim (NS) 255; *Re Hanlon* [1933] Ch 254.
12. (1875) 1 Ch D 399. See also the judgment of Ball C in *Duddy v. Gresham* (1878) 2 LR Ir 442.
13. *Perrin v. Lyon* (1807) 9 East 170.
14. *Duddy v. Gresham* (1878) 2 LR Ir 442; *Leong v. Cheye* [1955] AC 648, 660.
15. *Ryan v. Attorney General* [1965] IR 294, 313; *McGee v. Attorney General* [1974] IR 284, 301. Note also the comments of Gavan Duffy P in *Re McKenna* [1947] IR 277.

which might encourage the future separation of a husband and wife are void. So, in *Re Johnson's Will Trusts*[16] a trust which cut down the testator's daughter's interest to a nominal amount so long as she was married and living with her husband was considered to be void on that basis. This decision can be distinguished from that in *Re Lovell*,[17] where the object of the trust was found to be to make provision for a woman during her separation until she might return to her husband or remarry and where the parties are already separated no objection should arise.[18] However, in view of the constitutional status of the institution of marriage in this jurisdiction, it is likely that a strict attitude will be taken by the courts here towards any trust which might have the effect of directly or indirectly weakening the marriage bond.

Trusts Tending to Interfere with Parental Duties

Trusts which seek to weaken the ties between parents and children by requiring that children reside apart from their parents have been held to be void as being contrary to public policy. So, in *Re Boulter*[19] a condition in a gift to the testator's grandchildren which provided that it should be forfeited if either or both of them should live with or be under the custody or control of their father was held to be void as being contrary to public policy and tending to encourage the separation of parents from their children. In addition, trusts which interfere with parental duties in relation to the upbringing of their children will also be considered void on policy grounds. In *Re Borwick*[20] a condition subsequent in a trust which provided that an interest should be forfeited if the beneficiary should before attaining the age of 21 'become a Roman Catholic or not be openly or avowedly Protestant' was found to be void as it interfered with the exercise of parental duty in relation to the religious upbringing of the child. Some doubt was thrown on the validity of this approach by the decision of the House of Lords in *Blathwayt v. Baron Cawley*,[21] in which a clause in a trust which provided for forfeiture of an interest if the beneficiary should become a Roman Catholic was upheld. The majority of the House of Lords acknowledged that such conditions would tend to influence or interfere with parental responsibilities but took the view that they should not be categorised as contrary to public policy.

---

16. [1967] Ch 387. See also *Re Caborne* [1943] Ch 224. Although note the decision of *Re Thompson* [1939] 1 All ER 681 in which Bennett J came to the contrary conclusion.
17. [1920] 1 Ch 122.
18. *Wilson v. Wilson* (1848) 1 HLC 538.
19. [1922] 1 Ch 75. See also *Re Sandbrook* [1912] 2 Ch 471 and *Re Piper* [1946] 2 All ER 503 where the fact that the father was divorced did not affect the court's finding on this issue.
20. [1933] Ch 657. See also *Re Tegg* [1936] 2 All ER 878.
21. [1976] AC 397.

The validity of this type of condition has been considered by the courts in this jurisdiction on a number of occasions. In *Re Burke's Estate*[22] Gavan Duffy P held that a condition in the testatrix's will that his nephew should be educated in a Roman Catholic school to be selected at the absolute discretion of the trustees, 'however well meaning from the standpoint of an anxious benefactor' was inoperative as it tended to override the rights and duties of parents in relation to the education of their children provided for in Article 42 of the Constitution. Perhaps the most important authority in this area is the judgment of Dixon J in *Re Blake*[23] in which he had to consider the validity of a trust in favour of the testator's grandchildren but subject to a condition that they be brought up as Roman Catholics. Dixon J referred to the relevant English authorities and to Article 42 of the Constitution and stated as follows:

> This Article puts the matter on a different and higher plane in this country, as the parental right and duty is declared and guaranteed by our fundamental law. Under it, the State 'guarantees to respect the inalienable right and duty of parents to provide, according to their means, for the religious and moral, intellectual, physical and social education of their children.' It is clear that any attempt to restrict or fetter that right would be contrary to the solemnly declared policy and conceptions of the community as a whole and therefore such as the Courts established under that Constitution could not and would not lend their aid to.[24]

The effect of such a finding was considered in detail by Dixon J. The distinction between a finding of invalidity in relation to conditions precedent and subsequent had been outlined as follows by Gavan Duffy P in *Re Burke's Estate*:[25]

> The practical effect of the distinction is of the utmost importance: a gift made subject to a condition precedent fails altogether, as a rule, if the condition is found to be void, but if a gift is made subject to a condition subsequent which is found to be void or inapplicable, the condition disappears and the gift takes effect independently of the condition.

While Dixon J acknowledged that Gavan Duffy P had left open the possibility of there being an exception to the general rule in the case of conditions precedent, he concluded that the conditions in the case before him were void and unenforceable and that the gifts were dependent on their being carried out and were also void. Some doubt must be raised about such a conclusion in

---

22. [1951] IR 216.
23. [1955] IR 89.
24. *Ibid.* at 97.
25. [1951] IR 216, 224.

the light of the decision of Kenny J in *Re Doyle*, where it appears to have been stated that where a condition precedent to a gift is found to be in violation of the donee's constitutional rights the donee may take the benefit of the gift without complying with the condition. However, it should be pointed out that the condition in that case, which was found to be contrary to the provisions of Article 44.2.1° of the Constitution, was held in any event to be invalid on the grounds that it was impossible to perform.

VOIDABLE TRUSTS

Trusts falling within this category come into operation and will remain effective unless and until they are set aside in court proceedings. A trust may be voidable for a variety of reasons often because it comes into being as a result of mistake, misrepresentation, fraud, duress or undue influence. In addition a trust may be set aside where it amounts to an attempt to defraud a settlor's creditors or subsequent purchasers or where the settlor becomes bankrupt within a specified period of settling the property. In this context it is proposed to examine these latter situations, which are governed by specific statutory provisions, in more detail.

Settlements Defrauding Creditors

In practice a person may often be tempted to settle property, usually on his family or close associates, in circumstances where he fears that his creditors may otherwise succeed in obtaining control over his assets. However, as Fitzgerald B commented in *Smith v. Tatton*:[26] 'A man must be honest before he is generous' and section 10 of the Conveyancing Act (Ireland) 1634[27] provides that any gift or conveyance of property, real or personal made for the purpose of delaying, hindering or defrauding creditors is 'void' as against such creditors, although this phrase has been interpreted as meaning 'voidable'.[28] Section 14 of the 1634 Act goes on to provide that this provision will not extend to conveyances *bona fide* made for good consideration[29] without notice of any fraud. The general object of this legislation was

---

26. (1879) 6 LR Ir 32, 41. See also the comments of Jessel MR in *Re Butterworth* (1882) 19 Ch D 588, 598: 'a man is not entitled to go into a hazardous business, and immediately before doing so, settle all his property voluntarily, the object being this: "if I succeed in business, I make a fortune for myself. If I fail, I leave my creditors unpaid. They will bear the loss".'

27. 10 Chas 1, sess. 2, c.3. (The original equivalent in England was 13 Eliz., c.5).

28. *Re Eichholz* [1959] Ch 708.

29. This requirement has been interpreted to mean valuable consideration including marriage consideration, but natural love and affection does not suffice, see *Re Rorke's Estate* (1865) 15 Ir Ch R 316.

summarised by Palles CB in *Re Moroney*[30] as follows: 'The object of the statute was to protect the rights of creditors as against the property of their debtor. It was no part of its object to regulate the rights of creditors *inter se*, or to entitle them to an equal distribution of that property.' The extent of the fraudulent intent required by the statute is far from clear; in *Rose v. Greer*[31] Overend J stated that the class of fraud against which the statute is directed is 'one in which the debtor attempts to defeat his creditors by bogus or colourable transactions under which the debtor retains a benefit to himself'. While it was suggested by Pennycuick VC in *Lloyds Bank Ltd v. Marcan*[32] in the context of the then equivalent English provision,[33] that the word 'defraud' was not intended to be confined to cases involving actual deceit or dishonesty, Cairns LJ disagreed with this view when the matter was considered by the Court of Appeal[34] and said that fraud involves dishonesty, so that while deceit is not a necessary element, dishonest intention is required, at any rate when the conveyance is one for consideration.

However, the view expressed by Pennycuick VC seems to be more in accord with the position adopted in this jurisdiction. In *Re Moroney*[35] Palles CB appeared to accept that there might be cases falling within the ambit of the statute where no fraudulent intention actually exists in the settlor's mind but can be assumed as a matter of law from the consequences of his actions. At this point it is useful to set out the Chief Baron's comments in full:

> Therefore to bring a conveyance within the statute, first, it must be fraudulent; secondly, the class of fraud must be an intent to delay, hinder or defraud creditors. Whether a particular conveyance be within this description may depend upon an infinite variety of circumstances and considerations. One conveyance for instance, may be executed with the express intent and object in the mind of the party to defeat and delay his creditors, and from such an intent the law presumes the conveyance to be fraudulent, and does not require or allow such fraud to be deduced as an inference of fact. In other cases, no such intention actually exists in the mind of the grantor, but the necessary or probable result of his denuding himself of the property included in the conveyance, for the consideration, and under the circumstances actually existing, is to defeat or delay creditors, and in such a case, as stated by Mellish LJ in *Re*

---

30. (1887) 21 LR Ir 27, 62. See also the comments of O'Connor MR in *National Bank Ltd v. Behan* [1913] 1 IR 512, 516, to the effect that 'the deed must be fraudulent in its conception or execution'.
31. [1945] IR 503, 510.
32. [1973] 1 WLR 339, 344.
33. S. 172 of the Law of Property Act 1925. Subsequently replaced by s. 423 of the Insolvency Act 1986.
34. [1973] 1 WLR 1387, 1391.
35. (1887) 21 LR Ir 27.

> Wood LR 7 Ch App 302, the intent is, as a matter of law, assumed from the necessary or probable consequences of the act done.[36]

This view that it is not necessary to establish that the agreement was motivated by actual fraud provided that the necessary or probable result of the agreement was to defeat or delay creditors has recently been approved by Costello P in *McQuillan v. Maguire*.[37] A decree in favour of the plaintiffs against the first named defendant in relation to a building contract had been converted into a judgment mortgage over the latter's interest in a property. A month after the decree had been obtained, the second named defendant, who was the wife of the first named defendant, instituted proceedings under the Married Women's Status Act 1957 and an order was made by consent declaring that she was entitled to the entire beneficial interest in this premises. When the plaintiffs learnt of the order they instituted proceedings seeking a declaration that the first named defendant was at all material times the beneficial owner of the premises and that the judgment mortgage was well charged on that beneficial interest. The plaintiffs submitted that the order had been obtained by collusion and with the intention of defrauding them and argued that it should be set aside in accordance with the provisions of the Conveyancing Act (Ireland) 1634. Costello P referred to *Re Moroney* and reiterated that the court did not have to find that the agreement had been motivated by actual fraud in order to set it aside. If it could be shown that the necessary or probable result of the agreement was to defeat or delay creditors, it could be avoided. He concluded that the agreement entered into between the defendants in the proceedings taken under the 1957 Act was void as it had the effect both of hindering and delaying the payment of a debt due by the first named defendant to the plaintiffs. He therefore held that the plaintiffs were entitled to a well charging order over the first named defendant's 50% of the premises on the basis that the wife had a 50% beneficial interest by virtue of contributions she had made to earlier family homes.

The onus would appear to be on the party alleging fraud,[38] particularly where it appears that the transfer or conveyance of the property was made in a *bona fide* manner for good consideration. The latter point emerges clearly from the decision of the High Court in *Bryce v. Fleming*.[39] The first named defendant assigned lands to the second named defendant at a price which reflected the estimate which the parties placed on the value of the lands. The plaintiff had three days previously obtained judgment against the first named defendant and was a creditor of his to nearly half the value of the lands in question. The second named defendant stated in evidence that she had paid

---

36. *Ibid.* at 61-62.
37. [1996] 1 ILRM 395.
38. *National Bank Ltd v. Behan* [1913] 1 IR 512, 516 *per* O'Connor MR.
39. [1930] IR 376.

the full value of the lands and that she had no knowledge of the judgment which had been obtained against the vendor. The Circuit Court judge declared the deed void as against the first named defendant's creditors on the grounds that he did not believe the evidence of the second named defendant that she had no knowledge of the fraudulent nature of the transaction. On appeal the plaintiff's action was dismissed on the basis that the assignment was for valuable consideration and the evidence of the plaintiff did not establish that there was any knowledge of fraud on the part of the second named defendant nor did it show that she had sought to acquire the land other than as a *bona fide* purchaser.

So, even where a conveyance is for valuable consideration, this fact alone will not suffice to prevent the application of section 10.[40] This point was developed by Palles CB in *Re Moroney*[41] in the following manner:

> If, however, in such a case, the intent were not only to sell the property, but forthwith to abscond with the proceeds, so as in effect to withdraw the property from the fund available for the creditors without providing an equivalent, I should entertain no doubt that in such a case there would be an intention to defraud creditors, which, if the purchaser had notice of, would avoid the sale, and which, whether he had notice or not, would be an act of bankruptcy by the vendor.

However, it will clearly be more difficult to impugn the validity of a deed made for valuable consideration; as Turner LJ stated in *Harman v. Richards*:[42] 'those who undertake to impeach for *mala fides* a deed which has been executed for valuable consideration, have, I think, a task of great difficulty to discharge'. As Johnston J made clear in *Bryce v. Fleming*,[43] where there is a *bona fide* purchase for valuable consideration it cannot be impeached unless the purchaser is shown to be privy to the vendor's intention.

A further point to note is that the mere fact that an individual with debts is selling property is not necessarily evidence that he intends to defeat his creditors rather than to obtain the means to satisfy these debts.[44] *A fortiori*, knowledge of such a fact will not be a sufficient ground for imputing to a purchaser knowledge of a fraudulent intention on the part of the vendor. From a practical perspective a sale of this nature often provides the means necessary to satisfy existing debts; while the property itself ceases to be available for the purpose

---

40. *Cadogan v. Kennett* (1776) 2 Cowp 432, 434-435 *per* Lord Mansfield.
41. (1887) 21 LR Ir 27, 63.
42. (1852) 10 Hare 81, 89. See also *Re Johnson* (1881) 20 Ch D 389, 393; *Bryce v. Fleming* [1930] IR 376, 379-380, 385.
43. [1930] IR 376.
44. *Bryce v. Fleming* [1930] IR 376, 380 *per* Johnston J.

of satisfaction, the consideration derived from the sale can be regarded as a 'substantial equivalent'.[45]

Some uncertainty surrounds the question of whether a settlement entered into with the intention of defrauding future creditors may come within the ambit of these provisions. In *Stileman v. Ashdown*[46] Lord Hardwicke accepted that this could be the case: 'It is not necessary that a man should actually be indebted at the time he enters into a voluntary settlement, to make it fraudulent; for, if a man does it with a view to his being indebted at a future time, it is equally fraudulent, and ought to be set aside.'

This principle was confirmed in this jurisdiction in *Murphy v. Abraham*,[47] where it was held by Smith MR that a voluntary deed in the form of a post-nuptial settlement entered into by a trader prior to embarking upon a partnership arrangement was executed with a view to defrauding his future creditors and could be set aside. Subsequently, in *Smith v. Tatton*[48] Fitzgerald B concluded that there was no evidence of future indebtedness being in the contemplation of the grantor, although he seemed to accept that in principle at least, a deed might be impeached if this had been the case. He stated that there were two classes of cases in which a deed might be set aside on this ground, first where there were existing debts and secondly, where 'either by the provision of the deed or other circumstances, it is shown that future indebtedness was at least in the contemplation of the grantor, so as to point whatever other evidence there may be of fraud to future creditors.'[49] Doubt was cast on the validity of this principle by some of the *dicta* of the Irish Court of Appeal in *Re Kelleher*,[50] including the statement of Holmes LJ that once the debts of creditors existing at the date of a deed have been discharged, a later creditor cannot take advantage of what might have been relied on by previous creditors as an implied fraud on them. However, a closer reading of the decision would suggest that the decisive factor was the lack of any proof of an actual intention to defraud and it is likely that where such an intention can be established the principle laid down in *Murphy v. Abraham*[51] remains intact.

Finally, it appears to be well settled that merely preferring one creditor over another does not come within the mischief which the statute was designed to prevent[52] and that a debtor who gives a creditor security with the intention

---

45. *Re Moroney* (1887) 21 LR Ir 27, 63.
46. (1742) 2 Atk 477, 481 in relation to the initial equivalent English provision (13 Eliz, c.5). See also *Barling v. Bishopp* (1860) 29 Beav 417.
47. (1864) 15 Ir Ch R 371.
48. (1879) 6 LR Ir 32.
49. *Ibid.* at 43.
50. [1911] 2 IR 1, 9.
51. (1864) 15 Ir Ch R 371.
52. *Glegg v. Bromley* [1912] 3 KB 474, 484 *per* Vaughan Williams LJ.

of preferring him to other creditors does not possess the necessary illegal intention.[53]

Voluntary Settlements to Defraud Purchasers

Section 1 of the Conveyancing Act (Ireland) 1634 provides that any voluntary conveyance made with the intention of defrauding subsequent purchasers is void (interpreted as meaning voidable), as against subsequent purchasers for value, and section 3 of the Act goes on to exclude *bona fide* conveyances for good consideration from the ambit of the section. The meaning of the term '*bona fide*' in this context was considered by Hamilton P in *Re O'Neill*,[54] who said that it must be taken to mean 'without notice of the intention to delay, hinder or defraud creditors of their lawful debts, rights and remedies.'

This legislation was interpreted strictly from the point of view of the person conveying the property and as Monahan CJ stated in *Gardiner v. Gardiner*:[55] 'from the fact of the deed being voluntary, we are justified in drawing the inference that the deed was made with intent to defraud purchasers.' The corresponding English enactment[56] was similarly interpreted,[57] and as Ronan LJ commented in *Moore v. Kelly*:[58] 'this principle plainly treated as fraudulent perfectly honest transactions, and was found, particularly in the case of settlements making provision for families, to operate very harshly and unjustly.' As a result, the Voluntary Conveyances Act 1893 was passed which provided in the words of O'Connor MR in *National Bank Ltd v. Behan*:[59] 'that no voluntary conveyance, if in fact made *bona fide* and without any fraudulent intent, should thereafter be deemed fraudulent or convinous within the meaning of the Act 10 Chas. 1, Sess. 2, c.3, by reason of any subsequent purchase for value.' However, it was held in *Behan* that despite these provisions, the onus of proving the *bona fides* of a voluntary settlement still lay on the person seeking to uphold it. O'Connor MR held that as infants were unable to prove affirmatively the *bona fides* of a voluntary conveyance of lands executed in their favour by their father, the conveyance was void as against a subsequent purchaser for value. He stated that in his view there could be no doubt as to the onus of proof under the Act of 1893 and that the words 'if *in fact* made *bona fide* and without any fraudulent intent' seemed to clearly place the onus on the party seeking the protection of the statute. This would seem to be an unduly restrictive approach and serious doubts about its validity were voiced

---

53. [1912] 3 KB 474 492 *per* Parker J.
54. [1989] IR 544.
55. (1861) 12 ICLR 565, 575.
56. 27 Eliz c.4.
57. *Doe v. Manning* (1807) 9 East 59.
58. [1918] 1 IR 169, 181.
59. [1913] 1 IR 512, 517.

by O'Brien LC in *Moore v. Kelly*.[60] Although he referred to the *Behan* decision and said that he would never overrule the judgment of the Master of the Rolls unless he considered that he was 'absolutely bound to reach a different conclusion', he went on to comment as follows:

> [O]rdinarily, I should have thought that the person on whom the onus of proof would lie under 27 Eliz. c.4, once the irrebuttable presumption to which I have referred was swept away, was the person alleging fraud, just as under 13 Eliz., c.5, where an actual intent to defraud the grantor's creditors is alleged, the burden of proving such intent falls on the person alleging it.[61]

In view of the harsh and unjust operation of the earlier legislation to which Ronan LJ made reference this would certainly seem to be a fairer approach and while the decision of the Master of the Rolls in *Behan* was not formally overruled, it would seem likely that a court today would take such a step or that at the very least slight evidence indeed would suffice to establish that a transaction was *bona fide*.

Settlements by Bankrupts

Section 52 of the Bankruptcy (Ireland) Amendment Act 1872, which made provision for the setting aside in certain circumstances of settlements made by persons subsequently adjudicated bankrupt, was repealed[62] and replaced by section 59 of the Bankruptcy Act 1988.[63] Section 59 now provides that any settlement of property,[64] not being a settlement before and in consideration of marriage, or made in favour of a purchaser or incumbrancer in good faith and for valuable consideration, shall be void as against the official assignee if the settlor is adjudicated bankrupt within two years of the date of the settlement and, if the settlor is adjudicated bankrupt within five years of the date of the settlement, shall be void unless the parties claiming under the settlement prove that the settlor was, at the time of making the settlement, able to pay all his debts without the aid of the property comprised in it and that the interest of the settlor in such property passed to the trustee of the settlement on its execution.

As in the case of the sections considered above, the reference to the settlement being void as against the official assignee has been interpreted as

---

60. [1918] 1 IR 169.
61. *Ibid.* at 179.
62. By s. 6, Second Schedule of the Bankruptcy Act 1988.
63. See generally Sanfey & Holohan, *Bankruptcy Law and Practice in Ireland* (1991) pp. 121-124 and Forde, *Bankruptcy Law in Ireland* (1990) pp.130-134.
64. Defined in s. 3 of the Act of 1988 to include real and personal property.

meaning voidable and therefore valid unless steps are taken to have it set aside.[65] There is no requirement to prove any fraudulent intent on the part of the settlor and it is the mere fact of him becoming bankrupt within the period of time laid down in the statute which brings the section into operation.[66] To secure protection against its provisions as Hamilton P commented in *Re O'Neill*:[67] 'it is necessary that the conveyance should be both for valuable consideration and *bona fide*' or that the settlement should be one in consideration of marriage.

In *Re O'Neill* the bankrupt conveyed his interest in premises to his daughter for slightly below the market value less than two years prior to being adjudicated bankrupt. The official assignee applied to have the conveyance set aside on the grounds that it had not been entered into *bona fide* and for valuable consideration. Hamilton P stated that the onus was on the official assignee to establish as a matter of probability that the conveyance was made with intent to delay, hinder or defraud creditors of their lawful debts, rights and remedies and that it was possible for the court to infer such intent from the circumstances of the case. In relation to the question of on whom the onus lay to establish that the conveyance was not made in good faith or for valuable consideration, Hamilton P stated that without deciding this question finally, he was prepared to deal with the particular case before him on the basis that the onus was on the official assignee to establish a lack of good faith on the part of the bankrupt's daughter. He concluded that while she must be regarded as a purchaser for valuable consideration, she did not purchase the premises in good faith as she must have been aware of her father's financial position and of the fact that the object of the transaction was to hinder, delay and defraud his creditors.

One further point to note about the judgment of Hamilton P in *Re O'Neill* is that he accepted as applying with equal validity to the Irish legislation the statement of Stirling J in *Mackintosh v. Pogose*[68] to the effect that to come within the saving clause in the section, it is sufficient that the purchaser acts in good faith and it is not necessary that both parties should have so acted.[69]

The other ground on which the application of the section may be avoided is where the settlement is made 'before and in consideration of marriage'. It was confirmed in *Re Campbell*[70] that this wording cannot extend to a post-nuptial settlement not made in pursuance of an ante-nuptial agreement. It has been held in England that for a settlement to be regarded as being in

---

65. *Per* Palles CB in *Re Doyle* (1891) Court of Appeal, unreported, quoted in Kiely, *The Principles of Equity as applied in Ireland* (1936) pp. 70-71.
66. *Re Moore* (1897) 31 ILTR 5.
67. [1989] IR 544, 551.
68. [1895] 1 Ch 505, 509.
69. [1989] IR 544, 551.
70. (1878) 12 ILTR 163.

consideration of marriage, it must be made on the occasion of the marriage, must be conditioned only to take effect on the marriage taking place and it must be made by a person for the purpose of, or with a view to, encouraging or facilitating the marriage.[71] In addition, it was held by the Irish Court of Appeal in *Re Downes*[72] that the exception in relation to settlements made before or in consideration of marriage is not confined to settlements made on the marriage of the settlor and in that case was held to extend to a settlement made on the marriage of the settlor's sister.

While section 59 of the Bankruptcy Act 1988 essentially reproduces the important features of section 52 of the Bankruptcy (Ireland) Amendment Act 1872, there are a number of important changes to note. Section 52 only applied to traders, a distinction which was criticised[73] and not retained in section 59. The ten-year period originally specified was reduced to five years in section 59(1) and the relevant date from which the two and five-year periods specified are to be calculated is now the date of adjudication of bankruptcy, whereas formerly it was reckoned from the date when an act of bankruptcy was committed.[74] In addition, the phrase 'and that the interest of the settlor in such property passed to the trustee of such settlement on the execution thereof' was included so that a settlement to take effect in the future would fall within the section. In addition, section 59(3) renders void as against the official assignee any transfer of property made in pursuance of a contract or covenant for the settlement of property acquired after its execution unless the payment or transfer comes within certain conditions set out in the subsection.[75]

71. *Rennell v. IRC* [1964] AC 173, 202 *per* Lord Cohen. See also *Re Densham* [1975] 1 WLR 1519, 1527 *per* Goff J in the context of equivalent English legislation.
72. [1898] 2 IR 635.
73. See Bankruptcy Law Committee Report (1972; Prl. 2714) chapter 23.
74. *Re Mackey* [1915] 2 IR 347.
75. This subsection was inserted to meet the criticisms made in the Bankruptcy Law Committee Report (1972; Prl. 2714) chapter 23.10.1 (5).

CHAPTER 12

The Administration of Trusts

THE OFFICE OF TRUSTEE

Introduction

Wylie[1] has commented that 'the position of a trustee is an extremely exacting one and, all too frequently, a thankless one.' This statement is an accurate reflection of the view which might be expressed by many who agree to undertake such a role. Trustees are required to carry out duties and obligations which can often be of considerable complexity and in doing so are expected to display a high degree of honesty and integrity. Referring to the danger that the interests of innocent beneficiaries may be jeopardised by those appointed to safeguard them, Porter MR stated as follows in *Bank of Ireland v. Cogry Flax Spinning Co.*:[2]

> That is why it is so important to select an honourable and upright, as well as an intelligent and capable man for the office of trustee. If the selection is unfortunate, so may be the results.

Trustees are only entitled to payment for such endeavours if the trust instrument itself makes provision for remuneration and they are precluded from making any form of personal profit out of the affairs of the trust or as a result of placing themselves in a position where their own interests and those of the trust might conflict. By undertaking to act in this capacity, in addition to incurring the wrath of the beneficiaries should he fail to exercise his duties in a manner which they might consider appropriate, a trustee may also face the prospect of personal liability to account where he is found to have been in breach of duty.

In view of these considerations, it may reasonably be asked why any right-minded individual would ever agree to act as a trustee, and it is the onerous nature of the responsibilities which go with the office which is primarily responsible for the growth in the numbers of professional trustees. Traditionally, trustees have fallen into two categories: non-professional

---

1. *Irish Land Law* (3rd ed., 1997) p. 595.
2. [1900] 1 IR 219, 236.

trustees, who are often family members or close associates of the settlor or testator who agree to act out of a sense of duty, and professional trustees, usually banks and financial institutions, who undertake the role only in circumstances where suitable provision is made for their remuneration. Arguably it is preferable when creating a trust to ensure that a combination of these categories of trustees are appointed; it is often unwise to nominate only non-professional trustees,[3] for although they may and indeed should seek professional assistance where this is required, they may not always be aware of the circumstances in which this will be necessary.

Any person can be appointed a trustee in this jurisdiction, even a minor,[4] although in practice it is desirable to appoint a person who will be capable of carrying out the functions required of him. A corporation may act as a trustee provided that its memorandum and articles of association confer on it express authority to carry out this role. It is preferable that the trustees appointed reside in the jurisdiction but in special circumstances an exception may have to be made, and the court may sanction the appointment of persons resident outside the jurisdiction where there is no practical alternative.[5] While a beneficiary or the close relative of a beneficiary[6] may be appointed a trustee, arguably this is undesirable in practice in view of the potential conflict of interest which might result. However, there may be difficulties in finding sufficient suitable persons who do not stand to benefit from the trust to act and it has also been argued that provided a beneficiary does not act as a sole trustee, it may even be preferable to appoint such a person as they will have an added incentive to ensure that the affairs of the trust are effectively and profitably conducted.

There is generally no minimum number of trustees necessary: one trustee will suffice except where statute requires otherwise,[7] although for practical reasons it is more desirable to have two or more. In this jurisdiction there is no upper limit on the number of trustees who may be appointed,[8] but for reasons of administrative workability it is obviously undesirable to have more than a reasonable number to facilitate the process of decision-making and to avoid the machinery of the trust becoming unwieldy.

---

3. See e.g. *Turner v. Turner* [1984] Ch 100.
4. Although in England, s. 20 of the Law of Property Act 1925 provides that the appointment of a minor to be a trustee of an express trust shall be void.
5. *Crofton v. Crofton* (1913) 47 ILTR 24.
6. *Re Jackson's Trusts* (1874) 8 ILTR 174.
7. Two trustees are required under s. 39(1) of the Settled Land Act 1882 in order to give a receipt for capital money on a sale by a tenant for life unless the settlement authorises otherwise.
8. Note that in England, s. 34 of the Trustee Act 1925 restricts the number of trustees in trusts of land to four.

Appointment of Trustees

The first trustees are ordinarily appointed by the settlor or testator in the trust instrument and where this is a will, the executors and trustees will often be the same persons. Where none are appointed or where those nominated predecease the testator or refuse to act, the court has jurisdiction to appoint trustees.[9] These trustees will hold as joint tenants, so where one or more dies, the survivors continue to act as trustees and on the death of a sole trustee, the trust property will vest in his personal representatives pending the appointment of new trustees.

As regards the appointment of new or additional trustees, this power of appointment may be exercised by persons nominated for that purpose in the trust instrument in the circumstances laid down in that document. Usually, this power will be framed so that it is exercisable whenever the persons nominated deem it necessary but where limitations are imposed these may be strictly construed. In *Re Wheeler*[10] a power to appoint a new trustee in circumstances where an existing trustee was 'incapable' of acting was held not to be exercisable where an incumbent became bankrupt on the grounds that while he might as a result have been deemed 'unfit' to act, this did not mean that he was 'incapable' of performing his duties. In addition to any express power contained in the trust instrument, a statutory power to appoint new trustees is contained in section 10 of the Trustee Act 1893. This statutory power must be exercised in writing and in practice it is desirable that it is exercised by deed to facilitate the application of section 12 of the Act of 1893 which makes provision for the vesting of trust property in new or continuing trustees. Section 10(1) provides that this power can be exercised by 'the person or persons nominated for the purpose of appointing new trustees by the instrument, if any, creating the trust, or if there is no such person or no such person able and willing to act, then the surviving or continuing trustees or trustee for the time being, or the personal representatives of the last surviving or continuing trustee'. This power can be exercised where a trustee:

(i)   is dead, or

(ii) remains out of the jurisdiction for more than twelve months, or

(iii) desires to be discharged from his duties, or

(iv) refuses to act, or

(v)   is unfit to act, or incapable of acting.

This power is confined to the appointment of replacements for original or substituted trustees, although where trustee(s) are being replaced the number

---

9.   *Pollock v. Ennis* [1921] 1 IR 181.
10. [1896] 1 Ch 315.

may be increased. However, it should be noted that it does not confer a power to appoint additional trustees except in these circumstances and in this respect the law differs from that in Northern Ireland and England.[11]

In addition, section 25 of the Trustee Act 1893 confers a power on the court to appoint new or additional trustees whenever it is expedient to do so and would be 'inexpedient, difficult or impracticable so to do without the assistance of the court'. The procedure for bringing an application under section 25 is set out by Keane;[12] it must be brought by special summons grounded on affidavit if it is brought to the High Court,[13] or by civil bill if is made to the Circuit Court.[14]

Retirement of Trustees

A trustee may disclaim his appointment and refuse to take up the office at the outset and if he wishes to do this, to avoid any possible uncertainty, he should preferably express his intention by deed.[15] However once a trustee has accepted the office and has failed to disclaim it within a reasonable time, he can only retire in specified circumstances. First, he can retire if there is an express clause in the trust instrument permitting him to do so or if he receives the consent of all the beneficiaries, provided that they are all *sui juris* and between them entitled to the entire beneficial interest in the trust property. In addition, statutory provision is made for retirement by virtue of section 11 of the Trustee Act 1893 which lays down that provided there will be at least two trustees left to administer the trust, a trustee may by deed declare that he wishes to retire and if his co-trustees consent by deed, he will be permitted to do so. Alternatively, an existing trustee may retire as a result of the exercise of the statutory power to appoint new trustees provided in section 10. In addition, a trustee may seek a court order under section 25 of the 1893 Act which empowers the court to appoint new trustees for existing ones whenever it is expedient, or would be difficult or impractical to do so without the court's assistance.

Removal of Trustees

A trustee may be removed from his office where express provision is made for this in the trust instrument or by the beneficiaries where they are *sui juris* and between them absolutely entitled to the trust property. In addition, a trustee

---

11. See s. 35 of the Trustee Act (NI) 1958 and s. 36(6) of the Trustee Act 1925.
12. *Equity and the Law of Trusts in the Republic of Ireland* (1988) pp. 105-106.
13. Order 3, rule 11 of the Rules of Superior Courts 1986.
14. Order 46, rule 1 of the Rules of the Circuit Court 2001.
15. While disclaimer may be implied, in view of the limited circumstances in which a trustee may retire, it is preferable that an intention to disclaim should be unambiguously expressed.

may be removed where the court exercises the power conferred on it by section 25 of the Trustee Act 1893 to appoint a new trustee where an existing trustee refuses or is unfit to act. The court also has an inherent jurisdiction to remove trustees where they act dishonestly or incompetently or even where their conduct is deliberately obstructive. This point was confirmed by Murnaghan J in *Arnott v. Arnott*.[16] The defendant was removed from the position of trustee to which she had been appointed on the basis that the business, the subject-matter of the trust, was to be managed by the plaintiff in circumstances where her persistent non-co-operation rendered the trust virtually unworkable. Murnaghan J stated that the jurisdiction of the court to remove a trustee should be exercised if the welfare of the beneficiaries demanded it, even though no dishonesty or incompetence had been alleged or proved against the trustee in question. He said that the jurisdiction of the court was usually resorted to when a trustee has mismanaged a trust or has been proved dishonest or incompetent but the guiding principle to which all others must be subordinate was the welfare of the beneficiaries.

A further ground on which a court may exercise its inherent jurisdiction to remove a trustee is where there is a clear conflict of interest between the trustee's duty to the trust and his own personal interests. In *Moore v. McGlynn*[17] the defendant was discharged from further performance of the duties of trustee where he had set up a rival business in competition with that of which he was trustee for the benefit of the family of his deceased brother. Although Chatterton VC held that the new business should not be affected with a trust for the benefit of his brother's estate, he was satisfied that it would be improper for the trustee to continue in a position where his personal interests and his duty to the trust might conflict. As he stated: 'his new position disqualifies him from remaining any longer a trustee, and it would have been better for him to have procured his removal from trusteeship before setting up for himself. He should not be continued in a position where his duties and his self-interest may conflict.'[18] Conflict of interest also formed the basis for the decision of Carroll J in *Kirby v. Barden*,[19] in which the defendant's actions, both in retaining a gift of a questionable nature for herself and in acquiescing in giving up a claim to the property which should have formed part of the deceased's estate, appeared to have been driven by self-interest. While Carroll J concluded that the jurisdiction of the court to remove a trustee should be exercised with caution, in her view the circumstances of the case amply justified the defendant's removal both as trustee and personal representative.

The fact that the primary issue which the court should have regard to in

---

16. (1924) 58 ILTR 145.
17. [1894] 1 IR 74. See also *Kirby v. Barden* High Court 1995 No. 769 Sp (Carroll J) 12 March 1999.
18. *Ibid.* at 90.
19. High Court 1995 No. 769Sp (Carroll J) 12 March 1999.

deciding whether to order the removal of a trustee is the welfare of the beneficiaries has recently been confirmed by Barron J in *Spencer v. Kinsella*[20] in a judgment which, although ultimately failing to resolve some of the problems faced by the plaintiffs, did provide useful guidance in relation to the circumstances in which a trustee may be removed from his office. Showgrounds in Gorey were vested in trustees on trust so that they might be used as a sports ground, park or pleasure ground subject to conditions as to payment or otherwise to be prescribed by the trustees. In recent years the grounds had been used by a local football club and coursing club and the land had also been used for the grazing of sheep. Complaints against the trustees were made by the football club which had spent money on the repair and maintenance of the grounds, and it was alleged that they were neglecting their duties and that the grounds were being allowed to fall into a state of disrepair. The plaintiffs sought the removal of the trustees on the basis that they had persistently refused to act when called on to do so and submitted that the welfare of the beneficiaries required this course of action. They were supported in their claims by the second named defendant but the remaining trustees submitted that they had at all times acted in a *bona fide* manner and argued that the exercise of their powers should not be interfered with by the court unless they had acted *mala fide,* capriciously or outside the terms of the trust. Barron J accepted that the existing situation could not be allowed to continue and said that a reorganisation must take place, either with or without the assistance of the court. While he acknowledged that it was difficult to find local people who had no affiliation with any organisation seeking to use the grounds, he stated that 'in all cases of trust, it is a truism to say that no trustee should allow his interest to conflict with his duty'. Barron J referred to the *Arnott* case and said that a trust is set up for the welfare of beneficiaries and before determining whether or not any trustee should be removed it is necessary to determine whether his continuation in office will be detrimental to such welfare. He concluded that the welfare of the beneficiaries was being affected by the difficulties which had been brought to the court's attention and said that in view of the existing conflict of interest some of the trustees who found themselves in such a position of conflict should step down and allow a general reorganisation to take place. Barron J stated that what was required was the appointment of trustees who were as far as possible impartial as between the various users of the grounds. However, he decided not to exercise the powers of the court at that time and to adjourn the matter for six months to enable the administration of the trust to be placed on a proper footing.[21]

---

20. [1996] 2 ILRM 401.
21. Hamilton CJ in the course of a Supreme Court judgment delivered on 13 January 1999 (Supreme Court 1996 No. 357) stated that the matter was re-entered before Barron J on 11 November 1996 and that the order which he made on that date recited

Barron J's judgment is useful in that it confirms that the overriding principle to which the court must have regard in exercising its power to remove trustees is the welfare of the beneficiaries. This is also borne out by the decision of Carroll J in *M.K. v. J.B.*[22] in which she held, in refusing to remove a trustee, that there would be no grounds for doing so unless the latter's decision to sell a property was not for the welfare of the beneficiary, which in her opinion it would be. Clearly the court can act where although there has been no breach of trust or actual misconduct, the conflict of interest existing amongst the trustees is such that the trust can no longer function effectively.[23] From a practical perspective conflict of interest can be as damaging to the welfare of the beneficiaries of a trust as actual misconduct and by placing the interests of the beneficiaries at the forefront of the matters to which the court should have regard, the decision of Barron J should ensure that sufficient attention is given to this point. His pragmatic approach is to be welcomed and it is submitted that while it is important that trustees seek to work together to resolve their differences it is also crucial that the court retains a power to intervene where the welfare of the beneficiaries is not being adequately protected.

THE DUTIES OF TRUSTEES

Duties on Appointment

The first duties of a trustee once appointed are to ascertain the nature and extent of the property comprised in the trust and to ensure that he understands the terms of the trust instrument. As Kekewich J stated in *Hallows v. Lloyd*:[24]

> I think that when persons are asked to become new trustees, they are bound to inquire of what the property consists that is proposed to be handed over to them, and what are the trusts. They ought also to look

---

that the court was informed that the issues between the parties had been resolved save as to the costs of the proceedings. In its judgment, the Supreme Court allowed an appeal brought by the sixth named defendant, the Minister for Agriculture, Food and Forestry, in relation to the order for costs made against him by the trial judge.

22. High Court 1997 No. 550 Sp (Carroll J) 26 February 1999.
23. It is interesting to contrast this approach with that recently adopted by the Supreme Court in *Dunne v. Heffernan* [1997] 3 IR 431 in relation to the removal of an executor pursuant to s. 26(2) of the Succession Act 1965. Lynch J stated that an order removing an executor is a very serious step to take and that it is not justified because one of the beneficiaries appears to have felt frustrated and excluded from what he considered to be his legitimate concerns. In the view of Lynch J: 'It would require serious misconduct and/or serious special circumstances on the part of the [executor] to justify such a drastic step' (at 443). See also *Flood v. Flood* [1999] 2 IR 234.
24. (1888) 39 Ch D 686, 691.

into the trust documents and papers to ascertain what notices appear
among them of incumbrances and other matters affecting the trust.

Trustees are required to act in good faith and in a responsible and reasonable
manner in performing their functions and they must inform themselves, before
making a decision, of matters which are relevant to that decision.[25] It is
essential that a trustee is aware from the outset of the precise nature of the
powers conferred on him by the instrument e.g. in relation to investment, and
he should seek legal advice if there is any reasonable doubt about the ambit
of these powers.[26] A trustee must also ensure that the property which is subject
to the trust is under his control and where necessary he must arrange for the
property to be conveyed or transferred into the joint names of himself and his
co-trustees. He must collect in any assets which are part of the trust and ensure
that the trust fund is properly invested. In addition, a trustee should satisfy
himself that there is no evidence of a breach of trust committed by a previous
trustee which ought to be investigated or rectified. He must make all reasonable
inquiries in this regard, and if the circumstances suggest that such a breach
has occurred, he should take whatever steps may be necessary to remedy the
breach, or he may find himself liable also.

Duty to Safeguard the Trust Assets

It is generally accepted that in relation to the management and administration
of a trust, unpaid trustees are expected to use such due diligence and care as
an ordinary prudent man would use in the management of his own affairs.[27]
This obligation will be examined in more detail in the specific context of a
trustee's duty of investment but in this section it is proposed to consider it in
more general terms and also to consider the importance of preserving the
trust assets, and the circumstances in which a trustee may be indemnified in
relation to litigation.

The trustee's duty to safeguard trust assets has been interpreted as imposing
fairly strict standards and would seem to require him to obtain payment of
monies owing to the trust as soon as they become due. In *Re Brogden*[28] liability
was imposed upon trustees of a marriage settlement who, although they had
taken reasonable steps to obtain payment of a sum due, had stopped short of

---

25. *Per* Robert Walker J in *Scott v. National Trust for Places of Historic Interest or Natural
    Beauty* [1998] 2 All ER 705, 717.
26. In *Nestle v. National Westminster Bank plc* [1993] 1 WLR 1260, in which the plaintiff
    bank claimed to have had doubts about the precise scope of its investment powers,
    Dillon LJ stated (at 1265) that 'it was inexcusable that the bank took no step at any
    time to obtain legal advice as to the scope of its power'.
27. *Speight v. Gaunt* (1883) 9 App Cas 1, 19; *Re Lucking's Will Trusts* [1967] 3 All ER
    726, 733.
28. (1888) 38 Ch D 546.

instituting proceedings because of the effect which they feared this would have on a family partnership. As Lopes LJ stated when a trust is owed money, the trustee is bound to demand payment and if this demand is not met within a reasonable time, he must 'take active measures to enforce its payment, and if necessary, . . . institute legal proceedings'.[29] He continued by saying that he knew of nothing which would excuse not taking action 'unless it be a well founded belief that such action on his part would result in failure and be fruitless, the burden of proving such well-founded belief lying on the trustee setting it up in his own exoneration'.

A trustee is bound to do the best he can from a financial point of view for the beneficiaries and this principle can in certain circumstances, particularly in relation to the sale of trust assets, require him to act in a manner which an ordinary prudent business man would not deem appropriate.[30] So, in *Buttle v. Saunders*[31] Wynn-Parry J stated that trustees 'have an overriding duty to obtain the best price which they can for their beneficiaries'. However, he went on to say that it would be an unfortunate simplification of the problem to state that the mere production of an increased offer at no matter how late a stage in the negotiations would impose an obligation upon a trustee to accept this offer, and stated that 'trustees have such a discretion in the matter as will allow them to act with proper prudence'. Wynn-Parry J therefore accepted that there might be cases where a trustee could properly refuse a higher offer and proceed with the lower one, although he was satisfied that this was not such a case and the tenor of his judgment undoubtedly suggests that it will be difficult for a trustee not to accept the best offer from a financial point of view irrespective of ethical or other considerations.

If a trustee believes that it is necessary to institute or defend litigation in order to safeguard the trust assets, he would be well advised to seek the approval of the court before determining what course of action to take. On the one hand as noted above, Lopes LJ stated in *Re Brogden*[32] that where a debt is owed to the trust and has not been paid within a reasonable time the only thing which would excuse a trustee from not taking legal action would be a 'well-founded belief that such action on his part would result in failure and be fruitless'. On the other hand, there is also authority to the effect that a trustee can only be indemnified in relation to expenses properly incurred for

---

29. *Ibid.* at 574. The decision in *Ward v. Ward* (1843) 2 HL Cas 777 would suggest that an exception to this principle exists where the taking of legal proceedings would impose financial hardship on a beneficiary.
30. As Templeman J stated in *Re Wyvern Developments Ltd* [1974] 1 WLR 1097, 1106 in relation to the obligations of a fiduciary, in this case an official receiver: 'He must do his best by his creditors and contributories. He is in a fiduciary capacity and cannot make moral gestures, nor can the court authorise him to do so.'
31. [1950] 2 All ER 193. See Bodkin (1950) 14 Conv 228; Samuels [1975] Conv 177.
32. (1888) 38 Ch D 546.

the benefit of the trust and as Bowen LJ made in clear in *Re Beddoe*,[33] in this context the word 'properly' means 'reasonably as well as honestly incurred'. Bowen LJ went on to state as follows:

> While I agree that trustees ought not to be visited with personal loss on account of mere errors in judgment which fall short of negligence or unreasonableness, it is on the other hand essential to recollect that mere *bona fides* is not the test, and that it is no answer in the mouth of a trustee who has embarked in idle litigation to say that he honestly believed what his solicitor told him, if his solicitor has been wrong-headed and perverse.[34]

Similarly Lindley LJ stated that if a trustee brings or defends an action unsuccessfully and without the leave of the court, it is for him to show that the costs so incurred were 'properly' incurred and that while the fact that the trustee acted on counsel's opinion is a factor which ought to be in his favour, it will not provide him with indemnity.[35] The importance of acting on the basis of court authorisation if a trustee is to ensure that he will receive an indemnity has recently been reiterated in two first instance decisions. In *Alsop Wilkinson v. Neary*[36] Lightman J stated that a trustee's right to be indemnified extends in the case of a dispute with third parties to the costs of proceedings properly brought or defended for the benefit of the trust estate. However, he went on to say that '[v]iews may vary whether proceedings are properly brought or defended, and to avoid the risk of a challenge to their entitlement to the indemnity . . . trustees are well advised to seek court authorisation before they sue or defend'. In the view of Lightman J, provided trustees make full disclosure as to the strengths and weaknesses of their case, if they act as authorised by the court, their entitlement to an indemnity will be secure. Similarly in *Singh v. Bhasin*,[37] Alan Boyle QC sitting as a Deputy High Court judge, stressed that where a trustee omits to apply for court authorization, sometimes referred to as a *Re Beddoe* order, he defends an action at his own risk as to costs and may find at the conclusion of the proceedings that the court will hold that his conduct in so doing was unreasonable. He said that the court is entitled to examine the entirety of the trustee's conduct in defending

---

33. [1892] 1 Ch 547. See also *Re England's Settlement Trusts* [1918] 1 Ch 24 where Eve J stated that the trustee's failure to obtain any sanction from the court was 'grievously aggravated by his deplorable conduct' in prosecuting an action in the names of himself and his co-trustee without any authority from the latter. In the circumstances the court held that the trustee was not entitled to his costs out of the trust estate.
34. *Ibid.* at 562.
35. *Ibid.* at 558. See also *Stott v. Milne* (1884) 25 Ch D 710 and *Re England's Settlement Trusts* [1918] 1 Ch 24.
36. [1996] 1 WLR 1220.
37. Chancery Division, 24 July 1998.

the proceedings for the purpose of assessing whether it was reasonable to take this course and that matters which may be taken into account include the nature and merits of the proceedings brought and the legal advice on the basis of which the trustee took the steps which he did. Alan Boyle QC accepted the submission of counsel that a trustee cannot look to a trust fund for the costs incurred by him in consequence of a failure to act with the prudence and good sense of an ordinary prudent man and concluded that the trustee had acted unreasonably in defending the proceedings.

A further consideration which must be borne in mind where the trust fund is small and likely to be easily dissipated is that litigation is probably better avoided 'unless there is such a chance of success as to render it desirable in the interests of the estate that the necessary risk should be incurred'.[38] So in *Bradstock Trustee Services Ltd v. Nabarro Nathanson*[39] it was held that trustees had not failed in their duty to protect the trust estate when they discontinued litigation in circumstances where the trust fund was likely to have been exhausted in indemnifying them.

Duty to Invest

Trustees are under a duty to invest the trust property with a view to ensuring a steady income for the beneficiaries currently entitled to an interest while at the same time preserving the value of the capital for the benefit of those who may subsequently become entitled to an interest in the property.[40] They are under no obligation to consult the beneficiaries about their investment decisions, unless required to do so under the terms of the trust and 'should not be bound in any way to act on the wishes of the beneficiaries'.[41]

Some important principles must be noted at the outset. A trustee is only permitted to invest in authorized securities and even where he adheres to this requirement, he must display impartiality and act with ordinary prudence in deciding which investments to make. So the fact that a form of investment is authorized by the trust instrument or by statute will not absolve a trustee from liability if he does not exercise the requisite degree of care in deciding which investments to make.

The question of whether an investment is authorized is governed in the first instance by the terms of the trust instrument, which will usually include

---

38. *Per* Bowen LJ in *Re Beddoe* [1892] 1 Ch 547, 562.
39. [1995] 1 WLR 1405.
40. See *Stacey v. Branch* [1995] 2 ILRM 136, 142 *per* Murphy J.
41. *Per* Arden J in *X. v. A.* [2000] 1 All ER 490, 496. While Arden J clearly accepted that a trustee is under no obligation to consult, she noted that at the conclusion of his judgment in *Re Pauling's Settlement (No. 2)* [1963] Ch 576, 586, Wilberforce J had expressed the hope that the trustees would give consideration to suggestions made by the beneficiaries with regard to investments and would not object to any suggestion that was in reasonable terms.

an investment clause detailing the trustees' powers in this regard. Where a clause in the trust instrument expressly delimits the ambit of a trustee's power of investment, its provisions must be adhered to and investment in unauthorised securities will amount to a breach of trust.[42] However, in certain circumstances, the court may sanction the overriding of express directions as to powers of investment where these are found to be in conflict with a settlor or testator's implied intentions. So, in *Re Lynch's Trusts*[43] it was held by Johnston J that the court had jurisdiction to disregard a direction in a trust as to the lodgment of monies on deposit receipt and to direct these funds to be invested instead in suitable trustee securities. This finding was made as the predominant motive of the testator, as expressed in his will, was to make provision for the support and maintenance of his family and he concluded that the direction that the funds should remain on deposit receipt was subsidiary to this overall objective.

In the absence of an express investment clause, or subject to its terms, a trustee may invest the trust property in accordance with the statutory scheme laid down in Part I of the Trustee Act 1893 as amended by the Trustee (Authorized Investments) Act 1958. Section 3 of the Act of 1893 provides that this statutory power of investment is to be exercised according to the discretion of the trustees. Section 1 of the Act of 1958 as amended specifies what are authorised investments and section 2 of the 1958 Act empowers the Minister for Finance to vary this list. Until recently, the ambit of investments authorised by statute remained limited and was generally confined to investments such as Irish and British government securities, real securities, stock in semi-state bodies, debentures or debenture stock, in publicly quoted industrial and commercial companies registered in Ireland which met certain requirements, and in deposit accounts in specified financial institutions. However, the scope of authorised investments has been extended by statutory instrument and SI No. 28 of 1998 varies the list of investments set out in section 1 of the Act of 1958 by deleting those specified in the section and substituting those set out in the First Schedule to the order. These investments now include units or shares in certain unit trust or collective investment schemes, specified annuity and life assurance contracts and the equity of companies listed on the Irish Stock Exchange and other recognised exchanges which meet certain financial requirements. One interesting innovation is clause 4 of the Second Schedule to the order which provides that where any part of the trust fund is invested in equities, the trustee shall review those investments at intervals of not more than six months.[44] Further amendments have been effected by the Trustee (Authorised Investments) Order 1998 (Amendment) Order 2002[45] which provides that in making an investment of trust funds, a

42. *Rochfort v. Seaton* [1896] 1 IR 18; *Re Webber's Settlement Trusts* [1922] 1 IR 49.
43. [1931] IR 517.
44. See SI No. 327 of 1990, SI No. 75 of 1992 and SI No. 28 of 1998.
45. SI No. 595 of 2002.

trustee shall take due account of the nature of the liabilities of the trust, an appropriate diversification and liquidity of investments.

It is now quite common to authorize trustees to invest in such a manner as they think fit and in *Re Harari's Settlement Trusts*[46] a clause in a trust which gave trustees power to invest 'in or upon such investments as to them may seem fit' was held by Jenkins J to mean that the trustees should be empowered to invest in any investments which they honestly thought were desirable. Jenkins J said that to hold otherwise would be to read words into the settlement which were not there and that he saw no reason to impose any restriction on the plain and ordinary meaning of the words employed.

A power to invest in 'real securities' covers investment in mortgages of land,[47] but not in its purchase.[48] It should be noted that such a power does not authorise trustees to lend trust funds on the security of a judgment mortgage.[49] In addition, in relation to the investment in mortgages of land, Smith MR stressed in *Smithwick v. Smithwick*[50] that 'it may be that a trustee lending on a second mortgage should exercise greater caution than if there was no prior encumbrance. . . .' A degree of statutory protection is afforded to trustees who lend funds on the security of any property by section 8 of the Trustee Act 1893 which provides that no liability shall arise 'by reason only of the proportion borne by the amount of the loan to the value of the property at the time when the loan was made' provided that certain conditions laid down in the section are met.

It is important to stress that even where a trustee does not stray outside the ambit of investments authorised either by the terms of the trust or by statute, he must nevertheless observe certain standards in carrying out his duties in this regard. As O'Connor MR pointed out in *Re O'Connor*:[51] 'however unlimited the power of investment may be, the trustee remains subject to the jurisdiction of the court. The trustee has no power to act dishonestly, negligently or in breach of trust to invest on insufficient security'. O'Connor MR continued by saying that subject to the power of the court to compel a dishonest or grossly incompetent trustee to account, it is in the power of the settlor or testator to place funds in the hands of the trustee to be invested in the fullest sense of the word and it was held in the instant case that a clause which permitted the trustees to invest in property 'as they think most desirable, but not in British funds' authorized them to invest in freehold land in Ireland and England.

---

46. [1949] 1 All ER 430.
47. This extends to mortgages of certain leasehold land, see s. 5(1) of the Trustee Act 1893.
48. *Robinson v. Robinson* (1877) IR 10 Eq 189.
49. *Johnston v. Lloyd* (1844) 7 Ir Eq R 252.
50. (1861) 12 Ir Ch R 181, 196.
51. [1913] 1 IR 69, 75-76.

The standard of care and prudence which must be employed by a trustee in exercising his powers of investment has been considered by the courts on numerous occasions, although it has not always been expressed in a consistent manner. In *Learoyd v. Whiteley*[52] Lindley LJ stated in the Court of Appeal that a trustee would have to take not only such care as a prudent man would take if he had only himself to consider but the care that an ordinary prudent man would take if he were making investments for the benefit of those for whom he felt morally bound to provide.[53] When the matter reached the House of Lords, Lord Watson spoke along the same lines and stated that 'business men of ordinary prudence may, and frequently do, select investments which are more or less of a speculative character; but it is the duty of a trustee to confine himself to the class of investments which are permitted by the trust, and likewise to avoid all investments of that class which are attended with hazard'.[54]

These statements would suggest that the degree of care which a trustee might exercise in relation to the investment of his own money may be insufficient; a greater duty of care is required. However, despite the fact that these principles were apparently quoted with approval by Brightman J in *Bartlett v. Barclays Bank Trust Co. Ltd*,[55] a more flexible approach seems to have been applied in that case, at any rate as regards non-professional trustees. The defendant bank was trustee of a trust, the only assets of which were nearly all the shares in a family property company. It was thought that funds might be more readily raised to pay taxes due on the death of the life tenants if the company went public and that a public issue would be more successful if the company was also involved in property development. One speculative purchase resulted in large losses to the trust fund, and the plaintiff beneficiaries succeeded in their claim against the bank for breach of trust. Brightman J stated as follows:

> The cases establish that it is the duty of a trustee to conduct the business of the trust with the same care as an ordinary prudent man of business would extend towards his own affairs. ... That does not mean that the

---

52. (1886) 33 Ch D 347, 355.
53. In interpreting this obligation, Thomas J has recently commented in a decision of the New Zealand High Court in *Jones v. AMP Perpetual Trustee Co. NZ Ltd* [1994] 1 NZLR 690, 706 that: 'This duty includes the duty to seek advice on matters which the trustee may not understand, such as the making of investments, and in receiving that advice to act with the same degree of prudence. It is not enough to act in good faith and with sincerity. Consequently, although a trustee may take advice on investments, he or she is not bound to accept and act on that advice. They must, in addition to being honest and sincere in relation to the advice which is received, continue to act as an ordinary prudent person would act.'
54. (1887) 12 App Cas 727, 733.
55. [1980] Ch 515.

trustee is bound to avoid all risk and in effect act as an insurer of the trust fund. ... The distinction is between a prudent degree of risk on the one hand, and hazard on the other. Nor must the court be astute to fix liability upon a trustee who has committed no more than an error of judgment, from which no business man, however prudent can expect to be immune.[56]

A further important principle which was confirmed by Brightman J was that in his opinion a higher duty of care is expected of a professional trustee, such as a trust corporation which carries on the specialized business of trust management. This point had been made *obiter* by Harman J in *Re Waterman's Will Trusts*,[57] where he stated that a paid trustee is expected to exercise a higher standard of diligence and knowledge than an unpaid trustee. Brightman J concluded that a professional corporate trustee is liable for breach of trust if loss is caused to the trust fund because it neglects to exercise the special care and skill which it professes to have. He held that the bank had wrongfully and in breach of trust neglected to ensure that it received an adequate flow of information concerning the activities of the boards of the companies concerned and that it had failed in its duty whether it is judged by the standard of the prudent man of business or of the skilled trust corporation.[58]

The application of the standard of 'an ordinary prudent man of business' had more disturbing consequences from the point of view of the beneficiary in *Nestle v. National Westminster Bank plc.*[59] By virtue of the terms of a settlement made in 1922 the defendant bank, the successor to the original trustee, was given wide powers to invest in equities. However, the bank never obtained legal advice about the scope of its powers of investment and assumed that these were narrower than they in fact were. The plaintiff, the remainder beneficiary, contended that the trust fund which was worth approximately £269,000 when she became absolutely entitled in 1986 should have been worth well over £1 million by then if the fund had been properly invested. Hoffmann J rejected the plaintiff's claim and concluded that the bank had acted conscientiously, fairly and carefully throughout its administration of the trust. The Court of Appeal dismissed the plaintiff's appeal and concluded that the plaintiff had not succeeded in establishing that she had suffered loss. Legatt LJ stated that it had not been established that a prudent trustee, knowing the true scope of the power of investment and having conducted regular reviews, which the bank had not done, would have invested the fund in such a manner that it would have been worth more than it was when the plaintiff became

---

56. *Ibid.* at 531.
57. [1952] 2 All ER 1054, 1055.
58. [1980] Ch 515, 535.
59. [1993] 1 WLR 1260.

entitled to it.[60] The Court of Appeal applied the traditional test; as Legatt LJ stated: 'the essence of the bank's duty was to take such steps as a prudent businessman would have taken to maintain and increase the value of the trust fund. Unless it failed to do so, it was not in breach of trust.'[61]

Although the Court of Appeal did not find the bank liable, the judges did not agree with the trial judge's conclusion that the bank had acted conscientiously and as Legatt LJ commented: 'No testator, in the light of this example, would choose this bank for the effective management of his investment.'[62] Kenny[63] has rightly commented that it is a sad reflection on the present state of trust law that a bank which 'no testator ... would choose ... for the effective management of his investment' should be found not to be liable for mismanagement of the trust. The law in this area in England at any rate would seem to unduly favour the position of the trustee.[64] As Doyle[65] has commented there is no reported case in which a trustee has been found liable for a breach of trust arising from investment within the ambit of that authorized by the trust instrument or the general law where the trust capital has simply continued to erode as a result and he concludes that 'the burden of proof facing potentially litigious beneficiaries is prohibitively high.' Certainly in the case of professional trustees, the reasoning which surfaced in *Bartlett* of applying a stricter standard might be developed further to avoid a result such as that arrived at in *Nestle*.

The extent of the duty imposed on a trustee in relation to investment of trust property has recently been considered in this jurisdiction by Murphy J in *Stacey v. Branch*.[66] The plaintiff beneficiary brought a claim against the defendant trustee alleging a breach of trust on the grounds that the latter had not managed a trust property with the necessary degree of care and claimed specifically that if this house had been let over a period of 14 years rather than maintained by a caretaker, it would have yielded a substantial rental income. The trust deed conferred on the defendant the power to deal with this property 'as he in his absolute discretion shall think fit' pending the attainment

---

60. Similarly Staughton LJ stated that it must be shown that the bank's failure to appreciate the scope of its powers or to conduct periodic reviews led it to make decisions which it should not have made or to fail to make decisions which it should have made, and that loss thereby resulted.
61. [1993] 1 WLR 1260, 1283.
62. *Ibid.* at 1284. See Martin (1992) 142 NLJ 1279.
63. [1993] Conv 63, 67.
64. Watt and Stauch have commented [1998] Conv 352, 361 that the reasoning of the Court of Appeal in *Nestle* showed an 'erroneous conflation of the quite distinct processes of determining breach of trust and determining the lass caused by that breach'. In their view, the effect of this has been 'to leave the English courts unduly reluctant to review the exercise of investment discretions, no matter how imprudently discharged'.
65. (1991) 5 Trust Law Int 138, 142.
66. [1995] 2 ILRM 136. See Buttimore (1996) 14 ILT (ns) 48.

of 21 years by the plaintiff. Murphy J made it clear that words such as 'absolute discretion' would not necessarily relieve a trustee from his duty to exercise reasonable care and prudence. However, he was satisfied that the defendant's decision to place the caretaker in occupation of the premises was one made *bona fide* in the exercise of his discretion and he dismissed the plaintiff's claim. Murphy J also gave some consideration to the nature of a trustee's duty of investment in general terms and it is worth setting this *dicta* out in full.

> What is the nature of the duty imposed on a trustee? A trustee must, of course, invest trust funds in the securities authorised by the settlement or by statute. To invest in any other securities would be of itself a breach of trust; but, even with regard to those securities which are permissible, the trustee must take such care as a reasonably cautious man would take having regard not only to the interest of those who are entitled to the income but to the interest of those who will take in the future. In exercising his discretion a trustee must act honestly and must use as much diligence as a prudent man of business would exercise in dealing with his own private affairs; in selecting an investment he must take as much care as a prudent man would take in making an investment for the benefit of persons for whom he felt morally bound to provide. Businessmen of ordinary prudence may, and frequently do, select investments which are more or less of a speculative character; but it is the duty of a trustee to confine himself not only to the class of investments which are permitted by the settlement or by statute, but to avoid all such investments of that class as are attended with hazard.[67]

This statement which requires a trustee in selecting investments to exercise the care which a prudent man would take in making an investment for the benefit of persons for whom he felt morally obliged to provide imposes a relatively stringent standard on trustees. However, it can also be said that the degree of care which a prudent man would exercise in these circumstances has altered over the years;[68] as Panckhurst J has recently commented in the New Zealand decision of *Re Mulligan*,[69] 'prudence provides a flexible standard, one which will change with economic conditions and in the light of contemporary thinking and understanding'. Dillon LJ made a similar comment

---

67. *Ibid.* at 142.
68. There is certainly some evidence of a more pragmatic approach to the question of the degree of risk which a trustee may take in making investment decisions elsewhere in the common law world. As Thomas J stated in *Jones v. AMP Perpetual Trustee Company NZ Ltd* [1994] 1 NZLR 690, 707: 'Neither prophecy or prescience is expected of trustees and their performance must be judged, not by hindsight, but by facts which existed at the time of the occurrence'. Similarly in *Re Mulligan* [1998] 1 NZLR 481, 501 Panckhurst J stated that 'a trustee is neither a surety, nor an insurer of the fund for which he is responsible'.
69. [1998] 1 NZLR 481, 500.

in the course of his judgment in *Nestle v. National Westminster Bank plc*[70] to the effect that '[t]rustees should not be reckless with trust money but what a prudent man should do at any time depends on the economic and financial conditions at that time — not on what judges of the past, however eminent, held to be prudent in the conditions of 50 or 100 years before'.[71] Therefore there is probably merit in Curran's[72] suggestion that 'it could certainly be argued that some speculative investment e.g. hedging and support of an overall portfolio policy, would be perfectly acceptable today'.

Finally, it should be stressed that where the default on the part of the trustees, as in *Nestle* and *Stacey*, is due to lack of initiative rather than to speculative investment decisions, it would still seem to be extremely difficult for a beneficiary to succeed in establishing a breach of trust on the part of the trustee. Beneficiaries may legitimately have concerns that the law as it stands at present does not adequately protect them from the trustee who is guilty of inactivity or even neglect in relation to his investment duties. However, whether one views the law from the perspective of beneficiary or trustee, it is clear that any attempt to change existing principles will be problematic in view of the need to avoid encouraging trustees to engage in excessive speculation.

It will be interesting to see what impact the changes introduced by the provisions of the Trustee Act 2000 in England will have on the standards which had applied in that jurisdiction. Schedule 1 paragraph (1) of the Act of 2000 applies the statutory duty of care to powers of investment which requires that trustees 'must exercise such care and skill as is reasonable in the circumstances having regard in particular to any special knowledge or experience that he has or holds himself out as having, and if he acts as trustee in the course of a business or profession, to any special knowledge or experience that it is reasonable to expect of a person acting in the course of that kind of business or profession.'[73] Section 4 of the Act introduces the concept of 'standard investment criteria' which a trustee must have regard to in exercising any power of investment. These criteria are the suitability to the trust of investments of the same kind as any particular investment proposed to be made or retained and the need for diversification of trust investments in so far as is appropriate to the circumstances of the trust. In addition, a trustee is required to review trust investments from time to time and consider whether, having regard to the standard investment criteria, they should be varied. This provision should go some way towards ensuring that trustees cannot simply invest trust property at the outset and then fail to show any interest in their investments and will require them to carry out periodic reviews of their decisions. Section 5 of the Act of 2000 also requires a trustee to obtain and

---

70. [1993] 1 WLR 1260.
71. *Ibid.* at 1268.
72. (1996) 90 GILSI 340.
73. S.1 (1) of the Trustee Act 2000.

consider 'proper advice'[74] in relation to the exercise of his power of investment unless he reasonably concludes that in all the circumstances it is unnecessary and inappropriate to do so. Legislation along these lines might provide welcome clarification to the law in this jurisdiction and there is clearly growing unease about the message which decisions such as *Stacey v. Branch* may be sending to trustees.

Another question which arises in relation to investment is the extent to which trustees are entitled to take into account non-financial considerations in making investment decisions. In *Cowan v. Scargill*[75] it was made clear that trustees should not be influenced in their choice of investment by such considerations. A mineworker's pension fund was managed by ten trustees, five of whom were members of the National Union of Mineworkers. These five trustees refused to agree to a revised investment plan put forward on the basis, *inter alia*, that it contemplated increased overseas investment and investment in forms of energy such as oil and gas which were in competition with coal. It was held by Megarry VC that these trustees were in breach of duty in refusing to concur in the adoption of this investment plan. Megarry VC stated:

> Trustees may have strongly held social or political views. They may be firmly opposed to any investment in South Africa or other countries, or they may be opposed to any form of investment in companies concerned with alcohol, tobacco and armaments or many other things. In the conduct of their own affairs, of course, they are free to abstain from making any such investments. Yet under a trust, if investments of this type would be more beneficial to the beneficiaries than other investments, the trustees must not refrain from making the investments by reason of the views that they hold.[76]

It should be noted that Megarry VC seemed to accept that trustees might pursue an ethical investment policy provided that the financial implications of doing so were equally advantageous from the point of view of the beneficiaries.[77] Lord Nicholls, writing extra-judicially, has also accepted this point in the following terms:

---

74. This is the advice of a person who is reasonably believed by the trustee to be qualified to give it by his ability in and practical expertise of financial and other matters relating to the proposed investment, see s. 5(4) of the Trustee Act 2000.
75. [1985] Ch 270.
76. *Ibid.* at 287-288.
77. Megarry VC also pointed out that he was not suggesting that the benefit of the beneficiaries meant solely their financial benefit and said that if they hold strong views on certain moral and ethical issues, it might not be for their benefit to know that they were obtaining financial returns from sources which they would not consider morally acceptable. However, Megarry VC stressed that in his view cases in which such considerations might arise would be 'very rare'.

The range of sound investments available to trustees is so extensive that very frequently there is scope for trustees to give effect to moral considerations, either by positively preferring certain investments or negatively avoiding others, without thereby prejudicing beneficiaries' financial interests.[78]

The question of the extent to which trustees may pursue an ethical investment policy is clearly even more relevant in relation to charitable trusts and this issue has recently been considered by Nicholls VC in *Harries v. Church Commissioners*.[79] The plaintiffs sought declarations that the commissioners were obliged to have regard to the object of promoting the Christian faith and not to act in a manner which would be incompatible with that object when managing the assets of which they were trustees. The plaintiffs contended that the commissioners in making investment decisions attached overriding importance to financial considerations and that they were only prepared to take non-financial considerations into account to the extent that they did not significantly jeopardise or interfere with accepted investment principles. It was held by Nicholls VC in refusing the declarations sought that it was axiomatic that charity trustees were concerned to further the purposes of the trust of which they had accepted the office of trustee. When property was held by trustees for the purpose of generating money, *prima facie* the purposes of the trust were best served by the trustees seeking to obtain the best return which was consistent with commercial prudence and in most cases the best interests of the charity required that the trustee's choice of investments be made solely on the basis of well-established investment criteria. The circumstances in which charity trustees were bound or entitled to make a financially disadvantageous investment decision for ethical considerations were extremely limited and there was no evidence that such circumstances existed in the case before the court. Nicholls VC stated as follows:

> The law is not so cynical as to require trustees to behave in a fashion which would bring them or their charity into disrepute. ... On the other hand, trustees must act prudently. They must not use property held by them for investment purposes as a means for making moral statements at the expense of the charity of which they are trustees.[80]

The approach adopted in *Cowan* can be justified on the basis that if the criteria of the most sound decision from a financial point of view is qualified in any way, the court will lose the means of judging investment decisions on the

---

78. (1995) 9 Trust Law Int 71, 75.
79. [1992] 1 WLR 1241. See Buttimore (1995) 13 ILT (ns) 141.
80. *Ibid.* at 1247.

basis of an objective standard and will instead move into the realm of a purely subjective one. However, the judgment of Nicholls VC in *Harries* has been criticised by Nobles,[81] who argues that the investment policy of charitable trusts, like the manner in which they distribute funds, should be governed by the charitable purposes which they purport to further. He argues that: 'If trustees cannot make, or cannot be allowed to make, controversial moral judgments on the extent to which their investments give effect to their charity's purposes then they should not be able to make the same judgments when giving away its property. Conversely, if they can be trusted to make these judgments when giving away the charity's property, they can be trusted to make its investments on the same basis.'[82] There is an undeniable logic to this argument, but in practice it may prove far from easy to implement and oversee such an approach.

Duty to Maintain Equality Between Beneficiaries

A trustee is obliged to balance what may often be the competing interests of a life tenant and remainderman in relation to the trust property. As Panckhurst J stated in the decision of the New Zealand High Court in *Re Mulligan*:[83] 'It is elementary that a trustee must act with strict impartiality and endeavour to maintain a balance between the interests of life tenant and remaindermen. Put another way, a trustee must be even-handed as between income and capital beneficiaries.' Hoffmann J also acknowledged the importance of ensuring that a trustee acts in a fair manner in making investment decisions which may have different consequences for different classes of beneficiaries in the course of his judgment at first instance in *Nestle v. National Westminster Bank plc.*[84] However, he stressed that trustees must have a wide discretion in this regard and stated that he preferred the formulation that a trustee must act fairly rather than one which required strict equality between tenant for life and remainderman. As he stated: 'It would be an inhuman law which required trustees to adhere to some mechanical rule for preserving the real value of capital when the tenant for life was the testator's widow who had fallen upon hard times and the remainderman was young and well off'.[85]

It should be noted that in seeking to ensure that a fair result is achieved, a trustee may be obliged to convert certain types of trust investment into an alternative form and this in turn may necessitate apportionment of the beneficiaries' interests.

---

81. [1992] Conv 115.
82. *Ibid.* at 118.
83. [1998] 1 NZLR 481, 501.
84. Chancery Division, 29 June 1988.
85. *Ibid.* at 5.

Duty to Convert Trust Property

This duty arises specifically in two situations, first where there is an express trust for sale an obligation is imposed on a trustee to sell the property as soon as practicable. It should be noted that a mere power to sell the trust property is not sufficient to give rise to such an obligation to convert.[86] In addition, a duty to convert may arise under what is known as the rule in *Howe v. Earl of Dartmouth*,[87] which effectively provides that where residuary personalty is settled by will in favour of persons who are to enjoy it in succession, subject to a contrary provision in the will, all assets of a wasting, future or reversionary nature or which consist of unauthorized securities should be converted into property of a permanent or income bearing character.[88]

The effect of the rule was summarised by Walker LC in *Re Harris*[89] as follows:

> The general rule is, that where there is a general residuary bequest of personal estate, including chattels real, to be enjoyed by persons in succession, the Court puts upon the bequest the interpretation that the persons indicated are to enjoy the same thing in succession, and converts the property as the only means of giving effect to that intention.

The rule only applies to a residuary bequest in a will, not to a specific bequest nor where there is an *inter vivos* settlement on the basis that the settlor was assumed to have had an accurate idea of the state of the assets when he created the trust.[90] In addition, the application of the rule will be excluded where the will provides otherwise or where it was clearly the testator's intention that the property should be enjoyed *in specie*. The latter finding was made by Meredith J in *Re Abbott*[91] where he held that the testator had contemplated the trustees retaining the bulk of the property and must be presumed to have intended the tenants for life to enjoy it in the form in which it was left. In the circumstances, Meredith J was satisfied that the rule in *Howe v. Earl of Dartmouth* was excluded by virtue of the language employed by the testator himself. This can be compared with the decision in *Re Harris*,[92] where the Irish Court of Appeal found insufficient evidence of intention on the part of the testatrix that the property should be enjoyed *in specie*. Walker LC stated that the rule must be applied unless, 'upon the fair construction of the will, you find a sufficient

---

86. *Re Pitcairn* [1896] 2 Ch 199.
87. (1802) 7 Ves 137.
88. See *Hinves v. Hinves* (1844) 3 Hare 609, 611.
89. [1907] 1 IR 32, 35.
90. *Re Van Straubenzee* [1901] 2 Ch 779.
91. [1934] IR 189. See also *Alcock v. Soper* (1833) 2 My & K 699; *Re Sewell's Estate* (1870) LR 11 Eq 80 and *Re Fisher* [1943] Ch 377.
92. [1907] 1 IR 32. See also *Re Berry* [1962] Ch 97.

indication of intention that it is not to be applied'[93] and he held that the burden should be on the person seeking to exclude its application.

The purpose of the rule is effectively to maintain equality between present and future beneficiaries; to prevent the tenant for life from enjoying the benefit of unauthorized or wasting securities to the detriment of the remainderman and to prevent the latter benefiting from future or reversionary assets to the detriment of the tenant for life. The apportionment rules were considered by the Law Commission in England in a report published in 1982[94] and it was acknowledged that in practice the rules of apportionment are almost always excluded in well-drafted settlements. While its conclusions must be read in the light of more flexible statutory investment powers in both jurisdictions, it is worth quoting some of the comments contained in the report in relation to rules which existed then.

> It is quite clear that in present day investment conditions the rules both of conversion and apportionment pending conversion have little if any relevance. When they do apply they require, in effect, the sale of equities, other than those authorised by the Trustee Investment Act 1961, and re-investment in gilt-edged securities. At a time when investment in equities may be the only way in which the capital value of the fund can in fact be maintained the traditional theory that re-investment is necessary to protect those interested in the capital no longer holds good. Conversely, the yield on fixed interest investments is now such as to provide the tenant for life with an income which is as high as and may be higher than the average yield on unauthorised equities.[95]

Duty to Apportion

Where Duty to Convert Arises

Where a duty to convert arises in either of the above situations, in the absence of any indication that the tenant for life is to enjoy the income until the conversion is effected, a duty also arises to apportion the original property between the tenant for life and the remainderman pending conversion. Where the assets are of a wasting, hazardous or otherwise unauthorised nature, this is presumed to benefit the tenant for life at the expense of the remainderman as this property may produce a high level of income to the detriment of its capital value. In making any apportionment, the trustee should ensure that the beneficiary currently in possession only receives income equivalent to the current yield on authorised investments and that any additional monies should be added to the trust capital.

---

93. *Ibid.* at 35.
94. *The Powers and Duties of Trustees* (23rd Report) Cmnd 8733.
95. *Ibid.* paragraph 3.31.

In assessing when the capital should be valued for the purpose of calculating this yield, a distinction must be drawn between situations where there is a power to postpone conversion and cases where there is no such power. In the former case, the date of valuation is considered to be the date of the testator's death and in the latter case, if no sale is effected in the meantime, a date one year after his death is employed.[96] This principle is adopted on the basis that the testator's personal representatives are deemed to have an 'executor's year' in which to effect the administration of the estate. Whichever date is deemed to be the valuation date, the tenant for life is entitled to interest on the value of the assets at that date from the date of death until the date of the actual conversion.

The opposite problem to that referred to above in relation to wasting or hazardous securities arises in the context of future, reversionary or other non-income bearing assets. In the latter case, the life tenant will obtain no benefit from these types of security until the interest falls into possession and it may be necessary to sell such property and re-invest it in securities which will ensure a more equitable division as between the life tenant and the remainderman. The question of determining the manner of such apportionment is calculated in accordance with the rule in *Re Earl of Chesterfield's Trusts*.[97] The effect of this rule is well summarised by Wylie:[98]

> The trustees should calculate what sums invested at 4% interest at the date of the testator's death, accumulating at compound interest at that rate with yearly rests, would, after deduction of income tax at the standard or basic rate, produce the actual sum raised by sale of the future or reversionary interest. The sum so calculated should be treated as the capital and the difference between it and the sum received from the sale of future or reversionary interest should be paid to the tenant for life as income.

Keane[99] has suggested that there is no reason why the rate payable on judgment debts, currently fixed at 8%,[100] should not apply in this jurisdiction in relation to the application of this principle. It should also be noted that this rule will not apply where the settlor or testator manifests a contrary intention.

Duty to Apportion in Other Circumstances
A duty to apportion may arise in other circumstances, some of which will now be considered.

---

96. This distinction is illustrated in *Brown v. Gellatly* (1867) LR 2 Ch App 751.
97. (1883) 24 Ch D 643.
98. *Irish Land Law* (3rd ed., 1997) pp. 638-639.
99. *Equity and the Law of Trusts in the Republic of Ireland* (1988) p. 114.
100. Reduced from 11% by the Courts Act 1981 (Interest on Judgment Debts) Order 1989 (SI No.12 of 1989).

(a) *Under the Rule in Allhusen v. Whittel*[101]

The purpose of this rule is to achieve equity between the tenant for life and remainderman in relation to the payment of debts and other duties due out of an estate. Often debts will not be paid for a considerable period after the death of a testator and in the meantime the tenant for life will continue to enjoy the income from the estate, including that portion which is owed to creditors. The effect of the rule is to charge the tenant for life with interest on the monies subsequently used to meet whatever debts may be payable out of the estate and so put him in the same position as if these debts had actually been paid at the time of the testator's death. The manner in which this apportionment is achieved is set out in *The Modern Law of Trusts* as follows:[102] 'the rule requires a calculation of the average income of the estate from the date of death to the date of payment, taken net after the deduction of income tax at the basic rate.' It is important to note that the application of this rule may be excluded where the contrary intention is expressed by the testator.[103]

(b) *Under the Rule in Re Atkinson*[104]

This rule governs the manner in which an apportionment is made where an authorised mortgage security is sold and the proceeds received are insufficient to satisfy the amounts of the outstanding principal and interest in full. By virtue of the rule, these proceeds are apportioned between the tenant for life and the remainderman in the proportion which the amount due for arrears bears to the amount due in respect of the principal.[105] The circumstances in which the rule applies are still uncertain. It has been held that it applies to monies due under a holding of debenture stock,[106] but not to arrears of dividends on preference shares.[107]

(c) *Where Repairs or Improvements are Carried Out*

Where repairs which are necessitated by ordinary wear and tear and which can be considered merely as maintenance are effected to trust property, the cost of such work should come out of the income of the trust and must be borne by the tenant for life.[108] However, where work can be regarded as effecting a permanent improvement to property, it is considered that the cost

---

101. (1867) LR 4 Eq 295.
102. Parker and Mellows (7th ed., 1998, Oakley) at p. 583. See also *Corbett v. Commissioners of Inland Revenue* [1938] 1 KB 567, 584-585 *per* Romer LJ.
103. *Re McEuen* [1913] 2 Ch 704.
104. [1904] 2 Ch 160.
105. See also *Stewart v. Kingsale* [1902] 1 IR 496.
106. *Re Walker's Settlement Trusts* [1936] Ch 280.
107. *Re Sale* [1913] 2 Ch 697.
108. *Re Kingham* [1897] 1 IR 170; *Re Waldron and Bogue's Contract* [1904] 1 IR 240.

should be deducted from the trust capital,[109] and therefore this will have a greater effect on the interest of the remainderman.

(d) *Purchase or Sale of Shares Cum Dividend*

As a general rule, there will be no apportionment in relation to shares purchased or sold just before or after the payment of a dividend and the entire amount received is deemed to be capital. This may prove to be unjust, e.g. where shares are sold just before the dividend is declared the price reflects the amount which will be paid although if they had been retained until the payment was actually made the amount of the dividend would have been treated as income. This principle of non-apportionment may therefore be inequitable and it has been held that where it gives rise to a 'glaring injustice'[110] it may not be applied.

(e) *Distribution of Accumulated Profits in the Form of Bonus Shares*

It was decided by the House of Lords in *Bouch v. Sproule*[111] that such shares should be treated as capital except where a company has no power under its articles of association to create new shares in this manner, in which case they will be treated as income.

(f) *Distribution of Capital Profit*

Where a company makes a capital profit and distributes it in the form of a cash bonus or capital dividend, it is regarded as a distribution of income to which the tenant for life is entitled.[112] So, in *Re Meagher*,[113] where a company decided to allot stock to its shareholders in the form of a 'special capital profits dividend', it was held by Kingsmill Moore J that it should be treated as income and paid to the tenant for life.

Duty to Distribute

A trustee is under an obligation to ascertain the identity of those who are entitled under the trust instrument and to take the necessary steps to ensure that the trust property is distributed in accordance with its terms. In England, section 27 of the Trustee Act 1925 as amended provides that trustees may advertise for potential beneficiaries and provided that certain requirements

---

109. *Brereton v. Day* [1895] 1 IR 518.
110. *Re MacLaren's Settlement Trusts* [1951] 2 All ER 414, 420.
111. (1887) 12 App Cas 385. See also *Re Carson* [1915] 1 IR 321; *Hill v. Permanent Trustee Co. of New South Wales* [1930] AC 720, 730-732.
112. *Re Sechiari* [1950] 1 All ER 417; *Re Kleinwort's Settlements* [1951] Ch 860.
113. [1951] IR 100.

specified in the section are complied with, they may proceed to distribute the trust property amongst the beneficiaries whose identities are known to them. There is no equivalent statutory power in this jurisdiction, although section 49(2) of the Succession Act 1965 lays down a procedure whereby personal representatives of a deceased person may advertise for claimants and may distribute the estate amongst those who have lodged claims within the period specified. While trustees have no statutory power to assist them in carrying out this task, it would seem to be good practice for them to follow a similar course where doubts arise as to the identity of those entitled under the terms of a trust.

A beneficiary who is underpaid or who receives no payment at all has a right of action against the trustees for breach of trust, although the trustee in turn will have a right of recovery against any person who has been overpaid or paid in error. There is authority in England to support the proposition that where a trustee who is also a beneficiary underpays himself, he has no remedy but this has been criticised and it is unlikely that such a harsh principle would be followed in this jurisdiction.

Where a reasonable doubt exists about the respective claims of the beneficiaries a trustee may apply to the court for directions and will be protected from liability in this regard provided he follows these directions.[114] Such an application may be brought before the High Court by special summons grounded on affidavit and it is prudent for a trustee to take such a course of action where legitimate doubt exists about the manner in which the trust assets should be distributed.

In circumstances where the whereabouts or continued existence of a beneficiary are unknown, the court may authorise distribution of the trust property to proceed after a specified period of time. Such an order is known as a 'Benjamin order' and may be made after a period of seven years on the authority of the decision of Joyce J in *Re Benjamin*.[115] The testator's son disappeared in 1892 and under the will of his father, who died the following year, he was entitled to a share in the latter's estate if he survived the testator. Joyce J concluded that the son must be presumed dead and the court gave the trustees liberty to distribute his share on the basis that he had predeceased the testator.

The principles laid down in *Re Benjamin* were applied in *Re Green's Will Trusts*.[116] The testatrix's son went missing in 1943 while on a wartime bombing raid and was certified by the Air Ministry as presumed dead. She bequeathed the residue of her estate to trustees for her son's benefit and directed that if he had not come forward to claim the property by the year 2020 the trustees were

---

114. *Re Londonderry's Settlements* [1965] Ch 918.
115. [1902] 1 Ch 723.
116. [1985] 3 All ER 455.

to establish a charitable foundation for the benefit of cruelly treated animals. The court gave the executors liberty to deal with the estate on the basis that the son had predeceased the testatrix and made a Benjamin order, the effect of which was to enable the charity to enjoy the testatrix's estate as from the date of her death. This decision has been criticised by Luxton[117] on the grounds that such an order was contrary to the intention of the testatrix. However, from the point of view of the trustees, bringing an application to court is undoubtedly the most prudent course of action in such cases and while the order made may not always accurately reflect the wishes of a testator, it will at least have the advantage of absolving them from any personal liability.

An alternative to seeking a Benjamin order, which might prove a sensible option where the funds available are of a limited nature, is to take out a missing beneficiary insurance policy. This course was followed by the defendant trustee/beneficiary in *Re Evans*[118] in circumstances where the other beneficiary, her brother, had not been heard of for 30 years. Richard McCombe QC, sitting as a Deputy High Court judge, held that the premium payable on such a policy was a proper and allowable expense. He stated as follows:

> In my view, personal representatives, particularly of small estates, should not be discouraged from seeking practical solutions to difficult administration problems, without the expense of resort to the court. Further, in small intestate administrations, where frequently the representative will have a personal interest, sizeable sums should not have to be tied up indefinitely for fear of the re-emergence of a long lost beneficiary. The missing beneficiary policy does provide, at relatively small cost, a practical answer to such problems. Such a policy provides a fund to meet the claim of such a beneficiary in exoneration of the representative and of the overpaid beneficiary. The policy is to the advantage of all and is to some extent more effective than the limited protection provided by the more costly application to court for a Benjamin order.[119]

The policy taken out by the defendant only yielded up sufficient funds to cover the capital sum to which the plaintiff was entitled and the court also had to consider his claim to interest. In the circumstances, the court concluded that it would be wrong not to satisfy this claim to the extent to which it was capable of being realized out of property from the deceased's estate still at the defendant's disposal, although it was also held that the defendant should be relieved against the claim to the extent that it could not be satisfied out of the proceeds of sale of that property.

---

117. [1986] Conv 138.
118. [1999] 2 All ER 777.
119. *Ibid.* at 785-786.

Duty to Keep Accounts and Provide Information

A trustee is obliged to keep clear and accurate accounts of the trust property and a beneficiary is entitled to inspect these accounts although in theory if he wants a copy of them he must pay for them. This obligation to keep accounts arises independently of any question that a breach of duty may have occurred as was made clear by Chatterton VC in *Moore v. McGlynn*,[120] where he pointed out that the obligation arises merely by virtue of the relationship of trustee and beneficiary. It is not strictly necessary for a trustee to have these accounts audited although it may be prudent where the complexity of the trust demands it and it would usually be wise for a trustee to obtain professional assistance in this area where he does not possess the relevant expertise himself.

It has also been established that a beneficiary is entitled to inspect documents relating to the assets of the trust,[121] although it would seem that beneficiaries should only be permitted to have access to information relating to their interest in the trust property, so, for example, a remainderman would only be entitled to information relevant to capital transactions. The obligation on trustees to provide information is well-established,[122] and the extent of the entitlement was set out as follows in *The Law Relating to Trusts and Trustees*[123] and quoted with approval by Kenny J in *Chaine-Nickson v. Bank of Ireland*:[124]

> When a beneficiary has a vested interest in a trust fund so that he has a right to payment of the income, the trustees must at all reasonable times at his request give him full and accurate information as to the amount and state of the trust property and permit him or his solicitor, to inspect the accounts and vouchers and other documents relating to the trust.

There was some doubt about whether this entitlement extended to beneficiaries under a discretionary trust but this was resolved by Kenny J in *Chaine-Nickson*. The plaintiff was one of a number of potential beneficiaries under a settlement of property vested in the defendants as trustees on discretionary trusts. The plaintiff sought an order directing the defendants to give him particulars of matters relating to the administration of the trust. The defendants argued that in the case of a discretionary trust, none of the potential beneficiaries were entitled as of right to any information relating to the management of the trust. As Kenny J pointed out the logical result of this argument was that the trustees were not under an obligation to account to anyone in relation to their actions, a proposition he could not accept. He therefore concluded as follows:

---

120. [1894] 1 IR 74, 86.
121. *O'Rourke v. Darbishire* [1920] AC 581, 626 *per* Lord Wrenbury.
122. *Low v. Bouverie* [1891] 3 Ch 82, 99 *per* Lindley LJ.
123. Underhill (11th ed., 1959) p.401. (Now see 16th ed., 2003, Hayton).
124. [1976] IR 393, 396.

Legal principle and the one relevant authority [*Moore v. McGlynn*] establish that a potential beneficiary under a discretionary trust is entitled to copies of the trust accounts and to details of the investments representing the trust funds.[125]

The entitlements of potential beneficiaries under a discretionary trust were also considered by Neuberger J in his judgment in *Murphy v. Murphy*,[126] in which he referred to the fact that the decision in *Chaine-Nickson* has been accepted in the leading English textbooks as stating the correct position on this issue. Neuberger J held that the plaintiff was entitled to know the names and addresses of the trustees of settlements under which he was identified as a specific potential beneficiary although he was not entitled to such information in relation to settlements under which he was, along with the rest of the world, merely a potential beneficiary. He agreed that in relation to the former type of settlement, a potential beneficiary does have the right to ask the trustees for 'information as to the nature and value of the trust property, the trust income, and as to how the trustees have been investing and distributing it'.[127] However, it is clear from the judgment of Neuberger J that the extent of this obligation will depend on the nature of the discretionary trust and the number of potential beneficiaries. He stated that while a trustee of a discretionary trust must appreciate that he will have duties 'it would be most undesirable for this court to make orders which would be likely to result in trustees of discretionary private trusts being badgered with claims by many beneficiaries for consideration to be given to their claims for trust moneys, or for accounts as to how trust moneys have been spent: the duties of a trustee are, it may fairly be said, quite onerous enough without such added problems'.[128] Mitchell[129] has commented that these distinctions leave the law in a state of uncertainty since it cannot be confidently predicted whether the courts will hold that a given class of beneficiaries is so large as to make it undesirable to allow its individual members to enforce their rights. However, despite this element of uncertainty, the approach of Neuberger J is to be welcomed to the extent that it has clarified the potentially open-ended obligations which the decision of Kenny J in *Chaine-Nickson* might have been interpreted as imposing, irrespective of the size of the class of potential beneficiaries. While the obligations set out in *Chaine-Nickson* and *Murphy* may well be reasonable in relation to discretionary trusts of a relatively limited nature, these burdens could prove unduly onerous where the number of potential beneficiaries is large and it is useful that the courts have recognized this fact.

---

125. *Ibid.* at 399.
126. [1999] 1 WLR 282.
127. *Ibid.* at 290.
128. *Ibid.* at 293.
129. (1999) 115 LQR 206, 208.

It would appear on the authority of the decision of the English Court of Appeal in *Re Londonderry's Settlement*,[130] that trustees exercising a discretionary power are not bound to disclose to the beneficiaries the reasons which motivate them in reaching a decision as to the manner in which the trust property should be distributed. The trustees of a discretionary family trust decided to distribute the capital of the trust. The defendant, a daughter of the settlor, was dissatisfied with the provision made for her and her children and sought access to the minutes of the trustees' meetings, documents prepared for the meetings and correspondence entered into between those involved in the administration of the trust. The trustees only supplied her with copies of the intended appointments of capital and copies of the trust accounts, and sought clarification from the court in relation to the extent of their duty of disclosure. The Court of Appeal held that the trustees were not under an obligation to disclose the reasons for their decisions on the basis that they could not otherwise properly exercise their confidential role. As Danckwerts LJ stated:

> It seems to me that where trustees are given discretionary trusts which involve a decision upon matters between beneficiaries, viewing the merits and other rights to benefit under such a trust, the trustees are given a confidential role and they cannot properly exercise that confidential role if at any moment there is likely to be an investigation for the purpose of seeing whether they have exercised their discretion in the best possible manner.[131]

However, Danckwerts LJ continued by saying that this position might be otherwise if a case were made of lack of *bona fides* and it has been suggested that a beneficiary determined to discover the grounds on which a trustee's discretion has been exercised might do so by instituting litigation alleging that this discretion has been exercised *mala fides* and then obtaining an order for discovery.[132] The result in *Re Londonderry's Settlement* has been criticised on the grounds that it allows the trustees to be effectively unaccountable in the exercise of their decision-making functions in relation to the distribution of the assets of a discretionary trust.[133] There is some considerable merit in the principle that trustees in these circumstances should disclose, at least in outline, the reasons which have motivated them in coming to their decisions if only to avoid unnecessary allegations of bad faith but it remains to be seen how the courts in this jurisdiction will deal with these conflicting arguments.

---

130. [1965] Ch 918.
131. *Ibid.* at 935-936.
132. Megarry (1965) 81 LQR 192, 196. See also *per* Robert Walker J in *Scott v. National Trust for Places of Historic Interest or Natural Beauty* [1998] 2 All ER 705, 719.
133. See also *infra* p. 447.

Duty Not to Profit from the Trust

It is a well-established rule that a person who occupies a fiduciary position is not entitled to make a profit from that position unless expressly authorised to do so, or to place himself in a situation where his interest and duty may conflict.[134] As we have seen above,[135] this principle is strictly applied to the relationship between a trustee and beneficiary and a trustee is not entitled to retain any financial benefit which he has gained as a result of his fiduciary position. This point was reiterated by Lord O'Hagan C in *Armstrong v. Armstrong:*[136]

> I think it is plain that a trustee, so making a commodity of his position, and gaining a profit which but for it he would not have secured, must be held, on general principles and for the safety of *cestuis que trusts*, to retain that profit for the benefit of the trust estate.

In addition, the operation of this principle can be seen in relation to the issue of charging fees for work done on behalf of the trust and also arises where a trustee attempts to purchase trust property.

Remuneration and Expenses

As a general principle, a trustee is not entitled to remuneration for work carried out by him in his capacity as trustee.[137] This principle has been applied even where a trustee has expended considerable time and energy in performing the duties imposed upon him by the trust instrument.[138] However, it is not without exceptions and as Lord Normand commented in *Dale v. IRC*,[139] it does not mean 'that reward for services is repugnant to the fiduciary duty, but that he who has the duty shall not take any secret remuneration or any financial benefit not authorised by the law, or by his contract, or by the trust deed under which he acts, as the case may be.' Clearly where the trust instrument itself makes provision for remuneration, this will be paid and if a settlor or testator wishes to appoint a professional trustee, it is essential that satisfactory provision be made in this regard. Although such clauses are often strictly construed,[140] much will depend on the precise wording employed. It has recently been held

---

134. *Bray v. Ford* [1896] AC 44, 51 *per* Lord Herschell. See also *Re Drexel Burnham Lambert UK Pension Plan* [1995] 1 WLR 32, 37 *per* Lindsay J.
135. See *supra* Chapter 8.
136. (1880) 7 LR Ir 207, 218.
137. *Re Ormsby* (1809) 1 Ba & B 189.
138. *Barrett v. Hartley* (1886) LR 2 Eq 789.
139. [1954] AC 11, 27.
140. *Re Gee* [1948] Ch 284, 292 *per* Harman J.

in England that provided the instrument expressly authorises it, a trustee may employ a company which he controls to provide services for the trust and the company may be paid for such services.[141]

In addition, the court has an inherent jurisdiction to order that a trustee be remunerated for his services where no provision for payment has been made in the trust instrument or to allow a trustee to receive payment in excess of what was originally laid down or agreed. So, in *Re Duke of Norfolk's Settlement Trusts*[142] the Court of Appeal agreed to increase the rate of remuneration authorised by the settlor. It would appear that such payment will only be ordered by the court in fairly exceptional cases where the trustee's efforts have resulted in considerable profit accruing to the trust, as in *Boardman v. Phipps*,[143] where remuneration on a generous scale was permitted in recognition of the results achieved. Remuneration for trustees was also ordered pursuant to the court's inherent jurisdiction for past although not for future services in *Foster v. Spencer*[144] on the basis that the services rendered by the trustees were wholly outside their contemplation when appointed. In addition, Paul Baker QC, sitting as a Deputy High Court judge, stressed that the right of a trustee to remuneration for past services cannot depend upon the fact that, at the time he seeks it, his services are further required so that he is in a position to demand payment for the past as a condition of continuing in office.

A further exception to the general principle of no remuneration will also be made where a trustee makes an arrangement to this effect with all the beneficiaries, provided that they are *sui juris*. Where they are not all of full age and capacity, such as where some of the beneficiaries may be minors or as yet unborn, application must be made to the court to authorise any payment.

The position of a trustee who is also a solicitor gives rise to some difficulties. As a general rule such a person is not entitled to charge for his services and it has even been suggested that if he were, it might encourage the institution of unnecessary litigation.[145] However, where a solicitor/trustee acts for himself and his co-trustees in litigation relating to the trust and the costs of his so acting do not exceed the costs which would have been incurred had he acted for his co-trustees only, he is entitled to be paid these costs. This principle is known as the rule in *Cradock v. Piper*[146] and has been applied in this jurisdiction in *Re Smith's Estate*.[147]

A trustee is entitled to be reimbursed for expenses properly incurred in

---

141. *Re Orwell's Will Trusts* [1982] 1 WLR 1337.
142. [1982] Ch 61, 78 *per* Fox LJ.
143. [1967] 2 AC 46.
144. [1996] 2 All ER 672.
145. *New v. Jones* (1883) 1 Mac & G 685n.
146. (1850) 1 Mac & G 664.
147. [1894] 1 IR 60.

the administration and management of the trust. This principle was set out as follows by Chatterton VC in *Courtney v. Rumley*:[148]

> The principle upon which this Court acts in reference to the allowance of expenses to trustees is, that the trust property shall reimburse them all the charges and expenses incurred in the execution of the trust, and in this the Court will always deal liberally with a trustee acting *bona fide*. But when the costs or expenses claimed have been incurred through the misconduct or negligence of the trustee, he will not be allowed them.

This principle is given statutory confirmation by section 24 of the Trustee Act 1893 which provides that a trustee 'may reimburse himself, or pay or discharge out of the trust premises all expenses incurred in or about the execution of his trusts or powers.' As Chatterton VC made clear in *Courtney v. Rumley*, the fact that a trustee proves unsuccessful in litigation will not prevent him from being reimbursed provided that he is acting in good faith.[149]

Purchase of Trust Property

Subject to strictly limited exceptions, it is an established principle that a trustee may not purchase trust property from himself and his co-trustees because if this were permitted the trustee would effectively be both vendor and purchaser. This rule, sometimes referred to as the 'self-dealing rule' was summarised as follows by Megarry VC in *Tito v. Wadell (No. 2)*:[150] 'The self-dealing rule is (to put it very shortly) that if a trustee sells the trust property to himself, the sale is voidable by any beneficiary *ex debito justitiae*, however fair the transaction.' Thus any sale is voidable at the option of a beneficiary, who should take steps to have the transaction set aside within a reasonable time.[151] As Lord Kingsdown stated in *Smith v. Kay*,[152] in a portion of his judgment quoted with approval by Napier CS in *King v. Anderson*,[153] in the case of the trustee/beneficiary relationship, 'the Court presumes confidence put and influence exerted'. Therefore there appears to be an almost irrebuttable presumption in such cases that undue influence has been exercised and it is unlikely to be sufficient to establish that the trustee was acting honestly and that the price paid was a fair one. Equally, it has been established that the right of the beneficiaries to have a transaction of this nature set aside does not

---

148. (1871) IR 6 Eq 99, 106.
149. *Graham v. McCashin* [1901] 1 IR 404.
150. [1977] Ch 106, 241.
151. *Webb v. Rorke* (1806) 2 Sch & Lef 661, 672 *per* Lord Redesdale.
152. (1859) 7 HLC 750, 779.
153. (1874) IR 8 Eq 625, 628.

depend on the fact that the trustee has made a profit.[154] The strict manner in which the self-dealing rule is applied is well illustrated by the decision of the Privy Council in *Wright v. Morgan*.[155] Property was left to two trustees on trust for sale to only one of them. This trustee assigned his right to the other who retired from his office and then purchased the property at a price fixed by independent valuers. The Privy Council held that this sale must be set aside as only a sale to the other trustee had been authorised by the terms of the will.

As a general principle this rule cannot be evaded by selling the trust property to a relative or associate of the trustee or to a company controlled by him; at the very least in such circumstances the transaction will be closely scrutinised by the court to ensure that it is not merely a colourable device to preclude the application of the self-dealing rule. It would also appear that the principle applies where a trustee has recently retired,[156] although not where he has retired a considerable time before purchasing the trust property.[157]

The self-dealing rule was applied by analogy by Scott VC in *Kane v. Radley-Kane*[158] to a situation where a personal representative had appropriated shares in satisfaction of a statutory legacy due to her as the deceased's widow, without the consent of the beneficiaries or the sanction of the court. He stated that such an appropriation was 'in clear contravention of the self-dealing rule' and was equivalent to a purchase by the personal representative of the appropriated assets. Scott VC concluded that the appropriation could not stand against an objection by one of the beneficiaries and that the proceeds of the sale of the shares formed part of the assets of the estate for which the widow as personal representative was accountable.

There are three main exceptions to the principle that a trustee may not purchase trust property from himself and his co-trustees. First, he may do so where the trust instrument expressly permits this,[159] although any such authorisation will be strictly construed. Secondly, the court may sanction a purchase in a suitable case or thirdly the beneficiaries may consent provided that they are *sui juris* and all agree to this course of action. In addition, there are borderline cases where the court may feel that it is inappropriate to apply the self-dealing rule, as in *Holder v. Holder*.[160] There one of the executors of a will, who had renounced his executorship soon after his appointment and had taken little part in the administration of the estate prior to doing so,

---

154. *Ex p. Lacey* (1802) 6 Ves 625.
155. [1926] AC 788.
156. *Wright v. Morgan* [1926] AC 788.
157. *Re Boles & British Land Company's Contract* [1902] 1 Ch 244.
158. [1999] Ch 274.
159. *Sargeant v. National Westminster Bank plc* (1990) 61 P & CR 518.
160. [1968] Ch 353.

purchased trust property at an auction for a price above the reserve fixed by an independent valuer. The Court of Appeal declined to set aside the sale on the application of one of the beneficiaries. However, it would be fair to say that the circumstances of this case were exceptional and it would be incorrect to assume that this decision marks the beginning of any general trend towards a watering down of the self-dealing rule.[161]

However a less strict approach has always been adopted by the courts where a trustee purchases property from a beneficiary rather than from the trust itself, sometimes referred to as the 'fair-dealing rule'.[162] While a presumption of undue influence will arise because of the nature of the relationship, this is rebuttable and the onus lies on the trustee to show that the transaction should be upheld.[163] Megarry VC laid down this principle in *Tito v. Wadell (No. 2)* in the following terms:[164]

> [I]f a trustee purchases the beneficial interest of any of his beneficiaries, the transaction is not voidable *ex debito justitiae*, but can be set aside unless the trustee can show that he has taken no advantage of his position and has made full disclosure to the beneficiary, and that the transaction is fair and honest.

Similarly, in *Coles v. Trecothick*[165] Lord Eldon commented that a trustee may buy from a beneficiary provided that 'there is a distinct and clear contract, ascertained to be such after a jealous and scrupulous examination of all the circumstances' and provided that there is no evidence of fraud, concealment or of advantage being taken by the trustee of information acquired by him as a result of his position.

In such circumstances where a trustee is seeking to establish that he gave full value for the property, it will obviously be desirable that an independent valuation is obtained. In addition, in order to establish that a trustee did not take unfair advantage of the beneficiary, it may be advantageous to prove that independent legal advice has been given, although it has been established that a lack of such advice or an independent valuation will not necessarily prove fatal from the point of view of the trustee. In *Provincial Bank of Ireland v. McKeever*[166] it was stated by Black J that where a trustee takes a voluntary

---

161. See e.g. *Re Thompson's Settlement* [1985] 3 WLR 486, 497 *per* Vinelott J.
162. See generally Nolan 'Conflicts of Interest, Unjust Enrichment and Wrongdoing' in *Restitution, Past Present and Future* eds. Cornish *et al* (1998). As Nolan states at p. 95 a fiduciary faced with an action under the fair-dealing rule as opposed to the self-dealing rule can successfully defend the action by showing that he acted with 'objective' fairness.
163. *Thomson v. Eastwood* (1877) 2 App Cas 215, 236 *per* Lord Cairns.
164. [1977] Ch 106, 241.
165. (1804) 9 Ves 234, 247.
166. [1941] IR 471.

benefit from a beneficiary there is a presumption that the benefit was obtained by undue influence. However, he also made it clear that this presumption may be rebutted, irrespective of whether the beneficiary has had independent advice, if it is shown that the transfer was the result of the free exercise of an independent will. This point was also made by Costello J in *Smyth v. Smyth.*[167] The deceased gave a life interest in a field to his brother, who was one of the trustees of his will, and the remainder interest to his nephew. The nephew agreed to sell this interest to his uncle and subsequently sought to have the sale set aside on the grounds of undue influence and on the basis that as trustee the defendant should not have purchased the plaintiff's interest in this manner. Costello J confirmed that the onus of proving the *bona fides* of the transaction lay on the defendant and said that he was required to examine the surrounding circumstances 'with very great care' with a view to ascertaining whether any unfair advantage had been taken by the defendant. Costello J held that the price paid by the defendant was in fact a fair one and that the defendant had not sought to take advantage of his position as trustee or to influence the plaintiff's decision to sell. He further concluded that the defendant was not under any obligation to ensure that the plaintiff received independent legal advice nor was he under a duty to procure an independent valuation as in his view both the defendant and his solicitor were correct in their assessment that the price agreed was a fair one.

Duty Not to Delegate[168]

The general principle in relation to delegation by a trustee of his powers and functions was summarised by Lord Langdale MR in *Turner v. Corney*[169] as follows:

> [T]rustees who take on themselves the management of property for the benefit of others have no right to shift their duty on other persons; and if they employ an agent, they remain subject to the responsibility towards their *cestuis que trust*, for whom they have undertaken the duty.

The rationale behind the principle of non-delegation of a trustee's duties is that the office is viewed as one where confidence is placed in the abilities of the particular individual appointed and it is therefore expected that he should personally look after the interests of the beneficiaries. So, in *Re O'Flanagan and Ryan's Contract*,[170] where a testator appointed his wife as trustee of

---

167. High Court 1975 No. 4369P (Costello J) 22 November 1978.
168. See Jones (1959) 22 MLR 381, 381-385.
169. (1841) 5 Beav 515, 517.
170. [1905] 1 IR 280. See also *Carr v. Connor* (1929) 63 ILTR 185, 189 where Fitzgibbon J commented that a trustee is 'bound to exercise his own judgement'.

property to hold for herself and their children, it was held by Porter MR that she had no power to delegate this role.

It has been suggested that while trustees will often be required to take advice from appropriate experts, '[i]t is for advisers to advise and for trustees to decide'.[171] However, this proposition should be read with a degree of caution and the principle of *delegatus non potest delegare* cannot be applied inflexibly to the position of trustees. Indeed, it has long been recognised that a trustee may delegate in situations of 'legal necessity' or 'moral necessity'.[172] Provision may be made for delegation in the trust instrument, and provided that the delegation does not exceed what is authorised it will be permissible. In addition, it has been recognised that the proper administration of a trust would not be practicable if a trustee was not free to delegate the performance of certain functions to professional agents, such as solicitors and brokers. So, a trustee may employ a qualified professional person as his agent where the exercise of his office demands that these services be obtained and as Wylie[173] has commented, it may even in certain circumstances amount to a breach of trust not to delegate.

The general principle is that where an ordinary prudent man of business would employ an agent to act on his behalf, a trustee will be entitled to delegate his functions and will not be liable for the default of an agent employed in these circumstances.[174] In *Speight v. Gaunt*[175] the defendant trustee had employed a broker at the request of the beneficiaries to purchase stock. When the broker absconded with the monies provided for the purchase, the beneficiaries sought to make the defendant liable for breach of trust. It was held by the Court of Appeal and confirmed by the House of Lords that the defendant had acted prudently as a reasonable man of business would have acted in employing a broker to act in such a situation and that he was not liable.

A number of further points should be noted about the circumstances in which a trustee may delegate to an agent. First, a trustee must exercise his own discretion in appointing an agent, he cannot delegate the making of this choice.[176] So, in *Fry v. Tapson*[177] trustees did not exercise their own judgment

---

171. *Per* Robert Walker J in *Scott v. National Trust for Places of Historic Interest or Natural Beauty* [1998] 2 All ER 705, 717.
172. *Ex p. Belchier* (1754) Amb 218.
173. *Irish Land Law* (3rd ed., 1997) p. 610.
174. *Speight v. Gaunt* (1883) 22 Ch D 727, 739-740 *per* Lindley LJ; *Fry v. Tapson* (1884) 28 Ch D 268, 280.
175. (1883) 22 Ch D 727.
176. *Re Weall* (1889) 42 Ch D 674. Kekewich J pointed out that 'a trustee is bound to exercise discretion in the choice of his agents' but went on to state that provided he selects properly qualified persons he cannot be made responsible for their intelligence or honesty.
177. (1884) 28 Ch D 268. See also *Speight v. Gaunt* (1883) 22 Ch D 727, 756 *per* Lindley LJ.

in relation to the appointment of a valuer to advise them in a transaction where money was lent on a mortgage, but instead relied on the recommendation of their solicitor. This individual was in fact an agent of the mortgagor and when loss subsequently occurred, it was held that the trustees were liable as they had not made the decision in relation to who should be appointed themselves. It is also important to note that an agent should not be entrusted with responsibilities not normally undertaken by that class of agent[178] so, for example, a solicitor should not be employed to carry out work which should properly be within the remit of a broker's functions.[179]

In addition, even where an agent is properly appointed in the circumstances, a trustee must still exercise a reasonable degree of supervision over the agent's activities.[180] Some indemnity is afforded by section 24 of the Trustee Act 1893 which provides that a trustee shall be liable only for his own acts and defaults and not for those of any other trustee or banker or broker unless any loss occurs as a result of 'wilful default' on his part. The meaning of the latter term was considered by Lindley LJ in *Re Chapman*[181] where he commented that 'trustees acting honestly, with ordinary prudence and within the limits of their trust, are not liable for mere errors of judgment'. Subsequently in *Re Vickery*[182] in construing the phrase 'wilful default' in section 30 of the Trustee Act 1925, which replaced section 24 of the Act of 1893 in England, Maugham J said that the words implied, as suggested by Romer J in *Re City Equitable Fire Insurance Co.*,[183] 'either a consciousness of negligence or breach of duty, or a recklessness in the performance of a duty'.[184] However, this subjective approach has been criticized,[185] and the standard of the ordinary prudent man of business is probably preferable in this context.

A further relevant statutory exemption is provided by section 17 of the Trustee Act 1893 which lays down that a solicitor may be entrusted with the receipt of purchase money deriving from the sale of trust property and either a solicitor or banker may receive insurance monies. The validity of the power of delegation is dependent in the former case on the solicitor having custody of a deed containing a receipt for the money and in the latter case on the solicitor or banker having the insurance policy with a receipt signed by the

---

178. Trustees must ensure that they select persons who are 'properly qualified' to carry out the function at issue. *Per* Kekewich J in *Re Weall* (1889) 42 Ch D 674, 678.
179. *Rowland v. Witherden* (1851) 3 McN & G 568.
180. In terms of the degree of supervision required in such circumstances, trustees are expected to exercise the 'ordinary prudence which a man uses in his own affairs'; *Mendes v. Guedalla* (1862) 2 J & H 259, 277 *per* Page Wood VC.
181. [1896] 2 Ch 763, 776.
182. [1931] 1 Ch 572.
183. [1925] 1 Ch 407.
184. [1931] 1 Ch 572, 584.
185. See Stannard [1979] Conv 345 and Dal Pont [2001] Conv 376.

trustees. The effect of the section is that in these defined circumstances, a trustee will not be liable merely because he has delegated his functions, although subsection (3) goes on to provide that liability may be imposed where the trustees allow the monies received to remain in the hands of or under the control of the solicitor or broker for a period longer than is reasonably necessary.

The law in England in relation to the delegation of trustees' functions has recently been extended and clarified by the provisions of the Trustee Act 2000.[186] Trustees may now, subject to any restriction or exclusion imposed by the trust instrument or by other legislation,[187] authorize an agent to exercise any of their 'delegable functions'.[188] These constitute functions other than those listed in section 11(2), such as functions relating to the manner in which trust assets should be distributed or the power to appoint a person to be a trustee, but trustees may now delegate decision-making in relation to investments. A trustee is required to keep the arrangements under which an agent acts under review[189] but is not liable for any act or default of an agent unless he has failed to comply with the statutory duty of care laid down in the legislation in entering into the arrangement or in keeping it under review.[190] This requires that he must exercise such care and skill as is reasonable in the circumstances having regard in particular to any special knowledge or experience that he has or holds himself out as having and, if he acts as trustee in the course of a business or profession, to any special knowledge or experience that it is reasonable to expect of a person acting in the course of that kind of business or profession.[191]

It is fair to say that the present position in relation to delegation by trustees in this jurisdiction is far from satisfactory and clearly it needs to be addressed as a matter of some urgency. As Kenny has commented 'delegation of some or all of the acts of trusteeship is an inevitable consequence of modern trusteeship'[192] and legislation along the lines of that recently enacted in England would both clarify the law and ease the burden on trustees.

---

186. Formerly s. 23(1) of the Trustee Act 1925 provided that a trustee might employ an agent to do any act required to be done in the execution of the trust and that he should not be responsible for the default of such an agent if employed in good faith. In addition, s. 30(1) of the Act of 1925 provided that a trustee should not be liable for the acts or defaults of a co-trustee or agent or for any other loss unless this was caused by his own wilful default.

187. S. 26 of the Trustee Act 2000.

188. S. 11(1) of the Trustee Act 2000.

189. S. 22(1) of the Trustee Act 2000.

190. S. 23 and Schedule 1, paragraph 3 of the Trustee Act 2000.

191. S. 1(1) of the Trustee Act 2000.

192. [1997] Conv 372, 373.

THE POWERS OF TRUSTEES

Introduction

Before the intervention of statute in this area, where a trust instrument was being drafted it was necessary to ensure that sufficient powers were conferred on the trustees by the instrument to enable them to carry out their duties in the manner envisaged by the settlor or testator. The Trustee Act 1893 now confers a number of basic powers on trustees but this legislation was only intended to augment the powers conferred by the trust instrument, which will often still determine the precise extent of the trustees' powers. It is now proposed to examine some of the more important statutory powers conferred on trustees but it should be borne in mind that in the final analysis the terms of the instrument itself are still of overriding importance.

Power of Sale and to Give Receipts

A trustee may be authorised to sell trust property by virtue of an express power contained in a trust instrument or alternatively such a power may be implied e.g. in circumstances where the rule in *Howe v. Earl of Dartmouth*[193] applies. The only other circumstances in which a trustee may sell trust property is where he is authorised to do so by the court or where a power of sale is conferred on him by statute.

Where a trustee holds property on trust for sale or with a power of sale, statutory powers are conferred on him in relation to the conduct of the sale by section 13 of the Trustee Act 1893. The section provides that, subject to a contrary intention being expressed in the trust instrument, a trustee is empowered to sell the trust property in whole or in part and either by public auction or by private contract subject to such conditions as he thinks fit.

The overriding duty of a trustee selling trust property is to obtain the best price for the beneficiaries,[194] although it should be noted that section 14 of the Trustee Act 1893 provides that a sale may not be impeached by a beneficiary on the grounds that any of the conditions of sale were unduly depreciatory unless it appears that the consideration for the sale was thereby rendered inadequate. In such cases, the position of the purchaser is also protected unless it appears that he was acting in collusion with the trustee at the time the contract for sale was concluded.[195]

A further relevant power is contained in section 15 of the Act of 1893

---

193. (1802) 7 Ves 137. See *supra* p. 406.
194. *Buttle v. Saunders* [1950] 2 All ER 193, 195. See also *Re Cooper and Allen's Contract for Sale to Harlech* (1876) 4 Ch D 802, 815 *per* Jessel MR.
195. S. 14(2) of the Act of 1893.

which provides that a trustee who is either a vendor or purchaser may sell or buy trust property without excluding the application of section 2 of the Vendor and Purchaser Act 1874.

A statutory power is conferred on trustees by section 20 of the Trustee Act 1893 to give receipts and it provides that a written receipt given by a trustee for the money, securities or property sold is a sufficient discharge to the person paying and effectively exonerates him from being answerable for any loss or misapplication of the property.

Power of Maintenance

Express provision can be and often is made in the trust instrument empowering the trustees to apply the income of the trust property for an infant's benefit.[196] Statutory powers of maintenance are also conferred on trustees by section 43 of the Conveyancing Act 1881 which empowers them to use trust income towards the maintenance or education of infant beneficiaries in certain circumstances. In situations where this power is exercisable, trustees may pay maintenance to an infant's parent or guardian or otherwise apply the income for the maintenance, education or benefit of an infant. Section 43 can be applied where property is held on trust for an infant beneficiary for life or for any greater interest, whether absolutely or contingently, on attaining the age of 18 or on the occurrence of any specified event before attaining that age. However, if the vesting of the interest is contingent on reaching a greater age or on the happening of some future event, the statutory power cannot be employed.

A further limitation on this statutory power is that it only applies where the trust property 'carries the intermediate income' i.e. the income which arises between the time of the coming into effect of the trust and the time the infant attains his majority, or the contingency occurs. As a general principle, a future or contingent gift will not be regarded as carrying the intermediate income which could be applied for maintenance except where it is a gift of residuary personalty, as in such cases the income can go to no-one except the residuary legatee. However, other types of future or contingent legacies will only carry the intermediate income in limited circumstances, as set out by Ker.[197] First, they will be regarded as carrying the income where the testator was the parent of or, *in loco parentis* to, the infant beneficiary, except where the contingency is the attaining of some age greater than the age of majority,[198] or where the testator has provided another fund out of which the infant is to be maintained. So, in *Re Ferguson*[199] it was held by O'Connor MR that a

---

196. E.g. *Russell v. Russell* [1903] 1 IR 168.
197. (1953) 17 Conv 273, 276-278.
198. *Re Abrahams* [1911] 1 Ch 108.
199. (1915) 49 ILTR 110.

contingent specific bequest carried the intermediate income as the testator was *in loco parentis* and had made no alternative provision for the maintenance of the legatee before the bequest vested. The second exception is where the testator has manifested an intention that the infant is to be maintained as in *Re Churchill*,[200] where the testatrix had given a legacy to her grand-nephew and directed that any part of it should be paid towards his advancement in life or otherwise for his benefit. The third exception is where the testator segregates a fund for the legatee and is set out in the following terms by Chatterton VC in *Johnston v. O'Neill*:[201]

> It is, no doubt, the general rule that general legacies payable at a future day, even though vested, do not carry interest before the day of payment, except legacies given to a child by a parent, or a person *in loco parentis*. But to this general rule there are exceptions, one of which is, that where a fund is directed to be presently separated from the general personal estate for the purpose of providing for the future payment of certain legacies, it carries the interest accruing up to the time of payment, to the legatees, with the capital sum. In such cases, the rule that the interest follows the capital prevails, and the legatee gets his legacy with its interim accretions.

A statutory power to permit the court to make payments of income or capital is conferred by section 11 of the Guardianship of Infants Act 1964 which provides that an application may be brought by the guardian of the infant where such a payment is necessary for his maintenance or education. In addition, the court also has an inherent jurisdiction to make an order sanctioning the use of capital by trustees for the maintenance of infants where they have no other means of support.[202] In *Re O'Neill*[203] Maguire P directed that a payment be made out of the trust capital for the maintenance and education of the testator's children, although he made it clear that it was a jurisdiction which should only be exercised where it was really necessary. He stated:

> I must be satisfied that such a course is not only beneficial but necessary to the welfare of the minors. ... The jurisdiction to make an advance out of capital is not to be exercised lightly. Where a minor is actually destitute the way is clear, but where the minors, as here, are not destitute, the question of the existence of a sufficient element of necessity becomes a difficult problem.[204]

---

200. [1909] 2 Ch 431.
201. (1879) 3 LR Ir 476, 480-481.
202. *Robison v. Killey* (1862) 30 Beav 520, 521.
203. [1943] IR 562.
204. *Ibid*. at 564-565.

Power of Advancement

While 'maintenance' usually refers to the payment of income for the benefit of infant beneficiaries, the term 'advancement' is used to describe payments made out of the trust capital to a beneficiary before he becomes entitled to an interest under the trust. Traditionally, 'the word "advancement" meant ... the establishment in life of the beneficiary who was the object of the power or at any rate some step that would contribute to the furtherance of his establishment'.[205] A power to make advancements out of capital may be expressly conferred by the trust instrument.[206] In addition, as seen above, a statutory power exists under section 11 of the Guardianship of Infants Act 1964 whereby the court can sanction capital payments for the support of an infant beneficiary where an application is made by the infant's guardian.

Power to Compound Liabilities

By virtue of section 21 of the Trustee Act 1893, trustees may 'compromise, compound, abandon, submit to arbitration or otherwise settle' any debt or claim without being responsible for any loss occasioned by any act done by him in this regard in good faith. As Overend J stated in *Re Boyle*[207] in relation to this power, which is also conferred on executors and administrators: 'There is no question that an executor has power to compromise even a doubtful claim, if he *bona fide* believes it to be in the interest of the estate.'

Power to Insure

While trustees originally had no power to insure unless this was conferred by the trust instrument, section 18 of the Trustee Act 1893 provides that they may insure trust property 'against loss or damage by fire' to an amount not exceeding three-quarters of the full value of the property. In addition, section 18(2) provides that this power does not apply to any building or property which the trustees are bound to convey absolutely to any beneficiary on being requested to do so.

It should be noted that in England section 34 of Trustee Act 2000 now provides that a trustee may insure any property which is subject to a trust against risks of loss or damage due to any event and that a trustee may pay the premiums out of the trust funds.[208]

---

205. *Pilkington v. IRC* [1964] AC 612, 634.
206. *McMahon v. Gaussen* [1896] 1 IR 143; *L'Estrange v. L'Estrange* [1902] 1 IR 467.
207. [1947] IR 61, 69.
208. See paragraph 6.4 of Law Commission Report No. 260 1999 on *Trustees' Powers and Duties*.

LIABILITY OF TRUSTEES FOR BREACH OF TRUST

Extent and Measure of Liability

A trustee will be found to be acting in breach of trust if he fails to perform the duties required of him or if he acts in an unauthorized manner. A breach may occur in a variety of circumstances such as where trust monies are invested in unauthorised investments, where a trustee fails to distribute the trust estate to the beneficiaries in the correct proportions, or where he fails to exercise a proper degree of supervision over the management of the trust by his co-trustees. However, it will be necessary for the beneficiaries to establish conduct which in the opinion of the court amounts to a breach of trust.[209]

Where a trustee fails to comply with the duties imposed on him by the trust instrument he is liable to make good the loss to the trust estate or, where he makes an unauthorised profit for himself, even if this does not cause loss to the trust, he must account for it. As a general rule, a trustee is liable only in respect of the breaches of trust which he has himself committed and not those committed by his co-trustees, so liability is personal and not vicarious.[210] However, this indemnity will not apply where his conduct amounts to wilful default on his part, and inactivity on the part of a trustee in circumstances where he ought to have intervened can often be regarded as sufficient grounds for imposing liability.

A trustee is not liable for breaches of trust committed before his appointment unless there is evidence indicating such a breach which requires him to investigate further. It is therefore important that on appointment, a trustee takes whatever steps are necessary to ensure that the trust affairs are in order and investigates anything which causes him suspicion. When a trustee retires from a trust he remains liable for breaches committed by him during his term of office and his estate remains liable after his death. Where a breach occurs shortly after his retirement he will be liable if he retired in order to facilitate a breach of trust which he foresaw would take place or if he contemplated at the time that a breach of trust would be effected and decided to retire to avoid direct involvement. This issue was considered by Kekewich J in *Head v. Gould*,[211] where he held that to make a retiring trustee liable for a breach of trust committed by his successor, it must be proved that the breach committed was not merely the outcome of the retirement and new appointment but was contemplated by the former trustee when the retirement took place;

---

209. See *Carr v. Connor* (1929) ILTR 185 where Fitzgibbon J concluded at 191 that 'the plaintiffs had failed to prove that the defendant was guilty even of an error of judgment still less of any wilful default.'
210. *Townley v. Sherborne* (1634) J Bridg 35, 37.
211. [1898] 2 Ch 250.

as he said the former trustees 'must be proved to have been guilty as accessories before the fact of the impropriety actually perpetrated.'[212]

The measure of a trustee's liability where an unlawful profit has been made as a result of his breach of trust is that he should account for the profit.[213] It should be noted that the Privy Council has recently held that where such an unlawful profit has been made, a plaintiff is entitled either to an account of the profits made by the defendant in breach of his fiduciary obligations or to damages for the loss suffered by the plaintiff by reason of the breach; the plaintiff must make an election between these remedies.[214]

In other cases where there has been a breach of trust or fiduciary duty, the measure of a trustee's liability is the loss caused to the trust estate either directly or indirectly. Where the breach consists of a trustee making an unauthorized investment, the measure of damages will be the loss incurred by the trust in selling this investment if this is the course of action agreed on by the beneficiaries. Where trustees improperly retain an unauthorized investment, they will be liable for the difference between the price which the property would have fetched if sold at the proper time and the price actually received for it. This point is well illustrated by the decision of Romilly MR in *Fry v. Fry*.[215] A testator had directed that an inn should be sold 'as soon as convenient' after his death. The trustees refused an initial offer of £900 and nine years after the testator's death, the value of the property was greatly depreciated by the opening of a railway which deprived it of its coach traffic. The inn still remained unsold some 26 years after the testator's death. The estates of the trustees who had died in the interim were held liable for the difference between the original offer of £900 and the amount of the proceeds of the sale which the court directed should take place.

Where trustees improperly sell an authorised investment they may be liable either to account for the proceeds of sale or to repurchase the investment at its value at the date of the judgment.[216] In addition, where the trustees pay out trust funds to the wrong person, they will be liable to make good this amount so that the correct beneficiary can be paid.[217]

The principles relating to equitable compensation where loss has been caused as a result of a breach of trust or fiduciary duty have recently been considered in some detail by the House of Lords in *Target Holdings Ltd v.*

---

212. *Ibid.* at 274.
213. As the Privy Council made clear in *Attorney General for Hong Kong v. Reid* [1994] 1 AC 324 in such circumstances if assets are bought with trust monies, any increase in their value will be held on a constructive trust for the trust, whereas if they decrease in value the trustee will be personally liable in relation to such loss.
214. *Tang Man Sit v. Capacious Investments Ltd* [1996] 1 AC 514.
215. (1859) 27 Beav 144.
216. *Re Bell's Indenture* [1980] 1 WLR 1217.
217. See *Target Holdings Ltd v. Redferns* [1996] 1 AC 421.

Redferns.[218] As Lord Browne-Wilkinson commented:

> Equitable compensation for breach of trust is designed to achieve exactly what the word compensation suggests: to make good a loss in fact suffered by the beneficiaries and which, using hindsight and common sense, can be seen to have been caused by the breach.[219]

Lord Browne-Wilkinson stated that the equitable rules of compensation for breach of trust have largely been developed in relation to so-called traditional trusts, where the only way to properly protect the rights of the beneficiaries is to restore to the trust fund what ought to be in it. In such cases, he said that the basic rule is that 'a trustee in breach of trust must restore or pay to the trust estate either the assets which have been lost to the estate by reason of the breach or compensation for such loss'.[220] However, Lord Browne-Wilkinson stressed that there does have to be some causal connection between the breach of trust and the loss to the trust estate for which the compensation is recoverable. So, as the decision of the House of Lords made clear, a trustee will not be required to compensate for loss which would have occurred in any event even if there had been no breach of trust.[221]

Lord Browne-Wilkinson then went on to consider what the position would be where, at the time of the bringing of an action claiming compensation for breach of trust, those trusts had come to an end. In such circumstances, he stated, the court will not order restitution to be made to the trust estate, but rather will direct that payment of compensation be made directly to the beneficiaries. In such cases the measure of compensation will be the same, i.e. 'the difference between what the beneficiary has in fact received and the amount he would have received but for the breach of trust'.[222]

Another question which must be addressed is the date at which the actual loss to the trust should be assessed. Traditionally, it was accepted that the loss should be ascertained at the date proceedings commenced,[223] but Vinelott J disputed this in *Re Bell's Indenture*,[224] where he stated that the loss should be ascertained instead at the date of judgment. Further confusion was caused

---

218. [1996] 1 AC 421.
219. *Ibid.* at 439.
220. *Ibid.* at 434.
221. This so-called stringent test of causation or measure of loss has recently been applied by the Court of Appeal in *Swindle v. Harrison* [1997] 4 All ER 705 in the context of breach of fiduciary duty. See further Ho (1997) 11 Trust Law Int 72 and (1998) 12 Trust Law Int 66.
222. [1996] 1 AC 421, 435. See also *Swindle v. Harrison* [1997] 4 All ER 705, 717.
223. *Re Massingberd* (1890) 63 LT 296.
224. [1980] 1 WLR 1217, 1233.

when it was stated in *Jaffray v. Marshall*[225] that the trustees were liable to pay compensation at the highest intermediate value of the property between the date of the breach and the date of judgment. However, as a result of the consideration given by the House of Lords to this issue in *Target Holdings Ltd v. Redferns*[226] it now seems clear that liability is to be assessed at the date of judgment. As Lord Browne-Wilkinson stated:

> [T]he fact that there is an accrued cause of action as soon as the breach is committed does not in my judgment mean that the quantum of compensation payable is ultimately fixed as at the date when the breach occurred. The quantum is fixed at the date of the judgment at which date, according to the circumstances then pertaining, the compensation is assessed at the figure than necessary to put the trust estate or the beneficiary back into the position it would have been in had there been no breach.[227]

Finally, it should be noted that where a trustee is under an obligation to replace trust funds, he is charged with interest on the sum due. At common law this figure was 4% but the minimum rate now payable is 8% as prescribed by the Courts Act 1981 (Interest on Judgment Debts) Order 1989.[228]

Liability of Trustees Inter Se

Where two or more trustees are involved in a breach of trust, liability is joint and several, so each is liable in respect of the whole loss although all may not have been equally blameworthy.[229] In such circumstances, a decree against all the trustees involved may be enforced against one or more of them,[230] and those against whom execution is levied may claim contribution from the other trustees involved in the breach of trust. The effect of the operation of this principle is that while all the trustees may not be equally blameworthy, they may still be held to be equally liable. The fact that this is arguably not always fair in practice is well illustrated by the decision of the Court of Appeal in

---

225. [1993] 1 WLR 1285.
226. [1996] 1 AC 421. See Ulph (1995) 9 Trust Law Int 86; Nolan [1996] LMCLQ 161; Rickett (1996) 112 LQR 27; Capper [1997] Conv 14.
227. *Ibid.* at 437.
228. SI No. 12 of 1989.
229. As Panckhurst J stated recently in the decision of the New Zealand High Court in *Re Mulligan* [1998] 1 NZLR 481, 502 'it is elementary that a duty of diligence rests on each trustee' and that 'the starting point is that where a breach of trust has been committed, the trustees are jointly and severally liable to the beneficiaries for any loss caused by the breach' (at 511).
230. *Fletcher v. Green* (1864) 33 Beav 426, 430.

Bahin v. Hughes.[231] A testator gave a legacy to his three daughters on trust to pay the income to the plaintiff for life and after her death to her children. One of the daughters and the husband of another effected an unauthorized investment in leasehold property and when this security proved insufficient, the plaintiff sought to impose liability on all the trustees. The Court of Appeal held that they were jointly and severally liable and all equally responsible for indemnifying the beneficiaries. In the opinion of the court, the money had been lost just as much as a result of the default of the inactive trustees as by the innocent though erroneous action of their co-trustee. Cotton LJ remarked:

> It would be laying down a wrong rule to hold that where one trustee acts honestly, though erroneously, the other trustee is to be held entitled to indemnity who by doing nothing neglects his duty more than the acting trustee.[232]

It has been accepted that in limited circumstances where a breach of trust has occurred, a trustee may escape liability or may be entitled to indemnity from a co-trustee. Where one trustee acts in a fraudulent manner his co-trustees may be entitled to an indemnity. In addition, where one trustee alone receives the benefit of a breach of trust or where the breach reflects the fault of one trustee in his area of particular expertise indemnity may follow.[233] Similarly, where one trustee has exercised a controlling influence over the others which has effectively prevented his co-trustees from exercising independent judgment, they may successfully claim indemnity. This type of influence may be found to exist, e.g. where there is one professional trustee such as a solicitor although Kekewich J stressed in *Head v. Gould*[234] that there is no rule that 'a man is bound to indemnify his co-trustee against loss merely because he [is] a solicitor.' Certainly in that case where the co-trustee had been shown to be an active participant and not merely to have acted on the solicitor's advice, no indemnity could be obtained. Finally, where a trustee is also a beneficiary and has participated in a breach of trust, he must indemnify his co-trustees to the extent of his beneficial interest.[235]

---

231. (1886) 31 Ch D 390.
232. *Ibid.* at 396. Note that the provisions of the Civil Liability Act 1961 apply to a breach of trust. See the definition of 'wrong' in s. 2 and see also Part III Chapter 1 of the Act on the liability of concurrent wrongdoers.
233. *Per* Panckhurst J in *Re Mulligan* [1998] 1 NZLR 481, 502.
234. [1898] 2 Ch 250, 265.
235. *Chillingworth v. Chambers* [1896] 1 Ch 685.

Protection of Trustees from Personal Liability

A trustee who has committed a breach of trust may escape personal liability if he can establish certain circumstances. First, where the beneficiary has instigated, participated in or even consented to the breach of trust, the trustee will not be liable for any breach which occurs. Some of the factors which may influence the court in deciding whether the beneficiary's conduct will be such as to afford protection to the trustee were considered by Wilberforce J at first instance in *Re Pauling's Settlement Trusts*,[236] where he stated as follows:

> The court has to consider all the circumstances in which the concurrence of the *cestui que trust* was given with a view to seeing whether it is fair and equitable that, having given his concurrence, he should afterwards turn round and sue the trustees; that, subject to this, it is not necessary that he should know what he is concurring in is a breach of trust, provided that he fully understands what he is concurring in, and that it is not necessary that he should himself have directly benefited by the breach of trust.

A similar view has recently been expressed by Laskin JA, delivering the judgment of the Ontario Court of Appeal in *Gold v. Rosenberg*,[237] to the effect that in order for a beneficiary's consent to be valid, he must be capable of giving approval and must understand what is being approved. However, Laskin JA agreed that it was not necessary for the trustee to show that the beneficiary knew that the act or omission in question constituted a breach of trust.

A good example of a case in which a breach of trust was committed at the instigation of a beneficiary is *French v. Graham*.[238] Two trustees, one of whom was a solicitor, lent trust funds at the request of the tenant for life of a settlement on a security which proved totally inadequate. The non-professional trustee stood in the opinion of Brady LC in the 'ordinary position of a trustee who has been induced to commit a breach of trust at the request of one of his *cestuis que trust*' and was entitled to be indemnified by the tenant for life in respect of his liability for breach of trust. However, the Lord Chancellor was satisfied that the tenant for life had relied on the trustee solicitor advising him in the transaction in his professional capacity and as the latter had made no sufficient investigation of the title of the property involved, he was not entitled to be indemnified by the tenant for life.

The decision of a beneficiary to participate in or consent to a breach of

---

236. [1962] 1 WLR 86, 108. Approved by the Court of Appeal in *Holder v. Holder* [1968] Ch 353.
237. (1995) 129 DLR (4th) 152, 157.
238. (1860) 10 Ir Ch R 522. See also *Rutherfoord v. Maziere* (1862) 13 Ir Ch R 204.

trust will only usually[239] be relevant in this context where he is of full age and capacity and his participation or consent must have been freely given with full knowledge of the surrounding facts and circumstances. As Wilmer LJ stated in *Re Pauling's Settlement Trusts*[240] if the trustee can establish 'a valid request or consent by the beneficiary'[241] to an advance made in breach of trust, that will provide the trustee with a good defence against any claim by the beneficiary. In *Pauling* the trustees of a marriage settlement made a number of advancements to the children of the marriage with their mother's consent and although nominally paid to the children this money was applied to family purposes. The children subsequently brought an action claiming that these sums had been improperly paid out and the trustees relied on the consent and acquiescence of the beneficiaries to whom advancements had been made. However, in the view of the Court of Appeal this was not effective to absolve the trustees from liability in every case and it was held that some of the payments to the beneficiaries had constituted breaches of trust for which the trustees were liable.[242]

The court has an inherent jurisdiction where a beneficiary has been instrumental in effecting a breach of trust to require the beneficiary to indemnify the trustee in respect of the latter's liability to make good any loss incurred.[243] This principle was reiterated by Chitty J in *Sawyer v. Sawyer*[244] in the following terms:

> [E]ach person at whose instance the trustees have committed a breach of trust is liable to recoup the subject of that breach of trust to the trustees … it must be shown that the breach of trust was committed at the instance and request of the *cestuis que trust*. I make no distinction between instance and request, but it must be shown clearly that the breach of trust was instigated by them and that they were acting and moving parties to it.

However the proposition that 'a *cestui que trust* is bound to make good to the trustee every loss occasioned by an investment made with his privity' was rejected by Brady LC in *Browne v. Maunsell*,[245] and it would appear that

---

239. However in *Overton v. Banister* (1844) 3 Hare 503 the court refused to allow an infant who had fraudulently misrepresented her age to succeed in arguing that any assent was ineffective.
240. [1964] Ch 303.
241. *Ibid.* at 335.
242. Note that a statutory defence is now provided in England by s. 61 of the Trustee Act 1925 where the trustees have acted honestly and reasonably.
243. *Keays v. Lane* (1869) IR 3 Eq 1.
244. (1883) 28 Ch D 595, 598. Quoted with approval by Johnston J in *Anketill Jones v. Fitzgerald* (1930) 65 ILTR 185, 191.
245. (1856) 5 Ir Ch R 351.

where a beneficiary has merely consented to the breach of trust, his beneficial interest can only be impounded in this way where he has obtained a personal benefit from the breach. This power to impound a beneficiary's interest has now been given statutory authority by section 45 of the Trustee Act 1893 which provides that where it can be established that a beneficiary has instigated or requested or consented in writing to a breach of trust, the court may order that the interest of the beneficiary should be impounded with a view to indemnifying the trustee. This power will not normally be exercised in favour of the trustee unless it can be established that the beneficiary was aware at the time that the conduct which he instigated or consented to amounted to a breach of trust.

Even where a beneficiary is not involved prior to the breach being committed, a trustee may still be protected from liability where the beneficiary subsequently acquiesces in the breach or executes a release absolving the trustee from liability. As Lord Eldon stated in *Walker v. Symonds*:[246] 'either concurrence in the act or acquiescence without original concurrence will release the trustees' but he went on to state that this is only a general rule and that the court must investigate the circumstances which induced the concurrence or acquiescence. For acquiescence to be effective in this context, the beneficiary must be *sui juris* and have consented freely to the trustee's actions will full knowledge of the surrounding facts and circumstances and it appears that the onus lies on the party alleging acquiescence to prove facts from which the beneficiary's consent can be inferred.[247]

Similarly a release even of an informal nature may be effective to absolve a trustee from liability,[248] but it is essential that the beneficiary executed such a release with full knowledge of the facts and of the consequences of his actions.[249] Westbury LC summarised the position in *Farrant v. Blanchford*[250] as follows:

> Where a breach of trust has been committed, from which a trustee alleges that he has been released, it is incumbent on him to show that such release was given by the *cestui que trust* deliberately and advisedly with full knowledge of all the circumstances, and of his own rights and claims against the trustee. ...

A further issue which has attracted considerable judicial and academic attention in England recently is the extent to which an exemption clause in a trust

---

246. (1818) 3 Swans 1, 64. See also *Re McKenna's Estate* (1861) 13 Ir Ch R 239.
247. *Life Association of Scotland v. Siddal* (1861) 3 De G F & J 58, 77.
248. *Ghost v. Waller* (1846) 9 Beav 497.
249. *Thompson v. Eastwood* (1877) 2 App Cas 215.
250. (1863) 1 De G J & Sm 107, 119.

instrument may protect a trustee from liability.[251] The most important decision in this area is that of the Court of Appeal in *Armitage v. Nurse*[252] in which a clause in a settlement provided that no trustee should be liable for any loss or damage unless it was caused 'by his own actual fraud'. In upholding the trial judge's conclusion that the trustees were absolved from liability in the circumstances by this clause, Millett LJ expressed the view that it would exempt a trustee from liability 'no matter how indolent, imprudent, lacking in diligence, negligent or wilful he may have been, so long as he has not acted dishonestly.[253] While he agreed that there is an irreducible core of obligations owed by trustees to beneficiaries,[254] he did not accept that these core obligations included the duties of skill and care, prudence and diligence. In his view if a trustee acts honestly and in good faith it is sufficient, although he pointed out that a trustee who relied on the presence of an exemption clause to justify what he proposed to do would thereby lose its protection as he would be acting recklessly. Millett LJ concluded that none of the authorities referred to the court supported the proposition that it is contrary to public policy to exclude liability for gross negligence by an appropriately worded clause to that effect.[255] This is perhaps the most controversial aspect of the decision and Millett LJ himself acknowledges that there is a widely held view that exemptions clauses of this nature have gone too far and that professional trustees, who would not dream of excluding liability for ordinary professional negligence, should not be able to rely on a trustee exemption clause covering gross negligence.[256] It was subsequently held by the Court of Appeal in *Walker v. Stones*,[257] in which the exemption clause was described as not being materially different to that in

---

251. It should be noted that Schedule 1, paragraph 7 of the Trustee Act 2000 provides that the statutory duty of care 'does not apply if or in so far as it appears from the trust instrument that the duty is not meant to apply.'
252. [1998] Ch 241. See McCormack [1998] Conv 100 and McBride [1998] CLJ 33.
253. *Ibid.* at 251. It is arguable that this may be contrary to the view expressed by Lord Nicholls in *Royal Brunei Airlines Sdn Bhd v. Tan* [1995] 2 AC 378, 390 although as Sir Christopher Slade stated in *Walker v. Stones* [2001] QB 902, 941: 'It would be surprising if the court in *Armitage v. Nurse* had regarded itself as differing from *Royal Brunei Airlines Sdn Bhd v. Tan* without saying so or explaining why'.
254. See generally Hayton 'The irreducible core content of trusteeship' in *Trends in Contemporary Trust Law* ed. Oakley (1996) p. 47 *et seq.*
255. As McCormack comments [1998] Conv 100 the significance of *Armitage* lies in the fact that it lays to rest the proposition that a clause excluding trustee liability for gross negligence is incompatible with the fundamental basis of trusteeship. However, it should be noted that McCormack has expressed the view (at 110) that Millett LJ's interpretation of these authorities is open to question and that the *dicta* in the cases he refers to are certainly ambiguous.
256. See also Millett (1998) 114 LQR 214, 216.
257. [2001] QB 902. Leave to appeal has been granted, see [2001] 1 WLR 1341.

Armitage, that a solicitor-trustee[258] could not escape liability where he deliberately commits a breach of trust in the genuine belief that this course of action is in the interests of the beneficiaries, if no reasonable solicitor-trustee could have held that belief.

Hayton[259] has commented that 'there seems little reason to allow professional trustees, whether corporate or individual, in selling their skilled services to exempt themselves from liability for grossly negligent breaches of trust or even ordinarily negligent breaches.' In addition, the Trust Law Committee in *Trustees Exemption Clauses*[260] expressed the provisional view that a trustee remunerated for his services should not be able to rely on an exemption clause excluding liability for negligence and worse, at all events where the trustee cannot prove that prior independent advice was given to the settlor. Recently the Law Commission in its Consultation Paper on *Trustee Exemption Clauses*[261] has concluded that it does not consider that an outright prohibition of trustee exemption clauses is justified or necessary but has suggested that some legislative regulation is required.[262] The Commission proposed drawing a distinction between lay and professional trustees and suggested that lay trustees should in general continue to be able to rely on trustee exemption clauses.[263] It invited views on the suggestion that professional trustees should be unable to rely on an exemption clause where their conduct has been so unreasonable, irresponsible or incompetent that in fairness to the beneficiaries their conduct should not be excused and provisionally proposed that a professional trustee should not be able to rely on any provision excluding liability for breach of trust arising from negligence.[264] In addition, the Commission invited views on the suggestion that professional trustees should not be able to exclude liability for breach of trust where it is not reasonable for them to rely on an exemption clause by reference to all the circumstances including the nature and extent of the breach of trust.[265] While the issue of trustee exemption clauses has not yet received judicial consideration in this jurisdiction, it seems inevitable that given their proliferation an issue may arise in relation to their effectiveness. The proposal made by the Law Commission that a distinction should be drawn between lay and professional trustees in this regard seems an eminently fair and reasonable

---

258. Sir Christopher Slade said (at 939) that he was limiting this proposition to solicitor-trustees because he accepted that the test of honesty may vary from case to case, depending on among other things, the role and calling of the trustee.
259. *Commentary and Cases on the Law of Trusts and Equitable Remedies* (11th ed., 2001) p. 724.
260. (1999) paragraph 8.1.
261. Law Commission Consultation Paper No. 171 (2003).
262. Paragraph 4.19-4.20.
263. Paragraph 4.39.
264. Paragraphs 4.78 and 4.85.
265. Paragraph 4.86.

one but it remains to be seen whether the legislature in England will go as far as intervening to prevent professional trustees from relying on any provision excluding liability for breach of trust arising from negligence.

Finally, it should be noted that a trustee may be protected from an action for breach of trust by virtue of the provisions of the Statute of Limitations 1957. Section 43 provides that, subject to section 44, an action in respect of a breach of trust, not being an action in respect of which a period of limitation is fixed by any other provision of the legislation, shall not be brought against a trustee[266] after the expiration of six years from the date on which the right of action accrued. Section 44 goes on to provide that no limitation period fixed by the Act will apply to an action against a trustee where the claim is founded on any fraud or fraudulent breach of trust to which the trustee was party or where the claim is to recover trust property or the proceeds of trust property retained by the trustee or received by him and converted to his own use.[267] In *Murphy v. Allied Irish Banks Ltd*[268] the plaintiff succeeded in claiming interest on monies retained by the defendant following the sale of mortgaged property only for a period of six years from the date of the institution of proceedings. It was made clear by Murphy J in the course of his judgment that the fact that a trustee admits liability for trust moneys and is accountable for them does not prevent the statute running.

VARIATION OF TRUSTS

As a general principle a trustee must administer a trust according to the terms laid down in the trust instrument and any deviation will constitute a breach of trust.[269] Therefore a court will not, except in limited circumstances which will be considered below, sanction the performance of acts by the trustees which are not authorised by the trust instrument and it will not generally be possible to alter or vary the terms of a trust once it becomes effective.

The question of variation of the terms of a trust instrument after it has come into operation is one which has assumed increasing importance especially

---

266. See s. 2(2) of the Statute of Limitations 1957.
267. It was suggested by Fitzgibbon LJ in *Collings v. Wade* [1896] 1 IR 340, 349 that in this context 'fraud...must amount to dishonesty.' See also *Murphy v. Allied Irish Banks Ltd* [1994] 2 ILRM 220, 228 and *Jobling-Purser v. Jackson* High Court (Kinlen J) 27 November 2002 at 39.
268. [1994] 2 ILRM 220.
269. As Marshall JA has recently commented in the decision of the Newfoundland Court of Appeal in *Boy Scouts of Canada v. Doyle* (1997) 149 DLR (4th) 22, 63: 'It is, therefore, a basic tenet of law that, in the absence of authorization conferred upon them in the trust settlement, trustees may not appropriate to themselves the right to vary the terms of the trust settled upon them, or assume powers that have not been conferred upon them'.

in view of the need to adapt the terms of trusts to meet changing taxation requirements. As Lord Denning MR commented in *Re Weston's Settlements*:[270] 'Nearly every variation that has come before the court has tax avoidance for its principal object'. In addition, it may be necessary or in any event highly desirable to alter the original terms of a trust for a variety of other reasons and the courts must attempt to steer a path between giving effect to the intentions of a testator or settlor expressed in the trust instrument and seeking to envisage how these individuals might have wished the instrument to be altered in the light of changed circumstances.

Variation of the Terms of a Trust Without Court Approval

In certain situations the terms of the trust may be varied without court approval. Where the beneficiaries are all of full age and capacity and together are absolutely entitled to the trust property, they may terminate the trust and require that it be distributed in accordance with their directions, a principle sometimes referred to as the rule in *Saunders v. Vautier*,[271] although the decision in that case is expressed in slightly narrower terms.[272] There the testator bequeathed stock on trust to accumulate the dividends until a beneficiary attained the age of 25 and directed that the capital and the accumulated dividends should then be transferred to the beneficiary. When the latter reached the age of 21, he successfully claimed that he was entitled to call for the immediate transfer of the entire fund.

In practice this principle has been interpreted as meaning that any one or more adult beneficiaries who are of sound mind and entitled to the whole beneficial interest under a trust, can direct the trustees to transfer the trust property to them and put an end to the trust.

A further situation in which the terms of the trust may be varied without the sanction of the court is where an express power of advancement contained in the trust instrument is exercised by the trustees in order to secure a capital advance to the remainderman.

Variation of the Terms of a Trust With Court Approval

As a general principle a court will not permit trustees to deviate from the terms of a trust in performing their duties, although variation of a trust scheme may be sanctioned by the court in certain limited circumstances.[273] The need for court approval to vary the terms of a trust arises where there are unborn or

---

270. [1969] 1 Ch 223, 245.
271. (1841) Cr & Ph 240.
272. See *Wharton v. Masterman* [1895] AC 186, 198 *per* Lord Davey.
273. *Chapman v. Chapman* [1954] AC 429, 445 *per* Lord Simonds LC. See also *per* Lord Asquith at 469.

minor beneficiaries who cannot consent to a variation which might be desirable[274] e.g. from the point of view of reducing liability to taxation.

Emergency or Salvage Jurisdiction

The court has an inherent power to sanction variation of a trust instrument in cases of necessity to avoid the destruction of, or ensure the preservation of, trust property e.g. to effect essential repairs to a building to save it from collapse. This 'emergency or salvage' jurisdiction may be exercised where some crisis unforeseen by the settlor or testator has arisen and it is necessary for the trustees to vary the terms of the trust so as to enable them to take action where the consent of the beneficiaries cannot be obtained, often because they are not yet in existence or are under a disability. The most common reason for invoking this jurisdiction is to authorize the sale or mortgage of trust property for the purpose of effecting essential repairs to it. This principle was set out as follows by Gavan Duffy J in *Re Johnson's Settlement*:[275]

> Where trustees are not trustees for sale and have no power of sale or management, and where the limitations are equitable, I hold that the Court can as a last resort if no other way is open, apply the principle of salvage in order to sanction the expenditure out of capital of the money necessary for doing such repairs, constituting permanent improvements, as are essential to the preservation of the settled property.

In *Re Johnson's Settlement* the court authorized the trustee to mortgage settled lands for the purpose of raising money to effect repairs and in *Neill v. Neill*[276] Kenny J sanctioned the further mortgaging of a sheep farm over which the trust held a mortgage to raise funds for the continued running of the farm in a time of crisis. The ambit of this salvage jurisdiction has been extended to other types of emergency situations and perhaps the high watermark of this jurisdiction is the decision of the English Court of Appeal in *Re New*[277] in which the court authorized trustees to concur in a shareholders' scheme for the reconstruction of a company where the evidence showed that the scheme would be greatly to the advantage of all the parties involved. Romer LJ said

---

274. As Huband JA has commented in delivering the judgment of the Manitoba Court of Appeal in *Teichman v. Teichman Estate* (1996) 134 DLR (4th) 155, 157 in relation to the rule in *Saunders v. Vautier* 'unanimity [is] required, except that the court could consent on behalf of the beneficiaries who were minors or otherwise lacked capacity or who were as yet unborn, so long as the arrangement was for the benefit of those beneficiaries'.

275. [1944] IR 529, 533-534. See also *Bank of Ireland v. Geoghegan* [1955-56] Ir Jur Rep 7.

276. [1904] 1 IR 513.

277. [1901] 2 Ch 534.

that while as a rule the court has no jurisdiction to give sanction to the performance by trustees of acts not authorized by the terms of the trust it can intervene where the trustees have been embarrassed by an emergency. However, he stressed that: 'Of course, the jurisdiction is one to be exercised with great caution, and the Court will take care not to strain its powers.'[278] This decision has been criticised as being too liberal and it did not signify any general move to broaden the jurisdiction of the court in this area; as Kekewich J subsequently commented in *Re Tollemache*:[279] while the decision of the Court of Appeal was useful, 'it [did] not purport to enlarge the jurisdiction of the court'.

To Effect a Compromise of a Dispute

The court also has authority to sanction a variation in the terms of a trust in order to effect a compromise of disputes as between the claims of various beneficiaries. Before the decision of the House of Lords in *Chapman v. Chapman*,[280] the courts had accepted a fairly wide definition of the word 'compromise'. However, it was held by the majority of the House of Lords in *Chapman* that there must be a genuine dispute for this jurisdiction to be brought into effect and not merely a desire to alter the terms of the original trust. Lord Cohen dissented as Lord Denning MR had done in the Court of Appeal and held that the jurisdiction of the court in this context extended to effecting a compromise in a wide sense between the tenant for life and the remainderman. Partly as a result of this decision, legislation was introduced in England in the form of the Variation of Trusts Act 1958 which provides that a court may, if it thinks fit, approve an arrangement varying or revoking a trust or enlarging the powers of the trustees on the application of defined classes of beneficiaries or potential beneficiaries.[281] It remains to be seen whether, in the absence of similar legislation in this jurisdiction, our courts would adopt the more flexible approach of the minority in *Chapman*.

---

278. *Ibid.* at 545.
279. [1903] 1 Ch 457, 465.
280. [1954] AC 429.
281. As Mummery LJ has stated in the decision of the Court of Appeal in *Goulding v. James* [1997] 2 All ER 239, although the jurisdiction provided for in the Act has been invoked 'thousands of times' there have been 'remarkably few reported cases on its construction'. In *Goulding,* the court approved an arrangement varying the terms of a trust which was undoubtedly for the benefit of unborn beneficiaries although extrinsic evidence had been given to the effect that this variation would run contrary to the testatrix's original intentions. See further Luxton (1997) 60 MLR 719.

To Permit the Payment of Maintenance

Maintenance may be paid by virtue of the statutory power in section 43 of the Conveyancing Act 1881 or the court may permit maintenance to be paid out of interest directed to be accumulated.[282] A variation of this nature will be authorized on the grounds that a settlor or testator would not have intended the beneficiaries to be left without reasonable means. So, in *Re Collins*[283] a testator directed that the income of his real and personal property should be accumulated for 21 years and gave the accumulated property to his sister for life with remainder to her sons and their children. The court held that an annual sum be paid out of the income of the personal estate for the maintenance and education of the sister's sons. Pearson J stated as follows:

> Where a testator has made provision for a family ... but has postponed the enjoyment, either for a particular purpose or generally for the increase of the estate, it is assumed that he did not intend these children should be left unprovided for or in a state of such moderate means that they should not be educated properly for the position and fortune which he designs them to have. . . .[284]

Reform of the Law in Relation to Variation of Trusts

In its Report *The Variation of Trusts*[285] published in 2000 the Law Reform Commission recommended the introduction of legislation broadly similar to that introduced in England by the Variation of Trusts Act 1958. Section 1 of the draft legislation now provides that the court may, if it thinks fit, approve an arrangement varying, resettling or revoking a trust or enlarging, adding to or restricting the powers of trustees to manage or administer any trust property provided the arrangement would be for the benefit of those on whose behalf approval is sought. The court may approve an arrangement on behalf of (a) any person having an interest, whether vested or contingent, under a trust who by reason of infancy or incapacity is incapable of assenting, (b) any person unborn, (c) any person whose identity, existence or whereabouts cannot be established by taking reasonable measures or (d) any person having a contingent interest under a trust, other than a person to whom paragraph (a) applies. An application for an order approving such an arrangement may be made by a trustee, a beneficiary or 'such other person as the court sees fit'.

---

282. See *supra* pp. 426-427.
283. (1886) 32 Ch D 229.
284. *Ibid.* at 232.
285. LRC 63-2000.

LIKELY FUTURE DEVELOPMENTS IN RELATION TO THE
ADMINISTRATION OF TRUSTS

Lord Nicholls writing extra-judicially has commented that '[t]imes change
and with them the problems confronting trustees'.[286] The Law Commission
of England and Wales has also recently pointed out that 'trusteeship is an
increasingly specialised task that often requires professional skills that . . .
trustees may not have'.[287] As the range of choices in relation to investment of
trust funds has increased, so have the difficulties inherent in the management
of trust investments which is becoming an increasingly technical area requiring
specialist expertise. However, as was noted above, the circumstances in which
a trustee may delegate have not kept pace with such developments, with the
result that a trustee may find himself trying to make investment decisions
which he lacks the knowledge to make in a fully informed way.

Partly as a result of such factors, increasing numbers of professionals are
being appointed to act as trustees. This in itself leads to difficulties and as
Kenny has recently commented 'Equity's rules are unsuited to modern
professional trusts'.[288] As she points out, no professional trustee would act
unless paid for doing so and despite this fact trusts are still governed 'by rules
derived from a social era when trustees were generously donating their time
and skill to the administration of another's property'. Undoubtedly the tasks
performed by professional trustees require considerable skill and experience
for which they are well remunerated and as Kenny suggests, in view of this,
beneficiaries of modern trusts should be regarded as clients entitled to a high
level of service and standard of professionalism.

There have been suggestions made in the context of a trustee's duty to
invest to the effect that a higher standard of care is expected of a professional
trustee. So in *Re Waterman's Will Trusts*,[289] Harman J stated *obiter* that
a higher standard of diligence and knowledge is required and this was
confirmed by Brightman J in *Bartlett v. Barclays Bank Trust Co. Ltd*[290] in
which he said that a greater duty of care is owed by a professional trustee

---

286. (1995) 9 Trust Law Int 71. As Legatt LJ commented in *Nestle v. National Westminster Bank plc* [1993] 1 WLR 1260, 1281: '[I]n Victorian times . . . little was demanded of a trustee beyond the safeguarding of the trust fund by refraining from improvident investment. This process was no doubt also intended to save beneficiaries from trouble and anxiety, or what is now called "hassle"'.

287. Consultation Paper No. 146 on *Trustees' Powers and Duties* (1997) paragraph 1.1. The Commission commented that as a result of changes both in the way in which financial markets operate and the purposes for which trusts are now employed, the present law is no longer always adequate to enable trustees to administer a trust to the best advantage of the beneficiaries or the objects of the trust'.

288. (1996) 146 NLJ 348.

289. [1952] 2 All ER 1054, 1055.

290. [1980] Ch 515.

such as a trust corporation which carries on the specialised business of trust management. However, in *Nestle v. National Westminster Bank plc*,[291] while the defendant was a professional institution, Legatt LJ merely stated that 'the essence of the bank's duty was to take such steps as a prudent businessman would have taken to maintain and increase the value of the trust fund'.[292] When one considers the skill which a professional trustee professes to have and the fact that such a trustee will be financially rewarded, often quite substantially, for acting in this capacity, the reluctance of the Court of Appeal to impose a higher standard is surprising.

There have been some signs to indicate that the judiciary are aware that traditional principles developed in the context of family trusts are no longer adequate or suitable to deal with modern commercial trusts. The most useful statement to this effect is contained in the speech of Lord Browne-Wilkinson in *Target Holdings Ltd v. Redferns*[293] in the following terms:

> [I]n my judgment it is in any event wrong to lift wholesale the detailed rules developed in the context of traditional trusts and then seek to apply them to trusts of a quite different kind. In the modern world the trust has become a valuable device in commercial and financial dealings. The fundamental principles of equity apply as much to such trusts as they do to the traditional trusts in relation to which those principles were originally formulated. But in my judgment, it is important, if the trust is not to be rendered commercially useless, to distinguish between the basic principles of trust law and those specialist rules developed in relation to traditional trusts which are applicable only to such trusts and the rationale of which has no application to trusts of a quite different kind.

As Nolan has commented, drawing a distinction between different types of trusts might be justifiable in principle as it recognises that the relationship between trustee and beneficiary and therefore their correlative rights can vary widely from one context to another.[294] On the other hand Ulph argues that the unity of trust principles is already under threat due to the wide variety of contexts in which these principles operate and suggests that the approach in *Target* strains this unity even further.[295] Finally it should be noted that while the House of Lords concluded that traditional principles should not apply to the case before them, as Capper points out the *dicta* of Lord Browne-Wilkinson

---

291. [1993] 1 WLR 1260.
292. *Ibid.* at 1283.
293. [1996] 1 AC 421, 435.
294. [1996] LMCLQ 161, 163.
295. (1995) 9 Trust Law Int 86, 88.

offers little real insight into how the rules relating to commercial trusts should differ from those applicable to traditional trusts.[296]

One distinct area in which the established principles relating to the administration of trusts are clearly of doubtful utility is in relation to pension trusts. However, even in this context there has been considerable judicial debate in England about the efficacy of developing new principles which will take into account the different nature of such trusts. In *McDonald v. Horn*[297] Hoffmann LJ acknowledged that 'pension funds are a special form of trust' and in *Mettoy Pension Trustees Ltd v. Evans*,[298] Warner J pointed out that beneficiaries under a pension scheme are not volunteers and said that in construing the trust instrument it was important to bear in mind the origin of the beneficiaries' rights under it. However, in *Cowan v. Scargill*[299] Megarry VC stated that he could 'see no reason for holding that different principles apply to pension fund trusts from those which apply to other trusts'. This point was reiterated by Rattee J in *Wilson v. Law Debenture Trust Corporation plc*[300] where he commented that 'in general the principles applicable to private trusts as a matter of trust law apply equally to pension schemes'. In *Wilson* counsel for the plaintiffs submitted that in the case of a pension scheme, in the absence of express provision to the contrary, a trustee should be bound to give reasons for the exercise of the discretion conferred upon him as it would seem unreasonable that members of the scheme who had bought their interests could not see whether the trustee had exercised his discretion properly. However, Rattee J rejected this argument in the following terms:

> It would in my judgment be wrong in principle to hold that the long-established principles of trust law as to the exercise by trustees of discretions conferred on them by their trust instruments, in the context of which parties to a pension scheme such as the present entered into those schemes, no longer apply to them and that the trustees are under more onerous obligations to account to their beneficiaries than they could have appreciated when appointed, on the basis of the relevant trust law as it has stood for so long.[301]

Despite the rather restrictive terms of this judgment, it can be argued that the proposition put forward by counsel for the plaintiffs seemed eminently reasonable in the context of a pension scheme in which the 'beneficiaries' were individuals who had paid for their interest in the trust. The decision of

---

296. [1997] Conv 14, 22.
297. [1995] 1 All ER 961, 973.
298. [1990] 1 WLR 1587, 1618.
299. [1985] Ch 270, 290.
300. [1995] 2 All ER 337, 347.
301. *Ibid.* at 348.

the Court of Appeal in *Re Londonderry's Settlement*[302] to the effect that trustees are not obliged to disclose to the beneficiaries their reasons for acting seems out of touch with the commercial realities of modern pension trusts and it is likely that this question will be revisited. It should be noted that in England, section 35 of the Pensions Act 1996 now requires pension fund trustees to disclose their investment policy and this move towards greater accountability is clearly a desirable step.

Finally it is submitted that any piecemeal attempts at reform which can be effected by judicial decisions are likely to be insufficient to properly address the substantial practical difficulties facing trustees required to administer modern trusts. Furthermore it is clearly necessary to introduce a greater degree of accountability for the benefit of beneficiaries of certain types of trusts who are not volunteers and who are effectively paying for the trustees' services; as Kenny has argued such individuals should be regarded as 'clients, entitled to a high level of service'.[303] While there is some merit in the argument that for the sake of certainty the same principles should apply to all types of trust, it is submitted that such a view must yield to the reality that modern trusts are now called upon to fulfil many diverse functions. For this reason comprehensive legislation in this jurisdiction addressing these issues would clearly be desirable.

---

302. [1965] Ch 918.
303. (1996) 146 NLJ 348.

CHAPTER 13

Injunctions

INTRODUCTION

At common law the usual remedy where a plaintiff succeeded in his action was an award of damages; this form of relief was often inadequate or inappropriate and equity supplemented the legal remedies available by developing alternative types of remedy such as the injunction. An injunction is an order restraining the person to whom it is directed from carrying out a specified act or requiring him to perform such an act; it is a most flexible and versatile form of remedy and is used with increasing frequency today.

The injunction developed initially as a means of doing justice in cases where the traditional common law remedy of damages could not achieve such an aim. As the Court of Chancery grew in stature, the device of the injunction was even employed to restrain the enforcement of the judgments of the common law courts. This led to a bitter dispute between the two systems, a dispute which was resolved by the then King, James I, following the *Earl of Oxford's case*,[1] in favour of the Court of Chancery. A distinction has been drawn between the grant of equitable injunctions in the so-called 'exclusive jurisdiction', i.e. in circumstances where it is sought to protect an equitable right, for example the right of a beneficiary under a trust, and the grant of injunctions in the 'auxiliary jurisdiction' where the remedy is used to protect a legal right. Over a period of time this auxiliary jurisdiction became widely used and eventually power was given to the common law courts themselves to grant injunctions by the Common Law Procedure (Ireland) Act 1856.[2] Around this time jurisdiction was also given to the Court of Chancery to award damages in addition to or in lieu of an injunction by the Chancery Amendment Act 1858, known as Lord Cairns' Act, and from a procedural point of view the two systems grew even closer together. The enactment of the Judicature (Ireland) Act 1877 effectively brought about a fusion of procedure and section 28(8) provided that the court was empowered to grant

---

1. (1615) 1 Rep Ch 1.
2. The suggestion was made in the context of the equivalent English legislation, the Common Law Procedure Act 1854, that it resulted in the common law courts having more extensive jurisdiction in this area than the Court of Chancery; *Quartz Hill Consolidated Gold Mining Co. v. Beall* (1882) 20 Ch D 501, 509 *per* Baggallay LJ.

interlocutory relief 'whenever it was just and convenient to do so'. Debate has raged ever since, particularly in England, over the question of whether the Judicature Act and its successors effected any enlargement of the court's power to grant an injunction. In *Moore v. Attorney General*[3] Murnaghan J expressed the view that the Act 'extends the principles upon which jurisdiction was formerly exercised by the Court of Chancery' and Jessel MR commented in *Beddow v. Beddow*[4] that the courts now had unlimited power to grant an injunction whenever it was just and convenient to do so. However, the better view would seem to be that the legislation did not confer any additional jurisdiction on the court; as Brett LJ commented in *North London Railway Co. v. Great Northern Railway Co.*:[5] 'if no court had the power of issuing an injunction before the Judicature Act, no part of the High Court has power to issue an injunction now'. This view has been accepted by the House of Lords in England,[6] and despite the comment of Murnaghan J in *Moore* it would seem to be the logical conclusion to reach.

Injunctions may be classified in a number of ways, first as between those which impose negative and positive obligations. The most common form of injunction falls into the former category and is known as a prohibitory injunction, namely one which restrains the performance or continuance of a wrongful act. The latter form of order is known as a mandatory injunction and has the effect of requiring the performance of an act.

A further classification can be made between interim and interlocutory injunctions on the one hand and perpetual injunctions on the other hand. The former are granted prior to the trial of an action; an interim injunction is obtained for a limited period and will have effect only until a further order is made and is often, although not invariably, sought on an *ex parte* basis.[7] An interlocutory injunction will have effect until the final hearing of the action takes place and its purpose is to maintain the *status quo* between the parties as far as possible until the final determination of the issues in dispute by the court. A perpetual injunction on the other hand will only be granted at the trial of the action where a plaintiff has established a right and the actual or threatened infringement of that right by the defendant. In practice, the order

---

3. [1927] IR 569, 580. See also the *dicta* of Chatterton VC in *Cork Corporation v. Rooney* (1881) 17 LR Ir 191, 200.
4. (1878) 9 Ch D 89, 93. See also *Argyll v. Argyll* [1967] Ch 302.
5. (1883) 11 QBD 30, 36-37. See also *Day v. Brownrigg* (1878) 10 Ch D 294, 307 *per* James LJ.
6. *Gouriet v. Union of Post Office Workers* [1978] AC 435; *The Siskina* [1979] AC 210; *South Carolina Insurance Co. v. Assurance Maatschappij 'de Zeven Provincien' NV* [1987] AC 24.
7. Where a matter is particularly urgent a plaintiff may apply for such an order on an *ex parte* basis and such an order will generally continue until the next motion day when the defendant will have the opportunity of putting his side of the case.

amounts to a final determination of the issues in dispute by the court although it does not mean that the injunction will necessarily last perpetually as its name suggests.

Finally a distinction should be drawn between *quia timet* injunctions which are granted in respect of wrongs which are merely threatened or apprehended and other forms of injunction which are designed to prevent the continuance of a wrong or to guard against its repetition.

THE PRINCIPLES GOVERNING THE GRANT OF INJUNCTIONS

General Principles Governing the Grant of Perpetual Injunctions

Introduction

An injunction will only be granted to protect a right of the plaintiff whether a legal right deriving from the common law, an equitable right (e.g. the right of a beneficiary under a trust), a constitutional right, or a right deriving from a specific statutory power. The plaintiff must establish a sufficient interest in the protection of this right,[8] and an injunction will not issue to remedy mere inconvenience or where the interference with the plaintiff's rights is trivial. Traditionally it was thought that the grant of an injunction was limited to circumstances where a proprietary right had been infringed or threatened but this is certainly no longer the general rule. As Spry[9] has commented 'any attempt to found the jurisdiction to grant injunctions exclusively on the existence of property or proprietary rights is not justified'.

A further cardinal principle which must be borne in mind is that injunctions, like other forms of equitable remedy are discretionary in nature. So while a plaintiff may establish the infringement of a right and a *prima facie* entitlement to relief he may still be denied this relief on discretionary grounds. However, this discretion cannot be exercised in an arbitrary manner but rather in accordance with well established principles which have been considered in detail by the courts. So, as Evershed MR stated in *Pride of Derby and Derbyshire Angling Association Ltd v. British Celanese Ltd*:[10]

> It is, I think, well settled that if A proves that his proprietary rights are being wrongfully interfered with by B, and that B intends to continue his wrong, then A is *prima facie* entitled to an injunction, and he will be

---

8. *Maxwell v. Hogg* (1867) 2 Ch App 307, 311 *per* Turner LJ.
9. *The Principles of Equitable Remedies* (6th ed., 2001) p. 340.
10. [1953] Ch 149, 181.

deprived of that remedy only if special circumstances exist, including the circumstance that damages are an adequate remedy for the wrong that he has suffered.

It is now proposed to examine the operation of some of these discretionary factors in practice. It should be pointed out that many cases never progress beyond the interlocutory stage and in general the same discretionary principles operate irrespective of whether a perpetual or interlocutory order is being sought. The specific factors relevant to the grant of interlocutory relief will be considered in detail below.

The Inadequacy or Inappropriateness of Damages as a Remedy

Historically, the main reason for the intervention of the Court of Chancery was the inadequacy or inappropriateness of damages or other remedies at common law. Therefore in the context of the grant of an injunction, a plaintiff was required to satisfy the court that the right which he sought to protect was of such a nature that an award of damages would not leave him in all respects in as good a position as if he had obtained enforcement of this right. As Lindley LJ stated in *London and Blackwell Railway Co. v. Cross*:[11] '*prima facie* you do not obtain injunctions to restrain actionable wrongs, for which damages are the proper remedy'. This principle still operates today, although arguably in a slightly more modified form and no injunction will be granted where an injury can be properly compensated in monetary terms[12] but will only issue e.g to restrain a continuing nuisance or the breach of a negative obligation in a contract. However, the trend in some modern cases has been to move away from the traditional question of asking 'are damages an adequate remedy?' to 'is it just, in all the circumstances, that a plaintiff should be confined to his remedy in damages?'.[13]

It will often be considered just to confine a plaintiff to an award of damages where the wrongdoing of which he complains has ceased and is not likely to re-occur, and where his loss is quantifiable. However a question which has often arisen, particularly in the context of interlocutory applications, is the extent to which difficulties in quantifying a plaintiff's loss may make damages an inadequate form of relief. In *Yeates v. Minister for Posts and Telegraphs*[14] Kenny J commented that 'an injunction is granted before the hearing of an

---

11. (1886) 31 Ch D 354, 369. See also *Downey v. Minister for Education and Science* [2001] 2 IR 727.
12. In *Ryanair Ltd v. Aer Rianta cpt* High Court 2000 No. 801 (Kelly J) 25 January 2001 Kelly J stated that the fact that in the affidavit evidence before the court damages had actually been quantified was fatal to the applicant's claim for an interlocutory injunction.
13. *Evans Marshall & Co. Ltd v. Bertola SA* [1973] 1 WLR 349, 379 *per* Sachs LJ.
14. [1978] ILRM 22, 24.

action only when damages will not be an adequate remedy or when the assessment of damages will be extremely difficult'. This issue of difficulty in the quantification of damages was recently considered by the Supreme Court in *Curust Financial Services Ltd v. Loewe-Lack-Werk Otto Loewe GmbH*,[15] where Finlay CJ stressed that: 'Difficulty, as opposed to complete impossibility, in the assessment of ... damages should not, in my view, be a ground for characterizing the awarding of damages as an inadequate remedy.' In the circumstances the Supreme Court was satisfied that the quantum of damages could be assessed and that no interlocutory injunction should be granted. Clearly where wrongdoing is likely to continue into the future it may not be feasible to attempt to assess the measure of damages necessary to compensate a plaintiff and in such circumstances the grant of an injunction will often prove to be the only just remedy.

The Conduct of the Parties

The discretionary considerations which are taken into account by a court in deciding whether to grant an injunction relate not only to the nature of the right which a plaintiff seeks to enforce and to the potential consequences of the decision to grant or refuse relief, but may also include factors relating to the conduct of the person invoking the jurisdiction of the court, and to a lesser extent, the conduct of the defendant. In this regard, two of the maxims considered earlier are relevant, namely 'he who comes to equity must come with clean hands' and 'he who seeks equity must do equity'.[16] While these maxims should be treated with caution, they do reflect the general principles which operate in relation to a plaintiff's conduct.

Where an injunction is sought by a plaintiff in furtherance of the perpetration of fraud, a court will not hesitate to refuse relief but conduct falling far short of fraud may also disentitle a plaintiff to an equitable remedy. The effect of the maxim 'he who comes to equity must come with clean hands'[17] is such that where a plaintiff who has been guilty of some impropriety

---

15. [1994] 1 IR 450, 469. Quoted with approval by Kelly J in *Fitzpatrick v. Garda Commissioner* High Court 1996 No. 121 JR, 16 October 1996 at 14. See also the comments of Hamilton J in *Reno Engrais et Produits Chemiques SA v. Irish Agricultural Wholesale Society Ltd* [1976-77] ILRM 179, 184 and of Keane J in *Oblique Financial Services Ltd v. The Promise Production Co. Ltd* [1994] 1 ILRM 74, 79.

16. See *supra* Chapter 2.

17. For a statement of this general principle, see *Dering v. Earl of Winchelsea* (1787) 1 Cox 318, 319-320 where Eyre LCB stated: 'a man must come into a Court of Equity with clean hands; but when this is said, it does not mean a general depravity; it must have an immediate and necessary relation to the equity sued for; it must be a depravity in a legal as well as in the moral sense'. See also *Tinker v. Tinker* [1970] P 136, 143 *per* Salmon LJ.

or disreputable conduct seeks relief in the form of an equitable remedy, it may be refused by the court on discretionary grounds.[18] However, the court will decline to intervene on the basis of the 'clean hands' principle[19] unless there is a sufficient connection between the inequitable conduct and the subject matter of the dispute. As Scrutton LJ commented in *Moody v. Cox*:[20]

> Equity will not apply the principle about clean hands unless the depravity, the dirt in question on the hand, has an immediate and necessary relation to the equity sued for.

This proposition is well illustrated by *Argyll v. Argyll*,[21] where it was held by Ungoed-Thomas J that the alleged immorality of the plaintiff's conduct which had led to divorce did not deprive her of her entitlement to an injunction to restrain a breach of confidence by her husband. As Ungoed-Thomas J stated 'A person coming to equity for relief ... must come with clean hands, but the cleanliness required is to be judged in relation to the relief that is sought.'[22] The so-called 'clean hands' principle has been applied in a wide variety of situations where an injunction has been sought e.g. where the plaintiff's conduct has been 'unfair and unreasonable',[23] where he has sought to safeguard his rights by 'deplorable means',[24] where he has committed a breach of covenant,[25] or where he has attempted to mislead the court.[26] In some cases the conduct of the defendant may effectively cancel out any wrongdoing of the plaintiff, as in *Meridian Communications Ltd v. Eircell Ltd*[27] where Lavan J had rejected the plaintiff's application for an interlocutory injunction on the

---

18. See *Overton v. Banister* (1844) 3 Hare 503; *Gascoigne v. Gascoigne* [1918] 1 KB 223; *McEvoy v. Belfast Banking Co. Ltd* [1934] NI 67; *Smelter Corporation of Ireland Ltd v. O'Driscoll* [1977] IR 305; *Parkes v. Parkes* [1980] ILRM 137. The latter case illustrated the proposition that a plaintiff may be refused equitable relief where his conduct in relation to the transaction at issue has been less than honest even where this conduct has not directly prejudiced the defendant.
19. See generally Pettit [1990] Conv 416. Pettit suggests (at 424) that unclean hands seems to be a 'last resort defence' to be invoked where none of the so-called nominate defences are applicable but where it would be unconscionable for the plaintiff to be granted relief by the court.
20. [1917] 2 Ch 71, 87-88. The plaintiff's claim for rescission of a contract succeeded despite the fact that he had given a bribe to the vendor's solicitor, although admittedly in an unconnected matter.
21. [1967] Ch 302.
22. *Ibid.* at 332.
23. *Shell UK Ltd. v. Lostock Garage Ltd* [1976] 1 WLR 1187, 1199 *per* Lord Denning MR.
24. *Hubbard v. Vosper* [1972] 2 QB 84, 101 *per* Megaw LJ.
25. *Litvinoff v. Kent* (1918) 34 TLR 298.
26. *Armstrong v. Sheppard & Short Ltd* [1959] 2 QB 384, 397.
27. Supreme Court 2001 No. 109, 10 May 2001.

basis that it had not come to court with clean hands. However, on appeal McGuinness J concluded that neither party had been entirely free of fault and she stated that in the circumstances the court would not refuse relief on the grounds relied on by Lavan J.

This principle was also referred to by the Supreme Court in *Curust Financial Services Ltd v. Loewe-Lack-Werk Otto Loewe GmbH*,[28] in which the court had to consider whether the alleged breach by the plaintiff of an exclusive licensing agreement, consisting of its sub-contracting the manufacture of a product without the prior written consent of the first named defendant, should disentitle it to relief. As a general principle, Finlay CJ accepted that the court has a discretion, where it is satisfied that a person has come to court otherwise than with 'clean hands', to refuse equitable relief in the form of an injunction on that ground alone. However, he continued by saying that 'it seems to me that this phrase must of necessity involve an element of turpitude and cannot necessarily be equated with a mere breach of contract.'[29] Finlay CJ made reference to the fact that what might be established as a breach by the plaintiff of the agreement not to sub-contract, namely the entering into an arrangement with a third party for this purpose, might also be established as having been provoked by a wrongful repudiation on the part of the first named defendant of its own contractual obligations under the licensing agreement. He therefore concluded that it would be unreasonable that such conduct should disentitle the plaintiff to an injunction to which it would otherwise be entitled and this would suggest that the Supreme Court appears willing to take on board the flexible approach adopted in England in recent years towards the application of the 'clean hands' principle.

The application of the maxim 'he who seeks equity must do equity' can be seen where the court will decline to grant an injunction to a party who e.g. seeks to enforce contractual rights while at the same time refusing to perform his own contractual obligations or to give an assurance that he will do so in the future. This proposition is well illustrated by the decision of the Court of Appeal in *Chappell v. Times Newspapers*,[30] which concerned a dispute which had arisen between unions and employers in the printing industry. Following selective industrial action, the employers threatened to terminate their employees' contracts unless normal production was resumed. The plaintiffs, who were individual union members who had not personally been involved in any industrial action, sought an interim injunction to restrain their respective employers from terminating their contracts of employment, although they refused to give the undertakings sought by the employers not to engage in disruptive activities. The Court of Appeal refused to grant an interim injunction on the grounds that the plaintiffs had failed to establish that they themselves

---

28. [1994] 1 IR 450, 468.
29. *Ibid*. at 467.
30. [1975] 1 WLR 482.

intended to act equitably by abiding by the terms of their contracts of employment. As Lord Denning MR said 'it has long been settled both at common law and in equity that in a contract where each has to do his part concurrently with the other, then if one party seeks relief, he must be ready and willing to do his part in it.'[31]

The issue of the influence which the conduct of the defendant may have on the decision of a court to grant or withhold relief of this nature is one which has been considered less frequently. In *News Datacom Ltd v. Lyons*[32] in which the plaintiff sought an interlocutory injunction to restrain an alleged breach of copyright in software used to decode satellite television signals, Flood J said that the the mere fact that the conduct of one of the parties, in this case the defendant, might be questionable as a matter of ethics or morality was not a reason to grant relief in the absence of any other accepted grounds for making the order sought. However, in *Eircell Ltd v. Bernstoff*[33] the defendant's conduct seemed to constitute a significant factor in deciding where the balance of convenience lay. Barr J referred to what he termed the 'reprehensible' conduct of the defendants in seeking to intimidate other people and contrasted it with what he described as the 'fair and reasonable behaviour' of the plaintiff. In view of this and having regard to the fact that damages would not constitute an adequate remedy from the plaintiff's point of view, he concluded that the balance of convenience favoured the granting of the interlocutory injunction sought.

Laches and Acquiescence

The court may also refuse to grant an injunction on the grounds of laches or acquiescence. The defence of laches is said by Spry[34] to arise if two conditions are satisfied:

> [F]irst, there must be unreasonable delay on the part of the plaintiff in the commencement or prosecution of proceedings, and secondly, in view of the nature and consequences of that delay it must be unjust in all the circumstances to grant the specific relief that is in question, whether absolutely or on appropriate terms or conditions.

The length of the delay will be judged from the time the plaintiff had sufficient knowledge of the facts giving rise to the claim or where he had a reasonable suspicion of the infringement of his rights. Delay by itself is unlikely to bar a claim for equitable relief but when coupled with other circumstances, often

---

31. *Ibid.* at 502.
32. [1994] 1 ILRM 450.
33. High Court 1999 No. 10182P (Barr J) 18 February 2000.
34. *The Principles of Equitable Remedies* (6th ed., 2001) p. 431.

relating to the conduct of the plaintiff, it may be sufficient to lead to an equitable remedy being refused. Clearly once a plaintiff is appraised of the facts which would lead him to seek the intervention of the court he should proceed without undue delay and should not wait until the eleventh hour before bringing proceedings. This point was stressed by O'Hanlon J in *Lennon v. Ganly*,[35] in which he refused the plaintiff an injunction restraining the defendants from embarking on a rugby tour to South Africa, because, *inter alia* he had delayed until just before the tour was due to commence and because a considerable period of time had elapsed since news of it had first been announced. However, the courts will take a realistic view of what constitutes undue delay and unless it is of appreciable length or some serious prejudice has been suffered by reason of it, it will not be a bar to relief.[36]

The view was expressed by Budd J in *Cahill v. Irish Motor Traders' Association*[37] that delay by itself will not disentitle a plaintiff to an injunction to protect a legal as opposed to an equitable right unless the claim is barred by statute. This view would also seem to prevail in Australia where Deane J commented in *Orr v. Ford*[38] that '[l]aches is an equitable defence and is not available in answer to a legal claim'. However, the Court of Appeal in *Habib Bank Ltd v. Habib Bank AG Zurich*[39] drew no distinction between legal and equitable rights in this context and made it clear that the defence of laches can apply whenever an injunction is sought. Similarly, in *Gafford v. Graham*[40] Nourse LJ commented that he doubted whether a distinction ought to be made between a legal and equitable right when considering a defence of acquiescence. Whether this view would now find favour in Ireland remains to be seen, but it is likely that there will be a move towards the approach adopted in *Habib* in this jurisdiction also.

As Finnegan P made clear in *Criminal Assets Bureau v. P.S.*,[41] where a party has obtained an interim injunction he has an obligation to prosecute the proceedings promptly both in relation to the interlocutory injunction and the substantive action. He added that delay on the part of a plaintiff will entitle a defendant to seek to have the interim or interlocutory injunction discharged, although he stressed that an interim injunction which has been obtained by a plaintiff on an *ex parte* basis will be more susceptible to being discharged for

---

35. [1981] ILRM 84.
36. See e.g. *An Post v. Irish Permanent plc* [1995] 1 ILRM 336 where Kinlen J found that any delay in bringing an application for interlocutory relief was insufficient to influence the decision to grant relief. See also *Irish Shell Ltd v. Elm Motors Ltd* [1984] IR 200, 216; *Carrigaline Community Television Broadcasting Co. Ltd v. Minister for Transport, Energy and Communications* [1994] 2 IR 359.
37. [1966] IR 430, 449.
38. (1989) 167 CLR 316, 340 *per* Oliver LJ .
39. [1981] 1WLR 1265, 1285.
40. (1998) 77 P & CR 73, 80.
41. High Court 1997 No. 38R (Finnegan P) 12 April 2002.

delay than an interlocutory injunction. Similarly it would appear that a shorter period of inactivity will defeat a claim for an interlocutory injunction than is required to defeat an action for a perpetual injunction. This is a reflection of the fact that while the refusal of an injunction at the interlocutory stage does not preclude the plaintiff from ultimately obtaining the relief which he seeks, refusal at the trial stage will finally dispose of his claim. In *Howard v. Commissioners of Public Works in Ireland*,[42] which involved a claim for an interlocutory injunction to restrain the respondents from proceeding with development work on a proposed visitor centre and national park in the Burren, O'Hanlon J placed emphasis *inter alia* on the conduct of the parties. He concluded that the application should be refused because he believed that the balance of convenience lay in favour of allowing the work to proceed and because the applicants had delayed unduly in seeking the relief while the respondents had behaved in an 'irreproachable manner'.

Further consideration was given to the relevance of delay in the context of an application for an interlocutory injunction in *Newport Association Football Club Ltd v. Football Association of Wales Ltd*.[43] The plaintiffs, Welsh football clubs, sought an interlocutory injunction allowing them to play their home matches in Wales the following season as their revenue had decreased substantially as a result of sanctions preventing them playing there imposed by the defendant association due to the plaintiffs to participate instead in a league organised by the English Football Association. Jacob J commented that normally a party who has delayed for two years or more before applying for an interlocutory injunction will be refused it on grounds of delay as the final trial could have taken place by that time and the *status quo* is likely to have changed. However, Jacob J was satisfied that notwithstanding these points the case before him was a wholly exceptional one and he stated that if the injunction was not granted, there was a real risk that the plaintiffs would simply cease to exist. In addition, he adverted to the fact that this was not a case where the plaintiffs had been standing by for two years; during that time they had been actively seeking a solution to the problem and a reversal of the defendant's decision. Jacob J therefore concluded that while he took the delay into account, it was not enough to persuade him to withhold the injunction which he proposed to grant.

Acquiescence is described as arising in the following circumstances by Spry:[44] 'first, there must, on the part of the plaintiff, be an assent or lying by in relation to the acts of another person; and secondly, in view of the assent or lying by and consequent acts it must be unjust in all the circumstances to grant the specific relief that is in question.' Similarly, in *Archbold v. Scully*[45]

---

42. High Court 1992 No. 331JR (O'Hanlon J) 3 December 1992.
43. [1995] 2 All ER 87.
44. *The Principles of Equitable Remedies* (6th ed., 2001) p. 440.
45. (1861) 9 HLC 360, 383.

Lord Wensleydale said: 'if a party, who could object, lies by and knowingly permits another to incur an expense in doing an act under the belief that it would not be objected to, and so a kind of permission may be said to be given to another to alter his condition, he may be said to acquiesce.' The operation of the principle of acquiescence as a defence to a claim for an injunction can best be explained by reference to a number of examples. In *Sayers v. Collyer*[46] the plaintiff failed to obtain an injunction to restrain the use of a house as a beer shop in breach of covenant as he had been aware of this breach for a number of years and had even bought beer there himself. As Baggallay LJ commented 'I can hardly imagine a stronger case of acquiescence than this.'[47]

A good example of a case in which acquiescence barred a claim for an injunction but not a remedy in damages is the decision of the Court of Appeal in *Shaw v. Applegate*.[48] The defendant purchased property and covenanted not to use it as an amusement arcade and the vendor subsequently assigned the benefit of the covenant to the plaintiffs. Three years after the defendant had started to install amusement machines the plaintiff sought an injunction to restrain the breach of covenant. The Court of Appeal held that to deprive the possessor of a legal right of that right on the ground of his acquiescence the situation must have been such that it would be dishonest or unconscionable to seek to enforce it. Since the plaintiffs had been confused about whether the defendants' activities constituted a breach of covenant, it could not be said that the plaintiffs would be acting dishonestly or unconscionably in seeking to enforce their rights under the contract when they did. However, in view of the goodwill built up by the defendant over a period of years and the expenditure incurred by him, the court held that the appropriate remedy was damages and not an injunction. This can be contrasted with the approach taken by Nourse LJ in *Gafford v. Graham*[49] which concerned a claim for relief in respect of building works carried out by the defendant in breach of a restrictive covenant. The Court of Appeal was satisfied that the plaintiff had known of his rights and had made no attempt to complain for some three years after this building work had taken place; in these circumstances Nourse LJ stated that the plaintiff's acquiescence was a bar to all relief in respect of these matters.[50]

---

46. (1884) 28 Ch D 103.
47. *Ibid.* at 107.
48. [1977] 1 WLR 970.
49. (1998) 77 P & CR 73.
50. However, it should be noted that the Court of Appeal awarded damages in lieu of an injunction in respect of other building work where the plaintiff had acted promptly in complaining about it.

Effect on Third Parties

There have been judicial statements made suggesting that the courts in deciding whether to grant an injunction should have regard to the surrounding circumstances and to the rights of those who may be peripherally involved,[51] and that an injunction should not be granted where this will have the effect of 'very materially injuring the rights of third parties'.[52] However, Spry[53] has stated that 'it is not generally appropriate that specific private rights should be denied in order to give rise to an indefinite advantage to the general public' and this view has tended to prevail. The question was considered by the Supreme Court in *Bellew v. Cement Ltd*,[54] in which the majority of the court concluded that the general public convenience should not be taken into account in weighing up whether to grant relief in the form of an injunction. The plaintiffs sought an interlocutory injunction to restrain the defendants, who were the sole manufacturers of cement in the State, from carrying out blasting operations in a quarry which it was alleged constituted a nuisance. The defendants argued that in view of the importance of the defendants' products to the building industry and having regard to the fact that because of the impending long vacation blasting operations would have to cease for several months, an injunction should not be granted. It was held by the Supreme Court in granting the order sought that the plaintiff had made out a *prima facie* case[55] of nuisance and that the court was not entitled to take the public convenience into consideration when dealing with the rights of private parties. As Maguire CJ stated: 'This matter is a dispute between private parties and I think that the court should be concerned, only, to see that the rights of the parties are safeguarded.'[56] Black J dissented and stated that while the concept of public convenience cannot justify the refusal of a remedy for a nuisance, it is a different matter to say that it cannot, or ought not to, affect the way in which a nuisance should be dealt with.[57]

In England there have been conflicting authorities on this question, but more recent decisions would seem to support the view of the majority in *Bellew*.

---

51. *Wood v. Sutcliffe* (1851) 2 Sim (NS) 163, 165.
52. *Hartlepool Gas & Water Co. v. West Hartlepool Harbour & Rly Co.* (1865) 12 LT 366, 368.
53. *The Principles of Equitable Remedies* (6th ed., 2001) p. 402.
54. [1948] IR 61.
55. This was the accepted test in relation to the granting of an interlocutory injunction at the time. It has now been replaced by the requirement of establishing that there is a fair question to be tried. See *infra* p. 470.
56. *Ibid.* at 64.
57. Note that in *Wall v. Feely* High Court 1983 No. 7014P (Costello J) 26 October 1983, Costello J appeared to take the public convenience into account albeit to the limited extent of considering how this would affect the defendant local authority, although it did not ultimately influence his decision.

In *Miller v. Jackson*[58] the owner of a house situated beside a cricket ground sought an injunction to prevent the club continuing with its activities which involved a risk of injury from cricket balls landing on the property. While two members of the Court of Appeal agreed that these activities constituted a nuisance, Cumming-Bruce LJ agreed with the view of Lord Denning MR that an injunction should not be granted in these circumstances and that the plaintiff should be confined to a remedy in damages. In his view 'a court of equity must seek to strike a fair balance between the right of the plaintiffs to have quiet enjoyment of their house and garden without exposure to cricket balls occasionally falling like thunderbolts from the heavens, and the opportunity of the inhabitants of the village in which they live to continue to enjoy the manly sport which constitutes a summer recreation for adults and young persons, including one would hope and expect, the plaintiff's son.'[59] This view was unanimously disapproved of several years later by a differently constituted Court of Appeal in *Kennaway v. Thompson*.[60] The plaintiff sought an injunction to restrain a nuisance which consisted of excessive noise caused by power boat racing on a lake in the vicinity of her house. The Court of Appeal granted an injunction which greatly restricted the club's activities on the grounds that the public interest in allowing the racing to continue uninterrupted could not prevail over the plaintiff's entitlement to enjoy her home free from the tortious interference which this racing caused.

While the view expressed by the Supreme Court in *Bellew* and the Court of Appeal in *Kennaway* would seem to be the correct one, there has been some evidence of a tendency to look beyond the rights of the parties actually involved in an action in assessing whether to grant an injunction, particularly at the interlocutory stage. In *Howard v. Commissioners for Public Works*,[61] the applicants sought an interlocutory injunction to restrain the respondents from proceeding with development work on a proposed interpretative centre in the Burren. O'Hanlon J concluded that the evidence was sufficient to satisfy him that major disruption of a very serious kind would occur if the project were to be brought to a standstill. He said that he had no doubt that the financial loss would be very substantial, that the respondents might find themselves facing serious liabilities for breach of contract and that many people would lose their employment. In addition, O'Hanlon J was of the view that the loss and damage which would be sustained by the applicants if the interlocutory relief were refused did not fall within the category of what he could regard as irreparable damage and he concluded that the interlocutory order should be refused. While other factors, such as the conduct of the parties, were also referred to, it is difficult to avoid the conclusion that O'Hanlon J was influenced

---

58. [1977] QB 966.
59. *Ibid.* at 988.
60. [1981] QB 88.
61. High Court 1992 No.331JR (O'Hanlon J) 3 December 1992.

at least in part by the wider public convenience which involved primarily the employment prospects of those working on the project, in deciding to refuse the relief sought. Similarly, in *Dun Laoghaire Rathdown County Council v. Shackleton*[62] O'Sullivan J stated that, in reaching the conclusion that the plaintiff had made out a good cause of action and that interlocutory relief should be granted preventing an arbitrator from embarking on hearing a claim for compensation, he had been influenced by public interest considerations.

The question of whether the court could take into account the wider question of public convenience was raised also in *An Post v. Irish Permanent plc*,[63] but Kinlen J said that he would express no view on the matter at the interlocutory stage as it was one more properly to be determined at trial.

A related question is whether the activities of third parties should have any effect on the decision of a court to grant or refuse an injunction. Arguably this should not be a factor and the court should confine itself to an examination of the issues which affect the parties directly involved, although the approach adopted by Keane J in *Phonographic Performance (Ireland) Ltd v. Chariot Inns*[64] suggests that this will not always be the case. The plaintiff sought an interlocutory injunction restraining the defendants from permitting certain sound recordings from being played in public when the defendant refused to pay an amount claimed by the plaintiff by way of 'equitable remuneration' within the meaning of the Copyright Act 1963. Keane J concluded that there were 'unquestionably serious issues at stake between the parties involving difficult questions of law' and held that as more damage would be caused by refusing than by granting an injunction the order sought should be granted. However, in the course of his judgment, Keane J made reference to the fact that if the interlocutory injunction was refused and the plaintiff was ultimately successful, large sums would have to be recovered from other operators who might follow the defendants' example and refuse to pay and he said that it was unlikely, given the number of businesses involved, that all these sums would be recovered. While the conclusion reached by Keane J was probably correct in the circumstances, as Coughlan[65] has pointed out, the question should arguably have been decided solely by reference to the infringement of the plaintiff's rights allegedly committed by that defendant and the defendant could hardly be held accountable for the activities of independent third parties.

---

62. High Court 2002 No. 130P (O'Sullivan J) 23 January 2002.
63. [1995] 1 ILRM 336, 349.
64. High Court 1992 No. 4673P (Keane J) 7 October 1992.
65. [1993] EIPR D-10.

Jurisdiction to Award Damages under Lord Cairns' Act

While originally the Court of Chancery had no jurisdiction to award damages, the Chancery Amendment Act 1858 (Lord Cairns' Act) authorized the court in all cases where it had jurisdiction to grant an injunction or an order of specific performance to award damages either in addition to or in substitution for the other remedies. This power to award damages in equity declined in significance after the enactment of the Judicature Act which conferred jurisdiction on the courts to make an award of damages in any case where this could have been done previously by the common law courts. However, it is still necessary to rely on Lord Cairns' Act in circumstances where no entitlement to damages lies at common law; e.g. where the right in question is equitable in nature, or where a breach of the plaintiff's rights has not yet occurred and is merely anticipated.[66] The discretion granted by Lord Cairns' Act is similar to that exercised since the enactment of the Judicature Act to make an award of damages in lieu of granting an injunction and it does not seem necessary to draw any distinction in relation to the general principles involved.

An attempt to lay down a 'good working rule' in relation to the principles governing the award of damages in lieu of an injunction under Lord Cairns' Act was made by Smith LJ in *Shelfer v. City of London Electric Lighting Co.*[67] An electric lighting company caused considerable discomfort and annoyance to the lessee of premises by carrying out excavation work. At first instance Kekewich J held that while the defendants had created a continuing nuisance, damages should be the only remedy, although the Court of Appeal allowed the plaintiff's appeal against the refusal of an injunction. Smith LJ laid down the general principle that damages should only be awarded in lieu of an injunction or specific performance in the following circumstances:[68]

(1) If the injury to the plaintiff's legal rights is small,

(2) And is one which is capable of being estimated in money,

(3) And is one which can be adequately compensated by a small money payment,

(4) And the case is one in which it would be oppressive to the defendant to grant an injunction. ...

Smith LJ continued by saying that even where these four principles are satisfied, an injunction may still be awarded if the defendant has acted in reckless disregard of the plaintiff's rights. A further point stressed by Lindley LJ which is of particular importance is that the court in exercising this

---

66. *Johnson v. Agnew* [1980] AC 367, 400.
67. [1895] 1 Ch 287.
68. *Ibid.* at 322-323.

jurisdiction will not allow a wrong to continue simply because the wrongdoer is able and willing to pay for the injury he may inflict.

The application of the *Shelfer* principles did not immediately meet with universal approval in England, so, in *Fishenden v. Higgs & Hill Ltd*[69] Hanworth MR said that they were for guidance only and Romer LJ made it clear that if one of the four requirements was not fulfilled, it did not mean that an injunction must be granted. The Court of Appeal, while upholding a finding of nuisance with regard to interference with a right to light, held that in the circumstances damages were a sufficient remedy. However, more recently these principles have tended to be applied, as in *Kennaway v. Thompson*,[70] where the plaintiff sought an injunction to restrain power boat racing on a lake near her house. The Court of Appeal held that the principles in *Shelfer's* case applied and awarded her an injunction limiting the racing activities on the grounds that the injury to the plaintiff was not small or capable of estimation in monetary terms nor could the sum awarded by the High Court judge who had decided to award damages in lieu, be considered a small payment. Lawton LJ said that he considered that *Shelfer's* case was binding on him and stressed that in cases of continuing nuisance the jurisdiction to award damages in lieu should only be exercised in very exceptional circumstances. The 'good working rule' laid down in *Shelfer* was again applied by the Court of Appeal in *Jaggard v. Sawyer*[71] to support the conclusion that the plaintiff should have been awarded damages in lieu of an injunction in respect of a breach of covenant and trespass. However, Millett LJ made it clear that it should not be assumed that these principles will cover every potential situation and they should be applied where appropriate. As he commented: 'A.L. Smith LJ's check-list has stood the test of time; but it needs to be remembered that it is only a working rule and does not purport to be an exhaustive statement of the circumstances in which damages may be awarded instead of an injunction.'[72] Millett LJ added that the outcome of any particular case usually turns on the question of whether it would in all the circumstances be oppressive to the defendant to grant the injunction to which the plaintiff is *prima facie* entitled. This certainly seemed to form the basis for the decision of the Court of Appeal in *Gafford v. Graham*[73] where Nourse LJ applied the *Shelfer* principles and concluded in awarding damages in lieu of an injunction that it would be oppressive and therefore unfair to the defendant to grant an injunction. Finally, it should be noted as the decision in *Marcic v. Thames Water Utilities Ltd (No.2)*[74] makes clear,

---

69. (1935) 153 LT 128.
70. [1981] QB 88. See also *Jaggard v. Sawyer* [1995] 1 WLR 269, 277-278 *per* Bingham MR.
71. [1995] 1 WLR 269. See also *Ketley v. Gooden* (1996) 73 P & CR 305.
72. *Ibid.* at 287. See also *Marcic v. Thames Water Utilities Ltd (No.2)* [2002] QB 1003, 1008.
73. (1998) 77 P & CR 73.
74. [2002] QB 1003.

that the *Shelfer* principles only apply where it is the defendant who seeks to avoid an injunction being granted and not where the plaintiff seeks damages rather than an injunction.

The leading Irish authority in this area is *Patterson v. Murphy*,[75] in which the plaintiffs sought damages and an injunction arising out of alleged acts of nuisance caused by blasting and quarrying activities carried on by the defendants in a field adjoining their house. Costello J found that these activities did constitute acts of nuisance and held that the plaintiffs were entitled to an injunction. He said that the infringement of their rights was most serious; the injury which they had suffered and would continue to suffer if the nuisance were allowed to continue had been and would be considerable and he was satisfied that damages would not adequately compensate them. Costello J laid down a number of 'well established principles' on which the court exercises its discretion in deciding whether to grant an injunction and it is worth setting them out in full.

1. When an infringement of the plaintiffs' right and a threatened further infringement to a material extent has been established, the plaintiff is *prima facie* entitled to an injunction. There may be circumstances, however, depriving the plaintiff of this *prima facie* right but generally speaking the plaintiff will only be deprived of an injunction in very exceptional circumstances.

2. If the injury to the plaintiffs' rights is small, and is one capable of being estimated in money, and is one which can be adequately compensated by a small money payment and if the case is one in which it would be oppressive to the defendant to grant an injunction, then these are circumstances in which damages in lieu of an injunction may be granted.

3. The conduct of the plaintiff may be such as to disentitle him to an injunction. The conduct of the defendant may be such as to disentitle him from seeking the substitution of damages for an injunction.

4. The mere fact that a wrong-doer is able and willing to pay for the injury he has inflicted is not a ground for substituting damages.

Costello J distinguished the decision of Gannon J in *Halpin v. Tara Mines Ltd*,[76] in which the plaintiffs had been refused an injunction and awarded damages in respect of a nuisance caused by the defendant's prospecting activities. While he found that these activities had amounted to a nuisance, Gannon J was satisfied that the defendant had modified its operations and improved its working practices to such an extent by the time of the trial of the action that the court should decline to grant an injunction.

---

75. [1978] ILRM 85, 99-100.
76. [1976-77] ILRM 28.

While the point made by Lindley LJ in *Shelfer* that a court will not allow a wrong to continue simply because the wrongdoer is able and willing to pay for the injury he may inflict is an important one, where the wrongdoing is unintentional and the plaintiff has suffered no loss in its trading position, a remedy in damages may meet the justice of the situation. In *Falcon Travel Ltd v. Owners Abroad Group plc*[77] the plaintiff, a retail travel agent in the Wicklow and Dublin areas, sought an injunction against the defendants who had opened an office in this country on the grounds of alleged passing off. Due to the similarity in the companies' names confusion arose and there was bad publicity for the plaintiff on one occasion although in general their turnover increased because of the confusion. Murphy J accepted that while the defendant was aware of the plaintiff's business, he was satisfied that it had not intended to exploit its reputation or business. While it did not appear that the plaintiff's business had suffered, Murphy J accepted that the plaintiff had suffered damage in that its reputation had become submerged into that of the defendant and he concluded that the tort of passing off had been established. Although he said that an injunction would ordinarily be the most suitable means of protecting the plaintiff's property rights, he took into account the fact that the wrongdoing was unintentional and that the plaintiff had suffered no loss in its trading position as well as the fact that an injunction would involve the defendant in enormous expense. In view of these factors, Murphy J decided to exercise his discretion to award damages in lieu of an injunction, calculated with a view to organizing an advertising campaign to make it clear to the public that the plaintiff and defendant were separate businesses.

The Measure of Damages Under Lord Cairns' Act

The question of the measure of damages which can be awarded under Lord Cairns' Act is one which has provoked considerable uncertainty in England[78] and this controversy is not one which the courts in this jurisdiction have directly addressed. In *Johnson v. Agnew*[79] the House of Lords held that there was no difference in the measure of damages which could be awarded under Lord Cairns' Act and at common law, Lord Wilberforce stating that the Act 'does not provide for the assessment of damages on any new basis'.[80] However, no reference was made by the House of Lords in *Johnson* to the earlier decision of Brightman J in *Wrotham Park Estate Co. v. Parkside Homes Ltd*[81] in which

---

77. [1991] 1 IR 175.
78. Some of the factors which the courts will weigh up in assessing quantum are considered by Halpern [2001] Conv 453.
79. [1980] AC 367.
80. *Ibid.* at 400.
81. [1974] 1 WLR 798. It should be noted that *Wrotham Park* appears to have been approved by the Court of Appeal in *Stoke-on-Trent City Council v. W. & J. Wass Ltd*

he had considered the measure of damages to be awarded in equity in lieu of an injunction for breach of a restrictive covenant. As the plaintiff had sustained no loss, any damages which would have been awarded at common law would have been purely nominal,[82] but Brightman J concluded that a 'just substitute' for the injunction sought would be the sum which the plaintiff might have obtained in return for modifying the covenant.

Ingman has suggested that Brightman J's conclusion in *Wrotham Park* may have resulted from a misunderstanding as to what Lord Cairns' Act was intended to achieve.[83] In his view the primary object of the legislation was a purely procedural one and he asserts that it was 'never intended to change the substantive law so as to permit a court of equity to award damages on a different basis from that recognised at common law in a case where damages were available both in equity and at law.'[84] However it should be pointed out that in *Wrotham Park* damages would not have been available at law and for this reason, the decision may still be defended on its own facts.

Subsequently in *Surrey County Council v. Bredero Homes Ltd*,[85] in which the plaintiff only sought common law damages as the grant of an injunction had become impossible before proceedings were issued, the Court of Appeal expressed different views about the earlier decisions. Dillon LJ stated that in his opinion the award of significant damages in *Wrotham Park* was inconsistent with *Johnson* and said that the conclusion of Brightman J involved the assumption that Lord Cairns' Act had effected a substantive and not merely a procedural change in the law, a finding which ran contrary to what had been stated by the House of Lords. However, the majority of the Court of Appeal on an *obiter* basis expressed the view that the conclusion reached in *Wrotham Park* was a fair and just one in the circumstances.

More recently the Court of Appeal in *Jaggard v. Sawyer*[86] has addressed the question of whether it is possible to reconcile the earlier decisions. The Court of Appeal concluded that the trial judge had been correct to apply the *Wrotham Park* approach to the assessment of damages to compensate the plaintiff for a continuing breach of her rights, and it was clearly of significance to this decision that the damages included compensation for future injury. Millett LJ adverted to this fact when he stated that 'when the court awards damages in substitution for an injunction, it seeks to compensate the plaintiff for loss arising from future wrongs that is to say, loss for which the common

---

[1988] 1 WLR 1406 in which the House of Lords decision in *Johnson* was not referred to.
82. Although it should be stressed that on the facts of this case, as a restrictive covenant was involved, damages could only be awarded under Lord Cairns' Act.
83. [1994] Conv 110.
84. *Ibid.* at 120.
85. [1993] 1 WLR 1361.
86. [1995] 1 WLR 269. See also Ingman [1995] Conv 141.

law does not provide a remedy'. He also rightly pointed out that in *Johnson v. Agnew* the plaintiff was claiming damages for loss occasioned by a single, once-off, past breach of contract. He continued as follows:

> In my view Lord Wilberforce's statement [in *Johnson v. Agnew*] that the measure of damages is the same whether damages are recoverable at common law or under the Act must be taken to be limited to the case where they are recoverable in respect of the same cause of action. It cannot sensibly have any application where the claim at common law is in respect of a past trespass or breach of covenant and that under the Act is in respect of future trespasses or continuing breaches of covenant.[87]

The *Wrotham Park* principle which allows damages to be awarded in lieu of an injunction even where the plaintiff has sustained no loss has recently won the support of the House of Lords in *Attorney General v. Blake*.[88] Although the case did not involve the application of Lord Cairns' Act, the House of Lords, in holding that a claim for an account of profits might be made in a case of breach of contract, was required to consider whether a court might award substantial damages for an infringement when no financial loss flowed from such infringement. Lord Nicholls stated that in his opinion Brightman J had been correct in the conclusion which he had reached in *Wrotham Park* and that, in so far as the decision in *Surrey County Council v. Bredero Homes Ltd* was inconsistent with the approach adopted in the former case, the view of Brightman J was to be preferred. Lord Nicholls commented that: 'the *Wrotham Park* case, therefore, still shines, rather as a solitary beacon, showing that in contract as well as tort damages are not always narrowly confined to recoupment for financial loss.'[89] So, while the principle laid down in *Johnson v. Agnew* still applies, namely that where both common law and damages under Lord Cairns' Act are available their measure should be the same, it would appear that residual doubts about the conclusion reached in *Wrotham Park* have now been laid to rest and that where damages are available only under the Act more than a nominal amount may be awarded even where the plaintiff has sustained no loss.

---

87. *Ibid.* at at 291. It is interesting to note that while Millett LJ characterised the *Wrotham Park* decision as one concerning a single past breach of covenant (at 291), Bingham MR considered it to involve a 'continuing invasion' of the plaintiff's rights (at 281).
88. [2001] 1 AC 268.
89. *Ibid.* at 283.

Principles Governing the Grant of Interlocutory Injunctions

The essential aim of an interlocutory injunction is to preserve the *status quo* existing between the parties to an action until the trial of the issues in dispute can take place and it will have effect until the final determination of the rights of the parties by the court. The rationale behind the grant of such injunctions is primarily the need to protect the rights of a plaintiff by preserving the circumstances which exist at the time he institutes proceedings to prevent him suffering irreparable prejudice by reason of the delay which must necessarily occur between the institution of proceedings and the trial of the action. O'Higgins CJ summarised these principles as follows in *Campus Oil Ltd v. Minister for Industry & Energy (No. 2):*[90]

> Interlocutory relief is granted to an applicant where what he complains of is continuing and is causing him harm or injury which may be irreparable in the sense that it may not be possible to compensate him fairly or properly by an award of damages. Such relief is given because a period must necessarily elapse before the action can come for trial and for the purpose of keeping matters *in statu quo* until the hearing.

In practice the courts grant far more injunctions of an interlocutory than a perpetual nature as many disputes are resolved after the interlocutory stage and do not proceed to trial for various other reasons.[91] In certain circumstances, where the parties consent, the court may even treat the application for an interlocutory order as the trial of the action. While this procedure will inevitably lead to a more expeditious resolution of the issues to be determined, it will only be a suitable course to take where there is no dispute about the facts as an interlocutory hearing is conducted on the basis of affidavit evidence alone.

A further important preliminary point to note is that where an interlocutory injunction is sought, a plaintiff will almost invariably be required to give an undertaking as to damages and the court will have to be satisfied as to the plaintiff's ability to honour such an undertaking should this become necessary.[92] It would appear that the giving of an undertaking will only be dispensed with in 'special circumstances',[93] and it was stressed by Budd J in *Keenan v. CIE*[94] that such an undertaking is a *sine qua non* where a mandatory interlocutory injunction is sought. While it is required for the defendant's benefit to ensure that he can be recompensed if it is subsequently shown that no interlocutory order should have been made, it is given to the court and

---

90. [1983] IR 88, 105.
91. *Fellowes & Son v. Fisher* [1976] QB 122, 129 *per* Lord Denning MR.
92. *Brigid Foley Ltd v. Ellott* [1982] RPC 433, 435-436 *per* Megarry VC.
93. *Attorney-General v. Albany Hotel Co.* [1896] 2 Ch 696, 700 *per* North J.
94. (1963) 97 ILTR 54.

accordingly non-compliance with any undertaking given will constitute a contempt of court.

In principle a court may grant an injunction of an interlocutory nature whenever it is 'just and convenient so to do'[95] and it has been stressed that the remedy 'should be kept flexible and discretionary. ... and must not be made the subject of strict rules.'[96] However, in practice recognised guidelines have generally been applied by the courts in deciding whether to grant or refuse this form of relief. It has recently been acknowledged[97] that there is 'no significant difference' between the principles which apply to the granting or withholding of interlocutory injunctions in this jurisdiction and in England, with the proviso that in this jurisdiction a court cannot by its order abridge or in any way diminish the constitutional rights enjoyed by any of the parties to the action.

Traditionally, a plaintiff would be granted an interlocutory injunction only if he could establish a '*prima facie* case' i.e. a probability that he would succeed in his claim at the hearing of the action, and the effect of this requirement was that a plaintiff had to show that it was more likely than not that he would succeed. This test was accepted by the House of Lords in *J.T. Stratford and Sons v. Lindley*[98] and by the majority of the Supreme Court in *Esso Petroleum Co. (Ireland) Ltd v. Fogarty*.[99] However there was evidence of a different approach being suggested in some cases based on whether there was a fair or substantial question to be decided[100] and the *prima facie* test was criticized on the basis that it led to confusion as to the object sought to be achieved by this form of relief.

The *prima facie* test was finally rejected by the House of Lords in 1975 in favour of a less rigid requirement in the landmark decision of *American Cyanamid Co. v. Ethicon Ltd.*[101] The plaintiff sought and obtained an

---

95. Order 50 rule 6 of the Rules of the Superior Courts 1986.
96. *Hubbard v. Vosper* [1972] 2 QB 84, 96 *per* Denning MR.
97. *Oblique Financial Services Ltd v. The Promise Production Co Ltd* [1994] 1 ILRM 74, 76-77.
98. [1965] AC 269, 338 *per* Lord Upjohn.
99. [1965] IR 531, 538 *per* O Dálaigh CJ.
100. *Educational Co. of Ireland Ltd v. Fitzpatrick* [1961] IR 323, 337 *per* Lavery J and *Esso Petroleum Co. (Ireland) Ltd. v. Fogarty* [1965] IR 531, 541 *per* Walsh J.
101. [1975] AC 396. This test met with approval in a number of other common law jurisdictions, see further Kerr (1983) Ir Jur (ns) 34, 39, footnote 25. It is still generally applied in England, apart from in a number of exceptional cases. However, it should be noted that Laddie J has recently suggested in *Series 5 Software v. Clarke* [1996] 1 All ER 853, 865 that 'Lord Diplock did not intend . . . to exclude consideration of the strength of the cases in most applications for interlocutory relief.' He continued as follows: 'It appears to me that what is intended is that the court should not attempt to resolve difficult issues of fact or law on an application for interlocutory relief. If, on the other hand, the court is able to come to a view as to the strength of the parties' case on the credible evidence, then it can do so. . . . If it is apparent from that

interlocutory injunction to restrain the defendant from marketing surgical products in alleged infringement of the plaintiff's patent. The modified test propounded by Lord Diplock required a plaintiff to show that the claim was not frivolous or vexatious, in other words that there was 'a serious question to be tried', and where this was established, the court had to go on to consider the balance of convenience which involved assessing the probable implications for both parties should the relief sought be granted or refused. Lord Diplock stated that: 'It is no part of the court's function at this stage of the litigation to try to resolve conflicts of evidence on affidavit as to facts on which the claims of either party may ultimately depend nor to decide difficult questions of law which call for detailed argument and mature considerations. These are matters to be dealt with at the trial'.[102]

Although an assessment of where the balance of convenience lay involved consideration of a number of factors, the most important of these was recognised to be the question of the adequacy of damages.[103] The court was required to consider first, whether if no interlocutory order was made and the plaintiff were to succeed at the trial in establishing an entitlement to a permanent injunction, he would be adequately compensated by an award of damages. The court also had to consider whether the defendant would be adequately compensated by an award of damages if the decision went against him at the interlocutory stage but he was ultimately successful at the trial. In certain types of case, damages will almost inevitably not provide a sufficient remedy for a plaintiff so, for example, in *Pasture Properties Ltd v. Evans*[104] Laffoy J stated that 'it is axiomatic in trespass cases that damages are not an adequate remedy'. The court may also conclude that damages would not be an adequate remedy for either party and in such cases it may then consider whether on the facts the damage which would be suffered by the plaintiff should the court decline to make the order sought would on the balance of

---

material that one party's case is much stronger than the other's then that is a matter the court should not ignore. To suggest otherwise would be to exclude from consideration an important factor and such exclusion would fly in the face of the flexibility advocated earlier in *American Cyanamid*.'

102. *Ibid.* at 407. Quoted with approval by McCarthy J in *Irish Shell Ltd v. Elm Motors Ltd* [1984] IR 200, 224 and by Blayney J in *Ferris v. Ward* Supreme Court 1995 Nos. 333 & 334, 7 November 1995.

103. In *Smithkline Beecham plc v. Gentham BV* High Court 2002 No. 12824P (Kelly J) 28 February 2003 Kelly J suggested that the approach of treating adequacy of damages as an issue quite separate from the question of balance of convenience had been approved by the Supreme Court in *Westman Holdings Ltd v. McCormack* [1992] 1 IR 151, although this is open to some debate, see the *dicta* of Finlay CJ at 159. In the view of Kelly J, where a court is satisfied that damages would be an adequate remedy as in the case before him, that should conclude the matter and the court should not proceed to even consider the balance of convenience.

104. High Court 1997 No. 9351P (Laffoy J) 5 February 1999.

probability be greater than the damage suffered by the defendant should the court grant the interlocutory relief. [105]

If there is doubt as to the adequacy of the respective remedies in damages, the court may consider other factors, such as the taking of whatever measures would be necessary to preserve the status quo. The concept of the *status quo* was considered by Lord Diplock in *Garden Cottage Foods Ltd v. Milk Marketing Board*[106] where he said that 'the relevant *status quo* ... is the state of affairs existing during the period immediately proceeding the issue of the writ claiming the permanent injunction or, if there be unreasonable delay between the issue of the writ and the motion for an interlocutory injunction, the period immediately preceding the motion.' This interpretation is arguably correct although it has not always been strictly followed. In *Bayzana Ltd v. Galligan*[107] the plaintiff sought an injunction restraining the defendants from picketing a factory premises which it had bought with notice of the dispute. The majority of the Supreme Court concluded that there was a fair question to be tried and was satisfied that the balance of convenience favoured the plaintiff employers. However, McCarthy J in his dissenting judgment pointed out that in this instance the *status quo* to be preserved was that pertaining when the plaintiff became involved in the matter when it was aware of the dispute and of the picket and upheld the order of Hamilton P which merely restricted the number of pickets.

As McCracken J has recently commented in *Private Research Ltd v. Brosnan*:[108] 'Weighing heavily in favour of the plaintiff is the general rule that, where possible, the court should strive to maintain the *status quo*. However, this is only one element in considering the balance of convenience and there is no absolute rule that the *status quo* must be maintained'. In some cases, the balance of convenience will lie in favour of refusing an interlocutory injunction, notwithstanding that this may result in the alteration of the parties' respective positions. An example of this is the decision of McCracken J in *B. & S. Ltd v. Irish Auto Trader Ltd*[109] in which he refused to grant an injunction restraining the defendant from publishing, printing and distributing its magazine 'Auto Trader' in Ireland despite the plaintiff's claim that the tort of passing off had been established. McCracken J held that in view of the fact, *inter alia*, that the defendant had acted in a *bona fide* manner and that there was unlikely to be confusion between the parties' magazines, he was satisfied that the balance of convenience lay in refusing the relief sought notwithstanding that this altered the *status quo*.

---

105. *Local Ireland Ltd v. Local Ireland-Online Ltd* [2000] 4 IR 567. See also *Wright v. Board of Management of Gorey Community School* High Court 2000 No. 3038P (O'Sullivan J) 28 March 2002.
106. [1984] AC 130, 140.
107. [1987] IR 238.
108. [1996] 1 ILRM 27, 32.
109. [1995] 2 ILRM 152.

While these *American Cyanamid* principles received a mixed reception in this jurisdiction in the years immediately following the decision of the House of Lords,[110] they were approved in *Campus Oil Ltd v. Minister for Industry and Energy (No.2)*[111] and have been applied since in numerous decisions.[112] The plaintiff claimed a declaration that the obligation imposed on it by statutory instrument to buy a specified portion of its petroleum oil supplies from a state-owned refinery was contrary to Articles 30 and 31 of the EEC Treaty. The issue was referred to the European Court of Justice and the defendants sought an interlocutory injunction compelling the plaintiff to comply with the terms of the order pending determination of the plaintiff's claim at the trial of the action. It was held by Keane J in granting an interlocutory injunction that the probability of success at the trial was not the proper test to be applied by the court in deciding whether to grant such an injunction. Instead an applicant must establish that there is a fair question to be determined and that the balance of convenience lies on the side of granting the injunction. This finding was upheld by the Supreme Court and O'Higgins CJ stated as follows:

> In my view, the test to be applied is whether a fair *bona fide* question has been raised by the person seeking the relief. If such a question has been raised, it is not for the Court to determine that question on an interlocutory application; that remains to be decided at the trial. Once a fair question has been raised ... then the Court should consider the other matters which are appropriate to the exercise of its discretion to grant interlocutory relief. In this regard, I note the view expressed by Lord Diplock in *American Cyanamid Co. v. Ethicon Ltd.* I merely say that I entirely agree with what he said.[113]

These principles were re-iterated and applied by the Supreme Court in *Westman Holdings Ltd v McCormack*,[114] in which the plaintiff sought an interlocutory

---

110. See Kerr, *op. cit.* at 39-40. Note that in *TMG Group Ltd v. Al Babtain Trading and Contracting Co.* [1982] ILRM 343, 353, Keane J stated that 'insofar as the decision of the House of Lords in *American Cyanamid Co. v. Ethicon Ltd* suggests the application of different principles to applications of this nature, it does not represent the law in this country'. While they were applied at first with some reluctance by the Court of Appeal in *Hubbard v. Pitt* [1976] QB 142 and *Fellowes & Son v. Fisher* [1976] QB 122 they are now generally accepted in England.
111. [1983] IR 88. See also *Irish Shell Ltd v. Elm Motors Ltd* [1984] IR 200.
112. Some recent examples include *Connolly v. Byrne* Supreme Court 1997 No. 13, 23 January 1997; *D.G.S. Retail v. PC World* High Court 1997 No. 13388P (Laffoy J) 13 January 1998; *Clane Hospital Ltd v. VHI* High Court 1998 No. 3740P (Quirke J) 22 May 1998.
113. [1983] IR 88, 107.
114. [1992] 1 IR 151.

injunction to prevent the defendants, who had been employed by a company from which the plaintiff had bought a business, from picketing their premises. It was held by the Supreme Court that an interlocutory injunction granted to the plaintiffs should continue until the trial of the action. Finlay CJ said that while the loss which would be suffered by the plaintiff if it was refused an injunction but subsequently succeeded in establishing that the picketing was unlawful would be exclusively pecuniary loss, the combination of the inability on the part of some of the defendants to pay damages and the potential immunity from liability of the trade union, made it improbable that the plaintiff would, if refused an injunction, be able to obtain compensation. In addition, he found that the undertaking which the plaintiff must give in order to obtain the interlocutory injunction would be an adequate method of compensating the defendants in respect of any loss of wages which they might suffer and only their right to picket would remain uncompensated.

The following useful summary of the principles which the court should adhere to when considering applications for interlocutory relief is set out in the recent judgment of Quirke J in *Clane Hospital Ltd v. Voluntary Health Insurance Board*,[115] in which the plaintiffs sought an interlocutory injunction restraining the defendants from replacing their scheme of charges for medical services. He stated that the court should adopt the following sequence of issues for consideration:[116]

1. Whether or not the applicant has raised a fair, substantial[117] *bona fide* question for determination.

2. Whether, if the applicant were to succeed at the trial in establishing his right to a permanent injunction, he could be adequately compensated by an award of damages.

3. Whether, if the respondent were to be successful at the trial, he could be adequately compensated under the applicant's undertaking as to damages for any loss which he would have sustained by reason of the grant of interlocutory relief.

4. If either party or both have, by way of evidence, raised a real and substantial doubt as to the adequacy of the respective remedies in damages available to either party, then where does the 'balance of convenience' lie?

---

115. High Court 1998 No. 3740P (Quirke J) 22 May 1998.
116. *Ibid*. at 10.
117. On the same page of his judgment, Quirke J spoke in terms of the plaintiff establishing 'a fair *bona fide* question' and it is unlikely that he was deliberately seeking to make the test harder to satisfy by inserting the word 'substantial'. However, in view of the fact that the latter term did not appear in either the *American Cyanamid* or *Campus Oil* decisions, it is probably better omitted.

5. In some instances are there any 'special factors' (usually technical in nature) which may influence the exercise of discretion and the grant of the relief sought?

Quirke J concluded that the plaintiffs had raised a fair, substantial and *bona fide* question for determination, but he was satisfied that if the plaintiffs succeeded at the trial in establishing their right to a permanent injunction, they could be adequately compensated by an award of damages and in the circumstances, he decided to refuse the relief sought by the plaintiffs.

Recently in *Dunne v. Dun Laoghaire-Rathdown County Council*,[118] in which the plaintiffs sought interlocutory injunctions restraining the defendant from interfering with the remains of a castle which they claimed was a national monument, the Supreme Court again applied the traditional *Campus Oil* test, although Hardiman J stated that he considered that the plaintiffs had also met the higher standard of probability of success at trial, at least on the then state of the evidence. However, he went on to stress that the difficulty facing a court in dealing with any case on an interlocutory basis is that there is an ever present risk of doing an injustice to the party who ultimately succeeds and that it is necessary to balance the risks of injustice to the respective parties. He added that 'it is significant that, if no relief is granted, the court will be effectively deciding the issue by inaction, since the apprehended interference with the alleged national monument will be complete long before the action can be tried.'[119] On this basis it would be reasonable to conclude that if anything the court was suggesting that a less rather than more stringent test should be applied to the plaintiffs' case and there is nothing to indicate that the Supreme Court was advocating a return to pre-*Campus Oil* principles.

At this point it should be reiterated that an interlocutory injunction, like any other type of equitable remedy, is a discretionary form of relief and while the so-called '*Cyanamid* principles' have provided the basis for the exercise of the courts' jurisdiction in this area for some time, they should be regarded as guidelines[120] rather than rules which must be strictly adhered to. As Gray[121] has pointed out, in so far as Lord Diplock's formulation suggests that an applicant faces a series of hurdles and that once he has surmounted them he is guaranteed success, it is unfortunate. As she states, this approach goes beyond the provision of assistance to a judge in the exercise of his discretion and in fact amounts to a significant restriction of that discretion.

Lord Diplock himself acknowledged that there may be special factors which

---

118. [2003] 2 ILRM 147.
119. *Ibid.* at 27.
120. *Cayne v. Global Natural Resources plc* [1984] 1 All ER 225, 237 *per* May LJ. See also *Cambridge Nutrition Ltd v. British Broadcasting Corporation* [1990] 3 All ER 523, 535.
121. [1981] CLJ 307, 313.

should be taken into consideration in individual cases, although the fact that a trial is likely to take place within a short space of time is not one of them. This point was made by Kinlen J in the course of his judgment in *An Post v. Irish Permanent plc*,[122] in which the plaintiff sought an interlocutory injunction to restrain alleged passing off in relation to the use of the term 'savings certificate' by the defendant to describe a financial savings product which it was issuing in competition with the plaintiff. Kinlen J granted an interlocutory injunction as he found that there was a serious question to be tried and that the balance of convenience favoured the granting of the order and rejected the argument that the fact the matter was likely to be tried quickly was an important consideration.[123]

Circumstances in which a Departure from Cyanamid Guidelines Justified

It is now acknowledged that departure from the *Cyanamid* principles is justified in certain circumstances.[124] The most obvious of these is where the parties agree that the hearing of the interlocutory application will constitute the trial of the action. Other exceptions have developed and while it would not be wise to attempt to set these out in an exhaustive manner, the following situations have been recognised.

(i) Where there is no Arguable Defence to the Plaintiff's Claim

This principle is almost self-explanatory and as Scott J made clear in *Official Custodian for Charities v. Mackey*,[125] the *Cyanamid* principles are not applicable in a case where there is no arguable defence as there will clearly be no serious question to be tried in such a case. So e.g. where a plaintiff has clear title and the defendant's trespass is indisputable, the balance of convenience will play no part in the court's decision and the plaintiff may obtain an interlocutory injunction to restrain the trespass, even where it has caused no damage.[126] This principle has recently been confirmed by Keane J in *Keating & Co. Ltd v. Jervis Shopping Centre Ltd*[127] where he stated that: 'It is clear that a landowner, whose title is not in issue, is *prima facie* entitled to an injunction to restrain a trespass and . . . this is also the case where the

---

122. [1995] 1 ILRM 336.
123. Note that the case was settled prior to trial with the defendant giving an undertaking that it would not sell products bearing the name 'savings certificates'.
124. As Kelly J pointed out in *Reynolds v. Malocco* [1999] 2 IR 203, 209 'these principles have a wide but not a universal application'. See generally Martin (1993-94) 4 KCLJ 52.
125. [1985] Ch 168, 187.
126. *Patel v. W.H. Smith (Eziot) Ltd* [1987] 1 WLR 853.
127. High Court 1995 No. 9606P (Keane J) 1 March 1996.

claim is for an interlocutory injunction only'.[128] However, as Keane J pointed out, this principle is subject to the following qualification, set out by Balcombe LJ in the Court of Appeal decision in *Patel v. W.H. Smith (Eziot) Ltd*[129] as follows: 'However, the defendant may put in evidence to seek to establish that he has a right to do what would otherwise be a trespass. Then the court must consider the application of the principle set out in *American Cyanamid Co. v. Ethicon Ltd* in relation to the grant or refusal of an interlocutory injunction'. In the *Keating* case, Keane J stated that it was clear that the defendants were asserting a right to operate a crane in the airspace above the plaintiff's premises. In his opinion there was a serious question to be tried as to whether they had such a right and it followed that the plaintiff would not be entitled to an interlocutory injunction unless it could satisfy the court that damages would not be an adequate remedy. Keane J concluded that the plaintiff had not established that damages would be an inadequate remedy and decided for this and other reasons to refuse the injunction sought.

(ii) Where an Interlocutory Injunction is Sought in the Context of a Trade Dispute

The conclusions reached by the Supreme Court in both *Bayzana Ltd v. Galligan*[130] and *Westman Holdings Ltd v. McCormack*[131] made it clear that the common law position clearly favoured the employer where proceedings were brought seeking to restrain picketing by means of an interlocutory injunction. An employer could usually establish that the balance of convenience favoured the preservation of the *status quo* pending the trial of the action and the courts were often influenced by the potential inability on the part of some of the defendants to pay damages. In addition, they placed little emphasis on the loss of the defendants' right to picket, stressing instead that they could if necessary be subsequently compensated in respect of any loss of wages which they might suffer.[132]

Attempts have been made to redress this imbalance by means of legislation and section 19 of the Industrial Relations Act 1990 has qualified the effect of common law principles in the context of trade disputes. The effect of section 19(2) would appear to be that once a plaintiff establishes an entitlement to an interlocutory injunction by showing that there is a fair question to be tried,

128. *Ibid.* at 9.
129. [1987] 1 WLR 853, 859.
130. [1987] IR 238.
131. [1992] 1 IR 151.
132. As Keane J commented in *Nolan Transport (Oaklands) Ltd v. Halligan* High Court 1993 No.1008P, 22 March 1994 it was common knowledge that the use by employers of the procedure of seeking an interlocutory injunction 'meant that the use of what were otherwise legitimate methods sanctioned by law by trade unions of advancing their interests were effectively neutralised by the way in which the law operated'.

the court must consider whether the defendants can establish a fair case that they were acting in furtherance or contemplation of a trade dispute. If they can, the injunction will not be granted; if they cannot, the court will go on to consider as it does at common law, whether the balance of convenience favours the grant of an injunction.[133] This statutory provision can only be availed of by defendants where they have complied with the formalities laid down in the statute in relation to such matters as the holding of secret ballots and the giving of adequate strike notice and the consequence of failing to abide by such procedures is that the new restrictions on an employer's ability to obtain an interlocutory injunction do not apply.[134]

This point is well illustrated by a number recent decisions in which those involved in industrial action were unable to rely on the provisions of section 19 as they had failed to comply fully with the requirements contained in the Act. In *Nolan Transport (Oaklands) Ltd v. Halligan*[135] which concerned an application to restrain picketing, Keane J had to consider whether the defendants could invoke the statutory protection afforded to them by the section. He stated as follows:

> [I]t seems to me as a matter of first impression that the onus must be on the person resisting the injunction to establish that the provisions of section 14 of the Industrial Relations Act 1990 have been complied with, which seems to me to be crucial to the operation of the section. If the section has been complied with, then the Oireachtas goes on to provide for this unusual and special situation where the court must apply particular considerations to the granting of an interlocutory injunction, considerations which otherwise would not apply. Before a trade union is afforded the protection of section 19 of the Industrial Relations Act and, conversely, an employer is deprived of the protection that he would normally have at common law in relation to the obtaining of an interlocutory injunction in circumstances where his business is or could be affected, I would take the view that the court must be satisfied on the evidence before it that section 14 has been complied with.

In the case before him, Keane J said that he was satisfied that there was no evidence of sufficient weight to indicate that section 14 had been complied with and therefore the defendants could not rely on section 19(2) of the Act. He then went on to consider the application on the basis of the principles normally applicable to the granting of an interlocutory injunction and

---

133. See Kerr (1990) ICLSA 90/19-33.
134. See Kerr [1993] ELR xi.
135. High Court 1993 No.1008P (Keane J) 22 March 1994; [1999] 1 IR 128 (SC).

concluded that an injunction should be granted restraining the defendants from picketing other than in a peaceful manner.[136]

On appeal, Murphy J stated that he would find it difficult to escape the conclusion reached by Keane J that the onus lies on the party resisting an application for an interlocutory injunction to show that a secret ballot has been held in compliance with the terms of section 14 of the Act of 1990. In his view the express reference in section 19 to a secret ballot 'held in accordance with the rules of a trade union as provided for in section 14' suggests that those engaged in industrial action cannot rely on the protection afforded by the section unless the secret ballot has been held in accordance with the requirements laid down in section 14.

A similarly strict approach to the application of section 19(2) of the 1990 Act was taken both by the High Court and the Supreme Court in *G. & T. Crampton Ltd v. Building and Allied Trades Union*,[137] in which the plaintiff sought an interlocutory injunction to restrain the defendants from picketing its premises. The plaintiff argued that a precondition to the operation of section 19(2) of the Industrial Relations Act 1990 had not been complied with as there had been no effective secret ballot held sufficient to comply with the requirements of section 14 of the Act. Laffoy J granted the interlocutory injunction sought and the defendants appealed. The Supreme Court held that the trial judge had been entitled to come to the conclusion that a condition precedent to the implementation of section 19 had not been satisfied and upheld the conclusions which she had reached in deciding the matter on the basis of the principles set out in the *Campus Oil* case, namely that a fair question had been raised, that damages would be an inadequate remedy and that the balance of convenience lay in favour of granting the injunction.

In *Malincross Ltd v. Building and Allied Trades Union*[138] the plaintiff sought an interlocutory injunction to restrain picketing by the defendants at a building site, in circumstances where the employer with whom the defendants were in dispute no longer carried on business at the site. In relation to the question of whether the defendants might rely on the provisions of section 19(2) of the Act of 1990, McCracken J stated that he was satisfied that the union had held a secret ballot in accordance with its rules and that it had given the appropriate notice to the employer of its intention to take industrial action. However, an issue arose as to the extent to which the proposals in the

---

136. Keane J said that the dispute had been in existence for 'a very considerable time' and observed that the court's jurisdiction had only been invoked relatively late in the proceedings. Accordingly he said that he was not satisfied that it would be reasonable to restrain the defendants from picketing altogether and stated that, provided the picketing remained peaceful, as the defendants claimed that it was, they would not in any way be affected by the granting of the injunction.
137. [1998] 1 ILRM 431.
138. [2002] 3 IR 607.

ballot had to identify the nature of the industrial action, and specifically a question remained as to whether the ballot authorised the placing of pickets at a site when it ceased to be the company site of the employer. McCracken J stated that the sufficiency of the secret ballot is clearly a condition precedent to the right of the defendants to resist an interlocutory injunction under section 19(2). In his view the purpose of the Act appeared to be to ensure that, if a union is to be entitled to the protection of section 19, it must have the clear support of its members. He concluded that a serious issue remained as to the whether the picketing of the plaintiff's premises, once the employer had left those premises, was authorised by the ballot and that until that question had been determined, a condition precedent to section 19(2) had not been satisfied by the defendants. Accordingly, McCracken J felt obliged to apply the *Campus Oil* principles. He concluded that any loss or disadvantage which might be incurred by the defendants if an interlocutory order were granted would be far outweighed by the enormous damage which would be caused to the plaintiff should the injunction be wrongly refused. He was therefore satisfied that the balance of convenience strongly favoured the plaintiff and decided to grant the interlocutory injunction sought.

A slightly different point arose in *Daru Blocklaying Ltd v. Building and Allied Trades Union*[139] although the difficulty was still related to purported non-compliance with the secret ballot requirements imposed by section 14. Kelly J expressed the view that the ballot ought to have been conducted in circumstances where the entitlement to vote was accorded equally to all members whom it was reasonable at that time for the union to believe would be called upon to engage in industrial action. It appeared that only three persons had been balloted although it was accepted by the defendants that on the day the picketing commenced there might have been as many as nine people attending the picket. Kelly J stated that the union is obliged to ensure that all members whom it was reasonable for it to believe at the time of the ballot would be called upon to engage in the industrial action would be balloted and that there was no evidence before the court that this had been done. The onus lay on the defendants to satisfy the court as to compliance with the provisions of section 14 and he said that this onus was not discharged by a bald assertion that a ballot had been carried out in accordance with the rules of the union and the provisions of the Act. Kelly J concluded that the defendants had not discharged the onus of demonstrating full and complete compliance with section 14, particularly having regard to the choice of just three persons who were asked to ballot.

A number of points should be made in relation to these decisions and their consequences. First, as Purcell has commented, 'it is quite clear that the courts require a rigid application and strict adherence to the rules of the trade union

---

139. [2003] 1 ILRM 164.

introduced pursuant to section 14 [of the 1990 Act]'.[140] Secondly, it is clear from a number of these decisions that the onus is on the person resisting the injunction to show that the secret ballot procedure has been properly complied with.[141] For this reason trade unions should take care to ensure that they have not only complied with the necessary statutory requirements but that they will be in a position to establish this to the court. In most cases it should not be difficult for defendants engaged in legitimate industrial action to establish a fair case that they were acting in contemplation or furtherance of a trade dispute and as the caselaw illustrates, the main hurdle which must be overcome is establishing compliance with the statutory requirements in relation to the holding of secret ballots. It is interesting to note that, in the course of his judgment in *Nolan Transport (Oaklands) Ltd v. Halligan*,[142] Murphy J stated as follows:

> I am confident that the trade union movement will, if it has not already done so, arrange that the rules of all unions are amended so as to comply with the requirements of section 14 and, of equal importance, that secret ballots will be conducted not merely in accordance with the terms of such rules but also under professional and independent guidance which will guarantee that all appropriate conditions are complied with and facilitate the union in proving that such was the case.

However, as the subsequent decisions in *Malincross* and *Daru* illustrate, this advice does not appear to have been followed. Given the obvious advantage from the point of view of defendants of being able to rely on the provisions of section 19(2), some lessons should be learned from the strict approach taken by the court towards the application of the legislation.

(iii) Where an Interlocutory Injunction is Sought in Proceedings for Defamation or Where the Right to Freedom of Expression is at Issue

It would appear that a more onerous task faces a plaintiff seeking an interlocutory injunction to restrain publication of alleged defamatory matter, partly because of a traditional reluctance on the part of the courts to interfere unduly with an individual's right to freedom of expression,[143] a right given constitutional protection in this jurisdiction.[144] A further reason for such

---

140. (1998) 3 Bar Rev 239, 242.
141. *Nolan Transport (Oaklands) Ltd v. Halligan* High Court 1993 No. 1008P (Keane J) 22 March 1994; [1999] 1 IR 128 (SC) , *G. & T. Crampton Ltd v. Building and Allied Trades Union* High Court 1997 No. 7727P (Laffoy J) 20 November 1997 and *Daru Blocklaying Ltd v. Building and Allied Trades Union* [2003] 1 ILRM 164.
142. [1999] 1 IR 128, 161. See also the comments of O'Flaherty J at 136.
143. *Femis-Bank (Anguilla) Ltd v. Lazar* [1991] Ch 391.
144. Article 40.6.1.i of the Irish Constitution 1937.

caution is that, while a statement might appear defamatory, a defendant may intend to plead a variety of defences at the trial, including those of fair comment and justification,[145] or he may seek to establish that he is protected by privilege. The general principle was laid down by Lord Esher MR in *Bonnard v. Perryman*[146] in the following terms:

> [T]he subject matter of an action for defamation is so special as to require exceptional caution in exercising the jurisdiction to interfere by injunction before the trial of an action to prevent an anticipated wrong....Until it is clear that an alleged libel is untrue, it is not clear that any right at all has been infringed; and the importance of leaving free speech unfettered is a strong reason in cases of libel for dealing most cautiously and warily with the granting of interim injunctions.

The issue was considered by the Supreme Court in *Sinclair v. Gogarty*,[147] where Sullivan CJ stated that 'an interlocutory injunction should only be granted in the clearest cases where any jury would say that the matter complained of was libellous, and where if the jury did not so find, the court would set aside the verdict as unreasonable.' The Supreme Court held that imputations made in relation to the plaintiffs were clearly so defamatory that an injunction should be granted to prevent the continued sale of a book which contained these statements.

This question was also considered in *Connolly v. RTE.*[148] The plaintiff sought an interlocutory injunction to restrain further broadcasts by the defendant of material which she alleged was defamatory of her. The plaintiff claimed that if there was an issue to be tried and damages were not an adequate remedy, the balance of convenience should determine the question of whether to grant relief. The defendant argued that the principles laid down in *Campus Oil* did not apply and that the established law in cases of alleged defamation was that injunctions were 'very rarely granted'. Carroll J stated that there was no reason why both of these principles could not be applied and said that 'in considering the balance of convenience, the court must take into account the right to freedom of expression balanced against the plaintiff's right to a good name in the light of the law on injunctive relief in defamation cases.'[149] She concluded that, while she was satisfied that there was an issue to be tried and that damages would not be an adequate remedy, the balance of convenience favoured not granting an injunction and she said that it was preferable that

---

145. *Gallagher v. Tuohy* (1924) 58 ILTR 134. However, note the comments of O'Connor J in *Cullen v. Stanley* [1926] IR 73, 85 in this regard.
146. [1891] 2 Ch 269, 284.
147. [1937] IR 377, 384.
148. [1991] 2 IR 446.
149. *Ibid.* at 448.

the alleged libel should be tried by a jury. While Carroll J did not expressly agree with the defendant's contention that injunctions should rarely issue in such cases, it is implicit in the conclusion which she reached that it will be extremely difficult to establish that the balance of convenience favours the granting of interlocutory relief in defamation cases.

The principles laid down in *Bonnard v. Perryman* have recently been applied in England by the majority of the Court of Appeal in *Holley v. Smyth*[150] where it was held that the courts' discretion to grant an interlocutory injunction would not ordinarily be exercised to restrain a libel where the defendant had a defence or claimed justification unless the plaintiff had proved that the libel was plainly untrue. Auld LJ stated as follows:

> The courts' power to grant interlocutory relief to restrain a libel is discretionary . . . but is is a discretion that must be exercised with great caution.
>
> The discretion to grant such relief is guided by the statutory constraint in section 37(1) of the Supreme Court Act 1981 that it should be exercised only where 'it appears to the court to be just and convenient to do so'.
>
> Where there is a defence or claim of justification the discretion is further guided by the rule in *Bonnard v. Perryman* that it is not normally just or convenient to grant relief unless the plaintiff has proved that the libel is plainly untrue.[151]

Sir Christopher Slade stressed that 'neither the would be libeller's motive nor the manner in which he threatens publication nor the potential damage to the plaintiff is normally a basis for making an exception to the rule'[152] although he accepted that the court may be left with a residual discretion not to apply the rule in *Bonnard* in exceptional circumstances, one being where it is satisfied that the defamatory statement is clearly untrue.

The most recent decision in this area is that of Kelly J in *Reynolds v. Malocco*.[153] It contains a most useful summary of the principles to be applied where an interlocutory injunction is sought in defamation proceedings and in particular clarifies the effect which a plea of justification should have in this context. The plaintiff sought an interlocutory injunction to restrain the defendants from publishing an article about him which he alleged defamed him in two respects. He contended that the words in the article in the natural and ordinary meaning or by innuendo alleged, first, that he permitted the sale of drugs in his nightclub premises and was benefiting therefrom and secondly, that he was a homosexual. The first named defendant contended in relation to

---

150. [1998] 2 WLR 742.
151. *Ibid.* at 756-757.
152. *Ibid.* at 761.
153. [1999] 2 IR 203.

the first complaint that the words did not bear the meaning ascribed to them and argued that if they did, he would plead justification at the trial and asserted in relation to the second complaint that the words did not bear the meaning contended for. Kelly J referred to the *American Cyanamid/Campus Oil* principles and stated that they have a 'wide but not universal application' and that in 'a small number of cases special rules which are not encompassed by these principles apply'. He continued as follows:

> A plaintiff in an action such as this, in order to obtain an interlocutory injunction must show not merely that he has raised a serious issue concerning the words complained of but that there is no doubt that they are defamatory. Furthermore, if the defendant intends to plead justification or any other recognised defence, normally an injunction of this type will be refused.
>
> The jurisdiction to grant interlocutory injunctions to restrain publication of defamatory statements has been described as one 'of a delicate nature' which 'ought only to be exercised in the clearest cases' (see the judgment of Lord Esher MR in *Coulson v. Coulson* (1887) 3 TLR 846).[154]

Kelly J explained that the reason for the court's reluctance to grant interlocutory injunctions in cases of this nature is grounded in the importance attached to the right of free speech, a right now fortified by Article 10 of the European Convention for the Protection of Human Rights and Fundamental Freedoms. In his view he had to first ascertain whether the plaintiff's complaints were made out with the degree of clarity required to enable him to conclude that the words complained of were undoubtedly defamatory and if so, he then had to consider whether, in the light of the defendant's stated intention to plead justification in relation to the first allegation, an injunction could be granted. The reason he had to consider the latter aspect of the case was because of the principle laid down in *Bonnard v. Perryman* and approved by the Supreme Court in *Sinclair v. Gogarty* to the effect that, where a defendant in a libel action intends to plead justification, a court will not grant an interlocutory injunction to restrain publication of the statement complained of. The question then arose whether a bald statement of intent to plead justification was sufficient to debar a plaintiff who might otherwise be entitled to an injunction from such relief and in this regard Kelly J approved of the approach of the Supreme Court in *Cullen v. Stanley*[155] which allowed the court to examine the evidence adduced by the defendant in support of the justification plea so as to ascertain whether it had any substance or prospect of success. He did

---

154. *Ibid.* at 209-210.
155. [1926] IR 73.

not think that 'a rule which permits a defendant to in effect oust the ability of this Court to intervene by way of injunction in an appropriate case by the simple expedient of expressing an intention to plead justification at the trial of the action is consistent with the obligations imposed on the court under the Constitution'.[156]

Applying these principles to the first complaint, Kelly J concluded that the innuendo to the effect contended for by the plaintiff was clear and he stated that in the absence of a successful plea of justification a jury would say that the matter complained of was libellous, a verdict which he did not believe the Supreme Court would set aside as unreasonable. In relation to the question of a plea of justification he was satisfied that the first named defendant's averment did not go anywhere near demonstrating the existence of an arguable prospect of making out the defence. With regard to the second allegation, he also concluded that a jury would be entitled to find in the plaintiff's favour and it did not appear to him that such a verdict could be regarded as perverse. As there was no plea of justification made in relation to this complaint, it followed that in his view the plaintiff had made out a sufficiently strong case to satisfy the test required for the grant of an interlocutory injunction. However, Kelly J pointed out that it did not automatically follow that an injunction should be granted as such relief was of a discretionary nature. He repeated that the jurisdiction was 'of a delicate nature' and that the court must be circumspect to ensure that it does not unnecessarily interfere with the right to freedom of expression and stated that he did not want to set out in a hard and fast manner the factors which the court should take into account in the exercise of its discretion. In his view it was sufficient if he identified one issue of particular importance which had influenced the exercise of his discretion in the case before him and this was that it was unlikely that the plaintiff would be able to recover any damages from the defendants if the interlocutory injunction was refused but he later succeeded at the trial. In these circumstances Kelly J was satisfied that his discretion must be exercised in favour of granting an interlocutory injunction rather than refusing it.

It is submitted that the approach adopted by Kelly J is an eminently reasonable one and his attitude towards the effect of a plea of justification would seem fairer than the alternative view which involves accepting that a bald statement of intent to plead justification would be sufficient to debar a plaintiff who might otherwise have been entitled to an injunction from the benefit of such relief. His judgment also seems to achieve a reasonable balance between safeguarding the right to free speech by confirming that injunctive relief should only be granted in the clearest cases and ensuring that a plaintiff is not left without any remedy at all where the words complained of appear to be clearly defamatory.

---

156. [1999] 2 IR 203, 212.

Finally, it should be noted that Article 10 of the European Convention on Human Rights protects the right to freedom of expression and that sections 12(1) and (3) of the English Human Rights Act 1998 provide that, if a court is considering whether to grant relief which might affect the exercise of the convention right to freedom of expression, it should not restrain publication before trial unless it is satisfied that the applicant is likely to establish that publication should not be allowed. While it has generally been accepted that the right to freedom of expression will be safeguarded by a reluctance on the part of the courts to restrain publication pending trial, section 12(3) expressly provides for a different approach to that laid down in *American Cyanamid* as a number of decisions illustrate.

In *Douglas v. Hello! Ltd* [157] the Court of Appeal made it clear that section 12(3) requires the court to look at the merits of the case and not merely to apply the *American Cyanamid* test. As Keene LJ stated: 'Thus the court has to look ahead to the ultimate stage and to be satisfied that the scales are likely to come down in the applicant's favour'.[158] He noted that the jurisprudence of the European Court of Human Rights has been generally hostile to prior restraint by the courts[159] and that section 12(3) certainly makes it more difficult to obtain relief before trial where the right to freedom of expression is involved. Although the Court of Appeal was satisfied that the claimants had established that they were likely to be able to prove at the trial that publication should not be allowed, in the circumstances it was held that damages would be an adequate remedy and that the balance of convenience was against granting an injunction. In *Imutran Ltd v. Uncaged Campaigns Ltd*,[160] in which the claimant sought interim injunctions restraining the defendants from using or disclosing information contained in confidential documents, Sir Andrew Morritt VC considered the terms of section 12(3) and said that theoretically and as a matter of language 'likelihood' was slightly higher in the scale of probability than 'a real prospect of success'. However, he added that the difference between the two is small and that he could not believe that there would be many cases which would have succeeded under the *American Cyanamid* test but would fail as a result of the provisions of section 12(3).[161]

Subsequently in *Theakston v. MGN Ltd* [162] Ouseley J concluded that he had some difficulty in seeing how the approach required by section 12(3) could be other than that the claimant must show that it is more probable than not that he would succeed in obtaining an injunction at trial and said that if

---

157. [2001] QB 967.
158. *Ibid.* at 1008.
159. *The Observer v. United Kingdom* (1991) 14 EHRR 153, 191.
160. [2001] 2 All ER 385.
161. However, see *Cream Holdings Ltd v. Banerjee* [2003] EWCA Civ 103 Court of Appeal, 13 February 2003 paragraphs 56 and 103.
162. [2002] EWHC 137, 14 February 2002.

parliament had intended the relevant test to be whether the claimant had a real prospect of success it would have used that phrase.

However, more recently in *Cream Holdings Ltd v. Banerjee*[163] the majority of the Court of Appeal made it clear, in upholding the decision of the trial judge to grant an interlocutory injunction, that the test pursuant to section 12(3) is whether there is a real prospect of success convincingly established that a claimant would succeed at trial. Simon Brown LJ referred to the earlier decisions but pointed out that to date it had not been necessary to reach a clear view on this point and that it had not yet been authoritatively decided. In expressing a preference for the test of 'a real prospect of success, convincingly established' Simon Brown LJ stated that there is an important distinction between the *American Cyanamid* approach[164] and the threshold test required by section 12(3) because under the former test the court is concerned only to find a serious issue to be tried and is not required to resolve conflicts of fact or questions of law so as to gauge the merits of the claim. To this extent he said that he had some difficulty with the view expressed by the Vice Chancellor in *Imutran Ltd v. Uncaged Campaigns Ltd* to the effect that the difference between the tests is small. In his view there would indeed be a number of claims for injunctive relief which would fail under section 12(3) which would previously have succeeded because the court is now required to actually consider the merits and cannot grant relief unless satisfied on cogent evidence that the claim has a real prospect of succeeding at trial notwithstanding the defendant's conflicting right to freedom of expression. Arden LJ agreed that section 12(3) 'requires the court to envisage the outcome of the trial of the action' and stated that the court must consider the merits of a case and decide by reference to the merits whether the applicant has a real prospect of success in establishing that the publication should be restrained at trial. She added that she agreed with Simon Brown LJ that it was better to put the *American Cyanamid* test firmly to one side when applying section 12(3) of the Human Rights Act 1998.

While the decision in *Cream Holdings* is of purely academic interest in this jurisdiction, it nevertheless contains some interesting analysis of the distinctions between the test for the grant of interlocutory injunctions laid down in *American Cyanamid* and alternatives which provide for the examination of the merits of a case. Given the importance attached to the right of freedom of expression in the jurisprudence of the European Court of Human Rights[165] and its distaste for prior restraint, it is likely that these issues may well fall to be determined in this jurisdiction in the not too distant future.

---

163. [2003] EWCA Civ 103 Court of Appeal, 13 February 2003.
164. See also *per* Arden J at paragraph 103.
165. See e.g. *The Observer v. United Kingdom* (1991) 14 EHRR 153.

(iv) Where an Interlocutory Injunction is Sought to Restrain the Presentation of a Petition for the Winding Up of a Company

This exception has been accepted in England for some time,[166] and the approach taken there has recently been followed by the High Court in this jurisdiction. In *Truck and Machinery Sales Ltd v. Marubeni Komatsu Ltd*[167] the plaintiff sought an injunction to restrain the defendant from presenting a petition to wind the company up. Counsel for the plaintiff sought to rely on the *Campus Oil* principles and argued that the plaintiff had raised a serious question as to whether the sum claimed was due and owing by it and that the balance of convenience lay in favour of restraining the petition until the hearing of the action. Counsel for the defendant argued that in order to obtain such relief, the plaintiff would have to establish that the presentation of the petition was an abuse of process and that it was bound to fail or at least, that there was an alternative remedy available. Keane J stated that he was satisfied that the jurisdiction to restrain the presentation of a petition to wind up a company is one which should only be exercised with great caution. He referred to the principles set out by the Court of Appeal in *Bryanston Finance Ltd v. De Vries (No.2)*[168] and in *Coulson Sanderson & Ward v. Ward*[169] and said that he was satisfied that this was the approach which should also be adopted in this jurisdiction. He continued as follows:

> The constitutional right of recourse to the courts should not be inhibited, save in exceptional circumstances, and this applies as much to the presentation of a petition for the winding up of a company by a person with the appropriate *locus standi* as it does to any other form of proceedings. The undoubted power of the courts to restrain proceedings which are an abuse of process is one which should not be lightly exercised. In the context of winding-up petitions, I have no doubt that it should be exercised only where the plaintiff company has established at least a *prima facie* case that its presentation would constitute an abuse of process. In many cases, a *prima facie* case will be established where the plaintiff company adduces evidence which satisfies the court that the petition is bound to fail, or at the least, that there is a suitable alternative remedy. It would not be appropriate to apply the principles

---

166. *Bryanston Finance Ltd v. De Vries (No.2)* [1976] Ch 63.
167. High Court 1995 No. 6928P (Keane J) 23 February 1996.
168. [1976] Ch 63.
169. [1986] 2 BCLC 99. As Slade LJ had commented: '[T]he court should not, on the hearing of an interlocutory motion, interfere with what would otherwise appear to be the legitimate presentation of a winding up petition by someone qualified to present it unless the evidence before it is sufficient to establish *prima facie* that the plaintiff company will succeed in establishing that the proceedings sought to be restrained would constitute an abuse.'

laid down by the Supreme Court in *Campus Oil Ltd v. Minister for Industry and Energy (No.2)* in cases of this nature where it is the creditors' right to have recourse to the courts, rather than any right of the plaintiff company, which is under threat.[170]

Keane J concluded that the plaintiff company had failed to establish a *prima facie* case that the presentation of the petition would be an abuse of process or that it would be bound to fail. In addition, there was no alternative remedy open to the defendant and he held that the injunction sought should be refused.

(v) Where the Trial of the Action is Unlikely

It is now well-established that as a pre-requisite for the application of the guidelines in *American Cyanamid* it must be shown that a trial is in fact likely to take place. This principle was laid down in England by Lord Diplock in the decision of *N.W.L. Ltd v. Woods*,[171] where he stressed that *American Cyanamid* was not dealing with a case where the grant or refusal of an injunction would in effect dispose of the action finally in favour of whichever party was successful, and that where these circumstances exist an important additional element must be brought into the assessment of the balance of convenience. He continued as follows:

> Where ... the grant or refusal of the interlocutory injunction will have the practical effect of putting an end to the action because the harm that will have been already caused to the losing party by its grant or refusal is complete and of a kind for which money cannot constitute any worthwhile recompense, the degree of likelihood that the plaintiff would have succeeded in establishing his right to an injunction if the action had gone to trial is a factor to be brought into the balance by the judge in weighing the risks that injustice may result from his deciding the application one way rather than the other.[172]

This approach has been followed by the Court of Appeal in England in a number of cases. In *Cayne v. Global Natural Resources plc*[173] the plaintiff shareholders sought an interlocutory injunction to restrain the defendant company from implementing a merger agreement and proceeding with the allotment of shares prior to the company's impending annual general meeting. If the injunction was granted the balance of power in the company would remain the same until after the crucial vote was taken and the plaintiffs would

---

170. High Court 1995 No. 6928P (Keane J) 23 February 1996 at 20-21.
171. [1979] 1 WLR 1294.
172. *Ibid.* at 1307.
173. [1984] 1 All ER 225.

therefore obtain the result which they sought; on the other hand if the injunction was refused the votes of the new shareholders would ensure that the plan of the incumbent directors succeeded. As Kerr LJ commented 'the practical realities ... are that, if the plaintiffs succeed in obtaining an injunction, they will never take this case to trial'. May LJ stated that in a case such as that before the court where the grant or refusal of an injunction will effectively dispose of the action in favour of the successful party, the 'balance of the risk of doing an injustice' better described the process involved. The Court of Appeal concluded that in these circumstances it would not be appropriate to apply the *American Cyanamid* guidelines which were based on the assumption that a proper trial would determine the issues at a later stage, and instead justice required that the defendant should be entitled to dispute the plaintiff's claim at the trial of the action and if an injunction would preclude this it should not be granted at an interlocutory stage.

A similar finding was made by the Court of Appeal in *Cambridge Nutrition Ltd v. British Broadcasting Corporation*,[174] in which the plaintiff sought an injunction to prevent the broadcast of a TV programme about low calorie diets which focused particularly on its activities, claiming that the BBC had undertaken not to broadcast the programme until after an official report on the subject had been published. The nature of the programme was such that it was only suitable for transmission in its existing form before publication of the report and the defendant resisted the plaintiff's claim. As Kerr LJ stated: 'the subject matter concerns the right to publish an article, or to transmit a broadcast, whose importance may be transitory but whose impact depends on timing, news value and topicality.'[175] The Court of Appeal reiterated that where the decision on an application for an interlocutory injunction was the equivalent of giving final judgment the court should not grant the order merely because the plaintiff was able to show a good arguable case and the balance of convenience lay in favour of granting an injunction. Instead the court should assess the relative strength of each party's case before deciding whether the injunction should be granted. Kerr LJ stressed that the *American Cyanamid* principles were no more than a set of useful guidelines and 'must never be used as a rule of thumb, let alone as a strait-jacket'.[176] He concluded that the case before him was not an appropriate one for the application of these guidelines 'because the crucial issues between the parties do not depend on a trial, but solely or mainly on the grant or refusal of the interlocutory relief.' Similar issues were considered in the decision of the Court of Appeal in *Douglas v. Hello! Ltd*[177] in which the claimants sought an injunction restraining the defendants from publishing photographs taken at their wedding on the

174. [1990] 3 All ER 523.
175. *Ibid.* at 535.
176. *Ibid.* at 535.
177. [2001] QB 967.

grounds that any publication would be in breach of confidence. Keene LJ pointed out that the third named claimant, who had exclusive rights to the photographs, and the defendants which both published weekly magazines, were undoubtedly concerned with material whose topicality was crucial and said that in such cases where the parties are principally interested in the grant or refusal of the interlocutory relief, the court must look beyond conventional *American Cyanamid* principles and seek to establish where the balance of justice lies. In addition, in his view section 12(3) of the Human Rights Act 1998, which provides that where any relief might affect the Convention right to freedom of expression it should not be granted so as to restrain publication before trial 'unless the court is satisfied that the applicant is likely to establish that publication should not be allowed', requires the court to look at the merits of the case and not merely to apply the *American Cyanamid* test. However, the Court of Appeal concluded that, although the claimants were likely to establish at trial that publication should not be allowed, in its view damages were an adequate remedy and the balance of convenience came down against prior restraint.

A further example of a case where the decision at the interlocutory stage was crucial is that of *Lansing Linde Ltd v. Kerr*[178] where the Court of Appeal confirmed that a trial judge may properly take into account a plaintiff's prospects of success at trial where the grant or refusal of interlocutory relief will effectively determine the matter. In this case the plaintiff company sought an interlocutory injunction to enforce a clause in the defendant's contract of employment which stipulated that he would not work for any of its competitors for a period of 12 months after termination of his employment with the company. The defendant who occupied a senior position in the company had given six months' notice and a month later accepted the position of managing director of a competitor. It was held by the Court of Appeal in refusing the injunction that the trial judge had properly taken into account the plaintiff's prospects of success at the trial, having regard to the fact that it would not be possible to hold a trial before the period for which the plaintiff claimed to be entitled to an injunction had expired, or substantially expired, and that in those circumstances in was not enough to decide merely that there was a serious issue to be tried.

Recently an unsuccessful attempt was made in *Symonds Cider and English Wine Co. Ltd v. Showerings (Ireland) Ltd*[179] to further extend the list of situations in which the *American Cyanamid* principles should not be applied to all passing off actions on the grounds that in such cases the outcome of the interlocutory proceedings often determines the final outcome of the action. The plaintiff instituted proceedings alleging trade mark infringement and

---

178. [1991] 1 WLR 251. See also *Credit Suisse Asset Management Ltd v. Armstrong* [1996] ICR 882.
179. [1997] 1 ILRM 481.

passing off against the defendant and sought an interlocutory injunction restraining the defendant from selling its cider under the mark 'Golden Scrumpy' in cans similar to their own. It was submitted on the plaintiff's behalf that the principles by which the court should be guided in determining the application for interlocutory injunctions were those set out by the House of Lords in *American Cyanamid* as adopted by the Supreme Court in *Campus Oil*. However, counsel for the defendant submitted that the *American Cyanamid* guidelines had been significantly refined particularly in the field of intellectual property. He pointed to the fact that, in a passing off action such as this, the outcome of the interlocutory proceedings often determined the final outcome of the action and submitted that in such circumstances the court is justified in considering the substantive case. Laffoy J rejected this contention and said that having regard to the decision of the Supreme Court in *Westman Holdings Ltd v. McCormack*[180] – which applied the *American Cyanamid* principles – it was not open to her, assuming that the plaintiff established that there was a fair and *bona fide* question to be tried, to express any view on the strength of the competing submissions. She concluded that she was satisfied that the plaintiff had shown that there were fair issues to be tried but that the balance of convenience lay in favour of refusing the interlocutory relief. Subsequently in *Local Ireland Ltd v. Local Ireland-Online Ltd*[181] which also concerned a claim in relation to alleged passing off, despite the fact that counsel for both sides suggested that the outcome of the application for interlocutory relief was likely to determine the result of the dispute, Herbert J stated that having regard to the fact that there was no agreement to treat the hearing of the motion as the trial of the action, he was obliged to apply the *Campus Oil* principles.

The approach adopted in *Symonds* and *Local Ireland* would seem to suggest that the courts in this jurisdiction are still anxious to adhere to the *American Cyanamid/Campus Oil* guidelines unless there is good reason for departing from them. Laffoy J certainly showed a reluctance to extend the list of recognised exceptions to an entire class of proceedings, namely intellectual property disputes, although undoubtedly there may be individual cases falling under this heading in which the facts may warrant the conclusion being reached that the trial of the action is unlikely to take place and that a wider consideration of the merits of both parties' cases is therefore justified.

Whether Special Considerations Apply where the Presumption of Constitutionality is Involved

This question has been considered in a number of decisions which deal with such issues as seeking to restrain the ratification of a treaty or the

---

180. [1992] 1 IR 151.
181. [2000] 4 IR 567.

implementation of legislative provisions and an application to prohibit the exercise of a statutory power. In *Crotty v. An Taoiseach*[182] the plaintiff sought an interlocutory injunction to restrain the defendants from ratifying the Single European Act, a treaty which introduced a number of changes to the treaties establishing the European Communities, and also sought to challenge the constitutionality of the European Communities (Amendment) Act 1986. In delivering his judgment on the application for interlocutory relief, Barrington J stated that he must endeavour to follow the procedure laid down in *Campus Oil*, but added that the issues raised before him were of a constitutional nature 'in relation to which weight must be given to the presumption of constitutionality'. He stated that subject to this consideration, he had to direct his mind to whether the applicant had raised a fair question of law although he said that it appeared to him to be proper to attach a greater significance to the term a 'fair question of law' in the case before him than would be attached to that term in private litigation because of the existence of the presumption of constitutionality, which attaches to legislation and a similar presumption in favour of executive acts of the government. Applying these considerations, Barrington J was satisfied that the plaintiff had raised a number of fair and substantial issues for the court to decide and he concluded that the balance of convenience lay in favour of granting the injunction sought rather than refusing it.

In *Pesca Valentia Ltd v. Minister for Fisheries and Forestry*[183] the plaintiff sought an interlocutory injunction restraining the defendants from enforcing a term in a licence granted pursuant to the Fisheries (Consolidation) Act 1959 as amended which required that three-quarters of the crew of a trawler should be of Irish nationality. The Supreme Court had to consider whether any special principles applied to an application for an interlocutory injunction to prohibit the exercise of a statutory power presumed to be constitutional. Finlay CJ stated that he was satisfied that the presumption of constitutionality which applied to the legislation was material in relation to the determination by the court of whether the plaintiff had established a fair question to be tried at the hearing of the action. In addition, he was satisfied that the consequence arising from the making of an interlocutory injunction of preventing the executive from carrying out powers vested in it by a statute enjoying the presumption of constitutionality was a matter for consideration in assessing where the balance of convenience lay. However Finlay CJ stated that he was not satisfied that 'there is any special principle applicable to an application for an interlocutory injunction of this kind'. The Supreme Court dismissed the defendants' appeal against the grant of an interlocutory injunction, but varied the terms of the order.

---

182. [1987] IR 713.
183. [1985] IR 193.

A similar view has been expressed by Kelly J in *Controller of Patents, Designs and Trademarks v. Ireland*[184] in which a slightly different issue arose. The plaintiff sought, *inter alia*, an order restraining the defendant minister from implementing or bringing into operation sections 4 and 5 of the Intellectual Property (Miscellaneous Provisions) Act 1988 until further order of the court. Counsel for the defendants argued that where relief of this nature is sought it is not sufficient to establish that there is a serious issue to be tried and submitted that a stronger case than that had to be shown. The principal basis for this assertion was the fact that the legislation carried with it a presumption of constitutionality, but having referred to the *dicta* of Finlay CJ in *Pesca Valentia*, Kelly J stated that it seemed to him that the mere existence of the presumption of constitutionality in favour of the impugned legislation did not mean that new or different rules should govern the application. Instead he was of the view that he must weigh the presumption of constitutionality in the balance when deciding the question of whether a serious issue to be tried had been established and also in deciding where the balance of convenience lay. Applying these principles to the facts of the case before him, Kelly J concluded that the plaintiff had not established that there were any serious issues to be tried and said that in any event the balance of convenience would lie in favour of refusing the relief sought.

So, it would appear that the courts are of the view that no special principles are to be applied to applications for interlocutory injunctions where issues relating to the presumption of constitutionality are involved. However, it is also clear that at the very least this presumption must be weighed in the balance when deciding the question of whether a serious issue to be tried has been established. Whether Barrington J intended any more by his comment in *Crotty* that he would attach a greater significance to the term a 'fair question of law' in such cases has not been clarified and clearly some further judicial consideration of the issues involved would be welcome.

Principles Governing the Grant of Mandatory Injunctions

While a prohibitory injunction requires a defendant to refrain from doing certain acts, a mandatory injunction is one which compels a defendant to carry out an obligation or to perform a specified act. Traditionally, the courts were reluctant to grant an injunction of a mandatory nature and during the nineteenth century it was not uncommon to frame an injunction in terms which were prohibitory in form even though the order was mandatory in substance. This trend was reversed by the decision of *Jackson v. Normanby Brick Co.*[185] and now where a mandatory order is called for it will be framed in this form.

---

184. High Court 1998 No. 8283P (Kelly J) 31 July 1998.
185. [1899] 1 Ch 438.

Mandatory injunctions can be classified into two types, restorative and enforcing. The former type which is granted more frequently requires the party to whom it is directed to put right the consequences of his actions, e.g. by removing an offending structure. The enforcing mandatory injunction on the other hand requires the performance of some positive obligation, often of a continuing nature. To succeed in obtaining a mandatory order, particularly of the latter kind, it must be possible to specify with a sufficient degree of particularity precisely what action is required to comply with its terms and it must be quite clear 'what the person against whom the injunction or order is made is required to do or to refrain from doing.'[186] Maugham LJ laid down this requirement in *Fishenden v. Higgs and Hill Ltd*[187] in the following terms:

> I think a mandatory injunction, except in very exceptional circumstances, ought to be granted in such terms that the person against whom it is granted ought to know exactly what he has to do.

This statement was quoted with approval by Murphy J in *Bula Ltd v. Tara Mines Ltd (No.2)*,[188] in which he refused to grant mandatory interlocutory injunctions, *inter alia*, because in his opinion, if granted in the terms sought, the orders would not be certain enough in their terms to enable it to be ascertained whether the defendants were complying with the injunctions granted by the court.

In theory there appears to be no difference between the principles which apply to the granting of a mandatory and prohibitory injunction at the trial of an action[189] and it has been suggested that care and caution must be exercised by a judge in either case and that no greater degree of caution is required in deciding to grant a mandatory order.[190] However, it must be recognised that in practical terms, the making of a mandatory order will usually impose an additional degree of hardship or expense on a defendant and such factors may often influence a judge in deciding how to exercise his discretion. One English authority which suggests that an additional degree of caution is required in the context of mandatory orders is the decision of the House of Lords in *Redland Bricks Ltd v. Morris*.[191] Land owned by the respondents, who carried on the business of strawberry farming, was affected by subsidence caused by quarrying work undertaken by the appellant on adjoining property. It was

---

186. *Attorney-General v. Staffordshire County Council* [1905] 1 Ch 336, 342.
187. (1935) 153 LT 128, 142. See also *Redland Bricks Ltd v. Morris* [1970] AC 652, 666 where Lord Upjohn stated that the defendant must know what he has to do as a matter of fact not as matter of law. However note the comments of Staughton LJ in *Channel Tunnel Group Ltd v. Balfour Beatty Construction* [1992] QB 656, 678.
188. [1987] IR 95, 104 .
189. *Davies v. Gas Light & Coke Co.* [1909] 1 Ch 248, 259 *per* Warrington J.
190. *Smith v. Smith* (1875) LR 20 Eq 500, 504 *per* Jessel MR.
191. [1970] AC 652.

estimated that the cost of remedying the subsidence would be wholly disproportionate to the value of the land affected. The respondents were awarded damages and both prohibitory and mandatory injunctions to restrain further excavation, but the House of Lords, placing emphasis on the disproportionate cost of remedial work, allowed the appeal against the grant of a mandatory injunction. Lord Upjohn stated:

> A mandatory injunction can only be granted where the plaintiff shows a very strong probability upon the facts that grave damage will accrue to him in the future. ... It is jurisdiction to be exercised sparingly and with caution but, in the proper case, unhesitatingly.[192]

It was the view of Lord Upjohn that unlike in the case of a prohibitory injunction, the cost of the works which the defendant would be required to carry out must be taken into account except where the defendant has acted quite unreasonably. Where, as in the case before him, the defendant had acted reasonably, although wrongly, the cost of remedying his actions was a factor which should be taken into account. While these latter principles seem reasonable, Lord Upjohn's insistence on establishing a 'very strong probability ... of grave damage' has been criticised and it has been said that this view cannot be accepted without qualification.[193] Spry suggests the following alternative that 'whenever an injury to the plaintiff is shown, being an injury that might, before it took place, have been enjoined by a prohibitory injunction if the court thought fit, a mandatory injunction may be granted unless consequent prejudice to the defendant is so disproportionate that the course is unjust in all the circumstances'.[194]

While there may be no difference in theory between the principles which govern the grant of prohibitory and mandatory injunctions at trial, different considerations apply to the granting of mandatory as opposed to prohibitory injunctions of an interlocutory nature.[195] At the very least a plaintiff must show strong evidence of continuing or imminent prejudice before a court will make an order of this nature. In *Shepherd Homes Ltd v. Sandham*[196] Megarry J made it clear that the court is far more reluctant to grant a mandatory injunction than a prohibitory injunction and said that the 'case has to be unusually strong and clear before a mandatory injunction will be granted'[197]

---

192. *Ibid.* at 665.
193. Spry, *The Principles of Equitable Remedies* (6th ed., 2001) p. 547. See also Meagher, Gummow and Lehane, *Equity Doctrines and Remedies* (3rd ed., 1992) p. 617 where they comment that the decision 'scintillates with dubious propositions'.
194. *The Principles of Equitable Remedies* (6th ed., 2001) p. 547.
195. *Irish Shell Ltd v. Elm Motors* [1984] IR 200, 217 *per* Costello J.
196. [1971] Ch 340. See also *Locabail International Finance Ltd v. Agroexport* [1986] 1 WLR 657.
197. *Ibid.* at 349.

and the court must 'feel a high degree of assurance that at the trial it will appear that the injunction was rightly granted.'[198] Megarry J himself acknowledged that it was not possible to 'draw firm lines or impose any rigid classification' in this area and a more flexible approach was adopted subsequently by Hoffmann J in *Films Rover International Ltd v. Cannon Film Sales Ltd*,[199] where he said that the 'high degree of assurance' test does not have to be satisfied in every case before an interlocutory injunction of a mandatory nature may be granted. Hoffmann J pointed out that in an exceptional case, where withholding such an injunction would carry with it a greater risk of injustice than granting it, even where the court does not feel a high degree of assurance about the plaintiff's likelihood of succeeding at the trial, there cannot be any rational basis for withholding the injunction.[200]

There is still a degree of uncertainty in this jurisdiction about the test which should be applied in the context of mandatory interlocutory injunctions.[201] In *Bula Ltd v. Tara Mines Ltd (No.2)*[202] Murphy J said that while he agreed with much of what had been said by Megarry J in *Shepherd Homes Ltd v. Sandham*, he would be reluctant to accept the proposition that the granting or withholding of a mandatory interlocutory injunction should be related to or dependent on the strength of the applicant's case. This approach is in line with that adopted by the Supreme Court in *Campus Oil Ltd v. Minister for Industry and Energy (No.2)*,[203] in which O'Higgins CJ made it clear that the likelihood of success at trial should not be a factor in the granting of interlocutory relief generally although he did go on to say that such relief will only issue in mandatory form in exceptional cases, such as that before the court.

The trend in some other recent cases has been to emphasize the fact that mandatory interlocutory injunctions will only issue in very limited circumstances and reference has been made to the likelihood of a plaintiff succeeding at trial. In *Boyhan v. Tribunal of Inquiry into the Beef Industry*[204] Denham J declined to grant an interlocutory injunction of a mandatory nature in favour of the United Farmers Association directing that they should be granted full legal representation before the beef tribunal as she was satisfied that the limited representation granted to it by the tribunal was sufficient in

---

198. *Ibid.* at 351.
199. [1987] 1 WLR 670.
200. *Ibid.* at 681.
201. Note that where relief of an interlocutory nature is required, a plaintiff may seek an interlocutory mandatory injunction requiring it to specifically perform an agreement, see *Beshoff Brothers Ltd v. Select Service Partner Ireland Ltd* High Court 1998 No. 8102 P (O'Sullivan J) 28 July 1998.
202. [1987] IR 95. See also *de Burca v. Wicklow County Council* High Court 2000 No. 42JR (Ó Caoimh J) 24 May 2000.
203. [1983] IR 88.
204. [1992] ILRM 545. See also *O'Dea v. O'Briain* [1992] ILRM 364.

the circumstances. In the course of her judgment Denham J described a mandatory injunction as a 'powerful instrument' and said that in seeking 'this exceptional form of relief ... it is up to the plaintiffs to establish a strong and clear case — so that the court can feel a degree of assurance that at a trial of the action a similar injunction would be granted.'[205] In *Boyle v. An Post*,[206] while Lardner J decided to grant an interlocutory order of a mandatory nature directing An Post to pay the plaintiffs their wages after the payroll computer had to be shut down following the suspension of a number of staff, he stated that it was 'an exceptional case where one can say with assurance that at the hearing of the substantive action the plaintiffs are bound to succeed.'[207]

However, it should be noted that a much less restrictive approach was favoured by Carroll J in her judgment in *A. & N. Pharmacy Ltd v. United Drug Wholesale Ltd.*[208] The plaintiff, which had set up a new pharmacy in Limerick, sought a mandatory interlocutory injunction compelling the defendant, a wholesaler in its area, to supply it with non-generic pharmaceutical products. As a result of the refusal of the defendant and other major wholesalers to supply the plaintiff, it had been forced to import products from abroad at non-competitive prices. Carroll J held that there was a serious issue to be tried and that the balance of convenience favoured the plaintiff; in other words the ordinary test which it is accepted applies to interlocutory injunctions of a prohibitory nature had been satisfied. She found that it was likely that damages would not be an adequate remedy because the plaintiff would be forced out of business if it could not obtain the supplies it required and decided to grant a mandatory injunction of an interlocutory nature compelling the defendant to supply the plaintiff on a cash-on-delivery basis. Similarly in the recent decision of *Sheehy v. Ryan*,[209] Peart J appeared to grant an interlocutory injunction of a mandatory nature on the basis of the traditional *Campus Oil* principles. Although he made reference to the fact that 'in general the court is reluctant, save in truly exceptional circumstances to grant mandatory interlocutory relief', having regard to the fact that the plaintiff would be left without anything to live on if an order were not made, he held that her salary should be paid until the trial of the action or until further order of the court.

On balance it would appear that in recent decisions the courts have tended to favour the application of the traditional *Campus Oil* principles even in the context of mandatory relief and there has been some support for the proposition laid down by Murphy J in *Bula Ltd v. Tara Mines Ltd (No.2)*[210] that the granting or withholding of a mandatory interlocutory injunction should not be dependent

---

205. *Ibid.* at 556.
206. [1992] 2 IR 437.
207. *Ibid.* at 442.
208. [1996] 2 ILRM 46.
209. High Court 2002 No. 10338P (Peart J) 29 August 2002.
210. [1987] IR 95.

on the strength of the applicant's case.[211] However, it is also fair to say that it is unlikely that the balance of convenience will lie in favour of granting mandatory relief save in fairly exceptional cases and to this extent it is still accurate to assert that the courts are more reluctant to grant an interlocutory injunction where it is of a mandatory nature.

Principles Governing the Grant of Quia Timet Injunctions

While an injunction will generally issue on the basis of an infringement of a plaintiff's rights, an order known as a *quia timet* injunction may also be granted before any injury or damage has actually been sustained, in circumstances where the injury to the plaintiff is merely threatened or apprehended. As Lord Upjohn stated in *Redland Bricks Ltd v. Morris*:[212] 'to prevent the jurisdiction of the courts being stultified equity has invented the *quia timet* action, that is an action for an injunction to prevent an apprehended legal wrong, though none has occurred at present, and the suppliant for such an injunction is without any remedy at law.' This jurisdiction is preventative in nature and will be exercised either where a person threatens and intends to do an unlawful act, in which case the order is generally prohibitory in nature or where the plaintiff's rights have already been infringed and he alleges that this infringement will be repeated, in which case a mandatory injunction is the most likely remedy.[213]

Spry[214] suggests that the same general equitable principles are applied whether or not there has been a breach of the plaintiff's rights or merely a threatened violation of these rights: 'It may properly be said that wherever a court with equitable jurisdiction might enjoin an act if that act had been commenced, it may, in the exercise of its discretion, enjoin the act although it has not yet commenced, provided that its imminence is sufficiently clearly established in order to justify intervention in all the circumstances'. However, as he points out, the fact that no breach has as yet occurred is of relevance as it may be more difficult to establish that there is a sufficient risk of future injury to justify the immediate grant of an injunction.[215] Therefore it is important to consider how likely it is that injury will in fact occur and how severe the apprehended damage is required to be before a *quia timet* injunction will be granted. It is insufficient for a plaintiff merely to state that he harbours

---

211. *De Burca v. Wicklow County Council* High Court 2000 No. 42 JR (Ó Caoimh J) 24 May 2000.
212. [1970] AC 652, 664.
213. *Proctor v. Bayley* (1889) 42 Ch D 390, 398 *per* Cotton LJ; *Redland Bricks Ltd v. Morris* [1970] AC 652, 665 *per* Lord Upjohn.
214. *The Principles of Equitable Remedies* (6th ed., 2001) p. 378.
215. See e.g. *McGrane v. Louth County Council* High Court 1983 No. 28F (O'Hanlon J) 9 December 1983 where a *quia timet* injunction sought by the plaintiff to restrain the defendants from developing a rubbish dump was refused.

fears in this regard;[216] in the words of Chitty J in *Attorney-General v. Manchester Corporation*:[217] 'he must show a strong case of probability that the apprehended mischief will, in fact, arise.'

The onus of proof which lies on a plaintiff seeking a *quia timet* injunction has been considered in this jurisdiction on a number of occasions. In *Attorney General (Boswell) v. Rathmines and Pembroke Joint Hospital Board*[218] the plaintiff sought an injunction to restrain the defendant from building a smallpox hospital in a Dublin suburb. While there was conflicting expert evidence about the suitability of the site and the risk of the spread of disease, an injunction was refused on the ground that no real danger had been proved. Chatterton VC spoke in terms of having to establish 'a reasonable, well-grounded apprehension ... [of] substantial damage' and Holmes LJ warned against accepting 'as a measure of danger, the fears of the timid and unreasonable'. However, it was the statement of Fitzgibbon LJ which has been most frequently referred to and he stated:

> To sustain the injunction, the law requires proof by the plaintiff of a well-founded apprehension of injury — proof of actual and real danger — a strong probability, almost amounting to moral certainty, that if the Hospital be established, it will be an actionable nuisance.[219]

This passage was quoted with approval by Judge Fawsitt in the Circuit Court decision of *Radford v. Wexford Corporation*,[220] in which the plaintiffs failed in their application for a *quia timet* injunction to restrain the defendants from further proceeding with the construction of a public lavatory on a site adjoining the main street of Wexford town as they had not established a 'strong probability that the apprehended mischiefs will in fact arise'.

The slightly less stringent test of 'reasonable probability' was applied by Meredith J in *Independent Newspapers Ltd v. Irish Press Ltd*,[221] in which the

---

216. *Attorney-General for Dominion of Canada v. Ritchie Contracting & Supply Co.* [1919] AC 999, 1005 *per* Lord Dunedin.

217. [1893] 2 Ch 87, 92. See also *Litchfield-Speer v. Queen Anne's Gate Syndicate (No. 2) Ltd* [1919] 1 Ch 407, 412 where Lawrence J spoke of the plaintiff proving 'that he will certainly sustain substantial damage'.

218. [1904] 1 IR 161. See also *Attorney-General v. Nottingham Corporation* [1904] 1 Ch 673.

219. *Ibid.* at 171. This test seems to have been accepted by Finlay P in *C. & A. Modes v. C. & A. (Waterford) Ltd* [1976] IR 198 where he said that if the action before him was to be equated with an application for a *quia timet* injunction, which he did not necessarily so decide, the standard of proof laid down by Fitzgibbon LJ was the correct one. In the Supreme Court, Henchy J agreed that there were sufficient grounds for the conclusion that this onus of proof had been discharged in the circumstances, but concluded that he was satisfied that what the plaintiffs claimed was not a *quia timet* injunction.

220. (1954) 89 ILTR 184.

221. [1932] IR 615.

plaintiff company sought to restrain the defendant from publishing and passing off a newspaper with a title in which it claimed the property and goodwill. It was held by Meredith J that the plaintiff had failed to establish that damage would occur as it had not been able to show that the goodwill in the title was still an 'attractive force' and he refused to grant the injunction sought. Meredith J examined the onus which must be satisfied before a court would grant a *quia timet* injunction and said that it would not do so 'unless it is satisfied that there is a reasonable probability that what is threatened to be done is calculated in the ordinary course of events, or according to the ordinary course of business, to cause damage to the plaintiff'.[222] Subsequently, in *Whelan v. Madigan*[223] Kenny J spoke in terms of establishing a 'probability' *simpliciter* and granted a *quia timet* injunction to restrain the defendant from interfering with the plaintiffs' quiet enjoyment of their flats.

In view of the lack of consensus in relation to the degree of probability of injury required before a court will grant a *quia timet* injunction, perhaps the suggestion made by Russell LJ in *Hooper v. Rogers*[224] has much to commend it. He stated that 'the degree of probability of future injury is not an absolute standard: what is to be aimed at is justice between the parties having regard to all the relevant circumstances'.[225] In addition, it should be stated that the degree of probability of injury is not the only factor which should influence the court and the greater the damage or prejudice likely to be caused, the more justifiable the court's intervention will be.

Detailed consideration was given to the circumstances in which a *quia timet* injunction should be granted in the recent judgment of Geoghegan J in *Szabo v. ESAT Digiphone Ltd.*[226] The plaintiffs, who were schoolchildren attending a national school, sought *quia timet* injunctions to restrain the erection and operation of a mobile phone base station in the grounds of a garda station located beside their school. Geoghegan J referred to the test employed in *Attorney-General v. Manchester Corporation*, namely that the plaintiff must show 'a strong case of probability that the apprehended mischief will, in fact, arise' and stated that he was inclined to think that it went too far, although he did say that for a *quia timet* injunction to be granted, there would have to be 'a proven substantial risk of danger',[227] a view which he said was supported by the decision of the Irish Court of Appeal in the *Boswell* case. In that case, Walker LJ had also expressed the opinion that where there was conflicting expert evidence, the judge himself could not form a view as an

---

222. *Ibid.* at 631.
223. [1978] ILRM 136.
224. [1975] Ch 43.
225. *Ibid.* at 50.
226. [1998] 2 ILRM 102.
227. *Ibid.* at 110.

expert and if the conflict left him in doubt, he could not in a *quia timet* action decide that the case for the plaintiff had been made out.

Geoghegan J then went on to consider the correct principles to be applied in relation to applications for interlocutory *quia timet* injunctions and said that he would adopt the treatment of the subject in *Spry on Equitable Remedies*,[228] in which the author made it clear that there is no difference between the legal principles to be applied to interlocutory *quia timet* injunctions and any other kind of interlocutory injunction. However, as Spry pointed out in his consideration of *quia timet* injunctions in general, it should not be thought that it is never material that no breach of the applicant's rights has taken place at the time of the hearing of the application and if no breach has taken place, it may be more difficult to establish, as a matter of evidence, that there is a sufficient risk of a future injury to justify the immediate grant of an injunction. Geoghegan J concluded that it was highly improbable at the very least that any injury would ensue to the children before the hearing of the action and in these circumstances he did not think that it would be just or reasonable to grant a *quia timet* injunction.

The principles laid down by Geoghegan J in *Szabo* now seem firmly established and they have been applied in two more recent decisions. In *Ryanair Ltd v. Aer Rianta cpt*[229] Kelly J referred to Geoghegan J's acceptance of the proposition that there was no difference between the principles applicable to an interlocutory *quia timet* injunction and any other kind of interlocutory injunction, but that the fact that no breach of the plaintiff's rights had taken place as of the date of the hearing was of relevance because it might be more difficult to establish as a matter of evidence that a sufficient risk of future injury existed to justify the grant of such an injunction. Kelly J stated that in cases of this nature the court must balance the magnitude of the evil against the chances of its occurrence and he expressed the view that in order to grant a *quia timet* injunction there would have to be 'a proven substantial risk of danger'.[230] Kelly J concluded that in the case before him he was not satisfied that there was a sufficient risk of future injury to the applicant to justify the immediate grant of an injunction.[231] Similarly in *Garrahy v. Bord na gCon*[232] O'Higgins J stated that he would follow the approach of Geoghegan J in *Szabo* to the effect that there is no difference in the principles to be applied to interlocutory *quia timet* injunctions and any other kind of interlocutory

---

228. 4th ed., p.459. Now see 6th ed., 2001.

229. High Court 2000 No. 801 (Kelly J) 25 January 2001.

230. See also *Minister for Arts, Heritage, the Gaeltacht and the Islands v. Kennedy* [2002] 2 ILRM 94, 112.

231. The applicant's appeal from the decision of Kelly J which was solely concerned with the order for costs made against them was dismissed by the Supreme Court in a decision delivered on 26 October 2001.

232. [2002] 3 IR 566.

injunction, although he also accepted, like Geoghegan J, that it may be more difficult to establish as a matter of evidence that there is a sufficient risk of a future injury to justify the immediate grant of an injunction in the former case. On the facts, O'Higgins J concluded that the plaintiff had shown a proven substantial risk of danger and that he had also established a strong case of probability that the apprehended mischief would in fact arise, the test laid down in *Attorney General v. Manchester Corporation*.[233]

It is interesting to note that the notion of applying the *Campus Oil* guidelines has also been canvassed in a number of cases dealing with *quia timet* injunctions. In *Szabo* Geoghegan J said that he doubted whether their application was appropriate in a case such as that before him, but this was because he said there was something distasteful about balancing the convenience of the defendant in being able to carry on its business against alleged dangers to the health of the plaintiffs. In *National Irish Bank Ltd v. RTE*[234] Shanley J stated that he was deciding the interlocutory application before him on the basis of the principles in *Campus Oil*, rather than on the basis of the test laid down in *Boswell*, even though the application was of a *quia timet* nature. He explained that he was doing so because he was dealing with a situation where the defendant had actually conceded that its aim was to publish confidential information belonging to the plaintiff and, in his view, in such a case, the *Campus Oil* principles were 'a more appropriate guide than the more stringent burden' that the test in *Boswell* would impose.

However, it would appear that even if the courts no longer insist upon the test of 'a proven substantial risk of danger' being satisfied in every case in which a *quia timet* injunction is sought, it will nevertheless remain more difficult to obtain an injunction of this nature, not least because, as Spry has pointed out, if no wrongdoing has yet occurred, it will be more difficult to establish, as a matter of evidence, that there is a sufficient risk of a future injury to justify the grant of an injunction.

Finally, it should be pointed out that before a *quia timet* injunction will be granted against a defendant, it is important to establish that it is the defendant himself who has threatened to carry out the action in question. So, in *Celsteel Ltd v. Alton House Holdings Ltd*[235] the Court of Appeal set aside an injunction granted against a lessor, and left in place the injunction granted against the lessee, who was the party actually threatening to erect the car wash to which the plaintiff objected.

---

233. [1893] 2 Ch 87.
234. High Court 1998 No. 1306 P (Shanley J) 6 March 1998. Note that the Supreme Court upheld the refusal of an interlocutory injunction restraining the defendant from publishing information which the plaintiff asserted was confidential, see [1998] 2 ILRM 196.
235. [1986] 1 WLR 512.

SPECIFIC CIRCUMSTANCES IN WHICH AN INJUNCTION WILL BE GRANTED

To Restrain a Breach of Contract

While the usual method of enforcing a positive obligation in a contract is by an order of specific performance, an injunction may be granted to restrain the breach of a negative undertaking contained therein. It was suggested by Lord Cairns in *Doherty v. Allman*[236] that an injunction will issue to secure enforcement of a negative contractual obligation almost as a matter of course. He stated as follows:

> If parties, for valuable consideration, with their eyes open, contract that a particular thing shall not be done, all that a Court of Equity has to do is to say, by way of injunction, that which the parties have already said by way of covenant, that the thing shall not be done; and in such case the injunction does nothing more than give the sanction of the process of the Court to that which already is the contract between the parties. It is not then a question of the balance of convenience or inconvenience, or the amount of damage or of injury — it is the specific performance, by the Court, of that negative bargain which the parties have made, with their eyes open, between themselves.

However, it has been said that this statement is 'the starting point, not a summation of equity's attitude to negative stipulations'[237] and it must not be read without some qualification. In England it has been stated that it must be applied in the light of the surrounding circumstances of each case,[238] and wider discretionary considerations have been taken into account where an order of a mandatory nature has been sought. In *Shepherd Homes Ltd v. Sandham*[239] the plaintiff sought a mandatory injunction to compel the defendant to pull down a fence erected in breach of covenant. It was held by Megarry J in refusing the injunction that the court would exercise its discretion to withhold an injunction more readily if it were mandatory than if it were prohibitory and that even a blameless plaintiff could not as of right claim to enforce a negative covenant by means of a mandatory injunction. He commented that 'the enforcement of a negative covenant at the trial by a mandatory injunction is far more a matter of judicial discretion and not of right than in the case of a

---

236. (1878) 3 App Cas 709, 720.
237. Meagher, Gummow and Lehane, *Equity Doctrines and Remedies* (3rd ed., 1992) p. 568.
238. *Shaw v. Applegate* [1977] 1 WLR 970, 975 *per* Buckley LJ.
239. [1971] Ch 340. See also *Wrotham Park Estate Co. Ltd v. Parkside Homes Ltd* [1974] 1 WLR 798.

prohibitory injunction'[240] and that the statement of Lord Cairns, although it *prima facie* applies to mandatory injunctions, does not apply in its full width and is tempered by judicial discretion. This approach is in line with that put forward by Spry[241] who points out that it is clear that, in proceedings for specific performance to enforce the performance of positive obligations in a contract, considerations of hardship and other discretionary factors are relevant and may induce the court to refuse relief, so there is no reason in principle why the same considerations should not apply to proceedings to enforce contractual rights by injunction.

Where an interlocutory injunction is sought to restrain the breach of a negative covenant, there are conflicting authorities on the question of whether an injunction should issue as a matter of course. It has been held in England in *Hampstead & Suburban Properties Ltd v. Diomedous*[242] that the principle in *Doherty v. Allman* should apply where there is a 'plain and uncontested breach of a clear covenant.'[243] It seems to have also been accepted by the Supreme Court in *Dublin Port and Docks Board v. Britannia Dredging Co. Ltd*,[244] in which the plaintiff sought an interlocutory injunction restraining the defendant from removing dredging equipment from a site where it had undertaken to carry out work. The court held that as the defendant had agreed to this negative term and as it was satisfied that a breach of the covenant was imminent, an interlocutory injunction should be granted. Ó Dálaigh CJ concluded that the principle in *Doherty v. Allman* was accordingly applicable and said that the court was not concerned to examine either the balance of convenience or the amount of damage. In the circumstances where the parties had entered into a negative covenant, it was the duty of the court to hold the defendants to their bargain pending the trial.[245]

However, subsequently in *TMG Group Ltd v. Al Babtain Trading and Contracting Co.*,[246] Keane J distinguished the facts of the case before him from those in *Dublin Port and Docks Board* and stated as follows:

> The circumstances of the present case are wholly different: the defendants
> strenuously contend that neither of the transactions which the company
> proposes to enter into will constitute a breach of their contractual
> obligations under the shareholders' agreement. I do not think that Ó

---

240. *Ibid.* at 351. See also *Sharp v. Harrison* [1922] 1 Ch 502, 512 *per* Astbury J and *Charrington v. Simons & Co. Ltd* [1970] 1 WLR 725, 730.
241. *The Principles of Equitable Remedies* (6th ed., 2001) p. 586.
242. [1969] 1 Ch 248.
243. *Ibid.* at 259 *per* Megarry J. Although note the comments of Ungoed-Thomas J in *Texaco Ltd v. Mulberry Filling Station Ltd* [1972] 1 WLR 814, 831.
244. [1968] IR 136.
245. *Ibid.* at 147. Applied by Costello J in *Irish Shell Ltd v. Elm Motors Ltd* [1984] IR 200, 216.
246. [1982] ILRM 349.

Dálaigh CJ in the passages to which I have referred, was laying down any general principle that, in all cases where the plaintiff establishes a *prima facie* case of a breach of a negative stipulation in a contract, the court could disregard any question of the balance of convenience as between the parties. His observations were clearly confined to a case where one party to a contract was proposing to act in breach of a negative contract (and indeed to repudiate the whole contract) in circumstances where the court was not satisfied on the evidence that they were entitled so to do.[247]

Subsequently in *Irish Shell Ltd v. Elm Motors Ltd*[248] McCarthy J endorsed these views and said that save in the most exceptional circumstances, the determination of an application for an interlocutory injunction lies solely on a consideration of the questions of whether a fair case has been made out and where the balance of convenience lies. This question has recently been addressed again by the Supreme Court in *Premier Dairies Ltd v. Doyle*.[249] Delivering judgment in the High Court, Kinlen J held that the defendants, who had entered into distribution agreements with the plaintiff to deliver its products, should be held to the terms of the negative covenant contained in the agreements preventing them from competing with the plaintiff and he stated that the decision of the Supreme Court in *Britannia Dredging Co. Ltd* governed the case.[250] However, the defendants appealed against this order arguing, *inter alia*, that the clause in question was contrary to sections 4 and 5 of the Competition Act 1991. O'Flaherty J dismissed the appeal but it is interesting to note the comment which he made about the *Doherty v. Allman/ Britannia Dredging* principle. He was satisfied that if there had been no other factors in the case he would have held that it came 'four square within the *Britannia Dredging* decision'. However, O'Flaherty J stated that, as there was scope for an argument to be made as to the applicability of the Competition Act 1991 which he described as 'a rather complex piece of legislation which, so far, has not been judicially mined to any extent', it was not in his view appropriate to apply the *Britannia Dredging* principle to the case. O'Flaherty J accordingly went on to consider whether there was a fair case to be tried, which he was satisfied there was and to consider where the balance of convenience lay. While he disagreed with Kinlen J about the applicability of the *Britannia Dredging* principle, O'Flaherty J was satisfied that the former's conclusion that the balance of convenience favoured the plaintiffs was correct and for this reason affirmed his decision to grant the interlocutory relief sought. On balance the comments of McCarthy J in *Irish Shell Ltd*, referred to above,

247. *Ibid.* at 353.
248. [1984] IR 200.
249. [1996] 1 ILRM 363.
250. High Court 1995 No. 7008P (Kinlen J) 29 September 1995.

seem to reflect current practice and it is likely that *Britannia Dredging* may be interpreted as being confined to its own specific facts.

The jurisdiction of the courts to grant an injunction is wider than its jurisdiction to grant specific performance, and often a positive obligation in a contract may not be specifically enforceable.[251] It is therefore often of practical significance that even where a contract contains no express negative stipulation it may be possible to imply a negative undertaking which can be enforced by the grant of an injunction. As Lord Selborne stated in *Wolverhampton and Walsall Railway Co. v. London and North-Western Railway Co.*[252] in such circumstances the courts should look to the substance and not merely the form of the agreement and this approach has generally although not universally[253] been followed.[254] In *Catt v. Tourle*,[255] where a publican agreed to procure all his beer supplies from a specified source an injunction was granted restraining him from obtaining these supplies elsewhere. Similarly in *Metropolitan Electric Supply Co. v. Ginder*[256] the defendant agreed to take all his electricity requirements from the plaintiff for a specified period. The court construed the contract as an undertaking not to obtain electricity from another supplier and granted an injunction to restrain the defendant from doing so. This principle has also been applied in this jurisdiction in *Irish Shell Ltd v. Elm Motors Ltd*,[257] where injunctions were granted to compel the defendant to comply with the terms of covenants in a lease. As Costello J stated, once it was established that these covenants were enforceable it did not matter that they were expressed in the form of a positive rather than a negative obligation.

Particular Considerations which Apply to Contracts for Personal Services

In general the courts are reluctant to grant an injunction which would involve an element of ongoing supervision[258] and as Geoghegan J stated in *Ó Murchú*

---

251. The courts have traditionally displayed a reluctance to grant specific performance of part only of a contract. See *Ryan v. Mutual Tontine Westminster Chambers Association* [1893] 1 Ch 116, 125.
252. (1873) LR 16 Eq 433, 440.
253. See *Mortimer v. Beckett* [1920] 1 Ch 571 where Russell J laid emphasis on the positive form of the agreement in declining to grant an injunction.
254. See e.g. in relation to covenants affecting the use of land, *Tulk v. Moxhay* (1848) 2 Ph 774.
255. (1869) LR 4 Ch App 654.
256. [1901] 2 Ch 799. See also *James Jones & Sons Ltd v. Earl of Tankerville* [1909] 2 Ch 440.
257. [1984] IR 200.
258. However, note the decision of Costello P in *Wanze Properties (Ireland) Ltd v. Five Star Supermarket* High Court, 24 October 1997 in which he granted an interlocutory injunction compelling the defendant to comply with covenants in a lease requiring it to trade as a supermarket during usual business hours.

v. Eircell Ltd[259] they will be very slow to make orders of this nature in either service contracts or trading contracts because it will be difficult to assess whether they are being obeyed. A further compelling reason for the courts' reluctance to grant injunctions in respect of contracts for personal services is that as a matter of policy it is undesirable to force individuals to work together where a relationship of trust and confidence no longer exists between them. So, while it has been acknowledged that an injunction may be a useful remedy where the positive obligations in a contract are not specifically enforceable, it is also generally accepted, particularly in the context of contracts for personal services, that an injunction should not be granted where this would indirectly provide for specific performance of the positive terms of the contract. As Kenny J stated in *Yeates v. Minister for Posts and Telegraphs*[260] in the context of an application for an injunction which if granted would have indirectly amounted to specific performance, 'it is settled law that the courts never specifically enforce a contract for personal services'. Despite this principle on occasion the courts have permitted the issue of an injunction to restrain a negative undertaking in a contract for personal services which may indirectly cause the contract to be performed; as O'Flaherty J stated in *Capital Radio Productions Ltd v. Radio 2000 Ltd*[261] 'while a person cannot be forced to work against his will for someone he can, if in breach of contract, be *prevented* from working for anyone else.'

This principle is well illustrated by the decision of Lord St Leonards in *Lumley v. Wagner.*[262] The defendant undertook to sing at the plaintiff's theatre for a specified period and not to perform elsewhere during this time. Subsequently, the defendant agreed another contract for a larger fee with a third party and the plaintiff sought an injunction to restrain her from singing for this person. Lord St Leonards held that the plaintiff was entitled to an injunction to restrain the breach of the negative stipulation in the contract. The decision has been criticized on the basis that it amounted to the equivalent of ordering specific performance of the original contract, although as Lord St Leonards pointed out, the defendant could not have been compelled to fulfil this obligation. This approach was followed in *Warner Brothers Pictures, Incorporated v. Nelson,*[263] in which the defendant, Mrs Nelson, better known as the actress Bette Davis, agreed to act for a studio for a period of five years and undertook not to act for any other party during this time or to engage in any other occupation without the written consent of the studio. The plaintiff sought to enforce the obligation not to act for anyone other than itself and Branson J granted an injunction to restrain her from breaching this undertaking.

---

259. Supreme Court 2000 No. 336, 21 February 2001.
260. [1978] ILRM 22, 24.
261. Supreme Court 1998 No.128 & 129, 26 May 1998.
262. (1852) 1 De G M & G 604.
263. [1937] 1 KB 209.

He stated that where a contract of personal service contains negative covenants, the enforcement of which will not amount either to a decree of specific performance of the positive covenants of the contract or to a decree under which the defendant must remain idle or perform the positive covenants, the court will enforce those negative covenants subject to the consideration that an injunction is a discretionary remedy and the court in making an order of this nature may limit the terms of the injunction to what it considers reasonable in the circumstances. While an injunction covering all the negative covenants in the contract would have forced the defendant to perform her contract or to remain idle, that objection was removed by the limited form in which the order was sought. Branson J rejected the argument that the order made amounted to an indirect form of specific performance and said that while the defendant might be tempted to perform the contract in view of the fact that alternative work would be considerably less lucrative, she would not be driven to do so.

A related question is whether an employer can be compelled to continue to employ an employee and this issue was considered in *Page One Records Ltd v. Britton*.[264] The plaintiffs had contracted with a group of musicians known as 'the Troggs' that they would act as their manager for a period of five years and the group agreed not to employ anyone else during this time. When the plaintiffs sought an injunction to prevent the employment of another manager the court refused to grant an injunction on the basis that as a practical matter it would force the group to continue to employ the plaintiffs. Stamp J said that it would be tantamount to ordering specific performance of a contract of personal services and it would be wrong to put pressure on the defendants to continue to employ someone in a fiduciary capacity in whom they had lost confidence.

The approach adopted by Stamp J is in many respects preferable to that of Branson J in that it was unrealistic to expect the defendants in either case to give up their chosen careers and the alternative was that they would find themselves compelled to perform a contract of personal services. The Court of Appeal in England has recently confirmed this point and has re-asserted the view that an injunction should not be granted if its indirect effect would be to compel performance of a contract for personal services. In *Warren v. Mendy*[265] a boxer agreed that he would not be managed by anyone except the plaintiff for a three-year period but subsequently entered into a management agreement with the defendant. The plaintiff sought an injunction to restrain the defendant from inducing a breach of contract and from acting for the boxer. The effect of such an injunction would have been to restrain the boxer from receiving services from the defendant and would arguably have compelled him to perform his agreement with the plaintiff and the Court of Appeal held

264. [1968] 1 WLR 157.
265. [1989] 1 WLR 853. See McClean [1990] CLJ 28.

that no injunction should be granted. Nourse LJ commented that Branson J's approach in *Warner Brothers Pictures, Incorporated v. Nelson* was 'extraordinarily unrealistic' and stated as follows:

> [T]he following general principles are applicable to the grant or refusal of an injunction to enforce performance of the servant's negative obligations in a contract for personal services inseparable from the exercise of some special skill or talent. In such a case the court ought not to enforce the performance of the negative obligations if their enforcement will effectively compel the servant to perform his positive obligations under the contract. Compulsion is a question to be decided on the facts of each case, with a realistic regard for the probable reaction of an injunction on the psychological and material, and sometimes the physical, need of the servant to maintain the skill or talent. The longer the term for which the injunction is sought, the more readily will compulsion be inferred. ... An injunction will less readily be granted where there are obligations of mutual trust and confidence, more especially where the servant's trust in the master may have been betrayed or his confidence in him has genuinely gone.[266]

McCutcheon has stated that 'the practical consequence of *Warren v. Mendy* is to make it highly improbable that negative injunctions will be granted in sports cases, at least where the contract is for anything other than a short duration'[267] and has expressed the view that the approach of the English courts may be too lenient. In contrast he points out that the North American courts have placed a greater emphasis on ensuring that contracts of this nature are honoured and that individuals do not renege on their commitments simply because a more lucrative opportunity is presented to them.[268] There is clearly merit in his argument that 'if contractual obligations are to be taken seriously it is to be expected that the law would lean towards their enforcement rather than minimising the consequences of their breach to the wrongdoer' and it will be interesting to see whether the approach adopted in North America will ultimately be taken on board either in England or in this jurisdiction.

A limited exception to the general principle that employer and employee should not be forced to work together has been recognised where a relationship of mutual trust and confidence still exists between them. This is illustrated by the decision of the Court of Appeal in *Hill v. C.A. Parsons & Co. Ltd*,[269]

---

266. *Ibid.* at 867.
267. (1997) 17 LS 65, 74.
268. See e.g. *Washington Capitols Basketball Club Inc. v. Barry* (1969) 304 F Supp 1193; *Cincinnati Bangals Inc v. Bergey* (1974) 453 F Supp 129.
269. [1972] Ch 305. See also *Powell v. London Borough of Brent* [1987] IRLR 466 and *Robb v. Hammersmith* [1991] ICR 514.

where an injunction was granted against an employer to restrain an alleged wrongful dismissal after the employer had reluctantly been forced to terminate the contract of employment of an engineer who had refused to join a trade union. While arguably this amounted to indirect specific performance of a service contract, the majority of the court justified its decision on the basis that a relationship of mutual trust and confidence still existed between the parties. The employer in this case clearly still had confidence in his employee and had only acted in response to pressure from the trade union. This decision can be contrasted with that of the Irish High Court in *Yeates v. Minister for Posts and Telegraphs*,[270] in which the plaintiff civil servants, who had been suspended from their positions without pay when they refused to pass a picket placed on the premises in which they worked, sought interlocutory injunctions restoring them to their positions and giving them the right to remuneration. In this instance the employer clearly had lost confidence in the employees and had consciously wanted to suspend them. Kenny J refused the injunctions sought on the grounds, *inter alia*, that to restore the plaintiffs to their former positions would amount to specific performance of a contract for personal services which the court would not order on principle.

A subsequent decision which is out of line with those just considered is *Irani v. Southampton and South-West Hampshire Health Authority*,[271] in which Warner J granted an injunction to restrain the dismissal of an employee in circumstances where there were irreconcilable differences between him and a consultant but no complaints of professional incompetence. This result is less justifiable in that unlike in *Hill*, the employer actively sought the employee's dismissal and it is far from clear whether such an approach would be followed.[272] The better approach would seem to be that it is only in circumstances where the employer still retains trust and confidence in the employee that any order which will have the effect of obliging the parties to continue working together should be made. Similar considerations will apply in relation to trading contracts and as Geoghegan J made clear in *Ó Murchú v. Eircell Ltd*,[273] it will usually be impracticable and undesirable for two parties to be compelled to trade with one another when one does not want to carry on such trading.

Rather conflicting signals on this issue of whether the courts will intervene in cases of wrongful dismissal have been sent out in a number of recent judgments in this area. In *Courtney v. Radio 2000 Ltd*,[274] the plaintiff radio presenter sought a number of reliefs including an injunction restraining the defendant from implementing his purported dismissal until the trial of the

---

270. [1978] ILRM 22.
271. [1985] IRLR 203.
272. See Madden (1985) 3 ILT (ns) 134.
273. Supreme Court 2000 No. 336, 21 February 2001.
274. High Court 1997 No. 7903P (Laffoy J) 22 July 1997.

action and an order requiring the defendant to reinstate the plaintiff to his position pending the trial. The defendant submitted that the plaintiff was employed to present live broadcasts and given that trust and confidence no longer existed on its part, it would be inappropriate for the court to grant the reliefs sought. Laffoy J agreed that it would not be appropriate to make an order requiring the defendant to reinstate the plaintiff but decided that the balance of convenience lay in favour of granting an injunction restraining the defendant from implementing the purported dismissal until the trial of the action. She stated as follows: 'I consider that employment as a broadcaster, which is a high profile occupation, is in a special category and that the plaintiff might possibly establish at the trial of the action that this is one of the exceptional circumstances in which an injunction is the appropriate remedy in an employer and employee dispute. However, I express no view whatsoever on this issue'.

In *Martin v. Nationwide Building Society*[275] the plaintiff sought an order reinstating him in his position as branch manager of one of the defendant's offices and restraining the latter from appointing anyone other than the plaintiff to this position. Macken J acknowledged that where reinstatement has been sought at an interlocutory stage the authorities make it clear that if the employee does not enjoy the wholehearted support or confidence of his employer, the court will be very slow indeed to reinstate the employee pending the action. However, she stated that the case before her was not concerned with purported dismissal but with a suspension which had gone on for too long and the question was whether this suspension should be set aside because of the delay. Macken J concluded that the plaintiff had established a fair issue to be tried on the question of undue delay and that he would suffer irreparable loss and damage if relief were not granted. In the circumstances, even though she acknowledged that the defendant did not appear to have wholehearted trust in the plaintiff she decided to grant the interlocutory injunction sought. Relief of a similar nature was sought in *Howard v. University College Cork*[276] where the High Court considered an application made by the plaintiff for interlocutory injunctions restraining the defendant from taking any steps to remove her from her post as head of the Department of German at University College Cork or from appointing a person other than her to the post. O'Donovan J concluded that there were fair questions to the tried and made reference to the fact that if the plaintiff's role as head of department was terminated in advance of the trial and it was subsequently determined that this decision was unlawful, it would be extremely difficult if not impossible for a trial judge to assess a sum for damages which would adequately compensate the plaintiff for the injury to her reputation. O'Donovan J rejected the submission made by the

---

275. [2001] 1 IR 228.
276. High Court 2000 No. 3372P (O'Donovan J) 25 July 2000.

defendant that granting the interlocutory relief sought would cause the college irreparable harm and he concluded that the balance of convenience demanded that the status quo be maintained.

It would appear that in cases dealing with wrongful dismissal[277] the courts will generally be reluctant to order a plaintiff's reinstatement pending trial, although they may grant an injunction to restrain the appointment of a person other than the plaintiff to his position[278] or may prevent the advertising of a post which overlaps with the plaintiff's.[279] In addition, they may be willing to make an order that a plaintiff's salary should continue to be paid[280] and, as the judgment of Laffoy J in *Harte v. Kelly*[281] makes clear, orders of this nature will not be confined to situations in which a plaintiff can establish that he will face penury if an injunction is not granted. In those cases where an interlocutory injunction has been granted to restrain the purported termination of the plaintiff's employment[282] it has been usual to require a plaintiff to give an undertaking that he will perform such duties on behalf of the defendant as are reasonably appropriate pending the trial of the action. However, as Costello P made clear in *Phelan v. BIC (Ireland) Ltd*,[283] 'whether the defendants wish to avail of the plaintiff's services is entirely a matter for them' and in this way the court should be able to meet any criticism that it is effectively forcing parties to work together where there is no longer a relationship of trust and confidence between them.

A recent decision which appears to confirm that the courts will be unwilling to grant an interlocutory injunction requiring an employee's reinstatement pending trial, at any rate where relations between the parties have broken down to a significant degree, is *Moore v. Xnet Informations Systems Ltd.*[284]

---

277. The cases dealing with wrongful dismissal were distinguished by O'Higgins J in *Garrahy v. Bord na gCon* [2002] 3 IR 566 where he granted an injunction restraining the appointment of an individual to a full-time position which the plaintiff had been occupying on a part-time basis. While he stressed that it is 'a well-established principle in labour law that the courts will not order specific performance of a contract of employment' he stated that the case before him was not one dealing with wrongful dismissal and concluded that an interlocutory injunction was the appropriate remedy in the circumstances.

278. *Lonergan v. Salter-Townshend* [2000] ELR 15.

279. *Harkins v. Shannon Foynes Port Co.* High Court 2001 No. 433P (O'Sullivan J) 29 January 2001.

280. *Fennelly v. Azzicurazioni Generali* (1985) 3 ILT 73, *Shortt v. Data Packaging Ltd* [1994] ELR 251, *Boland v. Phoenix Shannon plc* [1997] ELR 113, *Phelan v. BIC (Ireland) Ltd* [1997] ELR 208, *Lonergan v. Salter-Townshend* [2000] ELR 15 and *Sheehy v. Ryan* High Court 2002 No. 10338P (Peart J) 29 August 2002.

281. [1997] ELR 125, 130. See also *Phelan v. BIC (Ireland) Ltd* [1997] ELR 208.

282. *Shortt v. Data Packaging Ltd* [1994] ELR 251, *Boland v. Phoenix Shannon plc* [1997] ELR 113 and *Phelan v. BIC (Ireland) Ltd* [1997] ELR 208.

283. [1997] ELR 208, 213.

284. [2002] 2 ILRM 278.

The plaintiff sought interlocutory injunctions restraining the defendants from taking any further steps to terminate his employment and requiring them to reinstate him in his position and pay him pending the trial of the action. O'Sullivan J stated that the plaintiff had raised fair questions for determination at the trial and concluded that the balance of convenience favoured granting an order directing the defendant to continue paying the plaintiff's salary and other benefits until the trial subject to an undertaking by the plaintiff to do any work he is required to do. However, while he was satisfied that the plaintiff had made out a fair argument that he had been wrongfully dismissed, having regard to the fact that relations between the parties had irretrievably broken down, O'Sullivan J stated that the balance of convenience did not favour an order directing the defendant to reinstate the plaintiff pending the hearing of the case.

Finally, it should be noted that it appears from the decision of the Supreme Court in *Parsons v. Iarnrod Eireann*[285] that the traditional relief at common law for unfair dismissal is a claim for damages and that other remedies which may be sought are in aid of this remedy and have no existence independent of it. This principle was applied by Roderick Murphy J in *Philpott v. Ogilvy & Mather Ltd*[286] in refusing the plaintiff's claim for an interlocutory injunction restraining the defendant from giving effect to his purported dismissal. In his view as the plaintiff had not claimed damages for wrongful dismissal the principle set out in *Parsons* applied. While the plaintiff might have sought an injunction in aid of any common law remedy claimed, in the circumstances such equitable relief had no independent existence and apart from a claim for damages there was no other free standing relief which could be claimed at law or in equity.

To Restrain the Commission or Continuance of a Tort

As Martin[287] makes clear, equity plays no part in determining whether a tort has been committed or threatened; that is purely a question of law but once it is established, a court may in its discretion grant or withhold an injunction on the basis of equitable principles.

Equity will commonly intervene and grant an injunction in the case of nuisance which is usually of a continuing nature and the remedy of an injunction will be the most appropriate form of remedy in the circumstances.[288] In relation to acts of public nuisance, i.e. acts or omissions which cause damage to the public generally, proceedings for an injunction may only be brought by the Attorney General either on his own motion or at the relation of an individual

---

285. [1997] ELR 203.
286. [2000] 3 IR 206.
287. Hanbury and Martin, *Modern Equity* (16th ed., 2001) p. 817.
288. See e.g. *Bellew v. Cement Ltd* [1948] IR 61; *Patterson v. Murphy* [1978] ILRM 85.

unless the individual can establish that he has suffered some special damage or that a private right of his has been infringed.[289]

An injunction is often sought to prevent a threatened or continued trespass to land, although if the trespass is of a trivial nature and involves no appreciable injury to the plaintiff,[290] an order will not be granted. Injunctions are also sought with increasing frequency in relation to alleged passing off,[291] and in the area of industrial relations. As noted above, the common law principles relating to the grant of an interlocutory injunction clearly favoured the employer where proceedings were brought seeking to restrain picketing by means of an interlocutory injunction and it remains to be seen whether the provisions of section 19 of the Industrial Relations Act 1990 will adequately redress this imbalance.[292]

The circumstances in which an injunction may be granted to restrain alleged defamation are difficult to define with precision, although as noted above the traditional reluctance on the part of the courts to interfere unduly with an individual's right to freedom of expression has been reflected in the rather onerous burden facing potential plaintiffs.[293]

To Restrain a Breach of Constitutional Rights

It is a well established principle that damages will lie in respect of a breach of constitutional rights,[294] and that the amount of such an award may vary, from exemplary damages where the State has deliberately and without justification infringed a person's constitutional rights,[295] to a purely nominal sum where the breach has caused no real damage.[296] However, it has also been recognised that an injunction will lie to restrain unconstitutional activities, such as in *Murtagh Properties v. Cleary*[297] where an injunction was granted by Kenny J to restrain the picketing of a licensed premises on the basis that it amounted to unlawful interference with the constitutional right of the employees who worked there to earn their livelihood. This approach was followed by O'Hanlon

---

289.	*Boyce v. Paddington Borough Council* [1903] 1 Ch 109, 113 *per* Buckley J.
290.	*Fielden v. Cox* (1906) 22 TLR 411; *Llandudno Urban District Council v. Woods* [1899] 2 Ch 705.
291.	See e.g. *Independent Newspapers Ltd v. Irish Press Ltd* [1932] IR 615; *C.& A. Modes v. C. & A. (Waterford) Ltd* [1976] IR 198; *Three Stripe International Ltd v. Charles O'Neill & Co. Ltd* [1989] ILRM 124; *An Post v. Irish Permanent plc* [1995] 1 ILRM 336; *Local Ireland Ltd v. Local Ireland-Online Ltd* High Court 2000 No. 7854P (Herbert J) 2 October 2000.
292.	See *supra* pp. 476-480.
293.	See *supra* pp. 480-486. *Sinclair v. Gogarty* [1937] IR 377, 384; *Connolly v. RTE* [1991] 2 IR 446 and *Reynolds v. Malocco* [1999] 1 ILRM 289.
294.	See e.g. *Meskell v. CIE* [1973] IR 121; *Hayes v. Ireland* [1987] ILRM 651.
295.	*Kennedy v. Ireland* [1987] IR 587.
296.	*Kearney v. Ireland* [1986] IR 116.
297.	[1972] IR 330.

J in *Parsons v. Kavanagh*,[298] in which the plaintiff, who operated a passenger bus service on a route pursuant to a statutory licence, sought an injunction to prevent the defendants operating a bus service without a licence on the same route. O'Hanlon held that having regard to the plaintiff's constitutional right to earn a livelihood, which carried with it the entitlement to be protected against any unlawful activity on the part of another person which materially infringed that right, the plaintiff was entitled to the injunction sought. Similarly in *Lovett v. Gogan*,[299] the Supreme Court granted an injunction restraining the defendants from operating an unlicensed coach passenger service in breach of the provisions of the Road Traffic Act 1932 on the basis that this activity constituted an actual and threatened interference with the plaintiff's constitutional right to earn a living by lawful means. However, it should be noted that Finlay CJ stressed that the plaintiff would be entitled to an injunction in such circumstances if he could establish that it was the only way of protecting himself from the threatened invasion of his constitutional rights. On the facts of the case before him, he was satisfied that an injunction was the only remedy which could protect the plaintiff given that the penalty which could be imposed on a person operating a passenger service without a licence was limited to £5 in respect of a continuing offence.

However, care should be exercised when the impugned activity constitutes a criminal offence, and the relevance of the statement made by Finlay CJ in *Lovett* becomes clear when one examines the judgment of Barron J in *O'Connor v. Williams*[300] in which the plaintiff taxi drivers sought an injunction to restrain the defendant hackney cab operators from carrying on their business in alleged breach of the Road Traffic (Public Service Vehicles) Regulations 1963, as amended, in a manner which the plaintiffs contended amounted to interference with their right to earn a livelihood. Barron J stated that the real issue was whether injunctive relief was the only way in which the plaintiffs could be protected from the invasion of their constitutional rights. He distinguished the decisions in *Parsons* and *Lovett* stating that in the case before him the defendants were only one of several firms operating a service allegedly in breach of the regulations and the penalties for breaches of the relevant regulations were substantial.[301] In his view the implementation of the criminal law was the most appropriate remedy and he refused the relief sought by the plaintiffs.

One area which has provoked a considerable amount of case law in this regard is Article 40.3.3 of the Constitution which provides that 'the State

---

298. [1990] ILRM 560.
299. [1995] 3 IR 132.
300. [2001] 1 IR 248.
301. In the view of Barron J the decision which was more relevant was that of the Supreme Court in *Incorporated Law Society of Ireland v. Carroll* [1995] 3 IR 145 in which the plaintiff's application for an injunction to restrain alleged breaches of the criminal law was refused.

acknowledges the right to life of the unborn and, with due regard to the equal right to life of the mother, guarantees in its laws to respect, and as far as practicable, by its laws to defend and vindicate that right'. In *Attorney General (SPUC) v. Open Door Counselling*[302] Hamilton P granted an order restraining the defendants from assisting pregnant women within the jurisdiction to travel abroad to obtain abortions by providing information relating to clinics where abortions are carried out or by referring them to such clinics. As he stated 'the courts will provide a procedure for the enforcement and protection of personal rights and the power of the courts in this regard does not depend on legislation. The public interest and the common good require that personal rights be respected, vindicated and protected.'[303] The Supreme Court rejected the defendants' appeal and Finlay CJ commented that the Attorney General, in whose name the proceedings had been brought, was an especially appropriate person to invoke the jurisdiction of the court to defend and vindicate the constitutional right in question. Further proceedings were taken in the case of *SPUC v. Grogan*,[304] in which the plaintiff sought an interlocutory injunction restraining the defendants from distributing certain information in relation to abortion services available outside the State. The Supreme Court allowed the plaintiff's appeal against the decision of Carroll J to refer questions of interpretation to the European Court of Justice without making any order in relation to the grant of the injunction. Finlay CJ said that the application for an interlocutory injunction consisted of an application to restrain an activity which had clearly been declared by the Supreme Court to be unconstitutional and laid down the following principles which in his view should apply in such cases. He stated:

> [I]t is clearly quite inappropriate to approach the exercise of the discretion to grant or refuse an interlocutory injunction, upon the basis of a supposed *status quo ante* consisting of activities which are constitutionally forbidden acts. The true principle which falls to be considered in this case in relation to the exercise of that discretion is the unqualified existence of the relevant provisions of the Constitution at the time of the application for an injunction which, in my view, having regard to the constitutional law applicable, replaces the ordinary concept of *status quo ante* arising in interlocutory cases. With regard to the issue of the balance of convenience, I am satisfied that where an injunction is sought to protect a constitutional right, that the only matter which could properly be capable of being weighed in a balance against the granting of such protection would be another competing constitutional right.[305]

---

302. [1988] IR 593.
303. *Ibid.* at 606.
304. [1989] IR 753.
305. *Ibid.* at 765.

Finlay CJ concluded that where the right sought to be protected is that of life, there could be no question of an entitlement in European Community law, as a corollary to the right to travel to avail of services, counterbalancing as a matter of convenience the necessity for an interlocutory injunction.

This line of reasoning was further developed in the controversial decision of *Attorney General v. X.*,[306] in which Costello J granted an injunction restraining the defendant and her parents from leaving the jurisdiction for a period of nine months or from arranging a termination of pregnancy, an order which was subsequently set aside on appeal by the Supreme Court.

To Protect Public Rights

An injunction may issue to restrain activities which are detrimental to the public generally. As a general rule such an injunction may only be sought successfully by the Attorney General, either acting on his own initiative, or at the relation of another who seeks to prevent infringement of a right. As an exception to this general principle, an individual may seek an injunction to restrain interference with a public right if this interference also amounts to an infringement of a private right or would cause special damage to this individual.[307] However the traditional principles in this area were thrown into some doubt by a number of decisions of the Supreme Court in the late 1980s such as *Crotty v. An Taoiseach*,[308] in which the plaintiff successfully sought an injunction to prevent the State ratifying the Single European Act, a treaty which introduced a number of significant changes to the treaties establishing the European Communities. In *SPUC v. Coogan*[309] the Supreme Court held that the Attorney General did not have an exclusive right to commence proceedings seeking to secure compliance with the provisions of Article 40.3.3° of the Constitution and that any citizen showing a *bona fide* interest and concern in its enforcement might do so. The Supreme Court held that the plaintiff, who was not in the position of an officious or meddlesome intervenient in the matter, had sufficient *locus standi* to maintain an action against individuals whom it claimed were acting in a manner contrary to Article 40.3.3° without being required to act in relator proceedings.

A question which has provoked considerable debate is whether an injunction may be granted to restrain the infringement of a public right even where a statutory remedy exists, in particular where the activity also constitutes a criminal offence. While the use of an injunction to restrain a breach of the criminal law has been described as a remedy of last resort,[310] it would appear

---

306. [1992] 1 IR 1.
307. *Lonrho v. Shell Petroleum Co. Ltd (No.2)* [1982] AC 173.
308. [1987] IR 713.
309. [1989] IR 734.
310. *Waverly BC v. Hilden* [1988] 1 WLR 246, 265 *per* Scott J.

that the Attorney General, in his role as guardian of the rights of the public, may obtain such a remedy. It has been stressed that an injunction will only be granted in these circumstances where the statutory remedy is inadequate and it has been established in England that an individual may not take such an action in the absence of interference with private rights or special damage. So, in *Gouriet v. Union of Post Office Workers*[311] the plaintiff failed to obtain an injunction to restrain a threatened boycott of postal communications between the UK and South Africa which amounted to a breach of the Post Office Act 1953 when the Attorney General declined to bring a relator action.

This issue has been considered in this jurisdiction on a number of occasions and in *Attorney General (O'Duffy) v. Appleton*[312] the Attorney General was granted an injunction in a relator action in which it was sought to restrain the activities of a company formed for fraudulent purposes contrary to the Dentists Act 1878. The most important decision in this area is that of Costello J in *Attorney General v. Paperlink*,[313] in which an injunction was sought to restrain the defendants from operating a courier service in breach of the statutory power of the minister under the Post Office Act 1908. Costello J accepted as correct the statement of Professor Casey[314] to the effect that 'it is possible for [the Attorney General] to obtain an injunction to restrain someone from acting in breach of a statutory provision even where his action constitutes an offence,' and also the following statement of Lord Denning MR in *Attorney General v. Chaudray*:[315]

> Whenever parliament has enacted a law and given a particular remedy for the breach of it, such remedy being in an inferior court, nevertheless the High Court always has reserve power to enforce the law so enacted by way of an injunction or declaration or other suitable remedy. The High Court has a jurisdiction to ensure obedience to the law whenever it is just and convenient to do so.

In the course of his judgment, Costello J laid down a number of important principles. He confirmed that the Attorney General has the right to seek an injunction to restrain a breach of statute, even where the statute prescribes alternative remedies including criminal sanctions. Costello J stressed that such a jurisdiction should only be exercised in exceptional circumstances and that the court must consider the adequacy of the alternative remedy but conceded that the fact that a criminal prosecution had not been brought did not in itself preclude the court from granting an injunction. Costello J was satisfied that

---

311. [1978] AC 435.
312. [1907] 1 IR 252.
313. [1984] ILRM 373.
314. *The Office of the Attorney General in Ireland* (1980) p. 149.
315. [1971] 1 WLR 1614, 1624.

there were exceptional circumstances justifying the granting of an injunction in the case before him and in answer to the defendant's argument stressed that the court was not trying a criminal charge but was merely exercising 'a distinct and different jurisdiction in civil proceedings'.

However, as the decision of the Supreme Court in *Incorporated Law Society of Ireland v. Carroll*[316] makes clear, the only party who may bring civil proceedings to enforce a public right is the Attorney General. As Blayney J stated there was no suggestion in the judgment of Costello J in *Attorney General v. Paperlink* that anyone other than the Attorney General could seek an injunction in the public interest to restrain an offence being committed in breach of statute.[317]

MAREVA INJUNCTIONS AND RELATED ORDERS[318]

Introduction

Traditionally, the courts would not grant an injunction to restrain a defendant from dealing with or dissipating his assets prior to the trial of an action.[319] However, a number of decisions of the English Court of Appeal in the mid-1970s resulted in a change in this position and now a 'Mareva' injunction may be granted to prevent a defendant from removing assets from the jurisdiction or from disposing of them within the jurisdiction in a manner likely to frustrate the plaintiff's proceedings. More recently it has been accepted that an injunction of this nature may even extend to assets held outside the jurisdiction on a worldwide basis.[320]

The genesis of Mareva injunctions can be traced to the decision of the English Court of Appeal in *Nippon Yusen Kaisha v. Karageorgis*,[321] in which Denning MR stated that 'it seems to me that the time has come when we should revise our practice'. The plaintiff shipowners let a number of ships to

---

316. [1995] 3 IR 145.
317. However, it should be noted that in his decision in the High Court in *Incorporated Law Society of Ireland v. Carroll* [1995] 3 IR 145, 163 Murphy J stated that the right to maintain civil proceedings in respect of a criminal wrong where a constitutional right is in jeopardy may be described as one of the exceptional cases referred to by Costello J in *Attorney General v. Paperlink* [1984] ILRM 373, 391 or as a distinct and separate exception to the rules laid down in that case. (See further *Parsons v. Kavanagh* [1990] ILRM 560 and *Lovett v. Gogan* [1995] 3 IR 132 considered *supra*.)
318. See generally Capper, *Mareva Injunctions* (1988) and Courtney, *Mareva Injunctions and Related Interlocutory Orders* (1998).
319. *Lister & Co. v. Stubbs* (1890) 45 Ch D 1.
320. *Babanaft International Co. SA v. Bassatne* [1990] Ch 13; *Deutsche Bank Atkiengesellschaft v. Murtagh* [1995] 1 ILRM 381; *Bennett Enterprises Ltd v. Lipton* [1999] 2 IR 221.
321. [1975] 1 WLR 1093, 1095.

charterers who defaulted after initially making some payments. Believing that the defendants had certain funds in London banks which would be sent out of the jurisdiction, the plaintiff sought an injunction to prevent this happening. The Court of Appeal held that where there is a strong *prima facie* case that a plaintiff is entitled to money from a defendant within the jurisdiction and the plaintiff has reason to believe that the defendant may remove these assets from the jurisdiction, the court may grant an interlocutory injunction on an *ex parte* basis restraining the defendant from disposing of these assets. This principle was confirmed several weeks later in *Mareva Compania Naviera SA v. International Bulkcarriers SA*,[322] the decision which gave its name to the form of injunction granted in these cases.

A Mareva injunction is interlocutory in nature and its usual purpose is to prevent the dissipation or removal of assets before the trial of an action, although it may be granted to prevent a defendant disposing of assets after the trial has taken place to avoid execution of a judgment. Ancillary orders may be granted to require a defendant to disclose information relating to his assets, although the privilege against self-incrimination[323] may be invoked to undermine the effectiveness of such orders.[324] The jurisdiction to grant such injunctions is of general application[325] and the courts are loathe to lay down any limitation in relation to the nature or subject-matter of proceedings in which they can be sought, although they tend to be employed predominantly in the commercial sphere. While in theory an order of an unlimited nature can be made, this will often be unnecessary and will inflict disproportionate hardship on a defendant, so in practice a limited order is usually granted which will at least allow retention of sufficient funds to provide for living expenses, or in the case of a company, the costs of its day-to-day running. It has been stressed that the courts should not be too ready to grant relief in the form of a Mareva injunction in the context of an ordinary *bona fide* business transaction, but intervention is justified where an asset is being disposed of at the undervalue to a creditor's detriment, even where an independent valuation has been obtained.[326]

A Mareva injunction operates *in personam*[327] to restrain the defendant from dealing with the assets to which the order relates and it gives the plaintiff no proprietary right over these assets nor priority over other creditors. Therefore the rights of a third party with an interest in an asset will not be prejudiced

---

322. [1975] 2 Lloyd's Rep 509.
323. Considered *infra* in the context of Anton Piller orders.
324. *Den Norske Bank ASA v. Antonatos* [1999] QB 271 and *Memory Corporation v. Sidhu* [2000] 2 WLR 1106.
325. [1982] QB 558, 584 *per* Kerr LJ in *Z. Ltd v. A-Z and AA-LL*.
326. *Customs and Excise Commissioners v. Anchor Foods Ltd* [1999] 1 WLR 1139.
327. Although note the rather ambiguous comments to the contrary of Lord Denning MR in *Z. Ltd v. A-Z and AA-LL* [1982] QB 558, 573.

and it was held by the English Court of Appeal in *Cretanor Maritime Co. Ltd v. Irish Marine Management Ltd*[328] that the plaintiff was not entitled to a Mareva injunction in relation to funds owed by the defendant where a debenture holder had appointed a receiver over those funds. However, once a third party has been notified of an injunction, he will be restrained from dealing with assets in a manner contrary to its terms otherwise he may be in contempt of court. It is therefore in the plaintiff's interest to notify any third parties such as banks who may be holding assets belonging to the defendant of the terms of the order as soon as it is made.

A number of guidelines for determining whether a Mareva injunction should be granted were laid down by Lord Denning MR in *Third Chandris Shipping Corporation v. Unimarine SA*[329] as follows:

(i)   The plaintiff should make full and frank disclosure of all matters in his knowledge which are material for the judge to know. ...

(ii) The plaintiff should give particulars of his claim against the defendant, stating the ground of his claim and the amount thereof, and fairly stating the grounds made against it by the defendant.

(iii) The plaintiff should give some grounds for believing that the defendant has assets here. ...

(iv) The plaintiff should give some grounds for believing that there is a risk of assets being removed before the judgment or award is satisfied. ...

(v)   The plaintiff must, of course, give an undertaking in damages — in case he fails in his claim or the injunction turns out to be unjustified.

A Mareva injunction will usually be sought on an *ex parte* basis and the plaintiff will be required to divulge all material facts to the court and failure to make sufficient disclosure may result in the Mareva injunction being subsequently discharged.[330] As Donaldson LJ commented in *Bank Mellat v. Nikpour*:[331]

The rule requiring full disclosure seems to me to be one of the most fundamental importance, particularly in the context of the Draconian remedy of the Mareva injunction. It is in effect, together with the Anton Piller order, one of the law's two 'nuclear' weapons. If access to such a weapon is obtained without the fullest and frankest disclosure, I have no doubt at all that it should be revoked.

---

328. [1978] 1 WLR 966.
329. [1979] QB 645, 668-669.
330. See *The Assios* [1979] 1 Lloyd's Rep 331 and *Bank Mellat v. Nikpour* [1985] FSR 87.
331. [1985] FSR 87, 92.

A court may vary a Mareva injunction where it is causing undue hardship to allow a defendant to draw down sufficient funds from frozen assets to discharge living expenses and legal fees[332] or upon application by a third party which is affected by the order made by the court.[333] The circumstances in which such a variation will be made were considered by Roderick Murphy J in *Superwood Holdings plc v. Sun Alliance and London Insurance plc*[334] in which the first named plaintiff sought to vary an existing Mareva injunction to pay the taxed costs of a third party. He referred to the *dicta* of Robert Goff J in *A. v. C.*[335] to the effect that the court must be satisfied that there are no other assets available to meet the debt and as Roderick Murphy J stated 'a condition required for such variation is that the applicant has no other funds available'.[336] He also accepted that the court may vary an injunction of this nature on grounds of hardship, either to the defendant himself or to third party creditors of the defendant who are entitled to be paid in the ordinary course of business.[337] While Roderick Murphy J stressed that the authorities relating to the initial grant of injunctive relief and those dealing with variation should be distinguished, he stated that the requirement of full and frank disclosure applies equally to both and in his view it had not been complied with in the circumstances of the application before the court. In addition, he pointed out that the application was not for a variation to enable the plaintiff to pursue a legal appeal in the future but was to facilitate payment of a debt incurred in relation to litigation against a third party in the past. Roderick Murphy J concluded that in the circumstances he would refuse the application for variation on the basis of the evidence before the court.

Prerequisites for the Granting of a Mareva Injunction

Although a Mareva injunction is a form of interlocutory injunction, it has been argued that the strength of the plaintiff's case is more important in Mareva proceedings than where other types of interlocutory order are sought,[338] and there is authority in England to the effect that 'a "good arguable case" is no doubt the minimum which the plaintiff must show in order to cross. ... the "threshold" for the exercise of the jurisdiction.'[339] This standard also seemed

---

332. *Director of Public Prosecutions v. E.H.* High Court (Kelly J) 22 April 1997. See also *Criminal Assets Bureau v. S.H.* High Court 1999 No. 235R (O'Sullivan J) 15 March 2000 where the court made an order varying the terms of a Mareva injunction to allow payment of legal expenses.
333. *Baltic Shipping Co. v. Translink Shipping Ltd* [1995] 1 Lloyd's Rep 673.
334. High Court 1989 No. 7315P (Roderick Murphy J) 25 July 2002.
335. [1981] 2 All ER 126.
336. High Court 1989 No. 7315P (Roderick Murphy J) 25 July 2002 at 8.
337. See also *Powerscourt Estates Ltd v. Gallagher* [1984] ILRM 123, 126.
338. See Capper, *Mareva Injunctions* (1988) p. 34
339. *The Niedersachsen* [1984] 1 All ER 398, 415.

to be required by McWilliam J in *Fleming v. Ranks (Ireland) Ltd*,[340] although he declined to grant a Mareva injunction on the basis of the facts before him.

The standard of proof required has been considered by the High Court in two relatively recent cases. In *Moloney v. Laurib Investments Ltd*,[341] in which the plaintiff sought a Mareva injunction pending the trial of her action against the defendant for damages for personal injuries, Lynch J concluded that the plaintiff had a 'stateable case' against the defendant company and said that it was not appropriate that he should seek to establish anything more regarding the issue of liability at the hearing of the application. However, in the circumstances, Lynch J doubted that the grant of the order sought would improve the plaintiff's prospects of enforcing a judgment in her favour, and having regard to his findings that the grant of such an injunction would cause very serious loss to the defendant which could not be made good if the company were ultimately successful and also bearing in mind the probable prejudice to the rights of its *bona fide* creditors, Lynch J declined to grant the relief sought.

This question was given more extensive consideration by Murphy J in *Countyglen plc v. Carway*,[342] in which he stressed that it would be wrong to require a plaintiff seeking a Mareva injunction to establish as a probability that his claim would succeed. The applicant company brought proceedings against the respondents seeking various orders including a declaration that they had been guilty of fraud and/or conspiracy to defraud, breach of trust and breach of duty and orders pursuant to section 12 of the Companies Act 1990 directing the respondents to repay sums which they had allegedly unlawfully and wrongfully removed from the company. The High Court granted an interim Mareva injunction and the issue of whether to grant an interlocutory order and ancillary relief then came before the court. Murphy J stated that he doubted that there was any significant difference between the expressions 'good arguable case' and 'substantial question to be tried', but he said that if such a distinction could be drawn he would prefer the latter formulation. He confirmed that the 'probability test' had been rejected by the Supreme Court in *Campus Oil* and stated 'in my view, it would be entirely inappropriate for the court on an interlocutory application to review such of the evidence as is available to it and attempt to forecast the outcome of the proceedings as a matter of probability or likelihood. What can and should be done is to determine that there is a fair and serious question to be tried.'[343] Murphy J stated that it was in relation to the risk of the defendant's assets being dissipated in advance of any judgment and also with regard to the general balance of convenience, that considerations different from those pertaining to conventional injunctions arose. On the basis of the evidence available to

---

340. [1983] ILRM 541, 546.
341. High Court 1993 No. 3189P (Lynch J) 20 July 1993.
342. [1995] 1 ILRM 481.
343. *Ibid.* at 487.

the court, Murphy J concluded that the proper inference to draw was that the defendants did have assets within the jurisdiction, that there was a real risk that these assets would be dissipated and that the defendants were not apprehensive of any real inconvenience being caused to them as a result of a Mareva injunction being granted and he made the order sought.

It is interesting to note that in *O'Mahony v. Horgan*,[344] which will be considered in more detail below, the Supreme Court seemed to favour the 'good arguable case' test. While Capper[345] suggests that it may be more difficult to establish this than that there is a serious or substantial question to be tried, he also says that the differences between the two tests should not be exaggerated.[346] In any event, as we will see, it is the other aspects of the proofs required to establish an entitlement to a Mareva injunction which clearly differentiate such applications from those in which an ordinary interlocutory injunction is sought.

A consideration of the balance of convenience between the parties will necessarily involve the weighing up of different factors to those which will normally be of relevance where an interlocutory injunction is sought. In the first instance, the plaintiff will not usually be seeking an injunction at trial, but rather an award of damages which the Mareva order is designed to safeguard. Similarly the question of the adequacy of damages as a remedy, which is often of considerable importance in deciding where the balance of convenience lies, will not be a factor. Instead the court will be required to weigh up the plaintiff's claim for relief against the likelihood of undue hardship or inconvenience being caused to the defendant. Finally, it should be borne in mind that a Mareva injunction, like any other form of equitable remedy, is granted on the basis of equitable principles and at the discretion of the court and will not be made in favour of a plaintiff whose conduct has been questionable in nature.[347]

Before a court will be satisfied that there is a real risk that a defendant is likely to frustrate the court's judgment by disposing of his assets, it will generally be necessary to establish either that they will be removed from the jurisdiction or that they will be dissipated within the jurisdiction.[348] Different considerations obviously apply to an extra-territorial Mareva injunction and these will be considered below. In relation to the risk of removal of assets from the jurisdiction, the defendant's domicile and place of residence or business may be of significance. In *Powerscourt Estates Ltd v. Gallagher*,[349] in which McWilliam J granted a Mareva injunction against the defendants,

---

344. [1995] 2 IR 411.
345. (1995) 17 DULJ (ns) 110.
346. *Ibid.* at 114.
347. *The Assios* [1979] 1 Lloyd's Rep 331, 334 *per* Shaw LJ.
348. See *Larkins v. National Union of Mineworkers* [1985] IR 671, 694.
349. [1984] ILRM 123. See Capper, *op. cit.*, p. 40.

the fact that they were directors of a group of companies many of which were located outside the jurisdiction was relevant as this would have facilitated the removal of assets from the jurisdiction of the Irish courts.

One of the most important issues which must be addressed in the context of Mareva injunctions is the extent to which it is necessary to adduce evidence that the defendant's intention is to frustrate the judgment of the court. This issue was considered by McWilliam J in *Fleming v. Ranks (Ireland) Ltd.*[350] A union issued strike notice and the first defendant announced that its mills would have to close. The plaintiff employees sought a Mareva injunction restraining the defendants from dealing with their assets so as to reduce their value below a certain level. McWilliam J stated as follows:

> I am of opinion that, to justify such an injunction, the anticipated disposal of a defendant's assets must be for the purpose of preventing a plaintiff from recovering damages and not merely for the purpose of carrying on a business or discharging lawful debts.[351]

McWilliam J concluded that the balance of convenience clearly favoured the defendants, both on account of the perishable nature of the goods which they sought to dispose of and having regard to the fact that any undertaking in damages given by the plaintiffs would be of little value. Subsequently, in *Powerscourt*, McWilliam J echoed this view when he stated that a Mareva injunction may be granted where 'it appears to the court that dispositions are likely to be made for the purpose of preventing a plaintiff from recovering the amount of his award, as distinct from conducting the normal business or personal affairs of the defendant'.[352]

This issue has also recently been addressed by the Supreme Court in *O'Mahony v. Horgan.*[353] The applicant had been appointed liquidator of a company of which the respondents were directors. Murphy J granted an interlocutory injunction to restrain the second named respondent from disposing of or dissipating a sum of money payable under an insurance policy. The Supreme Court allowed the appeal of the second named respondent. It held that before a plaintiff will be entitled to a Mareva injunction, he must establish that there is a likelihood that the defendant's assets will be dissipated with the intention that they would not be available to meet any decree ultimately made in the proceedings and found that this intention had not been established in the case before the court. Hamilton CJ stated that:

---

350. [1983] ILRM 541.
351. *Ibid.* at 546. Murphy J also drew attention to this point in *Countyglen plc v. Carway* [1995] 1 ILRM 481, 488 and said that McWilliam J had declined to make the order sought in the *Ranks* case as he accepted that there had been no intention of disposing of assets with a view to evading any obligation to the plaintiff.
352. [1984] ILRM 123, 126.
353. [1995] 2 IR 411.

[T]he cases establish that there must be an intention on the part of the defendant to dispose of his assets with a view to evading his obligation to the plaintiff and to frustrate the anticipated order of the court. It is not sufficient to establish that the assets are likely to be dissipated in the ordinary course of business or in the payment of lawful debts.[354]

Commenting on this decision, Courtney[355] has stated that the Supreme Court has clarified the fact that an applicant for a Mareva injunction must adduce specific evidence of 'the requisite intention' and he is of the view that this requirement will be given greater emphasis in the future. This view would certainly seem to be borne out by two recent High Court decisions. In *Production Association Minsk Tractor Works v. Saenko*[356] McCracken J quoted the above passage from *O'Mahony* and stated that he did not think that there was any evidence before him to establish an intention on the part of the defendants to dispose of assets with a view to evading their obligations to the plaintiff or frustrating the anticipated order of the court. He stressed that a Mareva injunction is 'an extremely drastic remedy' and concluded that the plaintiffs had not satisfied the criteria necessary to succeed in their application. Similarly in *OBA Enterprises Ltd v. TMC Trading International Ltd*[357] Laffoy J quoted the same passage from *O'Mahony* and concluded that in her view the plaintiffs had not adduced evidence to show, or entitle her to infer that the defendant was likely to dissipate its assets with the intention of evading its obligations, if any, to the plaintiffs.

In contrast, the approach of the English courts has tended to focus on the effect of the defendant's actions rather than on his intention. In *The Niedersachsen*[358] Kerr LJ accepted that no 'nefarious intent' was required and said that the plaintiff need only establish a real risk that a judgment in his favour would remain unsatisfied.[359] As Capper[360] has pointed out, it may be unrealistic to expect a plaintiff to be in a position to adduce evidence of a defendant's intentions in this regard in making an *ex parte* application and a more flexible approach may be necessary when a Mareva injunction is sought on this basis, as will usually be the case in practice. In a recent comment on the *O'Mahony* case Capper has reiterated this point stating that 'while the approach in the Irish cases reduces the risk of abuses of the Mareva jurisdiction

---

354. *Ibid.* at 419. Quoted with approval by O'Sullivan J in *Bennett Enterprises Inc. v. Lipton* [1999] 2 IR 221, 228. See also *Aerospares Ltd v. Thompson* High Court 1998 No. 13568P (Kearns J) 13 January 1999 at 4.
355. (1996) 3 Comm LP 3, 8.
356. High Court 1998 No. 869P (McCracken J) 25 February 1998.
357. High Court 1998 No.12535P (Laffoy J) 27 November 1998. See Courtney (1999) 6 Comm LP 39.
358. [1984] 1 All ER 398.
359. See also *Derby & Co. Ltd v. Weldon (Nos 3 & 4)* [1990] Ch 65, 76.
360. *Mareva Injunctions* (1988) p. 48.

it is unrealistic and unfair, especially on an *ex parte* application, to require plaintiffs to show that the defendant *intends* by the disposal of assets to defeat any judgment the plaintiff may obtain'.[361] Capper's suggestion 'that an intention may be inferred from the risk that assets will be disposed of for no good reason'[362] would seem to mitigate the harshness of this evidential requirement and it would seem fair to suggest that provided all the other procedural hurdles have been overcome, this requirement should be applied in a relatively flexible manner. Certainly a more pragmatic approach towards this question has been taken by O'Sullivan J in the recent High Court decision in *Bennett Enterprises Inc. v. Lipton*,[363] discussed in more detail below in the context of extra-territorial Mareva injunctions. He stressed that if any dissipation of assets were to occur in the ordinary course of business, this of itself would not justify the granting of a Mareva injunction and that the anticipated dissipation must be for the purpose of the defendant evading his obligation to the plaintiff. He then went on to state as follows:

> Equally, however, I consider that direct evidence of an intention to evade will rarely be available at the interlocutory stage. I consider it is legitimate for me to consider all the circumstances in relation to the case and I do not consider that this approach is in any way prohibited by or at variance with the principles set out in the Supreme Court judgment in *O'Mahony v. Horgan*.[364]

Initially the Mareva injunction evolved as a remedy against foreign-based defendants who possessed assets within the jurisdiction of the court and while it was thought at one time that such injunctions could only issue against foreign-based defendants, this limitation has been eroded by the courts.[365] So in both *Fleming v. Ranks (Ireland) Ltd*[366] and *Powerscourt Estates v. Gallagher*[367] McWilliam J accepted that the types of cases in which Mareva injunctions may be granted are not confined to those where the defendant is resident outside the State.

By virtue of the provisions of Article 31 of the EC Council Regulation on Jurisdiction and the Recognition and Enforcement of Judgments in Civil and Commercial Matters,[368] an application may be made to the courts of a Member

---

361. (1995) 17 DULJ 110, 117.
362. *Ibid.* at 119.
363. [1999] 2 IR 211. See Courtney (1999) 6 Comm LP 39.
364. *Ibid.* at 228.
365. See e.g. *A.J. Bekhor & Co Ltd v. Bilton* [1981] QB 923.
366. [1983] ILRM 541, 546.
367. [1984] ILRM 123.
368. Council Regulation (EC) No. 44/2001. This article effectively replaces Article 24 of the Brussels Convention on Jurisdiction and the Recognition and Enforcement of Judgments in Civil and Commercial Matters 1968.

State[369] for such provisional measures, including protective measures, as may be available under the law of that state, even if the court of another Member State has jurisdiction in relation to the substance of the matter. Section 13(1) of the Jurisdiction of Courts and Enforcement of Judgments Act 1998 provides that the courts in this jurisdiction have power to grant provisional, including protective, measures – which may include a Mareva injunction – where proceedings have been commenced or are about to be commenced in another contracting state, even where the plaintiff has no independent cause of action within this jurisdiction.[370] A similar provision, namely section 25(2) of the English Civil Jurisdiction and Judgments Act 1982, has recently been fairly broadly interpreted in *Credit Suisse Fides Trust SA v. Cuoghi*.[371] Millett LJ accepted that an ancillary jurisdiction ought to be exercised with caution and that care should be taken not to make orders which conflict with those of the court seised of the substantive proceedings. However, he did not accept that interim relief should be limited to that which would be available in the court trying the substantive dispute.[372] Although the worldwide Mareva injunction sought would not have been available in Switzerland, where the substantive action had been initiated, Millett LJ was satisfied that there was no danger of conflicting jurisdiction and concluded that it was not inexpedient to grant the protective measures sought. Bingham LJ reached the same conclusion and made the following useful comments about the relationship between the substantive proceedings and applications for protective measures:

> It would be unwise to attempt to list all of the considerations which might be held to make the grant of relief under s. 25 inexpedient or expedient, whether on a municipal or a worldwide basis. But it would obviously weigh heavily, probably conclusively, against the grant of interim relief if such grant would obstruct or hamper the management of the case by the court seized of the substantive proceedings ('the primary court') or give rise to a risk of conflicting, inconsistent or overlapping orders in other courts. It may weigh against the grant of relief by this court that the primary court could have granted such relief and has not done so, particularly if the primary court has been asked to grant such relief and declined. On the other hand, it may be thought to weigh in favour of granting such relief that a defendant is present in this

---

369. This regulation binds all Member States with the exception of Denmark and the Brussels Convention continues to apply to relations between Denmark and the other Member States.

370. This effectively reversed the finding of the Supreme Court in *Caudron v. Air Zaire* [1985] IR 716 that a Mareva injunction could not be claimed as primary relief in an action but only as an ancillary order. See also *The Siskina* [1979] AC 210.

371. [1998] QB 818.

372. See also *Motorola Credit Corporation v. Uzan* [2002] EWCA Civ 989 Court of Appeal, 26 June 2002.

country and so liable to effective enforcement of an order made *in personam*, always provided that by granting such relief this court does not tread on the toes of the primary court or any other court involved in the case. On any application under s.25 this court must recognise that its role is subordinate to and must be supportive of that of the primary court.[373]

This reasoning was considered by the Court of Appeal in *Refco Inc. v. Eastern Trading Co.*[374] in which protective measures were refused in circumstances where the court was satisfied that no Mareva relief would have been granted even if the substantive proceedings had been brought in England. Morritt LJ advocated first, considering whether the facts would warrant granting the interim relief sought if the substantive proceedings had been brought within the jurisdiction and, if the answer to that question was in the affirmative, then considering whether the fact that the court had no jurisdiction apart from under the section made it inexpedient to grant the relief sought.

Extra-Territorial Mareva Injunctions

One of the most significant developments in relation to Mareva injunctions in recent years has been the willingness of the courts to make such orders in respect of assets outside the jurisdiction on a worldwide basis.[375] Originally Mareva injunctions were of a more limited nature and as Dillon LJ commented in *Ashtiani v. Kashi*[376] 'the basis of the jurisdiction, as it seems to me, is clearly limited to the assets within the jurisdiction of this court'. The reasons for this practice were far from compelling,[377] and in a series of decisions in the late 1980s, the English Court of Appeal extended the scope of Mareva injunctions to cover worldwide assets. In *Babanaft International Co. SA v. Bassatne*[378] such an order was granted against the defendants who held assets in a number of foreign jurisdictions as well as in England and against whom judgment in the sum of $15 million had been obtained. Kerr LJ concluded that 'in appropriate cases, though they may well be rare, there is nothing to preclude our courts from granting Mareva type injunctions against defendants which extend to their assets outside the jurisdiction.'[379] However, he stressed that unqualified Mareva injunctions covering assets abroad can never be justified as they involve an exorbitant assertion of jurisdiction of an *in rem*

---

373. [1998] QB 818, 831-832.
374. [1999] 1 Lloyd's Rep 159.
375. See generally Capper (1991) 54 MLR 329.
376. [1987] QB 888, 899.
377. See Collins (1989) 105 LQR 262, 269.
378. [1990] Ch 13.
379. *Ibid.* at 28.

nature over third parties outside the jurisdiction of the court. It was therefore necessary to restrict such injunctions so as to bind only the defendant personally and to include a limiting proviso which made it clear that the order would not affect third parties.[380]

Extra-territorial Mareva injunctions are more likely to be granted after judgment has been obtained as the risk that such an order will be made in favour of a party who is wrongly asserting a cause of action is removed and it has been stressed that pre-judgment orders will be granted on a worldwide basis less readily than after trial.[381] In *Republic of Haiti v. Duvalier*[382] the Court of Appeal granted a pre-trial Mareva injunction against the assets of the defendants on a worldwide basis although Staughton LJ stressed that the cases in which it would be appropriate to grant such an injunction were 'rare — if not very rare indeed'.[383] The other notable feature of this decision is that the limiting proviso was extended to the effect that the order should not affect any third parties unless and to the extent that it is enforced by the courts of the state in which the defendants' assets are located. Similarly in *Derby & Co. Ltd v. Weldon*[384] the Court of Appeal granted a worldwide Mareva injunction prior to judgment in view of the large sums of money involved, the insufficiency of assets within the jurisdiction, the existence of foreign assets and the finding that there was a real risk that they would be dissipated before the trial. A point made by the Court of Appeal and subsequently reiterated by it in *Derby & Co. Ltd v. Weldon (Nos. 3 & 4)*[385] is that a Mareva injunction should be limited to assets within the jurisdiction of the court if these are sufficient to meet the plaintiff's claim. However, there will often be insufficient domestic assets or even none at all and the court stressed in the latter case that this will not be a bar to obtaining an order on a worldwide basis.

A further attempt was made by the Court of Appeal in *Derby & Co. Ltd v. Weldon (Nos. 3 & 4)* to clarify the position of third parties by putting forward a modified version of what had become known as the '*Babanaft* proviso'.[386] This new version of the proviso abolished what was seen as the rather artificial distinction drawn between legal and juridicial persons and gave the order extra-territorial effect over persons who were subject to the jurisdiction of the court making the order who had been given written notice of it and who were in a position to 'prevent acts or omissions outside the jurisdiction of this court

---

380. Although it should be noted that Kerr LJ suggested (at 37) that it might be better to add 'unless and to the extent that it is enforced by the courts of the states in which any of the defendants' assests are located.'
381. *Babanaft International Co. SA v. Bassatne* [1990] Ch 13, 40 *per* Neill LJ; *Republic of Haiti v. Duvalier* [1990] QB 202, 214 *per* Staughton LJ.
382. [1990] QB 202.
383. *Ibid.* at 215.
384. [1990] Ch 48.
385. [1990] Ch 65.
386. *Ibid.* at 84.

which assist in the breach of the terms of this order'. This modified proviso was developed further in the decision of *Baltic Shipping Co. v. Translink Shipping Ltd*[387] in which Clarke J suggested that in general and subject to the facts of a particular case, a proviso along the following lines should be adopted,[388] namely, that 'nothing in this order shall, in respect of assets located outside [the jurisdiction], prevent [the third party] or its subsidiaries from complying with…what it reasonably believes to be its obligations, contractual or otherwise under the laws and obligations of the country or state in which the assets are situated or under the proper law of any bank account in question.' This form of proviso, sometimes referred to as the '*Baltic* proviso' has been approved by the Court of Appeal in *Bank of China v. NBM LLC*[389] in upholding a decision to vary a Mareva injunction on the application of a third party by extending the proviso in this way. Tuckey LJ stated that the cases established two general principles, first, that the limits of the court's territorial jurisdiction and the principle of comity require that the effectiveness of freezing orders operating on third parties holding assets abroad should normally derive only from their recognition and enforcement by the local courts and secondly, that third parties amenable to the English jurisdiction should be given all reasonable protection. He concluded that the need to avoid unwanted extra-territorial jurisdiction and to provide reasonable protection for third parties affected by freezing orders will usually entitle them to have a proviso in the form set out above added unless the court considers that on the particular facts it is inappropriate.

The fact that Mareva injunctions may be made on a worldwide basis in this jurisdiction was confirmed by the High Court in *Deutsche Bank Atkiengesellchaft v. Murtagh*.[390] The plaintiff sought an order restraining the defendants from dealing with extra-territorial assets. Costello J was satisfied that 'the court has jurisdiction to restrain the dissipation of extra-territorial assets where such an order is warranted by the facts'. He said that it was well-established in England that a Mareva injunction may extend to foreign assets and that he believed the Irish courts had similar powers to avoid frustration of subsequent orders. It should be noted that the order made a month later by Murphy J in *Countyglen v. Carway*[391] was confined to assets of the defendants within the jurisdiction, but this was the extent of the order sought by the plaintiffs. His comment that a Mareva injunction should be restricted to assets

---

387. [1995] 1 Lloyd's Rep 673.
388. This suggestion was put forward by Saville J, the judge in charge of the Commercial Court, in his end of year statement on 30 July 1993. The relevant part of this statement is set out in *Baltic Shipping Co. v. Translink Shipping Ltd* [1995] 1 Lloyd's Rep 673, 675 and in *Bank of China v NBM LLC* [2002] 1 WLR 844, 849.
389. [2002] 1 WLR 844.
390. [1995] 1 ILRM 381.
391. [1995] 1 ILRM 481.

within the jurisdiction of the court must be viewed as purely *obiter* and it is unlikely that such an approach will be followed in view of the unequivocal approval given by Costello J to orders of an extra-territorial nature.

This is borne out by the approach adopted by O'Sullivan J in *Bennett Enterprises Ltd v. Lipton.*[392] The plaintiffs instituted proceedings against the defendants for breach of contract and sought, *inter alia*, an interlocutory injunction restraining the defendants from reducing the monies in certain trust funds below a stated sum. O'Sullivan J stated that it was clear that the defendants had no assets within the jurisdiction but he did not consider that the plaintiffs' alleged failure to establish that there were assets within the jurisdiction was necessarily fatal to their application. On the contrary, he said that he could see the logic in the observation of Donaldson MR in *Derby & Co. Ltd v. Weldon (Nos. 3 & 4)* to the effect that the fewer the assets within the jurisdiction the greater the necessity for taking protective measures in relation to those outside it. O'Sullivan J also pointed out that in *Babanaft* Kerr LJ had stated that 'some situations, which are nowadays by no means uncommon, cry out — as a matter of justice to plaintiffs — for disclosure orders and Mareva type injunctions covering foreign assets of defendants even before judgment.'[393] The plaintiffs accepted that any order which the court might make would be subject to the '*Babanaft* proviso' and O'Sullivan J concluded that he would make an interlocutory order as sought by the plaintiffs and stated that he would discuss with counsel the precise form of the order.

A further important aspect of Mareva jurisdiction which has particular relevance in the context of worldwide orders, is the power to make ancillary orders, for example requiring disclosure of the defendant's assets. This was adverted to by Ackner LJ in *Bekhor & Co. v. Bilton*,[394] where he stated that the court has power to make 'all such ancillary orders as appear to the court to be just and convenient, to ensure the exercise of the Mareva jurisdiction is effective to achieve its purpose'. Costello J also referred to this power to make ancillary orders in *Deutsche Bank Atkiengesellchaft v. Murtagh* and said that in a suitable case the court will grant a disclosure order requiring the defendant to swear an affidavit in relation to assets outside the jurisdiction. It is certainly in the context of worldwide orders that ancillary powers take on the greatest significance and it may even prove to be of more significant practical importance than the Mareva injunction itself. As Collins[395] has pointed out, if proper disclosure is made in relation to the defendant's foreign assets, the plaintiff will be able to seek an attachment order in relation to these assets in the relevant foreign jurisdiction. The Court of Appeal has recently re-emphasised the importance of disclosure orders in *Gruppo Torras*

---

392. [1999] 2 IR 221. See Courtney (1999) 6 Comm LP 39.
393. [1990] 1 Ch 13, 33.
394. [1981] QB 923, 940.
395. (1989) 105 LQR 262, 297.

SA v. Sheikh Fahad Mohammad Al-Sabah.[396] The plaintiff obtained a Mareva injunction against the defendant together with an ancillary order requiring him to disclose the nature and extent of his assets both in England and abroad. The court rejected the defendant's application to have the disclosure order discharged and reaffirmed the importance of orders of this nature. As Steyn LJ commented, without such ancillary powers, the Mareva injunction itself 'would be a relatively toothless procedure in the fight against rampant transnational fraud'.

Conclusions

In the final analysis the effectiveness of Mareva injunctions, particularly those of an extra-territorial nature, will depend on the extent to which the courts can guarantee their observance. It appears to have been accepted that it would be wrong in principle for the courts in one jurisdiction 'to impose or attempt to impose obligations on persons not before the court in respect of acts to be done by them abroad regarding property outside the jurisdiction' on the basis that this would amount to an attempt to claim an 'exorbitant' extra-territorial authority.[397] However, defendants and in particular third parties will often be outside the jurisdiction of the court which has made the Mareva injunction and so will not be amenable to control by that court. As Collins[398] has commented:

> In practice the remedy is likely to be most effective where the defendant is an individual present within the jurisdiction (or a company with offices within the jurisdiction) or if the defendant has a real interest in defending the substance of the English action or (as the case may be) in appealing the English judgment. It is possible that these are the only cases in which the remedy will be effective, and this may be regarded as a cynical but realistic, conclusion.

The far-reaching and often draconian nature of Mareva injunctions is more readily recognised today than when the jurisdiction was first exercised.[399] However, as against this, the sophisticated fraudulent endeavours which can often extend into numerous different jurisdictions are also becoming increasingly difficult to control. There have been some signs in a recent

---

396. 16 February 1994; (1994) 144 NLJ 932.
397. *Babanaft International Co. SA v. Bassatne* [1990] Ch 13, 44 *per* Nicholls LJ. See also the judgment of Neill LJ at 40.
398. (1989) 105 LQR 262, 296.
399. See e.g. the comments of Hamilton CJ in *O'Mahony v. Horgan* [1995] 2 IR 411, 418 and of McCracken J in *Production Association Minsk Tractor Works v. Saenko* High Court 1998 No. 869P (McCracken J) 25 February 1998 at 5 to the effect that a Mareva injunction is 'an extremely drastic remedy'.

decision of the English Court of Appeal that the judiciary are more willing at present to recognise the former consideration than the latter. In *Polly Peck International plc v. Nadir (No. 2)*,[400] while Millett J found that the plaintiff had shown an arguable case of liability and granted a Mareva injunction, the Court of Appeal concluded that the balance of convenience was against its continuance and discharged the order. Scott LJ stressed that the court will not grant a Mareva injunction before any liability has been established if the injunction would interfere with the normal course of the defendant's business particularly if the cause of action which it was sought to have protected, as in the case before him, was no more than speculative. In his view to grant a Mareva injunction in these circumstances would be 'not simply wrong in principle but positively unfair'.[401] Zuckerman[402] has commented that the approach of the Court of Appeal in *Polly Peck* restores the Mareva jurisdiction to its true basis as a measure against abuse rather than a form of security for the plaintiff. There appeared to be signs in the judgment of Lynch J in *Moloney v. Laurib Investments Ltd*[403] of a willingness to have regard to such considerations in that he appeared to place emphasis on the fact that the grant of the injunction sought would interfere with the normal course of the defendant's business and that it would cause serious loss which could not subsequently be made good if the defendant were ultimately successful. Signs of a more cautious approach are also evident in the Supreme Court decision of *O'Mahony v. Horgan*;[404] as O'Flaherty J commented: 'it needs to be emphasised that the Mareva injunction is a very powerful remedy which if improperly invoked will bring about an injustice, something that it was designed to prevent'. While it is arguable that the requirement of establishing an intention on the defendant's part to dispose of his assets with a view to evading his obligation to the plaintiff and to frustrate the anticipated order of the court imposes too great a burden on plaintiffs, the rationale behind such a requirement is understandable given the potentially far-reaching consequences of granting a Mareva injunction. What is clearly required in such cases is a careful balancing of the rights of both plaintiffs and defendants if this powerful legal weapon is not to be abused.

Anton Piller Orders

Anton Piller orders were developed as a means of dealing with cases where there is a serious risk that a defendant may destroy or otherwise dispose of material in his possession which may be of vital importance to the plaintiff if

---

400. [1992] 4 All ER 769.
401. *Ibid.* at 784.
402. (1992) 108 LQR 559, 561.
403. High Court 1993 No. 3189P (Lynch J) 20 July 1993.
404. [1996] 1 ILRM 161, 170.

he is to establish his claim at a trial.[405] An Anton Piller order requires the defendant to consent to a plaintiff, attended by his solicitor, entering his premises to inspect and if necessary take away any documents or articles specified in the order. As Scott J commented in *Columbia Pictures Incorporated v. Robinson*;[406] 'Anton Piller orders are used to prevent a defendant, when warned of impending litigation, from destroying all documentary evidence in his possession, which might, were it available, support the plaintiff's cause of action.'

Where appropriate an order may include directions that the defendant should provide discovery of documents or answer specified interrogatories. Such an order is obtained on an *ex parte* basis and applications are often heard *in camera*[407] as secrecy will be of the essence if the order is to have the required effect and if the defendant is forewarned he will in all likelihood take steps to frustrate the plaintiff's intentions.[408] As Smyth J made clear in *Microsoft Corporation v. Brightpoint Ireland Ltd*[409] the essence of an Anton Piller order is surprise and the publication of the existence of such an order in advance of its execution can weaken or deprive it of its element of surprise.

This remedy is of particular use in the context of the misappropriation of intellectual property, especially in the areas of infringement of copyright and patents and in relation to the exploitation of trade secrets. The practice of making orders of this nature developed in England in the mid 1970s,[410] and the jurisdiction to do so was confirmed by the Court of Appeal in *Anton Piller KG v. Manufacturing Processes Ltd*,[411] the decision which gave its name to the form of order. The plaintiffs claimed that the defendants were selling confidential information to their competitors which they had obtained in their capacity as selling agents for the plaintiffs' electrical equipment and sought access to documents located on the defendant's premises. The Court of Appeal made an *ex parte* order permitting the plaintiffs to enter the defendant's premises to inspect, remove or make copies of documents relating to the equipment. Lord Denning MR stated as follows:

It seems to me that such an order can be made by a judge *ex parte*, but it

---

405. As Paperny J commented in the decision of the Alberta Court of Queen's Bench in *Capitanescu v. Universal Weld Overlays Inc* (1996) 141 DLR (4th) 751, 757: 'The primary aim of such an order is to preserve evidence to ensure that the pending civil action is not frustrated through lack of evidence'.
406. [1987] Ch 38, 71.
407. S. 45(1) of the Courts (Supplemental Provisions) Act 1961 makes provision for this.
408. See the comments of Templeman LJ in *Rank Film Distributors Ltd v. Video Information Centre* [1982] AC 380, 418.
409. [2001] 1 ILRM 540, 545-546.
410. The first reported decision was in *EMI Ltd v. Pandit* [1975] 1WLR 302.
411. [1976] Ch 55, 61.

should only be made where it is essential that the plaintiff should have inspection so that justice can be done between the parties: and when, if the defendant were forewarned, there is a grave danger that vital evidence will be destroyed, that papers will be burnt or lost or hidden, or taken beyond the jurisdiction, and so the ends of justice be defeated: and when the inspection would do no real harm to the defendant or his case.[412]

In addition, Omrod LJ laid down three 'essential pre-conditions' which must be satisfied before an order of this nature will be granted; namely that the plaintiff must have an extremely strong *prima facie* case, the potential or actual damage must be very serious for the plaintiff, there must be clear evidence that the defendant has incriminating documents or articles in its possession and there must be a real possibility that these will be destroyed before any application *inter partes* can be made.

As Omrod LJ made clear in his judgment, the order operates *in personam* against the defendant and requires him to consent to its execution. While it is not equivalent to a search warrant and cannot be enforced by the plaintiff without the defendant's consent,[413] failure to comply with the order will constitute contempt of court. The terms of an order will usually require that in executing it, the plaintiff or his representatives afford the defendant the opportunity of obtaining legal advice provided that this is done forthwith. In assessing whether delay in complying with the terms of an order will constitute contempt, the courts may take a relatively lenient view, as in *Bhimji v. Chatwani*,[414] in which Scott J stressed that something more than 'a mere technical breach of the obligation to allow entry forthwith' must be shown.

One issue which has provoked controversy is the extent to which a defendant should be penalised for failing to comply with an Anton Piller which is subsequently set aside. In *Hallmark Cards Inc. v. Image Arts Ltd*[415] Buckley LJ stated that, while a defendant who refuses to comply with the terms of an order pending his application to have it set aside, is technically in contempt of court, he did not believe that such a defendant should be liable to any penalties if the order is subsequently discharged. However, in *Wardle Fabrics Ltd v. G. Myristis Ltd*,[416] Goulding J stressed that disobedience of an order constituted contempt even if it was later set aside and in the case before him he required the defendants to meet the cost of the plaintiff's motion for

---

412. *Ibid.* at 61.
413. As Lord Denning MR stated in *Anton Piller KG v. Manufacturing Processes Ltd* [1976] Ch 55, 61 if the defendants refuse the plaintiff permission to enter premises, the plaintiff must not force his way in but should bring this fact to the attention of the court.
414. [1991] 1 WLR 989, 1003.
415. [1977] FSR 150, 153. See also the judgment of Lord Donaldson MR in *WEA Records Ltd v. Visions Channel 4 Ltd* [1983] 1 WLR 721.
416. [1984] FSR 263.

contempt on an indemnity basis. While it cannot be disputed that failure to comply with the terms of an Anton Piller order in whatever circumstances technically amounts to contempt of court and should not be condoned, it is submitted that the courts should be slow to impose penalties where the order is subsequently set aside in view of the potential for abuse inherent in this far-reaching and often draconian form of relief.

In view of this potential for abuse, a plaintiff will be required to give certain undertakings to the court before an Anton Piller order will be granted and, as Browne-Wilkinson VC commented in *Tate Access Floors v. Boswell*,[417] failure to observe these undertakings 'should not be tolerated'. In view of the *ex parte* nature of the application, the plaintiff will be required to make full and frank disclosure of all material facts to the court and failure to do so may result in the order being discharged and a finding of liability in damages being made against the plaintiff. In *Microsoft Corporation v. Brightpoint Ireland Ltd*[418] Smyth J stated that an affidavit in support of an application for an Anton Piller order ought to err on the side of excessive disclosure because in the case of material which falls into the area of possible relevance, the judge and not the plaintiff should decide what is relevant.

As with other forms of orders of an interlocutory nature, the plaintiff will be required to give an undertaking in damages and where he has acted improperly, either in the manner in which he made his application or executed the order, the court will not hesitate to enforce this undertaking or to award both compensatory and aggravated damages. This point is illustrated by the judgment of Scott J in *Columbia Picture Industries v. Robinson*[419] in which the plaintiffs brought proceedings against the defendants for breach of copyright relating to an alleged video piracy operation. The plaintiffs obtained an Anton Piller order but failed to disclose all material facts in making their application and in executing it they removed items not included in its terms. The defendants then brought a motion seeking to have the order set aside and Scott J found that the plaintiffs and their solicitors had failed to make full and frank disclosure of all material matters to the court and had acted oppressively and in abuse of their powers in executing the order. He made a finding that no purpose would be served by setting aside the order as it had already been executed but held that the plaintiffs were liable in damages to the defendants who had ceased trading as a result. Scott J was clearly acutely aware of the potential for abuse inherent in Anton Piller orders as can be seen from the following extract from his judgment:

> [A] decision whether or not an Anton Piller order should be granted requires a balance to be struck between the plaintiff's need that the

---

417. [1991] Ch 512.
418. [2001] 1 ILRM 540, 545-546.
419. [1987] Ch 38.

remedies allowed by the civil law for the breach of his rights should be attainable and the requirement of justice that a defendant should not be deprived of his property without being heard. What I have heard in the present case has disposed me to think that the practice of the court has allowed the balance to swing much too far in favour of plaintiffs and that Anton Piller orders have been too readily granted and with insufficient safeguards for respondents.

The draconian and essentially unfair nature of Anton Piller orders from the point of view of respondents against whom they are made requires, in my view, that they be so drawn as to extend no further than the minimum extent necessary to achieve the purpose for which they are granted, namely the preservation of documents or articles which might otherwise be destroyed or concealed.[420]

In *Microsoft Corporation v. Brightpoint Ireland Ltd*[421] Smyth J had to consider, *inter alia*, an application brought by the defendant for reliefs arising out of the grant and execution of an Anton Piller order. On the facts Smyth J stated that he was satisfied that there had been full and proper disclosure by the plaintiff as to the circumstances of the case and that there was strong *prima facie* evidence of dishonest conduct by the defendants which indicated a strong probability that they would destroy records. In relation to the defendant's argument that the Anton Piller order had been oppressively executed, Smyth J stated that the conflict of evidence as to what had happened in the course of its execution could only be resolved by an oral hearing and that he was not disposed to set the order aside given this conflict. Smyth J concluded on the basis of the documentary evidence before him that the making of the Anton Piller order had been justified and that the subsequent conduct of the plaintiff in the case was not such as could be regarded as contemptuous or as to warrant the relief sought by the defendant.

Capper has commented on the options facing a defendant when confronted with an Anton Piller order which he believes should not have been granted.[422] First, he may refuse to allow the order to be executed until he has had an opportunity to apply to the court for its discharge. This may be a potentially dangerous course of action as the defendant's refusal to comply with the order immediately constitutes contempt of court, although if the application to discharge the order is successful this will not necessarily have serious consequences. The second possibility is to apply for the order to be discharged

---

420. *Ibid.* at 76. The views of Scott J were subsequently echoed by Hoffmann J in *Lock International plc v. Beswick* [1989] 1 WLR 1268, 1281 in which the latter stressed that there must be proportionality between the perceived threat to the plaintiff's rights and the remedy granted.
421. [2001] 1 ILRM 540.
422. (1998) 49 NILQ 210.

after it has been executed, which is what happened in the *Columbia* case. However, as Capper points out, this is often of questionable value as the damage will already have been done, and the defendant will usually simply be seeking to force the plaintiff to comply with his undertaking in damages. The third option, which can be pursued where a plaintiff fails to serve a statement of claim or otherwise proceed with the action after the execution of an order, is for a defendant to apply for dismissal of the plaintiff's action. This option was recently followed by the plaintiffs in the Northern Irish case of *Group 4 Securitas (Northern Ireland) Ltd v. McIldowney*[423] which was decided by Girvan J. The defendant succeeded in obtaining a dismissal of the plaintiffs' action following the execution of an Anton Piller order even though the plaintiffs were only two weeks late in delivering their statement of claim. Nothing of substance had been found as a result of the execution of the order and, as Capper has commented, 'in giving the plaintiffs precious little indulgence, Girvan J was clearly (and rightly it is submitted) influenced by a desire to warn practitioners and litigants against using the draconian remedy of the Anton Piller order in this way'.[424]

Another factor which has tended to swing the balance back in favour of defendants in recent years has been the increasingly frequency with which the privilege against self-incrimination has been invoked. This issue was considered by the House of Lords in *Rank Film Distributors Ltd v. Video Information Centre*,[425] in which it was held that a defendant could invoke this privilege to resist the making of an Anton Piller order. The appellants believed that unauthorised persons had pirated copies of their films and were selling videos of them and sought relief including Anton Piller orders which required the respondents, *inter alia*, to disclose certain information relating to these video cassettes. It was held by the House of Lords that disclosure of the information sought by the appellants would tend to expose the respondents to a charge of conspiracy to defraud and that there was no way in which the court could compel disclosure while at the same time protecting the respondents from the consequences of self-incrimination.[426]

---

423. [1997] NIJB 23.
424. (1998) 49 NILQ 210, 212.
425. [1982] AC 380.
426. In the area of copyright infringement, film companies have generally tended to choose the alternative method of informing the gardaí of their suspicions of video piracy, which is a criminal offence. Pursuant to s. 143 of the Copyright Act 2000, where a district judge is satisfied that there are reasonable grounds for suspecting that a copyright offence has been or is about to be committed, a warrant may be issued authorizing the gardaí to search premises and seize material. In practice, such a procedure is regarded as being preferable to seeking an Anton Piller order as it does not involve the copyright owner in any expense and entry can be enforced. In addition, in most video piracy cases, the defendant is unlikely to be in a position to pay damages even if the plaintiff succeeds in a civil action, and a criminal prosecution is perceived to be a more effective means of closing down the operation. It should be noted that

Lord Russell pointed out in the course of his judgment that because the privilege against self-incrimination could largely deprive the owner of copyright of his right to the protection of his property, legislation in this area would be desirable. This privilege was withdrawn in England by section 72 of the Supreme Court Act 1981 in proceedings to obtain disclosure of information relating to the infringement of rights in the area of intellectual property which provided that matters disclosed would not be admissible in evidence against the defendant in proceedings against him for a related offence.[427] However, the privilege can still be invoked in other forms of action and as the decision of Browne-Wilkinson VC in *Tate Access Floors v. Boswell*[428] shows, it can still provide a most effective weapon in a defendant's fight against the application of Anton Piller orders. In *Tate*, the plaintiffs alleged that the individual defendants who had formerly been senior employees of theirs had in the course of their employment fraudulently obtained large sums from the plaintiffs and had created the defendant companies specifically for the purpose of fraudulently invoicing the plaintiffs. The individual defendants had then allegedly authorized payments to the invoicing companies for their own benefit. The plaintiffs were granted worldwide Mareva injunctions against all the defendants and Anton Piller orders compelling the defendants to disclose their assets and permitting the plaintiffs to enter premises to search and seize relevant documents. The defendants sought to have these orders set aside and while Browne-Wilkinson VC refused to discharge the Mareva injunctions, he did set aside the Anton Piller orders against the individual defendants. He held that the privilege against self-incrimination could properly be invoked in a case involving discovery in a fraud action where, as in the case before him, on the facts alleged by the plaintiff there was a real risk that a defendant might be prosecuted for conspiracy in the jurisdiction and the documents and information sought by the order might be incriminating.[429] Browne-Wilkinson VC stated that it was not wholly clear from the decision in *Rank Film* whether

---

an order may also be made by the District Court on the application of a copyright owner under s. 132 of the Copyright Act 2000 authorising the gardaí to seize infringing copies or articles without warrant and in addition, pursuant to s. 133, a copyright owner, in limited circumstances and subject to certain conditions, may seize infringing copies or articles where it would be impracticable to apply to the District Court under s. 132.

427. See also s. 434(5) of the Companies Act 1985, s. 291 of the Insolvency Act 1986 and s. 2 of the Criminal Justice Act 1987 in England. As Lord Templeman commented in *A.T. & T. Istel Ltd v. Tully* [1993] AC 45, 55: 'Parliament has thus recognised the unsatisfactory results of the common law privilege against self-incrimination and has been willing to abrogate or modify that privilege'.

428. [1991] Ch 512.

429. It was accepted that there was no real risk of the corporate defendants which were overseas companies being prosecuted for conspiracy in England and it was held that the individual defendants could not object to the order made against the companies as there was no privilege against self-incrimination by a third party.

it had been held that the privilege against self-incrimination applied to the search and seizure aspects of an Anton Piller order. However, he confirmed that in the case before him, the privilege applied both to those parts of the order which required the defendants to produce and verify information and that part which required them to permit the plaintiffs to search their premises and seize material.

There have been signs of a growing judicial awareness in England of the 'profoundly unsatisfactory'[430] nature of this privilege and in *A.T. & T. Istel Ltd v. Tully*[431] the House of Lords, while acknowledging that it could only be altered by parliament, found that there was no reason to allow a defendant in civil proceedings to rely on the privilege, thus depriving a plaintiff of his rights, where the defendant's position could be adequately safeguarded by other means. In addition, it can be seen from the decision in *IBM (UK) Ltd v. Prima Data International Ltd*[432] that a plaintiff may avoid the difficulties which emerge from *Rank Films* and *Tate* where an Anton Piller order contains a proviso which clearly safeguards a defendant's right to claim the privilege and if the order is not executed until he has been told of this right and expressly declines to claim it. However in proceedings which do not come within the ambit of the statutory exceptions the risk that a defendant may be able to invoke successfully the privilege against self-incrimination to frustrate the plaintiff's attempts to safeguard evidence to support his claim will remain.[433] This problem is even more marked in this jurisdiction where the common law privilege against self-incrimination remains unaffected by legislation cutting down its effect. While there have been few cases involving Anton Piller orders in which written judgments have been delivered in this jurisdiction,[434] such orders are being sought with increasing frequency and legislative intervention to at least curtail the common law privilege may well be necessary if these orders are to be effective. The issue was raised but did not have to be determined in *Microsoft Corporation v. Brightpoint Ireland Ltd*[435] in which the defendant contended that the plaintiffs through their agents had failed to advise the defendant of its privilege against self-incrimination. However, given the assertion made on the defendant's behalf that the company was complying with the law, Smyth J stated that the issue of self-incrimination could not arise and he found that this was therefore not a basis for setting aside the Anton Piller order in the circumstances.

430. *A.T. & T. Istel Ltd v. Tully* [1993] AC 45, 53 *per* Lord Templeman. See also *Den Norske Bank ASA v. Antonatos* [1999] QB 271, 295 *per* Waller LJ.
431. [1993] AC 45.
432. [1994] 1 WLR 719.
433. See *A.T. & T. Istel v. Tully* [1993] AC 45.
434. See *Microsoft Corporation v. Brightpoint Ireland Ltd* [2001] 1 ILRM 540 and *Jobling-Purser v. Jackman* High Court 1992 No. 3808P (Carroll J) 27 July 1999.
435. [2001] 1 ILRM 540, 545-546.

In an English context, Dockray and Laddie[436] have suggested that unless the ambit of section 72 is extended, Anton Piller jurisdiction will to a large extent become incapable of being exercised and they comment that in their view something more than 'limited legislative tinkering'[437] is required. They quite rightly suggest that if legislation in this area is introduced it should also tackle the thorny question of potential abuse of this jurisdiction by plaintiffs and it would certainly appear that the 'inherently oppressive'[438] nature of the order is now more readily acknowledged by the judiciary. It is interesting to note that reference was made to some of their suggestions by Nicholls VC in *Universal Thermosensors Ltd v. Hibben.*[439] While the issues in the case relating to the oppressive manner in which an Anton Piller order granted to the plaintiff was executed had been settled during the course of the trial of the action, Nicholls VC clearly felt that the procedure lent itself 'too readily to abuse' and laid down a number of safeguards in relation to the execution of Anton Piller orders which he felt should be observed. In his view such orders should only be executed during working hours and if executed at a private house and where it is at all likely that a woman may be in the house alone, the solicitor serving the order must be, or must be accompanied by, a woman.[440] He also suggested that unless seriously impracticable, a detailed list of items removed from the premises should be prepared which the defendant should be given an opportunity to check at the time and that the order should not be executed at business premises in the absence of a responsible company representative unless there is good reason for so doing. Nicholls VC also recommended that, pursuing the suggestion made by Dockray and Laddie, judges should give serious consideration to the desirability of providing that the order should be served and its execution supervised by an experienced solicitor familiar with the workings of such orders other than a member of the firm of solicitors acting for the plaintiff and that a summary *inter partes* review of the manner in which the order is executed should then be conducted by the court. He concluded by saying that 'if plaintiffs wish to take advantage of this truly draconian type of order, they must be prepared to pay for the safeguards which experience has shown are necessary if the interests of defendants are fairly to be protected.'[441] Whether the suggestions made by Nicholls VC will be fully taken up in England remains to be seen, although as Davenport[442] has

---

436. (1990) 106 LQR 601.
437. *Ibid.* at 603.
438. *Bhimji v. Chatwani* [1991] 1 WLR 989, 1002 *per* Scott J.
439. [1992] 1 WLR 840.
440. Note that in Ireland there may be constitutional difficulties in executing an Anton Piller order at a private house in view of Article 40.5 of the Constitution which provides that: 'The dwelling of every citizen is inviolable and shall not be forcibly entered save in accordance with law.'
441. [1992] 1 WLR 840, 861.
442. (1992) 108 LQR 555.

commented they should 'if followed ... go far towards correcting some of the more undesirable features of the manner in which this draconian order has been put into effect.'

The issue of the type of guidelines which should be followed in executing an Anton Piller order has received little judicial attention in this jurisdiction, although in *Microsoft Corporation v. Brightpoint Ireland Ltd*[443] a point was raised in relation to whether the plaintiff should be required to provide a list of the items and documents seized. Smyth J commented that while it might have been a sensible thing at the time of the inspection for an agreed list or inventory of the items taken to have been made and signed, there was no obligation on the plaintiffs to provide a list as requested by the defendant. However, he said that as there was an obligation to preserve all copies of documents taken under the Anton Piller order, the furnishing of a list was a courtesy which should have been accorded. In this regard Smyth J stated that the law on this issue was properly put by Scott J in *Columbia Picture Industries Inc. v. Robinson*[444] where the latter had said that it is essential that a detailed record of the material taken should be made by a solicitor executing an Anton Piller order before the material is removed from the premises.

Bayer Injunctions

As Fox LJ stated in *Bayer AG v. Winter*,[445] 'the law in relation to the grant of injunctive relief for the protection of a litigant's rights pending the hearing of an action has been transformed over the past ten years by the Anton Piller and Mareva relief' and he added that 'the court should not shrink, if it is of opinion that an injunction is necessary for the proper protection of a party to the action, from granting relief, notwithstanding it may be, in its terms, of novel character'. The 'novel' injunctive relief to which the *Bayer* decision gave its name is an order which restrains a defendant from leaving the jurisdiction and will usually be granted in circumstances where an existing Mareva injunction or Anton Piller order has not been complied with. In the *Bayer* case the plaintiffs claimed that the defendants were distributing a counterfeit product and although the plaintiffs had obtained Mareva and Anton Piller injunctions they were afraid that the defendant would evade the effect of these orders by leaving the jurisdiction. The Court of Appeal held that it had jurisdiction to grant the order sought, Fox LJ stating that 'the court has a wide discretion to do what appears to be just and reasonable in the circumstances of the case.'[446] Fox LJ relied on the *dicta* of Cumming-Bruce LJ in *House of Spring Gardens Ltd v. Waite*[447] to the effect that 'the court has the power ... to take such steps as are

---

443. [2001] 1 ILRM 540, 545-546.
444. [1987] Ch 38, 76.
445. [1986] 1 WLR 497, 502.
446. *Ibid.* at 502.
447. [1985] 11 FSR 173, 183.

practicable upon an application of the plaintiff to procure that where an order has been made that the defendants identify their assets and disclose their whereabouts, such steps are taken as will enable the order to have effect as completely and successfully as the powers of the court can procure'. Fox LJ added that if such an order caused embarrassment or hardship to the defendant, he could apply to the High Court forthwith to seek its variation or discharge. He suggested that the order should be of very limited duration and should be in force for no longer than was necessary to enable the plaintiffs to serve the Mareva and Anton Piller orders which they had obtained and to endeavour to obtain from the defendant the information referred to in those orders.

It should be noted that it is clear from the decision of Wilson J in *B. v. B.*[448] that the power to grant a '*Bayer* injunction' is an ancillary jurisdiction. So, while the court may grant an order to restrain a debtor from leaving the jurisdiction as an aid to its established procedures for the enforcement of a judgment, this type of order may not be used as a freestanding enforcement procedure in it own right. Wilson J stressed that there was no general power to detain a foreign debtor within the jurisdiction until the debt was paid and refused to grant an injunction to a wife to restrain her husband from leaving the jurisdiction until he had paid a sum outstanding under a costs order made arising out of family law proceedings between the parties.

The principles set out in *Bayer* were considered and applied recently in this jurisdiction in *O'Neill v. O'Keeffe*.[449] The first named plaintiff had invested monies through the first named defendant who offered himself as a personal investment manager with particular expertise in trading foreign debt instruments through banks based in Switzerland. When the plaintiff sought repayment of his investment he failed to obtain it and he was apprehensive that his investment monies either had been or might be in the process of being dissipated or misappropriated altogether. On 1 February 2002, O'Higgins J made a number of orders on an *ex parte* basis including a Mareva injunction and an Anton Piller order to permit the plaintiff's solicitors to search a premises and seize listed items from it. Entry to the named premises to execute the Anton Piller order could not be effected. The plaintiff then sought to continue the existing reliefs and also sought an order that the defendant, whose whereabouts were unknown, be restrained from leaving the jurisdiction until a named date, and a further order that he deliver up his passport or other travel documents to the plaintiff's solicitors. Kearns J stated that it was clear from the decision in *Bayer* that the jurisdiction to make an injunction of this nature derived from the requirement to make court orders effective and was analogous to a disclosure order in aid of Mareva relief. However, he said that it went without saying that such relief could be granted in this jurisdiction

---

448. [1998] 1 WLR 329.
449. [2002] 2 IR 1.

only in 'exceptional and compelling circumstances'.[450] Any order of this nature was *prima facie* in breach of the constitutional right to travel, placing that right in abeyance for the specified period. However, Kearns J acknowledged that the right to travel might be curtailed in some instances and he referred to the decision of the High Court in *Lennon v. Ganly*[451] in which O'Hanlon J had stated that the defendants 'should only be restrained from exercising such right [to travel] if it was in some way unlawful for them to act in the manner in which they seek to act.' Kearns J stated that given that leaving the State with the intention of defrauding one's creditors was a criminal offence under section 124 of the Bankruptcy Act 1988, this requirement was capable of being met on the facts established on affidavit. He added that he was happy to adopt the criteria for granting such relief as enumerated by Courtney in *Mareva Injunctions*[452] where the author stated that such an injunction should only be granted where:

(1) The court is satisfied that there is probable cause for believing that the defendant is about to absent himself from the jurisdiction *with the intention* of frustrating the administration of justice and/or an order of the court.

(2) The jurisdiction should not be exercised for *punitive* reasons; a defendant's presence should be required in order to prevent a court hearing or process or existing order from being rendered nugatory.

(3) The injunction ought not to be granted where a lesser remedy would suffice.

(4) The injunction should be *interim* in nature and limited to the shortest possible period of time.

(5) The defendant's right to travel should be out-balanced by those of the plaintiff and the proper and effective administration of justice,

(6) The grant of the injunction should not be futile.

Kearns J concluded that he was satisfied that the case before him required the making of the orders sought both in relation to the restriction on the defendant leaving the country and in requiring him to hand over his passport. He added that a very substantial sum of money was unaccounted for in circumstances which gave rise to considerable suspicion and that he had a very real apprehension that the defendant might be about to absent himself from the jurisdiction with the intention of frustrating the orders of the court.

---

450. *Ibid*. at 7.
451. [1981] ILRM 84.
452. (1998) p. 457.

CHAPTER 14

Specific Performance

GENERAL PRINCIPLES

Where a court makes an order for specific performance, a party to a contract is compelled to carry out his contractual obligations.[1] As with the equitable remedy of the injunction, this remedy was developed by the Court of Chancery to provide relief where common law remedies were inadequate or inappropriate and is based on the principle that a person should be entitled to have that which he has contracted for rather than merely an award of damages. If a claim for specific performance is to be entertained, it is essential to prove that a valid and enforceable contract exists between the parties[2] for which consideration has been provided. The terms of this contract must also be sufficiently certain before a court will decree performance and the onus lies on the plaintiff to establish this.[3] At one time it was felt that the expression 'specific performance' presupposed the existence of an executory as opposed to an executed agreement.[4] However, the Privy Council has made it clear[5] that there is no reason why the 'equitable right to specific relief' should be governed by any different considerations in relation to executed as opposed to executory agreements and the distinction would not appear to be of practical significance in this jurisdiction.[6]

Specific performance of a contract will not be granted where the plaintiff has an adequate remedy at common law; as Lord Selborne stated in *Wilson v. Northampton and Banbury Junction Railway Co.*:[7] 'The court gives specific

---

1. See generally Farrell, *The Irish Law of Specific Performance* (1994) for a comprehensive examination of all aspects of this remedy. See also Jones and Goodhart, *Specific Performance* (2nd ed., 1996).
2. *Holohan v. Ardmayle Estates* Supreme Court 1966 No. 60, 1 May 1967 *per* Walsh J at 4.
3. *Williams v. Kenneally* (1912) 46 ILTR 292, 294 *per* Barton J.
4. *Wolverhampton and Walsall Rly Co. v. London & North-Western Railway Co.* (1873) LR 16 Eq 433, 439 *per* Lord Selborne LC.
5. *Australian Hardwoods Pty Ltd v. Commissioner for Railways* [1961] 1 All ER 737, 743 *per* Lord Radcliffe.
6. Keane, *Equity and the Law of Trusts in the Republic of Ireland* (1988) p. 244 and Farrell, *The Irish Law of Specific Performance* (1994) p. 3.
7. (1874) 9 Ch App 279, 284.

performance instead of damages, only when it can by that means do more perfect and complete justice.' It has come to be recognised that a more 'complete' form of relief can be afforded to a plaintiff by granting a decree for specific performance in certain types of situations e.g. in relation to a contract for the sale of land and that equally some forms of contract such as those that might involve a degree of supervision do not easily lend themselves to this type of remedy.

The Discretionary Nature of the Remedy

Like all equitable remedies, specific performance is granted only on a discretionary basis. So, the court has a discretion to refuse to make an order for specific performance where, e.g. a plaintiff comes to court otherwise than with clean hands.[8] However, the exercise of this discretion must not be arbitrary or capricious[9] and it is 'governed as far as possible by fixed rules and principles'.[10] This view has been echoed in numerous cases and as Romilly MR pointed out in *Haywood v. Cope*[11] 'what one person may consider fair another person may consider very unfair' and there must be some settled principles upon which to determine how this discretion is to be exercised. These points were well summarised as follows by Black LJ in *Conlon v. Murray*:[12]

> The remedy of specific performance still retains the character of an equitable remedy. It is not granted as of right but is a discretionary remedy which may be withheld in cases of a type where the court, having regard to the conduct of the parties and all the circumstances of the case considers in its discretion that the remedy ought not to be granted. This discretion is not, of course, the arbitrary discretion of the individual judge but is a discretion to be exercised on the principles which have been worked out in a multitude of decided cases.

---

8. *Kavanagh v. Caulfield* High Court 1999 No. 9769P (Roderick Murphy J) 19 June 2002 at 11.
9. *Smelter Corporation v. O'Driscoll* [1977] IR 305, 310-311.
10. *Lamare v. Dixon* (1873) LR 6 HL 414, 423.
11. (1858) 25 Beav 140, 151.
12. [1958] NI 17, 25. See also the *dicta* of Haugh J in *Nolan v. Graves* [1946] IR 376, 391 where he emphasised that the jurisdiction to grant specific performance must be exercised with discretion and care and the recent *dicta* of Lord Hoffmann in *Co-Operative Insurance Co. Ltd v. Argyll Stores (Holdings) Ltd* [1998] AC 1, 16 to the effect that the grant or refusal of specific performance remains a matter for the judge's discretion and that while there are no binding rules governing the exercise of this discretion, this does not mean that there cannot be settled principles to guide the court.

Despite his clear acceptance of the proposition that the discretion to grant or withhold the remedy of specific performance must be exercised in accordance with settled principles, Black LJ rejected the suggestion that the types of cases in which the remedy will be refused should be categorised in any rigid manner.

Before examining in more detail some of the categories of contract which may be specifically enforced by the court, it is worth considering a few general principles which are observed in deciding whether to grant relief. First, the courts have traditionally been loathe to grant specific performance of contracts which would require supervision, principally contracts to build and repair and contracts for services. While it has been accepted in both types of situation that this is not an inflexible rule,[13] it has certainly proved to be a relevant factor when a court is determining whether specific performance will lie.[14] Secondly, it is well accepted that an order of this nature will not be granted where to make it would be futile, e.g. if a plaintiff seeks specific performance of a lease for a term that has already expired,[15] or even where the lease is determinable by the defendant. Also for this reason, specific performance of a partnership agreement determinable at will would not be granted as it would not place the plaintiff in a more beneficial position. Similarly, in *Tito v. Wadell (No. 2)*[16] Megarry VC declined to make the order of specific performance sought by the plaintiff to replant specified portions of an island with particular crops as it was highly unlikely that they would grow successfully and because of problems relating to access, harvesting them would be difficult if not impossible. He concluded that he did not think that 'the court ever should, in its discretion, make an order which it is convinced would be an order of futility and waste'.[17]

Damages in Lieu of or in Addition to Specific Performance

Section 2 of the Chancery Amendment Act 1858, better known as Lord Cairns' Act, conferred power on the Court of Chancery to award damages either in addition to or in substitution for, specific performance. Since the enactment of the Judicature (Ireland) Act 1877 jurisdiction has been conferred on the courts to make an award of damages in any case where this could have been done previously under common law, and often where it is felt that an order of specific performance is not a suitable remedy in the circumstances, a plaintiff will have a claim for damages at common law. However it is in situations where a plaintiff may have no legal remedy that the jurisdiction conferred by

---

13. *Lift Manufacturers Ltd v. Irish Life Assurance Co. Ltd* [1979] ILRM 277, 280; *Hill v. C.A.Parsons & Co. Ltd* [1972] Ch 305.
14. See further *infra* pp. 561-569.
15. *Walters v. Northern Coal Mining Co.* (1855) 5 De GM & G 629, 639.
16. [1977] Ch 106. See particularly pp. 326-327.
17. *Ibid.* at 327.

Lord Cairns' Act is of such significance, e.g. where a contract for the sale of land has not been evidenced in writing as required by the Statute of Frauds but may be enforceable in equity because there have been acts of part performance.[18] In order for a court to exercise this jurisdiction, there must be present 'all those ingredients which would enable the Court, if it thought fit, to exercise this power and decree specific performance'.[19] It is important to stress that damages may not be granted in equity where there is no valid contract which could be specifically enforced but are usually awarded where the court decides on discretionary grounds that damages are a more appropriate form of relief. As Finlay CJ observed in *O'Neill v. Ryan (No. 3)*[20] there may well be cases where the courts will decide 'it is not fair to specifically perform this contract; we will award damages instead.' So where delay has occurred, insufficient to establish the defence of laches, a plaintiff may on discretionary grounds be confined to a remedy in damages.[21] Equally where specific performance is no longer possible where e.g. another agreement is accorded priority over that which a plaintiff seeks to enforce, damages will be the appropriate remedy.[22]

It seems clear from the decision of the House of Lords in *Johnson v. Agnew*[23] that where damages are available both at common law and under Lord Cairns' Act they should be assessed on the same basis. Finally it should be noted that damages may also be awarded in addition to an order of specific performance and this jurisdiction may be exercised whenever the court believes it to be necessary to do so.[24]

SPECIFIC PERFORMANCE OF PARTICULAR TYPES OF CONTRACT

Contracts for the Sale of Land

An order of specific performance is often sought in relation to contracts for the sale of land. While it cannot be said that a plaintiff is entitled to a decree in these circumstances because of the discretionary nature of the remedy, in practice an order will usually be granted provided that a valid contract which complies with the necessary statutory formalities exists, and it has been stated that the onus lies on the defendant to establish why the remedy should be

---

18. See *infra* pp. 554-558.
19. *Ferguson v. Wilson* (1866) 2 Ch App 77, 91 *per* Cairns LJ.
20. [1992] 1 IR 166, 196.
21. *White v. McCooey* [1976-77] ILRM 72; *Lark Developments Ltd v. Dublin Corporation*, High Court 1992 No. 2888 P (Murphy J) 10 February 1993 at 14-15.
22. *O'Connor v. McCarthy* [1982] IR 161, 178 *per* Costello J.
23. [1980] AC 367.
24. *Grant v. Dawkins* [1973] 3 All ER 897. See also *Duggan v. Allied Irish Building Society* High Court 1974 No 2302 P (Finlay P) 4 March 1976 at 16.

refused in such cases.[25] It is generally accepted that land is unique and will have a special value to a purchaser and that he cannot be adequately compensated by an award of damages which would enable him to buy other property instead.[26]

It is important to emphasise that to successfully seek an order of specific performance of a contract for the sale of land, it is necessary to comply with certain requirements. In the first instance there must be a valid contract made for consideration. Once this is established, there must be compliance with section 2 of the Statute of Frauds (Ireland) 1695 which requires that there be a note or memorandum in writing of the contract signed by the person to be charged or by someone authorised by him to do so,[27] or there must be some good reason why equity will not insist on compliance e.g. where to insist on compliance would facilitate a fraud or where sufficient acts of part performance can be established.[28] As Barron J stated in *Jodifern Ltd v. Fitzgerald*[29] in relation to contracts for the sale of land: 'In a claim for specific performance, a plaintiff must establish the making of an enforceable concluded agreement. Where the agreement is a verbal one, the plaintiff must establish not only the concluded agreement but also the existence of a note or memorandum of the agreement signed by the defendant or his agent.' However, as Henchy J made clear in the course of his judgment in *Lynch v. O'Meara*,[30] if the negotiations between the parties have not culminated in a contract, the plaintiff's claim for specific performance will fail, 'not for want of the statutory evidence necessary for the enforcement of a contract for the sale of lands, but simply in default of the existence of any such contract.'[31]

It is clear that there cannot be a concluded agreement unless everything which the parties intend to be covered by the contract has been either expressly or impliedly agreed.[32] Uncertainty has surrounded the issue of whether certain

---

25. *McCrystal v. O'Kane* [1986] NI 123, 132; *Broughton v. Snook* [1938] Ch 505, 513.
26. There is authority in Canada to support the view that where land is bought for investment or resale that an award of damages would provide adequate compensation, see Jones and Goodhart, *Specific Performance* (2nd ed., 1996) p. 130, n. 8. However authority in Australia, *Pianta v. National Finance and Trustees Ltd* (1964) 38 ALJR 232 and the dissenting judgment of Sir Garfield Barwick in *Loan Investment Corporation of Australasia v. Bonner* [1970] NZLR 724, 745, supports the view that the motive of the purchaser should be irrelevant to the question of whether specific performance should be granted. See also [1984] Conv 130.
27. As Ross J stated in *Lord Bellew's Estate* [1921] IR 174, 176 the purpose of the statutory requirement is to guard against fraud and provide for a 'definite kind of proof' before the agreement can be enforced.
28. It is necessary for the defendant to plead absence of writing, and technically speaking if he does not, it cannot act as a bar to specific performance.
29. [2000] 3 IR 321, 330.
30. Supreme Court 1974 No. 12, 8 May 1975. Quoted with approval by Geoghegan J in *Supermacs Ireland Ltd v. Katesan (Naas) Ltd* [2000] 4 IR 273, 288.
31. *Ibid.* at 4.
32. *Supermacs Ireland Ltd v. Katesan (Naas) Ltd* [2000] 4 IR 273, 288 *per* Geoghegan J.

matters, for example the the payment of a deposit, must be addressed in order for there to be a concluded and complete agreement. In *Boyle v. Lee*[33] Finlay CJ suggested that the amount of a deposit to be made is too important a part of a contract for the sale of land to be omitted from a concluded oral agreement unless the parties had agreed that no deposit would be paid. However, as Hardiman J pointed out in *Supermacs Ireland Ltd v. Katesan (Naas) Ltd*[34] this statement represented a considerable development of what the position in this regard had previously been and earlier decisions[35] suggested that it was not essential for a concluded agreement that there should be a stipulation in relation to a deposit. Hardiman J suggested that while there is no doubt that an agreement in relation to the matter of a deposit is usual in contracts for the sale of land, there was at least scope for the contention that a deposit may not be considered essential and he added that it was also arguable that the opinion expressed by Finlay CJ in *Boyle v. Lee* did not represent the view of the majority in that case. The better view would certainly seem to be that it is not essential that a term in relation to the payment of a deposit must invariably be included in order for there to be a concluded agreement and the crucial question must be whether everything that there is evidence the parties intended to include in the contract has been addressed.[36]

A further but less controversial issue is whether there must be agreement on a completion date in order for there to be a concluded contract. In his judgment in *Boyle v. Lee*[37] Egan J stated that 'it has long been established that where no time for performance is agreed the law implies an undertaking by each party to perform his part of the contract within a time which is reasonable having regard to the circumstances of the case'. Hardiman J agreed in *Supermacs Ireland Ltd v. Katesan (Naas) Ltd*[38] that this 'is a long standing and, to my knowledge, unchallenged statement of the law'.

It is important to distinguish the issues which arise in relation to the question

---

33. [1992] 1 IR 555, 571.
34. [2000] 4 IR 273, 279. Geoghegan J also considered the *dicta* of Finlay CJ in *Boyle v. Lee* [1992] 1 IR 555, 571 and stressed (at 286) that it was important to bear in mind that the former Chief Justice in considering the issue of agreement on a deposit was dealing only with the question of whether there was a concluded agreement and not with the question of whether there was a sufficient note or memorandum to satisfy the Statute of Frauds. See also the *dicta* of Geoghegan J in *Shirley Engineering Ltd v. Irish Telecommunications Investments plc* High Court 1997 No. 8063P, 2 December 1999 at 12 and of O'Sullivan J in *Higgins v. Argent Developments Ltd* High Court 1998 No. 13446P, 1 February 2002 at 19.
35. *Barrett v. Costello* High Court 1973 No. 703P (Kenny J) 13 July 1973; *Black v. Kavanagh* (1974) 108 ILTR 91.
36. So, as Geoghegan J pointed out in *Supermacs Ireland Ltd v. Katesan (Naas) Ltd* [2000] 4 IR 273, 286-287 if the evidence is that there is going to be a deposit but the amount of it is still to be negotiated, there cannot be a concluded agreement.
37. [1992] 1 IR 555, 593.
38. [2000] 4 IR 273, 280.

of whether a concluded agreement has been reached from those which must be addressed in considering whether there is a valid note or memorandum of the agreement to satisfy the requirements of section 2 of the Statute of Frauds (Ireland) 1695. As Geoghegan J stated in *Supermacs Ireland Ltd v. Katesan (Naas) Ltd:*[39] 'Only the "material terms" need be included in a note or memorandum for it to be sufficient but all the terms, whether they be important or unimportant, must be agreed before there can be a concluded agreement.'

In order to comply with the requirements of the Statute of Frauds, the note or memorandum must be in writing and signed by the person to be charged or by someone authorised by him to do so.[40] In addition, it must contain all the essential or material terms of the agreement,[41] and it has been suggested that what is essential or material in this context must be considered primarily from the point of view of the parties themselves.[42] The essential terms for the purpose of satisfying the statutory requirement have been described as 'the parties, the property and the consideration' but not the 'terms which the general law would imply'.[43] Consideration has been given in some cases to whether other terms, such as the amount of a deposit, should be required to be set out in a note or memorandum in order for it to be valid. While what is material must depend on the circumstances of any given case, in *Shirley Engineering Ltd v. Irish Telecommunications Investments plc*[44] Geoghegan J stated that he did not think that the amount of the deposit was an essential term in the sense that it had to be included in a note or memorandum. In addition, in *Supermacs Ireland Ltd v. Katesan (Naas) Ltd*[45] Geoghegan J stated that if there is an implied term as to a deposit it is well established that there is no need for it to be expressed in the note or memorandum. He added that even if there had been, which there was not, an express agreement as to the amount of the deposit, there would 'still be plenty of room for argument' that it does not have to be referred to in the note or memorandum as it might not be regarded in the circumstances as a material term.

---

39. [2000] 4 IR 273, 286.
40. Examples of cases where a sufficient note or memorandum has been held to exist include *McCarter & Co. Ltd v. Roughan* [1986] ILRM 447; *Kavanagh v. Delicato* High Court 1989 No. 7536P (Carroll J) 20 December 1996; *Higgins v. Argent Developments Ltd* High Court 1998 No. 13446P (O'Sullivan J) 1 February 2002.
41. [1992] 1 IR 555, 588, *per* O'Flaherty J; *Higgins v. Argent Developments Ltd* High Court 1998 No. 13446P (O'Sullivan J) 1 February 2002 at 20.
42. *Stinson v. Owens* N.I. High Court 1973 noted 107 ILTSJ 239, *per* Lord MacDermott LCJ quoted by Geoghegan J in *Shirley Engineering Ltd v. Irish Telecommunications Investments plc* High Court 1997 No. 8063P, 2 December 1999 at 13. As Geoghegan J stated, the authorities establish that 'essential terms' means in this context ' the kind of terms that would always be regarded as essential, together with any special added terms which the parties in the particular case regarded as essential.'
43. *Godley v. Power* (1961) 95 ILTR 135, 145.
44. High Court 1997 No. 8063P (Geoghegan J) 2 December 1999 at 12.
45. [2000] 4 IR 273, 297.

Another important prerequisite of a valid note or memorandum of an agreement is set out by Keane J in his judgment in *Mulhall v. Haren*[46] namely that either read alone or with other documents which can properly be read with it, it must contain a recognition, express or implied, of the existence of the oral contract sought to be enforced. Similar views were expressed by Finlay CJ in *Boyle v. Lee*[47] where he stated that a note or memorandum is not sufficient to satisfy the requirements of the statute 'unless it directly or by very necessary implication recognizes, not only the terms to be enforced, but also the existence of a concluded contract between the parties'.

A further related issue which has caused considerable controversy over the years is the effect of the inclusion of the words 'subject to contract' in any note or memorandum which is put forward to satisfy the requirements of the Statute of Frauds. Keane J put forward his view in *Mulhall v. Haren*[48] in the following terms: 'A letter, which expressly states that a transaction is "subject to contract" cannot be a sufficient note or memorandum, since the use of those words is normally inconsistent with the existence of a concluded contract.' He added that it was only in 'certain rare and exceptional circumstances' such as those which arose in *Kelly v. Park Hall School Ltd*[49] that the words could be treated as being of no effect. Subsequently in *Boyle v. Lee*[50] Finlay CJ reiterated this point stating that no note or memorandum which contains any term such as 'subject to contract' can be sufficient for the purposes of satisfying the statutory requirement even if it can be established with certainty that the expression did not form part of the original orally concluded agreement.[51] However, some doubt may have been cast on this position by the *dicta* of a number of Supreme Court judges in recent decisions. In *Supermacs Ireland Ltd v. Katesan (Naas) Ltd*[52] Hardiman J stated that it was plainly arguable that the use of the phrase 'subject to contract' did not preclude the existence of a 'done deal' between the parties. However, it should be

---

46. [1981] IR 364, 391. Quoted with approval by Morris J in *Aga Khan v. Firestone* [1992] ILRM 31, 43. See also the *dicta* of Barron J in *Jodifern Ltd v. Fitzgerald* [2000] 3 IR 321, 331 to the effect that 'there cannot be a valid note or memorandum in writing of an agreement when at the same time such note or memorandum denies that any such agreement exists'.
47. [1992] 1 IR 555, 574. See also *Shirley Engineering Ltd v. Irish Telecommunications Investments plc* High Court 1997 No. 8063P (Geoghegan J) 2 December 1999 at 11.
48. [1981] IR 364, 391.
49. [1979] IR 340.
50. [1992] 1 IR 555. See also the *dicta* of O'Flaherty J (at 588) that expressions like 'subject to contract' are *prima facie* a strong declaration that a concluded agreement does not exist.
51. *Ibid.* at 574. Finlay CJ added that in so far as the decision in *Kelly v. Park Hall School Ltd* [1979] IR 340 appeared to amend the note or memorandum by deletion by reference to the evidence of the oral agreements previously arrived at between the parties, it was not a decision which he thought the Supreme Court should follow.
52. [2000] 4 IR 273, 281. See also the *dicta* of Geoghegan J at 297.

borne in mind that the case before the Supreme Court concerned an application to dismiss a claim as being unsustainable and Hardiman J added that in so far as it was contended that the plaintiffs were estopped by the use of the phrase from asserting a completed agreement, this seemed to him to be a matter for evidence at the trial. In *Jodifern Ltd v. Fitzgerald*[53] Barron J suggested that while a party might head any letter or other form of writing with the phrase 'subject to contract' when he wished to negotiate but not enter into an enforceable contract, he added that if these words are not placed at the head of the letter but are contained in the body of the document 'it is a matter of construction of the writing as a whole whether it is intended to deny the existence of a concluded agreement.' However, in the next paragraph Barron J went on to say that there cannot be a valid note or memorandum of an agreement when at the same time the note or memorandum denies that any such agreement exists. Whether the overall effect of this *dicta* will be to undermine the clear statement of the Supreme Court's position on this question in *Boyle v. Lee* remains to be seen but it is obviously undesirable that this element of uncertainty has been reintroduced. One solution advocated by O'Flaherty J in *Boyle v. Lee*[54] is the amendment of the Statute of Frauds to provide that all contracts for the sale of land should be in writing.[55] However, in the meantime it is to be hoped that the uncertainty created by the *dicta* of the members of the Supreme Court in both *Supermacs* and *Jodifern* may be put to one side in a decision where the issue of the validity of a note or memorandum purporting to satisfy the requirements of the Statute of Frauds is central to the case.

Often where an oral agreement is reached between parties, there may be no sufficient note or memorandum to satisfy the requirements of the Statute of Frauds and equity is faced with the dilemma of insisting on strict compliance with the formalities or allowing alternative evidence of the agreement in order to prevent the perpetration of a fraud. It is a well-established principle that a statute may not be used as an instrument of fraud and in the exercise of this equitable jurisdiction, the courts will prevent a defendant from relying on non-compliance with the statutory formalities where to do so would amount to fraud. Equally, a plaintiff may be able to obtain specific performance in the absence of a sufficient note or memorandum of an agreement by invoking the equitable doctrine of part performance which allows a plaintiff to rely on his own actions as evidence of the existence of an agreement. The rationale behind the operation of this doctrine was set out by Chatterton VC in *Hope v. Lord Cloncurry*[56] where he stated as follows:

---

53. [2000] 3 IR 321, 331.
54. [1992] 1 IR 555, 589.
55. As in England, see the provisions of s. 2(1) of the Law of Property (Miscellaneous Provisions) Act 1989.
56. (1874) IR 8 Eq 555, 557.

The principle upon which the rule in cases of part performance was engrafted on the Statute of Frauds is, that it would be a fraud on the part of the person who had entered into an agreement by parol for a lease or sale, to turn around and say that it did not legally exist.

Similarly in *Lowry v. Reid*[57] Andrews LJ stated that the issue is 'whether the plaintiff has an equity arising from part performance which is so affixed upon the conscience of the defendant that it would amount to a fraud on his part to take advantage of the fact that the contract is not in writing.' The right to relief rests not so much on the contract as on what has been done in pursuance of it. There a mother undertook to make a will leaving her son two farms and thereby induced him to sell his farm to his brother. She made a will in those terms but subsequently revoked it leaving the plaintiff son with only a life interest. It was held that he was entitled to specific performance and that there were acts of part performance sufficient to take the case out of the reach of the statute.

It would appear, despite some suggestions to the contrary,[58] that the doctrine of part performance applies to all cases in which a court would entertain a claim for specific performance if the contract had been in writing and it is not confined to agreements for the sale of land.[59] This point would seem to have been confirmed in this jurisdiction by Palles CB in *Crowley v. O'Sullivan*.[60] However, in practice the vast majority of cases in which the doctrine will be relied upon concern contracts for the sale of land.

The point was made by the House of Lords in *Maddison v. Alderson*[61] that 'the acts relied upon as part performance must be unequivocally, and in their own nature, referable to some such agreement as that alleged.' A less strict requirement set out in *Fry on Specific Performance*[62] and approved by Andrews LJ in *Lowry v. Reid*[63] is that 'the operation of acts of part performance seems only to require that the acts in question be such as must be referred to some contract, and may be referred to the alleged one'. This view appears to have been accepted by the majority of the House of Lords in *Steadman v. Steadman*[64] where it was suggested that it would be sufficient if the acts of part performance in question were, on the balance of probabilities, referable to some contract and not inconsistent with the contract in fact entered into.

---

57. [1927] NI 142, 154-155. See also the *dicta* of Lord Redesdale in *Bond v. Hopkins* (1802) 1 Sch & Lef 413, 433.
58. *Britain v. Rossiter* (1879) 11 QBD 123.
59. *McManus v. Cooke* (1887) 35 Ch D 681, 697 *per* Kay J.
60. [1900] 2 IR 478, 489-92. See also *Lowry v. Reid* [1927] NI 142, 157.
61. (1883) 8 App Cas 467.
62. (6th ed., 1921), p. 278.
63. [1927] NI 142, 159.
64. [1976] AC 536.

This question was also considered by Keane J in *Silver Wraith Ltd v. Siúicre Éireann Cpt*[65] where he stated *obiter* that the acts should be 'unequivocally referable to the type of contract alleged'.[66] It has also recently been addressed by the Supreme Court in *Mackie v. Wilde*[67] in which Barron J gave detailed consideration to the circumstances in which the doctrine of part performance operates. In his view '[w]hat is required is that the acts relied upon as being acts of part performance be such that on examination of the contract which has been found to have been concluded and to which they are alleged to refer show an intention to perform that contract'.

In *Mackie* the plaintiff and the first named defendant were the owners of a joint fishery on rivers in Co. Donegal. The original rules for the operation of the fishery had been laid down in an indenture but the plaintiff was dissatisfied with the arrangements relating to the number of people who could fish on the rivers and the parties met with a view to reaching agreement about the number of annual licences and daily tickets which would be issued. Subsequently correspondence took place between the parties in which the plaintiff sought to obtain the defendant's written agreement to the limiting of the number of licences for the fishery. The plaintiff then instituted proceedings claiming that there was a binding agreement that each party would be limited to the granting of 25 annual licences and submitted that there had been part performance on foot of the agreement. Costello P held that a concluded agreement to this effect had been reached and that an additional term relating to the number of day tickets which could be granted had also been agreed upon. He therefore ordered that the first named defendant be restrained from issuing more than 25 annual licences and ten day tickets and this finding was appealed to the Supreme Court. The defendants submitted that the trial judge had been incorrect in finding that there had been a concluded agreement and that there were no sufficient acts of part performance to make the agreement enforceable. Barron J accepted the first submission and concluded that a concluded agreement had not been reached. It remained for him to consider whether there had been sufficient acts of part performance. He quoted extensively from the speech of Lord Simon in *Steadman v. Steadman* and from those of Lord O'Hagan and the Earl of Selborne LC in *Maddison v. Alderson* in relation to the nature of the doctrine and the acts which could be relied upon to constitute part performance. Barron J stated that ultimately the court is seeking to ensure that a defendant is not, in relying upon statute, 'breaking faith' with the plaintiff. He stated that the doctrine of part performance is based on three things; the acts on the part of the plaintiff which are said to have been in part performance of the concluded agreement,

---

65. High Court 1987 No. 6178 P (Keane J) 8 June 1989 at 12.
66. See Farrell, *op. cit.* pp. 138-140 for a more detailed consideration of this question.
67. [1998] 2 IR 578.

the involvement of the defendant with respect to such acts and the oral agreement itself. Barron J stated that ultimately what is essential is that:

(1) there was a concluded oral contract;

(2) the plaintiff acted in such way which showed an intention to perform that contract;

(3) the defendant induced such acts or stood by while they were being performed; and

(4) it would be unconscionable and a breach of good faith to allow the defendant to rely on the terms of the Statute of Frauds to prevent performance of the contract.[68]

Barron J stated that it is more logical to find out what the parties had agreed since in the absence of a concluded agreement there is no point in seeking to find acts of part performance. As noted above, he stated that the doctrine requires that the acts relied upon as being acts of part performance should be such that on an examination of the contract which has been found to have been concluded and to which they are alleged to refer, they show an intention to perform the contract. He also said that in the earlier cases it had been assumed that the acts of part performance must necessarily relate to and affect land and nothing which he had said should be taken to suggest a modification of that position. Barron J continued by saying that the detriment to the plaintiff must be the result of what the plaintiff does with the defendant standing by and not detriment to the plaintiff as a result of what the defendant does with the plaintiff standing by. Barron J concluded that there was nothing in what was alleged which would in any way render it a breaking of faith with the plaintiff for the defendant to plead the Statute of Frauds. He therefore held that even if there had been a concluded oral agreement as claimed, there were no acts on the part of the plaintiff which showed an intention to perform the alleged contract.

As Spry[69] has stated it should also be emphasised that 'an act of part performance must be judged, not in the abstract, but in the light of all the material circumstances, in order to establish whether it is sufficiently unequivocal'. The acts upon which a plaintiff seeks to rely in establishing part performance must be his own acts and not those of the defendant, although often an action such as the taking and giving of possession of land may be attributable to both parties. This is one of the most common acts of part performance in practice, and another common example, particularly in relation to an agreement for a lease, is the carrying out of improvements or alterations

---

68. *Ibid.* at 587.
69. *The Principles of Equitable Remedies* (6th ed., 2001) p. 280.

to property.[70] In *Starling Securities Ltd v. Woods*[71] McWilliam J held that entry onto land and the demolition of buildings thereon constituted sufficient acts of part performance.

While traditionally payment of purchase money was not a sufficient act of part performance,[72] this view must now be re-assessed in the light of the approach followed by the majority of the House of Lords in *Steadman v. Steadman*.[73] As Lord Reid stated: 'to make a general rule that payment of money can never be part performance would seem to me to defeat the whole purpose of the doctrine and I do not think that we are compelled by authority to do that.'[74] In that case the House of Lords held that payment of arrears of maintenance by a husband to his wife and the incurring of other costs such as those involved in the sending of a transfer agreement to her were sufficient acts of part performance of a compromise reached between the parties whereby she would sell him her interest in the family home. Subsequently, McWilliam J in his judgment in *Howlin v. Thomas F. Power (Dublin) Ltd*[75] said that he could not disagree with the reasoning of the majority in *Steadman* but stressed that the application of the doctrine was still confined to cases where it would be fraudulent or inequitable for a defendant to rely on the statute.

Finally, it should be noted that in England, the equitable doctrine of part performance is no longer recognised and section 2(1) of the Law of Property (Miscellaneous Provisions) Act 1989 now provides that contracts for the sale of land must be in writing. Some slight doubt on this issue remained as a result of the *dicta* of Neill LJ in *Singh v. Beggs*[76] in which he stated that the doctrine is an equitable one and 'it may be that in certain circumstances [it] could be relied on'.[77] However, as Swann[78] pointed out, it has generally been assumed that section 2 succeeded in giving effect to the policy of abolishing the doctrine of part performance;[79] as he comments 'the doctrine had become uncertain and confused and its abolition was a deliberate policy choice'.[80] The fact that the doctrine of part performance did not survive the enactment of section 2 of the Act of 1989 has been confirmed by Robert Walker LJ in the course of his judgment in *Yaxley v. Gotts*.[81]

---

70. *Rawlinson v. Ames* [1925] Ch 96.
71. High Court 1975 No. 4044P 24 May 1977.
72. *Clinam v Cooke* (1802) 1 Sch & Lef 22, 40-41; *Maddison v. Alderson* (1883) 8 App Cas 467, 478-9.
73. [1976] AC 536.
74. *Ibid*. at 541.
75. High Court 1977 No.736P (McWilliam J) 5 May 1978.
76. (1996) 71 P & CR 120.
77. *Ibid*. at 122. However, Neill LJ went on to reject the claim that the plaintiff's conduct could amount to part performance.
78. [1997] Conv 293.
79. See e.g. *Firstpost Homes Ltd v. Johnson* [1995] 1 WLR 1567, 1571.
80. [1997] Conv 293, 295.
81. [2000] Ch 162, 172. However, it should be noted that an oral contract relating to an

Before leaving this area, it is worth noting that specific performance may also be granted in relation to the assignment of a leasehold interest, or in relation to an option to purchase or re-purchase land. While traditionally specific performance of a lease of property for a short period or of a contractual licence to occupy land would not be granted, this would seem to no longer be the case. So in *Verrall v. Great Yarmouth Borough Council*,[82] the Court of Appeal granted specific performance of a contractual licence allowing the National Front to hold its annual conference in the defendant's hall.

Contracts for the Sale of Personal Property or to Pay Money

As a general principle a court will not exercise its discretion to award specific performance where damages would be an adequate remedy. Therefore as a rule specific performance will not be granted in relation to a contract for the sale of goods because a breach of such a contract will usually be adequately remedied by an award of damages. However it is important to stress that specific performance will not be refused merely because the object at the centre of the dispute is a chattel,[83] and where the item in question is of 'unusual beauty, rarity and distinction',[84] an order to enforce the contract specifically may be made. Often goods will fall into this category because of their rarity or antiquity, as for example, an Adam door in a house.[85]

A further question which it has been suggested a court should ask itself is whether the object in question is of 'peculiar and practically unique value'[86] to the individual concerned. This involves a more subjective approach which may not always be followed and perhaps a better test would be to ask whether an award of damages would 'place the disappointed buyer or seller in as good a position as delivery of the article or receipt of the price'.[87]

There is certainly authority to suggest that specific performance will be refused where the subject matter of the contract is an 'ordinary article ... of commerce and of no special value or interest'. This point was made by McCardie J in *Cohen v. Roche*[88] in which he refused to order specific performance of a contract to deliver up eight Hepplewaite chairs and held that the plaintiff's remedy should be confined to damages for breach of

---

interest in property was held by the Court of Appeal to be enforceable on the basis of a constructive trust under s.2(5) of the Law of Property (Miscellaneous Provisions) Act 1989 in circumstances where the doctrines of part performance or proprietary estoppel might previously have been relied upon.
82. [1981] QB 202.
83. *Falcke v. Gray* (1859) 4 Drew 651, 657-658.
84. *Ibid.* at 658.
85. *Phillips v. Lamdin* [1949] 2 KB 33.
86. *Behnke v. Bede Shipping Co. Ltd* [1927] 1 KB 649, 661.
87. *Dougan v. Ley* (1946) 71 CLR 142, 150 *per* Dixon J.
88. [1927] 1 KB 169, 181.

contract. McCardie J also appeared to lay emphasis on the fact that the chairs were bought by the plaintiff 'in the ordinary way of his trade for the purpose of ordinary resale at a profit'.[89] While arguably this fact may be relevant as it will often suggest that an alternative to the item or items contracted for may be readily available, this will not always be the case and the question of whether the goods at issue are freely available elsewhere would seem to be a better test. While this approach was not accepted by the Court of Appeal in *Societe des Industries Metallurgiques SA v. Bronx Engineering Co. Ltd*,[90] in which an order of specific performance was refused despite the urgent need for the object in question and the likely delay in procuring an alternative, it is submitted that if the question of the adequacy of damages is properly applied, the availability of the goods should be of primary concern. This approach was followed by Goulding J in *Sky Petroleum Ltd v. VIP Petroleum Ltd*[91] albeit in the context of the grant of an injunction, where he granted an interlocutory injunction to restrain the defendant from withholding supplies of petrol from the plaintiff at a time when these were limited and the plaintiff would have had little chance of finding an alternative supplier.

It should be noted that section 52 of the Sale of Goods Act 1893 confers a discretion on a court to order specific performance of a contract for the sale of goods provided these are 'specific' or 'ascertained'. It was suggested by Lord Hanworth MR in *Re Wait*[92] that the section adds nothing to the equitable jurisdiction of the courts in this area and an examination of the case law would tend to confirm this view. Certainly in *Sky Petroleum Ltd v. VIP Petroleum Ltd* Goulding J granted what amounted in substance to an order that a contract be specifically performed in respect of a commodity which might have been said to have been neither specific nor ascertained and the statutory power would seem to be in some respects less flexible than the equitable discretion which exists in this context.

The concept of free availability is also relevant in relation to contracts for the sale of shares or other securities. It would seem to be accepted on the authority of the *dicta* of Shadwell VC in *Duncuft v. Albrecht*[93] that a contract for the purchase of shares which 'are not always to be had in the market' and are therefore not readily obtainable may be specifically enforced. However this principle does not apply if 'anyone can go and buy them'[94] and damages will clearly be an adequate remedy where the purchaser can easily obtain the same amount of identical shares or securities elsewhere. One qualification to this principle is that even where the shares are freely available on the market,

---

89. *Ibid.* at 179.
90. [1975] 1 Lloyd's Rep 465.
91. [1974] 1 WLR 576.
92. [1927] 1 Ch 606.
93. (1841) 12 Sim 189, 199.
94. *Re Schwabacher* (1908) 98 LT 127, 128 *per* Parker J.

specific performance may be granted where the contract is for the sale of a quantity of shares which would give a controlling interest in a company,[95] or where it concerns a substantial holding which may alter the outcome of a takeover battle.[96]

As a general principle a contract to pay or lend money cannot be specifically enforced as damages will provide an adequate remedy.[97] However, where the contract is for the payment of an annuity or other periodic amount, or where the contract requires the payment of a sum to a third party, specific performance may be ordered.[98]

Contracts Requiring Supervision

Traditionally, the courts have been most unwilling to order specific performance of a contract which would require supervision on an ongoing basis; as Dixon J stated in *J.C. Williamson Ltd v. Lukey and Mulholland*:[99] 'specific performance is inapplicable when the continued supervision of the Court is necessary in order to ensure the fulfilment of the contract'. This principle could be said to underlie the courts' traditional reluctance to order specific performance of a contract to carry on a business,[100] and is also a significant factor where it is sought to enforce contracts to build and repair and for services.

One of the main authorities illustrating equity's dislike of granting specific performance of contracts requiring supervision is the decision of the Court of Appeal in *Ryan v. Mutual Tontine Westminster Chambers Association*.[101] The lease of a flat in a block of flats contained a covenant to the effect that the lessors should provide a porter who was 'constantly in attendance'. The lessors

---

95. *Dobell v. Cowichan Copper Co. Ltd* (1967) 65 DLR (2d) 440.
96. *Pernod Ricard Comrie plc v. FII (Fyffes) plc* High Court 1988 No. 8388 P (Costello J) 21 October 1988 and Supreme Court 1988 No. 345, 11 November 1988.
97. *Loan Investment Corporation of Australasia Pty Ltd v. Bonner* [1970] NZLR 724.
98. *Beswick v. Beswick* [1966] Ch 538. While there is some doubt about whether a contract to pay a lump sum to a third party as opposed to a periodic payment would be specifically enforced, the better view is that it should, as the plaintiff in these circumstances is liable to recover only nominal damages. It should also be noted that in England, the provisions of s. 1(5) of the Contracts (Rights of Third Parties) Act 1999 now provides that 'there shall be available to a third party any remedy that would have been available to him in an action for breach of contract if he had been a party to the contract (and the rules relating to damages, injunctions, specific performance and other relief shall apply accordingly).'
99. (1931) 45 CLR 282, 297-298. Quoted by Lord Hoffmann in *Co-Operative Insurance Society Ltd v. Argyll Stores (Holdings) Ltd* [1998] AC 1, 12.
100. *Co-Operative Insurance Society Ltd v. Argyll Stores (Holdings) Ltd* [1998] AC 1. However, see *Wanze Properties (Ireland) Ltd v. Five Star Supermarket Ltd* High Court (Costello P) 24 October 1997.
101. [1893] 1 Ch 116.

appointed a person who was frequently absent but the plaintiffs failed in their action for specific performance of the covenant on the basis that it would require 'constant superintendence by the court'.[102] More recent authorities would suggest that the difficulty of supervising the enforcement of contracts of this nature should not be a bar to specific performance but merely one of the factors to be taken into account in determining whether relief should be granted and a modification of the traditional position can be seen in the decision of Mervyn Davies J in *Posner v. Scott-Lewis*.[103] The defendants owned a block of flats and the terms of the lease between them and the tenants contained a covenant that they would employ a resident porter. The person employed as a porter ceased to be resident in the building and the plaintiff tenants brought an action for specific performance of the covenant. Mervyn Davies J agreed that the arrangements which had been made were insufficient to ensure compliance with the clause in the lease and held that there had been a breach of covenant. He stated that the requirement that the defendants employ a resident porter required little superintendence and decided to grant an order of specific performance in the circumstances. Mervyn Davies J listed the factors which in his opinion should be considered in deciding whether specific performance should be granted in such cases. First, it must be asked whether there is a sufficient definition of what has to be done in order to comply with the order of the court.[104] Secondly, the question of whether enforcing compliance would involve superintendence by the court to an unacceptable degree must be addressed, and thirdly, the prejudices or hardships which would be suffered by the parties if the order is made or not made must be considered. Therefore it would appear that where the terms of the obligation are sufficiently precisely defined and specific performance would seem to be the fairest remedy in the circumstances, it may be granted provided the order would not require an unacceptable degree of superintendence.

The issue of enforcing contracts which would require constant supervision has recently been examined in detail by the House of Lords in *Co-Operative Insurance Society Ltd v. Argyll Stores (Holdings) Ltd*.[105] The plaintiff landlord sought specific performance of a covenant in a lease requiring the defendant, which was the anchor tenant in a shopping centre, to keep its supermarket premises open for retail trade during usual business hours for the duration of the lease. The trial judge refused to order specific performance on the basis that there was a settled practice that an order which would require a defendant

---

102. *Ibid.* at 123 *per* Lord Esher.
103. [1987] Ch 25.
104. See also the *dicta* of Megarry VC in *Tito v. Wadell (No. 2)* [1977] Ch 106, 322 to the effect that 'the real question is whether there is a sufficient definition of what has to be done in order to comply with the order of the court'.
105. [1998] AC 1. See further Jones [1997] CLJ 488; Phang (1998) 61 MLR 421; McMeel (1998) 114 LQR 43; Tettenborn [1998] Conv 23; Luxton [1998] Conv 396.

to run a business would not be made but the majority of the Court of Appeal ordered that the covenant be specifically performed. Leggatt and Roch LJJ were satisfied that the contract defined the tenant's obligations with sufficient precision to enable it to know what was required to comply with the order and both seemed to be heavily influenced by the fact that the defendant had acted 'with gross commercial cynicism'.[106] Millett LJ, who dissented, was satisfied that the existence of a practice not to grant specific performance in such circumstances was beyond dispute and also pointed to the fact that to compel a defendant to carry on a business which it considered was not commercially viable would be to expose it to 'potentially large, unquantifiable and unlimited losses which may be out of all proportion to the loss which his breach of contract has caused to the plaintiff'.[107] The House of Lords allowed the defendant's appeal and reversed the decision of the Court of Appeal to grant specific performance of the covenant in the lease. Lord Hoffmann referred to the fact that the 'settled and invariable practice'[108] not to order a person to carry on a business had never been examined by the House of Lords[109] and proceeded to examine the rationale underlying it in some detail. He stated that the practice is not entirely dependant on damages being an adequate remedy[110] and that the most frequent reason given is that such orders would require constant supervision by the court. Lord Hoffmann pointed out that there has been some misunderstanding about what is meant by continued superintendence; supervision would in practice take the form of rulings by the courts and he said that it was the possibility of the court having to give an indefinite series of rulings in order to ensure the execution of the order which has been regarded as so undesirable. This was because the only means available to the court to enforce its order was punishment for contempt and this weapon was often so powerful as to be unsuitable as an instrument for resolving such disputes. Lord Hoffmann went on to distinguish between orders which require a defendant to carry on an activity such as running a business and orders which require him to achieve a result and stated that the possibility of repeated applications for rulings on compliance which arises in the former case does

---

106. [1996] Ch 286, 295 *per* Legatt LJ.
107. *Ibid.* at 304.
108. *Per* Slade J in *Braddon Towers Ltd v. International Stores Ltd* [1987] 1 EGLR 209, 213.
109. Phang has commented (1998) 61 MLR 421, 423 that the principle is 'so well entrenched . . . that it is seldom analysed and instead, is often repeated almost as a ritual incantation'.
110. McMeel has commented (1998) 114 LQR 43, 45 that both the dissenting judgment of Millett LJ and the speech of Lord Hoffmann make it clear that the true test is one of 'appropriateness of relief' and that the adequacy of damages is only one factor to be taken into account. Similarly Jones has stated [1997] CLJ 490 that 'the formula of "adequacy of damages" is a chameleon one; specific performance should be granted if it is the more appropriate remedy'.

not exist to anything like the same extent in the latter. A further objection, which would apply in either case, is the likelihood of imprecision in the terms of the order and if the terms cannot be precisely drawn, the possibility of wasteful litigation over compliance is increased. The fact that the terms of a contractual obligation are sufficiently definite to escape being void for uncertainty or to found a claim for damages does not necessarily mean that they will be sufficiently precise to be capable of being specifically enforced. A final point, which would be relevant to an order requiring a defendant to carry on a business, is that which was emphasised by Millett LJ, namely that it may cause injustice by allowing the plaintiff to enrich himself at the defendant's expense and the loss which the defendant may suffer through having to comply with the order may be far greater than the plaintiff would suffer from the contract being broken. He therefore concluded that: 'The cumulative effect of these various reasons, none of which would necessarily be sufficient on its own, seems to me to show that the settled practice is based upon sound sense'.[111] Lord Hoffmann stressed that the grant or refusal of specific performance remains a matter for the judge's discretion and that while there were no binding rules, this does not mean that there could not be settled principles which the courts would apply in all but exceptional circumstances. However, he pointed out that he could envisage cases of gross breach of personal faith, or attempts to use the threat of non-performance as blackmail, in which the needs of justice would override all the considerations which support the settled practice.

Academic reaction to the decision of the House of Lords has been mixed; while Jones concludes that 'on balance, the conclusion . . . is more to be welcomed than deplored',[112] Tettenborn has characterised it as 'an unfortunate failure to liberalise the rules of specific performance' and has expressed the view that it sits ill with the idea that it should be the function of the courts to ensure as far as possible that contracts should be performed rather than broken. As Phang has commented, the concept of constant supervision continues to constitute a major obstacle to the grant of specific performance in the context of continuous acts such as the running of a business.[113] However, as we shall see, in the context of obligations to achieve a result, which is what contracts to build or repair will often entail, lack of precision in the terms of the obligation has been the major stumbling block.

It should be noted that despite the decision of the House of Lords in *Co-Operative Insurance Society Ltd v. Argyll Stores (Holdings) Ltd*,[114] Costello P subsequently reached what was effectively the opposite conclusion in *Wanze*

---

111. [1998] AC 1, 16.
112. [1997] CLJ 488, 491.
113. (1998) 61 MLR 421, 432.
114. [1998] AC 1.

Properties (Ireland) Ltd v. Five Star Supermarket.[115] The defendant company held a lease of a premises in a shopping centre which contained a covenant that it would be used as a supermarket and that it would trade during usual business hours. In seeking an interlocutory injunction to enforce this covenant, the plaintiff submitted that the facts of the case before the court could be distinguished from those in *Argyll Stores*, in which the defendant had been running the supermarket business at a loss, and that it had made out a *prima facie* case that it would suffer very serious financial loss as a result of the defendant's decision to cease trading. Costello P made reference to the fact that in the case before him the defendant had taken a deliberate commercial decision to relocate its business to a new shopping centre being developed just 400 yards away.[116] In his view, it was open to the plaintiff to argue that the financial loss which the defendant would suffer as a result of being required to carry on business in the plaintiff's centre would be brought about by the defendant's own actions. In these circumstances Costello P decided to grant an interlocutory injunction to force the defendant to comply with the covenants in the lease requiring it to continue trading in the plaintiff's shopping centre during usual business hours, although he stressed that he was 'merely deciding that the plaintiff had made out a strong case that there was a reasonable probability that it would obtain the order it sought.'[117]

Breen[118] has raised the issue of whether the factual distinction between the two cases, i.e. between breaching a trading covenant on the basis of non-viability of a business as in *Argyll* and breaching a covenant in pursuit of a deliberate commercial decision to obtain higher profits elsewhere as in *Wanze*, is sufficient to warrant the different conclusions reached and she concludes that 'the compelling points raised by both Millett LJ and the House of Lords [in *Argyll*] remain to be answered by the Irish courts'.[119] It is in many respects unfortunate that the matter never proceeded to trial in *Wanze* as the case undoubtedly raised questions relating to the need for continuing supervision

---

115. High Court (Costello P) 24 October 1997.
116. However, it should be noted that in his dissenting judgment in the Court of Appeal in *Co-Operative Insurance Society Ltd v. Argyll Stores (Holdings) Ltd* [1996] Ch 286, 304 Millett LJ expressed the view that to compel a defendant to carry on a business 'which for his own commercial reasons he has decided to close down' might expose him to potentially large and unquantifiable losses which might be out of all proportion to the loss which his breach of contract had caused to the plaintiff.
117. Note that Girvan J granted a mandatory interlocutory injunction in *Ravenseft Properties Ltd v. Stewart's Supermarkets Ltd* Chancery Division (Girvan J) 6 May 1997 requiring the defendant to perform trading covenants in a lease where it had sought to close its supermarket business as its purchase figures had significantly declined when faced by competition from another shopping centre, although the order was to be reviewed by the court when the ruling of the House of Lords in *Co-Operative Insurance Society Ltd v. Argyll Stores (Holdings) Ltd* became available.
118. (1999) 50 NILQ 102.
119. *Ibid.* at 115.

of any order made which the court would in all likelihood have felt compelled
to address. Until the matter is clarified by the courts in this jurisdiction
considerable doubt surrounds the question of whether trading covenants of
the nature considered above will be enforced, although it should be said that
the underlying reasons for the conclusion reached by the House of Lords in
Argyll appear convincing.

Contracts to Build or Repair

By their nature building contracts will often be of an intricate and indefinite
nature involving the performance of a variety of different obligations. As
Porter MR noted in *Rushbrooke v. O'Sullivan*,[120] the attitude of courts of
equity towards their enforcement has not always been consistent, but the
predominant view has traditionally been that they should rarely be enforced
particularly as their uncertain nature would make it difficult for a court to
determine whether any order made has been complied with. In addition, it is
often argued that damages will be an adequate remedy where another builder
can be found to carry out the work. In practice the likelihood of obtaining
specific performance has tended to hinge on two main issues; primarily the
certainty of the terms of the contract and, to a lesser extent, the degree of
supervision which an order for specific performance would require.[121] One of
the most important decisions in this area is that of the Court of Appeal in
Wolverhampton Corporation v. Emmons,[122] where Romer LJ laid down the
principle that a court would order specific performance of a building contract
if three conditions were satisfied. First, the work in question must be defined
with sufficient precision in the contract; secondly, the plaintiff must have a
substantial interest in the performance of the contract and damages must not
be an adequate remedy and thirdly, the defendant must have 'by the contract
obtained possession of the land on which the work is contracted to be done'.
The plaintiff corporation sold land, which was part of a scheme for street
improvement, to the defendant who agreed to build houses on the land. The
court ordered specific performance of the covenant to build on the basis that
the conditions outlined above were satisfied and held that the plaintiff's interest
in having the contract specifically performed was such that it was not capable
of being compensated by damages.

The first of these principles formed the basis of the court's decision in
Rushbrooke v. O'Sullivan[123] in which Porter MR concluded that 'the exact
nature of the work to be done [had] not been so specifically defined or

120. [1908] 1 IR 232, 234.
121. See the comments of Goff LJ in *Price v. Strange* [1978] Ch 337, 359.
122. [1901] 1 KB 515, 525.
123. [1908] 1 IR 232.

ascertained as to justify a decree for specific performance'.[124] Similarly in *Redland Bricks Ltd v. Morris*[125] Lord Upjohn commented that 'the court must be careful to see that the defendant knows exactly in fact what he has to do and this means not as a matter of law but as a matter of fact, so that in carrying out an order he can give his contractors the proper instructions'. It has been stated that this requirement of sufficient definition does not mean that the contract must be so specific that it leaves no room for doubt,[126] and Spry[127] has suggested that the requirement should be that 'the obligations in question must be at least so clear that it will be possible for the court at any later application, upon the proper presentation of evidence, to determine whether the acts of the parties do or do not amount to due performance.' Provided the extent of the works which must be carried out to comply with the contract can be deduced from the evidence, it would seem that the courts have at times been willing to decree specific performance.[128]

The third requirement as laid down by Romer LJ has been qualified to a degree by Farwell J in *Carpenters Estates Ltd v. Davies*,[129] in which the latter stated that it was not essential that the defendant had obtained possession of the land by virtue of the contract at issue provided that he is 'in possession of the land on which the work is contracted to be done'. In this case the court granted specific performance of a covenant entered into by the defendant to lay sewers on her land as she was in possession of this land and the plaintiffs could not proceed to build houses on the land which she had sold to them without these works being carried out.

Clearly, where the defendant is in possession of the lands specific performance may often be the preferred option as the plaintiff could not employ another builder without committing a trespass. While his qualification of Romer LJ's requirement would seem quite acceptable, Farwell J appeared to go on to suggest that the mere fact that the defendant does not have possession of the land on which the work is contracted to be carried out should not necessarily be a complete bar to relief in the form of specific performance.[130] This statement is definitely questionable for, as Farwell J himself acknowledged,[131] if the defendant is not in possession of the land, it may be impossible for him to carry out the works.

The requirements laid down in *Wolverhampton Corporation v. Emmons* were applied to a situation in which a tenant sought to enforce a landlord's

---

124. *Ibid.* at 237.
125. [1970] AC 652, 666.
126. *Molyneux v. Richard* [1906] 1 Ch 34, 42 *per* Kekewich J.
127. *The Principles of Equitable Remedies* (6th ed., 2001) p. 115.
128. *Todd & Co. v. Midland Great Western Rly of Ireland Co.* (1881) 9 LR Ir 85.
129. [1940] Ch 160.
130. *Ibid.* at 165.
131. *Ibid.* at 164-165.

covenant to repair in *Jeune v. Queens Cross Properties Ltd.*[132] Tenants alleged that their landlord was in breach of a covenant to repair by failing to reinstate a balcony at the front of the property after it had partially collapsed. It was accepted by Pennycuick VC that the court had a power which should be carefully exercised to make an order against a landlord to do specific work under a covenant to repair and an order of specific performance was granted in the circumstances.

Clearly the courts will be more willing to grant specific performance in contracts to build or repair where there is no need for ongoing supervision of any order it may make. As Lord Hoffmann stated in *Co-Operative Insurance Society Ltd v. Argyll Stores (Holdings) Ltd*:[133] 'even if the achievement of the result is a complicated matter which will take some time, the court if called upon to rule, only has to examine the finished work and say whether it complies with the order'. This *dicta* was relied upon by Lawrence Collins QC, sitting as a Deputy High Court judge, in *Rainbow Estates Ltd v. Tokenhold Ltd*[134] where the plaintiff sought specific performance of a tenant's covenant to repair in circumstances where property was in a serious state of disrepair and there was no provision in the lease permitting the landlord to enter the premises to carry out repairs and no forfeiture clause for re-entry. Lawrence Collins QC made it clear that in his view a modern law of remedies requires specific performance of a tenant's repairing covenant to be available in appropriate circumstances and he stated that there were no constraints of principle or binding authority against the availability of that remedy. He added that the problems of defining the work and the need for supervision can be overcome by ensuring that there is a sufficient definition of what has to be done in order to comply with the order of the court. He therefore concluded, in granting the order sought, that subject to the overriding need to avoid injustice or oppression, specific performance should be available where appropriate in such cases, particularly if there is a substantial obstacle to the landlord effecting repairs and the condition of the premises may be deteriorating.

Finally, it should be said that while the result in cases such as *Jeune* and *Rainbow Estates* show an increased willingness to grant specific performance in cases of this nature, they should be treated with a degree of caution as the particular difficulties which faced the plaintiffs in these cases will not always be present. Equally, it should be stressed that the court must have sufficiently precise information before it about the works needed and their likely duration before it will grant an order requiring them to be specifically performed.[135] In addition, it should not be assumed that orders which require a defendant to

---

132. [1974] Ch 97.
133. [1998] AC 1, 13.
134. [1999] Ch 64. See Pawlowski and Brown [1998] Conv 495 and Bridge [1999] CLJ 283.
135. *Jan v. Torrance* [2002] EWCA Civ 431 Court of Appeal, 18 March 2002.

achieve a result as opposed to those which require him to carry on an activity will necessarily be enforced by specific performance. In the last analysis, as Lord Hoffmann commented in *Co-Operative Insurance Society Ltd v. Argyll Stores (Holdings) Ltd*, the grant or refusal of specific performance remains a matter within the judge's discretion and the level of precision which must be present if an obligation is to be enforced is difficult to predict with accuracy.

Contracts for Services

As a general principle, contracts which involve the performance of personal services will not be specifically enforced.[136] This is due partly to the fact that the courts would often be required to exercise a degree of supervision in relation to any order made[137] and partly due to a reluctance on the part of the judiciary as a matter of policy to compel individuals to work together in circumstances where the relationship of trust and confidence between them no longer exists. As stated above, McWilliam J accepted in the course of his judgment in *Lift Manufacturers Ltd v. Irish Life Assurance Co. Ltd*[138] that the principle that specific performance of a contract for services will not be granted is not a rigid one and he acknowledged that where there does not seem to be any reason for the court to supervise performance of the contract, this argument against enforcement cannot apply. However, it is generally accepted that from a policy perspective it is undesirable to force parties to fulfil obligations arising under contracts for the provision of services and, as an examination of the relevant authorities in this area will show, it is usually only where a relationship of mutual trust still exists between the parties that the courts will be willing to grant specific performance, or where circumstances require it, an injunction.[139]

These issues were examined in some detail by Megarry J in his judgment in *C.H. Giles & Co. v. Morris*,[140] where he commented that the so-called rule that contracts for personal services or involving the continuous performance of services will not be specifically enforced is plainly not absolute and without exception. He continued:

> I do not think that it should be assumed that as soon as any element of personal service or continuous services can be discerned in a contract the court will, without more, refuse specific performance. ... As is so often the case in equity, the matter is one of balance of advantage and

---

136. As McCutcheon has commented (1997) 17 LS 65, 66 there is a 'near universal reluctance' to order performance of a contract for personal services.
137. See *supra Ryan v. Mutual Tontine Westminster Chambers Association* [1893] 2 Ch 116; *Posner v. Scott Lewis* [1987] Ch 25.
138. [1979] ILRM 277.
139. See *supra* Chapter 13.
140. [1972] 1 WLR 307.

disadvantage in relation to the particular obligations in question; and the fact that the balance will usually lie on one side does not turn this probability into a rule.[141]

The *Giles* case concerned the issue of specific performance of a service agreement and the question arose whether the presence in the contract of a term in relation to the appointment of a third party prevented the court decreeing specific performance of the agreement. Megarry J accepted that there was a distinction between an order to perform a contract for services and an order to procure the execution of such a contract and held that on the facts, the contract was specifically enforceable. As Megarry J said, specific performance may be granted of an agreement to execute an instrument even if the obligations which that instrument creates would not be specifically enforced.

In relation to contracts of employment, the policy arguments against enforcement are strong where a relationship of mutual trust and confidence no longer exists between the parties. However, as the decision of the Court of Appeal in *Hill v. C.A. Parsons & Co. Ltd*[142] illustrates, in exceptional cases where such a relationship still subsists, the courts will enforce a contract of employment, in this instance by the grant of an injunction. In that case, the court granted an injunction restraining the dismissal of an employee where his employer had been coerced by a trade union into taking such a course of action when the employee refused to join the union and where the employer still retained confidence in the employee's ability to do his job.

DEFENCES TO AN ACTION FOR SPECIFIC PERFORMANCE

Introduction

Having considered some of the types of cases in which a court will grant specific performance, it is now necessary to examine the various defences which may be put forward when a claim for specific performance is made. It is important to point out that while some of these defences may provide an absolute bar to relief (e.g. the fact that the contract is an illegal one), the

---

141. *Ibid.* at 318. Quoted with approval by Goff LJ in *Price v. Strange* [1978] Ch 337, 359-360. As McCutcheon has commented (1997) 17 LS 65, 67 Megarry J's judgment displays a 'willingness to depart from the traditional rule and to order performance where problems of superintendence would not arise and where the possibilities of evasion are not such as to render the order vain'. However, he points out that the efforts of Megarry J have not provided a base from which a general jurisdiction to order performance in such circumstances has been developed.
142. [1972] Ch 305.

majority are of a discretionary nature and such defences will often be merely one of a number of factors which the court will be required to consider in deciding whether to grant relief. In addition, it is necessary to draw a distinction between two types of cases; first, those where even if the defence is successfully established the validity of the contract itself remains unaffected and the defendant may still be liable in damages (e.g. where the defence of hardship is raised). These cases should be distinguished from those in which the defence (e.g. mistake or misrepresentation) is sufficient to secure rescission of the contract.

Before examining these defences under various headings it is also necessary to stress that the types of cases in which specific performance will be refused do not fall into 'rigid categories'[143] and the following examination is not intended to be exhaustive.

Lack of Mutuality

It has traditionally been accepted that a court would not grant specific performance at the suit of one party when it could not do so at the suit of the other and that in order to obtain a decree of specific performance, the contract had to be mutually enforceable.[144] This point was summarised in the following manner by O'Connor LJ in *O'Regan v. White*:[145]

> Generally speaking, at any rate, it would not be even-handed justice to compel specific performance against the one party, where the same remedy would not be available against the other party in respect of matters to be by him performed under the contract.

The operation of this principle can be seen in relation to the situation in which an infant seeks to enforce specifically a contract into which he has entered. So, in *Flight v. Bolland*[146] a minor failed to obtain a decree of specific performance of a contract because such a decree could not be obtained against him. As Leach MR commented: 'It is a general principle of courts of equity to interpose only where the remedy is mutual.'

One question which has provoked considerable controversy is whether

---

143. *Conlon v. Murray* [1958] NI 17, 26.
144. However, it should be noted that it seems to have been accepted by Brady LC in *Fennelly v. Anderson* (1851) 1 Ir Ch R 706, 711 that lack of mutuality should not be a bar in cases arising under the Statute of Frauds and that a plaintiff may obtain specific performance of a contract signed by the defendant but not by him.
145. [1919] 2 IR 339, 393. See also his statement at 392 that 'equity will not aid one party to an agreement to have *in specie* that for which he bargained unless it can likewise aid (if necessary) the other party to have *in specie* that for which he bargained'.
146. (1828) 4 Russ 298.

the question of mutuality is to be determined at the time the contract is entered into or at the date of the judgment. The former approach was favoured by Fry[147] and by Meredith J in *Murphy v. Harrington*,[148] in which he stated that, in relation to the issue of mutuality, 'the material point in time to be considered is the time when the contract was entered into.' However, this point of view did not meet with the universal approval either of academic commentators,[149] or of members of the judiciary,[150] and the question was considered again by the English Court of Appeal in *Price v. Strange*.[151] The plaintiff and the defendant agreed that the former should carry out certain repairs to the defendant's property in return for a new underlease. When the plaintiff had completed half the work, the defendant refused to allow him to continue and repudiated the agreement. When the plaintiff sought specific performance of the agreement this was refused by the trial judge on the grounds that the contract was not capable of mutual enforcement at the time it was entered into.

However, the Court of Appeal did not agree with this conclusion. Buckley LJ stressed that the time at which the mutual availability of specific performance must be considered is the time of judgment and said that the correct principle is that 'the court will not compel a defendant to perform his obligations specifically if it cannot at the same time ensure that any unperformed obligations of the plaintiff will be specifically performed, unless perhaps, damages would be an adequate remedy to the defendant for any default on the plaintiff's part.'[152] However, perhaps the most important principle to emerge from the decision of the Court of Appeal, is that a lack of mutuality does not result in the court being deprived of jurisdiction to entertain a claim for specific performance but is rather a matter to be taken into account in deciding whether to exercise its discretion in favour of granting the remedy.[153] In this case, the Court of Appeal held that specific performance of the agreement should be granted subject to the defendant being recompensed for any repair work carried out by her and concluded that, in any event, the defendant had waived any defence of want of mutuality by allowing the plaintiff to start the repair work and in accepting the increased rent payable under the new underlease.

---

147. *Specific Performance* (6th ed., 1921) p. 219. 'A contract to be specifically enforced by the Court must, as a general rule, be mutual — that is to say, such that it might, *at the time it was entered into*, have been enforced by either of the parties against the other of them' (emphasis added).
148. [1927] IR 339, 344. See *Bayley v. Shoesmith's Contract* (1918) 87 LJ Ch 626.
149. Langdell (1887-88) 1 Harv LR 104; Saunders (1903) 19 LQR 341.
150. See the judgment of O'Connor LJ in *O'Regan v. White* [1919] 2 IR 339, 395.
151. [1978] Ch 337.
152. *Ibid.* at 367-368.
153. See also *Rainbow Estates Ltd v. Tokenhold Ltd* [1999] Ch 64, 69.

Misrepresentation

The fact that a contract was induced by reason of a misrepresentation will usually be a defence to an action for specific performance. Certainly any misrepresentation which justifies rescission will suffice and specific performance may even be refused where there is no right to rescind. This point was made by Jessel MR in *Re Banister*[154] where he stated as follows:

> I apprehend that the considerations which induce a Court to rescind any contract and the considerations which induce a Court of Equity to decline to enforce specific performance of a contract are by no means the same. It may well be that there is not sufficient to induce the Court to rescind the contract but still sufficient to prevent the Court enforcing it.

This point was reiterated by Lindley LJ in *Re Terry and White's Contract*,[155] where he said that 'a less serious misleading' of the defendant is sufficient to provide a defence in an action for specific performance than would be required to justify rescission. In practice successfully raising the defence of misrepresentation where specific performance is sought will be of less benefit to a defendant as he may still be liable in damages to the plaintiff whereas if rescission of the contract is granted this will not be an option.

In some cases, while a defendant in a specific performance action may have had good grounds for rescission, this right may have been lost for one reason or another,[156] and in these circumstances the misrepresentation should almost invariably still provide a good defence.

Misrepresentation will only provide a defence to an action for specific performance where it has induced the defendant to enter into the contract and he has been prejudiced as a result, although it may not be necessary to prove that the misrepresentation provided the sole motivation for the defendant's decision to enter into the agreement. It seems to have been accepted that even an innocent misrepresentation may suffice in this regard; as Brett LJ stated in *Re Banister*:[157] 'if there be a misrepresentation of facts however innocently made, the court of equity will not enforce the performance of the contract.' However, it would be fair to say that where the facts would never have warranted rescission or where the representation relates merely to a matter of opinion, a degree of caution should be exercised. Often where the misrepresentation can be classed as innocent in nature the question of whether it can provide a valid defence will depend on whether the court can find

---

154. (1879) 12 Ch D 131, 142.
155. (1886) 32 Ch D 14, 29.
156. E.g. as a result of the doctrine of laches or because the parties cannot be restored to their original positions.
157. (1879) 12 Ch D 131, 147.

evidence of fundamental unfairness in the transaction. This point can be deduced from the decision of the Supreme Court in *Smelter Corporation v. O'Driscoll*[158] in which the plaintiff claimed an order of specific performance in relation to a contract for the sale of lands. The plaintiff's agent had told the defendant in the course of negotiations that if she did not agree to sell, the local authority would acquire the lands compulsorily and although the agent believed this statement to be true, it was actually without foundation. The Supreme Court held that, while the plaintiff's agent had acted in a *bona fide* manner, by reason of the misrepresentation of the facts by the agent, the defendant had been under a 'fundamental misapprehension' as to the true position. O'Higgins CJ concluded that in these circumstances there was a fundamental unfairness in the transaction and that it would be unjust to grant a decree of specific performance. The general principles in this area are well summarised by Spry[159] as follows:

> If the defendant has entered into the material contract, or has elected not to rescind, in reliance on misleading statements or actions of the plaintiff, specific performance is refused either if circumstances of unfairness render it unreasonable to grant relief (and here it is generally of importance whether the plaintiff knew or ought to have known that his statements or actions might be relied upon) or if in view of the error or misunderstanding of the defendant and the hardship that may be suffered by him it is unreasonable to grant relief (and here it may be less important, though it is usually relevant, whether the plaintiff knew or ought to have known that his statements or acts would be relied upon), or if in view of both of these considerations it is unreasonable to grant relief.

A final point which should be made is that 'misrepresentation may arise as much from suppression of the material facts as from mis-stating them.' This point emerges from the judgment of Smith MR in *Geoghegan v. Connolly*,[160] in which he found that there had been such a suppression of the facts in the particulars of sale of property as to disentitle the plaintiff to a decree of specific performance.

Mistake

In certain circumstances, mistake will constitute a defence to an action for specific performance. In determining whether specific performance should be refused on this ground, the court will often be primarily influenced by the

---

158. [1977] IR 305.
159. *The Principles of Equitable Remedies* (6th ed., 2001) p. 162.
160. (1859) 8 Ir Ch R 598, 609.

unfairness or hardship caused by any misapprehension or mistake on the part of the defendant as to the nature of the contractual obligations.

The mistake may be of such proportions that it prevents a valid contract coming into existence at all; in these circumstances clearly no order of specific performance can be made. However, it is also necessary to consider the types of mistake, which although they do not prevent the contract being initially effective, may be of such a nature that a court will in the exercise of its discretion refuse to grant specific performance. Therefore specific performance may be refused where the mistake is not such as to render the contract void at law, or even where there is no right to rescind in equity. In other words, as we have seen above in the context of misrepresentation, a less serious mistake is sufficient to provide a defence to an action for specific performance than would be required to justify rescission.

There will also be types of mistake which are neither serious enough to justify rescission nor to provide a good defence in an action for specific performance. This can be seen from an examination of the decision of Murphy J in *Ferguson v. Merchant Banking Ltd*[161] in which the plaintiff claimed specific performance of a contract for the sale of land. The defendant company was being wound up and the official liquidator contested the plaintiff's right to have the contract performed. It was claimed that the agreement between the parties was for the sale of specified residential estates and ancillary lands and that it was never intended that a vacant site with development potential should be included in the sale. The defendant sought rescission of the contract or rectification thereof to give effect to what it argued was the true intention of the parties. While Murphy J accepted that a mistake had been made in that the official liquidator had not intended to dispose of the property with development potential, he found that there had not been a fundamental error nor an absence of agreement on any fundamental term. He concluded that whether the matter was viewed as one of fundamental mistake or absence of consensus, the defendant was not entitled to deprive the plaintiff of the benefit of the contract which he had entered into and in the circumstances held that he was entitled to an order of specific performance and the defendant's counterclaim was rejected.

Where a defendant seeks to rely on mistake as a defence, often a crucial question will be whether the plaintiff contributed in any way to the misapprehension or misunderstanding. Certainly where the plaintiff is aware of the mistake and seeks to take advantage of it a court will not grant specific performance in his favour. In *Webster v. Cecil*[162] a vendor offered property for sale for £1,250 instead of £2,250 as he had intended and the purchaser accepted the offer knowing that the former had made a mistake. Specific

---

161. [1993] ILRM 136.
162. (1861) 30 Beav 62.

performance of the sale was refused on the basis that the mistake had been clearly proved and the defendant had immediately given notice of it. Romilly MR therefore concluded that the court would not compel the defendant to sell property for much less than its real value. On the other hand, where the mistake is solely that of the defendant and the plaintiff has in no way contributed to it, the courts are unlikely to refuse specific performance. This point is illustrated by the decision in *Tamplin v. James*[163] where property was offered for sale by reference to plans which correctly described the area of the site. The defendant did not look at the plans and mistakenly assumed that a piece of land behind the premises was included in the sale and agreed to buy on this basis. The plaintiff was granted a decree of specific performance when the defendant failed to complete the purchase. As James LJ stated: 'for the most part the cases where a defendant has escaped on the ground of a mistake not contributed to by the plaintiff have been cases where a hardship amounting to an injustice would have been inflicted upon him by holding him to his bargain, and it was unreasonable to hold him to it. ... If a man makes a mistake of this kind without any reasonable excuse he ought to be held to his bargain.'[164]

This statement was quoted with approval by Costello J in *O'Neill v. Ryan (No. 3)*[165] in a judgment which confirms the point that where a plaintiff has in no way contributed to the mistake it would not be unjust or unreasonable to require the defendant to carry out his contractual obligations. The plaintiff had instituted various proceedings against a number of defendants including an action under section 205 of the Companies Act 1963, claiming oppression and seeking damages for wrongful dismissal, fraud, misrepresentation and conspiracy. He claimed that the respondents in the section 205 proceedings had offered to buy his shares in the company at a stipulated price and to pay his costs and sought specific performance of this agreement. The defendants resisted the claim contending that the agreement relied on had been entered into by mistake and that they had intended this offer to settle to apply to more than just the section 205 action and submitted that, as the parties had not been *ad idem*, there was no contract in existence which could be specifically enforced. Costello J said that he had to balance the hardship which the defendants contended they would suffer against the hardship which the plaintiff would be subject to if the contract was not specifically enforced. He held that a valid enforceable agreement had come into existence, that the plaintiff had in no way contributed to the situation which had arisen and concluded that the plaintiff was entitled to an order of specific performance. The conclusion reached by Costello J was upheld by the Supreme Court which held that he had properly exercised his discretion in granting specific performance.

While it would appear that even where the plaintiff has contributed to

---

163. (1880) 15 Ch D 215.
164. *Ibid.* at 221.
165. [1992] 1 IR 166, 192.

the mistake in an unintentional manner the defence may succeed,[166] it remains difficult to lay down any definite principles in relation to a situation where the plaintiff bears no responsibility for the mistake which has occurred. While specific performance has on occasion been refused where the mistake made is entirely attributable to the defendant,[167] the better view would seem to be that in such cases there must be other circumstances which would make it 'highly unreasonable' to decree performance of the contractual obligations. This approach is well set out by Lord Macnaghten in *Stewart v. Kennedy*[168] in which he acknowledged that while a court may refuse specific performance in cases of mistake not caused or contributed to by the plaintiff, it has acted in this manner because it would not be reasonable to compel the defendant to carry out his obligations.

In the last analysis perhaps the most realistic formula is that put forward by James LJ in *Tamplin v. James*,[169] namely whether a 'hardship amounting to an injustice' would be caused to the defendant by not allowing him to resist a decree for specific performance on the basis of the mistake which has occurred. Spry[170] has captured the essence of the cases where the mistake may not be sufficiently grave to justify rescission and yet may be serious enough to persuade the court to refuse to decree specific performance. In his view it is necessary not to regard the mistake or misapprehension as an independent discretionary factor, but rather to treat it as a matter which, together with other considerations such as hardship or unfairness, may make it inequitable to grant specific performance of a contract.

Hardship

In the exercise of its discretion, a court may refuse to order specific performance of a contract where to do so would inflict unnecessary hardship on the defendant, even where the plaintiff is not responsible for this. This fact was acknowledged by Budd J in his judgment in *Lavan v. Walsh*,[171] in which he said that it is well-established that a court 'will not enforce the specific performance of a contract the result of which would be to impose great hardship on either of the parties to it.'[172] However it was conceded by counsel in that case that the question of hardship should generally be judged at the time the contract is entered into and, as Budd J commented, proof of subsequent hardship would have to be 'strong and above suspicion'. This issue was further

---

166. *Denny v. Hancock* (1870) 6 Ch App 1.
167. *Malins v. Freeman* (1837) 2 Keen 25.
168. (1890) 15 App Cas 75, 105.
169. (1880) 15 Ch D 215.
170. *The Principles of Equitable Remedies* (6th ed., 2001) p. 157.
171. [1964] IR 87.
172. *Ibid.* at 102.

considered by the Supreme Court in *Roberts v. O'Neill*,[173] in which the plaintiff claimed specific performance of a contract for the sale of a licensed premises. The defendants claimed that to grant specific performance of the contract with the plaintiff would be to impose unreasonable hardship on them because of the large increase in the value of the property since the date of the contract. McCarthy J acknowledged that hardship might provide a good defence to an action for specific performance where an existing hardship was not known at the date of the contract. However, he clearly felt that subsequent hardship should operate as a defence only in exceptional cases:

> While recognising that there may be cases in which hardship arising after the date of the contract is such that to decree specific performance would result in great injury, there must be few such cases and, in my view, they should not include ordinarily cases of hardship resulting from inflation alone. To permit as an ordinary rule a defence of subsequent hardship, would be to add a further hazard to the already trouble strewn area of the law of contracts for the sale of land.[174]

In the circumstances the Supreme Court decided to grant a decree of specific performance and concluded that it was not a case in which the court should intervene to deny this remedy to a contracting party to what was 'at the time, a perfectly fair and proper transaction'.

However, it is clear from both the *Lavan* and *Roberts* cases that, where a serious injustice would otherwise result, supervening hardship may in an exceptional case provide a defence. A good example of the type of circumstances which might warrant such a conclusion is provided by *Patel v. Ali*,[175] in which the claim of a purchaser of a house to an order of specific performance against the vendor was resisted on the grounds of hardship. After the parties had entered into the contract the vendor became seriously ill, necessitating the amputation of her leg. To compound her difficulties she gave birth to a second child and her husband, who had been adjudicated bankrupt, was sent to prison for a time. Evidence was adduced that she relied greatly on the help of neighbours and of members of her family living nearby to cope with looking after the household and that to enforce specifically the contract for sale would cause undue hardship. Goulding J acknowledged that 'the court has sometimes refused specific performance because of a change of circumstances supervening after the making of the contract and not in any way attributable to the plaintiff'[176] and refused to grant an order in these circumstances and instead awarded damages to the purchaser.

---

173. [1983] IR 47.
174. *Ibid.* at 64.
175. [1984] Ch 283.
176. *Ibid.* at 287.

Clearly in deciding whether to exercise its discretion on this basis, the court must balance the hardship which the defendant contends he would suffer against the hardship which the plaintiff would sustain if the contract were not specifically enforced,[177] which may for example relate to the likelihood that the plaintiff may not be able to recover damages to compensate him for the defendant's wrongdoing.

The predominant view is that hardship which may be caused to third parties as a result of a decision to grant specific performance is a factor which may be taken into account by a court.[178] So, in *Conlon v. Murray*[179] Black LJ seems to have attached some weight at least to the fact that if the vendor's executors were compelled to proceed with a contract for the sale of her farm, her brother would have had nowhere to live. Whether hardship which may be suffered by the public generally will be relevant is less easy to predict but in either case the weight which a court will attach to it will depend largely on the probable extent of the hardship or prejudice which will ensue.

Closely related to the issue of the potential hardship which may be caused to the defendant are general considerations of unfairness which are more likely to concern the manner in which the plaintiff has behaved. So, where the plaintiff has acted in an unconscionable manner so as to take advantage of the weakness of a defendant's position, specific performance may be refused. A good illustration of the operation of this principle is the decision of the Northern Ireland Court of Appeal in *Conlon v. Murray* to which reference has just been made. The plaintiff brought an action for specific performance of a contract for the sale of a farm against the vendor which was continued against her executors after her death. The vendor was an elderly lady who had agreed to the sale in a distressed state without taking any time for reflection and without the benefit of independent advice. While Black LJ acknowledged that specific performance of a contract will not be refused on the sole ground that one of the parties had not received legal advice, he stated that in view of the 'extraordinary and unexplained haste' with which the transaction had been rushed through, the court should hesitate to decree specific performance. He said that it is well-established that there is a class of case in which a contract may be of such a nature that the court will not order it to be rescinded, but at the same time, having regard to the substantial justice of the case, will not order that it be specifically performed. In the circumstances, in the exercise of its discretion, the Court of Appeal refused to grant specific performance. This result can be contrasted with that arrived at by Murray J in *McCrystal v. O'Kane*[180] in which *Conlon* was distinguished and suggestions that the plaintiff

---

177. *O'Neill v. Ryan (No. 3)* [1992] 1 IR 166, 192. See also *Beshoff Brothers Ltd v. Select Service Partner Ireland Ltd* High Court 1998 No. 8102P (O'Sullivan J) 28 July 1998.

178. Although note the comments of Issacs J in *Gall v. Mitchell* (1924) 35 CLR 222, 230.

179. [1958] NI 17.

180. [1986] NI 123.

had taken unfair advantage of the defendant in concluding an agreement for the sale of land were rejected.

Laches or Delay

As a general principle, a plaintiff who delays unreasonably in bringing proceedings for specific performance may fail to obtain the relief which he seeks where by reason of his delay it would be inequitable to grant the remedy sought. It is important to stress that delay alone will probably be insufficient without some further element of prejudice and it will be necessary to show circumstances which, when considered in conjunction with the delay, would render the granting of a decree for specific performance unjust.

It is clear from the judgment of O'Connor J in *Guerin v. Heffernan*[181] that where a plaintiff intends to seek relief in the form of specific performance he is bound to proceed without delay; as he said: 'A man who sleeps on his rights does not find favour in a court of equity.'[182] There the defendant sought to repudiate a contract for the purchase of a farm and the plaintiff, after threatening to institute proceedings against him, did nothing for a period of over a year. O'Connor J concluded that during the intervening time the defendant might well have assumed that the plaintiff had abandoned his rights under the contract and had accepted the defendant's repudiation and held that on this basis the plaintiff was not entitled to relief in the form of specific performance.

It is difficult to lay down reliable guidelines about the length of delay which may disentitle a plaintiff to relief as the question is often governed by other factors such as the conduct of the parties. However, Spry[183] has stated that 'the general rule is that in order to establish that the delay of the plaintiff has been excessive it must appear that, in all the material circumstances, a reasonably assiduous person would have proceeded with substantially greater speed or diligence.' In *Lazard Brothers & Co. Ltd v. Fairfield Properties Co. (Mayfair) Ltd*[184] the plaintiff failed to issue proceedings for specific performance until over two years had passed since the contract had been concluded. Megarry VC said that if specific performance was to be regarded as a prize 'to be awarded by equity to the zealous and denied to the indolent' the plaintiff might not succeed, but this was not the case and in the absence of any evidence of any other prejudice or circumstances which would make it unjust to grant relief, he made the order sought. More recently it has been suggested by Aldous LJ in the decision of the Court of Appeal in *Frawley v.*

---

181. [1925] 1 IR 57.
182. *Ibid.* at 68.
183. *The Principles of Equitable Remedies* (6th ed., 2001) pp. 227-228.
184. (1987) 121 SJ 793.

Neill[185] that the modern approach in such cases should not require an inquiry as to whether the circumstances can be fitted within the confines of a preconceived formula derived from earlier cases. Instead the court should take a broad approach, directed to ascertaining whether it would in all the circumstances be unconscionable for a party to be permitted to assert his beneficial right.

Usually, unless the parties have stipulated otherwise, time will not be of the essence to a contract in equity so a plaintiff may still be entitled to an order for specific performance even after the date for performance of the contractual obligations has passed, although he might be liable for damages for breach of contract for failing to complete on time. However, where it is clear that time is of the essence, it is likely that a plaintiff will be entitled to relief in the form of an order for specific performance only in exceptional circumstances. Certainly a rigid approach to enforcing time stipulations in a contract has recently been taken by the Privy Council in *Union Eagle Ltd v. Golden Achievement Ltd*,[186] although a more flexible approach has been taken in a number of decisions of the High Court of Australia.[187] In *Union Eagle* relief in the form of specific performance was refused where a purchaser failed to complete a contract for the sale of property within the time stipulated by tendering the purchase price ten minutes after the time for completion had passed. It was clear as Lord Hoffmann stated that 'time was to be in every respect of the essence of the agreement' and in the circumstances the vendor declared that the contract was rescinded and the deposit paid by the purchaser forfeited. Lord Hoffmann referred to the dicta of Viscount Haldane in *Steedman v. Drinkle*[188] and stated that the courts in England, while ready to grant restitutionary relief against penalties, have been unwilling to grant specific performance where there has been a breach of an essential condition as to time.[189] While he acknowledged that the High Court of Australia has accepted that in exceptional cases, specific performance may be granted at the instance of a purchaser who is in breach of an essential condition in a contract,[190] in his view these decisions could provide no assistance to the purchaser in the circumstances of the case before the court. He stated as follows:

> There is no question of any penalty, or of the vendor being unjustly

---

185. Court of Appeal, 1 March 1999.
186. [1997] AC 515. See Thompson [1997] Conv 382, Heydon (1997) 113 LQR 385 and Stevens (1998) 61 MLR 255.
187. *Legione v. Hateley* (1983) 152 CLR 406; *Stern v. McArthur* (1988) 165 CLR 489.
188. [1916] 1 AC 275.
189. However, earlier authorities showed that specific performance might be granted where time was of the essence where e.g. a term providing for forfeiture of half the purchase price was regarded as a penalty, see *Re Dagenham (Thames) Dock Co.; Ex p. Hulse* (1873) LR 8 Ch App 1022.
190. *Legione v. Hateley* (1983) 152 CLR 406; *Stern v. McArthur* (1988) 165 CLR 489.

enriched by improvements made at the purchaser's expense, or of the vendor's conduct having contributed to the breach, or of the transaction being in substance a mortgage. It remains for consideration on some future occasion as to whether the way to deal with the problems which have arisen in such cases is by relaxing the principle in *Steedman v. Drinkle*, as the Australian courts have done, or by development of the law of restitution and estoppel.[191]

In the view of the Privy Council the case seemed to be one to which the full force of the general rule applied; as Lord Hoffmann stated: 'the fact is that the purchaser was late' and any suggestion that he was only slightly late was bound to lead to arguments over how late was too late which could only be resolved by litigation. In the circumstances he concluded that there was a need for a firm restatement of the principle 'that in cases of rescission of an ordinary contract of sale of land for failure to comply with an essential condition as to time, equity will not intervene'. It remains to be seen whether in the circumstances referred to by Lord Hoffmann above, for example where the question of a penalty arises, or where it appears that the vendor has been unjustly enriched by improvements made at the purchaser's expense, the courts in this jurisdiction might be prepared to take a more lenient approach.

Illegality

A contract which is illegal will be void and cannot be specifically enforced. As Jessel MR stated in *Sykes v. Beadon*[192] 'the principle is clear that you cannot directly enforce an illegal contract, and you cannot ask the court to assist you in carrying it out.' Where the illegality inherent in the contract involves criminal or immoral conduct, as a general principle it will invalidate the entire agreement, although where the illegal element is of a lesser nature, for example, a clause in restraint of trade,[193] the contract may stand if the portion which the courts will not enforce on grounds of public policy can be severed.[194] In addition, a contract which appears valid on its face but which if carried into effect might achieve an underlying illegal purpose or be contrary to public policy will not be enforceable. So, in *Wroth v. Tyler*[195] specific performance of a contract entered into by the defendant to sell his house to

---

191. [1997] AC 515, 523.
192. (1879) 11 Ch D 170, 197.
193. *S.V. Nevenas & Co. v. Walker* [1914] 1 Ch 413; *Goldsoll v. Goldman* [1915] 1 Ch 292. However, note the comments of Younger LJ in *Attwood v. Lamont* [1920] 3 KB 571, 595.
194. *Bennett v. Bennett* [1952] 1 KB 249, 260; *Goodinson v. Goodinson* [1954] 2 QB 118, 120.
195. [1974] Ch 30.

the plaintiff was refused in circumstances where the defendant's wife had the right not to be evicted from the property. The court was satisfied that if the order were made the plaintiff would be able to evict the husband and other members of his family apart from his wife and this would have the effect of splitting up the family which would be contrary to public policy.

As McWilliam J made clear in his judgment in *Starling Securities Ltd v. Woods*,[196] the courts in this jurisdiction will not grant specific performance of a contract where there is an underlying illegal purpose. On the facts of the case before him he found that the only interpretation he could put on the 'very peculiar method adopted to conduct these transactions' was that both parties were trying to conceal their true nature from the Revenue Commissioners and he concluded that he would not countenance such attempted fraud on the Revenue by enforcing performance of the contract. In addition, it is clear from the *dicta* of Finlay P in *Whitecross Potatoes (International) Ltd v. Coyle*[197] that the onus is on a defendant who asserts that a contract is illegal to establish as a matter of probability that it was at the time of its formation illegal in nature. This point has been reiterated in a number of recent decisions in which the question of relying on illegality as a defence to an action for specific performance has been considered. In *Whelan v. Kavanagh*[198] Herbert J stated that a party who has executed a contract which is regular and lawful on its face should not lightly be permitted to impugn it, particularly to his own advantage, by pleading illegality as a defence to a claim for specific performance. He stressed that the onus of proving such illegality lies firmly on the party raising it, although he stated that extrinsic evidence outside the terms of the written contract was admissible to prove, for example as in the case before him, a smaller 'real' consideration inconsistent with the agreement itself. Herbert J was satisfied that there had been no proof placed before the court to support the defendant's claim to this effect other than his own oral evidence which was unsupported by any document or reliable corroborative evidence. He concluded that this evidence was 'altogether unreliable' and affirmed the order of the Circuit Court granting specific performance of the agreement for the sale of the premises in question.

Similarly in *Kavanagh v. Caulfield*,[199] Roderick Murphy J reiterated that it is clear that the onus of proving illegality in a contract lies on the defendant. The parties had entered into a contract for the sale of a property, although the plaintiff claimed that the defendant had required her to pay a sum of money to a charity as an inducement to enter into the contract. In resisting the claim for specific performance, the defendant contended that if any agreement had been made, it was an illegal and unenforceable contract by reason of the fact that it

---

196. High Court 1975 No. 4044P (McWilliam J) 24 May 1977.
197. [1978] ILRM 31.
198. High Court 2000 No. 99CA (Herbert J) 29 January 2001.
199. High Court 1999 No. 9769P (Roderick Murphy J) 19 June 2002.

did not reflect the true price paid by the plaintiff for the premises and that it had been agreed that the additional sum would be paid to the charity with the intention that it would not be disclosed to the Revenue Commissioners. Roderick Murphy J stated that, in deciding whether to grant the relief sought, the court must examine the quality of the illegality relied upon by the defendant and must look at all of the surrounding circumstances. It must assess whether there had been an illegality of which the court should take notice, whether it would be an affront to the public conscience if, by granting the relief sought the court was seen to be indirectly assisting a criminal act, and it must also be satisfied that the contract has not been otherwise rendered ineffective. On the facts he concluded that the contract in the case before him was one which in accordance with the apparent intention of the parties at the time of its formation, could and would be carried out in a legal manner. He concluded, in granting an order for specific performance, that there was insufficient evidence to establish that the plaintiff intended to carry the contract out in an illegal fashion and that there was therefore no illegality such as to render it unenforceable.

Impossibility and Frustration

A court will not make an order of specific performance compelling a party to a contract to perform his obligations where it will not be possible for him to comply with the order which the court proposes to make; as Brewster LC stated in *Sheppard v. Murphy:*[200] 'a Court of Equity cannot compel him to do that which is impossible'. This point has been reiterated by Murphy J in *Neville & Sons Ltd v. Guardian Builders Ltd,*[201] where he commented that 'if a contract is discharged by impossibility then clearly no court could compel its performance'. However, as Brewster LC also made clear in *Sheppard*, a party cannot take steps to make performance of his contractual obligations impossible and then seek to rely on this as a defence.

A contract may be rendered impossible to perform by reason of frustration and the circumstances in which this may occur have recently been considered by the Supreme Court in *Neville & Sons Ltd v. Guardian Builders Ltd.*[202] The plaintiff and defendant entered into an agreement whereby the plaintiff contracted to build houses on a site owned by the defendant. It was accepted that the only means of ensuring effective access to the site would be by the construction of a new roadway which involved the acquisition of a strip of land owned by the county council. Difficulties arose in acquiring this land; the plaintiff sought specific performance of the agreement and the defendant contended that by reason of the difficulties which had arisen in relation to access to the site, performance of the contract had been rendered impossible

---

200. (1868) IR 2 Eq 544, 557.
201. [1990] ILRM 601, 616. Reversed by the Supreme Court [1995] 1 ILRM 1.
202. [1995] 1 ILRM 1.

or possible only in circumstances so different from those contemplated that both parties were relieved from further performance. Murphy J accepted that performance of the contract had been frustrated by intervening circumstances and held that the plaintiffs were not entitled to specific performance, although this decision was reversed by the Supreme Court. In the course of his judgment Blayney J quoted with approval[203] from the speech of Lord Simon in *National Carriers Ltd v. Panalpina (Northern) Ltd*[204] as follows:

> Frustration of a contract takes place when there supervenes an event (without default of either party and for which the contract makes no sufficient provision) which so significantly changes the nature (not merely the expense or onerousness) of the outstanding contractual rights and/or obligations from what the parties could reasonably have contemplated at the time of its execution that it would be unjust to hold them to the literal sense of its stipulations in the new circumstances; in such case the law declares both parties to be discharged from further performance.

Blayney J concluded that what had transpired could not be termed a supervening event which significantly changed the nature of the defendant's obligations and while it made performance of the contract more onerous, he was satisfied that the defence of frustration should fail.

Finally, it would appear that a party cannot rely on the doctrine of frustration to provide a defence where the contract has been frustrated by an event which he anticipated or should have anticipated.[205]

---

203. *Ibid.* at 7.
204. [1981] AC 675, 700. See also the judgment of Kenny J in *Browne v. Mulligan* [1976-77] ILRM 327, 332-333 in relation to the possible basis for the doctrine of frustration.
205. *McGuill v. Aer Lingus Teo* High Court 1981 No. 2238 (McWilliam J) 3 October 1983 at 13-14.

CHAPTER 15

Rectification

INTRODUCTION

Rectification is a discretionary equitable remedy which allows for the correction of an instrument which has failed to record the actual intentions of the parties to a contract.[1] This jurisdiction allows the court to rectify documents, such as deeds, in order to make them correspond with the pre-existing agreement of the parties. For example, in the case of a contract for the sale of land, where a deed did not reflect the agreement of the parties, equity would allow rectification so as to ensure that the final instrument gave proper effect to the prior contract. This jurisdiction is viewed as an exception to the parol evidence rule that oral evidence will not suffice to alter a written document.

It is important to stress that this does not constitute rectification of the contract, but only of the writing recording the contract. This point is well summarised in the following *dicta* of James VC in *Mackenzie v. Coulson*[2] that while 'Courts of Equity do not rectify contracts; they may and do rectify instruments purporting to have been made in pursuance of the terms of contracts'. Similar sentiments have been expressed in a number of recent decisions in this jurisdiction; in *Irish Life Assurance Co. Ltd v. Dublin Land Securities Ltd*[3] Griffin J commented that 'rectification is concerned with defects in the recording, not in the making, of an agreement' a statement echoed by Barron J in *McD. v. McD.*[4]

---

1. As Binnie J stated in the decision of the Supreme Court of Canada in *Sylvan Lake Golf and Tennis Club Ltd v. Performance Industries Ltd* (2002) 209 DLR (4th) 318, 330: 'The court's task in a rectification case is corrective, not speculative. It is to restore the parties to their original bargain, not to rectify a belatedly recognized error of judgment by one party or the other.'
2. (1869) LR 8 Eq 368, 375. See also the *dicta* of Buckley LJ in *Lovell and Christmas Ltd v. Wall* (1911) 104 LT 85, 93 that 'the court does not rectify contracts, but what it rectifies is the erroneous expression of contracts in documents.'
3. [1989] IR 253, 260.
4. [1993] ILRM 717, 722.

PREREQUISITES FOR RECTIFICATION

Originally, it was necessary to show that there was a valid and enforceable contract antecedent to the instrument sought to be rectified, and that such contract was inaccurately represented in the instrument. However, Clauson J suggested *obiter* in *Shipley Urban District Council v. Bradford Corporation*[5] that it was not necessary to find a concluded and binding contract between the parties antecedent to the agreement which it was sought to rectify provided that there was a common continuing intention with regard to a particular provision or aspect of the agreement. Thus if the parties were *ad idem* up to the point in time when they executed the formal instrument which, it transpired, did not correspond with their common agreement, the court might order rectification even though there was no concluded and binding contract between the parties up to the point when the formal instrument was executed. This approach was followed in this jurisdiction in *Monaghan County Council v. Vaughan*.[6] The plaintiff county council invited tenders for demolition work and the removal of valuable materials from a derelict site. Dixon J found that it was the clear intention of both parties that the defendant would pay for the right to carry out the works. Thus when the county council executed a contract which provided that the defendant should be paid for the demolition work, this was an instance of mutual mistake, as the parties had agreed on matters which were not reflected in the written contract. Dixon J rejected the argument that there could be no rectification because there was no antecedent agreement between the parties which was capable of being enforced and granted the plaintiff's claim for rectification.

The reasoning of Clauson J in *Shipley* was followed in England in *Crane v. Hegeman-Harris Co. Inc*,[7] where Simonds J stated that it was not necessary to find a concluded and binding contract between the parties antecedent to the agreement which it is sought to rectify provided there is a common continuing intention in relation to the particular provision of the agreement. Leaving aside questions about enforceability, doubts remained about whether an antecedent complete concluded agreement was necessary, particularly as a result of the views expressed by Denning LJ in *Frederick E. Rose (London) Ltd v. William H. Pim Junior & Co. Ltd*,[8] which were quoted with approval in this jurisdiction in *Lucey v. Laurel Construction Co. Ltd*.[9] The issue appears to have been resolved in England as a result of the judgment of Russell LJ in *Joscelyne v. Nissen*[10] where he stated that in his view the correct position was

---

5. [1936] Ch 375.
6. [1948] IR 306.
7. [1939] 1 All ER 662, 664.
8. [1953] 2 QB 450, 461-462.
9. High Court 1970 No. 3816 (Kenny J) 18 December 1970 at 10-11.
10. [1970] 2 QB 86.

that enunciated by Simonds J in *Crane* subject to the qualification that there should be some outward expression of accord between the parties. This question was also considered in Northern Ireland by Lowry LCJ in *Rooney and McParland Ltd v. Carlin*[11] where he laid down the following requirements which must be satisfied where the remedy of rectification is sought:

1. There must be a concluded agreement antecedent to the instrument which it is sought to be rectified; but

2. The antecedent agreement need not be binding in law (for example, it need not be under seal if made by a public authority or in writing and signed by the party if relating to a sale of land) nor need it be in writing: such incidents merely help to discharge the heavy burden of proof; and

3. A complete antecedent concluded contract is not required, as long as there was prior accord on a term of a proposed agreement, outwardly expressed and communicated between the parties, as in *Joscelyne v. Nissen*.

When the matter came before the Supreme Court in *Irish Life Assurance Co. Ltd v. Dublin Land Securities Ltd*[12] Griffin J said unhesitatingly that he would adopt what had been said by Russell LJ in *Joscelyne* and by Lowry LCJ in *Rooney* and pointed out that in *Lucey*, Kenny J did not appear to have been referred to the decision of Russell LJ. Griffin J concluded as follows:

> Applying those principles to the facts of this case, and bearing in mind the heavy burden of proof that lies on those seeking rectification, the question to be addressed is whether there was convincing proof, reflected in some outward expression of accord, that the contract in writing did not represent the common continuing intention of the parties on which the court can act. . . . [13]

As a result it would now seem to be firmly established that an antecedent concluded agreement is not necessary provided there is a common intention to include or exclude a particular term which continues until the contract is executed and which is made manifest by the parties in some way. However it is vital that this common intention can be ascertained with precision and a number of claims for rectification have failed on the grounds that the parties' exact intentions cannot be identified with sufficient certainty. This point

---

11. [1981] NI 138, 146.
12. [1989] IR 253.
13. *Ibid.* at 263. Quoted with approval by Murphy J in *Lac Minerals Ltd v. Chevron Mineral Corporation of Ireland* [1995] 1 ILRM 161, 172.

emerges from the decision of the Supreme Court in *Irish Life Assurance Co. Ltd v. Dublin Land Securities Ltd.*[14] The plaintiff company owned a large portfolio of ground rents and also valuable lands which had been made the subject of compulsory purchase orders. A contract of sale between the plaintiff and the defendant was drawn up and while it was the intention of the plaintiff to exclude the lands subject to the C.P.O.s from the sale, due to a mix-up in its legal department, they were included in the contract. The plaintiff's intention to exclude these lands was communicated to an agent of the defendant in a rather imprecise way but was not passed on to the defendant. The plaintiff sought rectification of the contract, while the defendant sought specific performance of the agreement in its original form. Keane J found that the defendant did not know of the plaintiff's intention to exclude the properties in question and dismissed the plaintiff's claim on the grounds that there was no common intention between the parties to this effect. On appeal, the Supreme Court upheld the order of the High Court. Griffin J said that the party seeking rectification must establish by convincing proof that the instrument does not reflect the common intention of the parties and held that the plaintiff had failed to discharge this onus as the oral reference to the properties by the plaintiffs lacked the precision necessary to enable the court to conclude what the common intention of the parties had been.

The lack of precision in relation to the alleged common intention was even more pronounced in the subsequent decision of Murphy J in *Ferguson v. Merchant Banking Ltd.*[15] The plaintiff claimed specific performance of a contract for the sale of land and the official liquidator of the defendant company contested the plaintiff's right to have the contract performed claiming that it was never the intention to include certain development lands in the sale. Murphy J commented that the case before him was far weaker from the defendant's point of view than that presented to the court by the plaintiff in *Irish Life Assurance Co.* In that case a conscious decision to exclude the lands in question had been made whereas in the case before the court, the liquidator simply did not know of the existence of the valuable vacant land. Murphy J also said that there was a striking similarity in that there was an 'absence of a pre-existing concluded agreement establishing the common intention of the parties with a sufficient degree of particularity'. He concluded that the bargain was too imprecise to constitute a contract and that the question of rectification of the agreement was wholly unstateable.

Lack of precision also proved to be fatal to the plaintiff's case in the decision of Barron J in *McD. v. McD.*[16] The plaintiff wife and defendant husband signed an agreement following negotiations to settle proceedings relating to maintenance and the distribution of their property and custody of their children.

---

14. [1986] IR 332 (HC); [1989] IR 253 (SC).
15. [1993] ILRM 136.
16. [1993] ILRM 717.

The plaintiff sought rectification of the agreement to include the fact that the husband had agreed to pay her costs in all outstanding legal proceedings between them. Barron J accepted that: 'In order to rectify the contract the court must be satisfied that there was a common and continuing intention and that the agreement as recorded does not represent [the parties'] common intention'[17] and continued that it 'must also be satisfied as to precisely what that common intention was.' Applying these principles, Barron J said that it was necessary for the evidence to show that there was a common intention that the husband should pay the wife's costs and also the precise nature of such costs. He did not believe that the evidence established either of these matters and said that even if there had been an agreement that the husband was to pay the wife's costs, it was clear from the drafting of the subsequent documents that there was no *consensus ad idem* as to the matters to be dealt with on taxation.

For rectification to be available it is necessary to establish that the instrument in question does not accord with the actual terms agreed by the parties and that if rectified it will do so. In this context it is important to distinguish the actual terms from those the parties might have stipulated if they had not been under some misapprehension about what they were agreeing upon. As Spry[18] has stated 'where there is no lack of conformity between the document and the concurrent intention, the basis for rectification does not exist' so an instrument which truly reflects what the parties agreed cannot be altered even though those involved laboured under a fundamental misapprehension about the consequences of their agreement. This point is well illustrated by the decision of the Court of Appeal in *Frederick E. Rose (London) Ltd v. W.H. Pim Junior & Co. Ltd.*[19] The defendant agreed to supply the plaintiff with 'horsebeans', both parties mistakenly believing that the term was synonymous with 'feveroles'. When the defendant subsequently supplied another type of horsebean which was less valuable in nature the plaintiff sought rectification of the agreement to refer specifically to the term 'feverole' but failed on the basis that the contract as recorded accurately reflected the actual terms agreed.

Finally, it emerges from the decision of Murphy J in *Lac Minerals Ltd v. Chevron Mineral Corporation of Ireland*[20] that a claim for rectification cannot succeed where it is not made by either of the parties involved in the original agreement, but by a party who although undoubtedly affected by it was in no sense privy to the manner in which it was negotiated, or the circumstances in which the error occurred. Murphy J concluded that the case law in the area demonstrated that while:

---

17. *Ibid.* at 722.
18. *The Principles of Equitable Remedies* (6th ed., 2001) at p. 612.
19. [1953] 2 QB 450.
20. [1995] 1 ILRM 161.

the action for rectification does not require that the parties to the litigation should be privy to the same contract, they must be privy to or affected by the same mistake in such a way that it would be unconscionable for the defendant in such proceedings to seek to rely on the document which erroneously recorded or mistakenly implemented the true agreement.[21]

UNILATERAL MISTAKE

As Griffin J stated in *Irish Life Assurance Co. Ltd v. Dublin Land Securities Ltd*[22] 'as a general rule, the courts only rectify an agreement in writing where there has been a mutual mistake i.e. where it fails to record the intention of *both* parties'. However, he went on to acknowledge that this statement must now be qualified somewhat and that a party who has entered into an agreement by mistake may be entitled to rectification if he establishes that the other party concluded the agreement with knowledge of this mistake.[23] This position had been accepted by Kenny J in his judgment in *Lucey v. Laurel Construction Co. Ltd*[24] in the following manner:

> The Court has jurisdiction to rectify a written agreement made between two parties only when either there is a mutual mistake made by the two parties in the drafting of a written agreement which is to give effect to a prior oral agreement or when one party sees a mistake in the written agreement and when he knows that the other party has not seen it and then signs the document knowing that it contains a mistake. . . .

Similar views were expressed by Pennycuick J in *A. Roberts & Co. Ltd v. Leicestershire County Council*[25] where he stated that 'a party is entitled to rectification of a contract on proof that he believed a particular term to be included in the contract and that the other party concluded the contract with the omission or a variation of that term in the knowledge that the first party believed the term to be included'. The plaintiff had undertaken to build a school for the defendant council. The agreement originally provided that the building should be completed within 18 months, but officers of the defendant changed the time for the performance of the contract to 30 months and the plaintiff signed without noticing the alteration. It was held that the defendant was aware of the mistake and rectification was ordered on this basis. This result can be contrasted with that arrived at in *Riverlate Properties Ltd v.*

---

21. *Ibid.* at 178.
22. [1989] IR 253, 260.
23. *Ibid.* at 261. See also *O'Neill v. Ryan (No. 3)* [1992] 1 IR 166, 185 *per* Costello J.
24. High Court 1970 No. 3816P (Kenny J) 18 December 1970 at 9-10.
25. [1961] Ch 555.

Paul.[26] The parties executed a lease prepared by the solicitors for the lessor which obliged the lessor to bear all the costs of exterior and structural repairs to the demised premises. Although the lessor had intended that the lessee should be liable to make a contribution towards this expenditure, neither the lessee nor her solicitor were aware of this. The lessor sought rectification of the lease, or if the lessee would not accept this remedy, then rescission. The Court of Appeal held that rectification should not be granted since the lessee neither directly nor through her solicitor knew of the lessor's mistake.

The circumstances in which the so-called doctrine in *Roberts* will apply were considered in some detail by the Court of Appeal in *Thomas Bates & Son Ltd v. Wyndham's (Lingerie) Ltd.*[27] The defendant tenant was aware of the plaintiff landlord's mistake in not including an arbitration provision in a rent review clause but did not draw its attention to it. The plaintiff realized the omission only when rent review was necessary although the defendant had at all times been aware of the mistake. The Court of Appeal ordered that an arbitration clause be inserted into the lease in accordance with the parties' original intention. Buckley LJ stated that for the doctrine to apply the following conditions must be satisfied:

1. One party, A, erroneously believed that the document to be rectified contained a particular term or provision, or mistakenly thought it did not contain a particular term or provision which mistakenly, it did contain.

2. The other party, B, was aware of the mistake and knew that it was due to an error on the part of A.

3. B omitted to draw the mistake to the notice of A.

4. The mistake must be one calculated to benefit B.

Buckley LJ commented that where these requirements are fulfilled, the court may regard it as inequitable to allow B to resist a claim for rectification to give effect to A's intention on the ground that the mistake was not a common one at the time of the execution of the document. One final observation made by Buckley LJ in *Bates* which is worth noting is his comment that while this 'inequitable conduct' may involve some element of sharp practice it depends more 'on the equity of the position'.

A useful summary of the circumstances in which the court will permit rectification for unilateral mistake is contained in the judgment of Binnie J in the decision of the Supreme Court of Canada in *Sylvan Lake Golf and Tennis Club Ltd v. Performance Industries Ltd*[28] in which he stated as follows:

---

26. [1975] Ch 133.
27. [1981] 1 WLR 505.
28. (2002) 209 DLR (4th) 318, 330.

The plaintiff must establish that the terms agreed to orally were not written down properly. The error may be fraudulent, or it may be innocent. What is essential is that at the time of execution of the written document the defendant knew or ought to have known of the error and the plaintiff did not. Moreover, the attempt of the defendant to rely on the erroneous written document must amount to 'fraud or the equivalent of fraud'.

In *Irish Life Assurance Co. Ltd v. Dublin Land Securities*[29] Keane J said that rectification could be granted in cases of unilateral mistake where it would be inequitable in the circumstances to allow the other party to retain a benefit derived from the mistake. In the case before him there was a mere unilateral mistake and no sharp practice or fraud on the part of the defendant. It would therefore not be equitable to grant rectification because the defendant was not aware of the plaintiffs' mistake when the contract was executed. A further example of circumstances in which a court can decree rectification of a document in a case of unilateral mistake is when the party who is not mistaken is guilty of fraud. Thus in *McCausland v. Young*[30] a son was held to have acquired a right to rectification of an instrument of re-settlement on the grounds that his father, who stood in a fiduciary relationship towards him, had failed to disclose the nature and effect of a forfeiture clause contained in the settlement.

THE ONUS OF PROOF

Clearly the rule that parol evidence is not admissible to add to or vary the terms of a written instrument does not apply to a claim for rectification as such a claim is based on the premise that the written agreement as recorded does not reflect the true intention of the parties. Oral evidence which expressly contradicts the terms of the written agreement may therefore be adduced and the onus lies firmly on the plaintiff to establish grounds for rectification. Traditionally it was accepted that 'much vigilance and caution' was required in such cases particularly where a claim was based entirely on oral evidence.[31] In *Fowler v. Fowler*[32] Lord Chelmsford LC stated that evidence of the clearest and most satisfactory nature was necessary and that 'something more than the highest degree of probability' was required which would leave 'no fair and

---

29. [1986] IR 332.
30. [1949] NI 49.
31. *McCormack v. McCormack* (1877) 1 LR Ir 119, 124.
32. (1859) 4 De G & J 250, 265. See also the *dicta* of Thurlow LC in *Countess of Shelburne v. Earl of Inchiquin* (1784) 1 Bro CC 338, 341 that 'strong irrefragable evidence is required'.

reasonable doubt' about the matter. Similar terminology was employed in this jurisdiction by Haugh J in *Nolan v. Graves*[33] where he spoke of an onus of proof 'beyond all reasonable doubt'.

More recently however, the tendency has been to move towards a more lenient approach to this issue. In *Joscelyne v. Nissen*[34] Russell LJ stated that in the view of the Court of Appeal it would be better to use the phrase 'convincing proof' without importing the phrase 'beyond all reasonable doubt' from the criminal law. The matter was also given some consideration by the members of the Court of Appeal in *Thomas Bates & Son Ltd v. Wyndham's (Lingerie) Ltd*[35] where Brightman LJ stated that the standard of proof required in an action for rectification to establish the common intention of the parties is 'the civil standard of balance of probability'. However, he continued by saying that as the alleged common intention will necessarily contradict the written instrument 'convincing proof' is required to counteract the intention of the parties as displayed in the instrument itself. In addition, he was of the opinion that the standard of proof should be no different in cases of unilateral mistake such as that before him, a suggestion which would seem to be in accordance with the view of Griffin J in *Irish Life Assurance Co. Ltd v. Dublin Land Securities Ltd*[36] where he spoke of the plaintiff establishing his case by 'convincing evidence'. In this case, Griffin J also gave consideration to the general standard required in cases where a plaintiff seeks to establish the common continuing intention of the parties. He said that bearing in mind 'the heavy burden of proof'[37] that lies on a party seeking rectification, the question which the court must answer is whether there was 'convincing proof' that the written instrument did not reflect the parties' intention.

Therefore, the position would appear to be very similar now both in this jurisdiction and in England, namely that while it has been accepted that the ordinary civil standard of proof should apply, the nature of the case being made inevitably demands that the proof adduced be 'convincing' in view of the fact that it will necessarily contradict the written agreement between the parties. This is in line with the approach adopted recently by the Supreme Court of Canada in *Sylvan Lake Golf and Tennis Club Ltd v. Performance Industries Ltd*[38] in which Binnie J spoke in terms of 'convincing proof' which he described as 'proof that may fall well short of the criminal standard, but which goes beyond the sort of proof that only reluctantly and with hesitation scrapes over the low end of the civil "more probable than not" standard'.

---

33. [1946] IR 376, 389.
34. [1970] 2 QB 86, 98. See also *Westland Savings Bank v. Hancock* [1987] 2 NZLR 21.
35. [1981] 1 WLR 505.
36. [1989] IR 253, 260-261.
37. *Ibid.* at 263. See also at 259.
38. (2002) 209 DLR (4th) 318, 333.

DISCRETIONARY FACTORS

Rectification as an equitable remedy is discretionary in nature. Haugh J has commented in *Nolan v. Graves*[39] that the jurisdiction of a court to grant rectification and specific performance 'is a delicate jurisdiction ... [which] must be exercised with discretion and care'. However an examination of the case law in this area would suggest that where a convincing case for a right to relief in this form is established, the remedy will only infrequently be withheld on discretionary grounds. The most obvious reason for this finding is that unlike other types of equitable remedy such as injunctions and specific performance, which may be withheld on discretionary grounds leaving the plaintiff to a remedy in damages, if rectification is refused the instrument in question remains effective in its original form and the plaintiff may have no remedy whatsoever.

One clear case in which rectification will not be granted is where a *bona fide* purchaser for value without notice has acquired some interest under the instrument which the plaintiff seeks to rectify.[40] In addition, an order will be withheld where granting it will serve no practical purpose e.g. where the obligations arising under the agreement have already been performed in accordance with the common intention of the parties. Other more general discretionary grounds may relate to the conduct of the parties, such as an absence of clean hands on the part of the plaintiff or laches or acquiescence on his part. Where a plaintiff has delayed unreasonably in seeking relief combined with circumstances which would make it inequitable or unjust to grant relief, such as where the defendant has altered his position on the basis of the plaintiff's statements or actions, relief in the form of rectification may be withheld. Equally even where the plaintiff has in no way been at fault, he may still fail to obtain a remedy on discretionary grounds where the court is satisfied that to make the order sought would cause undue prejudice or hardship to the defendant.

TYPES OF INSTRUMENTS WHICH CAN BE RECTIFIED

Various types of *inter partes* agreements such as leases[41] and share transfers[42] can be rectified. However, where statute requires that an instrument be registered, relief may be refused once this has been done, particularly where

---

39. [1946] IR 376, 391. See also the comments of Evershed MR in *Whiteside v. Whiteside* [1950] Ch 65, 71 that rectification is a discretionary remedy 'which must be cautiously watched and jealously exercised'.
40. *Smith v. Jones* [1954] 1 WLR 1089.
41. *Thomas Bates & Son Ltd v. Wyndham's (Lingerie) Ltd* [1981] 1 WLR 505.
42. *Re International Contract Co.* (1872) 7 Ch App 485.

a statutory mechanism exists for altering the document, and a court will not make an order rectifying the articles of association of a company.[43]

Rectification of a voluntary deed or settlement may be obtained where there is sufficient evidence to satisfy the court that the donor or settlor's intentions were not accurately recorded in the terms of the instrument. As Brightman J stated in *Re Butlin's Settlement Trusts*,[44] there is no doubt that 'the court has power to rectify a settlement notwithstanding that it is a voluntary settlement and not the result of a bargain'. So, in *Fitzgerald v. Fitzgerald*[45] the Irish Court of Appeal granted rectification of a marriage settlement to allow for the insertion of proper words of limitation where the deed itself afforded sufficient evidence of the parties' intention. While such applications will often be made by the settlor himself, a court may entertain a claim by a beneficiary although it will be unlikely to be successful if made during the settlor's lifetime if his consent to the alteration is not forthcoming.[46] However, where the settlor is dead and it is proved either from his instructions or otherwise that the deed was not drawn up in the exact manner which he intended, rectification may be granted.[47] The circumstances in which a court may grant rectification of a voluntary settlement on the application of the settlor, where a trustee does not consent, were considered in *Re Butlin's Settlement Trusts*,[48] but it is clearly necessary for such a trustee to have reasonable evidence to support his opposition to the making of an order before he will succeed.

It is generally accepted that a court has no jurisdiction to rectify a will apart from where as a matter of construction it finds that a manifest error has occurred.[49] In England, section 20 of the Administration of Justice Act 1982 provides that a will may be rectified where the instrument fails to give effect to the testator's intentions by reason of a clerical error or due to a failure to give effect to his instructions but there is no equivalent provision in this jurisdiction.

---

43. *Scott v. Frank F. Scott (London) Ltd* [1940] Ch 794.
44. [1976] Ch 251, 260.
45. [1902] 1 IR 477.
46. *Thompson v. Whitmore* (1860) 1 J & H 268.
47. *Lister v. Hodgson* (1867) LR 4 Eq 30, 34 *per* Romilly MR.
48. [1976] Ch 251.
49. *Re Bacharach's Will Trusts* [1959] Ch 245.

CHAPTER 16

Rescission

INTRODUCTION

The term 'rescission' can be used in a number of different contexts and it is important to appreciate this before examining the circumstances in which rescission in equity may be granted. Where one party has been in breach of a fundamental term of a contract, the innocent party may chose to either affirm it and sue for damages for its breach or, provided the breach goes to the root of the contract, he may treat this conduct as repudiation of the contract by the other party which relieves him from the performance of further contractual obligations and still allows him to sue for damages. This latter option of 'rescission' is a purely common law concept and the decision to pursue this course is essentially one for the innocent party to make. Alternatively the terms of a contract itself may confer on a party the right to terminate or 'rescind' it in certain circumstances e.g. on the occurrence of a specified event or where there is non-compliance with a condition precedent laid down in the contract.

Unlike the forms of rescission just described, rescission in equity involves the setting aside or avoiding of contracts and other instruments by the court, rather than as a result of a decision taken by a party to it where, as Pettit[1] states, 'the contract contains an inherent cause of invalidity' often in the form of mistake, misrepresentation or undue influence. If a court orders the rescission of a contract in the exercise of this equitable jurisdiction the contract is treated as being voidable *ab initio*, so while it is treated as valid until rescission is ordered, it is then retrospectively invalidated from its inception.

The circumstances in which a court will intervene in the exercise of its equitable jurisdiction were summarised by Henchy J in *Northern Bank Finance Corporation Ltd v. Charlton*[2] where he said that relief in the form of rescission 'will be granted when the court considers that it would be just and equitable to do so in order to restore the parties, at least substantially to their respective positions' before the vitiating conduct occurred, a point which was echoed by Griffin J in his judgment in the same case.[3] As he went on to say 'the primary

---

1. *Equity and the Law of Trusts* (9th ed., 2001) p. 670.
2. [1979] IR 149, 197.
3. *Ibid.* at 206. See also the comments of Denning LJ in *Solle v. Butcher* [1950] 1 KB 671, 696.

purpose of all proceedings for rescission, as contrasted with that of actions for damages, is to restore the *status quo* and bring back the original position by undoing all that has intervened between it and the present' and 'the object to be achieved by rescission is the restoration of *both parties* as nearly as may be to the position which each occupied before the transaction'. However, it should be noted that the attitude of equity towards the concept of *restitutio in integrum* in granting rescission is more flexible than that adopted by the common law and as Lord Blackburn commented in *Erlanger v. New Sombrero Phosphate Co.*:[4] 'the practice has always been for a Court of Equity to give this relief whenever, by the exercise of its powers, it can do what is practically just, though it cannot restore the parties precisely to the state they were in before the contract.'

GROUNDS FOR RESCISSION

Mistake

While mistake alone is capable of justifying the refusal of a decree of specific performance, it would be incorrect to assume that it will always automatically justify rescission. However, as Flanagan J stated in *Gun v. McCarthy*:[5]

> [W]here there being a clear undoubted mistake by one party in reference to a material term of the contract which he entered into with another, and the other party knowingly seeks to avail himself of that, and seeks to bind the other to the mistake, the law of this Court is, that it will not allow such a contract to be binding on the parties, but will give relief against it.

The type of mistake which will render a contract void in law was identified by Lord Atkin in *Bell v. Lever Brothers Ltd*[6] as one 'as to the existence of some quality which makes the thing without the quality essentially different from the thing as it was believed to be'. However, for many years a well established line of authority in England laid down the principle that equity would permit rescission of a contract on grounds of common mistake where the contract was valid at common law. While the Court of Appeal has recently held in *Great Peace Shipping Ltd v. Tsavliris Salvage (International) Ltd*[7] that there is no jurisdiction in equity to grant rescission of a contract on such grounds when it is valid and enforceable on ordinary principles of contract law, given

---

4.   (1878) 3 App Cas 1218, 1278-1279.
5.   (1883) 13 LR Ir 304, 310.
6.   [1932] AC 161, 218.
7.   [2002] 3 WLR 1617.

the controversial nature of the decision and the fact that the courts in this jurisdiction may prefer to follow the previous authorities on this issue,[8] it remains necessary to trace how this equitable jurisdiction has been developed and applied.

The starting point in examining the decisions in which relief was granted in equity on grounds of mistake in England is *Cooper v. Phibbs*.[9] An individual agreed to take a lease of a salmon fishery from the trustee of a settlement in circumstances where, unknown to both parties, it already belonged to him, and the House of Lords agreed to set aside the agreement subject to a lien on the fishery for such monies as had been expended on improvements. As Lord Westbury stated:

> [I]f parties contract under a mutual mistake and misapprehension as to their relative and respective rights, the result is, that that agreement is liable to be set aside as having proceeded upon a common mistake.[10]

This decision also illustrates the ability of equity to set aside a contract on such terms as the court sees fit to impose, in this instance involving the imposition of a lien, and shows the flexible nature of equitable rescission.

Perhaps the most extensive consideration of the circumstances in which rescission will be granted in equity on the grounds of common mistake is contained in the judgment of Denning LJ as he then was in *Solle v. Butcher*.[11] In that case a lessee leased a flat for a period of years on the basis of an erroneous assumption made by both parties, that it had been so completely reconstructed that it constituted a new flat and as such was no longer controlled by the provisions of the Rent Acts. In fact the maximum permissible rent was substantially less than that paid and the lessee sued to recover the overpaid rent. This action failed and the lease was set aside on the grounds of common mistake. Denning LJ stated as follows:

> It is now clear that a contract will be set aside if the mistake of the one party has been induced by a material misrepresentation of the other, even though it was not fraudulent or fundamental; or if the one party, knowing that the other is mistaken about the terms of an offer, or the identity of the person by whom it is made, lets him remain under his delusion and conclude a contract on the mistaken terms instead of pointing out the mistake.[12]

---

8. See *O'Neill v. Ryan (No. 3)* [1992] 1 IR 166, 185.
9. (1867) LR 2 HL 149.
10. *Ibid.* at 170.
11. [1950] 1 KB 671.
12. *Ibid.* at 692.

He continued:

> A contract is also liable in equity to be set aside if the parties were
> under a common misapprehension either as to facts or as to their relative
> and respective rights provided that the misapprehension was fundamental
> and that the party seeking to set it aside was not himself at fault.[13]

The suggestion made by Denning LJ that a contract which although not void
as a result of mistake at law, may nevertheless be voidable in equity, was
accepted by Goff J in *Grist v. Bailey*.[14] The plaintiff agreed to buy the
defendant's house at a reduced price because both parties mistakenly believed
that it was the subject of a protected tenancy. The plaintiff claimed specific
performance and the defendant counter-claimed and sought rescission of the
contract. Goff J held that although the mistake did not suffice to nullify the
contract at common law, equity could intervene. In relation to the statement
made by Denning LJ in *Solle* he commented that this could not be dismissed
as a 'mere *dictum*' and was in his judgment the basis of the decision and
therefore binding on him. Goff J said that the essential questions to be decided
were first, whether there had been a common mistake, secondly, whether it
was fundamental and thirdly, whether the defendant was at fault. He was
satisfied that in the case before him there had been a common mistake of a
fundamental nature. While Goff J said that it was not absolutely clear what
Denning LJ meant by the third requirement, namely that the party seeking to
take advantage of the mistake must not be at fault, clearly there must be some
degree of blameworthiness beyond the mere fact of having made a mistake.
In the circumstances he did not feel that the defendant was at fault to the
extent of disentitling herself to relief and he concluded that the plaintiff's
action should be dismissed on terms that the defendant would enter into a
new contract to sell the house at an appropriate price for vacant possession.

The reasoning in *Solle v. Butcher* was applied again by Denning MR in
Magee v. Pennine Insurance Co. Ltd[15] where he said that '[a] common mistake,
even on a most fundamental matter, does not make a contract void at law; but
it makes it voidable in equity'. Subsequently, in *Associated Japanese Bank
(International) Ltd v. Credit du Nord SA*,[16] while Steyn J accepted that a
contract affected by mistake in equity is not void but may be set aside on
terms, he added that in his view the principles enunciated by the House of
Lords in *Bell v. Lever Brothers Ltd*[17] clearly still governed mistake at common
law. More recent decisions showed an acceptance of the principles enunciated

13. *Ibid.* at 693. See also *Magee v. Pennine Insurance Co. Ltd* [1969] 2 QB 507, 514.
14. [1967] Ch 532.
15. [1969] 2 QB 507, 514.
16. [1989] 1 WLR 255, 266.
17. [1932] AC 161.

by Denning LJ in *Solle v. Butcher* and in *William Sindall plc v. Cambridgeshire County Council*[18] Evans LJ stated that it must be assumed that there is a category of mistake which is 'fundamental' so as to permit the equitable remedy of rescission and wider than the 'serious and radical' mistake which means that the agreement is void in law. In his view the difference may be that the common law rule is limited to mistakes with regard to the subject matter of the contract while equity can have regard to a wider and perhaps unlimited category of 'fundamental mistake'.

However, in the recent decision of the Court of Appeal in *Great Peace Shipping Ltd v. Tsavliris Salvage (International) Ltd*[19] Lord Phillips MR made it clear that the court found it impossible to reconcile *Solle v. Butcher* with the decision of the House of Lords in *Bell v. Lever Brothers Ltd* and stated that it was not possible to distinguish a mistake which was 'fundamental' from Lord Atkin's mistake as to quality which 'makes the thing contracted for essentially different from the thing that it was believed to be'. As Phillips MR stated:

> Thus the premise of equity's intrusion into the effects of the common law is that the common law rule in question is seen in the particular case to work injustice, and for some reason the common law cannot cure itself. But it is difficult to see how that can apply here....We are *only* concerned with the question whether relief might be given for common mistake in circumstances wider than those stipulated in *Bell v. Lever Brothers Ltd*. But that, surely, is a question as to where the common law rule should draw the line; not whether, given the common law rule, it needs to be mitigated by application of some other doctrine. The common law has drawn the line in *Bell v. Lever Brothers Ltd*.[20]

The Court of Appeal concluded that if coherence was to be restored to this area of the law it could only be by declaring that there is no jurisdiction to grant rescission of a contract on the ground of common mistake where the contract is valid and enforceable on ordinary principles of contract law. It is in some respects doubtful whether the courts in this jurisdiction would agree with the conclusion reached by the Court of Appeal in *Great Peace Shipping*. Certainly in *O'Neill v. Ryan (No. 3)*[21] Costello J referred to the decision of Denning LJ in *Solle* as establishing that a court may set aside an agreement in the exercise of its equitable jurisdiction even though it is not void on the grounds of common mistake. There are good grounds for arguing that this

---

18. [1994] 1 WLR 1016, 1042. See also *Clarion Ltd v. National Provident Institution* [2000] 1 WLR 1888; *West Sussex Properties Ltd v. Chichester DC* Court of Appeal, 28 June 2000 paragraph 42.
19. [2002] 3 WLR 1617.
20. *Ibid.* at 1660.
21. [1992] 1 IR 166.

equitable basis for intervention should be allowed to continue as it allows for the setting aside of a contract where the justice of the case requires it and also permits this to take place on terms which appear just to the court.

One question which has yet to be satisfactorily resolved is whether a court will grant rescission in a case of unilateral mistake or whether the mistake must be common to both parties before it will intervene. This issue was considered by Russell LJ in *Riverlate Properties Ltd v. Paul*[22] where the parties executed a lease prepared by the lessor's solicitors which obliged the lessor to bear all the costs of exterior and structural repairs to the premises. Although the lessor had intended that the lessee should be liable to make a contribution towards this expenditure, neither the lessee nor her solicitor were aware of this. The Court of Appeal accepted that the mistake was in no way attributable to anything said or done by the lessee and held that it was a case of 'mere unilateral mistake' which could not entitle the plaintiff to rescission of the lease. The opposite approach would seem to have been accepted in Ireland, at least in principle, although it is not clear whether the *dicta* to this effect will be followed. In *Monaghan County Council v. Vaughan*[23] Dixon J commented that 'unilateral mistake arises where one of two or more parties is not *ad idem* with the other party or parties, and there is therefore, no real agreement between them. In such a case rescission may be appropriate. . . .' This statement was referred to by Griffin J in the course of his judgment in *Irish Life Assurance Co. Ltd v. Dublin Land Securities Ltd*,[24] although as the Supreme Court was concerned solely with the issue of rectification in that case, no view was expressed on the circumstances in which the remedy of rescission would be granted.

Misrepresentation

A contract can be rescinded at common law and in equity where there has been a fraudulent misrepresentation. The most important Irish authority on the right to rescind in equity on grounds of fraudulent misrepresentation is *Northern Bank Finance Corporation Ltd v. Charlton*.[25] The plaintiff bank loaned the defendants a sum of money to facilitate their objective of acquiring control of a public company. When the defendants defaulted on the loan repayments, the plaintiff claimed the balance and interest and the defendants counter-claimed that they had entered into the original transaction because of the fraudulent misrepresentations of the plaintiff. In the High Court, Finlay P made an order dismissing the plaintiff's claim and allowing the defendants' counter-claim on the basis that the defendants had been induced by a fraudulent

---

22. [1975] Ch 133.
23. [1948] IR 306, 312.
24. [1989] IR 253.
25. [1979] IR 149.

misrepresentation to enter into the transactions. The Supreme Court agreed that the plaintiff's claim should be dismissed but the majority of the court held that the order of rescission granted by the High Court should be set aside because the principle of *restitutio in integrum* could not apply. Extensive consideration was given by a number of members of the Supreme Court to the circumstances in which rescission of a contract may be granted. O'Higgins CJ pointed out that in the case of a fraudulent misrepresentation, the fact that the contract has already been executed or the transaction completed is no bar to rescission unless *restitutio in integrum* has become impossible as a result. In his view it was the duty of the court to do what was 'practically just' in the circumstances, even though the precise restoration of the parties to their previous position was no longer possible. However, the majority view was to the contrary; as Henchy J put it an order of rescission would in the circumstances run counter to the object of the restoration of the *status quo ante*.

The principles which apply to rescission in cases of innocent misrepresentation are not as free from doubt.[26] The situation that arises where the contract has not yet been completed was examined in *Gahan v. Boland*.[27] Murphy J said that where a false representation was made, even though made in good faith and with no intention to mislead, rescission could be granted where the plaintiff could establish that 'the representation was made by the defendant with the intention of inducing the plaintiff to act thereon and secondly, that the plaintiff did in fact act or rely on the representation.'[28] This view was echoed by Henchy J in the Supreme Court where he stated that an innocent yet false representation could suffice where it was a material one made with the intention of inducing a plaintiff to act on it and where it was one of the factors which induced the plaintiff to enter into the contract. It would appear that it need not be the 'sole cause of the transaction' and it is enough that it provides a material inducement to enter into the obligations in question.[29]

It would appear that in circumstances where the contract is complete rescission will only be granted in cases of fraudulent misrepresentation. This point was made by Lord Selborne in *Brownlie v. Campbell*[30] in the following manner: 'it is not ... the principle of equity that relief should afterwards be given against [a] conveyance, unless there be a case of fraud, or a case of

---

26. As Keane J commented in *Doolan v. Murray* High Court 1990 No. 7753 P, 21 December 1993: 'An innocent misrepresentation . . . may afford grounds for rescission of a contract'.
27. High Court 1981 No. 4995P (Murphy J) 21 January 1983 and Supreme Court 1983 No. 37, 20 January 1984.
28. *Ibid.* at 14.
29. *Lecky v. Walter* [1914] 1 IR 378, 384 *per* O'Connor MR.
30. (1880) 5 App Cas 925, 937. Quoted with approval by O'Connor MR in *Lecky v. Walter* [1914] 1 IR 378, 385-386.

misrepresentation amounting to fraud, by which the purchaser may have been deceived'. This dicta was referred to by O'Connor MR in *Lecky v. Walter*[31] in holding that where a contract has been completed and there has been no fraud, but only an innocent misrepresentation, the agreement cannot be set aside.[32]

A further distinction which must be drawn between cases of fraudulent and innocent misrepresentation in the context of rescission, is that in the former case it is sufficient to show that the misrepresentation has been made 'as to any part of that which induced the party to enter into the contract which he seeks to rescind' whereas in the latter it is necessary to show that as a result there is 'a complete difference in substance' between what was contracted for and what was delivered.[33]

As a general principle, failure to disclose facts material to a contract will not constitute grounds for rescission unless by his silence a person implicitly alters the meaning of a representation previously made by him.[34] However, an exception to this general principle are contracts *uberrimae fidei* of which contracts of insurance and family settlements are the most common examples. In such cases failure to disclose any material fact may justify rescission.

Undue Influence

Gifts or agreements concluded on the basis of wholly inadequate consideration are liable to be set aside in equity where they have been given or made as a result of the exercise of undue influence over the donor or party of whom advantage has been taken. As Lindley LJ made clear in *Allcard v. Skinner*,[35] equity intervenes not to save individuals 'from the consequences of their own folly' but to prevent them from being victimised by others. He stated as follows in what has been described as a 'famous passage':[36]

> It would obviously be to encourage folly, recklessness, extravagance and vice if persons could get back property which they foolishly made away with, whether by giving it to charitable institutions or by bestowing it on less worthy objects. On the other hand, to protect people from being forced, tricked or misled in any way by others into parting with

---

31. [1914] 1 IR 378.
32. See also *Legge v. Croker* (1811) 1 Ba & B 506, 514.
33. *Kennedy v. Panama, New Zealand, and Australian Royal Mail Co. (Ltd)* (1867) LR 2 QB 580, 587. Quoted with approval by Joyce J in *Seddon v. North Eastern Salt Co. Ltd* [1905] 1 Ch 326, 333, by O'Connor MR in *Lecky v. Walter* [1914] 1 IR 378, 386 and by Fitzgibbon J in *Carbin v. Somerville* [1933] IR 276, 288.
34. *Oakes v. Turquand* (1867) LR 2 HL 325.
35. (1887) 36 Ch D 145, 182.
36. By Lord Scarman in *National Westminster Bank plc v. Morgan* [1985] AC 686, 705.

their property is one of the most legitimate objects of all laws; and the equitable doctrine of undue influence has grown out of and been developed by the necessity of grappling with insidious forms of spiritual tyranny and with the infinite varieties of fraud.[37]

In general the courts have shied away from any attempt to define precisely what constitutes undue influence; but it has been described as where a person has exercised 'unfair, undue and unreasonable mental control'[38] over another. Perhaps the most comprehensive formulation of the type of conduct which will amount to undue influence is that laid down by Lowry LCJ in *R. (Proctor) v. Hutton*[39] where he stated that 'the plaintiff must prove that an unfair advantage has been gained by an unconscientious use of power in the form of some unfair and improper conduct, some coercion from outside, some over reaching, some form of cheating.' Undue influence will therefore arise in circumstances where the defendant has caused the plaintiff's judgment to become clouded through the exercise of some form of domination and caused him to enter a transaction disadvantageous to him.

Presumed and Actual Undue Influence

Cases of undue influence have traditionally been divided into two broad categories, presumed and actual undue influence.[40] In cases of actual undue influence as Lord Browne-Wilkinson commented in *Barclays Bank plc v. O'Brien*,[41] 'it is necessary for the claimant to prove affirmatively that the wrongdoer exerted undue influence on the complainant to enter into the particular transaction which is impugned'. In addition, undue influence is readily presumed in the case of certain relationships of trust and confidence and in such situations the evidential burden shifts from the complainant to the other party.[42] As Lowry LCJ pointed out in *R. (Proctor) v. Hutton*[43] the undue

---

37. (1887) 36 Ch D 145, 182-183.
38. *Harris v. Swordy* High Court 1960 No 71 Sp (Henchy J) 21 December 1967 at 15.
39. [1978] NI 139, 146.
40. Although it should be noted that Lord Clyde has commented in *Royal Bank of Scotland v. Etridge (No. 2)* [2002] 2 AC 773, 816 that on the face of it a division into cases of actual and presumed undue influence appears to be illogical. However, in her judgment in *Carroll v. Carroll* [1999] 4 IR 241, 253 Denham J accepted this division. See also *Síodhacháin v. O'Mahony* High Court 2001 No. 13306P (Kearns J) 31 October 2002 at 40.
41. [1994] 1 AC 180, 189.
42. As Lord Nicholls stated in *Royal Bank of Scotland v. Etridge (No. 2)* [2002] 2 AC 773, 798 there are two prerequisites to this shift in the burden of proof; first, that the complainant reposed trust and confidence in the other party and secondly, that the transaction is not readily explicable by the relationship between the parties.
43. [1978] NI 139, 146.

influence is of the same nature in both cases, the difference being that in cases of presumed undue influence it is deemed to have been exercised until this presumption is negatived on a balance of probabilities by evidence.[44] The distinction between these two classes of cases was well summarised by Costello J, as he then was, in *O'Flanagan v. Ray-Ger Ltd*[45] as follows:

> The cases where a plaintiff seeks to set aside a gift or other transaction on the ground that it was procured by undue influence have been divided into two classes; firstly those in which it can be expressly proved that undue influence was exercised, in which circumstances the Court intervenes on the principle that no one should be allowed to retain any benefit arising from his own fraud or wrongful act; secondly those in which the relations between the donor and donee have at or shortly before the execution of a gift been such as to raise a presumption that the donor had influence over the donee.

Within the category of presumed undue influence, Slade LJ in *Bank of Credit and Commerce International SA v. Aboody*[46] identified two distinct cases. The first, which he termed class 2(A) was where certain relationships existed which as a matter of law raised the presumption that undue influence had been exercised and the second, class 2(B) related to cases where 'the complainant proves the *de facto* existence of a relationship under which the complainant generally reposed trust and confidence in the wrongdoer'. However, it should be noted that doubt was recently cast on the practice of adopting the so-called class 2(B) presumption by Lord Hobhouse in *Royal Bank of Scotland v. Etridge (No. 2)*[47] where he stated that 'it is not a useful forensic tool'. In his view where the relevant question is one of fact and degree and of the evaluation of evidence, the language of presumption is likely to confuse rather than assist.

Some of the types of relationship in which the presumption of undue influence arises were referred to by Jones LJ in the decision of the Northern Ireland Court of Appeal in *R. (Proctor) v. Hutton*[48] as follows 'solicitor and client, trustee and *cestui que trust*, doctor and patient or religious adviser and

---

44. It should be noted that in *Healy v. McGillicudy* [1978] ILRM 175, 178 Costello J stated that the authorities established that 'no presumption of undue influence, however, arises in the case of wills and the burden of proving undue influence in relation to wills always rests on the person alleging it'.

45. High Court 1980 No. 2858P (Costello J) 28 April 1983 at 18. Quoted with approval by Shanley J in *Carroll v. Carroll* [1998] 2 ILRM 218, 229. See also *Allcard v. Skinner* (1887) 36 Ch D 145, 171 *per* Cotton LJ.

46. [1990] 1 QB 923.

47. [2002] 2 AC 773, 822. See also the *dicta* of Lord Clyde at 816.

48. 30 April 1979 at 7.

pupil.' To this list could be added the relationships of parent and child and guardian and ward but not the relationships of husband and wife,[49] or the relationship which exists between engaged couples.[50] Some elucidation of the circumstances in which the presumption operates in the context of these various relationships is necessary. First, the case law suggests that where a person has assumed the role of adviser, whether in a legal sense or otherwise, even where the relationship has ended in the strict sense, the confidence which arises from it may still subsist in relation to matters previously within the scope of this arrangement.[51] Equally, in the context of the relationship of parent/child or guardian/ward, the presumption may continue even after the child has reached his majority or married,[52] or, provided some element of control remains, where the wardship has ceased,[53] although the view expressed by the English Court of Appeal in *Re Pauling's Settlement's Trusts*[54] was that it should not continue indefinitely. As Budd J made clear in *Gregg v. Kidd*,[55] the courts have never attempted to delimit the categories of relationship in which this presumption may arise as 'to do so would fetter that wide jurisdiction to relieve against all manner of constructive fraud which courts administering equitable jurisdiction have always exercised.'[56] In that case the plaintiff executor succeeded in having a voluntary settlement made by the deceased in favour of his nephew set aside on the grounds that the relationship between the testator on the one hand, and the nephew and his mother on the other hand, was such as to raise a presumption of influence which had not been rebutted.

One of the decisions most frequently referred to in this area of presumed undue influence is that of the English Court of Appeal in *Allcard v. Skinner*.[57] The plaintiff joined a sisterhood of nuns and made her will in favour of the superior of the order and also transferred large amounts of money and stock to her. When she left the order, she revoked her will but made no attempt to reclaim her property until five or six years later when she instituted proceedings

---

49. *Bank of Montreal v. Stuart* [1911] AC 120. See also *Royal Bank of Scotland v. Etridge (No. 2)* [2002] 2 AC 773, 797, 842.
50. *Zamet v. Hyman* [1961] 1 WLR 1442.
51. See *McMaster v. Byrne* [1952] 1 All ER 1362 in the context of a solicitor/client relationship.
52. *Lancashire Loans Ltd v. Black* [1934] 1 KB 380.
53. *Hylton v. Hylton* (1754) 2 Ves Sen 547.
54. [1964] Ch 303, 337.
55. [1956] IR 183, 194. So these categories can be added to as in *O'Sullivan v. Management Agency & Music Ltd* [1985] QB 428 where the presumption of undue influence was found to arise in a relationship between an inexperienced and unknown composer and performer and his manager.
56. See also the comment of Shanley J in *Carroll v. Carroll* [1998] 2 ILRM 218, 229 that 'the categories of relationship which will give rise to the presumption are never "closed"'.
57. (1887) 36 Ch D 145.

claiming that it had been transferred as a result of undue influence. The court held that the gifts were made by the plaintiff, who had received no independent legal advice, as a result of pressure which she could not resist and that they were recoverable in principle. However, the majority of the Court of Appeal held that in the circumstances, the claim was barred by laches and acquiescence.

Once a relationship giving rise to a presumption of undue influence is established, and it is shown that a 'substantial benefit'[58] has been obtained, the onus lies on the donee to establish that the gift or transaction resulted from the 'free exercise of the donor's will.'[59] As Dixon J put it in *Johnson v. Buttress*,[60] the evidence must establish that the gift was 'the independent and well-understood act of a man in a position to exercise a free judgment based on information as full as that of the donee.' The manner in which this presumption may be rebutted relates to two main issues; first, the question of whether independent legal advice has been received and secondly, whether it can be shown that the decision to make the gift or transfer was 'a spontaneous and independent act'[61] or that the donor 'acted of his own free will.'[62] Where independent legal advice has been given, it will tend to rebut the presumption of undue influence,[63] even where the donor is in a particularly vulnerable position *vis-à-vis* the donee.[64] On the other hand, while it would appear that it is not essential that independent legal advice be given in order to rebut the presumption,[65] the complete lack of any such advice may be a decisive factor in determining whether this will be achieved.[66] Black J made it clear in the

---

58. *Johnson v. Buttress* (1936) 56 CLR 113, 134. See also the judgment of Lowry LCJ in *R. (Proctor) v. Hutton* [1978] NI 139, 147 where he referred to the making of a 'substantial gift'.
59. *Gregg v. Kidd* [1956] IR 183, 196.
60. (1936) 56 CLR 113, 134-35.
61. *Re Brocklehurst's Estate* [1978] Ch 14. See also *Carroll v. Carroll* [1999] 4 IR 241, 264 and *Moyles v. Mahon* High Court 1997 No. 6357P (Smyth J) 6 October 2000.
62. *Gregg v. Kidd* [1956] IR 183, 196. See also *Inche Noriah v. Shaik Allie Bin Omar* [1929] AC 127, 135 and *Carroll v. Carroll* [1999] 4 IR 241, 254.
63. As Ward LJ stated in *Hammond v. Osborn* [2002] EWCA Civ 887 Court of Appeal, 27 June 2002 paragraph 49 'independent advice is....usually the crucial evidence going to the rebuttal of the presumption' although he went on the stress that it is not the only way in which the presumption can be rebutted, see *Inche Noriah v. Shaik Allie Bin Omar* [1929] AC 127, 135.
64. See e.g. *Leonard v. Leonard* [1988] ILRM 245 where a transfer by an vulnerable elderly lady to her son was upheld despite a claim of undue influence in circumstances where she had obtained proper independent legal advice. It should also be pointed out that MacKenzie J stated that he was satisfied that 'the coercion on [the plaintiff] was because of her situation and was not of [the defendant's] making'. In his view she was alone, afraid and unable to work the land and needed the company and support which transferring the land to her son would bring her.
65. *Provincial Bank of Ireland v. McKeever* [1941] IR 471, 485.
66. *McMakin v. Hibernian Bank* [1905] 1 IR 306.

course of his judgment in *Provincial Bank of Ireland v. McKeever*[67] that in certain circumstances even where independent advice has been given and rejected, the fact of it having been given may suffice to rebut the presumption of undue influence, although this will not always be the case, as it may only have been rejected as a result of influence exerted. In the view of Black J 'one cannot expect absolute disproof of undue influence' and he suggested that it is sufficient to establish 'a reasonable probability of the exercise of independent will founded upon adequate understanding'.[68] In *McKeever* the sons and widow of the deceased settlor were persuaded by trustees to execute a mortgage to secure an overdraft which these trustees had run up. Black J accepted that on the facts the presumption of undue influence had been rebutted although the only legal advice which they had received was from the trustees' solicitor, who was the sons' uncle. Black J stated that viewing the evidence as a whole, he was satisfied that the consequences of the mortgage transaction had been sufficiently understood and he allowed the claim of the plaintiff bank.

A useful recent summary of the relevant principles in this area is contained in the judgment of Shanley J which was upheld by the Supreme Court in *Carroll v. Carroll.*[69] The plaintiffs, who were the daughters and personal representatives of an elderly donor, sought to have a transfer of a pub and residential accommodation set aside on the grounds that it had been procured by undue influence and was an improvident transaction. After his wife's death, the donor had transferred the property to his son without disclosing this fact to his daughters. The donor and his son both subsequently died and tensions arose between the plaintiffs and the son's widow, the defendant, which led to the bringing of proceedings to have the original transfer set aside. The donor had discussed making the transfer to his son on two occasions with the solicitor who effected it, although the latter was in reality acting for both parties. While the donor was mentally alert at that time, he was subject to a number of physical infirmities which made him increasingly dependent on others. The plaintiffs submitted that the relationship between the donor and donee was such as to raise a presumption of undue influence, which they argued had not been rebutted. The defendant conceded that the relationship between the parties did give rise to a presumption of undue influence but submitted that it had been rebutted in the circumstances. In setting out the relevant legal principles, Shanley J stated that the law will not concern itself with insignificant transactions and that the presumption of undue influence will only arise where one party has derived a substantial benefit from the transaction. In relation to the circumstances in which the presumption may be rebutted, he stated as follows:

---

67. [1941] IR 471, 485. Although note the comments of Farwell J in *Powell v. Powell* [1900] 1 Ch 243, 246.
68. *Ibid.* at 485.
69. [1998] 2 ILRM 218 (HC); [1999] 4 IR 241 (SC). See Dwyer (2001) 36 Ir Jur 324; Hourican (2001) 6 CPLJ 18.

Where the presumption exists, it may be rebutted by evidence which establishes on the balance of probability that the transaction was the consequence of the exercise of the donor of his own free will and not the result of undue influence. Such evidence may be evidence that the donor had independent legal advice — or competent and honest lay advice.[70]

Shanley J concluded that he was not satisfied that the defendant had established as a matter of probability that the transaction was the result of the free exercise of the donor's will such as to rebut presumption of undue influence. Shanley J stated that while he accepted the evidence that the donor was mentally alert at the time he made the transfer, he was not satisfied that he had received the necessary independent advice, whether it was from a legal adviser or from a competent and qualified lay person, such as would persuade him that the transaction was made of his own free will. This conclusion was upheld by the Supreme Court, Denham J stating that, as the presumption of undue influence had been established and a substantial benefit obtained, the onus lay on the donee to establish that the transfer was the result of the free exercise of the will of the donor. In considering the submission made on behalf of the defendant that for the plaintiff to succeed it was necessary that there should be evidence that the donee had exercised undue influence on the donor, Denham J pointed out that this was not a case of actual undue influence but rather one in which the relationship between the donor and donee raised a presumption of undue influence. It was therefore necessary for the defendant to rebut the presumption and to this extent she expressed the view that the appeal had been argued on the basis of a mistaken approach to the law. Denham J stated that the facts and circumstances of the case had been fully considered and determined by the learned trial judge and she was satisfied that he was correct in his finding that it was not necessary to prove specific acts of undue influence by the donee. Instead the evidence had to be considered to see whether the presumption of undue influence had been rebutted and Denham J stated that she was satisfied that this had been done most carefully by Shanley J and that she would affirm his decision on this aspect of the appeal. In relation to rebutting the presumption of undue influence, Barron J stated that it has to be shown that the 'gift was the spontaneous act of the donor acting in circumstances which enabled him to exercise an independent will'.[71] He added

---

70. *Ibid.* at 229. While it was not relevant in the *Carroll* decision, it is interesting that Shanley J adopted the view of Lord Hailsham in *Inche Noriah v. Shaik Allie Bin Omar* [1929] AC 127, 135 that independent *legal* advice was not an essential element in rebutting the presumption and that independent advice from a suitably qualified person could suffice.

71. *Ibid.* at 264. Quoting from the judgment of Cotton LJ in *Allcard v. Skinner* (1887) 36 Ch D 145, 171.

that there is no one way in which the presumption may be rebutted and that the usual way is to show that the donor had advice from someone who was independent and who was aware of all the relevant circumstances, but that it is equally good to show that all the relevant facts are before the court and that these show that the donor was not in any way influenced in what he did by the donee. Barron J was satisfied that there could have been no independent advice given by the solicitor in the case before him as he was at best acting for both parties and he agreed with the conclusion reached by Denham J that the presumption of undue influence had not been rebutted in the circumstances.

It is important to stress that the presumption of undue influence does not arise in the context of all relationships which could be described as 'fiduciary' in nature,[72] and that whether a presumption will arise in a particular type of relationship may depend on the facts of the individual case. So, in *Lloyds Bank Ltd v. Bundy*[73] the presumption was held to apply to the relationship of banker and client in circumstances where a father had relied entirely on the advice of his bank manager in mortgaging his house as security for a guarantee relating to his son's debts. However, *Bundy* was distinguished by the House of Lords as turning on special facts in *National Westminster Bank plc v. Morgan*[74] in which a wife claimed that a bank manager had exerted undue influence over her to obtain her signature in relation to a mortgage agreement relating to the parties' house, which was concluded in order to secure a loan to her husband. The House of Lords was not satisfied that the relationship between Mrs Morgan and the bank went beyond the normal business relationship of banker and customer and held that the manager had never assumed a role which would raise the presumption of undue influence.

Undue Influence and Third Parties

The principles considered above also extend to cases where the party exerting influence does not benefit directly from his conduct and where the person over whom he has exercised this influence enters into obligations to a third party as a result. This issue has recently become very relevant in the context of obligations to financial institutions entered into by one party allegedly as a result of influence exerted over them by another and has generally arisen in the context of husband/wife relationships.

Several questions have arisen in this area; first, should the husband/wife relationship give rise to any presumption or should wives be treated as a 'specially protected class'? However, the primary focus of debate has been the circumstances in which the bank, in the absence of actual knowledge of

---

72. E.g. *Re Coomber* [1911] 1 Ch 723.
73. [1975] QB 326.
74. [1985] AC 686.

the debtor's improper conduct, will be fixed with constructive notice of this conduct.

In relation to the first of these questions, while it appears to be accepted that the relationship of husband and wife does not give rise to any presumption of undue influence,[75] there have been suggestions that wives constitute a special class which deserves protection in these circumstances. This approach was adopted by the majority of the Court of Appeal in *Barclays Bank plc v. O'Brien*[76] where Scott LJ made it clear that the likelihood of a husband exerting influence over his wife, which was the original justification for the 'tenderness of equity' towards married women who gave their property as security for their husband's debts, was still a relevant consideration.[77] This 'special equity' theory was referred to by Lord Browne-Wilkinson in the course of his speech in the House of Lords in *O'Brien* as meaning that 'equity affords special protection to a protected class of surety viz. those where the relationship between the debtor and the surety is such that influence by the debtor over the surety and reliance by the surety on the debtor are natural features of the relationship'. The approach adopted recently by Lord Nicholls in *Royal Bank of Scotland v. Etridge (No. 2)*[78] towards this issue was to confirm that no presumption of undue influence arises as a result of the husband/wife relationship, although he did state that the court will note as a matter of fact the opportunities for abuse which flow from a wife's confidence in her husband.

The approach of Scott LJ in *O'Brien* was accepted by Geoghegan J in the High Court in *Bank of Ireland v. Smyth*[79] in holding that the wife's consent to a charge over the family home was not a true consent and that the charge was therefore void. More recently the Supreme Court has suggested in *Bank of Nova Scotia v. Hogan*[80] that it may be possible to identify circumstances which would more readily raise a presumption in favour of a wife than any other third party. Murphy J stated that, notwithstanding the fact that the relationship between husband and wife has been held not to raise a presumption of undue influence, some special status does appear to have been accorded to wives in a number of decisions. He concluded that while the matrimonial relationship as such did not give rise to a presumption of undue influence,[81]

---

75. *Bank of Montreal v. Stuart* [1911] AC 120, 137; *Bank of Credit and Commerce International SA v. Aboody* [1990] 1 QB 923, 953; *Royal Bank of Scotland v. Etridge (No. 2)* [2002] 2 AC 773, 797, 842.
76. [1992] 3 WLR 593. See Dixon [1993] CLJ 24.
77. See also the reference made by Dixon J in the decision of the High Court of Australia in *Yerkey v. Jones* (1930) 63 CLR 649 to the 'invalidating tendency' applied by the courts to transactions between husbands and wives. See further Burton (1997) 4 Comm LP 120.
78. [2002] 2 AC 773, 797.
79. [1995] 2 IR 459.
80. [1996] 3 IR 239.
81. Although note that later in his judgment, Murphy J commented (at 249) that

in such cases a presumption might more readily be raised in favour of a wife than any outside party.

The circumstances in which a financial institution may be unable to rely on a guarantee provided by a wife or partner, even where it does not have actual knowledge of any improper conduct, has given rise to much debate. This involves a consideration of the circumstances in which a bank will be 'put on inquiry' and what steps it should take when in this situation. This in turn raises the issue of the content of the legal advice which should be given in such circumstances and the related question of the independence of this advice. These issues have been considered in numerous cases over the past decade, particularly in England, most notably in two decisions of the House of Lords in *Barclays Bank plc v. O'Brien*[82] and in *Royal Bank of Scotland v. Etridge (No. 2)*.[83]

In *Barclays Bank plc v. O'Brien* a wife had joined in a charge over the family home jointly owned by her and her husband as security for overdraft facilities extended by the plaintiff bank to a company in which the husband had an interest. The House of Lords found that as a general principle, where a wife was induced to stand as surety for her husband's debt as a result of his undue influence, misrepresentation or some other legal wrong, she had an equity against him to set aside the transaction and this right would be enforceable against a third party who had actual or constructive notice of the circumstances giving rise to the equity or for whom the husband was acting as agent. In the circumstances, it was held that the bank was fixed with constructive notice of the husband's wrongful misrepresentation and the wife was entitled as against the bank to set aside the legal charge on the matrimonial home securing the husband's liability to the bank. Lord Browne-Wilkinson said that constructive notice will exist when a creditor is put on inquiry e.g. by the fact that the transaction is not on its face to the financial advantage of the borrower, and if having been put on inquiry, the lender fails to take reasonable steps to ensure that the borrower understands the nature of the transaction. In terms of what amounts to taking reasonable steps, Lord Browne-Wilkinson stated as follows:

> [A] creditor will have satisfied these requirements if it insists that the wife attend a private meeting (in the absence of the husband) with a representative of the creditor at which she is told of the extent of her

---

'assuming, without deciding, that married women in this jurisdiction may in certain circumstances enjoy as against their husbands a presumption that undue influence was exercised. . . .'

82. [1994] 1 AC 180.
83. [2002] 2 AC 773. A number of commentators have written about this decision and its consequences, see Berg [1994] LMCLQ 34; Allen (1995) 58 MLR 87; Lawson [1995] CLJ 280; Sparkes [1995] Conv 250; Felhberg (1996) 59 MLR 675; Richardson (1996) 16 LS 368.

liability as surety, warned of the risk she is running and urged to take independent legal advice. If these steps are taken in my judgment the creditor will have taken such reasonable steps as are necessary to preclude a subsequent claim that it had constructive notice of the wife's rights.[84]

The alternative approach, namely the agency theory, was also considered by Lord Browne-Wilkinson although he criticised it as having developed in an artificial way. Essentially where it applies, the wrongdoing of the husband will be imputed to the creditor if the former can be regarded as being the agent of the latter in obtaining the wife's consent to the transaction.

It is important to note that in *O'Brien* the bank was held to have constructive notice of the husband's improper conduct because the use of the wife's interest to secure a loan to a company in which she had no interest was *prima facie* not to her advantage, a fact which immediately should have put the bank on inquiry. It was this fact which distinguished the result in *O'Brien* from that in *CIBC Mortgages plc v. Pitt*,[85] where the loan was on its face to both husband and wife for their joint benefit[86] and therefore not apparently to the wife's disadvantage. In *Pitt* the first named defendant persuaded his wife, the second named defendant, to execute a legal charge over their house in favour of the plaintiff in order to obtain a loan to purchase shares which he told her would improve their standard of living. After the stock market crash in 1987, the plaintiff brought proceedings for possession of the matrimonial home when the husband fell into arrears with the payments due under the loan. The Court of Appeal dismissed the wife's appeal against the finding of the trial judge in the plaintiff's favour and held that since the transaction was not manifestly disadvantageous to the wife, she could not establish undue influence and in any event since the plaintiff did not have any actual or constructive notice of any irregularity, the charge was valid as against the second named defendant. In the House of Lords, counsel for the wife argued that the Court of Appeal in *Bank of Credit and Commerce International SA v. Aboody*[87] had erred in extending the need to show manifest disadvantage to cases of actual as opposed to presumed undue influence. Lord Browne-Wilkinson agreed and said that he had no doubt that this requirement laid down in *National Westminster Bank plc v. Morgan*,[88] does not extend to cases of actual undue influence.[89]

---

84. [1994] 1 AC 180, 196-197.
85. See also the *dicta* of Lord Nicholls in *Royal Bank of Scotland v. Etridge (No. 2)* [2002] 2 AC 773, 804.
86. [1994] 1 AC 200.
87. [1990] 1 QB 923.
88. [1985] AC 686.
89. However, Fehlberg has argued (1994) 57 MLR 467, 473 that by effectively saying that the transaction must not on its face be to the financial advantage of the wife in order for constructive notice to arise, the 'manifest disadvantage' requirement rejected

However, the House of Lords held that as the transaction was not *prima facie* disadvantageous to the wife, the bank was not put on inquiry and was not affected by constructive notice of her husband's undue influence and could therefore enforce the security.

An important feature of the decision of the House of Lords in *Pitt* was the finding that a person who could prove the exercise of actual undue influence by another in carrying out a transaction was entitled as of right to have the transaction set aside as against the other without proof of manifest disadvantage. This had proved to be a major stumbling block for the plaintiff in *Bank of Credit and Commerce International SA v. Aboody*[90] where the Court of Appeal had held that a party who established that a transaction was induced by undue influence was not entitled to have it set aside in reliance on the doctrine without also proving that the transaction was manifestly disadvantageous to him.

However, the requirement of manifest disadvantage in cases of presumed undue influence has been an issue which has troubled the courts in England on a number of occasions in recent years. Millett LJ commented in *Dunbar Bank plc v. Nadeem*[91] that 'a person who can prove the exercise of actual undue influence by another in respect to a transaction is entitled to have the transaction set aside without proof of manifest disadvantage . . . [b]ut such proof is required when the exercise of undue influence is only presumed'. Similarly in *Cheese v. Thomas,*[92] although the requirement of manifest disadvantage was given a fairly flexible interpretation, it was nevertheless insisted upon by the Court of Appeal. Subsequently in *Barclays Bank plc v. Coleman*[93] Nourse LJ repeated that before a presumption of undue influence can be said to arise, a transaction must be shown to be manifestly disadvantageous to the party allegedly influenced.[94] However, he did concede that the views expressed by Lord Browne-Wilkinson in *CIBC Mortgages plc v. Pitt*[95] placed a serious question mark over the future of the requirement of manifest disadvantage in cases of presumed as well as actual undue influence.[96]

---

in *Pitt* is being resurrected in another guise. See also the comments of Lord Nicholls in *Royal Bank of Scotland v. Etridge (No.2)* [2002] 2 AC 773, 796.

90. [1990] 1 QB 923.
91. [1998] 3 All ER 876, 882. See also *Mahoney v. Purnell* [1996] 3 All ER 61, 82-83.
92. [1994] 1 WLR 129. See Mee [1994] LMCLQ 330; Chen-Wishart (1994) 110 LQR 173.
93. [2001] 1 QB 20. See Thompson [2000] Conv 444. The appeal was dismissed by the House of Lords [2002] 2 AC 773.
94. Nourse LJ stated that a manifest disadvantage must be one which is 'clear and obvious' and in deciding whether a transaction is manifestly disadvantageous an objective view must be taken of it and that view must be taken as at the date when the transaction is entered into. (at 33)
95. [1994] 1 AC 200.
96. It has been suggested by Thompson [2000] Conv 444 that Nourse LJ was effectively saying that it was only judicial courtesy which restrained Lord Browne-Wilkinson in

When the appeal in *Coleman* was heard by the House of Lords along with a number of others in *Royal Bank of Scotland v. Etridge (No. 2)*,[97] Lord Nicholls, while he acknowledged that the label 'manifest disadvantage' has been causing difficulty and can give rise to misunderstanding, did not accept that the requirement could be dispensed with. In his view in relationships where trust and confidence is reposed in another party, something more is needed before the law will reverse the burden of proof and 'when that something more is present, the greater the disadvantage to the vulnerable person, the more cogent must be the explanation before the presumption will be regarded as rebutted'.[98]

The issues of when a bank should be put on inquiry and what steps it should take when it has been have recently been addressed in some detail by the House of Lords in *Royal Bank of Scotland v. Etridge (No. 2)*.[99] In a number of cases wives charged their interests in their homes in favour of financial institutions as security for their husbands' indebtedness or the indebtedness of a company through which he carried on business. When the banks sought to enforce the charges, the wives raised the defence that they had signed them as a result of the undue influence of their husbands. The House of Lords heard a number of appeals together and set out the principles which should apply in such cases.[100] While Lord Nicholls acknowledged that the term 'put on inquiry' is strictly speaking a misnomer as the bank is not required to make inquiries but to take other steps, he stated that Lord Browne-Wilkinson's *dicta* in *O'Brien* has the effect that a bank is put on inquiry whenever a wife offers to stand surety for the husband's debts. The test in relation to the steps which a bank should take if put on inquiry where this applies to past transactions was as set out by Lord Browne-Wilkinson in *O'Brien* namely, that it should reasonably be expected to take steps to bring home to the wife the risk she is running and to advise her to take independent advice. In relation to future transactions, a bank will fulfil its obligations if it insists that a wife attends a private meeting with a representative of the bank at which she is told of the extent of her liability, warned of the risk she is running and urged to take independent advice. Lord Nicholls commented that the practice of banks generally is not to have a private meeting with the wife in such cases[101] and concluded that 'the furthest a bank can be expected to go

---

CIBC Mortgages plc v. Pitt from stating that the introduction of a requirement of manifest disadvantage was wrong.

97. [2002] 2 AC 773.
98. *Ibid.* at 779.
99. [2002] 2 AC 773. However, as Lord Hobhouse pointed out (at 822) situations will differ across a spectrum ranging from a very small risk to a risk verging on a probability and 'there has to be proportionality between the degree of risk and the requisite response to it'.
100. See generally Andrews [2002] Conv 456, Oldham [2002] CLJ 29, O'Sullivan (2002) 118 LQR 337, Bigwood (2002) 65 MLR 435, Breslin (2002) 9 Comm LP 35 and White (2002) 20 ILT 70.
101. See further Pawlowski and Greer [2001] Conv 229.

is to take reasonable steps to satisfy itself that the wife has had brought home to her, in a meaningful way, the practical implications of the proposed transaction'.[102] In addition, he stressed that he did not understand Lord Browne-Wilkinson to have stated in *O'Brien* that a personal meeting with the wife was the only way a bank could discharge its obligation to bring home to the wife the risks she was running.[103] This is in line with the approach previously adopted by the Court of Appeal in *Massey v. Midland Bank plc*,[104] in which a bank was found to have been put on inquiry by the circumstances in which a woman had agreed to provide security for an overdraft granted to a business venture in which a man with whom she had a long-standing relationship was involved. However, the Court of Appeal was satisfied that the bank had taken reasonable steps to ensure that her agreement had been properly obtained and held that it was not fixed with constructive notice of the misrepresentation made in this case. Steyn LJ commented that the guidance provided by the House of Lords in *O'Brien* 'should not be mechanically applied'[105] and that, provided the lender had taken alternative steps to achieve Lord Browne-Wilkinson's aim, failure to follow his guidelines precisely would not be fatal to the lendor's case. In this instance there had been no separate meeting between the surety and and creditor's representative unattended by the debtor but the creditor had required her to be independently advised. Steyn LJ was satisfied that she had received such independent legal advice[106] and that the creditor had therefore complied with the substance of Lord Browne-Wilkinson's guidance.[107]

---

102. *Ibid.* at 805.
103. However, note the *dicta* of Lord Hobhouse at 824 to the effect that Lord Browne-Wilkinson had stressed the need for the wife to be communicated with separately from her husband. Lord Hobhouse expressed the view that this was clearly appropriate since, if the purpose is to establish that the wife is acting freely, it is unlikely that an interview in the presence of the husband will achieve this if she has been improperly influenced by him.
104. [1995] 1 All ER 929. See Mee [1995] Conv 148.
105. *Ibid.* at 934. Steyn LJ stated that this guidance 'was intended to strike a fair balance between the need to protect wives (and others in a like position) whose judgmental capacity was impaired and the need to avoid unnecessary impediments to using the matrimonial home as security'.
106. However, it should be noted that earlier in his judgment (at 931) Steyn LJ mentioned that both debtor and surety had visited this independent legal adviser together and that the solicitor did not see the surety alone but explained the nature of the transaction to her and that she understood it. It should also be noted that Millett LJ has recently commented in the course of his judgment in *Credit Lyonnais Bank Nederland NV v. Burch* [1997] 1 All ER 144, 156 that independent legal advice is 'neither always necessary nor always sufficient' and that the result in such cases 'does not depend mechanically on the presence or absence of legal advice'.
107. This can be contrasted with the decision of the Court of Appeal in *TSB Bank plc v. Camfield* [1995] 1 All ER 951 where the bank was fixed with constructive notice of a husband's representation because it had failed in the view of the court to take

Turning to the issue of the content of any legal advice which a solicitor may give wives in such a situation, the speech of Lord Nicholls in *Royal Bank of Scotland v. Etridge (No. 2)*[108] also provides useful guidance on this point. In his view the *dicta* of the Court of Appeal in *Etridge (No. 2)* went too far and he stated that the content of the advice required from a solicitor before giving the confirmation sought by the bank will inevitably depend on the circumstances of the case. He added that typically the advice which a solicitor can be expected to give should cover the following matters as a core minimum.

(1) He will need to explain the nature of the documents and the practical consequences these will have for the wife if she signs them.

(2) He will need to point out the seriousness of the risks involved and discuss her financial means with her, including whether there are other assets out of which repayments might be made.

(3) He will need to state clearly that the wife has a choice and that the decision is hers and hers alone.

(4) He should check whether the wife wishes to proceed and whether she is content that he should write to the bank confirming that he has explained the nature of the transaction to her.[109]

Lord Scott also listed a number of issues which he felt a solicitor should generally address which included a requirement that he should explain to the wife that he may need to give the bank written confirmation that he has advised her about the nature and effect of the transaction and obtain her written consent to his doing so.

A further issue which has provoked debate is whether a financial institution is entitled to rely on the fact that a solicitor has undertaken his task of advising a wife in a sufficiently independent manner. In general the Court of Appeal has held that a bank is entitled to assume that the solicitor has given her appropriate advice[110] even in circumstances where he has also acted for the company, owned and controlled by the husband, to whom the loan had been made.[111] So, in *Barclays Bank plc v. Thomson*[112] Simon Brown LJ commented:

---

reasonable steps to ensure that the wife understood the nature of the charge. While the bank had stipulated that the wife should be given independent advice, in fact she was not separately advised from her husband, and the wife executed the charge under the false impression that it was for a limited amount.

108. [2002] 2 AC 773. It should be noted that Lord Hobhouse has pointed out (at 825) that there is a risk of confusion about what the role of a solicitor should be in such cases and he has suggested that problems may arise in ensuring that the solicitor is in possession of any relevant facts known to the bank.

109. *Ibid.* at 808.

110. *Bank of Baroda v. Rayarel* [1995] 2 FLR 376.

111. *Banco Exterior Internacional v. Mann* [1995] 1 All ER 936. See Dunn [1995] Conv 325.

112. [1997] 4 All ER 816.

'I can see no good reason whatever why a bank, perhaps conscientiously instructing solicitors to give independent advice to a signatory who might otherwise go unadvised, should thereby be disabled from relying on the solicitors' certificate that such advice has been properly given'. It should be noted that a differently constituted Court of Appeal effectively held a few months later in *Royal Bank of Scotland v. Etridge*[113] that a solicitor's certificate to the effect that he had explained the nature of the transaction to a surety wife was not conclusive. The essential difference between the reasoning employed in these two decisions is that in the view of Simon Brown LJ in *Thomson* the solicitor is regarded as acting exclusively for the surety when advising her, although he may well have been retained by the bank to do so, whereas in *Etridge*, Hobhouse LJ was satisfied that the solicitor was acting as the bank's agent in so doing.

The view in *Thomson* seemed preferable[114] and this has been confirmed by the approach adopted by a number of the members of the House of Lords in *Royal Bank of Scotland v. Etridge (No. 2)*[115] where Lord Nicholls stated that 'ordinarily it will be reasonable that a bank should be able to rely upon confirmation from a solicitor, acting for the wife, that he has advised the wife appropriately'. Lord Nicholls stressed that when accepting instructions to advise the wife the solicitor assumes responsibilities directly to her and that in every case he must consider carefully whether there is any conflict of duty or interest and whether it would be in the wife's best interests for him to accept instructions from her. If he decides to accept the instructions, his assumption of legal and professional responsibilities towards her 'ought, in the ordinary course of things, to provide sufficient assurance that he will give the requisite advice fully, carefully and conscientiously'.[116] Lord Scott expressed the view that the fact that a solicitor is acting for the bank in arranging for the completion of the security does not prejudice his suitability to advise the wife. Where he is also acting for the husband, in his view this presents 'a little more difficulty' and if there is some particular reason known to the bank for suspecting impropriety on the husband's part, the bank should insist on advice being given by a solicitor who is independent of the husband. This is in line with the view expressed by Lord Browne-Wilkinson in *Barclays Bank plc v. O'Brien*[117] where he stated that in an exceptional case where a creditor knows of additional facts rendering the presence of undue influence probable and not just possible, the creditor must insist that the surety be separately advised.[118] However, in *Etridge (No. 2)* Lord Scott concluded that where the

---

113. [1997] 3 All ER 628.
114. See Price (1998) 114 LQR 186, 187. See also Draper [1999] Conv 176, 183-190.
115. [2002] 2 AC 773, 806.
116. *Ibid.* at 810.
117. [1994] 1 AC 180, 197.
118. The decision of the Court of Appeal in *Credit Lyonnais Bank Nederland NV v. Burch* [1997] 1 All ER 144 would appear to be an example of this type of case. See Hooley

risk is no more than a possibility of impropriety, which he said would be present in all cases in which a wife provides a surety, there was no reason why the solicitor advising the wife should not also be the husband's solicitor and that a bank is entitled to rely on the professional competence and propriety of the solicitor in providing proper and adequate advice in such circumstances. A further aspect of Lord Scott's speech which should be noted is his view that knowledge on the part of a bank that a solicitor is acting for a surety wife does not, without more, justify it the assumption that the solicitor's instructions extend to advising her about the nature and effect of the transaction.[119] So, as the judgment of Jonathan Parker LJ in *UCB Corporate Services Ltd v. Williams*[120] makes clear, a bank cannot avoid being fixed with constructive notice of a wife's equity to set aside a transaction by relying on an honest belief that she was represented in the transaction by a solicitor.

A final question which must be addressed is the type of relationship to which the principles laid down in *Barclays Bank plc v. O'Brien* apply. Recently in *Royal Bank of Scotland v. Etridge (No. 2)* Lord Nicholls stated that in his view the only practical solution was to regard banks as being put on inquiry in every case where the relationship between the surety and debtor is a non-commercial one. This approach is a sensible and pragmatic one and resolves the uncertainty which had lingered following the decision in *O'Brien*. In the course of his speech in that case, Lord Browne-Wilkinson stressed that the guidelines which he was laying down were not restricted to cases involving spouses and said that they also applied 'if and only if, the creditor is aware that the surety is co-habiting with the principal debtor'.[121] This requirement of co-habitation was relaxed in *Midland Bank v. Massey*[122] where, although the parties had never married or co-habited, they had enjoyed a stable 'sexual and emotional relationship' for many years and had had two children together. Steyn LJ, while recognising that it would constitute an extension of the approach laid down by Lord Browne-Wilkinson, said that he had no doubt that 'in terms of impairment of [the surety's] judgmental capacity, this case should be approached as if she was a wife or co-habitee of [the debtor]'.[123] It

---

and O'Sullivan [1997] LMCLQ 17; Tijo (1997) 113 LQR 10; Chen-Wishart [1997] CLJ 60.

119. [2002] 2 AC 773, 844-845. See also the speech of Lord Hobhouse at 825.

120. [2003] 1 P & CR 168, 188. See also *Lloyds TSB Bank v. Holdgate* [2002] EWCA Civ 1543 Court of Appeal, 14 October 2002 paragraphs 28 and 38.

121. [1994] 1 AC 180, 198. Lawson has suggested [1995] CLJ 280, 282 that this should be interpreted as meaning that a creditor should be put on inquiry only if he is actually aware that the surety is co-habiting with the debtor as otherwise it would require creditors to act as 'busybodies'.

122. [1995] 1 All ER 929.

123. *Ibid.* at 933. The approach in *Massey* was in line with that adopted by Lord Nicholls in *Royal Bank of Scotland v. Etridge (No. 2)* where he stated that the principles will apply to unmarried couples, whether heterosexual or homosexual, where the bank is aware of the relationship and he agreed that cohabitation is not essential.

should also be noted that in *O'Brien*, Lord Browne-Wilkinson stated that the principles he was setting out applied 'where, to the creditor's knowledge, the surety reposes trust and confidence in the principal debtor in relation to his or her financial affairs'.[124] An example of such a relationship is that which existed between an employer and a junior employee in *Credit Lyonnais Bank Nederland NV v. Burch*;[125] as Nourse LJ commented: 'although the relationship between the debtor and the mortgagor was not that of persons living together but employer and employee, it may broadly be said to fall under *Barclays Bank plc v. O'Brien*' and the court proceeded to apply these principles in order to determine whether the bank should be fixed with constructive notice of the employer's wrongdoing.

Reaction to the decision of the House of Lords in *Royal Bank of Scotland v. Etridge (No. 2)* has been generally favourable, although there is a lack of consensus in relation to its likely impact. While the predominant view is that it has tipped the scales further in favour of lending institutions and against surety wives,[126] it has also been heralded as a decision which goes further than *O'Brien* in reducing the risk of undue influence.[127] The decision undoubtedly imposes a lower threshold of proof in relation to the circumstances in which a bank will be put on inquiry and ensures that the safeguards designed to protect the interests of those providing sureties will frequently be required to be satisfied.

However, the 'reasonable steps' which a bank must take to avoid being fixed with notice appear less onerous than those contemplated in *O'Brien* and provided the bank requires that the wife receives independent legal advice it may avoid liability. In a sense the responsibility has shifted to the solicitor advising the wife and overall it is probably fair to say that the principles laid down in *Etridge (No. 2)* are more favourable from the point of view of financial institutions than those laid down in *O'Brien*.

It remains to consider how the *O'Brien* principles have fared in Ireland where they have been considered in a number of decisions. The first of these, *Bank of Ireland v Smyth*,[128] arose in the context of a wife signing a consent form for the purposes of the Family Home Protection Act 1976 in circumstances where her husband had charged their house and land as security for all present and future liabilities owed to the plaintiffs. Counsel for the wife, the second named defendant, submitted that under the Family Home Protection Act 1976 a consent by a wife to a mortgage or charge in favour of

---

124. [1994] 1 AC 180, 196.
125. [1997] 1 All ER 144.
126. Andrews [2002] Conv 456, 469 and O'Sullivan (2002) 118 LQR 337, 350.
127. Oldham [2002] CLJ 29.
128. [1993] ILRM 790 (HC); [1995] 2 IR 459 (SC). See generally Sanfey (1994) 1 Comm LP 99; Doyle (1994) 88 GILSI 187; Sanfey (1996) 3 Comm LP 31; Mee (1996) 14 ILT (ns) 188; 209.

the bank was not valid unless the wife understood the nature and consequences of the transaction and in this regard relied on the decision of the Court of Appeal in *O'Brien*. Geoghegan J stated that he believed that decision represented the law in this jurisdiction also and applying the criteria laid down by Scott LJ in *O'Brien* he said that it was obvious that the bank manager was well aware of the husband and wife relationship with the consequent inherent likelihood of influence and reliance. In his view, the manager should have realized that what he had told the wife had been inadequate and that he had not taken sufficient steps to ensure that she fully understood the transaction; in particular he had not advised her to take independent legal advice. Geoghegan J concluded that, while there was a document purporting to be a consent there was in fact no consent within the meaning of the 1976 Act and that the charge over the property was therefore void. The Supreme Court dismissed the plaintiff's appeal and held that as the second named defendant's consent was not a fully informed one — she believed that the charge affected only the land and not the family home — it was invalid. Blayney J stated that as the bank ought reasonably to have made inquiries which would have revealed the wife's lack of consent, the bank was treated as having constructive notice of the facts that the enquires would have revealed. While Blayney J rejected the argument that the bank had a duty to explain the charge fully to the wife or to suggest that she should obtain independent legal advice, he stated that in order to protect its own interests, the bank should have taken these steps, since if they had it was unlikely that her consent could have been challenged.

Sanfey has commented that the merit of the Supreme Court decision is that a bank now knows exactly what it must do to prove that there was valid consent for the purposes of the Family Home Protection Act 1976.[129] However, he stresses that while the decision clarifies the position of banks and the spouses of debtors who have given consent to the creation of a security over the family home, its reasoning cannot be extended to the general situation where a spouse has acted as a guarantor of liabilities or created a charge over assets in respect of the other spouse's liabilities. Mee similarly comments that the Supreme Court decision throws little light on the impact of third party undue influence or misrepresentation on the validity of bank guarantees.[130] He puts forward the view that the requirement of informed consent might suggest a similarly paternalistic approach should be taken to bank guarantees but points out that Blayney J's invocation of the concept of constructive notice might indicate a preference for the notice-based approach adopted by the House of Lords in *O'Brien*.

Another recent decision which did provide the Supreme Court with the opportunity to consider the question of the effect of third party undue influence

---

129. (1996) 3 Comm LP 31, 34.
130. (1996) 14 ILT (ns) 209, 210.

or misrepresentation on the validity of bank guarantees was *Bank of Nova Scotia v. Hogan*.[131] The first named defendant borrowed money from the plaintiff on the security of equitable mortgages created over several properties which he owned. Subsequently, in return for releasing the security over two of these properties, the plaintiff took an equitable mortgage over a further property owned by the second named defendant, who was the first named defendant's wife. Prior to depositing the title deeds, a solicitor from a firm which had acted for the second named defendant and her husband in the past, and also for the bank from time to time, explained to her that the plaintiff would be entitled to sell the property in the event of her husband's default. When the plaintiff subsequently brought proceedings to enforce the security, the second named defendant alleged that the security had been improperly obtained. In finding for the plaintiff, Keane J concluded that the legal advice received by the second named defendant had been adequate in all the circumstances.

In considering the appeal brought by the defendants against this order, Murphy J said that while there was a similarity between the facts of the case before him and those in *Bank of Ireland v. Smyth*, the fundamental differences between them rendered the decision of little assistance, although he concluded that the decision of the House of Lords in *O'Brien* was 'both relevant and helpful'. Murphy J concluded that whilst the matrimonial relationship as such did not give rise to a presumption of undue influence, it might be possible to identify circumstances which would more readily raise a presumption in favour of a wife than any outside party. He pointed out the essential issue in this case was the dispute between the rights of the creditor and the wife and in relation to this, he was prepared to adopt and apply the principles of Lord Browne-Wilkinson in *O'Brien* referred to above. These were as follows:

> A wife who has been induced to stand as a surety for her husband's debts by his undue influence, misrepresentation or some other legal wrong has an equity against him to set aside that transaction. Under the ordinary principles of equity, her right to set aside that transaction will be enforceable against third parties (e.g. against a creditor) if either the husband was acting as the third party's agent or the third party had actual or constructive notice of the facts giving rise to her equity.[132]

Murphy J stated that even assuming — and he did not decide this issue — that married women in this jurisdiction might in certain circumstances enjoy a presumption as against their husbands that undue influence had been exercised, the fatal flaw in the case before him was that no undue influence

---

131. High Court 1991 No. 97 Sp (Keane J) 21 December 1992; [1996] 3 IR 239.
132. [1994] 1 AC 180, 195. Quoted with approval [1996] 2 IR 239, 248.

was exercised by the husband; the wife had no equity against him to have the transaction set aside and therefore she had no equity on which she could rely to defeat the claim of the bank. Even if such an equity had existed, Murphy J was still satisfied that the availability of appropriate legal advice to the wife would have afforded the bank a defence in relation to any claim made by her in respect of an equity to set aside the transaction. Furthermore, he was satisfied that there was no evidence to support the claim that the bank itself had exercised undue influence over the wife; the relationship did not give rise to a presumption of undue influence and there was no suggestion of dealings which would raise an inference of wrongdoing.

It was therefore accepted by the Supreme Court in *Bank of Nova Scotia v. Hogan* that where a wife furnishes a guarantee as security for her husband's debts as a result of his undue influence, misrepresentation or some other legal wrong, she has an equity against him to set aside the transaction which may be enforceable against a third party, who had actual or constructive notice of the circumstances giving rise to the equity or for whom the husband was acting as agent. While the facts of this case did not demand any detailed examination by the Supreme Court of the circumstances in which a bank may be deemed to have constructive notice of any wrongdoing, the *dicta* of Murphy J would certainly suggest that the availability to the wife of 'appropriate legal advice' would have been sufficient to enable the bank to reject any claim that they should have been fixed with notice of any impropriety.

The most recent decision in this jurisdiction to examine the issue of undue influence and its effect on third parties is that of O'Donovan J in *Ulster Bank Ltd v. Fitzgerald*[133] and while it does identify areas in which the law in this jurisdiction would seem to differ from that in England, it is in some respects an unsatisfactory decision in terms of laying down general principles. The plaintiff bank instituted proceedings claiming monies it alleged were owed to it by a company operated by the first named defendant on foot of guarantees executed by this defendant and his wife, the second named defendant. The second named defendant claimed that the guarantees were not enforceable against her on the grounds that she had no financial interest in them and that she had been persuaded to execute the guarantees as a result of undue influence exercised over her by her husband, a fact which she claimed the bank was or should have been aware of. The evidence of the bank manager was that the second named defendant's husband had not been present when he had explained the meaning of the guarantees to her and that he had told her 'that she could obtain legal advice' with regard to them, although she had signed them straight away. While O'Donovan J said that he was prepared to accept that the first named defendant may have exercised inordinate pressure on his wife to execute the guarantees, he concluded that he was not persuaded that

---

133. High Court 1999 No. 197S (O'Donovan J) 9 November 2001.

the plaintiff bank had constructive notice of the fact that the wife might have executed the guarantees as a result of her husband's undue influence, if indeed this had been the case. He said that a presumption of undue influence did not arise merely because the parties were husband and wife and that he had heard no evidence to suggest that the bank had any inkling that there might be difficulties between the spouses or that there was any other reason why the wife might not have been acting of her own free will when she executed the guarantees. O'Donovan J added that he did not accept that the wife did not have a financial stake in the business, as she and her family relied on the income generated by it. So, in the absence of any actual or constructive knowledge on the part of the bank that the wife was not a free agent when she executed the guarantees, he was satisfied that the bank was not under any obligation to take any special steps to ensure that she had obtained independent legal advice.[134] While O'Donovan J referred to the decisions in *Barclays Bank plc v. O'Brien* and *Bank of Ireland v. Smyth*, he appeared to distinguish them on the basis that in the case before him there was no threat to the wife's family home[135] and that she had a financial stake in the guarantees. In the circumstances, O'Donovan J therefore concluded that the guarantees were enforceable against the second named defendant.

A number of points can be gleaned from the decision of O'Donovan J which may be relevant in determining how the courts in this jurisdiction will approach cases of third party undue influence involving surety wives. First, O'Donovan J made it clear that the relationship of husband and wife did not give rise to any presumption of undue influence[136] and he seemed to suggest that a financial institution would only be put on inquiry if it was aware of additional information about the parties' relationship which would increase the risk of such influence. This is a much less onerous standard from the point of view of financial institutions than that put forward by the House of Lords in *Royal Bank of Scotland v. Etridge (No. 2)*[137] where Lord Nicholls stated that a bank is put on inquiry whenever a wife offers to stand surety for her husband's debts. Secondly, O'Donovan J's rejection of the wife's contention that as she had no financial stake in the business, and as the transaction was not on its face to her advantage, this should have put the bank on inquiry, as had been the case in *O'Brien*, again falls far short of the level of protection afforded to wives by the English decisions. It has been suggested that it may be implied from *O'Brien* that the bank will be put on inquiry even if it is aware that the wife has an indirect financial interest in a company[138]

---

134. O'Donovan J stated (at 9) that 'the courts are not required to intervene to protect a contracting party from ill-advised action'.
135. It is unclear why O'Donovan J purported to distinguish *O'Brien* on this basis.
136. *Ibid.* at 7 and 8.
137. [2002] 2 AC 773, 803.
138. Mee (2002) 27 Ir Jur 292, 300.

and in *Etridge (No. 2)* Lord Nicholls stated that this will be the case even where the wife has a shareholding in the company, whether nominal or equal to that of her husband, or where she is a director or the secretary of it.[139] A further issue which remains unclear as a result of O'Donovan J's conclusion that the bank was not put on inquiry, is whether the steps taken by it, namely private meetings at which the meaning of the guarantees had been explained and at which the wife had been told that she 'could obtain' legal advice, would have sufficed if it had been deemed to have been put on notice. Mee[140] has suggested that it is likely that the steps taken would probably not have been sufficient to satisfy the requirements laid down in *O'Brien* but it is undoubtedly safer to await a considered view on this issue in a case where the adequacy of the action taken by the financial institution will determine the outcome.

The rejection by O'Donovan J of some of the more important principles laid down in *O'Brien* and developed in *Etridge (No. 2)*, particularly in relation to the circumstances in which a financial institution will be put on inquiry, is beyond doubt. Clearly the approach adopted by him ensures that little protection will be afforded to surety wives who execute guarantees in these circumstances and a strong argument could be made that the balance has swung too far in favour of financial institutions. In these circumstances, and in view of the rather unsatisfactory nature of the recent decisions in this jurisdiction, it would seem that Mee's assertion that in this area 'English law represents a not unreasonable basis for the development of Irish law'[141] has much to recommend it.

Unconscionable Transactions

A transaction may be set aside in equity where one party is at a serious disadvantage by reason of poverty, ignorance or some other factor such as old age, so that unfair advantage may be taken of that party.[142] Equity will intervene particularly where a transfer of property is made for no consideration at all[143]

---

139. [2002] 2 AC 773, 804.
140. (2002) 27 Ir Jur 292, 302.
141. *Ibid.* at 306.
142. See generally Clark (1980) 31 NILQ 114; Capper 'Unconscionable bargains' in *One Hundred and Fifty Years of Irish Law* (1996) eds., Dawson, Greer and Ingram p. 45 *et seq.* As Nourse LJ commented in *Credit Lyonnais Bank Nederland NV v. Burch* [1997] 1 All ER 144, 151: 'Equity's jurisdiction to relieve against such transactions, although more rarely exercised in modern times, is at least as venerable as its jurisdiction to relieve against those procured by undue influence'.
143. Some doubt was raised about this point by the decision in *Langton v. Langton* [1995] 2 FLR 890, in which A.W.H. Charles QC expressed the view that the doctrine of unconscionable bargains does not apply to gifts. However, as Capper has pointed out [1996] Conv 308, 314 'the weight of principle and authority is against him' and he has recently commented (1998) 114 LQR 479, 492 that 'the better view . . . is that

or at an undervalue and where the transferee acts without the benefit of independent legal advice. The basis of this principle which was set out by Lord Hatherley in *O'Rorke v. Bolingbroke*[144] was summarised as follows by Gavan Duffy J in *Grealish v. Murphy*:[145] 'Equity comes to the rescue whenever the parties to a contract have not met upon equal terms'. A more specific summary of the circumstances which will warrant equitable intervention on this basis was provided by Kitto J in the Australian decision of *Blomley v. Ryan*,[146] namely: 'whenever one party to a transaction is at a special disadvantage in dealing with the other party because illness, ignorance, inexperience, impaired faculties, financial need or other circumstances affect his ability to conserve his own interests, and the other party unconscientiously takes advantage of the opportunity thus placed in his hands.' In *Blomley* a sale of a property at an undervalue was set aside in circumstances where the same solicitor had acted for both parties and where the vendor was elderly and poorly educated and the purchasers had taken advantage of his liking for rum. Similarly, in *McGonigle v. Black*[147] factors which were considered by Barr J as contributing towards what he regarded as an improvident transaction from the point of view of the vendor were 'a combination of bereavement, inability to cope, loneliness, alcoholism and ill-health', which made him vulnerable to manipulation.

According to Martin[148] three elements must be established before equity will intervene, and it is helpful to set these out. First, one party must be at a serious disadvantage to the other by reason of poverty, ignorance or otherwise, so that circumstances exist of which unfair advantage can be taken; secondly, the transaction must be at an undervalue; and thirdly there must be a lack of independent legal advice. One of the most comprehensive statements of the essential preconditions for setting aside a transaction on grounds of unconscionability is set out in the judgment of Peter Millett QC, as he then was in *Alec Lobb (Garages) Ltd v. Total Oil (Great Britain) Ltd*:[149]

---

gifts are equally subject to the doctrine of unconscionability and that this concept rather than one of unconscionable bargain should be used in future to avoid confusion'.

144. (1877) 2 App Cas 814, 823.
145. [1946] IR 35, 49. Quoted with approval by McLoughlin J in *Haverty v. Brooks* [1970] IR 214, 219 and by Denham J in *Carroll v. Carroll* [1999] 4 IR 241, 258-259.
146. (1956) 99 CLR 362, 415. See also the *dicta* of Fullgar J at 405 and of Sullivan MR in *Slator v. Nolan* (1876) IR 11 Eq 367, 386 where he spoke of undue advantage being taken 'by reason of distress or recklessness or wildness or want of care' and said that transactions resting on such unconscionable dealing would not be allowed to stand.
147. High Court Circuit Appeal (Barr J) 14 November 1988.
148. Hanbury and Martin, *Modern Equity* (16th ed., 2001) pp.863-864.
149. [1983] 1 WLR 87, 94-95. (Reversed in part [1985] 1 WLR 173). See also *Portman Building Society v. Dusangh* [2000] 2 All ER (Comm) 221, 230-231.

First, one party has been at a serious disadvantage to the other, whether through poverty, or ignorance, or lack of advice, or otherwise, so that circumstances existed of which unfair advantage could be taken. Second, this weakness of the one party has been exploited by the other in some morally culpable manner...And third, the resulting transaction has been not merely hard or improvident, but overreaching and oppressive. ... In short, there must, in my judgment, be some impropriety, both in the conduct of the stronger party and in the terms of the transaction itself . . . which in the traditional phrase 'shocks the conscience of the court' and makes it against equity and good conscience for the stronger party to retain the benefit of a transaction he has unfairly obtained.

In considering the first of these requirements it is clear that some unfair advantage must have been gained 'by an unconscientious use of power by a stronger party against a weaker'.[150] On the second point, as Hooley and O'Sullivan have confirmed: 'the courts have repeatedly stressed that it is not sufficient to show that a bargain was a harsh or unreasonable one — it must also be shown that the stronger party acted reprehensibly, exploiting the weaker position of the other party'.[151]

As regards the requirement of undervalue, Gavan Duffy J stated in *Grealish v. Murphy*[152] that a court will be 'very much slower to undo a transaction for value', although he stressed that the principles underlying intervention in either case remain the same. In *Noonan v. O'Connell*[153] a transfer of a half-share in a farm by an elderly man with limited mental capacity to his nephew for what appeared to be a nominal consideration was set aside, as was the disposition in *Slator v. Nolan*[154] by a man to his brother-in-law for what was also a grossly inadequate consideration. These decisions can be contrasted with that of Pringle J in *Nyland v. Brennan*[155] in which a sale by an elderly lady at a reasonable price was upheld, albeit in circumstances where she had received comprehensive and independent legal advice, and with the decision of McLoughlin J in *Haverty v. Brooks*[156] where he found that 'substantial monetary consideration' had changed hands.

The receipt of full and independent legal advice becomes increasingly important where the consideration paid is low or non-existent[157] or where one

---

150. *Morrison v. Coast Finance Ltd* (1965) 55 DLR (2d) 710, 713 *per* Davey JA. See also the *dicta* of Lord Brightman in *O'Connor v. Hart* [1985] AC 1000, 1024 where the concept of taking advantage of the weaker party's position was also stressed.
151. [1997] LMCLQ 17, 23.
152. [1946] IR 35, 49-50.
153. High Court 1986 No. 2135P (Lynch J) 10 April 1987.
154. (1876) IR 11 Eq 367.
155. High Court 1970 No. 1548P (Pringle J) 19 December 1970.
156. [1970] IR 214, 219.
157. As in *Moyles v. Mahon* High Court 1997 No. 6357P (Smyth J) 6 October 2000

party is negotiating from a position of relative weakness, although it will always be a factor which the court will consider in assessing whether a transaction has been improvident. In *Grealish v. Murphy*[158] the plaintiff, an elderly farmer, who according to the medical evidence was mentally deficient, executed a settlement transferring his farm to the defendant subject to a life interest in his favour and charging the land with a right of residence and support for the defendant during the plaintiff's lifetime. While Gavan Duffy J declined to set aside the settlement on the grounds of undue influence, he accepted that the transaction was an improvident one and that it should be set aside on this basis. Gavan Duffy J laid emphasis on the plaintiff's weakness of mind and the deficiencies in the legal advice which he had received, pointing to the fact that his solicitor had been unaware of all the material facts and had failed to give the plaintiff a full explanation of the consequences of the settlement or to appreciate the latter's limited mental capacity. Lack of proper legal advice also appeared to be an important factor in the decision of Morris J in *McQuirk v. Branigan*[159] in which he set aside a deed executed by an elderly lady transferring land to her grandson so that he could build a house on the site. It became necessary to give the grandson an area larger than had been previously envisaged to make the site large enough to accommodate a house and this effectively divested the plaintiff completely of her back garden. Morris J pointed to the total lack of independent legal advice or indeed any advice given to the plaintiff and set aside the transaction as an improvident one from her point of view. Similarly, in *Carroll v. Carroll*[160] Denham J concluded that in view of the omissions in relation to the legal advice given, taken in conjunction with the donor's frail health and lack of other assets, there was clear evidence on which the trial judge could have concluded that this was a case in which the transaction should have been set aside on grounds of its improvidence.

It should be pointed out that as the above consideration of the case law tends to show, there remains a degree of uncertainty about the exact requirements which must be established to support a claim of unconscionability. As Bamforth has recently commented: 'the cases tend to leave the relative importance and requirements of each element unarticulated'[161] and in his view there is still an unacceptable degree of imprecision in the case law. Hooley and O'Sullivan have also recently raised this issue and suggest that the *dicta*

---

where it was acknowledged by Smyth J that a transaction was on its face improvident because the plaintiff had disposed of his interest in property without valuable consideration. However, he concluded that the plaintiff had exercised a 'spontaneous act of free will' and had had the benefit of independent legal advice and declined to set aside the transaction.

158. [1946] IR 35.
159. High Court Circuit Appeal (Morris J) 9 November 1992.
160. [1999] 4 IR 241.
161. [1995] LMCLQ 538, 539.

of the members of the Court of Appeal in *Credit Lyonnais Bank Nederland NV v. Burch*[162] provides an excellent illustration of Bamforth's point that the juridicial basis and elements of unconscionability as a vitiating factor should be more precisely defined and rooted in principle.[163] Recent *dicta* suggests that a 'very strong case' will be required before the courts will intervene on the grounds that there was an unconscionable bargain. So, in *Singla v. Bashir*[164] Park J stated that the bargain has to be more than hard, unreasonable or foolish: it must be provided to be unconscionable in the sense that one of the parties has imposed the bargain in a morally reprehensible manner'.[165]

Finally one issue which has provoked considerable academic debate in recent years is whether the doctrines of undue influence and unconscionable transactions or unconscionability should continue to remain separate and distinct or whether they should be merged. It should be noted that the same facts will often cause a court to consider whether to grant relief under both or either heading,[166] and the two have even been combined on occasion.[167] Capper argues that the doctrines of undue influence and unconscionability are 'sufficiently similar in their objectives and effects that they can and may profitably be merged into one'[168] and that unconscionability as the broader of the two doctrines would allow undue influence to be subsumed into it. On the other hand Birks and Chin have argued that the two doctrines are fundamentally distinct and that the existing analytical distinctions should be preserved.[169] In their view undue influence is concerned with the weakness of the plaintiff's consent owing to his excessive dependence on the defendant, while unconscionability is concerned with the defendant's exploitation of the plaintiff's vulnerability. Certainly there are authorities in Canada[170] and Australia[171] which support the approach of Birks and Chin and while the courts in this jurisdiction have not directly addressed this question, it is certainly

---

162. [1997] 1 All ER 144.
163. [1997] LMCLQ 17, 22.
164. [2002] EWHC 883 (Ch) 13 May 2002.
165. See also the *dicta* of Simon Brown LJ in *Portman Building Society v. Dusangh* [2000] 2 All ER (Comm) 221, 229 where he concluded that the transaction, although improvident was not 'overreaching and oppressive' and that the claimant had not acted in a 'morally reprehensible manner'.
166. *Grealish v. Murphy* [1946] IR 35.
167. *McGonigle v. Black* High Court Circuit Appeal (Barr J) 14 November 1988 in which a transaction was set aside as being a 'grossly improvident' one brought about by undue influence.
168. (1998) 114 LQR 479, 480.
169. 'On the Nature of Undue Influence' in *Good Faith and Fault in Contract Law* eds. Beatson and Friedmann (1995) p. 57 *et seq.*
170. *Morrison v. Coast Finance Ltd* (1965) 55 DLR (2d) 710, 713 *per* Bull JA to the effect that while the doctrines are closely related they are 'separate and distinct'.
171. *Commercial Bank of Australia Ltd v. Amadio* (1983) 151 CLR 447, 461 *per* Mason J.

unlikely in the short term that they would take the step of seeking to merge the doctrines.

LOSS OF THE RIGHT TO RESCIND

Affirmation

If the party is aware of the facts giving rise to the right to rescind and nevertheless affirms the contract by taking some benefit under it he will be taken to have waived his right to rescind.[172] Where a person seeks to rescind a contract he must do so within a reasonable time or he may be taken to have affirmed the contract and in this context the doctrine of laches may operate to defeat a claim. As we have seen, this involves a substantial lapse of time coupled with circumstances which make it inequitable to allow the plaintiff to succeed in his claim. The manner in which laches may defeat an action to have an agreement set aside in the context of an improvident transaction is illustrated by the decision of Keane J in *J.H. v. W.J.H.*[173] As a result of delay by the plaintiff for four years and by reason of the time and money invested in the running of a farm by the defendant on the basis that the plaintiff had abandoned her claim, Keane J refused to grant the plaintiff relief although he held that the transaction in question was an improvident one which the courts would normally have set aside.

If Substantial Restitutio in Integrum is Impossible

As Lord Blackburn stated in *Erlanger v. New Sombrero Phosphate Co.*[174] 'as a condition to a rescission there must be a *restitutio in integrum*'. This principle was strictly enforced at common law but equity has taken a more flexible approach and as Lord Blackburn noted there is a considerable difference in the manner in which it has been applied at law and in equity. In the latter case it has not been applied as literally, the aim being to achieve practical justice even where precise restoration of the parties to their previous positions is no longer possible. The attitude of equity towards this concept was well summarised by Griffin J in *Northern Bank Finance Corporation Ltd v. Charlton*[175] as follows: 'Therefore, the rule is that rescission cannot be enforced if events, which have occurred since the contract and in which the representee has participated, make it impossible to restore the parties substantially to their previous position.'

---

172. See *Payman v. Lanjani* [1985] Ch 457.
173. High Court 1977 No. 5831P (Keane J) 20 December 1979.
174. (1878) 3 App Cas 1218, 1278.
175. [1979] IR 149, 206. See also the *dicta* of O'Higgins CJ at 183.

While any property or monies transferred under the contract must in theory be handed back, equity does not insist on precise restoration, and the wrongdoer may be asked to give up his profits in return for receiving compensation for work carried out in performance of his contractual obligations.[176] A further relevant factor may be whether the impossibility of restoring the parties to their previous positions is attributable to the nature of the subject matter of the agreement or whether it is due to the plaintiff's conduct.[177] Clearly where precise restoration of the parties is impossible the courts will take a more flexible approach if the plaintiff is not in any way responsible for this state of affairs.

Third Party Rights

A contract will not be rescinded where this will prejudice the rights of innocent third parties who have acquired an interest for value in the subject matter of an agreement. So where a *bona fide* purchaser for value without notice has acquired good title to the property in the interim, an action for rescission will not succeed.[178] However, where the third party is a mere volunteer, the right to rescind will not be lost.

---

176. See *O'Sullivan v. Management Agency & Music Ltd* [1985] QB 428.
177. *Carbin v. Somerville* [1933] IR 276, 289.
178. *Anderson v. Ryan* [1967] IR 34.

CHAPTER 17

Equitable Estoppel

INTRODUCTION

Estoppel is not an exclusively equitable concept and operates today both at common law and in equity. Two main aspects of equitable estoppel are recognised; promissory and proprietary estoppel[1] and both owe their origins to the concept of estoppel by representation.[2] The essential basis of the latter doctrine is the making of a representation by a person whether by words or conduct of an existing fact which causes another party to incur detriment in reliance on this representation. In these circumstances, the person making the representation will not be permitted to act subsequently in a manner inconsistent with that representation. This principle formed the basis of the decision of the House of Lords in *Jorden v. Money*[3] which limited the operation of estoppel to representations of existing fact rather than of a party's intentions. As Lord Cranworth stated:

> [I]f a person makes any false representation to another, and that other acts upon that false representation, the person who has made it shall not afterwards be allowed to set up that what he said was false.[4]

However, he continued by saying that he thought that the doctrine did not apply 'to a case where the representation is not a representation of fact, but a statement of something which the party intends or does not intend to do'. This approach was also followed in Ireland in *Munster & Leinster Bank Ltd v. Croker*[5] in which Black J agreed that this form of estoppel 'only applies to representation of existing facts'. While this reasoning did not appear to leave much scope for development, equity has eroded some of the limitations of this principle in a manner which shall now be examined.

---

1. See Pawlowski, *Proprietary Estoppel* (1996).
2. See generally Spencer-Bower and Turner, *Estoppel by Representation* (3rd ed., 1977).
3. (1854) 5 HLC 185.
4. *Ibid.* at 210.
5. [1940] IR 185, 191.

PROMISSORY ESTOPPEL

One of the guiding principles which arguably has circumscribed the development of the doctrine of promissory estoppel has been that it should not undermine the requirement of consideration. Its operation has been confined to situations where a pre-existing contractual relationship or at least a relationship which gives rise to legal rights and obligations exists.[6] For this reason promissory estoppel is often considered in a contractual context and a fuller treatment of it can be found in the leading texts in that area.[7] It is therefore proposed to briefly outline its early development and examine its main characteristics and later in the chapter to assess whether there is evidence of a move towards a unified doctrine of equitable estoppel.

While the effect of *Jorden v. Money*[8] appeared to be to limit the doctrine of equitable estoppel to representations of existing fact, the decisions of *Hughes v. Metropolitan Railway Co.*[9] and *Birmingham and District Land Co. v. London and North Western Railway Co.*[10] showed that equity would give relief to a person in circumstances where the truth or accuracy of a representation of future intention might be denied in an unconscionable manner. These decisions were in turn employed by Denning J in his landmark judgment in *Central London Property Trust Ltd v. High Trees House Ltd*[11] which can be regarded as the decision in which the foundations of the doctrine known as 'promissory estoppel' were laid. In the view of Denning J, where a promise is made which is 'intended to create legal relations and which, to the knowledge of the person making the promise, was going to be acted on by the person to whom it was made, and which is in fact so acted on'[12] the court should ensure that such a promise is honoured. This reasoning was relied on in this jurisdiction by Kenny J in his decision in *Revenue Commissioners v. Moroney*[13] in which he held that a father who had promised his sons that they would not have to pay the consideration referred to in a deed which they had signed was estopped from subsequently seeking this consideration.[14]

---

6. E.g. *Durham Fancy Goods Ltd v. Michael Jackson (Fancy Goods) Ltd* [1968] 2 QB 839, 847 *per* Donaldson J.
7. See e.g. Clark, *Contract Law in Ireland* (4th ed., 1998); Treitel, *The Law of Contract* (10th ed., 1999).
8. (1854) 3 HLC 185.
9. (1877) 2 App Cas 439.
10. (1888) 40 Ch D 268.
11. [1947] 1 KB 130.
12. *Ibid.* at 134. See also *Kenny v. Kelly* [1988] IR 457, 463 where Barron J concluded that these elements, necessary to establish a claim based on promissory estoppel, were satisfied in the case before him.
13. [1972] IR 372.
14. The Supreme Court dismissed the father's appeal but rested its decision on other grounds and made no comment on the estoppel argument.

While this '*High Trees*' principle appeared to be potentially far-reaching in effect, its scope was circumscribed by the subsequent decision of the English Court of Appeal in *Combe v. Combe*[15] where Denning LJ himself stated that it did not 'create new causes of action where none existed before. It only prevents a party from insisting upon his strict legal rights, when it should be unjust to allow him to enforce them, having regard to the dealings which have taken place between the parties.' It was also in the *Combe* decision that Birkett LJ adopted the now famous expression used by counsel that the *High Trees* doctrine was one which should be 'used as a shield and not a sword',[16] This reasoning was applied by Barron J in *Chartered Trust Ireland Ltd v. Healy*[17] where he held that estoppel could not confer a cause of action on a plaintiff. The *High Trees* principle also underpinned the decision of Kenny J in *Cullen v Cullen*.[18] The plaintiff purported to transfer his property and business to his wife in return for an undertaking that she would not seek to have him committed to a mental hospital. The plaintiff's wife won a portable house in a competition and gave it to her son. She suggested that he should erect it on the father's lands and the latter expressed the view that as he was transferring the property to his wife she could do as she liked. The son erected the house on these lands, rather than on his own as he had originally contemplated, and when the plaintiff instituted proceedings, *inter alia*, claiming injunctions to prevent the son trespassing on the land, the son counter-claimed for a declaration that he was entitled to the house and the site on which it was built. Kenny J held that he was satisfied that the son would have erected the house on his own property had the plaintiff not given his wife permission to erect the house on the disputed lands. However, he rejected the son's claim that he had acquired a right to compel the plaintiff to transfer the site to him although he held that the plaintiff was estopped by his conduct from asserting any title to the site.[19] As Kenny J stated: 'While the estoppel created by the plaintiff's conduct prevents him asserting a title to the site, it does not give [the son] a right to require the plaintiff to transfer the site to him: if I had jurisdiction to make such an order I would do so, but I do not think I have.'[20]

While the principle had certainly been employed in a defensive context in *Hughes v. Metropolitan Railway Co.*[21] as Jackson[22] has commented 'this does not imply that an action cannot be brought upon a representation' and he

---

15. [1951] 2 KB 215.
16. *Ibid.* at 224.
17. High Court Circuit Appeal (Barron J)10 December 1985.
18. [1962] IR 268. See Brady (1970) 5 Ir Jur (ns) 239.
19. At the end of a 12-year period the son could therefore bring an application under s. 52 of the Registration of Title Act 1891 for his registration as owner.
20. *Ibid.* at 292.
21. (1877) 2 App Cas 439.
22. (1965) 81 LQR 223, 142.

argues that any attempt to restrict the effect of such a representation to a defensive mechanism ignores the principle on which it is based, namely that a promise may be enforced. As Mason CJ pointed out in *Waltons Stores (Interstate) Ltd v. Maher*,[23] Denning LJ himself acknowledged in the *Combe* case that estoppel 'may be part of a cause of action' even if not a cause of action in itself. More recently there have been signs in England of a more flexible approach being taken to this traditional limitation on the operation of the doctrine and in *Re Wyvern Developments Ltd*[24] Templeman J rejected the argument that estoppel could not confer a cause of action and said that it applies whenever 'the promissor knows and intends that the promise will irretrievably alter his position on the promise'.[25]

Recent High Court decisions in Ireland show that there is a lack of consensus on this question and it would be fair to say that there has been little real analysis of the issues underlying it. In *Re J.R.*[26] Costello J appeared to hold that promissory estoppel could give rise to a cause of action and indeed was capable of creating proprietary rights. However, this approach is at odds with the *dicta* of O'Hanlon J in *Association of General Practitioners Ltd v. Minister for Health*,[27] in which he reasserted the traditional view that promissory estoppel should be regarded as providing a shield and not a sword. The question arose in the context of a claim by the plaintiffs based, *inter alia*, on the doctrine of legitimate expectation which Finlay CJ had described in *Webb v. Ireland*[28] as 'but an aspect of the well-recognised equitable concept of promissory estoppel'. Relying on the position as laid down in *Combe v. Combe*,[29] O'Hanlon J stated that 'the doctrine of equitable or promissory estoppel cannot create any new cause of action where none existed before'[30] and from this proposition he concluded that where a promise is made which is unsupported by consideration, the promisee cannot bring an action. While no detailed consideration was given by O'Hanlon J to this issue, his reiteration of the orthodox view of the limitations of the doctrine of promissory estoppel indicates at the very least that there is no coherent move towards broadening its parameters in this jurisdiction.

Another aspect of promissory estoppel which has provoked a degree of uncertainty is the need for a claimant to establish detriment. There have been suggestions made by Lord Denning to the effect that this is not an essential

---

23. (1988) 164 CLR 387, 400.
24. [1974] 1 WLR 1097.
25. *Ibid.* at 1104.
26. [1993] ILRM 657.
27. [1995] 2 ILRM 481.
28. [1988] IR 353.
29. [1951] 2 KB 215.
30. [1995] 2 ILRM 481, 492.

requirement,[31] however in *Lowe v. Lombank Ltd*[32] Diplock J disagreed with this viewpoint and said that any representation made to a person must be acted upon by him to his detriment before an estoppel can arise. Similarly in *Industrial Yarns Ltd v. Greene*[33] Costello J stated that to establish a claim of estoppel, 'the representor must show that what was said or done by the representor influenced both the belief and conduct of the representor to his detriment'. The approach adopted by Costello J in his recent judgment in *Re J.R.*,[34] would tend to confirm the need to establish detriment if a claim based on promissory estoppel is to succeed in this jurisdiction.

PROPRIETARY ESTOPPEL

Introduction

The basis of the doctrine of proprietary estoppel is to prevent a person from insisting on his strict legal rights where to do so would be inequitable having regard to the dealings which have taken place between the parties.[35] It developed as an exception to the formalities required for the creation of interests in land and the rationale behind the doctrine could be said to be the prevention of unconscionable behaviour. It should be noted at this point that while proprietary estoppel is almost exclusively invoked in the context of rights in or over land, it can extend to other forms of property.[36]

To invoke successfully the doctrine of proprietary estoppel, it is necessary to establish that an assurance has been given, that reliance has been placed by the other party on that assurance and that detriment has been suffered as a result. As Edward Nugee QC (sitting as a High Court judge) stated in *Re Basham*:[37]

> Where one person, A, has acted to his detriment on the faith of a belief which was known to and encouraged by another person, B, that he either

31. *W.J. Alan & Co. Ltd v. El Nasr Export and Import Co* [1972] 2 QB 189, 213. See also *Brikom Investments Ltd v. Carr* [1979] QB 467, 482.
32. [1960] 1 WLR 196. Adopted as a correct statement of the law in this jurisdiction by Murphy J in *McCambridge v. Winters* High Court 1983 No. 486Sp (Murphy J) 28 May 1984.
33. [1984] ILRM 15, 23 *per* Costello J. See also *Dunne v. Molloy* [1976-77] ILRM 266 in which Gannon J pointed to the fact that there was no evidence of any detrimental act done by the plaintiff either with the encouragement or knowledge of the defendant.
34. [1993] ILRM 657.
35. *Crabb v. Arun District Council* [1976] Ch 179, 187-188 *per* Denning MR.
36. E.g. *Re Basham* [1986] 1 WLR 1498.
37. [1986] 1 WLR 1498, 1503. Quoted with approval by Balcombe LJ in *Wayling v. Jones* (1993) 69 P & CR 170, 172 and by Carnwath J in *Gillett v. Holt* [1998] 3 All ER 917, 926 (reversed by the Court of Appeal [2001] Ch 210).

has or is going to be given a right in or over B's property, B cannot insist on his strict legal rights if to do so would be inconsistent with A's belief.

The assurance given, while it need not necessarily have been express, must have been made by the party with the intention that it should be relied on and a mere expression of opinion would be insufficient in this context. It will usually consist of encouragement by words or deeds but mere acquiescence or 'conscious silence'[38] may also suffice.

Reliance would seem to be established once it is shown that a representation 'was calculated to influence the judgment of a reasonable man'[39] and there is authority for the proposition that once an assurance on the part of the legal owner has been established, there is a presumption of reliance.[40] The concept of reliance was considered recently by Balcombe LJ in *Wayling v. Jones*[41] in which he stated that '[o]nce it has been established that promises were made, and that there has been conduct by the plaintiff of such a nature that inducement may be inferred then the burden of proof shifts to the defendants to establish that he did not rely on the promises' but he added that 'there must be a sufficient link between the promises relied upon and the conduct which constitutes the detriment'. A further interesting point was made by Robert Walker LJ in *Gillett v. Holt*[42] to the effect that where assurances given were intended to be relied on, and were in fact relied on, it was not necessary to find an irrevocable promise as it is the other party's detrimental reliance on the promise which makes it irrevocable.

Detriment will be suffered where the assurance on which reliance is placed is withdrawn and it is the fact of detriment having been suffered which will render it unconscionable for the legal owner to insist on enforcing his rights. While the detriment suffered by the claimant will usually involve expenditure of money or the building of premises on another's land, it would appear that this is not the only form of detriment which will suffice. In *Re Basham*[43] Edward Nugee QC stated that 'the expenditure of A.'s money on B.'s property is not the only kind of detriment that gives rise to a proprietary estoppel' and in *McCarron v. McCarron*[44] Murphy J commented *obiter* that 'in a suitable case it may well be argued that a plaintiff suffers as severe a loss or detriment by providing his own labours or services in relation to the lands of another

---

38. *Salvation Army Trustee Co. Ltd v. W. Yorkshire Metropolitan County Council* (1981) 41 P & CR 179.
39. *Brikom Investments Ltd v. Carr* [1979] QB 467, 483 *per* Denning MR.
40. *Greasley v. Cooke* [1980] 1 WLR 1306. See also *Gillett v. Holt* [2001] Ch 210, 228.
41. (1993) 69 P & CR 170, 173. See Davis [1995] Conv 409 and Cooke (1995) 111 LQR 389.
42. [2001] Ch 210, 228-229.
43. [1986] 1 WLR 1498, 1509
44. Supreme Court 1995 No. 181, 13 February 1997 at 13.

and accordingly should equally qualify for recognition in equity'. This view was confirmed by Kinlen J in *McGuinness v. McGuinness*[45] where he stated that the detriment must be substantial although not it is necessarily confined to monetary considerations and added that it must be tested against the principle that it would be unjust or inequitable to allow the assurance to be disregarded.

A comprehensive analysis of the manner in which the principle of detriment operates in the context of proprietary estoppel has recently been undertaken by Robert Walker LJ in *Gillett v. Holt*.[46] Referring to the judgment of Slade LJ in *Jones v. Watkins*[47] he said that there must be a sufficient causal link between the assurance relied on and the detriment asserted, that the issue of detriment must be judged at the moment when the person who has given the assurance seeks to go back on it, that whether the detriment is sufficiently substantial is to be tested by whether it would be unjust or inequitable to allow the assurance to be disregarded and that the detriment alleged must be pleaded and proved.[48] Robert Walker LJ stated as follows:

> The overwhelming weight of authority shows that detriment is required. But the authorities also show that it is not a narrow or technical concept. The detriment need not consist of the expenditure of money or other quantifiable financial detriment, so long as it is something substantial. The requirement must be approached as part of a broad inquiry as to whether repudiation of an assurance is or is not unconscionable in all the circumstances.[49]

Gray and Gray[50] have suggested three categories of situation in which proprietary estoppel may arise: cases where an imperfect gift is made, cases based on common expectation and cases of unilateral mistake. These categories are clearly not mutually exclusive as the effect of the operation of the doctrine may well be to perfect an imperfect gift even in cases where the basis for its operation can be said to be expectation or mistake. An examination of the case law in this area over the last century shows that attempts were made to restrict the cases in which proprietary estoppel could arise to those falling into the mistake category and such an approach undoubtedly restricted the growth of the doctrine. More recently it has come to be recognised that such

---

45. High Court 2001 Nos.145CA and 147CA (Kinlen J) 19 March 2002.
46. [2001] Ch 211. While Thompson [2001] Conv 78, 83 has welcomed the decision as taking 'a wider and more principled view of the concept of detriment' Wells [2001] Conv 13, 30 is more critical and suggests that the principles relating to detriment have not been clarified by it.
47. Court of Appeal, 26 November 1987.
48. See also *McGuinness v. McGuinness* High Court 2001 Nos.145CA and 147CA (Kinlen J) 19 March 2002 at 7.
49. [2001] Ch 211, 232. See also *Lloyd v. Dugdale* [2002] 2 P & CR 167, 177.
50. *Elements of Land Law* (3rd ed., 2001) p. 763.

categorisation is unnecessary and even unhelpful and a broader doctrine based on the general concept of unconscionability has evolved.[51] Nevertheless, it is still useful to build up a picture of how proprietary estoppel has developed by examining the case law by reference to these categories.

Where an Imperfect Gift is Made

While the general principle is that equity will not complete an imperfect gift,[52] in some circumstances the courts will allow the perfection of a gift in favour of a volunteer, usually in the context of a voluntary gift of realty. The main authority for this proposition is the decision of Lord Westbury in *Dillwyn v. Llewelyn*.[53] A son built a house on his father's land with the latter's consent and an informal memorandum was signed which showed that the father's intention was that it should be given to the son for this purpose. After the father died, it was held by the House of Lords that the father's intention to convey the fee simple estate would be carried into effect by the court, although the land had been left in trust for the benefit of third parties by virtue of the provisions of the father's will. Lord Westbury pointed out that a promise of a gift had been made and on the strength of that promise and with the father's knowledge, the son had incurred substantial expenditure on the land. He stressed that a voluntary agreement would not be completed by a court of equity in the case of a mere gift and that it was instead the subsequent acts of the donor which gave rise to the claim. This decision was stated by Kenny J in *Cullen v. Cullen*[54] to be authority for the proposition that 'a person claiming under a voluntary agreement will not be assisted by a court of equity but that the subsequent acts of the donor may give the donee a ground of claim which he did not acquire from the original gift'.

The principle laid down in *Dillwyn* was applied by the English Court of Appeal in *Pascoe v. Turner*.[55] The parties had lived together for a considerable period of time in a house owned by the plaintiff and when he moved out and went to live with another woman, he assured the defendant that she could remain in the house and that it would henceforth belong to her. On the basis of this assurance, the defendant carried out repairs and improvements to the property. When the plaintiff subsequently brought proceedings for possession, the Court of Appeal held that the fee simple estate in the house should be conveyed to the defendant.

---

51. Pawlowski has recently commented in the preface to his book *Proprietary Estoppel* (1996) that these three categories 'remain valid, notwithstanding the modern trend towards applying an underlying concept of unconscionability as the basis for proprietary estoppel claims'.
52. *Milroy v. Lord* (1862) 4 De GF & J 264.
53. (1862) 4 De GF & J 517.
54. [1962] IR 268, 282.
55. [1979] 1 WLR 431.

Similarly in *Smyth v. Halpin*[56] the plaintiff had asked his father to provide him with a site on the latter's land so that he could build a house for himself. The father's reply was to the effect that the family house would be his after his mother's death and why would he want two houses and suggested that the plaintiff instead build an extension onto the family home. The father made a number of wills during his lifetime but in the last of these he left the house to his wife for her life and thereafter to the second named defendant, one of his daughters. After the father's death the plaintiff instituted proceedings seeking, *inter alia,* a declaration that he was entitled to the reversionary interest in the property following the life interest in favour of his mother. Geoghegan J stated that the kind of proprietary estoppel invoked in this case has its origins in the decision of *Dillwyn v. Llewelyn* and that the same principles have been applied in a number of other English decisions, including *Pascoe v. Turner*. He stated that the plaintiff's clear expectation in this case was that he would have a fee simple interest in the entire house and concluded that the protection of the equity arising from the expenditure required that an order be made by the court directing a conveyance of that interest to him.

Common Expectation

Cases such as *Pascoe v. Tuner* and *Smyth v. Halpin* could equally be considered under the heading of 'common expectation', and the key feature in this class of case is the notion of reliance. So, proprietary estoppel may arise where parties have consistently dealt with each other in such a way as reasonably to cause one party to rely on a shared assumption that he would acquire rights in the other party's lands. The accepted classic formulation of this proposition was laid down by Lord Kingsdown in his dissenting speech in *Ramsden v. Dyson*[57] as follows:

> If a man, under a verbal agreement with a landlord for a certain interest in land, or, what amounts to the same thing, under an expectation, created or encouraged by the landlord, that he shall have a certain interest, takes possession of such land, with the consent of the landlord, and upon the faith of such promise or expectation, with the knowledge of the landlord, and without objection by him, lays out money upon the land, a Court of equity will compel the landlord to give effect to such a promise or expectation. ...
>
> If, on the other hand, a tenant being in possession of land, and knowing the nature and extent of his interest, lays out money upon it in the hope and expectation of an extended term or an allowance for

---

56. [1997] 2 ILRM 38.
57. (1866) LR 1 HL 129, 170-171.

expenditure, then, if such expenditure has not been created or encouraged by the landlord, the tenant has no claim which any Court of law or equity can enforce.

Lord Kingsdown's observations were approved of by the Privy Council in *Plimmer v. Mayor of Wellington*,[58] where the landowner rather than merely encouraging the expenditure actually took the initiative in requesting it. A licensee of land had, at the government's request, spent a considerable sum of money on extending a jetty and constructing a warehouse. When the jetty was compulsorily acquired it was held that the appellants had an equity arising from their expenditure on the land and were entitled to 'an indefinite, that is practically a perpetual' right to the jetty for the purposes of the original licence. Similarly in *Inwards v. Baker*[59] an estoppel arose on the basis of a common expectation that by reason of one party's expenditure on land, he should be entitled to an interest in it. A father had allowed his son to build a house at his own expense on the former's land, encouraging the son to believe that he would be allowed to remain there during his lifetime. When the father died, the Court of Appeal refused to allow the trustees of the father's will to obtain possession of the lands on the basis that the son had acquired an equity in the land by reason of his expenditure which bound the father and his successors in title. Instead, the court made an order that the son could remain in possession of the property as long as he wished to use the house as his home.

It is important to stress that before Lord Kingsdown's *dicta* will apply it is essential that the expenditure has been requested, or more commonly encouraged, by the landowner. As the second paragraph of Lord Kingsdown's statement makes clear, where the other party merely lays out money in the hope or expectation of acquiring an interest, which has not been encouraged by the landowner, no estoppel will arise. This point is well illustrated by the decision of the Privy Council in *Attorney General of Hong Kong v. Humphrey's Estate*.[60] It was agreed in principle between the Hong Kong government and a group of companies, which included the respondent, that the government would grant the group a lease of specific property in exchange for flats which belonged to the latter. The government took possession of the flats and fitted them out for civil servants but before the contract was concluded, the group withdrew from the transaction. When the government brought an action contesting the group's right to withdraw, the respondent sought a declaration that it was entitled to possession of the flats. The government contended that the group were estopped from withdrawing from what had been agreed in

---

58. (1884) 9 App Cas 699. The formulation set out by the Privy Council was quoted by Murphy J in *McCarron v. McCarron* Supreme Court 1995 No. 181, 13 February 1997 at 12.
59. [1965] 2 QB 29.
60. [1987] AC 114.

principle but the Privy Council rejected this claim. It was held that to found an estoppel it would have to be established not only that the government had acted to its detriment to the knowledge of the group in the hope that it would not withdraw from the agreement, but also that the group had created or encouraged a belief or expectation on the government's part that they would not withdraw, and that the government had relied on that belief or expectation. While it was accepted that 'the government acted in the confident and not unreasonable hope that the agreement in principle would come into effect,' it was held that the group had not encouraged or allowed a belief or expectation on the government's part that it would not withdraw from the agreement and that in the circumstances no estoppel arose.

The fact that a claimant must establish that the legal owner created or encouraged a belief that it would not change its mind was also of importance in the recent decision of *Taylor v. Dickens*.[61] While the plaintiff asserted that he was confident that the defendant would not revoke the provision in her will in which she had left him her house as she had promised, there was no evidence that she had created or encouraged this belief on his behalf.[62] As Milne has commented 'proprietary estoppel may prevent unconscionable conduct in respect of property, but it cannot operate unless there has been reliance on an encouraged belief in rights over that property'.[63]

The importance of the fact that any expectation or belief be created or encouraged by a landowner can also be seen from the decision of Blayney J in *Haughan v. Rutledge*.[64] The plaintiffs, who were trustees of an association which promoted harness racing, sought to lease the defendant's land for the purpose of holding races. The parties agreed that the defendant would let a field for a trial period and the plaintiffs would construct a racetrack on it. It was further agreed that if at the end of this period the plaintiffs left the property, they would pay no rent and the defendant would retain the benefit of the works carried out. A dispute arose and the defendant re-possessed the lands and the plaintiffs sought specific performance of the alleged agreement to grant a lease of the lands or alternatively an order requiring the defendant to let them into possession. Blayney J held that four conditions would have to be satisfied before an estoppel could arise, namely detriment, expectation or belief, encouragement and finally, that there be no bar to the equity. On the facts of the case before him, he held that the second and third requirements had not been satisfied. The second condition required that the plaintiffs had built the racetrack in the belief that they owned a sufficient interest in the land to justify

---

61. [1998] 1 FLR 806. See Thompson [1998] Conv 210.
62. As Gray and Gray have commented in *Elements of Land Law* (3rd ed., 2001) p.790 'detrimental reliance upon a self-generated expectation gives rise to no valid claim of estoppel'.
63. (1998) 114 LQR 555, 558-559.
64. [1988] IR 295.

the expenditure or that they would obtain such an interest and this had not been established. Blayney J added that even if he had been of the view that the plaintiffs had the required belief, he would not have been satisfied that this belief had been encouraged by the defendant. Blayney J referred to the *dicta* of Lord Kingsdown in *Ramsden* and said that the case before him came within the second limb of the latter's statement. He concluded as follows:

> I consider that the plaintiffs laid out money on the construction of the track in the hope and expectation that the defendant would continue to make lettings of the track to them, but as that hope and expectation was not created or encouraged by the defendant, the plaintiffs have no claim which can be enforced at law or in equity.[65]

Unilateral Mistake

Proprietary estoppel may also be invoked where one party has made an error as to the nature of his rights, the crucial factor being that detriment is suffered by the party who innocently relies on the mistaken assumption that he has rights in land. The following statement of Lord Cranworth in *Ramsden v. Dyson*[66] provides a summary of the circumstances in which estoppel can arise in such cases:

> If a stranger begins to build on my land supposing it to be his own, and I, perceiving his mistake, abstain from setting him right, and leave him to persevere in his error, a Court of equity will not allow me afterwards to assert my title to the land on which he had expended money on the supposition that the land was his own. It considers that, when I saw the mistake into which he had fallen, it was my duty to be active and to state my adverse title, and that it would be dishonest in me to remain wilfully passive on such an occasion, in order afterwards to profit by the mistake which I might have prevented.

However, he continued: 'If a stranger builds on my land knowing it to be mine, there is no principle of equity which would prevent my claiming the land with the benefit of all the expenditure made on it.' Therefore it is necessary that the person spending the money thought that he was building on his own land and that the real owner knew at the time that the landed in fact belong to him; no estoppel will arise under this heading where the 'stranger' knows that he has no rights over the land. This point is illustrated by the case of *O'Callaghan v. Ballincollig Holdings Ltd.*[67] The plaintiffs claimed that they

---

65. *Ibid.* at 303.
66. (1866) LR 1 HL 129, 140-141.
67. High Court 1987 No. E202 (Blayney J) 31 March 1993.

had acquired title to a house by adverse possession and this claim was rejected by the defendants and a notice to quit served. The plaintiffs sought a declaration of their title or alternatively a declaration that they had a lien on the house for monies spent on reinstating it while the defendant counter-claimed for possession. The plaintiffs' claim to a lien was based on the grounds of proprietary estoppel and unjust enrichment. They argued that the defendant had stood idly by while they had spent substantial sums of money reinstating the house and that this precluded it from recovering the property without compensating the plaintiffs for their expenditure. Blayney J was satisfied that this submission was not well founded; as long as the plaintiffs' tenancy continued to subsist, the defendant was not entitled to interfere and it was not a case of the defendant standing idly by. He quoted with approval the second limb of Lord Cranworth's *dicta* in *Ramsden* and concluded that the plaintiffs knew that they held the defendant's house as tenants and that they were reinstating a house to which the defendant was entitled subject to their tenancy. Therefore they could not prevent the defendant from claiming the house with the benefit of their expenditure on it.

An attempt was made to rely on Lord Cranworth's principle in *Wilmott v. Barber*[68] although on the facts it was clear that both parties were mistaken as to their legal rights and the claim of estoppel was rejected. Neither the plaintiff assignee of a lease nor the lessor had realized that the lease prohibited assignment of the lease without the lessor's consent. Fry J concluded that the lessor could not, by his action in acquiescing in the expenditure incurred by the lessee, be estopped from asserting his right to refuse consent to the assignment since at the date of the purported acquiescence, he was not aware of the right of veto. However, the judgment of Fry J is important in view of the restrictive effect which it had on the development of the doctrine of proprietary estoppel. He laid down the proposition that a person should not be deprived of his strict legal rights unless he has acted in a manner which would make it fraudulent to assert those rights, fraud in this context being dependent on establishing five necessary elements. These were as follows:[69]

1. The claimant must have made a mistake as to his legal rights.

2. The claimant must have expended some money or done some act on the faith of his mistaken belief.

3. The owner of the land must know of his own right which is inconsistent with the right claimed by the plaintiff.

4. The owner must know of the claimant's mistaken belief as to his rights.

---

68. (1880) 15 Ch D 96.
69. *Ibid.* at 105-106. Quoted with approval by Gannon J in *Dunne v. Molloy* [1976-77] ILRM 266, 268.

5.   The owner must have encouraged the claimant in relation to the
     expenditure incurred or other acts done, either directly or by refraining
     from asserting his legal rights.

These so-called five probanda came to be applied by the courts in cases where
a claim of proprietary estoppel was made irrespective of the basis of such a
claim and even where it did not involve a case of unilateral mistake. With a
few limited exceptions, the most notable being the decision of the Privy Council
in *Plimmer v. Mayor of Wellington*,[70] in which a distinction was made between
cases of unilateral mistake and common expectation, the courts often sought
to construe situations so that they fell within the requirements laid down in
Fry, even where there was no mistake made, and where this was not possible,
a claim might fail. So, in *Cullen v. Cullen*[71] Kenny J appeared to reject a
claim based on proprietary estoppel on this basis. In *Hopgood v. Brown*,[72]
Evershed MR recognised that these requirements should be limited to cases
of unilateral mistake and commented that they were not intended to be a
'comprehensive formulation of the necessary requisites of any case of estoppel
by representation.' However, because of the apparently general nature of the
probanda, their application resulted in a very restrictive view of the
circumstances in which estoppel could arise.[73] Nevertheless, by the 1980s the
courts had begun to recognise that the *dicta* of Fry J did not constitute a
formula which had to be rigidly adhered to, although the requirements
continued to be applied in cases which did not fall within the category of
unilateral mistake, albeit less frequently.[74]

A Move Towards a Test of Unconscionability

A view that the five probanda should be used as a guide rather than as a strict
requirement began to emerge in England during the 1970s. As Buckley LJ
commented in *Shaw v. Applegate*[75] where they were satisfied he had no doubt
that it would be dishonest or unconscionable for the owner of a right to insist
upon it, although he doubted whether it was really necessary to comply strictly
with all five requirements to establish unconscionability. Similarly in *Crabb
v. Arun District Council*[76] Scarman LJ although he did refer to the probanda
as a 'valuable guide'[77] expressed the view that it should be necessary to

---

70. (1884) 9 App Cas 699, 712.
71. [1962] IR 268.
72. [1955] 1 WLR 213, 223.
73. E.g. *E. & L. Berg Homes Ltd v. Grey* (1979) 253 EG 473.
74. See e.g. *Coombes v. Smith* [1986] 1 WLR 808; *Matharu v. Matharu* (1994) 68 P &
    CR 93. See Milne (1995) 58 MLR 412.
75. [1977] 1 WLR 970.
76. [1976] Ch 179.
77. *Ibid.* at 194.

establish that a defendant by asserting a right is taking advantage of a plaintiff in a manner which is 'unconscionable, inequitable or unjust'.[78] However, it was not until the judgment of Oliver J in *Taylors Fashions Ltd v. Liverpool Victoria Trustees Co. Ltd*[79] that any detailed consideration was given to the idea of a departure from the *Wilmott v. Barber* approach, although on the facts of that case the plaintiff's claim was rejected. Oliver J pointed out that in the example given by Lord Kingsdown in *Ramsden v. Dyson*[80] there was no room for the literal application of the probanda as the circumstances referred to did not presuppose a mistake but rather the fostering of an expectation in the minds of both parties. He said that more recent authorities seemed to support a much wider equitable jurisdiction to interfere in situations where the assertion of legal rights was found by a court to be unconscionable and suggested that the relevance of the probanda even in cases of unilateral mistake was now open to doubt. Oliver J concluded as follows:

> Furthermore, the more recent cases indicate, in my judgment, that the application of the *Ramsden v. Dyson* principle ... requires a very much broader approach which is directed rather at ascertaining whether, in particular circumstances, it would be unconscionable for a party to be permitted to deny that which, knowingly or unknowingly, he has allowed or encouraged another to assume to his detriment rather than to inquiring whether the circumstances can be fitted within the confines of some preconceived formula serving as a universal yardstick for every form of unconscionable behaviour.[81]

This more flexible approach was not applied universally in England in the years following the decision in *Taylors Fashions*,[82] although a Privy Council decision suggested that the strictures of the *Wilmott v. Barber* principles had been substantially relaxed and that the real question now seemed to be whether or not the assertion of strict legal rights would be unconscionable. In *Lim Teng Huan v. Ang Swee Chuan*[83] the parties entered into an agreement whereby the plaintiff acknowledged his consent to the building of a house by the defendant on land which they had originally purchased jointly[84] and agreed to exchange his share in the property for unspecified land which the defendant

---

78. *Ibid.* at 195.
79. [1982] QB 133.
80. (1866) LR 1 HL 129.
81. [1982] QB 133, 151-152.
82. See *Coombes v. Smith* [1986] 1 WLR 808.
83. [1992] 1 WLR 113.
84. Shortly after the purchase the land was transferred into the name of their respective fathers who both died within a number of years and the plaintiff therefore instituted proceedings as administrator of his father's estate.

expected to acquire. After the defendant had completed the house and gone into occupation of it, the plaintiff sought a declaration that he was the owner of half the land and the defendant counter-claimed for a declaration that he was entitled to the sole beneficial ownership of the plaintiff's share or alternatively sought an injunction to restrain the plaintiff from entering the land. At the trial the plaintiff abandoned his claim and the defendant's counter-claim was dismissed. The Court of Appeal allowed the defendant' appeal and the Privy Council subsequently allowed the plaintiff's further appeal in part, ordering that on the payment of compensation by the defendant, the plaintiff must transfer his half share in the land to the defendant. The Privy Council inferred that the defendant had completed construction of the house in reliance on the agreement made between the parties and found that it would be unconscionable for the plaintiff to renege on the assumption that the defendant would have a sole absolute interest in the land upon paying compensation to the plaintiff. The plaintiff was therefore estopped from denying the defendant's title to the whole of the land. Lord Browne-Wilkinson referred to the decision of Oliver J in *Taylors Fashions* and said that it showed that in order to found a proprietary estoppel, 'it is enough if, in all the circumstances, it is unconscionable for the representor to go back on the assumption which he has permitted the representee to make'.[85]

Despite the attractiveness of such a straightforward formula, there has been a definite lack of consistency in the approach adopted by the English courts since the decision in *Lim*. In *Matharu v. Matharu*[86] despite the fact that adopting a narrow approach did not affect the outcome in the case, Roch LJ seemed to lay down the requirement that the probanda must be satisfied in all cases if proprietary estoppel is to be relied upon and did not refer to the broader approach based on the notion of unconscionability. However, in *Lloyds Bank plc v. Carrick*[87] Morritt LJ made it clear that he agreed with the conclusion of Oliver J in *Taylors Fashions* that 'proof of all those elements or "probanda" is not necessary to found an estoppel.' Thompson, commenting on that decision, stated that 'it is to be welcomed as it continues the trend away from seeking to fit a flexible doctrine into a Procrustean bed, which is frequently not an appropriate thing to do, and should, it is hoped, prevent cases in the future being decided on a somewhat mechanical application of these probanda'.[88]

Subsequently in *Taylor v. Dickens*[89] Judge Weeks seemed decidedly hostile to a suggestion that the court might intervene merely where the assertion of

85. [1992] 1 WLR 113, 117.
86. (1994) 69 P & CR 93. See Milne (1995) 58 MLR 412 and Welsted [1995] Conv 61.
87. [1996] 4 All ER 630, 640.
88. [1996] Conv 295, 298.
89. [1998] 1 FLR 806. This decision has been criticised by Thompson [1998] Conv 210, 217 as representing 'an unduly narrow approach to the doctrine of estoppel'.

strict legal rights was found to be unconscionable, although he stopped short of seeking to adopt the formulation in *Wilmott*. In his view if one were to follow such an approach 'one might as well forget the law of contract and issue every judge with a portable palm tree. The days of justice varying with the size of the Lord Chancellor's foot would have returned'.[90] However, the decision in *Taylor v. Dickens* has met with considerable academic[91] and judicial criticism[92] and more recent decisions would suggest that the concept of unconscionability is central to the modern doctrine of proprietary estoppel.[93]

One of the most important decisions in this area is *Gillett v. Holt*[94] in which the plaintiff spent his working life as a farm manager for the first named defendant whom he also regarded as a friend. The first named defendant repeatedly promised the plaintiff that he would succeed to the farming business and the house in which the plaintiff and his family had lived for over 25 years. After relations between the parties deteriorated and the plaintiff was dismissed from his job, the first named defendant made dispositions of the property to the second named defendant in whose favour he also altered his will. Carnwath J dismissed the plaintiff's claim based on proprietary estoppel finding that the representations made could not be construed as an irrevocable promise and that the claim would in any event have failed because the plaintiff had not proved himself to have suffered sufficient detriment in reliance on the first named defendant's assurances to give rise to proprietary estoppel. However, it is interesting to note that Carnwath J did agree that the overriding principle was that a defendant should be held to his representation 'only if it would be unconscionable to go back on it' although he stressed that estoppel must be founded on an expectation, created or encouraged by the party alleged to be bound by it, in reliance on which the other party has acted to his detriment. The plaintiff's appeal to the Court of Appeal was allowed, Robert Walker LJ stating that where assurances were intended to be relied on and were in fact relied on it was not necessary to look for an irrevocable promise since it was the other party's detrimental reliance on the promise which made it irrevocable. In relation to the issue of detriment, Robert Walker LJ stated that the trial judge had not stood back and 'look[ed] at the matter in the round' and he was satisfied that if he had, he would have found that the plaintiff's case on this point was an unusually compelling one. Having found in the plaintiff's favour, the Court of Appeal concluded that the minimum equity to do justice to the plaintiff was to convey the farmhouse to him and award him a sufficient sum

---

90. *Ibid.* at 820.
91. Thompson [1998] Conv 210; Swadling [1998] RLR 220; Wells [1999] Conv 462.
92. *Gillett v. Holt* [1998] 3 All ER 917 (ChD); [2001] Ch 210, 227 (CA). Dixon [2000] CLJ 453; Thompson [2001] Conv 78; Wells [2001] Conv 13.
93. See also *Lloyd v. Dugdale* [2002] 2 P & CR 167, 179 and *Jennings v. Rice* [2002] EWCA Civ 159 Court of Appeal, 22 February 2002 paragraphs 21 and 44.
94. [2001] Ch 210.

of money to compensate him for his exclusion from the rest of the farming business. While the approach adopted by Robert Walker LJ illustrates the importance of the traditional elements of assurance, reliance and detriment, his judgment also shows an acceptance of the increasing importance of the principle of unconscionability. As he stated, proprietary estoppel cannot be treated as if it can be subdivided into three or four watertight compartments, so the quality of the assurance may influence the issue of reliance and the concepts of reliance and detriment are often intertwined. In his view 'the fundamental principle that equity is concerned to prevent unconscionable conduct permeates all elements of the doctrine. In the end the court must look at the matter in the round.'[95] Robert Walker LJ added that the requirement of detriment must be approached as part of a broad inquiry as to whether repudiation of an assurance is or is not unconscionable in all the circumstances and it is clear from the tenor of his judgment that he believed the concept of unconscionability to be fundamental to the imposition of liability. More recently in his decision in *Jennings v. Rice*[96] Robert Walker LJ adopted a similar approach towards this issue and said that the doctrine of proprietary estoppel only applies if the elements of assurance and detrimental reliance make it unconscionable for the party making the assurance to go back on it.

The concept of unconscionability also appears to be playing an increasingly important role in this jurisdiction, as is evident from decisions such as *McMahon v. Kerry Co. Council*[97] in which Finlay P stressed the importance of assessing the consequences of the actions of the parties both from the point of view of the plaintiff and of the defendant. The plaintiffs bought a plot of land for the purpose of building a school, however shortly afterwards they abandoned their plan and did not visit the site again for a further three years. They then discovered that the defendant council which had originally known of their purchase, was preparing to build on the land and, upon a complaint being made, the work ceased. Four years later the defendant built two houses on the site and the following year the plaintiffs discovered this and instituted proceedings to recover possession of the site. Counsel for the defendant relied on *Ramsden v. Dyson* but Finlay P concluded that the facts of the case did not fall within the principle laid down by Lord Cranworth LC in that case and said that there was no question of the plaintiffs remaining wilfully passive when the defendant commenced to build on their land. However, Finlay P held that in the circumstances, it would be unjust and unconscionable that the plaintiffs should recover possession and he held that that they were only entitled to the market value of the site without the houses and to damages. With reference to *Ramsden*, Finlay P stated that the principles of equity set out in

---

95. [2001] Ch 210, 225.
96. [2002] EWCA Civ 159 Court of Appeal, 22 February 2002. See also the *dicta* of Aldous LJ at paragraph 21.
97. [1981] ILRM 419.

that case depended 'not exclusively on the action or inaction of the plaintiff or on the state of knowledge but have regard also to the action of the defendant.' He continued:

> If a court applying equitable principles is truly to act as a court of conscience then it seems to me unavoidable that it should consider not only conduct on the part of the plaintiff with particular regard to whether it is wrong and wilful but also conduct on the part of the defendant and furthermore the consequences and the justice of the consequences both from the point of view of the plaintiff and of the defendant.[98]

Unconscionability also appeared to provide the key to the imposition of liability in *Carter v. Ross*[99] where Murphy J stated that the courts will hold a promisor to his promise even if made without consideration where it would be unconscionable to permit him to resile from the promise which he had made. The defendant had already transferred a field in which the plaintiff had built his house to the latter. Having considered a statement made by the defendant that he wanted the plaintiff to return to Ireland, Murphy J concluded that he doubted whether there had ever been an assurance given by the defendant so that his decision to leave his farm to a third party could be deemed to be unconscionable or unacceptable. In his view the plaintiff's claim to the rest of the defendant's farm was based on a 'very vague promise and on minimal detriment to the plaintiff' and he concluded that his claim must be dismissed.

The Extent of the Remedy

As Brennan J commented in the Australian decision of *Waltons Stores (Interstate) Ltd v. Maher*[100] 'the remedy required to satisfy an equity varies according to the circumstances of the case'. This point is particularly apt in the context of proprietary estoppel[101] where the remedy may vary from the conferring of a fee simple interest to the granting of a mere licence. Equally, in some circumstances, it may be inappropriate to grant a remedy which involves any right to occupy property and it may be possible for the court to satisfy the equity raised by an award of damages, e.g. where improvements have been carried out to a premises which are not substantial in nature. As Cooke has commented: 'One of the most striking features of estoppel in the context of property claims is the wide range of responses available to the

---

98. *Ibid.* at 421.
99. High Court (Murphy J) 8 December 2000.
100. (1987) 164 CLR 387, 419.
101. As Lord Denning MR commented in *Crabb v. Arun District Council* [1976] Ch 179, 189: 'Here equity is displayed at its most flexible'.

court'.[102] Examples of the forms of remedy which have been granted in circumstances where an estoppel is made out have already been seen. In some cases, such as *Smyth v. Halpin*[103] and *Pascoe v. Turner*,[104] an order that a fee simple interest in property be transferred has been made while in the others, such as *Inwards v. Baker*,[105] a claimant has been confined to a more limited interest: in that case an irrevocable licence to occupy the property for life.

In the decision of the Privy Council in *Plimmer v. Mayor of Wellington*[106] it was made clear that where an equity has been raised, 'the court must look at the circumstances in each case to decide in what way the equity can be satisfied' and in *Crabb v. Arun DC*[107] Scarman LJ commented that the court should formulate the remedy which it will confer in such cases in terms of the 'minimum equity' required to do justice to the claimant. In the latter case the plaintiff acted to his detriment in parting with a portion of his land without having secured a means of access to the rest of it on the basis of a belief encouraged by the defendant that he would be granted a right of way over the latter's land. The Court of Appeal held that an equity arose in the plaintiff's favour and that he was entitled to be granted a right of way free of charge.

Mason CJ made it clear in his judgment in *Commonwealth of Australia v. Verwayen*[108] that a central element of the doctrine of proprietary estoppel is that there must be proportionality between the remedy and the detriment which it is designed to avoid. This theme was developed by Hobhouse LJ in *Sledmore v. Dalby*[109] where he stated that to recognize the need for proportionality 'is to say little more than that the end result must be a just one having regard to the assumption made by the party asserting the estoppel and the detriment which he has experienced.' Some consideration was also given to the manner in which the equity that arose might be satisfied by Robert Walker LJ in his judgment in *Gillett v. Holt*.[110] Having referred to the *dicta* in *Plimmer* set out above, he stated that the court approaches its task 'in a cautious way' in order to achieve what Scarman LJ described in *Crabb* as the 'minimum equity'.[111] He added that the court's aim should be, having identified the maximum extent

---

102. (1997) 17 LS 258, 266.
103. [1997] 2 ILRM 38.
104. [1979] 1 WLR 431. See also *Lim Teng Huan v. Ang Swee Chuan* [1992] 1 WLR 113.
105. [1965] 2 QB 29.
106. (1884) 9 App Cas 699, 714. Quoted with approval by Denning MR in *Crabb v. Arun District Council* [1976] Ch 179, 188.
107. [1976] Ch 179, 198.
108. (1990) 170 CLR 394, 413.
109. (1996) 72 P & CR 196, 209. See also *Jennings v. Rice* [2002] EWCA Civ 159 Court of Appeal, 22 February 2002 paragraph 56.
110. [2001] Ch 210.
111. *Ibid.* at 235. See also *Flowermix Ltd v. Site Development (Ferndown) Ltd* Chancery Divison (Arden J) 11 April 2000 paragraph 37 and *Campbell v. Griffin* [2001] EWCA Civ 990 Court of Appeal, 27 June 2001 paragraph 30.

of the equity, to form a view as to what is the minimum required to satisfy it and do justice between the parties and that the court must look at all of the circumstances, including the need to achieve a 'clean break' so far as possible and to avoid or minimize future friction.

An important recent decision which fully explores the question of satisfying the equity is that of the Court of Appeal in *Jennings v. Rice*.[112] The claimant had worked for the deceased for many years on a part time basis as a gardener and subsequently ran errands and carried out maintenance work about the house for her. During the last three years of her life, he also slept at her house to provide her with security and helped to care for her, although he had not been paid for many years. The deceased died intestate despite having made representations to the claimant that her house would be his one day and that she would 'see him right'. The trial judge held that the claimant was entitled to an award of £200,000 pursuant to the doctrine of proprietary estoppel on the basis that this was the minimum necessary to satisfy the equity in the case before the court. The claimant appealed contending that he was entitled to the deceased's whole estate or at least to a sum equal to the value of her house and furniture but the Court of Appeal dismissed his appeal. In considering how the equity in this case should be satisfied, Aldous LJ stated as follows:

> The value of that equity will depend upon all the circumstances including the expectation and the detriment. The task of the court is to do justice. The most essential requirement is that there must be proportionality between the expectation and the detriment.[113]

Robert Walker LJ stated that it was no coincidence that the statements of principle in relation to this question referred to satisfying the equity rather than satisfying or vindicating the claimant's expectations and that the equity arises not from the claimant's expectations alone, but from the combination of expectations, detrimental reliance, and the unconscionability of allowing the benefactor to go back on the assurance. He added that while it may be the natural response of the court to seek to fulfil the claimant's expectations, if these are uncertain, extravagant or out of all proportion to the detriment which he has suffered, the court can and should recognize that the claimant's equity should be satisfied in another and generally more limited way. Robert Walker LJ expressed the view that it would be unwise to attempt any comprehensive enumeration of the factors relevant to the exercise of the court's discretion or to suggest any hierarchy of factors. However, he went on to say that they included misconduct on the claimant's part, particularly oppressive behaviour on the part of the defendant, recognition of the fact that people cannot be

---

112. [2002] EWCA Civ 159 Court of Appeal, 22 February 2002.
113. *Ibid.* at paragraph 36.

compelled to live peaceably together, alterations in the benefactor's assets and circumstances, the likely effect of taxation and to a limited degree other legal or moral claims on the benefactor or his estate. He concluded that 'the essence of the doctrine of proprietary estoppel is to do what is necessary to avoid an unconscionable result, and a disproportionate remedy cannot be the right way of going about that.'[114]

The decision in *Jennings v. Rice* is also important for its analysis of what have traditionally been labelled as the 'reliance-based' and 'expectation-based' models and because it appears to come down in favour of an intermediate approach based on the concept of proportionality. The question of whether the task of the court should be to compensate a claimant for the detriment which he has suffered or to fulfil the claimant's expectations is one which has provoked considerable judicial and academic debate. As Robertson[115] has commented:

> The court can protect the reliance interest in an estoppel case by compensating the claimant for the loss suffered as a result of his or her reliance on the relevant promise or representation. Alternatively, the court can protect the claimant's expectation interest, by providing a remedy which puts the claimant in the position he or she would have occupied had the relevant promise been fulfilled.

The reliance-based theory appears to have been accepted by Dixon J in the decision of the High Court of Australia in *Grundt v. Great Boulder Proprietary Gold Mines Ltd*[116] and has been expressly adopted in more recent decisions in that jurisdiction. As Brennan J commented in *Waltons Stores (Interstate) Ltd v. Maher*:[117] 'The object of equity is not to compel the party bound to fulfil the assumption or expectation; it is to avoid the detriment which, if the assumption or expectation goes unfulfilled, will be suffered by the party who has been induced to act or to abstain from acting thereon.' It has been suggested that the adoption of this 'reliance loss' theory would confuse and emasculate the law of estoppel,[118] although it has also been argued that a reliance-based approach has made equitable estoppel far more coherent.[119] In addition, the view has been put forward that it will only be in occasional cases that the choice between a reliance and expectation-based approach will be significant, although clearly where a claimant has suffered quantifiable detriment

---

114. *Ibid.* at paragraph 56.
115. (1998) 18 LS 360, 361.
116. (1937) 59 CLR 641.
117. (1988) 164 CLR 387, 423. See also *Commonwealth of Australia v. Verwayen* (1990) 170 CLR 394. However, note the comments of Gardner (1999) 118 LQR 438, 439.
118. Cooke (1997) 17 LS 258, 280-281.
119. Robertson (1998) 18 LS 360, 363.

disproportionate to the expected benefit the differences between the two approaches will be crucial.[120]

It has generally been the expectation-based approach which has found favour with the courts in this jurisdiction and in England as decisions such as *Re J.R.*,[121] *Smyth v. Halpin*[122] and *Pascoe v. Turner*[123] illustrate.[124] However, the reasoning adopted by the members of the Court of Appeal in *Jennings v. Rice*[125] shows that the traditional distinction between the two approaches is being reassessed. Robert Walker LJ stated that if the claimant's expectations are uncertain their specific vindication cannot be the appropriate test. Equally, a problem will arise if the court is not satisfied that the high level of a claimant's expectations is fairly derived from the assurances given, which may have only justified a lower level of expectation[126] and in such cases he suggested that the court should merely take the claimant's expectations as a starting point. Robert Walker LJ stressed that he did not mean that the court should abandon expectations completely and look to the detriment suffered by the claimant as defining the appropriate measure of relief and added that in many cases detriment may be even more difficult to quantify in financial terms than the claimant's expectations. He concluded that he agreed with the view expressed by Hobhouse LJ in *Sledmore v. Dalby*[127] that the principle of proportionality between remedy and detriment, emphasized by Mason CJ in *Commonwealth of Australia v. Verwayen*,[128] is also relevant in England. Commenting on the approach adopted in *Jennings*, and in *Campbell v. Griffin*,[129] a decision in which the need for proportionality was also emphasized, Pawlowski[130] has suggested that it confirms that 'the fundamental aim of proprietary estoppel is not necessarily to fulfil the claimant's expectations nor, for that matter, to compensate him for his detrimental reliance, but to satisfy the equity in a way which does justice to both parties having

---

120. *Ibid.* at 368.
121. [1993] ILRM 657.
122. [1997] 2 ILRM 38
123. [1979] 1 WLR 431.
124. In *Jennings v. Rice* [2002] EWCA Civ 159 Court of Appeal, 22 February 2002 Aldous LJ commented (at paragraph 30) that he did not believe it necessary to examine the Australian authorities which appeared to lean towards the view that an award should compensate the detriment suffered as they 'did not reflect the law of this country'.
125. [2002] EWCA Civ 159 Court of Appeal, 22 February 2002.
126. See also the comment of Thompson [2001] Conv 78, 85 to the effect that: 'The acts of reliance in question may be of considerably less value than the expectation and to fulfil the expectation in its entirety may be to overcompensate the claimant.'
127. (1996) 72 P & CR 196, 208-209.
128. (1990) 170 CLR 394.
129. [2001] EWCA Civ 990 Court of Appeal, 27 June 2001.
130. (2002) 118 LQR 519, 519-520.

regard to all the circumstances and, in particular, the need for there to be proportionality between the expectation and detriment.'

The Relationship between Proprietary Estoppel and Constructive Trusts

It has been accepted that there is a close relationship between the concepts of proprietary estoppel and constructive trusts, in that both involve the application of the equitable principle that it would be unfair to allow a party to enforce his strict legal rights when it would be inequitable to do so on the basis of the dealings which have taken place between the parties. In the course of his judgment in *Grant v. Edwards*[131] Browne-Wilkinson VC noted that the principles underlying proprietary estoppel are 'closely akin' to those laid down in *Gissing v. Gissing*[132] in relation to constructive trusts and in his view while the two principles have been developed separately, they 'rest on the same foundation'. As he stated:

> In both, the claimant must to the knowledge of the legal owner have acted in the belief that the claimant has or will obtain an interest in the property. In both, the claimant must have acted to his or her detriment in reliance on such belief. In both, equity acts on the conscience of the legal owner to prevent him from acting in an unconscionable manner by defeating the common intention.[133]

Undoubtedly 'a common theme can be discerned'[134] in cases of proprietary estoppel and constructive trusts; they both allow for the creation of informal interests in land and the concept of unconscionability appears to underlie them both.[135] Nourse LJ commented in *Stokes v. Anderson*[136] that 'there is no real reason for thinking that their assimilation would be unduly hindered by their separate development out of basically different factual situations', although in his view no such assimilation had yet taken place. However, it has also been pointed out there are important differences between the two doctrines, namely in relation to the timing of the interest created and the type of interest which will be acquired by a claimant.[137] While establishing a claim of estoppel may lead to the conferral of a less extensive property right than

---

131. [1986] Ch 638.
132. [1971] AC 886.
133. [1986] Ch 638, 656. See also *Banner Homes plc v. Luff Developments Ltd* [2000] 2 WLR 772, 781.
134. *Re Basham* [1986] 1 WLR 1498, 1504.
135. Hayton [1990] Conv 370.
136. [1991] 1 FLR 391, 399.
137. Warburton (1991) 5 Trust Law Int 9; Ferguson (1993) 109 LQR 114.

that which may arise where a constructive trust is imposed, equally it will often lead to a more far-reaching form of relief.[138] It is also clear that both doctrines developed with different aims; proprietary estoppel as a means of compensating detrimental reliance and giving effect to expectations, and constructive trusts as a flexible device for achieving justice in equity.[139]

A decision which broke new ground in linking the two doctrines is *Re Basham*[140] in which Edward Nugee QC appeared to hold that proprietary estoppel will give rise to a constructive trust. The decision is also significant in that it showed that a claim of proprietary estoppel may succeed on the basis of acts undertaken not in reliance on the fact that the claimant had existing rights but on the faith of an undertaking that such rights would be granted in the future. The plaintiff helped to run her mother and stepfather's business for many years on an unpaid basis on the understanding that she would inherit her stepfather's estate and she and her husband also expended considerable time and money looking after her stepfather. The stepfather died intestate and the plaintiff sought a declaration against two of his nieces who were administratrixs of his estate that she was entitled to the deceased's house and to his furniture and other property. Edward Nugee QC held in granting the declaration sought that the principle of proprietary estoppel was not limited to acts done in reliance on a belief relating to an existing right but extended to acts done in reliance on a belief that future rights would be granted. In addition, he accepted that estoppel could extend to non-specific property and held that since the plaintiff had established that she had acted to her detriment in reliance on the belief, which was encouraged by her stepfather, that she would ultimately benefit by receiving his property on his death, she was entitled to the residuary estate. Martin[141] raises the question that if the plaintiff satisfied the requirements for proprietary estoppel, why was it necessary to introduce the concept of the constructive trust into the equation and further points out that the reasoning in *Re Basham* has not won approval and has been characterized as 'somewhat dubious'.[142]

More recently there has been a return to the theme of the similarities between the doctrines of proprietary estoppel and constructive trusts, although as an analysis of the relevant decisions show, the equating of the concepts creates its own difficulties. In *Yaxley v. Gotts*[143] the Court of Appeal held that an oral agreement whereby the plaintiff was promised an interest in a house in exchange for carrying out work on it, although unenforceable under section

---

138. E.g. *Pascoe v. Turner* [1979] 1 WLR 431.
139. Note that in *Haslemere Estates Ltd v. Baker* [1982] 1 WLR 1109, 1119 Megarry VC rejected the argument that proprietary estoppel arises 'whenever justice and good conscience requires it'.
140. [1986] 1 WLR 1498.
141. [1987] Conv 211, 213.
142. Moore (2000) 63 MLR 912, 915.
143. [2000] Ch 162.

2 of the Law of Property (Miscellaneous Provisions) Act 1989, was nevertheless enforceable on the basis of a constructive trust pursuant to section 2(5) of the Act, which provided that nothing in the section affected the creation or operation of resulting or constructive trusts. While Robert Walker LJ acknowledged that the trial judge had made no finding in relation to the existence of a constructive trust, on the findings of fact it had not been disputed that a proprietary estoppel arose and in his view such findings equally provided the basis for the conclusion that the plaintiff was entitled to an interest under a constructive trust. Beldam LJ took a broader approach to the construction of section 2(5) and concluded that the provision 'effectively excludes from the operation of the section cases in which an interest in land might equally well be claimed by relying on constructive trust or proprietary estoppel'.[144] He ultimately held that the first named defendant held the property in question subject to a constructive trust in favour of the plaintiff giving the latter a 99 year lease in respect of the ground floor of the premises but added that the trial judge was entitled to reach the same conclusion by finding a proprietary estoppel in favour of the plaintiff.

In the course of his judgment Robert Walker LJ stated that 'at a high level of generality there is much common ground between the doctrines of proprietary estoppel and the constructive trust'[145] and that in the area of a joint enterprise for the acquisition of land, the two concepts collide. He concluded that the species of constructive trust based on common intention is established by what Lord Bridge described in *Lloyds Bank plc v. Rosset*[146] as an agreement or understanding reached between the parties and relied on and acted on by the claimant and that a constructive trust of this nature is 'closely akin to, if not indistinguishable from, proprietary estoppel'.[147] Thompson[148] has commented that the approach of Beldam LJ is to be preferred as in his view 'estoppel is a more flexible tool than the common intention trust which underlies cases such as *Grant v. Edwards*' both in terms of the remedies which are available and the type of behaviour necessary to give rise to an equity. It has also been suggested that while the members of the Court of Appeal appeared to consider it irrelevant whether the plaintiff in *Yaxley* succeeded on the basis of proprietary estoppel or a constructive trust, as in either case the result would be identical,[149] in another case the differences between the two

---

144. *Ibid.* at 193.
145. *Ibid.* at 176.
146. [1991] 1 AC 107, 132.
147. [2000] Ch 162, 180. See also *Lloyds Bank plc v. Carrick* [1996] 4 All ER 630, 640; *Mollo v. Mollo* Chancery Division, 8 October 1999 paragraph 42; *Beresford v. Williamson* [2002] EWCA Civ 1632 Court of Appeal, 25 October 2002 paragraph 10.
148. [2000] Conv 248, 252.
149. See also *Chan v. Leung* [2002] EWCA Civ 1075 Court of Appeal, 29 July 2002 paragraph 91.

doctrines could be significant.[150] Subsequently in *Jennings v. Rice*[151] Robert Walker LJ again spoke of circumstances in which proprietary estoppel may become indistinguishable from a constructive trust. Given the increasing frequency with which this type of statement is being made further thought should be given to the consequences of the elision of what have traditionally been perceived to be distinct doctrines and it seems inevitable that cases will occur where the distinctions between them will be material to the outcome.

The Relationship between Proprietary and Promissory Estoppel

Traditionally a distinction has been drawn between cases in which promissory and proprietary estoppel may arise,[152] although there have also been suggestions to the effect that making such a distinction is not helpful.[153] However, the courts in this jurisdiction have increasingly used these labels in what appears to be a rather indiscriminate manner and it is necessary to consider what significance, if any, attaches to this development.

One of the most controversial decisions in this context is that of Costello J in *Re J.R.*[154] The committee of an elderly ward of court, who was living in a psychiatric hospital and was unable to manage his own affairs, sought to effect the sale of his house which had fallen into a dilapidated state. He had been living there with the respondent for many years and she maintained that when she went to live with him he had represented to her that he would look after her and that she would be sure of a home for the rest of her life. In his will the ward left everything to the respondent and at the time of its execution said to her that it was no longer his house but their house and that it would eventually be her house. Costello J concluded that the respondent had acted to her detriment on the representation made to her at the time she went to live with the ward that thereafter she could be sure of a home in his house for the rest of her life. He said that accordingly she had made out a case of promissory estoppel as she had acted on the representation made to her. 'It would be plainly inequitable for the ward now to deny that she has a right to live in his house and it seems to me that she has an equity which entitles her to stay in the house rent free for as long as she wishes to which the court must give effect.'[155] Costello J said that the respondent could not claim any enforceable rights by virtue of the ward handing her the will and saying the house was theirs as the gift was an imperfect one which the courts could not enforce —

---

150. Moore (2000) 63 MLR 912, 915. See also Smith (2000) 116 LQR 11, 12.
151. [2002] EWCA Civ 159 Court of Appeal, 22 February 2002 paragraph 45.
152. For a useful analysis of the most significant differences between the two doctrines, see Mee (1998) 33 Ir Jur (ns) 187, 197-202.
153. *Crabb v. Arun District Council* [1976] Ch 179, 193 *per* Scarman LJ.
154. [1993] ILRM 657.
155. *Ibid.* at 663.

these actions did not confer an immediate beneficial interest under a constructive trust. Instead the ward had intended that she have a right to reside in the house during his life and ownership of it after his death. He concluded that the equity which the respondent had been able to establish was a right to reside in the house for her life. However, in the special circumstances of the case as the house was in a serious state of dilapidation, the respondent's equity could be satisfied by selling the house and buying another one suitable for her needs.

While the result achieved was clearly a fair and equitable one in the circumstances, there are a number of difficulties with the reasoning employed by Costello J. First he appears to hold that promissory estoppel is capable of creating proprietary rights. While it has long been accepted that proprietary estoppel may give rise to a cause of action,[156] it would appear to be a novel approach to suggest that promissory estoppel is equally capable of doing so and it is clearly impossible to reconcile with the *dicta* of O'Hanlon J in *Association of General Practitioners Ltd v. Minister for Health*,[157] in which he reasserted the traditional view that promissory estoppel should be regarded as providing a shield and not a sword.[158] Although a more flexible approach appears to have been accepted in Australia by a number of the judges in *Waltons Stores (Interstate) Ltd v. Maher*[159] and in *Commonwealth of Australia v. Verwayen*,[160] Coughlan's[161] comment that in *Re J.R.*[162] Costello J failed to address fully the implications of the step he was taking or to consider the relevant authorities is a fair one. In the context of the facts which were before the court in that case Coughlan's statement that 'it is difficult to envisage situations in which promissory estoppel will be of more utility than proprietary estoppel'[163] is particularly apt.

Similarly, Mee[164] has commented in relation to *Re J.R.* that 'it is not readily apparent why Costello J chose to rest his decision on promissory estoppel rather than proprietary estoppel' and this remark might equally be applied to a more recent decision in which the plaintiff sought to his assert his entitlement to rights over land arising out of assurances allegedly made to him. In *Carter*

---

156. *Inwards v. Baker* [1965] 2 QB 29, 38; *Crabb v. Arun District Council* [1976] Ch 179, 187 *per* Denning MR. See also the comments of Geoghegan J in *Smyth v. Halpin* [1997] 2 ILRM 38, 42 in which he pointed out that the granting of a remedy to the plaintiff would involve using estoppel 'as a sword and not merely as a shield'.
157. [1995] 2 ILRM 481.
158. See *Combe v. Combe* [1951] 2 KB 215, 224. But see the judgment of Gresson J in *Thomas v. Thomas* [1956] NZLR 785.
159. (1988) 164 CLR 387. See in particular at 404 *per* Mason CJ; at 420 *per* Brennan J.
160. (1990) 170 CLR 394.
161. (1993) 15 DULJ 188.
162. [1993] ILRM 657.
163. (1993) 15 DULJ 188, 189.
164. (1998) 33 Ir Jur (ns) 187, 218.

v. Ross[165] Murphy J concluded that the plaintiff's claim was based on a very vague promise and that there had been minimal detriment suffered and he concluded that there was no evidence to support a finding that promissory estoppel arose on the basis of the facts before the court. It should also be noted that in *McGuinness v. McGuinness*,[166] although it differed significantly from the decisions considered above in that estoppel was raised as a defence rather than a cause of action, Kinlen J also spoke in terms of promissory estoppel. He concluded that 'to establish promissory estoppel, [the defendant] must prove a material detriment in reliance on a promise of entitlement to land'.

LIKELY FUTURE DEVELOPMENTS

As Robert Goff J commented in *Amalgamated Investment & Property Co. v. Texas Commerce International Bank Ltd*:[167] 'Of all doctrines, equitable estoppel is surely one of the most flexible'. While there have been *dicta* suggesting that the distinctions between the concepts of proprietary and promissory estoppel are 'not ... helpful'[168] and recommending that the different species of estoppel should 'merge into one general principle shorn of limitation,'[169] it is questionable whether such an all-embracing doctrine based on the unifying concept of unconscionability would be desirable. Certainly Treitel[170] has suggested that such an approach would provide no basis on which a doctrine capable of yielding predictable results could be developed and Evans[171] has argued that there is no real authority to back up a development of this nature. As against this, recent *dicta* in a number of Australian decisions would suggest that there is 'but one doctrine of estoppel'.[172] In *Waltons Stores (Interstate) Ltd v. Maher*[173] Mason CJ stated as follows:

> One may therefore discern in the cases a common thread which links them together, namely the principle that equity will come to the relief of a plaintiff who has acted to his detriment on the basis of a basic assumption in relation to which the other party to the transaction has

---

165. High Court (Murphy J) 8 December 2000.
166. High Court 2001 Nos. 145CA and 147CA (Kinlen J)19 March 2002.
167. [1982] QB 84, 103. See also *Waltons Stores (Interstate) Ltd v. Maher* (1988) 164 CLR 387, 419.
168. *Crabb v. Arun District Council* [1976] Ch 179, 193 *per* Scarman LJ.
169. *Amalgamated Investment and Property Co. Ltd v. Texas Commerce International Bank Ltd* [1982] QB 84, 122.
170. *The Law of Contract* (10th ed., 1999) p.135.
171. [1988] Conv 346, 347.
172. *Commonwealth of Australia v. Verwayen* (1990) 170 CLR 394, 412.
173. (1988) 164 CLR 387, 404.

'played such a part in the adoption of the assumption that it would be unfair or unjust if he were left free to ignore it' *per* Dixon J in *Grundt v. Great Boulder Pty Gold Mines Ltd* (1937) 59 CLR 641 at p.675; see also *Thompson v. Palmer* (1933) 49 CLR 507 at p. 547. Equity comes to the relief of such a plaintiff on the footing that it would be unconscionable conduct on the part of the other party to ignore the assumption.

Similarly, in *Commonwealth of Australia v. Verwayen*[174] Mason CJ spoke of a single doctrine of estoppel which would provide that a court of common law or equity may do what is necessary to prevent a person, who has relied on an assumption as to a present, past or future state of affairs, which was induced by the party estopped, from suffering detriment in reliance on this assumption. While Lunney[175] accepts that there is no direct authority in England which supports a unified doctrine of estoppel based on unconscionability raising equities which can be enforced by the other party, he holds the view that the approach advocated in Australia represents a logical advance. Although it could be argued that the reasoning employed by Costello J in *Re J.R.* would support the view that such an approach may be accepted in this jurisdiction, it would probably be unwise to assume such a conclusion based on a judgment which does not fully address the implications of such a step.[176] Realistically then we are unlikely to see a unified doctrine of estoppel emerging in the near future either in this jurisdiction or in England.[177] Mee[178] suggests that 'there has been nothing resembling a carefully considered (or even conscious) decision to merge the estoppels in Ireland' and states that the present position in this jurisdiction appears to be that the doctrines of proprietary and promissory estoppel retain their separate identities.

Finally, it should be noted that over the past few years there has also been considerable debate about the manner in which the doctrine of proprietary estoppel will develop. Halliwell[179] acknowledges that traditional orthodoxy is being challenged and asserts that it is now necessary to recognise that 'the organising concept for the doctrine of estoppel is unconscionability'. Although decisions such as *Taylor v. Dickens*[180] are indicative of a reluctance to adopt

---

174. (1990)170 CLR 394.
175. [1992] Conv 239, 248-250.
176. Mee has commented (1998) 33 Ir Jur (ns) 187, 219 that 'one must conclude that *Re J.R.* was simply another example of an Irish judge reaching a conclusion which he regarded as just without paying much attention to strict legal doctrine'.
177. See generally *National Westminster Bank v. Somer International (UK) Ltd* [2002] 3 WLR 64, 81.
178. (1998) 33 Ir Jur (ns) 187, 219.
179. (1994) 14 LS 15. However, she suggests that any new doctrine of estoppel freed from traditional labels must still be distinguished from the form of equitable estoppel identified in the *High Trees* case which as she states 'has afforded a defence in circumstances of a gratuitous promise to vary contractual obligations being enforced.'
180. [1998] 1 FLR 806.

such an approach, more recent decisions do show a definite movement in this direction. A number of years ago Pawlowski[181] commented that while 'the modern approach is to explain the doctrine in terms of a general concept of unconscionability, the courts do require the estoppel claimant to prove the three essential elements (i.e. assurance, reliance and detriment) as a prerequisite to a successful claim'. This would still appear to be an accurate summary of the position being taken by the courts in England as the decisions of the Court of Appeal in *Gillett v. Holt*[182] and *Jennings v. Rice*[183] illustrate.

181. (1998) 114 LQR 351, 352.
182. [2001] Ch 210.
183. [2002] EWCA Civ 159 Court of Appeal, 22 February 2002.

CHAPTER 18

Tracing

TRACING AT COMMON LAW

At common law while a person who was wrongfully deprived of his property could follow it into the hands of another party, he could only do so in circumstances where this property was still identifiable and had not been mixed with other funds. Millett J has summarised the principles which apply to this form of tracing in his judgment in *Agip (Africa) Ltd v. Jackson*:[1]

> Tracing at common law, unlike its counterpart in equity, is neither a cause of action nor a remedy but serves an evidential purpose. The cause of action is for money had and received. Tracing at common law enables the defendant to be identified as the recipient of the plaintiff's money and the measure of his liability to be determined by the amount of the plaintiff's money he is shown to have received.

So at common law the legal owner of property was entitled to follow it into the hands of another even where it had changed in form provided that there was a means of identifying the asset in its original or converted form. As Lord Ellenborough stated in *Taylor v. Plumer*:[2] 'It makes no difference in reason or law into what other form, different from the original, the change may have been made'. He pointed out that 'the product of or substitute for the original thing still follows the nature of the thing itself, as long as it can be ascertained as such'[3] but this right to follow at common law will cease when the means of identifying the original is lost as, e.g. when the assets are converted into money and 'confounded into a general mass of the same description'. These principles were reiterated by the Court of Appeal in *Re Diplock*[4] where Lord Greene MR commented that the common law 'could only appreciate what might almost

---

1. [1990] Ch 265, 285.
2. (1815) 3 M & S 562, 575. For an alternative interpretation of what this decision establishes, see Smith [1995] LMCLQ 240.
3. *Ibid.* at 575.
4. [1948] 1 Ch 465, 518. See also the comment of Millett J in *Agip (Africa) Ltd v. Jackson* [1990] Ch 265, 285 that 'it can only follow a physical asset . . . from one person to another' (at 285).

be called the "physical" identity of one thing with another'. So the common law could treat money as identifiable provided it was not mixed with other money and could also treat as identifiable other kinds of property acquired with these funds alone.[5]

The inability of the common law to trace into a mixed fund is undoubtedly its greatest limitation and it means that it cannot assist a plaintiff in what is probably the most common situation in practice where a tracing remedy may be required, namely where a defendant has mixed the plaintiff's money with his own and subsequently gone bankrupt.[6] The other major limitation of this form of tracing is that because the common law did not recognise equitable rights and interests, a beneficiary could not follow trust property into the hands of a trustee.[7]

Consideration was given to tracing at common law by the English Court of Appeal in *F.C. Jones & Sons (Trustees) v. Jones*,[8] in which the plaintiff was held entitled to trace not only the property but also any profit made from it. As Nourse LJ commented, the decision went further than previous cases 'in that it holds that the action for money had and received entitles the legal owner to trace his property into its product, not only in the sense of property for which it is exchanged, but also in the sense of property representing the original and the profit made by the defendant's use of it'.[9] In considering the rules which apply to tracing at law and in equity Millett LJ stated as follows:

> There is no merit in having distinct and different tracing rules at law and in equity, given that tracing is neither a right nor a remedy but merely the process by which the plaintiff establishes what has happened to his property and makes good his claim that the assets which he claims can properly be regarded as representing his property. The fact that there are different tracing rules at law and in equity is unfortunate though probably inevitable, but unnecessary differences should not be created where they are not required by the different nature of legal and equitable doctrines and remedies. There is in my view, even less merit in the present rule which precludes the invocation of the equitable tracing rules to support a common law claim; until that rule is swept away unnecessary obstacles to the development of a rational and coherent law of restitution will remain.[10]

---

5. *Ibid.* at 518.
6. See Hanbury and Martin, *Modern Equity* (16th ed., 2001) p. 680-681.
7. See the judgment of Lord Greene MR in *Re Diplock* [1948] Ch 465, 519-520 where this and other limitations are discussed.
8. [1996] 3 WLR 703.
9. *Ibid.* at 714.
10. *Ibid.* at 712.

These views have recently been reiterated by Lord Millett in his speech in *Foskett v. McKeown*[11] where he added that given its nature there is nothing inherently legal or equitable about the tracing exercise and that there is thus no sense in maintaining different rules for tracing at law and in equity. However, Stevens[12] has argued that once the proprietary nature of tracing is accepted,[13] it should be recognized that the historic distinction between legal and equitable tracing cannot be abandoned and that the rules in each case differ because the incidents of ownership at common law and in equity also differ.

TRACING IN EQUITY

Introduction

While a trustee or constructive trustee may be personally liable to beneficiaries, where e.g. he has transferred the trust property to another in breach of trust and has disposed of the proceeds of sale, this remedy will be of little value if the trustee has insufficient assets to meet the claim. Where he no longer has the trust property in his possession and cannot meet any personal claim against him, the alternative of a proprietary remedy must be considered. It is also important to remember that a constructive trust can only be imposed where trust property becomes vested in a person in a manner which amounts to a breach of trust and where property is transferred to an innocent volunteer, no personal liability can be imposed. In both these situations the proprietary remedy of tracing will provide a means whereby a beneficiary may recover property which has been wrongly disposed of. As Lord Millett stated in *Foskett v. McKeown*:[14]

> A beneficiary of a trust is entitled to a continuing beneficial interest not merely in the trust property but in its traceable proceeds also, and his interest binds every one who takes the property or its traceable proceeds except a *bona fide* purchaser for value without notice.

The proprietary tracing process has a number of advantages; first, where the trustee is insolvent, the claimant will take in priority to his general creditors[15]

---

11. [2001] 1 AC 102, 128. See also the views expressed by Lord Steyn in *Foskett* at 113 and by Birks in 'The necessity of a unitary law of tracing' in *Making Commercial Law, Essays in Honour of Roy Goode* (1997) at p. 257.
12. [2001] Conv 94, 100.
13. As it was by Lord Millett and the other law lords in the majority in *Foskett*, Lord Browne-Wilkinson and Lord Hoffmann.
14. [2001] 1 AC 102, 127.
15. *Re Hallett's Estate* (1880) 13 Ch D 696.

and secondly, where trust property comes into the hands of an innocent volunteer, who takes subject to the trust but has neither actual nor constructive knowledge of it, the volunteer will not be liable as constructive trustee but a tracing remedy will lie against him. So the tracing remedy may lie against a person who is not personally liable as a result of a breach of fiduciary duty.

Recently tracing has taken on a new significance as a means of recovering the proceeds of international fraud. While, as we have seen, the common law cannot trace into a mixed fund, equity does not require the existence of a physical asset and can follow funds even where they have been the subject of electronic transfer.[16] As Lord Greene MR commented in *Re Diplock*:[17] 'Equity adopted a more metaphysical approach' and 'found no difficulty in regarding a composite fund as an amalgam constituted by the mixture of two or more funds each of which could be regarded as having, for certain purposes, a continued separate existence.'

Some debate has also recently developed about the nature of the tracing process.[18] In the course of his speech for the majority in *Foskett v. McKeown*,[19] Lord Millett stated as follows:

> Tracing is thus neither a claim nor a remedy. It is merely the process by which a claimant demonstrates what has happened to his property, identifies its proceeds and the persons who have handled or received them, and justifies his claim that the proceeds can be properly regarded as representing his property.

Lord Steyn, although he was in the minority, agreed that tracing was a process of identifying assets and that it belonged to the realm of evidence. However, Stevens[20] has questioned whether such an approach is consistent with the proprietary nature of tracing and given Lord Millett's approval of this proposition in *Foskett*, some doubt must remain about the latter's reasoning in this regard.

General Principles

Tracing in equity is usually sought where property has come into the hands of trustees and other persons in a fiduciary relationship. It is a remedy *in rem*, 'a claim to follow and recover property with which, in equity at all events, [a

---

16. Millett (1991) 107 LQR 71, 74.
17. [1948] Ch 465, 520. Quoted by Budd J in *Shanahan's Stamp Auctions Ltd v. Farrelly* [1962] IR 386, 436.
18. See generally Smith, *The Law of Tracing* (1996). See also O'Dell (1999) 21 DULJ 131.
19. [2001] 1 AC 102, 128. See also Grantham and Rickett (2000) 63 MLR 905.
20. [2001] Conv 94, 101.

person] had never really parted'.[21] The right to trace in equity also exists against third parties into whose hands the funds may have come. Although it does not extend to purchasers for value of the property without notice of the right to trace, it will apply to an innocent volunteer who comes into possession of the trust property. It should also be noted that traditionally it has been accepted that in order to pursue an equitable tracing remedy, a plaintiff should possess an equitable proprietary interest.[22]

The decision in which the parameters of tracing in equity were first explored in detail and which illustrated the potential for tracing into a mixed fund was that of the English Court of Appeal in *Re Hallett's Estate*.[23] As Atkin LJ was later to comment in relation to this decision:[24] 'if in 1815 the common law halted outside the banker's door, by 1879 equity had had the courage to lift the latch, walk in and examine the books'. In *Hallett* a solicitor had lodged funds from a trust of which he was trustee and those belonging to a client to his own bank account. He made various payments from and into the account and after his death it emerged that there were insufficient funds remaining to pay these monies back and to meet his personal debts. In an action brought to decide how his estate should be administered, the question arose whether the trust and the client could claim priority over the solicitor's general creditors. It was held by the Court of Appeal that the beneficiaries under the trust and the client were entitled to trace the misappropriated funds and that they were entitled to a lien or charge on the monies in the bank account in priority to the general creditors. One important principle to be derived from the judgment to which we shall return is that the solicitor was presumed to have spent his own money first and not to have drawn on the trust monies irrespective of the order in which these funds were paid into his account.[25] It should be noted that one aspect of the conclusion reached by Jessel MR in *Hallett* has recently been disapproved by Lord Millett in *Foskett v. McKeown*[26] where he noted that the former appeared to suggest that in the case of a mixed substitution, the beneficiary is confined to a lien. Lord Millett stated 'in my view the time has come to state unequivocally that English law has no such rule'[27] and that it conflicts with the principle that a trustee must not benefit from his trust.

It has also been established that the equitable tracing remedy is not confined to claims as between a trustee and beneficiary but will extend to any persons in fiduciary relationships and it has become clear that this relationship need

---

21. *Sinclair v. Brougham* [1914] AC 398, 418.
22. Although note the decision of the English Court of Appeal in *Aluminium Industrie Vassen BV v. Romalpa Aluminium Ltd* [1976] 1 WLR 676.
23. (1880) 13 Ch D 696.
24. *Banque Belge pour l'Etranger v. Hambrouck* [1921] 1 KB 321, 335.
25. See also *Carroll Group Distributors Ltd v. G. & J.F. Bourke Ltd* [1990] 1 IR 481, 484.
26. [2001] 1 AC 102.
27. *Ibid.* at 131.

not exist between the parties to the action. In *Sinclair v. Brougham*[28] a building society which had operated an *ultra vires* banking business was wound up and a dispute arose in relation to the respective claims of the shareholders and the depositors. The House of Lords found that there was a sufficient fiduciary relationship between the depositors and the directors of the building society 'by reason of the fact that the purposes for which the depositors had handed their money to the directors were by law incapable of fulfilment'.[29] It was held that the depositors had a right to trace the funds into the hands of the society and ranked *pari passu* with the shareholders as regards entitlement to the funds; as Viscount Haldane LC commented: 'I see no reason why either set of claimants should have priority over the other.' As Oakley has commented 'the decision was unquestionably authority for the availability of an equitable proprietary claim to the transferor of property under a transaction which is void *ab initio*'.[30] However, it should be pointed out that the decision in *Sinclair v. Brougham* was effectively overruled by the House of Lords in *Westdeutsche Landesbank Girozentrale v. Islington London Borough Council*,[31] which will be considered in more detail below, where the majority of the House of Lords held that an equitable proprietary claim is not available to a transferor of property under an *ultra vires* transaction which is void *ab initio*.

It was established in *Re Diplock*[32] that an innocent volunteer who receives money or property *bona fide* is in the same position as regards entitlement to this property as an equitable owner who has a right to trace.[33] Mr Diplock left the residue of his estate on trust for 'such charitable institutions or other charitable or benevolent object or objects in England as my executors may in their absolute discretion select'. The executors of the will thinking that it was a valid charitable gift paid out a large part of the residue amounting to over £200,000 to various charitable institutions. Subsequently, it became clear that the gift was not a valid charitable one,[34] and the next of kin, having exhausted their remedies against the executors, sought to recover these monies from the

---

28. [1914] AC 398.
29. *Per* Lord Greene MR in *Re Diplock* [1948] Ch 465, 540-541.
30. [1997] Conv 1, 2.
31. Lord Browne-Wilkinson described it as a 'bewildering authority' and commented that all the reasoning in the decision was 'open to serious objection'.
32. [1948] Ch 465.
33. As Lord Greene MR commented at 539: 'It would be inequitable for the volunteer to claim priority for the reason that he is a volunteer: it would be equally inequitable for the true owner of the money to claim priority over the volunteer for the reason that the volunteer is innocent and cannot be said to act unconscionably if he claims the equal treatment for himself.'
34. The use of the word 'or' was interpreted to mean that the words of the gift were wide enough to allow the trustees to dispose of the fund or an unascertainable part of it to non-charitable purposes.

charities. It was held by the Court of Appeal[35] that they were entitled to trace the funds into the hands of the charities which were innocent volunteers,[36] with whom they had to share rateably. So, as Lord Greene MR stated: 'Where the contest is between two claimants to a mixed fund made up entirely of moneys held on behalf of the two of them respectively and mixed together by the fiduciary agent, they share *pari passu*.'[37]

This view was reiterated by Lord Millett in *Foskett v. McKeown*[38] where he stated that innocent contributors must be treated equally *inter se* and that where a beneficiary's claim is in competition with the claims of other innocent contributors, there is no basis upon which any of the claims can be subordinated to any of the others. *Foskett v. McKeown*[39] has been described as 'without doubt the most important recent decision of the law of tracing'[40] and needs to be considered in some detail. A trustee fraudulently used money entrusted to him for a property development scheme to pay a number of the premiums on a life insurance policy. When the trustee died, a dispute arose in relation to entitlement to the death benefit on the policy. A majority of the House of Lords held that the purchasers in the property development scheme were entitled to a share of the proceeds of the policy proportionate to the premiums which had been paid out of trust monies,[41] although there was disagreement about the manner in which the proportions were to be calculated.[42] Lord Millett stated the 'basic rule' as follows:

> Where a trustee wrongfully uses trust money to provide part of the cost of acquiring an asset, the beneficiary is entitled *at his option* either to

---

35. The appeal to the House of Lords, (*sub nom Ministry of Health v. Simpson* [1951] AC 251) related only to the *in personam* claims of the next of kin.
36. Lord Greene MR went on to stress (at 544) that although 'equity may operate upon the conscience of a volunteer, it will not operate upon the conscience of a purchaser for value without notice.'
37. *Ibid.* at 539.
38. [2001] 1 AC 102, 132.
39. [2001] 1 AC 102.
40. Stevens [2001] Conv 94. See also Jaffey (2000) 14 Trust Law Int 194; Walker [2000] RLR 573; Grantham and Rickett (2000) 63 MLR 905; Rotherham [2000] CLJ 440; Berg (2001) 117 LQR 366.
41. This view is in line with the approach suggested by Ungoed-Thomas J in *Re Tilley's Will Trusts* [1967] Ch 1179, 1193 where he commented as follows: 'If…it appears that the trustee has in fact, whatever his intention, laid out trust moneys in or towards a purchase, then the beneficiaries are entitled to the property purchased and any profits which it produces to the extent to which it has been paid for out of trust moneys.'
42. While Lord Browne-Wilkinson and Lord Hoffmann held that the purchasers' shares should be calculated on a pro rata basis, Lord Millett suggested a more complicated approach, although he ultimately conceded that he would be content if the money were divided between the parties in the proportions in which they had contributed to the premiums.

claim a proportionate share of the asset or to enforce a lien upon it to secure his personal claim against the trustee for the amount of the misapplied money. It does not matter whether the trustee mixed the trust money with his own in a single fund before using it to acquire the asset, or made separate payments (whether simultaneously or sequentially) out of the differently owned funds to acquire a single asset.[43]

The alternative to claiming a proportionate share, namely a lien for the amount of the misapplied money, may be useful where the mixed fund is ultimately deficient. However, Lord Millett stressed that the right of a beneficiary to claim a lien is available only against a wrongdoer and those deriving title under him otherwise than for value; as he stated 'it is not available against competing contributors who are innocent of any wrongdoing'.[44]

It is the reasoning underlying the difference between the conclusions reached by the majority and minority in *Foskett* which has attracted most academic comment. While the majority clearly felt that tracing was a process of a proprietary nature, the minority were in favour of a restitutionary-based approach. Lord Millett stated that the purchasers sought to vindicate their property rights and not to reverse unjust enrichment and Lord Browne-Wilkinson agreed that '[w]e are not dealing with a claim in unjust enrichment'.[45] Similarly Lord Hoffmann stressed that the claim was 'not based upon unjust enrichment except in the most trivial sense of that expression'[46] and was instead the vindication of a proprietary right. However, Lord Hope placed emphasis on the fact that the beneficiaries of the policy had not been enriched by the payments made and he and Lord Steyn concluded that the purchasers were merely entitled to a lien to secure payment of the monies expended on the policy.

Another important recent case in this area is *Westdeutsche Landesbank Girozentrale v. Islington London Borough Council.*[47] The parties had entered into a ten-year interest rate swap agreement whereby the plaintiff paid a lump sum to the defendant and the defendant was then obliged to make 'interest' payments to the plaintiff. The House of Lords had held in *Hazell v. Hammersmith and Fulham LBC*[48] that such interest rate swap agreements were *ultra vires* the powers of local authorities and following this decision the council made no more payments to the bank. The Court of Appeal held that the bank was entitled to recover the balance owed as money had and

---

43. [2001] 1 AC 102, 131.
44. *Ibid.* at 132.
45. *Ibid.* at 110.
46. *Ibid.* at 115.
47. [1996] AC 669. See Cope (1996) 112 LQR 521; Jones [1996] CLJ 432; Oakley [1997] Conv 1; Birks [1997] RLR 3.
48. [1992] AC 1.

received and in equity on the basis of its equitable proprietary interest in the monies advanced and awarded compound interest on this sum. Before the House of Lords the council contested its liability to pay compound interest, the traditional view being that the existence of a claim in equity is a prerequisite to the award of compound as opposed to simple interest. The majority of the House of Lords adhered to this view and held that the type of interest payable depended on whether the bank had a continuing equitable proprietary interest in the sum advanced. They held, overruling *Sinclair v. Brougham,* that an equitable proprietary interest cannot exist in favour of a transferor of property under an *ultra vires* transaction which is void *ab initio* and concluded that as a result only simple interest should be awarded to the bank. The minority disagreed and held that equitable jurisdiction to award compound interest could exist even in relation to personal claims at common law and dismissed the council's appeal. Lord Browne-Wilkinson summarised the effect of overruling *Sinclair v. Brougham* in the following terms:

> [T]he law can be established in accordance with principle and commercial common sense: a claimant for restitution of moneys paid under an *ultra vires*, and therefore void, contract has a personal action at law to recover the moneys paid as on a total failure of consideration; he will not have an equitable proprietary claim which gives him either rights against third parties or priority in an insolvency; nor will he have a personal claim in equity, since the recipient is not a trustee.[49]

One of the few cases in which general equitable tracing principles have been considered in this jurisdiction is *Shanahan's Stamp Auctions Ltd v. Farrelly.*[50] A company which grouped investors into syndicates and used their funds to buy stamps went into liquidation. Some of these investors had been allocated to syndicates at the time and the liquidator sought directions from the court about priority of payments as between the general creditors and the syndicated and unsyndicated investors. Budd J held that at all material times a fiduciary relationship existed between the company and the investors and that both classes of investors were entitled to trace their money. The stamps allocated to the syndicates were held to be subject to a charge in favour of the syndicated investors for the amount of the investment and the remaining stamps were held by the company subject to a charge in favour of the unsyndicated investors on a rateable basis.

---

49. [1996] AC 669, 714.
50. [1962] IR 386.

Tracing into a Bank Account

Where the mixed fund in which trust monies have been lodged is an active bank account, in certain circumstances a principle known as the rule in *Clayton's case*[51] may apply. In theory it applies to competing claims of beneficiaries of different trusts and of beneficiaries and innocent volunteers and the effect of the rule is 'first in, first out'. So if a trustee pays £1,000 from one trust fund into a bank account and then pays a further sum of £1,000 from another fund into the account and later withdraws £1,000, the loss is borne wholly by the first trust on the basis of the principle of 'first in first out'. It is important to stress that the rule in *Clayton's case* will not apply to the type of situation which arose in *Re Hallett's Estate*[52] as the trustee was presumed to be acting honestly and to have drawn on his own money in the account first. This is sometimes referred to as the rule in *Re Hallett's Estate* and can be summarised as follows:[53] 'the trustee is presumed to be honest rather than dishonest and to make payments out of his own private moneys and not out of the trust fund that was mingled with his private moneys'.

However, this principle will not always be strictly adhered to where this would lead to injustice. In *Re Oatway*[54] a trustee withdrew misappropriated trust monies from a mixed fund and invested them and subsequently dissipated the remainder of the fund. Joyce J refused to apply the *Hallett* principle strictly as this would have led to the conclusion that the money withdrawn initially and invested was the trustee's own, and held instead that the beneficiaries were entitled to the assets represented by the investments.

Consideration was given by Budd J to the circumstances in which the rule in *Clayton's case* should be applied in *Shanahan's Stamp Auctions Ltd v. Farrelly*.[55] He accepted that the rule is generally applicable to determine the competing claims of beneficiaries, 'that is the first drawings out are to be attributable to the first payments in'.[56] He then went on to state that it may be that the rule does not apply beyond tracing in a bank account and that it may have no application to property acquired by means of a mixed fund.[57] However, Budd J was satisfied that on the facts of the case it could have no application

---

51. (1816) 1 Mer 572. See generally O'Dell (2000) 22 DULJ 161.
52. (1880) 13 Ch D 696.
53. *Per* Sargant J in *James Roscoe (Bolton) Ltd v. Winder* [1915] 1 Ch 62, 67. See also the *dicta* of Budd J in *Shanahan's Stamp Auctions Ltd v. Farrelly* [1962] IR 386, 428: 'If the person holding the money in a fiduciary capacity mixed it with his own the rule in *Clayton's case* does not apply; such person must be taken to have drawn out his own monies in preference to the trust monies. . . .'
54. [1903] 2 Ch 356.
55. [1962] IR 386.
56. *Ibid.* at 442.
57. Although he added that he would' prefer to deal with the situation, for safety's sake, as if the principle can properly be applied to the case of property acquired with such a mixed fund' (at 442).

as there had been a 'second mixing of the investor's funds into a second mixed amalgam of property'.

The rule in *Clayton's case* was applied in relation to some of the claims in *Re Diplock*[58] although Lord Greene MR did not seem to be suggesting that it should be automatically applied in such circumstances[59] and said that it was a 'rule of convenience based upon so-called presumed intention'.[60] Similar views were expressed by Woolf LJ in *Barlow Clowes International Ltd v. Vaughan*[61] where he made it clear that 'the rule need only be applied when it is convenient to do so and when its application can be said to do broad justice having regard to the nature of the competing claims.'[62] There companies which had promoted and managed certain investment plans ran into severe financial difficulties and the amount of money owed to investors far exceeded the funds available for distribution. The receivers sought directions as to how the assets in their hands should be distributed. The trial judge held that the rule of first in first out should be applied to the distribution of assets so that the investors who could trace into the funds were to be paid in the reverse order to that in which they had made deposits. The Court of Appeal was of the view that, while the first in first out rule would be applied where it provided a convenient method of determining competing claims as between several beneficiaries, where its application would be impractical or would result in injustice between the investors it would not be applied if a preferable alternative method of distribution was available. It was held that it would be contrary to the presumed intention of the investors to distribute the remaining monies in accordance with the first in first out rule so that those who had invested first could expect least. Instead, it was held that the available assets and moneys should be distributed *pari passu* among all the unpaid investors rateably in proportion to the amounts due to them regardless of the dates on which investors had made their investment.

The suggestion made by Woolf LJ in *Barlow Clowes* that the rule should only be applied where it can be said to do 'broad justice' has been heralded as 'a welcome relaxation'[63] of what has been labelled a 'capricious and arbitrary'[64] rule. Subsequently in *El Ajou v. Dollar Land Holdings plc*[65] Robert Walker J

---

58. [1948] Ch 465.
59. *Barlow Clowes International Ltd v. Vaughan* [1992] 4 All ER 22, 38 *per* Woolf LJ.
60. [1948] Ch 465, 554.
61. [1992] 4 All ER 22, 39.
62. Oliver has commented (1995) 9 Trust Law Int 78, 79 that 'it is at least clear as a result of the *Barlow Clowes* case that the rule in *Clayton's case* is a rule of convenience and not a rule of law, and accordingly it seems unlikely that the courts will use it where it is impracticable or likely to produce inequitable results'.
63. Goff and Jones, *The Law of Restitution* (6th ed., 2002) p. 110.
64. *Ibid.* at 108.
65. [1995] 2 All ER 213.

pointed out in that the members of the Court of Appeal in *Barlow Clowes* recognised that the rule may be applied as between rival claimants seeking to trace through an active bank account, although he did acknowledge that the court had accepted that it is 'perhaps *prima facie* not appropriate for those who have the common misfortune of being victims of a large scale fraud'.[66] Recently the approach adopted in *Barlow Clowes* has been endorsed by Lindsay J in *Russell-Cooke Trust Co. v. Prentis*[67] in which he commented that the modern view has been generally not to challenge the binding nature of the rule in *Clayton's* case but rather to permit it to be distinguished by reference to the facts of the particular case. Lindsay J expressed the opinion that it is clear from all three judgments of the Court of Appeal in *Barlow Clowes* that the rule can be displaced by even a slight counterweight and added 'indeed, in terms of its actual application between beneficiaries who have in any sense met a shared misfortune, it might be more accurate to refer to the exception that is, rather than the rule in, *Clayton's* case'.[68]

Further consideration was given to the rule in *Clayton's* case by Laffoy J in *Re Money Markets International Stockbrokers Ltd*[69] and while her decision has not fully clarified the circumstances in which the rule will be applied, it nevertheless gives a useful indication of current judicial thinking on the issue in this jurisdiction. The applicant instructed a stockbroking firm to buy shares on the Irish Stock Exchange on his behalf and the sum due was transferred and credited to the company's bank account several days before the settlement date. The following day the Irish Stock Exchange suspended the right of the company to transact business on the exchange and it was subsequently wound up and an official liquidator appointed. The liquidator acknowledged that the applicant's situation was different to that of other clients of the company as he had transferred monies to the company before the settlement date and these were identifiable in the client account of the company. It was agreed that the company stood in a fiduciary relationship to the applicant and that the funds transferred by the applicant to the company's account were held by the company as trust funds. These funds had been mixed with other funds and the dispute between the parties was in broad terms whether the rule in *Clayton's* case should be applied to determine who was entitled to the monies represented by the credit balance in the company's account.

Having referred to the decisions in *Shanahan's Stamp Auctions Ltd v. Farrelly* and *Barlow Clowes International v. Vaughan*, Laffoy J stated as follows:

> The conclusions I draw from the authorities are that, as far as this Court

---

66. *Ibid.* at 222.
67. [2002] EWHC 2227 (Ch) Chancery Division, 4 November 2002.
68. *Ibid.* at paragraph 55.
69. [1999] 4 IR 267.

is concerned, in the case of a current account such as the account in issue here where trust funds sourced from various beneficiaries are mixed or pooled in the account, it is settled law that as a general proposition the rule in *Clayton's* case is applicable in determining to whom the balance on the account belongs. However, the application of the rule may be displaced in the particular circumstance of a case, for instance, if it is shown or to be inferred that it does not accord with the intention or the presumed intention of the beneficiaries of the trust funds.[70]

Laffoy J stated that having regard to the uniqueness of the applicant's position, she did not think that applying equitable principles, the applicant should be bound by a *pari passu* distribution. She concluded that if the rule in *Clayton's* case was applied in determining entitlement to the monies, it was clear that the applicant would be entitled to repayment of the entirety of the funds transferred by him. Equally if the rule in *Clayton's* case was not applicable, in her view the equity of the applicant was superior to the equity of any other client creditor so that he could not be bound by a rateable distribution. Therefore, irrespective of whether the rule in *Clayton's* case was applied, Laffoy J was satisfied that an order should be made directing the liquidator to repay to the applicant the sum transferred to the company.

The decision in *Re Money Markets International Stockbrokers Ltd* has been welcomed as 'a good start on the journey towards the repudiation of the rule in *Clayton's* case'[71] and as upholding a strong tradition of the courts deciding cases having regard to the justice of the case as between the parties.[72] Whether the courts in this jurisdiction follow the approach adopted in other parts of the common law world in rejecting the application of the rule to the claims of competing contributors remains to be seen,[73] but it is clear that the application of the rule may now be easily displaced.

Traditionally, a beneficiary's right to trace into a mixed fund in a bank account only applied to the extent that the trust monies could be shown to be still there and if the account fell below the sum said to constitute the trust funds, they were then deemed to have been spent. This point is illustrated by the decision of Sargant J in *James Roscoe (Bolton) Ltd v. Winder*[74] where an agreement for the sale of the goodwill of a business provided that the purchaser should collect certain book debts and pay this money over to the vendor. The

---

70. *Ibid.* at 276-277.
71. O'Dell (2000) 22 DULJ 161, 198.
72. McGrath (2000) 5 Bar Rev 393, 395.
73. *Re Registered Securities Ltd* [1991] 1 NZLR 545, 553; *Keefe v. Law Society* (1998) 44 NSWLR 451; *Ontario (Ontario Securities Commission) v. Greymac Credit Corporation* (1989) 52 DLR (4th) 767 (see also (1986) 30 DLR (4th) 1 Ont CA); *Law Society of Upper Canada v. Toronto-Dominion Bank* (1998) 169 DLR (4th) 353.
74. [1915] 1 Ch 62.

purchaser collected some of these debts and paid part of the money amounting to about £455 into his own account. Subsequently, this balance was reduced to approximately £25 although by the time of the purchaser's death, the balance had risen again to just over £358. Sargant J considered the principles laid down in *Re Hallett's Estate*[75] and said that the general view of that decision was 'that it only applied to such an amount of the balance ultimately standing to the credit of the trustee as did not exceed the lowest balance of the account during the intervening period'.[76] He therefore concluded that the purchaser held the money as trustee but found that the charge was limited to the sum of around £25, which was the lowest intermediate balance after the money had been appropriated.[77]

It is clear from this decision that subsequent payments into an account will not generally be treated as repayments of the trust fund. However, this presumption can be displaced by evidence which establishes that the trustee intended to replace the misappropriated funds. So, in *Re Hughes*,[78] where a solicitor lodged funds to an account after the Law Society had initiated an investigation into his professional activities, Kenny J held that the only possible inference was that he had intended the lodgement to be a replacement for the monies he had withdrawn from the client account.

The question of whether it is possible to trace into an overdrawn bank account has recently been considered in both England and Ireland and the consensus is that it is not possible. In *Bishopsgate Investment Management Ltd v. Homan*[79] the liquidators of a company which was the trustee of the assets of pension schemes from which monies had been improperly paid into the bank account of another company sought to establish an equitable charge in priority to this company's other unsecured creditors. Their claim was rejected by the Court of Appeal on the basis that equitable tracing could not be pursued through an overdrawn and therefore non-existent fund. The same conclusion was reached by Murphy J in *PMPA Ltd v. PMPS Ltd*[80] in which the plaintiff had made an *ultra vires* payment of £450,000 to the defendant which the latter had lodged in an overdrawn account. Murphy J was satisfied that the plaintiff could not pursue a tracing remedy as the monies had been dissipated

---

75. (1880) 13 Ch D 696.
76. [1915] 1 Ch 62, 69.
77. It should be noted that the Ontario Court of Appeal has recently declined to apply the lowest intermediate balance rule in *Law Society of Upper Canada v. Toronto-Dominion Bank* (1998) 169 DLR (4th) 353, a decision criticised by O'Dell (2000) 22 DULJ 161, 188-194.
78. [1970] IR 237.
79. [1994] 3 WLR 1270. See Smith (1994) 8 Trust Law Int 102; Jones [1996] Conv 129. See also *Re Goldcorp Exchange* [1995] 1 AC 74.
80. High Court 1992 No. 702 Sp (Murphy J) 27 June 1994. See also *Carroll Group Distributors Ltd v. G. & J.F. Bourke Ltd* [1990] 1 IR 481, 486-7.

and no longer existed as such, although he concluded that the defendant had no right to these monies in the first instance and that the plaintiff was entitled to restitution. It would seem therefore that once the balance in an account falls below a certain level or becomes overdrawn, the capacity to trace is limited to the lowest intermediate balance and in the case of an overdrawn account, ceases altogether.

The Requirement of a Fiduciary Relationship

While the decision in *Re Hallett's Estate*[81] concerned the relationship of trustee and beneficiary, Jessel MR made it clear in the course of his judgment that he intended that the principles which he laid down should be extended to other types of fiduciary relationships.[82]

The requirement of a fiduciary relationship was also stressed by Kenny J in *Re Shannon Travel Ltd*,[83] where he stated as follows:

> The general principle is that when a person receives money as a trustee or as one occupying a fiduciary relation to another, the person who transferred the property or paid the money may recover the property and has a charge on the account to which the money or cheques have been lodged or on property on which the monies received have been spent provided that the property or money can be traced through the accounts of the debtor into the bank account etc., and provided that there is money to the credit of the account on which the charge can operate.[84]

In *Shannon*, Kenny J held that an equitable charge over a bank account containing funds held in trust by an insolvent was liable to abatement so that the liquidator's expenses and remuneration could be paid. This result is in some respects unsatisfactory as Kenny J failed to address adequately the question of why the proprietary remedy should be qualified in such a manner.

In England, as a result of the decision of the House of Lords in *Sinclair v. Brougham*,[85] it became clear that tracing in equity would extend to any persons in fiduciary relationships even where this relationship did not exist between the parties to the action.[86] This requirement of a fiduciary relationship was

---

81. (1880) 13 Ch D 696.
82. *Ibid.* at 709.
83. High Court 1970 No. 3849 P (Kenny J) 8 May 1972.
84. *Ibid.* at 8-9.
85. [1914] Ch 398.
86. However, note that in *Dublin Corporation v. Ancient Guild of Incorporated Brick and Stone Layers and Allied Trades Union* High Court 1991 No. 1556P, 6 March 1996 Budd J questioned (at 41) whether *Sinclair* was authority for the proposition

accepted unquestioningly by the Court of Appeal in *Re Diplock*[87] and it was regarded in principle as a pre-requisite by Goulding J in *Chase Manhattan Bank NA v. Israel British Bank (London) Ltd*,[88] although it would appear that this 'fiduciary element can be satisfied at the moment the payment is made'.[89] The plaintiff made a duplicate payment of $2,000,000 in error into another bank for the benefit of the defendant. The defendant's bank became insolvent and the question arose whether the plaintiff was entitled to trace this money into the bank's assets or whether it had prove with the other creditors. Goulding J held that the fact that the payment had been mistakenly made gave rise to a constructive trust and that the plaintiff was entitled to trace these funds.[90] He stated that it was common ground that a right to trace money paid by mistake exists in English law and re-iterated that 'an initial fiduciary relationship is a necessary foundation of the equitable right of tracing'.[91] However, it is hard to disagree with the criticism that Goulding J was effectively by-passing the requirement of a fiduciary relationship and he appeared to hold that the payment into the wrong hands itself gave rise to the relationship. His reasoning was approved by Carroll J in *Re Irish Shipping Ltd*,[92] in which a bank made a duplicate payment in error to the bank account in Citibank of Irish Shipping Ltd which subsequently went into liquidation. Citibank, the former bankers of Irish Shipping, claimed to be entitled to set off debts due by the company to them against the mistaken payment. However, it was held by Carroll J that where monies are paid by mistake into the account of a company such monies do not form part of the assets of the company at the date of the liquidation and she concluded that the bank which had made the duplicate payment was entitled to trace the money into the account.

Further comments were made about the requirement of a fiduciary relationship by Millett J at first instance in *Agip (Africa) Ltd v. Jackson*[93] where he stated as follows:

that a fiduciary relationship is essential before a claim to trace in equity may be established.

87. [1948] Ch 465.
88. [1981] Ch 105.
89. Collins (1994) 1 Comm L P 211, 213.
90. It should be noted that Lord Browne-Wilkinson in *Westdeutsche Landesbank v. Islington London Borough Council* [1996] AC 669, 715 stated that while he did not accept the reasoning of Goulding J, *Chase Manhattan* may well have been correctly decided. As Jones has pointed out [1996] CLJ 432, 434-5: 'The retention of the money once the [defendant] learnt of the mistake may well have given rise to a constructive trust'. However, Oakley has commented [1997] Conv 1, 3 that although the decision has not been formally overruled, 'it appears unlikely that an equitable proprietary claim will now be available to a transferor of money acting as a result of a mistake of fact'. See also Cope (1996) 112 LQR 521, 523.
91. [1981] Ch 105, 119.
92. [1986] ILRM 518.
93. [1990] Ch 265, 290.

The only restriction on the ability of equity to follow assets is the requirement that there must be some fiduciary relationship which permits the assistance of equity to be invoked. The requirement has been widely condemned and depends on authority rather than principle, but the law was settled in *In re Diplock* [1948] Ch 465. It may need to be reconsidered but not, I venture to think, at first instance. The requirement may be circumvented since it is not necessary that the fund to be traced should have been the subject of fiduciary obligations before it got into the wrong hands; it is sufficient that the payment to the defendant itself gives rise to a fiduciary relationship: *Chase Manhattan Bank NA v. Israel-British Bank London Ltd* [1981] Ch 105.[94]

More recently in *Boscawen v. Bajwa*[95] Millett LJ reiterated that '[i]t is still a prerequisite of the right to trace in equity that there must be a fiduciary relationship which calls the equitable jurisdiction into being'. However, a subsequent pronouncement which has been interpreted as having relevance to this issue is less clear, namely Lord Browne-Wilkinson's statement in *Westdeutsche Landesbank Girozentrale v. Islington London Borough Council*,[96] that their Lordships 'should not be taken to be casting any doubt on the principles of tracing as established in *Re Diplock*'. As Oakley has commented: 'Since it is generally thought that in this case the Court of Appeal interpreted *Sinclair v. Brougham* as establishing the controversial proposition "that an initial fiduciary relationship is a necessary foundation of the equitable right of tracing" this remark appeared to indicate that Lord Browne-Wilkinson was in favour of the requirement'.[97] As a result of Lord Browne-Wilkinson's statement Cope has commented that 'the extent to which a trust or other fiduciary relationship is still essential to maintain an equitable proprietary claim is not made clear'[98] and Jones has stated that '[t]he condition that there must be a fiduciary relationship to support an equitable proprietary claim is still alive but appears to be increasingly meaningless'.[99]

While the issue did not arise for decision in *Foskett v. McKeown*[100] because,

---

94. Fox LJ also suggested in delivering his decision in the Court of Appeal [1991] Ch 547, 566 that the requirement of a fiduciary relationship remained.
95. [1996] 1 WLR 328, 335. See Birks (1995) 9 Trust Law Int 124; Andrews [1996] CLJ 199.
96. [1996] AC 669, 714.
97. [1997] Conv 1, 3-4. However, Oakley went on to point out that at a seminar in Oxford in September 1996, Lord Browne-Wilkinson indicated that he had only made that remark to forestall any argument that the whole framework of equitable proprietary claims had been swept away and that he regarded the requirement of establishing a fiduciary relationship as wholly misconceived.
98. (1996) 112 LQR 521, 523.
99. [1996] CLJ 432, 435. Oliver has expressed the hope that the House of Lords will soon eliminate the fiduciary requirement, see (1995) 9 Trust Law Int 78, 83.
100. [2001] 1 AC 102.

as Lord Millett pointed out, even on the traditional approach equitable tracing rules were available to the plaintiffs, Lord Millett did express some views on this issue. He stated that there was no logical justification for allowing any distinction between the rules governing tracing at common law and in equity 'to produce capricious results in cases of mixed substitutions by insisting on the existence of a fiduciary relationship as a precondition for applying equity's tracing rules',[101] although he added that the existence of a fiduciary relationship may be relevant to the nature of the claim which the plaintiff can maintain, whether personal or proprietary.

There are certainly signs elsewhere in the common law world of alternative approaches being adopted towards this issue, as in New Zealand where it was suggested by Cooke P in *Elders Pastoral Ltd v. Bank of New Zealand*[102] that unconscionability is the key to establishing a right to trace in equity and not the presence of a fiduciary relationship.

The best summary of the likely approach of the courts in this jurisdiction to the question of the need to establish a fiduciary relationship is provided by Collins in the following terms:[103]

> The fiduciary relationship requirement may not be expressly abandoned but the definition of that relationship is proving sufficiently flexible that it no longer seems to represent a real bar to exercising an equitable tracing remedy if the other conditions for that remedy are satisfied.

Loss of the Right to Trace

In certain circumstances, many of which were referred to by the Court of Appeal in its judgment in *Re Diplock*,[104] the right to trace in equity may be lost. The first example is the obvious one that if the property has been dissipated it cannot be traced. As Lord Greene MR stated in *Re Diplock*:

> The equitable remedies presuppose the continued existence of the money either as a separate fund or as part of a mixed fund or as latent in property acquired by means of such a fund. If, on the facts of any individual case, such continued existence is not established, equity is as helpless as the common law itself. If the fund mixed or unmixed is spent upon a dinner, equity, which dealt only in specific relief and not in damages, could do nothing.[105]

---

101. *Ibid.* at 128.
102. [1989] 2 NZLR 180. See Watts (1990) 106 LQR 552.
103. (1994) 1 Comm LP 211, 214.
104. [1948] Ch 465.
105. *Ibid.* at 521.

Secondly, where property comes into the hands of a *bona fide* purchaser for value without notice, any equitable tracing claim will be extinguished,[106] and an alternative remedy must be pursued.[107] Thirdly, where it would be inequitable to allow a tracing claim to proceed, such a remedy will not be available. This will happen most frequently where a volunteer uses trust funds to alter or improve property already owned by him. This occurred in *Re Diplock* where some of the charities who received trust funds had used them to carry out improvements to their property. As Lord Greene MR stated: 'In the case of adaptation of property of the volunteer by means of trust money, it by no means necessarily follows that the money can be said to be present in the adapted property.'[108] In such circumstances, he concluded that the trust money could not be traced. The reasoning behind such an approach is that it would be inequitable to allow beneficiaries a charge over the property which would be enforceable by sale. This can be contrasted with the situation where a volunteer has purchased an asset with a mixed fund in which case there would be nothing inequitable in forcing a sale and dividing up the proceeds as he would recover what he invested.

Although there is little evidence of how it would operate in relation to equitable proprietary claims, it would appear that the defence of change of position should also be referred to.[109] In *Lipkin Gorman v. Karpanale Ltd*[110] Lord Goff stated that 'the defence is available to a person whose position has so changed that it would be inequitable in all the circumstances to require him to make restitution, or alternatively to make restitution in full'. He commented that whilst he recognised the different functions of property at law and in equity, in his view 'there may also in due course develop a more consistent approach to tracing claims, in which common defences are recognised as available to such claims, whether advanced at law or in equity'.[111] As Oakley[112] has commented, it is clear from this statement that Lord Goff envisaged the application of the defence of change of position to both legal

---

106. *Re Diplock* [1948] Ch 465, 539. It would appear that in Ireland the equitable right to trace is regarded as a mere equity and thus a *bona fide* purchaser for value of an equitable estate will take free of it. See *Re Ffrench's Estate* (1887) 21 LR Ir 283 and *Scott v. Scott* [1924] 1 IR 141 and see *infra* Chapter 2.
107. E.g. a claim against the trustees personally.
108. [1948] Ch 465, 546-547.
109. See generally Goff and Jones, *The Law of Restitution* (6th ed., 2002) Chapter 40; Nolan in *Laundering and Tracing* (1995) ed. Birks p. 135 *et seq.* and Birks in *Laundering and Tracing* (1995) ed. Birks pp. 323-332.
110. [1991] 2 AC 548, 580.
111. *Ibid.* at 580. However, Lord Goff stated that nothing should be said by him which would inhibit the development of the defence on a case by case basis and Lord Bridge commented that in acknowledging the defence for the first time, 'it would be unwise to attempt to define its scope in abstract terms'.
112. [1995] CLJ 377, 425.

and equitable proprietary claims, although for the present the principles which have been developed relate to the former situation.

It has been accepted that the defence while available to an innocent defendant is not open to a wrongdoer, or to a person who has changed his position in bad faith.[113] In this context it would seem that a defendant who ought to have been aware of the fact that the property in question did not belong to him may not be classified as innocent.[114] It would also appear from the decision of Clark J in *South Tyneside Metropolitan Council v. Svenska International plc*[115] that the change of position would have to occur after the receipt of the property, other than in exceptional cases, in order for the defence to operate.[116]

---

113. *Lipkin Gorman v. Karpanale Ltd* [1991] 2 AC 548, 580 *per* Lord Goff.
114. *South Tyneside Metropolitan Council v. Svenska International plc* [1995] 1 All ER 545, 569.
115. [1995] 1 All ER 545.
116. Jones has submitted [1995] Conv 490, 497 that the approach adopted in *South Tyneside* is an unduly restrictive one and suggests that '[n]one of the reasons given for narrowly limiting the scope of the defence to changes occurring after receipt are convincing'.

CHAPTER 19

Equitable Doctrines

THE DOCTRINE OF CONVERSION

Introduction

The doctrine of conversion is based on the maxim that equity looks on that as done which ought to be done.[1] It operates by regarding one form of property as being another because an obligation to convert it exists. The effect of the doctrine is that in certain circumstances the nature of property is notionally changed so that realty may be treated as personalty with the legal incidents of personalty and vice versa. The reasoning behind the doctrine is that where a person is under a duty to convert realty into personalty or personalty into realty, the property should not be regarded as still being in its original form because the individual concerned has failed to perform his obligations.

Traditionally, the doctrine had an important effect on the passing of property where an individual died intestate, because real estate devolved to the heir-at-law and personalty to the next of kin. However, the practical significance of the doctrine has greatly diminished since the enactment of the Administration of Estates Act 1959 and the Succession Act 1965 which abolished these principles, although it remains relevant where a testator makes separate residuary dispositions of his real and personal property.

The basis of the doctrine was outlined by Sir Thomas Sewell MR in *Fletcher v. Ashburner*:[2]

> [N]othing was better established than this principle, that money directed to be employed in the purchase of land, and land directed to be sold and turned into money, are to be considered as that species of property into which they are directed to be converted; and this in whatever manner the direction is given.

There are a number of situations in which the doctrine of conversion will be applied and these will be examined in turn.

---

1. *McDonnell v. Stenson* [1921] 1 IR 80, 86 *per* Ronan LJ.
2. (1779) 1 Bro CC 497, 499.

Trusts for Sale[3]

Where trustees are directed to sell or purchase realty and there is some person who can insist on their doing so, the property is treated as being converted from the moment when the instrument comes into force. So, in the case of a will, conversion takes place from the date of the testator's death and, in the case of a deed, from the date of its execution. However, as Stirling J stated in *Goodier v. Edmunds*[4] 'nothing short of an absolute and effective trust for sale can in equity create the conversion of realty into personalty'. In order to effect the conversion, the direction to sell or buy must be imperative and a trust for sale, which is mandatory and imposes a duty to sell and which produces an immediate notional conversion, must be distinguished from a power of sale, which merely confers a discretion to sell. As Porter MR stated in *McGwire v. McGwire*:[5] the question which arises is 'whether there is to be found in the settlement an express and imperative direction to convert [the property], or a trust for [its] conversion'. In this case, he concluded that no immediate conversion was effected or intended and that the lands which remained unsold should pass as realty. Similarly, in *Re Tyndall's Estate*[6] where a testator directed that after his wife's death his trustees should invest his residuary personalty in the purchase of realty, it was held by Gavan Duffy J that such a direction did not create an imperative trust for such a conversion. As a matter of construction, it must be shown that the testator intended the conversion to take place and as Sullivan MR made clear in *Norreys v. Franks*[7] this intention must be discerned from the language which he has employed.

It should be noted that in England the Trusts of Land and Appointment of Trustees Act 1996 abolishes the doctrine of conversion in relation to trusts for sale which are now replaced by a 'trust of land', in relation to which trustees have a power of sale, which may be exercised.[8]

Contracts or Conditional Contracts for the Sale or Purchase of Land

Where there is a valid contract to sell realty, the realty is treated as part of the

---

3. See Boyle [1981] Conv 108.
4. [1893] 3 Ch 455, 462.
5. [1900] 1 IR 200, 203. See also *Owen v. Owen* [1897] 1 IR 580 and the *dicta* of Chatterton VC in *McDonogh v. Nolan* (1881) 9 Lr Ir 262, 270.
6. [1941] Ir Jur Rep 51.
7. (1874) IR 9 Eq 18, 35.
8. Pettit submits (1997) 113 LQR 207 that the Act does not abolish the trust for sale completely and argues that s. 3 of the Act clearly assumes that a trust for sale can still exist. S. 3(1) provides: 'Where land is held by trustees subject to a trust for sale, the land is not to be regarded as personal property; and where personal property is subject to a trust for sale in order that the trustees may acquire land, the personal property is not to be regarded as land.'

vendor's personalty from the time the contract is concluded.[9] Traditionally it was accepted that a contract must be specifically enforceable in order for the doctrine to apply, but this would no longer appear to be the case.[10] Where a vendor dies before completion of the contract, his representatives must convey the realty or will be entitled to enforce specific performance against the purchaser, and the proceeds of the sale will form part of the vendor's estate as personalty. If a purchaser dies before completion, his interest passes to those entitled to his realty, but subject to the obligation to pay the balance of the purchase price.

This principle has been extended to conditional contracts. As Holmes LJ commented in *Re Sherlock's Estate*:[11] 'if the making of an absolute agreement to sell is fixed by judicial authority as the time of conversion, it seems to me that it is both logical and desirable to apply the same rule to a conditional agreement.' The most common example of such a conditional contract is where an option to purchase is created. The operation of this principle is illustrated by the decision of *Lawes v. Bennett*[12] in which a testator leased a farm to an individual for a period of seven years and gave him an option to purchase the reversion on giving written notice before a specified date. This individual assigned the lease to another party who exercised the option and paid the purchase money after the testator's death. It was held that the purchase money formed part of the testator's personalty. The effect of this so-called rule in *Lawes v. Bennett* is therefore that the exercise of an option to purchase after a testator's death will retrospectively convert the property into personalty.

The rationale behind the application of this principle is that a testator is presumed to be aware of the legal result which will flow from granting an option of this nature.[13] However, as the principle is based on the presumed intention of the testator, it will not apply where a contrary intention can be deduced. So as Johnston J stated in *Miley v. Carty*:[14] 'whenever in a will or codicil the testator indicates an intention that, notwithstanding a contract for

---

9. See *Hillingdon Estates Co. v. Stonefield Estates Ltd* [1952] Ch 627, 631 *per* Vaisey J.
10. Keane suggests that all that is necessary is that there is a 'valid contract for sale' (see *Equity and the Law of Trusts in the Republic of Ireland* (1988) p. 298) and the most recent edition of Wylie's *Irish Land Law* (3rd ed., 1997 p. 139) states that 'arguably all that is needed is a "valid" contract or "binding contract *simpliciter*"'. Pettit also points out (1960) 24 Conv 47, 64-65 that it is doubtful whether the availability of specific performance can be regarded as a satisfactory criterion for determining whether conversion should occur and concludes that 'there do not appear to be any decisions directly and necessarily based on the availability or non-availability of the remedy of specific performance'.
11. [1899] 2 IR 561, 608.
12. (1785) 1 Cox 167.
13. See *Miley v. Carty* [1927] IR 541, 543. See also *Weeding v. Weeding* (1861) 1 J & H 424.
14. [1927] IR 541, 544.

the sale of the lands, the devisee shall take whatever interest in the lands that the testator may have had at the time of his death, then that intention is to be carried out, and the general rule as established in *Lawes v. Bennett* is not to be followed.' In addition, it has been held that the application of the principle 'should be limited to cases where there was no specific disposition of the property made after the date of the contract giving the option to purchase'.[15] This point was made in the following terms by Page-Wood VC in *Weeding v. Weeding*:[16]

> When you find that, in a will made after a contract giving an option of purchase, the testator, knowing of the existence of the contract, devises the specific property which is the subject of the contract without referring in any way to the contract ... it is considered that there is sufficient indication of an intention to pass that property, to give the devisee all the interest, whatever it may be, that the testator had in it.

Therefore, in the case of a general or residuary devise, the rule operates even where the option cannot be exercised until after the death of the grantor but in the case of a specific devise of the property, it will not operate if the will is made subsequent to the creation of the option or contemporaneously with it. The exception operates not only where a specific devise is made after the granting of the option but also where a will is republished after such grant by the execution of a codicil. These principles are conveniently summarised in *Snell's Equity*[17] in the following terms:

> Where ... there is a specific devise, the operation of the rule depends on the relative dates of the will and the grant of the option. If the will was made before the option was granted, the devise is adeemed by the exercise of the option, just as if the testator had sold the land in his lifetime. But if the will was made or confirmed by codicil after the grant of the option, or substantially contemporaneously with it, the specific devisee is entitled to the proceeds of sale; for the testator will be taken to have been aware of the option and to have intended the devisee to take the property whether it was land or purchase-money.

Where the option can be construed as a gift subject to the payment of the purchase price, it may subsequently be exercised by the personal representatives of the lessee to whom the option was given in the first

---

15. *Duffield v. McMaster* [1896] 1 IR 370, 379.
16. (1861) 1 J & H 424, 431. Quoted with approval by Porter MR in *Duffield v. McMaster* [1896] 1 IR 370, 381 and by Palles CB in *Steele v. Steele* [1913] 1 IR 292, 305.
17. (29th ed., 1990, Baker and Langan), p. 493. This passage was omitted from the 30th edition.

instance.[18] Finally, the rule in *Lawes v. Bennett* will only be applied as between the competing claims of those entitled to the real and personal property of a grantor on an option and will not apply as between a vendor and purchaser.[19]

Order of the Court

Conversion may occur by reason of a court order directing that property should be bought or sold[20] and such conversion takes effect from the date of the order[21] and not from the date of the sale. This principle is illustrated by the decision of Monroe J in *Re Beamish's Estate*[22] in which he held that an order for sale of an unencumbered estate operated as a conversion into personalty.

An absolute order for the sale of realty made on the petition of an incumbrancer operates as a conversion of only so much of the lands as it is necessary to sell to discharge the incumbrance. This conclusion was reached by Ross J in *Sheane v. Fetherstonhaugh*[23] in which part only of an owner's lands had been sold to discharge incumbrances on the property. After his death the question arose whether the unsold lands had been converted by the order made by the court or whether they remained as real estate. As Ross J concluded: 'because only so much of the land is to be sold as is required for the discharge of incumbrances, no valid order can be deemed to exist for the sale of the remainder. ... It can never become operative in respect of the unsold lands'. In reaching this conclusion, Ross J distinguished his previous decision in *Re Stinson's Estate*[24] where he had held that if more property is actually sold than is necessary to pay off incumbrances, it must pass as personalty to the next of kin.

It should be noted that a court order will not always effect a conversion and section 67 of the Lunacy Regulation (Ireland) Act 1871 provides that any surplus remaining on the sale or mortgage of a lunatic's estate will be treated as if it were of the same character and nature as the property sold.[25] If an order is not made under this section, but is made in the ordinary course of the management of the estate of a person of unsound mind, conversion will be effected unless the court makes a direction to the contrary. However, where

---

18. *Belshaw v. Rollins* [1904] 1 IR 284.
19. *Re Sherlock' Estate* [1899] 2 IR 561.
20. Pettit suggests (1997) 113 LQR 207, 210 that the courts have treated such cases as analogous to the situation where there is a trust for sale but states that it is not a trust for sale and would not appear to come within the terms of s. 3 of the Trusts of Land and Appointment of Trustees Act 1996.
21. *Re Henry's Estate* (1893) 31 LR Ir 158, 165.
22. (1891) 27 LR Ir 326. See also *Steed v. Preece* (1874) LR 18 Eq 192.
23. [1914] 1 IR 268.
24. [1910] 1 IR 13.
25. See the *dicta* of Kennedy CJ in *O'Connell v. Harrison* [1927] IR 330, 337-338.

an order for sale is made outside the ordinary course of managing the estate, the property will retain its original character.

Partnership Property

Section 22 of the Partnership Act 1890[26] provides that unless the contrary intention appears, land which has become partnership property shall be treated as personalty and not as realty as between the partners themselves and those entitled to their estates. The reason for this provision is that on the dissolution of a partnership, the land will have to be sold to be divided amongst the partners.

Settled Land

Section 22(5) of the Settled Land Act 1882 provides that capital money arising from the disposition of property pursuant to the Settled Land Acts 1882-1890 is to be treated as realty.

Failure of Conversion

Where property is subject to a duty to convert but before or at the same time as the direction to convert becomes effective, a total failure of the objects of the conversion occurs, there will be a resulting trust of the property in its actual form. So, if A devises realty on trust for sale for the benefit of B and B dies before the sale takes place, a resulting trust of the property, which remains as realty, arises in favour of the settlor. However, where there is a partial failure of the objects for which conversion was directed, the outcome depends on whether the property is left by will or settled by deed. Where the direction to convert is contained in a deed, the property will result subject to the trust for conversion.[27] On the other hand, if the direction is in a will, it will go to the person entitled to the property in its unconverted form, although he will receive it in its converted form because the trustees will be under an obligation to carry out the objects which have not failed.[28]

---

26. It should be noted that s.22 has been repealed in England by the Trusts of Land and Appointment of Trustees Act 1996. Pettit argues (1997) 113 LQR 207, 210-211 that as the section effectively put a pre-existing equitable principle into statutory form, the pre-Partnership Act equitable rule may continue to apply. However, he points out that the effect of this repeal is not entirely clear, see further (1997) 113 LQR 207, 211.
27. *Griffith v. Ricketts* (1849) 7 Hare 299.
28. *Re O'Connor's Estate* [1923] 1 IR 142.

THE DOCTRINE OF RECONVERSION

In certain circumstances, property which has notionally been converted may be reconverted or theoretically returned to its actual physical form. Reconversion may either occur by act of the party or by operation of law.

By Act of the Party

Where a party is absolutely entitled to property and expresses the desire to take this property in its original unconverted form, it would make no sense for equity to compel the trustees of the property to convert it as the owner could immediately reverse this process. Therefore, on the basis that 'Equity, like nature, will do nothing in vain', the doctrine of reconversion intervenes. So, where beneficiaries who are of full age and capacity and between them absolutely entitled to trust property choose to take property in its actual form, notional reconversion occurs. The decision to reconvert may be expressly stated or it may be inferred from 'evidence of acts and circumstances'.[29] Minors and persons of unsound mind cannot make an election of this nature although where it is necessary to do so, the court may make the decision for such persons or sanction a decision already made.

Normally, 'all persons having interests must concur to effect conversion',[30] although in a limited manner a remainderman may elect to reconvert. Clearly, no election made by him can prejudice the interests of those with interests in possession and any decision made may be affected subsequently by any actual conversion which occurs before his interest falls into possession.

In the case of tenants in common, one of them may reconvert without the concurrence of the other(s) in the case of money to be invested in land,[31] but, it would appear not in the case of land to be converted into money on the grounds that land would not be as valuable if divided up in such a manner.[32]

By Operation of Law

Reconversion may also be effected by operation of law where property which has been notionally converted in equity becomes reconverted without any declaration or act of the party entitled. This will occur where, e.g. property which was subject to an obligation to convert comes into the possession of some person who is absolutely entitled, without having been converted, and

---

29. *Hart v. McDougall* [1912] 1 IR 62, 75 *per* Barton J. See also the *dicta* of Byrne J in *Re Douglas and Powell's Contract* [1902] 2 Ch 296, 312 to the effect that evidence may be derived from 'declarations or acts and conduct'.
30. *Hart v. McDougall* [1912] 1 IR 62, 72 *per* Barton J.
31. *Seeley v. Jago* (1717) P Wms 389.
32. *Holloway v. Radcliffe* (1857) 23 Beav 163.

he dies without making any declaration of intention in relation to it. The important factor here is that there must no longer be anyone who can enforce the obligation to convert and this is illustrated by the decision of Chatterton VC in *McDonogh v. Nolan*.[33] By virtue of a marriage settlement, a sum of money was vested in trustees for the purchase of realty to be held on certain trusts. The realty was never purchased and the parties' only son became absolutely entitled and died unmarried and intestate. It was held that the money should be regarded as personalty and therefore passed to his next of kin.

THE DOCTRINE OF ELECTION

Introduction

The doctrine of election can be explained in terms of the principle that 'a man shall not be allowed to approbate and reprobate',[34] in other words one cannot take a benefit and reject an associated burden. The doctrine comes into operation where a testator or donor purports to confer a benefit on a donee and in the same instrument purports to transfer some of this donee's property to a third party. A useful recent summary of the effect of the doctrine of election is set out by Histed in the following terms:[35]

> Where a beneficiary receives a gift under a will or deed which also disposes of some of his own property and where the circumstances of the case permit the court to conclude that the donor would not have wanted the beneficiary to receive the gift and keep his own property, then the court will imply a condition that the beneficiary so give up his property before receiving the gift.

As Walsh MR stated in *Williams v. Mayne*:[36] 'In giving effect to an election, the Court professess to enforce a duty; there being two benefits which it is inequitable in the party electing to claim together, it compels him, on the

---

33. (1881) 9 LR Ir 262.
34. *Re Lord Chesham* (1886) 31 Ch D 466, 473 *per* Chitty J. See also the comments of Lord Redesdale in *Birmingham v. Kirwan* (1805) 2 Sch & Lef 444, 449 that 'a person cannot accept and reject the same instrument' and of Lord Robertson in *Douglas-Menzies v. Umphelby* [1908] AC 224, 232 that 'it is against equity that any one should take against a man's will and also under it'.
35. (1998) 114 LQR 621, 634. Histed comments at 637 that the doctrine is based on the intention of the testator and the willingness of the court to imply a conditional gift where it can be convinced that the intention would be defeated without the condition being placed on the gift.
36. (1867) IR 1 Eq 519, 530.

condition of obtaining one, to relinquish the other.' This principle was more fully set out by Lord Hatherley in the course of his judgment in *Cooper v. Cooper*:[37]

> There is an obligation on him who takes a benefit under a will or other instrument to give full effect to that instrument under which he takes a benefit; and if it be found that that instrument purports to deal with something which it was beyond the power of the donor or settlor to dispose of, but to which effect can be given by the concurrence of him who receives a benefit under the same instrument, the law will impose on him who takes the benefit the obligation of carrying the instrument into full and complete force and effect.

This statement was quoted with approval by Ronan LJ in *Re Sullivan*.[38] In that case, a testator gave his wife a legacy of £3,000 to be paid in cash or out of his own or their joint shares as she should select. The Irish Court of Appeal held that the widow was bound to elect between the benefits conferred by the will and any claim to the stocks and shares invested in the joint names of herself and the testator.

It is important to distinguish such a situation from one in which the gift to the donee is expressly made conditional upon his transferring his property to a third party. Where this condition is not complied with, the gift to the donee cannot take effect and it will fall into residue.

The example provided by Hanbury and Martin[39] best illustrates the operation of the doctrine in practice. This is as follows:

> A is owner of Blackacre. T in his will devises Blackacre to B and bequeaths £10,000 to A. A cannot, of course, be compelled to transfer Blackacre to B. A is put to his election. This means that he can choose to take with the will or against the will. If A takes with the will, he will release Blackacre to B and get his £10,000. If A takes against the will, he will retain Blackacre but the £10,000 will be subject to an equity in B to claim compensation out of it to the extent of the value of Blackacre.

The doctrine has traditionally been described as being based on the implied intention of the testator or donor that effect should be given to every part of the instrument drawn up.[40] However, more recently the view has been expressed that the principle does not depend on 'a conjecture of a presumed

---

37. (1874) LR 7 HL 53, 70.
38. [1917] 1 IR 38, 42.
39. *Modern Equity* (15th ed., 1997) p. 852. This chapter was omitted from the 16th edition.
40. *Re Vardon's Trusts* (1885) 31 Ch D 275, 279 *per* Fry LJ.

intention'[41] and as Meagher, Gummow and Lehane[42] have pointed out 'any such intention will usually be fictional or constructive for it attributes to the donor knowledge of the situation he has created'. In practice where a contrary intention is expressed, the operation of the doctrine may be excluded, although it would not be sufficient merely to show that the testator or donor had not contemplated the circumstances which would give rise to an election. As Buckley LJ pointed out in *Re Mengel's Will Trusts*,[43] 'the case in which the testator frames his will with the conscious intention of bringing the doctrine into play must be very rare' and in the vast majority of cases it will come into effect due to an oversight or mistake on the testator's part.[44]

However, it is necessary to establish an intention on the part of the testator or donor to dispose of the property in question, although it is irrelevant that he did not realise that the property was not in fact his.[45] This point was considered by Porter MR in *Minchin v. Gabbett*[46] where he stated as follows:

> But the question is, what was the intention of the testator? and that is to be gathered from the whole will, not by speculating, but by an honest endeavour to discover what the testator meant, seeing the language used and what it fairly means. No doubt, in approaching such a question, the Court must *prima facie* construe the words as applying to an estate which the testator had, if the words will fairly apply to it, nay, more than that, in order to raise a question of election, it must be clearly seen that the words used point to an estate which is not the testator's own but another's.

This reasoning was developed by Porter MR in *Galvin v. Devereux*[47] in which it was held that the testatrix intended to dispose only of her own estate and interest in lands and not to dispose of property which was not her own, and that therefore no case of election arose.

Requirements for Election

The doctrine of election applies both to wills and deeds,[48] although it operates more frequently in relation to wills. In circumstances where it applies, the donee is faced with a choice; he may either take under the instrument, in

---

41. *Cooper v. Cooper* (1874) LR 7 HL 53, 67 *per* Lord Cairns. See also *Re Sullivan* [1917] 1 IR 38, 43.
42. *Equity Doctrines and Remedies* (3rd ed., 1992) p. 855.
43. [1962] Ch 791, 796-797.
44. *Ibid.* and see Crago (1990) 106 LQR 487, 489.
45. *Re Harris* [1909] 2 Ch 206, 209; *Re Sullivan* [1917] 1 IR 38, 43.
46. [1896] 1 IR 1, 12.
47. [1903] 1 IR 185.
48. *Birmingham v. Kirwan* (1805) 2 Sch & Lef 444, 449.

which case he may take the benefit of the gift to himself but must also consent to the transfer of his own property to a third party. Alternatively, he may take against the instrument, in which case he will retain his own property but will lose the benefit of the gift which the donor directed that he should have to the extent to which it is required to compensate the third party for failing to receive the donee's own property. As Sugden LC stated in *Hamilton v. Jackson*,[49] in these circumstances 'the property goes in compensation to the persons disappointed' and in the event of delay, such compensation may carry interest.[50] However, it should be noted that the obligation to compensate is only to the extent of the benefit derived; as Jessel MR pointed out in *Pickersgill v. Rodger*[51] no more compensation can be required than the value of the testator's own property given to the person called upon to elect, even though this may be inadequate to compensate for the disappointment.

As Crago[52] points out, whatever choice the electing party decides to make, he will not be as well off as the testator in all likelihood intended that he should be. Where the value of the benefit which he is given is no more than the value of his own property, then irrespective of whether he takes under or against the instrument he will derive no net benefit. Even where the value of the benefit is greater than that of his own property, he will only receive a benefit amounting to the difference between these two values. The only circumstances in which the donee will benefit as much as the third party to whom he must give his own property is where the gift made to him by the donor is worth at least twice the value of his own property.

In order to give rise to an election, the testator or donor must not only make a gift to the donee but must also *in the same instrument* make an effective disposition of the donee's property to a third party. It has been accepted in England that a will and any codicils to it will be regarded as the same instrument in this context[53] and a deed and a will have even been treated as one for this purpose. In *Re Woodleys*[54] Palles CB was satisfied that the two documents taken together 'carry out and effectuate one entire and indivisible intention', although he made it clear in the course of his judgment that had they been 'separate and independent', no question of election would have arisen.

The essentials for election were set out as follows by Jenkins LJ in *Re Edwards*:[55] 'there should be an intention on the part of the testator or testatrix to dispose of certain property; secondly, that the property should not in fact

---

49. (1845) 8 Ir Eq R 195.
50. *Re Saul's Trust* [1951] Ir Jur Rep 34.
51. (1876) 5 Ch D 163, 174. As Jessel MR stated: 'the obligation is only to the extent of the benefit [which the donee] derives: it cannot go beyond that'.
52. (1990) 106 LQR 487, 488.
53. *Cooper v. Cooper* (1874) LR 7 HL 53.
54. (1892) 29 LR Ir 304.
55. [1958] Ch 168, 175.

be the testator's or testatrix's own property; and, thirdly, that a benefit should be given by the will to the true owner of the property.' So in order for election to be necessary, it is essential that the donor has conferred a benefit on the donee with which he can compensate the third party if he elects to take against the instrument. As Loughborough LC commented in *Bristow v. Warde*:[56] 'in all cases there must be some free disposable property given to the person, which can be made a compensation for what the testator takes away.' In addition, in order for a case for election to arise, it is necessary that the donee's property be directly disposed of to a third party by the terms of the same instrument. This point was laid down as follows by Christian LJ in *Lewis v. Lewis*:[57] 'in order to raise a case of election, a testator must directly by his will assume to dispose of that which is not his; if he merely recites that it *has been* already disposed of in a particular way, and then proceeds to distribute his property on that assumption, and it turns out that he was mistaken, that does not raise a case of election.'

A further requirement is that the donee's property, which the donor purports to give to the third party, must be freely alienable. Election presupposes that the donee will have a choice and if his property cannot be alienated, he will not be required to make an election and will take the donor's gift free from any obligation. This point is illustrated by the decision in *Re Lord Chesham*.[58] A testator bequeathed his residuary estate to his eldest son and purported to dispose of chattels, in relation to which this son enjoyed a life interest but over which he had no power of disposition, in favour of his younger sons. It was held that the eldest son was not put to his election as he had no power to alienate this property and that he was entitled to take the residue of the testator's estate without compensating his younger brothers. However, in this context, it has been held that the application of the doctrine will only be excluded where the donee cannot by any relevant means comply with the testator's intentions and that it will apply even where the donee merely has a contingent interest in the property which he is required to alienate. So, in *Morgan v. Morgan*[59] it was held that the doctrine applied even where the interest in question was a remainder expectant on an estate tail. Equally, the doctrine will apply to property which is subject to a special power of appointment so 'as a general rule when the donee of a power purports to give the property, the subject-matter of the power, to a person not an object, and gives property of his own to the object of the power, the latter is put to his election, and cannot dispute the disposition of the trust property if he takes the benefit out of the

---

56. (1794) 2 Ves 336, 350.
57. (1876) IR 11 Eq 313. Quoted with approval by Palles CB in *Re Woodleys* (1892) 29 LR Ir 304, 313.
58. (1886) 31 Ch D 466. See also *Brown v. Gregson* [1920] AC 860.
59. (1853) 4 Ir Ch R 606.

donee's own property'.[60] However, the decision of the Irish Court of Appeal in *Re Handcock's Trusts*[61] clearly establishes that no obligation to make an election will arise in such circumstances where this would result in a violation of the rule against perpetuities.

A further important prerequisite for the application of the doctrine is that title to the electing party's property must arise independently of the instrument which gives rise to the need for the election to be made. So as James VC stated in *Wollaston v. King*:[62] 'the rule as to election is to be applied as between a gift under the will, and a claim *dehors* the will and adverse to it, and is not to be applied as between one clause in a will and another clause in the same will'. This principle seems to have been accepted in England,[63] although it was not applied by Neville J in the decision of *Re Macartney*[64] which has admittedly been criticised as 'unsatisfactory'[65] and 'aberrant'.[66] The better view would seem to be that no case for election arises where the electing party acquires title to both properties under the same instrument and this approach is supported by the *dicta* of Chatterton VC in *Sweetman v. Sweetman*[67] where he said that the property which the testator purported to devise to a third party must belong 'not by the will, but by an earlier title, to the person who is called upon to elect'.

Making an Election

Romilly MR expressed the view in *Worthington v. Wiginton*[68] that two requirements had to be satisfied in order for a valid election to be made under a will; first, there must be clear proof that the person making the election was aware of the nature and extent of his rights and secondly, it must be shown that having this knowledge, he intended to elect. Chatterton VC expanded these requirements in the following terms in the course of his judgment in *Sweetman v. Sweetman*:[69]

> The requisites for holding a party bound by an election as concluded are, I think, these: first, he must have a knowledge of his rights, that is

---

60. *Re Handcock's Trusts* (1888) 23 LR Ir 34, 46-47. See also *Moriarty v. Martin* (1852) 3 Ir Ch R 26 and *Fearon v. Fearon* (1852) 3 Ir Ch R 19.
61. (1888) 23 LR Ir 34. See also *Re McCormick* [1915] 1 IR 315, 319.
62. (1869) Lr 8 Eq 165, 174.
63. See e.g. *Bate v. Willats* (1877) 37 LT 221.
64. [1918] 1 Ch 300.
65. Pettit, *Equity and the Law of Trusts* (9th ed., 2001) p. 733.
66. Meagher, Gummow and Lehane, *Equity Doctrines and Remedies* (3rd ed., 1992) p. 853.
67. (1868) IR 2 Eq 141, 153.
68. (1855) 20 Beav 67, 74.
69. (1868) IR 2 Eq 141, 152-153.

to say, he must know that the property, which the testator attempted to give to another person, was not the testator's property, and that it would, upon the testator's decease, become independently of the testator's will, the property of the party called upon to elect. It must be known by him, as a matter of fact, that the testator had not the power to give the property which he purported to devise, and that it belongs, not by the will, but by an earlier title, to the person who is called upon to elect. Next he must know the relative values of the properties between which he is called upon to elect; and further, he must know, as a matter of fact, and not as a presumption of law, that the rule of equity exists, that he cannot, under such circumstances, take both estates, but must make an election between the two. And further, the Court must be satisfied that he made a deliberate choice with the intention of making it.

Election may either be express or may be implied from a party's conduct,[70] provided that a clear choice was made with a full knowledge and understanding of the issues involved. When an election is made it relates back to the date of the gift and so any compensation payable in the case of election against the terms of a will depends on the valuation of the property in question at the date of the testator's death. It would appear that where a specified time limit is laid down by the instrument within which election must be made, failure to do so within this time will be considered as election against the instrument. However, where no limitation is expressed, a person is unlikely to lose the right to make an election, even if he has knowledge of his right to do so, merely by reason of lapse of time unless serious prejudice would be caused to third parties as a result.

Disabilities, namely infancy or mental incapacity, will prevent a person exercising a right of election. In such cases an election will generally be made on behalf of the individual once the court has conducted an inquiry as to the most appropriate course of action to take,[71] although in the case of infants, the election may be deferred until majority is attained.

Conclusion

In practice the application of the doctrine of election may lead to rather anomalous results. Although the donee alone has an effective gift under a will, where the doctrine comes into operation, he will generally receive less of a net benefit than a third party to whom he must give either his own property or that which he appeared to be entitled to under the terms of the will, and in

---

70. Note that in *Padbury v. Clarke* (1850) 2 McN & G 298 it was found by Lord Cottenham LC that mere receipt of rents and profits of properties could not be construed as election. See also *Morgan v. Morgan* (1853) 4 Ir Ch R 606, 614.
71. *Moore v. Butler* (1805) 2 Sch & Lef 249, 266-267 *per* Lord Redesdale.

some circumstances he may receive no net benefit at all. It has been argued[72] that the doctrine is a 'mischievous' one which tends to defeat the testator's real intentions and that it is being applied in conditions which no longer correspond to those which may have justified its adoption in the first instance. Any application of the doctrine today will almost inevitably be as a result of a mistake made on the testator's part and the question must be asked whether equity should continue to intervene in a manner which arguably does not give effect to a testator's actual intentions and which so often produces an unfair result from the perspective of the person whom he expressly sought to benefit.

THE DOCTRINE OF SATISFACTION

This equitable doctrine is an illustration of the maxim that 'Equity imputes an intention to fulfil an obligation' and depends on a party's presumed intention to carry out an obligation. Where the doctrine of satisfaction applies, the act performed is of a different nature to that which it had been agreed should be carried out. The question which must be addressed is whether it can be presumed to have been intended to satisfy the original obligation. Cases in which the doctrine may operate are usually grouped into the following classifications.

1. Satisfaction of debts by legacies.

2. Satisfaction of portion debts by legacies.

3. Satisfaction (or ademption) of legacies by portions.

4. Satisfaction of legacies by legacies.

Satisfaction of Debts by Legacies

Where a testator leaves a legacy to a creditor the question arises whether the creditor can claim both the legacy and the debt. The position is straightforward if the legacy is expressed to be in reduction of the debt. However, even if there is no such stipulation, equity presumes that if a debtor leaves a legacy in his will to his creditor of a sum which equals or exceeds the amount of the debt without making any mention of it, the legacy should be treated as being in satisfaction of the debt.[73] The general principle in this area was set out by Trevor MR in *Talbot v. Duke of Shrewsbury*[74] as follows:

---

72. See Crago (1990) 106 LQR 487, 505.
73. *Garner v. Holmes* (1858) 8 Ir Ch R 469, 476.
74. (1714) Prec Ch 394, 394-395.

[T]hat if one, being indebted to another in a sum of money, does by his will give him as great, or greater sum of money than the debt amounts to, without taking any notice at all of the debt, that this shall nevertheless be in satisfaction of the debt, so as that he shall not have both the debt and legacy.

Being based on a presumption, the doctrine will not apply where there is an indication of a contrary intention. In practice the presumption may be rebutted where there are any reasonable grounds for doing so and the general trend has been to circumscribe the scope of the circumstances in which it may apply.[75] The doctrine has been held not to apply for a number of different reasons. First, the presumption of satisfaction of a debt by a legacy does not apply where a will contains a direction to pay the testator's debts.[76] Most well-drafted wills now contain such a direction and in practice the application of the doctrine is usually excluded on this basis. Secondly, its application may be excluded for reasons relating to the nature of the debt and the time when it was incurred. Because the doctrine is based on presumed intention, the debt must have existed before the making of the will.[77] In addition, it does not apply to a continuous running account where the debt would have been uncertain at the time of drawing up the will. So in *Buckley v. Buckley*,[78] the testator and another party were involved in ongoing business dealings and their practice was to settle their accounts from time to time. The amounts owed by the testator fluctuated after the date when the will was made and it was held by Porter MR that the testator's indebtedness to the other party at the time of his death was not satisfied by a legacy left in his will. As Porter MR stated:

The debt here was on a running account, to which the ordinary presumption of satisfaction of debts by legacies does not apply. … The reason is that the testator could not be presumed to know how the account would stand at his death and therefore he is not deemed to have intended the legacy in satisfaction of it without express words.[79]

Finally, it is important to stress that the presumption of satisfaction of a debt by a legacy applies only if the legacy is equal to or greater than the debt. In

---

75. See the comments of Stirling J in *Re Horlock* [1895] 1 Ch 516, 518 that 'no sooner was [the doctrine] established than learned Judges of great eminence expressed their disapproval of it, and invented ways to get out of it'. But note also the comments of Romer J in *Re Stibbe* (1946) 175 LT 198, 201.
76. *Re Manners* [1949] Ch 613, 618 *per* Evershed MR.
77. *Cranmer's Case* (1701) 2 Salk 508.
78. (1888) 19 LR Ir 544.
79. *Ibid.* at 558.

Ellard v. Phelan[80] where the testator owed small sums of money in respect of wages to his employees and left them more substantial legacies in his will, Ross J held that these bequests should be held to be a satisfaction of the sums owed by him at the time of his death. This can be contrasted with the situation which arose in *Coates v. Coates*[81] where it was held that where the amount of the legacy was less than the amount of the debt the presumption could not operate. Chatterton VC stressed in the course of his judgment that *pro tanto* satisfaction is not possible either in such cases; as he stated 'a legacy cannot operate in satisfaction of a debt of greater amount, even *pro tanto*'.[82] Therefore, it is even doubtful whether a legacy can be regarded as being in satisfaction of a debt which is for exactly the same amount but subject to the payment of interest.

The presumption will not apply where the legacy is of uncertain amount, and satisfaction is not possible where the gift under the will is the whole or part of the residue of an estate because its value cannot be definitely fixed. So, even where the residue of the testator's estate may clearly exceed the amount of the debt, such a gift will not be regarded as satisfaction of the debt. In *Re Keogh's Estate*,[83] the testator mortgaged his land and in his will directed that the mortgagees, who were relatives and had resided with him prior to his death, should be entitled to remain in his house for a year after his death. The testator also appointed them joint residuary legatees but Monroe J held that these benefits were not to be regarded as being in satisfaction of the mortgage debt.

In order for the presumption to apply, the legacy must be in every way as beneficial as the debt and where the legacy is different in character to the debt, this will not be the case. So in *Coates v. Coates*,[84] a bequest of the use of a house and furniture for life could not satisfy an obligation to pay a sum of money on a weekly basis. As Chatterton VC stated 'the nature of the gift must correspond with the nature of the obligation'.[85]

Satisfaction of Portion Debts by Legacies

The presumption in favour of the satisfaction of portion debts by legacies is an aspect of the principle that 'equity leans against double portions'.[86] The effect of the presumption is that where a father, or another person *in loco parentis* to a child undertakes to make a gift of a substantial nature or incurs

---

80. [1914] 1 IR 76.
81. [1898] 1 IR 258.
82. *Ibid.* at 261. See also *Reade v. Reade* (1880) 9 LR Ir 409.
83. (1889) 23 LR Ir 257.
84. [1898] 1 IR 258.
85. *Ibid.* at 261.
86. See *Keays v. Gilmore* (1873) IR 8 Eq 290, 295 *per* Sullivan MR.

an obligation to do so and subsequently makes provision in his will in the nature of a portion for this child, the portion debt is deemed to be satisfied by the obligation contained in the will. As Lord Cottenham LC stated in *Thynne v. Earl of Glengall*:[87] 'Equity leans in favour of a provision by will being in satisfaction of a portion by contract feeling the great improbability of a parent intending a double portion for one child, to the prejudice generally . . . of other children.'

A number of aspects of this principle require further elaboration. A 'portion' in this context means that the gift must be of a substantial nature, relative to the means of the parent and child, and intended to set a child up in life. As Jessel MR commented in *Taylor v. Taylor*:[88] 'I have always understood that an advancement by way of portion is something given by the parent to establish the child in life, or make what is called a provision for him — not a mere casual payment. . . .' The mere bestowing of a gift by a parent on a child will not suffice to make this gift a portion and equally a number of small gifts or advancements cannot be construed together as amounting to a portion.[89] The most common examples of a 'portion' would be a substantial gift made to a child on the occasion of his marriage or to enable him to set up in business.

The presumption of the satisfaction of portion debts by legacies in this context will only apply where the person making the provision for the child is his father or stands *in loco parentis* to him. Authority would suggest that it does not apply to provision made for a child by his mother[90] or other close relative unless that person can be considered to be *in loco parentis*. The exact interpretation of this phrase has caused difficulties,[91] but it is generally accepted as meaning where a person has assumed 'the office and duty of the parent to make provision for the child'.[92] In *Preston v. Greene*,[93] Meredith MR commented that 'the difference between a father and a mother is this, that in the one case there is a moral obligation to [advance the child] recognised in equity, while in the case of a mother the moral obligation is there, but the Courts of equity do not recognise it.' While it is unlikely that the courts in this jurisdiction would continue to approve of drawing a distinction between fathers and mothers in this context,[94] until the matter falls to be considered, no definite conclusion can be reached. Where a child's father is still alive it may be more difficult to establish that another individual is acting *in loco parentis*, although

---

87. (1848) 2 HL Cas 131, 153.
88. (1875) LR 20 Eq 155, 157.
89. *Suisse v. Lord Lowther* (1843) 2 Hare 424, 434 *per* Wigram VC; *Watson v. Watson* (1864) 33 Beav 574.
90. *Re Ashton* [1897] 2 Ch 574.
91. See e.g. *Fowkes v. Pascoe* (1875) 10 Ch App 343, 350 *per* James LJ.
92. *Powys v. Mansfield* (1837) 3 My & Cr 359, 377 *per* Lord Cottenham LC.
93. [1909] 1 IR 172, 177-178.
94. See also *infra* Chapter 7 in relation to the presumption of advancement.

it will be easier to do so where this individual is a close relative, and in *Pym v. Lockyer*[95] a grandfather was held to be acting *in loco parentis* to his grandchildren even though their father was still alive. The question of whether a person is acting *in loco parentis* must be answered on the basis of whether there has been 'the assumption of a parent's responsibility'.[96] While Barton J suggested in *Smyth v. Gleeson*[97] that the actions of a brother in making a gift to his older sister were more those of 'an affectionate brother' and said that it was at least doubtful whether the former has ever placed himself *in loco parentis*, he was prepared to assume for the sake of argument that this might have been the case. However, this can be contrasted with the decision of the Supreme Court in *Re Bannon*[98] where it was held that the facts proved did not support the inference that the testator stood *in loco parentis* to his nephew.

It would appear that the question of whether a portion debt may be satisfied by a legacy is one of intention to be determined from the terms of the instrument in the absence of evidence to the contrary. This point was made by Monroe J in *Re Battersby's Estate*[99] in the following terms:

> The question whether a portion given by a settlement is satisfied by a legacy in a subsequent will is entirely one of intention to be gathered in the absence of other evidence from the terms of the two instruments, subject to the consideration, that the presumption of law is against double portions. If the provision made by the later limitations are substantially the same, double portions will not be allowed; the parties entitled will be put to their election. If the limitations are widely different, the presumption is that the provisions were to be cumulative.

Unlike in the case of satisfaction of debts by legacies, *pro tanto* satisfaction is possible so if the legacy is of less value than the portion, it is deemed to be a satisfaction *pro tanto*.[100] Although the *dicta* of Monroe J in *Re Battersby*[101] might suggest otherwise, it is likely that this wider construction of *pro tanto* satisfaction would be applied in this jurisdiction.

As a general principle the property left by will must be of the same general nature as the property to which the beneficiary is entitled by virtue of the existing obligation and the interest in the property taken by the beneficiary must be as beneficial to him as this interest. While a greater degree of flexibility may be exercised than in the case of ordinary debts and legacies, generally

---

95. (1841) 5 My & Cr 29.
96. *Smyth v. Gleeson* [1911] 1 IR 113, 119. See also *Monck v. Monck* (1810) 1 Ba & B 298.
97. [1911] 1 IR 113.
98. [1934] IR 701.
99. (1887) 19 LR Ir 359, 363-364.
100. *Warren v. Warren* (1783) 1 Bro CC 305.
101. (1887) 19 LR Ir 359, 363-364.

speaking they 'must be of the same nature and attended with the same degree of certainty'.[102] So, in *Smyth v. Gleeson*[103] the presumption of satisfaction of a portion debt by a legacy was rebutted by the difference in certainty and value between the two benefits.

If the father or person *in loco parentis* has actually advanced a portion to a child and subsequently gives a legacy to the same child, the latter will not be regarded as satisfaction and the child will be entitled to take the benefit of the legacy. The reasoning behind this approach is clear, as, if the father has already given the child the gift in the nature of a portion, he would undoubtedly intend that child to benefit in addition from any provision made for him in a subsequent will.

Unlike in the case of ordinary debts, once it is found that the presumption applies, the child is put to his election between the gift under the will and the *inter vivos* portion obligation.[104]

Although designed to promote equality between children, the application of the doctrine of satisfaction has been criticised for penalising an only child in an unfair manner while not applying to more distant relatives of a testator. However, it has been expressly preserved by section 63(9) of the Succession Act 1965. The subsection provides that section 63, which requires that advancements made to a child must be taken into account when determining the child's share on an intestacy, is not to affect the principle of the satisfaction of portion debts by legacies.

Satisfaction of Legacies by Portions and the Doctrine of Ademption

This is essentially a case of ademption, meaning in this context the writing off of a legacy by an advance made during the intended legatee's lifetime. There are two aspects of this principle which must be considered; first the ademption of a legacy by a subsequent portion where the parties are father and child or where the donor is *in loco parentis*, and secondly the ademption of a legacy given for a specific purpose by a subsequent gift made during the donee's lifetime for the same purpose.

The principle of the ademption of a legacy by a portion was set out in the following terms by Lord Selborne LC in *Re Pollock*:[105]

> When a testator gives a legacy to a child, or to any other person towards whom he has taken on himself parental obligations, and afterwards makes

---

102. *Bellasis v. Uthwatt* (1737) 1 Atk 426, 427-428.
103. [1911] 1 IR 113.
104. See the *dicta* of Monroe J in *Re Battersby's Estate* (1887) 19 LR Ir 359, 363-364. This choice must be distinguished from the operation of the doctrine of election discussed above.
105. (1885) 28 Ch D 552, 555.

a gift or enters into a binding contract in his lifetime in favour of the same legatee then (unless there be distinctions between the nature and conditions of the two gifts) there is a presumption that both gifts were made to fulfil the same natural or moral obligation of providing for the legatee and consequently that the gift *inter vivos* is either wholly or in part a substitution for or an ademption of the legacy.

The operation of these principles can be seen in the decision of Sugden LC in *Barry v. Harding*[106] in which he held that an absolute gift in a will to a child would be adeemed by a portion of the same amount subsequently given on her marriage, even though this sum was settled on her and her husband. The presumption against double portions forms the basis for this principle, as was made clear by Sullivan MR in his judgment in *Curtin v. Evans*:[107]

> There is a presumption raised by the law against double portions; and accordingly, when a parent, or one standing *in loco parentis*, gives by will a sum of money to a child, and afterwards a like or greater sum is secured by a settlement on the marriage of that child, the law presumes the legacy to be adeemed.

However, Sullivan MR went on to stress that this principle is only a presumption and may be rebutted by evidence of intention to the contrary. He stated that the burden of proving the intention necessary to rebut the presumption rests on the person claiming the double portion and said that parol evidence will be admitted with a view to establishing whether the presumption is well founded. However, he stressed that where the claim rests on oral evidence, 'the Court ought to view and examine it with scrupulous care and great discrimination' and ought not to act on it unless it is free from suspicion and clearly shows the real intention of the person making the advancement.

Where a devise or bequest in the will is followed by a subsequent *inter vivos* gift to the same beneficiary, ademption may operate *pro tanto* if the amount of the gift is less than the value of the legacy.[108] The corollary of this principle is that where a child is left a legacy and is subsequently advanced a smaller sum, he can claim the balance under the terms of the will.[109]

If the portion is paid before the will is drawn up, there can be no question of ademption, as there will be no legacy in existence at the time to be adeemed.[110] Where ademption does take place, equity deems the devise or

---

106. (1844) 7 Ir Eq R 313.
107. (1872) IR 9 Eq 553, 557.
108. *Edgeworth v. Johnston* (1877) IR 11 Eq 326.
109. *Pym v. Lockyer* (1841) 5 My & Cr 29. See also *Re Pollock* (1885) 28 Ch D 522.
110. *Re Peacock's Estate* (1872) LR 14 Eq 236.

bequest in the will to have been cancelled. It is therefore no longer treated as being an operable part of the will and the beneficiary cannot claim under it. Thus, unlike in the case of the satisfaction of portions by legacies considered above, there can be no election between the will and the *inter vivos* portion and the beneficiary must take the latter.[111]

The legacy and the portion must be of the same general nature for the presumption of ademption to apply: e.g. there can be no ademption of a pecuniary legacy by a portion consisting of land.[112] However, this requirement will be less strictly applied than in the case of satisfaction and the presumption of ademption will only be displaced by more substantial differences in subject-matter.[113]

As noted above, the doctrine of ademption can operate in a more general context, and a legacy given for a specific purpose may be adeemed by a subsequent gift made during the donee's lifetime for the same purpose. The operation of this principle is well illustrated by the decision of *Griffith v. Bourke*.[114] A legacy was given to a parish priest for the purpose of erecting a new chapel. It was held by Porter MR that this legacy was adeemed by the gift of a like sum for the same purpose to the archbishop of the diocese by the testator during his lifetime. As Porter MR stated: 'Where there is a gift in a will for an expressed object and afterwards a donation by the testator in his lifetime for the *same* object, the law presumes that he did not intend that both should take effect but that the latter should be in substitution for the former gift.'[115] However, he went on to stress that the object in question must be clearly expressed and it must be plain that the reason for making the *inter vivos* gift was the same as that which motivated the testator to give the legacy; both gifts must be for the 'same identical object'.

It is the requirement of a specific purpose which distinguishes this form of ademption from the variety applying to father and child. A fairly liberal interpretation of the requirement of a specific purpose was given by the English Court of Appeal in *Re Pollock*[116] where Lord Selborne LC stated that the legacy may be adeemed by the subsequent gift where it is expressed to be made 'in fulfilment of some moral obligation recognised by the testator' even though this obligation is not of a kind which the law will recognise. In this case a testatrix bequeathed a sum of £500 to a niece of her deceased husband stating that she was doing so in accordance with the latter's wishes. Subsequently, during her lifetime, she paid the niece the sum of £300 and entered in her diary that this was a legacy from her uncle. It was held by Lord

---

111. See the *dicta* of Lord Cranworth in *Chichester v. Coventry* (1867) LR 2 HL 71, 87.
112. *Re Wall's Estate* [1922] 1 IR 59.
113. *Chichester v. Coventry* (1867) LR 2 HL 71, 87 *per* Lord Cranworth.
114. (1887) 21 LR Ir 92.
115. *Ibid.* at 95.
116. (1885) 28 Ch D 552.

Selborne LC that there was a presumption that the legacy was adeemed to the extent of £300.

Satisfaction of Legacies by Legacies

This process has been described as only 'superficially akin'[117] to the doctrine of satisfaction and is probably better described as an instance of construing a will so as to avoid duplication of legacies which a testator is not likely to have intended. The underlying principle is the desire of the courts to attempt to construe the testamentary documents so as to give effect where possible to the testator's actual intention.

Where two or more legacies are given to the same person either in the same will or more usually in a will and a codicil, the question arises whether these should be regarded as cumulative or substitutional. If the two legacies which are given to the same person are of the same value and are given in the same instrument, equity presumes that they are substitutional and the legatee can take one only.[118] However, where the two legacies given by the same instrument are for different amounts, the presumption is that they are cumulative. This point was made in the following terms by Smith MR in *Brennan v. Moran*:[119]

> [I]t is a rule of construction that; where two legacies are given by the same testamentary instrument to the same person, of different amount, the legacies are to be considered cumulative, unless a contrary intention appears on the will.

In addition, if the two legacies are given by different instruments, usually by a will and a codicil, it is presumed that they are cumulative irrespective of their value; as Smith MR stated in *Brennan v. Moran*[120] in such a case 'as the testator has given twice, he must *prima facie* be intended to mean two gifts'. This principle was re-iterated by O'Sullivan MR in *Quin v. Armstrong*[121] as follows:

> [W]here a testator by his will gives a benefit to a person, and by a codicil to his will gives a benefit to the same person, the presumption of law is that he means to give twice; and it lies on the party who disputes it to show why that construction of them should not be adopted.

---

117. Meagher, Gummow and Lehane, *Equity Doctrines and Remedies* (3rd ed., 1992) p. 765.
118. *Garth v. Meyrick* (1779)1 Bro CC 30.
119. (1857) 6 Ir Ch R 126, 130.
120. *Ibid.* at 130. See also *Walsh v. Walsh* (1870) IR 4 Eq 396.
121. (1876) IR 11 Eq 161, 168.

However, this presumption may be rebutted and the legacies may be regarded as substitutional if they are for the same amount and are given for the same motive. So, in *Re Armstrong*[122] it was held that the presumption that legacies given to the same person in a will and in a subsequent testamentary instrument are cumulative was rebutted by the testatrix's intention 'to take away one gift and leave . . . one gift instead of that one which is taken away'.[123]

Despite the guidelines laid down above, the question will ultimately be one of construction of the instruments concerned and as stated, the primary aim is to give effect as far as possible to the testator's intentions. So, in *Bell v. Park*[124] legacies in a second will were taken as being in substitution for those in the first because, on an overall reading of the instruments, it appeared that this was the intention of the testatrix. As Cherry LJ stated: 'Such gifts are undoubtedly *prima facie* cumulative, but it is always permissible to show by the terms of the two instruments that the gifts by the later document were intended to be substitutional and not cumulative'.[125]

If gifts are presumed to be cumulative parol evidence is not admissible to rebut this presumption. However, if gifts are presumed to be substitutional parol evidence is admissible.

THE DOCTRINE OF PERFORMANCE

This equitable doctrine is also based on the maxim that 'Equity imputes an intention to fulfil an obligation' and reflects the principle that 'a person is presumed to do that which he is bound to do'.[126] However, performance can be distinguished from satisfaction because while satisfaction involves fulfilling an obligation by means of an act different in form from the one originally contemplated, performance involves the carrying out of the obligation itself. So, where a person is under an obligation to carry out a particular act and subsequently does an act which can be considered as performance of his obligation, in certain circumstances equity will presume that this subsequent act was done in performance of the earlier obligation. This principle was stated in the following terms by Walker LJ in *Bannatyne v. Ferguson*:[127]

> The principle of performance is that when a person covenants to do an act, and he does that which may either wholly or partially be converted

---

122. (1893) 31 LR Ir 154.
123. *Ibid.* at 156.
124. [1914] 1 IR 158.
125. *Ibid.* at 174.
126. *Tubbs v. Broadwood* (1831) 2 Russ & M 487, 493 *per* Lord Brougham LC.
127. [1896] 1 IR 149, 179.

to or towards a completion of the covenant there will be a presumption that he had done the act with the intention to perform his covenant.

The situations in which the doctrine of performance operates can be divided into two categories.

By Act of the Party

The most common example of the operation of the doctrine by act of the party is where a person covenants to purchase land and settle it on certain trusts and subsequently purchases land but fails to settle it. In these circumstances, equity may consider that the purchase amounted to performance of the covenant and the land will be considered as being held on the trusts of the settlement. This point is illustrated by the decision of Talbot LC in *Lechmere v. Lechmere*.[128] Prior to his marriage, a husband covenanted to lay out £30,000 in the purchase of freehold land within one year of his marriage. These lands were to be conveyed to trustees and each purchase was to be approved by them. After his marriage but not within the time stipulated and without the consent of the trustees, the husband purchased various interests in land, some of a fee simple nature but others of a reversionary or leasehold character, and also contracted to purchase fee simple estates. The husband died intestate and was survived by his wife. It was held that the freehold land purchased and contracted to be purchased after his marriage, although not amounting to £30,000 in value, should go towards performance of the covenant. However, any lands purchased by the husband before the date of the covenant and the interests which were not of a fee simple nature could not regarded as having been purchased in performance of his obligations. This decision established that where the lands are of lesser value than the lands covenanted to be purchased, they will be considered to have been purchased in part performance of the obligation and it also shows that property of a different nature from that covenanted to be purchased will not be available for this purpose.

However, for the doctrine to apply in this context, the act done must be essentially the same as that which the individual has covenanted to do and in *Bannatyne v. Ferguson*[129] the Irish Court of Appeal held that the appointment of a jointure by deed was not performance of an obligation to secure an annuity.

The operation of the doctrine may have important practical consequences in this context because where a covenant to purchase or settle property in the future is deemed to be performed, it may create a specific charge or lien over the property.[130]

---

128. (1735) Cas t Talb 80.
129. [1896] 1 IR 149.
130. *Creed v. Carey* (1857) 7 Ir Ch R 295.

By Operation of Law

Where a person covenants to leave a sum of money to another person or covenants that his executors will pay that person such a sum and then dies intestate, with the other person taking a share in his intestate estate, that share may be regarded as performance, or *pro tanto* performance, of the covenant to leave money. While provision for this individual may be expressly made to be in substitution for any claim which the covenantee may have in relation to an estate,[131] the more common situation is that which arose in *Re Finegan's Estate*.[132] A husband executed a bond which provided that in the event of his death in his wife's lifetime, a sum of money was to be paid to trustees in trust for her. When he predeceased his wife leaving no issue it was held that the sum secured by the bond was to be regarded, in the absence of any contrary intention being expressed, as satisfaction *pro tanto* of the widow's share in her husband's estate. Where there is evidence of a contrary intention, the doctrine will not apply and the covenantee will be entitled to the benefit of the gift and the distributive share.[133]

---

131. See *Re Hogan* [1901] 1 IR 168.
132. [1925] 1 IR 201. See also *Blandy v. Widmore* (1716) 1 P Wms 323.
133. *Re Hood* [1923] 1 IR 109.

Index